D1518340

Handbook of Research Methods in Public Administration

Second Edition

PUBLIC ADMINISTRATION AND PUBLIC POLICY

A Comprehensive Publication Program

EDITOR-IN-CHIEF

EVAN M. BERMAN

Huey McElveen Distinguished Professor
Louisiana State University
Public Administration Institute
Baton Rouge, Louisiana

Executive Editor

JACK RABIN

Professor of Public Administration and Public Policy
The Pennsylvania State University—Harrisburg
School of Public Affairs
Middletown, Pennsylvania

Available Electronically

Principles and Practices of Public Administration, edited by Jack Rabin, Robert F. Munzenrider, and Sherrie M. Bartell

PublicADMINISTRATION*netBASE*

Handbook of Research Methods in Public Administration

Second Edition

Edited by

Kaifeng Yang
Florida State University
Tallahassee, Florida, U.S.A.

Gerald J. Miller
Rutgers University
Newark, New Jersey, U.S.A.

CRC Press
Taylor & Francis Group
Boca Raton London New York

CRC Press is an imprint of the
Taylor & Francis Group, an **informa** business

Auerbach Publications
Taylor & Francis Group
6000 Broken Sound Parkway NW, Suite 300
Boca Raton, FL 33487-2742

© 2008 by Taylor & Francis Group, LLC
Auerbach is an imprint of Taylor & Francis Group, an Informa business

No claim to original U.S. Government works
Printed in the United States of America on acid-free paper
10 9 8 7 6 5 4 3 2 1

International Standard Book Number-13: 978-0-8493-5384-0 (Hardcover)

This book contains information obtained from authentic and highly regarded sources. Reprinted material is quoted with permission, and sources are indicated. A wide variety of references are listed. Reasonable efforts have been made to publish reliable data and information, but the author and the publisher cannot assume responsibility for the validity of all materials or for the consequences of their use.

Except as permitted under U.S. Copyright Law, no part of this book may be reprinted, reproduced, transmitted, or utilized in any form by any electronic, mechanical, or other means, now known or hereafter invented, including photocopying, microfilming, and recording, or in any information storage or retrieval system, without written permission from the publishers.

For permission to photocopy or use material electronically from this work, please access www.copyright.com (http://www.copyright.com/) or contact the Copyright Clearance Center, Inc. (CCC) 222 Rosewood Drive, Danvers, MA 01923, 978-750-8400. CCC is a not-for-profit organization that provides licenses and registration for a variety of users. For organizations that have been granted a photocopy license by the CCC, a separate system of payment has been arranged.

Trademark Notice: Product or corporate names may be trademarks or registered trademarks, and are used only for identification and explanation without intent to infringe.

Library of Congress Cataloging-in-Publication Data

Handbook of research methods in public administration / editors: Kaifeng Yang and Gerald J. Miller.
-- 2nd ed.
p. cm. -- (Public administration and public policy series)
Originally published: New York : M. Dekker, c1999.
Includes bibliographical references and index.
ISBN-13: 978-0-8493-5384-0 (alk. paper)
ISBN-10: 0-8493-5384-X (alk. paper)
1. Public administration--Research--Methodology. I. Miller, Gerald. II. Yang, Kaifeng.

JF1338.A2H34 2007
351.072--dc22   2007018721

Visit the Taylor & Francis Web site at
http://www.taylorandfrancis.com

and the Auerbach Web site at
http://www.auerbach-publications.com

Dedication

Yang: Ivy Jade Yang
Miller: Milan W. Nelson II

Contents

Part III
Measurement and Data Collection 203

Part IV
Data Management 291

Preface

The need for more rigorous and systematic research in public administration has grown as the complexity of problems in government and nonprofit organizations has increased. This book describes and explains the use of research methods that will strengthen the research efforts of those solving government and nonprofit problems.

This book is aimed primarily at those studying research methods in masters and doctoral level courses in curricula that concern the public and nonprofit sector. Thus, students in programs in public administration, nonprofit management, criminal justice, nursing, and education, to mention a few, will be provided detailed information on conceptualizing, planning, and implementing research projects of many different types.

The book is also aimed at consumers of research reports. For example, government executives who fund research must be able to determine whether the research objectives set out in the project are properly conceptualized and whether the research methods chosen are appropriate to the objectives and concepts. This volume will inform such research consumers.

We would like to thank many anonymous peer reviewers for their critical reading of the chapters in this book. Other groups merit public attention. The first group has two members who served without anything but our thanks, and we thank them again in public—Professor Hindy L. Schachter, New Jersey Institute of Technology, and Professor Alfred Tat-Kei Ho, Indiana University-Purdue University Indianapolis. The second group is a group of methodologists who helped us by providing ideas for chapters, arguing with us about whether the quantitative–qualitative balance seemed right, and reviewing pieces of chapters or combinations of chapters or the entire manuscript. For these and the support of the book they represent, we thank you. The third group is comprised of the authors who appear here. Each of the authors worked incredibly hard to produce their best thinking and teaching ideas. All of them made suggestions about cross-indexing and ensuring that consistency was not forgotten. Many helped each other beyond what any editor could have asked. We thank each of you with enthusiasm.

Kaifeng Yang
Gerald J. Miller

Introduction

This handbook has multiple purposes, and they build on each other. First, the handbook provides a comprehensive survey of research methods used in public administration research, whether in government administration of public programs or in academic research aimed toward theory building and theory testing. Second, the authors document past uses of these methods in public administration. They link systematic research techniques to their uses in public administration literature and practice in the past and present. Third, the chapters explore potential emerging uses of methods in public administration. These chapters illustrate to students, faculty, and practitioners how various methods may be used to help answer emerging theoretical public policy and nonmarket organization management questions. Therefore, the handbook provides a reference on systematic research methods in public administration and (1) how they could aid in understanding traditional questions in public administration and (2) how students, researchers, and practitioners might use them to help answer emerging theoretical and practical questions.

This book can serve as the primary text in research methods courses in masters of public administration programs and the research methods sequence courses in PhD in public administration, public policy, and public management programs. These courses are surveys that must cover a vast amount of material and work done in public administration. This handbook can help by giving survey courses a focus—exemplary research already published—and will also be able to give students a practical introduction to almost every topic now taught in the research methods course.

This book has four significant strengths. First, the exposition here contributes to the improvement and sophistication of research and research methods used in public administration research wherever done, in the university, in the public agency, or among consultants and researchers funded by foundations and other such organizations. Second, it stands as a reference manual for researchers as they deal with various quandaries in carrying out their various projects. Third, the chapters expose doctoral students to the wide variety of methodologies available to them. Finally, we hope that the authors give masters students an awareness of the variety of methods available to them, and we also hope that the chapters provide a high level of comfort to students in using systematic methods, whether in understanding work they read or in their own research. Thus, the revolution of desktop computing and the Web have made powerful research methods readily available to current and future students. This handbook can increase their awareness and ease in dealing with those methods, both for understanding studies that they use in their jobs as well as in carrying out research projects.

The book follows the linear logic of many methods courses and the planning process in pursuing research projects on contemporary public administration problems. The logic allows eight groups of chapters:

1. Theory-based public administration inquiry
2. Research design
3. Measurement and data collection
4. Data management
5. Basic quantitative analysis
6. Advanced quantitative analysis
7. Other techniques
8. Reporting, presentation, and teaching

The first set of chapters reveals both the logic of inquiry and the practical problems of locating research in the context of existing research. The section starts with "The Logic of Inquiry in the

Field of Public Administration" by Norma M. Riccucci followed by Hugh T. Miller's "Theory," "Dealing with Multiple Paradigms in Public Administration Research" by Kaifeng Yang, Yahong Zhang, and Marc Holzer, and "Where Do Research Questions Come From and How Are They Developed?" by Sam J. Yeager. The section ends with "Writing a Literature Review: The Art of Scientific Literature" by Domonic A. Bearfield and Warren S. Eller.

Authors deal with the practical and difficult problems related to research design in the second section. Design alone stands as the big problem; therefore the section begins with Jonathan B. Justice's "Purpose and Significance of Research Design." James S. Bowman follows the opener with "The Research Problem, Method, and Serendipity: One Investigator's Journey." Special problems in design concern authors in the remaining chapters, with "Threats to Validity in Research Designs" by Nicholas A. Giannatasio; "Responsible Conduct of Social Research" by Phyllis Coontz; "Qualitative Research Methods" by Vache Gabrielian, Kaifeng Yang, and Susan Spice; "Comparative Research in Public Administration" from the perspective of history and institutions by Robert S. Kravchuk; and "Legal Research Methods" by Julia Beckett.

The complex problems of measurement and data collection follow in the chapters in the third section. An overview by Lung-Teng Hu and Dorothy Olshfski entitled "Describing and Measuring Phenomena in Public Administration" begins the section. Following the overview, Alana Northrop and Shelly Arsneault describe "Sampling and Data Collection." Detailed information on survey research follows with the chapters "Using the Survey as an Instrument of Inquiry in Research" authored by Sarmistha Rina Majumdar, "Questionnaire Construction" by Donijo Robbins, and Richard W. Schwester's primer on "Collecting Survey Data via Telephone." The section ends with a chapter on an often overlooked source for data in "Obtaining Archival and Other Existing Records" by Suzanne J. Piotrowski.

Concerning anticipating and solving data management problems, the chapter authors in the fourth section give practical, considered advice based on experience. "General Issues in Data Management" by Roslyn K. Chavda starts the section. Carmine Scavo follows with his chapter "Constructing Data Sets and Manipulating Data." The section's third chapter deals with very real, practical problems for researchers, "Managing Large-Scale Electronic Data for Public Administration Research" by Yu-Che Chen.

From basic to advanced quantitative analysis, the next two sections cover the fundamentals with substantial numbers of illustrations. The section on basic analysis has four chapters, in the first of which Kamal Chavda introduces basic concepts and ideas. An introduction and discussion, "Applying Matrix Algebra in Statistical Analysis," by Sarmistha Rina Majumdar completes the introductory set of chapters. Changhwan Mo's chapter on "Univariate Analysis" is followed by "Statistics for Nominal and Ordinal Data" by Michael Margolis, "Analysis of Variance" by Carmen Cirincione, and "Linear Correlation and Regression" by Leslie R. Alm and Susan G. Mason.

The following section on advanced analysis describes six techniques. The six are "Multivariate Regression Analysis," a chapter by Elizabeth A. Graddy and Lili Wang; "Multivariate Techniques for Dichotomous Dependent Variables" by Mack C. Shelley; the chapter on principal component analysis, factor analysis, and other clustering techniques by George Julnes; "Confirmatory Factor Analysis: A Practical Introduction" by David Coursey; an introduction to panel data analysis by Tae Ho Eom, Sock Hwan Lee and Hua Xu; and Dan Williams' "Forecasting Methods for Serial Data."

Public administration researchers have used a large number of unique analytic techniques to gain insight about the nonmarket sector's unique and knotty problems. In the seventh section, "Data Envelopment Analysis" by Patria De Lancer Julnes begins discussion on special techniques. The section presents "Content Analysis" by Chieh-Chen Bowen and William M. Bowen and "Meta-Analysis" by Chieh-Chen Bowen next. Five other chapters round off the section, with "Q Methodology" by Steven R. Brown and Dan W. Durning with Sally C. Selden, "Methods of Network Analysis" by Simon A. Andrew and Richard C. Feiock, "Economic Modeling" by Ronald John Hy and Jim R. Wollscheid, "Grounded Analysis" by Ralph Brower and Hong-Sang Jeong, and "Research Methods Using Geographic Information Systems" by Akhlaque Haque.

The research consumption problem concerns authors in the final section. The ultimate problem in research is impact, how researchers can overcome illusive, tricky, and sizeable barriers to influence other researchers, public and nonprofit decision makers, the citizens nonmarket organizations serve, and the foundations and grant-making institutions that make the enterprise of public administration research possible. In the ninth section, the groups to reach and convince of research's merits get attention in the five chapters: "Presenting Quantitative Research Results" by Jane E. Miller; "Styles of Scholarship in Public Administration" by Kyle Farmbry and Lamar Bennett; "Strategies for Effective Data Presentation" by Marc Holzer, Kathryn Kloby, and Aroon Manharan; "Influencing the Policy Process and Making Reports Usable to Citizens" by Kathe Callahan; and "Applying for Research Grants" by Neil DeHaan.

Contributors

Leslie R. Alm is professor and chair of the Department of Public Policy & Administration at Boise State University, and is the director of the master of public administration program. He has recently published articles in *American Review of Canadian Studies*, *The Social Science Journal*, and *State and Local Government Review*.

Simon A. Andrew is an assistant professor in the Department of Public Administration at University of North Texas in Denton. His recent articles include publications in the *International Journal of Public Administration* and in *Administrative Change: A Journal on Political and Administrative Development*.

Shelly Arsneault is an associate professor in the Department of Political Science at California State University, Fullerton. Her recent publications include work on rural welfare program administration and women in state legislatures. She received her PhD from Michigan State University.

Domonic A. Bearfield is an assistant professor at the George Bush School of Government and Public Service. He received his PhD in public administration from Rutgers University-Newark. His research focuses on improving the understanding of patronage, a concept central to the study of public sector human resource systems. He currently serves as the newsletter editor for the section for public administration of the American Political Science Association.

Julia Beckett is an associate professor in the Department of Public Administration and Urban Studies at the University of Akron in Ohio. She recently coedited *Public Administration and Law* and authored "Five Great Issues in Public Law and Public Administration" in the *Handbook of Public Administration*.

Lamar Vernon Bennett is a doctoral candidate in public administration and policy at The American University, School of Public Affairs in Washington, DC. He received his Masters of Public Administration from Rutgers University, New York. His research interests include urban education reform, public management, and performance measurement.

Chieh-Chen Bowen is associate professor and associate department chair in the Department of Psychology at Cleveland State University in Cleveland, Ohio. Besides her strong academic background in research methods and statistics in social sciences, her recent publications cover the areas of international human resource management, selection, and performance management.

William M. Bowen is professor and director of the PhD program in urban studies and public affairs in the Maxine Goodman Levin College of Urban Affairs at Cleveland State University. He has authored or coauthored approximately 40 scholarly articles and three books related to research-based decision making and problem solving in regional analysis and planning, especially in relation to economic development, environmental issues, and energy studies.

James S. Bowman is professor of public administration at the Askew School of Public Administration and Policy, Florida State University. His primary area is human resource management. He is author of over 100 journal articles and book chapters. Bowman coauthored, with Berman, West, and Van Wert, *Human Resource Management: Paradoxes, Processes and Problems* (2nd ed., Sage, 2006) and *The Professional Edge: Competencies for Public Service* (Sharpe, 2004). He is editor-in-chief of *Public Integrity.*

Ralph S. Brower is associate professor in the Askew School of Public Administration and Policy and Director of the Center for Civic and Nonprofit Leadership at Florida State University. His academic interests include nonprofit organizations, organization theories, and qualitative research methods.

Steven R. Brown is a professor of political science at Kent State University, where he has taught for 40 years. He is the author of *Political Subjectivity* (1980) and has been a author or coauthor of a hundred book chapters and scholarly articles, the most recent appearing in *Handbook of Decision Making* (2007), *Psycho-Oncology* (2007), and *Quality & Quantity* (2006).

Kathe Callahan is an assistant professor in the School of Public Affairs and Administration at Rutgers University-Newark. Her research focuses on citizen participation and performance measurement. Her most recent book, *Elements of Effective Government: Measurement, Accountability and Participation*, was recently published by Taylor & Francis.

Kamal Chavda is the assistant director of the University of New Hampshire's Survey Center, in Durham. He also serves as lecturer in the Department of Political Science. He received his PhD from Rutgers University-Newark.

Roslyn K. Chavda is an assistant professor in the Department of Political Science at the University of New Hampshire. Her research interests are in the area of the impact of regulatory activity on economic development. She received her PhD in public administration from Rutgers University.

Yu-Che Chen is an assistant professor in the Division of Public Administration at Northern Illinois University. His research and teaching interests are in e-government and collaboration. His recent works appear in the *International Journal of Electronic Government Research*, *Social Science Computer Review*, and IBM reports.

Carmen Cirincione was an assistant professor at the Department of Political Science, University of Connecticut when he wrote the chapter.

Phyllis Coontz is associate professor and director of the doctoral program in the Graduate School of Public and International Affairs at the University of Pittsburgh. She has published numerous articles on gender, crime, drug use, sports gambling, social control, gender bias, female criminality, and research ethics. She has a forthcoming book examining sports bookmaking and gambling policy in the United States and is the editor of another book on German social theory.

David H. Coursey is a visiting professor at the Decision Theater (www.decisiontheater.org), Arizona State University. He specializes in methods, e-gov, and general public management. His current research concerns issues in measurement theory.

Neil De Haan serves as the director of grants for Essex County College, Newark, New Jersey and teaches grants writing in the School of Public Affairs and Administration at Rutgers University-Newark in New Jersey. He has over 30 years of experience in grants writing and management. He received his PhD from Rutgers University-Newark.

Dan W. Durning is a senior research associate in the Carl Vinson Institute at the University of Georgia in Athens, Georgia. His research on Q methodology, participatory policy analysis, and city–county consolidation has been published in the *Journal of Policy Analysis and Management, Public Administration Quarterly, State and Local Government Review,* and other journals.

Warren S. Eller is a visiting assistant professor at the Bush School of Government and Public Service at Texas A&M University and serves as the managing editor of the *Policy Studies Journal.* His recent work includes publications in *Journal of Policy Analysis and Management, Public Administration Review,* and the *Journal of Politics.*

Tae Ho Eom is an assistant professor in the Department of Public Administration at Yonsei University, Korea. His research interests include government accounting and local public finance, especially, property tax reform and education finance. His recent work has been published in *Public Budgeting and Finance.*

Kyle Farmbry is an assistant professor in the School of Public Affairs and Administration at Rutgers University-Newark. He received his PhD from the George Washington University.

Richard C. Feiock is the Augustus B. Turnbull Professor of public administration and policy in the Askew School, Florida State University. His work appears in the leading scholarly journals of political science, public administration, and urban affairs. His recent books include *Institutional Constraints and Local Government: An Exploration of Local Governance, City-County Consolidation and Its Alternatives,* and *Metropolitan Governance: Conflict, Competition and Cooperation.*

Vache Gabrielian is a board member of the Central Bank of Armenia and teaches at American University of Armenia. For the last eight years he has been a member of the Public Sector Reform Commission of Armenia. He has written on public administration in transition countries, privatization, comparative public administration, and macroeconomic and regulatory issues.

Nicholas A. Giannatasio is professor and Chair of the Department of Political Science and Public Administration at the University of North Carolina at Pembroke. He is also the managing editor of the *Journal of Public Affairs Education* (JPAE), the official journal of the *National Association of Schools of Public Affairs and Administration* (NASPAA).

Elizabeth A. Graddy is professor and senior associate dean for faculty and academic affairs, the School of Policy, Planning, and Development at the University of Southern California in Los Angeles. Her research focuses on the private sector role in public service delivery, how industry and organizational structure affect performance, and how information asymmetry and uncertainty affect institutional design and effectiveness. She received her PhD from Carnegie Mellon University.

Akhlaque Haque is an associate professor of government and director of graduate studies in public administration at the University of Alabama at Birmingham. His area of research is in administrative behavior, public information management, and its implications in a democracy. His work has been widely published in reputable national and international journals.

Marc Holzer is the dean and Board of Governors Professor, School of Public Affairs and Administration, Rutgers University-Newark, New Jersey. He is the editor in chief of the *Public Performance and Management Review.* Among his recent books, he coauthored *Digital Governance in Municipalities Worldwide (2005),* and coedited *Citizen-Driven Government Performance* and the *Public Productivity Handbook (2nd Ed.).*

Lung-Teng Hu is an assistant professor in the Department of Public Policy and Management at Shih Hsin University in Taipei, Taiwan. He received his PhD from the School of Public Affairs and Administration at Rutgers University-Newark. His research interests include knowledge management in the public sector, e-government and e-governance, government performance measurement and management, as well as public personnel and human resource management.

Ronald John Hy is the dean of the College of Arts and Sciences at Texas A&M University-Kingsville. His research focuses on economic modeling of various tax and education finance issues. He received his PhD from Miami University.

Hong-Sang Jeong completed his PhD at the Askew School of Public Administration and Policy, Florida State University in 2006. He is currently a Research Fellow at The Korea Institute of Public Administration. His teaching and research interests include organization theory, organizational learning, organizational development, qualitative research methods, and emergency management.

George Julnes is an associate professor of psychology at Utah State University. He is a recognized leader in promoting context-appropriate quantitative methodology for informing public policy. His major works include the book *Evaluation* (2000; Mark, Henry, & Julnes) and volumes of *New Directions for Evaluation* coedited with E. Michael Foster (2001) and Debra Rog (2007).

Patria de Lancer Julnes is associate professor and director of the graduate program in the Department of Political Science at Utah State University. Her recent work includes the coedited *International Handbook of Practice-Based Performance Management*. She was cochair of the American Society for Public Administration's Center for Accountability and Performance.

Jonathan B. Justice is an assistant professor in the School of Urban Affairs & Public Policy, University of Delaware. His most recent scholarly publications and editorial projects have concerned business improvement districts, accountability and ethics, budgetary transparency, and performance budgeting. He received his PhD from Rutgers University-Newark.

Kathryn Kloby is an assistant professor of political science at Monmouth University. Her research focuses on public sector accountability, performance measurement, and citizen participation.

Robert S. Kravchuk is professor and chair, Department of Political Science, at the University of North Carolina at Charlotte. He is the coauthor of *Public Administration: Understanding Management, Politics and Law in the Public Sector*, and has published widely on public management in leading academic journals. He received the PhD from The Maxwell School of Citizenship and Public Affairs at Syracuse University.

Sock Hwan Lee is a PhD student in the School of Public Affairs and Administration at Rutgers University-Newark. His research interests include local public finance, performance management, and research methodology.

Sarmistha Rina Majumdar is an assistant professor in the MPA program, Department of Political Science at Sam Houston State University, Huntsville, Texas. She teaches research methods and public policies with a focus on transportation and the environment. Her recent work includes a paper on sustainable development and a book chapter on transportation.

Aroon Manoharan is currently pursuing his doctorate in public administration at the School of Public Affairs and Administration, Rutgers University, Newark. His research interests include public performance measurement and reporting, survey research, e-government, and public transit. He received his MPA from Kansas State University in 2005.

Michael Margolis is a professor of political science at the University of Cincinnati. Coauthor of *Politics as Usual: The Cyberspace "Revolution"* (2000) and *Toward a New Theory of American Electoral Psychology* (2006), his publications include books, articles, and essays on political parties, elections, public opinion, methodology, and modern democratic theory.

Susan G. Mason is a professor in the Department of Public Policy & Administration and the Department of Political Science at Boise State University. She received her PhD and MPPA at the University of Missouri-St. Louis.

Gerald J. Miller is professor of Public Administration, Rutgers, the State University of New Jersey in Newark and served as 2007 Fulbright Research Chair at the University of Ottawa's Centre on Governance, School of Political Studies. His research articles have appeared in *Public Administration Review*, *Policy Studies Journal*, *Public Budgeting & Finance*, and *the International Journal of Public Administration*. Among his books published, he has authored *Government Financial Management Theory*, coauthored *Public Budgeting Laboratory* (with Jack Rabin and W. Bartley Hildreth), and co-edited *Handbook of Public Policy Analysis* (with Frank Fischer and Mara Sidney) and *Handbook of Public Administration* (3rd ed. with Jack Rabin and W. Bartley Hildreth).

Hugh T. Miller is professor and director of the School of Public Administration at Florida Atlantic University. His books include *Postmodern Public Administration: Revised Edition* (with Charles J. Fox, 2007) and *Tampering with Tradition: The Unrealized Authority of Democratic Agency* (with Peter Bogason and Sandra Kensen, 2004). He also wrote the introduction to Transaction's 2006 republication of Dwight Waldo's classic *The Administrative State.*

Jane E. Miller is a research professor at the Institute for Health, Health Care Policy and Aging Research, and Bloustein School of Planning and Public Policy at Rutgers University. She is the author of *The Chicago Guide to Writing about Numbers* and *The Chicago Guide to Writing about Multivariate Analysis*, and numerous articles on socioeconomic differences in child health and access to health care.

Changhwan Mo is a research fellow at the Korea Transport Institute in South Korea. He is the author or coauthor of several articles in the area of public policy, budgeting, and globalization. He received his PhD from Rutgers University–Newark.

Alana Northrop is a professor of political science in the Division of Politics, Administration and Criminal Justice, at California State University, Fullerton. Over the past 20 plus years she has published a book, numerous articles, and book chapters on government use of information technology as well as works on the federal bureaucracy and the initiative process.

Dorothy Olshfski is an associate professor in the School of Public Affairs and Administration at Rutgers University-Newark in New Jersey. Her book, *Agendas and Decisions*, written with Robert Cunningham of the University of Tennessee will be published by SUNY, Albany Press in 2007.

Suzanne J. Piotrowski is an assistant professor in the School of Public Affairs and Administration at Rutgers University-Newark in New Jersey. Her recent work includes the book *Governmental Transparency in the Path of Administrative Reform*. She received a PhD in political science from American University in Washington, DC.

Norma M. Riccucci is a professor of public administration at Rutgers University-Newark in New Jersey. Among her recent books are *How Management Matters: Street-Level Bureaucrats and Welfare Reform*, and *Managing Diversity in Public Sector Workforces*. In 2005, she was inducted into the National Academy of Public Administration, and in 2006 she received ASPA's Charles H. Levine Award.

Donijo Robbins is an associate professor for the school of public & nonprofit administration at Grand Valley State University in Grand Rapids, Michigan, where she teaches graduate and undergraduate courses in public budgeting, financial management, and research methods. Professor Robbins received her PhD from Rutgers University-Newark.

Carmine Scavo is an associate professor in the Department of Political Science, East Carolina University. His recent published work has appeared in the *Journal of Public Affairs Education*, *The Municipal Yearbook 2006*, *Urban Affairs Review*, and *Public Administration Review* as well as in edited volumes.

Richard W. Schwester is Assistant Professor in the Department of Public Management at John Jay College of Criminal Justice, the City University of New York. His current research deals with housing appreciation, shared services, and municipal 311 systems. His most recent work deals with stadium financing and will appear in Public Budgeting and Finance.

Sally C. Selden is an associate professor of management at Lynchburg College. Professor Selden's teaching and research interests include public management, human resource management, and nonprofit management effectiveness. She is also a principal investigator for the Government Performance Project (GPP), a study of public management systems in all fifty states funded by The Pew Charitable Trusts. She was responsible for leading the academic team that graded the human resource management systems of state governments. She is the author of more than 50 articles, books, or book chapters.

Mack C. Shelley, II is a university professor of political science, statistics, and educational leadership and policy studies at Iowa State University. From 1999 to 2007, he served as coordinator of research and director of the Research Institute for Studies in Education. His research and teaching focuses on public policy and research methodology applied primarily to social science and to health and environmental topics.

Susan Spice is a doctoral student at the Askew School of Public Administration & Policy, Florida State University. Her research interests include nonprofit management, international development, and qualitative methods.

Lili Wang is a postdoctoral research associate at the Taubman Center for Public Policy and American Institutions of Brown University. Her recent work focuses on nonprofit studies and public policy.

Dan Williams is an associate professor of public affairs at Baruch-CUNY, School of Public Affairs located in Manhattan. His recent work includes "Shrinkage Estimators of Time Series Seasonal Factors and Their Effect on Forecasting Accuracy," which was awarded outstanding paper of 2003 by the *International Journal of Forecasting*. He also has examined the early history of performance measurement in the United States.

Jim R. Wollscheid is an assistant professor of economics in the Department of Economics and Finance in the College of Business at Texas A&M University-Kingsville in Texas. His research specialties include environmental and sports economics. He received his PhD from Southern Methodist University in economics.

Hua Xu is currently a PhD candidate at the School of Public Affairs & Administration of Rutgers University in Newark, New Jersey. He taught statistical methods at the economics department of Rutgers University. He received his MPA from the LBJ School at University of Texas in Austin.

Kaifeng Yang is an assistant professor at the Askew School of Public Administration and Policy, Florida State University. His research interests include public and performance management, citizen participation, e-governance, and organizational theory. He has published in various journals, including *Public Administration Review*, *Administration & Society*, *Public Performance & Management Review*, and *Public Integrity*, among others.

Samuel J. Yeager, professor of public administration in the Hugo Wall School of Urban and Public Affairs, Wichita State University, teaches organization theory and behavior, ethics, and computer applications.

Yahong Zhang is an assistant professor in the School of Public Affairs & Administration of Rutgers University-Newark, New Jersey. Her research interests include local government administration, institutions and organizations, and policy analysis. She received her PhD from Florida State University.

Part I

Theory-Based Public Administration Inquiry

1 The Logic of Inquiry in the Field of Public Administration

Norma M. Riccucci

CONTENTS

1.1 INTRODUCTION

The field of public administration, since its inception, has been beleaguered by questions surrounding its "identity." What is public administration? Is there a "theory" of public administration? Is public administration a discipline? Is public administration an art or a science, or both? These and other questions persist and dogmatize public administration from the standpoint of study, teaching, and practice.

At this point in the history of public administration, the debate over its identity may seem somewhat banal, hackneyed, and even immaterial (no pun intended). Public administration has a very rich intellectual heritage which guides its research, teaching, and practice. Few would question the legitimacy of public administration as a full-fledged discipline or field of study. Conflict and dissonance arise, however, over whether there is "one best way" or approach to public administration. Should the field, steeped in a scientific management tradition, be regarded as a "science"? Or, should public administration be predisposed to at least the "tools" of science, including its analytic methods? The "real" questions—normative ones to be sure—behind the debate revolve around how we should study public administration.

The purpose of this chapter is to examine the field of public administration through the lenses of the philosophy of science. In this sense, public administration is examined through ontological (nominalism versus realism), epistemological (antipositivism versus positivism), and methodological (ideographic versus nomothetic) underpinnings. Somewhat contiguous, ontology asks "what is reality" and "what is existence"; epistemology asks "what can we know" and "how do we know what we know"; and methodology asks "how should efforts to know be executed." The chapter begins by asking, "where on the disciplinary continuum of the arts and sciences does public administration fit?" It then posits that public administration can best be characterized as a "postnormal science," and thus operates in a realm where prediction and control are limited, politics and society are paramount and, consequently, complete objectivity is not possible. From here, it reviews the epistemological and methodological approaches which might best suit the discipline of public administration.

1.2 IS PUBLIC ADMINISTRATION A SCIENCE?

A question that scholars and practitioners continue to ask even today is whether public administration is an art or a science. From ontological and epistemological standpoints, one might approach

3

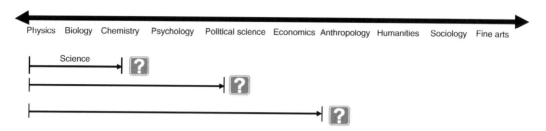

FIGURE 1.1 A disciplinary continuum: From science to art. (Adapted from Dempster, B., Toward a post-normal science: New (?) approaches to research, May 1998. *http://bethd.ca/webs/pnsresearch/index.html*, date accessed September 4, 2004.)

the question as it is depicted in Figure 1.1. Where exactly does public administration fit into this disciplinary framework? It seems axiomatic that public administration can never be a pure science in the sense of the physical or natural sciences (e.g., chemistry, astronomy, and physics). Rather, it is situated somewhere in between the universality of the natural sciences and the value-laden, postmodern world of the arts. And most would agree that public administration is a branch of the social sciences (Box, 1992).

A related question that has been grappled with repeatedly during the course of its history is "does public administration have a paradigm?" One way to approach this question is to substitute the word "science" for "paradigm" in Figure 1.1. In a very strict sense, public administration lacks a governing paradigmatic base. Granted, the concept of paradigm is very ambiguous, where even Kuhn (1962), who gave the concept credence in *The Structure of Scientific Revolutions*,* used the term in 21 distinct senses (Rainey, 1994; also see Lakatos and Musgrave, 1970).

If we think of paradigms in a broad sense, such as models, worldviews, bodies of thought, or even, as Kuhn propounded, as that which "attract(s) an enduring group of adherents," then public administration absolutely is guided by paradigmatic bases. Lan and Anders (2000, p. 155) make the case that public administration does have a paradigm, which "asserts that public administration differs from other types of management, private management in particular, in meaningful ways." They go on to say that the "foremost governing paradigm is publicness. Under this umbrella, a set of subparadigms (approaches) are competing with one another in guiding the inquiries of researchers" (Lan and Anders, 2000, p. 162).

Rainey (1994, p. 41, 48) argues that "we have no paradigm" but he goes on to say that "there is a degree of consensus ... on the validity and value of a focus on the public sector as a domain of inquiry." From a pure science perspective, we do not and cannot have a paradigmatic base, as Rainey aptly points out. However, as a community of scholars we do not like to admit this as it may serve to marginalize or lessen us as a field or a discipline (see Rosenbloom, 1983). Indeed, as Kuhn makes clear in one of his many usages of the concept, paradigms help scientific communities to bound their discipline; preparadigmatic disciplines, he purports, are "immature sciences." Thus, public admini-stration has sought to identify or formulate—albeit futilely—a governing paradigmatic base.

But Kuhn's contextual framework, as well as all of the examples he raises in his book, are grounded in the natural or physical sciences. Kuhn repeatedly points to Newtonian mechanics, Einsteinian dynamics, and Copernican cosmology to support his premise that paradigmatic disciplines are mature sciences. Perhaps Kuhn's hidden subtext was that only the natural sciences are or can be paradigmatic, and hence what he terms "normal sciences." According to Kuhn, normal science refers to a period in which routine "puzzle-solving" is conducted by scientists within a paradigm. His basic thesis in *The Structure of Scientific Revolutions* is that science progresses through

---

* The term paradigm had heretofore been used in certain forms of linguistics.

cycles, evolving not gradually toward truth, but through periodic revolutions or paradigm shifts. A scientific revolution occurs when scientists encounter anomalies that cannot be explained by the universally accepted paradigm within which scientific progress had heretofore been made. For Kuhn, a mature science develops through successive transitions from one paradigm to another through this process of revolutions. Once a revolution has occurred and the paradigm shifts, the field is once again returned to the period or cycle of normal science.

In the Kuhnian context then, public administration, as with any of the other branches of the social sciences, can only be preparadigmatic. This being the case, public administration might be better taxonomized not as a normal science, but rather as a postnormal science. This concept was conceived and articulated by Funtowicz and Ravetz (1992, 1993, and 1994) to address the existence of societal and ethical complexities in the environments we study. A postnormal science is one where objectivity is not always achievable. Environmental factors, particularly politics, interfere with the quest for objectivity, and, consequently, prediction and control are limited. A postnormal science, according to Funtowicz and Ravetz, is one that is relevant when high risks, uncertainty, and divergent values prevail. It urges new methods in the development and application of scientific knowledge, an extended peer community (i.e., one where a dialogue is created among all stake-holders, regardless of their official position or qualifications), and an extension of facts (Dempster, 1998; Sardar, 2000). Funtowicz and Ravetz (1992, p. 254), in effect, have called for a broader conception of science or "the democratization of science."

Interestingly, the notion of public administration qua postnormal science may have been proposed much earlier in the evolution of the field when scholars explicitly debated its scientificity. Simon, in his 1945 treatise, *Administrative Behavior* and related writings, emphatically professed that public administration is not a science per se, but could and ought to be studied scientifically. Simon was heavily influenced by the behavioral movement in the social sciences, which traces its historical roots to the philosophical movement known first as positivism, as advanced by Auguste Comte, and later logical positivism,* as advanced by the Vienna Circle. Public administration, according to Simon, should be based on fact: empiricism, measurement, and verification. Values, he claimed, have no place in the realm of public administration (Stivers, 2000).

But, many students of public administration observed a major fallacy in Simon's reasoning. One of his chief critics, Dwight Waldo (1948, p. 58) maintained that Simon and his followers unjustifiably sought "to place large segments of social life—or even the whole of it—upon a scientific basis." Waldo (1948, p. 182) argued that "administration is generally suffused with questions of value." Waldo went on to say that "a physical science problem is a problem of 'What is the case?' An administrative problem is characteristically a problem of 'What should be done?' Administrative study, as any 'social science,' is concerned primarily with human beings, a type of being characterized by thinking and valuing" (Waldo, 1948, p. 181, emphasis in original). Waldo, in fact, may have advanced the seminal concerns for the status of public administration as a postnormal science, one marked by great ambiguity in value and factual premises.

1.3 SEARCHING FOR THE TRUTH

If public administration is not a normal science, but rather a postnormal science, what should its approach to research be? How should scientific inquiry be carried out? This section looks at how various approaches to research postulate reality and truth. It asks, by what means do we arrive at the truth in public administration, or more broadly, the social sciences? Is it "scientific" methods that lead us to the truth? How do we know if or when we have arrived at the truth?

---

* For the purposes of this chapter, the terms positivism and logical positivism are used interchangeably, although logical positivism combines positivism with apriorism (i.e., where some knowledge can exist prior to experience).

Public administration is a field which has historically generated a rich body of qualitative research, often empirically based (e.g., descriptive; best practices; case studies). Even Simon, who strongly urged the field to adopt analytical tools and methods in the logical positivist tradition, contributed mainly descriptive and normative discourse to the field of public administration. Yet, the work of Simon has led to a broad reliance on, and acceptance of positivism in public administration. Although an important approach, it is only one of many which are appropriate for post-normal sciences, such as public administration. As noted earlier, the post-normal sciences operate with a different level of assumptions as compared to the normal sciences. For instance, unlike the normal sciences, which are assumed to be both certain and value-free, post-normal science, as Ravetz (1999, p. 647) points out, "makes 'systems uncertainties' and 'decision stakes' the essential elements of its analysis." He goes on to say that the insight leading to Post-Normal Science is that in the sorts of issue-driven science relating to environmental debates, typically facts are uncertain, values in dispute, stakes high, and decisions urgent. Some might say that such problems should not be called 'science'; but the answer could be that such problems are everywhere, and when science is (as it must be) applied to them, the conditions are anything but 'normal'. For the previous distinction between 'hard', objective scientific facts and 'soft', subjective value-judgments is now inverted. All too often, we must make hard policy decisions where our only scientific inputs are irremediably soft. In such contexts of policy making, there is a new role for natural science. The facts that are taught from textbooks in institutions are still necessary, but are no longer sufficient. For these relate to a standardised [sic] version of the natural world, frequently to the artificially pure and stable conditions of a laboratory experiment. The world is quite different when we interact with it, either destructively or constructively.... Contrary to the impression conveyed by textbooks, most problems in practice have more than one plausible answer, and many have no answer at all. (Ravetz, 1999, p. 649)

Table 1.1 provides a matrix comparing various approaches to research.* The matrix, although not definitive, seeks to illustrate the ontological, epistemological, and methodological bases for conducting research in the social sciences. It does not intend to promote one best way for researching matters concerning public administration but rather to generate a discussion around the utility of varied approaches to public administrative research. Some of the prominent philosophers and thinkers associated with the various approaches are also listed to encourage others to more fully explore the application of philosophic thought and science to public administration.

As indicated in Table 1.1, from an ontological standpoint, approaches to research range from positivism—where reality exists "out there" and is driven by immutable, universal, or natural laws that are completely independent of the researcher—to postmodernism, where reality is a social construction and is "in the eye of the beholder." It results from the interactions between the researcher and their world, and there is no single, objective truth (example, Guba, 1990; Fox and Miller, 1994; McSwite, 1996, 1997; Dempster, 1998; Lincoln and Guba, 2000; Miller, 2002). The ontologies are different, but no value can be ascribed to them; one is not better than the other. In fact, we conduct research on the basis of accepting specific ontologies. For example, postmodernist's sense of reality is governed by nominalism, where ideas have no objective realities, but rather are merely names; postmodernists know a pencil to be a pencil because the name tells them it is. For positivists, however, grounded in realism,[†] the reality of a concept is accepted without question and at face value.

---

* It should be noted that there is a degree of ambiguity in the use of ontological and epistemological concepts and propositions which emanate not only from the different branches of the social sciences but also from theological philosophies as well. That is to say, each of the disciplines within the social sciences as well as the varied theologies embraces the philosophy of science in distinct or unique ways. For example, antipositivism, a term introduced by Max Weber, was first used in the field of sociology to encourage researchers to create and use scientific methods that differed from those employed in the natural sciences. Others have equated the term antipositivism with deconstructionism (as conceived by Jacque Derrida) and postmodernism or relativism.

[†] I use the term "realism" as distinct from critical realism or other conceptions of realism (e.g., scientific realism, commonsense philosophical realism). Realism in the context here assumes that a thought- or mind-independent reality exists. Critical realism asserts that there is a reality "out there" but that our knowledge will always be limited and mutable because it is made up of the world, our perception of it, and us. For different and overlapping treatments of these concepts, see, for example, Little, 2000; Sayer, 2000; Niiniluoto, 1999; Leplin, 1984; Feyerabend, 1981.

TABLE 1.1
The Philosophy of Science: Comparing Research Approaches in the Social Sciences

	Postmodernism (Antipositivism)[a]	Rationalism	Empiricism	Positivism[b]	Postpositivism[c]
Ontology[d]	Nominalism; relativism; researcher and reality are inseparable, as are life and world	Researcher's mind is reality; mind comes from God	Researcher and reality are separate	Realism; researcher and reality are separate; universals exist and they are real	Critical realism; researcher and reality are one and the same
Epistemology	Knowledge is relative; objectivity does not exist; all truth is a social construction and is culture bound	Reason is chief source of knowledge; deduction; knowledge is innate; mind experience; intuition; *a priori* knowledge	Objective reality arises from introspective awareness; sense experience; *a posteriori* knowledge	Objective reality exists beyond the human mind; value neutrality; induction	Qualified objectivity; reality exists, but too complex to be fully understood or explained; empirical falsification
Methodology	Ideographic; hermeneutics; phenomenology; interpretation	Deductive; speculation; common sense reasoning	Observation; logically derived hypotheses; empirical testing of hypotheses inductive process of thought	Nomothetic; inductive; logically derived hypotheses; empirical testing of hypotheses; verification	Triangulation; modified experimental
Recording Technique	Qualitative	Qualitative	Qualitative and quantitative	Quantitative	Qualitative and quantitative
Philosophers and Thinkers	Max Weber (antipositivism); Jean-François Lyotard; Jacques Derrida; Michel Foucault; Sandra Harding; Nancy Scheper-Hughes	Plato; Descartes; Leibniz; Spinoza	Aristotle; Epicurus; Francis Bacon; John Locke; George Berkeley; David Hume	Auguste Comte; Rudolf Carnap; Wittgenstein; Otto Neurath; John Stuart Mill; Herbert Spencer	Karl Popper; John Dewey; Nicholas Rescher

[a]　See Weber, R., 2004, *MIS Quarterly*, 28, iii, especially p. iv for a comparison of the usage of terminology.

[b]　For the purposes here, positivism and logical positivism are treated alike, although strictly speaking logical positivism combines positivism with apriorism.

[c]　Postpositivism overlaps with postmodernism in that it has been used to refer to a group within political theory, mostly comprised of feminists and postmodernists.

[d]　Ontology generally refers to the nature of existence or being; however, it also encompasses the general features and relations of the entities which exist. It is in this latter context that ontology is used in this table.

Ontologies are ultimately based upon our belief system (e.g., positivists' belief that reality is out there or postpositivists' belief that we can never fully know). Thus, as Dempster (1998) points out, even positivism which, "is, generally taken to be an objective process...is based on core beliefs. Such beliefs, in turn, are reinforced by understanding gained through scientific study." In short, questions of ontology inevitably rest on beliefs.

Epistemology asks how do we know what we know. As many have pointed out (Bunge, 1983; Dempster, 1998), epistemological questions are closely linked to ontological considerations: How can we know something without first knowing whether (or believing) it exists? Epistemologies, like ontologies, take many forms. That is to say, we know something to be true through a variety of sources. For example, we experience them in our mind (rationalism) or empirically via our senses (touch, sight, etc.). Or, we know something to be true because we feel it or have been told it by a credible source (Fernández-Armesto, 1997). For postpositivists, truth or knowledge can only be gained through empirical falsification (Fischer, 1998). According to the imminent political and social philosopher Karl Popper (1963, 1977), falsification is a process of "conjectures and refutations." Hypotheses, propositions, or theories cannot be scientific unless there is the possibility of a contrary case. The process of accumulating knowledge involves formulating hypotheses and then trying to prove them wrong. In this sense, the hypotheses can never be proven correct because of the possibility that one or more experiments could prove them wrong. Thus, we can approximate, but never fully know reality.

For positivists on the other hand, there is no room for metaphysical speculation, reason, or innate ideas, as the rationalists called for. Truth and knowledge are gained through induction. Positivists maintain that logical and mathematical propositions are tautological and moral and value statements are merely emotive. The goal of knowledge under this approach is to describe the phenomena experienced (Riccucci, 2001, 2006). It should further be noted that positivism favors the distinction between pure and applied research. Although public administration is an applied field, positivists might argue that both applied research, which seeks application of knowledge and truths, and pure or basic research, where knowledge is pursued without concern for application, can be pursued.

Methodology is equally linked with ontologies and epistemologies. Indeed, methodology and hence, choice of method* and even recording technique depends upon our ontological and epistemological frameworks. So, conducting research in any of the social sciences involves not simply making choices about methodology but also hinges on the researcher's ontological and epistemological suppositions. Bunge (1983, p. xiv) points out that "methodology...is the discipline that studies the principles of successful inquiry, whether in ordinary life, science, technology or the humanities...it is descriptive and analytical, but in addition it is prescriptive or normative: It attempts to find out not only how people actually get to know but also how they ought to proceed in order to attain their cognitive goals."

For positivists, study must be nomothetic, inductive, and based on value-free, rationally derived, testable, and verifiable hypotheses. They maintain that "questions answerable through natural science methods of testing and confirmation are the only legitimately answerable questions, and the correct answers can only come from those methods" (Little, 2000, p. 5, emphasis in original). Postmodernists, on the other hand, subscribe to hermeneutics and phenomenology, where case studies and best practices research are highly valued. Postpositivists emphasize the importance of triangulation, multiple measures, and observations, each of which may possess different types of error; ultimately, multiple realities manifest simultaneously (Guba, 1990; Lincoln and Guba, 2000). Through the increased reliance on qualitative techniques, postpositivist methodology seeks to falsify, rather than verify hypotheses.

---

* Method and methodology are often used interchangeably. But some argue that methodology is the theory and analysis of how research should proceed—the practice of knowing—although method is simply the technique for gathering evidence (see, for example, Bunge, 1983; Harding, 1987; Guba, 1990; Dempster, 1998).

In sum, there are various ontological, epistemological, and methodological bases for conducting research in any of the social sciences. And, regardless to the approach, choice and subjectivity are invariably present. As Dempster (1998) points out, the challenge is "recognizing the gray areas that exist among and between [the various approaches to conducting research] ... tailoring research approaches to match characteristics of particular situations is not only valuable, but essential ... plural perspectives offer the potential for strong contributions to research."

1.4 SUMMARY AND CONCLUSIONS

Writing over 55 years ago, Dwight Waldo (1948, pp. 177–178) argued, in his pioneering work, *The Administrative State*, that "Empiricism and experimentalism, both have a prominent place in the methods of physical science. But there is much in scientific method which is nonempirical and nonexperimental. The close identification, in America, of science with empiricism seems to be the work of persons who espouse pragmatic philosophy, and have sought to give pragmatism the prestige of the 'philosophy of science'." Waldo effectively refutes the notion that there is one best way to approach the study of public administration (Stivers, 2000).

This chapter sought to illustrate that there is indeed a variety of approaches to study public administration. It argued that public administration can never be a pure science in the sense of the physical or natural sciences (e.g., chemistry, astronomy, and physics), is not governed by a paradigmatic base, and therefore, can never be a normal science. Public administration can be characterized as a postnormal science, lending itself to study from any number of ontologies, epistemologies, and methodologies. Each brings value toward the goal of strengthening research in public administration.

Stivers (2000) points out that some within the field of public administration continue to struggle in vain to make public administration more scientific, through the application of quantitatively based empirical research. But, as Thompson (1997, pp. 485–486) suggests, "positive public management research is hard to do. Unlike the subjects of the physical sciences, human beings make choices that confound our analytic designs ... management scholars can rarely show a straightforward unambiguous cause–effect relationship" (also see Adams and White, 1994; White et al., 1996; Stivers, 2000). This is not to say, of course, that there is no role for scientific method in public administration. Rather, it suggests that the contextual variables that surround the research question, along with the underlying assumptions that researchers make about ontology and epistemology, determine the suitability of the analytical tools.

Adams and White (1994) argue that method or technique sometimes overshadow other important considerations for research in public administration. They point out that

> when technique alone assumes paramount importance, it is an easy ... next step to omit a framework, or fail to address theory-building, among other pitfalls. Technique may even dictate the choice of topic (e.g., what problem can statistic X be applied to). One cannot help but wonder whether courses on research methods, often taught as 'toolkits' and divorced from the substantive content of the field, have fostered ... mindless empiricism. (Adams and White, 1994, p. 573)

Adams and White (1994, p. 574) conclude that the lure of "technique can replace theoretical reflection.... A fascination with technique and its use essentially drives out the larger substantive concerns within which the research problem is embedded." This proclivity, they argue, could ultimately lead to a "theoretical wasteland" in public administration.

In sum, the logic of inquiry in the field of public administration is multifaceted. As with any postnormal science, there is immense room for a diversity of perspectives. Moreover, values and beliefs (i.e., subjectivity) will always be extant. And, most importantly, striving to apply ontologies, epistemologies, and methodologies of the natural sciences will not produce better research and will not improve the field of public administration; they are, in effect, inappropriate.

REFERENCES

Adams, G.B. and J.D. White. 1994. Dissertation research in public administration and cognate fields: An Assessment of Methods and Quality. *Public Administration Review*, 54, 565–574.

Box, R.C. 1992. An examination of the debate over research in public administration. *Public Administration Review*, 52, 62–69.

Bunge, M. 1983. Epistemology and methodology I: Exploring the world. *Treatise on Basic Philosophy*, volume 5, Dordrecht, Holland: D. Reidel Publishing Company.

Dempster, B. 1998. Toward a post-normal science: New (?) approaches to research, *http://bethd.ca/webs/pnsresearch/index.html*, date accessed September 4, 2004.

Fernández-Armesto, F. 1997. *Truth: A History and a Guide for the Perplexed*. New York: St. Martin's Press.

Feyerabend, P. 1981. *Realism, Rationalism and Scientific Method*. New York: Cambridge University Press.

Fischer, F. 1998. Beyond empiricism: Policy inquiry in postpositivist perspective. *Policy Studies Journal*, 26, 129–146.

Fox, C.J. and H.T. Miller. 1994. *Postmodern Public Administration: Toward Discourse*. Thousand Oaks, California: Sage Publications.

Funtowicz, S.O. and J.R. Ravetz. 1992. Three types of risk assessment and the emergence of post normal science. In S. Krimsky and D. Golding (eds.), *Social Theories of Risk*. Westport, Connecticut: Praeger.

Funtowicz, S.O. and J.R. Ravetz. 1993. Science for the post-normal age. *Futures*, 25, 739–755.

Funtowicz, S.O. and J.R. Ravetz. 1994. Emergent complex systems. *Futures*, 26, 568–582.

Guba, E.G. 1990. *The Paradigm Dialog*. Newbury Park, California: Sage Publications.

Harding, S. 1987. Introduction: Is there a feminist method? In Sandra Harding (ed.), *Feminism and Methodology: Social Science Issues*. Bloomington, Indiana: Indiana University Press.

Kuhn, T.S. 1962. *The Structure of Scientific Revolutions*. Chicago: University of Chicago Press.

Lakatos, I. and A. Musgrave. 1970. *Criticism and Growth of Knowledge*. Cambridge, United Kingdom: Cambridge University Press.

Lan, Z. and K.K. Anders. 2000. A paradigmatic view of contemporary public administration research. *Administration & Society*, 32, 138–165.

Leplin, J. 1984. *Scientific Realism*. Berkeley, California: University of California Press.

Lincoln, Y.S. and E.G. Guba. 2000. Paradigmatic controversies, contradictions and emerging confluences. In Yvonna S. Lincoln and Norman K. Denzin (eds.), *Handbook of Qualitative Research 2nd edition*. Thousand Oaks, California: Sage Publications, pp. 157–213.

Little, J.H. 2000. Between positivism and relativism: A middle path for pubic administration. Paper presented at The 13th Annual Conference of the Public Administration Theory Network, Fort Lauderdale, Florida, January 28–29.

McSwite, O.C. 1996. Postmodernism, public administration, and the public interest. In Gary L. Wamsley and James F. Wolf (eds.), *Refounding Democratic Public Administration: Modern Paradoxes, Postmodern Challenges*. Thousand Oaks, California: Sage Publications, pp. 198–224.

McSwite, O.C. 1997. *Legitimacy in Public Administration: A Discourse Analysis*. Thousand Oaks, California: Sage Publications.

Miller, H.T. 2002. *Postmodern Public Policy*. Albany, New York: State University of New York Press.

Niiniluoto, I. 1999. *Critical Scientific Realism*. New York: Oxford University Press.

Popper, K. 1963. *Conjectures and Refutations: The Growth of Scientific Knowledge*. London, United Kingdom: Routledge.

Popper, K. 1977. *The Logic of Scientific Discovery*. London, United Kingdom: Routledge, 14th printing.

Rainey, H.G. 1994. On paradigms, progress and prospects for public management. *Journal of Public Administration Research and Theory*, 1, 41–48.

Ravetz, J.R. 1999. What is postnormal science? *Futures*, 31, 647–653.

Riccucci, N.M. 2001. The old public management v. the new public management: Where does public administration fit in? *Public Administration Review*, 61, 172–175.

Riccucci, N.M. 2006. The criteria of action in reforming and advancing the administrative state: How do we determine or know effectiveness? In Howard McCurdy and David H. Rosenbloom (eds.), *Revisiting Dwight Waldo's Administrative State*. Washington, DC: Georgetown University Press, pp. 55–70.

Rosenbloom, D.H. 1983. Public administrative theory and the separation of powers. *Public Administration Review*, 43, 219–227.

Sardar, Z. 2000. *Thomas Kuhn and the Science Wars*. Cambridge, United Kingdom: Icon Books, Ltd.

Sayer, R.A. 2000. *Realism and Social Science*. Thousand Oaks, California: Sage Publications.

Simon, H.A. 1945. *Administrative Behavior*. New York: MacMillan.

Stivers, C. 2000. *Bureau Men, Settlement Women: Construction Public Administration in the Progressive Era*. Lawrence, Kansas: University Press of Kansas.

Thompson, F. 1997. Book review of the state of public management. Donald F. Kettl and H. Brinton Milward (eds.), *Journal of Policy Analysis and Management*, 16, 484–507.

Waldo, D. 1948. *The Administrative State*. New York: The Ronald Press Company.

Weber, R. 2004. The rhetoric of positivism versus interpretivism, *MIS Quarterly*, 28 (March), iii–xii.

White, J.D., G.B. Adams, and J.P. Forrester. 1996. Knowledge and theory development in public administration: The role of doctoral education and research. *Public Administration Review*, 56, 441–452.

2 Theory

Hugh T. Miller

CONTENTS

This chapter focuses not on fact-finding or truth-seeking (the functions of methods) but on question-raising and redescription (the functions of theory). To oversimplify for the sake of brevity, although the method-oriented researcher seeks to get the facts right and find the truth, the theory-oriented scholar confronts established truths by reconciling incoherent elements of a theory into a more coherent narrative, by reinterpreting the findings, or by deploying new and different categories to reframe the question.

This chapter considers theory in three ways: (1) as a source of hypotheses and generalizable deductions, (2) as a narrative of reason, and finally (3) as one side of the infamous theory–practice gap. The now-standard understanding of theory (as a source of hypotheses) derives mostly from Karl Popper's (1959) notion that theory is a logical-deductive set of statements from which testable propositions can be drawn and then subject to tests of evidence.

2.1 THEORY AS HYPOTHESIS-PRODUCING, NOMOTHETIC GENERALIZATION

In a scientific sense, a theory is a coherent narrative capable of describing the world and perhaps even explaining the world and predicting the world's next turn. In its natural science aspirations, social theory would predict events before they happen, so precise would be its cause–effect linkages.

2.1.1 A COHERENT ACCOUNT OF THE FACTS

In everyday usage, theory sometimes lacks the prestige that it possesses in scientific disciplines. For example, the common expression, "That may work in theory, but not in practice" tends to dismiss theory as overly idealistic, speculative, or abstract. Other times theory is used as if it were synonymous with terms such as hunch or guess. Theory is often used synonymously with model, a term that emphasizes interrelations among observable phenomena. The formal dictionary definition of theory emphasizes the connecting of facts to one another through analysis. The idea behind theory in research is that generalizations declaring themselves to be descriptive of reality are phrased in a way that is testable.

Theory can be deployed to reinterpret the apparently obvious, common sense version of reality. For example, it is readily observable that the sun rises in the morning and sets in the evening. But this patently observable fact was put to a severe challenge by a new narrative developed in the 1500s when Nicholas Copernicus theorized that the earth rotated around the sun and also rotated on an axis fixed in a particular direction—hence accounting for seasons as well as the apparent rising and setting of the sun. Observables such as seasons and apparent star movement became coherent in Copernicus's theory. There had for centuries been speculation that the sun rather than the earth was at the center of things, but Copernicus's system was among the most complete and coherent alternatives. Galileo, making observations using what was at the time a new-fangled telescope, provided some empirical evidence to support the Copernican system. His observations indicated that, like the moon, Venus went through phases of lightness and darkness (e.g., full moon, half moon). Although these observations of Venus were not proof of Copernicus's theory, they strongly supported its plausibility. The understanding that Venus is a planet that rotates around the sun constitutes however a small portion of the physics or astronomy theory under consideration. But by peeling off testable hypotheses from the whole of the theoretical account, the scientific investigation of a theory's veracity can be enhanced (or possibly undermined) with empirical data.

Peeling off a testable hypothesis is accomplished by developing a construct. A construct is a concept taken from theory that is then tailored for testing in the empirical world. A phase (as in a phase of the moon) is a construct that urges the observer to pay attention to the pattern of light reflecting off a celestial object in orbit. The construct is further translated into categories or variables that can be observed, measured, or counted (e.g., full moon, new moon) through the use of some instrument (e.g., eye or telescope) capable of affirming the presence or absence of the phenomenon under investigation.

Creating indicators capable of connecting a theoretical construct to an observable presence is one of the most challenging and uncertain tasks for the researcher. In the social sciences, the correspondence between conceptual constructs and empirical reality is virtually always suspect or debatable. For example, the measurement problems associated with unemployment rate are under constant challenge on the grounds of validity even though unemployment rate is one of the more stable and consensual economic indicators.* Potential social science categories such as "drunk driver," "student," or "bureaucrat" are useful in many contexts, but they contain value and role prescriptions and are not simply neutral descriptors. The indicators actually used by practicing researchers are often merely a matter of negotiation and habit among the community of scholars and researchers working on the problem of unemployment or some other social problem or phenomena. Indicators and methods that tend to endure in the social sciences are the pragmatically useful ones. Because of the intangible nature of social phenomena, there is an implicit question mark at the end of any sentence claiming a connection between an indicator and a fact. Does a response to a survey questionnaire represent a fact?

2.1.2 THEORY/DATA VERSUS DATA/THEORY

In the philosophy of science, there has been a long discussion about the precedence of theory over data or vice versa. Is knowledge generated inductively through experience or deductively from theory? The debate has historically set empiricists apart from rationalists. Rationalism holds out the

---

* In the United States, for example, those who have been unemployed for long periods are systematically excluded from the count.

possibility of a priori knowledge, a mental understanding independent of sensory inputs. Empiricism emphasizes the importance of sensory inputs. For example, one must first observe the presence of tidal variation (high and low tide being empirical facts) before one can begin to theorize about it.

The critique of empiricism is that the logic of knowledge eventually devolves into an endless stream of sensory inputs, and they would not cohere in an intellectual sense. It is one thing when the sun shines, another thing when the wind blows, another thing when the cat crosses the street, and then an insect flew by—one danged thing after another. A world without theory is but a stream of sensory images—mindless empiricism to put it harshly. Moreover, rationalists would point out that we sometimes need a category to exist before we can see instances of it in the world. "Legislature," "prison," and "health insurance" might be examples of abstract concepts existing in the imagination before they eventually help to create empirical reality. Until we develop the vocabulary and categories, the realities cannot be described.

The critique of rationalism (as well as a priori reasoning, intuition, or revelation) is that there is no necessary contact with the observable world. This is a problem because knowledge of nature is not derived from scripture, or ideology, or from any official authoritative narrative, but from the experience of particular cases. Hence the particularity of the circumstances matter more than conformity to general rules, however logical they may be. Moreover, there is tremendous power in the use of empirical data. Empirical evidence can debunk one theory while affirming another.

Debunking a false theory with empirical data would bring a wonderful clarity to the knowledge-building project, but social questions are rarely resolved in so clear a manner. Nor is the distinction between empiricism and rationalism so clear-cut; the philosophical and scientific mainstreams adopt aspects of both. Following Popper (1959), theory is regarded as a coherent set of logical-deductive statements from which hypotheses are derived. Empirical tests that subject these statements to falsification protocols are then fashioned by researchers. A scientific test, then, is one that can show a statement to be false if indeed it is. Whether theory precedes data or data precedes theory depends on the circumstances of the investigation.

The excitement in knowledge building takes place at the point of collision between and among data and theories. Because the sun rises each day and sets each night, any intelligent observer might hypothesize that the sun revolves around the earth. How shocking it must have been to have one's perception of reality upended so thoroughly! The new theory advanced by Copernicus and Galileo changed the facts that were once self-evident. The facts of sunrise and sunset became nonfacts. Even so, new theory has a difficult time changing the language of the past even when the old theory has been displaced. We still speak of sunrise and sunset even though it would be hard to imagine an educated person who now believes that the sun is revolving around the earth.

The recent political conflict swirling around the theory of evolution is testimony to the difficulties faced by a theory that challenges widely held beliefs about reality. Religious believers in parts of the United States have attempted to force teachers of biology to offer a theory of creationism alongside the theory of evolution. The idea that random variation and natural selection of genetic mutations are what led to human differentiation from other primates runs profoundly contrary to many religious accounts of the origin of humans. Perhaps even more instructive than the conflicts between religion and science is that evolutionary theory itself has evolved over time. A short theory-building example is illustrative of how the norms of science generate knowledge—a surprisingly malleable product.

Isbell (2006) tracked the changes in those evolutionary theories that attempted to explain why primates have better vision than other mammals. Arboreal theory had it that our ancestral primates lived in trees, and those without excellent vision would fall out of trees and die at a higher rate. When challengers pointed out that other mammals such as tree squirrels without excellent vision lived in trees, the arboreal hypothesis retreated and a visual predation hypothesis emerged. In this account, primates need excellent vision because successfully stalking and grabbing their small prey requires it. But subsequent evidence showed that some primates find their prey using their ears or noses and not their eyes.

Recently, researchers have noticed that in primate brains the part of the visual system that has expanded the most is the region identified with the ability to distinguish nearby objects from their backgrounds and with the ability to see camouflaged objects. This is interesting. It means that the ability to see snakes, for example, might have proved functional to species survival.

Indeed, Isbell (2006) reports the species of monkeys with the sharpest eyesight tend to be those who live in closest proximity to venomous snakes. For example, the Malagasy lemurs, the primates with the least complex visual systems, live in Madagascar, a place where venomous snakes have never lived. Primates in Africa and Asia, where venomous snakes have been around for about 100 million years, have the best vision. Humans are descendants of that group. Could it be that African/Asian primates that failed to develop excellent vision were disproportionately killed by snakes? Isbell notes the observation made a century ago by P. Chalmers Mitchell and R.I. Pocock when they carried writhing snakes into a roomful of caged chimpanzees, baboons, and lemurs. The African/Asian chimpanzees and baboons were panic-stricken, chattering loudly, and retreating as high up and far away in their cages as possible. In contrast, the Malagasy lemurs, lacking sophisticated vision, were unperturbed. Hence, the snake theory of excellent human eyesight gains credibility.

This short example of theory building shows how an interaction of data and theory and a strong norm of openness to revision have contributed to the formidable power of evolutionary theory. Despite its prestige in the scientific community, evolutionary theory continues to call itself a theory—a testimony to the hesitancy, tentativity, and open-mindedness that exemplifies scientific inquiry. Whether the snake-detection hypothesis withstands future tests of theoretical coherence and empirical observation is, consistent with the spirit of inquiry, an open question.

Though it is important to distinguish between them, empirical data and theories may not be such completely distinct categories as philosophers once portrayed them to be. Instead of insisting that theory precedes facts, or that facts precede theory, it might be better to see the two as intimately related. Facts are described differently from different theoretical perspectives. One theory can detect facts that are invisible to another theory. Arboreal theory shed light on different empirical data than visual predation theory did. Some facts—that primates lived in trees—are important in arboreal theory but not in visual predation theory. Meanwhile, the snake-vision theory makes use of correlations between the presence of snakes and complexity of vision in primates, and the conversation shifts. Evolution is talked about less in terms of hunting and eating, as in visual predation theory, and more in terms of avoiding being killed. In all these cases, different facts were emphasized in different theories. Because of this interdependence between theory and fact, a theory and its facts may be thought of as a paradigm or as complementary elements of a narrative.

2.2 THEORY AS NARRATIVE

Facts do not always perform the theory-testing function we would like them to. Facts claim to be actual evidence, but they never speak for themselves. They are always reported by fallible human beings, of course. But even more important to appreciate is that these facts are reported from a perspective. There is no objective perch from which a social scientist has a view of the world that is incontrovertibly true, even though there may be a multitude of facts upon which most can agree. However, agreement on the facts is both enabled and limited by the language we speak, the culture we are from, the values we share, the points of view we have been exposed to, the race or class or gender conditions we have learned to cope with, and perhaps the academic discipline we were socialized into. In the social sciences, we easily become part of the scene we are investigating as the reports of our research can potentially change the behavior of the people we were studying. In applied fields, behavioral change is frequently the point of the investigation. Though it is quite apparent that the social sciences have not developed the prestigious theories found in astronomy or biology, it is also a more complicated research setting in that the subject, the social group or human being, may react to inquiries in unpredictable ways. The lesson of the so-called Hawthorne effect

(Roethlisberger, 1967) was that the investigator is part of the problem and thus interacts with the subject of inquiry. The presence of a researcher alters the behavior of the subjects of the study. Of course, social scientists nonetheless strive for a less partial view and seek to maintain a convincing distance from their subjects, but only on rare occasions can observers of social reality credibly claim an objective distance from their subjects. A methodology for a science that includes the observer as an integral part of the observation is still in the process of development under the various efforts taking place in qualitative research.

2.2.1 THE QUEST OF REASON

Empirical testing, whether qualitative or quantitative, is but one of many ways of subjecting a narrative to critique. Common in the social sciences too are logical tests of coherence and reason, critical tests of justice and fairness, political tests of interests and domination, and the applications of various ethical or moral criteria including efficiency, responsibility, kindness, and equal treatment. There are many rhetorical ways that theory can be undermined, affirmed, redirected, or ignored. The contest of ideas is rarely just about facts. It is also a matter of putting events and ideas into a framework so that the world seems less chaotic. Organizing events and ideas into frameworks is the work of theory building. This theorizing, narrative writing, data reporting, and story telling is very much a collegial enterprise, subject to peer review, critical consideration, and rebuttal.

Theory in the social sciences thus may be thought of as a narrative-creating enterprise that is subject to critical reflection among communities of inquirers. Hence, theorizing is storytelling but of a special sort—disciplined by reason and collegial criticism. This use of reason does not imply that humans are by nature rational; Sigmund Freud put an end to those speculations. Rather, the criterion of reason means that beliefs and knowledge claims must be justified using appropriate evidence, inferences, or language. The sort of storytelling that counts as theory is not the same sort of storytelling one finds in novels. Doctoral dissertations are frequently, though not always, structured into a story line that (1) states the research problem, (2) reviews the relevant literature, (3) discusses the procedures and methods employed to create a fair test of the hypothesis, (4) reports the findings, and (5) announces the conclusions, implications, and limitations. This structure regularly conveys useful information to attentive scholars who are interested in a particular area of inquiry, even though students of literature may find the plot line to be unimaginative. Many empirically oriented scholarly journals require a similar style of storytelling in the articles published.

In applied disciplines such as public policy or administration the prevalence of and need for sense-making narratives are especially pronounced. Here, the function of theory entails research-for-action. The weaving together of facts, metaphors, and values is a skill accomplished by a storyteller capable of interpreting the situation in preparation for actions or outcomes based on explicit end values.

2.2.2 METAPHORS

Rein (1976) regards the metaphor as the central element in storytelling. "This means that we must rely upon actions or events that appear to be analogous to situations we already know and that permit us to reason from the familiar to the unfamiliar. Familiar concepts are brought into unfamiliar situations, and in the process they transform the unfamiliar. The metaphor enables us to describe patterns and tease out lessons" (p. 75). Some metaphors that have now become standard usage in public administration include spoils system, administrative state, bureaucrat, chain of command, and red tape. In public administration or policy, the metaphor chosen is also suggestive of the action to be taken or the problem to be addressed.

Metaphors are often underappreciated as building blocks of theory, but understanding theory as narrative underscores the value of metaphors. The images and metaphors of a new theory may seem exotic at first, but over time they become part of ordinary language. Perhaps this is because metaphors are considered metaphors only when they are first introduced. Once upon a time it was not the case that rivers literally had mouths. The same was true of bottles, which now not only have mouths, but some even have necks. Now that the language has accepted the metaphors "mouth" and "neck" as literal reality for bottles, highways and the Panama Canal took it one step further and began developing bottlenecks of their own. Along with empirical facts and coherent logic, metaphors too should be regarded as a building block of theory. A metaphor has the potential to bring new understanding to a situation, to raise new questions, and to introduce a different perspective to the discussion.

According to Rorty (1991, p. 12), "there are three ways in which a new belief can be added to our previous beliefs, thereby forcing us to reweave the fabric of our beliefs and desires ..." These are (1) perception (functioning in service of empirical evidence), (2) inference (roughly synonymous with logical coherence), and (3) metaphor (a linguistic innovation).

> [1] Perception [empirical evidence] changes our beliefs by intruding a new belief into the network of previous beliefs. For example, if I open a door and see a friend doing something shocking, I shall have to eliminate certain old beliefs about him, and rethink my desires in regard to him. [2] Inference [logical coherence] changes our beliefs by making us see that our previous beliefs commit us to a belief we had not previously held ... For example, if I realize, through a complicated detective-story train of reasoning, that my present beliefs entail the conclusion that my friend is a murderer, I shall have to either find some way to revise those beliefs, or else rethink my friendship. (Rorty, 1991: p. 12)

Knowledge building is what Rorty calls reweaving the fabric of our beliefs and desires. If limited to perception and inference, knowledge building would not entail changing the language. Perception and inference can change the truth-value of a sentence, perhaps, but they do not add to our repertoire of sentences. To leave it at that would be to assume that the language we presently speak is all the language we will ever need. Therefore, the third way of theory building is metaphor. Metaphor is sometimes needed to move from one perspective to another one. Talk of "policy implementation" entails different connotations than talk of "public administration." Similarly, "public management" gathers in a set of ideas that varies, at least in emphasis, from "public administration." Empirical evidence and logical coherence alone might not be enough to accomplish the paradigm shift that Kuhn (1970) made famous. "[T]o think of metaphor as a third source of beliefs, and thus a third motive for reweaving our networks of beliefs and desires, is to think of language, logical space, and the realm of possibility as open-ended" (Rorty, 1991: p. 12). With metaphor, the building of knowledge is not always a matter of fitting data into pre-established categories. Metaphor is not a proposal to systematize; rather it is "a call to change one's language and one's life" (Rorty, 1991: p. 13).

This account of metaphor as a third vector of knowledge is at odds with its usual definition, which is that something has, in addition to its literal sense, another possibility that is expressed by metaphor. How does metaphor count as knowledge? Let us return to a previous point and again consider the linguistic innovation: "Once upon a time ... rivers and bottles did not, as they do now, literally have mouths" (Davidson, 1984: p. 246 cited in Rorty, 1991: p. 13). What once was metaphor has become literal. Language changes over time. Attaching an unusual metaphor like "mouth" to a river becomes second nature and eventually literal and no longer ridiculous. By expanding the language in this way, new metaphors can lead to new knowledge. They can help us redescribe our beliefs. Inquiry in the social sciences is mostly a matter of reweaving beliefs and redescribing ideas, not discovering the true nature of real objects.

To summarize, one upshot of the narrative understanding of theory is that to the normal knowledge-building components of (1) empirical facts and (2) logical coherence one can add (3) metaphor. This addition recognizes the power of analogies, categories, concepts, and interpretations to construct the reality we take to be true. Quite frequently, the concept precedes the reality. A female president of the United States and melting of the polar ice cap are two examples. Other times, we do not see empirical reality until a new conceptualization draws our attention to it.

Childhood obesity, corporate welfare, and bird flu are examples of facts that did not become acknowledged as such until a new conceptual category was introduced.

2.3 THEORY AND PRACTICE

There is a belief, widely shared in an applied field such as public administration, that there exists a gap between theory and practice. On the one hand there is the academy, and on the other is the real world of practice, or so the story goes. So next we consider (1) theory as something that gets applied to practice and (2) the theory–practice gap.

2.3.1 THEORY AS SOMETHING TO APPLY TO PRACTICE

It is commonplace for academicians in the field of public administration to justify their work as advice-giving to practitioners. Conferences of the American Society for Public Administration are sometimes conceptualized as an opportunity for practitioners to learn the latest theories so that their practices can be updated. The theorists at the conference, usually but not always academicians, have the opportunity to extend their ideas into the so-called real world. The underlying assumption of the exchange between theorists and practitioners is that theory is judged by its ability to help the practitioner do her or his job better. But consider the difference between single-loop learning and double-loop learning, made famous by Argyris and Schön (1974).

In single loop learning, people are able to alter their behavior and perhaps even improve things for a time based on feedback and data, but the effort is focused upon improving the status quo operations and practices; there is no questioning of the plans or values or goals upon which current practices are premised. In double-loop learning, the governing variables (goals, premises, values, theory in use, etc.) of the situation are put on the table for examination. In double-loop learning, the "why" of the task is examined, not merely the "how" of the task. Practitioners who insist that theorists help them do their jobs better may be unable or unwilling to engage in double-loop learning, especially in public administration where the tasks and the "why" are seemingly preset by elected officials. When practitioners in graduate school beseech their professors, "Skip the theory; just tell me how to do my job better" they do not want to engage in double-loop learning. They want to do what they have been doing all along, only better—single-loop learning. Theory that subjects itself exclusively to that criterion eventually becomes attenuated and flat.

By emphasizing practice to the complete neglect of theory, the field of public administration would adopt an intrinsically conservative approach. The bias toward action in practice can create inertia for doing things the same today as yesterday, but the bias for action need not rule out changing the way things are currently done. As new impasses come into view and make their presence known, continuing to do things the same old way is no longer acceptable. Problems multiply and expand when practitioners remain completely stuck in their ways, or are forced to perpetuate ineffective practices because of ideological commitments of higher-ups. Alternatively, as impasses come into view, the intellectual freedom to think anew demonstrates its worth and appeal. Theorizing here does not mean substituting one formulaic procedure for another, it means reflecting on situational contingencies from as many perspectives as possible.

A willingness to entertain multiple theoretical frameworks simultaneously is helpful in dealing with practical impasses. Neither academics nor reflective practitioners should be expected merely to affirm in-place practices. Though it is certainly a possibility that current practices are the best possible practices and that professors' theories do not take sufficient account of practical contingencies, it is also possible that resistance to new theory amounts to nothing more than an unexamined commitment to habit. Theoretical engagement is very often inspired by the curiosities and mysteries of important practical problems. It would be limiting to demand that theory not contradict practice or not confront status quo ways of doing things.

If there is a danger in being overly resistant to new ideas, a quite opposite worry about theory-applied-to-practice is that the theory is wrong but will not admit it. There is often justifiable concern that dogma, creed, and ideological commitment will lord themselves over actual events. Solutions that claim to be "one best way" or the "best practices" are suspect on these grounds. Being the best solution in one situation or even several does not make a universal principle. Doctrinaire policy prescriptions that demand to be put into place everywhere regardless of local contingencies frequently take on the characteristics of ossified theory that refuses to take account of falsifying evidence. Evidence gleaned from practice may undermine one's favored theory, but reason dictates a healthy respect for a considered distance from a matter instead of adopting a one-sided outlook. Additionally, evidence gleaned from practice makes the path between theory and practice a two-way street. Theory may be applied to practice, but practice informs theory as well.

2.3.2 THE THEORY–PRACTICE GAP

The term "practice," derived from the Greek *praktikos*, connotes experience, performance, proficiency, or repetition. Practice in its negative connotations is sometimes characterized by mind-numbing repetition, use of hackneyed clichés instead of animated language, or thoughtlessness rather than reflection.* Going through the motions of the daily drill does not necessarily help to confront the impasses brought about by changes in the environment, a new challenge to be met, or a new way of looking at things. The difference between a practitioner who has twenty years of experience and another who has one year of experience repeated twenty times depends on their comparative willingness to reflect. When everything changes but the old habits, unreflective practice will not get the job done. This is where theory comes in.

Thinking anew is what we do when the old ways no longer work the way we want them to. Reflection and critique on the part of practitioners are urgent concerns. Practitioners are on the scene involved in the world of action. Practical theory implies facility with conceptual frameworks, paradigms, and systems of thought. This sort of imaginative activity entails an ability to engage in discourse, to listen and read, and to articulate ideas—these are activities that thoughtful people have always done. Practice in these activities prepares the practitioner for the really tough questions, those for which there are no preprogrammed solutions. Theory that deals with the overly grand Being or Truth is rightfully perceived as perhaps too ultimate to be useful in critiquing daily practice. Theory that is relevant is not the sort that hovers over the practitioner like some sort of arrogance that knows it is right and that the world must be made to conform to it. Rather, practical theory is composed of concepts and logics that render the current impasse coherent and actionable.

An impasse, therefore, highlights the inadequacy of the way we have been doing things. The old ways no longer work because of ineffectiveness, a changed reality, or a new awareness that things might be different (Miller and Fox, 2007). At the moment of realizing this inadequacy of present practice, we can look at the old ways differently—as an old conceptualization that no longer suffices. Were it not for the fact that this conceptualization infiltrated itself into established practices of the familiar daily drill, it might be called "bad theory"—theory that does not work in practice.

But better than making simplistic judgments of good and bad, think instead of practice as "theory-in-place" and theory as "practice-to-be." The theory–practice gap can be resolved by thinking of theory and practice as two iterations of the same essential phenomenon. Theory as practice-to-be is waiting in the wings for that moment of impasse where it might be allowed on stage. Practice as theory-in-place is that set of ideas that have come to dominate in the order of things, if only temporarily.

---

* Terms such as span of control, unity of command, "works better costs less" are nominees for hackneyed phrases, along with Luther Gulick's so-called principles of administration, ridiculed by Herbert Simon as proverbs of administration.

2.4 SUMMARY

After introducing theory as a question-raising enterprise that is capable of redescribing reality, three main points about theory were presented: (1) theory is a thoughtful, rational, and intellectual integration of facts into a coherent narrative; (2) theory, as narrative, employs not only facts and logic but also metaphors; and (3) theory and practice are two facets of the same phenomenon: the understanding of appropriate action in the world in which we live.

2.5 EXERCISES

2.5.1 INTELLIGENCE AND REIFICATION

Stephen Jay Gould (1996) identified intelligence as a reified concept. In *The Mismeasure of Man*, touted as the definitive refutation to *The Bell Curve* (a book that ascribed social inequality to biological factors), Gould pronounced reification to be the major theme of his book: "in this case, the notion that such a nebulous, socially defined concept as intelligence might be identified as a 'thing' with a locus in the brain and a definite degree of heritability—and that it might be measured as a single number, thus permitting a unilinear ranking of people according to the amount of it they possess" (p. 269).

To make his case, Gould recalled the historical origins of mental tests. Charles Spearman in 1904 noticed that if two mental tests are given to a large number of people, there is almost always a positive correlation coefficient between them. Spearman theorized that the underlying structure was a two-factor dynamic. The common intelligence that correlated between two different mental tests was called general intelligence (g) and the residual variance peculiar to each test was called specific intelligence (s) that registered an intelligence specific to the test. As Gould notes, "Charles Spearman developed factor analysis—still the most important technique in modern multivariate statistics—as a procedure for deciding between the two- versus the many-factor theory by determining whether the common variance in a matrix of correlation coefficients could be reduced to a single 'general' factor, or only to several independent 'group' factors." (p. 287) He opted for the two-factor theory (Spearman, 1904, cited in Gould, 1996).

Although Spearman thought he had discovered the innate essence of intelligence in its fundamental and quantifiable thingness, Gould points out that general intelligence is nothing more than a series of correlations, an artifact of the measurement instruments (i.e., mental tests) and statistical procedures deployed. "We have known since the early days of mental testing—and it should surprise no one—that most of these correlation coefficients are positive: that is people who score highly on one kind of test tend, on average, to score highly on others as well. Most correlation matrices for mental tests contain a preponderance of positive entries. This basic observation served as the starting point for factor analysis. Charles Spearman virtually invented the technique in 1904 as a device for inferring causes from correlation matrices of mental tests" (p. 281).

Intelligence, in its scientific construction, is an artifact of a measurement protocol whose values are then correlated using factor analysis. Principal components of factor analysis are mathematical abstractions, not empirical realities. Hence intelligence is not an actual thing. Or as Gould puts it, "Spearman's g is not an ineluctable entity; it represents one mathematical solution among many equivalent alternatives" (p. 350).

The upshot is that research methods produce their own facts, in this case via factor analysis. The reification takes place when intelligence is identified as a thing, has a singular number ascribed to it, and is then used to rank people. General intelligence (g), as a series of correlations, contains no additional independent evidence beyond the fact of the correlation itself. Even though it is intoxicating to think that we might find the underlying essence of some phenomenon, it might be wiser to abandon the fixed idea of intelligence along with some of its crude corollaries (for example, innate stupidity as the cause of poverty).

Discussion: To reify is to treat an abstraction as if it were a concrete reality. What are some reified concepts in use in public administration? (Hint: Have you ever seen an organization?)

2.5.2 Precession of Simulacra

When Jean Baudrillard (1994) wrote about "the successive phases of the image" he provided a model for mind-expanding theorizing. The first phase of the image is that it is a reflection of a profound reality. That is, the image is taken to be reality itself, to represent a physical presence. The fable about the king's cartographers drawing up a map of the king's territory—in such detail that when it is finished it covers exactly the entire territory—is a humorous example of the first phase of the image (the map being the image). Mirrors and photographs are other representations that capture the aspirations of the first phase of the image to profoundly reflect the reality that is.

The second phase of the image is to denature a profound reality. Here Baudrillard refers to the early Christian iconoclasts who took strong exception to the excess of iconic representations of God, which had the effect of not merely obfuscating and masking God, but of effacing God and certainly not representing God. The second phase of the image begins the negation of a sign (an image, a symbol, an icon, a word or phrase) as a taken-for-granted representation of reality.

In the third phase of the succession, the image masks the absence of a profound reality. The image plays at being a representation of presence, but it is more like the sorcerer who summons the spirits at a séance. Despite the setting, the incense, the mood, the noises, and the symbols, there is no ghostly Being present.

In the fourth phase, the image no longer asserts its relation to reality. The simulation of reality has displaced the representation of it.

This framework has been used in the public administration literature to deconstruct the debate over privatization (Miller and Simmons, 1998).

1. Correspondence: In the first phase of the image, privatization is what it says it is, a movement to improve the efficiency and effectiveness of government.
2. Skepticism: In the second phase, privatization does not make things better; it makes things worse because of increased costs of contract oversight, increased incidences of corruption, and profiteering by corporate contractors.
3. Radical absence: In the third phase, privatization masks the absence of anything different taking place. "Private" practices transpire in much the same way as "public" practices. The way the work gets done changes not at all, although public expenditures continue to increase or decrease at the same rate as before.
4. Self-referential epiphenomenon: Finally, privatization is a simulation. Not representative of anything, privatization is a symbol that celebrates itself, its free market associations, and its businesslike imagery.

Exercise: Choose a public administration concept and try to describe it from the vantage point of each of the four phases of the image. Examples: Performance measurement; the budget; civil service reform; best practices; citizen participation.

2.5.3 Thought Experiments

1. Imagine a researcher entering an organizational culture to observe a subject with the intent of discerning the subject's understanding of appropriate conduct in this particular organizational setting. The researcher takes copious field notes to describe the subject's behaviors and utterances, including interview responses. Then, during the ongoing research project the subject decides to reflect to himself about his own sense of appropriate conduct in this particular organizational setting. The subject of the research is now studying the researcher for helpful clues about what the researcher's sense of appropriate conduct is.

Discussion question: Which inquiry is subjective and which is objective?

2. Thomas Hobbes' social contract theory imagines a state of nature in which we all have unlimited freedom. Among other freedoms, we can harm anyone we please. The result, says Hobbes, would be a war of all against all in which life is mean, brutish, and short. To avoid this calamitous scenario we agree with others to form a social contract whereby we all accept an obligation to respect one another's rights, give up some freedoms, and hand over power to a sovereign state.

   Discussion question: Hobbes' Leviathan was published in 1651. Despite being inspired by a warring English civil society, the main tenants of this theory (especially the social contract itself) were not based on empirical reality. Speculate on the role that social contract theory might have had on subsequent social reality.

3. Suppose that wireless technology was perfected to the point that your brain could be placed for safe keeping in a large pickle jar in your house, while your body went out and experienced the real world, communicating with your brain via wireless technology everything that went on.

   Discussion question: Assuming perfect signal strength, should your brain in the pickle jar trust your body for correct sensory inputs?

4. Bertrand Russell (1952), a famous atheist who nonetheless referred to himself as an agnostic, once wrote, "If I were to suggest that between the Earth and Mars there is a china teapot revolving about the sun in an elliptical orbit, nobody would be able to disprove my assertion provided I were careful to add that the teapot is too small to be revealed even by our most powerful telescopes." In other words, Russell would agree that just because one cannot find a needle in the haystack (or find God) does not mean there is *not* a needle in the haystack (or a God). His logic would not permit absolute disbelief.

Karl Popper (1959) would recognize this as a problem of falsifiability. For a statement to be scientifically meaningful, it should be empirically testable. The empirical test should be such that the statement could be disproved were it a false statement. Statements that are not potentially falsifiable through an empirical test do not contribute to science, according to Popper.

Conspiracy theories, which usually posit the existence of some behind-the-scene alliance of powerful people as the causal determinant of some social bad, often contain non-verifiable elements such as secret meetings, coded messages, or killings disguised as accidental deaths.

Discussion: There may exist a range of phenomena that is outside the reach of empirical verification. Speculate on what kinds of things may be in that range and whether they should count as knowledge.

REFERENCES

Argyris, C. and Schön, D.A. 1974. *Theory in Practice: Increasing Professional Effectiveness*. San Francisco: Jossey-Bass Publishers.
Baudrillard, J. 1994. *Simulacra and Simulation*. Ann Arbor: University of Michigan Press.
Davidson, D. 1984. *Inquiries into Truth and Interpretation*. Oxford: Clarendon Press.
Gould, S.J. 1996. *The Mismeasure of Man*. New York: W.W. Norton & Company.
Isbell, L.A. 2006. Snakes on the brain. *New York Times*. September 3, Section 4, p. 10.
Kuhn, T. 1970. *The Structure of Scientific Revolutions* (2nd. ed.) Chicago: University of Chicago Press.
Miller, H.T. and Fox, J.F. 2007. *Postmodern Public Administration: Revised Edition*. Armonk, New York: M.E. Sharpe.
Miller, H.T. and Simmons, J.R. 1998. The irony of privatization. *Administration & Society*. 30 (5): 513–532.
Popper, K.R. 1959. *The Logic of Scientific Discovery*. New York: Basic Books.
Rein, M. 1976. *Social Science & Public Policy*. New York: Penguin Books.

Roethlisberger, F.J. 1967. *Management and the Worker; An account of a Research Program Conducted by Western Electric Company, Hawthorne Works, Chicago.* New York: Wiley.

Rorty, R. 1991. *Essays on Heidegger and Others, Philosophical Papers Volume 2.* New York: Cambridge University Press.

Russell, B. 1952. Is There a God? commissioned by, but never published in, Illustrated Magazine (1968 Reprinted in *The Collected Papers of Bertrand Russell, Volume 11: Last Philosophical Testament, 1943–1968,* ed. John G. Slater and Peter Köllner (London: Routledge, 1997), pp. 543–548, quoted from S.T. Joshi, *Atheism: A Reader.* Downloaded August 30, 2006 from http://www.positiveatheism. org/hist/quotes/russell.htm.)

Spearman, C. 1904. General intelligence objectively determined and measured. *American Journal of Psychology.* 15: 201–293.

3 Dealing with Multiple Paradigms in Public Administration Research

Kaifeng Yang, Yahong Zhang, and Marc Holzer

CONTENTS

Many scholars agree that public administration lacks a governing paradigmatic base (Rainey, 1994; Riccucci, chapter 1 of this volume). Many would also agree that seeking and imposing a narrowly conceived paradigm may do more harm than good to the field by excluding viable, emerging alternatives (Frederickson and Smith, 2003; Rainey, 1994). In particular, public administration is both interdisciplinary and applied, so "no theory standing alone is capable of accounting for the complexity of the field" (Frederickson and Smith, 2003, p. 4).

The term "paradigm" is frequently used as a view of reality and an intellectual framework that specifies a discipline's proper domain, basic assumptions, appropriate research questions, and rules of inference (Arndt, 1985; Morgan, 1980). Paradigms are broadly equated with perspectives and theoretical lenses through which people perceive different pictures of the same world. In this sense, public administration does have a number of "great ideas," "clusters," or paradigms (Holzer, Gabrielian and Yang, 2006; Lan and Anders, 2000; Rainey, 1994). A paradigm mentality that strives for a dominant framework is unhealthy for a practical field such as public administration, but "letting a hundred flowers bloom" without knowing the family lineage of the flowers is equally problematic. If one is unaware of the differences and similarities among the flowers, he or she cannot fully appreciate the variety, nor could he or she treat every flower appropriately and make all of them bloom. The development of a scholarly discipline will benefit only "if clusters of researchers work together on similar research questions in similar ways, in constructive competition and communication with other such clusters" (Rainey, 1994). Theory development will be facilitated if public administration researchers are conscious about and readily reveal the theoretical lenses they use in their studies, as well as the assumptions, advantages, and disadvantages of the lenses. Although public administration theories are cumulative, useful, and increasingly sophisticated and reliable (Frederickson and Smith, 2003), their scientific rigor, theoretical or methodological, has long been lamented by scholars (Kettl, 2000; March, 1997; Whicker, Strickland and Olshfski, 1993). A better understanding of paradigms can help us design stronger studies and develop more practical and relevant solutions to the problems faced by society.

In this chapter, we treat the term "paradigm" in a broad sense to represent research clusters or theoretical lenses that share similar philosophies, focused problems, and approaches of inquiry. As Babbie (2005) states, "social science paradigms represent a variety of views, each of which offers insights the others lack while ignoring aspects of social life that the others reveal" (p. 34). We attempt to show how public administration students can benefit from the existence of multiple, conflicting paradigms in their own research. We begin with a brief introduction of the major categorizations of public administration paradigms, and continue with discussions as to how multiple paradigms can be bridged or connected in a research project. To better illustrate how our approach to paradigm dynamics helps improve public administration research, we use examples to demonstrate how to link the existence of multiple paradigms with the typical research process.

3.1 PARADIGMS IN PUBLIC ADMINISTRATION

Depending on the definition of paradigm, there are various categorizations. Social science, where public administration is usually located, is characterized by some general paradigms that represent different ways of looking at human social life. For example, Babbie (2005) identifies six major perspectives: early positivism (e.g., Auguste Comte), conflict paradigm (e.g., Karl Marx), symbolic interactionism (e.g., George Herbert Mead), ethnomethodology (e.g., Harold Garfinkel), structural functionalism (e.g., Talcott Parsons), and feminist paradigms (e.g., Simone de Beauvoir). This categorization is made at the metatheoretical level based on ontological and epistemological concerns. Similarly, Morgan's (1980) classification, which is very influential in management and organizational theory, includes four sociological paradigms: functionalism, radical structuralism, interpretivism, and radical humanism (see also Burrell and Morgan, 1979). This classification has been applied in research areas such as marketing (Arndt, 1985) and organizational culture (Martin, 1992). Although its assumption that paradigms are incompatible is rejected by many later writers, the use of ontology and epistemology to identify and differentiate paradigms is widely accepted (e.g., Gioia and Pitre, 1990; Lewis and Grimes, 1999; Schultz and Hatch, 1996).

The categorization in the business literature above is useful for public administration as well. In particular, organizational theory is an important research area for both business and public administration. From this perspective, the two disciplines share historical origins, key constructs, influential authors, and research approaches. More generally, since the 1970s, there has been a growth of postmodern, interpretive, critical, and feminist analysis of public administration (Fox and Miller, 1995; Stivers, 2002). Postmodern approaches have expanded our understanding of the complex public administration phenomena, although they often cause frustration for researchers who are concerned about the practical relevance of public administration. Indeed, applying a framework similar to Morgan's (1980) may help public administration researchers generate alternative understandings.

However, public administration resists clear classification due to its multidisciplinary nature (Holzer et al., 2006), and the major debates in specific public administration areas (e.g., budgeting, performance management, etc.) are often not organized around these metatheoretical distinctions. For example, PPBS (planning, programming, and budgeting system), ZBB (zero-based budgeting), and PBB (performance-based budgeting) may be viewed as three budgeting paradigms. In institutional analysis, the sociological view and the economic view may be considered two distinctive paradigms (Lewis and Grimes, 1999). Therefore, we further relax the definition of paradigm and include different schools of thought based on epistemological and methodological considerations.

Schools of thought are metaphors or foundations of inquiry (Morgan, 1980). For example, in his best-selling book, Morgan (1997) identifies eight metaphors in organization studies that view organizations as machines, organisms, brains, cultures, political systems, psychic prisons, flux, and transformation, and instruments of domination. He emphasizes that "all theories of organization and management are based on implicit images or metaphors that lead us to see, understand, and manage organizations in distinctive yet partial ways" (p. 4). A similar perspective is developed in the public administration literature by Lan and Anders (2000), who argue that public administration as a whole is a tier-one, paramount paradigm, under which there are at least six subparadigms or cognitive approaches: managerial, political, judicial, ethical, historical, and integrated. Under those approaches are different sub-subparadigms or areas of concentrations such as personnel management, finance and budgeting, and policy analysis and design. The six approaches can be summarized as in Table 3.1. The first three approaches are also identified and emphasized by other scholars such as Rosenbloom and Kravchuk (2005), who demonstrate clearly how the three perspectives differ with regard to values, cognitive approaches, and understanding of organizational structure, individuals, budgeting, decision making, and governmental function.

Each school of thought can be dealt with from different metatheoretical stances. For example, the concerns of the managerial approach can be analyzed from the stances of either functionalism or postmodernism. Moreover, depending on its focuses, the managerial approach can be further classified into different models. For example, Quinn and Rohrbaugh (1983) constructed a two-dimensional competing-values framework (flexibility versus control; internal versus external) that includes four models: open systems, rational goals, human relations, and internal processes. Quinn and Rohrbaugh (1983) argue that these models are to some extent mutually exclusive because they are conceptually distinctive and managers should not pay equal attention to all of them at a single time. These models are also complementary because managers must strike a balance between them, and should not emphasize one model to the exclusion of the others in a longer period. Such holistic approaches have been in the mainstream of organizational thought since at least the mid-1970s, when the public productivity movement was launched to synthesize different schools of management (Holzer et al., 2006).

Frederickson (1980), for example, recognizes five models of public administration based on a definition of theory as empirically based knowledge: classic bureaucratic (Gulick and Urwick), neo-bureaucratic (Simon), institutional (Lindblom), human relations (McGregor), and public choice (Ostrom). He argues for a sixth one, the "new public administration," which places a greater emphasis on humanistic, equitable, and democratic values, as opposed to the previous ones that focused primarily on efficiency and effectiveness. Later on, Frederickson and Smith (2003) systematically review the theories' origins, assumptions, arguments, and implications, identifying eight contemporary families of theories that have contributed significantly to the body of knowledge in public administration or have the potential to make such contributions: theories of political control of bureaucracy, theories of bureaucratic politics, theories of public institutions, theories of public management, postmodern theory, decision theory, rational choice theory, and theories of governance. Moreover, they compare the theories' performance on six dimensions: parsimony or elegance, explanatory capacity, replicability, descriptive capacity, predictive capacity, and empirical warrant.

There are other categorizations of schools of thought in public administration. Stillman (1995) identified six schools of the "refounding public administration" movement developed since the 1970s: (1) the reinventors—an eclectic approach catalyzed by Osborne and Gaebler (1992); (2) the communitarians—with emphasis on citizenship, family values, and civic participation; (3) the Blacksburg Manifesto refounders—who try to extend the meaning of public administration from mere management of public organizations to a larger and more legitimate understanding of it as a part of governance; (4) the interpretive theorists and postmodernists—with emphasis on the human condition in a society dominated by organizations; (5) the tools approach—with a leading theme that today, with the burgeoning of the not-for-profit sector in delivery of public services, there is no one best way of approaching the administration of services, even at the federal level; and (6) the new bureaucratic perspectives—with the main emphasis on bureaucratic accountability in a constitutional democracy (Holzer et al., 2006).

TABLE 3.1
Six Approaches to Public Administration Studies

	Managerial	Political	Judicial	Ethical	Historical	Integrated
Values/focuses	• Efficiency • Effectiveness • Economy	• Representation • Responsiveness • Accountability	• Legal rights • Legal privilege • Due process • Equity	• Morality • Ethics • Integrity	• Lessons from past	• Process of governing • Democratic values
Unit of analysis	• Individuals • Groups • Org. structures • Org. processes	• Individuals • Groups • Communities • Political institutions (structures and processes)	• Regulations • Laws • Legal processes	• Ethical procedures • Ethical standards	• Historical literature • Individuals events	• Anything relevant to governing
Core problems	• How to improve efficiency, effectiveness, and economy?	• How to achieve power and resource allocation?	• How to settle conflicts and achieve compliance?	• How to improve the substance and ethics of administration and society?	• How not to repeat past mistakes?	• How to understand and enhance public administration in a holistic way

Sources: Adapted from Lan, Z. and Anders, K.K., *Adm. Soc.*, 32, 138, 2000; Rosenbloom, D.H. and Kravchuk, R.S. in *Public Administration* (6th edn), McGraw Hill, New York, 2005.

Holzer, Gabrielian, and Yang (2006) argue that given the applied nature of public administration, it is important to discuss theories and ideas "not only from the viewpoint of their theoretical distinctiveness and rigor, but also from the viewpoint of their impact on the development of the field, the rhetoric that justified their embrace by the public, and the factors that shaped them" (p. 57). Accordingly, they outline five great ideas that shaped the field of public administration. The first idea is honest, nonpartisan, and businesslike government. This stream of thought was manifested in the progressive movement, which not only separated administration from politics but also started the relentless drive of looking to the private sector for best practices. Under the dichotomy logic, administration became politically neutral, and the elected body took the responsibility for democratic achievement through the policy-making process.

The second idea refers to classic management models, which relate closely to the first idea both theoretically and temporarily. Starting with the politics–administration dichotomy and assuming a business-like approach, the second idea emphasized machine-like efficiency in "getting the job done." The first idea focused on the political question of the place of public administration in society, whereas the second idea concentrated on a micro-concern—effective management of an organization premised upon the idea of clearly recognizable and scientific laws that describe reality. It gave rise to a number of universal principles of administration such as POSDCORB (planning, organizing, staffing, directing, coordinating, reporting, and budgeting). When Wilson and White were calling for a science of management, Frederick Taylor was conducting time and motion studies, trying to find the "one best way" to improve productivity. Between the world wars, Taylor's methodology to efficiently accomplish physical tasks was increasingly applied to the organization in a broad social context (e.g., Gulick). Fayol (1949) extended the notion of scientific management to the public sector by indicating that the basic elements of administrative organization are specialization, authority, hierarchy, division of labor, communication, standard procedures of operations, and management; the combination of these elements and the relationships between them define the organizational structure of government. The types of organizations defined by scientific management theorists fit with Max Weber's (1958) bureaucratic model. Weber's "ideal-type" bureaucracy consists of these elements: universal rules, use of written records, division of duties into spheres of competence, training for each position, selection on the basis of competence, hierarchical arrangement of offices, salary based on position, and tenure of office. This model of bureaucracy was accepted throughout public administration circles as a significant advancement for understanding both the whole of bureaucracy and the elements of modern government.

The third idea is politics and policy making. In contrast to the first two ideas, this idea rejected the politics–administration dichotomy, the administrative principles as proverbs, and the absolute neutrality of administrators, arguing that a theory of administration is necessarily a theory of politics. After World War II, a major trend in public administration has been the movement away from the idea of administrative neutrality and toward the idea of bureaucratic politics, which led to big research questions such as the following (Frederickson and Smith, 2003; Holzer et al., 2006): (1) To what extent do administrative processes, as opposed to democratic processes, determine public policy? (2) What is the role of bureaucratic power in representing and advancing the goals of particular clientele groups or organized interests? (3) How can an administrative body organized on nondemocratic lines be consistent with the notion of a democratic society? (4) How can a bureaucracy balance representativeness and administrative capacity? (5) How can the democratic system balance administrative capacity and its democratic control? Dwight Waldo, Paul Appleby, Philip Selznick, Graham Allison, Herbert Kaufman, George Frederickson, Kenneth Meier, Laurence Lynn, and Harold Seidman, among others, have contributed to the theory development of bureaucratic politics by addressing the questions above.

The fourth school of thought is human relations, which was formed following the Hawthorne experiments and the introduction of a sociological approach to organizations in the late 1920s and 1930s. The first two models were closed and concentrated primarily on a technical system of

organization, whereas the behavioral model recognized the equal importance of the social system—
a system comprised of informal, multidimensional, and nebulous networks of relationships between
individuals or groups within an organization. The research team of the well-known Hawthorne
experiments, via field research methodology, accidentally found that organizations serve the
purpose of "creating and distributing satisfaction among the individual members of the organization," in addition to creating goods or services (Roethlisberger and Dickson, 1939, p. 562). The
Hawthorne conclusions were reaffirmed in Chester Barnard's work. Frameworks such as the needs
hierarchy (Maslow), Theory X and Y (McGregor), the need for achievement (McClelland), equity
(Adams), expectancy theory (Vroom), and goal-setting (Locke and Latham) have been adopted and
extended by many public administration scholars to develop empirical hypotheses about a central
question, that is, why bureaucrats do what they do. For example, Wilson (1989) argues that several
factors drive the behavior of bureaucrats and bureaucracies: situational imperatives, peer expectations, professional values, and ideology. Wilson concluded that successful bureaucracies are those
in which executives have created a clear sense of mission, identified the tasks that must be achieved
to fulfill that mission, distributed authority within the organization according to those tasks, and
provided subordinates with enough autonomy to achieve the tasks at hand.

The fifth idea identified by Holzer, Gabrielian, and Yang (2006) is program effectiveness or
performance. As a result of growth of government programs with new missions, combined with the
rapid technological and demographic changes experienced since the turn of the twentieth century,
and, the shrinking of public resources, the effectiveness or performance of public organizations has
become a primary concern of public administration. By and large public administration began to view
itself as a synthetic field, one that has to balance competing, often contradictory, values and which is
open to continuous adaptation and improvement in pursuit of productive performance. This idea can
be related to the productivity movement, performance measurement, program evaluation, and even
governance. For example, Lynn, Heinrich, and Hill (2000) present a model of governance logic as
$O = f$ [E, C, T, S, M], where $O =$ outputs/outcomes; $E =$ environmental factors such as political
structures, levels of authority, funding constraints, legal institutions, and technological dynamism;
$C =$ client characteristics; $T =$ treatments or the primary work or core processes of the organizations
such as missions, objectives, and technologies; $S =$ structures such as organizational type, level
of coordination and integration, centralization of control, functional differentiation, administrative
rules and incentives, budgetary allocations, contractual arrangements, and institutional culture and
values; and $M =$ managerial roles and actions such as leadership characteristics, staff-management
relations, communications, decision-making tools, professionalism/career concerns, mechanisms of
monitoring, control, and accountability.

3.2 DEALING WITH MULTIPLE PARADIGMS

How should researchers deal with the existence of multiple paradigms? Although public administration scholars have realized that the discipline does not have a dominant paradigm and acknowledged the benefits of alternative theoretical perspectives, few have written about how to conduct
multiparadigm inquiry. In this chapter, we borrow from the organizational theory studies and
introduce the ways in which organizational theory scholars have written about multiparadigm
inquiry. As Pondy and Boje (1981) warned more than two decades ago, organizational theory
has increasingly faced a frontier problem of "how to conduct inquiry based on several paradigms"
(p. 84). Strategies such as metatriangulation (Gioia and Pitre, 1990), multiparadigm inquiry
(Lewis and Grimes, 1999), and paradigm interplay (Schultz and Hatch, 1996) have been proposed
to help researchers deal with the multiparadigm reality.

At least four types of stances can be identified with regard to the relationship between
competing paradigms, as shown in Figure 3.1. The first stance assumes incommensurability
between paradigms, as reflected in the strict Kuhnian conception that views the advancement of
science as a linear revolutionary process in which newer paradigms replace older paradigms.

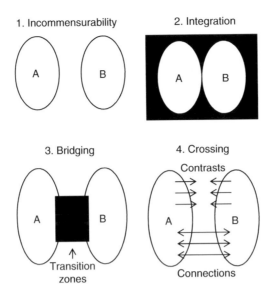

FIGURE 3.1 Four stances in dealing with competing paradigms.

Paradigms, thus seen, are radically or fundamentally different. In a multiparadigm reality, however, the first stance does not suggest a linear revolutionary process. Rather, it simply presumes that it is impossible or nearly impossible to communicate effectively between adherents to different paradigms. Therefore, although different paradigms help advance our understanding of the same phenomenon, these paradigms can only be separately developed and applied (Burrell and Morgan, 1979; Jackson and Carter, 1993).

Assuming incommensurability or nonpermeability, there are two analytical strategies that can be adopted. One strategy is sequential, where paradigms are applied one after another in a project. Paradigms are considered different but mutually complementary, rather than exclusive. Therefore, they are used sequentially as complements to reveal sequential levels of understanding within an integrated research project, enabling one paradigm to inform another (Schultz and Hatch, 1996). The influence between the paradigms, however, operates in one direction in a linear fashion: findings from one paradigm are recontextualized and reinterpreted in such a way that they inform the research from a different paradigm. Another strategy is parallel, where paradigms are applied on equal terms rather than sequentially. This strategy is usually used to emphasize differences and conflicts between paradigms rather than similarities. For example, Martin (1992) applies each of Burrell and Morgan's four paradigms separately to organizational culture research.

The second stance is an extreme opposite of the first. It assumes that there are no irresolvable tensions between paradigms, which can be integrated and submerged into a new paradigm (Reed, 1985; Willmott, 1993). In the process of constructing this new paradigm, researchers assess and synthesize a variety of contributions from competing paradigms, and ignore their differences. The old paradigms become part of the new comprehensive paradigm.

The third and fourth stances are positioned in between the first and the second ones. They agree on the assumption that paradigms are fundamentally different but nevertheless can be connected. In other words, the boundaries are permeable. The difference between the third and the fourth is that the third one, bridging, focuses on the transition zones between paradigms. As Gioia and Pitre (1990) argue, paradigms are not completely isolated because there are transition zones between paradigms. Within these transition zones, second-order theoretical concepts such as structuration (Giddens, 1976), negotiated order (Strauss, 1978), and organizing (Weick, 1979) can be used to bridge the paradigms. In comparison, the fourth stance, interplay, does not rely on those second-order theoretical concepts, nor does it conceptualize a transition zone. Instead, it argues that researchers should move back and forth between paradigms so that multiple views are held in tension. Contrasts and connections exist simultaneously between paradigms, and the tension between them should be maintained because oppositions are always defined in terms of one another (Schultz and Hatch, 1996).

For example, functionalism and interpretivism are two of the four paradigms identified by Burrell and Morgan (1979). The two perspectives have led to very different theories and arguments in organizational studies, such as those pertaining to organizational culture (Martin, 1992). Schultz and Hatch (1996, pp. 537–540) demonstrate that there are both contrasts and connections between functionalism and interpretivism in organizational culture studies.

Contrasts

- Analytical framework
  - Functionalism: the framework is predefined and universal, assuming that similar levels and functions of culture exist in all organizations.
  - Interpretivism: the framework is emergent and specific, assuming that opportunities for creation of meaning are unique to each cultural context.
- Model of analysis
  - Functionalism: categorical. Identifying cultural elements and discovering causal relations between them.
  - Interpretivism: associative. Constructing meanings and exploring the associations between them.
- Analytical process
  - Functionalism: convergent. Condensing and bringing elements of cultural analysis together.
  - Interpretivism: divergent. Expanding and enriching cultural analysis.

Connections

- Culture as pattern
  - Functionalism: culture as a pattern of values or basic assumptions.
  - Interpretivism: culture as a worldview or webs of significance.
- Culture as essence
  - Functionalism: discovering the deep level of culture makes it possible to decipher visible and espoused levels of culture.
  - Interpretivism: interpreting the symbolic expressions and representations of deep layers of meaning.
- Culture as static
  - Functionalism: predictable, linear, deterministic stage of development.
  - Interpretivism: interrelated, circular relations between interpretations and meaning.

Indeed, attending to both contrasts and connections may help advance public administration researchers' understanding of social phenomena. For example, the major thrust of the postwar (World War II) criticism came from a debate between those seeking to create a social science focusing on administration and those committed to a normative agenda for the field of public administration. Herbert Simon and Dwight Waldo were the two representatives of the debate. Simon (1947) preferred a logical positivist approach and argued that public administration should focus on facts and become a value-free science. Taking an opposing position, Waldo (1946) strived for development of a democratic theory of public administration, believing that public administration must give priority to the values of the democratic society, to normative theories rather than empirical theories advocated by logical positivists. The debate indicated that the prewar orthodoxy came under scrutiny (Dubnick, 1999), and the public administration field split into at least two largely different themes after World War II. One is Simon's tradition focusing on scientific management of public administration; the other is Waldo's tradition arguing for a normative agenda for democratic theory of public administration. By the 1960s, administrative sciences had developed into the scholarly extension of businesslike administration and organizational studies. Following Waldo, the theory of bureaucratic politics has been developed.

The relative detachment between the positivist approach and the normative approach reflects, to some extent, the Type-1 situation in Figure 3.1 (incommensurability). This detachment, although understandable and reasonable, was a partial reason for the lack of methodological rigor in many public administration studies. As a remedy, recent public management studies have emphasized linking public administration more closely to other disciplines such as political science and business administration (Moynihan and Pandey, 2005; Pandey and Wright, 2006; Whicker, Strickland and Olshfski, 1993), which have more developed positivist or functionalist frameworks. Whicker Strickland and Olshfski (1993) in arguing why public administration should remain aligned with political science, point out that in several decades public administration was largely nonempirical, unquantitative, and unscientific, despite its quantitative roots in scientific management (see also Kraemer and Perry, 1989). Recent studies show that the distance between normative theories and positivist theories are not insurmountable. For example, administrative discretion has largely been a descriptive and normative term in public administration literature, which has been concerned with questions such as whether more discretion should be granted to competent civil servants to produce more coherent policy making and what appropriate strategies to maintain both discretion and accountability. Huber and Shipan (2002) show, however, that a positivist theory of administrative discretion can and should be developed. They use the length of legislation as a viable dependent variable and demonstrate how policy conflict, bargaining environment, legislative capacity, and other nonstatutory factors determine the level of discretion in the area of Medicaid and medical assistance among state governments.

Lewis and Grimes (1999) provide a more operational guideline about multiparadigm inquiry. They emphasize paradigms as heuristics that help scholars explore theoretical and organizational complexity and extend the scope, relevance, and creativity of organizational theory. On the basis of a solid review of empirical organizational studies that included multiple paradigms, Lewis and Grimes identify three multiparadigm approaches. The first approach is a multiparadigm review, which emphasizes revealing the impact of theorists' underlying, and often taken-for-granted, assumptions on their understandings of phenomena. At least two techniques are associated with this approach: bracketing, which is to make different assumptions explicit and delineating paradigm distinctions (Burrell and Morgan, 1979), and bridging, which concentrates on transition zones that span paradigms (Gioia and Pitre, 1990). The second approach is multiparadigm research, which includes two techniques: sequential and parallel. The third approach is multiparadigm theory building, which can be realized by either metatheorizing or paradigm interplay. Metatheorizing refers to bridging as recommended by Gioia and Pitre (1990). This technique explores patterns that span conflicting paradigms treated as debating voices that deliver partial truth respectively. By juxtaposing paradigmatic explanations, the constructs of interest are translated to a metaparadigm level, and a theoretical reference system that links contrasting perspectives is developed (Gioia and Pitre, 1990). Paradigm interplay, in comparison, stresses the importance of recognizing both the similarities and differences between paradigms, emphasizing that paradigmatic insights and biases are most recognizable from opposing views.

Moreover, Lewis and Grimes (1999) detail the theory-building processes of metatriangulation, comparing it with the traditional induction process based on a single paradigm. The single-paradigm induction process of theory building is classified as including three phases: groundwork, data analysis, and theory building. The first phase, groundwork, further includes three substages:

specification of research question, review of relevant literature, and choice of data source. The second phase, data analysis, also contains three substages: design of analytical process, coding, tabulation, or exhibition of analyses. The final phase, theory building, has three substages as well: development and test of propositions, theory development, and evaluation of resulting theory. For each of the nine substages, Lewis and Grimes (1999) propose corresponding inductive activities that are based on multiple paradigms. The purpose of these activities is outlined; the activities are exemplified and applied to the study of advanced manufacturing technology (AMT).

3.3 TAKING ADVANTAGE OF MULTIPLE PARADIGMS IN PUBLIC ADMINISTRATION RESEARCH

In the following section, we discuss how public administration researchers can take advantage of multiple paradigms and conduct better research. We relate multiparadigm inquiry to the common quantitative research process: specifying research questions, reviewing literature, developing hypotheses, choosing methodology, and interpreting results (see Table 3.2). The discussions are based on the literature on multiparadigm inquiry in the area of organizational studies that are briefly summarized in the section above. We take the "crossing" or "interplay" stance (Type 4 in Figure 3.1) and assume that paradigms or major theoretical perspectives have both differences and linkages. However, we detach the analytical techniques from the four approaches in Figure 3.1. For example, sequential and parallel are two techniques used in the Type 1 approach in Figure 3.1, but they can also be used in the Type-4 approach. It must be stated here that we are not arguing that studies based on a single paradigm are less valuable. Advancement of specific paradigms can lead to advancement of multiparadigm research. We aim to address a practical question: how the existence of multiple paradigms might affect the common research process based on a single paradigm?

TABLE 3.2

Multiparadigm Studies and Common Quantitative Research Process

Research Processes	Multiparadigm Studies	Purpose
Research question	• Define phenomenon of interest instead of a narrow research question	Provide focus, but retain interpretative flexibility
Literature review	• Identify literature in different paradigms Bracketing or bridging the literatures • Evaluate the literatures from a multiparadigm perspective	Gain multiparadigm understanding and cognizance of home paradigm
Hypotheses	• Realize paradigmatic assumptions of the hypotheses • Use competing or complementary hypotheses based on different paradigms	Develop balanced hypotheses to fully examine the phenomenon
Methodology	• Collect data via multiple sources so that multiple paradigms can be examined • Design plans that use paradigms sequentially or in parallel • Multiparadigm coding when necessary	Design research that can use or test multiple paradigms
Results	• Interpret results from multiple perspectives	Make unbiased interpretation of the results

Source: Adapted from Lewis, M.W. and Grimes, A.J., *Acad. Manag. Rev.*, 24, 672, 1999.

3.3.1 RESEARCH QUESTION

Transforming broad topics to researchable questions is a starting point for most quantitative studies. An original research question is the foundation of the house of inquiry. A good and significant question should have the potential to contribute to knowledge and theory development, as well as managerial and policy practices. It is not surprising to see that most social science studies anchor their research question to a single paradigm, reflecting what Morgan (1980) calls puzzle-solving activities that "seek to operationalize the detailed implications of the metaphor defining a particular school of thought." Such activities, as Kuhn (1962) sees it, are characteristic of "normal science" where the legitimacy of a question depends on whether it fits or contributes to the dominant paradigm. In a postnormal science with competing paradigms, the legitimacy of the question may vary across paradigms. As a result, rather than defining the research question from a narrow perspective based on a single paradigm, multiparadigm inquiry concentrates on defining the phenomenon of interest so that interpretative flexibility can be enabled. This is particularly important for public administration as an applied field where helping understand and improve administrative performance regardless of theoretical perspectives is, at the very least, as important as validating or extending a single perspective.

For example, the issue regarding the performance of public service networks can be approached in different ways. A comprehensive list of factors that may help explain such performance can be identified such as the informal relational structure of the network (e.g., centrality and density), institutional arrangements (e.g., performance monitoring and oversight rules), network stability (e.g., network participant stability and personnel stability), network learning, social capital, managerial strategies (e.g., networking and managing upwards and outwards), and network contexts (e.g., resources and environments). It would be nice if all those aspects could be included and tested in a comprehensive model, but public administration scholars are often constrained in their ability to conduct such a large-scale project. Depending on their theoretical perspectives, they may narrow the topic in different ways. A positivist researcher who is more interested in examining the effects of managerial strategies would probably use network contexts as control variables, assuming that public managers can deliberately choose among alternative strategies based on rational calculations (e.g., Agranoff and McGuire, 2003; O'Toole and Meier, 1999). An interpretivist researcher, in comparison, would probably take network contexts more seriously, adopt qualitative designs, and examine the contexts affecting the emergence of managerial strategies and the social construction of performance (e.g., Granovetter, 1985). In the words of Berry et al. (2004), the contexts can be treated "not as noise that is incidental to the purposes of the network, but as everyday sources of meaning that guide and define the actions of the participants" (p. 549). These two lines of research, of course, can be integrated into a larger project. Public administration researchers need to be aware of the fact that how a question should be defined depends on their paradigmatic assumptions. When it is feasible, asking several questions from different perspectives would help us gain a more complete understanding of the phenomenon of interest.

Again, it is worth acknowledging that framing research questions from a multiparadigm perspective is not always more preferable than from a single-paradigm perspective. The background and purpose of the research matter in the choice. Nevertheless, one should remember that paradigmatic assumptions determine the big questions one thinks worth pursuing. For example, from the traditional managerial perspective that focused on organizational and behavioral analysis (the first model in Table 3.1 or the Ideas II and IV in Holzer, Gabrielian, and Yang (2006)), Behn (1995) identifies three big questions of public management: How can public managers break the micromanagement cycle? How can public managers motivate people? How can public managers measure achievement? In comparison, Neumann (1996) starts with the open systems theory and specifies three different big questions: What is the nature of a "public" organization? How is the public organization related to its environment? What does it mean to manage or to administer the public organization? Taking a different stance, Kirlin (1996) points out that Behn's argument is rooted in the managerial perspective of public administration and it ignores other perspectives including the political and legal ones (see Table 3.1). Rooted instead in a perspective of democratic polity, Kirlin (1996) puts forward seven big questions:

- What are the instruments of collective action that remain responsible both to democratically elected officials and to core societal values?
- What are the roles of nongovernmental forms of collective action in society, and how can desired roles be protected and nurtured?
- What are the appropriate tradeoffs between governmental structures based on function (which commonly eases organizational tasks) and geography (which eases citizenship, political leadership, and societal leaning)?
- How shall tensions between national and local political arenas be resolved?
- What decisions shall be "isolated" from the normal processes of politics so that some other rationale can be applied?
- What balance shall be struck among neutral competence, representativeness and leadership?
- How can processes of societal learning be improved, including knowledge of choices available, of consequences of alternatives, and of how to achieve desired goals, most importantly, the nurturing and development of a democratic polity? (p. 417)

3.3.2 Literature Review

In multiparadigm inquiry, literature in different paradigms should be identified, compared, end evaluated. This is particularly useful when the researcher attempts to develop a new theory or perspective. For example, in explaining and advocating the New Public Administration (NPA), Frederickson (1980) reviewed five public administration models that can be viewed as paradigms as loosely defined: classic bureaucratic model, neobureaucratic model, institutional model, human relations model, and public choice model. He used a bracketing technique by showing how the five models are different in terms of their empirical focus, unit of analysis, characteristics, and values to be maximized. However, the review also addressed bridging among the models as they overlap in various ways. Both the classic bureaucratic model (e.g., Gulick and Urwick) and the neobureaucratic model (e.g., Simon and March) emphasize the value of efficiency and economy, although the latter pays specific attention to rationality and productivity. Both the neobureaucratic model and the institutional model (e.g., Downs, Lindbloom and Thompson) adopt the positivist perspective and focus on decision making, but they emphasize different values—the latter stresses incrementalism, pluralism, and criticism instead of rationality, efficiency and economy.

Moreover, in comparing New Public Administration with traditional public administration models, Frederickson (1980) uses a technique similar to "bridging" that attends to transition zones between paradigms. Frederickson considers the new public administration and traditional models as two extremes, in between which are transitional positions. For example, although traditional models advocate for "leadership by authority," the New Public Administration prescribes "leadership by change facilitation," and the transitional position indicates "leadership by consent" (p. 55). For traditional models, "the problem is basically one of reform or change"; for the New Public Administration, "the problem is one of institutionalizing change procedures"; and for the transitional position, "change and reorganization should be encouraged" (p. 55). The book also offers similar comparisons with regard to the nature of change, uncertainty, responsiveness, and the relationship between technology and politics. In another well-articulated study, Frederickson (1996) compares the reinventing government movement and the new public administration. He sees the similarities between the two movements in terms of management and organization: "Both movements have as their impetus the need for change. Both are committed to responsiveness but in different ways. In new public administration, it is a professional public service dedicated to both efficiency and social equity; in reinventing government, it is the empowerment of individual customers to make their own choices" (p. 269). In the meantime, he points out the two movements differ in significant ways. New Public Administration, in his view, is more concerned with issues of rationality, epistemology, methodology, institutions, and politics than reinvention is. In addition, the two movements have a sharp difference in the values they espouse. Although reinvention emphasizes individual choice, incentive structure, competition, and market, "new public administration is concerned more with humanistic and democratic administration, concerned more with institution building and professional competence, concerned more directly with issues of politics and with matters of justice and fairness—broadly under the label of social equity" (p. 269).

Another excellent example is provided by Denhardt and Denhardt (2000) in outlining a theory of new public service and comparing it to old public administration and New Public Management. Denhardt and Denhardt demonstrate clearly how the three perspectives differ with regard to ten aspects: primary theoretical and epistemological foundations; prevailing rationality and associated models of human behavior; conception of the public interest; targets of public service responsiveness; role of government; mechanisms for achieving policy objectives; approach to accountability; administrative discretion; assumed organizational structure; and assumed motivational basis of public servants and administrators. For instance, in old public administration, the role of government is rowing (designing and implementing policies focusing on a single, politically defined objective) and the approach to accountability is hierarchical (administrators are responsible to elected officials); in New Public Management, the role of government is steering (acting as a catalyst to unleash market forces) and the approach to accountability is market-driven (administrators are responsible to customers); and in new public service, the role of government is serving (negotiating and brokering interests among citizen and community groups, creating shared values) and the approach to accountability is multifaceted (administrators are responsible to law, community values, political norms, professional standards, and citizen interests).

Reviewing the literature as suggested above may be a difficult and arduous task because authors rarely state their paradigm and often make the choice unconsciously. As Berry et al. (2004) comment on network research, they identify three traditions rooted in different disciplines: social network analysis (sociology), policy networks (political science), and public management networks (public administration). They point out that "until the last few years, there has been relatively little cross-fertilization across the research traditions, and it is often unclear whether authors in each research stream have intentionally disregarded or are simply unaware of the complementary research streams" (p. 540). Multiparadigm inquiry requires researchers to evaluate publications carefully, attending specifically to the use of terms and metaphorical language in the publications (Willmott, 1993). This also suggests that it may be beneficial to the discipline if researchers could make conscious a choice about paradigms and then state it explicitly in their articles.

3.3.3 Hypotheses

With multiple paradigms available for use, researchers should make explicit the paradigmatic assumptions of their hypotheses. At the least, they should be aware of the assumptions and associated limitations even when it is clear that they are dealing with a single-paradigm study. Whenever feasible, it is also beneficial to use competing or complementary hypotheses based on different paradigms so that a more complete picture can be drawn about the phenomenon of interest. This can be applied not only to quantitative studies, but also to qualitative studies that include qualitative propositions.

One classic example is offered by Allison (1971) in explaining the Cuban Missile Crisis with three models of decision making, which are used as three hypotheses or propositions to be tested. The first model, rational actor, views government decisions as the product of a single actor in strategic pursuit of self-interest. This model supports hypotheses that are related to the problem, the alternatives, the strategic benefits and costs, shared values and axioms, and internal pressures. The second model, organizational process, conceptualizes decision making as highly structured through standard operating procedures (SOP). It relates to hypotheses that are directed to concepts such as organizational implementation, organizational options, incremental change, long-range planning, administrative feasibility, and directed change. The third model, bureaucratic politics, argues that government actions are the product of bargaining and compromise among political players. This model entails hypotheses that are related to concepts such as power, parochial priorities, rules of the game, action-channels, and stakes and stands. In drawing the conclusion, Allison hinted that future studies should explain decision making with multiple models and associated hypotheses because the models can complement each other: "The best analysts of foreign policy manage to weave stands of each of the three conceptual models into their explanations... By drawing complementary pieces from each of these styles of analysis, explanations can be significantly strengthened" (p. 259). In this view, Model II is embedded in Model I, as the former "fixes the broader context, the larger national patterns, and the shared images," whereas the latter "illuminates the organization routines that produce the information, alternatives, and action" (p. 258). Similarly, Model III can be seen as embedded in Model II, as Model III "focuses in greater detail on the individual leaders of a government and the politics among them that determine major governmental choices" (p. 258).

In empirical quantitative studies, researchers often include hypotheses derived from different schools of thought to improve their model's explanatory power without explicitly acknowledging or realizing the multiparadigm nature of the hypotheses development. For example, Quinn and Rohrbaugh's (1983) competing-values framework gives rise to four organizational culture types: rational culture (rational goal model), group culture (human relations model), developmental culture (open systems model), and hierarchical culture (internal process model). These four types of organizational culture are all included as independent variables by Moynihan and Pandey (2005) in assessing how environmental factors and organizational factors affect government performance. In addition to the culture variables, their model includes other variables that reflect different models of the competing-value framework such as goal clarity (rational goal model), centralization (internal process model), and elected official support of agency (open systems model). Another example is offered by Yang (2006) in examining the conditions under which public managers will honestly communicate performance measurement results to other stakeholders. Yang (2006) develops hypotheses that are based on two contrasting perspectives of bureaucratic behavior: agency theory and culture theory. More generally, scholars have borrowed a variety of perspectives and approaches from other disciplines to study behavior of bureaucrats and bureaucracies. These perspectives fall into at least two categories: the rational choice school of which agency theory is a part and the human relations school of which culture theory is a part. Any explanation of bureaucratic behavior will necessarily involve hypotheses from both schools of thought.

3.3.4 METHODOLOGY

Given a multiparadigm reality, researchers should realize that it may be beneficial to adopt a mixed methodology, to collect data via multiple sources, and to code the data from multiple perspectives. The argument for mixed methodology is not new in the public administration literature. Qualitative methods such as case study, ethnography, hermeneutics, action research, and grounded theory are usually associated with interpretivist or constructivist paradigms. Quantitative designs such as experiments, quasi-experiments, and cross-sectional designs are often associated with positivist paradigms. The debate of qualitative versus quantitative methods has evolved in a way that corresponds to what we depict in Figure 3.1. Taking the incommensurability position, the segregationists argue that quantitative and qualitative paradigms are incompatible due to their mutually exclusive epistemological and ontological assumptions. Therefore, using different methods will lead to essentially different observations of the same phenomenon. Taking the second position in Figure 3.1, the integrationists, however, reject the dichotomy between the quantitative and the qualitative, attempting to integrate both methodologies for the same study. The quantitative and qualitative methods will support each other and enhance the credibility of the research. Taking the third or the fourth position in Figure 3.1, the eclectics acknowledge the two approaches have distinct assumptions, but both are valid and the situation will dictate which one should be used or whether both should be used as complementary elements.

We contend that qualitative and quantitative designs are complementary. Researchers can use a parallel strategy, simultaneously applying both designs. This is particularly useful when researchers first develop or explore a new paradigm because the parallel strategy minimizes the chances of confusion between paradigms (Schultz and Hatch, 1996). Alternatively, they can take a sequential route, applying the two types of designs one after another. A common sequence is that one starts with objective paradigms and follows with subjective paradigms, obtaining generalizable overviews first and then seeking more localized meanings. For example, in studying whether and how training is provided to local government employees with regard to citizen participation, Callahan and Yang (2005) used a national survey to collect quantitative data. The survey analysis led to some interesting questions, so they decided to purposefully select ten jurisdictions for follow-up interviews based on the level of training they provided and the nature of the comments they made in their open-ended responses. They randomly selected five large and five small jurisdictions from a group of 49 jurisdictions that indicated in the survey that they provided a lot of training or developed partnerships with citizens. They then conducted telephone interviews with the city managers and coordinators of neighborhood relations programs. One can also reverse the order, seeking subjective understandings of a new topic first and then designing quantitative studies. This sequence is often assumed in quantitative studies, but authors rarely show whether they went though the arduous qualitative research process before testing the quantitative models.

Public administration may benefit greatly from more conscious efforts to apply multiple paradigms in a research project. Take performance measurement research for example. One stream of studies is functionalist, describing how performance measurement systems should be established and what factors affect their effectiveness (e.g., De Lancer Julnes and Holzer, 2001; Wang and Evan, 2000). Another stream is critical or postmodern, arguing that performance measurement is a control gimmick employed by politicians as a discourse that can be misused (Fox, 1996; Radin, 2000). It would advance performance measurement research if the two approaches can be more carefully aligned or even integrated. In organizational studies, it is not rare that one uses a functionalist paradigm to highlight managerialist understandings and then follows with more critical views to expose fragmentation and conflict (Martin, 1992). The sequence can be reversed to start with critical views followed by functionalist perspectives.

Paradigms relate to data collection and coding. As Lewis and Grimes (1999) contend, "choosing a source of data for multiparadigm inquiry is controversial, since the question of what constitutes data is paradigm laden (Gioia and Pitre, 1990). Managing this dilemma requires collecting a metatheoretical sample: data interpretable from multiple-paradigm perspectives" (p. 679). For example, Martin (1992) collected extensive and unstructured interview data about organizational culture, which were analyzed through divergent theoretical lenses. In the meantime, with multiple paradigms in mind one is more likely to "see" the data with greater analytical depth. Multiparadigm coding typically involves a two-stage process: becoming intimate with the data and then imposing alternative spins. During the first step, researchers take detailed notes, developing first impressions of nuances and patterns of the data. During the second step, researchers "read" the data via each paradigm, enabling construction of the different insights (Lewis and Grimes, 1999). The application of each paradigm is a reconstruction process and a recoding process.

3.3.5 RESULTS

With a richer understanding of various paradigms, a researcher is more likely to develop insightful analysis because he or she is more likely to capture certain features and subtleties in the data and to avoid oversimplified interpretations (Glaser and Strauss, 1967). As Lewis and Grimes (1999) suggest, researchers can "immerse themselves within alternative paradigms, track down patterns in the data, and create contrasting accounts of the phenomenon of interest" (p. 681). In so doing, the resulting accounts may help researchers to juxtapose paradigm interpretations and gain a complete understanding of a common empirical referent (Reed, 1997). A simple example is that a 50 percent number can be counted either as half full or half empty depending on one's point of view. For example, in a study of managerial perceptions of privatization in a state department of transportation, DeHart-Davis and Kingsley (2005) find that better relationships between managers and contractors lead to more favorable perceptions toward privatization. This observation can be interpreted in different ways. As DeHart-Davis and Kingsley (2005) write, the implications of the results can be specified in different ways depending on one's view of privatization. If one is deeply concerned with the negative impact of privatization on the integrity of public administration, then he or she "may warn that public managers can be 'captured' by contractors, much in the same way that regulators are captured by their regulated communities" (p. 239). However, if one is a diehard advocate for privatization, then he or she "may view these study results as information for improving managerial acceptance of privatization. The implications...may be couched as advice to public executives, e.g., 'building relationships between consultants and mangers'" (p. 239).

3.4 CONCLUSION

Public administration researchers face multiple competing paradigms, broadly defined, and they have to deal with this reality in their own research. These paradigms complement one another, providing both alternative and overlapping insights toward the phenomenon of interest. Together they constitute a substantial body of knowledge for public administration research. Public administration students should take a "both...and" stance toward these paradigms rather than an "either ...or" stance. The "both...and" stance, however, should not be taken at the extreme to mean a "hands off" policy. It is not rare that students pay little attention to paradigmatic assumptions of published articles and their own work. They may justify this neglect by arguing that public administration does not really have a paradigm and such a paradigm may not be necessary. This chapter argues that paying attention to paradigmatic assumptions is important for theory advancement and practical problem solving. As Schultz and Hatch (1996) state, "it is impossible and illusionary to settle the paradigm issue once and for all...but it is equally naïve to think organization theorists are ready to transcend the need for paradigms completely. Rather, researchers need paradigms (or some other orienting device) to maintain and make use of the diversity that characterizes the field of organization studies" (pp. 552–553).

Kettl (2000) asserts that American public administration is struggling with three questions, one of which is how public administration can "ensure the systematic testing of its theoretical propositions and, therefore, advance the state of theory" (p. 30). Public administration has long been criticized for a lack of rigor in theory and research. Kettl argues that the question is difficult to solve partly because of conflicting theoretical approaches and partly because of the difficulty of providing rigorous practical advice on practical problems that ultimately depend on infinitely variable individual behavior. This chapter argues that a better understanding of multiparadigm inquiry may help us improve the theoretical and methodological rigor of public administration research.

END-OF-CHAPTER QUESTIONS

1. Select an empirical article from a major public administration journal, such as *Public Administration Review* and *Journal of Public Administration Research and Theory*. After reading the article, please answer the following questions: (1) Is the theoretical framework clearly stated in

the article? What is it? (2) Are hypotheses derived naturally from the theoretical framework? Would other theories or approaches lead to the same hypotheses? Can other theories or approaches lead to additional hypotheses that complement the current ones? (3) What methodology is employed by the author? Can alternative methodologies enrich the understanding of the topic? (4) Are the findings and implications consistent with the data and results? Is it possible to interpret the results in different, even opposite, ways?

2. Find and read the Morgan (1980) article, and be familiar with its framework. Then choose a research area of your interest, such as contracting, performance management, and leadership, and answer the following question based on your review of the literature in the research area: (1) Are all the four paradigms specified by Morgan reflected in the literature in this area of research? (2) If one or more paradigms are missing from the literature, what might be the reason? Can you think of meaningful ways to apply the missing paradigms to this area of research? (3) If one or more paradigms have been developed in the literature, are there any syntheses? If not, can you develop one?

REFERENCES

Agranoff, R. and McGuire, M. 2003. *Collaborative Public Management: New Strategies for Local Governments*. Washington, DC: Georgetown University Press.

Allison, G.T. 1971. *Essence of Decision*. Boston: Little Brown.

Arndt, J. 1985. On making marketing science more scientific: Role of orientations, paradigms, metaphors, and puzzle solving. *Journal of Marketing* 49(3), 11–23.

Babbie, E.B. 2005. *The Basics of Social Research*. Belmont, California: Wadsworth.

Behn, R.D. 1995. The big questions of public management. *Public Administration Review* 55(July/August), 313–324.

Berry, F.S., Brower, R.S., Choi, S.O., Gao, W.X., Jang, H., Kwan, M., and Word, J. 2004. Three traditions of network research: What the public management research agenda can learn from other research communities. *Public Administration Review* 64(5), 539–552.

Burrell, G. and Morgan, G. 1979. *Sociological Paradigms and Organizational Analysis*. Portsmouth, NH: Heinemann.

Callahan, K. and Yang, K. 2005. Training and professional development for civically engaged communities. *Innovation Journal* 10(1), 1–16.

DeHart-Davis, L. and Kingsley, G. 2005. Managerial perceptions of privatization: Evidence from a state department of transportation. *State and Local Government Review* 37(3), 228–241.

De Lancer Julnes, P. and Holzer, M. 2001. Promoting the utilization of performance measures in public organizations: An empirical study of factors affecting adoption and implementation. *Public Administration Review* 61(6), 693–708.

Denhardt, R.B. and Denhardt, J.V. 2000. The new public service: Serving rather than steering. *Public Administration Review* 60(6), 549–559.

Dubnick, M. 1999. Demons, spirits, and elephants: Reflections on the failure of public administration theory. Prepared for delivery at *The 1999 Annual Meeting of American Political Science Association, Atlanta*.

Fayol, H. 1949. *General and Industrial Management*. London: Pitman Publishing.

Fox, C.J. and Miller, H.T. 1995. *Postmodern Public Administration*. Thousand Oaks, California: Sage.

Fox, C.J. 1996. Reinventing government as postmodern symbolic politics. *Public Administration Review* 56(3), 256–262.

Frederickson, H.G. 1980. *New Public Administration*. University of Alabama Press.

Frederickson, H.G. 1996. Comparing the reinventing government movement with the new public administration. *Public Administration Review* 56(3), 263–270.

Frederickson, H.G. and Smith, K.B. 2003. *The Public Administration Theory Primer*. Boulder, Colorado: Westview Press.

Giddens, A. 1976. *New Rules of Sociological Method*. New York: Basic Books.

Gioia, D.A. and Pitre, E. 1990. Multiparadigm perspectives on theory building. *Academy of Management Review* 15, 584–602.

Glaser, B.G. and Strauss, A.L. 1967. *The Discovery of Grounded Theory: Strategies for Qualitative Research*. Chicago: Aldine.

Granovetter, M. 1985. Economic action and social structure: The problem of embeddedness. *American Journal of Sociology* 91(3), 481–510.

Heinrich, C. and Lynn, L., Jr. 2000. *Governance and Performance: New Perspectives*. Washington, DC: Georgetown University Press.

Holzer, M., Gabrielian, V., and Yang, K. 2006. Five great ideas in American public administration. In Jack Rabin, W. Bartley Hildreth and Gerald J. Miller (eds.), *Handbook of Public Administration (3rd edn)*. New York: Taylor and Francis pp. 49–102.

Huber, J.D. and Shipan, C.R. 2002. *Deliberate Discretion? The Institutional Foundations of Bureaucratic Autonomy*. Cambridge, United Kingdom: Cambridge University Press.

Jackson, N. and Carter, P. 1993. Paradigm wars: A response to Hugh Willmott. *Organization Studies* 14, 721–725.

Kettl, D.F. 2000. Public administration at the millennium: The state of the field. *Journal of Public Administration Research and Theory* 10(1), 7–34.

Kirlin, J.J. 1996. The big questions of public administration in a democracy. *Public Administration Review* 56(5), 416–423.

Kraemer, K.L. and Perry, J.L. 1989. Institutional requirements for academic research in public administration. *Public Administration Review* 49(1), 9–16.

Kuhn, T.S. 1962. *The Structure of Scientific Revolutions*. Chicago: University of Chicago Press.

Lan, Z. and Anders, K.K. 2000. A paradigmatic view of contemporary public administration research: An empirical test. *Administration and Society* 32(2), 138–165.

Lewis, M.W. and Grimes, A.J. 1999. Metatriangulation: Building theory from multiple paradigms. *Academy of Management Review* 24(4), 672–690.

Lynn, L.E., Heinrich, C.J., and Hill, C.J. 2000. Studying Governance and Public Management: Challenges and Prospects. *Journal of Public Administration Research and Theory*. 10(2), 233–261.

March, J. 1997. Administrative practice, organization theory, and political philosophy: Ruminations on the reflection of John M. Gaus. *PS: Political Science and Politics* 30(4), 689–698.

Martin, J. 1992. *Cultures in Organization*. Oxford, England: Oxford University Press.

Morgan, G. 1997. *Images of Organization (2nd edn)*. Thousand Oaks, California: Sage.

Morgan, G. 1980. Paradigms, metaphors, and puzzle solving in organization theory. *Administrative Science Quarterly* 25(4), 605–622.

Moynihan, D.P. and Pandey, S.K. 2005. Testing how management matters in an era of government by performance management. *Journal of Public Administration Research and Theory* 15(3), 371–392.

Neumann, F.X. 1996. What makes public administration a science? Or, are its "big questions" really big? *Public Administration Review* 56(5), 409–415.

Osborne, D. and Ted Gaebler. 1992. *Reinventing Government*. Reading: Addison-Wesley.

O'Toole, L.J. and Meier, K.J. 1999. Modeling the impact of public management: Implications of structural context. *Journal of Public Administration Research and Theory* 9(4), 505–526.

Pandey, S.K. and Wright, B. 2006. Connecting the dots in public management: Political environment, organizational goal ambiguity and the public manager's role ambiguity. *Journal of Public Administration Research and Theory* 16(4), 511–532.

Pondy, L. and Boje, D.M. 1981. Bring the mind back in. In W. Evan (Ed.), *Frontiers in Organization and Management*. New York: Praeger pp. 83–101.

Quinn, R.E. and Rohrbaugh, J. 1983. A spatial model of effectiveness criteria: Toward a competing values approach to organizational analysis. *Management Science* 29, 363–377.

Radin, B. 2000. The government performance and results act and the tradition of federal management reform: Square pegs in round holes? *Journal of Public Administration Research and Theory* 10(1), 111–135.

Rainey, H.G. 1994. On paradigms, progress, and prospects for public management. *Journal of Public Administration Research and Theory* 4(1), 41–48.

Reed, M. 1997. In praise of duality and dualism: Rethinking agency and structure in organizational analysis. *Organization Studies* 18, 21–42.

Reed, M. 1985. *Redirections in Organizational Analysis*. London: Tavistock.

Riccucci, N. 2007. The logic of inquiry in the field of public administration. In *Handbook of Research Methods in Public Administration*, K. Yang and G. Miller (Eds.). New York: Taylor & Francis pp. 3–11.

Roethlisberger, F.J. and Dickson, W.J. 1939. *Management and the Worker*. Cambridge, Massachusetts: Harvard University Press.

Rosenbloom, D.H. and Kravchuk, R.S. 2005. *Public Administration (6th edn)*. New York: McGraw Hill.

Schultz, M. and Hatch, M.J. 1996. Living with multiple paradigms: The cases of paradigm interplay in organizational culture studies. *Academy of Management Review* 21(2), 529–557.

Simon, H. 1947. *Administrative Behavior*. New York: The Free Press.

Stillman, R.J. 1995. The refounding movement in American public administration. *Administrative Theory Praxis* 17(1), 29–45.

Stivers, C. 2002. *Bureau Men, Settlement Women: Constructing Public Administration in the Progressive Era*. Lawrence, Kansas: University Press of Kansas.

Strauss, A.L. 1978. *Negotiations*. San Francisco: Jossey-Bass.

Waldo, D. 1946. *The Administrative State*. San Francisco: Chandler.

Wang, X. and Evan, B. 2000. Hypotheses about performance measurement in counties. *Journal of Public Administration Research and Theory* 11(3), 403–428.

Weber, M. 1958. Bureaucracy. In Gerth, H.H. and Mills, C.W. (eds.), *From Max Weber: Essays in Sociology*. New York: Oxford University Press, pp. 196–244.

Weick, K. 1979. *The Social Psychology of Organizing*. Reading, Massachusetts: Addison-Wesley.

Whicker, M.L., Strickland, R.A., and Olshfski, D. 1993. The troublesome cleft: Public administration and political science. *Public Administration Review* 53(6), 531–541.

Willmott, H. 1993. Breaking the paradigm mentality. *Organization Studies* 14, 681–719.

Wilson, J. 1989. *Bureaucracy*. California: Basic Book.

Yang, K. 2006. Will performance results be communicated honestly? Testing a political model. Presented at *The 3rd Sino-U.S. conference in Beijing*, June.

4 Where Do Research Questions Come from and How Are They Developed?

Samuel J. Yeager

CONTENTS

4.1   WHERE DO RESEARCH QUESTIONS COME FROM AND HOW ARE THEY DEVELOPED?

In *Alice's Adventures in Wonderland* Alice asks the Cheshire cat "Would you tell me, please, which way I ought to go from here?" "That depends a good deal on where you want to get to," said the cat. "I don't much care where . . ." said Alice. "Then it doesn't matter which way you go," said the cat. ". . . so long as I get SOMEWHERE," Alice added as an explanation. "Oh, you're sure to do that," said the cat, "if you only walk long enough." (Carroll, 2005, pp. 57–58). The researcher's quest, like that of Alice, is to make a journey of discovery. Making a research journey efficiently and effectively requires a sense of direction provided by a research question.

Most research projects start with a question. Identifying the research problem or defining the study question is the first and most important of eight steps in the research process described by McNabb (2002, p. 54). Similarly, Gail Johnson describes planning as the key to successful research and the first step in planning a research project is determining the question (2002, p. 27). Johnson believes that this step is so crucial to the success of a research project that if mistakes are made then "the research cannot be saved" (2002, p. 27).

What does the phrase research question mean? It is the focal question a research project is intended to answer. It is not a question developed for a survey or an interview protocol. Most research methods, survey research, and interviewing texts cover writing that type of question very well. Such questions are tools designed to help develop an answer to the research question.

Virtually every research methods text talks of research questions. Their authors acknowledge the importance of a research question as a guide for the research project. The research question helps define what is to be included in the project, and just as important what is to be excluded. Multiple authors of methods texts make this point (Johnson, 1997; McNabb, 2002, p. 73; Andrews, 2003,

p. 14; and Trochim, 2005). This guidance includes direction for the literature review, research design, method or methods of collecting data, selection of a sampling frame and sample, forms of analysis, and also influences how the results are written, and may affect decisions about where and how they are presented. These texts make this point well.

In contrast, a few authors of methods texts proffer some ideas about finding or creating research questions which is of some use, but many do not help the reader learn where research questions come from and how to develop research questions and subquestions. Usually, methods texts' coverage of research questions is limited to making the point about the importance of the research question. Once this is done they usually then suggest that the researcher can find research questions by reading the literature, talking with experts, and attending conferences. Usually the topic of research questions is not developed more than this and no examples are provided.

Although these ideas are useful, is it enough to suggest that research questions can be found by reading the literature, talking with experts in the field, and attending conferences? The author thinks not, because this level of coverage barely scratches the surface of the issue. Moreover, the preferred process of developing a research question varies from individual to individual researcher and it is only one topic in any methods text.

The process used by a specific researcher to develop a research question is highly individualistic and may be approached in different ways for different topics. What works best for one person may not work equally well for another. Researchers like all students learn in different ways and are interested in different things. How deductive or inductive an approach a researcher takes, or how they mix these approaches, varies considerably across individuals and projects too. Some researchers like to use research questions in their work although others prefer more formally stated hypotheses. How an individual approaches the issue of question development may evolve considerably over the life of their career. A student and, in turn, a young faculty member may struggle to find research questions. Later in their careers they may find research questions almost everywhere they look. The issue then is one of prioritizing and concentrating one's efforts on the questions the researcher believes are most important.

To be fair, development of a research question is only one of the many complex topics that research methods text must address as they survey the methodological field. For that matter a research methods text can barely touch the issue of research questions or virtually assume that they occur naturally in the research process, but cannot legitimately treat topics like survey research, interviews, and measurement issues that way.

Questions are our primary means of dealing with the unknown and of obtaining new information. A question frames the literature review. In fact, a literature review may reveal answers to the research question and eliminate the need for new research to answer a given question. This discovery could be a fortunate event in multiple senses, at a minimum because it saves time and energy. Similarly, a literature review may lead to studies of closely related questions. These are useful because they suggest perspectives, issues, questions, and research methods that a researcher can build on in their own work.

In addressing the question of where research questions come from this essay examines the following topics:

- Motivation to do research and decide on a research question
- Where do research questions come from?
- Types of research questions
- Explicit and implicit questions
- How are research questions framed?
- Creating, clarifying, and framing research questions
- How questions are framed determines their usefulness
- Every research question may contain subquestions
- Review by colleagues, practitioners, and clients
- Conclusion

4.2   MOTIVATION TO DO RESEARCH AND DECIDE
ON A RESEARCH QUESTION

One of several things the organization behavior literature tells us is that motivation spurs activity. So the question here is what spurs individuals to develop research questions and do research?

According to Gordon Tullock, curiosity is a motive for inquiry. The subject of inquiry is quite simply anything which anyone might be curious about or which might be practically useful (Tullock, 1966, p. 40). Similarly, Jean Johnson believes that "searching seems to be a result of our natural curiosity, our desire to find answers to problems, our urge to question what others have told us, or perhaps just our need to know more about the unknown" (Johnson, 1992, p. 3).

Tullock identifies two types of curiosity: induced and pure. Induced curiosity describes the motivation of university faculty "who do research and produce articles simply because that is the way they earn their living. They may actually have very little interest in the subject of their investigation and will abandon their researches without a single pang of regret if they are offered a better paying job doing something else" (1966, p. 29). Those who are genuinely curious are immersed in their vocation "so completely as seriously to limit all other activity.... Most of them are happiest when they are working.... Economic return, social, and professional status are of secondary importance." Tullock concludes that the most common condition is a "varying mixture of the [se] two pure cases" (1966, p. 29).

Tullock believes that "the particular curiosity which leads a scientist to undertake a given bit of research is always the outcome of [their] general curiosity" which leads a researcher to keep informed of developments in the whole field about which [they] are curious, "but... undertake specific investigations only when [they] see an opportunity for particularly fruitful discoveries" (Tullock, 1966, pp. 30–31). When a research project is finished they will hunt for and move on to the next project. In fact their new problem may be an outgrowth of a previous project. Some researchers will spend a significant portion of their career on a single research problem and its offspring. This is especially likely with difficult and complex problems. Normally a researcher's interests may shift considerably during their life (1966, pp. 32–34, 54).

All scientists are engaged in the discovery of the real world. "Inquiry may be inspired by... dissatisfaction with the state of knowledge" (Tullock, 1966, p. 28). So a researcher's efforts may be spurred by their reactions to existing research or lack of it. Researchers often try to think up a completely new approach to a problem (Tullock, 1966, p. 61). Research may lead to the development and application of a new theory. Even if this research effort is unsuccessful it will lead to the development of new knowledge which will affect their future work (Tullock, 1966, pp. 43–53, 177). This is learning and is a cumulative process. In sum, Tullock believes that knowledge of one's field, innovation, or creativity, and efforts to develop theory and apply it are all sources of research ideas. A healthy dose of curiosity may spur any or all of these activities. Tullock believes that there is a tremendous range of motives for and means employed in doing research. So what do others have to say about finding research questions?

4.3   WHERE DO RESEARCH QUESTIONS COME FROM?

Social scientists are in the business of describing and understanding the world around them of defining what it is, how things work, and ultimately, perhaps, how to improve them. And as for finding research questions they only need to interact with that world. The public administration literature talks of pracademics (Ospina and Dodge, 2005) and connectedness (Newland, 2000). Is finding research questions not part of what pracademics and connectedness are all about? Questions come from practice and practitioners can supply an endless variety of them either as individuals whom a researcher interacts with directly or though the formal RFP process. What is it that practitioners do? Why do they do it? How can they do it more effectively and efficiently? Well-known research works used this technique (Kaufman, 1960; Mintzberg, 1973). The author's experience is that practitioners are delighted to tell you about what they are doing. One only has to ask and most practitioners and politicians will take advantage of all the help they can get.

Questions also come from reading the literature on a regular basis and from doing a literature review. "Research topics can come from questions discovered in texts, in the professional literature, from classroom discussions, from hobbies and other outside interests, and, of course, from the life experience of the researcher" (McNabb, 2002, p. 63).

Andrews (2003) indicates that there are two common ways to develop research questions. "One is to work hard and fast, early in the project, to generate and refine your research question. The other is to let the research question emerge from the literature" (Andrews, 2003, p. 9). Developing a question early starts with a literature review and a decision about what aspect of the topic you want to focus on.

Researchers almost always stand on the proverbial shoulders of their predecessors. Why not take advantage of the work of others, get a running start so to speak, rather than reinvent the proverbial wheel. As Gordon Tullock points out that "new discoveries are based on older discoveries [and]... that the absence of these [earlier] discoveries would significantly reduce our present rate of progress" (1966, p. 24). So researchers build on the work of their predecessors and knowledge cumulates.

Strong motivations drive the researcher to do a literature review. This is described as one of the standard steps in the research process or good science in virtually every research methods text and course. Some authors of methods texts devote substantial attention to how a literature search and literature review should be done (Johnson, 1997), whereas others do not get into the nitty gritty deeply. To not do a literature review risks discovering that someone else has already done your study. For that matter the author believes that most researchers do not want to simply repeat exactly what a predecessor has done. A primary purpose of research is learning and doing new and different things. Besides, going where none have gone before is exciting for an academic, and perhaps more likely to result in a publishable manuscript.

In its simplest form, building on the work of another may start with a single study. Almost any study can be extended. This can be done in an endless variety of ways. Almost any study can be carried out in a different or larger setting, looking at additional things (variables) that may affect the result, and using different measures. Neuman (1997) suggests that the individual seeking a research problem might do any or some combination of the following:[1]

- Replicate a research project in a different setting or with a different population
- Consider how various subpopulations might behave differently in the same situation
- Apply an existing perspective or explanation to a new situation
- Explore unexpected or contradictory findings in previous studies
- Challenge research findings that fly in the face of what you know or believe to be true

Another source of ideas for new research questions is found in the suggestions for further research that is an expected part of any research presentation. Today, virtually every article contains suggestions for further research. These statements come in the direct form of suggestions of what needs to be done in future studies. Also, suggestions occur indirectly through statements recognizing limitations of the current study.

Alternatively, one can ask "What do these results contribute to theory?" "Do they support what we know or not?" "Do they extend it in some way?" Would-be researchers are taught to constantly question theory and these endeavors allow them to test findings and theory. If confirmation does not occur then the researcher faces the task of explaining why and modifying what is known. Because theory is always in a process of development, replication and extension efforts are good science. For example, Janet Kelly examines the theoretically important problem of the linkage between citizen satisfaction and service quality (Kelly, 2005). Specifically the issue is, "We don't know the relationship between the performance of government and improvement in citizen satisfaction with or confidence in government, though we assume it exists and that it is positive" (Kelly, 2005, p. 77).

Another way to find research questions is to reexamine a classic work in the field. Such is the case, for example, in recent reexaminations of Herbert Kaufman's *The Forest Ranger* (Carroll, Freemath, and Alm, 1996; Koontz, 2007; Luton, 2007; Martin and Toddi, 2004).

New theories are developed or old ones extended because old theory, despite some degree of longevity, proves to be either invalid or inadequate. Someone may introduce a new idea. In an effort to develop theory this type of endeavor can be based on drawing different works together in new and particular ways. One can take multiple studies and bring them together assembling them into a new whole, much the way a child builds something with Legos. For example, in part, Maslow's theory of motivation was assembled in this way (Maslow, 1970), and so too the theory of public service motivation (PSM; Perry and Wise, 1990).

Others then develop and extend these new ideas. For example, Perry and Wise extended motivation theory by developing the concepts and theory of public service motivation to better explain behavior they observed among people engaged in public service (1990). How can this concept and its subcomponents be measured? What does it mean? Does it apply? How can it be used? Is it valid? In fact, for example, at the end of their initial study Perry and Wise called for further research on public sector motivation (1990). Perry did substantial follow-up work on public service motivation focusing on measurement, antecedents of the construct, refinement of the theory, and ethics (Perry, 1996, 1997, 2000; Perry, Coursey, and Littlepage, 2005). And Wise incorporated the concept in a larger theoretical context (Wise, 2003).

Many other researches have used the PSM concept in a variety of different ways including measurement issues, conditions that foster PSM, gender differences, and productivity (Alonso and Lewis, 2001; Brewer and Facer, 2000; Bright, 2005; DeHart-Davis, Marlowe, and pandey, 2006; Houston, 2006; Miller and Whitford, 2007; Moynihan and Sanjay, 2007; Wright, 2001, 2007). Perry and Wise's, 1990 study has been cited 110 times (results from a Google Scholar search identifying the original 1990 study that indicated "Cited by 110') in other researches although this probably underestimates the actual amount of research being done, and a search for [Perry AND Wise AND "public service motivation"] produced 121 hits. And a broader search using the target [Perry AND Wise AND motivation] produced 5260 hits.

Rather than improve on or build on a single study, a researcher could use a literature synthesis to develop research questions. One way to go about this is by synthesizing the work of several other individuals by examining multiple studies. What does the body of evidence say about a topic or multiple subtopics? What answers do the studies consistently offer to research questions? What are the effect sizes of these studies? For example, Edwards et al. (2002) summarized the results of 292 empirical studies of methods designed to improve response rate to mail-back surveys. They provide substantial evidence of what works and what does not and provide subsequent investigators with ideas about what needs to be examined in future studies.

Similarly, meta-analysis could be used to develop similar questions from prior research. For example, a now-classic study examined earlier research reports to determine the effects of financial rewards, goal setting, participation, and job enrichment on employee motivation (Locke, Feren, McCaleb, Shaw, and Denny, 1980). Further work has been done to elaborate all four of these suggested means of stimulating employee motivation.

As mentioned earlier, existing lines of research can be extended in many ways. For instance, considering how various subpopulations might behave differently in the same situation is the basis for much research today. For instance, a large number of research studies exist that focus on issues involving race, gender, age, disability, religion, ethnicity, and cultural background. Gone are the days when such questions would not be asked but simply assumed away. The whole basis of ethnic studies and of feminist studies rests on the assumption of and demonstration of differences. Even without questions of discrimination there are a myriad number of issues because one can ask these kinds of questions about any research finding. For example, how might this apply to public service motivation? Is it the same for African Americans, Hispanics, Asians, and whites? Does it change with age? Do people become more or less altruistic with age? Is it the same for persons of different religious and cultural backgrounds? Do the disabled exhibit PSM? How do they compare with members of other groups? Overall, how do the values of members of these different groups come into play? And, how does PSM affect the attitudes and work behaviors of these different subgroups? A number of studies examine these questions.[2]

Answering the following questions may help the researcher select, define, and refine a research question:[3]

- Is this a worthwhile question?
- Is the question answerable?
- Are there ethical issues involved in research on this question?
- Is there a clear reason for asking this question?
- What is already known about this issue? This is the reason for conducting a literature review. Virtually all texts emphasize this.
- What assumptions exist in what is already known?
- How does the topic fit into the exploratory research categories you might use such as personal, sociological, political, historical, and scientific categories?
- Are you interested in this question? Do you care about it or not?
- Early on develop a wide range of potential questions and refine that list as your knowledge of the topic develops.
- Do you want to be known as a person who does or did research on this topic?
- Will this project help you develop in a desirable way? Each research project contributes to your knowledge and professional development and helps define who you are as a person.
- How have others conducted research on this issue? What theories and methods did they use? What problems did they encounter? This is the reason for conducting a literature review. Virtually all texts emphasize this.
- Who is requesting this research? Do they really know what they need to know or not? Will they be willing to work with you putting in the amount of time required to execute the project in an appropriate manner? Do they have a particular outcome they hope the research will support?
- Are there any mandates from policy makers involved?
- Does this research have political implications? Can this project potentially blowback on you and your employer?
- Who are the likely users of the research? What are they most interested in?
- In relative terms how easy will it be to answer this question?
- Do you have the resources necessary to answer this question including the expertise, time, money, and access to data sources? What are the resource requirements, data availability?

Questions posed by those sponsoring research may not be clear. For example, the questions in a public agency's RFP may not be clear and simple because the individuals who wrote the RFP did not spend sufficient time refining them or deciding what they really needed to know or think about how they were going to use the information collected. Questions in the RFP may not be specific enough to be researchable and may even be unrelated to what that public agency actually needs. One way to resolve the clarity of the problem is to confer repeatedly with stakeholders until they have defined in a clear, focused, and relevant manner what they need to know (Johnson, 2002, pp. 27–29; Patton, 1986).

This is an important issue because slightly altering a research question may change the focus of a project so much that different data is needed to answer it. This data may have to be collected and analyzed in entirely different ways. Alternative methods and analyses may drastically change the time and cost required to carry out a project. Gail Johnson provides a perceptive illustration of this issue.

If the legislature asks the transportation department "Can you evaluate a road construction project between several suburban communities and a large retail area in the central city?" this is rather vague.

There are several possible questions that have slightly different wording but suggest different data collection strategies:

- If the question is "What is the quality of the road?" the transportation department might want to bring in some engineering experts to determine the number and size of potholes in the roads.
- If the question is "How frequently is the road used?" the department may want to use a method to count the traffic.
- If the question is "How satisfied are citizens with the road?" then the department might want to gather data directly from citizens.
- If the question is "Has business at the retail center increased as a result of the roads?" then the department might want to collect sales data over time or ask the owners whether they think business has improved (Johnson, 2002, p. 28).

To help a group generate a list of questions, Michael Patton suggests a practical exercise. Meet with a group of key stakeholders, and ask them to complete ten times the blank in the sentence "I would like to know _____ about (name of program or object of study)." Then, divide them into groups of three or four people each and ask them to combine their lists together into a single list of ten things each group wants to know. Finally, get back together and generate a single list of ten basic things the group does not have information on but they would like to know, things that could make a difference in what they are doing. Follow-up sessions should be held to refine and prioritize these questions (Patton, 1986, pp. 75–77).

This is an important issue because slightly altering a research question may change the focus of a project so much that different data is needed to answer it. It may have to be collected and analyzed in entirely different ways. The data may change the time and cost required to carry out a project.

4.4 TYPES OF RESEARCH QUESTIONS

There are three general types of research questions and they focus on description, normative issues, and relationships. Descriptive questions do exactly that—they describe something. The researcher answers questions involving issues of who, what, how many, and how much. Normative questions focus on "what is" and compare it with "what should be." Relationship questions address relationships between variables and may be phrased in terms of association or covariance, or if the researcher is ambitious, cause and effect, or impacts or outcomes, and may predict future impacts. A single study might involve one single type of question or it could involve multiple, that is, all three types of questions (derived from Johnson, 2002 and Trochim, 2005).

4.5 EXPLICIT AND IMPLICIT QUESTIONS

Authors of articles in the public administration literature sometimes state research questions explicitly. A few authors even go a step further and develop explicit formal hypotheses to test. Other researchers address specific questions without stating them. They may tell the reader exactly what they are investigating but their questions are implicit in their text.

Supporters of explicit questions and hypotheses might say that it is easier to conduct research by starting with clearly stated questions. They might say that it is easier to present the results and easier for the reader to understand what the investigator is trying to communicate. Critics of this approach might claim that it can become just a matter of filling in an outline and can lead to a writing and presentation style that is too pedantic, stiff, and formal. A reviewer might look at a manuscript and state "It reads just like a government report."

Those who do not use explicit questions might indicate that they are doing the same thing as those who use questions and hypotheses—making clear what they are investigating. They might point out that they too are effectively communicating with their readers.

Another practice that researchers use is making statements that tell the reader explicitly what they are doing and why. These statements guide their research activities, manuscript preparation, and the reader.

Whether a researcher prepares a manuscript using explicit questions or not or whether a researcher uses statements indicating what they are doing seems to this writer to be a matter of personal preference and writing style. Given that substantive content is what matters most, these practices do not necessarily either add to or detract from the value of any researcher's work. Nevertheless, the author prefers starting with a question because it makes the research process easier for him and makes working with coinvestigators easier as well.

From a reader's perspective—when explicit questions are lacking, but appropriate informative content is present in the text—the reader can develop statements of the research questions investigated on their own. Examples of these practices are described in the following paragraphs.

A recent article by De Vita and Eric (2005) illustrates the development of subquestions. In fact, the first part of the title of this article contains an important subquestion—"Who gains from charitable tax credit programs? The Arizona model." This subquestion is intended to catch the reader's eye and get them to read the article. This article explores a new public finance or tax incentive phenomenon known as charitable tax credit programs at the state level. The authors explicitly identify and systematically address the following questions in their work:

How will program eligibility be defined?
Will taxpayers respond to the incentive?
Which organizations will benefit?
What are the implications for nonprofit fundraising and program accountability?

Unstated questions exist in this manuscript as well. One is "Why did states begin to offer charitable tax credit programs?" Another unstated question is "How many or which states use charitable tax credit programs?" These are factual questions that are easy to answer. The answers provide contextual background for the current study, but neither is a major research question, so they were left unstated.

Researchers might use both explicitly stated questions and specific statements in the research and presentation efforts. For example, Lewis and Brooks (2005) use both explicit questions and statements in their study entitled "A question of morality: Artists' values and public funding for the arts." Explicit questions include:

How did public funding for the arts briefly generate the kind of controversy typical of issues such as abortion, gay rights, and capital punishment?
Why was the NEA susceptible to having its existence framed as a legal sanction of right and wrong?

These are factual questions and they are worthy research questions. Recently, funding of the arts was and remains to some extent a highly contentious issue. Public perceptions and debate of this issue contain a tremendous amount of incomplete information, rhetoric, and bombast. The answers to Lewis and Brooks questions involve specialized information most people are unaware of. Answers are located in public records that these researchers examined in detail to find the facts.

To address these issues the investigators explored the history of federal funding for the arts, and details of the controversies leading to Congress repeatedly revisiting public support for the arts, government actions, and court decisions. They state "Despite congressional action, the National Endowment for the Arts (NEA) continued to generate controversy." That statement implies a question of "Why did controversy continue after Congress acted?"

The authors provide a multipart answer to this statement and their implied question. They focus on lawsuits, the objectionable activities of artists presenting in venues operated by less than a handful of organizations receiving NEA funding, NEA operations, local government decisions in response to public furor, federal court decisions addressing issues of censorship, and the issue of values shared within the artist community.

The second half of Lewis and Brooks' study begins with the statement, "But the controversy also continued because of artists' values." This statement presents a conclusion which might seem debatable if it were not based on the findings Lewis and Brooks examine two paragraphs later. They review some literature addressing the issue of values affecting decisions. This phenomenon is found in the representative bureaucracy literature. Finally, they examine literature both suggesting and denying that artists, the art community, and consumers of art have values that are different from the values of the general population. They do not state a specific research question, nor do they need to, because it is clear what they are speaking about. Nevertheless, the reader can create one. Thus

> Do the values of artists, members of the art community, and consumers of art differ significantly from the values of the general population?

Other researchers may not make much use of explicitly stated research questions in presenting their results. For example, Norris and Moon wrote an article whose title, "Advancing e-government at the grassroots: Tortoise or hare?" (2005), contains one of their research questions. To be more specific, one of the issues they investigate is how rapidly has e-government been adopted by local governments? However, they investigate more than this. Instead of single questions Norris and Moon developed a guiding framework for their study consisting of three dimensions. The "input dimension" consisted of organizational and environmental factors affecting the adoption of information technology. An "impacts" dimension focused on internal organizational processes, and another "impacts" dimension consisted of organizational outputs and outcomes. They use this framework to review the literature and it provides the structure for presentation of their findings.

In addition, Norris and Moon provide more detailed guiding statements throughout the findings section of their article. For example, "The input dimension includes local government adoption of e-government, the age of local government Web sites, and the development or evolution of local e-government measured by the transactional capabilities of local Web sites." Each of these specific statements could just as easily have been written as a question. For example, "To what extent have local governments adopted e-government?" Similarly, Norris and Moon state "Here, we have examined the perceived impacts of e-government on several aspects of local government administration." An alternative question might have read, "What are the perceived impacts of e-government on local government?"

Important questions sometimes arise as discoveries are made. For example, in addressing the issue of barriers to e-government Norris and Moon develop a question that naturally evolves from their findings. "These findings also show that... it [e-government] has produced relatively few impacts, and not all of them are in the positive direction indicated by the hype surrounding this new technology. The obvious question is, why?" They use this question to guide the remainder of their investigation. In this example, the simple direct question "why?" would be meaningless without the specific details provided by the sentence preceding it.

No doubt a variety of other formally stated questions could have been developed and addressed in Norris and Moon's study. Would they have improved it? Who knows? On the other hand the author wonders if questions did not exist at the beginning of this project and what appears in the article is just a matter of writing style. It seems that the following questions could have easily driven this research project even if they do not explicitly appear in the text: "What is the extent of e-government use among local governments?" "How sophisticated are these e-government Web sites?" and, "What factors foster or inhibit use of e-government?" or, "What factors foster or inhibit use of sophisticated aspects of e-government?"

Another source of research questions consists of the expectations that authors may include in their conclusions. For example, Norris and Moon's study of e-government (2005) contains several expectations about future trends in local e-government development. Two of those statements illustrate the point, "For the next few years at least, most local government Web sites can be expected to remain mainly informational with limited transactional capabilities." And, "as has been the case with IT in government in general, payoffs will lag adoption."

The following questions are suggested by Norris and Moon's expectations "How rapidly do local governments adopt e-government applications that have demonstrated payoffs?" or, "What are the payoffs that local governments realize from implementing e-government?" and, "Do local governments adopt applications that have demonstrated payoffs more quickly than other types of applications."

4.6   CREATING, CLARIFYING, AND FRAMING RESEARCH QUESTIONS

An initial draft of a research question may be too general and vague to be useful. Revision is necessary to focus it more sharply or clarify it. As more is learned about the topic, the process of question revision may require multiple iterations.

Basic types of questions that researchers start with include who, what, where, when, how, and why? Each type of question suggests a specific type of research focus such as those indicated in the following table.[4]

Question Frames and Their Focus

Question Frames	Focus
Who	Identification of actors, audience, users
What	Classification, specification
Where	Locations, context
When	Time, sequence, context
How	Action taken, process, method, operation
Why	Reason, cause, purpose
Cause	Temporal order, covariance, explanation
Can	Possibility, probability
Will	Probability, trend
Do	Performance, action
Which	Comparison

These question frames serve an orienting function in the process of creating research questions (Burton-Roberts, 1997, pp. 16, 219). But they are only a starting point because they have no specific, topic-related content. Additional material must be added to them to create useful questions.

O'Sullivan and Rassel give examples that are developed one step further: "The research question can be framed using questions that begin 'how many,' 'how much,' 'how efficient,' 'how effective,' 'how adequate,' 'why'" (1999, p. 17).

What practices can help an investigator develop and refine research questions? Leedy and Jeanne (2001) provide some useful suggestions.

State the problem clearly and completely. This involves writing the statement in a clear logical sentence. Use specific terms that have a precise meaning. The research question should have a clear focus and it should be clear what the limits of the question are.

Does the answer to the problem have the potential for providing important and useful information? Will the result be more than a simple exercise in gathering information, answering a yes/no question, or making a simple comparison?

A common difficulty in developing a research question consists of defining a solution into the problem statement. Bardach provides examples that illustrate this problem and how to avoid it. For example, "Don't say: 'There is too little shelter for homeless families'. " This implies one specific solution. A better research question is: "There are too many homeless families." Or, for example, "Don't say: 'New schools are being built too slowly'. " This problem statement implies a solution. A more effective alternative leads to exploration of many different solutions and evaluation of them on their merits. In light of these criteria, a better alternative is "There are too many schoolchildren relative to the currently available classroom space" (Bardach, 2000, pp. 6–8).

How questions are framed determines their usefulness in focusing a research project. This is usually an iterative process in which one problem after another is eliminated from the draft of a question until the researcher is left with a usable question. A series of questions and discussion of their revision illustrates this process starting with the following question:

Question 1: How rapidly do governments adopt IT applications?

As this question stands, it is too vague to be useful. The words or phrases "rapidly," "governments," and "IT applications" are too broad to give the research a clear enough focus to be useful. Thus

[vague] [type of government?] [type of IT?]
Q1: How *rapidly* do *governments* adopt *IT applications*?

Revision of a research question is an iterative process in which vague words are replaced with more specific ones and the focus is made more exact or sharpened. Here the general word "governments" is replaced with "local governments" and the general phrase "IT applications" is replaced with "e-government."

The focus on local government comes from the fact that the International City and County Managers Association (ICMA) already collects relevant data on IT and e-government at intervals from cities with populations greater than 20,000, and will sell it to a researcher for a reasonable price. This means two important things. It would probably not make sense to collect new data on your own and an investigation could reasonably be limited to those cities. This data provides the focus on e-government which is a hot topic in the public administration literature today.

[vague]
Q2: How *rapidly* do *local governments* adopt *e-government*
[what payoffs]?
applications that have *demonstrated payoffs?*

The second version still contains vague words such as "rapidly" and "demonstrated payoffs." The phrase "demonstrated payoffs" is derived from Norris and Moon's discussion in their conclusion.

Q3: "Are local government adoption rates for e-government applications that have
[a specific grouping factor]
proven to work successfully in other cities
[a specific measure]
faster than adoption rates of other e-government applications?"

The third version of the question focuses more narrowly on comparison of the adoption rates of e-government applications that have or have not been successful in other cites. Copying what works is one explanation for the spread of technology. This explanation may or may not explain the spread of specific e-government applications. Other factors such as size of a city, demand, and cost might limit the adoption rate too. Demonstrated payoffs could be measured in other ways as well such as cost-effectiveness (lower cost per transaction) or improved/lowered response times or lowered complaint rates as well.

Another way to focus this question might be to make it even more specific. For example, this question could be focused more tightly by specifying which aspects of e-government to examine. For example, if the question were limited to the adoption of full e-government portal capabilities the following question might result:

Q4: Does *city size impact* adoption of *e-government portal capability?*[5]

This question contains three issues. What is meant by city size? What is meant by impact? And, what is meant by e-government portal capability? City size can be measured in terms of population, size of budget, size of the IT budget, size of the IT budget relative to the total general operating fund and land area, and in other ways as well. Impact could be the relationship between two variables or one variable could be used to predict another. For example, do cities spend larger percentages of their budgets on IT to adopt more portal transaction capabilities? E-government portal capability could mean nonfinancial transactions, or financial transactions. So the question could be revised to make it more specific in the following manner:

Q5: Does city size impact adoption of the following e-government transactions?

One way to address this issue of e-government transactions in more detail might be to use subquestions, one per service, such as

Q6: Does city size impact adoption of permit application and renewal transactions through a Web portal?

Rather than address a series of similar questions, a single question could be asked if there were a single measure of transaction portal capabilities. One way to do this would involve data reduction and scale construction. This would start with survey data such as those collected by the ICMA in which respondents indicated all the different kinds of nonfinancial and financial services provided through their Web portal. Data reduction techniques could be used to create a scaled measure of transaction portal capabilities in local e-governments. A question like the following one could then be asked:

Q7: Does city size (percent of budget spent on IT) impact adoption of the e-government transaction portal capabilities (TPC scale)?

To be fair to the authors, Don Norris and Jae Moon did not ask these questions in their article because it would not have made sense to do so. The data distributions they report tell the reader that there were too few cities offering interactive transactions through their portals to support analysis of questions like these. Perhaps, the International City and County Manager's Association's latest e-government survey data collected in 2004 which became available for purchase in 2006 will support this type of analysis.

Every research question may contain subquestions. Leedy and Ormrod (2004) describe them as follows: Each subquestion should be a completely researchable unit. Each subquestion must be clearly tied to the interpretation of the data. The subquestions must add up to the totality of the problem. And, subquestions should be small in number. They suggest identifying subquestions by going through the following paper and pencil steps:

1. Copy the problem onto a clean sheet of paper, leaving considerable space between the lines.
2. Read the problem critically to discover the areas that should receive in-depth treatment before the problem can be resolved.
3. Make sure every subquestion contains a word that indicates the necessity to interpret the data within that particular subquestions (e.g., analyze, discover, compare). Underline that word.
4. Arrange the entire problem . . . into a skeletal plan that shows the research structure of the problem. You now have a structure of the whole research design (Leedy and Ormrod, 2004, p. 58).

The reader may have reacted to the words "paper and pencil" much like the author by thinking "I can do this paper and pencil process better with a word processor." So be it. Alternatively, they point out that one could use brainstorming software (Leedy and Ormrod, 2001).

More research questions and subquestions may be developed than can be examined in a single study. This problem can be resolved by prioritizing them to determine which ones to examine in a single study (McNabb, 2002, pp. 67–71).

4.7   REVIEW BY COLLEAGUES, PRACTITIONERS, AND CLIENTS

A specific technique suggested by many authors of methods texts is to consult other persons about your research question. To at least run the question by a colleague seems to be a minimum. One means of answering the question "why didn't I think of that" and avoiding the question "if only I had thought of that" is to run research questions by one's peers, practitioners, and clients. It never ceases to amaze the author how different people perceive disparate and sometimes contradictory things in the same words, and in a single situation. Feedback that begins with the words "have you thought about . . ." may prove invaluable.

4.8   CONCLUSION

Why should anyone care about where research questions come from and how they are developed? We should all care for two reasons. As consumers of research have clearly stated, focused research questions make the reader's task easier. As researchers, we should care because it makes the tasks of executing a research project and presenting it easier.

ENDNOTES

1. These items are lightly edited and reordered to facilitate this presentation.
2. Perry and Wise's own research and that of many other scholars address these issues.
3. These questions were developed by combining ideas from several research methods texts with ideas of the author (Andrews, 2003; Bardach, 2000; Booth, Colomb, and Williams, 2003; Johnson, 2002; Leedy and Ormrod, 2001; McNabb, 2002; O'Sullian and Rassell, 1999; Ragin, 1994; Trochim, 2005).
4. Adapted from Poggenpohl, 2000.
5. This question is derived from one of Norris and Moon's conclusions "adoption of Web sites is strongly related to local government size, measured by population".

REFERENCES

Alonso, P. and Lewis, G.B. 2001. Public service motivation and job performance evidence from the federal sector. *American Review of Public Administration* 31 (4): 363–380.

Andrews, R. 2003. *Research Questions*. London: Continuum.

Bardach, E. 2000. *A Practical Guide for Policy Analysis: The Eightfold Path to More Effective Problem Solving*. New York: Chatham House Publishers.

Booth, W.C., Colomb, G.C., and Williams, J.M. 2003. *The Craft of Research*, 2nd ed. Chicago: University of Chicago Press.

Brewer, G., Selden S., and Facer R. 2000. Individual conceptions of public service motivation, *Public Administration Review* 60 (3): 254–264.

Bright, L. 2005. Public employees with high levels of public service motivation: Who are they, where are they, and what do they want? *Review of Public Personnel Administration* 25 (2): 138–154.

Burton-Roberts, N. 1997. *Analysing Sentences: An Introduction to English Syntax*, 2nd ed. London: Longman.

Carroll, L. 2005. *Alice's Adventures in Wonderland*. New York: Sterling Publishing Co.

Carroll, F.O., Freemuth, J., and Alm, L. 1996. Women forest rangers: Revisiting Kaufman's "The Forest Ranger". *Journal of Forestry*. 94 (1): 38–41.

DeHart-Davis, L., Marlowe, J., and Pandey, S.K. 2006. Gender dimensions of public service motivation. *Public Administration Review* 66 (6): 873–887.

De Vita, C.J. and Twombly, E.C. 2005. Who gains from charitable tax credit programs? The Arizona model. *Public Administration Review* 65 (1): 57–63.

Edwards, P., Roberts, I., Clarke, M., DiGuiseppi, C., Pratap, S., Wentz, R., and Kwan I. 2002. Increasing response rates to postal questionnaires: Systematic review. *BMJ* 324: 1183–1185.

Houston, D.J. 2006. Walking the walk of public service motivation: Public employees and charitable gifts of time, blood, and money. *Journal of Public Administration Research and Theory* 16 (1): 67–86.

Johnson, G. 2002. *Research Methods for Public Administrators*. Westport, Connecticut: Quorum Books.

Johnson, J. 1992. *The Bedford Guide to the Research Process*, 2nd ed. Boston: Bedford Books of St. Martin's Press.

Johnson, J. 1997. *The Bedford Gride to the Research Process*, 3rd ed. Boston: Bedford Books of St. Martin's Press.

Kaufman, H. 1960. *The Forest Ranger: A Study in Administrative Behavior*. Baltimore: The Johns Hopkins University Press.

Kelly, M.J. 2005. The dilemma of the unsatisfied customer in a market model of public administration. *Pulic Administration Review*. 65 (1): 76–84.

Koontz, T.M. 2007. Federal and state public forest administration in the new millennium: Revisiting Herbert Kaufman's The Forest Ranger. *Public Administration Review* 67 (1): 152–164.

Leedy, P.D. and Ormrod, J.E. 2004. *Practical Research: Planning and Design*, 8th ed. Upper Saddle River, New Jersey: Prentice-Hall.

Lewis, G.B. and Brooks, A.C. 2005. A question of morality: Artists' values and public funding for the arts. *Public Administration Review* 65 (1): 8–17.

Locke, E.A., Feren, D.B., McCaleb, V.M., Shaw, K.N., and Denny, A.T. 1980. The relative effectiveness of four methods of motivating employee performance. In *Changes in Working Life: Proceedings of an International Conference on Changes in the Nature and Quality of Working Life, Sponsored by the Human Factors Panel of the NATO Scientific Affairs Division*. Duncan, K.D., Gruneberg, M.M., and Wallis, D., (Eds.). Chichester: John Wiley & Sons, pp. 363–388.

Luton, L.S. 2007. Digging deeply 47 years later: Herbert Kaufman's The Forest Ranger. *Public Administration Review* 67 (1): 165–168.

Martin, I.M. and Toddi, A.S. 2004. Using multiple methods to understand agency values and objectives: Lessons for public lands management. *Policy Sciences* 37 (1): 37–69.

Maslow, A. 1970. *Motivation and Personality*. New York: Harper and Row.

McNabb, David, E. 2002. *Research Methods in Public Administration and Nonprofit Management: Quantitative and Qualitative Approaches*. Armonk, New York: M.E. Sharpe.

Miller, G.J. and Whitford, A.B. 2007. The principal's moral hazard: Constraints on the use of incentives in hierarchy. *Journal of Public Administration Research and Theory* 17(2): 213–233.

Mintzberg, H. 1973. *The Nature of Managerial Work*, New York: Harper & Row.

Moynihan, D.P. and Pandey, S.K. 2007. The role of organizations in fostering public service motivation. *Public Administration Review* 67 (1): 40–53.

Neuman, WL. 1997. *Social Research Methods: Qualitative and Quantitative Approaches*, 3rd ed. Boston: Allyn and Bacon.

Newland, C.A. 2000. The public administration review and ongoing struggles for connectedness. *Public Administration Review* 60 (1): 20–38.

Norris, D.F. and Moon, M.J. 2005. Advancing e-government at the grassroots: Tortoise or hare? *Public Administration Review* 65 (1): 64–75.

O'Sullivan, E. and Rassel, G. 1999. *Research Methods for Public Administrators*, 3rd ed. New York: Addison Wesley Longman.

Ospina, S.M. and Dodge, J. 2005. Narrative inquiry and the search for connectedness: Practitioners and academics developing public administration scholarship. *Public Administration Review* 65 (4): 409–423.

Patton, M. 1986. *Utilization-Focused Research*, 2nd ed. Newbury Park: SAGE.

Perry, J.L. 1996. Measuring public service motivation: An assessment of construct reliability and validity. *Journal of Public Administration Research and Theory* 6 (1): 5–22.

Perry, J.L. 1997. Antecedents of public service motivation. *Journal of Public Administration Research and Theory* 7 (2): 181–197.

Perry, J.L. 2000. Bringing society in: Toward a theory of public-service motivation. *Journal of Public Administration Research and Theory* 10 (2): 471–488.

Perry, J.L. and Wise, L.R. 1990. The motivational bases of public service. *Public Administration Review* 50 (3): 367–373.

Perry, J., Coursey, D., and Littlepage, L. 2005. Morally committed public servants: Lessons for developing ethical public administrators. Paper delivered at Ethics and Integrity of Governance: The First Transatlantic Dialogue, Public Management Institute, Catholic University Leuven, Leuven, Belgium, June 2–5, 2005.

Poggenpohl, S.H. 2000. Constructing knowledge of design, part 2: Questions—An approach to design research. Paper presented at the 2nd Doctoral Education in Design Conference, La Clusaz, France, July 2000.

Ragin, C.C. 1994. *Constructing Social Research: The Unity and Diversity of Method.* Thousand Oaks, California: Pine Forge Press.

Trochim, W.M.K. 2005. *Research Methods: The Concise Knowledge Base.* Cincinnati, Ohio: Atomic Dog Publishing.

Tullock, G. 1966. *The Organization of Inquiry.* Durham, North Carolina: Duke University Press.

Wise, L.R. 2003. Bureaucratic posture: Building a composite theory of bureaucratic behavior. Paper presented at the 7th National Public Management Research Conference, Georgetown University October 11th 2003.

Wright, B.E. 2007. Public service motivation: Does mission matter. *Public Administration Review* 67 (1): 54–64.

Wright, B. 2001. Public-sector work motivation: A review of the current literature and a revised conceptual model. *Journal of Public Administration Research and Theory* 11 (4): 559–586.

5 Writing a Literature Review: The Art of Scientific Literature

Domonic A. Bearfield and Warren S. Eller

CONTENTS

5.1   WHAT IS A LITERATURE REVIEW?

The literature review is a comprehensive survey of previous inquiries related to a research question. Although it can often be wide in scope, covering decades, perhaps even centuries of material, it should also be narrowly tailored, addressing only the scholarship that is directly related to the research question. This is by no means an easy task. However, by using a systematic approach to previous scholarship, the literature review allows the author to place his or her research into an intellectual and historical context. In other words, the literature review helps the author declare why their research matters.

5.2   WHAT A LITERATURE REVIEW IS NOT?

A literature review is not simply an annotated bibliography or a glorified book review. An annotated bibliography is a detailed listing of the major books and articles on a specific subject, such as public sector human resources or leadership. Each listing is accompanied by a short commentary on the work's main points or arguments. Although an annotated bibliography is a great resource for discovering works to be included in your literature review, annotated bibliographies do not contain the level of critical insight expected of a literature review. It also does not attempt to synthesize the work as part of a larger argument.

In contrast, although a well-constructed book review may provide the type of keen critical analysis often found in literature reviews, the focus is generally on a single work or a small number of articles. In this sense, it lacks the scope and breadth of written knowledge needed for a sound review of the literature. Without sounding overly dramatic, the literature review should be seen as a grand enterprise, where the researcher attempts, in as concise a manner as possible, to reflect the major research developments on a specific subject.

5.3   WHAT IS THE PURPOSE OF THE LITERATURE REVIEW?

The literature review is used to serve several important functions in academic research. The review explains to the reader why a particular research question is important. Although a question may sound interesting, or it may invoke a bit of curiosity, to properly establish its importance the research must be placed into context. The literature review allows the author to explain how other scholars, both within their own discipline and outside of that discipline, have approached the question. What is the history of research on this question? What approaches have been used? What insights can be gained from the work of other scholars? Also, what are the challenges and dead ends? A well-constructed literature review should provide a panoramic view of the research question, which will help the reader understand why the question matters.

The literature review also gives the reader the historical background on a given subject. Fink (2005) notes that a literature review describes the most up-to-date scholarship on a subject, supports the need for additional research, discusses the quality of previous research, and explains important research findings. In addition, the literature review also provides clarity on a given subject by revealing long-standing conflicts and debates, reveals the interdisciplinary nature of research on a subject, and places the work in a historical context.

In this way, authors demonstrate to the lay reader what is known and not known on a given subject. A literature review often has to cover a vast amount of material in a very concise fashion. Because of this, authors have to make choices about what to include and what to leave out. It is helpful if the writer articulates why certain decisions were made, both revealing their grasp of the material, and explaining to the reader why some choices are more appropriate than others. In many ways, this is similar to the old axiom used in high school math "show your work." By showing your work, the author is given the chance to explain the logic behind their decisions. This helps to create a framework during the writing stage to keep the research focused. It also gives the reader insight into the writer's decision making process, making it easier to follow the key argument.

5.4 WHEN IS A LITERATURE REVIEW NEEDED?

Most academic research will contain a section dedicated to the review of the previous literature. Although it is often explicitly labeled as "The Literature Review," at other times it is not. It is our belief that a review of the previous literature should begin at the "idea stage," even before a specific research question has been developed. This is because many research projects begin not as a formal question, but as a reaction to something. Often that reaction is as simple as hearing or reading something that causes the researcher to think, "that sounds right," or, "that does not sound right." Although a layperson might be content to stop there, for a researcher this is often the genesis for future exploration and discovery. Or as they are fond of saying on the popular show MTV Cribs, "This is where the magic happens."

The magic begins with a cursory review of the literature to help the author become familiar with the topic. Although we will deal with this in greater depth later in the chapter, this initial assessment can reveal the latest research on the subject, the most up-to-date methods used to explore the subject, as well as scholarship in other fields and disciplines. Although later searches will be used to narrow and fine-tune, with this search the author should try to cast a wide net in hopes of learning as much as they can about the subject.

5.5 THE LITERATURE REVIEW—TWO APPROACHES

Although there are a variety of ways to think about how to conduct a literature review—with many approaches far more haphazard than others—it is important to remember that the goal is to conduct a systematic review of the literature. To help us achieve this goal, it is important to think in a systematic fashion from the beginning, instead of waiting until we have gathered a list of books and articles hoping for a pattern to emerge.

One way to approach the literature review is to consider it as an intellectual history on a particular subject. An intellectual history represents the history of scholarship in a given area, such as political science, philosophy, or public administration. Considered another way, it is a way to understand how a particular group of scholars has conducted research on a specific subject. Although it is understood that areas of study are not developed in a vacuum and that the walls between disciplines are often more porous than solid, the goal of an intellectual history is to focus on a particular unit of analysis, such as eras (e.g., progressive), disciplines (e.g., public administration), movements (e.g., civil service reform), etc. So, for example, an intellectual history of the concept of patronage in public administration would focus on the development of how patronage has been used and understood over time in the field of public administration. This could be done in a chronological fashion, revealing how the field has changed its thoughts about patronage over time.

The intellectual history approach is very popular, because it uses the disciplinary boundary to contain the scope of the exploration. So, although there may be research in other disciplines addressing a specific subject, if that literature does not amount to a substantial movement within the field of public administration, it would not be a part of the field's intellectual history. For instance, Van Wart's (2003) intellectual history of public sector leadership theory is an excellent example of this approach. Covering over 61 years of research, Van Wart details the exploration of the concept of leadership in *Public Administration Review*, the leading journal in public administration. Although the author also introduces the major themes found in the traditional study of leadership, what makes this approach an intellectual history is that it is done in the context of showing how the development of these themes influenced the study of leadership in public administration.

A contrasting approach would be to frame the literature review using the history of ideas. The history of ideas represents an attempt to transcend the boundaries of specific disciplines while focusing on a specific individual idea. As A.O. Lovejoy, the founder of the history of ideas concept explained:

> By the history of ideas I mean something at once more specific and less restricted than the history of philosophy. It is differentiated primarily by the character of the units with which it concerns itself... In dealing with the history of philosophical doctrines, for example, it cuts into the hard-and-fast individual systems, and, for its own purposes, breaks them up into their unit-ideas (Lovejoy, 1936).

This approach would try to explore the history of an idea as it developed across disciplinary boundaries, revealing both the similarities and contradictions of different approaches. So in this case, one might explore how the concept of patronage has been explored by researchers across disciplines during a specific period like the Progressive Era. Again, though the scope is wider in terms of the crossing of traditional academic boundaries, there is a constraint placed on the researcher in terms of time or by focusing on a specific aspect of a broader subject.

For instance, Spicer (2004) provides an excellent example of this approach with his exploration of the concept of the state. By examining how this concept has been used and understood over time, Spicer placed the concept in both a political and a social context that helps the reader clarify the multiple meanings of the term.

Both approaches represent a systematic way of organizing the initial literature search. Because the literature review has to communicate so much information, it is essential that the writer structures the search in a way that is clearly organized. Of course this is often easier said than done. Anyone who has attempted to conduct either an intellectual history of a field or the history of a well-known idea or concept knows how quickly this endeavor can spiral out of control. To guard against this, it is strongly suggested that the writer has at least a temporary set of boundaries to help guide the direction of the search. Again, it is understood that many of the boundaries that exist between disciplines, fields, and chronological time periods are porous, if not completely arbitrary; however, they still provide important markers for the person conducting an initial search. In either case, a well organized search will help the writer set the parameters for the rest of the paper.

5.6 WHEN DOES THE LITERATURE REVIEW START?

The actual beginning of a literature review is unclear. As mentioned earlier, the literature review starts before or while the question is being devised. It is very important to be mindful of what is being read and what it draws upon when searching for a paper topic. While reading, it is important to pay attention to (1) the type of journal that is being read, (2) the literature being cited, and (3) how this work ties in with other bodies of literature.

It is important to remember that there are several types of journals and the type of journal will assist the writer on where to go for follow-up literature. Every field of science, and most subfields, have specialized journals. Typical public administration journals include *Public Administration Review*, *Journal of Public Administration Research and Theory*, and the *Journal of Public Administration and Management*. Public administration specialty journals would include journals like the *Review of Public Personnel Administration*, which specializes in public personnel and human resources.

Area journals typically address broad questions that are of interest across the discipline, while specialty journals cater to more focused subsets. If the focus of the inquiry addresses broad theoretic questions, then the bulk of the research will probably be in area journals. Similarly, if the question is focused and more specific, specialty journals will be of more use.

A very easy way of identifying the important bodies of literature is to follow the citations in the material being read. While reading a book or article, the reader will notice the names that get repeated time and time again. This should be the first indication of material that should be read! In general we like to follow the rule of three, which is if a name appears more than three times it should be pulled and read. While this may sound straightforward enough, it is surprising how many times people do not read the seminal works of the question they are addressing.

Many different literatures have a high degree of overlap. For instance, management literature tends to overlap with policy implementation, public administration and business correlate pretty strongly, and a great deal of budgeting literature will share theories with public finance. It is very common while reading, to be reminded of previously read papers. Jotting things like this down in the margins while reading an article is a great way to identify your first steps in reviewing pertinent literature.

5.7   WHAT DO I NEED TO HAVE TO BEGIN A LITERATURE REVIEW?

In days past, writing a literature review was a far more arduous chore. While the task at hand has become somewhat easier with the advent of the electronic age, the expectations for the quality of a literature review from students have increased. Before the 1990s, and in some cases as late as the new millennium, a quality literature review required access to a library that held extensive collections on the topic at hand. Currently, the vast majority of research that was previously done in the bowels of dark library stacks can be done through electronic access. In fact, most colleges and universities offer remote access to limitless electronic holdings from commercial electronic indices. Even without university affiliation it is now possible (albeit expensive) to access vast stores of quality research. Given the current availability of information on the World Wide Web, the true challenge of producing a sharp literature review has changed from the ability to locate existing knowledge to being able to synthesize this literature into clear and concise prose.

It would seem then that there are only two basic requirements for performing a literature review: (1) access to existing literature and (2) a well formulated question. As simple as this may seem, the lack of a clear, well formulated question will confound the process of writing a literature review, and then probably lead to a very bad paper. We will leave the details of how to construct a good question for others, but we cannot overemphasize the importance of thinking through the variable of interest, outcome variable, and theoretic linkages between the two before beginning a paper.

5.8   WHAT ARE THE STEPS IN PERFORMING A LITERATURE REVIEW?

There exist several important steps in writing a literature review. Given that what is to be done is to review literature, the first and most important step is finding that important literature. Currently, electronic access is probably the source for the majority of literature cited in student research today. There are several different types of electronic access, and each offers different strengths and weaknesses.

5.8.1   GATHER SOURCE MATERIAL

5.8.1.1   Electronic Resources

First-line searches are typically done with either a search engine or an index. The search engine actually goes out and searches the World Wide Web for pages that reference the specified search criteria. Oftentimes, the types of searches can lead to a long and fruitless path. Bear in mind, that while the Internet offers a tremendous amount of information, there is no filter for this information. By this we mean that there is no check on the veracity of what is there. While some very bright, informed individuals poach research on the World Wide Web, it is also home to a great deal of "less than accurate" information. One notable exception is Google Scholar.

Indices, on the other hand, are searchable databases from known sources. Typically these sources are from refereed journals, official documents, or bona fide news outlets. JSTOR, one of the oldest scholarly journal indices, offers a list of the journals included. Other indices do one better. Blackwell Synergy offers not only full text access to all Blackwell journals but it also offers hyperlinks for the citations. The major downside to these types of indices is that they give the illusion of total coverage. What we mean is that a typical search on any of the commercially available indices will usually result in tens of pages of article listings. However, important literature, especially that which predates the electronic era, often can easily be missed. Also, topics that are reserved for specialty journals typically do not fare as well when searches are limited to electronic indices. Some popular indices include

Blackwell Synergy: http://www.blackwell-synergy.com/
ERIC: http://www.eric.ed.gov/ERICWebPortal/Home.portal
First Search: http://firstsearch.oclc.org/
JSTOR: http://www.jstor.org/
Lexis/Nexis: http://global.lexisnexis.com/us

5.8.1.2   Old School Library Usage

Before 1990, it was easy to tell when class papers were due at major universities. That would be the day that college professors and students fought for space at the large tables in the library. The advent of electronic access has all but done away with this seasonal trend. This is unfortunate, as some of the best access to information is still only available from a trip to the library. Often, one will be able to find information from state and local governments, which is unavailable online in the library. Older information, including government documents and reports, is often stored as microfiche which must be accessed in the library.

Unique information, not available online, is certainly a good reason to visit the library; however, it is not the best. The most important resource in the library offers its patrons are librarians. Ever since man first started storing knowledge, we have continually upgraded the storage, medium, and delivery of knowledge. For this reason, librarians always know the best way to locate information. Furthermore, they will often steer you to information you had not originally thought of. Librarians are masters of far more than the Dewey decimal system, and every researcher would be well served to be able to call at least one friend.

5.8.1.3   Find a Friend!

Ever noticed that senior professors seem to be far more prolific in their writing than the junior professors? There are several reasons for this: first and most obvious is that they have been doing it for a long time, and have read a fair amount of the literature extant. Second and somewhat less obvious is that there are just not that many academics in any specific area. This means that more senior professors likely know everyone who is active in research within their discipline. We should be clear here that when we say know we do not mean know of, but truly know. Through networking, conferences, and social events, most active scholars know everyone who publishes in their area. The long and the short of this is it is easier to remember what your friends are doing than someone you have never met. The third and final reason is that scholars tend to focus all their research in a very few areas. This means the longer you focus on a given literature, the better you get to know the literature. We are certainly not suggesting that senior professors should provide every reference needed to read on any given topic area, but any professor should be able to steer an interested party to the body of literature on a particular topic within their individual expertise.

It is not uncommon for researchers to consult one another about existing bodies of literature; however, a person does not have to be a professor to be able to suggest a place to start. As mentioned earlier, librarians are great for this. Another good source can be classmates or friends who do work in the same field. Remember, just because two people had the same classes does not necessarily mean they retain the same information.

5.8.1.4 Quality of the Literature

A good literature review does not just sum up everything that exists on a given topic. A good literature review summarizes and synthesizes all the literature that is pertinent to a given question. With this in mind, it follows that one must be able to identify good research from bad. In some cases this is more difficult than it sounds. Everyone who has ever watched late-night TV has certainly seen an infomercial. The interesting thing about infomercials is that it is often difficult to distinguish them from actual TV news programs. Obviously, this is a marketing ploy. Research can be similar in that often very bad research gets "packaged" in such a manner as to increase the face validity of the work. There are some rules of thumb, however, that can help to distinguish the good from the bad (and the ugly).

5.8.2 Literature Sources

5.8.2.1 Journals

When we speak of journals, we mean peer-reviewed, scholarly journals. A peer-reviewed journal is one where the manuscripts are sent out for reviews before publication. These reviews are double-blind. This means that neither the authors nor the reviewers know who the other is. This is done in an effort to ensure the quality of the research. Due to the laws of supply and demand, the research found in better journals faces a more scrutinizing review process. Typically, journals can be thought of as a fairly reliable source of scholarly research. It is important to remember all journals are not created equal. There are two easy ways to distinguish between good journals and the rest.

The first is by reputation. In the field of public administration there are journals heard referenced over and over again. This will include *Public Administration Review, Journal of Public Administration Research and Theory, Journal of Policy Analysis and Management, Journal of Public Affairs Education*, as well as others. One can have more confidence in the quality of research in these better-known journals than the research found in more obscure journals. One major reason for this is the demand for journal space. Each journal has a finite set of resources and can publish only as many articles every year. It follows then, that the more popular a journal becomes, the more manuscripts it receives every year. The larger the number of submissions received, the more selective a journal can be in what it chooses to publish.

The second way to distinguish between journals is to look up the ISI impact factor. These can be found on the ISI Web of Science Web site. The impact factor is a score which reflects how often manuscripts published in a journal are cited in other work. Although this is not a perfect measure, it does give a pretty good indication of the status of the particular journal with other researchers.

5.8.2.2 Books

Books are a good source of information, but they are typically more dated than journal articles. This is because it takes longer to write a book, and it takes longer to review a book. Bearing this in mind, one of the greatest strengths of a book is the coverage it can give to older subjects. Also, books can be a fantastic way to find a starting point in unfamiliar literature. There are also quality differences in books that can be identified by the type of publisher. The basic rule of thumb is that university presses are more academically rigorous than commercial presses. Also, some commercial presses are better than others. There are a number of good presses, including Lexington, McGraw-Hill, Wiley and Sons, and others that you will see repeatedly as classroom texts. Typically, these produce better scholarship than "prestige" presses.

5.8.2.3 Conference Proceedings

Many conferences now publish conference papers in either hard or electronic format. This is a good source of cutting-edge research, and often a good way to catch manuscripts before they go to journals. The easiest way to access conference proceedings is to go to the association Web site. The downside of conference papers is that they have not been through a peer review.

5.8.2.4 Dissertations

Dissertations are a good source of information on a given topic. Typically a dissertation will have a very thorough review of the literature on any given topic. Also, dissertations go through a rigorous reviewing process by the dissertation committee. Unfortunately all committees are not created equal, and it is important to see who the committee was. This information is usually contained within the bound dissertation.

5.8.2.5 Government Research

There is a great deal of government produced or sponsored research that never makes it to a refereed journal but is performed by world-class researchers. This is because the government is typically more interested in outputs and outcomes than the theoretical links, whereas scholarly research is done with the intent to understand theoretical linkages. Much of this is easily available on the Web. For instance, the Department of Education Web site has links to tremendous amounts of research on US schools. The same is true for almost every other large agency.

5.8.2.6 Internet Sources

Internet sources are a mixed bag at best. While there are some noteworthy research projects out there that will emerge from a general Web search (i.e., Yahoo, Google, Dogpile), the majority of what will result are either hits that are only tertiary to the given subject, or are dangerous. And by dangerous, we mean that they will be convincing enough that you might be inclined to take the site as a reliable source, only to find out later that the information was wrong.

5.8.2.7 Think Tanks

Research produced by think tanks can be very valuable, as long as one understands the system that produced the product. Think tanks produce research for clients or are based on an ideology. Bear in mind that ideologically driven research starts with a set of assumptions that are typically not altogether solid. For example, there exists literature on teen pregnancy that is built on the assumption that life begins at conception. While this is a truth in some religious beliefs, this is a subjective truth that has not been verified by science. The premise of science is that facts that cannot be substantiated objectively are not facts. Hence, research that builds on literature derived from this assumption would be faulty from the start. This is not to say that science is "better" or "worse" than metaphysics, only that the fundamental requirements for the two are starkly different and are not interchangeable.

5.9 KEEPING TRACK OF WHAT YOU LEARN

In the old days, the way you constructed a literature review was to read all sorts of information and take notes on note cards. This way one could write the paper from an outline, referencing your note cards as you went. Note cards could be grouped however necessary and the author could have multitudes of information directly available and searchable without having piles of source material lying around. In the end all one had to do was to order your note cards alphabetically and then type your bibliography when you were done. Fortunately, the electronic age has brought new technology that has made writing easier. Unfortunately, many people go from thought to page without much in-between.

Yes, writing papers is far easier now than it was even ten years ago; however, technology has marginalized some of the strong writing skills that were imperative in the past. Now, people tend to just write without notes and without any sort of outline. We strongly suggest that you do not write this way. Outlining is one of the most useful tools a writer can employ. Outlining allows the writer to map out where the paper is going and how it is going to get there. One can actually see the flow of the paper before it is written. This is important for two reasons; first, it ensures the paper actually gets to the intended destination, and second it helps the author compare the temporal flow of information.

As with most professors, we can normally tell when a paper is written without a roadmap. Often the paper wanders, exploring irrelevant item after irrelevant item. Occasionally, the literature review wanders so much, that it never really covers the topics that are seminal to the paper at hand. Needless to say, this is bad. Remember, good writing is not a gift and does not just happen. Good writing is a function of strong writing skills and practice. Start a literature review with an outline. From there, notes can even be cut and pasted into the appropriate sections. Additionally, one can even start adding in citations while writing, thus forming the bibliography on the fly. This can be done in two ways, either by simply typing the references at the end, or by using a program like EndNote, BibTex, ProCite, or RefWorks.

Referencing software like EndNote stores references and will automatically generate a bibliography based on the citations in the paper. Although this type of software has an additional up front cost, there is a huge payoff at the end. The software will change between styles automatically, and you never have to retype references. This means that if a fair amount of your work uses similar references, you do not have to enter those references again.

5.10   TEMPORAL ORDERING

Once the resources are collected and the outline created, the only thing left is writing. There are three basic parts to every literature review: the introduction, the body, and the conclusion. All three sections are equally important; however, if the reader's interest is lost in the beginning, it will be difficult to recapture their interest later on in the paper (if they read that far)! Another rule of thumb is to tell them what you are going to do, tell them what you are doing, and tell them what you have done.

5.10.1   BEGINNINGS AND ENDINGS

The introduction serves two main purposes. The first is simple: tell the reader what they are going to read. The second function of the introduction is to "set the hook." That is, the author's job is to set up the research question as an interesting puzzle. In the introduction it should be presented in as seductive a manner as possible. If the reader's interest is captured in the beginning, the paper will be easier to read. This quality has huge dividends whether the reader is looking for information, deciding to assign the paper as a reading, or grading it.

The conclusion is also straightforward in intent. A good conclusion tells the reader what has been done and emphasizes the "takeaway" points. In the case of a literature review for an empirical paper, the takeaway points will be why the existence of a relationship between your variables is important, both theoretically and substantively. This leaves only the body of the literature review.

5.10.2   THE BODY

There are several ways in which the body of a literature review may be presented. The job here is to decide which approach offers the clearest presentation of the material at hand. One common problem with writing a literature review is that when the author has read a really good literature review it becomes difficult to present the same material (with some additions) in a different format. Unfortunately, it can be very difficult to write in a similar presentation style as another author without lapsing into rewriting the paper with synonyms in the actual text. This is not acceptable and we strongly advise that if the material being reviewed is very similar to the work of an existing author, take the time to reframe it completely. Although this is more work, it removes any suspicion about "borrowed" work. Besides, if the material has already been presented in a given temporal flow, it may make the material accessible to a different audience by presenting it in a different fashion.

5.10.3 ARRANGING THE BODY

As discussed earlier, there are many logical ways to order a literature review. We previously discussed the differences between two types of approaches—an intellectual history and the history of ideas. However, there are additional approaches that one can consider. Among them are chronological, by topic, and methodological approaches (The Writing Center, 2006).

5.10.3.1 Chronological

A chronological approach tracks events through time. This approach is good if you want to trace the evolution of an event or theory, but may become confusing if there is a lot of information about a subject over a short period. For example, if an author wanted to trace the evolution of public administration, they could start with Wilson (1887) and finish with Frederickson and Smith (2003), hitting such greats as White (1926), Gulick (1937), Stillman (1987), and Kettl and Milward (1996) along the way.

5.10.3.2 Topic

Often, telling a tale as it happens is not the best way to emphasize specific events. The same is true with writing. Often it is more helpful to discuss the advent of a given phenomenon in terms of the components that drove it. For instance, Shafritz and Hyde (1997) offer the contents of their reader in both chronological and topical orders. The latter allows the reader to only read the sections dealing with human resource or organization theory. By seeing the development of the parts, it is easier to understand the development of the whole.

5.10.3.3 Methodological Approaches

While the first two approaches are more common, the constant expansion of methodological approaches is becoming ever more confusing in the field of public administration. If there are several sets of methodological approaches, it is often to group the literature by these approaches so the reader can compare apples to apples and so the author does not have to be redundant in the explanations of a technology. It is also common to blend these approaches to better tailor the discussion to the question at hand. Above all, there are a few points that should be universal in writing.

5.10.4 UNIVERSALS

5.10.4.1 Synthesize

Always work to be succinct in writing. It is the writer's job to synthesize the material, make sense of it, and make it one's own. There is nothing more valuable than a good literature review and little as punishing as a bad one. Unfortunately there is not much middle ground between the two. Think back to a young child trying to tell a story about a series of events that hurt its feelings. "Bobby said this, and Suzie said this and Frank said this, and Krystle said this, and Maggie said this . . . " It is truly hard to be compassionate when a story becomes this annoying. Far better would be something like, "Bobby, Frank, Maggie, and Krystle all agreed that . . . While Suzie and I think this . . . "; parsimonious, efficient, and effective (although it is difficult to get adults to speak so clearly at times, this is probably an impossibility for an emotional youth).

5.10.4.2 Keep Your Own Persona

There is nothing as bad as seeing a bad impersonator doing an impression of someone you like. By the same measure, it is terrible to read a paper that is trying to sound like someone they are not. This is probably one of the biggest shortcomings in writing today. Far too many people believe that they must write like the work they read, when in fact this is a horrible approach. Remember, the reader wants your personality and flavor. Some of the best scholars in the field are not great because they are great thinkers, but because they are great communicators. Emulate that quality instead of trying to impersonate someone else.

5.10.4.3 Provide Structure

Very few people can write so well that they do not need to impose structure in the writing. Structure guides your thought while you are creating and, more importantly, it helps the reader through the work. It also allows the reader to jump back to previous sections, provides natural stopping points, and gives an overview of the work. Earlier we advocated the use of outlines in your writing. We also suggest using the outline to create section headings. The really fun part of this is that using the headings feature in your word processor allows the author to jump around within the outline and make automatic tables and indexes.

5.10.4.4 Give Credit

Someone once said that if you copy from one it is plagiarism, but if you copy from many it is research. Although that is not exactly true, there is some merit to the saying. The most important thing to do is make sure everything used is cited. We cannot think of a reason to omit citations (with the possible exception that the author did not track them properly and has lost the reference). Err to the side of citing too much, and if in doubt, seek advice (you only have to cite advice if you are going to publish the paper).

5.10.4.5 Revise

Never expect that a first draft of anything is good enough. Make it a habit of writing papers well before due dates and take a break from the paper. Set it aside for a day or two so as to completely clear the mind, and then go back to it. The more fresh looks one can take at a paper, the better the final product will be.

5.10.4.6 Share the Pain!

Before sending anything anywhere for evaluation (be it a conference, class, or to a journal), one should at a minimum read the paper aloud. If the author is unable to do this, then the paper probably does not flow very well. An even better approach to evaluating writing is to have a friend read the paper aloud. This will let the author hear how the prose flows and allow them to identify where others will stumble on the writing. As well as improving your paper, this will create a way to gauge writing proficiency over time.

REFERENCES

Fink, A. 2005. *Conducting Research Literature Reviews*. Thousand Oaks: Sage.

Frederickson, G.H. and Smith, K.B. (Eds.). 2003. *The Public Administration Theory Primer*. Cambridge: Westview Press.

Gulick, L. 1937. Notes on the theory of organization. In L. Gulick and L. Urwick (Eds.), *Papers on the Science of Administration*, pp. 1–89. New York: Institute of Public Administration.

Kettl, D.F. and Milward, H.B. (Eds.). 1996. *The State of Public Management*. Baltimore: Johns Hopkins University Press.

Lovejoy, A.O. 1936. The great chain of being; a study of the history of an idea. Cambridge, Mass: Harvard University Press.

Shafritz, J.M. and Hyde, A.C. (Eds.). 1997. *Classics of Public Administration*. Fort Worth: Harcourt Brace.

Spicer, M. 2004. Public administration, the history of ideas, and the reinventing government movement. *Public Administration Review* 64(3), 353–362.

Stillman, R.J. 1987. *The American Bureaucracy*. Chicago: Nelson-Hall.

The Writing Center, U. o. N. C. a. C. H. 2006. Literature Reviews.

Van Wart, M. 2003. Public sector leadership theory: An assessment. *Public Administration Review* 63(2), 214–228.

White, L.D. 1926. *Introduction to the Study of Public Administration*. Saddle River: Prentice Hall.

Wilson, W. 1887. The study of administration. *Political Science Quarterly 2(June)*, 197–222.

Part II

Research Design

6 Purpose and Significance of Research Design

Jonathan B. Justice

CONTENTS

6.1 INTRODUCTION

The phrase "research design" denotes both a process and a product aimed at facilitating the construction of sound *arguments*. An argument is a logical structure that marshalls both evidence and reasons why that evidence supports some claim or point. A sound argument is one that supports its claim in a way which is, even in the eyes of a skeptical and well-informed audience, credible and useful to the greatest degree feasible given the resources we have available for gathering and analyzing evidence in support of that claim. Research involves using a transparent and systematic approach to conducting inquiries that answer questions and solve problems by means of claims that are supported well enough to be treated reasonably as knowledge rather than mere assertion. The process of designing research can be difficult and at times frustrating—messy, seemingly inefficient, nonlinear, and even repetitive. If we invest the time and effort to do research design well, however, the resulting plan for conducting research will allow us to be more orderly, efficient, and linear in amassing and interpreting evidence and using it to construct a sound argument. If we design research poorly or not at all, we may get lucky and be able to generate a valid argument anyway, or we may be unlucky and end up having conducted an investigation that fails to support a claim adequately. Well-designed research leaves less to chance and thereby reduces the risk of wasting time and effort on pointless research.

The *purpose* of research design, then, is to define the structure of an inquiry into a research problem that will produce a persuasive, valid, and demonstrably useful argument in the eyes of the researcher's audience, yet can feasibly be carried out within the bounds of the material and intellectual resources, and time, available. Like any kind of design, research design is a form of constrained problem solving, used to prescribe a way to use available materials to yield some desired product or outcome. For an engineer, the problem may be to design a bridge that can carry particular vehicles over a particular river at a particular height, and which also can be constructed within specified limits on cost and schedule. The bridge once constructed will solve the problem of how to get those vehicles over that river. For the researcher, the problem may be to design a research project that will provide the best possible—for a defined audience and application—answer to a question, or the best possible confirmation or disconfirmation of a claim, within resource limits. In public administration, the underlying problem may be a practical one confronting administrators or policy makers (e.g., whether to privatize trash collection) or a theoretical one confronting researchers (e.g., whether "rational choice" theorists' assumptions about human nature are correct).

The *significance* of research design is thus twofold. First, the quality of the design will be a determinant of the quality of the product. It is usually easier to produce a good bridge or a demonstrably sound argument if you start with a carefully thought-out design. Second, by narrowing inquiry to a specific combination of particular theories, frameworks, research question(s), evidence, methods of drawing inferences from evidence, and audience, the design determines what arguments can and cannot convincingly be made, what uses can and cannot reasonably be made of the research findings, and by whom. (Will the bridge be designed to carry pedestrians, trains, and bicycles, or only cars, trucks, and buses?) The process of design is a process of trading off competing values and purposes: perfection against feasibility, breadth against depth, accessibility to an audience of practicing managers versus some of the qualities sought by academic social scientists, parsimony versus realistic description, statistical (Yin, 2003, p. 10) generalizability versus fine-grained accuracy and relevance to a particular case, and so on.

In this chapter, I will emphasize the problem-solving aspects of research design in public administration (PA), as a somewhat iterative and often messy process which is used to solve the second-order problem of how to solve research problems by delineating credible and feasible procedures for investigation and argumentation in both the practice and study of PA. The nature of PA as both a field of scholarly inquiry and a field of professional practice dictates the use of a diversity of paradigms, designs, and methods of research according to the specific purposes and audiences at hand. Thus we should not rush to privilege one form or source of knowledge over another (Schmidt, 1993). The implication of this for the design and conduct of research in PA, however, is not that fundamentally different standards of reasoning and argumentation apply in different applications, nor that scholars need somehow to adopt less rigorous standards and procedures or are justified in so doing. Rather, it means that we should seek as researchers to employ, and as consumers of research to demand, logic, argumentation, and evidence that reflect the standards of validity and reliability, susceptibility to scrutiny, and willingness to yield to demonstrably better supported claims that we tend to associate with "scientific" research.

This should not be intimidating for students or practicing managers, however: the systematic approach and publicness of data and methods associated with "scientific" rigor are meant precisely to make it easier for us mortals to maximize the quality of our arguments. Applying scientific rigor to research requires using a tested set of procedural guidelines to channel as well as to stimulate creativity. Accordingly, a good, scientific (meaning systematic, explicit, and transparently presented) research design can make the construction of useful[1] knowledge in (and of) public administration easier than it would otherwise have been, for managers and students as well as for specialist researchers.

My primary agenda in this chapter, therefore, is to present the fundamental logic of research design for public administration as involving simply the work of devising a sound plan for constructing a good argument to support a claim that will be useful to some audience or audiences. I will try here to demystify some of the social-scientific jargon usually employed in courses in research design and methods by showing how it is related to the more general problem of devising adequate arguments to support claims presented to skeptical audiences. Audiences of administrators and audiences of academics may well have different standards of evidence and inference but these are differences in technique rather than in the underlying logic of inquiry. Further, I would suggest that administrative researchers and administrative consumers of research would do well to design and evaluate administrative arguments with the same degree of concern for making their assumptions and limitations explicit and their logics of inquiry systematic that academic researchers (are supposed to) employ.

Courses in research design, like the chapters in this volume, discuss scientific procedures in terms of such qualities as validity, reliability, inference, induction, deduction, levels of measurement, operations, instrumentation, and so on. In practice, this language can be understood as concerned with the fundamental structural elements of an argument: claims, evidence (or data), inferential warrants, and qualifications (see Booth et al, 1995, pp. 85–148, for an updated discussion of this general structure grounded in a classic essay by Toulmin [1958, pp. 94–145]). *Claims* are the points we want to make: our proposed solutions to problems; answers to questions; assertions about what our audience should be paying attention to, or choosing, or doing; or simple descriptive statements (e.g., Toulmin's "Harry is a British subject"). Evidence is the observable data on which claims are ultimately based ("since Harry was born in Bermuda"). Inferential *warrants* are the accepted or acceptable logical principles that allow us to justify particular claims on the basis of particular evidence: generally recognized or defensible theories and principles that allow us to draw conclusions on the basis of observations ("because those born in Bermuda are British subjects"). Warrants in turn may be supported by implicit or explicit *backing* that justifies the warrant itself ("on account of the particular legal provisions that make those born in Bermuda British"). *Qualifications* describe limits to the force or breadth of application of our claims: the evidence and warrants I am able to muster in support of my claim may not be conclusive, there may be individual exceptions to a general rule, or a rule may apply only to a degree or only under certain conditions or in certain settings ("presumably," "unless he has become a naturalized American"). Researchers will also try to anticipate any reasonable *rebuttals* that a skeptical and well-informed audience might offer (that Harry wasn't really born in Bermuda, that my reading of the law is incorrect, that Harry has in fact become an American, and so on). What distinguishes research-based arguments and claims from those based on faith or on mere assertion is the researcher's explicit attention to grounding them by means of adequate and soundly backed warrants in appropriate evidence, to anticipating and responding to reasonable rebuttals, and to honestly acknowledging their limitations.

Another distinguishing characteristic of research arguments is that they are formally structured as inquiries rather than solely as means to justify already decided-upon claims. Thus, the formal jumping-off point for a research-based argument will be a central *research question*. When your research argument is constructed in its final form, therefore, it must have a question as well as an answer (your claim), and answering the question must lead demonstrably to the key points and conclusion of your argument. Procedurally, however, you may begin either with a pure question, and find your way to an argument in the course of answering that question, or with a point you want or need to make.[2] In either case, answering the research question should solve, or at least elucidate, a problem that matters to your audience, and a research design provides the road map for an argument that will arrive at that solution. The purpose of research design is to devise procedures for constructing an argument, adapted to a particular audience for and problem of research, given the applicable constraints. The significance of research design is that it determines whether, by whom, and for what purposes your research results will be valued.

6.2 PURPOSE AND SIGNIFICANCE OF RESEARCH DESIGN

If research design is a problem-motivated process of planning for the construction of a sound argument, one that will address a significant problem in a manner that is "credible, useful, and feasible" (Hedrick, Bickman, and Rog, 1993, p. ix), the purpose of research design is related to the purposes of research itself. Most broadly, in academe and the "real world" alike, research is meant to contribute to a collective stock of credible and useful knowledge, whether within an organization, a profession, or a polity. Design decisions involve choices of standards or paradigms of correctness and usefulness and of ways to operationalize those standards by beginning with a suitable object of inquiry and employing procedures meant to conform to those standards in gathering and interpreting evidence. Research, and therefore research design, also involves persuasion as a requisite for usefulness: "Persuading people is an important part of research: you have to be able to have your results accepted by other people" (Bechhofer and Paterson, 2000, p. 42). This means that in designing research, we are trying to figure out how to create knowledge[3] that will be useful and credible for a particular purpose and audience. Accordingly, the broad problem of identifying a demonstrably relevant question and the means by which it can be meaningfully answered—a soundly reasoned argument adequately supported by appropriate evidence and warrants—may be decomposed into four primary subcomponents, related respectively to persuasiveness, usefulness, correctness, and feasibility.

Persuasion has at least two elements here. We must persuade an audience that our proposed answer or conclusion is correct and appropriate, according to their standards or to other standards they deem meritorious (or in some cases we may seek to persuade them that some other particular answer or class of answers is not correct or appropriate). We must also persuade them that this correct answer responds to the correct question and solves a real *problem*. This begins by anticipating the inevitable question from our advisors or bosses or constituents or journal referees, "So what?" One metaphor sometimes offered is that inquiry in an area of knowledge may be seen as a continuing conversation. We can join and contribute usefully to that conversation by adding something meaningful to what others have said, confirming or refuting previous assertions, or even starting an entirely new and demonstrably more profitable direction for the discussion.[4] But as is true in any conversation, it must be evident to our interlocutors that what we have to say is relevant to what they were talking about and that it actually adds something worth listening to.

Of course, if we succeed in providing an actionable answer that is persuasive for one or more target audiences, we should as a matter of both ethics and personal pride make every effort to ensure that it is as correct as we can make it. Although standards of correctness (validity and reliability of evidence, warrants, and backings) may be field-specific to some degree, this still means that we must have a standard beyond just personal taste or convenience by which to assess the correspondence of our measurements and conclusions to the actual state of the world.

Here is where I think the scientific method, once demystified, can be useful to practitioners as well as academics. What lets good academic research call itself "science" is really just systematization and explicitness of logic and procedure, rather than any fundamental difference in logical structure from the kind of reasoning appropriate to solving managerial problems. Using a systematic approach to constructing arguments aimed at solving problems increases the likelihood that we will use appropriate evidence and reasoning. Explicitness allows others to understand how and why we have reached a certain conclusion, and to form an independent assessment of its validity. If we are right, this reassures well-informed skeptics and makes our arguments more persuasive. If we are wrong, this allows well-informed skeptics to show why we are wrong. Ideally, this prevents us and others from acting on mistaken conclusions, and stimulates us to search for a better conclusion. Anticipating skeptical scrutiny, or even supplying that skepticism for ourselves, is also a valuable stimulus to more careful thinking in the design and construction of arguments: why do we think our evidence supports our conclusions, and how do we know that some other conclusion is not a better one. That is, "A sound argument, a well-grounded or firmly-backed claim, is one which will stand up to criticism" (Toulmin, 1958, p. 8).

Last but not least, a research design solves the problem of how to match our research goals (including standards of acceptable quality), questions, and procedures with the research resources available to us. In many cases, the early stages of research design may show us that that something we wanted to do in a research project simply cannot be done—at least not by us just now. Can we obtain a large enough sample to get a statistically significant result? Can we get the right kind of evidence to support a particular kind of claim? Do we know how to use the kinds of analytic techniques called for by a particular kind of research question or evidence? A research design is not just a logical scheme for constructing an argument. It is also a project plan, for managing the construction by balancing the desired level of quality (usefulness, persuasiveness, correctness) against the time and resources available.

The significance of research design thus flows directly from its purpose. The process of research design is in large part a process of figuring out just exactly what phenomena and facts we are concerned with, and what we are trying to learn and say about them, with enough precision and depth that we can articulate it convincingly to others. (It has a great deal in common with teaching preparation in this regard.) The design choices that result from that process determine what practical or theoretical problems you will address; what audiences you will be able to inform and persuade; what precise questions you will pose in trying to do so; what evidence you will employ; how you will analyze and interpret that evidence; what warrants and forms of argumentation and logic you will use; the correctness and usefulness of your work; and how likely you will be able to reach a sound conclusion–to get to the point, so to speak–before running out of time and other resources.

6.3 ELEMENTS OF RESEARCH DESIGN

Design in general solves the problem of planning and specifying with appropriate levels of clarity and detail how to construct some artifact (a bridge, a research paper, an organizational process, an organization, a policy, and so on) in such a way as to solve a specified problem or problems. Problem solving can entail outcome-related as well as procedural goals (carrying trains across a river, testing the adequacy of rational-choice theory, issuing building permits, governing a small town, reducing the number of out-of-wedlock births) and constraints (physical conditions; limits on the time, people, money, and other resources available; and the like). Research design, more particularly, solves the problem of figuring out how to perform a given instance of research in such a way as to make its results persuasive, useful, and correct to the greatest degree possible, given the potential competition among these three priorities and the inevitable reality of constraints on time and other resources available for the research. In other words, research design has two major aspects: first "specify precisely what you want to find out" and then "determine the best way to do that" (Babbie, 1995, p. 83) by gathering and interpreting data and constructing a sound argument grounded in that data as well as in the relevant ongoing conversations among the academics, managers, and other members of your audience.

Table 6.1 summarizes the procedures involved in constructing a sound argument through research. For convenience, it illustrates a conventional model of academic research: reviewing the extant literature relevant to a topic or problem, stating the research problem and questions in operational form, specifying hypotheses, identifying the unit of analysis or observation and sample, developing instrumentation for data collection, collecting data, reducing and analyzing data, and interpreting the results of data analysis. This is a handy convention and a common order of presentation for journal articles as well as many other forms of research report, but it should not be confused with the actual sequence of work in designing or executing a specific instance of research. For one thing, the format is implicitly based on the "hypothetico-deductive" model for testing established theories in empirical applications, although many research problems call for inductive (warrant-establishing in Toulmin's terms) rather than deductive (warrant-using) logic and procedures. Further, the process of designing research often is necessarily nonlinear and iterative: a central purpose of design is that it provides a setting in which we can rework our plans and assumptions before investing in the conduct of the research itself. This may involve moving from a choice of method that seems on consideration undesirable or infeasible back to the reformulation of the research problem, or from the identification of difficulties in devising instrumentation back to a reconsideration of the theoretical basis for an inquiry. Hedrick, Bickman,

TABLE 6.1
Purpose and Significance of Research Design throughout the Research Cycle

Research Procedures	Design Considerations			
	Usefulness	Persuasiveness	Correctness	Feasibility
Define research problem and questions	Provides "the focus of the research" (Hedrick, Bickman, and Rog, 1993)	Answers the audience's question, "So what"	Is the problem a meaningful one? Is the question appropriate?	Can the evidence and warrants required by the question be provided?
Gather evidence, part 1: Review previous work, to learn what is already (un)known, theoretically, and empirically (the "literature review")	What kinds of evidence and warrants might be (accepted as) relevant to the problem? Has it already been solved? Has it defied solution?	Which of the evidence and warrants previously used will work with your question and audience? What qualifiers and challenges may arise?	What kinds of research designs and data have proven (in) appropriate to generate valid, fully warranted or qualified, arguments and claims?	Avoid "reinventing the wheel" or choosing an unanswerable question. "Stand on the shoulders of giants" by fully using existing knowledge
Specify hypotheses	Additional focus, and basis for comparison	Do propositions make sense to the audience?	Basis for comparison to rival explanations	Make concepts and claims provable or falsifiable
Identify units of analysis/observation, and samples	How you know what exactly your work means and for whom	Audience may have expectations that favor particular approaches	Are selected units and sample appropriate to of the population or phenomenon at issue?	Will you have access to the required units? Will they yield the right data?
Gather evidence, part 2: Develop instrumentation ("research methods")	Instrument quality (both type and goodness) determines data quality	Audience may have expectations that favor particular instruments	Instrument quality (both type and goodness) determines data quality	Do you have (access to) the skills to develop the planned instruments?
Gather evidence, part 3: Observe and measure (collect "data")	Data availability and quality determine possibility of a claim	Data quality determines whether an audience will accept the data	Data quality determines validity of claims based on the data	Do you have the time and material resources to collect the data?
Gather evidence, part 4: Reduce and analyze data ("data analysis")	Type and quality of analysis determine what claims are warranted	Audience expectations influence legitimacy of analytic techniques	Appropriateness and quality determine strength of warrants	Do you have (access to) the skills and technology needed for analysis?
Interpret data and state claims and qualifications ("conclusion")	Do claims answer the research question, solve the research problem?	Do data and warrants hold up to scrutiny by the target audiences?	Do data, warrants, and claims hold up to well-informed skepticism?	Identify qualifications and (de) limitations

and Rog (1993, p. 13) provide an explicit model of the research design and planning process as involving an iterative cycle of choosing a research design and methods; carefully considering their feasibility in light of available time, money, and human resources; assessing trade-offs; and then reconsidering the design and methods, until a plan has been arrived at that balances the criteria of credibility, usefulness, and feasibility.

6.3.1 LURKING BELOW THE SURFACE: CAUSALITY AND VARIABLES

Although not all research is explicitly concerned with discovering or explaining cause-and-effect relationships, the notions of variables and causality, and the dimensionality of concepts, nevertheless underlie much if not all research. *Variables* are "logical groupings" of the quantitatively or qualitatively measurable characteristics (or "attributes") of the objects or units being studied or described, or of their environment and history (Babbie, 1995, p. 31). For example, households may be characterized according to the variable annual income, which can assume a large range of values (that is, it can vary) measured in dollars or other monetary units. *Dimensions*, in the context of social research, are "specifiable aspect[s] or facet[s] of a concept" (p. 114), problem or question. For example, the concept "well-being," could be understood as encompassing a number of dimensions, among which might be material well-being and social well-being, although social well-being itself might be further broken down into a number of subdimensions, such as a person's relationships with a variety of others (see de Vaus, 2001, pp. 25–27). "Cause" in this context signifies that a phenomenon exists, or possesses a particular attribute, as a result of the influence of some other phenomenon or attribute: why something is or is not, or possesses particular characteristics, and how it comes to be or to exhibit those characteristics. Thus we might predict that an individual's profession or occupation might be one cause of her income, which in turn might influence her degree of material well-being.

In the abstract, we can describe several kinds of variables in terms of their relationships with respect to a causal relationship of interest, as depicted schematically in Figure 6.1. Within a specific context, independent variables are the root causes in a relationship of interest, and dependent variables are those the values of which we are trying to explain or understand. Intervening variables may come in between, such that an independent variable affects the dependent variable indirectly, by directly influencing the intervening variable, which in turn influences the dependent variable. Thus some might seek to explain the persistent pay gap between men and women (see U.S. Department of Labor Bureau of Labor Statistics, 2006) by hypothesizing that sex influences career choices, which in turn influence wage and salary income. Moderating variables alter the relationship

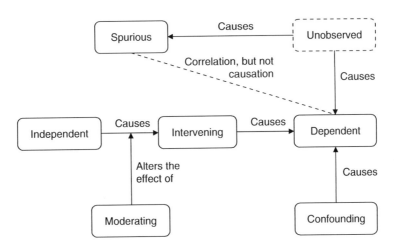

FIGURE 6.1 Schematic view of some types of variables in causal models.

between causes and effects, so that we might hypothesize that early socialization of girls influences their tendency to choose certain occupations. The former president of an Ivy League university might at this juncture suggest that an unobserved variable, the inherent genetic difference between men and women, is also at work here. Perhaps the university president was using a disparity in men's versus women's performance on a certain kind of test as an indicator of genetically based differences in ability, but another observer might argue instead that that test-score disparity is in fact a spurious variable. The test scores in question do not really measure anything causally related to income, he would say, but they do respond to sex discrimination in the construction of the tests. That same discrimination, he might continue, also causes wage differences, which is why there appears to be a correlation between the test scores and incomes. Finally, in examining any of these claims, we will also need to be on the lookout for the influence on income of a large number of likely confounding variables which might also influence the earnings of an individual or group, such as age, education, place of residence, economic cycles, access to educational and job opportunities associated with stereotypes and social networks, and so on.

Variables and their relationships are the fundamental building blocks of causal or explanatory research in particular, but exploratory and descriptive researchers must also attend selectively to the particular dimensions and variables of greatest interest and relevance for a particular research problem and audience. Otherwise, researcher and audience alike are in danger of becoming lost in a mass of undifferentiated detail, being distracted from important considerations by irrelevant ones, losing interest before getting to the important points, or simply running out of the time and space available for conducting, presenting, and receiving the research. One important way in which we can assess the relationships and relevance of phenomena, dimensions, and variables to one another is with reference to known or theoretically predicted causal influences. A researcher mindful of his audience's and his own limited time and attention will need to be selective, and so has a "social scientific [or administrative, we could add] obligation to select in some fairly systematic, that is, theory-laden manner" (Bechhofer and Paterson, 2000, p. 6) which aspects of a phenomenon of interest to attend to and describe.

6.3.2 Getting to the Point: Topics, Problems, Questions, Arguments, and Answers

The central tasks of what can be called the definitional stage of the research design process (Hedrick, et al., 1993, chapter 2) are to understand the problem, including its dimensions, objects, subjects, and relevant variables, and to formulate and refine the research questions to be answered. The process of designing research generally begins with at least a rudimentary idea of what people, objects, variables, and dimensions of a topic are of interest. Research undertaken by professional academic or managerial researchers is usually motivated by their perception that they need or want to solve a particular problem. One central purpose of research design, however, is to sharpen and narrow that focus still further, to render it feasible to conduct a meaningful investigation by stipulating an initial central research question or questions. "Meaningful" here signifies that we have selected dimensions and variables that have theoretical or practical significance for the researcher and her audience; that it is feasible for us to meet acceptable standards of usefulness, persuasion, and correctness given the resources available; and that both audience and researcher will be able to understand and make sense of the research process and its results. The significance of this narrowing and focusing work is that it is necessary for us to know what we are looking for, how to find it, when we have found it, and what we can or cannot and should or should not do with it once it is found.[5] In other words, how can we figure out what we are talking about with enough clarity and precision that we can design a way both to investigate it and explain it to others? This involves moving from broad topics to more specific problems,[6] from problems to research questions, from conceptual research questions to operational questions, and then eventually to a detailed set of plans for constructing an argument that will advance a claim adequately warranted by appropriate evidence.

Argumentation involves investigation, interpretation, and the presentation of the results of that investigation and interpretation in support of a claim, and all of this is a matter of research design. Investigation refers to the gathering of evidence (data collection) and its reduction and analysis. The quantity and quality of your evidence and its analysis are the foundation for advancing any claims about the natural or social world. Interpretation refers to making sense of the evidence, figuring out what it means, and thereby creating knowledge. Presentation is how we communicate meaningfully to others the process and results of our investigation and interpretation. Although we may denounce persuasive presentations based on dishonest or irrelevant evidence or interpretations as mere sophistry, even the most accurate data and reasonable conclusions are more compelling when presented well rather than haphazardly.

So in order to be whole—to have integrity, we could say—your research needs to have a research question motivated by a compelling research problem, but it also needs to result in an argument that connects that question with a defensible answer or claim. It may be motivated initially by a question intended to lead to an answer that can solve a problem of interest, or by a desire to demonstrate or test the appropriateness of what you believe may be the answer to a problem. If you start—in accordance with the conventionally espoused model—with a research question, you will then construct an argument from the process of answering that question. But you might just as reasonably start with a claim, and find your way to a suitable research question in the course of designing your strategy to marshal suitable evidence and warrants to support—or refute, because a responsible researcher must be open to this possibility as well—that claim with a valid argument.

6.3.2.1 Getting into the Conversation: Theories, Frameworks, and Previous Research

Whether you are beginning with a problem, a question, a hypothesis to be tested, or a claim to be justified, an assessment of what is currently known or unknown about that topic is an important early step in research design. This should include a structured literature review and other efforts to find out what others have already learned and are in the process of learning, what approaches they have used to create that knowledge, and (especially for theoretically oriented research) what major problems and opportunities there are for extending (or overturning) present knowledge. Literature reviews, queries to colleagues and recognized experts, professional conferences and their proceedings, and the Internet are sources of information about what theoretical and empirical approaches we might find useful or might be able to reject out of hand for our work, as well as of the answers to framing questions such as "What do we need to better understand your topic?" and "What do we know little about in terms of your topic?" (Creswell, 2003, p. 49, citing Maxwell, 1996).

One important purpose of a literature review is to help researchers formulate a theoretical framework for analyzing their topics and problems, grounded in an understanding of the most important dimensions and variables, and their causal relationships. This is true even for research that is not explicitly causal or concerned with theory testing or theorizing per se. If the problem is to describe or explore some phenomenon, a theoretical framework helps to focus that exploration and description on the most important dimensions and variables. If the research goal is to devise a way to correct some administrative or policy problem, it will be necessary to understand what has caused the problem, and what must change to solve the problem, as well as what consequences are associated with the problem and its solutions. Sound normative and explanatory theories help us figure out whether somebody else's "best practice" will be equally beneficial in our own setting, for example.

A second purpose is to understand what empirical research has already been done. First, this lets you find out what has been done and learned to date with respect to your topic or problem: what questions have already been asked, and what answers obtained? Second, you can examine previous research efforts with an eye to reverse-engineering them. What kinds of operational measures, data (evidence), and methods of analysis and interpretation (warrants) have been used? What evidence and analyses have proved most useful in answering particular research questions? Is specific data potentially available and appropriate for solving your own research problem? Or if you need to collect your own data, you can glean information about what kinds of data-gathering instruments proved most (and least) useful for the researchers who came before you. Alternatively, you might go further, and undertake an "integrative research review" (Cooper, 1989) to feel that you "own the literature" (Garrard, 2004); demonstrate mastery to a demanding audience; or justify a claim that none of those who went before you managed to capture the particular problem, question, evidence, or analytic approach you have.

6.3.2.2 Contributing to the Conversation: Research Problems and Questions

Once you have familiarized yourself with the relevant dimensions and variables of a problem and the key themes, theories, and methods used by others to pose and answer relevant research questions, you can begin to formulate your own contribution by bringing your particular problem to the ongoing conversation (or vice versa). At this point, the design task is to use the available accumulated knowledge, and your understanding of its gaps and limitations, to formulate and refine a researchable problem and questions in the context of the current state of the topic. This is true even if you have set out with a solution already in mind for which you wish to argue, rather than a problem for which you seek a solution. Figure 6.2 lays out a general design logic relating problems, questions, and other elements of research design in the form of a hierarchy. The actual sequence in which the components of a design are formulated and reformulated is, as we have noted, likely to be iterative and nonlinear, and may well put first things last. We can still describe a hierarchy, however, in which the logical strategies and procedural tactics of a research design are linked to a motivating research problem by means of one or more research questions. The point here is that research problems motivate research questions, and the detailed specification of particular research designs and methods is tailored to respond to those research questions: What do we need to know to solve the problem, and how can we go about satisfying ourselves and our audience that we have learned what it necessary and appropriate to our and their needs?

Types of research problems include (1) topics we believe are important but do not know yet know much about, (2) specific practical or theoretical problems we or our audience want to solve, and (3) phenomena for which available explanations are not satisfactory (Bechhofer and Paterson, 2000).[7] Research problems may involve fundamental theoretical puzzles, such as why "self-organized...regimes frequently outperform...regimes that rely on externally enforced, formal rules" in spite of theorists' predictions that such performance is impossible (Ostrom, 2000, p. 148), or descriptive projects intended to cure an audience's lack of awareness of important phenomena that should concern them (e.g., Harrington, 1962). Research problems may also involve basic challenges facing organizations, such as how a utility district can prevent its infrastructure from falling into disrepair, or how a research university can prevent repetitions of accounting anomalies that might jeopardize federal research funding.

Research as a means to solving administrative as well as theoretical research problems begins with a central research question, the starting point for focused inquiry in search of an answer. Research questions and arguments imply each other, and together they fundamentally define the purpose and significance of a particular research project or program. Thus a research design must include at least one suitable research question, and situate that question as the primary determinant of a plan for gathering and interpreting evidence, with the purpose of constructing a compelling argument leading to a point that answers the question. Whether the question is the actual starting point of inquiry (Why are self-governing regimes more effective?), or is selected as a means to try to reach a particular conclusion (What management practices will enable us to prevent infrastructure deterioration?), the research question and its associated propositions or hypotheses determine all that will follow: the type of research design employed; units of analysis and observation; sample; data requirements; methods of data collection and analysis; and thus the types of conclusions that can follow, the way in which those conclusions are warranted, and the extent to which they can be generalized to other samples and phenomena.

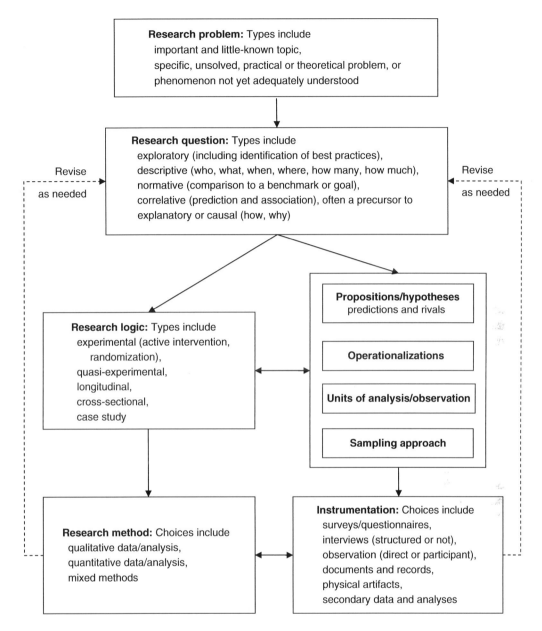

FIGURE 6.2 A hierarchy of design decisions.

Without duplicating the rest of this volume, I will note here that the soundness of an argument is highly dependent on the relevance and quality of the measurements and analytic methods we (plan to) use in research. The choice of measures and methods thus needs to be addressed by a research design, and must be based on the research problem and questions that motivate a particular study. A necessary early step in the process of selecting measures and methods is to make your research questions, hypotheses, and propositions *operational*—to express the relevant dimensions and variables in ways that allow measurement. If, for example, we set out to answer a descriptive or normative question such as "How good is our MPA program?" we might operationalize that question in any number of ways. One way might be to focus on the reputation of the program among academics (as the annual rankings produced by *U.S. News & World Report*)—"How highly do other academics rate the program?" Or we might focus on long-term career success of graduates. One of the many ways to define this could be in terms of their job satisfaction and salaries 20 years after graduation. Another operational expression of the question might be "How satisfied are students with each of their courses at the end of a semester?" One way to answer this last form of the question is by having students fill out the familiar end-of-course survey instruments. One task of research design, then, is to identify operational forms of research questions that can both contribute meaningfully to solving the motivating research problem and call for measurements that can feasibly be made and interpreted.

As Miles and Huberman (1994, pp. 22–25) observe, research questions are used not only to motivate arguments, but also to structure them as well, by narrowing research problems to deal with specific phenomena, units of analysis, research methods, analytic strategies, and instruments for gathering evidence (data). Toward this end, research questions need to be intimately linked to your literature review and to the theory or analytic framework you employ for your study, because those are key resources for understanding what variables and relationships among variables should be emphasized or have proved useful in previous research (or have been neglected to the detriment of previous research). In practice, it is common and reasonable to find that your development of a central research question will proceed in parallel with your review of the literature and the development of a theoretical framework for your research. Unless your project aims purely to test an obvious implication deduced from a settled theory, it is likely that you will proceed through multiple cycles of literature review, conceptual development, and research question formulation and reformulation. As you learn from the work of others how to understand your research problem conceptually and thus frame a suitable research question, you can also use the current version of your research question to focus your continuing review of the literature: What theories and themes, research designs, and data and methods of analysis have proved useful for grappling with questions like yours? What kinds of findings and interpretations have followed from which combinations of questions, designs, and methods, and how useful and credible have they proved to be for later research and practice (Galvan, 1999; Garrard, 2004)?

6.3.2.3 Designing a Strong Argument

The significance of research design is, as we have noted, that the combination of the many design decisions to be made will determine what kind of knowledge the research can create, and, together with the execution of the research, for what purposes and audiences and to what degree the argument and claims generated from the research will be useful and credible, or valid. In assessing research designs and arguments overall, we are concerned with two broad types of validity. *Internal validity* refers to the correctness of our claims: the extent to which the evidence and warrants used in an argument can actually support the claim offered, even in the face of skeptical challenges. *External validity* refers to generalizability of our claims: the extent to which the conclusions reached in a study can be expected to hold in other contexts or for instances other than the ones from which we gathered evidence.

The use of scientific research design logics and methods enhances the persuasiveness and correctness, and thereby much of the usefulness, of arguments aimed at explaining, predicting, or describing phenomena. Making assumptions and procedures explicit and internalizing the skepticism of a presumed audience helps us to improve the likelihood that we can demonstrate to others that our claims are well supported. First, we want to be able to show that the description (a form of claim) we offer is more accurate and relevant to our audience's interests than alternative descriptions they or competing researchers might come up with. Second, and for explanatory/causal or predictive even more than for descriptive research, our arguments should be designed to show that plausible alternative explanations (or predictions, interpretations, implications) are less likely than the ones we offer as our claims. Thus our designs must explicitly be prepared to let us eliminate the plausibility of rival explanations and descriptions.

Two central concepts or tools here are *comparison* and *control* (see Bechhofer and Paterson, 2000, for an extended treatment). We can determine that a particular independent variable or phenomenon causes something by comparing situations in which it is present to those in which it is absent, and observing whether a dependent variable differs in those situations in ways that we can attribute to the influence of the independent variable. If we are more oriented to description, we are still comparing our selection of phenomena and variables to describe against some competing set of phenomena and variables, even if the comparison is implicit. To be most probably persuasive and correct, we further need to control for alternative explanations, predictions, and descriptions—to show that any changes we detect in a dependent variable are more probably due to the relationship we claim, and are not in fact caused by some other factor. If, for example, we want to show that privatizing trash pickup saves money for cities, we would have to demonstrate that a change in costs does or would coincide with a change to or from privatized collection. We would also have to show, however, that the change cannot be more reasonably be attributed to other factors, such as changes in the general price level, the number of households served, the volume of trash generated per household, traffic congestion, and so on.

Among the logical strategies available, the pure *experiment* is "some kind of gold standard" for causal research designs (Bechhofer and Paterson, 2000, p. 13; also see de Vaus, 2001, for a good discussion of logical strategies in research design). This is because in an experimental design, the researcher is able to intentionally manipulate units of analysis to compare them across different values of the independent variable while controlling for values of rival explanatory and confounding factors. In administrative and policy research, both practical and ethical constraints often make it difficult to experiment, so researchers have developed a number of *quasi-experimental* designs that allow for comparison and control in circumstances where the researcher is unable to manipulate the objects of her attention (Campbell and Stanley, 1963; Cook and Campbell, 1979). For example, she might have a hard time convincing a selected city to privatize its trash collection to let her compare its costs to an otherwise identical (to achieve control) city. In public affairs and policy-related research, experimental and quasi-experimental designs often seek to use large samples, as a strategy for improving their validity. *Case study* designs, by contrast, examine one or a small number of cases in depth, aiming primarily at "analytic" rather than "statistical" validity (Yin, 2003, pp. 32–33) as criteria (for some examples of sampling strategies in small-sample and case-study research, see Miles and Huberman, 1994, pp. 27–34; Yin, 2003, pp. 40–53).

Designs further vary in the way they use time. *Cross-sectional* designs make comparisons across units of analysis at a single point in time, using observed correlations between dependent and independent variables at that one time as the basis for inferring a causal relationship, or taking descriptive characteristics at a given time as suitably representative of characteristics at the times of interest to the researcher and her audience. So our researcher might find a sample of cities that have privatized and compare them to cities that have not privatized, in terms of trash collection costs as well as various control factors. *Longitudinal* designs compare the characteristics of units of analysis over time. In this case, our researcher might try to measure trash collection costs for cities both before and after they privatized collection, or even to compare changes in costs over a time period for some cities that did and some that did not privatize. Longitudinal designs have some real advantages logically, because we normally presume that effects come after their causes in time: cost changes would normally be apparent after the event that caused them. But as a matter of feasibility, we may not always have the time or resources to follow cities over time, hoping that some will privatize their trash collection at some point.

Public administrators and academics might also want to generalize, in order to draw larger conclusions about the benefits (or lack thereof) of privatization. For instance, if it has been demonstrated that one or more cities included in a study saved money by privatizing trash removal, would that mean that City A also could enjoy cost savings if it privatized? Would all cities, or all cities of certain type or size, save money by privatizing? Is privatization simply more cost-effective for all services, or for all levels of government? Comparison and control are central to this problem of external validity as well. In particular, we will want to know whether the units of analysis on which the argument has been constructed are in the material respects representative of the other units to which we would like to extend (or deny) a particular claim. Again, experimentation, with random assignments of large "treatment" and "comparison" or "control" groups is often regarded as ideal, but not always feasible, for explanatory designs. Careful attention to variables, conceptual dimensions, the quality and relevance of measurements, the precise reasoning behind our inferential warrants, and any likely qualifications and rebuttals, all can help us strengthen the external validity of our arguments (or at least help us avoid making invalid generalizations).

6.3.2.4 Research Ethics and Writing

Ethical constraints on the manipulation of research participants are an important way in which social and life sciences differ from physical sciences. We do not generally accept the idea that research is likely to have benefits so great as to outweigh research procedures that cause harm to those from or about whom we gather data or construct arguments (see Miller and Salkind, 2002, section 3.8, for an overview). Although most research institutions have formal guidelines and procedures for protecting human subjects in research activities, individual researchers must themselves accept responsibility for upholding ethical standards in the conduct of research.

Creswell (2003) notes that researchers also need to consider ethical and rhetorical concerns with respect to stating the problem, describing the purpose of the research, data collection, data analysis and interpretation, and writing and dissemination. In general, the rules of thumb for the ethics of research design and its presentation are closely related to the principles embodied in the logical and procedural ideals of scientific inquiry: avoid misrepresentation (whether by commission or omission), strive for clarity, and make your procedures and conceptual frameworks explicit so that they can be subjected to careful scrutiny by your audience (and by yourself). Be clear about what your data is or will be, what kinds of inference can and cannot be drawn from such evidence, and what the limits and qualifications to your claims are likely to be. One way to design in an additional check on accuracy can be to plan on validating your data and interpretations by reviewing them with the participants in your research. Anticipate and try to forestall any potential for others to misuse your work, as well as dangers posed by your own conduct of the research. Note that for a skeptical and well-informed audience (our ideal audience) this promotes persuasiveness as well as correctness.

One useful device for improving both the ethical and logical quality, as well as the feasibility, of research design is the institutional review board (IRB). If you plan to collect data from or about human participants and are doing your research under the umbrella of an American university, you will probably have to have your plans for data collection, use, and retention reviewed by an IRB. Although the procedural ease or difficulty of negotiating IRB reviews and approvals varies from one institution to another, and the process can be difficult and time consuming in ways that at some times in some institutions are not obviously related to the protection of human subjects, IRB review requirements have considerable value for the research designer as well as the research participants. I have learned to love the IRB process not only because by protecting research participants it also reduces my potential liability for mistreating them, but also because it forces me to be explicit and clear in explaining my thinking about the logic and procedures of a research design. In preparing to secure informed consent from participants, I am compelled to state explicitly the purposes and sampling strategy of my research, the nature of the evidence I plan to gather and the instruments and analytic techniques I propose to use, why those choices are necessary and appropriate, and how long and for what additional purposes I plan to retain the data. That is, I have to write down in a form comprehensible to the members of the IRB many of the core components of a research design. In so doing I get a chance to think seriously about the design's validity and feasibility, as well as its ethical acceptability, in the eyes of a well-informed audience of skeptics.

Finally, think of writing and rewriting as a form of analysis, diagnosis, and quality control. Producing a clear, explicit, and complete design for research in written form makes it possible for others to evaluate a research design and offer advice for improvement, and it provides a useful mnemonic and benchmark for the researcher when the time comes to execute the research. If you cannot express it clearly and directly, it may not be "science" yet. Our inability to express something is frequently an indication that our logics of inquiry and argument have not been sufficiently worked out to allow for the clarity and precision with respect to research purposes and procedures that is a necessary precursor to systematic investigation. Until we understand what we plan to do, why, and with what anticipated outcome, clearly and explicitly enough to communicate it to others, especially if those others already share our interests and orientations (e.g., other faculty in our field, or fellow MPA students, or coworkers, or fellow legislators), we probably have not created a plan that will allow us feasibly to construct useful and relevant knowledge.

6.4   CONCLUSION

Research design is the creative phase of a research project. It involves transforming what may have begun as only a general interest or a vague concern into a specific research problem and questions compelling enough to justify the effort of producing and consuming research, and specific enough to be answered with a claim supported by a well-reasoned argument. It also involves devising a set of procedures by which you can answer that question correctly (as measured by validity, accuracy, precision, elimination of competing descriptions or explanations, and so on) and persuasively within the limits of time, money, and human resources available for the task. Research design is for many of us the most difficult aspect of research. But the cumulative wisdom of scientists and other systematic researchers has produced a body of technical knowledge that can provide us with the resources at least to make the problem of designing research a solvable one. It is worth the effort, because beginning with a good research design increases the likelihood of producing a finished research argument that is demonstrably correct, compelling but appropriately qualified, and useful—that is, one that makes a difference that justifies all the bother.

My major emphasis in this chapter has been that understanding the roles of research problems, questions, propositions, evidence, and warrants in forming a valid and robust argument is an essential starting point for the design of research. The process of designing a particular instance of research should begin by formulating a question (or a tentative claim) based on a problem that is demonstrably relevant to the interests of the researcher and the researcher's audience (dissertation committee, instructor, professional colleagues, boss, citizens who need to be alerted), so that the answer to the question (or the justification of the claim) will be genuinely useful, persuasive, and correct. Then operational specifications of the research questions, units of analysis, and suitable logic and instrumentation for testing the claims and answering the questions need to be identified. Methods of measurement and analysis must be matched to the problem, questions, dimensions, variables, concepts, and units of analysis and observation you have identified, to support a sound argument. As a researcher you can embrace skepticism, by explicitly taking into account plausible alternative explanations, descriptions, comparisons, and normative standards. In designing research, you are designing an argument, although you may well find that it leads to a claim other than the one you expected, once you follow it through.

The wide range of topics, problems, and audiences in public administration means that a bewilderingly large number of choices confronts the researcher, and that a variety of field- or subfield-specific standards for evaluating arguments may be applicable. This is a source of opportunity, if we do not allow ourselves to become overwhelmed. Taking a systematic approach to research design as the plan for a project that will construct an argument is one way to impose some order. Start with one or both of what you want to find out and what you want to tell others. Take into account your primary audience and its interests. Adopt a logically rigorous approach to designing your argument, even if you will eventually need to present it to an audience in a less systematic form. Take into account the available resources and time, and consider carefully any necessary revisions to the questions, propositions, methods, and qualifications you will use. By remaining focused on the centrality of a problem, a question, and the development of a sound argument that uses appropriate evidence and warrants to justify a claim, you can produce usable, credible knowledge, and avoid doing pointless research.

EXERCISES

This exercise can be done on its own, in the course of reading you would be doing anyway, or as part of the literature review as you are designing a research project. It involves simply "reverse-engineering" a research report (an article, chapter, book, or conference paper) to identify the elements of its research design. Identify each of the following elements, and critique them: Are they cogent? Do they all fit together into a coherent and sound argument? What ideas can you take for your own work? What would you have done differently? Why and how?

- Research problem: Does the researcher state or imply a problem that is sufficiently meaningful and significant (to some audience, even if not to you) that it justifies the effort of conducting (and reading about) the research? What type of problem is it (see Figure 6.2)?
- Research questions: Is there at least one research question stated, or implied clearly enough that you can state it yourself? Is it one that you would expect to lead to a useful answer, given the research problem? Is the operational version of the research question stated or implied in a way that allows the reader to understand what concepts, dimensions, variables, and measures can appropriately be used in answering the research questions? What type of question is it (see Figure 6.2)?
- Conversational context: Does the researcher demonstrate exactly how the research relates to previous research, either by taking advantage of it, and extending it, or by testing its conclusions, or by showing its deficiencies, or by showing that it has neglected the problem at hand?
- Claim: What points and claims does the researcher make?
- Data or evidence: What evidence is gathered and analyzed in support of the article's claims? Does the researcher use operational dimensions, variables, and measures appropriate to the research question?
- Warrants and methods: What inferential warrants are used to show that the researcher's evidence supports her claims? This includes the theories and conceptual frameworks used (implicitly as well as explicitly), the operational measures and instruments used for gathering evidence, and the techniques used for analyzing and interpreting the evidence gathered. Does the researcher explicitly state any backings for her warrants? What are they?
- Qualifications and rebuttals: Does the researcher explicitly acknowledge plausible rival explanations or claims and any important limitations of the research? How does she address them in the design or reporting of the research? Can you think of plausible rebuttals and qualifications that the researcher has not acknowledged or eliminated? Are they damaging to the argument? Why? How would you explain your concerns to the researcher?
- Argumentation: Diagram the argument's components. How compelling do you find the argument overall? Is it persuasive and evidently correct? Does it advance a useful claim?

ENDNOTES

1. And usefulness is precisely the point here. Research in public administration, whether for a scholarly article or for an advisory memo in a public organization, is fundamentally a problem-solving or problem-identifying exercise, aimed even if only indirectly at changing things for the better, "Otherwise,

why bother?" (to quote Aaron Wildavsky, 1961, p. 183, slightly out of context). In fact, it is precisely the normative aspect of scholarly research in PA that leads at least one researcher to argue forcefully for both greater rigor in research and separating the choice of research problems for academia from the concerns and expressed research agendas of practitioners (Meier, 2005).

2. When you start with a claim, a scientific approach will call for you to treat it as a hypothesis to be tested. You will then work to demonstrate whether and how a systematic investigation beginning with an appropriately defined question leads by means of a sound argument to that particular claim more than to plausible alternative claims.

3. The function of inquiry, after all, is precisely to create knowledge of or about the world. While extra-social realities and even much of *social reality* (Searle, 1995) can certainly be presumed to exist independently of a particular researcher's knowledge of them, that *knowledge* will itself be constructed, and usually through processes that include reference to others and to institutionalized forms of belief and understanding (Berger and Luckman, 1967). For example, it seems safe to say that the material natures and astronomical relationships of the sun, earth, and moon did not change when the Copernican concept of the solar system was developed (see the accessible account of this at www-history.mcs.st-and.ac.uk/Mathematicians/Copernicus.html), nor when Kepler ascertained that planetary orbits are elliptical rather than circular (see www-history.mcs.st-and.ac.uk/Biographies/Kepler.html). But certainly our knowledge of that reality was constructed differently at each juncture, and that in turn had implications for action in a number of human spheres.

4. Note that in all cases, I presume that an answer honestly presenting a null result is more useful than one which tortures the evidence or uses specious reasoning in order to seem more conclusive. It is useful for practitioners as well as researchers to know that a particular combination of question and methodology does not generate a definitive answer, or that a particular hypothesized answer is not supported by a particular body of evidence, or even that it is not presently feasible to answer a particular question or solve a particular problem. (Specialist researchers usually know this, and occasionally even some practitioners do as well.)

5. I am unable to resist offering an anecdote—perhaps apocryphal—from my days as a bookstore employee. A customer was reported to have approached a clerk in our vast and dusty store. He was looking for a book he had seen on a visit the previous week, and was able to describe its approximate size, color, and location on the sales floor. When asked, however, he was unable to recall the author, subject matter, or title of the book. On being informed that we could not readily locate the book for him without at least some of that information as well, the customer is reported to have exclaimed in dismay, "You mean, if I don't know what I want, you can't find it for me?"

6. For those whose research is initially prompted by a school assignment rather than by a strong desire to solve a particular theoretical or practical problem, Booth, Colomb, and Williams (1995; I prefer this edition, but others prefer the 2003 edition, and there is apparently a third edition in the works), provide a great deal of very useful advice about how to do this.

7. For a longer list of rationales, oriented specifically to scholarly research, see Miller and Salkind (2002, p. 13).

REFERENCES

Babbie, E. 1995. *The Practice of Social Research* (7th ed.). Belmont, California: Wadsworth Publishing Company.

Bechhofer, F. and Paterson, L. 2000. *Principles of Research Design in the Social Sciences*. London, New York: Routledge.

Berger, P.L. and Luckman, T. 1967. *The Social Construction of Reality: A Treatise in the Sociology of Knowledge* (Anchor Books ed.). Garden City, New York: Anchor Books.

Booth, W.C., Colomb, G.G., and Williams, J.M. 1995. *The Craft of Research*. Chicago: University of Chicago Press.

Campbell, D.T. and Stanley, J.C. 1963. *Experimental and Quasi-Experimental Designs for Research*. Chicago: Rand McNally College Publishing Company.

Cook, T.D. and Campbell, D.T. 1979. *Quasi-Experimentation: Design & Analysis Issues for Field Settings*. Boston: Houghton Mifflin Co.

Cooper, H.M. 1989. *Integrating Research: A Guide for Literature Reviews* (2nd ed.). Newbury Park, California: Sage.

Creswell, J.W. 2003. *Research Design: Qualitative, Quantitative, and Mixed Methods Approaches*. Thousand Oaks: Sage.

de Vaus, D. 2001. *Research Design in Social Research*. London: Sage.

Galvan, J.L. 1999. *Writing Literature Reviews: A Guide for Students of the Social and Behavioral Sciences*. Los Angeles, California: Pyrczak.

Garrard, J. 2004. *Health Sciences Literature Review Made Easy: The Matrix Method*. Sudbury, Massachusetts: Jones and Bartlett.

Harrington, M. 1962. *The Other America, Poverty in the United States*. New York: Macmillan.

Hedrick, T.E., Bickman, L., and Rog, D.J. 1993. *Applied Research Design: A Practical Guide* (Vol. 32). Newbury Park, California: Sage.

Maxwell, J.A. 1996. *Qualitative Research Design: An Interactive Approach*. Thousand Oaks, California: Sage Publications.

Meier, K.J. 2005. Public administration and the myth of positivism: The antichrist's view. *Administrative Theory & Praxis, 27*(4), 650–668.

Miles, M.B. and Huberman, A.M. 1994. *Qualitative Data Analysis: An Expanded Sourcebook* (2nd ed.). Thousand Oaks, California: Sage.

Miller, D.C. and Salkind, N.J. 2002. *Handbook of Research Design & Social Measurement* (6th ed.). Thousand Oaks, California: Sage.

Ostrom, E. 2000. Collective action and the evolution of social norms. *Journal of Economic Perspectives, 14*(3), 137–158.

Schmidt, M.R. 1993. Grout: Alternative kinds of knowledge and why they are ignored. *Public Administration Review, 53*(6), 525–530.

Searle, J.R. 1995. *The Construction of Social Reality*. New York: Free Press.

Toulmin, S.E. 1958. *The Uses of Argument*. Cambridge: Cambridge University Press.

U.S. Department of Labor Bureau of Labor Statistics. (2006, November 20). Women in the labor force: A databook. 2006. Retrieved December 12, 2006, from http://www.bls.gov/cps/wlf-databook2006.htm.

Wildavsky, A. 1961. Political implications of budget reform. *Public Administration Review, 21*(Autumn), 183–190.

Yin, R.K. 2003. *Case Study Research: Design and Methods* (3rd ed.). Thousand Oaks, California: Sage Publications.

BIBLIOGRAPHY

Giventer, L.L. 1996. *Statistical Analysis for Public Administration*. Belmont, California: Wadsworth.

Shields, P.M. 1999. Getting organized: A pragmatic tool for writing graduate papers. *Journal of Graduate Teaching Assistant Development, 7*(1), 5–17.

7 The Research Problem, Method, and Serendipity: An Investigator's Journey

James S. Bowman

CONTENTS

> Nothing so needs reforming as other people's habits
>
> Mark Twain

7.1 INTRODUCTION

A common question asked by graduate students—despite (or perhaps because of) taking a stand-alone research methods class is, "Do I have to do a survey for this assignment?" The standard response is that this cart-before-the-horse question is the wrong one. The right query, of course is, "What methodological tool is best suited to the problem?"

This essay describes the author's experience since 2000 in grappling with a critical issue confronting American governance: the fate of a priceless asset of democracy—the merit system—in an era of reform. Keenly aware that such an autobiographic approach creates a vulnerability to charges of narcissism, there is no delusion that this case study is any better or worse than that of others. The difference is that an unexpected opportunity was afforded to record the deeds. Still, the Twain epigram above contains a double entendre in the context of this work: not only is the merit system open to criticism, but also this chapter.

The narrative proceeds chronologically, but was encountered in a nonlinear, opportunistic manner. Consistent with past efforts, there was no grand research strategy, no way to know in the beginning the direction that the work would take. Indeed, this is the first time in the writer's career (including two books, six anthologies, and scores of articles and book chapters) that a sustained, half-dozen year effort was devoted to a single, if multifaceted, applied research subject. With greater intellectual foresight on this rapidly developing current issue, it is possible that a creative research program could have been divined at the outset. It is a manner of speculation, however, whether the results would have been superior or inferior to those examined below.

What took place was that targets of opportunity appeared and serendipity, if not providence, prevailed in the tasks undertaken. The journey demonstrates the utility of understanding various dimensions of a problem before selecting the right investigatory tool to probe them in depth. Although recognizing that different research strategies may influence the definition of a problem, choosing the method first and then seeking a subject to explore doubtlessness would have led to frustration, false starts, dead ends, and few publications. The sophisticated use of a technique can be admired, but one's efforts are wasted if the problem to which it was applied is inappropriate, obscure, or trivial. Methods are to be valued, but not to the point that they become ends in themselves (McNabb, 2002).

The chapter proceeds by first briefly describing the background of the topic, including the catalyst for the body of work that would develop. It then explains the selection of the disparate research approaches employed. They were driven, at least in retrospect, by a series of logical questions, the answers to which produced more questions and methods to comprehend the phenomenon analyzed. It would be unusual in examining a complex matter that a single method would suffice. The conclusion articulates a set of implications that may be helpful in thinking about the conduct of inquiry. The chapter closes with two problems (and possible solutions) as well as ideas for instructors who may wish to use the material herein for classroom discussion.

7.2 BACKGROUND

This section traces the antecedents of contemporary civil service reform, describes an event that proved to be the stimulus for the research, and identifies intriguing oddities and ironies that sustained the work as it progressed.[1]

A triad of enduring values—representativeness, neutral competence, and executive leadership—historically have characterized, with different degrees of emphasis, the history of public service (Kaufman, 1956). Although representativeness was the dominant value during much of the 1800s, the passage of the 1883 Pendleton Act meant that neutral competence became the principle civil service value throughout American government for most of the twentieth century. The Act sought to eliminate the graft and corruption of that characterized patronage-based, scandal-ridden spoils system. Reformers believed government should be operated in a business-like manner; a merit system, therefore, was needed to block capricious political influences in the appointment and removal of personnel. Public administration could be responsible and efficient only if civil servants were selected on the basis of qualifications and insulated from partisan intrigue by career service tenure. The moral and economic virtue of shielding public employees from predatory partisan pressures was self-evident for generations of citizens; it was seldom necessary to explain, much less defend, the merit system.

Yet "bash the bureaucrat," "run government like a business," and "government is the problem, not the solution" attitudes became increasing pervasive in American political culture in the latter decades of the last century. The New Public Management movement—an ideology emphasizing deregulated, decentralized, downsized organizations driven by market-style imperatives—propelled change. As a consequence, executive leadership would emerge as the dominant value in the management of the civil service by the dawn of the new millennium. Fueled by entrepreneurial strategies, budget cutbacks and devolution, reformers impacted merit systems across the nation by expanding management prerogatives and restricting employee rights[2] (Condrey and Maranto, 2001; Nigro and Kellough, 2006). Accordingly, the defining characteristic of the modern civil service—neutral competence with its protection from political interference—has been significantly eroded in many jurisdictions.

The corpus of work discussed here focuses on the Florida civil service reform known as "Service First," not simply because the research site was a convenience sample, but because this mega state is a national social and political trendsetter. The spur for the program—and the present research—was the publication of *Modernizing Florida's Civil Service System: Moving from Protection to Performance* by the Florida Council of One Hundred (2000), a group with close ties to the governor's office, who argued that the state government was long overdue for organizational transformation.

Contending that the merit system had changed from protecting the public to protecting employees without regard for performance, Service First was announced in the governor's 2001 state of the state address. In line with the Council's report, it was assumed that there was no reason that public workers should be treated any differently from employees in nonunionized private companies. The most contentious part of the reform was the conversion of 16,300 career service middle managers to Selected Exempt Service, thereby abolishing their job security. As Bush's top priority for the legislative session, the program was passed and went into effect that summer.

In short, the civil service reform movement in Florida (and elsewhere around the country) has been successful in achieving a multitude of changes, including employment at will, in recent years. Change advocates believe that differences between the public and private sector should be reduced by "running government like a business" and in so doing seek fundamental, nonincremental, reforms (see, for example, Ingraham and Moynihan, 2000).

As shown in Exhibit 1, many intriguing aspects, surprising events, odd ironies, dastardly deeds, unexamined premises, execrable actions, and puzzling paradoxes characterize the Florida reform. Not unlike the student who wants to do a survey before identifying a research subject, proponents of change also have a reform solution in search of a problem. The creation, passage, and implementation of Service First took place in a highly charged political atmosphere that assumed supremacy

---

Exhibit 1
Intriguing Aspects of Civil Service Reform in Florida

- The state's prereform personnel system was one of the most productive in the nation based on the number of employees compared to population.
- The negative aspect of the business management model was embraced (ready termination of employees), but not its positive dimensions (competitive compensation, the right to strike).
- The governor argued that because partisanship, cronyism, nepotism, and favoritism could corrupt the merit system, job safeguards designed to prevent such problems should be abolished.
- The only independent expert to examine Service First prior to legislative passage was a labor mediator Special Master, mandated by law to give the lawmakers nonpartisan advice when collective bargaining negotiations break down. He concluded that, "There was no factual evidence brought forward to show that the (existing) system was broken or dysfunctional" (Special Master's Report, 2001, p. 58) and that Service First would become "Service Worst" because the elimination of job protections although simultaneously seeking the most qualified staff "is not logical and will not work" (Special Master's Report, 2001, p. 74). The legislature rejected the recommendations and abolished the Special Master role in resolving future labor-management impasses.
- A Department of Transportation contract inspector observed that, "I have been involved in the private sector that Jeb [Bush] so wants to emulate, and if someone proposed a complete overhaul of an existing system without showing any facts or figures to back them up, like the governor is doing, they would earn a quick ticket to 'downsizing' " (Cotterell, 2001a, p. 2E).

(continued)

Exhibit 1 (*Continued*)
Intriguing Aspects of Civil Service Reform in Florida

- Unions who had endorsed Bush were exempted from Service First coverage. They argued that their members needed job protections when making public safety and medical decisions, and without them there would be considerable difficulty in recruiting and retaining quality personnel. Other unions, whose members had critical regulatory responsibilities but had not supported the governor in the 1998 election, were unsuccessful in making similar argument.
- The governor's "efficiency czar" resigned in protest the day the bill was signed into law. She argued that she was unable to "slow down the headlong rush to privatize, computerize, and downsize" state jobs, a reckless process that lacked analysis or justification. She was especially concerned about Service First and its expansion of the employment-at-will doctrine to careerists. "I was 'at will' . . . and you can't voice your opinion or be critical" in such an environment" (Cotterell, 2001b, p. 2A).
- Although some prominent abuses have been reported, widespread abuse (insofar as such things can be readily documented) apparently has not occurred, perhaps because of practical difficulties of hiring large numbers of employees in a downsizing era and persuading people to work for below-market government salaries. An underlying, key reason may be that old-fashioned job patronage is much less appealing to campaign contributors than "pin stripe" patronage found in the award of lucrative government contracts.
- Despite the value in documenting program successes, no evaluative metrics were written into the legislation. Rather, officials believed that employees would take more pride in their work, and that supervisors would report enhanced staff performance. There was a sense that the policy solved the problem, and attention shifted to other, more important, issues.
- There remains a determined belief in the inherent superiority of business management practices, with its current emphasis on executive leadership at the expense of merit-based neutral competence, despite the continuing corporate management problems of the Enron era (Labaton, 2006).
- Critics pointed out that a return to the spoils system of the nineteenth century is a questionable way to the meet the challenges of the twenty-first century.

of corporate values in the government. The results provided sufficient policy and academic motivations to sustain interest in the subject over the years. Accordingly, how and why the work evolved is examined next.

7.3 RESEARCH APPROACHES TO PUBLICATION OUTLETS FOR THE TOPIC

"It is impossible to observe and record everything," Hubert Blalock reminds us, "and even if we could, we wouldn't know what it all meant" (1964, p. 8). There is no such thing as an error-free approach. Work undertaken is determined by assumptions not only about the reality one seeks to comprehend but also by the method selected (Creswell, 2003). One's ontological (the nature of reality as objective or subjective), epistemological (the investigator as independent from or interactive with what is being researched), and axiological (the subject as value-free or value-laded) positions must all be considered.

The narrative in this section proceeds as each project was completed, not when published (release dates varied depending upon journal and book publisher backlogs). The tasks were premised on answers to questions raised, and influenced the choice of research strategies considered germane to the questions. The principle work products are categorized by their methodology: descriptive, normative, empirical, theoretical, literary, case study, comparative, and program evaluation (viz., theory-building is not the sole goal of research, especially in applied work). As a capstone, this review concludes with a discussion of how some of the works were collected for symposia and anthologies.

7.3.1 Descriptive Approach

Initial research interest in the topic, originating in late 2000, was an effort to ask the question, "What is it?" because the transformation of the entire state personnel system was proposed by the Florida Council of One Hundred and endorsed by the governor, comprehension of its ramifications had to be grasped. Subsidiary, implicit questions emerged such as "What problem did the original merit system seek to solve?" "Why are reformers introducing changes now?" and "What might be the consequences of new legislation?" The thrust of any such effort, then, is largely descriptive to gain information, knowledge, and understanding of the subject at hand.

Following a literature search on the merit system (the results of which would prove to be quite useful for this and future papers), it was evident that primary sources (government documents, newspaper articles and, critically, interviews) would form the basis of the inquiry. The decision was made, accordingly, that in-person interviews would be conducted with a representative sample of key stakeholders ($n = 28$). They included legislative members and staff, union officials, interest group representatives, the press, state managers, an illuminating, if time-consuming, process (although focus group methodology might have been more efficient, it was not seen as feasible because of scheduling difficulties or perhaps desirable due to potential "posturing" by participants).

A drawback in this sort of exploratory field work is that although it is fundamental to further research, it alone may not result in a publishable manuscript. An invitation to write a chapter in a civil service reform state-of-the-art reader (Nigro and Kellough, 2006), however, did provide an outlet as well as a reason to form a study team including another public administration scholar and a law professor. The manuscript was prepared during 2001–2002, first as an American Political Science Association 2002 convention paper and then revised for the book. Problems with anthologies, it can be noted, include the difficulty in locating publishers willing to support edited collections, the challenge in assembling authors in a timely fashion, and delays in publication.

7.3.2 Normative Approach

As more was learned about the nature of Service First, the research question changed from "What is it?" to "What does it mean?" Prescriptive work can be logically distinct from descriptive efforts because it suggests a commitment to particular values. But unless prescription is informed by reality, it is reduced to an unenlightened ideology thereby losing its moral force. Thus, concurrent with the descriptive book chapter, normative views on Service First developed and were presented in several venues. The author wrote several letters to the editor in the state capital newspaper as well as an op-ed essay, published as a point-counterpoint feature opposite the vice-chairman of the Florida Council of One Hundred (Bowman and Hoffman, 2001). In addition, four other public administration professors were recruited from different Florida universities to contribute to a critical appraisal of Service First (Bowman et al., 2001) that appeared in the *Public Administration Times*. Finally, a speech was delivered at the January, 2002 Florida Personnel Association meeting.[3]

Professional service activities such as these may not or cannot be translated into a journal article. In seeking to build upon this work, it was fortuitous, therefore, that a suitable outlet was identified. Thus, the central work product of the normative phase of the research was a solo-authored piece (Bowman, 2002) in a quarterly that publishes articles dealing with labor issues. In the polemic tradition, this critique of radical reform in Florida examined how private sector employment techniques were being used to corporatize state government.

An attraction of the normative course of action is that such armchair pieces are much more interesting to write than expository essays. The problem is that they cannot be done well without first doing the descriptive work. And, although prescriptive efforts are more engaging than narrative methods, they are also often more challenging and time consuming to write than, say, empirical papers. Indeed, having devoted considerable time and energy to Service First by this time, the author was ready to move on to other projects—not the least of which was a coauthored book on a related topic (discussed later). However, one of the virtues of coauthorship is that colleagues create opportunities that may not be immediately evident. Thus, book chapter coauthor Sally Gertz (with her husband in the Florida State School of Criminology) had access to resources to support a statewide empirical study of employees impacted by reform.

7.3.3 EMPIRICAL APPROACH

If the normative strategy poses the question, "What does the author think?", then the empirical strategy (at least in this instance) asks, "What do the affected officials think about the problem?" Put differently, the previous approaches are especially helpful in defining the process by which the problem emerged, whereas a quantitative method is most useful in understanding the extent and scope of the problem. Information is gathered and transformed in the first two strategies whereas survey research is concerned with generating data (Brewer and Hunter, 1989). This new project, then, seemed like an excellent chance to confirm, reject, or modify earlier findings from the inductive descriptive and normative publications (the former focused on policymaking officials and the latter emphasized the writer's understanding of those data). To assist with the survey, the authors recruited another colleague, Russell Williams.

Details of the methodology employed are found in the article (Bowman et al., 2003), but a 38-question structured telephone survey was administered by professional callers to a random sample of 457 employees (margin of error: 4.7 percent) who became exempt personnel under Service First. The objective was to gauge attitudes of those who play a key role in determining the ultimate success of the program: middle managers. There was no attempt to ascertain if the reform was needed or valid. The survey was supplemented by interviews with knowledgeable political actors and observers.

When the data collection, analysis, and write up were completed, one team member suggested that the manuscript be submitted to a leading general journal in the profession. Several others believed that the scope of the work was more appropriate for a specialized outlet, a judgment that turned out to be correct after the initial periodical rejected the piece. Unfortunately the accompanying reviews did not provide ideas for revisions, but the quarterly that did accept the study offered suggestions for improvement. The survey was the subject of a detailed press story (Cotterell, 2003), perhaps because many respondents seriously questioned Service First; the newspaper article included equivocal comments from a Bush Administration spokeswoman. *Government Technology* magazine also ran a lengthy feature reporting the questionnaire data because of its interest in whether employees in technology agencies should have civil service protections (Peterson, 2003).

Once again the present writer was prepared to devote time to other issues, but a different book chapter coauthor suggested that Service First might be further illuminated by the use of stakeholder theory. Thus, the research question shifted from the earlier ones to, "Is the topic theoretically interesting?" The findings were initially presented at the 2003 Western Political Science Association convention. The resulting article (West and Bowman, 2004) reflects the stakeholder literature which distinguishes between three types of research (Jones and Wicks, 1999): descriptive (focusing on how organizations manage employees), instrumental (emphasizing personnel as a means to achieve collective goals), and normative (stressing that staff have a right to be treated not merely as a means to an institutional end). In applying stakeholder analysis to the Florida reform, therefore, these approaches provided the framework for the study, and the discussion concluded with the implications of the findings for theory and practice. Although the manuscript was relatively "easy" to write (basic data had been collected earlier), the present author was ready to attend to other research—until yet another colleague from one of the previous projects offered an intriguing idea.

7.3.4 LITERARY APPROACH

Like the stakeholder article, this one (Bowman and Williams, 2007) was preceded by a conference paper (the 2004 American Society for Public Administration meeting). The point of departure for the study was the constant tension existing between efficiency and effectiveness in American public administration as reflected in the civil service reform controversies. Typically, although antagonists juxtapose the competing values of business management and public service, the debate is often not joined as positions become entrenched and sheer political power prevails. In such situations insights from another time and place can provide a perspective on issues and events. Thus, the research question for this project was, "Do insights from literature shed light on the topic?"

The case in point was philosopher and poet George Santayana (1863–1952) who lived during the era when the patronage-based spoils system gradually gave way to the merit-based civil service. Perhaps best known as the author of the adage, "those who cannot remember the past, are condemned to repeat it," he was a prolific and engagingly lyrical writer who penned many other insightful observations. Santayana possessed the uncanny ability to express complex concepts in a succinct aphoristic style that could, in the words of one biographer, "at once fix a point and transfix an opponent."

The authors agreed that this characteristic could be of assistance in understanding the increasingly rancorous reform debate. The manuscript made the case that Santayana's work provides an apt lens to assess the controversy. When it was not accepted by one journal, it was sent to another and received a "revise and resubmit" recommendation. At that point, the coauthor decided not to proceed, and granted the present writer permission to keep trying (as well as lead authorship if successful). After some changes, largely based on deleted material from an earlier draft, it was accepted.

7.3.5 CASE STUDY APPROACH

As time passed, Bowman and West considered doing an update of the 2001 statewide research that examined the impact of reform on affected employees one year after its passage. The question was, "After attitudinal surveys, what do scholars often say is needed to better understand a phenomenon?" The answer is that they make appeals for qualitative case studies to obtain in depth knowledge typically unavailable from surveys.

Between late 2004 and spring 2005, over fifty 10–45 minute, semistructured telephone interviews were conducted with pertinent staff in three departments representing the broad range of governmental distributive, regulatory, and redistribution functions. Respondents were chosen from agency-supplied randomized lists, one-half located in state capital headquarters (home to a substantial proportion of the workforce) and one-half in Miami-Dade county field district offices (home to the state's largest population center).

Questioning generally paralleled relevant topics included in the earlier survey so as to enable rough comparisons. However the findings were not expressed in percentage terms because qualitative research is an emergent design wherein the researcher seeks the interviewees' meanings and interpretations, nuanced and tacit knowledge (Creswell, 2003). In addition to these confidential interviews, the authors conducted semistructured, in-person interviews in February–June, 2005 with departmental human resource managers in central or district offices ($n = 3$), selected gubernatorial staff, legislative personnel, as well as current and former agency personnel ($n = 5$). These sessions lasted approximately 45–75 minutes each and also focused on the program implementation issues.

A potential problem with qualitative methods is the difficulty in generalizing to a larger environment. Yin (2002) suggests examining the context in which actions take place and using multiple sites to increase generalizability, a reason why several departments were selected for this research. One limitation of this work is its reliance on telephone interview data; despite guarantees of anonymity, information was not easily obtained from some subjects due to the sensitive nature of the topic[4] (also see Exhibit 2, Problem 1), a problem not encountered in the face-to-face sessions with other stakeholders. In addition, with few exceptions, potentially important secondary material such as departmental publications and raw personnel data did not contain relevant information to help document the case studies.

Despite such concerns, it proved possible to achieve a reasonable understanding of each agency under Service First, thus enabling an evaluation of the reform's impact some four years after it was passed into law. Preliminary results were discussed at the 2005 American Society for Public Administration conference. They were also the subject of a favorable newspaper story as well as negative reactions from high-level political officials (Cotterell, 2005), which generated a number of telephone calls for copies of the study from the governor's office on down. The published article (Bowman and West, 2006c) was part of a symposium edited by the authors (discussed below).

7.3.6 INTERNATIONAL COMPARATIVE APPROACH

Heretofore most of the investigation by the present author into civil service reform was focused on the American experience. On the basis of an opportunity to participate in 2005 international conference on ethics and governance, Bowman and West decided to examine the reform movement in an international context, with particular attention to a key aspect of the changes—employment at will. The research question was "How do American reforms compare to those in Europe?" The convention paper probed the origin and nature of at-will employment, as well as its ethical implications, followed by a review of its application (including its functional equivalents) in the United States and in Europe, and closed with conclusions about the future of public service. Typical problems in comparative work (e.g., availability and access to data) may affect reliability and validity of research, problems that might be addressed by recruiting knowledgeable coauthors if readily available. The final version of the manuscript (Bowman and West, 2007a) followed the format noted, but in response to referees limited the international component to the United Kingdom.

7.3.7 PROGRAM EVALUATION APPROACH

Civil service reforms continued to expand in the states (Hays and Sowa, 2006) as well as at the national level, particularly as the controversial, new personnel systems in the departments of defense and homeland security were being deployed—and were suggested as templates for the rest of the federal government. The rise of at-will employment (and related personnel techniques) is seen by proponents as a way to reenergize the bureaucracy and by opponents as a return to the spoils system. There are compelling, competing grounds in the debates over the merit system, and an overall assessment of these contentions would certainly be useful.

Because work is a chief source of income, involves a substantial personal commitment, and is a key source of social status for most people, the part it plays in the well-being of society is clear (Lawrence, 1999). Stated differently, evaluating the efficacy of the terms of employment in achieving human well-being is critical. The most serious form of justification, then, is to determine the moral worth of an issue; ethical argument plays an important role in clarifying a problem. Thus, the question for this project was, "Is at-will employment ethical?" A chapter in the present writer's coauthored book alluded to earlier (Bowman et al., 2004) contained an appropriate analytical device, a model of ethical action, to conduct the appraisal.

The framework, known as the "ethics triangle," recognizes the complementarity and interdependence of the imperatives in three schools of thought based on teleology, deontology, and virtue ethics (discussed in Bowman et al., 2004). Although each point of the triangle provides a lens to clarify and reframe different aspects of an issue, a narrow, overreaching application of a single approach at the expense of the other philosophies produces an insufficient evaluation. Although a synthesis developed from triangulation analysis may not supply a definitive judgment, it does tease out the underlying logic by which decisions are justified and provides the satisfaction that the problem has been fully examined. The employment-at-will doctrine was scrutinized, accordingly, using the three perspectives (Bowman and West, 2007b).

7.3.8   CAPSTONE: JOURNAL AND BOOK COLLECTIONS

In the midst of the research program discussed here, Bowman and West sought to encourage work in civil service reform in other state governments by developing a journal symposium and a subsequent anthology. The guiding question was, "What is happening in other jurisdictions?" To address this concern, an agreement was made with a periodical, and national call for papers, inviting the use of any methodology, was issued in 2004. Approximately two dozen proposals were received and 12 authors commissioned by the guest editors; 11 papers were submitted and refereed. In the interim, the journal changed editors and the new individual refused to accept the terms of the agreement. Through the course of telephone calls and correspondence, it became evident that the obligation made in the name of the publication would not be fulfilled.

Discussing the problem with the person's immediate superior, the journal's sponsors and relevant professional associations were contemplated, but not pursued. Despite obvious professional misconduct, success was not guaranteed as appeals likely would have been time consuming and delay publication in the journal (or some other outlet if the appeals failed). Forgiveness was granted believing that the editor's behavior would nonetheless have consequences: a group of well-known scholars, and perhaps their colleagues, would not submit work to the journal in the future, thereby possibly hastening a change in editorship.

With the articles in hand, the pressing issue was how to make the best of an untoward situation—viz., the challenge was to find ways to fulfill the guest editors' promises to the contributors. One of the editors discussed this turn of events with an editor of another journal. Not only was useful advice received, but also, after review of the materials, a commitment was made to publish one-half of the manuscripts as a special symposium (Bowman and West, 2006a). Because an obligation remained with the authors of the remaining papers, a different outlet was contacted and it also agreed to use them in a second symposium (Bowman and West, in press).

During this process, the editors continued to seek commercial publishers who might be interested in the symposia papers. Proposals were sent to five companies, serious consideration was received from several, and a contract would be signed with one firm (Bowman and West, 2006b). In short, although the initial plans for the work were thwarted in an ethically dubious manner, the guest editors were able to find periodical and book outlets for the contributors. Serendipity, present at various times during this research, seemed to be notably present in producing the edited collections.

7.4   CONCLUSION: IMPLICATIONS AND PROBLEMS

The substance of research is, of course, more interesting than its methodology, but techniques are of interest to the extent that they fulfill their purpose: to illuminate the problem. As discussed above, this research project employed many different methodological approaches to understand civil service reform in Florida and elsewhere. Readers who have come this far likely have formed tentative lessons from the narrative which they are encouraged to share with the author. What follows are some implications that can be overlain on them. Some may seem obvious, especially to the experienced academician, but what is obvious is often over looked.

1. Have a compelling research topic. There are many questions to study, but only those that are desirable (carrying social weight), feasible (doable within given constraints), and scientific (grounded in the literature) are worthy of attention. In the present case, only the most naive, uncaring, or foolish think that people, and how they are treated at work, are unimportant. This is especially true for government, given the critical role the public service performs in American governance. Indeed, having a fascinating subject matter will attract attention from conference organizers, the press, journals, and book publishers.

2. Divine different ways to think about the topic and the most productive research strategies to explore it. To do this effectively, as discussed in this chapter, it is evident that one must be well-versed in the subject, and be pragmatic about it. Every issue has methodological as well as substantive components, but one should resist getting locked into a fixed position. What is important for improving understanding of a problem is not the result of any particular investigation, but the accumulation of evidence from different studies. A key part of inquiry is to consult others, as intellectually exciting ideas are the lifeblood of a scholar. The result will not only be sage advice but could also produce a fruitful coauthor relationship.

3. Make your own luck in working with colleagues engaged in research. That is, the present writer was asked to coauthor as much as he asked others to work with him. Whether through graceful providence or good fortune, opportunities will arise for an active, visible investigator. If multiauthorship results, then clear understandings about who will do what and when should reduce any misconceptions that might otherwise develop.

   In the research enterprise described here, lead authorship was generally assumed by the individual who originated the idea for the paper, had ready access to local source material, or took responsibility for preparing the first complete draft manuscript. More importantly, all contributors seemed to operate under the assumption that more would be accomplished if no one worried about getting credit (or blame). Indeed, ordering of authors' names for the articles, chapters, and books was seldom discussed.

4. Do not be surprised if the subject matter continues to generate new research ideas. A truly enticing issue will spawn additional work, as answers to research questions are never complete or certain; knowledge is provisional, in principle problematic, and therefore subject to further investigation. The topic at hand, for instance, may be of particular interest in the wake of the next gubernatorial election. A 10th anniversary study of Service First in 2011 might be attractive for the authors, to say nothing (assuming dramatic advances in medicine) of the 100th anniversary of the program in 2101.

5. Seek diverse journal outlets. Other things being equal and for a number of reasons, it is better to publish, say, three articles in three periodicals than three articles in one. Although ultimately deciding where to submit work may be an educated guess, it should be informed by such oft-used factors as the periodical's mission statement, audience, rigor, the contents of past issues, and advice from peers. Sending manuscripts out with only a causal consideration of such concerns, or mailing them to the "best" outlet no matter what, is dubious strategy and a potential waste of the profession's resources. The choice of journals for the research discussed here was guided by the need to seek those with a demonstrated interest in human resource management or state government. Much of this work was not seen as apropos for highly theoretical or general public administration periodicals.

6. Do not assume that book publishers are interested in edited collections. Many are simply not attracted unless substantial sales are expected from very large classes. This is even more so when the material is previously published journal articles. If a publisher is found who can reach a relatively small, and still profitable, audience, the finished book manuscript may not necessarily be handled in a timely manner, competitively priced, or well marketed. Experiences by the author and others suggest that some presses are extraordinarily slow in production, set high prices on books, or engage in only minimal advertising.

7. Stay humble and be flexible. Whatever successes were recorded during this research project, the unexpected can and does occur. Journals that arguably should be interested in a subject may not be, editors can be capricious, referees can be demanding, and book publishers may have different concerns than authors. In such circumstances, rejections are inevitable, even desirable. Exert control over the things that are within one's control, and the odds on the uncontrollable factors will be improved.

In sum, an engrossing topic, one that lends itself to multiple research strategies, likely will attract others, yield additional research, and be suitable for diverse publication outlets. An old proverb says, "Man plans, God laughs." It follows that it is useful to retain perspective on these "lessons," as little is guaranteed in academic research.

To conclude the chapter, several problems in the conduct of inquiry are offered (Exhibit 2) as well as an instructor's class discussion guide (Exhibit 3). The problems are provided to apply the material from the case study narrative above and to build upon its lessons; ways to address the issues involved

---

Exhibit 2
Problems in the Conduct of Inquiry

To apply the chapter material, two research problems are shown below (see endnotes 5 and 6 for possible solutions). The first is a difficulty in gaining entree to sources, a concern of all students, but initially encountered in professional degree programs, if not before. The second illustrates the linkage between the research question, study design, and investigatory method, a concern of particular importance for doctoral students.

Problem One: Information Access
In qualitative research, rich data sources frequently prove to be interview sources. A problem arose in the course of the work on Service First wherein sources either refused to consent to an interview or agreed to participate but were reluctant to be forthcoming in their responses.

In the 2003, empirical study discussed in the text of chapter, an architect of Service First in the governor's office informed one of the authors that he was not available "before, during, or after" the legislature session for an interview. There seemed to be a view among some Administration officials that information was a proprietary asset, and that secrecy was prized and transparency frowned upon.

The followup 2006 case study experienced difficulties with rank-and-file employees and one department executive. Specifically, selected staffs were concerned about the purpose of the study, whether the agency and their universities authorized it, and if the interview was confidential (and whether they would be quoted). Many stated that they had to close their door before continuing. Several others said that the investigators had to obtain permission from their superior for a confidential interview. One person agreed to participate only after reviewing one of the author's published articles on a related subject. Although a number of interviewees were relatively at ease, cautious answers to some queries, such as "I'd rather not say" or "No comment," were common. In addition, a key executive, who had promised to participate, later declined because of an agency leadership change.

Question: What should be done to cope with such problems?

Problem Two: Research Question/Design/Method Nexus
Certainly the most difficult part of any project is defining the problem to be examined. Once that is accomplished, then research design can be developed, and an appropriate methodological tool utilized to implement the design. Perhaps the single most useful lesson from the chapter is the need to consult with others. The student then can test her ideas against their views on the issue and then accept or reject them as warranted. The point is that much of the work

---

(*continued*)

Exhibit 2   (*Continued*)
Problems in the Conduct of Inquiry

described in the text would not have been undertaken without the assistance of colleagues in generating possible research strategies. The same likely will prove true as students discuss issues with his or her Ph.D. committee and fellow students. It is understood that a solo researcher can create valuable work, but eventually it will be reviewed by someone, a faculty committee or journal referees. It seems prudent to get feedback on one's efforts sooner rather than later.

In any case, it will be assumed here that the challenging task of problem definition has been accomplished (considerations in developing a manageable research topic can be found in any "how to write a dissertation" guidebook). Formulating the proposed work involves a variety of crucial design issues (e.g., research site, time frame, the nature of source material, and so forth). A critical question as part of research design is the selection of the most appropriate technique to explore the topic (this may not be immediately apparent, especially if other parts of the proposal do not address design issues in some depth).

Consistent with the thrust of this book, a key concern is the *use* of an appropriate method. That is, it will be assumed that the student and his or her confidants have indeed selected a specific tool which will be the most efficacious in conducting the research. The next, critical step is to ensure that its utilization is fully realized.

Question: Using survey research as an example of an appropriate methodology for the subject of the dissertation, how can one ensure that it is employed in the most effective manner?

are found in the final endnotes.[5,6] The first exercise identifies a practical issue in gaining access to sources, and is perhaps most useful for professional degree students. The second conundrum illustrates the nexus between the research question, design, and method, a concern of particular importance for doctoral students. In dealing with these two cases, be encouraged by Einstein's quip: "The most incomprehensible thing about the world is that it is comprehensible." A problem, whether

Exhibit 3
Instructor's Guide

For those desiring to use this chapter in classroom discussion, a number of concerns can be highlighted. Einstein was once quoted saying, "The perfection of means and the confusion of ends characterize our age." Technologically savvy students may find methods at least as interesting as the substance of research. The chapter is a reminder that such a focus is a mistake, as methods, no matter how seductive, are merely tools to understand a subject.

With that in mind, students should be encouraged to tackle any topic of professional relevance that will sustain their interest. Indeed, lacking a well-grounded understanding of the problem inhibits the choice of a method to investigate it. The issue explored in this chapter was an on-going one, a selection not without risk as the researcher is at the mercy of events. Still, such a topic likely will be attractive to journals and their audiences.

A second matter to note is that students should join the community of scholars. At a minimum, this means sharing ideas and draft papers, but whenever coauthorship is feasible it should be pursued. Not only will this likely result in work superior to solo-authored pieces, but also it may produce opportunities for future collaboration. Coauthorship (like studying contemporary issues) is not without risk, but when skillfully handled the benefits exceed the drawbacks.

Exhibit 3 (*Continued*)
Instructor's Guide

A third concern worthy of mention is that as a topic develops and as drafts are written, students should be strategic in their choice of publishing outlets. A keen familiarity with a diversity of journals, supplemented by advice from others, will enhance the probability of receiving acceptance letters. Sending manuscripts to editors on the grounds of expediency (e.g., "It will be accepted quickly because it is a minor periodical") or simply to get ideas (i.e., "I know that this quarterly will reject the paper, but I will get some good comments") are not recommended. There are other ways to get feedback on one's work and being published promptly in a third-tier outlet may be self-defeating.

Finally, students should be prepared not only for acceptance letters but also for untoward surprises. One's very best work may not be so recognized by referees or editors. Assuming that reviewer critiques and editor letters provide sound reasons for rejection, a lot can be learned from anonymous comments on papers. This may be an even more reliable source for a "revise-and-resubmit" decision, which might be seen as a conditional acceptance pending improvements in the paper. Either way, what appears to be a stumbling block may simply be a stepping stone to success.

---

found in the exhibit or in one's own work, is a chance to do your best. "The greater danger is not that our aim is too high and we miss it," said Michelangelo, "but that it is too low and we achieve it."

ENDNOTES

1. Small parts of this paper, as well as selected examples, are adapted from the author's coproduced work cited in the references.

2. By the turn of the century, a variety of federal departments (e.g., Federal Aviation Administration, Internal Revenue Service, General Accountability Office, National Aeronautics and Space Administration) had received full or partial waivers from Title 5 of the U.S. Code defining the merit system. In the wake of September 11, 2001, the Transportation Security Agency established at-will employment for its personnel, and subsequently the departments of Homeland Security and Defense were authorized to create new human resource management systems. The Bush Administration is seeking congressional approval to use these approaches as templates for government wide change.

   At the state level, major reform examples also exist. In 1996, Georgia law mandated that all new civil servants be hired on an at-will basis, and in 2001 Florida eliminated job tenure for most incumbent middle managers (and made it easier to discipline remaining career employees and harder to appeal adverse actions). South Carolina and Arkansas recently abolished their merit systems; less dramatically, a number of states (e.g., Indiana, Delaware, Kansas) are reclassifying career service positions to unclassified ones as a consequence of reorganizations, reductions-in-force, or retirements.

3. Perhaps more proactive "pracademic" work could have been undertaken, such as testifying before legislative committees or doing pro bono research for public interest groups. Regarding the former, the way the Service First bill was handled in the legislature produced charges of stacked committees, one-sided hearings, and limitations on amendments and floor debates, thereby constraining opportunities to be involved in that arena.

   Concerning the latter, the state chapter of a prominent good government group was contacted. The author was unsuccessful in demonstrating that a proto-Spoils System program like Service First was directly germane to their objectives. The sense seemed to be it was an "inside baseball" employment issue that its membership would see an obscure matter. A well-known trainer of state employees, for instance, also downplayed the reform, in a conversation with the author, in light of more immediate issues confronting Florida.

4. A particularly worrisome instance occurred when an executive agreed to participate, but withdrew because of a change of agency leadership. Two strategies were used after it became apparent that the individual

definitely would not consent to a confidential interview. First, because the study design included respondents from both the capital area and the Miami district, one of the investigators was successful in accessing the district counterpart of the central office manager. Second, the authors identified a recently retired official from the department who not only explained why the person refused to participate (the new secretary "locked things down as much as possible" and "was known to be vindictive, so why take any chances granting interviews with outsiders?"), but also proved to be a very revealing source. More broadly, the Law of Large Numbers offers some confidence that the information gained from multiple, numerous sources may be accurate. In addition, and despite the above comments, many interviewees were, in fact, expansive in their responses.

5. Response to Problem One (Exhibit 2). There are at least four strategies to be considered in dealing with access-to-informant problems. First, in design of the project there should be an effort, such as a pilot project, to ascertain the extent to which respondents are likely to participate. Second, and most important, the investigator must consult a representative sample of stakeholders concerned with the issue (e.g., employees, supervisors, legislators, interest groups, union representatives, citizens), to obtain diverse perspectives and provide an opportunity to cross-check findings. Third, when some sources are not forthcoming, prepared follow-up probes are needed to prompt replies. Fourth, because these may not always be successful in eliciting additional information, large jurisdictions typically are populated by many knowledgeable people. Substitute participants may be located through such techniques as the "snowball" reputational method.

6. Response to Problem Two (Exhibit 2). The easy reply to the question posed in the Exhibit is that one's textbook from a general methods course should be sufficient in doing a survey, especially if supplemented by advice from others. It is startling, however, the number of times that a landmark survey research resource is not identified at the outset as a source of proven designs, and to thereby keep opportunity costs in line with available resources. Too many proposals, for example, do not recognize the significance of: a carefully crafted cover letter, a reader-friendly questionnaire, an appropriate number of follow-ups, tests for nonrespondents, and other seemingly basic requirements. As well, the advantages and drawbacks of a postal questionnaire versus an online survey may not be fully considered.

Fortunately, there is a valuable book, based on empirical data, which demonstrates the strengths and weaknesses of various approaches. Consulting this work reduces apprehensions, avoids as much guesswork, wishful thinking, and idiosyncratic preferences as possible, and provides some confidence that the investigation will be successfully conducted. The volume in question is Dillman's (2000) second edition of his 1974 survey research classic. Although there are other useful methods books, it would be a mistake not to peruse this one.

REFERENCES

Blalock, H. (1964). *Casual Inferences in Non-Experimental Research*. Chapel Hill: University of North Carolina Press.

Bowman, J. (2002). Employment at will in Florida government: A naked formula to corrupt the public service. *Working USA, 6,* 90–102.

Bowman, J. and Hoffman, A. (2001). Reforming state government point-counterpoint: Sizing up state workers, *Tallahassee Democrat*, 1E, February 25.

Bowman, J. and West, J., Eds. (2006a). Symposium: Civil service reform today. *Review of Public Personnel Administration*, 26, 2 (entire issue).

Bowman, J. and West, J., Eds. (2006b). *American Public Service: Radical Reform and the Merit System*. New York: Taylor & Francis.

Bowman, J. and West, J. (2006c). Ending civil service protections in Florida government: Experiences in state agencies. *Review of Public Personnel Administration, 26,* 139–157.

Bowman, J. and West, J. (2007a). Removing employee protections: A "see no evil" approach to civil service reform. In J. Maesschalck, L. Huberts, and C. Jurkiewicz (Eds.), *Ethics and Integrity in Governance*, pp. 000–000. United Kingdom: Edward Elgar.

Bowman, J. and West, J. (2007b). Lord Acton and employment doctrines: Absolute power and the spread of at-will employment. *Journal of Business Ethics, 74,* 000–000.

Bowman, J. and West, J., Eds. (in press). Symposium: American civil service reform. *International Journal of Public Administration*.

Bowman, J. and Williams, R. (2007). Civil service reform, at-will employment, and George Santayana: Are we condemned to repeat the past? *Public Personnel Management, 37*, 65–78.

Bowman, J. et al. (2001). Back to the future: Reforming or deforming state government? *Public Administration Times*, March 9, 5.

Bowman, J. et al. (2003). Civil service reform in Florida state government: Employee attitudes one year later. *Review of Public Personnel Administration, 32*, 286–304.

Bowman, J. et al. (2004). *The Professional Edge*. Armonk, New York: M.E. Sharpe.

Brewer, J. and Hunter, A. (1989). *Multimethod Research: A Synthesis of Styles*. Newbury Park, California: Sage.

Condrey, S. and Maranto, R. (2001). *Radical Reform of the Civil Service*. New York: Lexington Books.

Cotterell, B. (2001a). Bracing for change. *Tallahassee Democrat*, 1E, February 7.

Cotterell, B. (2001b). State "efficiency" czar resigns in protest. *Tallahassee Democrat*, 1A, May 15.

Cotterell, B. (2003). Survey knocks service first. *Tallahassee Democrat*, 1B, March 16.

Cotterell, B. (2005). Mixed reviews for service first. *Tallahassee Democrat*, 1B, August 28.

Creswell, J. (2003). *Research Design: Qualitative, Quantitative, and Mixed Methods Approaches*. 2nd ed. Thousand Oaks, California: Sage.

Dillman, D. (2000). *Mail and Internet Surveys: The Tailored Design Method*. New York: Wiley.

Florida Council of One Hundred (2000). *Modernizing Florida's Civil Service System: Moving From Protection To Performance*. Tampa: The Council, November.

Hays, S. and Sowa, J. (2006). A broader look at the "accountability" movement: Some grim realities in state civil service systems. *Review of Public Personnel Administration, 26*, 102–117.

Ingraham, P. and Moynihan, D. (2000). People and performance: Challenges for the future of public service—the report from the Wye River Conference. *Public Administration Review, 60*, 54–60.

Jones, T. and Wicks, A. (1999). Convergent stakeholder theory. *Academy of Management Review, 24*, 206–222.

Kaufman, H. (1956). Emerging conflicts in the doctrines of public administration. *American Political Science Review, 50*, 1057–1073.

Labaton, S. (2006). Four years later, Enron's shadow lingers as change comes slowly. *New York Times*, January 5.

Lawrence, J. (1999). *Argument for Action: Ethics and Professional Conduct*. Aldershot, United Kingdom: Ashgate.

McNabb, D. (2002). *Research Methods in Public Administration and Nonprofit Management*. Armonk, New York: M.E. Sharpe.

Nigro, L. and Kellough, J. (Eds.) (2006). *Civil Service Reform in the States*. Albany: SUNY Press.

Peterson, S. (2003). Scrapping the civil service. *Government Technology, 16*(13), 10, 32–36, 40–42, 64.

Special Master's Report (2001). In the matter of fact finding between the state of Florida and the American federation of state, county, and municipal employees council 79 Hearings and Special Master Recommendations, *Tallahassee*, March 12–14.

West, J. and Bowman, J. (2004). Stakeholder analysis of civil service reform in Florida: A descriptive, instrumental, normative human resource management perspective. *State and Local Government Review, 36*, 20–34.

Yin, R. (2002). *Case Study Research: Design and Methods*. 3rd ed. Thousand Oaks, California: Sage.

8 Threats to Validity in Research Designs

Nicholas A. Giannatasio

CONTENTS

8.1 INTRODUCTION

In the framework of everyday conversation, there seems to be little distinction made between the terms reliability and validity. When we discuss reliability we are describing a quality of something or someone that is "dependable" or "trustworthy." Validity has some similar connotations as reliability. When one tries to conceptualize something as valid, we often conform this term with similar sounding synonyms as those used for reliability and possibly include sound, telling, or cogent. Yet, most people would not make the distinction between a scale that measures weight as being reliable or valid. Although we would accept either reliability or validity in this context, validity implies much more than reliability. Validity implies logic and well-grounded principles of evidence; and, if one were to place reliability and validity on a continuum, they would occupy opposite poles. In research, such is the case. Researchers want their measurements to be reliable, but often, as in some case studies, reliability cannot be assured to the degree the researcher feels is warranted. On the other hand, validity must be assured. This chapter attempts to clarify the distinction between reliability and validity in research design. If one understands validity and is able to conceptualize its distinction from reliability, the research design will be stronger, more sound, and ultimately more convincing.

This topic also presents logistical considerations of "what comes first, the chicken or the egg"; and, from what context, framework, or paradigm does one look at the chicken and the egg? Does one come up with an experimental design and then look for what would threaten the validity of the design? Or, should one be aware of threats from internal and external issues before the research design is developed? In both cases the answer is simply yes. Therefore, whether we start with explaining threats to validity or the components of a research design, both topics—validity and design—are prominent in their importance to quantitative and qualitative methods and data analysis. Notwithstanding, the equal footing of validity and design, this chapter will discuss validity as a prologue to a discussion of research design, and place both validity and research design in the framework of positivism.

8.2 POSITIVISM

There is much debate in the social sciences about positivism. Auguste Comte, the French philosopher and the founder of the positivist school, adapted his theory as one that excluded speculation and was based on positive facts and phenomena. Positivism is a valuable reference point for all schools of thought, because it is the most dominant framework of rational, comprehensive, and empirical experimental designs that are the closest that the social sciences come to the "hard" sciences. Threats to validity of research designs in experimental and observational settings, experimental designs, preexperimental designs, and quasi-experimental designs, the topic of this chapter, communicate positivism. Positivism looks to the past for causality to advise the decision maker on future considerations. Simply put, if a city manager needed to make a decision about whether a new fire station needed to be placed in a growing area of town, the manager would most likely look at historical facts, such as the number of fire alarms answered by existing fire stations in the proposed district, response time to those fires, multiple alarm fires in those districts that may have been caused by a slow response time allowing the fire to escalate, the cost of present fire stations, and their predicted impact on the tax burden of new fire stations. These are positivistic facts that often influence the decision process. The debate begins to rage when detractors of positivism affirm that positivists only consider the descriptive side, the facts of the issue, and ignore the value side, the normative issues that may raise questions of whether an additional fire station may save someone's life. Indeed, scholars such as Durning (1993), Denardt (1993), Bobrow and Dryzek (1987), and Kaplan (1963) feel that positivism provides little help in determining public policy and most likely is the root of the problem in acquiring the knowledge necessary for decision and policy making. Furthermore, positivism implies an all-or-nothing type of approach to the future of policy actions, i.e., X_1 through X_n causes Y. Therefore, the decision must include all factors of X. The problem with this aspect of positivism is that it may contain internal contradictions that can paralyze the practical realization of the analysis (Bobrow and Dryzek, 1987). These contradictions include self-negation, described by Kaplan (1993) as self-defeating, in that general laws as prescribed by positivists will at some time in the future be negated by other laws. An example of this self-negation is how Darwinian evolution negates religious fundamental beliefs in creation. A further contradiction is that the positivistic world view is one of cause and effect and this determinism is too insulated.

Decision makers and policy scientists realized that the parochial approach of positivism had to be adjusted. However, there was hardly a total, realistic intention to "throw the baby out with the bath water."[1] Rather, positivism became a tool, one of many others, to be used as appropriate. Popper in the 1930s realized that some aspects of the positivistic approach were necessary in what he termed "piecemeal social engineering," where an all-or-nothing approach is not needed but rather a piecemeal, moderate, cautious intervention (Bobrow and Dryzek, 1987). Lindblom and Cohen (1979) described a path to what they refer to as "usable knowledge" that included scientific (positivism) and ordinary knowledge (common sense, causal intuitiveness, etc.) Hermeneutics, forensic policy analysis, and pragmatism use positivistic approaches to weave their narrative case. Fischer (1995) describes a discursive method of policy analysis where a consensus must be reached on each level. In Fischer's model, the first level includes positivistic verification before proceeding with a higher level of discourse.

The point of the newer approaches to analysis is not that positivism is dead, nor is it the ultimate tool in the social sciences, but it remains a prominent, viable tool, part of a total "tool box" of analytical tools where verification of programs need an empirical interpretation as part of the argument of analysis.

8.3 DEFINITION OF TERMS

The following three basic definitions are the beginning of the discussion, not the end; nevertheless, they are the point of reference for this chapter's discussion:

Validity: Simply put, are we comparing "apples to apples?" A measure is valid if it really measures what it is supposed to measure. For example, a valid measure of reading scores would be one where those with high reading ability scored high and those with low reading ability scored low.

Threats to validity: Those internal and external factors that may prevent one from measuring what one wants to measure or obscure the relationship between the dependent and the independent variables. For example, the Hawthorne effect, or testing effect (Campbell and Stanley, 1963), if not controlled, would affect the results of scores.

Furthermore, respondents, realizing they are being tested, may give responses based on what they may feel the researcher is looking for.

Experimental design: The experimental design is a research design where one can manipulate the independent variable to see if this manipulation causes changes in the dependent variable. The purpose of the experimental design is to eliminate all competing hypotheses so that the only hypothesis left is the experimental hypothesis. A subgroup of experimental designs are pre-experimental designs (Campbell and Stanley, 1963). These experiments are ones that involve a one-time study or a single pretest, or a pretest/posttest study, and are a subgroup of the experimental design.

Quasi-experimental design: It may be impossible to eliminate all competing hypotheses from the experimental hypothesis, manipulate the independent variable, or randomly assign conditions to the dependent variable. Therefore, one can only come relatively close to an experimental design; or, the researcher is only able to achieve a quasi-experimental design.

In the social sciences, experimental designs are difficult to achieve. Experimental designs are found in laboratory settings where it is easier to manipulate an independent variable. An example of an experimental design would be a chemical experiment where the effects of a reagent or catalyst, the independent variable, are manipulated to see the result of this manipulation on the compound, the dependent variable, what the reagent is intended to affect.

Social science quantitatively operates in the quasi-experimental arena. Independent variables usually cannot be manipulated and it is difficult, if not impossible to eliminate all contending hypotheses.

With a conceptual picture of two types of experiments—experimental, where one can manipulate the independent variable and eliminate all competing hypotheses and quasi-experimental, where one cannot manipulate the independent variable, eliminate all the competing hypothesis, or randomly assign subjects to conditions—both experimental and quasi-experimental research designs must measure what we want them to measure in order for them to meet the test of validity.

8.4 MEASUREMENT VALIDITY

Figure 8.1 places validity in a framework of types of validity and threats to this framework in a positivistic universe.

Figure 8.1 is a representation of how validity exists in a positivistic universe consisting of internal and external validity, where validity is segmented into questions of accuracy based on content, face value, criterion, and construct. The universe of validity is threatened from extraneous factors that affect internal validity, the left side of the illustration, and external validity, on the right side. Campbell and Stanley (1963) presented the eight factors that threaten internal and four factors that threaten external

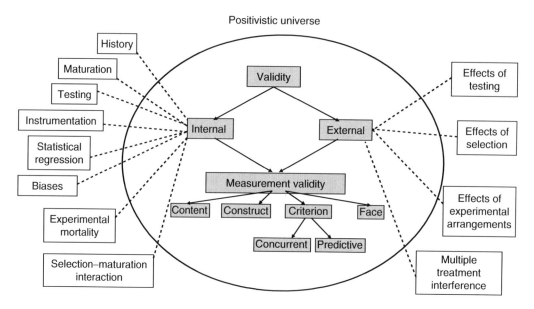

FIGURE 8.1 The validity framework and concomitant threats.

validity of experiments based on Campbell's earlier work "Factors affecting the validity of experiments" (*Psychology Bulletin*, 1957). All threats to internal and external validity remain applicable 50 years later, and will be presented with examples appropriate to public administration.

However, a distinction should be made at the outset of any discussion of validity; validity is not reliability. Notwithstanding various tests for reliability of empirical methods, the retest method, alternative form method, the split halves method, and the internal consistency method (Carmines and Zeller, 1979),[2] a measurement can be reliable but not valid. A measurement tool can give reliable, consistent measurements but not measure exactly what one wants it to measure and therefore fail the test for validity.

For example, the state highway patrol was monitoring car speed on the interstate and, unknowingly, the radar gun they were using was defective and only measured car speeds up to 68 miles/hour, i.e., if a car was going through the speed zone at 55 miles/hour the radar gun would read 55 miles/hour. However, if a car passes through the zone at 75 miles/hour, the radar gun would only read 68 miles/hour. The state police measured speed for 24 hours and consistently measured speeds that were reliable and consistent, but they were not valid.

Our measurement tool may also give us consistent, reliable measurements, but validity could be compromised. For a measurement tool to be valid the tool must measure what it is supposed to measure. The police radar speed gun must be able to measure all speeds, not just speeds up to 68 miles/hour.

To conclude the discussion of reliability, it is important to note that reliability is secondary to validity. If the measurement tool is not valid, its reliability cannot be considered.

Campbell and Stanley (1963) describe two types of validity: internal and external validity. At the beginning of Campbell and Stanley's discussion of validity it is clear that "internal validity is the sine qua non" (1963, p. 5)—the essential validity—the essence of the experiment. Internal validity is examined when the researcher examines the question: Did the independent variable cause the expected corresponding change in the dependent variable? An example of internal validity using fire stations would be the answer to the question: Did an increase in fire stations cause a decrease in multiple alarm fires in the new district? Or, did an increase in police on beat patrol cause a concomitant decrease in crime?

In contrast to internal validity, which is specific to the experiment, external validity asks the question of generalizability, or to what extent can the findings of an experiment be applied to different groups, settings, subjects, and under what conditions can this experiment be generalized. Campbell and Stanley (1963) explain external validity by comparing it to inductive reference, in that it is never completely answerable (p. 5).

In the example of reading scores, an experimental finding may be as follows:

Students in New York City public high schools with an enrollment in excess of 3000 have lower reading scores than public high schools in the same city with less than 3000 enrollment. However, this experiment may not be able to be duplicated in Newark, Chicago, or Los Angeles. In short, although high enrollment in New York City public schools may cause lower reading scores it might not have the same effect in another area of the country.

Furthermore, external validity does not rule out the possibility that although more police on beat patrol may reduce crime under one set of circumstances, less crime may reduce the amount of police on beat patrol in another set of circumstances—a case where the independent variable in experiment A becomes the dependent variable in experiment B.

The important question that persists when one examines experimental validity is as follows: Does the measurement tool measure what it is supposed to measure? This question is predicated on matters of precision and accuracy. The accuracy of the measurement tool involves several types of validity questions.

Face validity: Face validity is the simplest type of validity. It answers the question: Does the measurement tool appear to measure what we want it to measure? For example: If we wanted to measure customer service department effectiveness at the internal revenue service, we would not measure the eating habits, secretarial skills, or the amount of graduates from accredited graduate schools of accounting in the customer service department because "on the face of it" these items tell us little, if anything at all, about customer reaction to customer service.

Face validity, being a simple measure of validity, is also the most innocuous measure of validity. Face validity alone is not sufficient to meet accuracy tests of validity.

Content validity: Content validity asks the question: Is the measurement that is being taken a subset of a larger group of measurements that represent the focus of the study? Although similar to face validity, it is a more sophisticated test for validity. An example of content validity can be shown in our study of internal revenue customer service's department.

In this study we want to determine if the customer service representative was accommodating to the taxpayer. If a survey instrument was to be used to determine customer satisfaction, the survey could ask one question: Were you satisfied with your contact with the internal revenue customer service department? Though this question may be adequate in some cases, most likely the question might attract many negative responses because the customers' needs might not be totally satisfied, or conversely, affirmative answers might not give you the information you will need to make changes in customer service. A better approach would be to measure responses to questions that come from a subset of customer satisfaction. For example, the IRS might inquire if the customer service representative

- Answered the phone in a certain length of time following your connection to the department.
- Did they identify themselves to you?
- Did they inquire about your problem?
- Did they give you a satisfactory answer?
- If they did not know the answer, did they say that they would get back to you?
- Did they return with an answer in a timely manner?

These are typical questions that would meet the question of content validity for customer service.

In the same example, a question that would not meet the criteria of content validity would be as follows: Did you submit your income tax return in a timely fashion? Not only would this question not meet the content validity criteria of customer service, but if used in a survey of the IRS's customer service department, it may illicit negative responses to the relevant questions.

Criterion validity: There are two types of criterion validity—concurrent and predictive. Concurrent validity is used to question the validity of a subset of questions that are already verified by content validity. This subset may be created to save time during the actual questioning during a survey. Consider, for example, a survey given to motorists at a bridge toll booth. The motorist can bring the survey home and return it on the next pass over the bridge. However, the decision makers would like a faster and more immediate response to the survey instrument. They decide that they will have the bridge police set up a safe area past the toll booths and before the entrance to the Interstate. Police will assist surveyors in detaining random cars so that motorists can be asked the survey questions. Any anxiety caused by the police detaining the motorist is immediately relieved when the motorist finds that he is only being detained to answer a few questions. To ultimately get their cooperation, the motorists are told that their names will be entered in a raffle for a free dinner-for-two at a local restaurant. Before this plan can be initiated, the survey planners realize that the motorists can not be detained to answer the current questionnaire. This would delay traffic, and slow down the process, limiting the number of motorists who can be questioned, and possibly incur the wrath of the detained motorist. The survey planners decide to create a significantly shorter survey instrument from the original questionnaire that will meet face and content validity questions and give them the information that they need to meet the criteria of the survey.

Predictive validity: This validity asks the question: Does the test that is being administered have some predictive relationship on some future event that can be related back to the test administered? In the fire station experiment of determining alarm response time to newly developed areas of a township, we can determine that fire stations within a certain radius of housing developments decrease response time to alarms, whereas fire stations outside this radius increase response time. In this instance, the fire station experiment has predictive validity if we use the results of this experiment as a predictor of future fire station placement in the community. The future placement of fire stations relates the result of the experiment back to the test, and the test can be related to the placement of the fire stations.

Construct validity: This validity relates back to general theories being tested; aptitude tests should relate to general theories of aptitude, intelligence tests should relate to general theories of intelligence, etc. For example, in the bridge repair experiment, the county engineers realize that certain heavy equipment must be utilized by mechanics hired by the county. They want to give aptitude tests for potential hires to reduce their liability during construction. The assumption is made that the engineers, or those creating the aptitude test for using heavy equipment, understand what constitutes aptitude for using heavy equipment during bridge construction. The test to measure aptitude—the construct validity—must relate back to general theories of aptitude, to measure the individual's capacity to operate heavy equipment and not general theories of heavy equipment.

8.5 THREATS TO RESEARCH DESIGN VALIDITY

Threats to internal and external validity are variables—different from the independent variable—that affect the dependent variable. When one explains the methodology of their research design, they must address how well they understand the threats to validity, how they confront the threats from these variables, or how these threats are controlled. These threats, or extraneous variables, which need to be addressed in the experimental design (Campbell and Stanley, 1963), will be presented as an introduction to each threat to validity, as listed in Campbell and Stanley's *Experimental and Quasi Experimental Designs for Research* (1963).

8.5.1 THREATS TO INTERNAL VALIDITY

*History—the specific events occurring between the first and second measurement in addition to the experimental variable.**

---

* The epigraphs in Section 8.5.1 are by Campbell and Stanley (1963, p. 5).

When events occur that fall outside the boundaries of the experiment that could affect the dependent variable, internal validity has been threatened by history. History is a potential problem when studies are conducted in natural settings (O'Sullivan and Rassel, 1995). History is impossible for the experimenter to control for; rather, threats to the experiment's validity due to history need to be explained when discussing causality. History threatens validity when we can ascertain that an event, other than the independent variable, may be associated with the dependent variable. The following example illustrates threats to validity from history.

In a study of the adequacy of existing fire stations done during the course of one year, we may find that the existing fire stations were not adequate as evidenced by the number of multiple alarm fires (requiring more than one group of responders to extinguish). In this case, the relationship we are looking for is that the number of multiple alarm fires is negatively related to the number of fire stations in a district. However, during the course of the year when the data was collected, the summer was exceptionally hot and there was a drought. The drought lasted for approximately five weeks; nevertheless, it was also a period when the temperature was higher than normal. Because the area encompassed large expanses of rural and undeveloped areas, numerous brush fires occurred. Due to the stage of drying that the brush was in, the fires spread rapidly and soon required a second or third fire station to respond.

In the above example, the results were affected by the extraneous variable history. It is impossible to control the extraneous variable—weather, and the effect that the weather had on drying and the spread of fires. The study's validity is threatened, but not totally invalid. In this case, if one explains the effect of history and that the threat to validity is actually a contingency that districts should be prepared for, the study still has merit.

Maturation—the processes within the respondents operating as a function of the passage of time per se (not specific to the particular events), including growing older, growing hungrier, growing more tired, and the like.

When changes occur naturally over a period in the groups being studied, the threat to validity is called maturation. Commonly, studying children, or any group that may go through rapid physical and social changes, affects the validity of the experiment. Typically studies of education of a cohort group may occur over a period of years. For example, a study of reading skills of children in the primary grades is undertaken. Students will be tested over a period of six years from kindergarten through grade five. Students will be tested five months into the kindergarten school year and then at the end of kindergarten. Subsequently, reading skills will be tested every year at the end of the school year.

In this example, maturation is expected to occur. The question that maturation compels us to ask is, without the educators teaching reading skills (the independent variable) would we receive similar changes in the improved reading scores (the dependent variable) without the effect of the independent variable? Children grow rapidly both socially and physically, and this rapid growth, the maturation in both physical and social contexts, may have an effect on the experiment.

Testing—the effects of taking a test upon the scores of a second testing.

In an experiment where a group is given a pretest before the introduction of the independent variable, the pretest sensitizes a group to experimentation and their response to the independent variable may be attributed to the pretest and not the independent variable. The administration of the posttest, which shows the effect of the independent variable, must be reviewed in the following context: Did the pretest effect change in the dependent variable? In short, could a pretest group associate questions from the pretest to the experiment and affect the results by consciously or unconsciously taking that experiment to that end; or, as a result of the pretest and what they remember from it, i.e., the experimental or control group are "good test takers," the group does better on the posttest because their test-taking abilities affect causality and not the effect of the independent variable.

A more interesting way of illustrating the effects of testing is what has become commonly known as the Hawthorne Effect. An experiment that was begun to test workplace efficiency at the Hawthorne Electrical Plant soon became the basis of the organizational development theories of administration. The essence of Hawthorne was that the employees who were being tested performed better—were more efficient despite workplace conditions being more and then less favorable—because they knew that they were being tested. Researchers who have tried to duplicate this experiment have been unsuccessful and have repudiated the validity of Hawthorne. To the extent that other researchers have disavowed the Hawthorne experiments based on validity, there is merit; however, to the extent that they reject Hawthorne as a lesson for organizational development, they are mistaken.

Notwithstanding Hawthorne, the following public administration example shows the effect of testing threats to validity in terms of pretest and posttest knowledge.

A city may be looking for ways to streamline trash collection and at the same time reduce personnel costs. Other cities, such as New York, found that the introduction of a "two-man truck" (as opposed to a three-man truck) reduced costs and was an effective means of collecting trash. At a city council meeting the mayor proposes the New York model as one that might work in their city. The city council, at their public meeting, decides to do a study in one of the city's sectors. However, there was concern that the increased costs and maintenance required on the new trucks may not offset the savings in personnel costs. They decided that they would do efficiency and cost measurements under the current system, while awaiting an order for two two-man trucks. The local newspaper reporter, covering the council meeting, reports the results of the council meeting in the next day's edition.

Within two weeks, efficiency experts are dispatched with the sector's two trash-teams. Aware that they are being tested, and conscious of the purpose of the study, the men outdo themselves collecting the trash. When the new trucks arrive and a posttest is administered, production and efficiency did not improve, which was anticipated by the council, and the savings in personnel costs of one less man on the two-man trucks did not offset the cost of the new trucks and the anticipated maintenance on the vehicles.

Obviously, the fact that subjects became aware that they were to be studied and the concomitant realization that their livelihood may be threatened affected the results of the experiment. In this case, the pretest, as well as information that the groups would be tested, threatened the validity of the experiment and skewed the results.

Instrumentation—in which changes in the calibration of measuring instrument or changes in the observers or scores used may produce changes in the obtained measurements.

When changes occur in the interpretation of the dependent or independent variable, or the methodology changes during the interval from the pretest to the posttest, these changes are interpreted as threats to validity from instrumentation. It is not unusual that during the course of a social science experiment threats to the validity from instrumentation occur.

For example, during a meeting of the local school district, a principal was concerned that shortly after lunch it seemed that students participated less in activities designed to foster participation. The principal's theory was that the lunch provided by the district was not healthy and the amount of fats and empty calories used in the diet were the major factor for this lack of participation. To illustrate his point, the principal brought with him a nutritionist who attested to the fact that the essence of the school lunch program was "junk food." The board decided that a study should be commissioned to determine if there was a relationship between school lunches and the level of participation in school activities after lunch. The study was to encompass the school term from September to June. Contacts were made with the school district in the next county, which had more nutritionally sound meals, to act as a control group. After the study was in effect for three months the same nutritionist presented her case in front of the state senate. Shortly after her presentation, a bill was introduced, passed by the state legislature, appropriate vendors found, and statewide nutritionally sound meals were mandated in all the school districts. However, the commissioned study continued in the school district in question and the final result of the study was that there was little correlation between the lunch meal and the level of participation.

Between the beginning of this study and the end, a change occurred—the state's mandate that nutritionally sound meals be served—which may have affected the validity of the experiment. Instrumentation threats to validity are common when studies examine issues that can be affected extraneously by changes in laws or the court's interpretation of existing laws.

Statistical Regression—operating where groups have been selected on the basis of their extreme scores.

Statistical regression threatens validity when the study chooses to include in the experiment an outlier score—a score higher or lower than expected—at the time of the pretest. The expectation of such a score is that if the subject is evaluated again, the score on the next test will be substantially lower or higher than the previous test, i.e., their scores will regress toward the mean. However, if choices of subjects for the study were based on pretest outlier scores, and one does not consider statistical regression, validity is threatened. Notwithstanding the essence of validity—the test measures what we want it to measure, where those with high abilities score high, and those with low abilities score low—it would not be unusual to make errors in experimentation by not considering statistical regression.

In this example, the commissioner of human services wanted a breakdown of the department's community mental health partial treatment centers so that a decision could be reached on closing some of the least-utilized facilities and privatizing the rest. For the last quarter, due to incidental reasons, the Fairfax Community Mental Health Center showed a decrease in admissions, substantially lower than their previous trends. The Fairfax Center had been operating for approximately ten years, and always maintained a high new-patient census. However, this decrease in new admissions was assumed to be the result of population shifts and better utilization of new treatment modalities. Based on the low admission rate for new patients and the recent increase in new drug utilization, a decision to close Fairfax was reached. Fairfax community leaders were not in any hurry to temper the Department of Human Service's decision as the community mental health center was a continual cause of discontent within the community. Shortly after Fairfax closed, the community witnessed an increase in the homeless population, crime, and the suicide rate.

The above is a typical example of not considering statistical regression as a threat to validity. Fairfax Community Mental Health Center was experiencing some type of "blip" in their admission rate. The low admission rate represented an outlier score that was too low. Had the Fairfax admission rate been viewed for the ensuing three months, the rate would most likely revert or regress to Fairfax's historical mean admission rate.

Biases—resulting in differential selection of respondents for the comparison groups.

Bias or selection is a threat to internal validity when the subjects, cases, scores, etc., are not chosen randomly. On the face of it, biases are something that we inherently avoid so as not to appear prejudiced. However, the threats to validity from bias and all other threats to internal validity can occur with or without the researcher being aware of these threats. Biases occur when we choose comparison groups that are uniformly different from each other. Our results then become affected by our biases so that the results obtained would not have been obtained if the differences between the experimental and control group were less extreme. The following example of an invalid study is one where the researcher purposely biased the experiment.

Baby formula companies have often lobbied for state infant nutrition programs to bolster product sales. In one such state, pressure from the American Academy of Pediatrics Council on Nutrition lobbied state legislators saying that such programs limit the use of breast milk as the primary choice of nutrition for babies. Seeing that this pressure from the pediatric community might limit the power base of the agency by eliminating the program, there was a need to show program success. Analysts in the Department of Health in favor of the continuation of the Infant Nutrition

Program decided to conduct a study investigating the relationship between infant morbidity and participants in the program and using an experimental control group of infants who were not participants in the Infant Nutrition Program and who were identified by the health department as those who were born of crack-addicted and HIV-positive mothers.

In the above case, the stark difference between the experimental and control group is so systematic that this difference or selection process has replaced the independent variable—participation in the Infant Nutrition Program—with the threat to validity—bias, which would be the factor that had the ultimate effect on the dependent variable—infant morbidity.

Experimental Mortality—or differential loss of respondents from the comparison groups.

The threat to internal validity that makes the researcher more concerned with those experimental subjects who leave or drop out of the study rather than remain in the study until completion is called experimental mortality. Further, experimental mortality includes those subjects who are misplaced in the control group, i.e., those subjects who at one time before the experiment or during the course of the experiment were exposed to part of the experimental treatment, a stage or effect of the independent variable, and then incorrectly assigned to the control group. Whether a dropout or a misplaced, exposed member of the control group, the experimenter must ask if the experiment would have been any different if those who dropped out had remained, or if those who were incorrectly assigned to the control group were assigned to the experimental group. Regarding the dropouts, the researcher must not only inquire how his results would have been different, but also if there is an effect of the independent variable treatment that caused the subject to drop out. There are obvious examples of both dropouts and incorrect assignment that can be applied to any pharmaceutical test on a new drug. Dropouts can be described by a pharmaceutical experiment where the effects of the drug during the course of the experiment caused the subject to leave. In this case, the researcher must determine if an unfavorable treatment reaction affected the dropout; if that subject had stayed to the end of the experiment, how would it affect the experiment's results; could the person have been exposed to some earlier derivative of the drug, its natural or chemical form that would have sensitized the subject to the drug?

Selection Maturation Interaction—which in certain of the multi-group quasi experimental designs . . . is confounded with . . . the effect of the experimental variable.

Selection maturation interaction is what can be described as "design contamination" (O'Sullivan and Rassel, 1995), "diffusion or imitation of treatments" (Jones, 1985), and other sobriquets. At the least, it is contamination of either the control or the experimental group that negates the effect of the experiment unless one is doing research on the effects of contamination. Benignly, selection maturation, or contamination, is related to the threat to validity from "testing". This occurs when the experimental groups guess the purpose of the experiment and gravitate toward that end. Malignantly, contamination occurs when one group tells another group what they are experiencing or what they believe the experiment is about, and this cross-contamination places the experiment in the validity danger zone.

For example, a long-time problem in education is the use of a testing model to evaluate teaching performance through a testing instrument given to their students. Recently, education researchers had developed a testing instrument that would eliminate 65 percent of the variance. School districts throughout the country are excited about this development. Politicians who feel that teachers are overpaid and not productive enough are eager to see the results of the experiment. The teachers' union feels that a test of this type is just another ploy to adversely affect contract negations to their constituency. Before the test is administered, a thorough description of the examination is picked up by the press, and considering the hot political issue the test has developed into, they publish the story and various follow-up pieces. Teachers, unions, and families discussing the test with students, constituents, and children have sensitized the students to the issue. In many schools, teachers who believe they have an idea of the sum and substance of the test discuss the test in the classroom. Students' impressions are influenced and the scores on this test show that teachers are performing well.

These threats to internal validity have been augmented and altered to include other threats that are merely variations on a theme. Compensatory rivalry and compensatory equalization (Jones, 1985) are variations of contamination. Similarly, selection maturation interaction (Campbell and Stanley, 1963), where one group finds out that the other group is being treated better than they are being treated, is also one of the variations. Essentially the basis of internal validity are these eight, all others are derivatives with different "spins."

8.5.2 THREATS TO EXTERNAL VALIDITY

As mentioned previously, external validity focuses on how well the experiment can be generalized or applied to different groups or, how we can refer the results of one experiment to the hypothesis of another similar experiment. Again, as in discussions of internal validity, Campbell and Stanley's (1963) descriptions of these threats are presented as benchmarks for interpretation. Sometimes the differences between the threats to internal validity and external validity are subtle and it is important to direct one's focus on the nuances of their differences.*

> *The Reactive or Interactive Effect of Testing—in which a pretest might increase or decrease the respondent's sensitivity or responsiveness to the experimental variable and thus make the results… unrepresentative of the effects of the experimental variable for the unpretested universe….*

Testing, which is also an internal threat, differs from testing as an external threat because, internally, testing affects the subjects as a result of a pretest that changes behavior. External validity is threatened by testing when the successful outcome of the program can only be replicated by the administration of a pretest. Without the pretest, the experiment cannot be generalized.

For example, participants in a county maternal and child health clinic were studied to determine if they knew when to bring their child in for care. The pretest tested their knowledge of child health and disease. The mothers were then given child-health classes tailored to meet their requirements based on the pretest. The result of the classes reduced infant morbidity and mortality in the county. Other counties wanted to initiate this program of education to achieve the same result. The educational programs were initiated without the administration of a pretest and the education classes were lectures that were not tailored to educational needs. Child morbidity and mortality were not reduced in the other counties.

In the above example, the experiment was not able to be generalized because the interpretation of the effect of the treatment, the independent variable, was education. By not giving the pretest in the other counties and merely initiating a program of education without evaluating needs of the target population, external validity defeats the pertinence of the general application of the experiment elsewhere.

> *The Interaction effects of the selection biases and the experimental variable.*

When an experiment produces results that show a relationship between the dependent variable and the treatment, despite the fact that biases were used in determining participation, the experiment may still be internally valid, in the context of the original experiment in that there is some commonality between the two groups. However, when the experiment is repeated elsewhere, the use of a significantly different control or experimental group, more or less applicable, produces disconcerting results.

For example, in New York City, an experiment was conducted to examine the relationship between firemen's heath in fire stations where there are many more alarms and in less busy fire stations. It was determined on the basis of this study that there was little correlation between those firemen's health in busy fire stations and the less busy fire houses. When the study was duplicated in less populated urban areas, the opposite results were obtained.

---

* The epigraphs in Section 8.5.2 are by Campbell and Stanley (1963, p. 6).

In this experiment, selection biases are a result of the assignment of firemen to busy or less busy fire stations. In New York, where there are many fire stations in both busy and less busy areas, younger firemen are assigned to the busier fire stations and firemen who are older and have been through assignments in busy fire stations, have been placed in the less busy stations. As a result of this bias, older firemen who may have developed poorer health over the years are being compared to younger firemen who are generally in good health. In other cities where there are much less fire stations there is little choice as to assignment and firemen may stay in one station for their entire tenure as firemen.

Reactive Effects of Experimental Arrangements—which would preclude generalization about the effect of the experimental variable upon persons being exposed to it in non-experimental settings.

When the experimental arrangement—the situation in which the experiment is being conducted—is so clinical or controlled that the duplication of the experiment in nonclinical surroundings is virtually impossible, then the experiment is threatened by the threat to external validity of the arrangements themselves. This threat also applies to the situations where testing validity is threatened in that the subjects know that they are being tested and alter their behavior accordingly as in Hawthorne or in the following case.

Residents of a community are told that they are to pilot a program of community policing initiatives to lower crime in the area. The residents of the community are individually visited by the members of the township's police department and the program is explained to them. The residents are to report any suspicious cars or people they see in their community to a special police telephone number. The residents are enthused about this experiment and the new relationship with a formally aloof police department that the experiment is effecting. The residents perform exceptionally well and community crime is reduced. Other townships decide on the basis of this experiment to implement their own test of community policing. However, the lack of partnership between police in the other townships and the community—the lack of special arrangements—shows that community policing programs make little difference in reducing crime.

Multiple Treatment Interference—likely to occur whenever multiple treatments are applied to the same respondents because the effects of prior treatments are not usually erasable.

When experimental treatments are applied to a group of subjects, they affect the participants in the study and cannot be undone. When this occurs and other independent variables are applied to the same group, the effect of the previous independent variable affects the reaction to the new independent variable. When efforts to duplicate the experiment are attempted without the previous experimental treatment given to the original group, the experiment cannot be duplicated. In the case of the community policing, if the original test community was also the community used to test volunteerism in reporting the location of trash and refuse along the community streets to develop a cleaner, more attractive community, the effect of this treatment may have influenced their participation in community policing.

This discussion of validity is one that should raise the level of consciousness of the researcher that there are threats to all experimentation which have to be considered in the research design. These threats must be considered early in the design process. Constantly throughout the experiment, attempts to control and limit these threats are what makes the experiment more valid and applicable in settings other that the experimental and observational environment.

8.6   EXPERIMENTAL DESIGNS

Experimental designs offer researchers the format for inferring a relationship between a theory and the application of that theory. The relationship between the dependent variable can be an association or a correlation but more often than not the relationship cannot show true causality—the cause leads to the effect—in the strict sense of the word. Even in total, clinical, experimental research, randomness threatens causality (Blalock, 1964). Furthermore, if all attempts to control for random selection are observed, total randomness is always questioned. This phenomenon is increasingly demonstrated more in quasi-experimental designs than in experimental designs; nevertheless, it appears to be more accurate to refer to the relationship between variables as an association, a relationship, or a correlation, especially in the social sciences, rather than refer to the relationship between the dependent and independent variables as one of cause and effect.

Often designs are expressed using symbols of

R = randomly chosen subjects

O = the observation or the measurement of the effect on the dependent variable

X — the independent variable

Although looking at combinations of these symbols in describing experiments presents some confusion on the part of the student, there is little alternative to presenting a diagram of the research designs in this way. However, when a description of the experiment is plainly given, the diagram of the experiment eventually presents a visual representation of which design is desired.

Furthermore, it is important to note that experimental designs and variations and derivatives of those designs are numerous, and often the researcher uses different combinations of designs to investigate a phenomenon or prove a theory. It would be unduly cumulative to present all of the combinations that could be created and, at the same time, some combination would invariably be omitted.

The following designs are listed and described using the typical R, X, O format. The threats to validity and the internal and external controls, the strength of the experimental design over the threats to validity, are also identified.

8.6.1 PREEXPERIMENTAL DESIGN

One-Shot Case Study[3]

X O

Threatened Internally by	Threatened Externally by	Controls Internally
History	Selection interaction	None
Maturation		
Selection bias		**Controls Externally**
Mortality		None

As the design states, a one-shot case study does nothing more than observe the effect of the independent variable. It reports nothing more than some contrast or difference in a group attributed to some treatment. There is little scientific value to the one-shot case study; it is at risk from most relevant threats to validity; it does not control any threats. Other than a bearing from where to begin a discussion of experimental design, one-shot case studies offer little utility in the social sciences other than single "snapshots" of a group at one point in time.

One-Group Pretest–Posttest Design

O X O

Threatened Internally by	Threatened Externally by	Controls Internally
History	Testing interaction	Selection bias
Maturation	Selection interaction	mortality
Testing		
Instrumentation		**Controls Externally**
Selection maturation interaction		None
Mortality		

With its numerous threats to validity, the one-group pretest–posttest design is just slightly better than the one-shot study or as Campbell and Stanley state "… enough better than Design 1 [One-Shot Case Study] to be worth doing when nothing better can be done" (1963, p. 7).

An example of the one-group pretest–posttest design is the study of reading skills development, where a group is tested and then after some of time the same group is tested again.

	Static-Group Comparison X O ——— O		
Threatened Internally by	**Threatened Externally by**	**Controls Internally**
Selection bias	Selection interaction	History
Maturation		Testing
Selection maturation interaction		Instrumentation regression
		Controls Externally
		None

Static-group comparison studies are done where two groups are observed, one receiving the effect of the independent variable and the other group not experiencing the treatment. Static-group comparisons are useful when comparing program participants—children who have participated in operation "Head Start"—with the reading level of those who did not participate in the head start program. The single accomplishment of the static-group comparison is that it establishes the effect of the independent variable.

8.6.2   The Classical Experimental Design

Notwithstanding the preexperimental designs where there are drawbacks that often preclude the use of these designs to protect research from threats to validity, the experimental designs offer more insulation from internal and external threats and are more appropriate as a research design. For this discussion the focus is on those experimental designs that have the following features:

- Reflect a random selection of subjects and there is no significant difference between an experimental and control group.
- A pretest that measures the dependent variable is given to the experimental and control groups.
- Both experimental and control groups will experience equal conditions except for the treatment of the independent variable.
- The researcher controls the amount of treatment to the experimental group.
- A posttest is given after the exposure to the treatment to both the experimental and control groups.
- Changes due to the dependent variable and the differences between the dependent variable effect on the experimental and control group, evidenced by the posttest, are attributed to the independent variable (adapted from O'Sullivan and Rassel, 1995).

	Pretest–Posttest Control Group Design R O X O ——— R O O		
Threatened Internally by	**Threatened Externally by**	**Controls Internally**
None	Selection interaction	History
		Maturation
		Testing
		Instrumentation
		Regression
		Selection bias
		Mortality
		Selection interaction
		Controls Externally
		No external threats noted

The pretest–posttest control group design is also referred to as the classical experimental design. It is the most commonly used experimental design. This design enables the researcher to choose experimental and control groups of randomly assigned subjects. One group receives the experimental treatment while the control group does not. After the introduction of the independent variable, both groups are observed again. Differences between the experimental and control groups are attributed to the effect of the independent variable.

From the beginning of this research design—the assignment of random subjects to experimental and control groups—threats to validity are being controlled. If the selection is truly random, then biases, regression toward the mean, and all other internal threats are initially controlled in the experiment. However, as the experiment progresses over time, it is practically impossible to control for maturation and maturation interaction. The following example is a description of a pretest–posttest control group design.

A random selection of mothers at the local community health station were chosen to test if there were differences in satisfaction levels between the random group of mothers who were in the experimental group and those in the control. The study wanted to determine if they could eliminate, as a cost-containment technique, nurses at the intake level and run the clinic with ancillary health-professionals, nurse practitioners, and doctors. The experimental group was to be interviewed by a nurse to take a history of the current complaint, whether this was a "well-baby care" visit, or a "sick-baby" visit and answer any questions the mother may have about her child. After the initial visit by the nurse, the nurse practitioner or the doctor would come into the room to examine or treat the child. The control group would not receive the nurses' visit. Both groups would receive a pretest one month after being enrolled as patients. Then the independent variable would be introduced, and a posttest on both groups for customer satisfaction.

Solomon Four-Group Design

R O X O
R O   O
R   X O
R   O

Threatened Internally by	Threatened Externally by	Controls Internally
None	None	History
		Maturation
		Testing
		Instrumentation
		Regression
		Selection bias
		Mortality
		Selection interaction
		Controls Externally
		Testing interaction

The Solomon four-group design is the first experimental design presented that controls, to some extent, threats to generalizability or duplication. The design is set up where the component of the pretest–posttest control group design makes up the first two randomized groups. In addition to this experimental and control group, a third group is added that is not given a pretest but is exposed to the independent variable, and a fourth group that is given neither the pretest nor exposure to the independent variable. In the example of eliminating nurses at a clinic, there would be a group of clients who were not given the pretest for customer satisfaction but received the previsit by the nurse, and a fourth random group that received neither the pretest nor the experimental treatment of the nursing previsit.

Posttest Only Control-Group Design R X O R O		
Threatened Internally by	**Threatened Externally by**	**Controls Internally**
None	None	History
		Maturation
		Testing
		Instrumentation
		Regression
		Selection bias
		Mortality
		Selection interaction
		Controls Externally
		Testing interaction

The posttest only control-group design is also known as the randomized posttest design (O'Sullivan and Rassel, 1995). This design also protects the experiment from the same threats to internal and external validity as the Solomon four-group design. The posttest only control-group design also presents the same opportunity for generalization as the Solomon design. However, there are times when it may not be practical, feasible, or possible to administer a pretest. The option of a pretest is removed when we are studying large groups of subjects, there are no pertinent questions to be asked in a pretest, or there is not adequate funding to administer a pretest to the experiment's participants. Furthermore, the application of a pretest takes enormous time and may not be of value. Consider the following example.

The federal government was considering changing the style of uniforms for the Air Force. Since the end of World War II, there was much discontent among members of the Air Force that the uniforms were drab and generally lacking in the type of military style that may be found in the other branches of the military. Although the discontent over the uniforms ebbed and flowed over the years, recently, recruitment quotas were consistently below expected levels and it was thought that changing the uniforms would enhance recruitment. To see if the new uniform would increase recruitment, new recruits, from random cities on the West Coast, were given the new uniforms, while new recruits from random cities on the East Coast were issued the old uniforms. The result of the experiment was that recruitment quotas were met on the West Coast but remained at a continuous low level on the East Coast.

This posttest design experiment is one that illustrates the point that it would be difficult to administer a pretest to every adult eligible to join the Air Force; nevertheless, the posttest was able to show that there was an association between the independent and dependent variables.

8.7   QUASI-EXPERIMENTAL DESIGNS

The experimental design is predicated on the ability for the researcher to be able to manipulate the independent variable, the ability to randomly assign subjects and the experimental treatments, and to eliminate competing hypothesis in their experimental research so that only the working hypothesis remains to be proved or disproved by the experiment. Once the research leaves the controlled environment of the laboratory or other controlled environment, the amount of control that the researcher normally has in experimental settings is virtually unrealizable. When the researcher is unable to randomly assign, manipulate the treatment, or eliminate competing hypothesis, the experimental design that remains is quasi-experimental.

The quasi-experimental design is one where the researcher is left to design the best possible alternative to the experimental design including as many components as possible from experimental designs. The creation of a quasi-experiment and the inability to assign random sampling open the experiment to threats to external validity. The inability of generalizing results brings fields like public administration into the argument of whether public administration and other related social science disciplines are truly a science. The use of the quasi-experiment also leads to inertia in disciplines as the findings are difficult to duplicate, or when others attempt to duplicate the experiment, their findings are different or explain less of the variance than the original experiment. Nevertheless, the social sciences tool for doing research largely involves a research design that is quasi-experimental.

Interrupted Time Series

$$O \quad O \quad O \quad O \quad X \quad O \quad O \quad O \quad O$$

Threatened Internally by	Threatened Externally by	Controls Internally
History	Testing interaction	Maturation
		Testing
		Regression
		Selection bias
		Mortality
		Selection interaction
		Controls Externally
		None

The interrupted time series is a design that enables the researcher to make multiple observations of a group before and after the introduction of the independent variable. The independent variable is not usually introduced by the public administration researcher; rather, this design is one that observes changes in groups that cannot be attributed to time when an independent variable was introduced by some agency, law, or action, which in the researcher's view would have caused a change to occur in the group observed.

Consider for example, a researcher has the hypothesis that stricter drug laws are associated with increased state prison populations. The researcher defines a period before the enactment of stricter drug laws to observe yearly prison populations. The independent variable—the stricter drug laws—is introduced, and the prison populations are observed for a period of years after the introduction of the laws.

Notwithstanding other variables that would need to be controlled, the above example illustrates the utility of an interrupted time series. Finally, in public administration, and in some other social sciences, the interrupted time series takes a snapshot of some past time. The use of this technique in the present would have to entail a dependent variable that would be affected in a very short period or the researcher must be committed to studies that will encompass an expanse of past, present, and future time.

Equivalent Time Samples Design

$$X_1 \, O \quad X_0 \, O \quad X_1 \, O \quad X_0 \, O$$

Threatened Internally by	Threatened Externally by	Controls Internally
None	Testing interaction	History
	Reactive effects of arrangements	Maturation
	Multiple interference	Testing
		Instrumentation
		Regression
		Selection bias
		Mortality
		Selection interaction
		Controls Externally
		None

An interrupted time series design does not offer the researcher the option of testing the effect of the independent variable on the test population over a period more than once. In contrast, the equivalent time sample design allows the researcher to do a time series experiment with repeated introductions of the independent variable. However, as the table illustrates, the treatment is introduced (X_1) and the observation taken; after a lapse of time, the observation is taken without the effect of the treatment (X_0). In this manner the researcher can observe the effect with and without the independent variable on the same population, varying the amount of observations and length of time of the experiment. The benefits of this quasi-experiment are that the effect of the independent variable may be transient or reversible (Campbell and Stanley, 1963).

The equivalent time sample is useful in the social sciences in education, the workplace, or in any environment where the effect of the experimental treatment can be exposed and withdrawn.

Quasi-experimental designs continue to evolve with variations on the presented examples. For example, the equivalent materials design takes the model of the equivalent time sample design and augments it with a materials aspect as an independent variable. At each point where the independent variable (X_1) is introduced, materials become the independent variable and these materials can be varied from points X_1 and X_0. The equivalent materials design does control for threats from interactive arrangements and the design would be diagrammed as (Campbell and Stanley, 1963).

$$M_a \, X_1 \, O \quad M_b \, X_0 \, O \quad M_c \, X_1 \, O \quad M_d \, X_0 \, O$$

As shown above, the materials (M_a through M_d) are not the same materials; rather, they change at different time points in the experiment.

A variation of the equivalent time series design are panel studies, where one group is examined at different times for the effects of different or multiple independent variables.

The nonequivalent control group design is similar to the experimental pretest–posttest control group design. The difference is simply that randomness is not required; as previously mentioned, the inability to assign random subjects qualifies the design as quasi-experimental. The nonequivalent control group design, the most common quasi-experimental design, is diagrammed as

$$\begin{array}{ccc} O & X & O \\ \hline O & & O \end{array}$$

The random sampling in pretest–posttest is replaced by an experimental and control group that is not determined by similar characteristics, i.e., the experimental and control groups are similar in all characteristics except for the exposure to the independent variable. However, they are not so similar that the pretest can be dispensed with (Campbell and Stanley, 1963). Understandably, the nonequivalent control group design cannot control internally for selection interaction, nevertheless, this type of design is useful to compare similar, defined groups that the researcher identifies as the two groups that must be tested. For example, an education study of third grade students might compare the two classes in one school without examining the subjects for like characteristics. In this way all third graders are examined, i.e., they are similar enough—not identical—and appropriate for the nonequivalent control group design.

8.8 SUMMARY

What would a house look like if one were just to buy wood, nails, and tools, and were to start building that house without plans on how they were to build it? For the reason that a builder would not proceed in this manner, neither should the researcher. This chapter offered the basic information on experimental design and threats to validity—the tools one needs to conceptualize a plan for research. Having all the knowledge about experimental models offers little help if that knowledge remains on the pages in this handbook. It is hoped that in the manner that threats and designs were presented that one will be able to conceptualize threats and designs. At first, this may seem difficult, but do not give up at that point, or think it is impossible—you are just not used to doing it. Over time that will change. Nevertheless, if one is serious about research, one must conceptualize these models and be aware of the threats to those models. When these concepts are discernible, and an idea, problem, or question for research presents itself, devising a research design comes naturally. Finally, being fluent in experimental design will give the researcher the confidence needed to defend their research in all environments.

EXERCISES

1. Describe different scenarios where reliability and validity differ. For example (as described within) the radar gun being reliable but not valid.
2. Conceptualize the relationship between independent and dependent variables within an experiment that uses a preexperimental design, classical experimental design, and a quasi-experimental design. Then, set up an experiment using each type of research design. Label each variable (*X*) and observation (*O* and *RO*) in the design with real-life examples. Then write a brief narrative explaining the experiment.
   Example:
   Classical experimental design: Pretest–posttest control group design

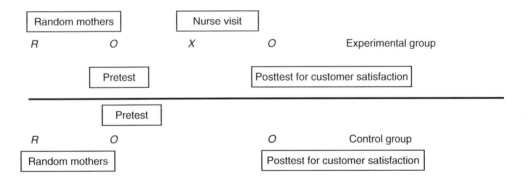

   Narrative:
   A random selection of mothers at the local community health station were chosen to test if there were differences in satisfaction levels between the random group of mothers who were in the experiment group and those in the control group.
3. In the above exercise, pick an internal and external threat to validity (if applicable) and describe the effect on the experiment.

ENDNOTES

1. There have been approaches to policy analysis that have disdained any type of positivistic approach, post-modernism being the most striking example. However, post-modernism in its detraction of positivism is even more contradictory, i.e., using logic to denigrate logic, etc.
2. Reliability testing methods are discussed in various texts. In Carmines and Zeller's *Reliability and Validity Assessment*, Sage, 1979, the authors present models of reliability. The retest method is where the same test is given to the same group of people after a period of time. The Alternative Form Method is similar to the retest but an alternative test is given after a period of time. The Split Halves method is where the test instrument is divided into two halves. The scores of each half are correlated to test reliability. The Internal

Consistency method test reliability at the same time and without splitting or alternating tests. It uses Cronbach's alpha formula: $\alpha = N/(N-1)\ [1 - \Sigma\sigma^2\ (Y_i)/\sigma^2_x]$.

3. All titles for Preexperimental, Experimental, and Quasi-Experimental Designs are from Campbell, D.T. and Stanley, J.C. 1963. *Experimental and Quasi-Experimental Designs for Research,* Houghton Mifflin Co., Boston., unless otherwise noted.

REFERENCES

Bobrow, D.B. and J.S. Dryzek. 1987. *Policy Analysis by Design*, Pittsburgh: The University of Pittsburgh Press.

Carmines, E.G. and R.A. Zeller. 1979. *Reliability and Research Assessment*, Thousand Oaks: Sage.

Campbell, D.T. and J.C. Stanley. 1963. *Experimental and Quasi-Experimental Designs for Research*, Boston: Houghton Mifflin.

Denardt, R.B. 1993. *Theories of Public Organizations*, Belmont: Wadsworth.

Durning, D. 1993. Participatory policy analysis in a Georgia state agency. *Journal of Policy Analysis and Management*, 12(2): 297–322.

Fischer, F. 1995. *Evaluating Public Policy*, Chicago: Nelson Hall.

Jones, R.A. 1985. *Research Methods in the Behavioral and Social Sciences*, Sunderland: Sineaur Associates.

Kaplan, A. 1963. *American Ethics and Public Policy*, New York: Oxford University Press.

Lindblom, C.E. and D.K. Cohen. 1979. *Usable Knowledge*, New Haven: Yale University Press.

O'Sullivan, E. and G.R. Rassel. 1995. *Research Methods for Public Administrators*, White Plains: Longman.

BIBLIOGRAPHY

Blalock, H.M. 1964. *Causal Inferences in Non-Experimental Research*, New York: W.W. Norton.

Cook, D.T. and D.T. Campbell. 1979. *Quasi-Experimentation: Design Analysis Issues for Field Settings*, Boston: Houghton Mifflin.

Dickenson, M. and G. Watson. 1976. *Political and Social Inquiry*, New York: Wiley.

Howard, G.S. 1985. *Basic Research Methods in Social Science*, Glenview: Scott Foresman.

Keppel, G. 1973. *Design and Analysis: A Researcher's Handbook*, Englewood Cliffs: Prentis Hall.

Patton, M.Q. 1990. *Qualitative Evaluation and Research Methods*, Thousand Oaks: Sage.

Rutman, L. 1984. *Evaluation Research Methods*, Thousand Oaks: Sage.

Spector, P.E. 1981. *Research Designs*, Thousand Oaks: Sage.

9 The Responsible Conduct of Social Research

Phyllis Coontz

CONTENTS

9.1   THE CASE OF PROFESSOR HWANG WOO-SUK

Until December 2005, Professor Hwang Woo-Suk of Seoul National University was a world renowned and highly respected stem-cell researcher. He had published three landmark articles in the prestigious journals Science and Nature reporting that he had successfully created human embryonic stem cells by cloning. Professor Hwang's esteemed career began to unravel when members of his research team alleged that he had fabricated his data. In response to these allegations Seoul National University convened an internal review panel to examine his data. On December 23, 2005, the review panel reported that Professor Hwang had intentionally fabricated the results of his stem cell research (*The New York Times*, December 23, 2005). For a summary of the panel's Final Report, go to www.geocities.com/giantdeli/art/CellNEWS_Hwang_clonging_th.html.

Professor Hwang's misconduct was found to be so egregious that the panel stated that Hwang's research deceived the "scientific community and the public at large" and mandated a "severe penalty." In May 2006 Korean prosecutors indicted Professor Hwang on charges of fraud, embezzlement, and breaching the country's bioethics law.

Professor Hwang's misconduct represents an extreme case of ethics violations. At the same time it represents an example of what Babbie calls the "politics of research" (2001, p. 481). The politics of research refers to the political climate and public debate generated by controversial research. In this case there has been widespread public debate on stem cell research, especially with regard to the techniques used to create and use stem cells. At issue in this debate is the current state of the technology for starting a stem cell line because it requires the destruction of a human embryo or therapeutic cloning. Opponents of stem cell research equate the destruction of embryos with destroying life. Because stem cells need to be extracted from existing stem cells (from the surplus of existing stem cells or frozen embryos left over from in-vitro fertilization clinics) and the extraction process kills the embryo, opponents see the process tantamount to destroying life. They also claim that the research constitutes a form of experimentation on human beings.

Proponents argue that such research is medically worthy because it holds greatest promise for alleviating suffering from disease since the development of antibiotics. Because over 100 million Americans and approximately two billion humans worldwide suffer from diseases that could be more effectively treated with stem cells and possibly even cured (including heart disease, Parkinson's, Alzheimer's, diabetes, and some forms of cancer), proponents argue that the research can eventually save hundreds of thousands of lives.

The political context of research is largely fueled by competing values and ideologies. Because values and ideologies vary by social and cultural contexts there is great variation around the world with respect to the way the public perceives stem cell research. For example, government funding of research on embryonic stem cells is currently authorized in the United Kingdom, France, Japan, South Korea, and other countries. It was halted in the United States when President Bush vetoed legislation that would have lifted prohibitions against federal funding for stem cell research (on September 24, 2005) because it "crossed a moral boundary that our decent society needs to respect."

Beyond the political context of the research conducted by Professor Hwang is the issue of the *ethics of research*. The ethics of research deal with the methods researchers use in conducting research—*is it true*, i.e., does it correspond to reality; *is it fair*, i.e., has the researcher respected the rights of human subject, colleagues, and funding agencies; and *is it socially responsible*, i.e., does the research improve the human condition (Pimple, 2001)? Research ethics encompass how research is conducted and whether researchers have acted responsibly in accordance with scientific norms. Public trust in science is built upon the truthfulness of the scientific community. Whenever that trust is violated, questions naturally arise about whether science is true, fair, and morally worth funding. Professor Hwang had been awarded $33 million in government funding and an additional $6.4 million in private donations for his research (The New York Times, May 12, 2006). Although Professor Hwang's misconduct has not lead to a moratorium on stem cell research, it has shaken the public's trust in science. Society needs to have confidence that what scientists tell us is true.

Although the federal government has responded to some aspects of research misconduct with policies and regulations, it is the scientific community itself that regulates the conduct of researchers through an informal code of scientific norms. Because the PhD is a research degree, doctoral programs in universities and colleges have traditionally provided the apprenticeships for the next generation of scientists. It is during this experience that the majority of doctoral candidates learn about the accepted methodologies of good research and responsible research (Zuckerman, 1977). Although scientists have relied on each other to safeguard the integrity of the research process, such informal oversight is becoming less and less viable as a vehicle for socializing young researchers. This is because the research enterprise itself has changed dramatically over the last three decades. Gone is the era of single-investigator projects. Today research is carried out in what can only be thought of as a "research industrial complex." That is, researchers and their respective institutions are dependent on funding from governmental agencies, industry, and private foundations. Consider that in 1995 alone, federal allocations for research were estimated at $73 billion (Mervis, 1995). The "complex" is made up of networks of researchers, institutions, government, and organizations. Thus the research that takes place is conducted in multi-purpose, formal, competitive, and highly diversified environments that involve working on complex problems with teams of multi-disciplinary and multi-layered researchers dependent on outside funding.

Without systematic training in research ethics, students, postdoctoral fellows, technicians, and even junior faculty are left to learn about ethical research practices on their own. The aim of this chapter is to facilitate this learning process by providing an overview of what constitutes ethical research. I have organized this chapter into two broad ethical areas. The first focuses on the norms of the scientific community and summarizes the responsibilities that researchers have for ethical research. The second section reviews the policies and regulations that apply to the protection of human subjects in the United States and Institutional Review Board (IRB) requirements that apply to all government funded research.

9.2   NORMS OF THE SCIENTIFIC COMMUNITY

As indicated earlier, the scientific community has historically relied upon itself to regulate the conduct of research. This informal system consists of a set of shared principles and accepted research practices thought to be necessary for safeguarding the "integrity" of science and the validity of scientific findings. Broadly stated the scientific enterprise entails the systematic investigation and modeling of parts of the world or the universe. Such investigation is designed to lead to what the sociologist, Robert Merton, referred to as "certified knowledge" (1973, p. 267). The principles of collegiality, honesty, objectivity, and openness are woven throughout a set of universally accepted norms that have been characterized by Merton in the acronym CUDOS (Merton, 1973). These norms include the following:

Communalism which refers to the expectation that discoveries will be freely shared and dedicated to the community of scientists.

Universalism which refers to the expectation that scientists should judge empirical claims according to impersonal criteria without regard to the identity of the author.

Disinterestedness which refers to the expectation that scientists will subordinate their own biases and interests to the advancement of knowledge.

Organized skepticism which refers to the expectation that scientists will subject empirical claims to systematic scrutiny and validation.

Added to these norms are the principles of *originality*, *individualism*, and *independence*. Merton believed that these norms functioned together and created a community wherein the contributions generated by the scientific process contributed to a larger body of "scientific" knowledge that was useful for solving society's problems. But like the behavioral norms of any community, the fact of their existence does not translate into universal compliance (Zuckerman, 1977). Although scientists are expected to disseminate their discoveries through published papers and reports read by the larger community, the research itself is vetted through a process of the peer review of the published work. In publishing findings, the researcher describes the methods used to produce the results. Reviewers give their imprimatur that the research meets the standards of "science." Recognition and respect of peers are the researcher's reward for passing through the review process and adhering to the scientific community's norms (Merton, 1973:270–271).

Because the keystone for receiving recognition and respect from peers rests with the dissemination of research findings, misconduct usually appears in published papers and research reports (Burk, 1995:311). A paper may present fabricated methods by describing experiments that were never conducted, observations that were never performed, and calculations that were never made (Zuckerman, 1977). This is referred to as "forging" the data. In some disciplines, peers will not accept the findings without physical proof of the experiment. When physical evidence is expected, it may also be fabricated. In addition to forging data, data may also be deliberately manipulated or falsified to support conclusions that are incorrect. These practices have been termed "cooking" or "trimming" the data (Babbage, 1969). Cooking data involves selecting only those data that fit the research hypothesis. Trimming the data refers to the practice of massaging the data to make them look better than they are. Attempts at "replicating" the study serve as a "check" against faulty research practices. And when a researcher engages in cooking and trimming the results reported will be unreliable and unable to be reproduced. Another form of dishonesty is plagiarism. This involves taking the words or data of another without attribution.

There are other instances of misconduct that do not rise to the level of scientific fraud described above. Zuckerman refers to these less serious violations as violations of "scientific etiquette" (1977, pp. 119–120). These violations include such things as claiming authorship on a paper when little or no contribution has been made; excluding subordinates from authorship when they have made a contribution; generating a large number of publications that focuses on the same issue from a single research effort; and finally taking advantage of the peer review process by "poaching" the ideas of others and incorporating them into one's own work.

Scientists are generally held in high esteem and the public tends to think of them as well intentioned along with the universities with which they are affiliated. The status accorded scientists is related to the role that research and development play in maintaining a healthy economy and improving the human condition. Interestingly, when scientific fraud and deception are exposed, scientists around the world have tended the "circle the wagons" by minimizing extent of the misconduct or characterizing the incident as aberrant and isolated fueled by stress, bad judgment, or moral corruption. As the article from *The New York Times* in Figure 9.1 below illustrates with regard to Professor Hwang, the scientific community responded to misconduct with a caveat about ways to improve the review process. Had such improvements been in place, the fraud "may" have been prevented.

November 29, 2006 The New York Times
Journal Faulted In Publishing Korean's Claims

By Nicholas Wade

Fraudulent stem cell reports that shook the scientific world could have been prevented by extra review procedures, according to a panel appointed by Science, the journal that published the claims.

Donald Kennedy, the editor of Science, said the journal would accept the panel's major findings.

The South Korean researcher Dr. Hwang Woo-Suk reported in Science in 2004 that he had generated embryonic stem cells from an adult human cell, the necessary first step in proposed schemes for growing replacement tissues from a patient's own cells. In a second report, in 2005, he claimed he could perform this step routinely and efficiently, using very few human eggs.

Both reports proved to be fabrications, and the journal formally retracted the papers in January.

The fraud came to light not through any of the formal checking procedures in the scientific process, but because a whistle-blower in Dr. Hwang's lab spoke to the South Korean television station MBC.

Like other scientific journals, Science has long taken the position that its reviewing procedures work well but cannot be expected to detect deliberate fraud, and therefore no change is necessary.

But the spectacular nature of the fraud prompted deeper than usual soul-searching on the part of leading journals.

After reviewing the paper record of how the Hwang reports were handled, a panel led by John I. Brauman, a chemist at Stanford University, yesterday recommended four changes in Science's procedures.

A risk-assessment method should be developed to flag high-visibility papers for further review, the panel said. Also, authors should specify their individual contributions to a paper, a reform aimed at Dr. Hwang's stratagem of allowing another researcher, Gerald Schatten of the University of Pittsburgh, to be lead author of one of the reports even though Dr. Schatten had done none of the experiments.

The panel advised online publication of more of the raw data on which a scientific report is based. It also suggested that Science, Nature and other leading journals establish common standards for reviewing papers to prevent authors bent on deceit from favoring journals with laxer standards.

The panel states in its report that these measures "would have detected" Dr. Hwang's fraud.

But in a news conference, Dr. Brauman retreated from that statement, saying only that they "might have" uncovered it.

FIGURE 9.1 The scientific community's equivocal response to ethical misconduct.

The federal government got involved in regulating scientific conduct in the 1970s and 1980s after several cases of faked and fabricated research were discovered at several prestigious universities. This publicity drew attention to what had previously been handled on an informal basis. In response to several disclosures of fraud, Congress passed the *Health Research Extension Act of 1985*. This act gave the federal government the authority to regulate the research it funds. In 1989, the Department of Health and Human Services (DHHS) established the Office of Scientific Integrity (OSI) and the Office of Scientific Integrity Review (OSIR) to augment the 1985 Health Research Extension Act. The Office of Research Integrity (ORI) replaced these two offices in 1993. In addition to the authority to respond to scientific misconduct, the ORI took on the responsibility of promoting responsible research practices. For a review of the ORI's policies and regulations, visit their Web site at: http://ori.hhs.gov/.

Although the number of cases involving scientific misconduct has increased over the years, until recently the extent of it was thought to be minimal. According to the findings of a recent study of scientists that were funded by the NIH, more than a third of those surveyed admitted to misconduct within the last three years of the survey's publication (Martinson, Anderson, and de Vries, 2005). Specifically, of the 3247 early and mid-career researchers who responded, less than 1.5 percent admitted falsifying data or plagiarism. But 16 percent reported changing the design methodology or results of a study in response to pressure from a funding source; 13 percent admitted overlooking others' use of flawed data; and 8 percent reported they had circumvented minor aspects of requirements regarding the use of human subjects (Martinson, et al., 2005, p. 737). The authors suggest that

> U.S. scientists engage in a range of behaviours extending far beyond FFP (fabrication, falsification, and plagiarism) that can damage the integrity of science.... [W]ith as many as 33 percent of our survey respondents admitting to one or more of the top-ten behaviours, the scientific community can no longer remain complacent about such misbehaviour

The extent of ethical misconduct strongly underscores the failure of the scientific community to adequately correct the problem. Although the ORI proposed requiring ethics training for all researchers receiving funds from DHHS in 2000, systematic training has remained at the proposal level because of protests and resistance to the idea by universities and researchers. Although more and more universities are electing to provide ethics training for researchers, the findings of the Martinson, et al. study underscore the failure of the informal mechanism for training budding scientists.

9.3   THE TREATMENT OF HUMAN SUBJECTS AND THE EVOLUTION OF THE IRB

The Nuremberg Trials revealed the atrocities committed by the Nazis during World War II and resulted in The Nuremberg Code of 1949, which set forth 10 moral, ethical, and legal principles that apply to medical experimentation on humans. It was The Nuremberg Code that first established the concept of "voluntary consent" in human experimentation and has since served as a model for developing and assessing ethical practices in the social and behavioral sciences.

A more complex code for protecting human subjects is found in the World Medical Association's Declaration of Helsinki. The Declaration has been amended five times, most recently in 2000 and remains the standard for medical research. The Helsinki code focuses specifically on medical research and acknowledges the multiple sources of vulnerability that must be taken into account to protect human subjects. The principles making up this code may be viewed at www.wma.net/e/policy/b3.htm.

In 1979, the Department of Health, Education, and Welfare (now known as the Department of Health and Human Services) issued the Belmont Report. This report contains a set of ethical principles that apply to researchers and include the following:

Respect for persons: This principle incorporates the belief that individuals should be treated as having autonomy and that those with diminished autonomy (e.g., minors, prisoners, those mentally incompetent) are entitled to protection.

Beneficence: This principle conveys the obligation of researchers to "do good" and that human subjects are to be protected from harm. Researchers are also obliged to maximize the benefits of their research.

Justice: This principle ensures that the selection criteria for participation are not based on gender, race, easy availability, manipulability or compromised. Thus the benefits from research should be available not only to the wealthy and privileged, but also to the poor and less advantaged.

The full text of the Belmont Report may be obtained by visiting www.hhs.gov/ohrp/humansubjects/guidance/belmont.htm.

Although worldwide concern for the ethical treatment of human subjects dates back to the Nuremberg Trials, a catalyst for the recent concern over the treatment of human subjects in the United States is the Tuskegee Syphilis Experiment. For forty years between 1932 and 1972, the U.S., Public Health Service (PHS) conducted an experiment on 399 black men in the late stages of syphilis. These men were never given a diagnosis of their disease and they never gave informed consent to participate in the study. These men were poor and illiterate sharecroppers from Alabama. The men were told that they were being treated for "bad blood." The study was of the treatment and natural history of syphilis and was designed to monitor how syphilis affected blacks compared to whites. By 1947 penicillin has become the standard treatment for syphilis, but the Tuskegee scientists withheld penicillin from these men along with information about the disease, e.g., how it spreads, and about penicillin as a treatment for it.

Of course, the true nature of the study had to be kept secret from the subjects to ensure their cooperation. Encouraged by the prospect of free medical care, these unsuspecting men became human guinea pigs. The men were prescribed a series of the so-called remedies but in such small dosages as to have little effect on the disease. The men were also subjected to painful and potentially dangerous spinal taps. By the end of the experiment 28 of the men had died directly from syphilis. A hundred more were dead of related complications, 40 of their wives had been infected, and 19 of their children had been born with congenital syphilis. By the time the experiment was brought to the attention of the media in 1972, news anchor Harry Reasoner described it as an experiment that "used human beings as laboratory animals in a long and inefficient study of how long it takes syphilis to kill someone." Then on May 16, 1997 President Clinton formally apologized for the experiment to the eight remaining survivors. President Clinton stated that "The United States government did something that was wrong—deeply, profoundly, morally wrong; it was an outrage to our commitment to integrity and equality for all of our citizens...". The full text of President Clinton's apology may be viewed at http://clinton4.nara.gov/textonly/New/Remarks/Fri/19970516-898.html.

According to Diener and Crandall (1978) the ethical treatment of human subjects applies to potential harm, informed consent, privacy and confidentiality, and deception. To cause harm or injury to others (physical and psychological), to coerce someone to engage in activities against their will, to invade the privacy of others without their permission, or to mislead or deceive participants of research are all actions that violate the trust between the researcher and the participant.

9.4 POTENTIAL HARM TO HUMAN SUBJECTS, INFORMED CONSENT AND PRIVACY AND CONFIDENTIALITY

Although physical harm to participants in social research is highly unlikely people can be harmed personally (e.g., by being embarrassed or humiliated), psychologically (e.g., by losing their self-esteem or by being forced to reveal something about themselves that they would not ordinarily share with others), and socially (e.g., by losing trust in others or suffering a blow to their reputation or status). Almost any type of research that might be done carries the risk of harming others in some way. Determining potential risks is not always apparent at the outset of a study and can surface at some later point after the study has begun. Some participants may be at higher risk for harm than others.

What measures can researchers take to minimize risks to participants of social research? Researchers have the obligation to inform participants of foreseeable risks or possible discomforts prior to the startup of a study and to give participants ample time to think about the implications of their participation. Researchers can screen participants for psychological harm that could be exacerbated by participation in the research. If stress or potential discomfort is a possible or anticipated outcome, measures need to be taken to assess the degree of risk or discomfort anticipated from the study. A common way of neutralizing stressful effects from participation in research is by debriefing participants and the study and providing them with procedures for contacting the principal investigator should problems develop.

Federal regulations require that researchers give special consideration to protecting the welfare of what are classified as protected populations. These include: children and minors, prisoners, pregnant women and fetuses, the institutionalized mentally disabled, the elderly, and the economically or educationally disadvantaged. For more detailed information about protected populations visit the following Web sites:

www.hhs.gov/ohrp/children
http://grants1.nih.gov/grants/guide/notice-files/not98-024.html
www.hhs.gov/ohrp/irb/irb_chapter6htm#g2

There are two underlying principles involved in informed consent. One is the belief that participants have the right to choose whether to participate in research without fear of coercion or pressure. This ensures that participation in the research is voluntary. The other principle is based on the belief that participants have the right to be given information that is relevant and necessary for deciding whether or not to participate in the research. Federal regulations require that participants sign a written consent form when more than "minimal risk" is anticipated. According to federal regulations, "minimal risk" refers to risk that is no greater than what can be expected in daily life.

According to Westin, privacy refers to "the claim of individuals, groups, or institutions to determine for themselves when, how, and to what extent information about them is communicated to others (1968, p. 7). Sieber expands this to include confidentiality and argues that confidentiality "refers to agreements between persons that limit others' access to private information" (1982:146). Thus privacy refers to persons and confidentiality refers to information.

Deception is perhaps the most controversial aspect of the treatment of human subjects because it is widely used and there is a lack of consensus about whether it is appropriate. The most common way that participants are deceived involves intentionally misleading them about the purpose of the research. The frequent use of deception in research was documented by Adair et al. (1985) who found that 58 percent of the empirical studies published in three leading social psychological journals used deception. Deception has been justified by professional associations like the American Psychological Association when alternative procedures are not available or when methodological requirements necessitate it (APA, 1990, pp. 394–395).

With the advent of computerized databases, the potential for invading an individual's privacy has grown. Medical information is now governed by the Privacy Rule of the Health Insurance Portability and Accountability Act (HIPAA) and restricts the release of medical records. If the research involves the disclosure of sensitive topics (e.g., HIV status, drug use, or immigration status) and the information will not be anonymous, researchers should apply to the Department of Health and Human Services for a Certificate of Confidentiality, which will protect the data from subpoena. It should be noted that research data is not privileged and can be subject to subpoena. Returned surveys and questionnaires, notes, field records, and files can be accessed by the federal government under certain administrative provisions, such as the Freedom of Information Act and the Federal Property and Administrative Services Act. Gelles reminds us that "[R]esearchers who engage in research that deals with illegal, sensitive or taboo topics run the risks of being forced to turn over material they pledged would be kept confidential, of engaging in legal battles, or of spending time in jail for contempt of court" (1978, p. 422).

When conducting research in a foreign country, the researchers should keep in mind that foreign governments vary in the approaches to research ethics. The Council of Europe developed research guidelines in 1985 that were reinforced by the European Union in 1990. Collaborative efforts between the World Health Organization and the Council for International Organizations of Medical Sciences generated proposed international guidelines for human subjects research to be used throughout the world. These guidelines reflect the principles expressed in the Declaration of Helsinki and include the following:

- Prior approval by an independent review board
- Obtaining informed consent from prospective subjects
- Favorable risk to benefit ratio
- Equitable selection of subjects
- Protection of data confidentiality
- Privacy of subjects

Numerous world organizations have emphasized that special attention should be given to research conducted by researchers from First World countries on human subjects from Third World countries. Attention needs to be given to the particular culture in which the research is being conducted especially with respect to obtaining informed consent. When international research is funded by the federal government the same procedures and protection should be accorded to human subjects as is provided to human subjects of domestic research.

Public concern with human subject experimentation was heightened with the revelation of the research practices employed in the federally funded Tuskegee experiment. The Tuskegee scandal led to congressional hearings, demands for greater research oversight, and eventually new legislation and federal regulations. Congress passed the National Research Act in 1974. The Act required that institutions receiving Department of Health, Education, and Welfare research funds establish "Institutional Review Board[s] . . . in order to protect the rights of the human subjects. . . . " Government estimates indicate that between 3000 and 5000 IRBs now operate across the country.

IRBs are mandated to review proposed research projects involving the use of human subjects. This initial review generally consists of an examination of the proposed research design and protocol, informed consent documents, and any advertising or other recruitment devices. The IRB may vote to approve the project, to approve it with required modifications, or to reject it. To approve a project undergoing initial review, federal regulations require IRBs to determine that (1) risks to subjects are minimized through the use of a sound research design; (2) risks to subjects are reasonable in light of anticipated benefits to the subjects and the importance of the knowledge to be gained; (3) subjects are selected equitably; (4) informed consent will be obtained from subjects and documented; (5) when appropriate because of safety concerns, a plan is in place to monitor incoming data from subjects on the protocol; (6) there are adequate protections for protecting subjects' privacy and confidentiality; and (7) appropriate precautions are in place when particularly vulnerable subjects, such as children, prisoners, or the mentally disabled, will participate. As indicated earlier, IRBs are to follow additional procedures, and consider other safeguards, when the research involves "protected populations." Individual researchers are required to submit a written protocol to the IRB that describes the proposed research (including dissertation proposals) and outlines the measures that will be used to protect the rights of participants.

Funding agencies award research funds to institutions rather than individual researchers. This practice makes institutions accountable for the use of funds and for overseeing the conduct of research (Andersen, 1988). The presumption is that misconduct will be discovered at the institutional level through IRB oversight. In addition to IRB oversight, misconduct investigations can also be undertaken by the ORI. In some cases, ethical violations may be turned over to local or federal prosecutors for criminal prosecution. We saw in Professor Hwang's case that the Korean government initiated criminal sanctions against Professor Hwang.

Ethical violations may also lend themselves to prosecution under civil law. In the United States the relevant statute under civil law is the civil False Claims Act. The civil provisions of this act carry a fine of $5,000–$10,000 per violation, plus treble damages (refers to the costs of the misconduct plus damages of three times that amount). Although civil cases are rarely used in cases of ethics violations, Friedman suggests that they may become more common simply because the stiff competition to receive government funding encourages researchers to "leapfrog" funds (1992). This refers to doing the proposed research in advance to apply for funding and then using the money for the proposal to use on the next research project. This practice could constitute a false claim under the False Claims Act.

Increasingly, questions are being raised about the "objectivity" of the IRB process, particularly with respect to conflicts of interest among IRB members, their institutions, and industry. Conflicts of interest can occur when primary interests are eclipsed by secondary interests. The primary interest of IRBs is to ensure the rights, safety, and welfare of human subjects—all other interests, e.g., financial gain, professional status, power, or recognition, are secondary. To maintain the commitment to protecting human subjects, federal regulations require that each IRB should have at least five members with varying backgrounds (to ensure the adequate review of research proposals). To provide a cross-section of expertise, members must include at least one nonscientist (such as a lawyer, an ethicist, or a member of the clergy), at least one member not affiliated with the research institution, and members who are competent to review specific research activities.

The concern over the potential conflict of interest between IRB members and the relationships with industry rests with the belief in the "integrity" of the researcher and scientific results. The potential to undermine this belief is present when there are no clear policies that define when an IRB member's financial or other industry relationship is a conflict of interest. A recent study published in the New England Journal of Medicine found that 36 percent of all IRB members (a sample of 893 IRB members from 100 major research institutions) reported having at least one relationship with industry within the past year (Campbell, et al., 2006, p. 2321). Fifteen percent reported that at least one proposal came before their IRB within the prior year that was sponsored by a company with which they had a relationship or by a competitor of that company. Perhaps more troubling is the finding that more than half of the IRB members in this study reported that their IRBs did not have a formal procedure for disclosure of relationships with industry.

9.5 CONCLUSION

The scientific enterprise does not occur in a vacuum. Within the context of a "research industrial complex" today's researcher is faced with professional, social, and political pressures that generate myriad ethical challenges. We lose sight of the fact that although social scientists study problems and issues that impact people and affect the way they live, they are members of the same communities on which they do research and are shaped by values and beliefs that affect their worldview. Ethical principles and standards, although they exist informally, do not constitute a checklist of "dos" and "don'ts" useful when dealing with obvious ethical dilemmas. The real challenge comes from the embedded ethical dilemmas that arise as a result of the unforeseen, hidden, and conflicted aspects of complex research environments. The novice researcher is responsible for internalizing and abiding the principles that distinguish the scientific enterprise from other activities and at the same time must learn how to navigate the regulatory and bureaucratic apparatus that provides ethical oversight to research. Lest we forget, researchers are no longer accountable to just their peers, but also to those who support them—the public and the elected representatives of the public. Ethical violations harm the public and erode the public's trust in science by diverting scarce tax dollars on worthless research (Andersen, 1988; Burk, 1995).

In extreme cases, the public may be physically harmed by ethical violations. Reliance on informal norms to regulate the conduct of researchers, although necessary, is no longer sufficient for preserving scientific integrity. Informal norms have increasingly been replaced by legal strictures, financial oversight, and bureaucratic provisions (Alberts and Shine, 1994).

KEY TERMS

Politics of research	Cooking data
Research industrial complex	Trimming data
Communalism	Scientific etiquette
Universalism	Health Research Extension Act
Disinterestedness	Office of Research Integrity
Organized scepticism	Tuskegee experiment
Forging data	The Belmont Report
The Declaration of Helsinki	The Nuremberg Trials
Protection of Human Subjects	Protected populations
Informed consent	Confidentiality
HIPPA	IRBs
Privacy	False Claims Act

CLASSROOM EXERCISES

Case Study 1

Researchers are gathering data on newly arrested male and female inmates for a study of drug abuse history. The study has received approval from the IRB and the researchers have obtained a Certificate of Confidentiality. The interview schedule they will be using asks about drug use history, employment history, educational background, and family relationships. All participants are fully informed of their rights, including the protection of their privacy and have signed a formal consent form.

During the interview process, a researcher is startled when the interviewee unexpectedly begins talking about having abused his youngest child

What should the researcher do, having been told this information?

Possible scenarios for discussion

A. Because the interviewee has been given assurances of privacy, the researcher just lets the interviewee talk about his involvement in child abuse and ignores it.

B. The researcher decides that the potential harm of the abuse to the interviewee's child outweighs the responsibility to protect the participant's privacy and the researcher notifies authorities about the child abuse.

Case Study 2

In an effort to understand what it means to live with a serious disease, researchers in the Nursing School are planning to study patients who have been diagnosed with HIV/AIDS and are being treated for their disease. They believe that learning more about how patients with a serious disease learn to manage their disease will ultimately improve the way other patients manage serious diseases.

Because they are looking for volunteers from a select group of people who have been diagnosed with HIV/AIDS and are being treated for it, they decide to post a flyer in two nearby hospitals describing the study. The flyer gives details of how to contact the researchers using a private telephone answering service. The researchers are not confident that they will be able to recruit enough subjects through posting the flyer. What are the best ways to recruit subjects for this study?

Possible scenarios for discussion

A. Because the researchers work in both hospitals, they are worried that they may inadvertently encounter patients they see as recruits. They decide that all patients they see at the hospital are eligible for participation in the study.

B. Researchers decide to place ads in the local newspapers and to ask physicians and health care workers to identify patients who meet the study's inclusion criteria to contact the researchers.

Case Study 3

A political science instructor is vehemently opposed to the war in Iraq. She decides to administer a questionnaire in all of her classes to see what political science students think about the war. She wants to use the findings for a publication on attitudes about the war among college students. She debates whether she should administer the questionnaire during class time or simply hand it out after class. A colleague suggests that she administer the questionnaire in classes she does not teach, but if she did that the project would take much longer than she wants to spend on it. What should she do?

Case Study 4

After entering data on a research project, the researcher discovers that half of the study's surveys have been incorrectly coded. He goes to the project's principal investigator and informs him. The principal investigator looks at the miscoded questions and tells the researcher to ignore the miscodes. The data is analyzed and published in an academic journal. The researcher knows that the results are misleading because of the miscoded data. What should the researcher do?

Exercise

Review the IRB guidelines at your university/college. Have the students take the tutorial and exam for certification.

REFERENCES

Adair, J.G., Dushenko, T.W., and Lindsay, R.C. 1985. Ethical regulations and their impact on research practice. *American Psychologist*, 40: 59–72.

Alberts, B. and Shine, K. 1994. Scientists and the integrity of research. *Science*, 266 (December), 1660–1661.

American Psychological Association. 1981. *Ethical Principles of Psychologists*. Washington, D.C.

Andersen, R. 1988. The federal government's role in regulating misconduct in scientific and technological research. *Georgetown Journal of Law and Technology*, 3: 115–121.

Babbage, C. 1969. *Reflection on the Decline of Science in England and on Some of Its Causes*. London: Gregg International.

Babbie, E. 2001. *The Practice of Social Research*. Belmont, California: Wadsworth/Thomson Learning.

Burk, D. 1995. Research misconduct: Deviance, due process, and the disestablishment of science. *George Mason Independent Law Review*, 3: 305–350.

Campbell, E., Weissman, J., Vogeli, C., Clarridge, B., Abraham, M., Marder, J., and Koski, G. 2006. Financial relationships between institutional review board members and industry. *The New England Journal of Medicine*, 355: 2321–2329.

Diener, E. and Crandall, R. 1978. *Ethics in Social and Behavioral Research*. Chicago: University of Chicago Press.

Friedman, P. 1992. Mistakes and fraud in medical research. *Law, Medicine, and Health Care*, 20: 17–25.

Gelles, R. 1978. Methods for studying sensitive family topics. *American Journal of Orthopsychiatry*, 48: 408–424.

Martinson, B., Anderson, M., and deVries, R. 2005. Scientists behaving badly. *Nature*, 435: 737–738.

Merton, R. 1973. *The Sociology of Science*. Chicago: University of Chicago Press.

Mervis, J. 1995. Hitting the president's target is mixed blessing for agencies. *Science*, 266 (October): 211.

Sieber, J.E. (ed.). 1982. *The Ethics of Social Research: Surveys and Experiments*. New York: Springer-Verlag.

Pimple, K. 2001. The six domains of research ethics: A heuristic framework for the responsible conduct of research. Paper presented at The Ninth Annual National Textile Center Forum, Myrtle Bedach, South Carolina.

Westin, A.F. 1968. *Privacy and Freedom*. New York: Atherneum.

Zuckerman, H. 1977. Deviant behavior and social control in *Science in Deviance and Social Change*, E. Sagarin (ed.). Beverly Hills, California: Sage.

10 Qualitative Research Methods

Vache Gabrielian, Kaifeng Yang, and Susan Spice

CONTENTS

10.1 INTRODUCTION

In recent years, there has been resurgence in the use of qualitative research methods in social sciences. Once the preferred method for research in social science, qualitative methods in the mid-twentieth century were supplanted by quantitative methods, in large part due to the fact that computers made it much easier to do extremely complex mathematical calculations quickly and accurately. However, qualitative research methods are reclaiming their place in social science inquiry. Public administration scholars are also increasingly engaging in qualitative research (e.g., Abolafia, 2004; Brower and Abolafia, 1996, 1997; Carr and Brower, 2000; Charmaz, 2006; Frederickson and Frederickson, 2006; Kelly and Maynard-Moody, 1993; Maynard-Moody and Musheno, 2006; Yanow, 1999). Unfortunately, with some exceptions, many qualitative public administration studies lack methodological rigor or credibility, which suggests a great need to train students with rigorous qualitative methods (Brower, Abolafia, and Carr, 2000; Lowery and Evans, 2004; Perry and Kraemer, 1994).

This chapter offers an introduction to qualitative research regarding its definitions, purposes, types, uses, and its quality criteria. It is not to provide a comprehensive coverage and full classification of qualitative methods, nor is it to lay down a practical guide for conducting qualitative research. Readers interested in broader coverage of qualitative research may refer to books such as *The Sage Handbook of Qualitative Research* (Denzin and Lincoln, 2005a) and *The Landscape of Qualitative Research: Theories and Issues* (Denzin and Lincoln, 2003b; see also McNabb, 2002; Ritchie and Lewis, 2003). Readers interested in more in-depth explanations and how-to guides may look to books such as *The Strategies of Qualitative Inquiry* (Denzin and Lincoln, 2003a) or *Qualitative Inquiry and Research Design* (Creswell, 2006; see also Marshall and Rossman, 1995; Miles and Huberman, 1984, 1994), or to volumes addressing specific qualitative research methods or techniques (e.g., Glasser and Strauss, 1967; Rubin and Rubin, 2005; Strauss and Corbin, 1990). There are also some volumes that try to combine the encyclopedic coverage with examples and illustrations of each research technique (Somekh and Lewin, 2005).

10.2   WHAT IS QUALITATIVE RESEARCH

10.2.1   DEFINITIONS

"Qualitative methods" often serve as an umbrella term for a variety of methods and techniques that could not, for various reasons, be "quantified." Examples of these reasons are inability to formulate fuzzy concepts, small number of observations, study of unique events, and losing essence in coding the situation. Specifically, qualitative methods are often used to indicate three related concepts: (1) qualitative research epistemologies that are nonpositivistic; (2) qualitative research strategies that aim more toward interpreting or revealing meanings rather than generalizing causal relationships; and (3) qualitative research techniques that are not operationalized with numbers (e.g., interviewing). The three concepts overlap, but they are different. For example, qualitative techniques can be applied in a research based on a positivistic paradigm (e.g., ethnography applied to structuralist anthropology); research based on a constructivist paradigm can employ simple quantitative techniques (e.g., tabulations or frequency counts) or more rigorous quantitative techniques (e.g., Q-methodology). It is also important to note the qualitative–quantitative dichotomy in research methods is not very accurate: what is not quantitative is not necessarily qualitative and vice versa— it can be classified just as "ordinary knowledge" (Cohen and Lindblom, 1979).

There is no consensus as to what exactly qualitative research methods are. Nor is there unanimous agreement on their inherent characteristics, underlying epistemology (if any), compatibility with quantitative methods, fields of human (scientific) inquiry they relate to, or questions they answer. Even for the champions, the term assumes different meanings in different historical contexts and generic definitions are often quite broad and can cover a very large realm. Denzin and Lincoln (2005b, p. 3), for example, define qualitative research as a "situated activity that locates the observer in the world," where the researchers are "attempting to make sense of, or interpret, phenomena in terms of the meanings people bring to them" in natural settings.

On the other hand, qualitative research is often being defined through its relation to quantitative research. As a recent National Science Foundation report notes, one should view qualitative/quantitative divide "as a continuum rather than as a dichotomy" (Ragin, Nagel, and White, 2004, pp. 9–10) and derive from the "middle range of the qualitative–quantitative continuum" a minimalist definition of qualitative research that involves an in-depth, case-oriented study of small number of cases, an aim of a detailed knowledge of specific cases, trying to uncover how things happen, and a primary goal of "making the facts understandable," placing less emphasis on deriving inferences, thus prompting a trade-off between intensive and extensive knowledge.

Quantitative methods originated from the natural sciences such as physics and chemistry. They are objective and can be used to establish causal relationships generalizable to a wider population. Qualitative methods, on the other hand, were rooted in arts and humanities and clinical research, with an emphasis on the interpretation of human cognition and action (even if it is applied to only one person). The qualitative approach sometimes helps develop new theories, as the research is not bounded by old theories but guided by what the researcher observes. This is very different from the quantitative approach that stresses hypothesis testing based on theoretical deduction. Many qualitative researchers view the positivist approaches as an ivory-tower type enterprise that aims more at proving existing dogmas than solving actual problems or introducing new theories.

Qualitative research is sometimes seen as research based on in-kind rather than in-degrees differences (Caporoso, 1995). Thus, qualitative variation (differences across categories such as types of government) is not a variation of magnitude as is quantitative variation (differences across the quantities of the same variable, such as income). It is a loose assortment of complex and interconnected concepts, terms, and assumptions that crosscut disciplines, fields, and subject matters and assume different meanings in different historical contexts (Denzin and Lincoln, 2005b). For the purposes of this chapter, the term suggests any combination of the following: ethnography; participant observation; ethnology; textual, hermeneutic, semiotic, and narrative analysis; analysis through symbolic interactionism; ethnomethodology; psychoanalysis; feminist inquiry; phenomenology; phenomenography; deconstruction; action research and participatory action research; and case studies.

Perhaps the most important facet of qualitative research is the researcher himself or herself. As Lincoln and Guba (1985) argue, human beings possess unique qualities as instruments of research—they have the capacity to respond to a wide range of hints, to make often unpredictable mental associations and references, to see phenomena from a holistic perspective while detecting atypical features, to process data on the spot, and to test out new knowledge immediately. Many qualitative researchers speak of the importance of what Glasser (1978) labeled as "theoretical sensitivity," which is defined by Strauss and Corbin (1990) as "the attribute of having insight, the ability to give meaning to data, the capacity to understand, and capability to separate the pertinent from that which isn't" (p. 42). Theoretical sensitivity can stem from mastery of the literature as well as from professional and personal experience.

Qualitative research often implies multiple methodologies. The diversity of methodologies is often called bricolage, and the researcher a bricoleur—a "Jack of all trades or a kind of professional do-it-yourself person" (Levi–Strauss, 1966, p. 17). This often implies triangulation—the act of bringing more than one data source or more than one perspective to bear on a single point. Admittedly, triangulation is not only for qualitative researchers. It has been increasingly used in quantitative studies as well. Nevertheless, triangulation seems to be particularly important for qualitative researchers who attempt to understand multiple meanings and realities.

Based on this, many researchers distinguish between research techniques (tools) and methods (strategies of inquiry). In this view, research method is qualitative if its intent and focus is on interpretation and understanding rather than explanation and prediction. Understanding is seen as more contextual and specific, whereas explaining is seen more like laying down law-like patterns of phenomena under investigation that will apply in the future and similar situations as well. In essence, this line of reasoning is an argument for defining qualitative research as a paradigm of research with certain assumptions about ontology (reality), epistemology (knowledge), and methodology (tools). Such an argumentation rejects the definition of qualitative research as addiction to methods (that many would dismiss as "soft" science) and tries to picture qualitative research as an expression of nonpositivist scientific paradigm. This brings us to examination of competing paradigms of scientific inquiry.

10.2.2 Underlying Paradigms of Qualitative Inquiry

Despite some opposing arguments (Miles and Huberman, 1984, 1994), qualitative research is seen by many as antipositivistic inquiry geared toward understanding rather than explaining. This perception relates to researchers' assumptions about appropriate ontology and epistemology, which are often used to differentiate research paradigms. As Guba and Lincoln (2005) define, a paradigm is a set of basic beliefs (or metaphysics) that deals with ultimates or first principles. It represents a worldview that defines, for its holder, the nature of the world, the individual's place in it, and the range of possible relationships to that world and its parts. Guba and Lincoln (1994) compare four alternative inquiry paradigms (Table 10.1).

The positivistic perspective assumes that, given similar structures and incentives, people behave similarly; that there is a clear separation between the researcher and the research participants because the researcher does not influence the participants' behavior; that the researcher can observe the participants' behavior; that by having a control group or controlling for individual characteristics the researcher can correctly test the hypothesis concerning the benefits of a program; and that the application of the research findings to the society at large will solve the problem the program is addressing.

The postpositivistic perspective, as Guba and Lincoln (1994) use the term, requires similar designs as from the positivistic perspective. The only difference, perhaps, would be that the former has greater tolerance for error—the findings would be probable, rather than established and verified laws; they would be considered true until falsified. Qualitative research may be employed to augment what is essentially a positivistic design. For example, some (or all) aspects of participant behavior that cannot be quantified easily will be given to independent experts who, based on unstructured interviews, will grade them according to certain scales, which will later be statistically analyzed. Here the process of interpretation is explicitly incorporated into the research design.

The critical perspective attacks the premise that there is no link between the researcher and the participants. Because the participants know they are participating, their behaviors are affected and become less authentic (the Hawthorne effect). Therefore, the critical perspective is not value-free, but explicit about the values and actively advocating an emancipatory empowerment ethic. Critical qualitative researchers do not aim to assess whether certain incentives influence behaviors, but to understand what causes the behavior—to determine the existing structures that shape undesirable behaviors and to correct the structures. The correction or change can be achieved through a dialogue between the investigator and the participants, which educates and emancipates the participants and transforms unjust structures. For example, the positivistic approach studies the impact of welfare benefits on teen pregnancy by manipulating welfare benefits (e.g., changing benefits, duration, and eligibility) and then observing the behavioral differences. The critical approach, however, requires the researcher to work with teenage girls to understand and transform their awareness of their potential and their prospects as well as improving the conditions that induce undesirable behavior (e.g., poverty and education). This emancipatory action stimulus is part of the criteria by which the qualitative research is evaluated. Consequently, critical research may be better used with a local focus rather than global ambitions.

The constructivist approach asserts that there are multiple realities that are constructed by actors in each particular environment. For example, in examining success in higher education, a constructivist may argue that one cannot compare the experiences (and thus their understanding of the world and their logic of action) of minority students in an urban state university and students from prep schools and Ivy League colleges. Education, grades, and a host of other variables may have different meanings for both groups of students. As a result, although a positivist researcher may ask whether the characteristics of a professor (age, gender, number of publications, tenure, the ability to entertain, etc.) have an impact on the grades achieved by students, a constructivist does not assume any variable beforehand but expects the answers will emerge during the investigation through hermeneutic or dialectical interaction between and among the investigator and respondents.

This four-paradigm classification above is neither exhaustive nor final. Although positivism is fairly accurately represented, the definitions of other schools of thought are still a subject of controversy. Even positivism is not an obvious creed to which many researchers subscribe. For example, Huberman and Miles (1994)—perhaps the best-known "positivistic" qualitative researchers—see themselves as realists or transcendental realists, rather than positivists. The consensus is even less with other schools of thought.

TABLE 10.1
Basic Beliefs (Metaphysics) of Alternative Inquiry Paradigms

Item	Positivism	Postpositivism	Critical Theory et al.	Constructivism (Naturalism)
Ontology	Naive realism—reality is real and apprehendable	Critical realism—reality is real, but only imperfectly and probabilistically apprehendable; it should be approximated as much as possible, but cannot be fully captured	Historical realism—reality consists of crystallization (reified) structures (that are real for all practical purposes) that over time were shaped by social, political, cultural, economic and ethnic, and gender factors	Relativism—there are multiple realities that are constructed, experiential, local, specific, and dependent for their form and content on the individuals or groups holding the constructions
Epistemology	Dualist (clear separation between the knowing subject and examined object of the study with no influence in either direction) and objectivist; findings are true	Modified dualist (clear separation between the knowing subject and examined object of the study with no influence in either direction) and objectivist; critical tradition; findings probably true	Transactional/subjectivist (interactive link and mutual influence between the investigator and the investigated object); findings are value-mediated	Transactional/subjective (interactive link and mutual influence between the investigator and the investigated object); findings are literally created as the investigation proceeds
Methodology	Experimental/manipulative; (propositions are stated in form of hypotheses and are subject to empirical or logical verification; confounding conditions are controlled); methods employed are chiefly quantitative	Modified experimental/manipulative; critical multiplism (hypotheses are not verified but tested against possible falsification); discovery is reintroduced as an element in inquiry; there is a drive to include qualitative methods and do research in more nature settings	Dialogic/dialectical; the dialog between the investigator and the subjects of the inquiry must be dialectical to transform ignorance and misapprehensions (accepting unjust status quo as immutable) into more informed consciousness (seeing and showing how the structures can be changed)	Hermeneutic/dialectical; social constructions can be elicited and refined only through interaction between and among investigator and respondents; constructions are interpreted through hermeneutic techniques, with an aim of creating more informed and more sophisticated new consensus
Inquiry aim	Explanation; prediction and control	Explanation; prediction and control	Critique and transformation; restitution and emancipation	Understanding and reconstruction
Nature of knowledge	Verified hypotheses established as facts or laws	Nonfalsified hypotheses that are probably facts or laws	Structural/historical insights	Individual reconstruction coalescing around consensus
Quality criteria	Internal validity (isomorphism of findings with reality); external validity (generalizability); reliability (stability and replicability); objectivity (does not depend on observer)	Internal validity; external validity; reliability; objectivity	Historical situatedness; erosion of ignorance and misapprehensions; action stimulus	Trustworthiness (credibility, transferability, dependability, and confirmability) and authenticity (fairness, enrichment, education, stimulation to action and empowerment)

Source: Adapted from Guba, E.S. and Lincoln, Y.S., in *Handbook of Qualitative Research*, N.K. Denzin and Y.S. Lincoln (eds.), Sage, Thousand Oaks, California, 1994, 105–117. Reprinted by permission of Sage Publications.

Nevertheless, more people would agree that qualitative research has increasingly become more interpretive and geared more toward understanding than explaining, with more frequent contestation and fragmentation of the research programs and methodologies (Denzin and Lincoln, 2005a, Atkinson, 2005, Best, 2004), and diverging cultural traditions (Flick, 2005). In social sciences, by the mid 1970s, with more and more serious defeats of positivism and its various offshoots, there was an increasing popularity of new trends (e.g., phenomenology, hermeneutics, semiotics, poststructuralism), and given the ability of qualitative methods to work with much richer and more holistic data which positivism failed to explain, qualitative methodologists began to be more explicit in their interpretivist leanings. Since the mid-1980s, postmodernism has deconstructed and questioned nearly every major assumption inherent in research (gender bias, ethnic bias, colonialist bias, political bias, historical bias, etc.). Particularly, the skeptical school of postmodernism sees no truth but the demise of the subject, the death of the author, and the play of words and meanings (Rosenau, 1992). It questions the ability of qualitative researchers to capture lived experience and to accurately represent such an experience. Some even argue that qualitative research may have gone to another extreme by reflecting every major contradiction of postmodernism, which could undermine the very enterprise of scientific inquiry (Atkinson, 2005).

Overall, it is clear that qualitative research methods are increasingly more interpretivist, relativist, and constructivist. Indeed, the term "qualitative research" increasingly means attitude and substantive focus rather than specific, nonquantitative techniques. Still, one cannot claim in the field of qualitative research methods that postmodernism or constructivism reigns. For example, Miles and Huberman's (1984, 1994) "realist" sourcebook of qualitative methods is very popular. Huberman and Miles (1994) give the best rationale, which we are aware of, for "cohabitation" of realist and constructivist approaches to qualitative research, and identification of qualitative research as a field not determined by epistemology. They argue that "there do appear ... to be some procedural commonalities, in the sequential process of analyzing, concluding, and confirming findings in a field study format. ... [T]he researcher shifts between cycles of inductive data collection and analysis to deductive cycles of testing and verification" (Huberman and Miles, 1994, p. 438).

10.3 QUALITATIVE VERSUS QUANTITATIVE RESEARCH

It is important to note that the qualitative–quantitative dichotomy in research methods is not very accurate. First, what is not quantitative is not necessarily qualitative and vice versa. For example, although renowned economists Coase and Hirschman did not employ statistical or mathematical techniques and did not operate with empirical data in some of their classic studies, one still cannot call the logic or the method they employed "qualitative" as described above. Rather, this type of technique is often called "ordinary knowledge" (Lindblom and Cohen, 1979). Second, the qualitative and quantitative approaches cannot be separated absolutely. For example, Kritzer (1996) identifies three levels at which interpretive processes operate in quantitative research, while Collier (2005) talks about statistical rationale for qualitative research.

Nevertheless, there has long been a debate regarding the quantitative–qualitative relationship. Many people take a purist position, asserting that because qualitative research is in the domain of nonpositivistic paradigms, it would be absurd to mix it with positivist quantification. For instance, what is the purpose of generalizing the social experience of people suffering from a rare disease in the Amish community in Pennsylvania to the population of the United States? How can you compare the meanings that are attached to public space by adolescent Navajo Indians with that of teenagers from New York's Upper East Side? Are there any lessons to be learned from, say, the Manhattan project if it was a one-of-a-kind project that will never recur? This posture does not deny the right of existence to quantitative methods; rather it points out that qualitative researchers are answering different questions by employing different logic. A slightly different position is that regardless of whether quantitative and qualitative methods are epistemologically incompatible, qualitative research produces complete and practical knowledge by itself. Although its results can be used later in quantitative studies (say, to test generalizability), there is absolutely no need to make qualitative researchers engage in both types of research for the same program (Morse, 1996).

Qualitative researchers in public administration often take the above perspectives and differentiate between qualitative and quantitative research regarding ontology, epistemology, axiology (value base), rhetorical style, and methodology (analytic process, research design, goals of sampling, basis for conclusions, etc.). Table 10.2, based on a review of the recent public administration literature (Brower, Abolafia, and Carr, 2000; McNabb, 2002; Rubin and Rubin, 2005), summarizes the typical differences proposed, with qualitative research being more interpretivist and constructivist. However, such a strict differentiation is rather simplistic.

Many authors argue that qualitative and quantitative approaches are complementary. Some point to the fact that quantitative research is not "purely" empirical. Even the most rigorous quantitative research uses interpretation as well. Kritzer (1996), for example, identifies three levels of interpretation in quantitative research. The first level involves the interpretation of statistical results (e.g., what is R^2? Is there a lowest threshold for explained variance? How good is satisfactory?). The second level involves the use of statistical results to identify "problems" in the data and analysis (e.g., what is indicated by regression coefficients that are large in absolute terms, but have the "wrong" sign and fail to achieve statistical significance? Does that indicate no link, or opposite relationship? Is it the result of collinearity? How should outliers be identified?). The third level involves connecting statistical results to broader theoretical patterns, which is closely tied to contextual elements such as substantive theory, data collection or generation, and peripheral information available to the analyst. Interpretation is always political; it is a problem of

---

TABLE 10.2
Purist Position on Differences between Qualitative and Quantitative Research by Some Researchers

Dimensions	Qualitative	Quantitative
Ontology	Multiple realities subjectively derived from participants' local, everyday, emergent experiences	A single, objective reality "out there"
Epistemology	Researchers interact with participants or studied phenomena	Researchers are detached and independent of the variables under study
Axiology (value bases)	Researchers and participants are value-laden and biased	Researchers and participants are value-free and unbiased
Rhetorical style	Personal voice often in present tense	Impersonal voice often in past tense
Analytical process	Largely inductive	Largely deductive
Basis for conclusions	Evidence from naturally occurring, local experiences	Relationships derived from replicable, numerical data
Causality explanations	Idiographic; emergent, unfolding process of interconnected actions	Nomothetic; relations among static variables
Research design	Emergent, improvisational, and openness of meaning	Static design; meanings closed before study begins
Types of research questions	Marginal or hard-to-study settings and groups; ambiguous phenomena; open-ended questions	Specifiable, measurable variables and relationships
Goal of sampling	Explanatory power; variation and richness	Generalizability and representativeness

Sources: Based on McNabb, D.E., in *Research Methods in Public Administration and Nonprofit Management: Quantitative and Qualitative Approaches*, M.E. Sharpe, Armonk, New York, 2002; Rubin, H.J. and Rubin, I.S., *Qualitative Interviewing*, Sage, Thousand Oaks, California, 2005; Brower, R.S., Abolafia, M.Y., and Carr, J.B., *Admin. Soc.* 32, 363, 2000.

language and communication, even if the language is mathematical in form. Therefore, Kritzer (1996) concludes that the lines between quantitative and qualitative social science are less clear than often presumed.

Another view does not see any way of resolving differences between competing epistemologies, because it is a matter of belief (Olson, 1995). For example, interviews (a qualitative technique) can be used in a controlled experiment. Whether interviews are seen as representing the particular contextual beliefs of interviewees or as representing an objective truth that can be generalized is a matter of one's subscription to a certain epistemology and does not depend on the value-neutral tool of the interview itself. Researchers should be aware of the choices they are making and understand how this implies their stance on epistemological and methodological issues. The argument is for more reflexive research, and the researcher is urged to constantly question the epistemology and ontology of the research and their own rather than rigidly adhere to certain pre-established principles.

Most applied researchers would agree that qualitative and quantitative methods are fully compatible and answering different questions. They concentrate less on epistemologies and differentiate qualitative and quantitative methods focusing on more pragmatic criteria, such as the level of measurement, size of the N, use of statistical tests, and thick versus thin analysis (Collier, Seawright, and Brandy, 2004), or "the analysis of qualitative data" or "the qualitative analysis of data" (Ryan, 2005). This chapter takes the position that qualitative and quantitative research traditions complement and enrich each other, and can be combined (Ragin et al., 2004), or more accurately, matched (Smith, 2004) in different ways. The task of the researcher should be the open-minded consideration of all research alternatives suitable for the particular problem at hand. During the process of analysis the researcher should constantly question his or her personal bias and the ontology and epistemology of research inquiry as well as examining the data and testing theory. Qualitative research tends to be explicitly interpretive and more suited for certain tasks such as establishing meanings, clarifying concepts, and proposing hypotheses. The demarcation lines between qualitative and quantitative domains of research are not very clear, and neither of them have inherent prominence over the other.

10.4 STRATEGIES OF QUALITATIVE INQUIRY

A comprehensive classification of research strategies in behavioral sciences is provided by McGrath (1981), who distinguishes eight research strategies along two continua: obtrusive–unobtrusive research operations and universal–particular behavior systems. None of the research methods maximizes more than one of the three conflicting goals of behavioral research: precision, generality, and concreteness or faithfulness to a real situation (Figure 10.1). Most of the qualitative research fits what this classification calls field studies, with its primary concern being faithfulness to the situation.

Despite numerous attempts at classification of qualitative methods, there is no general consensus on their boundaries and contents. Jacob (1987, 1988) identifies six major domains of qualitative research in education: Human ethnology, ethnography of communication, ecological psychology, holistic ethnography, cognitive anthropology, and symbolic interactionalism. Atkinson, Delamont, and Hammersley (1988) identify seven: symbolic interactionism, anthropology, sociolinguistics, democratic evaluation, neo-Marxist or critical ethnography, ethnomethodology, and feminist research. Marshall and Rossman (1995) add action research to the list. Janesick (1994) mentions 18 possible research strategies such as oral history, microethnography, literary criticism, etc.

The categorization is complicated by the fact that people have different opinions over the relationship between methods of inquiry and methods of data collection. Some see the two as independent of each other, whereas others claim that research strategies often dictate data-collection methods (Marshall and Rossman, 1995). There is also some confusion about methods, with some authors considering frequently mentioned research strategies as topics of study rather than methods. For example, Stake (1994) sees case studies not as "methodological choice, but a choice of object to

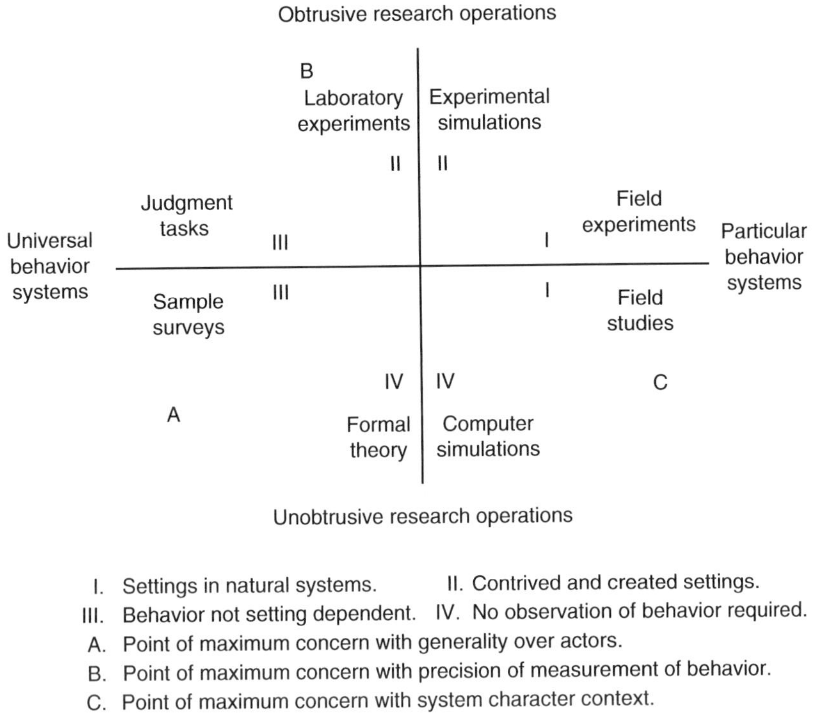

Obtrusive research operations

```
                          B
                     Laboratory │ Experimental
                     experiments │ simulations

                          II    │  II

             Judgment                        Field
               tasks                      experiments    Particular
Universal              III              I                 behavior
behavior  ─────────────────────────┼───────────────────  systems
systems      Sample    III              I      Field
             surveys                          studies

                          IV    │  IV                    C

               A          Formal │ Computer
                          theory │ simulations
```

Unobtrusive research operations

   I. Settings in natural systems.   II. Contrived and created settings.
 III. Behavior not setting dependent. IV. No observation of behavior required.
  A. Point of maximum concern with generality over actors.
  B. Point of maximum concern with precision of measurement of behavior.
  C. Point of maximum concern with system character context.

FIGURE 10.1 McGrath's (1981) classification of research strategies. (From McGrath, J., *Am. Behav. Scientist*, 25, 179, 1981. Reprinted with permission of Sage Publications.)

be studied" (p. 2236), adding that case studies can be both quantitative and qualitative. The same logic applies to a biographical method, which is more an object than a method for studying a phenomenon, although some biographies may give more insight into particular phenomena than scores of rigorous studies. Feminist studies similarly are bound not by methodology but by their focus and sensitivity to women's issues—thus they can be considered cultural studies, ethnographies, ethnomethodologies, etc.

10.5 QUALITATIVE RESEARCH PROCESS

Before we describe types of qualitative methods, it is important to identify the stages of qualitative inquiry in general. Morse (1994b) provides us with useful insights, referring to four cognitive processes:

1. Comprehending, which means "learning everything about a setting or the experiences of participants" (p. 27). This step is not finished until "the researcher has enough data to be able to write complete, coherent, detailed, and rich description" (p. 27). When overlaid on concrete research design, this step parallels data gathering (e.g., conversation and dialogues in phenomenological analysis).
2. Synthesizing, which is "the merging of several stories, experiences, or cases to describe a typical, or composite pattern of behavior or response" (p. 30). The equivalent of this process in research design will be the actual method employed (e.g., content analysis and saturation of categories in ethnography).
3. Theorizing, which is "the process of constructing alternative explanations and of holding these against the data until a best fit that explains the data most simply is obtained" (p. 33). In research design, this will be the phase of laying down the end result of the research—i.e., connecting

specific phenomena in the study (e.g., for ethnoscience it will be developing linkages between categories and putting them in a taxonomy).

4. Recontextualization, which is the "development of emerging theory so that the theory is applicable to other settings and to other populations to whom the research may be applied" (p. 34). This step generalizes the results of particular research in abstract terms (e.g., development of substantial and formal theory in grounded theory approach).

After identifying these cognitive processes, Morse (1994b) argues that the "way each process is applied, targeted, sequenced, weighed, or used distinguishes one qualitative method from another and gives each method its unique perspective" (p. 34). Morse (1994a) identifies the following phases of developing qualitative research design:

1. Stage of reflection
   a. Identification of the topic
   b. Identifying paradigmatic perspectives
2. Stage of planning
   a. Selecting a site
   b. Selecting a strategy
   c. Methodological triangulation
   d. Investigator preparation
   e. Creating and refining the research question
   f. Writing the proposal
3. Stage of entry
   a. Sampling
   b. Interview techniques
4. Stage of productive data collection and analysis
   a. Data management techniques
   b. Ensuring rigor of the data
5. Stage of withdrawal
6. Stage of writing

The first stage involves the search for a research topic, which may come from sources such as personal experience, discrepancy in literature and research findings, project assignment, etc. (Morse, 1994a; Strauss and Corbin, 1990). The more important issue here, however, is not where the topic comes from but the researcher's awareness of his or her motives that may result in a bias when studying a particular phenomenon (Morse, 1994a). Reflection on the researcher's epistemological paradigm, as well as on his or her "posture" in qualitative research, is important for qualitative research. For example, Wolcott (1992) identifies three postures in qualitative research: (1) theory driven (i.e., based on certain broad theory, such as cultural theory in ethnography); (2) concept driven (i.e., based on certain concept within a theory, such as the concept of care in clinical ethnography); and (3) reform focused (i.e. political project with predetermined goals, such as feminist research).

The next issue, site selection, can be illustrated as case selection. As Stake (1994) argues, a case study is not a methodological tool but a choice of object to be studied. Stake (1994) identifies three main types of cases. The first type refers to intrinsic case studies, for which a particular case is studied because of the researcher's inherent interest in the case. A tragedy like the Challenger disaster may be studied because the researcher is interested in learning why this particular disaster occurred. The second type includes instrumental case studies, for which a particular case is examined to "provide insight into an issue or refinement of theory." For example, Lijphart (1975) studies the social cleavages in the Netherlands to falsify the pluralist theory, posited by David Truman and others, that cross-cutting social cleavages decrease the level of social peace and destabilize the democratic government. The third type includes collective case studies, for which the researchers study a "number of cases jointly in order to inquire into the phenomenon, population, or general condition." Mintzberg (1973) provides such a study, observing five executives in five different types of organizations. Mintzberg recognizes that managers in real life engage in activities that go beyond those described in the literature (e.g., planning, organizing, coordination, and control). He records managers' everyday activities and groups them into ten functions.

There are always features that make a particular case unique. Stake (1994) identifies six features based on which the researchers should gather information: (1) the nature of the case; (2) its historical background; (3) the physical setting; (4) other contexts, including economic, political, legal, and aesthetic; (5) other cases through which this case is recognized; and (6) those informants through whom the case can be known. Site (case) selection is especially important if one holds to a positivistic paradigm because, to arrive at one best explanation for a phenomenon it is instrumental to have the case that provides the richest (or most essential) information.

Perhaps the most important issue in research design is choosing a particular strategy for pursuing the research topic. Yin (1984) proposes three questions for selecting the soundest research strategy: What is the nature of the research question? Does the research require control over behavior or should it be naturalistic? Is the phenomenon contemporary or historical? The key issue is for the researcher to identify the research question and make clear in what aspect of the phenomenon they are interested. Yin (1984) identifies three types of research questions (exploratory, descriptive, and explanatory) and five distinct research strategies (experiments, surveys, archival analysis, histories, and case studies).

Marshall and Rossman (1995) add predictive questions as the fourth type of research question, with explanatory questions seeking to explain the phenomenon under study while predictive questions try to study the consequences of the phenomenon. Marshall and Rossman (1995) further add field studies, ethnographies, and in-depth interviews as three additional research strategies. They find that particular qualitative methods often define data-collection methods, and propose a heuristic guide for selecting research strategy and data-collection methods for specific research questions. According to them, experimental and quasi-experimental research designs are best suited for predictive questions, with qualitative research more appropriate for other questions (most notably for exploratory questions). We add action-oriented and critical questions to the guideline and reproduced it below (Table 10.3).

10.6   FOUR MAJOR TYPES OF QUALITATIVE RESEARCH STRATEGIES

Assuming, for the sake of simplicity, that qualitative research is confined to exploratory, critical, and descriptive inquiries (or designs), there is still one question looming. Which strategy (or method or tradition) of qualitative research does one use if one wants to explore a specific topic? Can they be triangulated? Morse (1994a, p. 233) lists several major types of qualitative research strategies, describing for each strategy typical research questions, underlying paradigms, methods of data collection, and data sources. Based on Morse (1994a), we discuss the essential attributes of four qualitative research strategies (Table 10.4). We limit our discussion to some main types of qualitative research that, in our view, are most relevant for public administrators in general.

As Morse (1994a, p. 233) advises, it is often useful to imagine what one wants to find out "by projecting the research outcome, the researcher may begin to conceptualize the question, the sample size, the feasibility of the study, the data sources, and so on." Following her example, we sketch what the four research strategies would yield in a mock project entitled "Managing a nonprofit organization" (Table 10.5). It has to be noted that for the purposes of methodological triangulation, more than one qualitative method can be used in a research project. It is also important to remember that the four methods identified here are not all-agreed-upon procedures that are "carved in stone." Each of them is rather a family of similar methods than a concise methodology.

TABLE 10.3

Types of Research Questions

Types	Purpose of the Study	Research Question
Exploratory	To investigate little-understood phenomena To identify/discover important variables To generate hypotheses for future research	What is happening here? What are the salient themes, patterns, and categories in participant's meaning structures? How are these patterns linked with one another?
Explanatory	To explain the forces causing the phenomenon in question To identify plausible causal networks shaping the phenomenon	What events, beliefs, attitudes, and policies are shaping this phenomenon? How do these forces interact to result in the phenomenon?
Critical	To uncover implicit assumptions and biases (and structures) on which the predominant argument (narrative) rests	What are the assumptions about human nature, society, reality, and type of knowledge that define the existing views on the phenomenon? Are they right? Are they fair?
Descriptive	To document the phenomenon of interest	What are the salient behaviors, events, beliefs, attitudes, structures, and processes occurring in this phenomenon?
Action-oriented	To change the phenomenon by educating and mobilizing people involved in it and affected by it	What events, beliefs, attitudes, and policies are shaping this phenomenon? How the target group (people needing help) see the phenomenon? How can they change it?
Predictive	To predict the outcomes of the phenomenon To forecast the events and behaviors resulting from phenomenon	What will occur as a result of this phenomenon? Who will be affected? In what ways?

Source: Adapted and amended from Marshall, C. and Rossman, G., in *Designing Qualitative Research*, Sage, Thousand Oaks, California, 1995, 41. With permission.

10.6.1 PHENOMENOLOGY

Phenomenology attempts to reveal the essential meaning of human actions. Introduced into the social sciences by Schutz (1967), elaborated upon by Husserl (1970), and further developed by Heidegger (1972), phenomenology has been applied successfully to the study of bureaucracy and public administration (Hummel, 1994a,b). At least two schools of phenomenology can be identified: (1) eidetic (descriptive) phenomenology, based on Husserl's "transcendental subjectivity" and (2) hermeneutic (interpretive) phenomenology, based on Heideggerian ontology (Ray, 1994). Others sometimes distinguish phenomenography as a different branch of phenomenology (Marton, 1994). Very often, phenomenology is included in larger groupings of hermeneutic-interpretive research methods (Diesing, 1991). The very brief description below lists some common features of their methodology.

In phenomenology, comprehension is achieved first of all by reflecting upon one's own experiences. Then in-depth interviews and conversations are carried out with subjects aiming to bring forth experiential descriptions of phenomena. These conversations are tape-recorded, transcribed, and thoroughly examined. Descriptive words and phrases are highlighted and studied. Data from other relevant sources can also be used. The principal means for combining data is the process of conducting thematic analyses by identifying common structures of the particular experience. Van Maanen (1990) proposes four "existential" guidelines for phenomenological reflection: lived space, lived body, lived time, and lived human relations. The result of phenomenological research is an abstract reflective statement purified through several iterations of writing. Ray (1994)

TABLE 10.4
Comparison of Four Major Types of Qualitative Research Strategies

Strategy	Disciplinary Traditions	Type of Question	Primary Method	Other Data Sources	References
Phenomenology	Philosophy	Questions about meaning: what is the meaning of a person's experience? How do group members cope with various phenomena?	Audiotaped "conversations"; written anecdotes of personal experiences; in-depth interviews	Phenomenological literature; philosophical reflections; art; poetry	Van Maanen (1990); Hummel (1994a)
Ethnography	Anthropology	Questions about culture: what are values and beliefs of this group? What is accepted behavior? What is not acceptable?	Participant observation; unstructured interviews; field notes	Documents, records; pictures; social network diagrams; maps; genealogies	Atkinson (1992); Jorgensen (1989)
Grounded theory	Sociology Social psychology	Questions about process: what theory is embedded in the relationships between variables? Is there a theory of change?	Interviews (tape-recorded); participant observation; coding	Memos; diary	Glaser and Strauss (1967); Strauss and Corbin (1990)
Action research	Social psychology Education	Questions about critique: what are participants' perceptions and implicit models of thought and action? How can we emancipate group members? What inhibits change?	Interviews (audio- and video-recorded); conversations	Observation	Argyris et al. (1985); Torbert (1991)

Source: Adapted and amended from Morse, J.M., in *Handbook of Qualitative Research*, Sage, Thousand Oaks, California, 224. With permission.

TABLE 10.5
Comparison of Four Major Types of Qualitative Research Strategies for the Hypothetical Project "Managing a Nonprofit Organization"

Strategy	Type of Question	Participants/Informants/Sources	Sample Size	Data-Collection Methods	Type of Results
Phenomenology	What is the meaning of managing a nonprofit organization?	Managers of nonprofit organization; autobiographies and biographies	About 5–6 participants or until saturation	In-depth conversations	Reflective description of the experience of "what it feels like to manage"
Ethnography	What are the activities the manager engages in? How does he or she relate to others?	Managers, assistants, secretaries, other subordinates, clients, funders, various documents	About 30–50 interviews or until saturation	Participant observation; unstructured interviews; "shadowing"; examination of calendars, organization charts, etc.	Description of manager's daily activities, routines, relationships with subordinates and clients
Grounded theory	What is the essence of specific actions (e.g., is the observed act of writing planning, information processing, or communicating?) In what context did it occur?	Managers, secretaries; assistants; clients; diaries, calendars; organization charts; plans; phone bills	About 30–50 interviews or until saturation	Interviews (tape-recorded); participant observation; coding (open and axial); writing and analyzing memos; drawing schemata	Description of sociopsychological aspects of managing—what action/interaction is more likely under different stimuli and in different situations
Action research	What are the perceptions of the manager and his/her subordinates about his/her work? How different are they from his/her activities? How the practice can be changed to make it more efficient and just?	The manager and his or her subordinates in one organization; clients	About 15–25 interviews or until saturation	Interviews (audio- and video-recorded); conversations; observation	Arriving to enlightenment (reflection) for manages so they can detect their shortcomings and take a corrective action

argues that "affirmation and credibility of phenomenological research can be best understood by Heidegger's (1972) concept of truth as unconcealment and Ricooeur's idea that truth of the text may be regarded as the world it unfolds" (p. 130).

10.6.2 ETHNOGRAPHY

Historically originating from cultural anthropology, ethnographic approaches to social research have been applied in numerous fields such as social and cultural anthropology, sociology, human geography, organization studies, educational research, and cultural studies (Atkinson and Hammersly, 1994). Ethnography and participant observation can be understood as the description of one group's culture from that group's perspective. As with phenomenology, ethnography is not an agreed-upon precise body of methodology. Boyle (1994) discusses four types of ethnographies (classical or holistic; particularistic; cross-sectional; ethnohistorical). Muecke (1994) discusses classical, systematic, interpretive, and critical directions in ethnography. Some authors consider ethnomethodology (Garfinkel, 1967) as a part of this tradition whereas others see ethnomethodology more as a hermeneutic practice (Holstein and Gubrium, 1994). Nevertheless, there is more agreement on the term participant observation, which is essentially the method or technique of ethnography. Although participant observation and ethnography are not exactly the same, they are often used synonymously.

Jorgensen (1989) fairly accurately summarizes the essence of participant observation: "[Participant observation] focuses on human interaction and meaning viewed from the insider's viewpoint in everyday life situations and settings. It aims to generate practical and theoretical truths formulated as interpretive theories ... involves a flexible, open-ended, opportunistic process and logic of inquiry through which what is studied constantly is subject to redefinition based on field experience and observation" (p. 23). In addition, participant observation "concentrates on in-depth description and analysis of some phenomena. Participation is a strategy for gaining access to otherwise inaccessible dimensions of human life and experience" (Jorgensen, 1989, p. 23).

10.6.3 GROUNDED THEORY

Firstly articulated by Glasser and Strauss (1967), the grounded theory approach shares many features with other types of qualitative researches regarding sources of data, data gathering, analyzing techniques, and possible uses of quantitative techniques. However, it has a uniquely explicit emphasis on theory generation. Evolving theory (i.e., propositions about the nature of relationships between phenomena that are examined) is iteratively validated against the data (i.e., being grounded in the data) until a substantive theory emerges that relates the concepts and their properties and dimensions in a systematic manner. Grounded theory is not an all-agreed-upon research strategy, although disagreements in this approach are of much lesser magnitude than in other approaches. The research question in a grounded theory study is a statement that identifies the phenomenon to be studied. The researcher should rely on his or her ability to recognize what is important in the data and to give it meaning. Readers interested in more details may read the chapter on grounded theory in this handbook (Chapter 40), or for a more detailed guidance, consult Strauss and Corbin (1990).

10.6.4 ACTION RESEARCH

Action research is a research strategy that studies action with three goals: making that action more effective and efficient; empowerment and participation; and developing scientific knowledge. Action research is again a family of methods rather than a precise research methodology, and is often covered under the title of participative research. Chein, Cook, and Harding (1948) identify four varieties of action research: diagnostic, participant, empirical, and experimental. Reason (1994) identifies three main approaches to participative inquiry: cooperative inquiry, participatory action research, and action science and action inquiry. Deshler and Ewert (1995) identify five fields of practice that have contributed to this participatory action research: action research in organizations, participatory action research in community development, action research in schools, farmer partici-patory research and technology generation, and participatory evaluation.

As one can conclude from the above, action research is a different research strategy in different environments. Students of public administration are more familiar with the following three varieties of action research: action research as a form of organizational development (e.g., Argyris, Putham, and Smith, 1985), as participatory evaluation (e.g., Guba and Lincoln, 1989), and as participatory action research in community development (e.g., Whyte, 1991). For example, as to action research and organizational development, French and Bell (1995) write that "action research is essentially a mixture of three ingredients: the highly participative nature of OD [Organizational Development], the consultant role of collaborator and co-learner, and the iterative process of diagnosis and action" (p. 7). Six types of activities are usually involved in this type of research, including (1) a preliminary diagnosis, (2) data gathering from client group, (3) data feedback to the client group, (4) exploration of the data by the client group, (5) action planning by the client group, and (6) action taken by the client group with an OD practitioner acting as facilitator throughout the process. Consequently, "widespread participation by client group members ensures better information, better decision making, and action taking, and increased commitment to action programs. ... Action research yields both change and new knowledge. ... The client group learns what works and what doesn't work" (French and Bell, 1995, p. 7).

10.7 QUALITATIVE DATA COLLECTION AND ANALYSIS

Marshall and Rossman (1995) identify 15 techniques of qualitative data collection and analysis: participant observation, interviewing, ethnographic interviewing, elite interviewing, focus group interviewing, document review, narratives, life history, historical analysis, film, questionnaire, proxemics, kinesics, psychological techniques, and unobtrusive measures. These techniques can be broadly grouped under three categories: observation, interviewing, and documentary analysis. Due to space limitation, we only sketch the contours of the three broad categories and briefly discuss data management and qualitative software.

10.7.1 DATA MANAGEMENT

Huberman and Miles (1994) define data management as "the operations needed for a systematic, coherent process of data collection, storage and retrieval" (p. 428). One should design the data man-agement system long before the actual data collection starts. Following Levine (1985), Huberman and Miles (1994) distinguish five general storage and retrieval functions that should be addressed in the data management system: (1) formatting (physical layout of the materials and their structuriza-tion into types of files), (2) cross-referral (linkage across different files), (3) indexing (defining codes, organizing them into a structure, an pairing codes with specific parts of database), (4) abstracting (condensed summaries of longer material), and (5) pagination (numbers and letters locating specific materials in-field notes).

10.7.2 INTERVIEWING

Interviews can be distinguished along three dimensions: (1) type of questions (structured, unstruc-tured, or semistructured), (2) number of interviewees questioned simultaneously (individual or group), and (3) selection of interviewees (random or specialized). The most popular form is random, one-on-one, individual interview, very often using structured or semistructured questionnaires. Polls, surveys, and censuses are examples of such interviews (Babbie, 1990). One-on-one, face-to-face, in-depth unstructured interviews are often called ethnographic interviews (Fontana and Frey, 1994).

There is more than one type of group interview—focus groups, brainstorming, Delphi tech-nique, etc. (Fontana and Frey, 1994), of which the focus group is the most common. Focus groups, in essence, are six to twelve individuals who have some knowledge or experience of the topic the researcher is interested in, and whose thinking on the matter is stimulated and enhanced by group dynamics and interaction. The result is rich and detailed perspectives on the topic that the researcher draws from discussions in several groups. Finally, interviewees can be selected randomly (as for surveys), and selectively, as in focus groups, because they are thought to have greater knowledge of the subject. In this case, the researcher may engage in specialized or elite interviewing.

There may be other classifications of interviews—postmodern, gendered, creative, phenomeno-logical, etc. (Fontana and Frey, 1994; Marshall and Rossman, 1995). Usually, different styles of interviews require different techniques. For example, in structured interviews the researcher should be more neutral, while in an ethnographic interview he or she should be more "involved"—trying to engage in conversation, elicit answers, and be empathetic. The answers are not treated as simple texts, but are analyzed in conjunction with the respondent's body language, use of interpersonal space, tone of voice, and flow of speech. In ethnographic interviews it is important to locate the "key informants," establish rapport with respondents, and understand their culture and language (including body language and cultural norms) (Fontana and Frey, 1994). And finally, there are ethical considerations involved in interviewing—issues of anonymity, privacy, and consent, among others (Punch, 1994; Fontana and Frey, 1994).

10.7.3 OBSERVATION

Observation "entails the systematic noting and recording of events, behaviors, and artifacts (objects) in the social setting chosen for study" (Marshall and Rossman, 1995, p. 79). Sometimes, observation is seen as more general activity into which the participant observation also fits. Sometimes it is classified as different from participant observation by the different levels of involvement of the researcher. Subscribers to the latter view distinguish the following levels of engagement in observation: complete observer, observer as participant, participant as observer, and complete participant. They call observation only the first level. The important point here is not rigid classification but the researcher's clear understanding of his or her position and potential biases because of that position.

Observation also requires activities that are inherent in other methods of data collection (e.g., interviewing), such as gaining access to the social setting, establishing rapport with the people in the setting, and so forth. Observation proceeds in two stages: (1) unfocused and descriptive and (2) focused, when research questions become clearer (Jorgenson, 1989; Adler and Adler, 1994). Observation works best through triangulation—e.g., having multiple observers and verifying observations with document analysis, interviews, etc. For the researcher, observation also entails the same types of ethical considerations as interviewing.

Adler and Adler (1994) identify five observational paradigms or research traditions that are clearly associated with observational methods: (1) formal sociology, focusing on structures according to which social interactions are patterned; (2) dramaturgical sociology, which is concerned with how people construct their self-presentations and act according to that in front of others; (3) studies of public realm, which "address the issues of moral order, interpersonal relations, norms of functioning, and norms of relating to strange individuals and different categories of individuals"; (4) auto-observation; and (5) ethnomethodology, with focus on how people construct their everyday lives.

10.7.4 TEXTUAL AND ARTIFACT ANALYSIS

Written texts and artifacts constitute what Hodder (1994) calls mute evidence. Lincoln and Guba (1985) distinguish between records (texts attesting some sort of formal transaction, such as contracts) and documents (texts created largely for personal reasons, such as diaries). Records (e.g., census records, archival materials) are a widely used source of data in public administration. Artifacts are pieces of material culture that characterize the social setting (e.g., a three-piece suit indicates a formal social setting whereas shorts and a t-shirt indicate an informal setting).

There are several methods for analyzing texts. The most common, perhaps, is content analysis, which constitutes a separate chapter in this handbook (Chapter 35). Other types of document analysis include (1) narrative analysis, that is, examining the form of a narrative in conveying meaning and (2) poststructuralist and postmodern deconstruction, which is the practice of "taking things apart," of showing that the meaning of a particular text is indeterminate and can be rendered differently in a different semiotic system (sign system). Artifacts are generally analyzed through situating them in a context and analyzing their function in that social setting (e.g., the role of clothing in showing socials status).

10.7.5 DATA ANALYSIS

Data gathering continues until researchers achieve theoretical saturation (Glasser and Strauss, 1967; Morse, 1995)—i.e., when the generic features of their new findings consistently replicate earlier ones. Data analysis can be conceptualized as three linked subprocesses: (1) data reduction—i.e., choosing the conceptual framework, research questions, cases and instruments, and further condensing the data by coding, summarizing, clustering, writing up; (2) data display—condensed and organized layout of the data that permits conclusion drawing or action taking; and (3) conclusion drawing or verification—i.e., interpreting, drawing meaning from data (Miles and Huberman, 1984, 1994). As Huberman and Miles (1994) point out, "these processes occur before data collection, during study design and planning, during data collection as interim and early analyses are carried out; and after data collection as final products are approached and completed" (p. 429). The process of data analysis is not completed in one decisive step, but is iterative, with consecutive inductive and deductive reasoning in each pattern identification–verification cycle.

Qualitative data analysis can be enhanced by modern technology. There are many qualitative software tools on the market that significantly enhance the process. Richards and Richards (1994), after discussing qualitative analysis potential of general-purpose software packages (such as word-processing and relational database management systems), classify special-purpose qualitative analysis into the following categories: (1) code-and-retrieve software (e.g., Ethnograph), (2) rule-based theory-building systems (e.g., HyperRESEARCH), (3) logic-based systems (e.g., AQUAD), (4) index-based software (e.g., NUD.ISTTM), and (5) conceptual network systems (e.g., ATLAS/ti). NUD.ISTTM, for example, allows one to code (index) and retrieve units of records (e.g., sentences or paragraphs), write memos about records in dialog boxes that can be easily retrieved with the records, systematically orders codes into trees (or hierarchies), searches for text patterns in documents, systematically relates (compares) different codings, etc.

Computer programs for qualitative analysis are also discussed in Kelle (1995) and Weitzman and Miles (1995). A German consulting Web site QUARC (2007) classifies qualitative research software into (1) text retrievers and text managers (e.g., Sonar Professional, FolioVIEWS), (2) rule-based systems (e.g., HyperRESEARCH), (3) logic-based systems (e.g., AQUAD), (4) classic code-and-retrieve programs (e.g., The Ethnograph, winMAX), (5) "theory builders," including the (i) index-based-approach (Nud*ist) or (ii) conceptual network-builders, which in turn are classified into code-and-retrieve (Atlas.ti) and specialized graphical display (e.g., Inspiration, Decision Explorer) systems. The Website also compares Atlas.ti, The Ethnograph, QSR Nud*ist, and winMAX on their features regarding data entry, coding, retrieval of coded segments, visualization, quantitative elements, and teamwork.

Qualitative research has a proper place on the Internet as well. In addition to class curricula and articles on occasional home pages and on-line journals (e.g., Qualitative Report), there is now a repository of qualitative data—ESDS QUALIDATA (provided by the University of Essex) that, just like ICPSR, can be accessed electronically on distance (QUALIDATA, 2007). Researchers depositing qualitative datasets for the public use should be aware of ethical concerns, such as informed consent and confidentiality, among others.

10.8 THE QUALITY OF QUALITATIVE RESEARCH

There are no universally accepted criteria for judging the soundness and goodness of qualitative research. All discussions on the matter draw from the criteria for mainstream (i.e., quantitative) research that includes internal and external validity, reliability, and objectivity. Positions on the matter vary. Some suggest establishing practical guidelines for using existing criteria with qualitative research. Others assert the existing criteria should be amended and modified for qualitative research. Still others argue the criteria should be abandoned and new criteria be formulated. The criteria of judgment used reflect the epistemological paradigms of the researchers—from a pragmatic approach of complementing the accepted "positivistic" criteria to denying them at all. Generally, the criteria proposed specifically for qualitative research are articulated within nonpositivistic paradigms.

Huberman and Miles (1994) propose that a good qualitative manuscript should report the following contents: (1) sampling decisions made, both within and across cases; (2) instrumentation and data-collection operations; (3) database summary and size, as well as the method by which it was produced; (4) software used, if any; (5) overview of analytic strategies followed; and (6) inclusion of key data-displays supporting main conclusions. Strauss and Corbin (1990) argue that judgments of research quality should center around three issues: (1) validity, reliability, and credibility of the data; (2) adequacy of the research process; and (3) empirical grounding of research findings. They offer a set of criteria against which a grounded theory study can be judged in terms of the theory-generation aspects of the research: (1) Are concepts generated? (2) Are concepts systematically related? (3) Are there many conceptual linkages and are the categories well developed? (4) Is much variation built into the theory?

Lincoln and Guba (Guba and Lincoln, 2005; Lincoln and Guba, 1985) offer two sets of criteria for qualitative research: trustworthiness (credibility, transferability, dependability, and confirmability) and authenticity (fairness, enrichment, education, stimulation to action, and empowerment). Trustworthiness parallels the criteria in the positivistic-quantitative paradigm. Specifically, credibility is the counterpart of internal validity, which can be achieved by carefully identifying the setting of the research, the population, and the underlying theoretical framework. Second, transferability parallels external validity and denotes the applicability of one set of findings to another context. This is usually problematic in qualitative research, but it can be improved by two strategies: explicitly stating theoretical parameters of the research (so that other researchers can decide upon generalizing the approach to their settings) and triangulation of the research methodologies. Third, dependability is similar to reliability and concerned with the consistency of the research—i.e., how the researcher accounts for changing conditions in the phenomena and changes in design. However, dependability is different from the positivist understanding of replicability because the social world is always constructed and thus replicability is a problem. Finally, conformability relates to objectivity or neutrality of the research. The criterion is "Do the data help to confirm the general findings and lead to the implications?" (Marshall and Rossman, 1995, p. 145). The researcher can never eliminate his or her bias, but should adopt strategies to provide a balance for bias in interpretation, such as playing devil's advocate for one's research partner, a constant search for negative instances, etc. The second set of criteria Guba and Lincoln present is about authenticity, including fairness, ontological authenticity (enlarges personal constructions, educative authenticity (leads to improved understanding of constructions of others), catalytic authenticity (stimulates to action), and tactical authenticity (empowers action).

King, Keohane, and Verba (1994) argue that both quantitative and qualitative research have the same underlying logic of inference. While valuing the role of interpretation in clarifying and defining concepts as well as idea and hypothesis generation, they insist that for evaluation of these hypotheses the logic of scientific inference applies. Therefore, qualitative researchers should also ask questions such as: How many observations are enough for valid inferences? How do you measure and improve data when you have already established the concepts? How valid is the generalization? Or perhaps, the question can be formulated as: How do you build an empirically sound theory on the basis of small number of often unique observations? They insist on situating every research inquiry in the framework of a broader theory to test for generalizability—i.e., bring the issues of internal and external validity to qualitative research. A single case study, for example, can contribute to theory greatly if it disproves (falsifies) a predominant theory. More generally, King and his collaborators argue the single case was useful because it was a part of research program and it was compared against other observations (perhaps gathered by other researchers).

Critics argue that King, Keohane, and Verba (1994) maintain the "positivist" criteria for goodness of research (internal and external validity, reliability, and objectivity) and do not mention alternative criteria proposed for qualitative research (e.g., credibility; transferability; dependability and confirmability; and empathy proposed for constructivist paradigm). Although they leave room for qualitative research (hypotheses generation and concept definition and clarification), their attempt still may be seen as emphasizing "the third part of scientific inquiry, the rigorous testing of hypotheses, almost to the exclusion of the first two—the elaboration of precise models and the deduction of their (ideally, many) logical implications—and thus point us to a pure, but needlessly inefficient, path of social scientific inquiry" (Rogowski, 1995, p. 467; see also Brady and Collier, 2004; George and Bennett, 2005). Some researchers argue that even such a proposed division of labor is not very accurate, because "the evaluation of theory with qualitative data is not inherently antithetical to qualitative research." But to do so, "qualitative projects must be designed with the goal of theory testing in order to achieve this important objective" (Ragin et al., 2004, p. 16). While others complain about unsubstantiated association of standards and rigor only with confirmatory and hypothesis-driven research (Ryan, 2005).

There are two other issues to which qualitative researchers should pay attention—the questions of ethics and "the art and politics of interpretation." The ethical issues include informed consent, deception, privacy, harm, identification, and confidentiality, among others. Researchers should be aware of all the issues in the context of a research project, and make sure that they follow the established codes of conduct. Discussing the issue of interpretation, Denzin (1994) holds that "the age of putative value-free social science is over," and "any discussion of this process must become political, personal and experiential." Whether subscribing to this view or not, one must be aware of the tendency that Denzin predicts: a proliferation of "race-, ethnicity-, and gender-specific" interpretive communities and epistemologies. An equally important issue is how research findings are communicated to scholars, governments, communities, and individuals. Especially in action-oriented interventionist research, it is very important to tell stories that "subjects" or partners may be willing to listen to.

Marshall and Rossman (1995, pp. 146–148) present a practical checklist of 20 questions to help judge the quality of qualitative research. Although not necessarily applicable to all research situations, these guidelines give a good understanding of the criteria employed to judge qualitative research. With some abridgment, they are as follows:

1. Method is explicated in detail so that a judgment can be made about the method's adequacy.
2. Assumptions and biases are expressed.
3. Research guides against value judgments in data collection and analysis.
4. There is evidence from raw data demonstrating the connection between the findings and the real world; and it is done in an accessible and readable manner.
5. Research questions are stated and answered, and answers generate new questions.
6. Relationship with previous research is explicit, and the phenomena are defined clearly.
7. Study is accessible to other researchers, practitioners, and policymakers.
8. Evidence is presented that the researcher was tolerant to ambiguity and strove to balance his or her biases.
9. Report recognizes limitations of generalizability and helps the readers to find transferability.
10. It should be a study of exploration and not reasserting theories from literature.
11. Observations are made of a full range of activities over a full cycle of activities.
12. Data is preserved and available for reanalysis.

13. Methods are devised for checking data quality (e.g., informants' knowledgeability, ulterior motives) and for guarding against ethnocentric explanation.
14. In-field work analysis is documented.
15. Meaning is elicited from cross-cultural perspective.
16. Ethical standards are followed.
17. People in the research setting benefit some way.
18. Data-collection strategies are the most adequate and efficient available. The researcher is careful to be reflexive and recognize when he or she is "going native."
19. Study is tied into "the big picture." The researcher looks holistically at the setting to understand the linkages among systems.
20. Researcher traces the historical context to understand how institutions and roles have evolved (Marshall and Rossman, 1995, pp. 146–148; reprinted by permission of Sage Publications, Inc.)

10.9 QUALITATIVE RESEARCH AND PUBLIC ADMINISTRATION

Research methods of public administration have been influenced by those in political science and economics, both of which are more concerned with generalizations. Subsequently, there is an overwhelming dominance of quantitative methods as tools of inquiry in university curricula. However, there is also quite an impressive share of theory-generation in the field that has been achieved through use of nonquantitative methods—usually a case study or deductive reasoning based on nonstructured or incomplete data. As opposed to political science, which is more concerned with the role of institutions in society, public administration has a micro-focus, the study of organizational life, which it shares with sociology, anthropology, and psychology. Despite the increasing quantification in public administration research, most insights still rise from traditional nonquantitative studies. Very often there is an interesting gap between the rhetoric and practice of public administration research. Although the rhetoric is predominantly quantitative and statistics-oriented, the practice relies heavily on qualitative methods (Yeager, 1989).

The first textbook on research methods in public administration, Pfiffner's *Research Methods in Public Administration* dates back to 1940. Although it adopts a positivistic approach, it is at ease with the rudiments of both quantitative and qualitative research strategies, and is a little bit skeptical toward the former. He argues that although hypothesis testing is achieved through classification, comparison, and analogy, formulating the hypothesis is a more creative and less structured process, where it is "legitimate to resort to imagination, supposition, and idealization, even though they may result in barren hypotheses" (Pfiffner, 1940, p. 10). In his critique of quantitative methods, Pfiffner (1940) holds to a rather balanced view: "Good quantitative work must be based on good qualitative work. This does not mean that no statistical treatment should be attempted until perfection is reached as to the collection of data. ... What is necessary is that the quantitative researcher realize the limitations of his data and select his hypotheses accordingly" (p. 168). In other words, "If the data are admittedly crude, one should look for an underlying trend rather than attempt refined treatment" (p. 168).

Some of the techniques Pfiffner describes, such as work flow and charting techniques and personnel classification are not considered (and perhaps justly so) in the domain of research methods now. But Pfiffner does discuss something that is, by and large, ignored in today's public administration research methods textbooks—the human factor in the research process. The book covers issues ranging from "handling politicians" to "handling the 'hothead'" to "wangling"— "the use of influence, suggestion, button-holing, politics and expediency to obtain action" (Pfiffner, 1940, p. 130). He includes chapters devoted to interviewing, field data studies, and biographical method. He also pays more attention to the process of research design and planning than modern textbooks. Without doubt, new research methods textbooks are much more sophisticated statistically and offer better tools for operationalizing research variables, but they miss the practical, people- and organization-oriented research agenda of Pfiffner. Pfiffner (1940) writes: "The social scientist who feels inferior in the presence of the physicist, chemist, or engineer, should remember that a great share of their knowledge is based on accepted practice rather than precise measurement" (p. 18).

This line of thought in the 1980s and 1990s was pursued with great eloquence by other public administration scholars. Discussing the experiments as endeavors to control extraneous variables, Bailey (1994) convincingly shows similarities between case studies and experiments: "The outcome of an experiment, then, is essentially a hypothesis, and each experiment is, in reality, a case study. A set of case studies can be used to challenge dominant theories or for applied research projects in fields (medicine, engineering, etc.) that are derived from 'pure' disciplines" (p. 187). She also discusses how criteria of scientific rigor can be applied to case studies. Behn (1992) points out that even physicists use empirically nonproven concepts in their theories: "Many of the observations that they [physicists] use to create reality are only indirect. Neutrinos exist—just like gravity exists—not because they are observed directly, but because something is observed that should happen if neutrinos or gravity exist. The only advantage that neutrinos and gravity have over other realities—over, say, angels—is that the mathematics that the physicists have invented ... can be used to make very specific predictions ... and that these predictions are confirmed by observations" (p. 111). Behn (1992) convincingly legitimizes the exploratory, meaning-seeking nature of the research in the field of public administration: "The reality of the managerial world is created by those who write about the world ... those who are most persuasive in their writings—those who use metaphors that others find most evocative of the managerial world they 'know'—define managerial reality" (p. 418). As a result, Behn (1992) concludes that "Research in public management—just like research in physics—is a search for meaningful metaphors" (p. 418).

Although issues of comparison with natural sciences have been raised since the formative years of public administration as a discipline, issues of epistemology in public administration (as in social sciences in general) have only been discussed since the 1970s. Mitroff and Pondy (1974) identify three inquiry systems: Leibnizian inquiry (deductive, formal reasoning), Lockean inquiry (inductive reasoning), and Kantian inquiry (trying to reconcile the two former systems). White (1994) identifies three research approaches (explanatory, interpretive, and critical) and discusses their implications for public administration studies. Adams (1994), White and Adams (1994), Farmer (1995), and Fox and Miller (1995) discuss public administration from the postmodern perspective. Bureaucracy has been studied from phenomenological (Hummel, 1994a,b), critical (Denhardt, 1981), and postmodern (Farmer, 1995; Fox and Miller, 1995) perspectives. A good source for debate over the nature of research in the discipline of public administration in the 1980s is the *Public Administration Review* articles collection edited by White and Adams (1994), *Research in Public Administration: Reflections on Theory and Practice*, as well as articles in *Administrative Theory and Praxis*, and sometimes, *Administration and Society*.

Increasingly, the arguments for new, more inclusive criteria to judge the research in public administration are taking hold in the discipline. As opposed to radical postmodern conception, criteria derived from positivism are not seen as completely wrong, but rather incomplete. As White (1994) argues, "The growth of knowledge in public administration can be satisfied by interpretive and critical research as well as explanatory research. ... [R]eflection on each mode of research is called for to discover what norms, rules, and values pertain to each. The norms and rules will constitute the method of each mode of research, while the values will indicate criteria by which to judge the truth of each type of knowledge" (p. 57). He further writes, "Practical reasoning is fundamentally a matter of interpretation and criticism. It is very much a political endeavor requiring the giving of reasons why one rule should be followed rather than another, or why one criterion should be met rather than another. The growth of knowledge in public administration is based on this type of argument" (p. 57).

Nevertheless, the range of qualitative methods used in public administration studies is limited (mostly case studies) and the use of those methods lacks rigor as found in other disciplines such as business and sociology (Brower, Abolafia, and Carr, 2000; Lowery and Evans, 2004; Perry and Kraemer, 1994). Lowery and Evans (2004) conclude that in articles published in major public administration journals, "the distinction between positivist and interpretivist/constructivist paradigms is not well understood. A limited range of theoretical paradigms and research methods are employed. The conventions that attend to qualitative research methods are rarely followed ..." (p. 312).

Aiming to improve qualitative methods in public administration research, Brower, Abolafia, and Carr, (2000, pp. 391–392) develop a useful assessment guideline: (1) authenticity, which requires authors to make their role visible in the interpretive process and to present in detail procedures used in data collection and provide thick, rich descriptions (copious use of natives' words/behaviors, particulars of everyday life, and aspects of setting and surroundings); (2) plausibility, which requires authors to connect with the reader by legitimizing their research methods, using the first person plural pronoun, normalizing the atypical, smoothing contestable findings, differentiating findings as a singular contribution, and building dramatic anticipation in describing research methods; (3) criticality, which requires authors to create unique impressions about the subject, to stimulate readers to reexamine taken-for-granted assumptions (by deliberate reflection, recognition, and examination of competing views, imagination of new possibilities, or illumination of the researchers' surprise and differentness from natives), and to provide analysis of both the frontstage and the backstage (presenting both formal and informal activities and views from dominant or less powerful participants, accounting for both the bright and the dark sides, and integrating the differences in perspective); (4) adequacy of theorization, which requires a formally stated research question, appropriate research design, and sound analysis that relates to existing theories and uncovers subtleties in the data. It indicates that authors have to tease out nuances in the data and develop the full theoretical potential of data examples.

Before we conclude, we briefly point to several recent publications that employed thorough qualitative research methods. Frederickson and Frederickson (2006) study the federal implementation of Government Performance and Results Act (GPRA) in the context of hollow state, employing a qualitative, comparative case study research methodology and grounded theory analysis. They explain that "qualitative research techniques were chosen because GPRA is relatively new and because the body of extant research ... is still relatively limited ... there have simply not been enough aggregated quantitative data over enough years to sustain reliable generalizations based on statistical analysis" (p. 195). They suggest that the research approach fit the research questions surrounding "the processes by which federal health care agencies, representing a diversity of policy tools and third-party service providers, either successfully or unsuccessfully develop performance measures and plans to collect data for those measures" (p. 198). They further state that the use of cross-case analysis is "to expand the basis of information, to bolster the validity of and add confidence to findings" (p. 198), referring to the quality criteria proposed by Miles and Huberman (1994). With the thorough approach, Frederickson and Frederickson (2006) are able to create new theories and link the GRPA implementation with the level of third-party policy implementation, the nature and quality of network articulations, the characteristics of goals, the level of goal and policy agreement, the level of centralization of policy implementation, the level and character of client and stakeholder support, and professional identity.

Maynard-Moody and Musheno (2006), using storytelling and narrative, provide a thorough, stimulating, direct examination of the reality of street-level bureaucrats. The book is based on a substantial qualitative research: three years of fieldwork, 157 stories collected from 48 front-level workers at 5 research sites in 2 states. The book reports 36 stories from teachers, cops, and rehabilitation counselors, each of which was selected to illustrate significant theoretical points and to offer a vivid sense of street-level reality. Maynard-Moody and Musheno (2006) use the stories to address issues such as occupational identities, the nature of street-level work, organizational and social divisions among street-level workers, and normative decision making and discretion. The authors not only provide the details about their method in an appendix but also discuss, in a comprehensive manner, the strengths and weaknesses of story-based research.

10.10 CONCLUSION

Qualitative research is a general term denoting a host of research strategies and techniques that should be specified based on the research context. Generally geared to exploratory, descriptive, and interpretive tasks of scientific endeavor, they are invaluable tools of research. Different traditions of qualitative research have established procedures and criteria of goodness, and qualitative research designs should conform to the requirements of a particular tradition. Although researchers may use triangulation and try to explain the phenomenon from different perspectives, this should be done very carefully, without jeopardizing the integrity of each strategy, and clearly integrating them at the meta-level. Although the criteria for evaluating qualitative research may not be accepted across all of the domains of social science, for each research design there are criteria of soundness that have been established though systematic practice in that particular subfield. Finally, qualitative research requires constant reflection. The researcher should strive to distinguish and analyze his or her biases—if not to balance them, at least make them as explicit as possible.

REFERENCES

Abolafia, M.Y. 2004. Framing moves: Interpretive politics at the federal reserve. *Journal of Public Administration Research & Theory* 14(3), 349–370.

Adams, G.B. 1994. Enthralled with modernity: The historical context of knowledge and theory development. In J.D. White and G.B. Adams (Eds.), *Research in Public Administration: Reflections on Theory and Practice*. Newbury Park, California: Sage, pp. 25–41.

Adler, P.A. and Adler, P. 1994, Observational techniques. In N.K. Denzin and Y.S. Lincoln (Eds.), *Handbook of Qualitative Research*. Thousand Oaks, California: Sage, pp. 377–392.

Argyris, C., Putnam, R., and Smith, D.M. 1985. *Action Science*. San Francisco: Jossey-Bass.

Atkinson, P. 2005. Qualitative research—Unity and diversity, *Forum: Qualitative Social Research,* FQS 6(3), Art. 26. Also available at http://www.qualitative-research.net/fqs/

Atkinson, P., Delamont, S., and Hammersley, M. 1988. Qualitative research traditions: A British response to Jacob. *Review of Educational Research* 58, 231–250.

Atkinson, P. and Hammersly, M. 1994. Ethnography and participant observation. In N.K. Denzin and Y.S. Lincoln (Eds.), *Handbook of Qualitative Research*. Thousand Oaks, California: Sage, pp. 248–261.

Atkinson, P. 1992. *Understanding Ethnographic Texts*. Newbury Park, California: Sage.

Babbie, E. 1990. *Survey Research Methods*, 2nd edition. Belmont, California: Wadsworth Publishing.

Bailey, M.T. 1994. Do physicists use case studies? Thoughts on public administration research. In J.D. White and G.B. Adams (Eds.), *Research in Public Administration: Reflections on Theory and Practice*. Newbury Park, California: Sage, pp. 183–196.

Behn, R.D. 1992. Management and the neutrino: The search for meaningful metaphors. *Public Administration Review* 52, 409–419.

Best, J. 2004, Defining qualitative research. In C.C. Ragin, J. Nagel, and P. White (Eds.), *Report on the Workshop on Scientific Foundations of Qualitative Research*. Washington, DC: National Science Foundation.

Boyle, J. 1994. Styles of ethnography. In J. Morse (Ed.), *Critical Issues in Qualitative Research Methods*. Newbury Park, California: Sage, pp. 159–185.

Brady, H.E. and Collier, D. (Eds.) 2004. *Rethinking Social Inquiry: Diverse Tools, Shared Standards*. Lanham, Maryland: Rowman & Littlefield.

Brower, R.S. and Abolafia, M.Y. 1997. Bureaucratic politics: The view from below. *Journal of Public Administration Research and Theory* 7, 305–331.

Brower, R.S. 1996. Procedural entrepreneurship: Enacting alternative channels to administrative effectiveness. *American Review of Public Administration* 26, 287–308.

Brower, R.S., Abolafia, M.Y., and Carr, J.B. 2000. On improving qualitative methods in public administration research. *Administration & Society* 32(4), 363–397.

Caporoso, J.A. 1995. Research design, falsification, and the qualitative–quantitative divide. *American Political Science Review* 89(2), 457–460.

Carr, J.B. and Brower, R.S. 2000. Principled opportunism: Evidence from the organizational middle. *Public Administration Quarterly* 24, 109–138.

Charmaz, K. 2006. *Constructing Grounded Theory*. London: Sage Publications.

Chein, I., Cook, S., and Harding, J. 1948. The field of action research. *American Psychologies* 3, 43–50.

Collier, D. 2005. A statistical rationale for qualitative research? Paper Prepared for the *NSF Workshop on Interdisciplinary Standards for Systematic Qualitative Research*, Washington, DC. May 2005. http://www.wjh.harvard.edu/nsfqual/Collier%20Paper.pdf

Collier, D., Seawright, J., and Brady, H.E. 2004. Qualitative versus quantitative: What might this distinction mean? In C.C. Ragin, J. Nagel, and P. White (Eds.), *Report on the Workshop on Scientific Foundations of Qualitative Research*. Washington, DC: National Science Foundation, pp. 71–76.

Creswell, J. 2006. *Qualitative Inquiry and Research Design: Choosing among Five Approaches*. 2nd edition. Thousand Oaks, California: Sage.

Denhardt, R.B. 1981. *In the Shadow of Organization*. Lawrence, Kansas: University of Kansas Press.

Denzin, N.K. 1994. The art and politics of interpretation. In N.K. Denzin and Y.S. Lincoln (Eds.), *Handbook of Qualitative Research*. Thousand Oaks, California: Sage, pp. 500–515.

Denzin, N.K. and Lincoln, Y.S. (Eds.) (2005a). *The SAGE Handbook of Qualitative Research*. 3rd edition. Thousand Oaks, California: Sage.

Denzin, N.K. and Lincoln, Y.S. (2005b). Introduction: The discipline and practice of qualitative research. In N.K. Denzin and Y.S. Lincoln (Eds.), *The SAGE Handbook of Qualitative Research*. Thousand Oaks, California: Sage, pp. 1–42.

Denzin, N.K. and Lincoln, Y.S. (2003a). *Strategies of Qualitative Inquiry*. 2nd edition. Thousand Oaks, California: Sage.

Denzin, N.K. and Lincoln, Y.S. (2003b). *The Landscape of Qualitative Research: Theories and Issues*. 2nd edition. Thousand Oaks, California: Sage.

Deshler, D. and Ewert, M. 1995. Participatory action research: Traditions and major assumptions. Available at http://munex.arme.cornell.edu/parnet/tools/tools1.html, May 25, 1995.

Diesing, P. 1991. *How Does Social Science Work?* Pittsburg, Pennsylvania: University of Pittsburg Press.

Farmer, D.J. 1995. *The Language of Public Administration: Bureaucracy, Modernity and Postmodernity*. University of Alabama Press.

Flick, U. 2005. Qualitative research in sociology in Germany and the U.S.—State of the art, differences and developments. *Forum: Qualitative Social Research*, FQS 6(3), Art. 23. Also available at http://www.qualitative-research.net/fqs/

Fontana, A. and Frey, J.H. 1994. Interviewing: The art of science. In N.K. Denzin and Y.S. Lincoln (Eds.), *Handbook of Qualitative Research*. Thousand Oaks, California: Sage, pp. 361–376.

Fox, C.J. and Miller, H.T. 1995. *Postmodern Public Administration*. Thousand Oaks, California: Sage.

Frederickson, D.G. and Frederickson, H.G. 2006. *Measuring the Performance of the Hallow State*. Washington, DC: Georgetown University Press.

French, W.L. and Bell, C. 1995. *Organizational Development: Behavioral Science Interventions for Organization Improvement*. 5th edition. Englewood Cliffs, New Jersey: Prentice Hall.

Garfinkel, H. 1967. *Studies in Ethnomethodology*. Englewood Cliffs, New Jersey: Prentice Hall.

George, A.L. and Bennett, A. 2005. *Case Studies and Theory Development in the Social Sciences*. Cambridge, Massachusetts: MIT Press.

Glasser, B. and Strauss, A. 1967. *The Discovery of Grounded Theory: Strategies for Qualitative Research*. Chicago: Aldine.

Glasser, B. 1978. *Theoretical Sensitivity*. Mill Valley, California: Sociology Press.

Guba, E.S. and Lincoln, Y.S. 1994. Competing paradigms in qualitative research. In N.K. Denzin and Y.S. Lincoln (Eds.), *Handbook of Qualitative Research*. Thousand Oaks, California: Sage, pp. 105–117.

Guba, E.S. and Lincoln, Y.S. 2005. Competing paradigms in qualitative research. In N.K. Denzin and Y.S. Lincoln (Eds.), *Handbook of Qualitative Research*. Thousand Oaks, California: Sage, pp. 105–117.

Guba, E.S. and Lincoln, Y.S. 1989. *Fourth Generation Evaluation*. Newbury Park, California: Sage, pp. 105–117.

Heidegger, M. 1972. *On Time and Being*. New York: Harper and Row.

Hodder, I. 1994. The interpretation of documents and material culture. In N.K. Denzin and Y.S. Lincoln (Eds.), *Handbook of Qualitative Research*. Thousand Oaks, California: Sage, pp. 393–402.

Holstein, J.A. and Gubrium, J.F. 1994. Phenomenology, ethnomethodology and interpretive practice. In N.K. Denzin and S. Lincoln (Eds.), *Handbook of Qualitative Research*. Thousand Oaks, California: Sage, pp. 262–273.

Huberman, A.M. and Miles, M.B. 1994. Data management and analysis methods. In N.K. Denzin and S. Lincoln (Eds.), *Handbook of Qualitative Research*. Thousand Oaks, California: Sage, pp. 428–444.

Hummel, R. (1994). *The Bureaucratic Experience*. New York: St. Martin's Press.

Husserl, E. 1970. *The Crisis of European Sciences and Transcendental Phenomenology*. Evanston, Illinois: Northwestern University Press.

Jacob, E. 1988. Clarifying qualitative research: A focus on traditions. *Educational Researcher* 17, 16–24.

Janesick, V. 1994. The dance of qualitative research design: Metaphor, methodolatry and meaning. In N.K. Denzin and Y.S. Lincoln (Eds.), *Handbook of Qualitative Research*. Thousand Oaks, California: Sage, pp. 209–219.

Jorgensen, D.L. 1989. *Participant Observation: A Methodology for Human Studies*. Thousand Oaks, California: Sage.

Kelle, U. (ed.) 1995. *Computer-Aided Qualitative Data Analysis*. Newbury Park, California: Sage.

Kelly, M. and Maynard-Moody, S. 1993. Policy analysis in the post-positivist era: Engaging stakeholders in evaluating the economic development districts program. *Public Administration Review* 53(2), 135–142.

King, G., Keohane, R., and Verba, S. 1994. *Designing Social Inquiry: Scientific Inference in Qualitative Research*. Princeton University Press.

Kritzer, H.M. 1996. The data puzzle: The nature of interpretation in qualitative research. *American Journal of Political Science* 40(1), 1–32.

Levine, H.G. 1985. Principles of data storage and retrieval for use in qualitative evaluations. *Educational Evaluation and Policy Analysis* 7(2), 179–186.

Levi-Strauss. C. 1966. *The Savage Mind*. London: Weidenfeld and Nicolson.

Lijphart, A. 1975. T*he Politics of Accommodation: Pluralism and Democracy in the Netherlands*. Berkeley, California: University of California Press.

Lincoln, Y.S. and Guba, E.S. 1985. *Organizational Theory and Inquiry: The Paradigm Revolution*. Newbury Park, California: Sage.

Lindblom, C. and Cohen, D. 1979. *Useable Knowledge*. New Haven: Yale University Press.

Lowery, D. and Evans, K.G. 2004. The iron cage of methodology. *Administration & Society* 36(3), 306–327.

Marshall, C. and Rossman, G. 1995. *Designing Qualitative Research*. Thousand Oaks, California: Sage.

Marton, F. 1994. Phenomenography. In T. Husen and T.N. Postlethwaite (Eds.), *International Encyclopedia of Education*. London: Pergamon Press, pp. 4424–4429.

Maynard-Moody, S. and Musheno, M. 2006. *Cops, Teachers, Counselors: Stories from the Front Lines of Public Service*. Ann Arbor: The University of Michigan Press.

McGrath, J. 1981. Dilemmatics: The study of research choices and dilemmas. *American Behavioral Scientist* 25(2), 179–210.

McNabb, D.E. 2002. *Research Methods in Public Administration and Nonprofit Management: Quantitative and Qualitative Approaches*. Armonk, New York: M.E. Sharpe.

Miles, M.B. and Huberman, A.M. 1984. *Qualitative Data Analysis: A Sourcebook of New Methods*. Beverly Hills, California: Sage.

Miles, M.B. and Huberman, A.M. 1994. *Qualitative Data Analysis: A New Sourcebook of Methods*. Beverly Hills, California: Sage.

Mintzberg, H. 1973. *The Nature of Managerial Work*. New York: Harper and Row.

Mitroff, I.I. and Pondy, L.R. 1974. On the organization of inquiry: A comparison of some radically different approaches to policy analysis. *Public Administration Review* 34, 471–479.

Morse, J.M. 1996. Is qualitative research complete? *Qualitative Health Research* 6(1), 3–5.

Morse, J.M. 1995. The significance of saturation. *Qualitative Health Research* 5(2), 147–149.

Morse, J.M. (1994a). Designing funded qualitative research. In N.K. Denzin and Y.S. Lincoln (Eds.), *Handbook of Qualitative Research*. Thousand Oaks, California: Sage, pp. 220–235.

Morse, J.M. (1994b). Emerging from the data: The cognitive process of analysis of qualitative inquiry. In J. Morse (Ed.), *Critical Issues in Qualitative Research Methods*. Newbury Park, California: Sage, pp. 23–43.

Muecke, M. 1994. On the evaluation of ethnographies. In J. Morse (Ed.), *Critical Issues in Qualitative Research Methods*. Newbury Park, California: Sage, pp. 187–209.

Olson, H. 1995. Quantitative "versus" qualitative research: The wrong question. Internet WWW page at URL: http://www.alberta.ca./dept/slis/cais/olson.htm

Perry, J.L. and Kraemer, K.L. 1994. Research methodology in public administration review. 1975–1984. In J.D. White and G.B. Adams (Eds.) *Research in Public Administration: Reflections on Theory and Practice.* Thousand Oaks, California: Sage, pp. 93–109.

Pfiffner, J.M. 1940. *Research Methods in Public Administration.* New York: The Ronald Press Company.

Punch, M. 1994. Politics and ethics in qualitative research. In N.K. Denzin and Y.S. Lincoln (Eds.), *Handbook of Qualitative Research.* Thousand Oaks, California: Sage, pp. 83–98.

QUALIDATA 2007. WWW document. Available http://www.essex.ac.uk/qialidata, January 2007.

QUARC 2007. *Qualitative Research & Consulting.* A WWW Web site, available at http://www.quarc.de/english.html

Ragin, C.C., Nagel, J., and White P. 2004. *Report on the Workshop on Scientific Foundations of Qualitative Research.* Washington, DC: National Science Foundation. Also available at URL: http://www.nsf.gov/pubs/2004/nsf04219/nsf04219.pdf

Ray, M.C. 1994. The richness of phenomenology: Philosophic, theoretic and methodologic concerns. In J. Morse (Ed.), *Critical Issues in Qualitative Research Methods.* Newbury Park, California: Sage, pp. 117–133.

Reason, P. 1994. Three approaches to participative inquiry. In N.K. Denzin and Y.S. Lincoln (Eds.), *Handbook of Qualitative Research.* Thousand Oaks, California: Sage, pp. 324–339.

Richards, T.J. and Richards, L. 1994. Using computers in qualitative research. In N.K. Denzin and Y.S. Lincoln (Eds.), *Handbook of Qualitative Research.* Thousand Oaks, California: Sage, pp. 445–463.

Ritchie, J. and Lewis, J. 2003. *Qualitative Research Practice.* Thousand Oaks, California: Sage.

Rogowski, R. 1995. The role of theory and anomaly in social-science inference. *American Political Science Review* 89(2), 467–470.

Rosenau, P.M. 1992. *Post-Modernism and the Social Sciences.* Princeton University Press.

Rubin, H.J. and Rubin, I.S. 2005. *Qualitative Interviewing.* Thousand Oaks, California: Sage.

Ryan, G.W. 2005. What are standards of rigor for qualitative research? Paper Prepared for the NSF Workshop on Interdisciplinary Standards for Systematic Qualitative Research, Washington, DC: May. URL: http://www.wjh.harvard.edu/nsfqual/ryan%20Paper.pdf

Schutz, A. 1967. *The Phenomenology of Social World.* Evanston, Illinois: Northwestern University Press.

Smith, R.C. 2004. Complementary articulation: Matching qualitative data and quantitative methods. In C.C. Ragin, J. Nagel, and P. White (Eds.), *Report on the Workshop on Scientific Foundations of Qualitative Research.* Washington, DC: National Science Foundation, pp. 127–132. http://www.nsf.gov/ pubs/2004/nsf04219/nsf04219.pdf.

Somekh, B. and Lewin, C. (Eds.). 2005. *Research Methods in the Social Sciences.* London: Sage.

Stake, R.E. 1994. Case studies. In N.K. Denzin and Y.S. Lincoln (Eds.), *Handbook of Qualitative Research.* Thousand Oaks, California: Sage, pp. 236–247.

Strauss, A. and Corbin, J. 1990. *Basics of Qualitative Research.* Newbury Park, California: Sage.

Torbert, W.R. 1991. *The Power of Balance: Transforming Self, Society, and Scientific Inquiry.* Newbury Park, California: Sage.

Van Maanen, M. 1990. *Researching Lived Experience.* Albany, New York: Sate University of New York Press.

Weitzman, E.A. and Miles, M.B. 1995. *Computer Programs for Qualitative Data Analysis: A Software Sourcebook.* Newbury Park, California: Sage.

White, J.D. 1994. On growth of knowledge in public administration. In J.D. White and G.B. Adams (Eds.), *Research in Public Administration: Reflections on Theory and Practice.* Newbury Park, California: Sage, pp. 42–59.

White, J.D. and Adams, G.B. 1994. Making sense with diversity: The context of research, theory and knowledge development in public administration. In *Research in Public Administration: Reflections on Theory and Practice.* Newbury Park, California: Sage, pp. 1–22.

Whyte, W.F. (Ed.) 1991. *Participatory Action Research.* Newbury Park, California: Sage.

Wolcott, H.F. 1992. Posturing in qualitative inquiry. In M.D. Lecompte et al. (Eds.), *The Handbook of Qualitative Research in Education.* New York: Academic Press, pp. 3–52.

Yanow, D. 1999. *Conducting Interpretive Policy Analysis.* Thousand Oaks, California: Sage.

Yeager, S.J. 1989. Classic methods in public administration research. In J. Rabin, W.B. Hildreth, and G.J. Miller (Eds.), *Handbook of Public Administration.* New York: Marcel Dekker, pp. 683–794.

Yin, R.K. 1984. *Case Study Research: Design and Methods.* Newbury Park, California: Sage.

BIBLIOGRAPHY

National Science Foundation. 2004. *Workshop on the Scientific Foundations of Qualitative Research.* Washington, DC: National Science Foundation. http://www.nsf.gov/pubs/2004/nsf04219/nsf04219.pdf

National Science Foundation. 2005. *Workshop on Interdisciplinary Standards for Systematic Qualitative Research.* Washington, DC: National Science Foundation. Also available at URL: http://www.wjh.harvard.edu/nsfqual/

11 Comparative Research in Public Administration: A Historical-Institutionalist Perspective

Robert S. Kravchuk

CONTENTS

11.1 INTRODUCTION

The basic problem of comparative analysis is to generalize from similarities and differences between and among objects of interest, in this case, administrative structures, policies, and procedures in different countries. Researchers would like to be able to make colloquial statements about the administrative institutions that they observe in different contexts. Insofar as this chapter is fundamentally concerned with the logic of comparative public administration research, several pertinent issues arise: "how to compare seemingly disparate things? Are administrative institutions in different countries so unique that they defy comparison? What guiding principles can the researcher turn to? How has such research been conducted in the past? Are there any useful examples?"

The case study approach has been dominant throughout the development of comparative public administration. Case analysis is a necessary step in the research enterprise, in that all hypothesis testing and generalization is preceded by "thick description." Case studies generally focus on particular countries or regions, and on some aspect of their administration (i.e., elites, careerists, finances, or policy issue). Case studies may be cross-sectional, and therefore highly descriptive, or longitudinal, in which case they will follow some particular aspect of the public administration across time. Our focus in this chapter is not on specific issues of research design, however, but on strengthening comparative research by recognizing and overcoming certain cultural and methodological biases that researchers may bring to their work.

Comparative research is particularly susceptible to such bias. Przeworski and Teune (1970) observed over three decades ago, "many books on techniques of research are so involved in presenting specific procedures and techniques that neither their justifications nor their implications are discussed." This chapter, then, is explicitly concerned with the implications of doing comparative public administration research, and the justification of a particular mode of doing comparative research which this author recommends to the reader's attention: *Historical Institutionalism*.

11.2 A BRIEF HISTORY OF COMPARATIVE PUBLIC ADMINISTRATION'S EXPANDING DOMAIN

Writing in 1962, and with the benefit of a half-century of hindsight, Fred Riggs (1962), one of the founding figures of the field, discerned three trends in the comparative study of public administration from 1912 to 1962. The main trend was a de-emphasis of the normative element in writings on administrative methods and techniques, in favor of greater empirical description of actual administrative practices in different regional and cultural contexts. A second trend was a movement from an idiographic approach, manifest in the many individual country case-studies that had dominated the field, towards a more nomothetic (i.e., general law seeking) approach. The field was increasingly concerned with similarities and differences between administrative approaches to certain common problems encountered by all governments. Riggs's third trend was in the direction of an "ecological approach" to comparative study, which viewed administrative institutions as embedded in, and their functioning colored by, the indigenous social systems of which they formed parts. The latter trend is, perhaps, best represented by Riggs's own work (1961). The country case study approach remained dominant throughout the 1980s (Barrington, 1980) and 1990s (Tummala, 1994), however.

11.2.1 EARLY FOCUS ON WESTERN BUREAUCRACIES

The starting point for most early—and far too many contemporary—studies of comparative public administration has been the bureaucracy (Siffin, 1957). Traditional public administrationists have tended to concentrate on bureaucratic functions, structures, methods, and procedural routines (Berger, 1957a; Heady, 1959, 1966, 1984). Their political science contemporaries have focused more on the recruitment, training, and roles of administrative elites (White, 1930; Chapman, 1959; Presthus, 1959a,b, 1961; Armstrong, 1973; Dogan, 1975; Peters, 1978; Suleiman, 1978; Campbell and Szablowski, 1979; Aberbach et al., 1981; Burns, 1994). Most of these studies have been either elaborate country case-studies, or collections of country cases, with editors' "integrating essays" seeking to discern commonalities and differences, and proposing explanations for them. Most have been descriptive or anecdotal in nature, though some have been based on surveys of bureaucratic officials (Berger, 1957b).

A central focus of many early comparative studies—and it is a research locus that persists to this day—was on Western European developments, most notably the Prussian bureaucracy (Rosenberg, 1958), the French system of prefectures (Chapman, 1953), the British civil service (Brown and

Steel, 1970), and the state-building (Barker, 1944). Europe was a logical point of departure, insofar as American public administration had always had strong academic links to European universities. Woodrow Wilson's founding essay (1887), after all, reflected the future president's interest in the possible transference of German administrative practices to the American context. Following World War II, American public administrationists paid increasing attention to administrative realities in parts of the world beyond Europe.

The overriding objectives of American foreign policy to rebuild the war-torn regions, and to alleviate poverty in other regions served as the spur to greatly expanding the domain of comparative public administration research. Consequently, many prominent post-war studies focused on patterns of bureaucracy in various cultures (Meyer, 1957), and the problems and prospects of development administration (Riggs, 1964; Waldo, 1964; Montgomery and Siffin, 1966; Braibranti, 1969; Gant, 1979). Although such studies proved to be interesting in themselves, comparative public administrationists were straining to generalize their country-specific findings to other countries and contexts. The need for such generalization was pointed out in Robert Dahl's seminal 1947 article on *The Science of Public Administration* (Dahl, 1947). Comparative analysis in public administration had largely been separated from its American counterpart, and conducted in isolation. Integrating the two in a meaningful way has been a perennial challenge for comparative public administration.

11.2.2 LINKAGES BETWEEN BUREAUCRACY AND POLITICAL DEVELOPMENT

An important and timely contribution to development of model-building in comparative public administration—and broadly across all of political science—was David Easton's 1953 book, *The Political System*, a classic work in the behavioral revolution in social science. Embracing a systems model of interaction, Easton conceived of political actors and institutions, including the bureaucratic organs of the state, as engaged in many series of exchange relations with one another, and with the larger social system. Inputs valued by the bureaucracy were transformed into outputs valued by the external environment. The transformation of system inputs into outputs took place within the "black box" of the bureaucracy. Unfortunately, the innards of the box in such studies largely remained opaque, including their internal politics. An over-emphasis on the formal attributes of administration—a research attitude bequeathed many years before by Max Weber (1949)—left the vital informal interactions between administrators, clienteles, and political officials under-researched. Informal power still is power, and modern scholars generally agree that, in many instances, it can be the determining factor (Giddens, 1984; Perrson, 1996).

The result was that comparative public administration continued its search for meaningful comparisons, but now sought greater sophistication by again expanding the domain of inquiry to explore linkages between bureaucracy and political development, as well as the stages of social and economic development that engendered particular types and modes of bureaucracy (Heady and Stokes, 1962; Binder, 1971; Jacoby, 1973). During this period, Fred Riggs found the stages of social development to be such compelling determinants of bureaucratic development that he went as far as to devise an entirely new lexicon—that of the "prismatic society"—to employ in studies of what he regarded as a unique subject matter: the stages of political and administrative development (Riggs, 1964, 1973). During the same period, and obviously influenced by the same intellectual currents that prompted Almond and Verba's classic study of *The Civic Culture* (1963), Joseph LaPalombara and collaborators (1963) worked to link bureaucratic development generally to processes of political development—democratization, specifically. The main thrust of their findings was that political development should precede efforts to improve the public administration if unwarranted increases in bureaucratic power—perhaps reinforcing the pathological tendencies of authoritarian regimes—was to be avoided. The focus at this time remained on the bureaucracy, however, in its more or less classical, Weberian form. Indeed, Ferrel Heady's widely read textbook (1966, 1984) is a paradigm example of the original bureau-centric approach to comparative public administration.

11.2.3 COMPARATIVE POLICY PROCESSES AND OUTCOMES

In the early 1970s, and on the heels of the New Public Administration movement in the United States (Marini, 1971), comparative public administration refocused the research enterprise, again expanding its domain. At this time, public administration as a field recognized the need to strengthen administrative capabilities as a prelude to economic growth and development (Riggs, 1971). Less developed countries it was held, were hampered by administrative incapacity, incompetence, and corruption. Such factors were regarded as obstacles to the formulation and implementation of rational policy in the public interest. Consequently, several researchers widened the scope of research to examine policy processes and policy outcomes, all with an eye towards improvement (Dror, 1968; Heclo, 1974; Heidenheimer et al., 1975; Ashford, 1978; and Ashford et al., 1978).

11.2.4 LATE TWENTIETH CENTURY TRENDS: CONVERGENCE AND NEW PUBLIC MANAGEMENT

Political scientist Keith Henderson in 1983 described the "new role for comparative public administration" as extending beyond interpretation and application to "a quest for worldwide study of public administration" (Henderson, 1983, p. 99). To realize this vision, Henderson proposed to incorporate non-Western administrative experiences into prevailing conceptual frames, to move towards "a total public administration study universe." He would make a central feature of comparative public administration the study of administrative history, noting that, "history provides a humbling account of growth and decline which places all of modern Western development as a moment in time." For, he asks, how else are we to make sense of "the origins of administrative ideas and institutions, similarities, and differences in dealing with perennial problems, successes, and failures of administrative action, and global trends?" (Henderson, 1983, p. 108).

Beginning in the 1990s, studies of administrative developments across the globe have focused increasingly on the worldwide spread of new public management (NPM) reforms (Caiden, 1991; Barzelay, 1992, 2001; Kettl, 2000). These studies focus on the recent trends towards convergence in the use of NPM methods, most prominently in British Commonwealth countries, but not limited only to these countries. It is not too much to say that NPM has become an international phenomenon (Hood, 1991). There is some consensus among researchers that the widespread adoption of modern information technology, dissemination of knowledge through the internet, specifically, and the increasing educational qualifications of public administrators have contributed to a convergence in these methods and processes across the globe.

The worldwide spread of economic rationalism, which is being driven forward by recent policy successes of the ideology of free markets, also is driving a certain convergence in administrative practices, as politicians and senior government officials increasingly embrace the main tenets of free market economics. Pusey (1991) certainly sees a spreading economic rationalism as the main driving force behind Australia's recent reforms. Zifcak (1994) traces the adoption of certain corporate practices in Australia and the United Kingdom (notably, strategic planning, program budgeting, and methods of financial management improvement) to a spreading affinity for economic rationalism.

NPM can be an amorphous subject. Nonetheless, there are certain core beliefs, principles, and features that can be identified. In summary form, NPM is based on the belief that the public service is inefficient (but not inherently so); that the best international practices of NPM can be transplanted effectively across borders with little loss in their potency; and that the administrative methods of successful private sector concerns may be self-consciously emulated by public sector organizations. The explicit decision to improve the public service is a defining feature of the NPM. Barzelay (2001), in fact, proposes re-situating public management as a field within public policy, in recognition of the explicit choices that various governments have made in the last two decades to improve their administrative capabilities. He terms the new field "public management policymaking" (PMP).

Public management policies are to be studied as "authoritative means intended to guide, constrain, and motivate the public service as a whole" (Barzelay, 2001, p. 6). In Barzelay's view, the recent literature on the adoption of NPM in various countries may be viewed as research into the dynamics of PMP.

Barzelay argues for a more systematic and unified approach to comparative research. The unity is to be provided by a common commitment to doing what is essentially policy research. Given the rather haphazard development of comparative public administration over the last six decades, this writer can only agree that, "shifting the emphasis of NPM scholarship from trend spotting to policy research is arguably long overdue" (Barzelay, 2001, p. 10). To this end, however, Barzelay recommends what is all too familiar: definition of case outcomes; selection of explanatory frameworks; and use of comparative methods. There is little specificity as to which "comparative methods" he would recommend, however. Further, his writings on PMP cite little of the historical work on comparative public administration. He appears to see PMP as largely isomorphic with NPM: For research purposes, he defines NPM as comprised of the core experiences of the United Kingdom, Australia, and New Zealand as a "benchmark case group" (Barzelay, 2001, p. 55). It is clear that he is seeking a basis for making valid comparisons, but one suspects that his preferred approach too narrowly delimits the domain of inquiry. The approach and methods of historical institutionalism, discussed following the next section, hold greater potential to recognize and overcome the problems of comparative inquiry which are far too easily dismissed in his writings on the subject.

Like Henderson (1983), this author does not see in the current convergence a "full-circle retreat to 'universal principles' of [administrative science in] the pre-World War II period" (1983, p. 114). Admittedly, there is an inherent normative element to the NPM literature. But convergence appears as an empirical reality, whose driving forces must be subjected to further research. Unfortunately, in the zeal to collapse all of public management into the field of public policy, Barzelay all but ignores the rather "thorny" problems of comparative analysis discussed immediately below. A close examination of the genuine theoretical and practical problems associated with doing high-quality, meaningful comparative research leads one more in the direction of the literature of comparative politics, rather than towards public policy analysis. The following section makes the case.

11.3 "THORNY" LOGIC OF COMPARATIVE INQUIRY

According to Przeworski and Teune (1970), the basic problem of comparative research is to access a "meta language" that is capable of evaluating statements concerning the comparability of social phenomena across social systems (i.e., countries, regions, cultures, and time). In comparative administrative inquiry, researchers seek to be able to make general colloquial statements about administrative phenomena. This implies that observations can be expressed in terms of general laws that transcend cultures, geographic regions, and time. On the way to achieving this rather lofty goal, comparativists must meet and overcome the difficulties and dangers of generalizing across time and space. These difficulties and dangers involve the three interrelated problems of ahistoricity, comparability, and reification.

11.3.1 AHISTORICITY PROBLEM

In an extreme view of comparative analysis, the specific circumstances of countries and cultures are presumed to have little significance in reaching generalizations about specific features which they may have in common, such as policy-making processes, fiscal practices, civil service recruitment and training. This implies that such studies are, in an important sense, ahistorical. A more common view is that research findings are at least partially relative to the nations, cultures, and histories that produced them, and of which they are parts. This does not imply in the least the more radical view that only indigenous factors are relevant, and that, therefore, truly comparative research is not possible. A more middle-of-the-road approach generally is advisable, where researchers seek generalizations, but recognize the effects of significant relevant features that condition the results.

11.3.2 COMPARABILITY PROBLEM

The very idea that social, political, and administrative phenomena may not be comparable rests on the suspicion (or the belief, in some cases) that social reality is infinitely diverse, that categories of analysis are incomplete or subject to misapplication, and as a consequence, that observations are misunderstood or misclassified. Przeworski and Teune observe that these difficulties "lead some to conclude that social reality can be 'understood' only within the context in which it is observed, and can never be explained by general lawlike statements" (1970, p. 12).

Context is important, perhaps even crucial. Geographies, cultures, and histories condition the observed behavior of institutions and the individuals who populate and animate them. The relative importance of structures versus choices, or that of institutions versus individuals, for instance, will vary considerably as a function of cultural climate, geography, and historical circumstances. As a practical matter, researchers will still seek to make comparisons, but also to explicitly recognize the effects of significant relevant factors that may affect the reported results, conclusions, and implications of the research.

11.3.3 REIFICATION PROBLEM

A common theoretical objection against generalizing across disparate cases (countries, regions, cultures) is that all social phenomena are to an extent unique, some more than others. Consequently, the explanatory power of general concepts varies considerably across social systems. Difficulties reach their most extreme form when the conceptual or linguistic equipment of researchers from one culture is inadequate to describe the state of affairs that prevails in another culture. Researchers will therefore attempt to make sense of their observations by substituting (in most cases, inadvertently, and unconsciously) their own culturally conditioned and historically specific theories and concepts. This raises the danger that certain indigenous features of the systems under study—some of which may be crucial to the research question—may be ignored, disregarded, misunderstood, or missed altogether.

Such a reification of concepts, projecting the familiar into an alien context, is a potentially serious problem in all spatiotemporal research (Prezeworski and Teune, 1970, p. 10), Researchers can strive to control for their biases, or at least to be more explicit about their (otherwise implicit) intellectual commitments. The degree of bias introduced by the researcher will obviously depend upon how well studied and understood the particular subject of interest may be. Consequently, researchers will need to know as much as they can about their subject's history, environment, and so forth, before they begin. Comparativists are therefore best advised to seek to understand the indigenous language, culture, and history first, nourishing themselves intellectually on the previous work of others. This is in order that they might avoid carelessly applying principles and perspectives that are inherently insensitive to local realities.

It is well to keep in mind that, in Riggs's conception, only empirical, nomothetic, and ecological studies can truly be considered to be "comparative" (Riggs, 1962, p. 15). In comparative scholarship, then, the research goal can be seen as being two-staged. First, researchers seek to develop theories that will explain a given phenomenon in one or more social systems. Then, where different theories may explain what is substantively the same phenomenon in two different societies (or the same society in two different time periods), the second-stage goal is to develop a more complete theory. The emergent theory would be one that encapsulates both sets of results, it is hoped, without sacrificing the richness of the social texture in which each one is woven.

11.4   CONDUCTING COMPARATIVE RESEARCH: THE HISTORICAL-INSTITUTIONALIST APPROACH

One of the serious shortcomings of comparative public administration research over the last six decades has been that the logic of comparative analysis—so central to any genuinely comparative approach—has been so little developed. Comparative public administration has had largely to borrow concepts which have been more rigorously developed elsewhere in the literature, particularly in comparative politics. A marriage between comparative public administration and comparative politics was, perhaps, presaged four and a half decades ago by Alfred Diamant (1960). Diamant argued that, as a subset of political authority, administrative authority must be studied within the context of a typology of regime types (not necessarily Weber's), with their varying institutions of government.

It should be axiomatic that modern comparative public administration research must take its subject matter as it is, in all of its inherent complexity. The state administrative organs of advanced industrial countries exhibit a high degree of institutional diversity that is not observed in less developed societies. Increasing social complexity has given rise to the functional differentiation of state institutions, which themselves have become more complex, precisely in response to their environments. It is the fundamental point of this chapter that relevant features of this institutional richness must be captured in comparative public administration research.

11.4.1   INSTITUTIONS MATTER

The foundation for any institutional analysis is the general proposition that institutions, in the long run, will generally matter more than individuals. This is not a wholesale negation of "great (wo)man theories of history." History is replete with courageous individuals who impress us with their exploits and achievements. However so, researchers must fairly judge the choice set that circumstances have presented to such individuals. To wit: despite his image in the public mind, if Mikhail Gorbachev had not presided over the Soviet collapse, someone else would have. [Note: Gorbachev was General Secretary of the Communist Party of the Soviet Union, then President of the USSR, from 1984 until the dissolution of the USSR in 1991.] The die was cast for Gorbachev, not by him. Consequently, historical institutionalists will focus on evolving patterns of governing institutions, which are conditioned on—and in many ways determined by—the historical contingencies which are specific to a given society, or specific to several distinct societies in the case of truly comparative analysis (Orren and Skowronek, 1995). In this vein, comparativists seek to explore structural processes of institutional development, as implied by the work of Comte, Durkheim, and Weber.

Comparative institutionalists recognize that all governments face similar challenges: borders must be defended, public order maintained, justice administered, social programs delivered, children educated, and taxes collected. Governments meet these challenges in vastly different ways, however (Steinmo et al., 1992). Here arises the broad diversity of institutional arrangements that comparativists observe and embrace. Taking governing institutions as the basic units of analysis, the method brings to bear "questions of temporality . . . to the center of analysis on just how institutions matter" (Orren and Skowronek, 1994, p. 312). Other authorities to note the importance of history—and, specifically, administrative history—include Nash (1969), Gladden (1972), Jacoby (1973), and Waldo (1980). Questions of continuity and change are viewed as being of critical importance, especially as regards the examination of persisting patterns of political behavior, which simultaneously open and close future opportunities for development and change.

11.4.2   INSTITUTIONAL ANALYSIS HAS APPEAL

Several key features of institutional analysis are particularly appealing. First among them is the proposition that institutions have a critical role in social science research. Institutions are worthy objects of study in their own right. Institutions viewed as "bundles" of rules and roles channel, focus, and consolidate choices and behaviors in critical ways. Second, the historical development of institutions warrants attention. The choice sets provided to decision makers and other actors is subject to evolution and change, perhaps in unanticipated ways. Third, states and state institutions are not merely the agents of society, nor even of the political elite, but have some degree of autonomous existence. The most fundamental observation of historical institutionalism, then, may be that states and governing institutions are not merely agents of society, but are, in fact, autonomous actors in many ways. This is not a new observation (Morstein Marx, 1946, 1957, 1963). What is new is self-consciously situating institutions at the very center of the research enterprise.

11.4.3 INSTITUTIONAL ANALYSIS IS DYNAMIC

Behavioral regularities do not quite persist across time and space. Issues involving continuity and change are very difficult to address using only static forms of analysis. A historical approach will be more sensitive to the dynamics of change. Institutional analysis is not nearly as fluid as it may seem, however. Historians remind us that the critical differences between and among societies may be understood with reference to choices made (perhaps not consciously)—and distinctive patterns which were largely set—quite early in a given regime's development. For mature regimes, many basic institutions emerged in the early modern era (Poggi, 1978, 1990). These choices have manifested themselves in different ways, and placed many governments—even geographically adjacent states—on somewhat different evolutionary paths.

In his brilliant work tracing the formation of national states in Western Europe from a set of common conditions from around the year 1500, Charles Tilly (1975) has referred to this as a process of "different exits from common conditions." Tilly's "different exits" are, in fact, diverse institutional responses to particular needs. The degree of diversity observed depends on many factors. As governments have invested in development of certain institutional capacities, they have likewise underinvested in others. This means that relevant research questions will involve not only the long-term observation of events, but also of non-events. Choices ruled out by institutional evolution, inertia, and drift also are important factors worthy of study.

11.4.4 CHANGE HAPPENS

Historically, we observe at least two general processes of change. The one occurs where governing institutions evolve according to a prevailing set of institutions and norms for some (perhaps long) period of time. Such stable, "normal" development is most amenable to study using historical institutionalist methods. The second change process consists of rather short periods of rapid, discontinuous (and perhaps revolutionary) change which results in establishment of new sets of institutions and prevalent norms. Historical change may therefore be seen in terms of a "punctuated equilibrium" model, largely along lines consistent with Kuhn's theory of scientific paradigm change, but also popularized by Gould and Eldredge (1993) in the field of biological evolution, and True, Jones, and Baumgartner (1999) in their study of public policy dynamics.

The contemporary comparativist's task in analyzing change is to, first, understand Tilly's notion of different "exits" in terms of distinctive evolutions from common (or nearly common) conditions. Such differences may be explored, for instance, within Gilpin's (1981) threefold typology of actors, structures and the processes of interaction that characterize institutions. Second, during the current era that we are living through—which can be described as a period of rapid and discontinuous change of the sort described by Johnson (1966)—it is particularly important for comparativists to seek fresh understandings of the processes that drive discontinuous change, but also the internal and external forces that will propel institutions towards new states of social and political equilibrium.

Intermittent periods of significant change in governing institutions—where change is both dramatic and rapid—generally result from the disruption of existing institutions, deriving from so-called accidents of history, such as natural disaster, war, or some other exogenous shock (Diamond, 1997). The period of regime change that gripped the whole of Eastern Europe and the former USSR, during the period demarcated (roughly) from the beginnings of the Solidarity government in Poland through the Bosnian civil war, marks such a period of rapid, substantive change. The struggles of these regimes since the mid-1990s to restore a more normal state of internal politics and external relations with other countries may be interpreted as efforts to attain a new equilibrium, through changes in their institutional architectures (Filippov et al., 2004).

11.4.5   AN EXAMPLE OF DISCONTINUOUS CHANGE

The political and economic restructuring that commenced in the early 1990s in the new states of the former Soviet Union placed unprecedented demands on vestigial administrative and governance structures, which had been developed under markedly different conditions (communism), and which were intended to serve largely different purposes (coordination of the command economy). Consequently, much of the new comparative research on the former USSR explores current and evolving governmental reforms and policies, and their effects (both intended and unintended) in light of these governments' expressed goals and objectives, and all within the context of the continuities and discontinuities with the previous regime (Elster et al., 1998; Suleiman, 1999; Nunberg, 1999; Manning and Parison, 2004).

The vestigial remnants of former socialist regimes (i.e., the persistence of the nomenklatura, former communists holding high public office, overly burdensome social security and national defense sectors, civil society deficits) imparted certain inertial tendencies to subsequent events, whereby many unfortunate aspects of the former regime tended to persist, or even worsen under successor regimes in Russia and Ukraine (e.g., overly centralized, executive-centered, secretive, prone to corruption, etc.). Such persistent qualities form the basis for understanding and interpreting political, commercial, and administrative developments since the collapse of communism.

11.4.6   AN APPLICATION TO COMPARATIVE FISCAL POLICY

In the early 1990s, political scientist Sven Steinmo employed historical institutionalist methods to explain observed variation in how different Western countries finance their governments (Steinmo, 1993). The problem essentially turned on how different institutional structures, politics, and procedures combine with social preferences concerning the quantity and mix of government services, to determine an equilibrium political solution. Steinmo observed that introducing concrete institutions into the analysis places the entire problem of understanding the funding of government within a historical context rich in cultural influences.

Steinmo's work also highlights a distinct advantage of comparative study for understanding domestic politics and policy. In the case of countries with robust governing institutions, like those of the U.S. fiscal system, structures and procedures are so much a part of the phenomenon itself that it is difficult to separate out the preferences and strategic behaviors of the various interest groups without resorting to comparative study. Consequently, although Steinmo studied only the Swedish and British cases along with the American case, even this limited case set served to highlight contrasts, incongruities, and disparities among them. What Steinmo's approach and method permits is a more direct means to reveal the general cultural preferences for certain kinds of fiscal outcomes in these countries.

The focus on institutions does not mean that citizens, politicians, and administrators are excluded from the analysis. Rather, the sets of choices of these actors are viewed as determined by and large by institutional factors. It is in institutions, then, that "individuals interpret their self-interest and define their policy preferences." In what Steinmo calls the "institutionalization of bias" (with apologies to Schattschneider, 1960), the sources of budgetary outcomes are embedded in state governing and administrative institutions. The sources of bias are various constitutional structures, election procedures, interest group politics, bureaucratic routines and procedural norms, and so on.

The specific features of the governing institutions in various countries set the stage for the often dramatic differences in their politics and outcome, even though, as Steinmo notes, "what is being fought over is remarkably similar" among them (Steinmo, 1993, p. 9).

In his work, by tracing different patterns of fiscal outcomes from common paths, Steinmo provides an account of the institutional roots of complexity of the American tax system, the relative stability of Swedish tax burdens and yields, and the historical "roller coaster" of British taxes. The study stands as a powerful and compelling demonstration of both the power of comparative analysis, and of the crucial role that institutions play in determining fiscal outcomes.

11.5 CONCLUSION

The usual issues and concerns regarding valid description and scientific inference are present in comparative research: accuracy, validity, reliability, generality, parsimony, and causality. Theories improve with continuing research, and over time. Comparative research in this regard is therefore much like any other research. Comparative research must also confront disparate cultures, histories, and geographies. Ensuring the validity, reliability, and equivalence of comparisons across regions and nations is inherently challenging (Merritt and Rokkan, 1966). All models in comparative research are, to one degree or another, under-specified. This does not mean, however, that meaningful research is not possible; indeed, it argues for the intensification of the comparative research effort.

Comparative analysis seeks to generalize across geographical space, culture, and time, taking care not to introduce alien factors. This requires recognizing the presence of the three interrelated problems of ahistoricity, comparability, and reification. Modern comparative public administration research must take its subject matter as it is, in all of its inherent complexity. The institutional foundation of the modern public administration provides an "underlay," as it were, that permits comparative analysis across time and space. Institutional analysis takes as its starting point the proposition that institutions generally matter more than individuals. All governments face similar challenges: borders must be defended, public order maintained, justice administered, social programs delivered, children educated, taxes collected. Governments meet these challenges in vastly different ways, giving rise to the broad diversity of institutional arrangements we observe.

Institutionalism recognizes that states and state institutions have some degree of autonomous existence. That is, they are agents unto themselves. The dynamic study of institutions thus has great appeal, especially in framing processes of social—and institutional—continuity and change. It can assist in reaching fresh understandings of the processes that drive discontinuous change, but also the internal and external forces that propel institutions towards new states of social and political equilibrium. Institutional analysis is therefore presented in this chapter as an analytically rigorous, and academically respectable method for making sense of an inherently difficult subject matter.

PROBLEMS

1. Problems of comparison sometimes affect even the most basic issues and items. A good example is the comparison of U.S. state governments to small countries. In many respects, the American states resemble small countries. California, for example, with a population of roughly 35 million souls, is larger than Canada, Belgium the Czech Republic, Denmark, Finland, Greece, Hungary, Ireland, the Netherlands, Norway, and Portugal. Scan the data in Tables 11.1 and 11.2 in the accompanying Excel files. Notice that California's 2002 Gross State Product (GSP) of 1.364 trillion dollars was more than 10 percent of the U.S. total, and larger than the Gross Domestic Products (GDP) of Canada, Mexico, Italy, Korea, Sweden, and Switzerland. Of the member countries of the Organization for Economic Cooperation & Development (OECD), only the U.S., Japan, France, Germany, and the United Kingdom have larger economies. To explore this, and other kinds of comparisons, complete the following basic tasks.

TABLE 11.1
U.S. State Governments Data Summary

State	Population in Thousands, July 2002	Gross State Product in Billions of U.S. Dollars, 2002	Total Revenue in Millions of U.S. Dollars, 2003[a]	Per Capita Personal Income, 2000
All U.S. states	287,985	10,412.2	1,295,659	30,547
Alabama	4,480	123.8	19,099	25,778
Alaska	641	29.7	6,924	31,954
Arizona	5,438	173.1	17,927	26,378
Arkansas	2,707	71.2	11,805	23,858
California	34,988	1,363.6	195,545	32,478
Colorado	4,498	181.2	13,806	33,446
Connecticut	3,458	167.2	18,241	42,104
Delaware	806	47.0	5,041	33,259
Florida	16,678	522.3	55,213	29,173
Georgia	8,582	307.4	29,874	27,870
Hawaii	1,234	43.8	6,808	29,826
Idaho	1,344	38.3	5,493	25,132
Illinois	12,587	486.2	44,423	31,858
Indiana	6,155	203.3	24,553	27,910
Iowa	2,934	97.8	12,973	28,342
Kansas	2,712	89.9	10,402	28,575
Kentucky	4,089	121.6	18,377	25,698
Louisiana	4,475	134.4	19,438	25,580
Maine	1,297	39.0	6,801	28,348
Maryland	5,442	202.8	21,801	36,399
Massachusetts	6,412	287.2	30,371	38,768
Michigan	10,039	347.0	50,077	29,635
Minnesota	5,024	199.3	25,596	33,259
Mississippi	2,866	68.6	13,393	22,861
Missouri	5,681	187.1	22,024	28,387
Montana	910	23.9	4,608	24,908
Nebraska	1,727	60.6	7,285	29,065
Nevada	2,168	82.4	8,351	30,981
New Hampshire	1,275	46.1	5,207	34,352
New Jersey	8,576	377.8	46,078	38,333
New Mexico	1,855	53.4	9,848	24,291
New York	19,165	802.9	118,275	35,454
North Carolina	8,313	301.3	30,043	27,124
North Dakota	634	20.0	3,359	29,120
Ohio	11,405	385.7	49,905	29,049
Oklahoma	3,487	95.3	14,919	26,051
Oregon	3,522	115.1	19,252	27,796
Pennsylvania	12,324	424.8	49,459	30,928
Rhode Island	1,069	37.0	5,856	31,285
South Carolina	4,103	122.3	19,669	25,200
South Dakota	760	25.8	3,000	28,617
Tennessee	5,790	191.4	20,564	27,828
Texas	21,722	775.5	82,621	28,029
Utah	2,337	73.6	11,534	24,675
Vermont	616	19.4	3,639	30,392

(continued)

TABLE 11.1 (*Continued*)
U.S. State Governments Data Summary

State	Population in Thousands, July 2002	Gross State Product in Billions of U.S. Dollars, 2002	Total Revenue in Millions of U.S. Dollars, 2003[a]	Per Capita Personal Income, 2000
Virginia	7,286	288.8	28,185	32,903
Washington	6,066	234.0	29,661	32,738
West Virginia	1,805	45.3	9,766	23,995
Wisconsin	5,439	189.5	25,165	29,824
Wyoming	499	20.3	3,403	31,817

Sources: From U.S. Census Bureau, http://www.census.gov/govs/www/statetax.html (revised 27 April 2005); U.S. Bureau of Economic Analysis Survey of Current Business, July 2005, and Internet site at http://www.bea.doc.gov/bea/regional/ gsp/and http://www.bea.doc.gov/bea/newsrelarchive/2005/gsp0605.pdf\ (released 23 June 2005); For population data: U.S. Census Bureau, http://www.census.gov/popest/archives/2000s/vintage_2001/CO-EST2001-12/CO-EST2001-12-00.html.

[a] Duplicate intergovernmental transactions are excluded.

TABLE 11.2
OECD Country Data Summary, 2002

Country	Population, in Thousands	Gross Domestic Product (GDP), in Billions of U.S. Dollars	General Government Revenue as percent GDP
Canada	31,373	724.3	41.2
Mexico	101,398	648.6	n.a.
United States	287,941	10,417.6	32.6
Australia	19,641	425.3	36.8
Japan	127,435	3,904.8	30.3
Korea	47,615	548.9	32.3 (2002)
New Zealand	3,939	60.5	43.4 (1997)
Austria	8,084	207.8	50.9
Belgium	10,333	251.8	50.5
Czech Republic	10,201	73.8	42.8
Denmark	5,374	173.9	57.4
Finland	5,201	135.5	54.4
France	59,678	1,457.4	50.2
Germany	82,456	2,017.0	45.0
Greece	10,988	135.0	45.3
Hungary	10,159	65.6	43.4
Iceland	288	8.7	44.9
Ireland	3,917	122.8	33.1
Italy	57,474	1,219.0	45.6
Luxembourg	446	22.6	46.7
Netherlands	16,149	437.8	45.9
Norway	4,538	190.3	57.6
Poland	38,232	198.0	n.a.
Portugal	10,380	127.5	43.2
Slovak Republic	5,379	24.5	45.3
Spain	41,314	686.1	39.9

TABLE 11.2   (*Continued*)
OECD Country Data Summary, 2002

Country	Population, in Thousands	Gross Domestic Product (GDP), in Billions of U.S. Dollars	General Government Revenue as percent GDP
Sweden	8,925	243.6	58.1
Switzerland	7,285	276.2	35.6
Turkey	69,626	184.2	n.a.
United Kingdom	59,322	1,571.4	39.4
OECD Total	1,145,090	26,558.6	
G-7 Nations	705,679	21,311.5	
Euro Zone Countries	306,419	6,820.4	
European Union 15	380,040	8,809.2	

Source: From Organization for Economic Cooperation & Development, OECD in Figures 2004 and 2005 Editions. Available online at http://www1.oecd.org/publications/e-book/0104071E.PDF#search=% 22 OECD%20in%20Figures%202004%22.

a. Is comparing U.S. state economies with the economies of foreign countries a valid one-for-one comparison? How do GSP and GDP differ from one another? (You can check the relevant definitions on the website of the U.S. Commerce Department's Bureau of Economic Analysis.) What aspects of a national economy are not present in a state economy? Are the institutions of economic management the same? How do they differ? Be brief.

b. Compare the data on the size of the government sectors in the case of U.S. states in Table 11.1 with the wealthy nations of the OECD in Table 11.2. What can you learn from comparing revenues as a percent of GDP or GSP? Is there any additional information that you would want to know before reaching any hard conclusions about how large and extensive are the governments of the American state in comparison with the OECD countries? (In other words, on the basis of a numerical comparison, is it meaningful to conclude that one government is, for instance, two times the size of another one?).

2. Comparing the sub-national tax systems of two countries can be extremely treacherous. There may be many differences that can combine to confound the researcher's best efforts to make valid comparisons. Following is a sample of some of the sources of difficulty: the taxes that are employed vary broadly; the items which are subject to taxation are at least partly a function of the country's history; there may be in place a rather arcane structure of taxes that are assigned or shared between the national, regional, and municipal authorities; the types and amounts of intergovernmental transfers may be quite unique; tax administration may be decentralized or not, and can be highly selective, or even downright corrupt; finally, the tax regime may be highly unstable, and subject to frequent change by the legislature.

   A useful illustration of the difficulty making comparisons would be to compare the sub-national tax structures of the United States and Russian Federation. Complete the following tasks, using the data that is provided in Tables 11.3 through 11.6 in the accompanying Excel data files.

a. A reasonable starting point would be to calculate the percentage shares of the various taxes that are collected. Create pie charts for both the US states and Russian regions, indicating the relative shares of various taxes that are collected for a given year, say, 2003. Does this comparison provide you with any useful information or insight?

b. Much can be learned from discerning the relative authority of federal and regional officials to set tax rates, determine the items that are subject to taxation, and allocate tax proceeds between the national, federal, and local levels. A summary of such authority over the Russian sub-national tax system in 2003 is provided in Table 11.5. You may rely upon what you

TABLE 11.3

U.S. State Governments Revenue Summary, By Source, 1990–2003

Revenue Item	Total (Millions of Dollars)				Per Capita (Dollars)[a]			
	2000	2001	2002	2003	2000	2001	2002	2003
Total Revenue	1,260,829	1,180,305	1,097,829	1,295,659	4,489	4,145	3,820	4,464
General revenue	984,783	1,049,298	1,062,305	1,112,349	3,506	3,685	3,696	3,833
Taxes	539,655	559,679	535,241	548,991	1,922	1,966	1,862	1,892
Sales and gross receipts	252,147	258,018	262,361	273,811	898	906	913	943
General	174,461	179,319	179,665	184,597	621	630	625	636
Motor fuels	29,968	31,026	31,968	32,269	107	109	111	111
Alcoholic beverages	4,104	4,167	4,249	4,399	15	15	15	15
Tobacco products	8,391	8,644	8,902	11,482	30	30	31	40
Other	35,222	34,863	37,576	41,065	125	122	131	141
Licenses	32,598	32,866	35,391	35,863	116	115	123	124
Motor vehicles	15,099	15,141	15,641	16,009	54	53	54	55
Corporations in general	6,460	6,384	5,842	6,129	23	22	20	21
Other	11,039	11,341	13,908	13,725	39	40	48	47
Individual income	194,573	208,079	185,697	181,933	693	731	646	627
Corporation net income	32,522	31,687	25,123	28,384	116	111	87	98
Property	10,996	10,430	9,702	10,471	39	37	34	36
Other	16,819	18,597	16,967	18,529	60	65	59	64
Charges and miscellaneous	170,747	183,998	191,641	201,741	608	646	667	695
Intergovernmental revenue	274,382	305,621	335,423	361,617	977	1,073	1,167	1,246
From Federal Government	259,114	288,309	317,581	343,308	923	1,013	1,105	1,183
Public welfare	147,150	165,800	181,517	196,954	524	582	632	679
Education	42,086	45,760	51,103	56,362	150	161	178	194
Highways	23,790	27,894	29,641	29,481	85	98	103	102
Health and hospitals	14,223	16,426	17,875	19,559	51	58	62	67
Other	31,865	32,428	37,445	40,951	113	114	130	141
From local governments	15,268	17,312	17,842	18,309	54	61	62	63
Utility revenue	4,513	6,930	11,935	12,518	16	24	42	43
Liquor store revenue	3,895	4,092	4,288	4,518	14	14	15	16
Insurance trust revenue[b]	267,639	119,985	19,301	166,274	953	421	67	573
Employee retirement	230,166	79,527	−25,244	110,839	820	279	−88	382
Unemployment compensation	23,260	23,221	26,960	35,191	83	82	94	121

Source: U.S. Census Bureau, 1990, State Government Finances, series GF, No. 3; thereafter, <http://www.census. gov/govs/www/state03.html>.

[a] 1990 based on enumerated resident population as of April 1 of that year.
[b] Includes repayments.

TABLE 11.4

Russian Federation Regional Revenue Summary, By Source, 2000–2003

Revenue Item	Billions of Russian Rubles				Per Capita			
	2000	2001	2002	2003	2000	2001	2002	2003
Total Revenue	1,129	1,342	1,644	1,929	7,711	9,210	11,325	13,344
Enterprise Profit Tax	221	300	291	356	1,508	2,059	2,004	2,463
Personal Income Tax	147	253	358	456	1,004	1,736	2,466	3,154

TABLE 11.4   (Continued)
Russian Federation Regional Revenue Summary, By Source, 1990–2003

Revenue Item	Billions of Russian Rubles				Per Capita			
	2000	2001	2002	2003	2000	2001	2002	2003
Value-Added Tax (VAT)	85	2	0	0	580	14	0	0
Excise Taxes	35	40	49	90	239	275	338	622
Sales and Imputed Taxes	47	66	77	77	321	453	820	532
Property Tax	63	88	119	136	430	604	820	941
Other Tax Revenues	143	123	205	214	977	844	1,412	1,480
Nontax Revenue	61	86	125	175	417	590	861	1,211
Budgetary Funds[a]	203	142	125	105	1,387	975	861	726
Transfers (Net)[b]	123	242	293	322	840	1,661	2,018	2,227
Memorandum: Rubles per US Dollar	28.2	30.1	31.8	29.5				
Population (thousands)	146,405	145,710	145,167	144,558				
	(Est.)	(Est.)	(2002 Census)	(Est.)				

Source: For 2000–2003 Data: International Monetary Fund, Russian Federation: Statistical Appendix, Country Report 05/378, October 20, 2005; available at: <http://www.imf.org/external/pubind.htm>; Per capita data are the author's calculations.

[a] Including all territorial road funds.
[b] Including net budgetary loans.

TABLE 11.5
Russian Regional Taxes and Fees, 2003

Tax	Tax Imposed by	Tax Rate Determined by	Revenue Distribution
Enterprise Profit Tax	Federal Bodies	Regional Bodies within Limits Established by Federal Legislation	Percentage Distribution Defined in Annual Federal Budget Law [For 2003: 50 percent to the regions; 50 percent to the central government]
Personal Income Tax	Federal Bodies	Federal Bodies	For 2003: 100 percent to Regional Budgets
Property Tax	Federal Bodies	Regional and Local Bodies within Limits Established by Federal Legislation	100 percent to Regional and Local Budgets
Excise Taxes on Alcoholic Beverages	Federal Bodies	Federal Bodies	100 percent to Regional Budgets
Excise Taxes on Motor Fuels	Federal Bodies	Federal Bodies	60 percent to Regional Budgets
Fee for Needs of Instructional Institutions	Regional Bodies	Regional Bodies	100 percent to Regional Budgets
Sales Tax	Regional Bodies	Regional Bodies within Limits Established by Federal Legislation	40 percent to the Regions; 60 percent to Budgets of Municipalities within Each Region
Payments for the Use of the Forest Fund: (a) Forest Duty (b) Rental Income	Federal Bodies	Regional Bodies Set Specific Rates; Minimum Rate is Defined by Federal legislation	For 2003: 50 percent of Revenues in Excess of the Minimum Rate Accrues to the Federal Budget

(*continued*)

TABLE 11.5   (*Continued*)
Russian Regional Taxes and Fees, 2003

Tax	Tax Imposed by	Tax Rate Determined by	Revenue Distribution
Transport Tax	Regional Bodies	Regional Bodies within Limits Established by Federal Legislation	100 percent to Regional Budgets

Source: Center for Fiscal Policy at: <http://english.fpcenter.ru/>.

Note: Excluding an array of relatively minor taxes, such as: Natural Resources tax, Gambling tax, Various Licensing and registration Fees, Water Use Fees, Green Tax, Fauna Use Tax, and the Unified Agricultural Tax.

TABLE 11.6
Russian Tax Sharing Rates, 1991–2002

	Enterprise Profits Tax	Personal Income Tax	Value Added Tax	Excise on Alcohol	Energy Tax	Excises on Domestic Consumption
1991 Basic Law on Principles of Taxation	100 percent Regional	100 percent Regional	100 percent Federal	50 percent Equal Shares	n.a.	n.a.
1992: 1Q	47 percent Federal 53 percent Regional	100 percent Regional	Ad hoc Negotiations	50 percent Equal Shares	100 percent Federal	n.a.
1992: 2Q–4Q	41 percent Federal 59 percent Regional	100 percent Regional	80 percent Federal 20 percent Regional	50 percent Equal Shares	100 percent Federal	n.a.
1993	31 percent Federal 69 percent Regional	100 percent Regional	80 percent Federal 20 percent Regional	50 percent Equal Shares	100 percent Federal	n.a.
1994: 1Q	37 percent Federal 63 percent Regional	100 percent Regional	75 percent Federal 25 percent Regional	50 percent Equal Shares	100 percent Federal	100 percent Regional
1994: 2Q–4Q	37 percent Federal 63 percent Regional	100 percent Regional	75 percent Federal 25 percent Regional	50 percent Equal Shares	100 percent Federal	100 percent Regional
1995	34 percent Federal 66 percent Regional	10 percent Federal 90 percent Regional	75 percent Federal 25 percent Regional	50 percent Equal Shares	100 percent Federal	100 percent Regional
1996	34 percent Federal 66 percent Regional	10 percent Federal 90 percent Regional	75 percent Federal 25 percent Regional	50 percent Equal Shares	100 percent Federal	100 percent Regional

TABLE 11.6   *(Continued)*
Russian Tax Sharing Rates, 1991–2002

	Enterprise Profits Tax	Personal Income Tax	Value Added Tax	Excise on Alcohol	Energy Tax	Exises on Domestic Consumption
1997	34 percent Federal 66 percent Regional	100 percent Regional	75 percent Federal 25 percent Regional	50 percent Equal Shares	100 percent Federal	100 percent Regional
1998	34 percent Federal 66 percent Regional	40 percent Federal 60 percent Regional	75 percent Federal 25 percent Regional	50 percent Equal Shares	100 percent Federal	100 percent Regional
1999: 1Q	37 percent Federal 63 percent Regional	14 percent Federal 86 percent Regional	75 percent Federal 25 percent Regional	50 percent Equal Shares	100 percent Federal	100 percent Regional
1999: 2Q–4Q	37 percent Federal 63 percent Regional	14 percent Federal 86 percent Regional	85 percent Federal 15 percent Regional	50 percent Equal Shares	100 percent Federal	100 percent Regional
2000	37 percent Federal 63 percent Regional	14 percent Federal 86 percent Regional	85 percent Federal 15 percent Regional	50 percent Equal Shares	100 percent Federal	100 percent Regional
2001	31 percent Federal 69 percent Regional[a]	1 percent Federal 99 percent Regional	100 percent Federal	50 percent Equal Shares	100 percent Federal	100 percent Regional
2002	31 percent Federal 69 percent Regional[b]	100 percent Regional	100 percent Federal	50 percent Equal Shares	100 percent Federal	100 percent Regional

Source: Jorge Martinez-Vazques, "Asymmetric Federalism in Russia: Cure or Poison?" International Studies Program Working Paper 03–04 (December 2002), Andrew Young School of Policy Studies, Georgia State University. Available online at: <http://isp-aysps.gsu.edu/papers/ispwp0304.html>.

[a] In 2001 a local Enterprise Profits Tax was introduced; the reported regional share includes the municipal 5 percent.

[b] In 2002 the local Enterprise Profits Tax rate was 2 percent; the reported regional share includes the municipal 2 percent.

know about the independence of U.S. state and federal tax systems. Based on the information in this table, are the U.S. and Russian sub-national tax systems comparable? How are they different? How would research comparing the U.S. and Russian sub-national tax systems be affected by the apparent legal and institutional differences between them?

c. A critical question for many comparative tax studies would concern the relative stability of the revenue stream. The Russian tax system traditionally shares the yields of the most ample revenue sources between the central government, and the regions, on an originazation basis (i.e., if the Enterprise Profits Tax is shared 69:31 in favor of the regions, then 69 percent of the tax collected, say, in the Volgograd region would accrue to that region's government). Using the time series data which is provided in the accompanying table, what implication for the stability of Russian regional revenues would the changing sharing rates hold for Russia's regions? Are U.S. state revenues more stable? Does it matter? Why or why not?

REFERENCES

Aberbach, J.D., Putnam, R.D., and Rockman, B.A. 1981. *Bureaucrats & Politicians in Western Democracies.* Cambridge, Massachusetts: Harvard University Press.

Almond, G. and Verba, S. 1963. *The Civic Culture.* Princeton, New Jersey: Princeton University Press.

Armstrong, J.A. 1973. *The European Administrative Elite.* Princeton, New Jersey: Princeton University Press.

Ashford, D. (Ed.) 1978. *Comparing Public Policies: New Concepts and Methods.* Beverly Hills, California: Sage.

Ashford, D., Katzerstein, P., and Pemple, T.J. (Eds.) 1978. *Comparative Policy: A Cross-National Bibliography.* Beverly Hills, California: Sage.

Barker, E. 1944. *The Development of Public Services in Western Europe, 1660–1930.* London: Oxford University Press.

Barrington, T.J. 1980. *The Irish Administrative System.* Dublin: Institute of Public Administration.

Barzelay, M. 1992. *Breaking through Bureaucracy: A New Vision for Managing in Government.* Berkeley, California, New York: University of California Press.

Barzelay, M. 2001. *The New Public Management: Improving Research and Policy Dialogue.* Berkeley, California, New York: University of California Press.

Berger, M. 1957a. Bureaucracy East and West. *Administrative Sciences Quarterly, 1,* 518–529.

Berger, M. 1957b. *Bureaucracy and Society in Modern Egypt.* Princeton, New Jersey: Princeton University Press.

Binder, L. 1971. *Crises and Sequences in Political Development.* Princeton, New Jersey: Princeton University Press.

Braibranti, R. 1969. *Political and Administrative Development.* Durham, North Carolina: Duke University Press.

Brown, R.G.S. and Steel, D.R. 1970. *The Administrative Process in Britain.* London: Methuen & Co., Ltd.

Burns, J.P. (Ed.) 1994. *Asian Civil Service Systems: Improving Efficiency and Productivity.* Singapore: Times Academic Press.

Caiden, G.E. 1991. *Administrative Reform Comes of Age.* Berlin, New York: Walter de Gruyter.

Campbell, C. and Szablowski, G. 1979. *The Super Bureaucrats: Structure and Behavior in Central Agencies.* New York: New York University Press.

Chapman, B. 1953. *Introduction to French Local Government.* London: George Allen & Unwin.

Chapman, B. 1959. *The Profession of Government.* London: George Allen & Unwin.

Dahl, R. 1947. The science of public administration: Three problems. *Public Administration Review, 7 (1947),* 1–11.

Diamant, A. 1960. The relevance of comparative politics to the study of comparative administration. *Administrative Science Quarterly, 5,* 87–112.

Diamond, J. 1997. *Guns, Germs, and Steel.* New York: W.W. Norton & Co.

Dogan, M. (Ed.) 1975. *The Mandarins of Western Europe: The Political Role of Top Civil Servants.* Beverly Hills, California: Sage.

Dror, Y. 1968. *Public Policymaking Reexamined.* San Francisco: Chandler Publishing Co.

Easton, D. 1953. *The Political System.* New York: Alfred A. Knopf.

Elster, J., Offe, C., and Preuss, U.K. 1998. *Institutional Design in Post-Communist Societies: Rebuilding the Ship at Sea.* Cambridge, England: Cambridge University Press.

Filippov, M., Ordeshook, P.C., and Shvetsova, O. 2004. *Designing Federalism: A Theory of Self-Sustainable Institutions.* Cambridge, United Kingdom: Cambridge University Press.

Gant, G. 1979. *Development Administration: Concepts, Goals, Methods.* Madison, Wisconsin: The University of Wisconsin Press.

Giddens, A. 1984. *The Constitution of Society.* Cambridge, England: Polity Press.

Gilpin, R. 1981. *War and Change in World Politics.* Princeton, New Jersey: Princeton University Press.

Gladden, E.N. 1972. *A History of Public Administration.* London: Frank Cass.

Gould, S.J. and Eldredge, N. 1993. Punctuated equilibrium comes of age. *Nature, 366 (6452),* 223–227.

Heady, F. 1959. Bureaucratic theory and comparative administration. *Administrative Sciences Quarterly, 3 (4),* 509–525.

Heady, F. 1966. *Public Administration: A Comparative Perspective.* Englewood Cliffs, New Jersey: Prentice-Hall, Inc.

Heady, F. 1984. *Public Administration: A Comparative Perspective,* 3rd ed. New York, Basel: Marcel Dekker, Inc.

Heady, F. and Stokes, S.L. (Eds.) 1962. *Papers in Comparative Public Administration*. Ann Arbor, Michigan: Institute of Public Administration, The University of Michigan.

Heclo, H. 1974. *Modern Social Politics in Britain and Sweden*. New Haven, Connecticut; London: Yale University Press.

Heidenheimer, A.J., Heclo, H., and Adams, C.T. 1975. *Comparative Public Policy: The Politics of Social Choice in Europe and America*. New York: St. Martins Press.

Henderson, K. 1983. *The Study of Public Administration*. Lanham, Maryland: University Press of America.

Hood, C. 1991. A public management for all seasons? *Public Administration, 69 (1)*, 3–19.

Jacoby, H. 1973. *The Bureaucratization of the World*. Berkeley, California: University of California Press.

Johnson, C. 1966. *Revolutionary Change*. Boston, Massachusetts: Little, Brown & Co.

Kettl, D.F. 2000. *The Global Public Management Revolution: A Report on the Transformation of Governance*. Washington, DC: The Brookings Institution.

Kuhn, T.S. 1962. *The Structure of Scientific Revolutions*. Chicago, Illinois: University of Chicago Press.

LaPalombara, J. (Ed.) 1963. *Bureaucracy and Political Development*. Princeton, New Jersey: Princeton University Press.

Manning, N. and Parison, N. 2004. *International Public Administration Reform: Implications for the Russian Federation*. Washington, DC: The World Bank.

Marini, F. (Ed.) 1971. *Toward a New Public Administration: The Minnowbrook Perspective*. Scranton, Pennsylvania: Chandler Publishing Co.

Merritt, R.C. and Rokkan, S. 1966. *Comparing Nations: The Use of Quantitative Data in Cross-National Research*. New Haven, Connecticut: Yale University Press.

Meyer, P. 1957. *Administrative Organization: A Comparative Study of the Organization of Public Administration*. London: Stevens & Sons.

Montgomery, J.D. and Siffin, W.J. (Eds.) 1966. *Approaches to Development: Politics, Administration and Change*. New York: McGraw-Hill.

Morstein Marx, F. (1946, 1957). *The Administrative State*. Chicago, Illinois: University of Chicago Press.

Morstein Marx, F. 1963. *Elements of Public Administration*, 2nd ed. Englewood Cliffs, New Jersey: Prentice-Hall, Inc.

Nash, G.D. 1969. *Perspectives on Administration: The Vistas of History*. Berkeley, California, Institute of Governmental Studies, University of California.

Nunberg, B. (Ed.) 1999. *The State After Communism: Administrative Transitions in Central and Eastern Europe*. Washington, DC: The World Bank.

Orren, K. and Skowronek, S. 1994. Beyond the iconography of order: Notes for a "New Institutionalism". In Dodd, L.C. and Jillson, C. (Eds.), *The Dynamics of American Politics: Approaches & Interpretations*. Boulder, Colorado: Westview Press, pp. 311–330.

Orren, K. and Skowronek, S. 1995. Order and time in institutional study: A brief for the historical approach. In Farr, J., Dryzek, J.S., and Leonard, S.T. (Eds.), *Political Science in History: Research Programs and Political Traditions*. Cambridge, United Kingdom: Cambridge University Press, pp. 296–317.

Perrson, K. 1996. The structure of informal power and its impact on local development in connection with the process of European integration. In Kobayashi, K. and Kita, H. (Eds.) *Exploring Sustainability*. Tottori, Japan: RPRG Press.

Peters, G. 1978. *The Politics of Bureaucracy: A Comparative Perspective*. New York: Longmans.

Poggi, G. 1978. *The Development of the Modern State: A Sociological Introduction*. Stanford, California: Stanford University Press.

Poggi, G. 1990. *The State: Its Nature, Development and Prospects*. Stanford, California: Stanford University Press.

Presthus, R.V. 1959a. The Social Bases of Bureaucratic Organization. *Social Forces, 38*, 103–109.

Presthus, R.V. 1959b. Behavior and Bureaucracy in Many Cultures. *Public Administration Review, 19*, 25–35.

Presthus, R.V. 1961. Weberian v. Welfare Bureaucracy in Traditional Society. *Administrative Science Quarterly, 6*, 1–24.

Przeworski, A. and Teune, H. 1970. *The Logic of Comparative Social Inquiry*. Malabar, Florida: Robert E. Kreiger Publishing Company.

Pusey, M. 1991. *Economic Rationalism in Canberra*. New York: Cambridge University Press.

Riggs, F.W. 1961. *The Ecology of Public Administration*. New Delhi: Asia Publishing House.

Riggs, F.W. 1962. Trends in the comparative study of public administration. *International Review of Administrative Sciences*, 28, 10–20.

Riggs, F.W. 1964. *Administration in Developing Countries—The Theory of Prismatic Society*. Boston, Massachusetts: Houghton Mifflin Company.

Riggs, F.W. 1971. *Frontiers of Development Administration*. Durham, North Carolina: Duke University Press.

Riggs, F.W. 1973. *Prismatic Society Revisited*. Morristown, New Jersey: General Learning Press.

Rosenberg, H. 1958. *Bureaucracy, Aristocracy and Autocracy: The Prussian Experience 1660–1815*. Cambridge, Massachusetts: Harvard University Press.

Schattschneider, E.E. 1960. *The Semisovereign People*. Hinsdale, Illinois: Dryden Press.

Siffin, W.J. (Ed.) 1957. *Toward the Comparative Study of Public Administration*. Bloomington, Indiana: Indiana University Press.

Steinmo, S. 1993. *Taxation and Democracy: Swedish, British, and American Approaches to Financing the Modern State*. New Haven, London: Yale University Press.

Steinmo, S., Thelen, K., and Longstreth, F. (Eds.) 1992. *Structuring Politics: Historical Institutionalism in Comparative Analysis*. Cambridge, United Kingdom: Cambridge University Press.

Suleiman, E. 1978. *Elites in French Society: The Politics of Survival*. Princeton, New Jersey: Princeton University Press.

Suleiman, E. 1999. Bureaucracy and democratic consolidation: Lessons from eastern Europe. In Anderson, L. (Ed.), *Transitions to Democracy*. New York: Columbia University Press, pp. 141–167.

Tilly, C. (Ed.) 1975. *The Formation of National States in Western Europe*. Princeton, New Jersey: Princeton University Press.

True, J.L., Jones, B.D., and Baumgartner, F.R. 1999. Punctuated equilibrium theory: Explaining stability and change in American policymaking. In Sabatier, P.A. (Ed.), *Theories of the Policy Process*. Boulder, Colorado: Westview Press, pp. 97–115.

Tummala, K.K. 1994. *Public Administration in India*. Singapore: Times Academic Press.

Waldo, D. 1964. *Comparative Public Administration: Prologue, Problems and Promise*. Chicago, Illinois: Comparative Administration Group, American Society for Public Administration.

Walso, D. 1980. *The Enterprise of Public Administration*. Novato, California: Chandler & Sharp Publishers, Inc.

Weber, M. 1949. *The Methodology of the Social Sciences*. New York: The Free Press.

White, L.D. 1930. *The Civil Service in the Modern State*. Chicago, Illinois: University of Chicago Press.

Wilson, T.W. 1887. The study of administration. *Political Science Quarterly, 2 (June)*, 197–222. Reprinted in 56 (December, 1941), 481–506.

Zifcak, S. 1994. *New Managerialism: Administrative Reform in Whitehall and Canberra*. Buckingham, England: Open University Press.

12 Legal Research Methods

Julia Beckett

CONTENTS

12.1   INTRODUCTION

Although the emphasis in public administration and public management textbooks has been on management, law is a foundation for democratic governance. Public administration involves implementing policies and programs that are delegated to it by law. The sources of legal obligations, duties, and restrictions for public administrators include constitutions, statutes, administrative regulations, executive orders, treaties, and court decisions. American government operates under the rule of law. Locating the sources of these legal obligations and restraints through legal research is useful to students and public administrators.

Administrators and policy analysts should have a general understanding of techniques and tools of legal research to understand their duties and to understand how policies change. Legal research and analysis are the foundational skills of the judiciary and the legal profession. These skills are taught in law school and honed in practice, but there are strategies, techniques, and design considerations from legal research that have practical applications for public administration. Often the questions that arise in legal practice are about disputes and are in preparation for advocacy. Other times the questions arise in proactive advice on the legality of an action. Practice involves real questions, real disputes that require opinions, decisions, and action. Public administration and policy analysis share this practice and action orientation.

This chapter explains how legal research techniques can assist students and practitioners of public management and public policy analysis. It undertakes this task by considering these areas: research strategy; preliminary research considerations; starting points; unfamiliar areas and general overviews; statutory provisions and enacted law; locating a specific case; locating cases regarding an issue; controlling law; iterative process and interpretation; and legal sources as data.

12.2 RESEARCH STRATEGY—AUTHORITY OR DATA

Law is dynamic and this affects the research strategy. Law changes with the enactment of statutes and the promulgation of regulations. These enactments are formal statements of policy. Law changes when courts interpret enacted law or when appellate court decisions determine whether to follow, distinguish or overrule common law precedent. "[A] reasonably competent public official should know the law governing his conduct" *Harlow v. Fitzgerald*, 457 U.S. 800, 819 (1982). This is a matter of constitutional competence (Rosenbloom, Carroll, and Carroll, 2000). The general public is expected to follow the law, or as the saying goes "ignorance of the law is no excuse."

What you want to know and the type of data available are important aspects of every research strategy. Some considerations include: How will the information be used? Is the subject of research for a program evaluation or for a research paper? In social science research, the two major types of research are quantitative research using statistical analysis and qualitative research. Legal research can be considered more like qualitative research. There are some distinctive aspects of legal research, including the resources, the mode of analysis, and the technical language of legal documents. Legal research techniques and resources are used for the practice of law to locate legal authority, and they are used in public administration and policy research.

Legal research and analysis is a skill used by a profession. Lawyers conduct research in response to a problem involving a question about what is the controlling legal authority—the socially binding rule—for a given situation. Legal research is conducted to resolve a dispute or to provide advice for operations or policy. Research for legal authority is part of the preparation for advocacy, in litigation or in alternative dispute resolution forums. Understanding the factual situation, the evidence and circumstances is also essential for lawyers. Clients request and pay lawyers for advice based on legal research and analysis. Thus most legal research, unlike basic science or much academic social science research, is purposive and practical. There are real-life consequences to this applied research.

Legal research is used by scholars to analyze the development of rules and social norms, or to critique legal decisions or advocate changing policy. For example, the approach of analyzing a selection of Supreme Court decisions was used by Frederickson (1990) to consider how court decisions impose social equity obligations on administrators; Rosenbloom (2000) showed how the administrative state is subject to constitutional duties as defined by the court; and Lee (2004) examined the judicial requirements of reasonableness. In other articles, the legal structure and obligations of corporations and partnerships are compared to public entities (Beckett, 2000) and the common law and equity doctrines are linked to administration (Green, 2001).

Legal scholars, social scientists, historians, and linguists use the techniques and resources of legal research. They may consider links between administrative law and the processes affect administration. For example, the process and politics of rulemaking have been a frequent subject of inquiry, and in this context both the statutory delegation of authority and legal challenges to the rules have been analyzed. Questions of compliance and development of regulations are raised (DeHart-Davis and Bozeman, 2001; Shapiro, 2002). Rules may be seen as tools of administrative process or indications of policy (West, 2005). Concerns of legalistic behavior or rigid adherence to rules have been analyzed (Kagan, 1991) and one case study shows developing alternative dispute resolution techniques can improve agency operations (see, Carnevale, 1993).

Comparing and analyzing legislation can be part of the research design in evaluating the development of a policy. For example one research design included evaluating government regulatory process controls found in legislation in a number of states (Shapiro, 2002). The text and statutes may be evaluated in relation to fiscal concerns such as budgeting, and income tax laws and regulations (Saxton, Hoene, and Erie, 2002).

Landmark cases and appellate decisions have been studied regarding public policy and management. For example, the public law litigation strategy of interest groups suing to change government policy and practices (Schuck, 1983) has been studied in relation to structural reform of agencies (Bertelli, 2004) and in changes in policy and administrative practices in schools, prisons, and social services (Frederickson, 1990). Often litigation involving government has been studied more with the focus of how individuals and interest groups can change policies through the courts. Government can also develop policies through a series of administrative adjudications under the Administrative Procedure Act (West, 1982). But government may also set policy through litigation as well, for example the states' attorneys general suing tobacco companies (Derthick, 2005).

Understanding the types of factual situations that give rise to government enforcement of law, or in the lawsuits against government, can provide insight into practices, but the logic of precedent and stare decisis means that appellate decisions on a given topic are not a measure of central tendency or typical practices. Instead, the logic of appellate review requires that parties appealing a case raise a new question of law or seek a change in the existing law. This means appellate cases focus on legal questions regarding precedent and interpretation of law rather than factual issues. This logic of precedent and judicial review means that the appeals raise exceptions to the current laws or present situations that have not been considered before. When there is a cluster of reported opinions in a particular area this does not necessarily mean that there is a common problem; for lawyers, rather, it means that law relating to this area is unsettled. This makes published court opinions rarely amenable to quantitative research methods.

Legal resource may provide data for research involving understanding government actions or policy development. The primary documents of legal research—published cases, published laws and rules, and the published legislative histories—can serve as data for a qualitative research project. Using materials from legal research would be an unobtrusive approach to gathering data. But, before developing this type of design, the researcher should understand how legal authority is developed, collected, and categorized.

12.3 PRELIMINARY RESEARCH CONSIDERATIONS

Law is recorded in books. For the legal profession, legal research is the search for authority that is recorded in volumes of official statutes and court decisions. The established tradition of legal research is library research. Constitutions, statutes, rules, and regulations are published. Case decisions are published. To locate these published materials, researchers need a basic understanding of the system of cataloging and citation, and the tools of cross-referencing. Many of the published resources and effective tools are compiled by private publishers. The same type of information may be available through the internet, but not for free; this legal information is available by subscription and high fees. Even in this day and age of internet, many law libraries are accessible only to those who pay membership fees. This chapter will use examples based on commonly available library resources and some public access Web-based resources.

There are different search strategies to locate materials. Some individuals may want to locate a statute or ordinance that provides the delegated authority to an agency. Others may want to go beyond the sentence or paragraph of information provided in a text book and to read the entire decision of a prominent case. When the citation to the case, statute or rule is known, locating the specific materials is a matter of pulling the book from the shelf, or entering the citation into the online legal search engine. This requires a basic understanding of the legal citation format and the legal resource materials. If the citation is incomplete, or if there is a general area of interest, this requires knowledge of general legal resources and finding aids.

Locating the materials involves knowing what types of books to look for and knowing how to find materials in those volumes. Citation systems provide concise and consistent ways to reference and locate materials. Understanding legal citation and style are detailed in the *Bluebook*, now in its 18th edition (2005). In addition to explaining how to cite legal materials in briefs and legal publications, the listings of types of publications may provide additional resources to explore, the *Bluebook* also includes discussions of how to cite materials such as United Nations materials or unpublished government papers. These guidelines can help a person decipher an unfamiliar citation found in a legal periodical.

Legal citation follows the general form of volume or chapter number, series or publication, page or section number. For example the case quoted above, *Harlow v. Fitzgerald*, 457 U.S. 800, 819 (1982), is found in volume 457 of the series the U.S. Supreme Court Reporter at page 800. The quote is found on page 819, and the case was decided in 1982. Harlow brought the appeal to the Supreme Court. Many times state cases and lower court federal cases include the location of the court in the parenthesis with the date. Often times, cases included parallel citations, or the location where the case can be found in different publishers reporters. The sections for statutes may change and so the form is slightly different. For statutes and rules, the numbering system does not use the book volume number and page; instead, the title, chapter or sub-chapter of the code is given first followed by the name of the series, and then the section of the code is given rather than page number. For the example of 42 U.S.C.A. §1983: the title is 42, the series is the *United States Code Annotated* and the section is 1983.

Cases are collected in multi-volume sets of reporters and statutes are published in multi-volume codes. Some common abbreviations for federal case reporters: U.S., S.Ct, and LEd2d contain U.S. Supreme Court opinions produced by different publishers. The F2d or F3d reporters contain Federal appellate court opinions. The F.Supp. contains opinions on questions of law by federal trial courts. State court opinions may be published by one of the dominant publishers, such as West or BNA, or by smaller publishers.

In legal research, publishers typically provide explanatory materials and research aids in the introductory materials in the front of the volumes. Materials include editor's introduction, table of abbreviations, table of contents, indexes, annotations, and updates. The editor may explain the method and terms for categorizing materials and this helps in locating similar materials. These basic tools can be very useful and should not be overlooked. Being able to examine these explanatory materials is one benefit of starting the research in a library.

12.4 STARTING POINTS

Lawyers conducting research look for the relevant, applicable, and controlling law. They use a process that includes repeating the research probe in a number of sources. There are a cluster of preliminary questions in legal research design. What jurisdiction is involved? What is the substantive area of law that defines rights and obligations? Does the research need to consider cases, statutes, rules, or constitutions or some combination of these? What are the legal procedures that need to be followed? Where does someone begin to look for the types of legal authority the situation may involve? There are a number of places to start to locate authoritative law, and jurisdiction is a good starting point.

Jurisdiction is important. Statutes and judicial precedents are authoritative only within the jurisdiction that issued them. In the American system that is divided between state and federal jurisdictions this means that there are multiple laws that must be evaluated. Although there are legal issues and problems that are predominately federal or state, often there are areas of overlapping jurisdiction. This leads to complexity in research and in application. Knowing what jurisdiction applies helps focus research on the applicable series of publications or specifies the starting page in search engines.

Determining what the legal issues are the next major focus for legal research. The concern is substantive legal authority and how it is categorized. Substantive issues may include: What can an agency do if a contractor fails to provide services? Is an agency liable for negligence when an employee exceeds the scope of one's responsibility? Can the residents of a nursing home challenge the decertification by the agency? Finding and interpreting the substantive legal authority is the complex and this is specialized knowledge that is developed both in law school and in legal practice. The following section discusses resources that can provide a general overview.

12.5 UNFAMILIAR AREAS AND GENERAL OVERVIEWS

Lawyers through education and experience have learned generally the way law is classified and categorized, but there may be times when an area is unfamiliar to them. In this situation, rather than starting with statutes or cases, it can be useful to begin with sources that can provide a general overview.

Consider the following situation and list some of the legal concerns it may raise. A local government operates a landfill as part of its trash pickup services and public health responsibilities for its citizens. The government wants to limit the landfill deliveries to local haulers only.

This simple scenario may involve various administrative and political concerns, and there are a number of legal issues as well. This scenario involves local governmental authority expressed in state law. It involves issues of state or local regulations. It also involves questions regarding hazardous waste disposal that are categorized under environmental laws. These areas seem to be clear enough. Yet this situation also involves constitutional issues that were raised in a series of cases. In an article in *Public Administration Review*, O'Leary (1997) explained the Supreme Court has held that to limit landfill access to only local haulers violates the U.S. Constitution commerce clause because trash was related to interstate transportation.

Suppose a student wanted to follow up on the O'Leary article and learn more about the general law relating to local governments or environmental law, or suppose a student wants to learn more about employment or labor law. There are general legal materials that give overviews of law and provide references and citations to other materials. What if the student wanted to look up these cases O'Leary discussed to see if there were more recent cases on this topic? What if a student wants to review other cases or statutes that are mentioned in books or articles? How is this done? Some strategies to locate sources or conduct more specific searches are discussed below.

For the trash hauling scenario, overviews of the law relating to local government regulation of health, safety, and welfare, including trash pickup and landfills, may be of interest. A good starting place is to go to a law library and use a legal encyclopedia to get a general overview of law. The two general legal encyclopedias are *American Jurisprudence* (2005) or *Corpus Juris Secundum* (Mack and Kiser, 2005) (commonly called AmJur and CJS, respectively). Both encyclopedias give overviews of law and may provide references to cases from individual states. They take slightly different approaches; CJS provides general information about the established law and AmJur provides more information for litigation. Both are published by West and use the Key Number® classification and cross-referencing system. West is now the major publisher for legal materials. Using its key number system gives access to materials in digests, annotations, and cases, and it is an important locator tool in legal research.

Beginning with an encyclopedia can inform a student about the settled substantive law. It can give a researcher insight into the way law is categorized, indexed, and classified. It can inform a student of legal terminology as well. Like many professions, law has its distinct language and terms; because legal research involves so many technical terms an essential reference tool is a legal dictionary.

Other general law library sources include specialized multivolume treatises that explain an area of law and provide references that help locate more specific source materials. There are treatises on many areas including local government, environmental, employment, tax, administrative law and other topics. Three other types of overview materials may be helpful: restatements of law, hornbooks, and uniform laws. The restatements and hornbooks are used by law students because they summarize established common law doctrine in areas such as property, contracts, and torts. Uniform laws have been developed by committees of lawyers for states to adopt. There are also many law review journals that include articles related to a research interest; law review articles include analysis, explanation, and normative positions or advocacy regarding legal and policy concerns.

There are other helpful books that contain concise overviews of legal areas that are developed for students and the general public. These range from the West "Nutshell Series" that are often used by law students to the NOLO publications that are written to help the general public handle legal matters. For instance, there is a *Legal Research in a Nutshell* (Cohen and Olson, 2003). There are books providing greater detail on legal research and analysis. Some university and law school Web pages provide information on legal research, and there are a number of Web pages of differing quality that provide information on law.

12.6   STATUTORY PROVISIONS AND ENACTED LAW

Policy is enacted through legislation and rules, and policy may be found in administrative interpretation of legislation. There may be questions of constitutional authority and the constitutional text. Thus locating applicable provisions of enacted law may be part of a research strategy. Most enacted laws are codified, but other information may be contained in the session laws. Consider the following: Although many are familiar with the concept of equal opportunity in employment either as commonly understood or as explained in public personnel texts, a student may wish to research how equal opportunity policy originated and evolved. There are many legal sources that may be useful for this problem. The research strategy may include reading the executive orders, attorney general opinions, and legislation that used the term "equal opportunity." Even after finding these sources, a researcher may want to locate and read cases that have considered "equal opportunity" in specific contexts to understand the different ways the term has been presented by litigants and to understand how the courts have applied the term.

One starting point to locate legislation online is USA.gov. This general portal has links to many federal and state Web sites that may include current legislation, statutes, and constitutions. A quick visit to this site shows there is enormous variability of what is available. Recent bills and acts can be found on Congressional Web pages–which is the Library of Congress Thomas site [http://thomas.loc.gov/]. One caution, "recent" usually means within the last three years. Another source of Federal codified statutes is at the site of the Office of the Law Revision Counsel [http://uscode.house.gov/]. Both of these federal sites can be searched using general and advance search strategies.

Finding statutes on the Web may not be the most efficient or effective research approach, especially if there is a common phrase used as the primary search term. Even when the section of statute can be directly located, the result may be misleading if the researcher does not consider the broader chapter in the code. One problem of searching online is that it may be difficult to read the entire statute because many Web-based statutes often display only one small section, and they are not constructed to browse through preceding and succeeding sections or subsections of a chapter. It is possible to browse federal statutes on the Office of the Law Revision Counsel site. The useful annotations to statutes are compiled by private publishers and so they are not available on free Web sites.

Using statute books has advantages. It is easy to see how the titles are organized: for instance, Title 42 in the U.S. Code includes Public Health Safety and Welfare Section 1983 included in Chapter 22, Civil Rights. Thus, the interrelated chapters and sections may be easier to understand in bound volumes. The typical format for a chapter in codified statutes includes a statement of public purpose of the act in the first section; this is followed by a definition section and then a number of substantive sections of the act. Reviewing or skimming the chapter may provide helpful and essential information in understanding the section. In the American system, interpreting a statute is not limited simply to reading one section of a statute, but includes considering other sections of title or chapter. Skimming neighboring sections of the statute may reveal other relevant portions of the law.

A visit to a law library to use annotated statutes provides a wealth of information and cross-references. The entire set is available and so it is easy to move between sections. The information contained in an annotated statute book includes: (1) the legislative history of when the law was passed or amended and often a reference to the page in the session law volume; (2) references to catalog cross-reference system such as West Key Numbers; (3) references to authoritative law review articles; (4) annotations or articles in other legal works such as encyclopedias; (5) indexes with categories for cases; and (6) abstracts of cases that considered the statute. Legal researchers also check the pocket parts of published volumes. Because statutes are often amended or revised, the publishers annually print "pocket parts" or paperback volumes that include updates in the laws and the annotations.

When a person knows the full citation, it is fairly easy to locate enacted statutes online; state and federal governments include statutes in their official Web pages. Sometimes statutes are also available on public access legal Web pages. Often there is a set of state and the federal codified statutes at the local library for larger cities and at college libraries. The noncodified statutes, such as session laws, can be found in law libraries. Law school libraries and State Supreme Court libraries often have statutes for all states. However, city or county ordinances and codes often are simply not available online. Sometimes they are not at a public library. It may take a few phone calls and a visit to City Hall or the city prosecutor's office to locate a copy of the city ordinances.

12.7 LOCATING A SPECIFIC CASE

Students may want to find a specific case. For instance, oftentimes there is a landmark opinion that is fairly well-known or influential cases are mentioned in textbooks. To understand the policy or administrative issues, a person will want to locate these decisions of the court. For instance, many know that *Brown v. Board of Education* is credited with prohibiting race-based discrimination in public schools. Perhaps a student wants to know more about the case because it was mentioned in a class or because a researcher read Henderson's *Public Administration Review* article (2004). Reading the decision may provide insight into: how the case came to the court; what the court Considered to be the legal issue; how the court rejected the precedent; how the court interpreted the Constitution as a source of policy; and how the court delayed providing a remedy until after another hearing. Supreme Court opinions are located in reports in a law library and on web sites.

Locating that decision online may not be as efficient as expected. Entering the phrase *Brown v. Board of Education* in a general Web browser will produce an enormous number of hits, so searching the U.S. Supreme Court's Web page may seem like a better strategy. From the Firstgov.gov portal, a person can go to the Federal Judiciary Page and then to the Supreme Court Page. After examining the official U.S. Supreme Court Web page a student will note that it is ineffectual resource because only recent cases are available here (from the last three years) and cases that are published in the official reports are not there. However, Supreme Court decisions are often available on other public access Web sites (such as Findlaw.com). Unfortunately, decisions from lower Federal Courts or States may not be as available on public access Web sites.

Consider this search example: The problem is how to find the *Brown v. Board of Education* case. One site in July, 2007 that allows searches for and displays of full text Supreme Court decisions is Findlaw. [http://www.findlaw.com/casecode/supreme.html]

Enter the search for "Brown v. Board" in the Party Name Search category.

This leads to the FindLaw page and comes up with the following results and links to the opinion for each citation. The following list includes the results from the party name search, but which one of these is the landmark decision?

Brown v. Board of Education, 344 U.S. 1 (1952)
Brown v. Board of Education, 344 U.S. 141 (1952)
Brown v. Board of Education, 347 U.S. 483 (1954)
Brown v. Board of Education, 349 U.S. 294 (1955)
Labor Board v. Brown, 380 U.S. 278 (1965)
South Carolina State Board of Education v. Brown, 393 U.S. 222 (1968)

In the above example the search results show multiple entries. It is common on a word search to get at least two citations for a case searching the parties' names for a Supreme Court case. This is because the first cite is normally the short opinion issued when the Supreme Court agreed to hear the case, or where the court granted certiorari. Connecting to the first case listed (344 U.S. 1) and reviewing the order shows that the case was not just an appeal of one case but that there were a number of appellate cases joined together under the heading *Brown v. Board of Education for Topeka*. The second citation for 1952 (344 U.S. 141) was on a procedural matter whether the State of Kansas would appear as a party. It is in the 1954 opinion that the court overruled the "separate but equal" doctrine of *Plessey v. Ferguson* (1896), and the court then continued the case to allow the parties time to brief and argue for a remedy. An opinion about the remedy is reported in the 1956 opinion. In short, all of the *Brown v. Board of Education* captioned cases included listed above are part of the famous controversy. A lawyer reading these cases would look for the legal issue, the existing precedent, and then the holding or the legal doctrine following from this case. Another point about the search results is that other cases fit the search criteria; the last two cases included both Brown and Board in the parties' names. This illustrates how search criteria sometimes produce irrelevant results.

Some of the public access legal Web browsers allow a person to search with more specific information, such as the citation or the date. The advantage is, of course, that it may produce the specific decision. In the above example, a narrow search would have missed the later consideration and decisions of the Supreme Court. For legal researchers, merely finding the one case is not seen as sufficient to consider whether the case is valid authority. Legal researchers also want to know if the decision was reconsidered, if it was overturned or modified. They want to know the controlling law and so they check Shepard's citators, as explained below.

12.8 LOCATING CASES REGARDING AN ISSUE

Often lawyers start with a question about whether some factual scenario is legal or if there is any law that affects a given situation. Then instead of starting with a section of a statute or a lead case, the researcher must locate applicable law. Finding relevant statutes may require checking numerous terms and browsing through sections of the statute book. Using a general resource like an encyclopedia or treatise may provide cases that seem to be old. However, the citation to an old case often means the decision is the best presentation of the legal doctrine; this means the case has an established and enduring precedent, not that it is outdated. The next step to finding relevant case law in a library involves searching by topic using digests, which are multivolume series of abstracts organized by jurisdiction and topics.

Finding common law precedent involves a search strategy of defining the issue within existing categories and using finding aides called digests. Each state and federal jurisdiction has individual digests. Digests catalog and summarize cases. Like legal encyclopedias, there are chapters and titles and subject headings. Individual cases are summarized in headnotes that provide a partial case abstract regarding a narrow legal issue. Headnotes are editorial materials and they are not legally binding; they are, instead, finding aides to locate applicable cases. The dominant classification for digests is the West Key Numbers.

The publishers of reporters include editorial materials along with the official case opinion that may be useful for understanding the law or finding additional materials. Editorial materials include a "syllabus" which is a summary of the entire opinion. There are headnotes for issues included in the case and there is often information about the parties, the lawyers representing them and the judges that heard the case. None of this material is part of the official opinion, but the syllabus can be helpful in skimming the case for relevance, and the headnotes serve as a way to locate other cases in the digests.

Legal researchers can scan the digests and case summaries for possible primary and secondary source materials. Primary materials are the cases that can serve as binding legal authority; primary cases are from the jurisdiction where the dispute arose, or from courts that govern the issues in the dispute; sometimes this can be federal, state, or both. If a case is from a court outside the jurisdiction, it is secondary authority, meaning that at best the opinion is advisory. The search then turns to reading the cases to locate decisions that address the same facts or the same legal issues, or both. Lawyers first carefully read the cases and statutes, and then they will determine what authority is most pertinent to the situation. If a case is located for the jurisdiction that has the same facts and legal issue, then it is controlling. But often a search results with either the facts or legal issue being different. Then the process of reasoning by analogy is used to make comparisons to the similarities and differences. The most relevant and pertinent cases are then included as authority either to advise a client or as part of a legal argument before a court. When advice is given to a client it may be in the form of a written memorandum or opinion. Typically, the controlling law and legal authority are included in a motion or brief to the court.

12.9   CONTROLLING LAW

For lawyers, legal research is not simply locating one source such as a section of an act or one landmark case. Instead, the search is first to locate relevant law and then to continue the search to establish that in the dynamic legal environment no amendments or court interpretations have superceded the statute and that no relevant case interpretation has overridden, distinguished, or modified the legal doctrine. Lawyers talk about this as "making sure that the case or statute is still good law." The concern in law for jurisdiction and primary sources are a search for the controlling authority. When courts in another jurisdiction have considered the same factual and legal issue, the decision is only advisory for legal research purposes.

In addition to locating cases through statutory annotations and from digests, legal researchers also use commercial citators both to determine if a case is still valid and to provide a resource to locate other cases. Shepard's is the dominant publisher of these citator services and conducting a citation search is called "Shepardizing." Shepard's compiles and updates citations to cases in an abbreviated and distinctive style. At the beginning of each volume of Shepard's includes the key and codes and it explains how to use the citation. The Shepard citators are arranged by the volume, reporter, and page number. The referenced case is identified by the parties' names, e.g., *Brown v. Board of Education*, and then it is followed by a list of truncated citations that only include the volume, reporter abbreviation and page. The information for the referenced case begins with parallel citations to where the same case was published in other reporters, and then it will include citations of case history for the same case, which explains (in code) if the same case has been appealed or reconsidered. These case history citations are followed by cites to law review articles or annotations, and then there are lists of other cases that cite a portion of the opinion. Searching a citator service or Shepard's will reveal if a case is overturned, distinguished, followed or broadly cited. There are series of Shepard's organized by reporter. There are Shepard's citations for Federal statutes and rules. Although there may be a short lag in the printed volume from the online subscription services, Shepard's also keeps current through pocket parts and paperback volumes.

12.10   ITERATIVE PROCESS AND INTERPRETATION

In legal research, the evaluation of published cases—normally appellate legal decisions—involves, separation of factual situation and legal discussion. It is essential to know the legal context and general framework. Then there is a search for the controlling law. The process is interpretive and iterative. The legal opinion has consequences as well. The facts are distinctive to the individual parties of the dispute and the question of law raised by the parties result in a decision. Thus the purpose of every legal decision is neither scholarly nor hypothetical. It involves making a choice between competing parties that often have persuasive arguments supported by legal doctrine. Yet once the court issues a decision, it applies to the general public until it is overturned by statute or by case law: this is precedent.

The research strategies used in law involve an iterative process of searching multiple sources both for the controlling authority—the relevant law—and also to determine that this controlling authority has not been modified or replaced. The possibility of overlapping authority between

Federal and state laws is often a consideration in legal research. All these complexities result in lawyers often issuing legal opinions of what is legal and what is not settled law. For government, the legal opinions issued by the Attorney General interpreting a legal situation are binding. These opinions also may explain the appropriate administrative procedure. These opinions are resources for researchers interested in bureaucracy or policy development.

Since there are a number of possible sources of authority—cases, statutes, and rules—the legal research norm involves checking and cross checking materials. Doing the legal research in a law library can be an advantage of pulling books and comparing the different sections or the different cases. Because many of the finding aids online are expensive, a trip to a law library may suit a student budget better.

When lawyers read cases, they are attentive to the legal issue or issues in the case, the court's explanation or rationale that includes precedent and authority to consider the issue, and to the holding which is the authoritative statement of the law of the case. Within a decision by the court, there may be "orbiter dictum" or discussion and analysis by the judge that is not essential for the legal resolution of the case. However, for social scientists and historians, the facts of a case and the dictum may provide important insights about government actions and services, about what issues judges consider important, about conflicting values, and about societal attitudes.

12.11 LEGAL SOURCES AS DATA

In social science research, the use of case study is often used to understand a situation or a social construct. So the questions may be: what is the story and what does it mean? Supreme Court decisions may be used as the factual basis for this type of analysis and discussion. At other times, case studies are used to probe situations, and a selection of published cases may be data regarding similar situations. Locating and comparing cases from several states or different courts may provide insights. Management cases are used in public administration to analyze decision making and using a published court opinion may provide an alternative view of decision making practices and priorities.

Legal sources may be considered part of the data for a study that includes either qualitative or quantitative approaches to research. As the earlier discussion and examples demonstrate, it is more common to use appellate cases and legal materials in a qualitative manner. Public policy or management articles may focus on how a landmark case affects administrators or imposes obligations on them (see, Frederickson, 1990; Rosenbloom and O'Leary, 1997; and Rosenbloom, 2000). This narrative and interpretive approach is common. Sometimes a legal decision emphasizes the importance of public management practices rather than considering the legal holding in a case. For example, Grumet (1982) discussed the impact of a case where individual residents cannot sue regarding nursing home licensing and instead regulators are expected to protect the interest of the public and residents. In this article, the obligations and responsibilities of the regulators towards the public was left to agency determination.

There are also qualitative and statistical analyses of data from agency enforcement actions or from trial court cases involving government. In evaluating litigation there can be a number of elements to consider: the parties involved, the legal rulings from the judge, and the final decision in the case. Occasionally, trial court cases or administrative complaints are the data used in a research design that has a large enough sample for quantitative analysis. These are complaints which are at the fact-finding level, rather than an analysis of appellate decisions, codified statutes, or rules. For example, changes in the number and types of Equal Employment Opportunity Commission (EEOC) discrimination complaints have been studied (Meier, Pennington, and Eller, 2005). Another example is how regulatory hearings process and petitions for permits were analyzed relating to staff recommendations and public participation (Rosener, 1982).

Research using data from the hearing (or fact-finding) level involves an understanding of legal practice, procedure, and terminology. There are two general models that can be used to consider legal situations or materials as data for analysis. The first situation may involve selecting a number of cases from examining the dockets of cases at an agency enforcement level or court trial level. In an example of this type of research, Rosener (1982) considered a group of petitions before the hearing board through the entire decision process. The analysis considered petitions, staff reports, public hearings, public participation, and reported outcomes. To conduct this sort of research, there may be limited types of material that are available to the general public; the researcher often needs the access to documents controlled by an agency, and although, in theory, these are public documents, often matters of litigation or enforcement can be kept confidential under open records of laws until the dispute is resolved. Thus, cooperation with an agency may be a necessary prerequisite to study, and to gain access there may be conditions imposed on the researcher.

Second, although many hearings may be "on the record" this does not mean that the records are maintained in a manner that is amenable to study. Hearings on the record may mean that the hearing was tape-recorded and the tape was kept only until the period for an appeal lapsed. A hearing on the record at a court trial often means that a court recorder is taking shorthand of the proceedings, but these notes are only transcribed if a party pays for them. Transcripts may be prepared for appeals, but as a matter of course, these are not produced. Finally, a research must go to the court or agency of record to gain access to these materials.

Studying the number of complaints filed regarding a particular action or activity may be difficult. In looking at cases where a government is sued, the cases are brought against a particular official, so when someone is aggrieved about Social Security benefits, they sue Secretary Shalala or Secretary Bowen. This can make tracking down cases difficult. Second, under rules of pleadings, a complaint must include a general statement of the claim, the facts that support it and the relief requested. This means the allegations can be general and this may make it difficult to trace and code from the time of the complaint to the termination of the case. The legal stage of gathering evidence and data is called discovery, but most of the information gathered is exchanged between parties and is not kept in the court files and there is no public access.

Following a complaint through to a clear resolution of the case may be difficult as well. It can take years for civil trial case to go from the date of filing to the verdict from the jury or judge. Cases may be dismissed for technical reasons (e.g., filed too late) or by agreement of the parties. Courts often encourage settlements. Learning the resolution of settlements can be difficult because parties often agree to confidential agreements or settle without admission of liability. Thus, the ability to present a clear conclusion of winning or losing may be troublesome. Obtaining and interpreting the legal data requires careful planning and execution in the research design.

A second type of in-depth study concerns how litigation may affect the management of public programs. Although it is often noted that court decrees add expenses to the budgets, it is less often recognized that there is an underlying problem of governance that leads to finding of negligence or failure to follow the law before a remedy was imposed. Some of the most difficult cases have been where courts have supervised administrative processes to alleviate past discrimination. In an exceptional and impressive study of the networks, the problems, and judicial management of public services, Wise and O'Leary (2003) included interviews, court documents, public records, budgets, and student performance. The methods and legal resource materials used in this study are worth systematically evaluation (or deconstruction) to show how qualitative and legal sources can be integrated into a study of policy and management.

12.12 CONCLUSION

Legal research methods are closely linked to a profession, but they are also relevant and important to governance. Lawyers are trained in locating and analyzing legal materials. The information in a judicial decision does relate to development of law, and the tradition judges use is to educate and explain their reasoning through the rationale in the decision. Lawyers are schooled on how to distinguish the legal issue from the irrelevant language—the orbiter dicta. They read and interpret statutes and rules according to the conventions judges require in court cases. Judges expect administrators to act within the law and to make efforts to understand the law. Legal research skills aid in finding these legal authorities.

The public understanding of law is often different from lawyers. Often it is the story of what happened or the drama of who won that is reported in the press. The dicta may be quoted and remembered because it includes a pithy quote, like Justice Potter Stewart's concurring opinion discussing how difficult it is to define hard core pornography, by saying "I shall not today attempt further to define the kinds of material I understand to be embraced within that shorthand description; and perhaps I could never succeed in intelligibly doing so. But I know it when I see it, and the motion picture involved in this case is not that." (*Jacobellis v. Ohio*, 378 U.S. 184, 197 (1964)). Balancing this common sense understanding to the requirements of legal interpretation is a challenge in public policy and public management.

Administrators and legislators may be faced with defining terms, interpreting, and applying policy. How law is used and affects administrators is an interesting and important part of governance. Including legal resource materials as part of research design for public management and public policy considerations provides depth. Legal research techniques and resources can provide data, concepts, contexts, and insight into policy and administration. In conclusion, understanding legal research skills and practices can provide valuable information in designing and conducting research about governance.

EXERCISES

1. Consider what information is available on the U.S. Supreme Court's official Web page
   A. What information is available for the most recent term Supreme Court Term at their official site? [http://www.supremecourtus.gov/opinions/opinions.html]
      (a) list of cases
      (b) schedule of arguments and decisions
      (c) briefs
   B. For the Supreme Court how many years of decisions are available on this site? Is it more or less than the last 3 years?
2. Locating federal statute by a phrase
   A. If you search the Office of Law Revision Counsel [http://uscode.house.gov/] for the phrase "equal opportunity" how many documents do you think you will locate?
      (a) fewer than 200
      (b) between 200–500
      (c) between 500–1000
      (d) more than 5000
   Even reviewing 200 documents can be time-consuming, and so developing and using a search strategy that is more specific, or relates to a specific act saves time. (7992 documents were found when the search was conducted in July, 2007.)
3. Access to the local laws
   A. Locate your city's Web page and look for the following information: Is the text of city charter available online? Are the local ordinances available online? Or is there information on the city's Web site that says where the printed versions can be found?
   B. Locate your public library's Web page. Conduct a search to see if the City Ordinances are available in print at the main branch.
4. What legal decisions are discussed in your text books? Can you locate copies of these on line? Are they still valid precedent?

REFERENCES

American jurisprudence: A modern comprehensive text statement of American law, State, and Federal, 2nd ed. 2005. St. Paul, Minnesota: West Publishing.

Beckett, J. 2000. The government should run like a business mantra. *The American Review of Public Administration, 30,* 185–204.

Bertelli, A.M. 2004. Strategy and accountability: Structural reform litigation and public management. *Public Administration Review, 42,* 28–42.

Bluebook: A uniform system of citation, 18th ed. 2005. Cambridge, Massachusetts: Harvard Law Review Association.

Carnevale, D.G. 1993. Root dynamics of alternative dispute resolution: An illustrative case in the U.S. Postal Service. *Public Administration Review, 53,* 455–461.

Cohen, M.L. and Olson, K.C. 2003. *Legal research in a nutshell, 8th ed.* St. Paul, Minnesota: Thomson/West.

DeHart-Davis, L. and Bozeman, B. 2001. Regulatory compliance and air quality permitting: Why do firms overcomply? *Journal of Public Administration Research, 11,* 471–508.

Derthick, M.A. 2005. *Up in Smoke: From Legislation to Litigation in Tobacco Politics, 2nd ed.* Washington, DC: CQ Press.

Frederickson, H.G. 1990. Public administration and social equity. *Public Administration Review, 50,* 228–237.

Green, R.T. 2001. Common law, equity, and public administration. *The American Review of Public Administration, 32,* 263–294.

Grumet, B.S. 1982. Who is "due" process? *Public Administration Review, 42,* 321–326.

Harlow v. Fitzgerald, 457 U.S. 800, 1982.

Henderson, L.J. Jr. 2004. *Brown v. Board of Education* at 50: The multiple legacies for policy and administration. *Public Administration Review, 64,* 270–274.

Jacobellis v. Ohio, 378 U.S. 184, 1964.

Kagan, R.A. 1991. Adversarial legalism and American government. *Journal of Policy Analysis and Management, 10,* 369–406.

Lee, Yong, S. 2004. The judicial theory of a reasonable public servant. *Public Administration Review, 64,* 425–437.

Mack, W. and Kiser, D.J. 2005. *Corpus juris secundum: A complete restatement of the entire American law as developed by all reported cases* [1658 to date]. St. Paul, Minnesota: West Publishing.

Meier, K.J., Pennington, M.S., and Eller, W.S. 2005. Race, sex, and Clarence Thomas: Representation and change in the EEOC. *Public Administration Review, 65,* 171–179.

O'Leary, R. 1997. Trash talk: The Supreme Court and the interstate transportation of waste. *Public Administration Review, 57,* 281–284.

Plessey v. Ferguson, 163 U.S. 537, 1896.

Rosenbloom, D.H. 2000. Retrofitting the administrative state to the Constitution: Congress and the Judiciary's twentieth-century progress. *Public Administration Review, 60,* 39–46.

Rosenbloom, D.H. and O'Leary, R. 1997. *Public Administration and Law, 2nd ed.* New York: Marcel Dekker.

Rosenbloom, D.H., Carroll, J.D., and Carroll, J.D. 2000. *Constitutional Competence for Public Managers: Cases and Commentary.* Itasca, Illinois: F.E. Peacock Publishers.

Rosener, J.B. 1982. Making bureaucrats responsive: A study on the impact of citizen participation and staff recommendations on regulatory decision making. *Public Administration Review, 42,* 339–345.

Saxton, G.D., Hoene, C.W., and Erie, S.P. 2002. Fiscal constraints and the loss of home rule: The long term impacts of California's Proposition 13 fiscal regime. *The American Review of Public Administration, 32,* 423–454.

Schuck, P.H. 1983. *Suing Government: Citizen Remedies for Official Wrongs.* New Haven, Connecticut: Yale University Press.

Shapiro, S. 2002. Speed bumps and roadblocks: Procedural controls and regulatory change. *Journal of Public Administration Research, 12,* 29–58.

United States Code Annotated. (2002, as amended). St. Paul, Minnesota: West Publishing.

West, W. 1982. The politics of administrative rulemaking. *Public Administration Review, 42,* 420–426.

West, W. 2005. Administrative rulemaking: An old and emerging literature. *Public Administration Review, 65,* 655–668.

Wise, C.R. and O'Leary, R. 2003. Breaking up is hard to do: The dissolution of judicial supervision of public services. *Public Administration Review, 63,* 177–191.

Part III

Measurement and Data Collection

13 Describing and Measuring Phenomena in Public Administration

Lung-Teng Hu and Dorothy Olshfski

CONTENTS

Measurement plays an important part in the work of both practitioners and researchers in public administration. As managers, we know that the portion of the work that is measured is the portion of the work that gets attended to. As researchers, especially those using a quantitative design, we know that the first consideration in any evaluation of our work is the appropriateness of the measures used in the research. What we choose to measure illustrates what is valued in a particular situation. So measurement is a particularly important consideration because it captures the assumptions made by both practitioner and researcher about what really matters in the managerial activity or the research effort.

This chapter discusses the important issues surrounding measurement itself. First, we will examine the grouping of variables into constructs which is the way that abstract concepts are operationalized. Then, the central methodological considerations of validity and reliability will be examined, followed by other secondary considerations that impact measurement. Finally, we offer some suggestions for designing good measures.

13.1 FUNDAMENTAL CONCERNS IN MEASUREMENT

13.1.1 OPERATIONALIZATION

The primary concern of measurement is to transform the abstract concepts that we attempt to examine in public administration into measurable constructs or variables. This transformation is called operationalization. Some things are easily measured. Demographic variables are used many times in social science research as independent variables. Gender, age, race, education level, and income level appear to be easy to measure, and sometimes they even are so. But consider race as a variable; is race a self-reported variable or is it a scientific question that is answered by genetic or genealogical analysis? Even variables that seem easy to measure can sometimes be tricky. How central the variable is to your analysis will determine how specific or precise the method to elicit that variable must be.

Grouping variables into a manageable data set require that the analysis identifies acceptable groups. For example, income can be grouped as under $50,000 and over $50,000 and that would be appropriate in some instances. But other times a more gradated scale would be more useful: less than $15,000, between $15,001 and $25,000, between $25,001 and $35,000, and so on. Again, whether the researcher uses dichotomous variables or a gradated scale depends upon the question under analysis and how important the variable is to answering the research question. On the other hand, it is prudent to gather finer gradations in data early because categories can be collapsed later if a more refined listing of the variable becomes unnecessary.

However, much research is concerned with concepts that are not easily measured with a single question. Important public administration concepts such as organizational culture, trust, commitment, or prejudice are not readily captured. In these cases, measurement attempts to grasp the underlying unobservable concept by substituting observable attitudes or behaviors that are associated with the concept under study (Carmines and Zeller, 1979; Guion, 1980). Thus, the concept must be defined operationally in terms of observable attitudes or behaviors. An operational definition of an attitudinal concept is usually based on the subject's response to a number of questions designed to tap the variable under study (Sirkin, 1995). These questions are then combined to form an index or a scale.

And here, some concepts that require a surrogate measure are sometimes simple to operationalize. Speed is captured by miles per hour or keyboarding facility is measured by words per minute. Sometimes, a vague concept could be captured by a simplified measure. The National Election Studies constantly track Americans' political trust by asking a single question: "How much of the time do you think you can trust the government in Washington to do what is right?" Sometimes, it is more difficult: quality health care might be captured by mortality rates, access to a professional in a timely manner, number of patients per health care professional, infant mortality, and the list goes on. But with the problematic health care measurement example as with many other elusive concepts, our efforts frequently fall short. Quality health care has so many characteristics largely dependent upon who is being asked that it is unlikely that a mutually agreed upon group of variables will be accepted by everyone. Nurses, doctors, administrators, and patients each have distinct definitions of quality care (Puran, 2004). Ultimately, the researcher decides what variables to include. The list of selected variables that compose the concept is called the construct. The choice of variables used to operationalize the concept serves as the basis for evaluating its validity. The key question is: does the construct measures what it is supposed to measure? Or rather, is it a valid construct?

13.1.2 VALIDITY

Validity of measurement means that the manner used by the researcher to capture the concept under investigation truly captures that concept. Or, is the researcher measuring what is said to be measured? Validity is a slippery measurement requirement because there is no lists of criteria, if fulfilled, guarantee validity for a concept (Cunningham and Olshfski, 1985).

If the concept itself can only be captured by identifying quantifiable attitudes or behaviors in the environment that accompany that concept, some important considerations may be neglected because the behaviors or attitudes may not be easily seen or reported. For example, if the measurement of corruption only includes number of public officials charged with a violation, then the researcher would be missing all those who have not been caught. In fact it might be that the more corrupt the system, the fewer the number of captured violators so that less corrupt states may, in fact, have more captured violators. The validity of the measure (convictions) would be critical in this situation in determining whether the measure is of any use. Validity can be evaluated in different ways: face validity, content validity, criterion validity, construct validity, predictive validity, and concurrent validity.

Face validity focuses on the extent to which knowledgeable individuals would agree that the measure adequately captures the concept under examination (Sirkin, 1995). It is a largely subjective validity measure as it only asks whether the scale or index makes sense to an outside observer.

Content validity, also called logical validity, involves a more careful definition of the domain of behaviors or attitudes to be measured by a test, and seeks to ensure that all the important items that make up the concept under review are included in the measure (Allen and Yen, 1979). Content validity is widely used in psychology and education. The pertinent question is: is the measure internally complete and consistent? Here, the researcher is concerned that the content of measurement definitely reflects the domain that is to be measured or tested. A test to determine who is to be promoted on a police force is content-valid if the test items cover the full range of knowledge that a qualified police officer needs to know to adequately function in that position. Researcher judgment plays the most important part in determining face validity and content validity. They are more subjective and less empirical than the type of validity to be discussed next.

Criterion validity focuses on the ability to demonstrate a significant correlation between the measure being used by the researcher and objective measures of the concept. This type of validity can be further divided into concurrent validity and predictive validity. For example, criterion validity demands that the standardized tests used for university admission, such as the SAT or GRE, be correlated with the students' performance in the program. The tests will have concurrent validity if the association is made in the present time but not necessarily with the same groupings of individuals: entering students with high scores are judged positively because most graduating students who had high test scores performed well in their programs. Predictive validity allows the passage of time to factor into the criterion validity considerations, did the students who scored well on the SATs or GREs upon entering the program actually perform well in their programs? With predictive validity, the problem is finding an acceptable criterion that is not contaminated by other factors that will occur over time. Criterion-related validity may not be applied to all measurement procedures in social science, as not every abstract concept has an appropriate criterion for assessing a measure of it (Carmines and Zeller, 1979).

Construct validity is concerned with the ability of the measure to work well within the theoretical demands of the researcher's model (Sirkin, 1995). Construct validity demands that the construct (the scale or the index) be successfully used to generate predictions in accordance with theoretical expectation, not only by the initial investigator but also by others who are examining similar activities or events. For example, does the conservatism scale under examination accurately predict to an individual's attitude toward gun control, but does it also predict to the individual's attitude toward abortion? If it does, the construct gains supportive evidence of having construct validity. Establishing construct validity for a measure requires a pattern of consistent findings involving different researchers using the same measure but employing different theoretical structures across a number of different studies. Carmines and Zeller (1979, p. 23) suggested three steps to establish construct validity: (1) specify the theoretical relationship between measured concepts, (2) examine the empirical relationship between the measures of concepts, and (3) interpret the empirical evidence and demonstrate the extent to which the theoretical relationship between the concepts is demonstrated by the measures. But additionally, point to other research findings that support the findings of the present study. The establishment of construct validity is theory-driven.

Criterion validity and construct validity are not judgment based and can be empirically tested using techniques that measure association and correlation. The different measures of validity answer different parts of the question "does it measure what it is supposed to measure?" Judgment based validity measures are important for determining the integrity of the concept: is the operationalization of the construct complete and thorough? The empirically tested measures of validity look to the internal construction of the construct and ask whether it is internally consistent and does it satisfy theoretical predictions. However, just because a measure is valid that does not necessarily mean that it is reliable.

13.1.3 Reliability

A measure is reliable if it consistently produces the same results over repeated tests and it is free of measurement errors. Reliability has two components: test–retest reliability and internal consistency. Test–retest reliability measures the consistency of an individual's response to a test over time. If the same group of people takes the same test at two different times and the results of the tests do not change, then the test–retest reliability requirement is satisfied. Vague or ambiguous wording of questions may be the cause of an unsatisfactory result. The internal consistency of a measure focuses on whether the items that make up the construct are all getting at some overall aspect of the construct being measured. The way to gauge this reliability measure is to divide in half the items used to construct an index or scale, score the subsections of the measure, and then correlate the results. If the individual scores positively on one subset of the test, he or she should also score positively on the other subset. Clarity and specificity are the strongest supports for a reliable measurement instrument. Babbie (2003) has pointed out a tension between reliability and validity. The specificity required of reliability sometimes overshadows validity concerns and robs concepts of their "richness of meaning."

13.2 OTHER CONSIDERATIONS CONCERNING MEASUREMENT

The ranking of criteria to evaluate a choice of measurement strategy will be different for the academic (who is concerned with elaborating on theory) and the practitioner (who is concerned with performance of the governmental unit). Validity and reliability are of major concern to each, but both researchers and practitioners have other considerations in their choice of measures.

Accuracy: The truthfulness of the respondents and the care taken to record the data into a useable format focus attention on accuracy. Reliability does not insure accuracy. Careful attention to detail, both in question design and data entry, helps ensure that accurate information is elicited and recorded.

Precision: The degree of refinement and exactness of the measure refers to precision. The social science requirements for precision are not as high as in the physical sciences. The math must be precise if aiming a rocket at Saturn because a thousandth of an inch may mean the difference between hitting the target and sailing through space forever. Clearly defining poverty is a less precise activity, but a consideration nonetheless.

Cost: All research activities have a cost associated with them. In most situations, the cost considerations are money and time. Limitations imposed by time and money usually require the researcher to make trade-offs among data collection methods, sample size, and method of data analysis. Furthermore, the target of your measurement activities also will consider the cost of complying with the measurement request. From the researchers' standpoint, questionnaire length will influence response rate: a long involved questionnaire may elicit a low response. The practitioner should consider how the measurement activity fits within the normal work load of the participating employee; extended measurement requirements superimposed on a normal work day may reduce compliance. And the practitioner should also consider the cost of not conducting research into productivity, customer satisfaction, or efficiency because documenting success can have a positive impact on funding, accountability, and performance.

Timeliness: Most important to the practitioner, but also a consideration to the researcher, is measuring the behavior or activity being examined at a time when it will be of most use to those using the analysis. Timeliness is complicated by the amount of time it takes to get the measure designed and tested before any application of the measure is possible.

Simplicity or parsimony: The measurement of a concept should be understandable to the audience. A short statement of expected cause and effect is preferable to a long extended discourse about the research plan. The easier it is to understand the measurement activity, the easier it will be to communicate the measurement process and the results of that process to the target audience. And the easier it will be to elicit compliance with the request for completing the test.

Ease of execution: The issue of ease of execution considers not only the cost of measuring, but also the convenience of the respondents in using the measuring instrument. If the measuring instrument is complicated to understand, difficult to use and answer, or hard to explain, then the respondents may either misunderstand the questions in the instrument, or withhold their cooperation.

Utility: The measurement activity should be undertaken for a good reason and that reason should be communicated to the subjects of the measurement. For practitioners this is particularly important, because many times measurement is directed by legislation or another outside agency, so the linkage between compliance and enhanced productivity may not be obvious. The researcher must be concerned that those who are the recipients of the request for data are convinced that the purpose or potential outcome of the project is worth their efforts.

13.3   DESIGNING GOOD MEASURES IN PUBLIC ADMINISTRATION

There is no perfect measure. And given that the goals of public programs are generally vague, multi-faceted, sometimes contradictory, and without agreement among the stakeholders involved in the process, it is not surprising that the process of measuring attitudes, behaviors, outcomes, efficiencies, performance, and so on is complicated.

Yet, we offer some basic considerations regarding measurement that will be helpful in designing good measures.

No single instrument can tell the whole story. Because the research questions that are important to public administration are complex, not easily manipulated, and in some cases not subject to direct observation, there is no best and perfect measuring instrument. Every data collection strategy and every measurement design have its own strengths and limitations. Almost any discovery identified by any single measurement only depicts parts of the whole picture. Having several sets of measures is a safer way to proceed. Triangulation is the use of several different research methods to examine the same phenomenon, and it is a very valuable research strategy.

Consider the task of measuring the effectiveness of a single secondary school: test scores are a convenient measure but they only portray one aspect of schooling. Other measures to consider would be the satisfaction of the stakeholders (the students, parents, taxpayers, and teachers), organizational climate measures including an examination of the physical plant, and success rate of the students as they continued with their education. And even with these diverse measures we would still be missing some other ingredients that create a really good school, like, athletic activities open to all students, the presence of diversity among the students and staff, access to state supported meals for qualified students, and the availability of programs that cultivate creativity and stimulate curiosity. A single instrument will only give you one slice of the reality that you are examining.

The design of the measurement instrument should be problem- or purpose-driven rather than instrument-driven. The research question is the primary consideration in determining what research strategy to employ. The method should be appropriate to the question, it should be cognizant of the level of analysis, and the researcher has a duty to explain the fit between the research question, the data, and the method of analysis (Wright, Manigault, and Black 2004). Using a survey questionnaire with scales to see the success of a homelessness project may be problematic because the core issue of such project is the behavior change of homeless people as well as the burden reduction for their families. Tracing the behavioral adaptation of the homeless and their families is certainly a more difficult project than simply administering a questionnaire survey to public officials. But for the results to be meaningful the measuring tool must be able to capture the intricacies of the problem being studied.

The instrument may be valid and reliable but it may be directed at solving the wrong problem. A type III error is solving the wrong problem. Managerial problems are largely defined by the person in the position to focus the attention of those involved in the situation. In this way, managerial problems are subjective; they are only a problem if they are identified as such. It is the researcher's task to portray the significance of the problem to the readers and to argue that out of all the problems that could be identified as the one that requires redress; this is the problem that demands attention. And the measurement instrument being used is the correct one to focus on the problem. Cost–benefit analysis is a well-developed method for assessing value in the workplace; however, it would be a misuse to apply that tool to measure the impact of a workplace diversity program. The impact of a diversity program which aims at the values of fairness and equity may not be suited to a comparison of costs (calculable) to benefits (largely unclarified).

Measure twice; cut one. Measuring is costly, time-consuming, and troublesome. Before the activity begins, make sure that the instrument is not flawed. Pretest the instrument before the actual study begins. The test might have all kinds of problems and they will not be apparent until the test is taken for a practice run. Problems that a pretest might discover are: unclear directions, an unmanageable time requirements, confusing choices for the test-taker, ambiguous question construction, or unnecessary overlap among the elements of the test.

13.3.1 Some Practical Strategies

Here, we elaborate some practical strategies regarding measurement design for both the practitioner and researcher in public administration. The practical strategy, RESULTS, is listed below:

Refine (R): As the purposes of public programs are quite vague, ambiguous, even conflicting, before starting any measurement and evaluation design, it is critically important to keep refining the evaluation purpose, study intention, and problems or questions that are the subject of the inquiry. Given the interest in the effect of privatization on improvement in government productivity, for example, the research question concerned with governments' investments in contract-management capacity and its consequences (Brown and Potoski, 2003) is certainly more specific and manageable than merely considering the effectiveness of contracting-out strategy on governmental cost saving. The more specific the problem or question is, the easier it will be for the researcher to proceed.

Evaluate (E): After refining the problem that is to be the subject of the analysis, then managers and researchers need to evaluate the accessibility of the target of the measurement. The targets may be populations, such as maltreated women, high school dropouts, or general citizens, or targeted behaviors or attitudes like leadership, reciprocal behavior with colleagues, or commitment to the organization. The selection of the measuring instrument and the validity of research result are highly related to the accessibility of measuring targets. If the targets are inaccessible, like CIA operatives, then the selection of proxy inevitably becomes another critical consideration in measurement. It should be noted that the utilization of a proxy or a substitute as indirect measure is not always welcome, and the misuse of substitute measure may certainly distort research findings.

Screen (S): After the measuring issue and target are specifically identified, the screening and selection of proper measuring instrument and alternatives becomes the focus of attention. The screening and selection of an appropriate and feasible instrument should accommodate the goals of research question and problem to be addressed, as well as the accessibility and the willingness of measuring targets to participate. The research question dictates the methodology and the range of measurement options available. When seeking to understand the attitudes and behaviors of high school dropouts, we may choose to conduct telephone survey with those students and their parents, or undertake a personal visit and interview with the students and their parents. Alternatively, we might access public opinion regarding their satisfaction with the performance of their elected officials using an anonymous survey, or we might conclude that anonymity is less important than the assessments of the local opinion leaders. What is found depends upon what and how the questions are poised to the target groups.

Utilize (U): If possible, the best way to measure is to utilize a tested and validity-proven measuring instrument. To find such instrument, efforts in reviewing past studies and literatures are absolutely necessary. Sometimes, the frequency of use of a given measuring instrument can be used to help verifying its validity. But this strategy may be problematic, because some frequently used instruments were misused by the researcher. Consequently, careful scrutiny demands that the researcher checks to insure that the source of the measures was specified and the indicators of reliability and validity were indicated (Wright et al., 2004). Further it might be necessary to revise the measuring instrument to adapt it to the researcher's present context. Here are two examples of research that have used measures developed elsewhere: Moon (2000) explored the drivers of organizational commitment by adapting measures developed in previous research and Van Ryzin and colleagues examined citizen satisfaction with local government services by adapting a commonly used measure, the American Customer Satisfaction Index model (Van Ryzin et al., 2004).

Leverage (L): If a tested and validity-proven measuring instrument is unavailable, then developing a new instrument becomes the consideration. Leveraging associated theories, models, and pervious findings as a base to develop a preliminary instrument is a desirable course. Leverage involves a two-part action. One is building up the conceptual framework for the research based upon theory, because research that is informed by theory will focus the design of the measuring instrument and will more likely advance what we know about the concept under investigation. The other aspect of leverage is operationalizing the conceptual framework into measurable variables using the work of other researchers or related theories whenever possible. An example of this is the study by Chun and Rainey (2005), who develop a conceptual framework of goal ambiguity based upon theories of bureaucracy, public policy, public organization, and management. Their four dimensions of goal ambiguity utilized preexisting indices and measures drawn from performance measurement and public policy literature.

Test (T): As the original instrument is developed, pretests and adjustments are necessary and required to insure that the measurement is reliable and valid for the research or evaluation purpose. An elegant questionnaire is worthless if it does not operate as intended. No matter how good you think the instrument is, it will only be improved by asking others to comment on it. It is especially helpful if those who are used to test the instrument are familiar with the issue being studied or they possess characteristics that are close to the target population.

Synergy (S): As mentioned previously, no instrument is perfect and capable of addressing the whole problem. Hence, using multiple approaches such as quantitative and qualitative instruments to address the same set of issues from different angles is an important consideration. For example, one can use in-depth interviews or focus-group interviews to explore a single case, and the things learned from the case study can be generalized to the larger test audience. Findings coming from multiple sources and approaches can provide complementary understandings of the issue, as well as helping to avoid unexpected errors or biases resulting from single measurement.

13.4 CONCLUSIONS

The quality of the measurement is critical to the value of any study. In this chapter, we discussed fundamental requirements of measurement. There is no best practice that can fit all cases in terms of measuring and explaining phenomena in the social sciences. The basic considerations and rules illustrated in this chapter should be a useful guide to thinking about the measurement process.

QUESTIONS

1. Ensuring measurement validity is an important task for researchers and practitioners, why is it so important and what are the different ways to determine the validity of a measure?
2. In addition of ensuring validity for a measure, it is important to be sure that the methods used to measure are also reliable. Why does reliability matter and what are the different ways to determine the reliability of a measure?
3. What would be some practical strategies that you might use to ensure that your measurement activities are valid, reliable, and useful for the project at hand?

REFERENCES

Allen, M.J. and Yen, W.M. 1979. *Introduction to Measurement Theory*. Monterey, California: Brooks/Cole.

Babbie, E.R. 2003. *The Practice of Social Research*. 10th ed. New York: Wadsworth.

Brown, T.L. and Potoski, M. 2003. Contract-management capacity in municipal and county governments. *Public Administration Review, 63*(2): 153–176.

Carmines, E.G. and Zeller, R.A. 1979. *Reliability and Validity Assessment*. Newbury Park, California: Sage.

Chun, Y.H. and Rainey, H.G. 2005. Goal ambiguity in U.S. federal agencies. *Journal of Public Administration Research and Theory, 15*(1): 1–30.

Cunningham, R. and Olshfski, D. 1985. Objectifying assessment centers. *Public Personnel Administration, 5*(3): 42–49.

Guion, R. 1980. On trinitarian doctrines of validity. *Professional Psychology*, 11: 385–398.

Moon, M.J. 2000. Organizational commitment revisited in new public management: motivation, organizational culture, sector, and managerial level. *Public Performance & Management Review, 24*(2): 177–194.

Puran, A. 2004. *Measuring Quality in the Health Care System*. Unpublished Ph.D. dissertation. Rutgers University, Newark, New Jersey.

Sirkin, R.M. 1995. *Statistics for the Social Sciences*. Thousand Oaks, California: Sage.

Van Ryzin, G.G., Muzzio, D., Immerwahr, S., Gulick, L., and Martinez, E. 2004. Drivers and consequences of citizen satisfaction: An application of the American customer satisfaction index model to New York City. *Public Administration Review, 64*(3): 331–341.

Wright, B.E., Manigault, L.J., and Black, T.R. 2004. Quantitative research measurement in public administration. *Administration and Society, 35*(6): 747–764.

14 Sampling and Data Collection

Alana Northrop and Shelly Arsneault

CONTENTS

One starts with a research topic then develops hypotheses and identifies the variables to be measured. Now it is time to plan the data collection.

First, one needs to decide from whom the data will be collected. Data can come from a wide variety of units of analysis. These units can be people, cities, counties, countries, departments, and corporations.

Second, one needs to decide if she needs to do a census or a sample. A census is information that comes from all the units of analysis in a list. Obviously, if the list of units is all citizens in a country, that list is very large. Just consider the resources that the United States expends every ten years to do a census of its population. Census 2000 cost the government $6.5 billion. Given the magnitude of data collection involved in doing many censuses, sampling is a common alternative form of data collection.

Sampling means collecting data from a smaller number than the whole list of units. The need to do a sample instead of a census is driven by the answers to several questions. Does one have the time to collect information from all the units? Does she have the resources to collect information from all the units? And, most importantly, is it necessary to collect information from all the units for what one wants to learn from the data?

When one only collects data from a subset or sample of the complete list, the question arises whether or to what extent does the sample look like the whole universe. The ability to answer this question is the difference between probability samples and nonprobability samples. Probability samples are samples chosen from the universe by random without the researcher having any role in choosing which units are sampled and which are not. Nonprobability samples are samples in which the researcher does play a role in choosing which units from the complete list or universe end up in the sample for data collection. The topic of this chapter is sampling and data collection. We will describe the different types of probability and nonprobability samples, the advantages of each, and the special problems involved in data collection, such as the critical issue of achieving a high response rate.

14.1   DEFINING THE THEORETICAL POPULATION

Before deciding whether to sample or what kind of sample to do, one must clearly define the theoretical population. To define the theoretical population, one specifies from what units data will be collected in terms of time, territory, and other relevant factors.

14.1.1   UNIT OF ANALYSIS

Data can be collected from individuals, groups, or social artifacts. Individuals are human beings, whether adult citizens or employees in city hall. Groups represent collectivities, such as cities, counties, countries, or departments. If one wants to know how an employee feels about a different work schedule or how a citizen evaluates the delivery of city services, the data is collected from each individual. Thus, the individual is the unit of analysis. If one wants to know the population of a city or the mortality rate of a hospital, the data is collected from each city or hospital. In these cases, the unit of analysis is the group and not the individual because only a group can have a population or a mortality rate. To find out whether data collection should be focused on the individual or group, one asks on what variables he wants to collect data. If the variables are characteristics of individual people, then the unit is individuals; and if the variables are characteristics of groups of people, then the unit is groups.

The last kind of unit of analysis is social artifacts. An artifact is any object made by people with a view to subsequent use. Examples of social artifacts are laws, books, buildings, computers, etc. A study of fire risk factors might use buildings as the unit of analysis. Buildings could be evaluated by such characteristics as number of stories, square footage, business use, and type of roofing material.

14.1.2 Time

The unit of analysis must be defined in terms of time. Should data be collected as of one point in time or over a period of time? Data that is collected as of one point in time is called cross-sectional. For example when the Gallup Poll asks adult Americans to rate the president's performance, it is doing a cross-sectional analysis of public opinion that describes how the public evaluates the president as of a set date. When a news agency compares several of these cross-sectional polls, data is being compared over more than one point in time, and such data is called longitudinal.

Whether to do a cross-sectional or longitudinal study depends on resources and why one is collecting data. The State of California draws cross-sectional samples of names on initiative petitions because it only cares if enough legal signatures have been collected as of a certain date. Initiative drives are given 150 days to collect the required number of registered voters' signatures. Enough names are either collected by that date or not. In contrast, a study of the effectiveness of community policing on the crime rate involves looking at the crime rate at more than one point in time, both before the introduction of community policing and after, which would be longitudinal data.

There are three kinds of longitudinal studies: trend, panel, and cohort. A trend study collects data from different units at more than one point in time. The previously mentioned Gallup poll is an example of a trend study because the same citizens are not interviewed more than once. A panel study collects data from the same units at more than one point in time. If one were doing the community policing evaluation, they would need to do a panel study, collecting data from the same city or cities at more than one point in time. It would only make sense to look at the same city's crime rate before and after the introduction of community policing.

A cohort study falls in between a panel and a trend. In a cohort study, different units are studied but the units have something in common. Typically, what the units have in common is age or shared experience in a training program. A study of different police academy classes would be a cohort study. The classes could be compared as to their rates of officer involved shootings or complaints of sexual harassment.

In general, longitudinal data collection produces better quality data than does cross-sectional. Obviously, data that is collected at more than one point in time can indicate whether findings vary over time, which cross-sectional data cannot. Cross-sectional data is perfectly fine when one needs to know only about one point in time, such as the initiative petitions example or a city surveying households about whether to build a senior citizen center or not. Cross-sectional studies are also quite acceptable when the variables that are being measured are known to be stable, such as the square mileage of a city and population density.

A panel study is better than a trend when the theoretical population is heterogeneous. Studying different units from populations with great variations can give very different results than studying the same units. For example, the poverty rate in the United States has stayed fairly stable since the 1960s. Using trend data, we cannot tell whether or not it is the same people who fall below the poverty level. Thus, the data does not allow us to know whether there is a permanent underclass. Using panel data, we could tell that although the poverty level stayed the same, the people who comprised that group changed a lot, so a permanent underclass would be an inaccurate description.

14.1.3 TERRITORY

A theoretical population defines the units to be studied in terms of time and also territory. Territory literally refers to governmental boundaries. So if one wanted to study households, he needs to specify households in which city or state. If he wanted to study adult citizens, he needs to specify adult citizens living within distinct territorial boundaries, such as west of the river in the city of Hartford, Connecticut.

14.1.4 OTHER RELEVANT FACTORS

Here is the catchall consideration in defining theoretical populations. If we were doing a study for Washington State's highway patrol on drivers who speed, a useful theoretical population would be all licensed drivers in the state as of July 1, 2007. We have identified the right unit, which is individual. We have stated a date, so we know we will only collect data from people who lived in the state as of that date. We have also stated a territory, the state of Washington. The other relevant factor specified is that we will only collect data from licensed drivers. If the unit of analysis is individuals, typically one needs to limit the population by setting a minimum age limit or status, such as licensed driver or employee. Two year olds are not very helpful survey respondents, even though they can be accident victims. Studies of employees should consider limiting the theoretical population to only full-time employees who have passed their probationary period.

14.2   WHETHER TO SAMPLE OR NOT

One should now have a well-defined theoretical population. Look at it. Does the theoretical population involve under 200 employees or does it involve 50,000 households? The rule is if the population is under 200, one does a census. Essentially, there is no way to do a probability sample on populations under 200 and have any useful error rate. Still, resources may force one to sample when the population is under 200 but beware of the increase in error.

If the population is over 200 do not automatically consider a sample. Although time and money can be saved by doing a sample, there can be political costs that are too high. For instance, consider studies that want to survey employees about their satisfaction with benefits, work schedules, or training programs. If the list of employees is above 200, those study directors would still be well advised to survey all employees. Probability theory is all fine and good about drawing conclusions from a sample to the universe. Employees, though, want their individual voices heard on many matters and will not understand why they were not chosen to do so. The same can be said about voters or citizens if we are talking about a local area issue, such as building a new school or fire house in the neighborhood.

There are also theoretical populations above 200 in size that are rarely sampled because collecting data from all of them is so easy. The case of congressional districts comes to mind. Data from districts is so readily available that there is negligible time and staff savings gained by using a sample for data collection. The decision comes down to whether the time and staff savings are significantly large enough to outweigh the error and political risk that comes from drawing a sample versus doing a census.

14.3   PROBABILITY SAMPLING

The theory of probability sampling was first explained by a Swiss mathematician Jacques Bernoulli (1654–1705). He argued that a small, randomly chosen sample would look like the entire population. There would be a difference between the characteristics of the sample and the population, but it would be small and calculable. Thus, probability samples are distinguished by the fact that they are chosen randomly from the populations and that how they differ from the populations can be expressed by a calculable error rate.

Many American television viewers have absorbed this argument. Broadcasters frequently report survey results, results based on a random survey of adult Americans. For example, broadcasters report that 63 percent of Americans say employer penalties are the most effective approach to reducing illegal immigration and then go on to say that the margin of error for the survey was ± 3 percent. We, the television viewers, interpret the report as saying between 60 and 66 percent of us believe that employer penalties are the most effective way to reduce illegal immigration. This interpretation is essentially correct. Few viewers could go on to explain the assumptions behind the data, such as respondents to the survey were randomly chosen and that there is another error rate besides the one reported. Still, Bernoulli's description of probability sampling has laid the basis for data collection that is so common in the United States that the average citizen cannot escape its effects. From news reports to telephone market surveys to product labeling, Americans are the recipients of data collected from probability samples.

There are four types of probability samples: simple random sample (SRS), systematic sample, stratified sample, and a cluster sample. If one has a list of the theoretical population to begin with, she can do any of the first three types. If she does not have a list of the theoretical population, then she must consider doing a cluster sample or redefining one's theoretical population so that a list exists. In other words, if one's theoretical population is all households in the city of Fullerton as of October 1, the city can provide her with such a list because it provides water service to all households. Thus, one can do a SRS, stratified sample, or systematic sample. However, if the city bills landlords for water usage for apartment complexes because each apartment does not have its own meter, then no list of the theoretical population is available from the city. If this is true, consult with the central Post Office in the area to see if they can direct one to a firm that has a list of addresses. If still no luck, then a cluster sample is one's only respectable option.

The quality of the sample rests on the quality of one's list of the theoretical population. The list should be up-to-date. The list also should describe the population about which one wants to draw conclusions. If apartment renters are left off the list of households, then the conclusions one draws from the sample of households only represents home owners and home renters. This may not be a problem if apartments make up less than 5 percent of the city's households. The point is one needs to critically evaluate whether a list is available that adequately reflects the theoretical population. The list one uses to draw a sample from is called a sampling frame.

14.3.1 SIMPLE RANDOM SAMPLE

Many research designs and most statistics assume that the data is collected by means of a simple random sampling. Thus, SRS is the ideal type of sample in theory. It may not be the most appropriate one to do in practice. We need to discuss how to do the different samplings before we can expand on this point.

To do a SRS, one must have a sampling frame, which is the list of the theoretical population. Then, take the following steps:

1. Number every unit on the list. It does not matter whether one starts numbering from one or one thousand. But it is easier if one uses the typical numbering system of 1, 2, 3, etc.
2. Obtain a random number chart. They are in the appendixes of most statistics books.* Many popular computer software packages such as Excel, SPSS, and Stata also include a random number generator function. See also the Research Randomizer Web site for a tutorial on how to assign random numbers (Urbaniak and Plaus, 2006).
3. Decide on how to read the chart. One can start anywhere on the chart. Because it is random, there is no pattern to the appearances of the numbers. One can read rows left to right or

---

* RAND Corporation printed a book of random digits (1955).

right to left. One can read columns down or up. One can also read diagonals, but this way is very hard when reading more than one digit.

4. Decide how many digits to read. One reads the number of digits equivalent to the number of digits used to number the sampling frame. If one's list was numbered from one to nine, read one digit. If one's list was numbered from one to 99, read two digits. If one's list was numbered from one to 902, read three digits (see Appendix A).

5. Now read the appropriate number of digits on the random number chart. For example, if I was supposed to read three digits and the first numbers I read on the chart were 777, 939, and 961, then the units with those numbers in my sampling frame have made it into the sample. If no one in my sampling frame had one of those numbers, then I ignore the number and keep reading the random number chart (see Appendix A). I read as many numbers from the chart as I need to get the number of units I wanted in my sample. Do not choose extra names to compensate for refusals or failures to respond. Enlarging the sample size for this purpose does not work. Return rate is based on the number of surveys completed as compared to the number attempted.

As one can imagine, if one is reading five digits and needs to get a sample of 1000, reading a random number chart could make one's eyes hurt. The solution is to computerize one's list and use a random number generator. That way the computer chooses the sample. For instance, the random selection procedure within the widely used SPSS software package can select a SRS.

Entering all the names in one's sampling frame into the computer may not be worth the time trade-off, though. If that is the case, then a systematic sample may be the solution to any eye-strain problem.

14.3.2 SYSTEMATIC SAMPLE

Again, one must begin with a list or sampling frame to do this second type of probability sample. Here is a list of steps to be followed.

1. Number each unit listed in the sampling frame. This time, start with the whole number one and continue in normal numbering fashion until running out of units to be numbered.

2. Divide the size of the sampling frame by the number of units one wants in the sample. For example, if one has 1000 employees and needs 250 in his sample, divide 1000 by 250. The result is 4. This is referred to as the sampling interval. In other words, one out of four units in the sampling frame will be chosen to be in the sample.

3. Go to a random number chart. Read as many digits as are in the sampling interval. In our example that would be one digit. Start reading anywhere on the random number chart, looking for the first number between one and the sampling interval to appear. Ignore numbers on the random chart that do not fall within that range. So in our example we are looking for the first number to appear between one and four. Whatever it is becomes the random start. So if we read a zero and then a three, our random start is three. If we read a six and then a two, our random start is two. Let us assume we got a two.

4. The unit in the sampling frame with the number two assigned to it is chosen for the sample. Now add the sampling interval to the random start. Four added to two gives a six. Now the unit in the sampling frame with the number six assigned to it is chosen for the sample. Keep adding the sampling interval to the last number and one will select the numbered units in the sampling frame that will be in the sample. In the example, 2, 6, 10, 14, 18, 22, 26, 30, 34, 38, 42, 46, 50, etc., will be the units chosen from the sampling frame for the sample. When one runs out of numbers in the sampling frame, one will have exactly the right number of units wanted for the sample. This was accomplished with just using the random number chart once, so no eye strain.

Obviously, a systematic sample is easier to choose than a classic simple random sample. So why ever use a SRS? There is one problem with a systematic sample, but it is not always a problem. If the sampling frame has a cycle to the order of units, then a systematic sample can pick up that cycle and actually increase sampling error compared to a SRS. So one needs to inspect the sampling frame to make sure there is no cycle to the order.

What do we mean by cycle? Let us assume one's list is made up of Boy Scout troops, each with fifteen scouts. The first name on the list of each troop is the oldest boy in the troop. If the random start had been a one and the interval a fifteen, the resulting sample would be made up of the oldest boy in each troop. The first boy to be chosen for the sample would be number one, the oldest boy in the first troop. The second boy to be chosen for the sample would be number sixteen, random start one plus the interval of 15. This means that the second boy to be chosen for the sample would be the oldest boy in the second troop. Continuing with adding the interval of fifteen, the oldest boy in each troop ends up in the sample. The result is a randomly chosen sample with a marked bias to over representing the characteristics and opinions of older boy scouts. The aim of probability sampling is to reflect the population or sampling frame not to distort it. Thus, if there is a cycle, a repeatable order to how the units' names are listed in the sampling frame, do not use a systematic sampling method. Of course, if the cyclical order of the list, if one does exist, has no relevance to the aims of the study or to any variables being measured, then there is no increase in error rate created by systematic sampling. That assumption, though, may be hard to prove. Hence, if there is a cycle to how units' names are listed in one's sampling frame, refrain from using a systematic sampling method. Opt for doing a SRS.

14.3.3 STRATIFIED SAMPLE

To do a stratified sample, one not only needs a list of the theoretical population but also to know at least one variable about each unit in the list. This information must be available before beginning data collection. So it is not enough just to have a list of the names of the units. One must initially also know something about them. For example, if one's sampling frame is a list of all current full-time employees of the maintenance department, personnel department could provide a list of names and also for each name an age, income, position title, how long they had worked for the city, whether they belonged to the union or not, etc. All the latter information are variables that can be used to divide the personnel list into strata before one draws a sample. If one's sampling frame is a list of all counties in the state of Illinois, information exists in various resource books about the population size of the counties, the median income, political party registration, ethnic make-up, etc. These latter variables or characteristics of the counties can be used to divide the county list into strata before any sample is drawn.

The reason one wants to be able to divide the sampling frame into strata or units with something in common is that it reduces sampling error. The result is a sample for the same cost as a SRS or systematic but one that is a more accurate representation of the theoretical population. The logic behind this reduction in error is that there can be no sampling error if one is choosing units for the sample from a group in which each unit looks exactly alike. So if one were choosing a sample of police cars from a list of all police cars delivered on August 1 to one's city, no matter which car was selected it would be a 2007 Crown Victoria. But if one were randomly choosing a sample of cars from a list of all cars delivered on August 1 to the city, one might not get a single Crown Victoria because only the police department ordered that make and model. The resulting sample would not reflect the variation of kinds of cars delivered to the city as of August 1.

Here is how to draw a stratified sample. Begin with a list of units and at least one known variable on each of the units. Let us assume the researcher is a supervisor in the maintenance department and wants to devise a routine maintenance schedule for the city-owned vehicles. To do so, the supervisor wants to check on past maintenance records of the vehicles, how often they had a routine inspection, and how often they were sent to the yard with problems. Because the city owns over a thousand vehicles, the supervisor decides to do a sample. A stratified sampling technique is possible because one knows which department was assigned each vehicle. The researcher orders the list of all city vehicles by department. Thus, there is a stratum or group of vehicles assigned to the mayor's office, a stratum of vehicles assigned to refuse, a stratum assigned to police, a stratum assigned to parks and recreation, etc. Then one does a SRS or a systematic sample within each stratum. So if police have 100 vehicles, number the vehicles and randomly choose which vehicles' records will be inspected (see Appendix B).

Vehicles chosen by a SRS would be determined by reading three digits in a random number chart. Again ignore any random number that does not match a police car's number. To choose a systematic sample of police cars, determine the sampling interval (i.e., divide the number of police cars by the number of cars one wants in one's sample from this department). Then find the first number between one and the sampling interval to appear when reading the random number chart. The police car with that number is selected for the sample. Add the sampling interval to the random start number and select the police car with that number. Continue adding the sampling interval to the last number chosen, and you will get a sample of cars in the police department. To get the sample of all city-owned vehicles, repeat this procedure for each department or stratum. Note that the sample will likely end up with a vehicle from every department in the city. A department will not be represented only if it has fewer vehicles assigned to it than the sampling interval. There is no way, though, that a stratified sample does not reflect the population's strata, in this case departments with assigned vehicles.

14.3.3.1 Proportional or Nonproportional

An issue in stratified sampling is how many units to select from each stratum. Because the aim of sampling is to choose a sample that looks like the theoretical population, one normally wants her stratified sample to look like the sampling frame in terms of the variable on which she stratified. If the police department has 20 percent of the city-owned vehicles and the refuse department has 30 percent, 20 percent of the sample should be chosen from the police stratum and 30 percent from the refuse stratum. This is called proportional stratified sampling. The researcher samples each stratum in proportion to its size in the sampling frame. If she wants 100 vehicles in the sample, 20 or 20 percent would need to be chosen randomly from the police vehicle list and 30 or 30 percent from the refuse list. In this way the sample would perfectly reflect the distribution of city-owned vehicles assigned by department. Only through stratified sampling can one insure this perfect department representation. Using a SRS or systematic method for choosing the vehicles normally will result in a sample of vehicles that is close to the actual department vehicle assignment but not as close as using a stratified. The stratified sample therefore reduces sampling error on the variable used to divide the units into strata.

A stratified sample also reduces the sampling error on any other variables that may be related to the strata's variable. For example, not only does stratification reduce error on choosing police cars for the study, but it also reduces error on another variable, how many drivers per car. All police cars are driven by different people because of the 24 hour nature of police work. In contrast, in other departments cars are often assigned to an individual; these cars have only one driver. Cars driven by different drivers may experience the need for more frequent maintenance than cars driven by the same driver. As the supervisor, one would want to see if this is true. The suggested stratified sample would allow one to assess more accurately this factor.

The aim of sampling is to choose a sample that accurately reflects the population's characteristics. This is the logic behind proportional stratified sampling. There are instances, though, when it may be worthwhile to do nonproportional sampling. If one or more of the strata are so small that none or less than five units from that stratum would be chosen through proportional sampling, then one may wish to over sample that stratum. To over sample a stratum, just select more units from that stratum than you would through proportional sampling. The presumption is that those very small strata are of interest to the study's purpose. If only one car is assigned to a department, it may not make sense to make sure that car ends up in the sample. Then again, if that one car is assigned to the mayor, you may want to sample that car to insure that the mayor is never left on the side of the road with a disabled car. Cities with small but politically active Latino populations or senior citizens may want to over sample the Latino or senior citizen strata to understand more accurately the concerns of that group.

Of major importance, whenever using the whole sample to state findings, the researcher must restore the over sampled strata to their size in proportion to the population. One uses nonproportional sampling to learn about the strata individually, never to learn about the population as a whole. To draw conclusions about the population, he must use proportional sampling. If he has used nonproportional sampling of a stratum and wishes to also speak about the whole population, he must weight the over sampled stratum back to its proper proportion of the population.

To over sample Latino school children, for example, randomly select more of their names from the school provided lists than their proportion of all public school children. This data allows one to talk about Latino school children. When one wants to talk about all public school children, one needs to weight the Latino children back to their proportion of the school population and combine the data with the data from the other strata. If Latino's are 8 percent of the school population but twice that amount have been sampled, multiply the Latino responses by one-half to weight their responses back to their proper proportion. Now one has a proportional sample again.

In sum, nonproportional sampling should be considered when a stratum is too small in size to adequately analyze with the sample N that one would have gotten if one used just a proportional stratified sample. The point is that one would not use the inflated N of the strata when looking at that full sample.

14.3.4 Choice of Strata Variables

What variable to stratify on is an important consideration. Sampling error is only reduced if the variable on which one stratifies is related to the purpose of the study. If one wants to sample employees on their benefit packages, choose a variable to stratify on that which can affect their opinions of benefits, such as sex, age, or department. Female employees may be more interested in whether they can use sick days for personal business or if child care is available on the premises. Older employees may be more interested in retirement benefits, and safety employees may be more concerned with disability rules and paid survivor insurance.

More than one variable can be used in dividing the sampling frame into the strata. The more variables used, the less sampling error. The addition of a second variable at least doubles the number of stratum and so complicates the choosing of the sample. If one were stratifying on sex and whether or not the employee was safety personnel, one would have four strata: female safety personnel, female nonsafety, male safety, and male nonsafety. One reduces sampling error to the extent that the second variable is related to the study's purpose and is unrelated to the first variable. So do not choose a second variable to stratify on if it is highly associated with the first one even if it is related to the study's purpose. Therefore, one probably does not want to stratify on sex and safety personnel status in the example if safety personnel tend to be overwhelmingly male and nonsafety overwhelmingly female. The addition of sex as a second stratifying variable will not reduce one's error much but will increase the effort involved in drawing the sample.

14.3.5 Cluster or Multistage Sample

A cluster sample is the only choice if one does not have a list of the theoretical population, and it involves too many resources to get such a list. For example, there is no list of all adult Americans, except the U.S. census that very quickly gets out of date and access to actual names is severely limited for many years. There are also not lists of all adults in any city or county or state in the

United States. To obtain such a list is beyond the resources of any governmental unit besides the federal government, and the federal government only does its population census because it is mandated in the U.S. Constitution. In fact, in the past there has been discussion in the Bureau of the Census to substitute a probability sample for the census. The Census Bureau currently uses a sample to check on the accuracy of the census. It first used a sample in 1850 when 23 counties were sampled to check on marital and educational trends in the U.S. society. Clearly, a sample would be less costly. A sample would also be more accurate, especially given the low mail response rate to the 1990 and 2000 censuses. The hitch is getting around the wording of the Constitution.

Back to our question, what to do if one cannot get a list of her theoretical population? First, she can redefine the theoretical population so a list is possible. Change "all adult citizens" to "all registered to vote citizens." Now a SRS, systematic, or stratified sample is possible. The problem is that she may have to redefine the theoretical population to such an extent that the then available list is inappropriate for her purposes. If this happens, she should consider doing a cluster sample before considering a nonprobability kind of sample.

To do any kind of probability sample one needs a list of units from which to sample. This is also true of a cluster sample. A cluster sample involves drawing at least two samples or, put another way, a cluster sample is drawn in at least two stages.

To illustrate, one wants to draw a sample of all adults living within two miles of a proposed baseball stadium. These would be the people most likely to feel the effects of the stadium in terms of traffic, noise, litter, and lights. No such list exists. One might consider redefining the theoretical population to households within the two mile limit. The city has access to a list of dwelling units. However, someone on the city council objects because she is concerned about voters' reactions to the stadium, and households do not represent potential voters. Back to the drawing board, the list of registered voters is rejected as a sampling frame because it would be unrepresentative of actual voters, especially when a hot issue increases late registration and turnout. Finally, the city council accepts that the only way to find out how adult citizens feel about the stadium is to do a cluster sample. The money is allocated with the proviso that interns are used to do the enumeration.

To carry out this cluster sample, a list of city blocks in the two mile radius of the proposed stadium is developed by the planning staff. A SRS or a systematic sample of those blocks is drawn. This is the first stage of the cluster sample. Next, to get a list of the right units, adult citizens, interns are sent to the selected blocks and literally go door to door, writing down the names of all residents 18 years or older. Hospitals, nursing homes, and institutions like halfway houses are traditionally left out of the enumeration. Residents of such facilities are considered transients, and many would be incapable of responding to the subsequent interviewer or mailed questionnaire.

Using the new list of adults gathered by the interns, a SRS or a systematic sample is drawn of the respondents to be sampled for their reactions to the proposed baseball stadium. This second sampling is the second stage of the cluster sample.

As you can probably tell, a cluster sample is more expensive and time consuming to do than the first three kinds of probability samples because a cluster sample involves sending staff or volunteers to areas to develop a list of the right units. Still, it is the only type of probability sample that is possible if no appropriate list of the theoretical population exists.

The sampling error rate can be computed for a cluster sample just as it can be for the other kinds of probability samples. A cluster sample involves higher error, though, because at least two samples are drawn. To compensate for the higher error rate in a cluster sample, one can increase one's sample size by 50 percent.

14.3.6 RANDOM DIGIT DIALING

Telephones are a quicker and cheaper way to gather information than door-to-door interviews. The old method of obtaining a telephone survey via a phone book, however, faces two difficulties today: unlisted numbers and cell phones. For example, by 2004 in both the United States and abroad, more people had cell phones than land-line telephones (Rosen, 2004). In particular, younger people and renters are less likely to have land-lines, leading to possible under-sampling of people in these demographic categories. As a result, the phone book is a very inaccurate list to use for a sampling frame. So random digit dialing, a form of a cluster sample, is used. Note that cell phones do not present a problem for studies relevant to government issues—at least not yet. Currently cell-phone-only users are not very engaged in government and are not a dominant segment of the government workforce.

Random digit dialing is undertaken in the following way. First, one develops a list of the area codes, only if more than one area code is used in the area one wants to survey. One then develops a list of the central-office codes in each area code. The central-office codes are the first three digits of the seven digit phone number. To choose which phone numbers will be called, randomly choose an area code then randomly choose a central-office number. Given that both these numbers are three digits, one would read three digits off the random number chart. Then one needs to randomly choose a four digit number to get a full phone number.

When a phone number is dialed, one then randomly chooses which adult in the household will be asked to answer the questionnaire. This is the second sampling stage. The interviewer has to ask whoever answers the phone how many adults there are in the household and then must randomly choose who in that household is asked to answer the questions. Lists based on sex and age can be used to avoid household enumeration. One randomly chooses combinations of sex and age groups to interview from phone number to phone number. For example, on one call the interviewer asks to speak to the oldest adult female in the household, and on the next phone call the interviewer asks to speak to the second oldest adult male in the household. Asking to speak to the adult in the household whom most recently had a birthday can also be used to pick respondents.

A major problem with random digit dialing is the number of phone numbers which are inoperative numbers. Phone companies, where possible, do assign new numbers in groups of sequential numbers. If this is true in the area being sampled, then once an operating phone number has been found by the above random method one can randomly select more random numbers around the operating number as long as one stays within ± 100 units. If the working number is 999-2424, for instance, we might also select 999-2456 or 999-2392.

Conducting a telephone survey is complicated. One might want to seriously consider at least hiring a sampling expert or a survey firm to design the sampling procedure. There are also other major issues, such as training the interviewers and supervising their work and establishing a callback procedure for calls in which no one is home or the right respondent is unavailable at that time.

14.3.7 FUTURE CITIES' SAMPLING DESIGN

Innovative sampling designs are rare. They are variations of SRS, systematic, and stratified. Even a cluster sample is a multistage SRS or a systematic sample. A unique stratified sampling design was developed in the 1970s at the University of California, Irvine (Kraemer et al., 1981). The aim was to draw a sample of cities that would reflect not the current characteristics of cities but the characteristics of possible future cities. Sampling theory presumes one wants to draw a sample to describe the current theoretical population. In other words, data is collected from the sample at one point in time to learn about the theoretical population as of the same point in time. The aim of the future cities' design departs from this typical intention behind sampling.

The design was developed so that the researchers could answer what would happen to cities if they did x, x being a policy relating to computerization. To stratify they needed to know about computer policy in each city. No such information existed, so a survey was done of all cities over 50,000 in population, asking extensive questions about computer policies. From this survey six policy variables were chosen on which to stratify the cities. Note that the sampling frame was being divided into strata based on combinations of six variables, not one variable as described above in detail. Each of the six variables was dichotomized, so they each had two categories. The possible strata or combinations of six variables with two categories are 64. Resources limited the study to site visits to only 40 cities although there were 64 strata. So 40 strata were randomly chosen, and a city from each of these 40 strata was then randomly chosen.

The result was a stratified sample that represented possible variation on computing policy not current variation. From this sample, the researchers would be able to collect data that could answer what would happen if cities had this computing policy or that one. A more typical sampling method might not have picked cities for the sample that had a certain type of policy because that policy would have been rare or rare in combination with other policies. Hence, a typical sample would not have allowed researchers to discuss the effects of rare policies.

This innovative sampling method was expensive and time consuming because a survey of the theoretical population had to be carried out to find information about each unit to be able to stratify. Drawing the actual sample from this information was also time consuming because of the large number of strata and the fact that not all strata were represented by a real city. A further complication was obtaining permission to study the city's operations from various officials in each city chosen for the sample.

14.3.8 Sampling the Role and Not the Person

Another innovation in sampling design is sampling the role and not the person. This approach is particularly appropriate for longitudinal data collection in organizations. People leave organizations or change their positions in organizations. Thus, it is not always possible or appropriate to ask the same respondent questions at a second point in time. Thus, if one were conducting an evaluation of a training program or a change in policy, one does not necessarily have to sample the same person at each point of time in data collection.

The key is getting data from the person who holds a particular job that has a perception of the effects of the policy. Asking employees about their morale before and after a policy change requires only that the employees still work for the organization and hold the same job responsibilities so that they are affected in the same way. It does not require that they be the same individuals.

Moreover, the size of one's sample would be greatly reduced if one had to sample the same people where there is high job turnover. By sampling the role and not the person, sample size can be maintained at the two points in time.

14.3.9 Sampling without Replacement

One issue in probability sampling that has not been addressed is sampling without replacement. Probability sampling presumes each unit in the sampling frame has an equal chance of being chosen for the sample. If each unit has an equal chance of being chosen, then there are no biases in selecting the sample. However, this assumption is often violated. A number can appear more than once in the random number chart. Thus, when using the random number chart to select a SRS, a unit in the sampling frame could be selected twice. It does not make sense to interview the same individual twice. So in practice, if a number is selected more than once, that repeat number is ignored. One is actually throwing numbers out of consideration for the sample once they have been selected. The result is that the units in the sampling frame do not have equal chances of being chosen for the sample.

To illustrate, if there are 200 numbers in the sampling frame and a sample of 20 is desired, each unit in the sampling frame has a one out of ten chances of being chosen. This is before the first random number is chosen. Once a random number is chosen and cannot be chosen again, the remaining 199 units in the sampling frame have slightly more than one out of ten chances of being chosen. Every time a number is selected and then retired, the chances of being selected for the other units change.

But importantly, when the sample is small compared to the size of the sampling frame, there is a negligible error introduced by throwing numbers out of consideration once selected. Systematic sampling avoids this error all together.

14.3.10   REPORTING SAMPLE DESIGN

Although it is critical to include in one's report the sampling method and all its essential characteristics, it may not always be appropriate to impose this information at the beginning of the report.
One should consider his audience. If the report is prepared for public officials or public dissemination, the sampling information should be put in an appendix. In fact, major publications, like the
Gallup Poll Monthly, reserve a section under the title "Design of the Sample" at the end of each
issue. This enables them to present the findings without the burden of a long, technical introduction.
However, putting the information in an appendix may increase suspicion about the quality of the
data. If this is possible, one may want to explain where the information can be found when not
introduced in the beginning of the report.

For academic audiences, it is crucial to describe one's sample design in the beginning to acquire
support and recognition from one's research colleagues, who would not consider any of one's claims
unless properly informed on the quality of the data. The *Public Opinion Quarterly* and the *Public
Administration Review* strictly enforce such up-front reporting in every published article.

14.4   NONPROBABILITY SAMPLING

Probability samples can be expensive and thus beyond the reach of researchers and organizations.
There may also not be the need to go to the trouble and expense of doing a probability survey.
Nonprobability samples are an alternative. The key distinction between probability samples and
nonprobability samples is that in the first the researchers have no influence over which units in the
sampling frame end up in the sample; the opposite is true in the latter. It is also true that only in
probability samples it is possible to compute sampling error, i.e., to what extent does collecting data
from the sample differ from collecting data from the whole sampling frame.

14.4.1   JUDGMENTAL OR REPUTATION SAMPLE

A judgmental or reputation sample is a common kind of sample. Many articles in the *Public
Administration Review* are based on studies from one state's experiences or a few cities'. The
state or cities are chosen based on their reputations for success or, sometimes, very costly failure in
policy making. For example, if one hears that a city has really reduced its trash collection costs, one
would likely want to talk with that city and find out how. If a city similar to one's own has made a
major advance or suffered a severe loss, it might be beneficial to explore why. Thus, based on
reputation, one seeks out certain units or samples from which to gather data. This form of data
collection makes sense because it fits with people's logical tendencies to learn from example.

There may be other cities, though, which were even more successful or less successful. Using
the reputation approach, one may actually be learning from cities whose experiences are totally
unique and unable to be guideposts. The lessons learned would therefore be misleading. That is the
weakness of a reputation sample. There is no way to know how representative or typical the
experiences of the sample units are. Therefore the "best practices" approach is not without
debatable weaknesses. The strengths of a reputation sample are that limited resources can be
expended and an in-depth understanding of a situation can be undertaken.

14.4.2   CONVENIENCE SAMPLE

A convenience sample involves choosing units to study that are readily available to the researcher.
Many articles in the *Public Administration Review* and much research in the field are still based on
samples of convenience. Studies done by government employees based on their work experiences
are studies of convenience. Academics find it convenient to study cities that are located near their
universities.

A sample of convenience is the least likely to reflect the larger theoretical population. Although a reputation and a convenience sample may seem similar, they are not. Unlike a convenience sample, the reputation sample is chosen on a criterion independent of the researcher, its reputation. Still, it is true that like a reputation sample a convenience sample is less expensive than a probability sample and allows for in-depth study.

To improve the quality of a convenience sample, one can vary the time and place for selecting the units. This is a good idea if the units of analysis are individuals. Then one can collect data from individuals at different points of time in different cities or departments or classes. For instance, if a manager wanted to assess students' satisfaction with classes offered by the Parks and Recreation Department, it would be wise to survey students in different classes in different sessions. One could vary the time by both time of day (morning, afternoon, evening, weekend) and by session (spring, summer, winter).

14.4.3 QUOTA SAMPLE

A quota sample is an important kind of nonprobability sample. It is used often in marketing research and election polls. It also bears a similarity to a stratified sample. In a quota sample the researcher sets quotas on key variables that will shape who is chosen for the sample. The quotas are characteristics of the theoretical population. For example, if one knows the sex and age and racial make-up of the population, she then sets the same ratios for the sample. So if 10 percent of the population is African-American, she sets the quota of 10 percent African-American for the sample.

The advantage of a quota sample over other nonprobability samples is that a quota sample insures that the sample looks like the theoretical population on the variables on which quotas have been set. However, the researcher gets to choose who ends up in the sample within the quota framework. So if one were standing outside a supermarket doing a quota survey, one would be more likely to approach the smiling male over 35 than the male who is moving fast and avoiding eye contact even though he is also over 35 and thus meets the quota. The introduction of biases by the researcher in selecting who ends up in the sample within the quotas is why quota sampling is a nonprobability sample.

Like the first two kinds of nonprobability samples, a quota sample is cheaper than a probability sample of the same size. It can also present good data. The quality of a quota sample rests on choosing good variables on which to set quotas. The best variables are ones highly related to the purpose of the study. So if one wants to know residents' reactions to building a skateboard park, set quotas on variables that are likely to affect reactions, such as residence's proximity to the park and whether a household has children under 16. Information gathered from such a quota sample would be an excellent supplement to public hearings. The quota sample could balance the bias inherent in using public hearings to gauge wider public sentiment. Moreover, the quota sample can provide the additional information for far less cost and in much faster time than a probability sample could.

The quality of a quota sample also rests on how the units are chosen within the quota allowances. The researcher could give the interviewers a list of one digit random numbers. The interviewers choose who is interviewed using the numbers and not whom they personally would pick. So within the quota of a white, female, under 30, the interviewer can only approach the woman who fits that description and the random number. If the random number is three, the interviewer can only approach the third woman who fits the quota description. The random numbers are used similarly to pick respondents within the other quotas.

14.4.4 VOLUNTEER SAMPLE

A volunteer sample is another type of nonprobability sample, but one that is more common in other fields such as medical research. Sample members are self-chosen; they nominate themselves for the sample, following some form of public announcement. Like the other types of nonprobability samples, there is no way to know if the sample is at all representative of the theoretical population.

Clearly, a sample based on volunteers looks different from the theoretical population because the sample are the only ones interested in participating.

Volunteers are more motivated for a variety of reasons. In medical research, volunteers may be more seriously ill than the wider theoretical population suffering from the disease. Hence, such volunteers may be less likely to respond to treatment because the disease has progressed beyond the point of help. Accordingly, the treatment being evaluated may look less successful than it would if tested on a more representative sample.

Programs can also look more successful. In 1995, the Army did a study to see if women were capable of doing very heavy military tasks, involving lifting a 100 lb weight. Using female volunteers from various occupations, the Army measured their strength before a training program and then after completing the program. The results showed a dramatic increase in the volunteers' abilities to lift 100 lb. The impressive success of the program may be distorted though. The volunteers were likely much more motivated to be faithful to the training and give it their best than a group of women who were required to do so. Many of the volunteers had never exercised before. Some had just had children and wanted to get back into shape. The study did show women can do heavy military tasks like loading trucks and marching under the weight of a full backpack. The study does not show that all or many female recruits would respond as well to a weight training program and thus be able to load trucks.

Often, cities want citizen input so that a strategic plan can be developed. Surveys can be published in one or two of the city's newspapers and placed in every public library. This would be an example of a volunteer sample that tries to get at a wide segment of the population by using multiple ways to gather respondents. In this case, a random segment of citizens can also be surveyed. The volunteer sample makes sense as a complement to the probability sample for political reasons. Specifically, volunteer samples can serve a valuable purpose by giving citizens or consumers or clients an outlet to express their opinions. Individuals not selected in a random sample can feel that they are being ignored. By supplementing random samples with volunteer samples, an important outlet for discontent is provided. Political discontent may thereby be reduced. Such an approach may also increase acceptance of reports based on the data analysis.

Sometimes, a volunteer sample makes sense because the public policy being evaluated is based on volunteer participation. Consider school magnet programs, which are programs that select students who volunteer for the programs. The students and their parents want to participate because the programs promise specialized advanced schooling in academic areas. To accurately evaluate school magnet programs, one should take a random sample of programs and a random sample of students in the programs. But if one wanted to do in-depth interviewing of students and parents, a random sample might be too costly and might suffer from a low response rate. The option is to ask for volunteers in the program. Using volunteers from a volunteer-based theoretical population is less susceptible to the unique error of self-selection inherent in volunteer samples.

In sum, the profession looks with great skepticism on volunteer samples. We do believe a case can be made for them, but only under unusual circumstances such as that just described.

14.5 HOW BIG A SAMPLE

There are a variety of factors that shape how big a sample is needed. Resources both in terms of staff and budget have to be balanced against getting the kind of data that is needed. The kind of data that is needed depends on the required accuracy of the conclusions, the detail of the analysis, and the political needs of who gets the report.

14.5.1 SAMPLING ERROR

The issue of how much sampling error can be tolerated only applies to probability samples. Remember that the difference between probability and nonprobability samples is that only in the former can one say how much the sample differs from the theoretical population. This is because only probability samples are chosen randomly. Random selection of samples involves two kinds of errors, one is confidence interval and one is confidence level.

14.5.1.1 Confidence Interval

This type of random sampling error is the best known and is now consistently reported in news stories. Confidence interval is expressed as a $\pm$ percentage. So if the confidence interval is ± 3 percent, it would mean that the data from the sample fall within the ± 3 percent range as compared to what the results would be using the whole theoretical population. More concretely, if a president's approval rating is 37 percent according to the latest Gallup sample, the president's rating is actually between 34 and 40 percent among all adults.

Confidence interval dictates sample size. The less error one wants, the larger the sample. Because larger samples eat scarce resources, it is important to set the interval according to how much error is needed to draw conclusions. If there is a controversial ordinance proposed which appears to divide the community, a smaller interval should be chosen. This way the results of the survey can be used to drive the decision whether to approve the ordinance or not, reflecting the public will be the goal.

Often, though, surveys are done that are more exploratory in nature. If one wants to know what public service areas citizens consider problematic, then ballpark results are just fine. It does not really matter whether 10 or 12 percent of the citizens surveyed think parks are a problem, the point is it is a low percentage. So what if the interval error is $\pm$ even 5 percent. One would still know that only a small percentage feels parks are a problem.

Determining the interval is based on how accurate one needs the results to be. 7 percent is probably the widest one would want to set the interval. 7 percent is actually a 14 percent range of error, which is getting large enough to cause serious distortion of data results. The Gallup Poll organization will not do surveys with confidence intervals larger than 5 percent.

Consider that the food packaging error rate for calories is set at 20 percent. What this means is that a serving portion of 100 calories could really be as low as 80 or as high as 120. If one were on a strict diet, this error rate might be too large to allow for weight loss, or at the other end of error it might be too large to allow for faithful dieting without serious feelings of starvation.

14.5.1.2 Confidence Level

Confidence interval cannot be understood without knowing confidence level. The two random sampling errors are interpreted together. Confidence level refers to the percentage of time that the sample differs from the theoretical population within the confidence interval. It is not true that the sample looks like the theoretical population always within the $\pm$ percentage set as the interval.

For example, in the 2004 presidential election the national random sample for exit polls had a margin of ± 1 percent. The exit polls showed that John Kerry had an insurmountable lead and would win the Electoral College vote with 309 to George W. Bush's 174. As we all know the exit polls were wrong and Bush won the Electoral College and the election itself.

Confidence level is expressed as a percentage. It can range from 1 percent to 99 percent. Realistically, confidence level should never fall below 90 percent, 95 percent being the most common. So if the confidence level is 95 percent and the interval is 3 percent, then in 95 samples out of 100 the sample will differ from the theoretical population by ± 3 percent. There is a 5 percent chance that the sample differs from the theoretical population by more than ± 3 percent.

Confidence level dictates sample size along with confidence interval. The higher the confidence level, which means the more accurate, the larger the sample must be. Like one's decision about how big an interval should be, the size of the confidence level should be dictated by how accurate the data needs to be.

Once a confidence level and interval have been chosen, one refers to established tables or Web sites such as The Survey System (2003) to know how big a sample is required for those error rates. If one's population is less than 10,000, there are tables based on the size of the population that one references. If one's population is 10,000 or larger, then population size does not affect how big a sample is required. One merely finds where the confidence level and interval bisect in the table and reads the sample size.

To get an idea how error rates affect sample size for populations over 10,000, consider these examples. If the confidence level is 95 percent and the confidence interval is 1 percent, the sample size is 9604. If one changes the interval to 3 percent, the sample size changes to 1067. If one changes the interval to 7 percent, the sample size goes down to 196, a big saving in time and survey costs. If one raises the confidence level to 99 percent but keeps the interval at seven, the sample size becomes 339. Keeping the 99 percent level but lowering the interval to three results in a sample size of 1843.

Perhaps the easiest way to understand the relationship between confidence interval, confidence level, and sample size is to use online tools provided by sites by The Survey System or the UCLA Department of Statistics (2005). One simply inputs the sample and population size that one is using, and within seconds the sample's confidence level is calculated. This tool is also useful in determining how large a sample one needs to obtain given a chosen confidence interval and level desired for the study.

Polling organizations tend to sample between 400 and 1200 adults for congressional districts or statewide surveys (Goldhaber, 1984). They use a 95 percent confidence level but vary the interval between 3 and 5 percent. Cost considerations are the major factors affecting sample size. In those districts or states that are very homogeneous, such as Wyoming, polling organizations find the smaller sample size quite acceptable because there is less random sampling error within homogeneous populations than within heterogeneous populations.

The random sampling errors presume 100 percent response rate. One will likely not achieve close to that ideal. With less than 100 percent response rate, error increases, but one cannot know how much the increase has been. People who respond to surveys do not look like the non-responders. There is a difference in the time one is willing to invest and interest in the topic of the survey. Therefore, because response rate is not randomly occurring, the researcher does not mathematically know how the sampling errors have changed. Importantly, this means the researcher cannot start with an intended sample of 1000 with 95 percent confidence, ± 3 percent, and when 600 surveys are returned, restate the error as 95 ± 5 percent.

14.5.1.3 Detailed Analysis

The above explanation of sampling error applies to interpreting data based on the whole sample. What if one is also interested in learning about subgroups in the sample? For example, one may want to know not only how the whole state feels about a law but also how the Latino population feels. When the Latinos are separated from the sample, then analysis is being done on a smaller sample. Sample size corresponds to confidence level and interval. So if one lowers the sample size, one raises the error. Therefore, to maintain the same confidence level and interval, one needs to increase the initial sample size to allow for analysis of the Latinos within the accuracy level predetermined. Or if one does not increase sample size, then interpretations of subgroups must take into account their higher sampling error.

An interval of 3 percent in national samples applies to data based on the whole sample. Breaking the sample into regions of the country to find out about how adults in the West or South feel results in error of about ± 5 percent. Analyzing different religious groups results in widely varying error because the sizes of the groups are so different. The error for Protestants will stay within the 3 percent range, whereas the error for Jews is 18 percent, plus or minus. The Jewish data would be all but worthless. If one wanted to learn anything about the Jewish population, he would have to increase sample size.

Sometimes analysis gets down to just having units in subgroups of the sample to analyze. Every year the U.S. Justice Department samples 100,000 people. This incredibly large sample is necessary so that the Department can analyze crimes by sex of victim, age, time of day, type of crime, location such as suburb versus central city, etc. To do such analysis requires breaking the sample down into many different groups; just one such group would be female afternoon rape victim over sixty-five, living in central city. The Justice Department needs an incredibly large sample just to increase the chance that it will have such a person in the sample. For statistical analysis reasons one really wants at least five such bodies for each group. So if one wants to analyze a sample in terms of 50 subgroups, then one would need a 250 person sample just to get five in a group. Of course, one only needs a 250 person sample if he assumes all group memberships are evenly distributed and randomly occurring. The latter two assumptions never apply, so he needs an even bigger sample.

In sum, if one is going to do detailed analysis within subgroups of the sample, one needs to consider a larger sample size. The number of subgroups as well as the size of the subgroups in proportion to the size of the theoretical population affects how much the sample size should be increased.

14.5.2 WHO ASKED FOR THE DATA

Sample size does depend on how much error can be tolerated in probability samples. In both probability and nonprobability samples, there is another important consideration. The person or group who asks for the data to be collected has a personal sense of what would be an adequate sized sample. This sense may be unconnected to sampling theory or, rather, may reflect a lack of understanding of sampling theory. City councils have been known to reject out of hand that a sample of 400 could possibly represent their citizenry. As an employee or outside consultant, one can politely lecture the council why 400 would be adequate. If this fails, try the numbers game. Point out to the council what a 5000 person sample would cost and what a 400 person sample would cost.

Do not underestimate the importance of what is an adequate sample size for those who asked for the data in the first place. Even if those who asked for it understand the sampling error arguments, they may still want a much larger sample for political reasons. They may think that their constituents would not trust a survey's results based on 400 people when there are 500,000 of them. This is a very strong argument for using a larger sample. Data based on a sample is only as good as people think it is. The best stratified sample with a 2 percent confidence interval is no good if the users or readers of the data think it is not large enough to be trusted.

14.5.3 RESOURCES

The above factors determine the size of the sample that is needed. Once one has the number, the reality of the budget needs to be faced. Time and money are scarce resources. One may neither have the time nor the money to collect data from as many units as one would want. It is time then to adjust sample size to reflect the resources available.

Time is a prime consideration. Data is collected for a reason. Perhaps data is needed before the next Board of Education meeting or by the June 16th council meeting. Data collection must be completed before that date. Reports are often ignored or paid less attention to if delivered on the day of a big meeting. Data drawn from a probability sample is probably important and thus should be circulated in report form two weeks before a meeting that will make decisions related to that data. Data drawn from a nonprobability sample varies in importance, depending on how many resources have been expended to collect it. Important data that can affect big decisions should be circulated two weeks before the appropriate meeting. Less important data can be circulated closer to the meeting date.

Another time consideration also has to do with the length of time to collect the data. Independent of when the data is needed is the actual time spent collecting the data. Data's accuracy is affected by the length of time it takes to collect. Sampling theory presumes all data is collected at the very same time. This means that surveys of individuals presume that all individuals answered the survey at the very same time. This assumption is impossible to meet. No organization has enough interviewers to make the phone calls or visits at the same time.

There is also no control over when a respondent fills out a mail surveyor even when distributed at work. There are exceptions, such as surveys of police officers that are done during watch meetings. The rule of thumb is that surveys of individuals should be completed within six weeks. After that time too many other factors could influence responses to trust that the responses of people surveyed the first day would be the same as their responses if interviewed the last day.

The rule of thumb if the unit of analysis is an organization is three months. A classic characteristic of an organization is its resistance to change. Therefore, organizations are expected to be less changeable than individuals, and data can be collected over a longer period of time.

Finally, there is the issue of money. Does the budget allow for data to be collected from the predetermined sample size? One needs to consider the production of questionnaires, mailing or interviewing costs, data cleaning and analysis costs, production of reports costs, etc. If one cannot afford the size of sample needed based on sampling error or views of who asked for the data, reconsider the initial needs. Beware. Increasing sampling error to get a smaller sample size may result in unusable data. This is the challenge of sampling, balancing resources against the quality of data needed.

14.6   RESPONSE RATE

Sample size normally is not the same as number of units actually studied. Mail surveys have very low initial response rates, 5 to 20 percent returned. Telephone and interview surveys can also suffer from low response rates. Surveys that are filled out in a room with supervision will have good response rates.

What is a good response rate? A response rate of at least 85 percent is excellent. Response rates between 70 and 85 percent are considered very good. Over 60 percent is considered acceptable. Response rates between 50 and 59 percent are questionable. Below 50 percent is just not scientifically acceptable. Thus, a very low response rate is simply a waste of resources.

For example, the U.S. Agriculture Department regularly surveys citizens about what they eat. The data is used to regulate school lunches, food stamps, food labels, and pesticide exposures. This data is very important for it not only affects the health of millions of Americans, but it also affects the spending of millions of dollars. The 1987–1988 food consumption survey was badly flawed due to its low response rate. Although the contractor randomly sampled 9000 households, only 34 percent of the households responded. With two-thirds of households not represented in the data, the federal government was left with data that did not represent the consumption patterns of most Americans.

In contrast, the Gallup Poll has an 88 percent response rate to its telephone interviews (personal interview, 1996). This is twice the industry average and, obviously, is a great response rate. Gallup attributes its high response rate to the prestige associated with being a respondent to a Gallup poll. Thus, who is sponsoring or conducting a study contributes to the likelihood of responding and thereby the usefulness of the data.

Response rate is particularly important for anyone doing research for professional publication. Journal editors and reviewers are unlikely to publish work with a response rate below 50 percent. One should, therefore, be diligent in attempts to improve one's response rate (see below). Occasionally, obtaining a better response rate is impossible because one is doing exploratory research, is using a new theory or approach or has applied a theory from another discipline. In such a case, the researcher must be able to explain the low response rate and document that any biases relevant to the topic due to the low response rate have been thoroughly examined.

In sum, response rate is critical to usefulness of data. There are a number of things that can be done to increase the likely response rate: envelope features, good cover letter, quality of questionnaire, postage, incentives, media blurbs, and follow-up.

14.6.1 ENVELOPE OR E-MAIL FEATURES

If mail delivery is necessary, then the first step in getting a high response rate is getting the respondent to open the envelope. If the survey is being distributed to people in an organization, use the type and color of envelope used for important notices. To illustrate, many offices use a large brown envelope that can be reused over and over again by just crossing out the old name on it. This type of envelope is used for a variety of regular office communications. It does not signal that the contents are important or that they need to be read promptly. Do not use this type of envelope. Instead, use the envelope that personnel use to send out important notifications, such as promotion and benefit announcements. Employees recognize this latter type of envelope as containing important information in need of prompt attention. Thus, the respondents will very probably open it and do so quickly.

If the U.S. mails are to be used, the envelope should not have a bulk rate stamp. Many people throw out mails by just looking at the envelope. Bulk rate stamps indicate mass mailings, which are unsolicited and often sales' pitches. Commemorative stamps look nice and do not send up such a red flag.

The envelope should be addressed, whenever possible, to the name of the household or household member. An envelope addressed to "occupant" is another "please throw me away" indicator. It is important to note that it is just fine to use mailing labels on the envelopes.

A return address can also encourage or discourage the recipient from opening the envelope. Government or university addresses are good. Envelopes with the names of charities or some nonprofit groups can be viewed as solicitations and therefore thrown away without being opened. But, according to the ethical standards of the American Association of Public Opinion Research, one does need to be honest. In addition, if research is being supported by a federal grant, the researcher is required to inform the respondent exactly how the data will be used.

If e-mail is to be used, one must remember that people are prone to delete items from unrecognized senders. Because of this, mass e-mail surveys are unlikely to yield good response rates. Intra-organizational surveys sent from the e-mail of a well-recognized organizational member, the city manager for example, will encourage the best response to the e-mail survey format.

It may be worthwhile to put a phrase alerting the recipient about the contents on the bottom of the envelope or in the e-mail subject line. Of course, this works only if it ties into a widely felt interest in the topic. "Important Survey Inside" does not always do it. "Benefits Survey" would work if the respondent were an employee or government aid recipient.

14.6.2 GOOD COVER LETTER, E-MAIL, AND PHONE INTRODUCTION

Once one gets the addressee to open the envelope or e-mail, one has to get her interested in filling out the questionnaire. The cover letter is key. Again, many people look at the letter and within reading just the first few lines make the decision to toss or continue reading. Therefore, the cover letter must give a good first impression.

The cover letter should be on letterhead. It should also be a very well spaced and short letter, one page maximum. Moreover, the letter, whenever possible, should use the respondent's name in the salutation. The letter should be signed with a signature and a title. More than one signature can be used if it encourages completion. For example, a survey being conducted by the Maintenance Department should bear the signature of the department head and the mayor or city manager.

In the very first sentence one needs to foster the respondent's interest in reading further. By stating why the survey is important and important to them, one taps into their interest. If more motivation is needed, mention the bribe or incentive next. This is especially important in a survey that is being sent out to a wide community audience.

The letter needs to be honest about who is sponsoring the survey. Normally, this is done in the first sentence as one is trying to tap into the respondent's interest. Statements such as "the city council and mayor want your input into whether or not the city should build a stadium" get right to the point of both sponsorship and interest in participating.

Now, if the respondents make it past the first paragraph, one still has to persuade them to fill out the survey. To do so, it is necessary to assuage some qualms they might have. Explain why they were chosen for the study and if the data is confidential. Also point out how little of their time the survey will take by saying a true estimate. An example would be "this survey will take only ten minutes of your valuable time." (see also, Leeuw and Hox, 2004.)

Always in the last paragraph there should be directions about how to get the survey back to the office and a stated date of arrival. For example, "Please return the survey in the enclosed self-addressed envelope by September 15," or for e-mail, "Please submit your survey by replying to this e-mail by March 30." In this last paragraph, one should also thank the respondent and give a phone number, e-mail address, and name of a person they can call if they have any questions. Just by giving the respondent an option to check on the survey increases response rate and does not necessarily subject the organization to a flood of calls. Although few people will call or e-mail, there should still be a trained staff member prepared to receive and address any inquiries.

Obviously, the cover letter or phone introduction needs to be directed at the language level of the respondent. It should also have a "friendly" style.

14.6.3 QUALITY OF QUESTIONNAIRE

Questionnaire construction is treated in a later chapter of this handbook. A well-constructed questionnaire not only produces useful data but also affects response rate. It is important that the questionnaire is easy to follow as well as simple to read. Otherwise, respondents may just quit filling out the questionnaire and never return it. Well-spaced questions, clear directions between sections, consistent set up of questions, and response alignment all help to increase response rate.

The actual length of the questionnaire is also a factor that can affect response rate. There are no tried and true rules on what length questionnaire produces what response rate. Too many other factors affect response rate, such as the design features and interest of respondent in the survey.

14.6.4 POSTAGE

In the envelope feature's section above, commemorative stamps were recommended for the envelope addressed to the respondent. There is also the issue of return postage if the U.S. mail is being used. First, always provide the respondent with a return envelope, which has already been addressed and stamped. Second, a commemorative stamp on the envelope will again increase response rates. It seems that respondents feel a subtle pressure to return surveys when the envelopes have a stamp on them.

The use of a stamp on the return envelope does increase response rates but not dramatically. Therefore, weight the cost differential of using stamps versus business reply. With stamps, one has to pay for each one whether or not they are used by respondents to mail the survey back. In contrast, with business reply the post office only charges for questionnaires returned. The post office does charge a little extra for this service, so that the additional cost needs to be factored in one's decision to use stamps or business reply. Do not forget that if stamps are used, someone has to stick them on the envelopes.

14.6.5 INCENTIVES

Incentives are rewards to encourage response. Whether monetary or material, incentives are effective ways to increase response rates. Incentives can be provided with the surveyor upon return of the survey. They work best when the incentives are included with the survey. True, including the incentive with the survey is more expensive. The inclusion, though, works as a subtle contractual obligation, i.e., "we gave you this, you now must do the survey." In contrast, when receiving the bribe depends on the return of a completed survey, the respondent does not need to feel remorse when they throw away the demanding piece of mail that requests work for a small reward.

Monetary rewards do not have to be large to increase response rates. In fact, a dollar included with the questionnaire so the respondent can buy a cup of coffee (but not at Starbucks) to drink while they fill out the survey works well. Monetary rewards are not always appropriate or even legal if the sponsoring agency is public. The legal issue is whether it is acceptable to give a monetary benefit to only the sample population and not the whole population.

Moreover, monetary compensation may not always be the best reward because some people's time may be more valuable than the small monetary incentive. Furthermore, depending upon who is being polled, money may be misjudged or even unnecessary. When people are concerned about an issue and are eager to make their opinions' known, there may be no need for extra spending on such incentives. For example, when polling employees on work related issues that could affect their environment, a bribe may not be necessary to increase response rates. Of course, there may be other reasons for offering an incentive, such as showing respect for the employee's time.

Many material rewards are also possible. The key is that the reward must appeal to the entire sample population. If the sponsoring agency is the library, bookmarks can be included with hours or important city phone numbers listed. A water agency might use a hard water tester. An all purpose incentive is the refrigerator magnet on which numbers, information or pictures can be printed.

It is also possible to include coupons as the incentive. Parks and recreation might include a coupon of dollars off next class or team sign-up. This reward would work well if the sample were all past students or sport participants. If the city has an annual fair, free admission coupons work well if the survey is conducted close to the event.

Coupons do not have to cost the sponsoring agency anything. Local businesses often are willing to provide the coupons as a goodwill gesture or form of advertising. But be careful that the business has no relevance to the aim of the study. One does not want the incentive to introduce a bias. Also be careful that the solicitation of coupons from one business is not considered favoritism, that is, if there is a rival business in the city, for example.

Finally, offering to supply the respondents with a brief summary of the study's results can be used as a motivation. One could mention that a link to the report will be on the organization's Web page when the results are final. This form of incentive may be most useful for an elite sampling population, such as city managers, police chiefs, or civic leaders. This reward for responding should not be used if the summary mailing or e-mail would occur so far in the future that the respondents may not even remember doing the survey or find the results useful.

14.6.6 MEDIA BLURBS OR PRENOTIFICATION

Another technique that can be used to increase response rates is prenotification. One to two weeks before the receipt of the survey one can contact respondents by mail, phone, or e-mail, alerting them that they have been selected to participate in the study. For instance, a brightly colored mailing or picture postcard is likely to be read and get the respondent's attention.

A cheaper form of prenotification would be to use media blurbs announcing the upcoming survey. The choice of media outlet depends on the sample population. If the sample population is the general community, newspapers or the city's cable channel can be used. If the sample population is concentrated in an organization or a building, such as employees, then bulletin boards, e-mail, or newsletters are useful. If the sample population is members of a group that gets newsletters or periodic mailings, these outlets can provide prenotification.

14.6.7 FOLLOW-UPS

A major technique used to increase response rates is doing follow-ups. After the initial questionnaire has been distributed, reminders to return the questionnaire should be done. Reminders can be in the form of a postcard, letter, telephone call, e-mail, fax, or a complete redistribution. The method used for reminders depends upon budget and access to information, such as phone numbers.

If one has kept track of who has returned the questionnaire, follow-ups need only be done to those who have not responded. By putting an office code on the questionnaire, one can keep track of who has and has not responded. Thus, reminders can be sent only to those who have not responded.

Follow-ups should be done in two week intervals. The first reminder would go out two weeks or ten business days after the questionnaire distribution. The reminder should stress the importance of the study and also thank the respondent if they have already responded. It is also important to provide a number to call if the respondent has misplaced the questionnaire so a replacement can be sent.

If after the first follow-up, the return rate is over 80 percent, one may decide to stop collecting data or do one final follow-up. Return rates lower than 50 percent demand a second if not third follow-up. Remember that the worth of the data depends upon achieving as high a response rate as possible, 60 percent or higher is a must. Expect to get about half the return rate in the second follow-up as in the first. So if one got 40 percent in the first follow-up, the second follow-up should produce about 20 percent return.

The last follow-up, if more than one, differs from earlier follow-ups in that a questionnaire as well as a reminder message may be included. Depending on budget and time passage since initial questionnaire distribution, it may be wise to include a questionnaire with the last reminder. After a month, it is likely that the initial questionnaire is lost. For e-mail questionnaires, of course, budget is far less a concern.

Telephone reminders are tricky. They not only require access to phone numbers but also require trained staff to do the calls. Each staff member making the calls should operate from a set script. The script should include the purpose of the study, who is sponsoring it, and its importance. Staff should have pleasant, friendly voices.

If a telephone reminder is possible, one might want to consider giving the respondent the option of doing the survey over the phone. Again, there must be a set script to work from so each staff member responds to respondents' questions the same way. Offering this option requires that the staff go through some training about phrasing of the survey questions. A supervisor should also oversee the calls and verify responses by calling back a few respondents. Unfortunately, a study indicated that inviting the respondents to complete their questionnaires by phone did not significantly increase the response rate (Dillman et al., 1994).

Finally, a sample chosen by random digit dialing requires special follow-up considerations. One must keep track of each number called and list those where one got no response or when one needs to call at a different time for the proper respondent to be available. One should have different time slots available for call backs. Try to cover a morning, afternoon, early evening, and an evening, i.e., 9 AM TO 12 PM, 12 PM TO 4:30 PM, 4:30 PM TO 6:30 PM, AND 6:30 PM TO 9 PM.

14.6.8 DEMOGRAPHIC ANALYSIS AS A CHECK ON RESPONSE BIAS

When response rate is less than 100 percent, there is the possibility that those who responded are different from those who did not. If possible, one needs to check for the extent of such a bias on the study's main variables. To do this, one needs to know some characteristic of the sampling population, such as the percent that are male or female or the percent that are union or nonunion members. Then one sees to what extent the sample reflects that actual percent. If one finds that the sample has a higher or lower percent of men or women for example, one needs to analyze the responses of the two sexes to some key questions. If they are significantly different, then there is an important response bias.

If a response bias exists, then one has two strategies to pursue in presenting one's data. First, one can weigh the sample to correct for the bias in response. In other words, if one has more women in the sample than in the sampling population, the women's answers are weighted less than men's.

This is just like weighting in nonproportional sampling, which is discussed earlier in the chapter. Second, one can present all findings within the subgroups, in this case male and female.

One should be on the look out for response bias during data collection. An early analysis of the first wave of returned questionnaires may signal how critical multiple follow-ups are to the quality of the sample. Special messages can be put in the reminders to elicit more responses from the under represented group too.

14.6.9   DATA COLLECTION IN DIFFERENT COUNTRIES

Even though one may need to collect data from units in countries other than the United States, do not rush out to book plane tickets (Taylor, 1995). One may be able to collect the data in this country or use data already collected.

For example, one might be able to collect the data desired from foreigners right at one's fingertips.

Foreign students at nearby U.S. campuses can provide a sufficient population for a sample. Be aware that the sample is foreign nationals but within the United States, which may create a bias and thus be inappropriate but not always.

A pharmaceutical company interested in flooding Europe with its new cough syrup turned to European born and raised students who had been in the United States for less than two years. By contacting foreign language departments and the Office of International Education at local universities, lists of appropriate students were obtained. Using the lists, the company drew a sample and had the selected students try out their European taste buds on the American cough syrup.

When one really needs the data to come from another country, one should always consider the resources that the country may have to offer. Many countries carry out a census of their population every ten years. Although the censuses are mostly demographic information, they often also cover other topics.

Another possibility is a research center or a university in the foreign country that also is interested in the same topic. They may have data or be willing to help in the data collection.

If it turns out that no existing data is relevant, one should probably resort to a local agency to conduct the survey. There are too many cultural differences that can affect data collection in different countries. Language nuances, types of incentives, how many people have phones or unique addresses, and even whether voter or household lists are available to nongovernment employees are some of the issues that show why one needs a native agency or professional to guide the survey.

Some final words of wisdom on data from foreign countries should be offered. It is amazing what is considered unacceptable in the United States but perfectly normal in other countries. For example, quota sampling has been regarded as unacceptable in the United States for 50 years. But many countries like Mexico, France, and the United Kingdom routinely use quota samples. Amazingly, in those countries quota sampling has worked well in public opinion polling. Random digit dialing is considered the only acceptable telephone interviewing sampling method in the United States. Yet, many countries do not use it.

14.7   CONCLUSION

The theme of this chapter has been sampling and data collection. There are many important issues to address in doing both. In the end, the quality of the final research report rests on the quality of one's data collection. The ability to do certain statistical analyses is also dependent on the data collection, particularly sample size. Once data is collected, though, there continues to be challenges to the quality of one's research. A large, probability sample done overtime sounds like great data. These data must be accurately transformed to a computer file to maintain their integrity. The problems faced in constructing data sets is the topic of the next chapter.

PROBLEMS

1. Older adults who exercised at least three times a week were much less likely to develop dementia than those who were less active, according to a study financed by the National Institutes of Health and the U.S. Department of Health and Human Services. The research, reported in the Annals of Internal Medicine, was conducted by Dr. Eric B. Larson and colleagues at the Group Health Cooperative (GHC), the University of Washington and the VA Puget Sound Health Care System in Seattle, Washington (Larson et al., 2006). The researchers followed 1740 GHC members age 65 or older for an average of 5.2 years between 1994 and 2003. When the study began, the participants—all of whom were tested and found to be cognitively normal—reported the number of days per week they engaged in at least 15 minutes of physical activity. Their cognitive function was then assessed, and new cases of dementia were identified, every two years. By the end of the study, the rate of developing dementia was significantly lower for those who exercised more—three times weekly, compared with those who exercised fewer than three times per week—a 32 percent reduction in risk.

    If you were an administrator for the U.S. Department of Health and Human Services, how would you evaluate this data in regard to sampling issues?

2. In spring 2006, the Californian Independent Field Poll organization did a poll of 1070 registered voters in the state. The poll found that 37 percent of the registered voters approved of Governor Arnold Schwarzenegger's performance in office and 40 percent approved of the state legislature's performance. The poll had a margin of error of 3 percent, 95 percent of the time
    a. Identify each of the following:
       Population, sample, level of confidence, confidence interval, unit of analysis
    b. Is this a random, voluntary, or convenience sample, and how do you know?
    c. If this study was a stratified sample and not a SRS, would you have more or less confidence in it and why?

APPENDIX A: READING A RANDOM DIGIT CHART

How Many Digits to Read?

1. If theoretical population has less than 10 units, read one digit.
    <u>5</u> <u>4</u> <u>7</u> <u>9</u> <u>3</u> <u>3</u> <u>0</u> <u>6</u> <u>4</u>
2. If theoretical population has between 10 and 99 units, read two digits.
    <u>5 4</u> <u>7 9</u> <u>3 3</u> <u>0 6</u> 4
3. If theoretical population has between 100 and 999 units, read three digits.

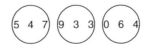

Where to Start to Read Chart?
The answer is anywhere.
    If one decides to read rows and is looking for three numbers between 1 and 12, then the numbers would be
54 79 33 <u>06</u> 41 99 43 96 95 34
<u>01</u> 49 35 <u>20</u> 27 92 63 20 67 <u>02</u>

APPENDIX B: ILLUSTRATION OF LIST OF THEORETICAL POPULATION FOR SRS VERSUS STRATIFIED SAMPLE

Theoretical Population: All city-owned vehicles as of August 1, 2007.

1	2001 Ford Crown Victoria
2	2002 Ford Crown Victoria
3	2002 Ford Crown Victoria
4	2005 Ford Crown Victoria
5	2004 Chevrolet Suburban
6–105	2006 Dodge Charger

Stratified: Numbered list of all city-owned vehicles stratified by city department.

Police	Mayor's Office	Parks and Recreation	Refuse
1–100. 2006 Dodge Charger	1. 2001 Ford Crown Victoria 2. 2005 Ford Crown Victoria	1. 2002 Ford Crown Victoria 2. 2004 Chevrolet Suburban	1. 2002 Ford Crown Victoria

APPENDIX C: PUBLIC ADMINISTRATION ARTICLES USING DIFFERENT SAMPLING METHODS

Simple Random Sample:
J. Rivera and P. de Leon. 2004. Is greener whiter? Voluntary environmental performance of western ski areas, *The Policy Studies Journal*, 32:417–437.

Stratified Random Sample:
T.L. Brown and M. Potoski. 2003. Contract-management capacity in municipal and county governments, *Public Administration Review*, 63:153–164.

Stratified Sample:
G.J. Miller, S.J. Yeager, W.B. Hildreth, and J. Rabin. 2005. How financial managers deal with ethical stress, *Public Administration Review*, 65:301–312.

Convenience Sample:
K. Thurmaier and C. Wood. 2002. Interlocal agreements as overlapping social networks: Picket-fence regionalism in metropolitan Kansas city, *Public Administration Review*, 62:585–598.

Volunteer Sample:
S.H. Mastracci, M.A. Newman, and M.E. Guy. 2006. Appraising emotion work. Determining whether emotional labor is valued in government jobs, *American Review of Public Administration*, 36:123–138.

Judgmental or Reputation Sample, note: the choice of city was based on reputation, not the inclusion of individual officers:
M.M. Brown and J.L. Brudney. 2003. Learning organizations in the public sector? A study of police agencies employing information and technology to advance knowledge, *Public Administration Review*, 63:30–43.

Census Sample:
S. Kim. 2002. Participative management and job satisfaction: Lessons for management leadership, *Public Administration Review*, 62:231–241.

APPENDIX D: ADDITIONAL READINGS ON SAMPLING AND DATA COLLECTION

D. Andrews, B. Nonnecke, and J. Preece. 2003. Electronic survey methodology: A case study in reaching hard-to-involve Internet users, *International Journal of Human-Computer Interaction*, 16:185–210.

S.J. Best and B.S. Krueger. 2004. *Internet Data Collection*, Thousand Oaks, California: Sage Publications.

M.A.I. Bulmer, P.J. Sturgis, and N. Allum. 2006. *The Secondary Analysis of Survey Data*, Volume I, Thousand Oaks, California: Sage Publications.

M.P. Couper. 2000. Web surveys: A review of issues and approaches, *Public Opinion Quarterly*, 64:464–494.

N.D. Glenn. 2005. *Cohort Analysis: Second Edition*, Thousand Oaks, California: Sage Publications.

G.B. Markus. 1979. *Analyzing Panel Data*, Thousand Oaks, California: Sage Publications.

REFERENCES

D.A. Dillman, K.K. West, and J.R. Clark. 1994. Influence of an invitation to answer by telephone on response to census questionnaires, *Public Opinion Quarterly*, 58:557.

E. de Leeuw and J.J. Hox. 2004. I am not selling anything: 29 Experiments in telephone introductions, *International Journal of Public Opinion Research*, 16:464–473.

G.M. Goldhaber. 1984. A Pollsters' Sampler, *Public Opinion*, 53:47–50.

K.L. Kraemer, W.H. Dutton, and A. Northrop. 1981. *The Management of Information Systems*, Columbia University Press, New York.

E.B. Larson, L. Wang, J.D. Bowen, W.C. McCormick, L. Teri, P. Crane, and W. Kukull. 2006. Exercise is associated with reduced risk for incident dementia among persons 65 years of age and older, *Annals of Internal Medicine*, 144:73–81.

Personal interview with Tom Reiger at Gallup Poll, Irvine California, March 1, 1996.

C. Rosen. 2004. Our cell phones, ourselves, *The New Atlantis*, 6:26–45.

The Survey System 2003. Sample size calculator. Retrieved August 16, 2006 from World Wide Web: http://www.surveysystem.com/sscalc.htm

H. Taylor. 1995. Horses for courses: How different countries measure public opinion in very different ways, *Public Perspective* (February/March): 3–7.

UCLA Department of Statistics. 2005. Calculators. Retrieved August 16, 2006 from World Wide Web: http://calculators.stat.ucla.edu

G. Urbaniak and S. Plaus. 2006. Research randomizer. Retrieved August 16, 2006 from World Wide Web: http://www.randomizer.org

15 Using the Survey as an Instrument of Inquiry in Research

Sarmistha Rina Majumdar

CONTENTS

The survey methodology is widely used in research. It helps to probe individuals' opinions, attitudes, behavior, and preferences in a social setting and collect information on demographics and various other topics that are of interest to researchers. According to Converse (1987), the survey instrument is like a telescope whose focus can be adjusted, broadened, or narrowed depending upon the needs of the researcher. The versatility in application of this instrument accounts for much of its popularity in the field of social science. In public administration, researchers frequently use the survey methodology to collect information on work values and organizational commitment among individuals in public organizations, people's opinions on public policies and to gauge the level of their satisfaction with public goods and services. In contingent valuation of those public goods like wilderness areas whose social values are difficult to assess, the survey methodology is often relied upon to collect information from the public for valuing such goods (Weimer, 2005, p. 73).

In administrative studies, the survey methodology can be easily incorporated into a quasi or a nonexperimental research design. It can be utilized to collect information from administrators and citizens to examine a policy or a program's effectiveness and to address managerial and other concerns in an organization. For example, information on children's test scores in mathematics, reading, and science collected through a national survey of schools can be utilized to determine the effectiveness of The No Children Left Behind Act and make decisions about its renewal in subsequent years (Dillon, 2006). Time series analysis of census data proves useful in studying the trend of activities that may range from crime and privatization of prisons to productivity in public organizations. In evaluation of public programs, surveys serve as an important tool in assessment of outcomes and in detection of weaknesses in the mechanism of service delivery.

In this chapter, some of the important features of the survey methodology have been discussed. Starting with a brief history of the method, efforts have been made to provide information on the essential elements of a survey, that is, from development of research questions to sample selection, modes of data collection, response rate, and ethics in survey research. Also, attempts have been made to answer questions about length of survey questionnaire, duration of surveys, and an acceptable response rate. It is important to keep in mind that any well planned survey can yield valuable information and help to generate both theoretical and empirical insights into administrative practices and policies.

15.1 BRIEF HISTORY

The use of surveys dates back to early times. In 1880, Marx, the German political sociologist, designed a lengthy questionnaire to investigate the exploitation of workers by employers. Even Weber used it in his study of religious ethic. In the twentieth century, its use expanded upon improvements in various aspects of the methodology. For example, the U.S. censuses made important contributions in sampling and data collection techniques. The commercial polling firms of Gallup, Roper, Harris, and others through their privately funded surveys helped to develop the sampling techniques and improved the format of the survey. Researchers like Samuel A. Stouffer helped to develop scientific methods of empirical research and Paul F. Lazarsfeld popularized the application of surveys in understanding of social phenomenon like an economic depression and its impact on population (Babbie, 1998, pp. 38–39). Over the years, the methodology has improved considerably as a result of ongoing research activities at various survey research institutes and universities in different parts of the world (House et al., 2003).

15.2 STAGES OF A SURVEY

There are several stages in a survey and each stage is interrelated to the other. Weaknesses in any one stage can lead to a flaw in the survey design and make it difficult to fulfill the objectives of the study. Thus, the development of the survey, stage by stage is considered to be critical in the data collection process. In the following sections, the various stages of the survey have been discussed.

15.2.1 OBJECTIVES

In a survey based research project, the researcher must first decide what is the actual purpose of the survey. Once the intents or the aims of the survey research have been established, the objectives need to be clearly and precisely stated. The statement of objectives requires reiterations and can be time consuming. It is worth investing time in such an endeavor as well defined objectives help to lay the foundation for the next stage, that is, development of the research questions for the study. Also, objectives of a survey help to effectively communicate with sponsors and respondents and attract the attention of those who might be interested in subject of the study.

15.2.2 RESEARCH QUESTIONS

The research question helps to identify variables and collect both specific and concrete information related to those variables. In fact, the research question provides the direct link between the abstract concept in objectives and the raw data that is collected through a survey. Like the objectives, the research question needs to be stated as clearly as possible. It is often done through a process of reiterations of statements until one is satisfied with the exact wordings and the meanings they convey. In any study, the research question provides the much needed direction and coherence and also helps to determine the unit of analysis in a study. In addition, it helps to mark the boundaries of a project, maintain focus and guide the entire data collection and analysis process (Punch, 2003).

15.2.3 Unit of Analysis

In a study, the unit of analysis needs to be identified prior to collection of information. In a survey, the unit of analysis can range from individuals to any element that is of interest to the researcher. For example, in a survey of citizens, the individual is the unit of analysis. In another survey, designed to collect information on crime rates of cities, the city becomes the unit of analysis. A survey can have more than one unit of analysis. For instance, in a survey designed to collect information on graduation and drop out rates of high schools in a school district along with that of household income of high school students, several units of analyses can be identified. They include the high schools in a school district, high school students and their households. In such a complex survey, each unit needs to be identified in advance and the data needs to be organized in such a way that they facilitate analysis at a later stage.

Information obtained from a survey can be utilized to describe the components of a sample. For example, in a survey of cities, information obtained on crimes and average household income can help to describe these cities in terms of their safety and wealth status. Sometimes a controversy might exist over the selection of unit of analysis. For example, in performance measurement of local governments, some scholars advocate the use of citizens' satisfaction surveys. These surveys help to provide a voice to citizens and give them the opportunity to make informed judgments about local services (Miller and Miller, 1991, p. 8). Other scholars disagree and prefer the survey of qualified administrators for several reasons. First, citizens' judgments are flawed due to their lack of knowledge about production and provision details of services provided by local governments (Lyons et al., 1992). Second, citizens' evaluations are more subjective in nature and often do not match with that of actual agency records (Percy, 1986, p. 67). Third, there exists the tendency among citizens to rate services lower than administrators of local governments (Melkers and Thomas, 1998). In contrast, qualified administrators tend to base their assessments on objective internal measures of service quality (Lovrich and Taylor, 1976). But a later study (Swindell and Kelly, 2000) on performance measurements in local governments has recommended the use of both units of analysis as they provide equally valuable information in such a scheme of measurement.

15.2.4 Sample

The word 'sample' refers to the subset of a population. A sample is created from a sampling frame from which elements are selected to be included in a sample. The sampling frame or the source of information (example, a list of names) has to be checked for omissions and repetitions of information. A survey sample can be a simple, single stage sample, with no difference between the sampling unit and the element. For example, public transit bus riders surveyed at a bus stop. If the researcher conducts the same survey at selected counties of the state, in few townships, at specific bus stops and only of daily commuters, the sample becomes more complex. In such a sample survey, four levels of sampling units can be identified—the counties, townships, bus stops, and daily commuters. The last unit, the daily commuters constitute the elements of the survey.

A sample can be either a probability or a nonprobability sample. In a probability sample, all members of the population have an equal chance of being selected. The randomness in the selection process helps to avoid both conscious and unconscious bias in element selection (Babbie, 1998). Sometimes a nonprobability sample may lack representativeness if it is selected by the researcher on the basis of some prior knowledge about the population. The latter type is used when probability sampling is expensive or when precise representativeness is not a requirement of the study.

In drawing a sample from a population, there exist the possibility of committing both sampling and nonsampling errors. The sampling error is the expected error in estimating a parameter from any given sample design. It can be calculated either before drawing a sample or afterwards and often the standard error serves as the measure of sampling error (based on theoretical sampling distribution). The size of the sampling error affects the accuracy of the estimate. A nonsampling error arises due to flaws in the survey design or faulty implementation and can lead to a bias in the study (O'Sullivan et al., 2003).

15.2.5 SURVEY DESIGN

The design of a survey is largely determined by the survey's purpose. If a survey is aimed at single time description and determination of relationships between variables, a cross sectional survey can be used. For instance, by selecting a sample from some larger population, a cross sectional survey can help to understand whether there exist gender differences if any, among adults in their attitudes towards smoking of tobacco. A longitudinal survey permits the analysis of data over a period of time. It can be used to collect explanatory or descriptive data at different points in time and observe a change in a variable over a fixed period of time.

A longitudinal survey can be designed either as a trend, cohort, or panel study. In a trend study, samples are drawn from a population and studied over a long period of time. Each time a sample is selected new members are included in it. In a trend study, the comparison of results of several surveys conducted at different periods of time helps to obtain descriptive information about the general population. For example, a researcher can use a trend study to observe changes if any, among university students' attitude towards smoking tobacco over the last two decades.

A cohort study can be used to collect information from a group that has experienced the same significant event within a specific time period (O'Sullivan et al., 2003, p. 37). In a cohort study, samples are drawn at different time periods from the same group or cohort of individuals, organizations or other units of analysis. Every time a sample is drawn from a cohort new members are included in the group, which makes it difficult to identify those individuals that undergo changes and establish a time sequence for such changes. To address the problem, a panel study can be conducted, where the same panel or sample is studied over a fixed period of time. Panel members are asked the same questions at regular intervals of time. The comparison of their answers makes it possible to observe and track changes among these individuals and provide suitable explanations for such changes over a specific period of time (Babbie, 1998).

15.2.6 QUESTIONNAIRE

The questions in a survey are directly related to the research question. In development of a survey questionnaire, the variables for which information needs to be collected have to be identified followed by their operational definition. The operational definition of a variable is directly linked to its conceptual definition and helps in collection of relevant data for that variable. For example, the conceptual definition of the variable, 'education,' can be operationalized as educational attainments of adults after high school education. With this definition in mind, relevant questions can be asked to collect information through a survey.

A survey questionnaire can contain both questions and statements and they should be relevant to the topic. The questionnaire can be developed in its entirety or by using borrowed questions and statements from previous studies that are similar. There also exists the option of using only a part of an existing question and making modifications in it by adding personal ideas and words to it. The advantage of previously used questions is that, it facilitates comparison of past and present results (Punch, 2003, p. 32).

In a survey questionnaire, the wording of questions requires both time and patience. All questions and statements should be worded in such a way that they do not display any personal bias or offend anyone. For example, the question, 'do you think the police failed to reduce crime in the city,' and provided with the response categories of agree, strongly agree, disagree, strongly disagree and no opinion should be avoided for aforementioned reasons. Keeping the response categories intact, the same question can be reworded as 'do you think that the police helped to control crime in the city?' The rewording should be done without making changes in the original intent of the question.

Survey questions can be both close and open-ended. In close-ended questions, the response categories are exhaustive, that is, include possible responses expected from respondents. They are also mutually exclusive, implying that only one category can be selected as the answer to a question. The number of close-ended questions in any survey exceeds the number of open-ended questions. The latter's popularity can be partly attributed to their usefulness in maintaining uniformity in response categories. For example, survey response categories of strongly agree, moderately agree, moderately disagree, strongly disagree and do not know can be used in several questions to collect information. The maintenance of unity in response categories facilitates the transfer of information directly from the survey sheet to the data entry form.

In writing a survey report, the criterion of exhaustiveness is difficult to maintain. It is not possible to report findings on all the response categories for all the questions in a report. So, there exists the tendency to group response categories into few groups leading to the loss of information. For example, grouping of the two response categories 'somewhat agree' and 'strongly agree' into a single category of 'agree' leads to some loss of information on the various levels of agreement observed among respondents in a survey. Also, in answering close-ended questions with multiple response categories, many respondents tend to select the middle option rather than the two extremes at the ends (Schwarz et al., 1985; Tourangeau et al., 2000, p. 232). In structuring of responses in a survey, a problem commonly encountered is the lack of space to accommodate all the possible categories of responses. For example, in a survey question aimed at probing respondents' preferred mode of commute to work all the available modern options cannot be listed in a survey question-naire. Only few popular options are presented to respondents that might reflect personal bias of the researcher and lead to overlooking of others. To address such a problem, sometimes the last option is listed as 'others (explain).' Despite the presence of such an option, many respondents simply ignore it and try to fit their answers into a given list of options even though the fit might not be perfect (Babbie, 1998, p. 128).

The open-ended questions of a survey provide respondents with the opportunity to answer questions in their own words (Fowler, Jr., 2002, p. 91). These questions require the provision of more space to answer them and more information can be obtained from such questions. Also, open-ended questions are more suited for posing opinion or belief questions and can help to obtain both exact and factual information. For example, the opinion question, 'do you think that networking with other organizations has helped your organization,' can help to obtain facts on networking from a survey of managers in public organizations. Similarly, open-ended questions can be asked to obtain exact information about age, income, education, number of years worked in an organization along with others in a survey. In answering exact questions, individuals always do not provide the actual numerical figures. Instead, they round off number and create their own grouped categories. For instance, instead of reporting exact income figures, individuals prefer to round them. Such a tendency to round of numbers can be attributed to various reasons that might range from difficulties in recalling an exact answer to privacy reasons or even lack of exact knowledge. A disadvantage with rounding of numbers is that, it makes it difficult to define the special characteristics of a sample with exact figures (Tourangeau et al., 2000, pp. 232–233).

In a survey questionnaire, the open and close-ended questions should be spaced in such a way that they are spread out and not squeezed together to fit a page. Their placement should be logical and sequential to help ensure the smooth transition from one topic to another and aid respondents in recollection of past events and facts. Any random placement of questions can easily confuse respondents and can make it difficult even for a researcher to make meaningful interpretations at a later stage in the study. Also, survey questions should be clear, short, and unambiguous. They should not contain any abbreviations to prevent any kind of misinterpretation.

A survey researcher should avoid using complex or double barreled questions. The following question, "do you think that the city should spend less money on street improvements and more on local schools?" is a complex question and is difficult to answer. In the question, two problems have been identified but only a single solution has been offered. Some respondents might agree or disagree with such a notion although others would leave the question unanswered as they might think of other solutions to address those two problems.

Often the length of a survey questionnaire influences the response rate and quality of data. If a survey questionnaire is too long, respondents with a busy schedule are likely to ignore or skip questions. Also, tired or bored respondents are likely to provide unreliable answers (O'Sullivan et al., 2003, p. 186). Hence, the number of questions to be included in a survey is a matter of judgment. The length of the survey questionnaire can be determined by a pilot test. If a survey takes more than 20 minutes to complete, it is most likely to pose a problem. Shorter questionnaires tend to have a higher response rate and yield more valid responses (Punch, 2003, p. 35).

In a face-to-face or telephone interview, a question that is frequently asked is, 'how long will it take to complete the survey?' The decision to participate in the survey often rests on the time estimate provided. Based on my personal experiences in interviewing of public and private sector officials, I noticed that they are reluctant to spend more than 30 minutes in answering survey questions in their regular week day schedule. Further, all questions on demographics should be placed at the end of the questionnaire. If they are placed at the beginning of the survey, respondents are most likely to ask, "What does my gender or level of education have to do with the topic of the survey?"

15.2.7 Pretests and Pilot Study

A pretest is an initial test of one or more components of a survey. A pretest helps to reveal many hidden problems prior to the administration of a survey. For example, if a researcher decides to pretest a sample that was reasonably easy to conceive in paper, the problems associated with drawing the actual sample become evident in such a process. Review of these problems provides information about the actual feasibility of the design along with an estimate of the time and cost involved in creation of such a sample.

Pretesting can be done in multiple stages to minimize obstacles in the data collection process. In pretesting of a survey questionnaire, ambiguous questions can be detected, which is often followed by a decision either to revise or drop them because of their complex nature. Also, pretesting helps to decide on the mode of delivery of the final survey. That is, whether it should be self administered, mailed, electronically delivered or interviews be conducted of selected individuals in a study. In pretesting of a data collection process, the researcher gets an idea of all tasks involved in administration of a survey. For example, if a researcher chooses to mail the questionnaire, pretesting helps to list the various steps involved from getting the questionnaire ready to mailing them to respondents. Often pretesting of the analysis process helps to reveal shortcomings in the data collection process. Any missing data on a variable can be easily linked to the failure to include pertinent questions for that variable. Thus, multiple pretests are necessary to make changes and revisions in a survey and these tests usually precede a pilot study.

A pilot study can be regarded as a mini survey. It involves testing of the entire research instrument in a form similar to the one that is used in the final survey and it is guided by three objectives: what should be the format of questions, how lengthy should the survey questionnaire be, and how can the data collection process be made more efficient without violating any ethical issues. Usually, a pilot study is conducted on a small sample, which can be chosen using the same process for selection of the final sample. If overlapping is a serious concern in the pilot study, then the sample can be drawn from the remainder of the population only after the final sampling has been done.

Those items that have not been pretested should not be included in a pilot study. An exception to this is the inclusion of more questions than were intended to be included in the final survey. Such an exception is based on the assumption that pretesting of questions is not sufficient enough to determine the right method of obtaining data for research purposes.

A pilot study helps to make the necessary adjustments in the final questionnaire. Even though a pilot study costs money and is time consuming, it is risky to eliminate it especially in a large project. Thus, when budgets, time, and other constraints pose serious obstacles, the risks of failure can be reduced by pretesting selected components and conducting a miniature pilot study.

15.3 DATA COLLECTION

Data collection requires the selection of a mode of data collection and development of a data collection form where the raw data is entered. The choice of any particular method of data collection is often based on its appropriateness in answering the central research question in a study. A data collection form requires planning in advance and assignment of codes to variables to reduce the possibility of making errors in the transfer of data to a statistical program for detailed analysis (Salkind, 2006).

15.3.1 METHODS OF DATA COLLECTION

Technological advancements have brought about significant changes in methods of data collection. Until the 1970s, much of the data were collected through face-to-face interviews or by mailing questionnaires. Later, increase in the number of telephone subscribers led to telephone interviews. Currently, with more people gaining access to the internet it is now possible to survey people online. Each method of data collection has its own advantages and disadvantages. The choice of any particular mode is determined by the availability of funds, time available and its appropriateness in answering the central research question. Each method has been discussed separately in the following paragraphs.

Survey by mail is a very common method of data collection. It involves the sending of a detailed cover letter explaining the purpose of the project and a questionnaire addressed to individuals selected to participate in the survey. The cover letter explains the purpose of the survey and provides assurance of confidentiality, which makes the respondent more comfortable in answering questions. A mail survey is more suited for collection of information on sensitive topics. The questionnaire must be self-explanatory. If respondents do not understand the questions or if answering the survey is too time consuming, they are most unlikely to return the survey. To elicit a higher response rate to a survey, both monetary and nonmonetary incentives could be included in the initial request. Even repeated follow-up attempts can prove to be effective. Also, the salience of the topic plays an equally important role in evoking a high response rate. For example, a survey sent to university students asking about their opinions on changes in the grading system is most likely to have a quick and a high response rate.

In a mail survey, it usually takes eight to ten weeks to collect data depending upon the sample size and the geographic distribution of the population. The cost of mailing the questionnaire includes that of the stationary, printing, and postage for both mailing and returning the survey. A response bias commonly evident in a mail survey is that, one subgroup is more or less likely to cooperate than others. Such a bias may arise from lack of education, physical limitations in reading or writing, age or other disabilities, complete lack of interest in the topic and geographical distribution of the sample. Sometimes it is possible to assess the potential response bias in a mail survey from the topic of the survey and its geographic distribution. For example, from a list of names and addresses, it can be predicted whether more males or females are likely to respond to a specific topic or whether residents in small townships are more likely to respond than city respondents.

Surveys conducted online share similarities with mail surveys. Even though it is a relatively new method of data collection, it is gaining in popularity as more individuals are subscribing to Internet services. Advantages of an online survey include collection of data at a minimal cost and within a short period of time. In selection of a sample for an online survey, respondents are selected from a sampling frame that includes a long list of names and addresses of internet users. Selected individuals receive a cover letter that is electronically mailed. The initial cover letter informs them about the importance and purposes of the survey, sponsorship of the survey if any, assures confidentiality and provides detailed instructions to complete the survey. To prevent nonsampled individuals from responding and multiple responses from selected individuals, each respondent is provided with a personal identification number (PIN) to gain access to the online questionnaire. Sometimes it is buried in the website address of the survey and the respondents have to click on to it to answer the questions.

On completion of an online survey, a thank you letter is sent to respondents in appreciation of their voluntary participation and for providing valuable information for research purposes. In this type of survey, technical problems are common and can range from lack of updated computer products to difficulties in accessing the website. Also, if respondents are not computer literate, they are unable to respond to the online questions. In such cases, the researcher lacks control over the response situation unlike in mail surveys. To enhance the overall response rate of internet surveys, repeated electronic mailings of reminders with link to the survey questionnaire and sometimes incentives are used.

A telephone survey is the most widely used method of survey. It is often used to access a geographically diverse population and can save both money and time. Telephone numbers can be selected at random from telephone books or created from an existing number by substituting the last four digits of the phone number with random numbers (random digit dialing). In a telephone survey, trained interviewers ask questions in a consistent manner and record the answers. The quality of the information collected depends upon the duration of interviews, order, and complexity of questions and on skills of surveyors in keeping the respondents engaged in answering the questions. Usually, a telephone interview lasts for 20 to 30 minutes depending upon the characteristics of the study population, length of questionnaire, motivation of individuals to respond, and on the skills of interviewers to persuade selected individuals to participate. The response rate of a telephone survey is considered slightly better than that of a mail survey even though, administrators, managers, and other professionals prefer mailed surveys over telephone interviews. The aged and less educated people prefer telephone surveys as telephone interviewers aid these respondents in answering questions not only by reading and repeating them but also by clarifying meanings when requested by respondents. Also, from the initial efforts in dialing numbers, it is easy to detect those that cannot be reached and those that refuse to participate (O'Sullivan et al., 2003, pp. 175–186). Further, it is much convenient to initiate contact by telephone than through other methods, establish a rapport with respondents, and in convincing them to complete the interview by making them believe in the relevance of the research topic and its impact on our lives.

In telephone surveys, there exists the flexibility to schedule an interview at a more convenient time. But in this mode of data collection, interviewers do not have control over the response situation. Even when a convenient time may be scheduled for a telephone survey, the location of the telephone and the presence of some other person in that room may make the respondent uncomfortable and reluctant to answer questions. The estimated cost of a telephone survey is more than a mail survey but less than that of a face-to-face interview and there exists a bias in the sampling frame. In the United States, 95.5 percent of households have telephones, but unlisted numbers and greater use of cellular phones currently pose a problem in selecting a sample. Researchers have to make special requests to concerned authorities for release of information on unlisted telephone numbers. Such efforts add to the time and cost of the survey. Also, modern technologies that enable blocking of calls, display of caller identity, answering machines, faxes, and other features pose problems in reaching respondents in a timely manner.

In a face-to-face interview, respondents are asked questions by interviewers in a relaxed atmosphere. These interviewers are trained to conduct interviews and are required to travel to initiate contact with respondents. Visual and other aids are used in the data collection process and to probe respondents for additional information. The expenses incurred in training and traveling and when combined with others make this mode of data collection the most expensive one. This method is used when complex and more open-ended questions need to be asked and respondents require much longer time to respond.

In this mode of survey, the face-to-face contact with respondents helps to establish a rapport with respondents. The appearance, manner, and facial expressions of interviewers do have an impact on the response rate. It is more difficult to refuse a person face-to-face than over the telephone or by not responding to a mail survey. If respondents cannot understand questions, interviewers can clarify their meanings and go over the various response choices. Interviewers also exert control over the response situation. For example, if a respondent feels uncomfortable in answering questions in the presence of others, interviewers can suggest moving to another place for greater privacy. Also, interviews can be conducted at locations that are accessible and convenient to respondents, which help to ensure their cooperation. A disadvantage of this method of data collection lies in accessing those respondents who live in unsafe neighborhoods, apartment complexes, and in remote areas (Czaja and Blair, 2005).

15.3.2 CODING OF DATA

Information collected through a survey is entered into a data entry form. The data should be organized in it in such a way that it is easy to understand and can be easily accessed any time for statistical analysis. A data entry form can be created using a spreadsheet like that of Excel, SPSS, and other statistical software. In the form, each variable is listed in a column and the responses from individuals are entered into rows, case by case. The entry of information requires the coding of data. For close-ended questions in a survey, responses are usually numerically coded and respondents are required to choose an option either by circling or putting a check mark against it for each question item. Answers to open-ended questions also need to be coded for analysis. These codes can be either developed after review of overall responses or be predefined and responses can be assigned to coded categories.

In a survey, if information is sought on a variable, example race, list different types and assign a code to each type. In entering data, do not combine codes as this would make the data lose some of its value. For example, the combination of codes for gender ($1 =$ male and $2 =$ female) and race ($1 =$ whites and $2 =$ nonwhites) into a code of 11 to represent a white male or 22 to indicate a female nonwhite, neither help to create a meaningful variable nor make it possible to separate the variables for analysis at a later stage. Thus, data should be entered into exclusive and exhaustive categories to prevent confusion and facilitate analysis (Salkind, 2006, p. 149).

15.4 RESPONSE RATE

The response rate is calculated as a percentage of the sample that has answered the questions. It helps to evaluate the data collection effort and can vary from one method of data collection to another. In any survey, some nonresponse is inevitable. To reduce the nonresponse bias, pertinent information about the survey including its importance and how it might affect selected individuals in a sample should be presented to respondents to generate interest in the topic of the survey. Also, more than one attempt should be made to establish contact with selected individuals either by post, electronic mail, telephone, or fax. The response rate of mail surveys is low and usually two to four attempts are made to contact individuals. For example, in a study aimed at understanding how cities help social entrepreneurship, city managers' and chief administrative officers in 544 U.S. cities with populations over 50,000 were surveyed by mail. After a pilot study and three rounds of mailings, only 202 responses were received, yielding a response rate of 37.1 percent (Korosec and Berman, 2006, p. 450). In writing a survey report, a nonresponse rate that exceeds five percent should be mentioned along with any discerned pattern in nonresponse that is, if certain categories of selected individuals refrained from answering survey questions (Czaja and Blair, 2005, p. 209, 253).

The response rates of different types of surveys vary. In a telephone survey, the average response rate is estimated to be 60 percent or less. Also, 3–20 attempts are made to contact individuals. For example, in a telephone survey on recycling and garbage collection in Madison (Wisconsin), 1330 residents were selected using postal zip codes. Initial dialing of their telephone numbers revealed that 4.7 percent had disconnected lines, 4.2 percent did not receive waste disposal services from the city of Madison, and 51.7 percent did not answer or were otherwise unavailable. A total of 301 individuals agreed to be surveyed over the phone, yielding a response rate of 57.3 percent (Jamelske and Wessling, 2005, p. 105). In face-to-face interviews, it is difficult to achieve a response rate higher than 70 percent (Brehm, 1993; O'Sullivan et al., 2003). If the sample size is small sometimes a higher response rate may be possible. For example, in my study of a local government that partnered with a private company to produce biodiesel (Majumdar, 2005), I used the snowballing approach to create a convenient sample which included 12 individuals from a total population of 20 people that were directly involved in decision making and implementation of the project. Because the mayor and city manager helped in selection of individuals for the study, their recommendations made all these individuals cooperate and thereby raised the response rate to nearly 100 percent.

The response rates of major American national surveys have been declining over the last four decades (Steeh, 1981; Brehm, 1993). Such a trend is partly attributable to representation of certain demographic groups in misleading numbers. Based on results from two leading, academic national public opinion surveys, Brehm (1993) has showed that the young and old adults, males, and people with higher income levels are underrepresented although those with lowest education levels are over represented. Also, people living in large cities and working longer hours are less likely to participate in a survey compared to those living in small towns (Smith, 1983; Fowler Jr., 2002, pp. 42–43). Additionally, there exist the tendency among respondents not to answer questions that are not of relevance to them (O'Sullivan et al., 2003).

The varied trends in response rates lead to a commonly asked question, 'what is an acceptable response rate?' According to Babbie (1998, p. 182), a response rate of at least 50 percent is often considered adequate for analysis and reporting. But in the field of public administration, there appears to be no agreed upon standard for a minimum acceptable response rate. Because administrators, city and county officials and others in various government positions and departments receive multiple requests to respond to surveys from academic, professional, and government organizations, they are often overwhelmed and annoyed (O'Sullivan et al., 2003, p. 199) by such requests and sometimes fail to respond. Under such circumstances, even a study with a low response report is acceptable and can make important contributions. For example, in a study aimed at examination of intergovernmental relations since 9/11, city and county officials in the state of Florida were surveyed by mail. A total of 1979 surveys were mailed out of which 414 usable surveys were returned, yielding a return rate of 21 percent. Despite the low response rate, survey findings showed evidences of improvements in intergovernmental cooperation as a result of the passage of federal and state mandates after 9/11 (Caruson and MacManus, 2006, pp. 522–525).

Efforts to improve a survey's response rate can lead to the use of monetary and nonmonetary incentives or more than one method of data collection. The latter method of mixing of modes helps to access those people who cannot be reached by a single mode. For example, if a respondent cannot be reached by telephone, the survey questionnaire can be faxed, electronically mailed, or posted. An important issue in such a multimodal method of data collection is the comparability of data across modes. Because answers to some questions might vary with the mode used in collection of data, it is important to check that the data is comparable when mixing modes.

In any survey, when all efforts to increase the response rate prove futile, the researcher has to accept the low response rate (Krosnick, 1999). A low response rate does not necessarily indicate that the results are inaccurate. Research has revealed that surveys with very low response rates can be more accurate when compared with surveys with much higher response rates. For example, Visser et al. (1996) compared the survey results of forecasts of outcomes of Ohio statewide elections over a 15 year period. Results showed that mail surveys with a response rate of about 20 percent predicted outcomes more accurately than telephone surveys with a response rate of about 60 percent. Also, high response rates or additional efforts aimed at correction of composition bias in a survey sample do not necessarily produce more accurate results. A Pew Research study (1998) has shown that the substantive conclusions of a study remain unaltered even with an increase in response rate. In those cases, where the substantive findings have changed, researchers have been unable to prove whether the findings were more accurate with the higher or lower response rate. Thus, a low response rate does not necessarily imply a large amount of nonresponse error (Krosnick, 1999, p. 540).

15.5 ETHICS IN SURVEY RESEARCH

Survey research like any other research project is guided by ethical guidelines. Ethical principles provide directions to the researcher right from the inception to the end of the project. They help to make sure that no one suffers from any adverse consequences as a result of the survey. Thus, the researcher has ethical obligations towards respondents in administration of the survey, in writing the final report, and making it available for public use. Additional guidance on ethical research practices can be sought from the professional code of conduct of the American Association for Public Opinion Research (Babbie, 1998), available at the organization's website http://www.aapor. org/pdfs/AAPOR_Code_2005.pdf

A researcher in meeting ethical obligations towards respondents or the voluntary participants of a survey has to provide them with adequate information about the project. The respondents should be made aware of the name of the organization conducting the study, sponsorship if any, and a brief description of the purpose of the study. Prior to administration of a survey, the researcher should promise confidentiality of responses and assure that they will not suffer negative consequences for their decisions either to participate or not to participate in the survey. Also, respondents need to be informed that they can skip any questions that they may not want to answer and can request a copy of the final report. The mode of conveying such information will vary with the type of data collection method used in a survey based research project. For instance, if telephone surveys or face-to-face interviews are to be conducted, such information can be verbally conveyed to respondents or included in the cover letter that can be either mailed, sent over the internet or faxed (Fowler, 2002).

Ethical principles guide the employment of interviewers and use of their services. A researcher cannot compel interviewers to visit unsafe places as part of their job requirements. Instead, they should be informed of the various options that are available in establishing contact with respondents in difficult situations (Czaja and Blair, 2005). Also, the researcher should provide them with full and accurate information about the research. This would prevent interviewers from being either deceptive or misleading in conducting interviews. Further, in preparation of the final report, the researcher has ethical obligations towards readers in the academic community and the public. Any weaknesses in the study and its impact, if any, have to be discussed. All negative findings along with positive ones should be reported. Also, any unexpected findings ought to be included in the final report for investigation in the future.

15.6 CONCLUSION

The survey methodology is a reliable method of data collection. Surveys can yield valuable information for exploratory purposes or descriptive reports. Surveys require much planning and the questionnaire needs to be designed and developed with time and patience. The final format of the survey should be always checked for flaws as undetected errors can prove to be costly and increase the risk of failure of the project. The time and money invested in a survey project can never be considered a waste as it helps to build a database and makes possible the primary and secondary analysis of data at a later and convenient date.

The flexibility allowed by the survey methodology in the choice of data collection method enables its application in various research projects and to suit all types of budgets and time schedules. But like any other methodology, the survey methodology has its own weaknesses too. Surveys can fail to capture the required information due to their faulty designs, misreporting by respondents, and failure to reach respondents in a timely manner. Also, the response rate of a survey depends on the choice of topic, sampling strategy used and on the mood of respondents. To minimize these problems and to utilize this tool to its maximum potential in the data collection process, a survey should be conducted on those topics that command attention and interest of the population. Also, the administration of a survey requires great persistence and use of social skills to reach out to individuals and appeal to their sense of responsibility for participation in a study. It is equally important to disseminate the information obtained from a survey to create awareness about problems and in drawing the attention of those that are responsible and capable of making relevant changes in administrative practices and policies.

EXERCISES

1. In recent years, the popularity of surveys has immensely increased. Both citizens and public administrators are deluged with requests to participate in different kinds of surveys. Most of these surveys cite compelling reasons for participation that are sometimes difficult to ignore. Explain the ubiquitous use of surveys in the modern era and comment on the response rate of surveys.
2. Last year, the Kirkland Independent School District funded a smoking cessation program for students in high schools. This year, reduction in school budget has called for the elimination of few accessory programs like the aforementioned one. The district superintendent is in a dilemma and has asked his assistant to collect information to help him decide whether or not to renew the smoking cessation program. Imagine you are that assistant and you have decided to use the survey instrument to collect information on the usefulness of the smoking cessation program to educators, students, and their family members.
   a. Develop a research question and at least two relevant hypotheses.
   b. Provide an outline of the steps that should be undertaken in design and development of a survey.
   c. Design a short survey questionnaire and comment on the sample selection process.
   d. What role do ethics play in the design and administration of the survey?
   e. Do you think that using a mixed mode in collection of information can help to enhance the response rate of the survey?

REFERENCES

Babbie, E. 1998. *Survey Research Methods*, California: Wadsworth Publishing Company.
Brehm, J. 1993. *The Phantom Respondents: Opinion Surveys and Political Representation*, Ann Arbor, Michigan: University of Michigan Press.
Caruson, K. and MacManus, S.A. 2006. Mandates and management challenges in the trenches: An intergovernmental perspective on homeland security, *Public Administration Review, 66*(4), 522–536.
Converse, J.M. 1987. *Survey Research in the United States: Roots and Emergence, 1890–1960*, Berkeley: University of California Press.
Czaja, R. and Blair, J. 2005. *Designing Surveys: A Guide to Decisions and Procedures*, California: Pine Forge Press.
Dillon, S. 2006. Schools slow in closing gaps between races, *The New York Times*, online version, accessed on November 20, 2006 at htttp://www.nytimes.com/2006/11/20/education/20gap.html
Fowler, F.J. Jr. 2002. *Survey Research Methods*, 3rd Ed., California: Sage Publications.

House, J.S., Juster, T.F., Kahn, R.L., Schuman, H., and Singer, E. 2003. *A Telescope on Society*, Ann Arbor, Michigan: The University of Michigan Press.

Jamelske, E.M. and Wessling, S. 2005. Assessing the support for the switch to automated collection of solid waste with single stream recycling in Madison, Wisconsin, *Public Works Management and Policy, 10*(2), 101–118.

Korosec, R.L. and Berman, E.M. 2006. Municipal support for social entrepreneurship, *Public Administration Review, 66*(3), 448–462.

Krosnick, Jon A. 1999. Survey research, *Annual Review of Psychology, 50,* 537–567.

Lovrich, N.P. Jr. and Taylor, G.T. 1976. Neighborhood evaluation of local government services: A citizen survey approach, *Urban Affairs Quarterly, 12*(2), 197–221.

Lyons, W.E., lowery, D., and DeHoog, R.H. 1992. *The Politics of Dissatisfaction: Citizens, Services and Urban Institutions*, Arming, New York: M.E. Sharp.

Majumdar, S.R. 2005. Innovative Texas partnership aims to attain clean air, *PA Times, 28*(10), 1–2.

Melkers, J. and Thomas, J.C. 1998. What do administrators think citizens think? Administrator predictions as an adjunct to citizen survey, *Public Administration Review, 58*(4), 327–334.

Miller, T.I. and Miller, M.A. 1991. *Citizen Surveys: How to Do Them, How to Use Them, What They Mean?* Washington DC: ICMA.

O'Sullivan, E., Rassel, G.R., and Berner, M. 2003. *Research Methods for Public Administrators*, fourth edition, New York, Longman.

Percy, S.L. 1986. In defense of citizen evaluations as performance measures, *Urban Affairs Quarterly, 22*(1), 66–83.

Pew Research Center. 1998. Opinion poll experiment reveals conservative opinions not underestimated, but racial hostility missed, accessible at http://www.people-press.org/resprpt.htm

Punch, K. 2003. *Survey Research: The Basics*, California: Sage Publications.

Salkind, N.J. 2006. *Exploring Research*, New Jersey, Pearson, Prentice Hall.

Schwarz, N., Hippler, H.J., Deutsch, B., and Strack, F. 1985. Response scales: Effects of category range on reported behavior and subsequent judgments, *Public Opinion Quarterly, 49,* 388–395.

Smith, T.W. 1983. The hidden 25 percent: An analysis of nonresponse in the 1980 General Social Survey, *Public Opinion Quarterly, 51,* 75–83.

Steeh, C. 1981. Trends in nonresponse rate, *Public Opinion Quarterly, 45,* 40–57.

Swindell, D. and Kelly, J.M. 2000. Linking citizen satisfaction data to performance measures: A preliminary evaluation, *Public Performance and Management Review, 24*(1), 30–52.

Tourangeau, R., Rips, L.J., and Rasinski, K. 2000. *The Psychology of Survey Response*, Cambridge University Press.

Visser, P.S., Krosnick, J.A., Marquette, J., and Curtin, M. 1996. Mail surveys for election forecasting? An evaluation of the Columbus Dispatch Poll. *Public Opinion Quarterly, 60,* 181–227.

Weimer, D.L. 2005. The potential of contingent valuation for public administration practice and research, *Journal of Public Administration, 28,* 73–87.

16 Questionnaire Construction

Donijo Robbins

CONTENTS

16.1 INTRODUCTION

A seemingly modern day marvel, survey research, at least in forms of counting, dates back to ancient (B.C.) times with the first known survey (i.e., census) under Caesar. The improvement of research techniques coupled with the advancements in technology, allows for easy access to people so to generate any and every kind of data. Qualitative and quantitative information is everywhere; many of the statistics reported on the news, read in papers, or seen on the web originate from questionnaires. For example, the federal government determines crime statistics, population estimates, and unemployment rates using phone survey instruments; local news stations conduct their own web or phone polling; and graduate students are interviewed as they graduate.

Regardless of how the information is collected and beyond an appropriate response rate that is representative of the population, the design of the questionnaires must achieve the following:

- The survey should cover the scope and purpose of the research.
- Each question on the survey must be valid—worded so to measure what we say we are measuring.
- Each question must be reliable—uniform and consistent.
- The response format for each question should be appropriate.
- The design should be logical.
- Human subjects must always be protected.

Researchers use surveys to measure the variables, concepts, and phenomena of interest. From the research topic of interest, the researcher should make a list of the variables that are necessary to explore or describe the topic of interest. The researcher need not make a list of survey questions at this time; rather the focus is on conceptualizing and operationalizing the concepts into meaningful and measurable variables. The researcher must also decide the target population and the appropriate sample size. Before the development of the survey, the researcher should have his plan of action stating the purpose of the research and list of the relevant variables to be measured, and what lies ahead in the project; for example, the type of survey to be used, the level of measurement for the appropriate statistical tests, and the rationale of the study.

In the end, surveys produce good statistics through proper sampling techniques and valid and reliable questions and survey design. Much of the literature on survey construction seems to focus less on the validity and reliability of the questions, and more on improving the response rate and response quality. Moreover, this literature is inconclusive at best. Although a high response rate is recommended, an argument could be made that as long as the participants and nonparticipants are representative of the population sampled and random in nature, a 20 percent response rate is just as relevant, revealing, and generalizable as a 70 percent response rate. The focus of this chapter, however, is on the construction of a valid and reliable survey, not on improving response rates. Unfortunately, there is no set format to construct questionnaires; just guidelines requiring knowledge of the subject being studied, measurement theory, research methodology, and common sense.

16.1.1 Types of Surveys

One of the first steps in survey construction is deciding the type of survey to use. The amount of time and money available to the researcher generally dictates this decision. There are two different types of surveys, interviews (face-to-face interviews or phone interviews) and self-administered surveys (mail, e-mail, on-site, or web-based surveys). Each is constructed differently to fit the nature of the study and has advantages and disadvantages which affect the reliability and validity of the questionnaire, the responses, and its results.

Although both are interviews, the questionnaires used in face-to-face interviews are much different than those used with phone interviews. Typically, face-to-face interviews are longer, use open-ended questions which allows for deeper inquiry and follow-up questions, and are performed by well-trained interviewers. On the other hand, phone surveys, usually conducted by trained interviewers, generally are quick, force a choice which enables a quick response and speedy coding. A first glance at some phone questionnaires might suggest anything less than a rapid interview, but phone surveys are created to assist the interviewer with both reading the survey and coding the responses. For example, the federal government's crime victimization survey is 12 pages long, but contains 48 questions.[1] Distributing a self-administered 12-page survey would probably receive a low response rate; the thickness and weight of the envelope alone may cause respondents to throw away the survey even before opening it. Phone surveys have many pages because of the design and layout, many use combinations of follow-up questions and skip-patterns; two mechanisms that should be limited or avoided in self-administered surveys.

Questionnaires used for interviews are constructed to help the interviewer whereas self-administered surveys are created to improve participant motivation and increase response rates. Table 16.1 presents the variations among the different types of questionnaires. All types of surveys should use valid and reliable questions. Web-based surveys are probably the cheapest and most efficient way to obtain survey data. The population base, however, is smaller and less diverse than those reached by phone or mail. In addition, the lack of a paper trail reduces the researcher's ability to verify responses where error is suspected.

TABLE 16.1

Differences among Types of Surveys

	Interview	Phone Survey	Mail Survey	Web Survey
Type of question	Open	Closed	Closed	Closed
Skip-patterns	Yes	Yes	Limited or avoided	Not necessary
Response set bias	Limited	Limited	Increases	Increases
Type of data	Mostly qualitative	Mostly quantitative	Mostly quantitative	Mostly quantitative
Data entry error	Yes	Yes	Yes	Yes
Length of survey	Long	Short	Short	Short
Interviewer	Well trained	Well trained	Not present	Not present
Interviewer effects	Yes	Yes	No	No
Cost	Expensive	Expensive	Inexpensive	Inexpensive

16.2 RELIABILITY AND VALIDITY

Measuring valid and reliable variables means asking the appropriate questions that will correctly measure the phenomenon of interest. In addition, the respondents should interpret these questions the same way. To help with the development of valid and reliable questions, the researcher should look through the relevant literature and pre-existing questionnaires that survey similar ideas. Moreover researchers improve reliability and validity by using small, focused discussion groups, properly worded questions, and appropriate response categories, which are indicative of the type of data to be collected.

Validity reveals how well the construct is captured in the measurable variable and how well the measure measures or holds up. Questions are reliable if they are interpreted the same way by those participating in the study and yield the same result repeatedly assuming the phenomenon has not changed from the first measurement to second. That is, it is repeatedly consistent or dependable generating accurate information at an aggregate level. There is more to reliability than consistency, however. Other researchers should yield the same finding for the same phenomenon; the results should be uniform. In sum, a reliable measure is one where the same results (equivalent) are generated repeatedly (consistent), in different situations and by different researchers (uniform).

Inconsistent conditions from an uncontrolled setting create errors and threaten the strength of reliability of even the best, most consistent, uniform measure. For example, some measures are irrelevant when we consider the knowledge level of respondents. Asking people about the quality of the local lake when they do not use the lake—no knowledge of the lake—creates unreliable data. Researchers control for this by adding options like "don't know" or "have not used the lake" to questionnaires. The same applies to truth telling. A respondent may consistently report her age as 39 when she is really 45—creating unreliable data. Finally, a participant's response may depend on his ability to fit in; to be socially acceptable. Social desirability bias is generally found in psychological and medical research, however. Beyond asking multiple questions about the same concept, a researcher can do little to minimize dishonest responses. In any event, these conditions create errors in the individual data points. If there are many individual data points that are unreliable, then the overall reliability of the measure is affected. In the end, the researcher has to ask, what percentage of respondents will guess or lie, and can the measure be improved so as to control for these conditions?

Although researchers cannot prove reliability, they can estimate it using a few different techniques. Methods such as the test–retest method, parallel forms, and the inter-rater technique are simple mathematical approaches used to estimate the reliability of one-question one-concept measures. Researchers using multiple questions to measure one concept (i.e., an index) rely on sophisticated statistical approaches such as the split-half method or the alpha coefficient to estimate reliability. Each method reveals reliability issues and helps the researcher improve reliability prior to administering the questionnaire.

Like reliability, measurement validity cannot be proved, but evidence can be provided to suggest that it is as close as possible to concept. Researchers test the theory of their measures by validating the goodness of their fit through different types of validity—face, content, criteria, or construct.

These methods, to test reliability and validity of measures, are done in the pretesting stages of the questionnaire. Questionnaire reliability and validity are manifested in question wording and response format; and respondent motivation through the layout of the survey.

16.3 QUESTION DEVELOPMENT: WORDING AND RESPONSE FORMATS

Question development is the most important issue when creating a valid and reliable survey. Questions that are unclear, have vague meaning or definitions, or inappropriate response formats result in useless information. The survey questions asked must be related directly to the variables, their definitions, and the research questions or propositions of interest. In addition, researchers should not ask irrelevant or useless questions—those that do not reflect the population of interest or are beyond the focus of the study; for example, there is no need to ask respondents their highest level of education obtained to date, when the population of interest is undergraduate students: they all would hold a high school diploma. Finally, do not ask questions just to ask and later determine their use; this wastes the time of the researchers and respondents.

Some variables are easier to measure than others are. Most variables of interest in policy, management, and administration, however, are those that are difficult to measure, like satisfaction with or quality of services. Each is relative to the respondent's interpretation of what the definition of satisfaction or quality is. Researchers sometimes replace magnitude with frequency. Rather than asking about the satisfaction of the park, researchers ask respondents how often they visit the park; visits are related to satisfaction—the more satisfied, the more visits. When variables are complex, multiple questions are used to improve researchers' ability to establish reliability and validity.

Reliability and validity depend on question/statement wording as well as the available responses; without straightforward, unambiguous wording and meaningful responses, respondents will not understand or interpret the question or statement correctly; this threatens reliability and validity. These threats are minimized by writing good questions and using appropriate response formats. No matter how perfect the question, however, error exists because of uncontrolled conditions, knowledge, and understanding levels, as well as truth-telling abilities of respondents; these factors are beyond the control of the researcher.

Consider the following statement with yes and no as the two possible responses, "I enjoy using the local park." Is this statement straightforward and unambiguous? On the surface, yes, it seems to be clear, but consider the two responses—yes and no—a respondent's interpretation of no could be different from another's. If a respondent answers, "no," does this mean he does not enjoy using the park or that he does not use the park? In the end, differences in answers should be attributed to the differences among respondents' personalities, behaviors, opinions, characteristics, or self-classifications not different interpretations.

16.3.1 QUESTION WORDING

Question writing is easy, writing a reliable and valid question is difficult. The question may seem straightforward, easy to understand, and unbiased to the researcher, but that is because the researcher wrote it; its meaning makes sense. Questions like "Do you exercise?" "Do you eat out?" "When did you visit the public museum?" seem like good questions. They are not; they are too vague. What is exercise or eating out, and what does "when" mean? Besides vagueness, researchers should avoid the following when writing questions: jargon, abbreviations, ambiguity, biasness, leading, future intentions, memory recall, assumptions, double negatives, and double-barreled questions.

The questions should be simple, clear, specific, and unambiguous. If terms or concepts are ambiguous, then define the concept prior to asking the question. For example, if respondents are asked, "When did you last visit the public museum?" responses will vary considerably. What constitutes "when" to one person may not mean the same to another person; they could say last year, last month, when I was 12, or 1995. "Do you frequently talk to your neighbors?" is another example of a vague question. What does frequently mean? Every day? Once a week? To improve the ambiguity, researchers use precise questions without being overly wordy; for example, "In what year did you visit the public museum?" or "On average, about how many times a week do you talk to your neighbors?" Where concepts are difficult to measure with one question or statement, multiple questions are used; this helps verify that respondents understand. Again, question development relates to the phenomenon of interest; to improve the public museum question, researchers may want to know frequency of visits in the last year and could ask, "In the past year, how many times did you visit the public museum?"

Biased or leading questions typically provide respondents with information they may not know and then ask a question or series of questions. For example, this question is leading and biased, "It has been estimated that Americans pay some 35–40 percent of their earnings each year in federal taxes. Do you believe this level of taxation is too high, too low, or about right?" How might most participants respond now, knowing that perhaps 40 percent of their income goes to the federal government? The preponderance of data would most likely be "too high." "Did you know the city uses renaissance zones?" is a leading question also. If the respondent did not know before the question was asked, he knows now.

Loaded questions generally include adjectives such as prestigious, respected, and verbs like forbid, prohibit, and allow. For example, the following is a loaded question: "Do you support the efforts made by our prestigious organization, through our respected Data Analysis Center, to provide unbiased analysis?" Loaded questions distort responses and create biased responses.

Asking respondents about future intentions or past experiences or behaviors threatens data reliability. For example, a question like, "Do you expect to visit the museum in the next two years?" depends on a number of external factors that are most likely beyond the respondent's control. Memories are not useful either when it comes to answering survey questions. When questions of past experiences are asked, respondents will more than likely guess or approximate the answers.

Some questions make assumptions about respondents. For example, "Do you drive to work?" assumes the respondent drives a vehicle and has a job. Unless researchers are certain that their assumptions are valid, screening and contingency questions could be used to assist with getting the appropriate information. For example, we could ask

Are you currently employed?
  ☐ No
  ☐ Yes

If yes, how do you get to work?
  ☐ Own, personal vehicle
  ☐ Public transportation
  ☐ Taxi
  ☐ Bicycle
  ☐ Walk
  ☐ Other, please specify _____

A few respondents who answer yes might accidentally skip this list. To make the questionnaire shorter and to avoid the contingency questions, the first question is eliminated and "I am currently unemployed" is added to the list of options:

How do you get to work?
- ☐ I am currently unemployed
- ☐ Own, personal vehicle
- ☐ Public transportation
- ☐ Taxi
- ☐ Bicycle
- ☐ Walk
- ☐ Other, please specify _____

Questions or statements using negatives or double negatives—those using the word "not"— should be avoided. Respondents might overlook the word "not" and read the question the opposite way or not understand the meaning of a double negative question. For example, "Do you not support a program that does not support senior citizens?" Respondents may be confused and answer one way but actually believe the contrary.

Double-barreled questions are those questions that ask two or more questions at the same time. For example, "when tuition increases are you more likely to drop out of school and look for a job?" In this example, some may drop out of school but not look for a job, whereas others stay in school and look for a job. Generally, when the word "and" is included, the question is most likely a double-barreled question; researchers should reword the question such that only one item is asked per question.

16.3.2 Response Formats

Question response formats are either open-ended, where the respondent writes a response, or closed-ended, where the participant selects a response from a list. What question format should the researcher use? Question development depends on what is being measured and the type of survey used.

Open-ended questions are useful because they allow unanticipated answers to be obtained. Respondents are free from any constraints and the answers given represent how respondents interpret the question. Open-ended questions can potentially allow for specific and precise answers although the responses may be random and inconsistent. For example, an open-ended question asking, "When did you visit the public museum?" leaves room for a large response variation— when I was four; in 1980; when I was in fourth grade—because this question is both open and vague. Open questions are useful when researchers want to probe for deeper meaning, rely on exploratory research, or when the response is so simple but the list of options is far too long to provide, for example, year of birth or occupation. When open questions require lengthy responses the amount of time it takes to answer increases. These types of questions are more appropriate for interviews than self-administered questionnaires where respondents are likely to either skip these questions or not participate altogether. Furthermore, respondent's written communication skills may affect the reliability of the answer; leaving the researcher guessing what the participant intended to say. Finally, open-ended questions where extended explanations are warranted are often difficult to code, which makes statistical analyses and generalizations virtually impossible.

Closed questions, on the other hand, are those with a nonoverlapping, exhaustive list of provided responses. Sometimes, though, exhaustive lists are difficult to create; for example, occupation. The list for occupations could be rather lengthy. The researcher should consider an open-ended question or broad categories; this decision depends on the purpose of the research.

Closed questions require less skill and effort and take less time to answer, which means the questions are easier to code and analyze. When the response categories are valid and reliable, the questions will be interpreted the same way because a constant frame of reference is supplied to all respondents.

A constant frame of reference, however, does not guarantee valid and reliable questions, or universal understanding and interpretation by all respondents. For example, True or False "I sometimes ride the bus." False could mean either the respondent never rides the bus or always rides the bus; the response depends on the respondent's interpretation of what the true and false options imply. In addition, the responses options may be inappropriate. Consider the following question with strongly agree, agree, neutral, disagree, and strongly disagree as responses: "I have made a purchase over the Internet." The responses are not appropriate for this question; the possibilities should be yes, no, and perhaps do not remember. Closed questions are more advantageous than open-ended questions because closed questions are uniform, more reliable, and easier to interpret.

Some options may have been left off the list unintentionally. Where closed questions are used, the list of options should also include a "don't know" or "no opinion" choice when respondents are asked to rate (i.e., level of agreement) a response. Sometimes the respondent may lack the knowledge of the topic being studied; for example, asking respondents to rate the quality of the public transit system—very good, good, average, poor, very poor when respondents have never used public transportation. Rather than forcing them to choose a rating, "don't know" or "haven't used public transit" are added to the list of responses. These responses allow researchers to analyze the unavailable knowledge base of the sample.

16.3.3 CLOSED-QUESTION FORMATS

Closed questions vary and so do their response options; each depends on what is being measured. Response formats use as few as two options and as many as ten or more; in every instance, the list must be exhaustive and nonoverlapping.

Binary or dichotomous responses are where there are only two possible options; for example, male or female, yes or no, single or married, or agree or disagree. Where researchers want additional information, the response list is expanded to multiple responses that are either nominal or ordinal. If a researcher wants to know more about marital status, then additional nominal categories are added; for example, many surveys list: single, married, separated, divorced, and widow or widower. Reliability problems arise from respondents' perception of martial status; a divorced respondent may characterize himself as single. Where reliability problems exist, question wording or responses ought to be changed.

Levels of agreement are important to understand and rate a phenomenon, like the quality of a service. In this instance, an ordinal, bi-polar, also known as a Likert scale, list is provided. The list offers a balanced number of options which are exhaustive and nonoverlapping; for example, strongly agree, agree, disagree, and strongly disagree; or very good, good, average, poor, very poor. An unbalanced list like excellent, great, very good, good, average, and poor, produces biased and unreliable information. The number of options included in the response list depends on the question wording, the target population, and the phenomenon of interest, should be balanced, nonoverlapping, and include a neutral or don't know option.

Scaled responses like a one to five scale where one is very poor and five is very good are common for rating and ranking but sometimes confusing to respondents. For example:

Example 1. Using a Scale of 1 to 5 Where 1 Is Very Poor and 5 Is Very Good; Please Rank Order the Following City Services

_____ Recycling service
_____ Trash collection
_____ Street sweeping
_____ Street maintenance
_____ Street lighting

Example 2. Using a Scale of 1 to 5 Where 1 Is Very Poor and 5 Is Very Good; Please Rate Each of the Following City Services

_____ Recycling service
_____ Trash collection
_____ Street sweeping
_____ Street maintenance
_____ Street lighting

In example 1, some respondents might think they are all very good or good and use fours and fives. More clarification is necessary in Example 1 such that each number is used only once. Some participants may skip one or two options in Example 2, particularly when the list is long; therefore, the list should be changed. Each option should become its own question or statement with the rating listed next to or under it. For example:

Example 3. Using a Scale of 1 to 5 Where 1 Is Very Poor, 2 Is Poor, 3 Is Average, 4 Is Good, 5 Is Very Good, Please Circle the Number That Best Represents the Quality of Each of the Following City Services

Recycling service	1	2	3	4	5
Trash collection	1	2	3	4	5
Street sweeping	1	2	3	4	5
Street maintenance	1	2	3	4	5
Street lighting	1	2	3	4	5

Example 3 has an increased potential for response set bias. Response set bias is where participants experience survey fatigue (i.e., boredom) and simply circle the same option again and again, for example all 3s, without really reading the questions or statements. Although most of the literature on response set bias is inconclusive, the shorter the survey and response set, the lower the probability of response set bias.

Another popular closed-question format is the "check all that apply" format. For example, the Greater Grand Rapids 2001 Community Report Card asked residents the following:

Example 4. In the Past Year, Have You Felt That You Were Discriminated Against for Any of the Following Reasons? (Check All That Apply)

☐ Race or ethnicity   ☐ Disability
☐ Sex/gender   ☐ Sexual orientation
☐ Age   ☐ Appearance
☐ Religion   ☐ Economic status

Like Example 2, Example 4 suffers from similar problems—respondents may overlook an option or two, particularly when the list is long. Changing Example 4 to be like Example 3, where each option is listed with a yes and no response set is likely to decrease the likelihood of skipping an option, but increases the potential for response set bias. For example:

Example 5. In the Past Year, Have You Felt That You Were Discriminated Against for Any of the Following Reasons? (Check One Box On Each Line.)

Race or ethnicity	☐ Yes	☐ No
Sex/gender	☐ Yes	☐ No
Age	☐ Yes	☐ No
Religion	☐ Yes	☐ No
Disability	☐ Yes	☐ No
Sexual orientation	☐ Yes	☐ No
Appearance	☐ Yes	☐ No
Economic status	☐ Yes	☐ No

Visual arrangement, where the anchors are on each end of a continuous line and respondents place an X on the line representing their opinion, is another format, but not recommended. For example:

Strongly agree	———————X ————————————————	Strongly disagree
Most likely	————————————————————————X ———————	Not at all likely
1	————————————————— X ———————	10

This approach has many problems, particularly with data coding. Unless a ruler is used, the researcher is left to his own devises guessing how to code the placement of the X.

Besides using scales in response categories which is appropriate for one question, survey questions can be written in such a way to create measurement scales. Scaling is where researchers rely on a series of questions to assess a phenomenon numerically, for example, Thurstone and Guttman scales. A Guttman or cumulative scale asks a sequence of questions on the same topic where the subsequent question is progressively more detailed or personal. Respondents are asked to select the statement with which they agree. These scales are more popular among psychologists and sociologists, often difficult to create, and less desirable than response scale formats like a Likert scale.

16.3.4   CODING

Researchers code—enter into a database—responses using numbers. Coding data is more an art than science. These numbers could be simple labels, for example numbers representing political party affiliation, or robust data, such as monthly property tax revenue. In any event, the measures are either discrete or continuous; meets the criteria for one level of data—nominal, ordinal, interval, or ratio—and is always mutually exclusive and exhaustive. Understanding data, their definitions, capabilities, and inabilities, allows researchers to create accurate and precise measurements and determines the appropriate type of statistical test.

Numbers used to code information are either discrete or continuous. Discrete, or categorical, numbers are characterized by whole numbers; that is, no data points are represented between each number. These measures—nominal and ordinal level data—are used as labels and beyond counting the number and calculating the percents of each category, mathematical operations (means, standard deviations) are inappropriate—although conducted by many researchers—and do not make sense. Continuous measures, on the other hand, embody continuity—there is no interruption between the whole numbers—and is the highest level of data classified as interval or ratio level data. The data and the number of increments between each whole number are infinite and arithmetic operations are appropriate and make sense.

It is important to understand the validity and reliability of measures in the context of the different levels of data. Asking respondents to report their income in ratio levels via an open-ended question results in response bias; most people do not know the exact figure so they round or guess. Accuracy is lost where rounding or guessing exists. Sometimes, then, there is a tradeoff between precision of measures and accuracy of data: the more precise—specific—the measure, the less accurate the data. To compensate for the loss of accuracy, closed questions with categorical data ranges are used; for example, rather than asking respondents to write out their annual income, categorical ranges are listed. This approach limits mathematical operations, does not eliminate errors associated with rounding or the lack of knowledge, but does help reduce reliability errors. In the end, understanding the different levels of data is not enough, researchers must also understand the relationship between the different levels of data and the appropriate type of data analysis—what type of data can be used when—so as to formulate valid and reliable questions.

Coding nominal and ordinal responses generally starts with one and ends with the number of total options; however, coding sometimes depends on the statistical tools and analyses. For instance, some researchers label the attributes of gender using one and zero rather than one and two, when using regression. The same is true for yes and no response formats. Rather than coding one and two, researchers may use one and zero when they want to create a scale or index. If researchers are unsure as to which statistical tool will be used, and numbers are entered inappropriately, most statistical software packages allow data manipulation enabling code changes.

Coding rating data, like all data, depends on the statistical analysis. Generally, when the survey question or statement is positive, then the higher or better rating is coded with the highest number of the list of options. For example, when a strongly agree to strongly disagree scale is used with agree, neutral, and disagree in the middle, and the question is positive—the city is safe; the schools are good—strongly agree is coded a five and strongly disagree a one. When the survey question is negative, the coding process is reversed assigning strongly agree a one and strongly disagree a five.

Including options like "don't know" or "no opinion" does not change the coding process or rating scale. Most researchers assign higher numbers like 98 and 99, but 6 and 7 are fine too, because these numbers do not affect the data analysis. Researchers are interested in those with an opinion; those without are dropped from the analysis. This is not to suggest that these data points are not entered or deleted altogether, they are still important to understanding who does not have an opinion and why this is the case.

16.4   QUESTIONNAIRE LAYOUT

The layout and design of the questionnaire is more relevant for self-administered surveys, response rates, and a certain extent the reliability of measures, rather than the validity of measures. Questionnaires used in the interviews are arranged for the interviewer's convenience, whereas self-administered surveys are conducive for participants. This section focuses on the layout of self-administered questionnaires.

16.4.1   LAYOUT

Although most of the literature regarding increasing response rates for self-administered surveys is inconclusive, it is typically suggested that the physical appearance must be attractive and professional looking, convenient to use and easy to follow and read. Surveys should be printed on white paper. The title of the survey should be at the top followed by simple, yet explicit, instructions. The printing should be large enough to read, and the researcher should never try to put as many questions on one page as possible. A cluttered survey will look too complex, be too difficult to read, and reduce response rates; therefore, maximize the "white space." There should also be enough space available for respondents to provide answers to open questions. The researcher should provide necessary instructions throughout the questionnaire, particularly where sections or response scales change or skip or contingency patterns are used. Skip-patterns should be kept to a minimum, however. Questionnaires are not guessing games for respondents; any increase in time and effort that a respondent has to put into filling out a survey will reduce response rates. Therefore, respondent motivation is improved by an attractive looking questionnaire.

16.4.2   QUESTION ORDER

Opening questions should be simple, pleasant, interesting, and nonoffensive. Sensitive questions should never be placed at the beginning of the questionnaire. Although no perfect place for these questions exists, a rule of thumb is to place sensitive questions toward the middle of the questionnaire, where the questions are most relevant to the questionnaire, and at a point where it is assumed the respondent has become comfortable and confident with the survey.

Boring questions and demographic or personal questions (i.e., race, gender, age, and income) are placed toward the end of the questionnaire. Boring questions early on make the survey uninteresting and create disinterest. In addition, asking personal questions in the beginning may irritate respondents; that is, they may presume the survey is too personal and stop participating. If placed toward the end, the respondent has had time to become comfortable with the survey, will feel less offended by such questions, increasing the probability of answering the question.

The sequence of questions should be logical and organized by topics like opinions, habits, experiences, knowledge, demographics, and the like. Question order does have the potential to create biased responses where a question asked or information provided early-on may influence the response to latter questions. This is particularly common when leading or biased questions are used. In addition, questions or statements using the same response-set format repeatedly create bias. Much of these types of response biases are avoided when questions maintain objectivity and when the questionnaire is tested prior to administering.

16.4.3 Cover Letters

For mail and web surveys, a cover letter explaining who the researcher is, the researcher's affiliation, and the research project itself is received better and increases response rates. The researcher only needs to explain why the research is being done; the purpose of the research should be explained but nothing else. The researcher should never attempt to explain the relationship that is hypothesized; attempting to explain this may influence respondents to answer questions a particular way.

In addition, human subjects are told where and when to return the survey, who to contact if they have questions, and that their responses are very important to the research. Finally, in all types of survey participants must be told about potential risks, if any exist; that responses are confidential; and that they can stop participating at any time with no adverse consequences. Researchers must never assume the respondent is familiar with their rights as human subjects protection must be ensured. The U.S. Department of Health and Human Services (HHS) offers helpful tips on informed consent, particularly what to include.[2] Most colleges and universities provide this same information. In either case, consent must be obtained and in a noncoercive manner. The federal government's regulation code (45CFR46) lists eight basic elements of informed consent that must be provided when consent is necessary:

1. A statement of the study, its purpose, the amount of time the subject can expect to be involved, a description of the procedures, identification of any experimental procedures.
2. A description of risks.
3. A description of the benefits.
4. A disclosure statement of alternative treatments that maybe more beneficial to the subject.
5. An explanation of how confidentiality will be maintained.
6. Where more than minimal risk is involved, details should be provided about compensation and available medical treatments should injury occur.
7. Contact information of whom subjects can call on to find out more about the research and subjects' rights.
8. A narrative explaining that participation is voluntary and no consequences exist for not participating.[3]

When using surveys that pose no risk to participants, informed consent forms typically are not used. In this case, the respondent's action connotes informed consent; the subject either fills out and returns the survey—consent—or does not fill out the survey and tosses it in the trash. Where more than minimal risk exists, a consent form is always necessary and each respondent must sign the form before participating.

16.5 FINAL STAGES

The final stages of questionnaire construction consist of pretesting and administering the survey, creating a codebook, and entering and analyzing the data. After the questions have been developed and constructed logically into a working questionnaire, the next step is to test the questionnaire. Testing prior to administering the survey allows the researcher to discard any uncertainties and ambiguities that were not apparent prior to the pretest. Pretesting is a way to increase and to reinforce the reliability and the validity of the questions. Like every other step involved in the questionnaire construction process, there is no predetermined way, just guidelines, to pretest surveys.

A number of pretest options are available, for example giving a draft questionnaire to colleagues, friends, and relatives, or to a small sample (i.e., focus groups) that mirrors the target population. Testing the survey on a similar population is most popular and ensures that the questions are interpreted the same way and mean the same thing to all respondents.

Once the questionnaire has been pretested and the necessary changes made, the survey is ready to be administered via the sampling method determined prior to constructing the survey. Once the interviews are conducted or the self-administered surveys are returned, the next step is for the researcher to code the responses. Once again, there is no set way to code responses, especially open-ended questions. This part of the process is up to the researcher, and begins with the development of a codebook. This codebook provides the definition of the question, the question number, the type of data, and the coding information. Next, the information is entered where variables are in the columns of the spreadsheet or database and the individual observations are in rows. Web-based surveys and phone interviews using a database interface skip this step; they are more efficient with data entry. Once a respondent clicks the appropriate answer or phone interviewer enters the information, the information is entered; and there is no additional coding. Data entry errors exist with all surveys, however. After the coding and entering process, researchers clean up the data by looking for missing entries or incorrectly coded information. This is possible only with paper and pencil surveys. If no paper trail exists, like with web-based surveys and phone interviews using database interfaces, then researchers are unable to reduce data entry error.

16.6   CONCLUSION

Valid and reliable questionnaires are not easy to construct. The construction process requires time, common sense, and an understanding of the research, measurement theory, the data to be gathered and analyzed, and the target population. A good survey is one that covers the scope and purpose of the research, asks valid and reliable questions, uses appropriate response formats, is professional looking, and does not harm human subjects. After constructing the survey, the researcher should ask, "is the question biased, leading, or loaded; double barreled; based on memory recall; too general or too wordy; presumptuous; about future intentions; a double negative; or full of jargon and abbreviations." If the answer to any of these questions is yes, changes are necessary. Next, researchers ask, "are the responses to the questions equally balanced; understandable; nonoverlapping; or exhaustive." If the answer is no, changes are necessary. Finally, when finished with the survey, researchers should step back and ask, "If I received this survey would I participate because it looks professional, makes sense, and is an important research topic?" If the impartial answer to all these questions is a resounding yes, the survey is ready.

EXERCISES

1. Determine what is wrong with the following questions and rewrite the question so it is valid and reliable.
   a. In your trip to the city, how often do you use public transportation or carpools to reduce traffic congestion or pollution?
      ☐ Always
      ☐ From time to time
      ☐ Never

b. Do you or your family recycle on a regular basis?
  - ☐ Strongly agree
  - ☐ Agree
  - ☐ Neutral
  - ☐ Disagree
  - ☐ Strongly disagree
c. What is your age?
  - ☐ 18–22 years old
  - ☐ 22–27 years old
  - ☐ 27–33 years old
  - ☐ 33–40 years old
  - ☐ Over 41 years old
d. Overall, how would you rate the care the patient received while under our care?
  - ☐ Excellent
  - ☐ Very Good
  - ☐ Good
  - ☐ Fair
  - ☐ Poor
e. Do you regularly provide help for a parent or elderly friend of relative?
  - ☐ Yes
  - ☐ No

2. Write a cover letter that conveys the importance of the survey and the subject's involvement, and addresses the rights and protections of human subjects.

ENDNOTES

1. See http://www.ojp.usdoj.gov/bjs/pub/pdf/ncvs104.pdf for the survey.
2. The tip sheet can be found at http://www.hhs.gov/ohrp/humansubjects/guidance/ictips.htm.
3. Department of Health and Human Services. (2005, June 23). Code of Federal Regulations, Title 45 Public Welfare, Part 46 Protection of Human Subjects. www.hhs.gov/ohrp/humansubjects/guidance/45cfr46.htm. Accessed October 24, 2005.

BIBLIOGRAPHY

Buckingham, A. and Saunders, P. 2004. *The Survey Methods Workbook: From Design to Analysis*. Cambridge, United Kingdom: Polity Press.

DeVellis, R.F. 2003. *Scale Development: Theory and Applications*. Second edition. Thousand Oaks, California: Sage Publications.

Dillman, D.A. 1978. *Mail and Telephone Surveys*. New York: Wiley.

Dillman, D.A. 2006. *Mail and Internet Surveys: The Tailored Design Method*. New York: Wiley.

Fink, A. 2006. *How to Conduct Surveys: A Step-by-Step Guide*. Thousand Oaks, California: Sage.

Fowler, F.J. 1995. *Improving Survey Questions: Design and Evaluation*. Thousand Oaks, California: Sage.

Groves, R.M. 2004. *Survey Errors and Survey Costs*. New York: Wiley.

Rea, L.M. and Parker, R.A. 2005. *Designing and Conducting Survey Research: A Comprehensive Guide*. San Francisco: Jossey-Bass.

Sudman, S. and Bradburn, N.M. 1974. *Response Effects in Surveys: A Review and Synthesis*. Chicago: Aldine Publishing Company.

17 Collecting Survey Data via Telephone: A Primer

Richard W. Schwester

CONTENTS

17.1 INTRODUCTION

Quantitative survey research entails asking certain individuals to answer a predetermined set of questions. Survey data is typically collected by mail, face-to-face interviews, or telephone interviews. Although the Internet is emerging as a method of collecting survey data, it presents specific difficulties, particularly the digital divide between those with web access and web-related skills and those without such resources. Collecting survey data via telephone simply entails verbally asking questions and corresponding answer choices to an individual designated as the unit of observation. In theory, of course, this appears rather straightforward. There are, however, a number of issues that a researcher must consider to effectively and efficiently self-administer a questionnaire via telephone. This chapter is framed within the context of my doctoral dissertation research experiences whereby I sampled 1200 individuals throughout the Baltimore and Cleveland metropolitan areas, having successfully completed 676 telephone interviews. The purpose of this chapter is to provide researchers with practical insights regarding the process of collecting survey research data via telephone. Special emphasis is placed on novice researchers, especially graduate students who, all too often, must muddle through this arduous yet fruitful process with little guidance.

17.2 ADVANTAGES OF TELEPHONE SURVEYS

There are several advantages to administering a questionnaire via telephone. All things being equal, telephone surveys typically elicit higher response rates compared to mail surveys (Babbie, 1990). A telephone survey of rank and file individuals will most likely generate a higher response rate than a mail survey of the same target population. This holds true for more specialized target populations as well, which in the field of public administration may include upper-level managers and other public personnel. A higher response rate reduces the likelihood of what is known as nonresponse bias. The notion of nonresponse bias is based upon the understanding that the opinions of nonrespondents, to some extent, differ systematically from those who have participated in the data collection process. A low response rate may jeopardize the representativeness of a survey, and therefore its generalizability to a larger population (McCarty, 2003; Singleton and Straits, 1999). Some have expressed concern that the widespread use of answering machines and voicemail systems may lower response rates by increasing the likelihood of call screening by potential respondents. However, research suggests that households using answering machines may be more accessible than households where there is no answering machines (Tuckel and Feinberg, 1991; Xu, Bates, and Schweitzer 1993). According to Piazza (1993), nonresponse due to answering machines and voice mail systems can be minimized by calling respondents on Saturday before 12:00 P.M. and Sunday through Thursday from 6:00 P.M. to 10:00 P.M.

Moreover, telephone surveys afford the interviewer centralized control over the quality of the data collection process, which is not the case for mail surveys. The interviewer has the opportunity to provide clarification should a respondent have a question about a specific question-naire item. For example, the purpose of my doctoral dissertation was to examine the "public good externalities" of Baltimore's Oriole Park and Cleveland's Jacobs Field. These public good exter-nalities included civic pride, the enhancement of each city's reputation and national identity, in addition to Oriole Park and Jacobs Field's patrimonial benefit to future generations. An inherent challenge regarding my research was that these so-called public good externalities are overly abstract and therefore more difficult for one to conceptualize. As a result, a small but significant proportion of respondents had questions as to what was actually meant by "civic pride" or the other public goods for that matter. By conducting telephone interviews, I had the opportunity to explain that the notion of civic pride was synonymous with simply feeling good about living in the Baltimore or Cleveland area.

In addition to clarification, telephone interviews allow researchers to probe should a respondent give an answer that does not correspond to a predetermined set of answer choices. For example, I presented Baltimore and Cleveland metropolitan area residents with the following: "It is appropriate to use public tax dollars to finance the construction of sports stadiums and arenas." Closed-ended response choices ranged from strongly agree to strongly disagree. Some respondents, however, did not choose an appropriate option, offering instead a response such as "I don't think that is appropriate." Given the ability to probe, I rebutted in this instance by asking, "Would you say that you disagree or strongly disagree that it is appropriate to use public tax dollars to finance the construction of sports stadiums and arenas." The ability to clarify and probe undoubtedly increased the reliability of my data.

17.3   DISADVANTAGES OF TELEPHONE SURVEYS

Telephone surveys are inherently more invasive compared to mail surveys. Mail surveys can be completed more anonymously and at a time more convenient for the respondent. Moreover, researchers are somewhat limited in the amount of data that can be collected via telephone as opposed to other mediums. This is largely attributable to what is known as "response fatigue," which is more pronounced with telephone surveys (Lavrakas, 1993). Dillman (1978) notes that telephone respondents tire more quickly compared to other mediums, as they rely solely on their sense of hearing to comprehend the questions and answer choices. This could compromise the integrity of the data collection process. Even though the questionnaire used for my research contained only 17 items, it was evident that a significant proportion of respondents began to grow weary toward the end. This highlights the importance of being as brief as possible, in addition to placing the most important questionnaire items at the beginning of the interview. Leave the demographic and personal information questions for the end given that these items can be answered, in most cases, with little effort.

Telephone interviews are further susceptible to "reduced channel capacity," which occurs given the absence of a visual component to data collection via telephone. Reduced channel capacity suggests that an individual's cognitive abilities may be somewhat compromised given that survey questions and answer choices are presented through an "audio-only medium" (Groves, 1990). According to Lavrakas (1993, p. 6), "a major disadvantage of telephone surveying, even when well executed, is its limitations on the complexity and length of the interview." Reduced channel capacity underscores the importance of minimizing questionnaire complexity.

Response fatigue and reduced channel capacity may foster what is referred to as "satisficing." According to Krosnik (1999, p. 548), satisficing occurs when a respondent manages to answer the questionnaire items without "expending substantial effort." In other words, respondents that are satisficing do not rely on their cognitive abilities, nor do they actively complete the questionnaire purposively. These individuals are mechanically completing the task. In more extreme cases, satisficing emerges in the form of random guessing and an inordinate number of neutral or "I don't know" responses. In an effort to decrease instances of satisficing, survey instrument questions and corresponding closed-ended answer choices should be designed to minimize complexity and ensure brevity. For example, five-point Likert scales may be better suited than seven- or ten-point scales, even though increasing the number of scale categories yields a higher correlation coefficient when conducting multiple regression analysis. My doctoral research relied upon multiple ordinal measures to operationalize my dependent and primary independent variable. Given, however, that the data was being collected via telephone, as opposed to mail or face-to-face interviews, I was forced to present my questionnaire items as succinctly and simplistically as possible. My questionnaire items were designed specifically for a telephone survey. Consider the following items presented to Baltimore metropolitan area respondents:

1. It is appropriate that the construction of Oriole Park cost each Maryland resident approximately 42 dollars.
   Strongly agree
   Agree
   Unsure (neutral)
   Disagree
   Strongly disagree
2. How important is Oriole Park to the amount of civic pride you have in Baltimore?
   Very important
   Somewhat important
   Not important
   Unsure (neutral)

Had I conducted a mail survey, questionnaire items one and two could have been structured somewhat differently. Consider items three and four, which are better suited for a mail survey:

3. It is appropriate that the construction of Oriole Park cost each Maryland resident approximately 42 dollars.

1	2	3	4	5	6	7	8	9	10

   Strongly disagree   Strongly agree

4. On a scale of one to ten, with ten representing the greatest amount of importance, how important is Oriole Park to the amount of civic pride you have in Baltimore?

1	2	3	4	5	6	7	8	9	10

   Low importance   High importance

Even though questionnaire item one effectively measures the level of support for public stadium subsidies in the context of per capita tax liability, and item two examines the importance of civic pride as a public good benefit of Baltimore's Oriole Park, questionnaire items three and four are preferable in that they will engender greater response variability. Social science research is predicated on examining the relationships among multiple variables, which require data variance. Compared to questionnaire items one and two, items three and four would enable a researcher to gather data with greater response variability, thereby allowing one to better examine bivariate and multivariate relationships. When designing a telephone survey questionnaire, it is important to weigh the pros and cons of using more complex questionnaire items that allow for the collection of more variable but potentially less reliable data, versus less complex questionnaire items that yield less variable but more reliable data. Striking the proper balance is a matter of judgment. This underscores the importance of carefully pretesting one's questionnaire.

It is also important to note that how a questionnaire item is structured (thus how a variable is operationalized) significantly impacts one's inferential statistical method. Items three and four could be treated as interval measures, and therefore ordinary least squares (OLS) regression analysis is appropriate. Items one and two, however, are ordinal measures, and as such an alternative to OLS regression must be used, such as logistic regression, probit analysis, and discriminant analysis.

17.4 PREINTERVIEW PREPARATION

Practical considerations concerning preinterview preparation involve arranging for a controlled environment with which to conduct telephone interviews. Background noise could be a distraction for both the interviewer and the respondent. Another necessary preinterview preparation is rehearsal. Simply, interviewers should practice reciting their questionnaire items and option choices. When doing so, be aware of your tone and the pace with which you recite your questionnaire. Your tone should be energetic yet natural, and your pace should be fast enough to keep things moving expeditiously, but not too fast so as to make the respondents ask you to reread the question or option choices. It is important that the questionnaire items be presented as if one were engaged in a casual conversation. In other words, avoid being mechanical. Be pleasant, energetic, and natural. Sufficient consideration should be given to interview rehearsal throughout the pretest phase of the research.

Another preinterview consideration centers on anticipating potential questions or problems that a respondent may have with certain questionnaire items. Although the questionnaire pretest will address the bulk of these concerns, there are likely to be some respondents in need of further clarification. It is therefore important that a researcher be able to explain each questionnaire item in a way that differs from the sheer text. In other words, it is important to be able to define key questionnaire concepts in multiple ways. This is especially critical for researchers who present overly complex or abstract concepts. For instance, when asked, "how important is Oriole Park to the amount of civic pride you have in Baltimore," a few respondents questioned what I meant by civic pride. Having anticipated the possibility of such instances, I was able to clarify the meaning of civic pride by rephrasing the initial question to: "How important is Oriole Park in making you feel good about Baltimore?" The key is to simply anticipate potential problems and be prepared to address these problems in an effort to better ensure that the data collected is as reliable as possible.

17.5 CONVINCING RESPONDENTS TO PARTICIPATE

By and large, individuals tend to prefer face-to-face and mail surveys rather than telephone surveys. Face-to-face surveys are preferred given the personal contact a respondent has with the interviewer, which allows the interviewer to build a rapport with the respondent rather quickly. Mail surveys are inherently more convenient and less invasive than telephone surveys (Groves, 1990). Knowing this, the introductory sequence is especially critical in terms of persuading individuals to participate via telephone, as refusals to participate tend to occur after the first few sentences of the introduction

(Barriball, Christian, While, and Bergen, 1996). According to Oskenberg and Cannell (1988), the vast majority of telephone survey refusals occur at some point during the introductory sequence. This calls attention to the importance of the first 30 to 60 seconds of interviewer–respondent contact. A survey introduction should strive to accomplish the following within the first 30 seconds of contact:

- Establish credibility and trust.
- Convey the nature of the research.

The proliferation of evening telemarketing calls, and the subsequent backlash against such practices, has made survey research via the telephone more challenging. It has become more difficult for social researchers to establish trust and credibility when people are conditioned to be skeptical of anyone probing for information via telephone. Increasing concerns over identity theft have further compromised a researcher's ability to conduct telephone surveys. It is therefore imperative that an interviewer not only introduces him or her by full name, but also streses his or her affiliation, especially if it is with an academic institution.

It is imperative that a prospective survey respondent understands not only who the interviewer is, but also what he or she is researching. The interviewer must be able to explain that nature of his or her research as succinctly and cogently as possible. It is important to avoid technical language or esoteric research jargon that could potentially confuse or alienate potential respondents. The purpose of my doctoral research was to examine the public good externalities of Baltimore's Oriole Park and Cleveland's Jacobs Field in the context of a public financing question. In other words, I sought to examine the extent to which Oriole Park and Jacobs Field offer metropolitan area residents public goods benefits, and whether such benefits justify government's role in subsidizing stadium projects. Framing my research in this manner to potential respondents would have succeeded in eliciting a low response rate. A better approach would entail the following:

"I am doing some research about Baltimore's Oriole Park, and I am asking local residents how they feel about having their tax money used to pay for the stadium's construction."

Thus, my full introduction read:

"Hello, my name is Richard Schwester and I am a graduate student at Rutgers University in New Jersey. I am doing some research about Baltimore's Oriole Park, and I am asking local residents how they feel about having their tax money used to pay for the stadium's construction. May I have a moment of your time to ask you a few questions?"

Often, the initial 30 second introduction will not convince an individual to participate. A researcher may hear phrases such as "I don't really have time for this," "I don't really know much about that," or "I'm not interested." Such phrases signal the need for further and immediate persuasion. If a potential respondent conveyed a lack of interest or knowledge about my research, then I stressed its importance and potential usefulness in an effort to persuade these individuals to participate. Individuals who feel that the information being gathered is potentially useful are, in my experiences, more likely to expend the necessary effort and avoid satisficing. Given that my research dealt with the public financing of sports stadiums, I often conveyed to respondents that I hoped my research would better inform policy-makers as to how people want their tax money spent. I further stressed that citizens, all too often, complain that there are very few outlets for average people to express their views, thus contributing to the perception that elected officials and decision-makers do not really care what people truly think. I consequently tried to portray myself as being a voice for people (albeit a small voice), as someone who was trying to find out whether the government should spend money on sports stadiums. I tried to personalize my research as much as possible for those reluctant to participate.

For individuals reluctant to participate citing a lack of time, I stressed the brevity of my survey, informing reluctant respondents that I would need between five and ten minutes of their time. It is important to be ethical in this regard. If you have a questionnaire that can be completed in less than 15 minutes, then emphasize this. Less ethical researchers will mislead respondents about the length of the questionnaire, having the understanding that once the interview begins a respondent will rarely stop in the middle of it.

Additionally, I stressed the importance of a respondent's participation. My experiences have shown me that if a potential respondent understands that their opinions are critical, then they are more likely to participate. This can be accomplished by informing reluctant respondents that they have been carefully chosen and that their views represent thousands of people. This is consistent with Cialdini's (1988) "scarcity principle," which assumes that people will place greater value on opportunities that are available to only a chosen few. Should an individual still refuse to participate, it is reasonable to ask for a day and time that is more convenient to the respondent (see Figure 17.1).

Also, students should feel free to experiment with less traditional techniques of securing cooperation. For instance, one may want to experiment with different voice tones or inflections. Marketing and telecommunications experts often refer to "using your best voice" (Finch, 2000). Students should experiment with using different tones and accentuating different words within the introduction in the hopes of finding a most favorable "voice."

An important and sometimes overlooked issue is that even though a researcher may have randomly sampled telephone numbers via random digit dialing (RDD) techniques or through systematic sampling methods when using a telephone directory, the person that answers the telephone should not be automatically designated as the unit of observation. For a telephone survey to be truly random, a researcher must randomly select a person within a given household. There are two primary ways in which this is done: the Kish and birthday methods for random selection within a household.

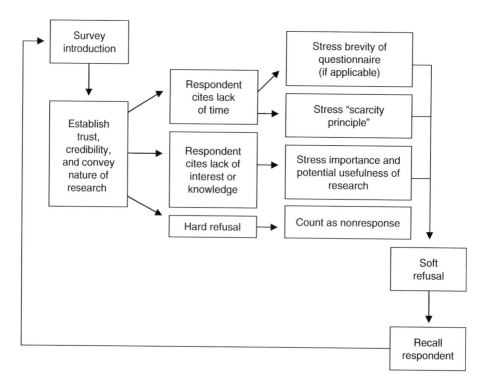

FIGURE 17.1 Securing respondent cooperation.

The Kish method entails having the interviewer identify all eligible respondents within a given household by age and gender. Each eligible respondent is then rank ordered as per the following rule: the oldest male in the household would be ranked one, the second oldest male would be ranked two, followed by the oldest female, the second oldest female, and so forth. For example, a household consisting of a father, mother, son, and daughter, all of whom are eligible respondents, would be ranked in the following order: father = 1; son = 2; mother = 3; daughter = 4. Subsequent to rank ordering all eligible respondents, the interviewer consults one of eight selection tables to determine which member of the household should be interviewed. The Kish method requires the collection of personal information shortly after contact with a household member, which could engender an unusually high nonresponse rate (Lavrakas, 1993).

The birthday method simply entails asking which member of the household has the "next upcoming birthday" or which household member had the "last birthday." This individual is designated as the unit of observation. There is some concern that the birthday method for random selection introduces a higher probability of respondent mis-selection compared to the Kish method. Research conducted by O'Rourke and Blair (1983) indicated that 90 percent of individuals identified the appropriate household member when using the birthday method. Lavrakas, Stasny, and Harpuder (2000) found that 75 percent of individuals correctly identified the appropriate household member when using the "next upcoming" birthday method, while Lind, Link, and Oldendick (2000) found an 80 percent accuracy rate using the "last" birthday method.

When choosing a method of random selection within a household, one must take into account the accuracy of such a method, coupled with the degree of invasiveness and consequently the likelihood of nonresponse. Researchers using the birthday method must be prepared for a higher degree of respondent misselection compared to the Kish method. However, the birthday method is widely used given that it is less time consuming and invasive, which will reduce the likelihood of nonresponse bias.

The need to randomly select individuals within a given household means that a researcher must essentially accomplish two tasks: (1) convince the person that answers the phone to tell you who in the household is the "appropriate" unit of analysis and then (2) convince that individual to participate.

17.6 DEALING WITH REFUSALS

The inevitability of survey refusals is a fact that researchers must reconcile. The invasive nature of telephone surveys means that refusals may prove to be unpleasant and sometimes personally distressing experiences. A researcher will encounter individuals who, more often than not, refuse to participate in a polite or semipolite manner. Others, however, will refuse in a verbally abusive and caustic manner. Try not to be discouraged when this happens. When a potential respondent does in fact refuse, one should not necessarily classify this individual as a nonresponse. That is to suggest that there are two types of refusals: soft and hard. A soft refusal can be characterized as someone who refuses in a relatively polite or semipolite manner, usually citing a lack of time or interest. These individuals are characterized as soft refusals simply because there is possibility that they could be persuaded to participate at a later date. In other words, recall soft refusals. Hard refusals are very unlikely to be converted. These individuals, by and large, are indignant and refuse to participate in all surveys. These individuals should not be recalled. Figure 17.1 shows my thought process for securing respondent cooperation. By no means is this exhaustive, as this simply represents how I dealt with reluctant participants and both soft and hard refusals. The importance of Figure 17.1 is that it represents a thought-out and tangible plan, which will increase one's likelihood of persuading people to participate.

17.7 CONCLUSION

This chapter draws on my doctoral dissertation research experiences whereby I sampled 1200 individuals throughout the Baltimore and Cleveland metropolitan areas, having successfully completed 676 interviews via telephone. Recall that there are several advantages to collecting survey research via telephone, most notably a higher response rate compared to mail surveys and greater quality control over the data collection process. There are, however, a number of concerns that a researcher must address when conducting telephone interviews. Response fatigue and reduced channel capacity are inherent challenges to telephone surveys, which can impact the reliability of one's data given the increased likelihood of satisficing. These challenges underscore the importance of designing one's questionnaire as succinctly and simplistically as possible. Keeping a questionnaire brief reduces the likelihood of response fatigue, although less complex questionnaire items allow a respondent to better compensate cognitively given that telephone questionnaires are presented through an audio-only medium.

A sometimes overwhelming task of conducting telephone surveys is persuading individuals to participate. Low response rates engender nonresponse bias, which compromises the representativeness of the sample and consequently the generalizability of one's findings. When attempting to convince individuals to participate, keep in mind the importance of the introduction. It is imperative that a researcher establishes credibility and trust and conveys the purpose of the research within the first 30 seconds of contact. Building a rapport with a potential respondent is the key. Many respondents will stress a lack of time, interest, or knowledge about your research. In other words, these individuals are trying to refuse politely. A significant proportion of these individuals can be convinced to participate if persuaded further, such as stressing the importance of the research, its personal relevance to the respondent, or the scarcity principle. Others will refuse altogether. Recall that all refusals are not created equal, and therefore one should differentiate between a hard and soft refusals and act accordingly.

Convincing complete strangers to dedicate time to your research endeavors proves far more difficult in practice than theory. This underscores the importance of practice and perseverance. Preinterview preparation will greatly enhance one's chances of success, and thus researchers should dedicate substantial effort during the pretest phase to cold calling individuals to practice the art of securing cooperation. Furthermore, refusals will happen, and some individuals will feel the need to be caustic. Try not to be discouraged, and continue to persevere.

EXERCISES AND PROBLEMS

1. Find a questionnaire that was used for a mail survey and rewrite that questionnaire so as to make it better suited for administration via telephone. Be sure to consider the length and complexity of the questionnaire items and response categories in the interest of collecting more reliable data by reducing the likelihood of response fatigue and satisficing.

2. Using a telephone directory or random digit dialing, administer a survey questionnaire to 30 randomly selected households. Special emphasis should be placed on securing cooperation. Be sure to concentrate on establishing trust and credibility, and conveying the nature of the questionnaire within the first 30 to 60 seconds of contact with a potential respondent. Prior to cold calling individuals, diagram a flow chart that shows how specifically you will deal with reluctant participants and soft refusals.

REFERENCES

Babbie, E. 1990. *Survey Research Methods*. Belmont, California: Wadsworth Publishing Company.
Barriball, L.K., Christian, S.L., While, A.E., and Bergen, A. 1996. The telephone survey method: A discussion paper. *Journal of Advanced Nursing*. 24, 115–121.
Cialdini, R.B. 1988. *Influence: Science and Practice*. Glenview, Illinois: Scott Forsman.
Dillman, D.A. 1978. *Mail and Telephone Surveys: The Total Design Method*. New York: John Wiley & Sons.
Finch, L. 2000. *Telephone Courtesy and Customer Service* (Third Edition). Boston, Massachusetts: Thomson.
Groves, R.M. 1990. Theories and methods of telephone surveys. *Annual Review of Sociology*. 16, 221–240.

Krosnik, J.A. 1999. Survey research. *Annual Review of Psychology.* 50, 537–567.

Lavrakas, P.J. 1993. *Telephone Survey Research Methods: Sampling, Selection, and Supervision.* Newbury Park: Sage Publications.

Lavrakas, P.J., Stasny, A., and Harpuder, B. 2000. A further investigation of the last birthday respondent selection method and within-unit coverage error. *Proceedings of the Survey Research Method Section, American Statistical Association*, 890–895.

Lind, K., Link, M., and Oldendick, R. 2000. A comparison of the accuracy of the last birthday versus the next birthday methods for random selection of household respondents. *Proceedings of the Survey Research Method Section, American Statistical Association*, 887–889.

McCarty, C. 2003. Differences in response rates using most recent versus final dispositions in telephone surveys. *Public Opinion Quarterly.* 67, 396–406.

O'Rourke, D. and Blaire, J. 1983. Improving random respondent selection in telephone surveys. *Journal of Marketing Research.* 20, 428–432.

Oskenberg, L. and Cannell, C. 1988. Effects of interview vocal characteristics on non response. In R. Groves, P. Biemer, and L. Lyberg (Eds.). *Telephone Survey Methodology.* New York: John Wiley & Sons, 257–272.

Piazza, T. 1993. Meeting the challenge of answering machines. *Public Opinion Quarterly.* 57, 219–231.

Singleton, R.A. and Straits, B.C. 1999. *Approaches to Social Research.* Oxford: Oxford University Press.

Tuckel, P.S. and Feinberg, B.M. 1991. The answering machine poses many questions for telephone survey researchers. *Public Opinion Quarterly.* 55, 200–217.

Xu, M., Bates, B.J., and Schweitzer, J.C. 1993. The impact of messages on survey participation in answering machine households. *Public Opinion Quarterly.* 57, 232–237.

SUGGESTED READINGS

Frey, J.H. 1989. *Survey Research by Telephone.* Newbury Park: Sage Publications.

Gorden, R.L. 1969. *Interviewing: Strategy, Techniques, and Tactics.* Homewood, Illinois: Dorsey Press.

Kahn, R.L. and Cannell, C.F. 1967. *The Dynamics of Interviewing.* New York: John Wiley & Sons.

Swindell, D. and Rosentraub, M.S. 1998. Who benefits from the presence of professional sports teams? The implications for public funding of stadiums and arenas. *Public Administration Review.* 57(1), 11–20.

18 Obtaining Archival and Other Existing Records

Suzanne J. Piotrowski

CONTENTS

Archival and other existing records are underutilized data sources in public administration research. The purpose of this chapter is to define these types of data sources and explore how they could be better incorporated in public administration research. These records include textual records, microforms, electronic records, still pictures, motion pictures, sound and video recordings, and cartographic and architectural records. Archives are "important organizational records preserved permanently because they reflect what an organization did and how it went about doing it" (National Archives and Records Administration, 2004, p. 5). Other existing records include those that are not permanently preserved or archived but nonetheless may be valuable to researchers.

Archival and other existing records are types of unobtrusive measures. This chapter includes a brief explanation of unobtrusive measures and a summary of the key issues surrounding the use of these measures. Although unobtrusive measures encompass a wide range of sources, this chapter focuses specifically on records which can be used as analytical data sources. Also discussed are the different avenues of access to such data.

Archival and other existing records can be found in private and government archives, depository libraries, and can be accessed through formal mechanisms such as freedom of information acts. Researchers are encouraged to look widely for access to appropriate data and many already are incorporating these sources into their work. Within my own work on management reform and transparency, I have incorporated archival and contemporary records into a larger case study design utilizing interviews, a survey, and a formal content analysis (Piotrowski, 2007). Other examples include a series of articles on the quality of doctoral dissertations in public administration resulted from a content analysis of Dissertation Abstracts International (Cleary, 1992, 1998; McCurdy and Cleary, 1984). Classic management textbooks (Duncan and Ginter, 1993) and collective bargaining agreements (Carnevale, 1993) have both served as data sources for scholars. Movies and other fictional work have been successfully incorporated into public administration research (Lee and Paddock, 2001; McCurdy, 1995). Electronic sources, such as local government Web sites (Holzer and Kim, 2004), have increasingly been analyzed in public administration research. Historical Congressional Records, floor speeches, and federal legislation have played prominently in public administration and political science scholarship (Hall, 2002; Light, 1997; Rosenbloom, 2000). Enterprising public administration scholars will continue with traditional data sources but will also look elsewhere for increasingly creative data sources that could help them appropriately answer their research questions.

18.1 UNOBTRUSIVE MEASURES

Unobtrusive measures are alternatives to more common data collection means, such as interviews or surveys. The term "unobtrusive measures" refer to "data gathered by means that do not involve direct elicitation of information from research subjects. Unobtrusive measures are 'nonreactive'; in the sense that they are presumed to avoid the problems caused by the researcher's presence" (Lee, 2000, p. 1). By not directly interacting with the research subject and using alternative avenues to collect data, a researcher is more likely to find evidence of actual behavior as opposed to reported behavior. Scholars in fields such as cultural studies have embraced unobtrusive measures. This type of data is seen as one way to study questions larger than those based on individuals and move to questions relating to the interaction of power, knowledge, and social order (Hesse-Biber and Leavy, 2004, p. 314).

Few books define a method of research to the same degree as *Nonreactive Measures in the Social Sciences* (Webb, Campbell, Schwartz, Sechrest, and Grove, 1981). If any social science research text could be described as having a cult following, it would be this one. The book was originally published in 1966 under the title, *Unobtrusive Measures* (Webb, Campbell, Schwartz, and Sechrest, 1966). This witty and informative book concludes with two extremely short chapters. *A Statistician on Method*, chapter 11, consists entirely of just one quotation:

> We must use all available weapons of attack, face our problems realistically and not retreat to the land of fashionable sterility, learn to sweat over our data with an admixture of judgment and intuitive rumination, and accept the usefulness of particular data even when the level of analysis available for them is markedly below that available for other data in the empirical area. (Binder, 1964, p. 294 quoted in; Webb et al., 1981, p. 329).

Webb and his colleagues embraced this idea of using "all available weapons of attack" in research. The book actually developed out of a lecture series where the challenge was to come up with innovative data sources. The last chapter in the book, *Cardinal Newman's Epitaph*, is even shorter than the proceeding one, and consists of one short sentence: "From symbols and shadows to the truth" (Webb et al., 1981, p. 330).

Webb and his coauthors encouraged readers not only to rely on interviews and surveys, but also to incorporate other types of data into their work to help answer their research questions. Common examples of unobtrusive measures include written, visual, and audio-visual records, material culture, physical traces, and simple observations. Interviews, questionnaires, manipulative experiments, and psychometric tests are not unobtrusive measures (Kellehear, 1993, p. 5). The possible inclusion of unobtrusive measures in a research project should be a function of both the theoretical approach and research question.

This book chapter focuses on "retrieved data," one category of unobtrusive measures (Lee, 2000). Retrieved data includes personal and societal records, both those that are continuous in nature (such as birth records) and episodic (such as a correspondence). Although the primary focus of the chapter is on textual data, photographs also play a role in research, though arguably a less prominent role in public administration research than in sociology or anthropology research. Like other forms of research, the use of photographs is not unbiased or objective but using them can show characteristics and attributes that are difficult to document otherwise (Posser and Schwartz, 2004).

18.2   ADVANTAGES AND DISADVANTAGES OF UNOBTRUSIVE MEASURES

A key advantage of unobtrusive measures over other types of methods, such as questionnaires or interviews, is that they can better represent actual rather than self-reported behavior. For example, unobtrusive measures are also safer to carry out than some other forms of research, such as door-to-door interviews. Typically they are easily repeatable and are nondisruptive to the subjects they are studying. Access to unobtrusive measures is usually easier than other forms such as interviews, which may involve multiple consent agreements. These methods are inexpensive to apply and may be used for longitudinal analysis (Kellehear, 1993, pp. 5–7).

Unobtrusive measures are not without their disadvantages though. Archival sources in particular are prone to distortion either through purposeful omission or tradition. Personal diaries will likely not be fully complete. Because of tradition, recorded data may be misleading, such as having suicide statistics recorded as other causes. Unobtrusive measures, including physical traces and observations, are also prone to misinterpretation because the researcher's point of view is almost certainly that of an outsider. Unknown intervening variables can cause a researcher to be misled. Because unobtrusive measures may not have as wide an application as other methods, an over-reliance on them can be a disadvantage (Kellehear, 1993, pp. 6–8).

18.3   EVIDENTIARY VALUE OF RECORDS

Records or materials that survive are likely the ones thought by archivists, librarians, administrators, colleagues, or family members of the originators to be the most important or significant. Archives receive material through voluntary donations from individuals and organizations, as well as required contributions from government agencies. We can never be 100 percent certain of what material is missing or what framework was used to decide which pieces to keep and which to discard. Archives only have a limited amount of space and inevitably cannot accept all possible donations or keep all of the material they do accept. Unflattering administrative documents may not make their way to official archives as administrations change. Public officials may create material with an eye on their legacy, thus obscuring their real motivations. Library material may be misplaced and lost for years. A researcher should be aware that the texts they are viewing are only a fragment of what was originally produced and that intentionally, or not, the complete set of records is unavailable. If possible, relying on triangulation by validating the records with other sources will enable a researcher to have more confidence in their conclusions. Even when sources on their face seem reliable and valid, such as the *New York Times Index*, this is not always so, therefore a critical look at the data is imperative. One study found there to be variations in classification schemes and subject headings between years of the *New York Times Index* due to the changing nature of longstanding issues (Althaus, Edy, and Phalen, 2001).

Researchers should be aware of their own biases when using archival material. "Scholars are not immune from the general tendency to attach particular significance to an item that supports their pre-existing or favored interpretation and, conversely, to downplay the significance of an item that challenges it" as George and Bennett (2005, p. 99) argue. To combat these biases, archival documents can be viewed as purposeful communication. When interpreting and assigning significance to what is communicated in a document, a researcher "should consider *who* is speaking *to whom, for what purpose* and *under what circumstances*" (emphasis in original George and Bennett, 2005, p. 100). The application of this framework will allow an analyst to better understand the purpose of the document and how it relates to other evidentiary material.

18.4   MIXED METHODS

Archival and other existing records can be used in conjunction with both qualitative and quantitative methods. The use of mixed methods in research projects has recently gained renewed popularity. Public administration and public policy scholarship has successfully incorporated archival data and in-depth interviews into single research designs (Baum, 2005; Berry et al., 2000; Bigelow and Stone, 1995; Gotham, 2001; Greenfield et al., 2004). Archival and textual data can be used both in a mixed or single method project. One leading set of authorities has argued, "Unobtrusive measures are frequently used in multimethod qualitative designs to augment data from field research or interviewing; however, the growth of cultural studies has caused many qualitative researchers to use unobtrusive measures as a stand-alone method" (Hesse-Biber and Leavy, 2004, p. 307). The case study design has a rich history in public administration research, and some have described them as "intellectual gold" and inherent to knowledge accumulation in our field (Jensen and Rodgers, 2001, p. 244). Case study research in particular lends itself to the use of archival data (George and Bennett, 2005; Yin, 2003).

18.5   ETHICAL CONSIDERATIONS

Researchers must be conscious of real or perceived ethical questions associated with their project. If there is question of harm coming to individuals because of the project, a researcher has an obligation and if often required to go through an institutional review board process. Some archival data may deal with personal information; thus, issues of informed consent must be considered. It has been argued that an increased adherence to the doctrine of informed consent may have resulted in a decline in the use of some unobtrusive measures, such as nonparticipant observation (Page, 2000). Archival documents, due to their largely historical nature, are less fraught with issues of consent than many other types of data.

The following sections contain discussions on the different sources of archival and other existing records including different types of archives, the Federal Government Printing Office, depository libraries, and administrative document requests.

18.6   ARCHIVES

Archives are a rich source of documents, pictures, maps, and other materials. The use of archival data, including census records, can confirm or refute previously generally accepted conclusions (Ayala and Bergad, 2002). There are multiple types of archives including the United States National Archives, Presidential Libraries, and state and local government, private and university archives. In practice, there is not a strict delineation between archives and libraries, and many archives are housed within libraries (Meyer, 2005). Also some published material, such as legislative records, which are typically housed in depository libraries are also housed in archives (see National Archives and Records Administration, 2004, p. 9). Although increasingly documents are being scanned and made available online, the overwhelming majority can only be accessed through visits to the archives. Because of this, archival research can be resource and time intensive.

18.6.1   THE NATIONAL ARCHIVES AND PRESIDENTIAL LIBRARIES

The United States National Archives and Presidential Libraries both hold material that is particularly useful for public administration research which is historical in nature. The National Archives maintains hundreds of millions of records. Only a small fraction of documents and material created by the federal government are stored at the National Archives. For legal and historical reasons, only about one to three percent of all records are kept forever. Records housed at the archives include textual documents, aerial photographs, architectural and engineering drawings, charts, electronic data files, maps, microforms, motion pictures, sound recordings, still pictures, and video recordings (National Archives and Records Administration, 2004, p. 3). The National Archives has facilities throughout the country with the main archives in the Washington DC metro area. The different facilities specialize in particular collections. For example, the National Archives Building in downtown Washington DC includes material on genealogy, American Indians, the New Deal, and the District of Columbia. The College Park, Maryland facility houses motion picture, sound, and video records and the John F. Kennedy Assassination Records Collection (National Archives and Records Administration, 2004). Federal census, public land, passenger arrivals, and naturalization records are commonly accessed for genealogical research (National Archives and Records Administration, revised 2006).

The Presidential Libraries system is overseen by the National Archives and Records Administration. The Presidential Library system began with Herbert Hoover and includes 11 presidential libraries and the Nixon Presidential Materials. See Table 18.1 for a listing of the libraries. The term Presidential Libraries is actually a misnomer. Although these organizations are referred to as libraries, in fact they function as museums and archives of documents and material culture. The Presidential Libraries are governed by the Presidential Libraries Acts of 1955 and 1986, the Presidential Records Act of 1978, the Presidential Recording and Material Preservation Act of 1974, the Freedom of Information Act, and relevant Executive Orders.

Research at Presidential Libraries can uncover a more nuanced and accurate understanding of presidential actions than was previously understood (Conley, 2003). Included in the libraries are official presidential records, personal papers of the family members, associates, and friends, as well as audio and visual collections. When looking for presidential material, a researcher should first decide what content ideally is desired and then determine which of the libraries may hold that material. Although the overwhelming majority of material in Presidential Libraries is not available online, the libraries do offer online indexes. Using these resources can give researchers an idea of what type of material they might find in a physical search of a Presidential Library. Researchers should consider using online resources and contacting an archivist before planning a visit. Some grant funding is available to visit the presidential libraries to conduct research. If travel to a presidential library is impossible, a limited amount of material, such as documents or videos, can be ordered and shipped.

TABLE 18.1
Presidential Libraries and Their Locations

Herbert Hoover Library	West Branch, Iowa	http://hoover.archives.gov
Franklin D. Roosevelt Library	Hyde Park, New York	http://www.fdrlibrary.marist.edu
Harry S. Truman Library	Independence, Missouri	http://www.trumanlibrary.org
Dwight D. Eisenhower Library	Abilene, Kansas	http://eisenhower.archives.gov
John F. Kennedy Library	Boston, Massachusetts	http://www.jfklibrary.org
Lyndon B. Johnson Library	Austin, Texas	http://www.lbjlib.utexas.edu
Nixon Presidential Materials	College Park, Maryland	http://nixon.archives.gov
Gerald R. Ford Library	Ann Arbor, Michigan	http://www.fordlibrarymuseum.gov
Jimmy Carter Library	Atlanta, Georgia	http://www.jimmycarterlibrary.gov
Ronald Reagan Library	Simi Valley, California	http://www.reagan.utexas.edu
George Bush Library	College Station, Texas	http://bushlibrary.tamu.edu
William J. Clinton Library	Little Rock, Arkansas	http://www.clintonlibrary.gov

18.6.2 State and Local Archives

All States, including the District of Columbia, have state archives (Council of State Archivists, 2005). State archives have an enormous amount of information, not all of which is directly from state agencies and may include a limited number of private documents and local government records. As every state archive has a different mix, experience has shown it is best to check with the particular archive before beginning a search. Most likely, archives will only have an abbreviated listing of their holdings online and a researcher may know that the needed material is available only after a physical visit. Some local governments establish their own archives, while others establish relationships and arrangements with libraries, historical societies, state archives, or other organizations (Council of State Archivists, 2006).

A researcher will undoubtedly find historical information on state government agencies and commissions in a state archive. Using documents available from a state archive, a researcher could trace the evolution of an administrative function over time to conduct the genealogy of an agency. A history of management reforms at the state level could be researched using agency, commission, and gubernatorial records. Scholars of public administration might be interested in the gubernatorial discussions surrounding a historical piece of legislation. Towns typically keep their own records but defunct towns will most likely have deposited their meeting minutes and administrative records in the state archives. Historical research using state archival data could be done on highway authorities, special commissions, and state universities.

18.6.3 Other Archives

Governments are not the only organizations that support archives. There are private archives and those held at universities. For example, the Rockefeller Archive Center is a division of The Rockefeller University. Private archives may be particularly helpful when trying to gain information on individuals who once worked for or with government or nonprofit organizations. For example, the Rockefeller Archive is useful for research on the New York Bureau of Municipal Research. Many businesses also keep archives to preserve key documents concerning their companies' history (The Society of American Archivists, 2006).

18.6.4 Practical Tips on Using Archives

Researchers should try to give themselves plenty of time to conduct an archival search. It is typically best to arrive at the archive early in the day because it may take considerable time to locate the material needed. An archivist will need to assist you in locating the material wanted. Archives differ from libraries in that researchers cannot retrieve material themselves. When planning, consider that a search will likely take longer than expected. Researching earlier periods may take less time than more recent time periods because there are likely to be fewer documents available.

If at all possible, a researcher should conduct preliminary research before arriving at an archive. For example, knowing the bill number to a piece of relevant legislation will make a search significantly easier. Similarly, if a researcher can identify organizations, individuals, and multiple search terms associated with the topic, the research will go smoother. One possibility is for a researcher to visit a depository library to look for published reports on the topic to facilitate the development of the list of search terms for use in the archival search.

Although government agencies may allow researchers to use handheld scanners or portable photocopiers to duplicate administrative documents, archives typically do not. Individual archives differ on photocopying policies. Some will let the researcher make the copies, while others will do it immediately for a researcher. Still others will make copies for a researcher but it may take many months to receive the documents. There are other practical things to consider when visiting an archive. A researcher will have to check-in with the receptionist, store any bags, and limit what they bring into the manuscript reading room. Pencils, notepads, and laptop computers are generally acceptable. Some may allow a researcher to bring a camera but will not allow the use of the flash.

18.7 GOVERNMENT PRINTING OFFICE

To access material and information regarding all three branches of the federal government, the U.S. Government Printing Office (GPO) is an excellent place to start. Dating back to 1813, the GPO is the primary, centralized resource for published government information, both in hard copy and electronic forms. The mission of the GPO is to ensure that the public has access to government information. Although the GPO is based in Washington DC, it has a Web site which carries an enormous amount of searchable information (www.gpo.gov).

The GPO takes orders for printed copies of thousands of publications. Some of the best sellers include the United States Statistical Abstract, a Surgeon General's report on second hand tobacco smoke, and a Department of Agriculture field book for describing and sampling soils. Approximately a quarter of a million titles are available online through *GPO Access*. The publications on *GPO Access* are searchable and are the official, published versions. Examples of online resources include the 9/11 Commission Report, the Congressional Record, select Congressional Hearings and Reports regarding the Challenger Space Shuttle Accident, the Plum Book (that identifies presidentially appointed positions in the federal government), and weekly compilations of presidential documents.

18.8 DEPOSITORY LIBRARIES

The federal government and most states have depository library systems. As of 2004 two states, Alabama and Maryland, were the only ones without a government depository program in practice. Both of these states have laws establishing state depository programs but these states have not funded these programs (Smith, 2004, p. 5). Three general characteristics mark a depository library program:

- A governing body deposits copies of its publications in geographically distributed libraries for the use of the public;
- The publications on deposit do not become the property of the library in which they are housed, but continue to belong to the governing body which deposited them;
- In return for the free use of these depository materials, libraries that participate in the program agree to meet certain standards, to provide physical facilities to house the publications, and to assist the public in using them (Smith, 2004, p. 5).

Unlike archives which generally have large holdings of unpublished material, depository libraries primarily hold published records, reports, books, monographs, research, and legislative material. Depository libraries are a good place to start for background material before the beginning of an archival search. States may have one central depository library and branch libraries located throughout the state with abbreviated holdings.

The Federal Depository Library Program is run out of the U.S. GPO. There are over 1300 federal depository libraries throughout the country. Federal government documents are provided to designated depository libraries, which in turn provide the public with free access to those documents. The majority (fifty-two percent) of federal depository libraries are academic libraries. Public libraries (nineteen percent), academic law libraries (twelve percent), community college libraries (five percent), state and special libraries (five percent), federal and state court libraries (three percent), and federal agency libraries (four percent) have all also been designated as federal depository libraries (Federal Depository Library Directory cited in American Library Association, 2004).

18.9 ADMINISTRATIVE DOCUMENT REQUESTS

Government archives and depository reading rooms are not the only means of accessing government documents. Many contemporary documents are available directly from federal, state, and local governments. There are two avenues to accessing these documents: proactive information released by governments or document requests. Governments may release contemporary information to local libraries. An even more readily accessible source of documents is a government's Web site. Among other products, formal reports, budget documents, and meeting minutes may all be posted online.

Federal agencies have both electronic and physical reading rooms. The Electronic Freedom of Information Act (EFOIA) requires agencies to post frequently requested documents online in electronic reading rooms (Electronic Freedom of Information Act, 1996). Although not all agencies follow the intent or the spirit of the law, a significant amount of information is accessible through these sites (see U.S. Department of Justice, 2006). The FBI's electronic reading room has hundreds of frequently requested files of individuals. Among scores of others, a researcher can find agency files on John Lennon, Malcolm X, and Pablo Picasso for example.

18.9.1 FEDERAL FREEDOM OF INFORMATION ACT

If a document is not immediately available, there are other avenues of access. Many governments will provide a researcher with documents or reports based on an informal request via email or the telephone. If an informal request does not provide results, a formal request can be made. When dealing with the U.S. federal government, the Freedom of Information Act (FOIA, 1966) can be invoked. One book on unobtrusive measures notes that the FOIA as: "An additional and potentially powerful weapon" (Lee, 2000, p. 104).

There are ethical considerations concerning documents received from governments. Although there are legal privacy provisions governing what type of material can legally be released, at times information on individuals is by mistake released. In some instances, it is possible to piece together information concerning an individual through triangulation. For example, a document may have a person's name redacted but refer to that individual elsewhere by their administrative title. In such a case, with a little research, the individual can be identified. Such triangulation violates the intent to preserve privacy in the FOIA. Moreover, researchers can damage a person's reputation, or in the case of classified information, possibly a person's safety by publishing inappropriately released information.

Nevertheless, this avenue of collecting data is largely free of ethical pitfalls because the administrative officers vet the material before release. Also, this type of data is relatively cheap to obtain. These positives are offset by the inevitable bureaucratic delays and possibility of getting mountains of documents, many one finds of limited value, to sort through.

Unless they are in the interest of the public at large, your neighbor's FBI files or tax returns will not be retrievable. Personal privacy is not the only reason why documents can be exempt from release through the federal FOIA. The nine FOIA exemptions are:

1. Classified national defense and foreign relations information
2. Internal agency rules and practices
3. Information that is prohibited from disclosure by another law
4. Trade secrets and other confidential business information
5. Inter- or intra-agency communications that are protected by legal privileges
6. Information involving matters of personal privacy
7. Certain information compiled for law enforcement purposes
8. Information relating to the supervision of financial institutions
9. Geological information on wells

If a request is denied, the federal agency will cite which exemptions were used for the denial.

Date

Agency FOIA Officer
Name of agency or agency component
Address

Dear _____:
Under the Freedom of Information Act, 5 U.S.C. subsection 552, I am requesting access
to [identify the records as clearly and specifically as possible].

If there are any fees for searching for or copying the records, please let me know before
you work on my request. [Or, please supply the records without informing me of the cost
if the fees do not exceed $_____ which I agree to pay.]

If you deny all or any part of this request, please cite each specific exemption you think
justifies your refusal to release the information and notify me of appeal procedures
available under the law.

Optional: If you have any questions about handling this request, you may telephone me
at _____(home phone) or at _____(office phone).

Sincerely,

Name
Address

FIGURE 18.1 Sample FOIA request letter.

At the federal level, there are different categories of requestors, which equate to different fee schedules charged for search, retrieval, and photocopy costs. A request letter should state the researcher's affiliation and whether he or she is conducting academic research. If appropriate for the project, sending the FOIA request on academic letterhead will likely yield better results and reduced fees. See Figure 18.1 for a sample federal FOIA request letter. The U.S. Department of Justice, which is the agency charged with deciding and implementing FOIA policy, publishes information on how to file an FOIA request and whom to address the letters (see www.usdoj.gov/04foia).

18.9.2 STATE FREEDOM OF INFORMATION ACTS

Every state has the equivalent of the federal FOIA and they are usually referred to as either a state's freedom of information or an open public records act. The state FOIAs apply to both the state and local governments. Some states have formal mechanisms of appeal if a request is not filled or denied, while others require a requestor to go to court. More information on state laws appears on the Reporter's Committee for Freedom of the Press (www.rcfp.org) and the National Freedom of Information Coalition (www.nfoic.org) Web sites. The Reporter's Committee for Freedom of the Press has an online guide on how to use the federal FOIA, as well as an Open Government Guide which is a compendium of information on all of the states' freedom of information and open meeting laws. The National Freedom of Information Coalition is a coalition of state organizations which support the public's right to oversee government through access to documents.

18.9.3 PRACTICAL TIPS ON WRITING FOI REQUESTS

From my experience I have learned that when writing an FOI request it is best to be as specific as possible. FOIA officers, the individuals who fill FOIA requests at the federal level, and municipal clerks frequently complain about extraordinarily broad requests. For example, it is impossible for someone at the State Department of fill a request for all documents concerning the defense contractor Halliburton. A researcher should specify which time period they are concerned with, as well as key phrases to expedite a search. Under most FOI laws, governments do not need to create a document that they do not already possess. As a practical matter, this means that a researcher may need to write multiple requests and compile the significant information into a dataset themselves. For example, if a researcher was interested in the names, titles, and salaries of all the individuals who work for an organization, and the information was not already available from one file, he or she would need to make two requests. The first request would be for the names and titles of all employees. The second request would be for the names and salaries of employees. The researcher would then have to compile the data into one file.

Delays are an inevitable part of freedom of information requests. In practice, most requests take longer than the statutorily specified amount of days. When possible, requestors should build into their research schedule extra time to compensate for delays. At the federal level, there are some requests in the queue that are over ten years old (The National Security Archive, 2006). The simpler the request, the quicker it will be filled. Also, breaking up requests into smaller, more manageable pieces work to ensure that the entire request will not be held up because of one document that an agency either chooses not to release or has difficulty locating.

A researcher should clearly state in a request letter how much they are willing to pay in fees. By stating up-front how much you are willing to pay, it hastens the process. A researcher should specifically ask the FOIA officer to contact them if the fees are expected to exceed a stated amount. To facilitate contact, a researcher should provide full contact information including phone numbers and an email address in a request letter.

18.10 SUMMARY

Archival and other existing records can, and are, currently used in public administration scholarship. These records can be accessed through federal and state archives, presidential libraries, depository libraries, the U.S. Government Printing Office, and administrative document requests. This type of data can be used as the sole data source for a project, or it can combined with other data sources in a mixed method research design. Students and scholars of public administration are encouraged to take the time to access archival data and administrative records and incorporate them into their research.

EXERCISES

1. Spend some time learning about your state's freedom of information act. One good resource to use is the Reporter's Committee for Freedom of the Press Web site (www.rcfp.org). Identify a topic of interest and three local governments from which to request information. Write freedom of information requests to these governments requesting the same documents. Take note of how long the requests take to be filled, and the quality and variety in the responses. How does this variation affect your research project?

2. Find out if your university has an archive. If your university does not have an archive, locate another archive in the area. Pick a relevant research topic and conduct a search of the archives. One example may be to research the evolution and history of the public administration education at your university. Begin by developing a list of key terms and names, and identify a time frame for your search. Reflect on your experience.

3. Identify a research topic, preferably one on which you are already working. Spend some time thinking of three ways you could use archival and other existing records as part of the research design.

REFERENCES

Althaus, S.L., Edy, J.A., and Phalen, P.F. 2001. Using substitutes for full-text news stories in content analysis: Which text is the best? *American Journal of Political Science, 45*(3), 701–723.

American Library Association. 2004. Depository libraries by type: 2004. Retrieved October 21, 2006, from http://www.ala.org/ala/godort/godortfactsheets/2004deplibs.htm.

Ayala, C.J. and Bergad, L.W. 2002. Rural Puerto Rico in the early twentieth century considered: Land and society, 1899–1915. *Latin American Research Review, 37*(2), 65–97.

Baum, J.R. 2005. Breaking authoritarian bonds: The political origins of the Taiwan administrative procedure act. *Journal of East Asian Studies, 5*, 365–399.

Berry, F.S., Brower, R.S., and Flowers, G. 2000. Implementing performance accountability in Florida: What changed, what mattered, and what resulted? *Public Productivity and Management Review, 23*(3), 338–358.

Bigelow, B. and Stone, M.M. 1995. Why don't they do what we want? An exploration of organizational responses to institutional pressures in community health centers. *Public Administration Review, 55*(2), 183–192.

Binder, A. 1964. Statistical theory. In P.R. Farnsworth, O. McNemar, and Q. McNemar (Eds.), *Annual Review of Psychology, 15*, 277–310.

Carnevale, D.G. 1993. Federal service 2000: Staff training and labor-management cooperation. *International Journal of Public Administration, 16*(6), 865–889.

Cleary, R.E. 1992. Revisiting the doctoral dissertation in public administration: An examination of the dissertations of 1990. *Public Administration Review, 52*(1), 55–61.

Cleary, R.E. 1998. The public administration doctoral dissertation reexamined: An evaluation of the dissertations of 1998. *Public Administration Review, 60*(5), 446–455.

Conley, R.S. 2003. George Bush and the 102nd Congress: The impact of public and "private" veto threats on policy outcomes. *Presidential Studies Quarterly, 33*(4), 730–750.

Council of State Archivists. 2005. FY2004 survey of state archives and records management programs. Retrieved October 20, 2006, from http://www.statearchivists.org/reports/2004-survey/index.htm.

Council of State Archivists. 2006. National project seeks to preserve valuable local government records. *"Closest to Home" Archival Programs for Local Government Records*. Retrieved October 20, 2006, from http://www.statearchivists.org/lga/documents/2006–09–12-cosa-lgatfnews.pdf.

Duncan, W.J. and Ginter, P.M. 1993. Recurring themes in management thought: What every manager should know about management history. *International Journal of Public Administration, 16*(10), 1569–1586.

Electronic Freedom of Information Act, 110 Stat. 3054, 1996.

FOIA (Freedom of Information Act) (80 Stat. 250) codified in 1967 (81 Stat. 54; 5 U.S.C. 552), 1966.

George, A.L. and Bennett, A. 2005. *Case Studies and Theory Development in the Social Science*. Cambridge: MIT Press.

Gotham, K.F. 2001. A city without slums: Urban renewal, public housing, and downtown revitalization in Kansas City, Missouri. *American Journal of Economics and Sociology, 60*(1), 285–316.

Greenfield, T.K., Johnson, S.P., and Giesbrecht, N. 2004. The alcohol policy development process: Policy-makers speak. *Contemporary Drug Problems, 31*(Winter), 627–654.

Hall, T.E. 2002. Live bureaucrats and dead public servants: How people in government are discussed on the floor of the house. *Public Administration Review, 62*(1), 242–251.

Hesse-Biber, S.N. and Leavy, P. (Eds.). 2004. *Approaches to Qualitative Research: A Reader on Theory and Practice*. New York: Oxford University Press.

Holzer, M. and Kim, S.-T. 2004. Digital governance in municipalities worldwide: An assessment of municipal web sites throughout the world. National Center for Public Productivity.

Jensen, J.L. and Rodgers, R. 2001. Cumulating the intellectual gold of case study research. *Public Administration Review, 61*(2), 235–246.

Kellehear, A. 1993. *The Unobtrusive Researcher: A Guide to Methods*. St Leonards, New South Wales, Australia: Allen & Unwin.

Lee, M. and Paddock, S.C. 2001. Strange but true tales from Hollywood: The bureaucrat as movie hero. *Public Administration and Management, 60*(4).

Lee, R.M. 2000. *Unobtrusive Methods in Social Research*. Philadelphia: Open University Press.

Light, P.C. 1997. *The Tides of Reform: Making Government Work 1945–1995*. New Haven: Yale University Press.

McCurdy, H.E. 1995. Fiction and imagination: How they affect public administration. *Public Administration Review, 55*(6), 499–506.

McCurdy, H.E. and Cleary, R.E. 1984. Why can't we resolve the research issue in public administration? *Public Administration Review, 44*(1), 49–55.

Meyer, L.M. 2005. Boxes of "stuff": Enhancing patron access to archival collections within the library. *Colorado Libraries* (Summer), 38–39.

National Archives and Records Administration. 2004. *That National Archives in the Nation's Capital: Information for Researchers General Information Leaflet 71.* Washington, DC.

National Archives and Records Administration. (revised 2006). *Using Civilian Records for Genealogical Research in the National Archives Washington, DC, Area, Reference Information Paper 110.* Washington, DC.

Page, S. 2000. Community research: The lost art of unobtrusive methods. *Journal of Applied Social Psychology, 30*(10), 2126–2136.

Piotrowski, S. 2007. *Governmental Transparency in the Path of Administrative Reform.* Albany, New York: State University of New York Press.

Posser, J. and Schwartz, D. 2004. Photographs within the sociological research process. In S.N. Hesse-Biber and P. Leavy (Eds.), *Approaches to Qualitative Research: A Reader on Theory and Practice* (pp. 334–349). Philadelphia: Oxford University Press.

Rosenbloom, D.H. 2000. *Building a Legislative-Centered Public Administration, 1946–1999.* Tuscaloosa: University of Alabama Press.

Smith, L.L. 2004. An overview of state depository library programs. *Louisiana Libraries* (Winter), 5–7.

The National Security Archive. 2006. A report on federal agency FOIA backlog. Retrieved December 1, 2006, from http://www.gwu.edu/~nsarchiv/NSAEBB/NSAEBB182/executive_summary.pdf

The Society of American Archivists. 2006. Business archives in North America. Retrieved October 22, 2006, from http://www.archivists.org/saagroups/bas/Intro_bus_arch.asp

U.S. Department of Justice. 2006. FOIA reading rooms. Retrieved October 21, 2006, from http://www.usdoj.gov/oip/04_2.html.

Webb, E.T., Campbell, D.T., Schwartz, R.D., and Sechrest, L. 1966. *Unobtrusive Measures.* New York: Rand-McNally.

Webb, E.T., Campbell, D.T., Schwartz, R.D., Sechrest, L., and Grove, J.B. 1981. *Nonreactive Measures in the Social Sciences* (2nd ed.). Boston: Houghton Mifflin Company.

Yin, R.K. 2003. *Case Study Research: Design and Methods* (3rd ed.). Thousand Oaks, California: Sage Publication.

Part IV

Data Management

19 General Issues in Data Management

Roslyn K. Chavda

CONTENTS

19.1 INTRODUCTION

Data management is essential to the success of the quantitative analysis process; it is also the first and most basic set of tasks in the analytical process. Effective data management brings order to a data set so that it can be properly and successfully analyzed. Good data management also demonstrates a deep and thorough understanding of the research matter and salient ancillary issues thereby creating confidence in the various analyses. By contrast, ineffective or poor data management calls into question all analyses done with the affected data.

So, what is data management? Data management comprises a group of operations designed to prepare data for analysis and proper storage. These operations include research design/data organization; data collection; codebook creation; data entry and checking; data cleaning and editing; and data storage, retention, and destruction. Data can be defined as measurements, observations, or any of the other products of research activity.

19.2 RESEARCH DESIGN/DATA ORGANIZATION

One might ask the necessity for organizing data before it is collected. In Chavda's 2004 study of the factors that impact the entry into and exit out of regions of business firms, there were a number of independent variables to be considered. Imagine that you are the principal researcher on this project who is investigating how the myriad of tax incentive instruments impact the geographical location of business firms. You wrestle with your theory, struggle through the development of your research question, and go on to your hypothesis generation. Later, after you have gone through the various steps of research design and data collection and management, you are ready to quantitatively analyze your data. To fully investigate all of the potential relationships between the independent and dependent variables, you must have properly and fully specified your model and your research instrument. Your research instrument must have included all potential independent variables. These relationships must be anticipated before data collection. If these relationships are not anticipated at the time of the design of the research instrument, it becomes impossible to perform all appropriate and quantitative analyses because of missing or ill-specified questions.

For example, going back to the earlier example, if one of the researcher's hypotheses is that the availability of low-interest loans positively impacts the presence of business firms, your research instrument may support this question. But, what if you want to do an additional analysis? What if you want to do analyses that you had not anticipated during the design of your research instrument? What if your variables are measured at the wrong level (ordinal versus ratio) for the type of analysis that you now want to perform? These are all data management issues that must be addressed during the research design/data organization phase.

During the research design/data organization phase, Chavda (2004) realized that there were a number of variables that impacted the entry and exit of business firms and was careful to include variables such as firm type (e.g., manufacturing, financial services, or high technology), firm size, whether the firm was publicly traded, etc. This enabled her to go beyond the original hypotheses and learn whether a firm being publicly traded has an impact on the exit or entry of a business firm. Additionally, measuring her variables at the highest level possible (ratio versus nominal) enabled her to ask more sophisticated questions and do higher level analyses. The salient point here is that in the research design/data organization stage, you must anticipate as of now unknown data needs. In order for the research instrument to yield the best, most appropriate data, a researcher must try to anticipate future needs before data collection occurs.

19.3 DATA COLLECTION

There are a number of research instruments that are used to collect data. Interviews are often used to garner information on important public administration issues. Interviews can be done in person or on the telephone. However, one of the most widely used research instruments in quantitative public administration research is the survey instrument. Survey instruments can be administered in person, by mail, or via the Internet.

Remember that each step of the data management process is not only designed to prepare data for analysis and proper storage, but also to get answers to the research question and to build knowledge in the discipline. The researcher is not simply organizing to organize. She organizes to maximize the probability that she will get answers to her questions, test her hypotheses, and learn something from the data. The data collection stage is crucial in achieving these aims.

At this point in the process, the researcher knows her research question, the guiding theory, and has developed hypotheses. She has also started assembling her research instrument by deciding which variables are important, which variables might be important, and which other variables are interesting, but not particularly important. Further, she has started constructing survey questions that will collect important data in a format that will allow her to do a wide variety of quantitative analyses appropriate to her research question.

Close-ended questions are those with a list of researcher-generated responses from which to choose. Close-ended questions are extremely useful when doing quantitative analysis because the responses to close-ended questions are easier to code and quantitatively analyze. "How likely would you be to move in response to an offer of a no-interest loan?" is a question that Chavda had on her 2004 survey. The survey item was a close-ended question with a five-point Likert scale response. The five possible responses ranged from very likely to very unlikely. Questions with "yes/no" answers are also close-ended. One problem with close-ended questions is that the researcher controls the choices that are available to the respondent.

Another question on the 2004 Chavda survey was: What are some of the tax-based incentives that would move you that are not currently being offered to you? In contrast to the earlier question, this question is an open-ended question. Open-ended questions allow respondents to answer freely, thus limiting researcher-imposed constraints, impressions, and perspectives. Open-ended questions also allow respondents to elaborate upon their answers, interpret the

questions in their own way, and provide other useful, previously missed, or overlooked information. One problem with using open-ended questions in quantitative research is that although they
often yield very useful information for the study, they do not yield information that is easily
quantifiable.

Finally, when deciding how to construct the survey instrument, each question's level of
measurement must be taken into account. Level of measurement is important because it determines
the types of quantitative analyses that can be done with your data. For instance, the four different
levels of measurement that are commonly taught are nominal, ordinal, interval, and ratio.

Nominal is the lowest level of measurement. Measuring a variable at the nominal level means
that two or more categories exist such as Republican, Democrat, Independent for the variable
political party or Northeast, South, Midwest, West for the variable geographic region. A number
is then assigned to each category. An example of measuring at the nominal level would be to have a
variable that asks the respondent to classify an organization as public, private, or non-profit. To
quantitatively analyze this question, each potential answer in the classification scheme must have a
number (e.g., public $= 1$, private $= 2$, and non-profit $= 3$). It is important to note that the assignation
of numbers to categories is completely arbitrary. The assigned numbers have no meaningful, logical,
or quantitative relationship to the categories. It would have been just as acceptable in our earlier
example if we had labeled non-profit $= 1$, private $= 2$, and public $= 3$. In fact, letters, pictures, or
symbols would be equally appropriate identifiers for each category. The only two requirements in
measuring at the nominal level are that the categories must be exhaustive and mutually exclusive.
When a variable has been measured at the nominal level, there are few statistical analyses that can
be performed. A few of the analytic operations that are appropriate for this level of measurement are
the creation of a frequency distribution, the calculation of a mode, Pearson's chi-square, and a cross-
tabulation of two nominal-level variables.

The next higher level of measurement is ordinal measurement. Ordinal measurement is distinguished from nominal primarily by the fact that the numbers assigned to the categories now have
some meaning. In ordinal measurement, the numbers assigned to the categories have the function of
ranking the categories on a variable. As the numbers that are assigned to the categories increase, the
amount of the measured variable increases. For example, for the variable "transparency," categories
may be: not meeting any requirements for transparency $= 1$, meeting some minimum requirements
for transparency $= 2$, and meeting all requirements for transparency $= 3$. One valuable feature of
this level of measurement is that there does not need to be a meeting of the minds on exactly how
much of the variable is represented in each category. It is enough to know in the transparency
example that in a comparison of category 2 to category 1, there is more of the characteristic
transparency in category 2 than in category 1. When a variable has been measured at the ordinal
level of measurement, there are statistical analyses that are appropriate for this level of measurement. First, any statistical operation that is appropriate for the analysis of a nominal-level variable is
also appropriate for the analysis of an ordinal-level variable. Other statistical operations that
are appropriate for ordinal-level variables are the calculation of the median, ordinal regression,
Kendall's tau-b, and Goodman and Kruskall's Gamma.

Variables measured at the next level of measurement are measured at the interval level.
An interval-level variable is characterized by having order as well as known and equal distance
between categories or numbers. Probably the most well-known example of an interval-level variable
is Fahrenheit temperature. However, before we expound on interval-level variables, let us bring in
the fourth and highest level of measurement: ratio. Ratio and interval variables are remarkably
similar except for the fact that ratio-level variables have a true zero-point. By contrast, interval-level
variables lack a true zero-point. For example, $0°F$ does not mean that there is a lack of heat.
However, in the case of a ratio-level variable, zero dollars of income mean that a respondent has an
absolute lack of income. Similarly, zero children mean that a respondent has no children. The ratio
level of measurement is often used in quantitative public administration research as these variables
are the most flexible out of all of the other choices and lend themselves to a number of different

quantitative analyses. Higher order levels of analyses such as correlation analysis, multiple regression, and path analysis are appropriate for both interval- and ratio-level data.

After the construction of the research instrument, the instrument is then administered in the manner considered most appropriate for the study. Data collection is discussed in greater depth elsewhere in the handbook.

19.4 CREATING A CODEBOOK

Creating a codebook is the next step in the data management process. A codebook is simply a numerical dictionary. The overriding goals of creating a codebook are to organize the data and communicate those decisions to people who are unfamiliar with the data, how it was developed, and its possible quirks and nuances. Depending on the form of your data, number of cases, and number of variables, you could have thousands and thousands of unruly and disorganized digits (see Figure 19.1). Thus, organization of these digits is imperative. Communication of these decisions is also important. Thanks to increased computing power, the Internet, and the ability to save large datasets on small media, it is possible and probable that researchers will increasingly share datasets. But once the dataset gets to the new researcher or the data analyst, without a codebook, the dataset is just a mass of unusable digits. In this instance, a data user can use the codebook as a numerical dictionary to decipher or "look up" the numbers that are his data.

The first step in creating a codebook, after assigning an identification number to each case, is to detail for the codebook the length and position of each variable. For example, the first two columns in Figure 19.1 are the case identification numbers.

Now if we switch to viewing item 1 in the codebook (Figure 19.2), we see that the first variable is called "id," is two digits long and occupies the first two columns of the dataset. That brings us to the next step in creating a codebook, which is detailing all valid responses for each variable. The codebook for the variable id includes 00 to 99 as valid responses. Another piece of information that a codebook offers is the coding scheme for close-ended questions or the number that corresponds with the categories. For example, item 2 in the codebook tells the researcher or someone reviewing the raw data that a response of 1 means that the respondent is female. Conversely, in looking at the data, one of course also knows that cases that have a 2 in the third column are those with a male respondent. The rationale for assigning these numbers is that the variables can now be analyzed quantitatively.

Creating a codebook also serves a number of other objectives. First, a codebook can tell a person who is unfamiliar with the dataset how the researcher deals with missing data. In item 2, the researcher can assign the number 4 to indicate that the respondent failed to answer the question or that the data is missing. Similarly, in item 3, assigning 9 as the code to indicate missing data would be appropriate. A codebook is also useful in communicating how a researcher has chosen to deal with multiple responses to a query. For example, in answer to an item asking whether a

Data set

```
0115000012789023457890652433849509847373633764537438858575638389909586674890
0221000265644075839837326363734894900509575374388585756383899095867489012009
0323034523990177493575747837476357350070909587436373489490005095753743885857
0424000017532028374763573500709095873637348949000509575374388585756383899095
0514000034761043764537438858575638389909586748907998812236373489490005095753
0622000027876053637348949000509575374388585756383899095867489012909586748901
0715001234070040070909587656440758398373263637348949000509573637348949005095
0812000078540080070909587363734894900050957537438858575638389907438858575638
0918000007341163673489490005095753743885857563838990958674890127438858575 63
```

FIGURE 19.1 Example of a data set.

Codebook

Item 1: column(s) 1 through 2, 2 digits, id number, valid responses 00 to 99

Item 2: column(s) 3, 1 digit, gender, valid responses 1, 2, 8 or 9, 1=female, 2=male, 8=multiple responses, 9=missing or unreadable response

Item 3: column(s) 4, 1 digit, race, valid responses 1, 2, 3, 4, 5, 6, 7, 8 and 9, 1=American Indian/Alaskan Native only, 2=Asian only, 3=Black only, 4=Native Hawaiian/Other Pacific Islander only, 5=White only, 6=2 or more races, 7=no identification, 8=multiple responses, 9=missing or unreadable response

Item 4: column(s) 5 through 13, 9 digits, income, valid responses 000000000 through 999999999, missing or unreadable response=000000098

Item 5: column(s) 14, 1 digit, student, valid responses 0, 1, 8, or 9, 0=not a university student, 1=university student, 8=multiple responses, 9=missing or unreadable response

Item 6: column(s) 15, 1 digit, education, valid responses 1, 2, 3, 4, 5, 6, 7, 8, or 9, 1=less than a high school diploma, 2=GED or high school diploma, 3=some college credits, 4=college degree, 5=some graduate school credits, 6=graduate degree, 7=doctoral degree, 8=multiple responses, 9=missing or unreadable responses

Item 7: column(s) 16, 1 digit, ...

FIGURE 19.2 Example of a codebook.

municipality's pension fund is managed by a public firm or a private firm, a respondent might check both choices. In this instance, instead of not entering these responses, the researcher can assign and enter a code such as 8 that indicates that the respondent gave multiple responses to the query.

In both of the aforementioned instances, when performing statistical analyses using computer statistical analysis software programs (e.g., SPSS, SAS, STATA, R, S-PLUS, etc.), these programs can (and should) be programmed to remove (or leave out) observations that are really not data but are codes indicating missing data or multiple responses. Therefore, when choosing codes to represent missing data and multiple responses to a question, make certain that you choose appropriate codes for the variable. If the study is a survey investigating the attitudes towards government of Social Security recipients, you might not want to use 99 as the missing data code for the variable age. Why? You might actually have respondents who are 99 years old.

A codebook can also communicate how a researcher has dealt with exceptions and odd data. One example of odd data would be, if in a study of state level of Chief Financial Officers in response to a query about salary, a respondent reported that she had a salary of $1,234,567,890. Depending on the research question, hypotheses, other cases, and various other factors, a researcher may choose to code this unusually high salary as $999,999. In other words, all salaries over $999,999 would be treated equally as (1) they are extremely unusual and (2) for the researcher's purposes, there may be little discernible difference between the respondent who makes $999,999 a year and the respondent who makes $1,234,567,890 a year.

Finally, a codebook details and communicates how a researcher has chosen to deal with open-ended questions. There are three main requirements when creating codes for open-ended questions. The first is that to analyze open-ended questions, the researcher must enable all responses to be categorized. In other words, there must be a category for every potential response. The second is that a sufficient level of detail must be maintained. This means that there cannot be too few categories. Finally, in coding open-ended questions, the categories into which the open-ended questions are coded must remain meaningful. This requirement means that there cannot be too many categories. An example that illustrates these concerns follows. In answer to the question, "What is your race?" respondents may give a number of different responses including Asian, Indian, Black, African-American, Pakistani,

Asian Kenyan, White, Latino, Hispanic, White, Native American, Anglo-American, Cheyenne, American, Burmese, White Dominican, Chickasaw, and Black Barbadian. To address the first requirement, the researcher would make certain that every possible answer would be covered by the coding scheme. This is generally accomplished by thoroughly understanding the research subject matter thus making it possible for the researcher to anticipate and code for potential responses. In Figure 19.2, you will note that there are six separate and distinct categories into which the researcher may put the above 17 responses. There are even codes for multiracial people and those who do not want to racially identify themselves. To address the second requirement that a sufficient level of detail be maintained, we have separated the categories into separate, recognizable, and significant groups that reflect a common way that people group themselves. In other words, our categories go beyond the Black, White, and other groups that a researcher might have used earlier in the century. To address the third requirement, we have only to make certain that we do not have too many different categories. Although, the point of asking an open-ended question is to get an unforced and unscanned answer from a respondent, the researcher still wants to be able to compare one group or case to another. The final coding scheme for this variable might look something like this:

1 = American Indian/Alaskan Native only: Native American, Chickasaw, Cheyenne
2 = Asian only: Asian, Indian, Pakistani, Asian Kenyan, Burmese
3 = Black only: Black, African-American, Black Barbadian
4 = Native Hawaiian/Other Pacific Islander only
5 = White only: White, Anglo-American, White Dominican
6 = Two or more races
7 = No identification: Latino, Hispanic, American
8 = Multiple responses
9 = Missing or unreadable response

If instead of the six categories that we currently have in the example, we were to have upward of twenty in an effort to capture every nuance during our quantitative analysis, our coding scheme would become less effective. In this example, the data analyst might have a few categories without data. There might be other categories with one or two pieces of data. But, going back to our overarching goal, which is to organize our data, how would this coding scheme help our data management and analysis efforts?

Finally, it should be noted that there will always be judgment calls when developing the coding scheme and then again when coding the actual data. In the above example, in some cases nationality is used as a proxy for race (e.g., Pakistani for Asian). In another case, nationality is not used as a proxy for race and is actually put into the "no identification" category. The importance is that the researcher is consistent in her philosophy and in how she implements the rules that she has created.

19.5   DATA ENTRY

In today's world of computers and software packages that are designed to assist with the capture of data, data entry is now simpler and more efficient than it was in the past. Data entry can be defined as the point in the process when you input your data. In other words, you sit down with your 765 surveys and manually enter the data for each case. Or if you have the capability and financial resources, you read the data into an electronic file by a scanner. Perhaps even easier is the downloading of the data captured by web surveys. This part of the process is sometimes seen as so simple that it is often contracted out.

Regardless of how you choose to enter your data, there are two conventions that must be followed. First, each completed or partially completed survey or interview must be recognized as a case. The electronic and paper cases will be identified with a number. Before the data from each paper survey or interview is entered, mark it with the same number given to the electronic case. In the instance of the electronic case, the identifier will probably be the first variable so that the researcher or data analyst can quickly and easily verify that the data being entered is a reflection of the data which is on the paper. Secondly, during data entry, each case entered will have the same number of variables, irrespective of whether respondents answered all questions or not. In cases where questions have gone unanswered or the answers are illegible, look to your codebook for the code that corresponds with missing data.

Before and after the data has been entered, the researcher can maximize the probability that the raw data is accurately represented by the dataset. One way is to use a statistical analysis software package that disallows data that do not conform to the codebook. For example, if you use the statistical analysis software package SPSS to analyze your data, before entering your data, you can "tell" SPSS the acceptable values or range of values for each variable.

In Figure 19.3, you will notice that the GSS survey has a variable "religious preference." The GSS-defined answers are Protestant = 1, Jewish = 2, Catholic = 3, None = 4, Other = 5, Do not Know = 8, and Not Applicable = 9. If the person entering the data mistakenly attempts to enter a nondefined or invalid value such as 6 for this variable, SPSS would beep and refuse to enter the data. This safeguard is also available on the other popular statistical analysis software packages. During data entry, the researcher or data entry person should also periodically and systematically visually verify that the research instruments and electronic record match.

19.6 DATA CLEANING AND EDITING

It is not possible to put too much emphasis on ensuring that your data is clean (i.e., free of input errors). With the great expense of resources (both time and money) that go into research, it is imperative that something as trivial as the failure to verify data accuracy not diminish the integrity of your project. Thus, the goal of this step in the data management process is to minimize errors

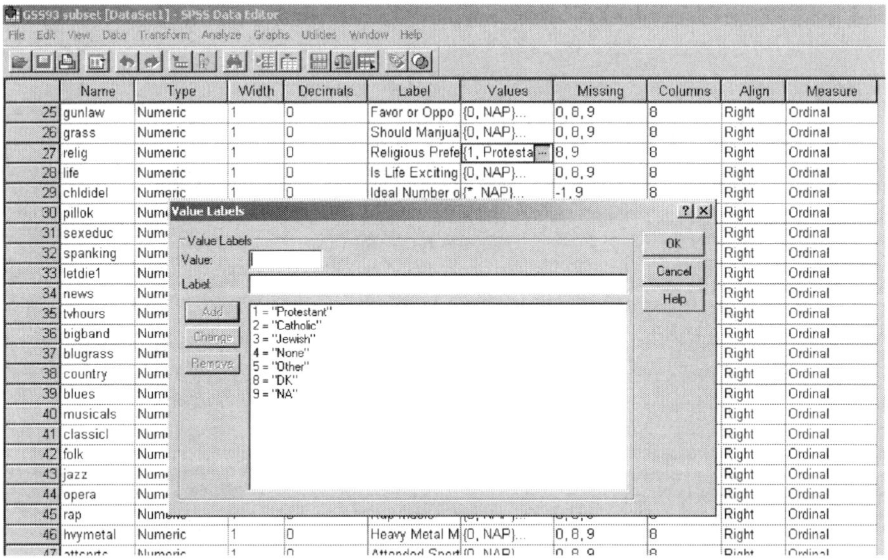

FIGURE 19.3 Example of value definitions in SPSS.

and verify data accuracy. There are three common ways of checking your data in electronic form for accuracy.

The first way that you can combat data inaccuracy is to use a feature offered by your statistical analysis software package. If the data entry person chose not to use the statistical analysis program to block invalid values before inputting the data, the researcher or data analyst can still use the program to find invalid values. An operation as simple as running a frequency distribution can tell you if you have observations that are outside the acceptable range (e.g., for the variable gender, male $= 1$ and female $= 2$, your frequency distribution however shows that there are four cases with a 0 for gender). Another way to ensure data accuracy is to randomly select cases to see if the observations of the particular case or answers to various questions are consistent with each other. An example would be a case that has a question about whether a respondent has children (yes/no question), and another question requesting that the respondent specifies the number of children. If the data file shows that the answer to the first question is no, then the response to the second query should be zero. So, a response of "4" should send up a red flag to the researcher. Finally, the quickest and most low-tech way to ensure that your data is clean is to visually check it. This technique will obviously only work with data sets of a manageable size.

19.7 DATA STORAGE, RETENTION, AND DISPOSAL

Data storage, retention, and disposal are important in the data management process for legal, ethical, and professional reasons.

Data collected as part of research is usually the property of the sponsoring institution. For example, as an employee of an economic development office you might conduct a study on why citizens move from jurisdiction to jurisdiction. The ED office pays you to produce the work and as a result the work and more importantly the data is the property of the organization. As such every researcher should know (1) who owns their data and (2) what the rules and regulations are regarding storage and security, retention, and disposal of data. The organization and regulations that generally govern these matters are your organization's institutional review board (IRB) as authorized by the United States Office for Human Research Protections. The specific regulation is codified at Title 45 Part 46 of the Code of Federal Regulations, Protection of Human Subjects (45 CFR 46).

One reason that proper and effective data storage, retention, and disposal are important is because in the social sciences, we often collect sensitive information about our research subjects. In any study it is probable that respondents report items, behaviors, thoughts, and tendencies that they might not want to share with the general public. Sometimes, data has identifiers that make it possible to connect the case with the individual. Respondents probably rarely think about it, but what researcher wants to be known as the one who accidentally revealed something that should have been confidential? Thus, good research practices dictate that the researcher or the person responsible for the data, handle and store the data and eventually destroy the data in a responsible manner.

Data storage impacts the paper copies of all research instruments, signed consent forms, all electronic data, as well as all notes related to the project. When considering how and for how long data should be stored, after consulting the organization's IRB, the researcher should take into account the type of data in anticipating security issues and possible mishaps. Electronic data and paper data have different vulnerabilities. However, data should be stored in both electronic and paper forms. This creates a backup in case of a mishap. And whether the data is stored electronically or in paper form, there must be some security. Most currently used software programs have security programs embedded in them. And paper documents can be kept locked in a fireproof file cabinet. Additionally, consent forms and identifiers should be kept as per IRB regulations.

Finally, the researcher's IRB or research sponsor should communicate as to how long the data should be kept and in what manner it should be destroyed.

19.8 CONCLUSION

In conclusion, effective data management is complex and multifaceted but not difficult. In fact, it makes most of the work on the research project easier as it disentangles relationships, assumptions, and separates the flotsam from the jetsam. Effective data management brings a sense of order to the research project so as to maximize the probability that the project will yield reliable results. Good data management also helps to fully maximize the resources allocated to a project.

BIBLIOGRAPHY

Babbie, E. 2003. *Adventures in Social Research: Data Analysis Using SPSS*. Thousand Oaks, California: Sage Publications.

Babbie, E. 2005. *The Basics of Social Research*. Stamford, Connecticut: Thomson.

Babbie, E. 2006. *The Practice of Social Research*. Stamford, Connecticut: Thomson.

Chavda, R.K. 2004. Public sector incentive programs and locational characteristics: Do preferences differ by industry? Unpublished dissertation.

King, G. 1995. Replication, replication. *PS: Political Science and Politics*, *28*, 444–452.

Montgomery, A. and Crittenden, K.S. 1977. Improving coding reliability for open-ended questions. *Public Opinion* Quarterly, *41*(2), 235–243.

Stevens, S.S. 1951. Mathematics, measurement, and psychophysics. In S.S. Stevens (Ed.), *Handbook of Experimental Psychology*. New York: John Wiley.

20 Constructing Data Sets and Manipulating Data

Carmine Scavo

CONTENTS

20.1 INTRODUCTION

The word data is often used in very general ways—get me the data on Jones; I'm collecting data on my ancestors; we need some data to support this grant application. These uses of the word data are far too general to be useful in the context of this chapter. We will thus utilize a much more limited definition of the word. In the words of Clyde Coombs, psychometrician and author of the classic text, *A Theory of Data*, "Data may be viewed as relations between points in space."[1] This use of the word data assumes a mathematical framework that makes the gathering of data, construction of data sets, and the manipulation of data much more logical and understandable, and so we will adopt that definition of data in this chapter. This chapter begins by looking at data, how it is collected and prepared for analysis. The chapter then looks at how data sets are typically structured, how data can be manipulated, changed, recalculated, and so on. Later, the chapter looks at the advantages and disadvantages of using precollected, archived data rather than collecting data for oneself. And last, the chapter looks at ways that data can be reformatted, recalculated, and otherwise changed to fit the user's needs.

20.2 NATURE OF DATA

Data can be thought of as observations about events in the real world. A data set can be thought of as a set of observations, one or more for each unit in which we are interested. Units can be individuals, nations, states, communities, neighborhoods, census tracts, or any other unique entity in which we are interested. Typically, a data set is structured as a matrix, each line representing a different unit or case and each column representing a different observation or variable.[2] For example, each unit or case may be a person for whom data has been collected. Each column would represent an observation on this person, gender, for example. One column in the matrix would have a code—a number or letter—which would designate whether the individual was a male or a female. A unit or case might be a large city in a data set of U.S. cities with populations over 100,000. A range of nine columns in the data set might contain each city's 2000 population as gathered by the U.S. Bureau of the Census. A range of nine columns would be required because the largest U.S. cities—New York, Los Angeles, Chicago, Philadelphia—have populations over one million but under ten million. The smallest sized cities would have only the six farthest right columns occupied with numbers—because their populations would be slightly larger than 100,000—whereas the largest cities would have numbers in all nine columns.[3] Although the numbers designating the population of a large city have their own intrinsic meaning, other numbers in a data set might not. If we had collected data on the gender of individuals surveyed about quality of city services in a large city, we might code female as "1" and male as "2." Naturally, there is no intrinsic meaning in these codes; male could just as easily have been "1" and female "2." What is important here, however, is telling the computer what code has been utilized to signify male and what code has been utilized to signify female.

20.3 SCALING

The numbers used in a data set will be part of one of the measurement scales that social scientists use—nominal, ordinal, interval, or ratio. Nominal scales are those in which observations that share the same value are assigned the same code. Ordinal scales are those in which the order of numbers assigned reflects an underlying ordering in the observations. Interval level scales are those in which differences between the codes reflect differences between the observations. Ratio level scales are those in which differences and ratios between the codes reflect differences and ratios between the observations.[4] Consider the following example from a survey on quality of city services:

How satisfied or dissatisfied are you with the job that the city Fire Department is doing?

1. Very satisfied
2. Somewhat satisfied
3. Somewhat dissatisfied
4. Very dissatisfied

The variable constructed to map this question into our data set would have codes ranging from 1 to 4 and each of these codes would be associated with the statement in the example. The scale is ordinal meaning that Very Satisfied indicates a higher level of satisfaction than Somewhat Satisfied, etc., but we do not know how much higher a level of satisfaction answering Very Satisfied conveys than answering Somewhat Satisfied. The actual numbers assigned to each of the responses to the question above are, in essence, arbitrary. Rather than coding the responses from 1 to 4, they could have been coded from -2 to $+2$ (omitting 0) or from 10 to 40, if we counted by tens rather than by ones. Or we could code the responses in the opposite direction—1 would be Very Dissatisfied; 2 Somewhat Dissatisfied; and so on. Measurement theory is the branch of social science that is concerned with scaling. Much of this theory was developed by the psychologist S.S. Stevens.[5] Perhaps the best explanation of Stevens' work is an article by Sarle[6] who explains that the various scales used to code data are defined by the permissible transformations that can be performed on the data without changing the data's underlying meaning. Thus:

Nominal level scales can undergo any one-to-one or many-to-one transformation. Thus, if we were coding ethnicity and had established codes as 1 White; 2 African-American; 3 Asian; 4 Hispanic; 5 Other, we could recode this variable by changing the ordering of the codes (2 could become Hispanic and 4 African-American, etc.) or by "collapsing" the scale—1 might remain White while 2, 3, and 4 would be recoded into a new category of Non-white.

It should be apparent that information about the exact nature of an individual's ethnicity is lost when the latter data transformation is undertaken.

Ordinal level scales can undergo any transformation that monotonically increases. Monotonicity is a scaling concept meaning that each category must be greater than or equal to the category that preceded it (of course, if the scale is decreasing, then each category must be less than or equal to the category that preceded it). Thus, all of the transformations for the data on fire service satisfaction undertaken above are permissible because the scale is ordinal.

Interval level scales can undergo what are known as affine transformations. These are transformations that allow the origin (the zero point) and the unit of measure to change. An example of an interval level scale and an affine transformation to it is the Fahrenheit scale of temperature and the transformation of degrees Fahrenheit into degrees Celsius. This transformation changes both the unit of measure and the origin through the formula $C = 9/5F + 32$.

Ratio level scales are rare in public administration and social science, but more common in the physical sciences. A ratio level scale is actually an interval level scale with a "true" zero. This indicates that the unit of measure is arbitrary but the origin is not. Permissible transformations are any which change the unit of measure but preserve the origin. An example is the conversion of length from the English system (feet, yards, etc.) to the Metric system (centimeters, etc.)

The question about fire services above is one in which each individual logically would choose only one response to the question. There are, however, other types of questions that allow for more than one response in surveys; these are commonly known as multiple response variables. Consider the following questions taken from a recent survey of individuals living in communities near a wild refuge designated by the U.S. Fish and Wildlife Service (USFWS) for reintroduction of red wolves.[7]

- Please consider the following hypothetical situation. Suppose the USFWS was accepting donations to a "Red Wolf Recovery Trust Fund." The money would be used by wildlife managers to pay for the reintroduction of the red wolf into the Alligator River National Wildlife Refuge. Would you and your household be willing to donate $1.00 every year to the trust fund?
- If you choose not to donate, what are your reasons? (Check all that apply.)
  - Do not feel the program is worthwhile.
  - Do not support red wolf recovery.
  - I feel the red wolf poses a threat to livestock.
  - I feel the red wolf poses a threat to people.
  - Some other reason. Specify.

The second question poses a problem because there is no unique single response to the question; in fact, respondents are asked to respond with as many answers as they feel are appropriate. In this situation, a single variable for the question is not appropriate but five variables for the five possible responses are. Each variable might contain a code of 1 if the respondent checked that response or 0 if he or she did not. There would thus be five columns of data—composed of ones or zeroes—in the data set for the five variables into which the data for this question was mapped.

Often, students have a problem in conceptualizing data, especially when the situation is like the one just described. Variables in the data set are not simply the questions in the survey; the data is not simply the responses to the questions. Variables are "observable characteristics that can have more than one value."[8] As such, variables can be questions in a survey (because, presumably, responses to these questions would have more than one value) but variables can also be the actual responses themselves, if we choose to code those responses as 1 if the respondent answered "yes" to the question and 2 if the respondent answered "no." Thus, we can conceptualize this latter variable as the presence or absence of agreement with the specific response to the question. If agreement is present, a 1 is coded; if agreement is absent, a 0 is coded.

This latter form of a dichotomous variable—one which is conceptualized as the presence or absence of an attribute, where presence is coded as 1 and absence is coded as 0—is known as a dummy variable. Dummy variables are particularly useful in social science applications for two reasons. First, any variable coded at any level of scaling can be converted into a dichotomous dummy variable. And second, by the definitions established above, dummy variables are coded at the interval level. A good example of this is religion which is typically coded from survey data at the nominal level. A simple coding of a question concerning religious preferences might resemble: 1 Protestant, 2 Catholic, 3 Jewish, 4 Other. There is no underlying ordinality to this scale and so the assumption must be made that the variable is measured at the nominal level. We can, however, change this variable into a four dichotomous dummy variables—Protestant, Catholic, Jewish, and Other. The new variable Protestant would have a code of 1 for every individual who had responded Protestant to the original religious preference question and 0 for all other respondents. The new variable Catholic would have a code of 1 for every individual who had responded Catholic to the original religious preference question and 0 for all other respondents, etc.

The major reason that dummy variables are useful in research applications goes beyond the scope of this chapter but suffice it to say that certain of those applications—in particular multiple regression—assume that the variables to be analyzed were measured at least at the interval level. By converting variables measured at the nominal level to dummy variables we are meeting the assumptions of the desired statistical application.[9]

20.4 READING DATA

Computer programs that analyze data need to know where data is located in a data set, what the allowable codes are for the variable in question, what each of those codes signifies, how to handle a code that might be out of the range of allowable values, and what terminology to attach to each of the numerical codes and to the variable itself. So, in the above example, the computer program that would analyze the data on satisfaction with fire services would need to know that the information on the question of satisfaction with the city's fire department exists in column 67, that it occupies only one column in the data set, and that only codes of 1 through 4 are allowed in this field. The program might also be told to set all other codes—those not in the range of 1 through 4—to missing. The computer would also need to be told to attach the terminology of Very Satisfied to the code 1, Somewhat Satisfied to the code 2, etc. And last, the computer program would need to know that the variable under which these codes exist is entitled something like "Satisfaction with City Fire Services." All of these instructions on reading data would appear as a series of statements which, depending on what type of computer one would be working with, could either be typed in one at a time, constructed from a series of menus and also run individually, or assembled into a file which could then be run as a whole against the data. Interactive computing systems allow for one or the other of the first two of these ways of reading in instructions for defining data. In some personal computer versions of computerized data-analysis packages such as SPSS, STATA, or SAS, or in the server versions of these, the computer program allows the user to type in and run individual statements. In other versions of these programs, the user can highlight commands in menus and also run these commands individually. Although this interactivity has great advantages in analyzing data, it is not particularly an efficient way to operate when reading in and defining data initially. For this latter operation, running a series of statements as a "batch" file has great advantages. Running as a batch file simply means to create a series of statements that do all that one would like to define the data and then to run this file against the data all at once. First and foremost among advantages of using a batch file to define data is the development of a history of what one has done. It is very easy to make a mistake when defining data—constructing a scale that runs high to low rather than low to high; defining gender as 1 and 2 when it should have been defined as 0 and 1, etc.—and these mistakes are not easily caught if a copy of the various files used to construct the data set was not saved. And those files are far harder to retrieve and read when the user worked interactively rather than in a batch-type mode. The simplest mistakes do not often show up until the data is analyzed at which point sense needs to be made out of some counter-intuitive finding such as men reporting they have been sexually harassed in the workplace more often than women reporting such harassment. The "explanation" for this finding might easily be a data error that coded gender oppositely from what was intended. The actual discovery of this error would be nearly impossible without being able to look back at the files that were used to create the data set originally.

The assembly of all of the instructions to define data is sometimes called a dictionary. In older data-analysis programs such as OSIRIS, the dictionary and data file actually existed separately from each other—they were separate files that needed to be used together. One supplied the instructions to read the data; the other supplied the actual raw data. Each time the data was read into a computer, the instructions would be read in first and then these would tell the computer how to read the data. This is like reading the raw data in each time one wanted to analyze the data. More recent data-analysis programs only require a separate dictionary and data file to be read in the first time the data is read into the computer. After this, the data is typically saved as a special file that can be easily read by that data-analysis package. This special file combines the dictionary and data into one file and formats that file in such a way as to optimize disk space for the computer being used. These latter files have special names—system files, internal files, etc. to designate that they are to be used only with the specific data-analysis package in question. Many computer packages automatically assigned special extensions to system files so that the user can recognize them as files to be used only with that data-analysis package. The major advantages to using systems or internal files to store data are ease of use, speed in reading data in and out, and minimization of disk space to store the file.

As noted above, raw data files look like large matrices formatted with variables as columns and observations or cases as rows. If there were a very large number of observations on any unit in a raw data file, we might want to have more than one row of data for each case. In the past, when computerized data was stored on cards, data sets with more than one row (or record) of data per case were very common because each record was limited to 80 columns. With modern computers, data is typically stored on CD's, hard drives, USB drives, or other external media, which can handle records with lengths up to tens of thousands of columns. Nevertheless, many analysts like to divide data sets up into shorter records because many computer monitors can only display 80 or slightly more columns at any one time. Another reason for storing data with multiple records per case might be if one had several sets of observations on each individual. For example, data on satisfaction with city services might have been collected from a sample of city residents in two separate surveys, one conducted before a major reorganization, and one after the reorganization had been accomplished. In this case, one might want to store the first set of observations as one record and the second as a separate one. The major point to be made here is that if this were done, the computer program that was to read the data would need to be told that there actually were two records per case. If not, the program would read each record as a separate case, resulting in double the number of cases and half the number of variables than were supposed to be in the data set.

Once data is stored as a systems file or internal file, additional data can be added fairly easily. A wide variety of data input devices make this addition of data simple and economical; the choice of which specific hardware or software to use is typically dictated by the type of project being conducted and the personal experience and preferences of the analysts involved in the project.

Scanners are one kind of device that are being used to automate the inputting of data. One kind of scanner is a screen that is programmed to accept a wide variety of data formats. For example, this kind of scanner could be used to read newspaper columns—the column is placed on the scanner, the cover is closed, and a few buttons are pushed—and to develop a data set of the actual words in the column. This technique has been used by researchers to conduct "content analyses" of various print journalism sources (newspapers, magazines, and so forth) in which the number of times certain words or phrases are used is counted and analyzed. A scanner might also be programmed to read other sorts of documents, such as blueprints. The blueprint thus becomes data for a data-analysis program to examine. For example, a study of county courthouses might begin with the hypothesis that the design of courthouses impacts the fairness of trials—courthouses where the jury might ride the same elevator as the defendant or where the jury could see the defendant entering the courthouse from the county jail might lead the jury to develop negative impressions of the defendant before the trial begins. By analyzing blueprints of country courthouses and comparing those to decisions of juries in those counties, the role of courthouse design issues could be ascertained, and recommendations for retrofitting courthouses could be developed.

Scanners are efficient devices for inputting large amounts of data because they read entire pages of words, pictures, or images at a time. Scanners (and the software that supports the scanning process) do, however, have certain disadvantages. First, even very sensitive scanners make mistakes in reading data. A scanner with a 95 percent rate of reading individual letters correctly will still most likely read five out of each one hundred letters incorrectly. Given that there are some three hundred words on a given typewritten page, this would lead to a fairly large number of errors per page. Scanners with greater than 99 percent correct reading rates are now becoming the norm, but even here the user must expect that a number of errors will occur in the scanned page. Second, the error rate increases dramatically as the print quality in the scanned document declines, so bad photocopies of documents present challenges to even sophisticated scanners and scanning software. Older scanners also seem to be better at scanning some kinds of print fonts than others. James Fallows, for example, reports that the scanner and accompanying software that he routinely used in the 1990s to scan newspaper articles is much more successful scanning the *Wall Street Journal* than the *Washington Post.*[10]

A second type of scanner that is more sensitive and thus makes fewer errors is the more familiar bar code scanner often used to read prices in grocery or other stores. These scanners recognize the bars in the field as individual pieces of data and add them to a preexisting data set. Of course, for such a system to work properly, bar codes must be set up and installed on each "item" to be later input as data and each bar code must be originally defined through a data definition statement when the data set is initially set up. Although computer programs exist to write bar codes, a person must still begin the process by writing the instructions that originally set up the codes. This labor-intensive process would appear to be cost-effective only if large numbers of individual items to be added to the data set were identical to each other, in an inventory situation, for example. Where individual items are unique, each would have its own bar code and it is thus difficult to see how any cost or labor savings could be obtained.

Last, there are now a variety of web-based data input applications that allow users to create a form and have respondents input information on their own. Using a predeveloped template, the information the user inputs is saved as a data record and becomes part of a data set. This type of application is widely used in web-based surveys and by both the private and public sector in collecting demographic and other information from those who register online for various activities or purposes.

20.5 RULES OF THUMB FOR CONSTRUCTING DATA SETS

Several lessons can be drawn from the discussion of reading data above. In collecting data and preparing it for input into a computerized data-analysis package, there are several rules of thumb that should be followed:

1. Although the computerized data-analysis package into which the data is read will not need to know what level of scale has been used to measure the variable, knowledge of scaling is integral in reading and analyzing data. Thus, attention needs to be paid to how the data is scaled, coded, and input into the computer when the data is being prepared for input. This will allow for efficient data-analysis after the data is ready for use.

2. All of the permissible data transformations for each of the scales noted above allow for data to be "collapsed"; that is data can be transformed from more specific measurements to less specific measurements. It is important to note that the opposite is not true—data cannot be transformed from less specific measurements to more specific. It is possible to recode exact income data for families into larger categories, but it is not possible to recover exact income data for families from data originally coded as larger categories. For this reason, data should always be gathered using the most specific measurements possible—given practical constraints. Income is typically a difficult variable to gather data on in surveys because many people do not like to divulge their income (particularly when the questions are asked by governmental entities!). Thus, asking the question "What is your family income?" will typically result in a large number of respondents refusing to answer the question and another large number answering that they simply do not know. Many techniques have been developed to "trap" individuals into divulging their income on surveys. One asks the respondent an initial question akin to: "Is your income above or below $30,000?" and then proceeds to ask further questions (above or below $50,000?) to categorize income. A second technique displays a list of income categories to the respondent and asks "Into which of these categories would you say your family income falls?" It is important to note that both of these techniques will most likely result in larger number of respondents answering the questions (a net plus) but will sacrifice the specificity of the income measure (a net minus). Therefore, care must be taken in setting up the categories for questions like this so that the resulting data is useful for analysis. Imagine the problem of taking an income question worded like either of the two techniques above that was used in a city-wide survey and using that question unchanged for an in-depth survey of poverty neighborhoods in the same city.

3. In the design of the data set, care should be taken to make the data compatible with other data sets that have been constructed by the agency for which the data is designed or compatible with the demands of other agencies or data archives. Although this may seem a minor point in the initial stages of a data-gathering project, a small amount of investment in compatibility in early stages will save major problems in reformatting data after the data set has been constructed and analyzed. Often, state and federal agencies have very restrictive requirements on how they want data collected by local governments or private contractors to be formatted when that data is archived with the parent agency.

20.6 USES OF DATA

Typically, data will prove most useful in documenting the existence of problems that public administrators are interested in. But data also has other important uses for the public administrator. Typically, policy analysis texts teach a six step method of analyzing public problems—problem identification and validation, development of evaluation criteria, development of alternative solutions, analysis of solutions in the light of evaluation criteria, display of results, and recommendations.[11] Data on the existence of a given problem would be necessary in determining how extensive a problem exists and whether the problem was worsening. Thus, data is necessary in validating and identifying a given problem, but data would also be extremely useful in each of the additional five policy analysis steps. The application of this idea can be best pursued through an example.

As a manager in a large city's public works department, you receive a memo from your supervisor directing you to look into the situation concerning potholes in city streets. Residents of the city are complaining of the existence of a larger-than-normal number of potholes which seem to have appeared after the particularly harsh winter your city experienced. What kinds of data on potholes would you begin looking for? How would you begin gathering these data? What would you do with the data?

First, note that the question of potholes is deceptively simple—deceptive because it more than likely is not the mere existence of potholes that city residents are complaining about. Most problems have both an objective and a subjective component[12] and the existence of potholes is no exception to this rule. Although the city may or may not actually have more potholes this spring than it has experienced before, city residents might perceive a larger number of potholes because the winter was so harsh and the local newspaper just ran a series of stories on pothole problems in neighboring states. Thus, the kinds of data to be gathered initially divide into objective data on the actual existence of potholes in city streets and subjective data on the perceptions of city residents about the existence of potholes. In pursuing the first type of data, one would most likely try to establish a sampling frame of city streets—it would probably be impossible to count all the potholes in all the streets in the city—and then to count, as inexpensively as possible, the number of potholes on those streets. In pursuing the second type of data, one would most likely want to conduct a survey of city residents by taking a sample of the population and asking them questions about the existence of potholes this year in comparison to past years and so on. These two kinds of data would provide a valuable base line in looking at this problem. If the department had collected similar data in the past, comparisons between the observations this year and those from past years could be made to identify whether the problem actually was worse, or whether there was more of a perceptual (subjective) problem. In deciding how to address the pothole problem, very different potential solutions would suggest themselves depending on whether the problem was documented as more of an objective or more of a subjective problem. But the need for data to examine this problem has only begun. Although data is certainly necessary to document the problem, to determine if it is getting worse, to compare this city with other cities, etc., data would also be necessary in the later stages of the policy analysis process. For example, a survey of experts in the field might be desirable to determine what kinds of evaluation criteria they would advocate in analyzing the policy problem. The survey of experts itself represents a data collection task and would have its own analysis—think, for example, of what statistic might be used to summarize the consensus of opinions of a group of experts. Would a Delphi technique, in which a survey was conducted and analyzed and the results then summarized and made available to the experts for comments and modification of their opinions be useful? In determining how actually to analyze the alternatives that were isolated in this policy problem against the evaluation criteria chosen, policy texts often advocate weighting the criteria such that some are more important than others in the final mathematical analyses. How would one determine how to assign these weights? The naive policy analyst might do this through intuition, a method which is virtually scientifically indefensible. A much better way would be, again, to survey experts in the field, and collect data on their opinions on how important the various criteria are. Weights can be easily calculated from the data collected from the policy experts.

20.7 WHERE DATA COME FROM

Data can come from a wide variety of sources. These sources can be divided initially into those where the data is collected specifically for the individual project and those where the data has been collected by somebody else but are being used for the project currently underway. Collecting one's own data to address problems in policy analysis and public administration has great advantages. Often, the types of problems that public administrators are interested in are limited—bounded both geographically and temporally—resulting in needs for data that are specialized for one or a small number of situations.[13]

In the pothole scenario developed above, it would have been difficult for the analyst to proceed in any other way than to gather the data for himself or herself. But this method of collecting specialized data has at least two major disadvantages. First, collecting one's own data has costs in terms of money, time, and effort. Mounting a survey of potholes in a large city can take a few weeks to accomplish, would need personnel assigned to conduct the survey, and would require the efforts of somebody to design the sample and conduct at least minimal training sessions with those who would conduct the survey. And then there are the necessary tasks of processing the survey data into computer-readable files, and so forth, all of which will also add to the cost, time, and effort of answering the question for which the data was collected. Second, the mind set that is developed by collecting specialized data to address one unique problem is one that is self-perpetuating. As long as public administrators operate in this fashion, there will not be large data archives from which other public administrators can profit.

This last point is worth pursuing in some detail. To conduct a survey of city services in a large U.S. city, one would want to collect data on such things as whether city residents think they are getting a good deal on the taxes they pay, on which departments they think are doing a good job and which need improvement. Many cities conduct such surveys on a regular basis; some such as Birmingham, Alabama have acquired a reputation as being particularly activist in conducting citizen surveys.[14]

For the purpose of answering the particular question concerning a specific city's needs, collecting particularized data might be exactly what one would want to do. In order to do so, a sample of city residents would need to be isolated through a scientifically defensible sampling scheme, questions that tap the relevant dimensions on which data was to be collected would need to be developed, the interview instrument would need to be tested for such things as length of interview, proper interpretation of questions, etc., and then the survey would need to be conducted. It might be discovered that 55 percent of those surveyed thought that taxes in this city were too high and that the sanitation and police departments were specifically identified as not performing their functions very effectively. After the report was submitted to the city manager and the city council, questions most likely would arise as to how this city compared to other cities in the state or other cities of similar population in other states. Given the individualized nature of the data project described, this question could not be answered with any great confidence and a second, comparative data-gathering project might be necessary to come up with the council's questions on this topic.

Imagine a different scenario for this project. After being assigned the survey project, the analyst calls a data archive and asks the librarian (or better yet, accesses their web site and personally looks for relevant studies) for information on the types of surveys that other cities have recently conducted. After looking at the half-dozen or so studies, the analyst isolates questions using those in the previous studies as models. This eliminates the step of pretesting the questionnaire for format (although, most likely, the questionnaire would still need to be pretested for time). The cost for accessing the data archive would, most likely, be small (or covered by a subscription that would allow unlimited access for a given length of time) but in return for access to the archive, one would be required to archive the data generated in the current study with the facility. The efficiencies in the latter mode of operation are clear; many hours of developing wording for questions to make them unbiased and clear in meaning become unnecessary. The analyst would know that the questions that he or she is using have been utilized in other studies and so have a degree of support in the academic community or among experts in survey research. This would greatly lower the overhead in conducting surveys for public administration and public policy uses. And data generated in other geographical settings become available so that any localized study can be compared with other localities or (possibly) national samples to validate the findings one might obtain. In addition, since the data was generated using the same question wordings, possible challenges stemming from differing wordings or formats become moot.

Such data archives are now either in existence or in the planning stages at various universities and other facilities around the United States and in other nations. Several large survey-oriented archives have been available for perusal for free or for nominal costs for some time and the developers of these archives have recently put them online so that they can be accessed through the Internet. Some large, national surveys are archived at their own survey house's website, but virtually all of the large national surveys are archived either at the Inter-university Consortium for Political and Social Research (ICPSR) Web site described below or at one of a number of other websites mainly associated with universities.[15]

The ICPSR is a membership-based organization that archives and disseminates questionnaires and data. Although the typical member of ICPSR is a university, local, state, and national government agencies also are members. Membership carries with it free access to the archive, along with technical assistance in accessing and utilizing the data stored there. ICPSR is housed at the University of Michigan; its governing board is composed of researchers from universities in the United States and abroad. ICPSR not only houses a great deal of survey data from such diverse sources as the American National Election Study, ABC, CBS, NBC, *The Wall Street Journal*, *The New York Times*, CNN, etc., but also houses data from the Department of Justice, The Department of Health and Human Services, and the Census Bureau.

The National Opinion Research Center (NORC) at the University of Chicago has been conducting the general social survey (GSS) for many years and has developed an archive of questions and data from that series of national surveys. The GSS asks questions from a number of disciplines—sociology, economics, psychology, child development, political science—and so can provide a wealth of information for those looking for possible question wordings or for base-line data on which to compare their own jurisdictions. The GSS is also archived at ICPSR and the archive there not only allows for retrieval of question wordings and data, but allows users to obtain marginals (frequency distributions) of questions and simple cross-tabulations over a computer link.

In the past several years, several researchers have suggested that state and local governments, who conduct large numbers of surveys typically monitoring citizens' opinions of the services governments offer, begin to develop a common standard set of questions and data formats to lower the overhead in the conduct of such surveys. With a common set of questions and formats, a state and local government data archive could be more easily (and less costly) established. Although such a data archive has been proposed by several different individuals in several different venues, it is still only in the planning stages.

As noted above, survey data is not the only kind that has been archived. The largest data archive in the United States is that maintained by the U.S. Census Bureau. The uses of Census data are numerous. Granting agencies typically require extensive documentation of a problem in order for an applicant to be considered for financial support. Census data is adaptable for such uses, although the actual steps that one must go through to make the data amenable for use in a grant application are not as simple as one might think. Consider the following example:

> A city manager has been receiving a large number of complaints from residents of two neighborhoods that abut the central business district of a city of 200,000. The residents are complaining that their neighborhoods are deteriorating, or at least are not keeping up with other neighborhoods it the city. The manager wants to be able to address the residents' complaints and to seek financial assistance from the Federal Department of Housing and Urban Development (HUD) if the data show that there are substantial, addressable, problems in these neighborhoods.

The manager turns the project over to a senior analyst and asks for the analyst's staff to collect data to address the economic, social, and physical state of these neighborhoods and the change in all three of these over time. The analyst, in receiving the manager's memo, knows that the necessary data is available through the Census Bureau. The analyst also knows that Census data is available from online sources directly from the U.S. Census Bureau (www.census.gov), from data archives such as ICPSR, etc., or in paper format through the extensive series of volumes that the Census Bureau publishes (and that are housed at the local university library).

The analyst's first steps in gathering the data would most likely be to think of what possible indicators of deterioration might be utilized in this situation. He or she would know that multiple indicators are better than single ones, and would also know that data needs to be gathered to determine if economic, social, or physical deterioration were occurring. The analyst develops an extensive list of indicators to research and begins to look at Census holdings to see: (1) if data on these indicators is available; (2) if these data was gathered over time; and (3) to see if the data on indicators that was gathered over time were defined in similar enough ways as to make over time comparisons meaningful.[16]

The analyst assigns the best graduate student intern working in the department to gather the data. At this point a problem occurs. The graduate student knows that there will not be data on all of the indicators that the analyst is looking for; the graduate student also knows that on only some of these indicators will there be data from more than one Census. But those are only minor problems; the major problems that hit are, first, that the city's definition of the neighborhoods under question and the Census Bureau's definition of a Census tract are not the same. And second, the Census Bureau constantly updates its definition of tracts and blocks which makes overtime work difficult. Consider these two points separately.

First, definitions of neighborhoods are difficult to develop. Residents of a given neighborhood subjectively know what geographic areas they consider to be in their neighborhood but these subjective definitions are often not shared with a large number of their neighbors, and the subjective definitions also often do not translate well onto city maps of the neighborhood. In addition to this, whatever subjective definition that can be developed for a given neighborhood will most likely not be exactly described in the most available U.S. Census data, the data sets that describe U.S. Census tracts. Census tracts are developed by the Census Bureau in conjunction with local government officials and researchers at local universities, and data from Census tracts is the basic building block on which most Census analyses are based but, at best, a given Census tract is only a statistical approximation of a neighborhood. Data on smaller units—Census blocks, for example—is also available through a variety of sources, and this data can be used to develop a finer approximation of a neighborhood, but this data is difficult to work with because one would need to know exactly what Census blocks are contained in a given neighborhood and then to build up the neighborhood data set from its component Census block data. Although this is not an inherently difficult task—and the actual process will be described later in this chapter—it is not one that an analyst would typically undertake for a single study. Several cities—Cincinnati is a notable example—have developed statistical approximations of neighborhoods from Census data and make this data available to both city departments and outsiders for research purposes, thus reducing the need to develop individualized data sets for particular projects.

Second, the Census Bureau is not consistent over time in its definition of a given Census tract.[17] Census tracts are adjusted for each census as neighborhoods, cities, and states gain or lose population from one U.S. Census to the next. These adjustments are attempted with a bias toward preserving the status quo, but often the changes that are made are large. Again, it is possible to recompute the data for a given Census tract from its underlying block structure and thus to make data from more recent censuses conform to those of the past, but the further back in history one wishes to go, the more changes will be necessary and the more time, effort, and money will have to go into developing the data set necessary to answer the initial question. At times this may be absolutely necessary. For example, if a researcher interested in population growth in cities wanted to disentangle "natural" growth (growth as a result of childbirths and in-migration) from growth as a result of annexation,[18] the researcher could attempt to match Census tracts from the original city (preannexation) with current Census tracts that approximated those and measure population only in these tracts.

At best, then, Census data can only yield an approximation of the data necessary to answer the question about neighborhood decline. Depending on how close the Census tract definitions for the city in question are to the underlying neighborhood structure of that city, the statistical approximation would be either close or distant. Given an unlimited amount of time, resources, and money, the Census data could be recalculated to yield an exact match to the city's neighborhoods, but for most public administration research tasks, time, resources, and money are almost the exact opposite of unlimited on all three dimensions.

The most important point to be drawn from this discussion is that although Census data is potentially a very useful source of data for state and local public administrators, the structure of the

Census data makes them difficult to use for certain purposes. The U.S. Census Bureau is extremely conscious of the confidentiality of its data; they simply refuse to make data available for small enough units that information about individual citizens can be inferred from the larger unit of analysis. If the Census Bureau errs in reporting data, it errs on the side of caution; data drawn from small units that researchers would be interested in is simply not released to respect individual privacy. Census tracts contain thousands or tens of thousands of individuals whereas Census blocks contain hundreds or thousands of individuals. In such large amalgamations, individual privacy is protected.

Geographical Information Systems (GIS) programs overcome many of the difficulties just mentioned in analyzing census data over time. GIS combines a data-analysis program with a mapping program and allows the analyst to draw maps shaded by various demographic or social characteristics. The incidence of crime, placement of underground storage tanks, and many other kinds of information can be plotted on maps that include bus routes, school districts, rivers, and so on. If the GIS program used by the local government above had been originally programmed with data at the Census block level, the analyst could have easily built up new definitions of neighborhoods from the preexisting block data and plotted these new definitions on maps to see if they were the same as the previous definitions of neighborhoods. GIS is a remarkable and powerful tool being used by local governments to make data analysis much easier and more accessible to employees and citizens. However, remember that both the promise and limitations of GIS are in the data used by the program—the better the data, the better the results. In computer days of yore, the acronym GIGO was developed—garbage in, garbage out. This means that bad results often come from bad data whereas good results can only come from good data.

20.8 MANIPULATING DATA

Once a data set has been constructed, the data in it, and the very structure of the data set itself, can be manipulated to fit the needs of the analyst. Because the manipulation of individual variables and the manipulation of the data set itself are quite different in concept, these are examined individually below.

20.9 SCALE OR INDEX CONSTRUCTION

Individual variables can be recoded, as described above, by reversing scales, collapsing data from many categories into fewer, and so on. These manipulations are fairly simple; the necessity for undertaking such manipulations should be self-evident. More complicated manipulations involve such things as scale or index construction, in which several individual variables are combined into a scale that summarizes the components.

Many scales are constructed as simple additive indices in which the responses to underlying questions are simply summed into an aggregate score. For example, a researcher in economic development might have isolated a number of mechanisms that economic development practitioners could possibly use in their quests to develop their communities. These mechanisms might have been sent out in questionnaire format to local government economic development practitioners throughout the state and the respondents asked to check off which mechanisms they had used to attempt to develop their communities. The resulting questionnaires could then be coded 0 where the respondent had not attempted one of the mechanisms, and 1 where the respondent had. By simply summing across all the questions, the researcher could construct an additive index of economic development activity in a given community—the higher the number, the greater degree of activity the community would be presumed to have undertaken.[19]

But this scale would be less informative than one which was theory driven. A different approach to constructing the same scale would be to start with some implicit or explicit theory of economic development and use that theory to assist in constructing whatever scales one might need. For example, one might want to divide all of the mechanisms identified in the survey described above into those that are supply driven and those that are demand driven and to construct scales of each of these by only summing the answers to questions under each category.

A more sophisticated scaling technique that has enjoyed some popularity in social science research is to use a data reduction technique such as factor analysis to organize one's data and then to construct scales using the factors identified by the computer program. For example, James Perry and William Berkes used factor analysis to examine strike behavior by local government employees. Their work isolated two factors—local employee status and past strike behavior—from a list of seven variables. The two factors were then used to predict the likelihood of strikes in other localities.[20] Factor analysis programs typically yield two sets of coefficients for each variable—a score of how highly each variable "loads" on a given factor and a set of factor scores. The first of these is a measure of how highly correlated each variable is with the latent variable that is being measured by the factor and thus provides useful information about the factor structure in the data. The second coefficient—the factor score—can be used to create a scale in which each of the components is not equivalently weighted. When creating the scale, the scores for each of the individual variables are multiplied by the factor score and then summed, resulting in a scale in which some of the variables contribute more toward the final index value more than do others. Some analysts find this weighted scale to be a more accurate measure of the underlying latent variable than a simple summing of the variables loading highly on a given factor.[21]

A second way of combining individual variables into a composite index or scale is to standardize each of the variables. This can be done in a variety of ways but one common one is converting the data to z-scores and then to sum the z-scores. This procedure is often used when the individual variables are measured on vastly different metrics or when one wishes to create a summary scale from a series of sub-scales of varying size. For example, in my own work on citizen participation, four sub-scales measuring the types of mechanisms cities used to foster citizen participation—information gathering mechanisms, open government mechanisms, neighborhood empowerment mechanisms, and citizen coproduction mechanisms—were standardized and summed to create a holistic citizen participation scale. The standardization procedure was necessary because each of the four sub-scales varied in how it was measured—citizen coproduction ranged from zero to nine while information gathering ranged from zero to four.[22] Without standardization, the scales with more categories (coproduction) would determine the outcome of the overall scale more heavily than would the scales with fewer categories (neighborhood empowerment).

A second use of this procedure would be where the composite variables are measuring vastly different items. One example given by Ken Meier and Jeff Brudney constructs a measure of performance for a city's garbage collection crews on the basis of two variables—tons of trash collected and number of complaints phoned in by residents. As can be seen, it would be impossible to sum tons of trash and numbers of complaints to arrive at a useful scale because the two items are measured on such different scales (metrics). The solution to this problem is to convert each of the two variables to its z-score analogue by subtracting the mean from the raw score and dividing by the standard deviation. The resulting standardized scores are by definition measured on a common metric and thus the scores can be summed to arrive at a usable summary index.[23]

Thus, one can see that scale or index construction is data manipulation because new data is being created from old data. In performing such manipulations, one important point must be stressed: once the scales or indices have been constructed and the analyst is satisfied with how they are performing, the new variable or variables must be saved—added to the data set—before one exits the computer program. Not saving the newly created variables is one of the most common errors in computerized data-analysis, and committing this error means that all of the steps undertaken to construct the index or scale must be gone through again. Because some scale or index construction is quite extensive and complicated, it is easy to see why the analyst would not want to repeat the procedure unnecessarily.

20.10   CREATING NEW DATA SETS FROM EXISTING ONES

At times, a data analyst will want to recast an entire data set by changing the unit of analysis, in essence creating a new data set. For example, in an early work looking at constituency influence on members of Congress, Warren Miller and Donald Stokes[24] aggregated the 1958 American National Election Study by Congressional District. They calculated a statistic (the mean) for responses on policy questions for individuals in Congressional Districts and compared those scores with members of Congress from those same districts. A data set where the individual was the unit of analysis was transposed into one where the Congressional District (and its member of Congress) was the unit of analysis. This technique can be used fruitfully in a variety of situations which are of interest to those involved in public administration. Several of these might be the aggregation of a survey of housing for a municipality into the municipality's composite neighborhoods to compare housing needs across neighborhoods, the aggregation of samples of individual bureaucratic encounters with the public into agency statistics to compare performance across public agencies, or the aggregation of individual electoral support for an education-related bond referendum into neighborhoods to ascertain comparative support for such issues.

In each of these and other situations, aggregating the data up to a higher level of analysis is a fairly easy task; of course, disaggregating data into lower levels of analysis is virtually impossible for many of the same reasons identified under Section 20.5 above.

In order to allow for aggregation, several important points should be stressed when gathering data:

First, in order for any aggregation to occur, the variable that one would want to aggregate on must be present in the data set. Although this sounds trivial, it is extremely important. If one wants to aggregate individual level data up to the Congressional District, a variable containing information about Congressional Districts must be present in the data set. Only then can the computer be instructed to aggregate the cases under each of the Congressional Districts coded.

Second, a statistic must be chosen to summarize the individual data at the group or aggregate level. In the Miller and Stokes example above, the mean was used to summarize the individual policy preference data at the Congressional District level. The median could also have been easily used. In fact, if one considers the sum to be a statistic, all of the discussion above on Census tracts can be thought of as creating a new Census tract data set from its constituent Census block structure. It should be apparent that the choice of a statistic is more than individual whim and should be driven by well-supported statistical theory and practices.

Third, it is important to keep in mind the nature of sample data and what happens to the representativeness of samples when one changes the unit of analysis. The American National Election Study used by Miller and Stokes in the example above is a representative national sample of the American electorate, but it is not a representative sample of any individual Congressional District in the United States. By aggregating individual responses by Congressional District, calculating the mean across those individuals, and using this statistic as an indicator of district opinion on policy issues, Miller and Stokes were probably pushing their data too far. There were very few cases in several Congressional Districts, making the samples in those districts far from representative. In statistical terms, the small samples in some Congressional Districts would result in very large standard errors, casting doubt on the validity of statistics calculated for those districts.

All popular computerized data-analysis programs such as SAS, STATA, or SPSS allow data to be aggregated in the ways described above. The actual command structure to accomplish the data transformations is fairly simple but does require a certain amount of experience with the program to get things to work the way the user would like. To accomplish such transformations efficiently, it is usually necessary to consult somebody experienced in the data-analysis program in which the work is being performed.

20.11 CONCLUSION

Data is available to researchers and practitioners in the field of public administration from a wide variety of sources. Whether one wishes to gather data specifically to address a certain problem or to use archived data gathered by somebody else, there is enough data to satisfy even the most ardent seeker. The important questions concerning data are those involving applicability or use, preservation, and sensitivity.

All data-gathering exercises must be guided by some theory of the applicability or use to which the data will be put. Simply gathering data on subjects on which the researcher or practitioner is interested is, at best, an inefficient use of resources. All data gathering has a cost—whether that cost be monetary, human, administrative, or whatever. And thus, all data gathering should be driven by at least implicit cost/benefit considerations. Is a new study necessary? Are there already published, relevant data that is available to us at no or moderate cost? Will that data suffice for the purposes of the current project? All of these are questions that should drive the data-gathering task. Often, public administrators who are new to the field will propose a study (a data-gathering task) to address a problem their agency is facing. Although new studies might be necessary to address such problems, it is often forgotten that there is a wealth of data available for a wide variety of sources which might already address the problem.

When quantitative data-analysis first began to be taught in the social sciences in the 1940s, some strict practitioners in the field taught their students to gather data for a specific task, calculate the statistics they wanted from the data, check the statistics against the preexisting hypotheses they had developed, and then destroy the data set so that they would not be tempted to go back and recalculate statistics or do something else that might compromise the practitioner's strict view of the scientific research process. In such an environment, archiving data was not anything that anybody cared about or advocated. In more recent times, considerations about what to do with data after it has been used for the specific purpose intended to carry much heavier weights. Public agencies throughout the United States and in other countries routinely keep files—computerized or paper—of the results of past studies so that any new work in the field can be compared to past results and to reduce the overhead of the research task by keeping researchers from recreating the wheel. Whether these archives are public or not is unimportant; what is important is that they are accessible by people who need to use them—researchers in the agency who are conducting current research, for whom past research would make their jobs easier. Thus, questions about the format of data sets, the nature and format of questions asked in surveys, etc. become important when one looks at data gathering with archiving as a goal.

Last, data is sensitive simply by its nature. Surveys, for example, sometimes ask sensitive questions of respondents, and to get the respondents to answer these questions frankly, confidentiality is promised. These promises of confidentiality often lead to different—at times "better"—data than if confidentiality was not promised. For example, victimization studies—studies where respondents are asked if they have been a victim of a crime—often use a random digit dialing (RDD) telephone sampling scheme. When RDD is used, the interviewer does not know to whom he or she is speaking and this is often communicated in the course of the interview. This form of confidentiality leads to much higher estimates of the rate of certain sensitive crimes—especially rape and sexual assault—than do analyses of crimes reported to the police. Society's understanding of crime has changed dramatically because victimization studies have been used to augment reported crime as a source of data on crime. But what would happen to these gains in the understanding of crime if respondents suspected that researchers were not treating the data as confidential? It would not take much to trace the phone numbers obtained through a RDD sampling scheme and obtain the names, addresses, etc. of the individuals who had been interviewed, and a nefarious survey organization could make good use of this information—perhaps attempting to sell crime deterrents to people who had been victimized. Or what would happen if a respondent found that the results of a study in which she had participated were reported in such detail that anybody with any passing familiarity with her case could identify her? What keeps this from happening to any extent is a common understanding among the research community about the confidentiality of data. This confidentiality is what allows survey data to be taken seriously; if individuals suspected that the data they were supplying governments, survey houses, corporations, etc. was going to be used in ways that were less than confidential, our faith in survey data would be seriously undermined. Thus, any data-gathering task that involves gathering data from individuals must guarantee the individuals' confidentiality. Failure to do so is courting disaster, both for the individual study and for the research community as a whole.

QUESTIONS

In the attached dataset:
1. What does code 0 mean for the variable that is labeled "gender?"
   Male
2. What does code 1 mean for the variable that is labeled "children?"
   Has Children
3. At what level (interval, ordinal, or nominal) are the variables labeled "gender" and "children" measured?
   Because both are coded 0 or 1, they are interval level variables. With only one interval between the two codes for the variables, they are by definition, interval level variables.
4. At what level (interval, ordinal, or nominal) is the variable labeled "importance of after school programs" measured?
   Ordinal
5. If you were going to recode the seven variables that rate the importance of various United Way programs into "Positive," "Neutral," and "Negative," what current codes would compose the new category "Positive?" Which ones would compose "Neutral?" And which would compose "Negative?"
   1, 2 = Positive
   3 = Neutral
   4, 5 = Negative
6. The three unrecorded "most important problem" questions can be used to develop a multiple response variable (how you would do this would depend on which statistical analysis program you are using). What are some possible bases for the new multiple response variable?
   Total number of respondents who mentioned an answer
   Total number of answers given
7. Do the recoded "most important problem" categories look reasonable to you? Could you develop a different recoding system for these variables?
8. Develop a table that displays the recoded "most important problem" multiple response variable by gender of the respondent where the base of the table is the total number of respondents.

| | | | Gender | | Total |
			Male	Female	
Most Important	Education/youth	Count	15	26	41
Problem		% within var1	50.0%	56.5%	
	Economy/jobs	Count	15	19	34
		% within var1	50.0%	41.3%	
	Drugs/alcohol	Count	6	13	19
		% within var1	20.0%	28.3%	

			Gender		Total
			Male	Female	
Crime/domestic violence		Count	2	13	15
		% within var1	6.7%	28.3%	
Elderly		Count	6	11	17
		% within var1	20.0%	23.9%	
Families/pregnancy		Count	4	6	10
		% within var1	13.3%	13.0%	
Health/medical/health care		Count	6	6	12
		% within var1	20.0%	13.0%	
Other community issues		Count	20	20	40
		% within var1	66.7%	43.5%	
Total		Count	30	46	76

Note: Percentages and totals are based on respondents.

9. Develop a table that displays the recoded "most important problem" multiple response variable by gender of the respondent where the base of the table is the total number of answers respondents have given to these three questions.

			Gender		Total
			Male	Female	
Most Important Problem	Education/youth	Count	15	26	41
		% within var1	20.3%	22.8%	
	Economy/jobs	Count	15	19	34
		% within var1	20.3%	16.7%	
	Drugs/alcohol	Count	6	13	19
		% within var1	8.1%	11.4%	
	Crime/domestic violence	Count	2	13	15
		% within var1	2.7%	11.4%	
	Elderly	Count	6	11	17
		% within var1	8.1%	9.6%	
	Families/pregnancy	Count	4	6	10
		% within var1	5.4%	5.3%	
	Health/medical/health care	Count	6	6	12
		% within var1	8.1%	5.3%	
	Other community issues	Count	20	20	40
		% within var1	27.0%	17.5%	
Total		Count	74	114	188

Note: Percentages and totals are based on responses.

ENDNOTES

1. C.H. Coombs, *A Theory of Data* (New York: John Wiley and Sons, 1964), p. 1.
2. It should be apparent that what we are discussing here is specifically what behavioral researchers call R methodology. R methodology involves seeking commonalities among variables across individual units. A different methodology—Q methodology—has been identified and advocated by W. Stephenson most clearly in his book. *The Study of Behavior: Q-Technique and Its Methodology* (Chicago: University of

Chicago Press, 1953). Q methodology seeks to represent an individual's subjective view of reality; it has very different data needs and quite different data-gathering tools than those described here. See S. Brown, *Political Subjectivity: Applications of Q Methodology in Political Science* (New Haven: Yale University Press, 1980) for a good explication of Q methodology and how it differs from R methodology. Also, see F. Kerlinger, *Foundations of Behavioral Research*, 2nd edition (New York: Holt, Rhinehart, and Winston, 1973), chapter 34, pp. 582–600.

3. In most computer applications commas would not have to be entered into the data. The computer program would do this automatically or could be told where to insert the commas.
4. W.S. Sarle, Measurement theory: Frequently asked questions, *Disseminations of the International Statistical Applications Institute*, 4th edition (Wichita: ACG Press, 1995), pp. 61–66.
5. S.S. Stevens, On the theory of scales of measurement, *Science*, 103: 677–680, 1946.
6. Sarle, 1995.
7. See W.R. Mangun, N. Lucas, J.C. Whitehead, and J.C. Mangun, Valuing red wolf recovery efforts at Alligator River NWR: Measuring citizen support, in *Wolves of America Conference Proceedings* (Washington, DC: Defenders of Wildlife, 1996), pp. 165–171.
8. E. O'Sullivan, G. Rassel, and M. Berner. *Research Methods for Public Administrators*, 4th edition (New York: Longman Publishers, 2003), p. 13.
9. There has been some controversy about using variables measured at the ordinal level in multiple regression applications. While statistical purists insist that only interval or ratio level variables should be used in multiple regression applications, other texts have adopted the rule that the ordinary least squares (OLS) regression model is robust enough to support analysis of ordinal level scales provided that there are a fairly large number of categories in the scale (typically, five or more) and that the analyst is willing to assume that the differences between the scale categories are approximately equal. L. Giventer, for example, in *Statistical Analysis for Public Administration* (Belmont, California: Wadsworth, 1996, p. 404) states flatly, "A variable having an ordinal level of measurement with an implicit underlying scale can be treated mathematically as if it has an interval level of measurement."
10. J. Fallows, Recognizable characters, *The Atlantic Monthly*, pp. 110–115, February, 1994.
11. See C. Patton and D. Sawicki, *Basic Methods of Policy Analysis and Planning*, 2nd edition (Englewood Cliffs: Prentice-Hall, 1996).
12. See C. Scavo, Racial integration of local government leadership in southern small cities: consequences for equity relevance and political relevance, *Social Science Quarterly*, 71(2): 362–372, 1993.
13. W. Dunn, *Public Policy Analysis: An Introduction*, 3rd edition (Englewood Cliffs, Prentice-Hall, 2003).
14. See C. Scavo, The use of participative mechanisms by large U.S. cities, *Journal of Urban Affairs*, 15(1): 93–110, 1990.
15. The Institute for Policy Research at the University of Cincinnati, for example, provides a data archive consisting mainly of data sets obtained from ICPSR, NORC, the International Survey Library Association (Roper studies), and the U.S. Census Bureau. Other universities—Yale, the University of Wisconsin, several of the University of California campuses, and others—maintain data archives focusing on various aspects of public administration, public policy, or other social science–related areas.
16. The Census Bureau did not, for example, publish data on female-headed families until 1990 when interest in these families among researchers and others warranted such publication. Attempting to develop tracking data for this indicator is thus futile, because the data literally does not exist before 1990.
17. To be fair to the Census Bureau, they do work extensively with state and local governments and researchers from area universities in making adjustments to Census tracts so that the changes from one Census to the next are more-or-less incremental in nature. There are, however, instances in which incremental change is impossible and only large-scale change in the Census tract structure for a geographical area can accommodate the population changes that have occurred.
18. Because annexation rates vary tremendously by state and region, comparisons of city population growth rates that seek to make assumptions about natural population increases would be required to make the types of statistical approximations described here.
19. See P. Eisenger, *The Rise of the Entrepreneurial State: State and Local Economic Development in the United States* (Madison, Wisconsin: University of Wisconsin Press, 1988); R. Hanson, and M. Berkman, A meteorology of state economic climates, *Economic Development Quarterly*, 5(3): 213–228, 1991; and L. Reese, Categories of local economic development techniques: an empirical analysis, *Policy Studies Journal*, 21(3): 492–506, 1993, on the use of additive indices in economic development research.

20. See J. Perry and W. Berkes, Predicting strike behavior, *Western Political Quarterly*, Spring, pp. 501–517, 1979.
21. See E. O'Sullivan, G. Rassel, and M. Berner 2003, *Research Methods for Public Administration*, 4th edition (New York: Addison Wesley Longman, 2003), pp. 304–305 for examples of this approach.
22. The four sub-scales described were first developed by Elaine Sharp in her book, *Urban Politics and Administration: From Service Delivery to Economic Development* (New York: Longman, 1990).
23. K. Meier and J. Brudney, *Applied Statistics for Public Administration*, 3rd edition (Belmont, California: Wadsworth, 1993), pp. 113–115.
24. See W. Miller and D. Stokes, "Constituency influence in Congress," in *Elections and the Political Order*, A. Campbell, W. Miller, P. Converse, and D. Stokes, Eds. (New York: John Wiley and Sons, 1966), pp. 351–372.

21 Managing Large-Scale Electronic Data for Public Administration Research: An Information System Approach

Yu-Che Chen

CONTENTS

21.1   INTRODUCTION

One distinct issue in public administration research concerns the growth in the availability, size, and complexity of research data in digital format. In an effort to maintain compliance with the 1996 Paperwork Reduction Act, federal agencies have made available to the public a large amount of information in electronic format. For example, Census of Government, a branch of the U.S. Census Bureau, has made available downloadable electronic files on federal, state, and local governments. At the state and local levels, we see similar efforts at making public information available online to better inform citizens about various policy issues. For example, state governments can easily inform interested citizens about the number of computers in each school in the state. Moreover, think tanks and foundations have also joined the bandwagon; they aim to disseminate research data to better inform the public and they want to empower research communities seeking to engage in evidence-based dialogue. The Pew Charitable Trusts is one of many such organizations active in these endeavors. Advancements in information and communication technologies (ICTs) enable these organizations to create, store, and disseminate information on a large scale. The expansion of increasingly detailed information on public administration will likely continue into the next decade.

ICTs also afford individual researchers more computing power and analytical tools, which heretofore have been the preserve of large research institutions. Thus, individual researchers are demanding that more detailed and raw data be made available.

The growth in digital data and maturing of ICTs present opportunities as well as challenges to researchers who study public administration. Researchers now have the ability to merge various data sources to answer new and more complex questions. For example, researchers can merge census data, emergency management information, and data on the population of disabled persons in the State of Mississippi to identify the most effective course of actions for evacuating the most vulnerable segment of the population during hurricanes or other calamities. The growth of Internet technology has made collaboration across space and time easier. This has made possible joint efforts in public administration research, particularly studies that track and analyze in digital format government-held data and public services.

However, challenges in digital data management abound. A particular challenge throughout the research process concerns protecting confidentiality and privacy. When a host of research team-members have easy access to digital data across several sites, wholesale loss of sensitive personal data becomes a real vulnerability. Thus, researchers have to meet increasingly stringent requirements to ensure the protection of data.

Yet another challenge concerns accessing and managing the massive data typically stored in a relational database. Government agencies may let researchers directly access their Oracle databases, but this requires at least a rudimentary knowledge of SQL language for data extraction. Moreover, the sheer size of a data load consisting of thousands, or tens of thousands of records may render ineffective flat-file systems (in which all data is packed into one large data table). Such scenarios are particularly apt to occur when data is stored in a specialized relational database.

Merging data from various sources and at different levels of aggregation presents another challenge. Datasets, such as the names of cities, may be entered differently by different sources. In fact, the unique identifiers used in each database are rarely identical across data sources. It is the researcher who must find ways to integrate thousands of such unassimilated records. Should there be a need for visualization, the complexity of data integration increases many fold. For example, when specific organizations need to be linked to individual geospatial identifiers (longitude/latitude), other data sources must have the same ID to overlay information for matching organizations. Thus, data quality assurance has become more difficult as the scale and complexity of the data have increased. A large data project may easily involve a team of ten or more researchers and research assistants entering, modifying, and updating data. Without a strict protocol, data-entry errors and loss or misplacement of digital files are likely to occur.

Adopting an information system perspective confers several advantages over the single flat-file model. This perspective places emphasis on key components such as software, hardware, data, network (telecommunication) infrastructure, and people.* Thus, the information system perspective is more comprehensive; it encompasses all the elements of building and managing a large-scale electronic research database. In contrast, the conventional single research file perspective (i.e., SPSS) tends to ignore the "human side" of the equation, missing out on the convenience that database programs offer for data quality assurance and access control. Second, an information system perspective helps prioritize and classify digital assets. Information made available through the system must support organizational objectives such as managing relationships with citizens or customers. Digital assets included in the information system can be prioritized based on their ability to help serve citizens.

Third, an information system approach can help the researcher design a process that maintains data integrity and confidentiality. This process would govern who can get what data and the

---

* The present author adopts a wider vision of information systems. Typically, the term "information system" connotes only the implementation of data, hardware, software, and telecommunication infrastructure within a clearly defined system boundary (Laudon and Laudon, 2002). In contrast, my more expansive view seeks to include end-users and system administrators, with the aim of capturing the wider set of social-technical and business management dimensions.

conditions under which data can be shared. Ensuring such a process in place has become a standard requirement for the human subject review of some university institutional review boards. Fourth, the information system perspective is fundamentally adaptive. Such a perspective would enable easy updating of existing data, fluid merging of newly available datasets, and easy manipulation to respond to emerging questions and new environmental conditions.

The remainder of this chapter will proceed in sequence with the main stages in developing and implementing a large-scale research information system. The discussion begins with identifying goals for the information system and "taking stock" of information resources relevant to the objectives of the system. Next, the design of the information system is correlated to the type of users who will have access to information and the kind of information to be included. The resulting conceptual map of the information system then serves to guide the next step, the development of the database that will be at the core of the information system. Next, implementation of the information system is discussed. Implementation encompasses not only the management of rights and privileges associated with the building and subsequent use of the system, it also includes data migration from the existing system (usually paper-based) to the new system, and collection of new data. Once the system is fully populated with data, the researchers and owners of the information system should enforce quality assurance measures to ensure data integrity. The final step prior to making the system available for all user-groups focuses on enhancing the interface and improving data manipulation and presentation functionality.

Finally, it should be noted that the discussion in this chapter incorporates a running case study that will be used to dynamically illustrate how various components of an actual research information system might function in unison. The simultaneous presentation of each phase of the running case study will also serve to exemplify each step in the research information system building process.

A brief introduction will help set the stage. The running case study presented below focuses on a research information system built in collaboration with several government entities of the state of Iowa. The primary objectives center on understanding how government entities at the local and state levels in Iowa can collaborate, and how to improve such collaboration. With this information system the researchers will be able to clarify certain facets of government collaborations conducted under formal agreements, including the participants of the collaborations, and the extent, type, and effectiveness of collaboration. Furthermore, this research database will have a service function. Part of the research data will be made accessible online to citizens and public managers in Iowa. As determined early on, a spatial representation of in-state collaboration will help researchers, interested citizens, and the public understand the extent, type, and effectiveness of collaboration.

21.2 AN INFORMATION SYSTEM APPROACH

This chapter uses an information system approach to address the challenges of managing digital data. This approach applies insights from information system design and development. Moreover, each point in the discussion will be illustrated with a running case study. Managing the design and implementation of a large-scale research database is in essence managing an information system that has data, software, hardware, telecommunication network, and people components. Certain issues will prove relevant across each stage of the process, though they will vary in degree of importance depending on the stage being discussed. For example, although the protection of confidentiality should be integrated into each step of the process, at the design stage, the focus is on hardware and software solutions. Likewise, at the data collection and entry stage, access management protocol is comparatively more critical.

21.2.1 SETTING GOALS AND TAKING STOCKS

The first step in designing a large-scale digital research information system entails setting goals. The goal-setting process is usually incorporated into grant writing because a large research information system project requires a significant amount of resources that can be better allocated if certain steps can overlap. Grant writing already requires that the principal investigators prove that the proposed information system should meet emerging information needs. Typically, a large-scale project not only serves the need of researchers building the system, but it should also serve the needs of likely users of information such as citizens and policy makers. For example, a rural policy information initiative which integrates data from various federal agencies and focuses on small rural communities would certainly have in mind researchers, public managers, and citizens in those communities.

The goals of the research information system project must identify those who would potentially benefit from the availability of the data and account for the projected costs. Goals must be specific enough to delineate the scope of the project; they should project a time line and specify entities covered in the system. In the running case study, for example, the Intergovernmental Collaborative Service Agreement (IGCSA, a.k.a. "28e agreements") states that citizens, policy makers, and public managers, in addition to public administration researchers, will benefit from the project. (So-called "28e agreements" are named after item 28(E) of the Iowa Codes which governs the writing of government collaborative agreements.) More specifically, the information system provides (1) a database searchable online by 28e agreement type and participating government type (e.g., county, small town, large city); (2) downloadable copies of actual 28e agreements; (3) a GIS-based spatial representation of 28e agreements; and (4) for a sample of selected 28e agreements, an in-depth management report that discusses why and how an agreement is effective (or ineffective) based on personal field interviews with participating 28e agreement managers. Citizens and policy makers can search for intergovernmental collaborative arrangements across the entire state for any service, such as fire protection or road work. They can obtain a copy of the agreement for their jurisdiction or any other jurisdiction in Iowa. They can also use the GIS visualization to generate quick communication and management lessons aimed at promoting the effectiveness of collaborative agreements. The 28e agreements that will be digitized for storage in the system will go back to 1993, as directed by IOWAccess, the funding agency for this project.

Next, in view of the project goals, information assets have to be identified and classified. The perspective taken here is information-centric. People, data, hardware, software, and the telecommunication infrastructure—these all form the information system and they must be included in the equation. All these components, for example, would be essential for a research project on civic engagement with the use of information technology. Such a project might involve citizens using handheld devices to report neighborhood problems directly to a city's central database. Citizens would then be responsible for taking digital photos and filling out forms on the handheld devices. Researchers would be responsible for developing the forms and making sure that the systems run properly. Data would be in text, video, and even audio, and it would flow from several sources: the city, a separate geographic information system application, and the government census. Such a project would also require hardware and specialized software, as well as fiber-optic broadband access for data transmission. Moreover, for this type of project, researchers would need to have an inventory of the digital assets (such as data files, and databases) that will be generated or used in the course of the research project. With such a vast amount of data and a variety of data formats, some prioritization scheme would be needed for storage and access.

In this case, data of high research value would be of the type that could link a specific neighborhood with its unique demographic characteristics and log of reported problems. More safeguards would then be required for such high-value and frequently accessed data. Of course, the protection of confidentiality should go hand-in-hand with the classification of digital assets. Here the protection of privacy should accord with the risk-management principles commonly used in the information security field. To strike a balance between information privacy and access to government information, researchers would have to conduct de-identification of sensitive information and take control of access and linkage (Duncan and Roehrig, 2003).

In large projects, researchers tend to integrate both primary and secondary sources of data. For example, a research project studying economic development at the local level might examine not only community organizations, but also social, political, economic, and management capacity. Such a project would need to gather data from various sources and conduct its own data collection. Census data, census of government data, and ICMA surveys would likely serve as sources of secondary data if the project is to capture some measure of the social, economic, and management capacity. The coherence of community organizations and the role of community organizations in economic development would probably be best investigated through field interviews and surveys. The required data elements would determine what information would be captured in the database.

The Intergovernmental Collaborative Service Agreement (IGCSA) project provides a useful example of the process of "taking stock." First, according to the purpose of the project, the researchers conducted a survey of existing information assets and stewards. Information on formal collaboration among governments in the state was drawn from the office of the Secretary of State, which held a repository of 28e agreements. The electronic index file of these agreements is maintained by the Secretary of State and contains basic information such as filing date, subject, description, document locator, and expiration date. A complete list of data fields and sample records are provided in Figure 21.1. This index file extends from the current date back to 1965, the year when the first agreement was filed. For agreements received after year 2000, scanned versions are available in TIFF format. These TIFF files are tagged with a document locator. At the project start in 2004, there were over 11,000 agreements indexed from 1965 to July 2004.

Other information assets include directory information for all governmental units in the state of Iowa, including over 370 school districts. This information allows the information system to pin-point a particular governmental participant. The directory information can also identify key contact personnel should more detailed information on the management of agreements be needed. Other potential sources of information that can be added to the system are Census of Government data.

ID	Filing Date	Subject	Description	Expiry	Print Flag	BarCodeNumber	DocLoc
10316	8/27/2002	Elk run road reconstruction	This agreement is made between the city of Elk run heights, Iowa and Black hawk county, Iowa. Whereas, the parties shall have varying degrees of responsibility for the design, payment and construction of subdrains and pavement replacement to replace the said existing pavement hereafter referred to as division I.	12/31/2004	True	M020108	000010316M020108
10512	10/1/2002	Tobacco enforcement	The parties of Iowa alcoholic beverages division and Pottawattamie county sheriffs office have entered into this agreement for the purpose of providing and funding tobacco enforcement activites.		False	M020514	000010512M020514
10644	11/25/2002	Mutual law enforcement aid agreement	This agreement between Dubuque county and city of Farley. The purpose of this agreement is to provide for mutual law enforcement aid		True	M021078	000010644M021078
7072	2/23/1998	Fire protection agreement	By and between Cascade community fire truck association and the Board of trustees of Whitewater township for the purpose of providing fire protection for approximately 94.4% of Whitewater Township or that portion set forth on the addendum attached to this agreement		False	M013380	000007072M013380

FIGURE 21.1 Sample records of the index file for 28E agreements.

To achieve the goals of the IGCSA, the researchers will need to acquire more information about the management of these intergovernmental service agreements. The process of "taking stock" helps the researchers discover what is already available and what is still to be collected. Through this process the researchers also mapped out the stewards of key sources of information. For example, surveys conducted to understand the impetus and management of collaborative agreements constitute an additional primary data source that can be mined. Public managers responsible for collaborative agreements can serve as possible sources of management insights.

21.2.2 User-Centric Conceptual Design

One current standard in information system design is the "use-case" approach, as applied in object-oriented system analysis and design (Hoffer, George, and Valacich, 2002). The advantage of this approach is that the researcher can concentrate on what the intended system must do, rather than the details of how the system is to be implemented. This allows for better communication among programmers, systems analysts, and end-users; as a group they would focus on "what" the system is designed to do rather than technical details on "how" to do it (Coad and Yourdon, 1991). Moreover, the object-oriented approach is more adaptive and robust because of its modular way of dealing with a complex system and addressing consistency in system analysis, design, and programming.

The use-case approach is based on the idea that an information system is best defined according to the various ways that information can be used (use cases) by certain types of information users (actors). A use case represents, therefore, a sequence of activities that an actor can perform via the information system. For example, a use case for a financial management system might encompass the entire set of activities required in compiling a quarterly financial report. Note, moreover, there is a difference between information users and actors as defined in the use-case approach. An information user is a person who uses information, whereas, an actor represents the role that an information user can play. For example, a researcher as an information user can play at least two different roles (i.e., be two different actors). She can assume the role of a system administrator (an actor) who has the privilege of making systemwide changes to the system. The other role she can play is that of the data-entry worker, who can only enter data into the system. According to this approach, a research information system will have at the least several standard actors: the system administrators who decide who can have access to what information with what specific privileges, the researchers who can perform more intrusive changes and updates to data tables, whether as a whole or by adding data fields, and the data-entry worker who can only enter data into the system.

A good example of the application of this approach can be seen in the public use and hosting of the IGCSA project. Through this example we can see how the use-case approach can effectively communicate the functions of the intended system. The system can be summarized according to three actors and the use cases associated with each actor. Figure 21.2 is an illustration of the conceptual design of the system.

With appropriate authorization, there are three main roles, or actors, an information user can play. These are the "citizens actor," "public administrators actor," and "system administrators actor." With the "citizens actor" the user can search the information system for all agreements by date, service type, and jurisdiction ("search" use case). With the "public administrators actor" the user can file agreements online ("online filing plus registration" use case), provided that an online account with the Secretary of State is activated. For example, a public manager in the state of Iowa (as an information user) can play the role of citizens actor and public administrators actor. Finally, with the system administrators actor the user can make systemwide changes as well as update and set access privileges for all other information users ("authorization" use case).

In terms of visualization of the project, the software MS VISIO is one among many tools that the researcher can utilize to create use-case scenarios in the conceptual design of an information system. Such software addresses the complexity that usually plagues the process of generating an effective strategy for meeting the needs of system end-users. Due to limited space, this discussion

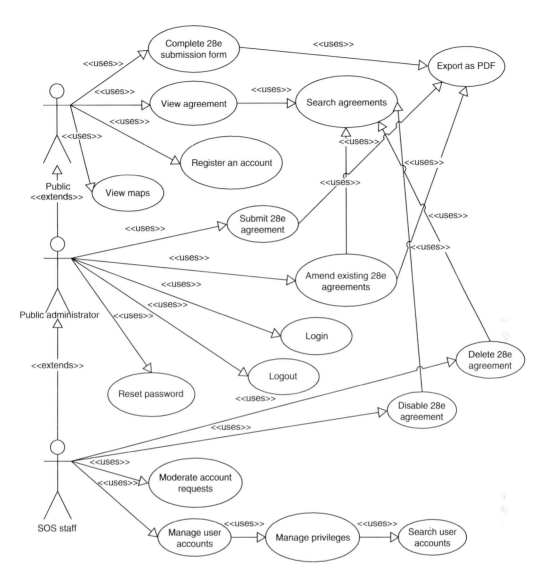

FIGURE 21.2 A draft use-case design for citizens' and public managers' use of collaborative service delivery information.

will not treat in detail the issue of use-case design and the utilization of software to produce use-case diagrams (similar to the one found in Figure 21.2). Nevertheless, it should be clear that the use-case approach provides an organized way of discussing the needs of information users and how such needs can be translated into various actor roles they can play.

An integral part of user-centric conceptual design involves determining how information in the information system is to be accessed and the confidentiality implications of granted access. The researcher must apply a system perspective when conceptually delineating the telecommunication and collaborative environment within which information and data are to be stored and accessed. Moreover, the issue of information access and confidentiality will vary depending on whether information is to be channeled through dedicated local desktop access with password control, or through general Internet access without authentication. Also, the various roles the information user can play will also have to be factored in. For example, in the IGCSA project, researchers located at home or at the office have full access to a password-protected server space containing research files and analysis results, as well as index and image files (with the setup of a virtual private network). Research assistants responsible for data-entry on site may enter and update individual records into a database by sitting at a local computer. From their office, system administrators have full access to the production Web server and database server. The public has search-only access, which is used to view 28e agreements over the Internet.

Mapping uses and access methods constitute the foundation for developing information security measures that protect confidentiality. A risk-based approach can minimize damages resulting from leakage or misuse of information. Personal and sensitive information (i.e., social security number, medical information) should receive the maximal protection, whereas security measures for public information can be comparatively relaxed. Authentication, network security, and access control are ways of protecting confidentiality. In the case of IGCSA, access privileges assigned to citizens, public administrators, system administrators, and researchers form the framework of system use and access. As 28e agreements are considered public records, there is no need for authentication to search the 28e information. On the other hand, the submission of a 28e agreement involves authentication to ensure that the filer of the agreement is legitimate. For research information systems holding sensitive personal information such as social security numbers or medical information, an elevated level of access control is necessary.

At this stage, the conceptual design must address how information can be shared among users located at multiple sites and how to safeguard against unfettered access. For information systems that need online analytical process capability, a Web-to-database functionality should be established. This would include functionality such as search, update, and modification of records in the system. For an information system whose primary purpose is to share files (read-only), a password-protected server space is sufficient. For example, should a research collaborator located at a different campus require convenient access through the Web with proper authentication, that collaborator would have unfettered access to raw data as well as final research datasets.

One related challenge of working with large-scale electronic data is the issue of evolving changes to the data. A common problem that often arises is when multiple authors work on different versions of datasets, thus causing time wastage. A convenient way of handling collaboration across campuses can be deployed with the use of either an FTP site or an online course environment, such as "blackboard" or "WebCT." Both types of environment would let researchers and team members share data and information according to access control. To accommodate a large-scale research information system, a dedicated server space used in conjunction with the project can help in archiving and securing critical raw research data.

21.2.3 DESIGN THE DATABASE IN SUPPORT OF THE INFORMATION SYSTEM

The development of the research database should meet the information needs of the research project as articulated in the use case. As large information systems used for public administration research often utilize publicly available government data, data merge is quite common. To maintain integrity in the data-merge process, researchers and information system analysts require more details about the data being drawn from multiple sources. Such details are usually called metadata. This "data on data" contains information on the individual files, programs used to create those files, and the creation and modification dates of the files. For research purposes, the metadata should also include information on the methods used for data collection, the people and organizations involved, the time period covered by the files, and any changes in the data definition.

Before designing the database, the database designer must address a deeper level of detail concerning information resources identified in the first stage discussed above. The designer requires detailed information down to each data field and possibly data records. Such required details include, but is not limited to, data field definition, field length, and data type. Knowing all the possible values that the data field can encompass will help the designer develop a validity check— phone number data, for example, can consist of only 10 digits. For another example, in the original data files from the Secretary of State, agreement ID numbers consist of only five digits or less. Any value over five digits can be identified as probably a data-entry error.

One key design consideration for a large public administration research information system involves merging primary and secondary data sources. This challenge is typically addressed by the use of a common identifier. This identifier should be able to capture the level of aggregation (unit of analysis) that the researcher would need for analysis.* Resolving problems related to disparate identifiers is challenging and usually labor-intensive. Almost each data collection organization has its own identification system. For example, the surveys conducted by the International City/County Management Association (ICMA), a major source of information for public administration research, have a unique identification system for each city or county included in its database (i.e., iMISID for e-government surveys). That system differs from the one in use by the Census of Government, another major source of information. This system does not have a unique ID for each government unit at the local level. To uniquely identify a local government, the researcher would have to combine the State Code, Type of government, County Code, Governmental Unit number, Supplemental Code and the Subcode contained in Census of Government public use data files.

Although inconsistencies in the identification systems of two or more data sources are numerous, one of the few viable common identifiers is the name field for cities. However, possible inconsistencies in spelling and other variations in naming conventions may make merging tasks rather labor-intensive. For example, the "Town of Yarmouth" may be identified in one data file as, "Town of Yarmouth," whereas another file might say, "Yarmouth, Town of." Thus, automation of the match would encounter much difficulty. Another problem arises when the name of a city is captured in two data fields, one designating the type of government (i.e., city) and the other simply giving the name (i.e., "Des Moines" for "city of Des Moines"). Typos and other incidentals further add to the complexity of merging multiple sources of information.

One standard solution for merging data from multiple sources involves expanding on an existing national database and classification system, selecting the most comprehensive system that can encompass all the possible entities or organizations that will register in the database. For example, if a researcher needed a national database, the Census of Government system can be modified with assignment of a new ID number to each government unit. Working with a comprehensive list, the researcher can expand the research information system and further integrate information from additional sources. For the IGCSA system, the researcher adopted a similar approach by having a new ID number for each government included in the database. This ensures consistency across various sources of information such as directory information from city and county associations.

At the design stage, care needs to be given to data definition standards. For each data element, the database designer needs to specify in detail data types and length of data field, perhaps even delimiting the range of values a specific field can accept. The goal here is to preserve data integrity, particularly for data being drawn from multiple sources. For example, if each township requires a county designation that can correlate to a position on a map of Iowa, then the county designation would be a numeric field accepting values of 1 through 99, because there are 99 counties in the state. This is similar to running a check on data of a different format while importing it into a relational database environment.

A database design is essentially relational when a common data definition needs to be established for linking and merging purposes. The point of having a relational database is to minimize redundancy while maximizing efficiency and accuracy in data-entry, deletion, and updating for a large electronic research database. The basic design includes the specification of the entity that may be any object such as classification of cities (i.e., form of government, urban influence index) or characteristics of cities (i.e., population, medium household income, etc.). For example, in the

---

* Scavo (1999, p. 139) in Miller and Whicker (1999) emphasizes the importance of choosing the variable for identifying the individual unit of analysis and for aggregation purpose. For example, if one wants to aggregate everything to the level of Congressional District, a unique identifier is needed for each individual district.

IGCSA project, governmental units, such as townships, fire districts, school districts, cities, counties, and state agencies, constitute an entity. The other main component of the design is relationships between entities. This captures the business rules governing the creation and management of data. For example, although each city has one official address, it may have one or many partners for economic development (i.e., chamber of commerce). This stage generates a conceptual data model usually referred to as the entity-relationship (E-R) diagram with attributes.

The investment of time at this stage is worthwhile for a large-scale research database; the design process compels the researcher to generate a clear inventory of all the data fields and a clear definition of business rules stipulating what values each field can take and how data is to be processed. Moreover, such a relational database design can serve as a foundation for large-scale data analysis using other statistical and visualization software programs. For example, Pajek, a social network analysis software built on the logic of relational database, is aimed at easing the management of large amounts of data (de Nooy et al., 2005). MS Access supports the design of E-R diagrams, and there are many alternative software programs available for designing relational databases. The discussion here focuses on an abbreviated version of database design, concentrating on main concepts. For more technical guidelines on database design, refer to the list of additional readings under the heading "database design."

The second step centers on developing a logical model with efficient and well-defined data table structures (Hoffer, Prescott, and McFadden, 2002). The process of normalization fosters improvements in efficiency and accuracy in functions such as adding, deleting, and modifying data. There are several general rules and concepts associated with normalization. First, each data field for a particular data table should be unique. For example, "last name" should have its own field, separate from "first name." The IGCSA collaboration database capturing the contact information of agreement managers also separates the last name and first name fields.

Second, for each table that is made up of one or more fields in the table a primary key is required. The role of the primary key is to uniquely identify each record in the data table. For example, in the IGCSA project, each agreement has an agreement ID that is assigned during initial registration with the Secretary of State. The researcher created an ID field for the entities that are currently participating in an agreement and those that could potentially participate in an agreement. They all receive an entity ID. Alternatively, an agreement can be uniquely identified by the combination of filing date, subject, and description.

Third, each data field should be functionally dependent on the primary key. Functional dependency depicts a particular relationship between two attributes (data fields). When every valid value A uniquely identifies value B, we can say there is a functional dependency of B on A. Normalization is based on the concept of functional dependency. Adhering to this rule will get the database to the first normal form. The second normal form is attained when each data field in the table—other than the ones used for primary key—depends on the whole key when the key is a composite of several data fields. For example, the Census of Government's public use data file, as mentioned earlier, requires a composite key to uniquely identify a local government. The higher the form of normalization, the more structured the database. A more structured database has a higher level of data integrity and less data redundancies. The highest form of normalization is the third normal form.* Third normal form is where all other nonkey fields are dependent exclusively on the whole primary key. For more technical details and step-by-step instructions on how to conduct normalization, the reader can refer to works listed in additional readings under database design.

Spatial data is increasingly becoming a part of database design. Database designers will need advance data merging plans that can incorporate the linkage of entities of interest with correlating geographic coordinates. The growth and maturity of geographic information systems (GIS) makes it

---

* Sometimes, the database designer may want to roll-back to the second normal form for some practical purpose, such as improving the performance of processing physical records.

easier to effectively communicate a complex phenomenon in pictures. This is especially critical in public administration directed at emergency management and development of infrastructure. Base maps and shape files are usually publicly available; and researchers can integrate them into the project to enhance visualization. For example, the IGCSA project capitalizes on Iowa State University's expertise in geographic information systems and ready-to-use base maps. Cities participating in collaborative service agreements are shown on a map, and lines connecting the cities are labeled according to the kind of services jointly provided by the parties. Newer versions of GIS software such as ArcGIS or ArcInfo can work with relational databases to perform queries. However, it is still the responsibility of the database designer to develop a unique identifier that will link geographic data and other sources of data. Finally, here an additional challenge is the need for the aforementioned metadata that makes possible integrating and interpreting results.

21.2.4 Research Information System Management and Implementation

Access and privilege management is of concern when multiple people have access to a large electronic database. By taking an information system approach, the researcher can tackle this issue directly and ensure the protection of sensitive information, thereby fostering trust from the public and funding agencies. Confidentiality, of course, is a high priority for public organizations. The typical setup of access and privilege management usually stipulates that one or two people serving as system administrators can perform blanket changes in the database such as the structure of the database and data definitions. In contrast, most users should only be able to engage in data-entry, deleting, or updating. This would avoid unintentional or intentional change of data structure.

Much of data retrieval for research purposes or basic viewing can be conducted through establishing queries. The use of queries is adaptive in nature. Having separate queries prevents users from changing records and provides the convenience of offering customized information in real-time. Even a primarily desktop database management software program such as MS Access features a structure that sets access privileges for research information system administration, data-entry, and other roles.

The implementation of access and privilege management is an integral part of an information security system that can protect privacy and confidentiality. An accepted piece of wisdom in the information security field views people as the "weakest link" in information security. For example, it is the casual attitude to password information or laptop access by a chief financial officer that could potentially result in the most severe damage for a company. Such a scenario is even worse than a firewall with limited defense capabilities. As the core of the information system, the database should be protected by security measures that maintain vigilant watch over physical and remote access. The level of sophistication of the security scheme would vary according to the size and access to the core database. At minimum, security measures should be based on a complete map that charts who has what access to what information via what kind of access (Internet or secure access). The security system might consist of a scenario as simple as password access for two researchers in a locked room with a desktop computer. On the other hand, a complex system may require a security scheme featuring remote access to a database server, with different personnel having different levels of clearance for accessing and changing data.

A complete protection of privacy and confidentiality requires a life-cycle approach to research data. Life-cycle stewardship begins with data collection and continues with entry and update, sharing and use of data, and ends with finally archiving or destroying data. Researchers and database designers must have in mind a clear chain of custody for the data passing through the possession of multiple personnel. The best approach lies in maintaining a protocol that can govern the protection of confidentiality. For example, the protocol may stipulate that the research team cannot share any confidential information with personnel outside the team, or data cannot be shared with such personnel absent the de-identification of participants.

One inevitable aspect of managing a large electronic database is the turnover of personnel. Knowledge transfer and documentation, as well as the discontinuing access privileges, become important as personnel move in and out of the project as it progresses. In an academic environment, for example, Master's level graduate students may stay on the project for only a year, even while a large research project may extend through two to three years. Thus, without adequate documentation and knowledge transfer, the project may experience a significant delay in implementation. Researchers would have problems finding files, or distinguishing files with the most updated information. The history of changes in the data files and the reasons for such changes—both of which are critical to understanding data validity—may get lost during personnel transitions.

21.2.4.1 Data Generation, Collection, and Migration

Using the information system approach, researchers can economize data collection and data-entry. For primary data collection, the information system approach can help capture the data more efficiently. For projects with online surveys, a web-to-database design can directly capture online surveys into the database. In this scenario, much of the labor goes into designing the Web interface, ensuring that the survey results are inputted directly into the database. Alternatively, researchers can use retail software or commercial Web site services to capture online survey results. At a minimum, a well-defined database is a structured environment that helps researchers to think through the data elements. Such a database would also ease the importing of data into a unified environment.

Data-entry can be made more efficient when approaching it from an information system perspective. As most research projects use text information embedded in government forms, it is sometimes more efficient to use OCR technology and supporting software to capture directly into the database hand-written information appearing in predefined fields. This importing process is more efficient than manual data-entry, especially when thousands of forms are concerned. An alternative method can use Web forms to connect directly to the information system. For example, for future updates to the IGCSA project data, users can input basic information into the database via Web forms.*

Predefined data-entry forms, coupled with careful development and training, can go a long way in ensuring data quality. This strategy reinforces the requirement that the preceding stage of database design must pay close attention to each data field in terms of the valid values it can assume. Data-entry forms (either generated through programmed interface or using form features of database software such as MS Access) allow for consistent input of data format as well as validation rules to avoid potential data-entry errors (e.g., social security numbers can only have nine total digits, with two intervening dashes). Also, for example, validation rules can be implemented to check political party affiliations. Using drop-down boxes with limited choice arrays is yet another way to improve both the efficiency and accuracy of data-entry. For example, the IGCSA system captures information on the type of organizations involved in agreements, and the system features a classification system with a limited set of possibilities (i.e., city, county, state agencies).

Moreover, the process of developing data-entry forms will improve when researchers work with users who will be responsible for entering data into the system. Paying attention to usability issues for end-users can yield handsome dividends. Training is an integral part of using an information system; it can streamline data-entry and improve data-entry accuracy. Data-entry can sometimes be fraught with cases of ambiguity and such cases require that people who enter data make judgments. The training session is precisely the opportunity when the researchers can identify such issues and

---

* In the IGCSA project, OCR is not a viable option to automate the capture of data on existing forms into the information system because this would require a standardized form. The 28e agreements do not have a standard format for all filers.

seek effective remedies. Training also helps personnel, who use the forms for data-entry, to gain greater familiarity with navigating the system.

The guidelines developed in the preceding stage, as part of the effort to protect privacy and information security, can be used to direct data-collection and data-entry activities. Here, the focus should be on translating these guidelines into protocols for data collection and entry. For example, a confidentiality statement can be displayed on the first page of an online data collection procedure (i.e., online survey), to inform the potential respondent about the protection of personal data. Protocols for data-entry and storage may stipulate that a log-in for each session of data-entry would be required. Storage requirements may demand that sensitive information can only be accessed via a locked box or a password-protected environment.

21.2.4.2 Data Quality Assurance

In a large research project generating tens, or even hundreds of thousands of research records, data quality assurance can be a challenging task. If each record should contain at least ten or more data fields, then the researcher must keep track of some millions of data cells. Manually dredging through the database record-by-record, or cell-by-cell, is neither feasible nor conducive to data accuracy. If multiple individuals are responsible for data-entry, identical records may get entered twice, even three times, especially when the start and end of records for a series of data-entry workers become blurred. Inadvertent duplication can also appear in secondary data sources either due to data quality issues or longitudinal data, where one jurisdiction may appear two times or more. For example, in the IGSA project, one 28e document may have two document locators (the primary key) assigned to it.

For an information system built on a relational database, the basic strategy for identifying duplicates is to formulate a SQL query to identify duplicate records. In a simpler scenario, identification may only involve pinpointing the duplication of names of the jurisdiction. SQL language has proven quite flexible at performing this task. In the IGCSA case study, one potential problem concerns the duplication of the participation of a particular entity in an agreement; this might arise when some agreements are inadvertently entered more than once. The SQL language identifies those duplicates by finding relationships between a participant and a particular agreement that appears more than once in the entity-agreement table.* In a more complex situation, the query may involve more than two or three data tables. An example would be the task of finding a registered agreement that involves more than two identical participants. For those unfamiliar with SQL, MS Access has a built-in query "wizard" for identifying duplicates in the database. This wizard helps the researcher identify the data field containing suspect items appearing to be duplicates, and the researcher can also choose more than one data table at a time.

With a list of duplicates, the researcher has an opportunity to identify the source of the problem and thus begin to develop the best strategy to remedy it. First, however, the researcher must examine the nature of the found duplication. A possible remedy might require recoding some of the records. If removal is deemed the best strategy, then the next step is to remove those duplicates. If the information system design and implementation strategy previously formulated in the preceding steps are carefully adhered to, then the number of duplicate records should be limited. In such a case, manually deleting duplicate records would be feasible. If the duplication occurs in one data table—where duplication is defined as identical value assumed for each data field in the table—then Excel offers an alternative strategy. First, the researcher must export the entire data table into an

---

* The SQL command for MS Access is below. For other database systems, the syntax follow a similar structure but slightly different in the commands
SELECT EntityAgreementTable.agreement_id, EntityAgreementTable.entity_id
FROM EntityAgreementTable
WHERE (((EntityAgreementTable.agreement_id) In (SELECT [agreement_id] FROM [EntityAgreementTable] As Tmp
GROUP BY [agreement_id] HAVING Count(*) > 1)))
ORDER BY EntityAgreementTable.agreement_id;

Excel-readable format (ASCII, comma delimited, etc.). Once Excel has the data file open, the researcher can use the "data → filter → advanced filter" command sequence to copy and paste the old data fields to an unused part of the data sheet. The paste criterion can be specified as "non-duplicate" by checking the "nonduplicate" box.

Furthermore, in a large electronic research information system, missing records are other likely possibilities that should be addressed. Missing records can occur as a result of various reasons, for example, problematic index files, duplications in data-entry, errors in coding, and so forth. When a system has missing records this scenario is a reflection of various data quality issues defined in the business rules for the information system. For the IGCSA example, each agreement should have at least two involved participants. But sometimes, perhaps due to oversight during data-entry, a missing record problem occurs and only one participant is entered into the database. At other times, the source of confusion may lie in miscoding, for example, when both participants are coded as a single entity (e.g., an agreement between an association of a worker compensation program and the very members of that association).

For an information system based on a relational database, the generic solution to missing records and other data quality issues should be approached through SQL. This approach can be taken for both identification and remedial actions. Although specific syntax varies depending on the database, the generic language is rather similar. Developing the SQL queries for data quality should accord with the business rules of the included data. In the IGCSA case, for example, each registered agreement should have at least two participants. Thus, the SQL query is used to identify agreements that have one or less participants. The general strategy is then to select records in the agreement table which has one or fewer participants identified in the entity-agreement table (that specifies the relationship between participating entities). This helps to identify the missing records. Moreover, the SQL strategy is rather flexible. Researchers can also identify entities in the master list which do not have corresponding agreements. MS Access also has a wizard that lets researchers formulate queries for missing records.

The method of updating the missing records depends on the nature of the problem. In the case of a single typo, a manual update of that individual record is sufficient. However, if the missing records result from systematic problems, an update query would be more efficient. For example, were an entity to get misclassified then it would be simple to update the classification. For most problems, then, the relational database offers a straightforward solution because it is designed to minimize work and reduce problem areas.

21.2.4.3 Data Manipulation and Presentation

A relational database employing on an information system approach has the power to perform complex data aggregation and presentation. For a large electronic database, data aggregation performed manually down to the level of a specified unit can prove dauntingly labor-intensive. Aggregating the number of computers for all the schools in a school district for an entire state, for example, can be extremely time-consuming and inefficient, not to mention should the scope have to be expanded to encompass the entire country. In a relational database, the generic solution to data manipulation is the use of SQL language. If each record contains information on the school district a school belongs to and the number of computer it has, then the general strategy would be to sum up the values in the "number of computers" data field per school district.* In the IGCSA case study, researchers can aggregate up to the county levels for all the agreements that have been signed by jurisdictions in their respective counties.

---

* Below is the MS Access syntax used to do aggregation
  SELECT School_Tech.District, School_Tech.[District Name], Sum(School_Tech.Computers) AS TotalNoofComputers, Sum(School_Tech.[Computers with Internet Access]) AS Total No_of Online Computer, Count(School_Tech.[School Name]) AS TotalNo_ofSchools
  FROM School_Tech
  GROUP BY School_Tech.District, School_Tech.[District Name]

Flexibility is another key feature of the information system approach. As the basic database structure remains the same, researchers can design customized research data sets and reports to meet evolving information needs. A query will allow the researchers to concentrate on a limited number of data fields directly pertinent to a particular research project. Once the core database is updated, executing the same query will generate an updated version of the data set. This approach is more time efficient for a system with a large number of data fields (i.e., 50 or more). Changes to the query can be easily done. Moreover, results of the query can be imported into statistical software such as SPSS for further statistical investigation. For example, in the IGSCA project, by selecting agreements that have at least one state agency and one government unit at a different level of government (i.e., federal or local) researchers can easily use queries to identify intergovernmental agreements among different levels of government (vertical cooperation in service delivery).

Moreover, often researchers need to communicate and share results. Reporting either raw or aggregated data can be flexible tasks when an information system is in place. For example, MS Access has a graphic user interface (GUI) that eases the designing and generation of customized reports. The IGCSA project has a strong service component and a reliance on public managers to update the system. It has a Web form for searching agreements recorded in the system. These searches generate queries on-the-fly into the MS SQL database, which serves as the core of the information. Some researchers may, if they wish, use tools familiar to them to conduct data manipulation and presentation. Meanwhile, the information system still serves as the core information source, the central source that provides data for additional or advanced analysis conducted with other software. Thus, this system is the master data source. It can integrate, back into the system, the results of statistical analysis. For example, the system can be made to label jurisdiction attributes that are considered important (statistically significant) for success in collaborative service delivery. The system also has the advantage of being able to effectively communicate with multiple usergroups. The IGCSA system makes it easy for public managers and citizens to understand the pattern and extent of collaborative service delivery.

21.3 CONCLUSION

This chapter describes how to take an information system approach in the development and management of a large electronic research database. The information system approach provides a systematic way of addressing complex issues such as the protection of confidentiality, merging of data, and ensuring of data integrity. Moreover, this approach improves automation of the data input and updates tasks which would otherwise be labor-intensive. The information system approach begins with the identification of research project objectives and proceeds to the identification of information resources that will help achieve those objectives. Next, the researcher is recommended to apply the use-case concept to the conceptual design of the system, while considering closely the telecommunication infrastructure involved. Then, the researchers and system designers should develop a supporting database for the proposed information system.

To researchers and students involved in the development and management of large electronic databases, this chapter offers tools and methods that will improve their effectiveness and efficiency. The researchers are not required to be able to complete the physical design of the information system and the supporting database. Rather, the goal of the chapter is to provide rudimentary knowledge that will help researchers work more effectively with information system analysts and programmers in their tasks of identifying relevant issues and addressing these issues through a structured process of group collaboration.

Investing the time and energy required in building such an information system should be premised on the need for future growth and further evolution of the research information system. So long as knowledge (research data) remains the main competitive edge for researchers, such a project should prove to be a worthwhile investment in the long term. Researchers will find that many issues are easier to address when they are properly recognized at the design phase. Incorporating spatial and network information at an early stage of the research information system design will likely pay dividends.

EXERCISES

1. In this exercise, the student develops and completes a worksheet that addresses key issues in developing and designing a large research information system. Please use the methods and the list of issues suggested in the chapter. The student should research the details of the project. More specifically, the worksheet must address the following components: (a) a research project statement including research and information objectives; (b) an inventory of information resources both internal and external to your organization; (c) a set of related issues that surrounds the collection, integration, and sharing of information such as confidentiality, information security, and so forth; and (d) a strategy based on the information system perspective that addresses those issues.

2. In this exercise, the student employs use-case design to develop the conceptual framework of a research information system. The use-case approach is an efficient way to communicate with all the people involved in the design and development of the system, including end-users, system analysts, programmers, and researchers. The approach also helps the researcher identify opportunities to improve and adapt the system in response to changing environments and user needs. Please apply the guidelines for use-case design mentioned in the chapter. At minimum, the use case should specify the roles and privileges of the actors and what functions each actor can perform within the information system.

REFERENCES

Coad, P. and Yourdon, E. 1991. *Object-Oriented Design*. Englewood Cliffs, New Jersey: Prentice-Hall.

de Nooy, W., Mrvar, A., and Batagelj, V. 2005. *Exploratory Social Network Analysis with Pajek*. Cambridge, New York: Cambridge University Press.

Duncan, G. and Roehrig, S. 2003. Mediating the tension between information privacy and information access: The role of digital government. In *Public Information Technology: Policy and Management Issues*, Garson, G. David (Ed.). Hershey, London: Idea Group Publishing.

Hoffer, J., George, J., and Valacich, J. 2002. *Modern Systems Analysis and Design* (3rd ed.). Upper Saddle River, New Jersey: Prentice Hall.

Hoffer, J., Prescott, M., and McFadden, F. 2002. *Modern Database Management*. Upper Saddle River, New Jersey: Prentice Hall.

Laudon, K. and Laudon, J. 2002. *Management Information Systems: Managing the Digital Firm*. Upper Saddle River, New Jersey: Prentice Hall.

Miller, G.J. and Whicker, M.L. 1999. *Handbook of Research Methods in Public Administration*. New York: Marcel Dekker, Inc.

Scavo, C.P.F. 1999. Constructing data sets and manipulating data. In *Handbook of Research Methods in Public Administration*, Miller, G.J. and Whicker, M.L. (Eds.). New York: Marcel Dekker, Inc.

Viescas, J. 1999. *Running Microsoft Access 2000*. Redmond, Washington: Microsoft Press.

ADDITIONAL READINGS AND RESOURCES

READINGS ON DATABASE DESIGN

Standard textbooks on database design or information system design should contain sufficient details for the design of relational database for further study. Examples include

Rob, P. and Coronel, C. 2004. *Database Systems: Design, Implementation and Management* (6th ed.): Course Technology.

Hoffer, J., George, J., and Valacich, J. 2002. *Modern Systems Analysis and Design* (3rd ed.). Upper Saddle River, New Jersey: Prentice Hall.

Hoffer, J., Prescott, M., and McFadden, F. 2002. *Modern Database Management*. Upper Saddle River, New Jersey: Prentice Hall.

Books on MS Access by Microsoft usually have a section on the basics of database design. For instance, Part II of Viescas's (1999) book is about building a relational database.

RESOURCE SITES

Census of Government
    http://www.census.gov/govs/www/cog2002.html
Community Information Resource Center
    http://circ.rupri.org/

Part V

Basic Quantitative Analysis

22 Introduction to Data Analysis

Kamal Chavda

CONTENTS

22.1 INTRODUCTION

Once the researcher has collected and cleaned the data, the analysis can begin. The research process typically places data analysis after a statement of the research questions, a review of the literature, presentation of the hypotheses, and description of the data and the methods to be used. However, the methods used for data analysis are limited on the one hand by the knowledge of the researcher, and on the other by elements of the research design itself. Thus, the methods used for analyzing data vary depending on whether the data is collected through an experimental or quasi-experimental (e.g., survey) design; whether the variables to be analyzed are quantitative (continuous or discrete) or qualitative/categorical (nominal or ordinal); whether the study is cross sectional or longitudinal; whether the data is obtained from a sample or from a population; and if the data comes from a sample, whether the sample size is large or small.

Fortunately, there are some analytic procedures that are common in most quantitative research designs. For example, large datasets are more easily interpreted when they are represented in tables or graphs, or summarized through numeric measures such as the mean. Collectively, we refer to these procedures as descriptive statistics, and they form the major focus of this chapter. The explanations in the chapter are accompanied by relatively simple examples, based on very small datasets, which allow the reader to easily understand the concepts. More often than not, however, researchers have to work with large datasets. To conduct their analyses, they use specialized software programs such as SPSS, SAS, or STATA. The Appendix uses a dataset of 222 cases to demonstrate how to use SPSS to conduct the analyses discussed below under Section 22.2.

Often, researchers want to do more than describe variables in a dataset. They want to identify relationships between variables. There are many techniques available to social scientists who want to study these relationships. As mentioned above, there are also many factors to consider in selecting the appropriate method. Section 22.3 briefly discusses some of the methods of choice based on the types of variables under study. The goal here is not to explain step by step how to carry out the analyses, but to provide short descriptions of the techniques and make the reader aware of what some of his or her options are based on the variables' levels of measurement.

22.2 DESCRIPTIVE ANALYSIS

22.2.1 FREQUENCY DISTRIBUTIONS AND GRAPHS

22.2.1.1 Frequency Distributions and Graphical Displays of Qualitative Variables

Once cleaned, the data set can be presented in tabular or graphical form to reveal its main characteristics. If the variable of interest is nominal or ordinal—collectively referred to as categorical or qualitative variables—then the frequency distribution simply lists the categories of the variable and the number of observations in each one. As an example, Table 22.1 shows the distribution of the variable "status" based on the following hypothetical responses from ten individuals, who were asked about their status in college:

Senior; Senior; Freshman; Junior; Junior; Sophomore;
Freshman; Sophomore; Senior; Freshman.

The frequency distribution table can also include the relative frequency of each category as well as a percentage of the relative frequency. The relative frequency is the frequency of a category divided by the total number of observations. To arrive at the percentage, we multiply the relative frequency by 100.

In addition to displaying categorical variables in this tabular form, the researcher can use a bar chart to display the data. In a bar graph, the categories of the variable are represented by equally spaced intervals along the horizontal axis, while the frequencies are represented on the vertical axis. Figure 22.1 displays the college status variable in a bar chart.

22.2.1.2 Frequency Distributions and Graphical Displays of Quantitative Variables

Just as we can display a categorical variable in tabular or graphical form, we can show the main characteristics of a quantitative variable in a similar way. By quantitative, we refer to continuous and discrete variables. To illustrate how to construct the frequency distribution table of a quantitative variable, we will use the example of a common demographic variable, age. Age is a continuous

TABLE 22.1
Frequency Distribution of College Status

Status	Frequency	Relative Frequency (Frequency/Sum of Frequencies)	Percentage (Relative Frequency × 100) (%)
Freshman	3	3/10 = 0.3	0.3 × 100 = 30
Sophomore	2	2/10 = 0.2	0.2 × 100 = 20
Junior	2	2/10 = 0.2	0.2 × 100 = 20
Senior	3	3/10 = 0.3	0.3 × 100 = 30
	$N = 20$	Sum = 1	Sum = 100

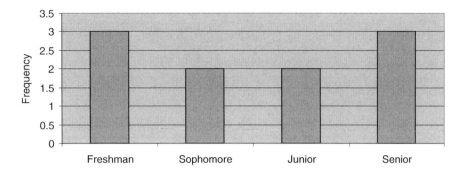

FIGURE 22.1 Bar chart of college status.

variable that can range from zero to more than one hundred. The researcher must first divide this range into a chosen, arbitrary number of classes. The class width is then calculated as

$$\text{Class width} = (\text{maximum value} - \text{minimum value})/\text{number of classes}$$

The frequency distribution table then lists each class and the number of values that belong to each. Table 22.2 below lists the ages of 20 office employees:

If we decide to group these values of age into four classes, we find that the class width is

$$(60 - 18)/4 = 10.5$$

For the sake of convenience, we can round this number to 10. As 18 is the lowest value in the dataset, we use it as the lower limit of the first class. The upper limit of this class is $18 + 10 = 28$. The lower limit of the second class is 29, and its upper limit is $29 + 10 = 39$, and so on. Table 22.3 lists all four classes and the corresponding frequencies, or total number of values in the dataset that fall within each class.

As with qualitative variables, we can calculate the relative frequencies and percentages of each class of the quantitative variable. These calculations are displayed in the third and fourth columns of Table 22.3. With quantitative variables, we can also add a cumulative percentage column to the frequency distribution table. The cumulative percentage for a given class is the percentage of values that fall in that class plus all the percentages in the classes below.

We use histograms to display quantitative variables in graphical form. Histograms are similar to bar charts but classes, rather than categories, are displayed on the horizontal axis. The vertical axis represents the frequency of each class. Figure 22.2 shows the histogram for the variable age.

TABLE 22.2
Ages of Office Employees

Employee	Age	Employee	Age
1	18	11	50
2	45	12	23
3	60	13	42
4	21	14	41
5	27	15	35
6	34	16	30
7	36	17	23
8	29	18	48
9	54	19	51
10	46	20	22

TABLE 22.3
Frequency Distribution Table of a Continuous Variable, Age

Age	Frequency	Relative Frequency (Frequency/Sum of Frequencies)	Percentage (Relative Frequency × 100) (%)	Cumulative Percentage (%)
18–28	6	6/20 = 0.3	0.3 × 100 = 30	30
29–39	5	5/20 = 0.25	0.25 × 100 = 25	25 + 30 = 55
40–50	6	6/20 = 0.3	0.3 × 100 = 30	30 + 25 + 30 = 85
51–61	3	3/20 = 0.15	0.15 × 100 = 15	15 + 30 + 25 + 30 = 100
	$N = 20$	Sum = 1	Sum = 100	

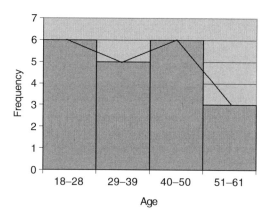

FIGURE 22.2 Histogram for age distribution.

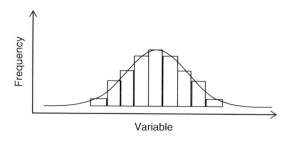

FIGURE 22.3 Normal curve (symmetric).

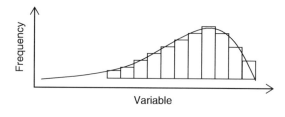

FIGURE 22.4 Negatively skewed frequency curve skewed to the left (asymmetric).

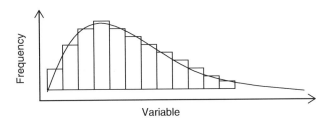

FIGURE 22.5 Positively skewed frequency curve skewed to the right (asymmetric).

An important distinction between bar charts and histograms is that in the latter, the bars have no gaps between them, representing the continuity of the classes. In addition to the bars in the histogram, the researcher can draw a polygon by joining the tops of each bar as shown in Figure 22.2. When the dataset is large and the classes are numerous with small widths, the frequency polygon looks more like a curve and is referred to as the frequency distribution curve. The frequency distribution curve can take various shapes. Figures 22.3 through 22.5 provide examples of three commonly encountered frequency curves.

Obviously, when we deal with large datasets, it is difficult to create frequency distribution tables, bar charts, or histograms and frequency curves manually. Fortunately, statistical software programs such as SPSS can quickly generate these graphs and tables for us. The Appendix shows how to do this.

22.2.2 NUMERICAL SUMMARY MEASURES

22.2.2.1 Measures of Central Tendency

In addition to visualizing the characteristics of variables through graphs and charts, an essential first step in data analysis is the examination of summary measures. These may be divided into two types: (1) measures of central tendency give us an idea about the center of the frequency distribution curve or histogram and (2) measures of dispersion provide clues about the spread of the frequency distribution curve or histogram.

22.2.2.1.1 Mean
The mean of a given quantitative variable—we cannot calculate means for qualitative variables—is obtained by dividing the sum of all values of that variable by the total number of values:

$$\text{Mean} = (\text{Sum of all values})/(\text{Number of values})$$

As an example, the average age of the employees in Table 22.2 is

$$\frac{735}{20} = 36.75$$

Although the mean is a commonly used summary measure, we should note that it is sensitive to outliers. In other words, just a few very small or very large values in a dataset will tend to skew the mean. For instance, the U.S. Census (2005) reports that the average homeownership rates in 2005 of four Northeastern states were

New Jersey—70.1 percent
Pennsylvania—73.3 percent
Connecticut—70.5 percent
Maryland—71.2 percent

Thus, the mean homeownership rate for these four states is

$$\frac{285.1}{4} = 71.3 \text{ percent}$$

If we add the homeownership rate of New York (55.9 percent) to this calculation, the mean rate for the five states is

$$\frac{341}{5} = 68.2 \text{ percent}$$

We can see that New York's homeownership rate, which is substantially lower than the others and may be considered an outlier, significantly reduces the mean rate.

22.2.2.1.2 Median

Once the values of a given variable have been arranged in an ascending or descending order, the value of the middle term is called the median. The median divides the dataset into two equal parts, such that half of all the values are greater than the median, and half are lower than the median.

The middle term of the dataset is the $\left(\frac{n+1}{2}\right)$th term.

To illustrate how to calculate the median, let us consider the following values of income from seven individuals:

55,000   43,000   27,000   34,000   76,000   82,000   45,000

We first have to order these values of income in an ascending or descending order:

27,000   34,000   43,000   45,000   55,000   76,000   82,000

Next, we have to find the middle term in the dataset: $\left(\frac{7+1}{2}\right) = 4$th term.

Thus, the median is the value of the 4th term. In this example, the median value of income is 45,000 dollars. Half of the individuals earn more than 45,000 dollars, while half earn less. If a dataset has an even number of observations, then the median is the average of the values of the two middle terms. Unlike the mean, outliers do not influence the median. This is why the median is a better measure of central tendency when analyzing data known to have outliers.

22.2.2.1.3 Mode

A third measure of central tendency is the mode. The mode is simply the most frequently occurring value of a given variable. The mode of the variable "age" in Table 22.2 is 23, because it has the highest frequency, $f = 2$. The mode has an advantage over the mean and the median because it can be used to describe qualitative variables. Unlike the mean and the median, however, the mode is not always unique. The categorical variable "college status" in Table 22.1 has two modes: the categories "freshman" and "senior," because they both occur with the highest frequency, $f = 3$. The variable "college status" is said to be bimodal.

22.2.2.2 Measures of Dispersion

Although the mean, median, and mode give us a sense of the center of a distribution, measures of dispersion help us understand the spread of a variable's distribution. For example, if a professor finds that her students' mean mid-semester grade is 80 percent, she may conclude that the students are progressing well. However, her conclusion may not be justified if there is a large variation in her students' grades: some students could be doing very well, whereas others may be failing and may need extra attention. Let us suppose that that her eight students obtained the following grades:

80   86   70   80   79   75   92   78 percent

The mean grade is indeed 80 percent. In this case, the variation in grades is relatively small: the professor may rest easy that her worst performing student had a mid-semester grade of 70 percent and that a little more work should help that student improve his performance.

On the other hand, the following eight scores also result in a mean of 80 percent:

57   100   100   47   100   98   39   99 percent

Here the distribution of the scores is much wider, with three students at risk of failing and five students performing brilliantly. If the professor did not have the individual grades in front of her and relied exclusively on the mean, median, or the mode, she would not get a full picture of the grade distribution.

To understand the variation in a variable's values, we can examine its range, variance, and standard deviation, jointly known as the measures of dispersion.

22.2.2.2.1 Range
The range is simply the result of subtracting the smallest value of a variable form the largest value:

Range = (largest value − smallest value)

In the example above, the first set of grades has a range of $(92 - 78) = 14$. The second set of grades has a range of $(100 - 39) = 61$. This is in keeping with our observation that the second set of grades has a wider distribution. Although the range is easy to calculate, it is sensitive to outliers. In addition, when working with large datasets, the range is not a very good summary measure because it relies on just two values of a variable.

22.2.2.2.2 Variance
The variance is the average squared deviations of a variable. The formula for the variance of a population is

$$\sigma^2 = \frac{\sum (x - \mu)^2}{N}$$

where
σ^2 is the population variance
$\Sigma(x - \mu)^2$ is the sum of squared deviations
$(x - \mu)$ is the deviation between the mean and the values of the variable
N is the size of the population

The formula for the variance of a sample is

$$s^2 = \frac{\sum (x - \bar{x})^2}{n - 1}$$

where
s^2 is the sample variance
$\Sigma(x - \bar{x})^2$ is the sum of squared deviations
$(x - \bar{x})$ is the deviation between the mean and the values of the variable
n is the sample size

The unit of the variance is the squared unit of the variable.

22.2.2.2.3 Standard Deviation
Because of the difficulty in conceptualizing the variance (its units are the squared units of the variable), the preferred measure of dispersion is the standard deviation. The standard deviation is simply the square root of the variance; it gives us an idea of how closely or how loosely clustered the values are in relation to the mean. A high standard deviation suggests that the values of a variable are widely spread (the frequency distribution curve would thus be flatter and wider). A low standard deviation indicates that the values are closer to the mean (the frequency distribution curve would be narrower with a high peak around the mean). The unit of the standard deviation is the same as the unit of the variable under study.

The population standard deviation is noted:

$$\sigma = \sqrt{\sigma^2} = \sqrt{\frac{\sum (x - \mu)^2}{N}}$$

The standard deviation of a sample is written:

$$s = \sqrt{s^2} = \sqrt{\frac{\sum (x - \bar{x})^2}{n - 1}}$$

We can illustrate the calculation of the variance and standard deviation using the two sets of mid-semester grades we used at the start of Section 22.3:

Set 1: 80   86   70   80   79   75   92   78 percent
Set 2: 57   100   100   47   100   98   39   99 percent

From the discussion under Section 22.3, we know that these are the grades of an entire classroom. We will therefore use the formula for the population variance. We already know that the mean grade of this dataset is 80 percent. We now have to calculate the sum of squared deviations of Set 1:

$$\sum (x - \mu)^2 = (80 - 80)^2 + (86 - 80)^2 + (70 - 80)^2 + (80 - 80)^2 + (79 - 80)^2$$
$$+ (75 - 80)^2 + (92 - 80)^2 + (78 - 80)^2$$
$$= 0 + 6^2 + (-10)^2 + 0 + (-1)^2 + (-5)^2 + 8^2 + (-2)^2$$
$$= 36 + 100 + 1 + 25 + 64 + 4 = 230$$

We can now calculate the variance:

$$\sigma^2 = \frac{\sum (x - \mu)^2}{N} = \frac{230}{8} = 28.75$$

We can also calculate the standard deviation of the grades:

$$\sigma = \sqrt{\sigma^2} = \sqrt{28.75} = 5.36 \text{ percent}$$

For Set 2, the sum of squared deviations is 5184 and the variance is 72 percent. The much larger standard deviation of Set 2 confirms our earlier observation that Set 1 has a much smaller spread than Set 2, even though both have the same mean.

The standard deviation can also be used to find the percentage of values that fall within a certain interval of the mean. Mann (2001) provides a discussion of how the standard deviation can be used in this way. As with frequency distribution tables and graphical displays, measures of central tendency and dispersion are difficult to calculate manually when the dataset is large. The Appendix demonstrates how to generate these statistics with SPSS.

22.3 RELATIONSHIPS BETWEEN VARIABLES

Organizing variables in tables, graphing them, and examining their descriptive measures provide the researcher with a good picture of the dataset. These techniques are referred to as univariate analyses because the variables are studied one at a time. Some research designs only require such univariate descriptive analyses.

Often however, researchers want to examine relationships between two or more variables. We refer to the study of these relationships as bivariate analysis if it involves two variables. Multivariate analysis refers to the study of relationships between more than two variables. In bivariate or multivariate analysis, researchers want to know if changes in the values of one variable lead to changes in the values of another. We may want to know if the variables are simply related to each other (association), or if changes in the values of one cause changes in the values of another (causation). If variables in a dataset are related to each other, we may want to know what the strength of that relationship is. We may also want to know the direction of the relationship: do

TABLE 22.4

Cross-Tabulation of Gender and Drinking Problem

| | | | Drinking Problem | | |
			Yes	No	Total
Respondent's sex	Male	Count	9	407	416
		%	2.2	97.8	100.0
	Female	Count	8	588	596
		%	1.3	98.7	100.0
Total		Count	17	995	1012
		%	1.7	98.3	100.0

the values of the variables increase or decrease at the same time as in a positive relationship? Or do they change in opposite directions, as in negative relationships?

There are many techniques available to social scientists who want to know the answers to these questions. Which one to adopt depends on the variables' levels of measurement (nominal, ordinal, discrete, or continuous). Although the aim here is not to review in detail these techniques, the rest of this chapter provides a nonexhaustive list of methods commonly used by researchers to examine relationships between different types of variables.

22.3.1 RELATIONSHIPS BETWEEN QUALITATIVE VARIABLES

Relationships between qualitative variables (nominal or ordinal) are usually examined through the use of tables known as cross-tabulations. The tables list the categories of one variable in rows and the categories of the second variable in columns. The cells in these tables show the frequency and percentage of cases that fall into each of the possible two-category combinations. As an example, let us examine the relationship between the two nominal variables "gender" and "drinking problem" (Table 22.4).

Note that the percentages are always calculated so that the categories of the independent variable (in this case gender), add up to 100 percent. Table 22.4 suggests that a larger percentage of men have a drinking problem compared to women (2.2 versus 1.3 percent). However, it is very important to remember that this conclusion is based on one sample of 1,012 individuals. We cannot make the claim that in general, or in the larger population, men are also more likely to have a drinking problem than women. Indeed, the result we have found could be due to chance: if we had picked a different sample, we may or may not find a similar relationship between "gender" and "drinking problem."

We can certainly hypothesize that the relationship between "gender" and "drinking problem" also holds true in the general population. To test such a hypothesis, we would use inferential statistics: these are tests of hypothesis that help us determine whether we can make inferences about a population based on observations we make in a sample. More specifically, hypothesis tests allow us to answer the question: "what is the probability that the relationship we observed in a sample occurred by chance?" Mohr (1990) provides a fuller treatment of hypothesis testing.

The hypothesis test associated with cross-tabulations is the chi-square (χ^2) test. The results of the chi-square test for the data in Table 22.5 are presented below. The test was conducted using

TABLE 22.5

Chi Square Test of Significance for Gender/Drinking Problem

	Value	Degrees of Freedom (df = Number of Rows − 1)	Sig. (2-Sided)
Pearson chi-square	1.000	1	0.317

SPSS. The level of significance (0.317) suggests that there is a 0.317 probability that the relationship between "gender" and "drinking problem" observed in the sample occurred by chance. This probability is considered to be too high. We conclude that the relationship between "gender" and "drinking problem" is not statistically significant (i.e., it is not likely to be true in the general population). In general, we only claim that a relationship is statistically significant (or true in the population) if the probability that it occurred by chance is less than 0.05. Schacht and Aspelmeier (2005) and Agresti (1996) provide a good overview of the chi-square statistic.

22.3.2 RELATIONSHIPS BETWEEN QUANTITATIVE VARIABLES (DISCRETE OR CONTINUOUS)

Linear regression analysis (Berry and Feldman, 1985; Lewis-Beck, 1980; Schroeder, Sjoquist, and Stephan, 1986) is a commonly used method to model relationships between quantitative variables. A simple linear regression allows us to estimate the effect of one variable (the independent variable) on another (the dependent variable). As the name implies, a simple linear regression models this relationship as a straight line. By estimating the equation of this line, including its slope and y-intercept, the analysis gives us an indication about the strength and direction of the relationship. The regression equation also allows us to predict values of the dependent variable for given values of the independent variable.

Multiple regression analysis is conceptually a little different from what we have described above. Indeed, the multiple regression equation does not represent a line, but rather a plane. In its application, however, multiple regression analysis is very similar to simple linear regression. The difference here is that we seek to predict the value of a dependent variable based on given values of *several* independent variables. By using multiple independent (or explanatory/predictor) variables, the researcher aims to explain a higher proportion of the variance in the dependent variable. To put it differently, multiple regression tries to make the predictions of the dependent variable more accurate by taking into account the effects of as many theoretically relevant independent variables as possible.

One note of caution before selecting linear regression to model relationships is that many relationships are nonlinear; the researcher should therefore have a theoretical basis for expecting that a linear model will be the best fit for his or her data. In addition, the researcher can use bivariate scatterplots to get a rough idea about the form of a relationship. Scatteplots are graphs in which the dependent variable is represented on the y-axis and the independent variable is represented on the x-axis. Each case in the dataset is then represented by a point on the graph.

22.3.3 RELATIONSHIPS BETWEEN QUANTITATIVE AND QUALITATIVE VARIABLES

Linear regression analysis may still be the method of choice in modeling relationships where the dependent variable is quantitative, and one or more of the independent or predictor variables are categorical (qualitative). In this case, we can transform the categories of the qualitative variable into dummy variables. For example, let us assume that a dataset contains the variable "gender" with the two categories male and female. We can transform the category "male" into a dummy variable with the values 0 if the person is not male, and 1 if the person is male. Similarly, we can transform the category "female" into a dummy variable with the values 0 if the person is not female, and 1 if the person is female. We can then use either one of the two dummy variables as a predictor in a regression analysis. It is important to note that we only need to enter one of the two dummy variables into the regression equation because they both contain the same information (entering both into a regression would lead to multicollinearity).

As another example, let us assume that a dataset contains the variable "race" with the following categories: African American, White, Asian, Hispanic, and Native American. Here again, we can create binary dummy variables for each category (0 if not African American, 1 if African American; 0 if not White, 1 if White, etc.). In the regression analysis, however, we would only enter four of the five dummy variables; the fifth category would serve as a reference or comparison group. In general then, when we want to use a categorical variable as an independent variable in a regression equation, we can transform the categories into dummy variables and enter one less dummy variable into the regression equation than there are categories (Hardy, 1993).

A linear regression equation is not appropriate when the dependent variable is categorical. In such cases, and specifically when the dependent variable has only two categories (i.e., it is dichotomous), we can use logistic regression analysis (Hosmer and Lemeshow, 1989). Logistic regression provides estimates of odds ratios for each of the independent variables in the model. For example, if we want to study which factors are likely to contribute to a heart attack, we could study a sample of individuals, some of whom have suffered a heart attack, some who have not. Whether or not a person has had a heart attack would be the dependent dichotomous variable. We might hypothesize that subjects with higher body weights are more likely to have had a heart attack. In that case, body weight is an independent variable. The relationship between these two variables can be modeled by a logistic regression, which would give us the factor by which the odds of having a heart attack increase when body weight increases by one unit.

Unfortunately, logistic regression is not applicable when the qualitative dependent variable has more than two categories. In such cases, the researcher may be able to model relationships between quantitative independent variables and the categorical dependent variable using discriminant analysis (Hubert, 1994; Kachigan, 1991). Discriminant analysis generates discriminant functions, which are similar to regression equations, with weights assigned to each predictor variable. However, rather than using the equations to predict the value of the dependent variable (as with quantitative dependent variables), discriminant functions are used to predict which category of the dependent variable a case belongs to given that case's values on the independent variables. For example, we may want to know which factors distinguish members of different political parties. The dependent variable in this case is party affiliation. Let us assume that it has three categories: Democrat, Republican, and Independent. We can use predictor variables such as income and education in a discriminant model that would help us discriminate between the three categories of the dependent variable. If income and education are good discriminators of party affiliation, we would be able to predict a person's party affiliation based on his or her income and education. Of course, we could also find that income and education are not good discriminators of party affiliation. Alternatively, we may find that they discriminate well between Democrats and Republicans, but not between these two groups and Independents.

22.4 CONCLUSION

Data analysis is one of the most important (and perhaps most exciting) aspects of the research process. This chapter provided an introduction to the mechanics of that process.

We first reviewed the collection of procedures known as descriptive statistics. These included the graphical and tabular presentation of variables, as well as calculating and interpreting measures of central tendency and dispersion. The examples we used were purposely simple to facilitate understanding. Of course, in the real world of research, especially in the social sciences where we most often deal with quasi-experimental designs, sample sizes are large. It would be difficult, if not nearly impossible, to carry out all the analyses by hand. The Appendix to this chapter provides a step-by-step tutorial on using SPSS with a large dataset to generate the statistics we have reviewed.

This chapter also illustrated a number of methods used by social scientists to study the relationships between variables. Although there are a multitude of bivariate and multivariate techniques available to the researcher, we narrowed down the list to those that are most frequently used in the field of public administration. We organized this discussion around the types of variables being studied. Although the discussion of individual methods was necessarily limited, we hope that the reader gets a sense of where to begin the search for the most appropriate technique for his or her research design.

PROBLEMS

1. The following numbers represent the revenue in millions of dollars at the end of three years that a city would gain for undertaking various projects. A negative sign indicates a net loss for the first three years of the project's implementation.

   150   −15   26   26   45   47   64

   a. Calculate the mean, median, mode, range, variance, and standard deviation for this data set.
   b. Identify any outliers in the dataset; omit the outliers and recalculate the mean and the median. Which of these summary measures changes the most when you drop the outliers?

2. The following sample represents the time in minutes taken by a group of students to complete an exam:

   34   56   32   21   9   27   54

   a. Find the mean, median, mode, range, variance, and standard deviation.
   b. Construct the intervals [mean − s; mean + s]; [mean − $2s$; mean + $2s$]; [mean − $3s$; mean + $3s$].
   c. How many observations fall into each interval?

Appendix: Descriptive Analysis with SPSS

The following demonstrations of how to generate tables and graphs using SPSS are based on the attached dataset "Innovation in Local Government Survey." The dataset includes responses from 222 individuals. All but the first two variables are characteristics of the respondents. The first two variables, "incgrow" (percentage growth in median income over ten years) and "govtype" (type of government), are characteristics of the city from which the respondents were selected.

A.1 FREQUENCY DISTRIBUTION AND GRAPHICAL DISPLAYS OF QUALITATIVE VARIABLES

From the data editor window of SPSS, select "Analyze" from the toolbar, scroll down to "Descriptive Statistics," and click on "Frequencies" (Figure 22.A1).

FIGURE 22.A1 Descriptive statistics for qualitative variables, SPSS Step 1.

From the list of variables in the left pane of the dialog box, select the second variable, "type of government," which is a categorical (nominal) variable, and click on the arrow to place the variable under the "variables'" list (Figure 22.A2).

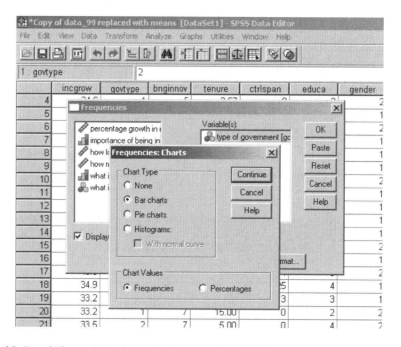

FIGURE 22.A2 Descriptive statistics for qualitative variables, SPSS Step 2.

Next, select the "Charts" option and select the button next to "Bar charts." Note that in the bottom of the dialog box, under "chart values," the default selection is "frequencies." For this example, we will chart the frequencies in the bar chart, but it is also possible to chart percentages. Once the selection has been made, click on "continue." This leads us back to the Frequencies dialog box (Figure 22.A3).

FIGURE 22.A3 Descriptive statistics for qualitative variables, SPSS Step 3.

From this box, click on "OK." The SPSS output window opens with the following tables and charts (Figure 22.A4):

Frequencies

Statistics

Type of government

N	Valid	222
	Missing	0

Type of government

		Frequency	Percent	Valid Percent	Cumulative Percent
Valid	Mayor/council	70	31.5	31.5	31.5
	Council/manager	152	68.5	68.5	100.0
	Total	222	100.0	100.0	

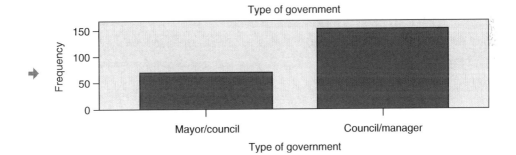

FIGURE 22.A4 Descriptive statistics for qualitative variables, SPSS Output.

We can see that of the 222 cases, 152 respondents come from council or manager type cities, whereas 70 (or 68.5) percent live in mayor or council type of cities.

A.2   FREQUENCY DISTRIBUTION, GRAPHICAL DISPLAYS, AND SUMMARY NUMERICAL MEASURES OF QUANTITATIVE VARIABLES

To obtain the frequency distribution of a quantitative variable, we follow the same steps as above: from the data editor window, we select "Analyze," "Descriptive Statistics," and "Frequencies." This time, we will select the first variable, "percentage growth in median income over ten years in the city," which is a continuous variable. From the charts option, we select "Histograms" instead of "Bar charts," and we also select the box next to "with normal curve." After clicking on "continue," we get back to the Frequencies dialog box (Figure 22.A5).

From the frequencies dialog box, we now select the "Statistics" button.

In the Statistics dialog box, under "Central Tendency," we select the Mean, Median, and Mode. Under "Dispersion" we select Std. Deviation, Variance, and Range. We can then click on "Continue" and return to the Frequencies dialog box (Figure 22.A6). Once we select "OK," the SPSS output window displays the frequency distribution table, which is rather long and not reproduced here. The output also contains the following table and histogram (Figure 22.A7):

From the histogram, we can see that the distribution of median income growth is not quite symmetrical: there is a small cluster of values near the higher end of the x-axis (around the 100

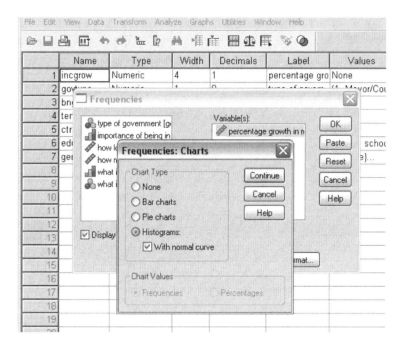

FIGURE 22.A5 Descriptive statistics for quantitative variables, SPSS Step 1.

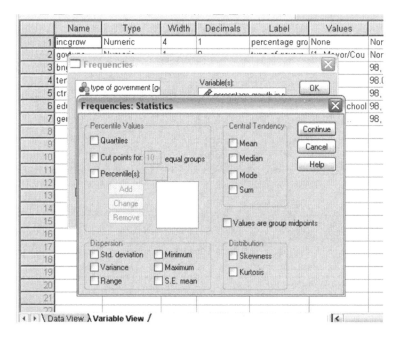

FIGURE 22.A6 Descriptive statistics for quantitative variables, SPSS Step 2.

Frequencies

Statistics

Percentage growth in median income over ten years in the city

N	Valid	222
	Missing	0
Mean		44.675
Median		42.400
Mode		28.2[a]
Std. Deviation		15.1169
Variance		228.520
Range		82.3

[a] Multiple modes exist. The smallest value is shown

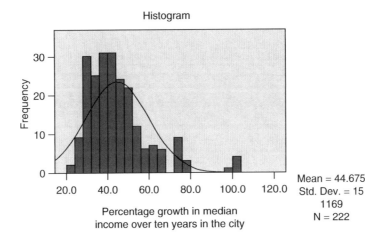

Histogram

Mean = 44.675
Std. Dev. = 15.1169
N = 222

FIGURE 22.A7 Descriptive statistics for quantitative variables, SPSS Output.

percent mark) that skew the frequency curve to the right. Without looking at the statistics, we know that in a distribution that is positively skewed, the mean has the highest value; the mode has the lowest value; and the median is in-between the two. We can also see from the histogram that the mode is not unique: there are multiple values near the 40 percent mark with the highest frequency.

Looking at the numerical measures of central tendency, we can see that the mean (44.7 percent) is indeed higher than the median and mode. The standard deviation (15.1 percent) also suggests that there is a fair amount of variation in median family income growth between the cities. This conclusion is also supported by the high value of the range: there is an 82 percentage point difference between the cities with the lowest and highest growth rates.

REFERENCES

Agresti, A. 1996. *An Introduction to Categorical Data Analysis*, New York: John Wiley & Sons.
Berry, W. and Feldman, S. 1985. *Multiple Regression in Practice*, Newbury Park, California: Sage Publications.
Hardy, M. 1993. *Regression with Dummy Variables*, Newbury Park, California: Sage Publications.
Hosmer, D. and Lemeshow, S. 1989. *Applied Logistic Regression*, New York: John Wiley & Sons.
Hubert, C. 1994. *Applied Discriminant Analysis*, New York: Wiley & Sons.
Kachigan, S. 1991. *Multivariate Statistical Analysis: A Conceptual Introduction*, New York: Radius Press.

Lewis-Beck, M. 1980. *Applied Regression: An Introduction*, Newbury Park, California: Sage Publications.

Mann, P. 2001. *Introductory Statistics*, 4th ed., New York: John Wiley & Sons.

Mohr, L. 1990. *Understanding Significance Testing*, Newbury Park, California: Sage Publications.

Schacht, S. and Aspelmeier, J. 2005. *Social and Behavioral Statistics: A User Friendly Approach*, 2nd ed., Boulder, Colorado: Westview Press.

Schroeder, L., Sjoquist, D., and Stephan, P. 1986. *Understanding Regression Analysis: An Introductory Guide*, Newbury Park, California: Sage Publications.

U.S. Census Bureau 2005. Housing Vacancies and Homeownership Survey. http://www.census.gov/hhes/www/housing/hvs/annual05/ann05t13.html

23 Applying Matrix Algebra in Statistical Analysis

Sarmistha Rina Majumdar

CONTENTS

23.1 INTRODUCTION

Algebra is a useful branch of mathematics. It is mainly concerned with the generalization of arithmetic and deals not only with numbers but also with letters that may represent a large variety of numbers. Algebraic functions can range from simple addition, subtraction, multiplication, and division to complex ones that involve a combination of the aforementioned functions. In an algebraic equation, the unknown letters can be solved and checked by replacing them with numerical values. This makes it possible to balance the equations and solve all those problems that are expressed in algebraic terms (Pine, 1992).

23.2 LINEAR EQUATIONS AND GRAPHS

Linear algebra when applied to linear equations enables the expression of a complex system of equations in a simplified form (Dowling, 1992). A linear equation is considered as a first degree equation, that is, each variable is of the first degree and can be expressed as a straight line on a graph (Hall and Bennett, 1985). For example, $2m = 12$ is a linear equation because m has an exponent of 1. But the equation $s^2 = 16$ is not a linear equation as the exponent of s is 2. It is therefore not an equation of the first degree. A linear equation may have more than one variable, for example, $6x + 2 = 5y + 8$ where the two variables are x and y.

In solving linear equations, like in any other equations, the first step involves simplification of the equation. This requires the elimination of fractions and parentheses. Second, it requires the

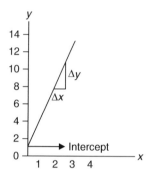

x	y
0	1 (0,1)
1	4 (1,4)
2	7 (2,7)
3	10 (3,10)
4	13 (4,13)

FIGURE 23.1 Plotting a graph with x and y values.

isolation of terms of the specified variable as a single term of that equation, and finally, solving the equation by factoring out the specified variable followed by division of its coefficient (Hall and Bennett, 1985).

In a linear equation, the analytical relationship that may exist between the two variables can be expressed in the form of a straight line by using the Cartesian coordinate system (Pine, 1992). If there exist two unknown variables x and y, the relationship between the variables in an equation for example, $y = 3x + 1$ can be plotted on a graph by plotting the values of y against x, provided we know or have chosen a numerical value for x.

In the equation $y = 3x + 1$, we choose the values of x as shown below, the corresponding values of y can be easily calculated and plotted on the graph as a straight line (Figure 23.1).

In the graph shown in Figure 23.1, the point where the straight line intersects the y axis is called the intercept. At this point the value of $y = 1$ for the line $y = 3x + 1$.

23.2.1 WHY WE NEED TO KNOW MATRIX ALGEBRA?

Matrix algebra refers to a set of rules with systematic implications for making deductions with matrices as elements. Seeing a chapter on matrix algebra in a research methods book, a question that is most likely to arise among readers is "why do we need to know matrix algebra when statistical softwares are available to perform complex statistical analysis?" True, sophisticated softwares are available to conduct statistical analysis and apparently it may seem to be a waste of time working out problems by hand. But the step-by-step procedures of matrix algebra offer greater insight into the analytical process. When we download a data file into statistical software and select appropriate commands to perform different types of analysis, we do not gain any understanding of how the program actually works (Freeman, 1961, p. 435). In order to understand the various processes used in statistical analysis of data, knowledge of the basic principles of matrix algebra can prove to be useful.

Principles of matrix algebra are widely used in psychological testing, economics, and business studies. In the field of administrative studies, we do not find its wide-scale application but it can be used to examine the structure of covariance or correlation matrices through principal component and factor analysis (Lawley et al., 1962, p. 209) or to investigate relationships among variables through regression analysis. All these methods can be worked out by hand (if sample size permits) by applying the principles of matrix algebra. Also, matrix algebra can prove to be useful in verifying answers that are produced by statistical softwares. Even regression diagnostics like auto-correlated errors can be checked using matrices (Polasek, 1984, p. 340).

Matrix algebra can be learned by anyone with a basic knowledge of high school algebra and basic statistics. In fact, learning matrix algebra does not require the knowledge of advanced mathematics. It can be learned either in a classroom setting or those who are interested in it can acquire knowledge on their own by reading elementary textbooks written on the subject and solving problems using the principles of matrix algebra. Knowledge of matrix algebra helps one to comprehend the logic of each step in the process of calculation and derivation of answers in both simplex and complex statistical analysis of data.

In this chapter, attempts have been made to introduce the basic principles of matrix algebra and create awareness of its utility in complex statistical analysis. Matrix algebra can specially prove to be extremely useful to those individuals who may not have quick and immediate access to costly statistical software and need to conduct statistical analysis for various reasons. In such cases, matrix algebra can be applied to solve problems and produce results that are accurate. Thus, its knowledge can save money from buying an expensive software that would not be used that much.

23.3   WHAT IS MATRIX ALGEBRA?

A matrix refers to a rectangular array of numbers that are arranged either in the form of a chart or a table. The basic axioms of mathematics are applied to matrix algebra (Hammer, 1971). Matrices provide the means to store information in an orderly and organized way. To denote matrices, capital letters are usually used. In a matrix, the numbers, parameters, or variables are referred to as elements. The numbers are usually placed in horizontal rows and in vertical columns. In data matrices, the rows represent entities and the columns represent attributes (Horst, 1963). In a matrix, the row number precedes the column number and the number of rows (r) and columns (c) defines the order of the matrix ($r \times c$).

A *zero* matrix can be a matrix of any size where each cell entry is zero. See matrix X. A *diagonal matrix* is similar to a zero matrix (Hammer, 1971) except that the leading diagonal cells from top left to bottom right may not have zero, as seen in matrix Y.

$$X = \begin{pmatrix} 0 & 0 & 0 \\ 0 & 0 & 0 \\ 0 & 0 & 0 \end{pmatrix} \quad Y = \begin{pmatrix} 3 & 0 & 0 \\ 0 & 0 & 0 \\ 0 & 0 & 2 \end{pmatrix}$$

The *identity* matrix is a scalar matrix where the diagonal value is 1 as seen in matrix M.

$$M = \begin{pmatrix} 1 & 0 & 0 & 0 \\ 0 & 1 & 0 & 0 \\ 0 & 0 & 1 & 0 \\ 0 & 0 & 0 & 1 \end{pmatrix}$$

In a *square* matrix, the number of rows is the same as that of the columns. If a single column dominates a matrix such that its dimensions are $r \times 1$, it is a column vector. Similarly, if a matrix has only a single row with dimensions $1 \times c$, it is a row vector. A *transposed* matrix is one where the rows of A can be converted to columns and the columns of A to rows. A transposed matrix is denoted by any capital letter, such as A' in the example below.

Examples:

$$A = \begin{pmatrix} 1_{11} & 2_{12} & 5_{13} \\ 3_{21} & 4_{22} & 0_{23} \end{pmatrix} \qquad A' = \begin{pmatrix} 1 & 3 \\ 2 & 4 \\ 5 & 0 \end{pmatrix} \qquad B = \begin{pmatrix} 4 & 0 & -8 \\ -5 & 2 & 3 \\ 1 & -4 & 7 \end{pmatrix}$$

$r \times c = 2 \times 3$ (general matrix) $r \times c = 3 \times 3$ (square matrix)

$$C = \begin{pmatrix} 5 \\ 2 \\ 1 \end{pmatrix} \qquad\qquad D = (1 \quad 3 \quad 5 \quad 2) \qquad C' = (5 \quad 2 \quad 1)$$

$r \times c = 3 \times 1$ (column vector) $r \times c = 1 \times 4$ (row vector)   Transposed matrix of C

In a general matrix A with the dimensions of 2×3, the subscript refers to the placement of numbers or elements. The first subscript of a number in a matrix identifies the row and the second number identifies the column. For example, the second number in the matrix A is 2_{12}. The subscript refers to the position of the number, which is located in the first row and second column.

23.4   ADDITION AND SUBTRACTION OF MATRICES

In the addition and subtraction of matrices A and B, the matrices should be of the same order. Each number in addition of matrices $(A + B)$ or in subtraction of matrices $(A - B)$ is obtained by either adding or subtracting the corresponding entries in A and B. If the matrices are not of the same order or dimension, then $A + B$ or $A - B$ cannot be identified.

Examples:

Addition of Matrices

$$A = \begin{pmatrix} 8 & 3 \\ 10 & 4 \end{pmatrix}_{2\times2} + B = \begin{pmatrix} 1 & 2 \\ 5 & 3 \end{pmatrix}_{2\times2} = \begin{pmatrix} 8+1 & 3+2 \\ 10+5 & 4+3 \end{pmatrix}_{2\times2} = \begin{pmatrix} 9 & 5 \\ 15 & 7 \end{pmatrix}_{2\times2}$$

Subtraction of Matrices

$$C = \begin{pmatrix} 5 & 8 \\ 9 & 6 \end{pmatrix}_{2\times2} - D = \begin{pmatrix} 4 & 1 \\ 6 & 5 \end{pmatrix}_{2\times2} = \begin{pmatrix} 5-4 & 8-1 \\ 9-6 & 6-5 \end{pmatrix}_{2\times2} = \begin{pmatrix} 1 & 7 \\ 3 & 1 \end{pmatrix}_{2\times2}$$

23.5   MULTIPLICATION OF MATRICES

In matrix algebra, scalar multiplication involves the multiplication of every number in the matrix with any simple number $(3, -2, 0.01)$ or a scalar. The product of scalar multiplication $k(A)$ when $k = 2$ is

$$A = \begin{pmatrix} 1 & 3 \\ 9 & 7 \end{pmatrix}_{2\times2} k(A) = \begin{pmatrix} 2(1) & 2(3) \\ 2(9) & 2(7) \end{pmatrix}_{2\times2} = \begin{pmatrix} 2 & 6 \\ 18 & 14 \end{pmatrix}_{2\times2}$$

Vector multiplication in matrix algebra involves the multiplication of a row vector A by column vector B. One of the prerequisites is that each vector should have the same number of elements so that each element in one vector can be multiplied with the corresponding element in the other vector.

Example:

$$A = (1 \quad 2 \quad 5)_{1\times3} \quad B = \begin{pmatrix} 3 \\ 6 \\ 7 \end{pmatrix}_{3\times1} \quad AB = 1(3) + 2(6) + 5(7) = 3 + 12 + 35 = 50$$

23.6 INVERSE MATRICES

The inverse of a matrix is used to solve equations and to find a curve that best fits the data (Bonney and Kissling, 1984, p. 722). Inverse matrix is a square (same number of rows and columns) and a nonsingular matrix that satisfies the relationship

$$AA^{-1} = A^{-1}A$$

An inversed matrix can be obtained by applying the formula

$$A^{-1} = \frac{1}{|A|} \text{Adj } A$$

Thus, in linear algebra, inverse matrix performs the same function as the reciprocal in ordinary algebra (Schott, 1997).

In inversion of the given matrix A, the following steps are important:

$$A = \begin{pmatrix} 5_{a11} & 3_{a12} & 6_{a13} \\ 4_{a21} & 2_{a22} & 7_{a23} \\ 8_{a31} & 5_{a32} & 3_{a33} \end{pmatrix}$$

$$A^{-1} = 1/|A|\text{Adj } A$$

(a) Evaluation of the determinant by taking the first element of the first row, i.e., a_{11}, and mentally deleting the row and column in which it appears. Then multiply a_{11} by the determinant of the remaining elements. For example

$$|A| = a_{11} \begin{pmatrix} 2_{a22} & 7_{a23} \\ 5_{a32} & 3_{a33} \end{pmatrix} + a_{12}^{(-1)} \begin{pmatrix} 4_{a21} & 7_{a23} \\ 8_{a31} & 3_{a33} \end{pmatrix} + a_{13} \begin{pmatrix} 4_{a21} & 2_{a22} \\ 8_{a31} & 5_{a32} \end{pmatrix}$$

$$= a_{11}(a_{22}a_{33} - a_{23}a_{32}) - a_{12}(a_{21}a_{33} - a_{23}a_{31}) + a_{13}(a_{21}a_{32} - a_{22}a_{31})$$

$$= 5(6 - 35) - 3(12 - 56) + 6(20 - 16)$$

$$= -145 + 132 + 24 = 11$$

(b) Finding the cofactor matrix by replacing every element a_{ij} in matrix A with its cofactor $|C_{ij}|$. Then finding the adjoint matrix, which is a transpose of the cofactor matrix. Thus, the cofactor matrix is

$$C = \begin{pmatrix} \begin{vmatrix} 2 & 7 \\ 5 & 3 \end{vmatrix} & -\begin{vmatrix} 4 & 7 \\ 8 & 3 \end{vmatrix} & \begin{vmatrix} 4 & 2 \\ 8 & 5 \end{vmatrix} \\ -\begin{vmatrix} 3 & 6 \\ 5 & 3 \end{vmatrix} & \begin{vmatrix} 5 & 6 \\ 8 & 3 \end{vmatrix} & -\begin{vmatrix} 5 & 3 \\ 8 & 5 \end{vmatrix} \\ \begin{vmatrix} 3 & 6 \\ 2 & 7 \end{vmatrix} & -\begin{vmatrix} 5 & 6 \\ 4 & 7 \end{vmatrix} & \begin{vmatrix} 5 & 3 \\ 4 & 2 \end{vmatrix} \end{pmatrix} = \begin{pmatrix} -29 & 44 & 4 \\ 21 & -33 & -1 \\ 9 & -11 & -2 \end{pmatrix}$$

$$\text{and Adj } A = C' = \begin{pmatrix} -29 & 21 & 9 \\ 44 & -33 & -11 \\ 4 & -1 & -2 \end{pmatrix}$$

$$\text{Thus } A^{-1} = \frac{1}{11} \begin{pmatrix} -29 & 21 & 9 \\ 44 & -33 & -11 \\ -4 & -1 & -2 \end{pmatrix} = \begin{pmatrix} -29/11 & 21/11 & 9/11 \\ 44/11 & -33/11 & -11/11 \\ -4/11 & -1/11 & -2/11 \end{pmatrix}$$

23.7   LINEAR EQUATIONS IN MATRIX ALGEBRA

Matrix algebra enables the expression of linear equations in simple and concise forms. For example, the equation given below can be expressed in a matrix form:

$$3x_1 + 2x_2 = 10$$

$$5x_1 + 4x_2 = 27$$

$$\text{Matrix form} = AX = B$$

where
(coefficient matrix) $A = \begin{pmatrix} 3 & 2 \\ 5 & 4 \end{pmatrix}$ (solution vector) $X = \begin{pmatrix} X_1 \\ X_2 \end{pmatrix} = $ (vector of constant term)
$B = \begin{pmatrix} 10 \\ 27 \end{pmatrix}$.

23.8   MATRIX INVERSION OF LINEAR EQUATION

If there are two unknowns in a linear equation, matrix algebra can be used to solve for the unknowns as shown below:

$$3x + 2y = 14$$

$$4x + 5y = 28$$

The same equation can be expressed in the following matrix form:

$$\begin{pmatrix} 3 & 2 \\ 4 & 5 \end{pmatrix} \begin{pmatrix} X \\ Y \end{pmatrix} = \begin{pmatrix} 14 \\ 28 \end{pmatrix}$$

Inverse the matrix and now $X = A^{-1}B$.
Inverse of A where $|A| = 3(5) - 2(4) = 7$. The cofactor matrix of A is

$$C \begin{pmatrix} 5 & -4 \\ -2 & 3 \end{pmatrix}$$

and Adj $A = C' = \begin{pmatrix} 5 & -2 \\ -4 & 3 \end{pmatrix}$

Thus, $A^{-1} = 1/7 \begin{pmatrix} 5 & -2 \\ -4 & 3 \end{pmatrix} = \begin{pmatrix} 5/7 & -2/7 \\ -4/7 & 3/7 \end{pmatrix}$

Then substituting in $X = A^{-1}B$ and simply multiplying matrices, we get

$$X = \begin{pmatrix} 5/7 & -2/7 \\ -4/7 & 3/7 \end{pmatrix} \begin{pmatrix} 14 \\ 28 \end{pmatrix} = \begin{pmatrix} 10 & -8 \\ -8 & 12 \end{pmatrix} = \begin{pmatrix} 2 \\ 4 \end{pmatrix}$$

Solving for x, we get $x = 2$ and $y = 4$.

23.9   APPLICATION OF INVERSE MATRIX IN REGRESSION ANALYSIS

A simple regression analysis is used to determine if there exists a linear relationship between a dependent variable (y) and an independent variable (x) (Searle and Willett, 2001, p. 285). In a simple regression equation, the dependent variable is usually regressed against the single independent variable. A simple regression equation can be expressed as

$$y = a + bx + e$$

where

$a =$ sample intercept (constant) represented by the value of dependent variable (y) when independent variable (x) is zero

$b =$ slope of a line, expressed as a ratio of change in the dependent variable (y) as a result of change in the independent variable (x)

$e =$ error ($n \times 1$ vector of random errors)

Consider a case, where a researcher is interested in finding out if there exists a relationship between cities expenditure (y) in recycling programs (in thousands of dollars) and their population (x) in thousands. Data is collected from a small sample of five cities and is presented in Table 23.1.

Using the above equation for a simple regression analysis, the following equations can be derived:

$$25 = a + b_1(65) + e_1$$

$$33 = a + b_2(70) + e_2$$

$$39 = a + b_3(67) + e_3$$

$$35 = a + b_4(55) + e_4$$

$$45 = a + b_5(68) + e_5$$

In applying the least squares method to determine linear relationship between y and x, we need to determine the two unknowns, a and b, such that

$$\sum_i (y_i - a - b_1 x_i)^2$$

Then the equation for the five cases (n) needs to be solved. Using the minimization process, two linear equations can be derived with the two unknowns, a and b:

$$(1) \quad (n)a + \left(\sum_{i=1}^{n} x_i \right) b_1 = \sum_{i=1}^{n} y_i$$

$$(2) \quad \left(\sum_{i=1}^{n} x_i \right) a + \left(\sum_{i=1}^{n} x_i^2 \right) b_1 = \sum_{i=1}^{n} x_i y_i$$

TABLE 23.1

Data on Variables for Simple Regression Analysis

City	Expenditure on Recycling (y)	Population (x)
1	25	65
2	33	70
3	39	67
4	35	55
5	45	68

For the data given above with $n = 5$,

$$\sum_{i=1}^{n} x_i = 325$$

$$\sum_{i=1}^{n} x_i^2 = 21263$$

$$\sum_{i=1}^{n} y_i = 177$$

$$\sum_{i=1}^{n} x_i y_i = 11533$$

The normal equations can be expressed as

$$5(a) + (325)b = 177$$

$$325(a) + (21263)b = 11533$$

and in matrix form as

$$\begin{pmatrix} n & \sum x_i \\ \sum x_i & \sum x_i^2 \end{pmatrix} \begin{pmatrix} a \\ b \end{pmatrix} = \begin{pmatrix} \sum y_i \\ \sum x_i y_i \end{pmatrix} \text{ or } \begin{pmatrix} 5 & 325 \\ 325 & 21263 \end{pmatrix} \begin{pmatrix} a \\ b \end{pmatrix} = \begin{pmatrix} 177 \\ 11533 \end{pmatrix}$$

Now, inverse the above equations using the same principle used in matrix inversion. The inverse of A where $|A| = 5(21263) - 325(325) = 690$. The cofactor matrix of A is

$$C\begin{pmatrix} 21263 & -325 \\ -325 & 5 \end{pmatrix}$$

and Adj A = C′ = $\begin{pmatrix} 21263 & -325 \\ -325 & 5 \end{pmatrix}$

Thus A^{-1} = 1/690 $\begin{pmatrix} 21263 & -325 \\ -325 & 5 \end{pmatrix} = \begin{pmatrix} 21263/690 & -325/690 \\ -325/690 & 5/690 \end{pmatrix}$

Multiplying the matrices we get

$$\begin{pmatrix} 21263/690 & -325/690 \\ -325/690 & 5/690 \end{pmatrix} \cdot \begin{pmatrix} 177 \\ 11533 \end{pmatrix} = \begin{pmatrix} 22.2116 \\ 0.2029 \end{pmatrix}$$

where $a = 22.2116$ and $b = 0.2029$.

Plot the graph by solving the regression equation for all the five cases.

23.10 EIGENVALUES AND EIGENVECTORS IN A MATRIX EQUATION

A square matrix has an eigenvalue and an eigenvector. The eigenvalue (λ) of a matrix A can be any number derived by solving the characteristic or determinantal equation in which $|A - \lambda I| = 0$ (Namboodiri, 1984). Consider matrix A expressed as

$$A = \begin{pmatrix} 7 & 2 \\ 2 & 1 \end{pmatrix}$$

$$|A - \lambda I| = \left| \begin{pmatrix} 7 & 2 \\ 2 & 1 \end{pmatrix} - \lambda \begin{pmatrix} 1 & 0 \\ 0 & 1 \end{pmatrix} \right| = \begin{vmatrix} 7 - \lambda & 2 \\ 2 & 1 - \lambda \end{vmatrix}$$

The characteristic equation is

$$\begin{vmatrix} 7 - \lambda & 2 \\ 2 & 1 - \lambda \end{vmatrix} = 0$$

When the above equation is multiplied, it becomes

$$(7 - \lambda)(1 - \lambda) - (2)(3) = 0$$

which is the same as

$$\lambda^2 - (8)(\lambda) + 3 = 0$$

Solve the above equation using the quadratic equation's principle.

$$\lambda = 1/2 \left[8 \pm \sqrt{\{(8)^2 - 4(3)\}} \right]$$
$$= 1/2[(8 \pm 7.2)]$$
$$= 7.6, 0.4$$

The eigenvalues (λ_1 and λ_2) obtained are 7.6 and 0.4. Associated with the eigenvalues are the eigenvectors. The eigenvector for each eigenvalue can be determined using the following equation (Hammer, 1971).

$(A - \lambda_1 I)v_1 = 0$ where 0 is a null vector
Thus, $Av_1 - \lambda_1 I v_1 = 0$
Therefore, $Av_1 = \lambda_1 v_1$
Apply the same equation to find the eigenvector associated with the eigenvalue of λ_2.
$(A - \lambda_2 I)v_2 = 0$ where 0 is a null vector
Thus, $Av_2 - \lambda_2 I v_2 = 0$
Therefore, $Av_2 = \lambda_2 v_2$
From the above equation, when $\lambda_1 = 7.6$

$$A - \lambda_1 I = \begin{pmatrix} 7 - 7.6 & 2 \\ 2 & 1 - 7.6 \end{pmatrix} \begin{pmatrix} v_1 \\ v_2 \end{pmatrix} = \begin{pmatrix} 0 \\ 0 \end{pmatrix}$$
$$-0.6v_1 + 2v_2 = 0$$
$$v_1/v_2 = 2/0.6$$

From the above equation when $\lambda_2 = 0.4$

$$A - \lambda_2 I = \begin{pmatrix} (7 - 0.4) & 2 \\ 2 & (1 - 0.4) \end{pmatrix} \begin{pmatrix} v_1 \\ v_2 \end{pmatrix} = \begin{pmatrix} 0 \\ 0 \end{pmatrix}$$

Now solve for v_{12} and v_{22}

$$2v_1 + 0.6v_2 = 0$$
$$v_1/v_2 = -0.6/2$$

Now the eigenvector matrix can be written as $\begin{pmatrix} 2 & -0.6 \\ 0.6 & 1 \end{pmatrix}$

Normalize the matrix of eigenvectors to keep the same scale (Hammer, 1971, p. 150). This can be done by dividing the numbers in each row by the square root of the sum of squares of numbers in each column. See example,

$$\begin{pmatrix} \dfrac{2}{\sqrt{[(2)^2 + (0.6)^2]}} & \dfrac{-0.6}{\sqrt{[(0.6)^2 + (1)^2]}} \\ \dfrac{0.6}{\sqrt{[(2)^2 + (0.6)^2]}} & \dfrac{0.2}{\sqrt{[(0.6)^2 + (1)^2]}} \end{pmatrix}$$

The matrix of eigenvector $= \begin{pmatrix} 0.96 & -0.28 \\ 0.28 & 0.96 \end{pmatrix}$

From the above matrix, the two eigenvector values are 0.96 and 0.28.

23.11 DETERMINING PRINCIPAL COMPONENTS USING EIGENVECTORS

Principal component analysis is a multivariate technique used for examination of relationships among several quantitative variables. It involves linear combinations of data, which is followed by calculation of principal components. Usually the principal components (p) are computed using as weights the elements of the eigenvectors of the matrix of sum of squares and products, also known as the covariance matrix. In such calculations, the eigenvectors are taken in their unit norm, that is, the sum of squares of elements of equal unity (Namboodiri, 1984).

Consider the test scores of five applicants in two exams (Table 23.2). The given data is deviations from the means. In order to represent the data in a matrix form, first calculate the sum of squares for each category and then add up the product of the two categories.

The sum of the two squares and the sum of the product of the two categories A and B can be expressed in the matrix form as

$$= 1/5 \begin{pmatrix} 50 & 20 \\ 20 & 10 \end{pmatrix}$$

$$= \begin{pmatrix} 10 & 4 \\ 4 & 2 \end{pmatrix}$$

To obtain the eigenvalues of the above matrix, subtract $-\lambda$ from the two sums of squares to get the characteristic equation, as seen below:

$$B = \begin{pmatrix} 10 - \lambda & 4 \\ 4 & 2 - \lambda \end{pmatrix}$$

TABLE 23.2

Test Scores of Applicants Taking Exam

Applicant	Test A	Squares of Test A	Test B	Squares of Test B	Product of Test A and B
1	−3.0	9.0	−2.0	4.0	6.0
2	−4.0	16.0	−1.0	1.0	4.0
3	0.0	0.0	0.0	0.0	0.0
4	4.0	16.0	1.0	1.0	4.0
5	3.0	9.0	2.0	4.0	6.0
Total		50.00		10.00	20.00

or

$$(10 - \lambda)(2 - \lambda) - (4)(4)$$

Multiplying the above numbers yields the following characteristic equation:

$$\lambda_2 - 12\lambda + 4 = 0$$

Solve the characteristic equation using the quadratic equation's principle

$$\lambda = 1/2 \left[12 \pm \sqrt{(12)^2 - 4(4)} \right]$$
$$= 1/2[12 \pm 11.3]$$
$$= 11.65 \text{ and } 0.35$$

The eigenvalues are 11.65 (λ_1) and 0.35 (λ_2).
Using the above eigenvalues, solve for the eigenvectors.
For the case where $\lambda_1 = 11.65$

$$A - \lambda_1 I = \begin{pmatrix} 10 - 11.65 & 4 \\ 4 & 2 - 11.65 \end{pmatrix}$$
$$= \begin{pmatrix} -1.65 & 4 \\ 4 & 9.65 \end{pmatrix} \begin{pmatrix} v_{11} \\ v_{21} \end{pmatrix} = \begin{pmatrix} 0 \\ 0 \end{pmatrix}$$

When $-1.65v_{11} + 4v_{21} = 0$

$$v_{11}/v_{21} = 4/1.65$$

For the case where $\lambda_2 = 0.35$

$$A - \lambda_2 I \begin{pmatrix} 10 - 0.35 & 4 \\ 4 & 2 - 0.35 \end{pmatrix} = \begin{pmatrix} 9.65 & 4 \\ 4 & 2 - 0.35 \end{pmatrix} \begin{pmatrix} v_{12} \\ v_{22} \end{pmatrix} = \begin{pmatrix} 0 \\ 0 \end{pmatrix}$$

when $4v_{12} + 1.65v_{22} = 0$

$$v_{12}/v_{22} = -1.65/4$$

The eigenvector matrix is $\begin{pmatrix} 4 & -1.65 \\ 1.65 & 4 \end{pmatrix}$

Normalize the matrix of eigenvectors:

$$\begin{pmatrix} \dfrac{4}{\sqrt{(4)^2 + (1.65)^2}} & \dfrac{-1.65}{\sqrt{(-1.65)^2 + (4)^2}} \\ \dfrac{-1.65}{\sqrt{(4)^2 + (1.65)^2}} & \dfrac{4}{\sqrt{(-1.65)^2 + (4)^2}} \end{pmatrix}$$

The new matrix (Y) of eigenvectors is

$$Y = \begin{pmatrix} 0.9 & -0.4 \\ 0.4 & 0.9 \end{pmatrix}$$

TABLE 23.3

Components Derived Using Matrix Algebra

Individual	First Component	Second Component
1	−0.35	−0.30
2	−0.40	−0.25
3	0	0
4	0.40	−0.07
5	0.35	0.06
Sum of squares	0.565	0.161

The eigenvectors are 0.9 and 0.4. Based on the linear combination of eigenvectors, the first applicant's test scores from test A and B can be expressed as

$$[-3.0 \ -2.0]\begin{pmatrix} 0.9 \\ 0.4 \end{pmatrix}$$

$$[-3.0 \ -2.0]\begin{pmatrix} 0.4 \\ 0.9 \end{pmatrix}$$

In order to determine the principal components, find out the two components. Multiply the deviation values from the means for tests A and B by the eigenvector values of 0.9 and 0.4 and add them up to obtain the first component values. For the second component value, repeat the same procedure using the eigenvector values of −0.4 and 0.9. Sum up the squares for both the components. See Table 23.3.

Review the sum of squares of the two principal components. It is evident from Table 23.3 that the sum of the squares of the first component is higher than that of the second. So, it can be concluded that the first principal component collectively captures much of the information in the data set. Thus, the first component can be selected as the most effective linear combination of data.

23.12   CONCLUSION

Matrix algebra can be used in both simple and complex statistical analysis of data. Its application in any type of statistical analysis, first, requires the arrangement of data in the form of a matrix. Once a matrix has been created, various mathematical functions like addition, subtraction, or multiplication can be performed. A matrix can also be transposed or inversed as required. The matrices formed can be used to test a linear hypothesis as in regression analysis or to determine the most effective linear combination of data as in principle component analysis. Thus, with a wide range of applications, knowledge of matrix algebra can be an asset to anyone doing research in any field of social science including public administration.

PROBLEMS

1. Add the matrices A and B and C and D.

$$A = \begin{pmatrix} 4 & 2 \\ 1 & 3 \end{pmatrix} + B\begin{pmatrix} 2 & 4 \\ 5 & 3 \end{pmatrix}$$

$$C = \begin{pmatrix} 4 & 0 & 2 \\ -3 & -1 & 5 \\ 2 & 7 & 6 \end{pmatrix} + D = \begin{pmatrix} -1 & 4 & 0 \\ -2 & 1 & -3 \\ -4 & -1 & 3 \end{pmatrix}$$

2. Subtract the matrix E from the matrix of M.

$$M = \begin{pmatrix} 3 & 5 \\ 4 & 1 \end{pmatrix} - E = \begin{pmatrix} 2 & 3 \\ 0 & 1 \end{pmatrix}$$

3. From the given matrix, find out the eigenvalues and eigenvectors.

$$\begin{pmatrix} 0.6 & 0.4 \\ 0.4 & 0.7 \end{pmatrix}$$

4. Using the data in the given table, perform a simple regression analysis using the principles of matrix algebra.

Case	(y)	(x)
1	30	66
2	35	67
3	40	50
4	20	58
5	15	48

5. An analyst is interested in identifying the most effective linear combination of variables through principal component analysis in his report on recidivism. From the given values presented below, select the component that captures effectively the most information.

Variables	First Component	Second Component
Duration of stay in prison	0.25	0.29
Education	0.36	0.40
Age of offender	0.25	0.05
Criminal records	0.41	0.33
Charges of misbehavior in prison	0.52	0.15

REFERENCES

Bonney, G.E. and Kissling, G.E. 1984. On the inverse of a patterned covariance matrix, *Journal of the American Statistical Association*, 79(387), 722–723.

Dowling, E.T. 1992. *Introduction to Mathematical Economics*, New York: Mcgraw Hill Inc.

Freeman, G.H. 1961. The analysis and interpretation of experimental results, *The Incorporated Statistician*, 11(1), 33–56.

Hall, J.W. and Bennett, R.D. 1985. *College Algebra with Applications*, Boston: Prindle Weber and Schmidt.

Hammer, A.G. 1971. *Elementary Matrix Algebra for Psychologists and Social Scientists*, Pergamon Press, Australia.

Horst, P. 1963. *Matrix Algebra for Social Scientists*, Holt, Rinehart & Winston, Inc., San Francisco.

Lawley, D.N. and Maxwell, A.E. 1962. Factor Analysis as a Statistical Method, *The Statistiction*, 12(3), 722–723.

Namboodiri, K. 1984. *Matrix Algebra: An Introduction*, Sage Publications, California.

Pine, C. 1992. *The Algebra Project*, Rutgers University, New Jersey.

Polasek, W. 1984. Regression diagnostics for general linear regression models, *Journal of the American Statistical Association*, 79(386), 336–340.

Schott, J.R. 1997. *Matrix Analysis for Statistics*, John Wiley & Sons, New York.

Searle, S.R. and Willett, L.S. 2001. *Matrix Algebra for Applied Economics*, John Wiley & Sons, New York.

24 Univariate Analysis

Changhwan Mo

CONTENTS

This chapter begins by introducing several tabular and graphical formats that can be used for organizing, summarizing, and presenting numerical data. After that, we briefly examine univariate measures, such as central tendency and dispersion, which deal with one variable at a time. Having collected data for analysis, we have several options for addressing them. We will investigate those options and see their aspects.

24.1 FREQUENCY DISTRIBUTION

Organizing and presenting a set of numeric information are among the first tasks in understanding a problem. As a typical situation, consider the values which represent the travel time to work of 57 employees in a large downtown office building. The times are given in minutes and each value represents an employee's average time over ten consecutive work days. The mere gathering of this data together is no small task, but it still needs further work for utilizing them as useful information. These raw numbers should be summarized in an organized way.

The easiest way to organize a set of data is to construct an array. An array is a list of data with the numerical values ordered from low to high (or high to low). Arrays are often used to help make the overall pattern of the data apparent. However, if the number of values is large, construction of the array may have to be done on a computer, and even then, the array may turn out to be so large that it is difficult to comprehend.

A more useful way to summarize a large set of data is to construct a frequency distribution. A frequency distribution is a tabular summary of a set of data that shows the frequency or number of items that fall in each of several distinctive classes. A class is an interval of values within the overall range of values spanned by the data. Then we count the number of observations that fall into each of these classes. By looking at such a frequency distribution we can readily see the overall pattern of the data.

A frequency distribution is also known as a frequency table. To construct a frequency distribution, we must do the following tasks:

1. Select the number of classes.
2. Choose the class interval or width of the classes.
3. Count the number of values in the data set that falls in each class.
4. Display the results in the form of a chart or table.

TABLE 24.1

Frequency Distribution of Commuting Time

Class (Time in Minutes)	Frequency (Persons)	Relative Frequency (Proportions)	Percentage Frequency
20–29	10	0.175	17.5
30–39	12	0.211	21.1
40–49	17	0.298	29.8
50–59	15	0.263	26.3
60–69	3	0.053	5.3
Total	57	1.00	100.0

There are no best rules for constructing frequency distributions because no one can fit all situations. Table 24.1 shows an example of frequency distribution which summarizes the travel time to work of 57 employees in an office. Its class interval is all equal ten minutes and there are five classes.

The number of observations in any class is the class frequency. The total number in all classes is the sum of individual class frequencies. We sometimes wish to present the data in a relative frequency distribution. The relative class frequencies, or proportions, are found by dividing the class frequencies by the total number of items. A percentage distribution is determined by multiplying the relative class frequencies by 100 to convert them to percentages. For example, when a class frequency is 17 and total number of frequencies is 57 as in Table 24.1, the relative frequency is 17/57, or 0.298, and the percentage frequency is 0.298 × 100, or 29.8 percent.

Frequency distributions are valuable aids for organizing and summarizing sets of data and for presenting data in such a way that the characteristics of data are shown clearly. Sometimes, however, we require information on the number of observations whose numerical value is "less than" or "more than" a given value. As you see at Table 24.2, this information is contained in the cumulative frequency distribution. We can convert a percentage distribution into a cumulative percentage distribution by adding the percentages, starting either at the top or at the bottom of the distribution.

Graphics are an effective tool to help people understand the characteristics of data, and they are beneficial for the presentation and analysis of data. The statistical graphical forms are as follows: line charts, bar charts, histograms, combination charts, and pie charts. Line charts use lines between data points to show the magnitudes of data for two variables or for one variable over time. Bar charts are used to show the sizes of data for different qualitative categories or over time. Histograms are similar to bar charts, but there is no empty space between bars. Usually the horizontal axis denotes class interval and the vertical axis shows class frequency according to each class interval. Combination charts use lines and bars, or use other charts together, to show the dimensions of two or more data values for different categories or for different times. Pie charts can be used effectively to show

TABLE 24.2

Cumulative Frequency Distribution

Time (1 min)	Percentage Frequency	Cumulative Frequency
Less than 30	17.5	17.5
Less than 40	21.1	38.6
Less than 50	29.8	68.4
Less than 60	26.3	94.7
Less than 70	5.3	100.0

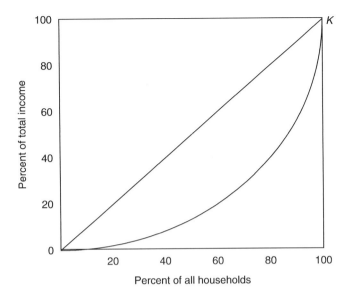

FIGURE 24.1 The Lorenz curve.

the proportions or percentages of a total quantity that correspond to several qualitative categories. It is recommended to be less than five.

In addition, we introduce a useful graphic form: the Lorenz curve. It is usually used for highlighting the extent of equality or inequality of income distribution in economics (Kohler, 1977). Consider the distribution of money income among U.S. households, including among them unattached individuals as well as families of two or more persons. We draw a square which measures the percentage of total money income received on the vertical axis and the percentage of households on the horizontal axis. According to each income level from the lowest to the highest, households are arranged from left to right (Figure 24.1).

Consider a straight line from the bottom left corner at 0 to the top right corner at K. This diagonal line means perfect equality, because it represents the position the Lorenz curve would hold if the same portion of money income went equally to each household. If all households in the country shared total income equally, it would be true that 40 percent of the households shared 40 percent of total income, that 60 percent of the households shared 60 percent of total income, and so on. In fact, the difference of income between the poor and the rich seems to become larger and larger. Thus, the line of actual inequality exists lower than that of perfect equality. The difference between actual inequality and perfect equality determines the Lorenz curve, in other words, the curved line of inequality from 0 to K.

We saw how tabular and graphical forms of presentation may be used to summarize and describe quantitative data. These techniques help us to distinguish important features of the distribution of data, but most statistical methods require numerical forms. We can get these numerical expressions through arithmetic calculations on the data, which yield descriptive measures or descriptive statistics. The basic descriptive statistics are measures of central tendency or location and measures of dispersion or scatter. The mode, median, mean, and weighted mean are presented as measures of central tendency. The range, mean deviation, variance, standard deviation, and coefficient of variation are explained as measures of dispersion.

24.2 MEASURES OF LOCATION (CENTRAL TENDENCY)

In most sets of data, we usually see that there is a particular tendency for the observed values to cluster themselves around some specific values. Central tendency refers to this phenomenon.

Some central values are likely to have characteristics of the whole data. We use these values to represent a set of data because the central values usually position the "middle" point of a distribution.

The mode is the most frequently occurring value in a set of data. The mode is generally not a useful measure of location. For example, assume that we collect the temperature data (Fahrenheit) of six winter days in New York City: 49, 7, 11, 18, 22, and 49. Although one value (49) does occur more than once, there is no guarantee that this value will in any way show the central tendency of the data set.

The median is a number that splits an ordered set of data in half. It is applied, specifically, when the values in a set of data have been arranged in a numerical order from the lowest to the highest. If there are an odd number of values in the data set, then the median (M_d) is the value in the middle position. In the case of an even number of values in the data set, it is the mean of the two values in the central positions. Consider the temperature data in New York City which have six values. When you wish to know the median of this data, it is calculated like this:

$$M_d = \frac{18 + 22}{2} = 20$$

The most common measure of central tendency is what the normal persons call an average and what the statisticians call a mean. The word "average" in life has all kinds of different meanings such as a baseball player's batting average, a student's grade point average, and a man's appearance as average. Generally the term "average" in statistics refers to the arithmetic mean. Simply, the mean of n numbers is their sum divided by n. Because it will be desirable to have a formula which is always applicable, we state it with formal expression. For a given population of N values, $X_1, X_2, X_3, \ldots, X_N$, the population mean is denoted by μ and the mean for a population of N data values is their sum divided by N, or

$$\mu = \frac{1}{N} \sum_{i=1}^{N} X_i$$

However, we often have to use sample values for estimating the mean of a larger population because of the time and cost involved in using the entire population. For instance, suppose we are interested in estimating the mean temperature of all winter days in New York City (NYC) by using the sample of six winter days, which we already utilized for calculating the mode and the median. Then we perform the same type of calculation as the mean for a population data, but we divide by the sample size n (as opposed to the population size N), and we call it sample mean which is denoted by $\overline{X}$.

$$\overline{X} = \frac{1}{n} \sum_{i-1}^{n} X_i$$

Applying the equation of sample mean to the temperature data, we find $\overline{X} = 1/6(49 + 7 + 11 + 18 + 22 + 49) = 26$. It means that the average winter temperature in NYC may be 26°, but we are not sure this sample mean can be regarded as a population mean because the sample number is only 6.

When we compute the simple arithmetic mean of a set of numbers, we assume that all the observed values are of equal importance, and we give them equal weight in our calculations. In a situation where the numbers are not equally important or not equally proportioned, we can assign each a weight that is proportional to its relative importance and calculate the weighted mean $(\overline{X}_w)$. Let $X_1, X_2, X_3, \ldots, X_N$ be a set of data values, and let $w_1, w_2, w_3, \ldots, w_N$ be the weights assigned to them. The weighted mean is calculated by dividing the sum of the multiplication of the values and their weights by the sum of the weights:

$$\overline{X}_{\text{w}} = \frac{\sum X_i w_i}{\sum w_i}$$

For example, the average salaries of elementary school teachers in Oregon and Alaska were $23,000 and $20,000, and there were 1000 and 200 elementary school teachers in these states. When we want to find the average salary of elementary school teachers in these two states, we should calculate a weighted mean because there are not equally many school teachers in the two states. The solution is as follows:

$$\overline{X}_{\text{w}} = \frac{(23,000)(1,000) + (20,000)(200)}{1,000 + 200} = 22,500$$

Thus, the average salary of elementary school teachers in these two states is $22,500.

24.3   MEASURE OF DISPERSION

When we wish to know about the variation or scatter among the values, we calculate a measure of dispersion. Suppose that in a hospital each patient's pulse rate is taken four times a day, and that on a certain day, the records of two patients show the same mean of pulse rates. Patient A's pulse rate is quite stable, whereas that of patient B varies widely. Patient A's records show 71, 73, 73, and 75, whereas those of patient B are 48, 70, 81, and 93. When we calculate the means of both patients' rates, they are the same (73). Although they have the same mean of pulse rates, it does not necessarily mean that they are identical in their health condition. Thus, a doctor might pay more attention to patient B than patient A. This example illustrates the importance of measuring dispersion in descriptive statistics. In this section, we will deal with four measures of variation: range, mean deviation, variance, and standard deviation.

The range is the difference between the largest and smallest values in the data, or

$$\text{Range} = X_{\text{Largest}} - X_{\text{Smallest}}$$

When we apply the formula of range, we can see that the temperature data set of NYC has a range of $49 - 7 = 42$. Usually, it is not a satisfactory measure of variation for several reasons. First, its calculation uses only two of the observed values regardless of the number of observations available. In this sense, the range is inefficient in that it "wastes" or "ignores" data. Second, the range is sensitive to sample size. As the number of observations is increased, the range generally tends to become larger. Third, the range may vary widely. It is the least stable of our measures of dispersion for all but the smallest sample sizes.

The mean deviation measures variation using distances between each data point and the population mean. When a data set is tightly clustered around the mean, distances will be small. When the data set is spread out widely, these distances will be large. When we have a population of N number, $X_1, X_2, X_3, \ldots, X_N$, whose mean is μ, then we might be tempted to think that the average, or mean, of these distances should provide a good measure of dispersion. If we just add the distances without addressing the fact that about half of the distances will be positive and half will be negative, we will always get one answer: zero. By eliminating the signs of these distances, we can solve this problem in two ways: first, we may simply ignore the signs by taking the absolute value, or we may square the distances. If we ignore the signs of the distances $(X_i - \mu)$, we have the mean deviation:

$$\text{Mean deviation} = \frac{1}{N} \sum_{i=1}^{N} |X_i - \mu|$$

In the above formula, $|X_i - \mu|$ is the absolute value of $X_i - \mu$, that is, just $X_i - \mu$ with the sign converted to $+$ (positive) if it happens to be $-$ (negative). However, the mean deviation does not have the mathematical properties because of artificially ignoring the signs of the distances. Thus, we are looking for a better procedure to eliminate the sign on the deviation around the mean by squaring the distances of each $X_i - \mu$.

Suppose that we use the square of the deviations instead of the absolute value as a measure of deviation. In the squaring process the negative signs will disappear; hence, the sum of the squares of the deviations from the mean will always be a positive number. Although the sum of squares provides a measure of dispersion, it is usually more convenient to use the mean of the squared deviations as a dispersion measure. This mean of squared deviations for population data is called the population variance (σ^2).

$$\sigma^2 = \frac{1}{N} \sum_{i=1}^{N} (X_i - \mu)^2$$

The variance for a population of N data values, X_1, X_2, $X_3, \ldots, X_N$, is the sum of the squared deviations for the values from their mean μ divided by N.

The population standard deviation σ of the numbers in a population of size N is the square root of the variance. The standard deviation for a population of N data values, X_1, X_2, $X_3, \ldots, X_N$, is the square root of the population variance, or

$$\sigma = \sqrt{\frac{1}{N} \sum_{i=1}^{N} (X_i - \mu)^2}$$

In Section 24.2, we made a distinction between μ, the mean of population, and $\overline{X}$, the mean of sample. Although the methods for calculating these means are shown to be the same, the different notations used to distinguish whether our data set was a population or a sample selected to represent a population.

The same type of symbol distinction is made between the population standard deviation σ and the sample standard deviation s. In addition, we must change the formula to divide by degrees of freedom ($n - 1$) for the sample data rather than the population size (N). When dealing with a sample of size n, we lose a degree of freedom for each parameter in the formula because we must estimate from sample data. If our data set is a sample and we wish to estimate a sample variance s^2, we can find it after the sample mean $\overline{X}$ is calculated at first. The variance for a sample of n data values, X_1, $X_2, \ldots, X_n$, is the sum of the squared deviations for the values from their mean $\overline{X}$ divided by the degrees of freedom, $n - 1$, or

$$s^2 = \frac{1}{n-1} \sum (X_i - \overline{X})^2$$

Applying this formula to the temperature data set of NYC again, we can calculate the sample variance because we already know the sample mean ($\overline{X}$) is 26:

$$s^2 = \frac{1}{6-1} \left\{ (49 - 26)^2 + (7 - 26)^2 + (11 - 26)^2 + (18 - 26)^2 + (22 - 26)^2 + (49 - 26)^2 \right\}$$
$$= 1724/5 = 344.8$$

It means that 344.8 is an average squared distance of any observation in the data set from the mean.

The standard deviation is always the square root of the variance. Thus, we define the sample standard deviation s as the square root of the sample variance, or

$$s = \sqrt{\frac{1}{n-1} \sum (X_i - \overline{X})^2}$$

When we apply this equation to the temperature data, we find $s = \sqrt{344.8} = 18.57$. It means that an average distance from the mean is 18.57.

There are only two differences between the formulas for the population and sample standard deviation. First, in the equation of population standard deviation, we use the mean μ, whereas in the equation of sample standard deviation, we use $\overline{X}$. Second, in the population equation for σ we divide the sum of squared deviations by N, but in the sample equation we divide it by $n-1$. Why do we have to use $n-1$ instead of n? In addition to the formal rationale of adjusting for degrees of freedom lost by estimating μ with $\overline{X}$, we can intuitively say that the spread of values in a sample will typically be less than the spread in the population (Watson et al., 1993). In the case of estimating the population standard deviation by using a sample data set, it is desirable to adjust our calculations to complement the smaller range in the sample. In other words, the sample standard deviation s^2 becomes a better estimator of the population variance σ^2 when we use $n-1$ rather than n. There are n squared deviations from the mean in a sample of n data values, but only $n-1$ of the deviations are free because of the limit that the sum of the deviations from the mean is 0 as explained in the earlier discussion of the mean deviation. Additionally, we generally use s as the estimator of σ because the standard deviation is the square root of the variance.

What does the standard deviation tell us? A data set with a large standard deviation has much dispersion with values widely scattered around its mean, and a data set with a small standard deviation has little dispersion with the values tightly clustered around its mean. If the bar chart for a set of data values is shaped like a bell or, in other words, shows normal distribution, we can say that

1. About 68 percent of the values in the population will lie within ± 1 standard deviation from the mean.
2. About 95 percent of the values will fall within ± 2 standard deviations from the mean, which means that about 95 percent of values will be in an interval ranging from 2 standard deviations below the mean to 2 standard deviations above the mean.
3. About 99 percent of the values will lie within ± 3 standard deviations from the mean.

For instance, when a stock traded on the New York Stock Exchange has a mean price of $50 and a standard deviation of $3 for one year, we are sure that 95 percent of the prices lies between $44 and $56 because this interval is $\mu \pm 2\sigma$. This conclusion is based on an assumption that the distribution of prices is approximately symmetrical.

How can we select measures of central tendency and dispersion? If the distribution is equally symmetric, then the $\overline{X}$, mode (M_o), and M_d will all coincide. When the distribution is not symmetric or is skewed, the mean, median, and mode will not match together. It is not unusual that some frequency distributions are skewed to the left or to the right. The mean is sensitive to outliers, a few extreme values, but outliers typically have little or no effect on the median. To the temperature data set of NYC, if we add one extreme value (89), the new data set is 49, 7, 11, 18, 22, 49, and 89. By using it, when we calculate the median and the mean, they are 22 and 35, respectively. As a result of adding an outlier, the mean has affected a lot from 26 to 35, whereas the median does not change so much from 20 to 22. Therefore, when the data is skewed or contains extreme values, we can say that the median provides a better measure of central tendency.

In the case of dispersion measures, the range is particularly sensitive to outliers. Due to mathematical properties possessed by the variance and standard deviation, we more often use them to describe the dispersion in a set of data values.

A descriptive statistic that combines the standard deviation and the mean is called the coefficient of variation. The coefficient of variation (CV) is useful for comparing between two number sets of rather different magnitudes. Its formulas are as follows:

$$CV = \left(\frac{\sigma}{\mu}\right) \times 100 \quad \mu > 0 \text{ [for a population]}$$

$$CV = \left(\frac{s}{\overline{X}}\right) \times 100 \quad s > 0 \text{ [for a sample]}$$

Although the standard deviation depends on the original units of measurement, CV is a unitless figure that expresses the standard deviation as a percentage of the mean (Freund and Simon, 1995). For instance, the lengths of certain distances may have a standard deviation of 1000 m or 1 km, which is the same, but neither value really tells us whether it reflects a great deal of variation or very little variation. Let's see another example for further understanding. At a hospital, patient A's blood pressure, measured daily over several weeks, averaged 199 with a standard deviation of 12.7, whereas that of patient B averaged 110 with a standard deviation of 9.5. When we want to find which patient's blood pressure is relatively more consistent, we calculate the coefficient of variation because their means are different.

$$CV_A = \frac{12.7}{199} \times 100 = 6.38 \quad CV_B = \frac{9.5}{110} \times 100 = 8.6$$

At first glance, it appears that patient B's blood pressure is relatively consistent because its standard deviation is smaller than that of patient A. When we compare CV_A and CV_B, however, we can conclude that patient A's blood pressure is relatively more consistent than that of patient B because CV_A is smaller than CV_B.

24.4 CONCLUSION

The univariate measures refer to measures of central tendency and dispersion. When we summarize data by using univariate analysis, it should be noted that it has a disadvantage of losing critical information. For minimizing the loss of information, analysts usually use different univariate measures together. As shown in Table 24.3, we can generally say that these descriptive statistics are best fit to different levels of data. However, it does not necessarily mean that only these different levels of data are applicable to specified descriptive statistics.

In addition, univariate analysis is important because multivariate analysis, which examines several variables such as factor analysis and multiple regression, starts from the basic logic of these descriptive statistics.

TABLE 24.3
Measures of Descriptive Statistics and Level of Data

Measures of Central Tendency	Measures of Dispersion	Minimum Level of Data Required
$\mu, \overline{X}$	σ^2, σ, s, s^2	Interval/ratio
M_d	Range	Ordinal
M_o	Frequency distribution	Nominal

EXERCISES

Please calculate the answers for these questions, show your calculations, and interpret your results properly.

1. A police officer in New York City (NYC) collects data from a five-period sample about the mean arrests per police officer in 2006: 10, 7, 5, 13, 15. Calculate (a) mean and (b) standard deviation.

2. In recent years, the average salaries of elementary school teachers in NYC, United States and in Seoul, South Korea were $40,500 and $36,000 respectively. If there were 500 and 700 teachers in each city, respectively, what is the average salary of all the elementary school teachers in the two cities?

3. Assume we collect temperature data, Fahrenheit, during ten winter days in Seoul, South Korea: 27, 17, 21, 21, 7, 28, 19, 19, 21, 80. (a) Calculate mean, median, and mode. (b) Which one is a better measure of central tendency? Why?

REFERENCES

Freund, J.E. and Simon, G.A. 1995. *Statistics: A First Course*. 6th Ed. Englewood Cliffs, New Jersey: Prentice-Hall.

Kohler, H. 1977. *Scarcity and Freedom: An Introduction to Economics*. Lexington, Massachussetts: Heath and Company.

Watson, C.J., Billingsley, P., Croft, D.J., and Huntsberger, D.V. 1993. *Statistics for Management and Economics*. 5th Ed. Boston, Massachussetts: Allyn and Bacon.

25 Statistics for Nominal and Ordinal Data

Michael Margolis

CONTENTS

25.1 OVERVIEW

Despite the growth of sophisticated techniques for multivariate analysis, contingency tables remain a common means for reporting results in both the popular and professional literature. There is good reason for this: contingency tables give readable overviews of the data, and they also illuminate differences among nominal categories or trends across ordinal categories. Furthermore, through cross-tabulation within categories of control variables, they can be used to characterize multivariate relationships.

    This chapter takes the perspective that the principal purpose for using these tables should be to enhance or otherwise clarify information about relationships among variables of interest. Testing for the statistical significance of these relationships is not an end in itself. Rather, public administrators and policy analysts should supplement such tests with measures that help explain political events, public policies, or other political phenomena of concern to themselves, their clientele, elected officials, or the citizenry in general. Testing whether or not statistically significant relationships exist among nominal or ordinal variables can provide useful information, but the samples of data that are tested often fail to satisfy the formal assumptions required for applying the statistical tests. Moreover, even when relationships prove to be statistically significant, they may be substantively insignificant. In many cases, therefore, using measures of association to characterize and compare the nature and strength of bivariate relationships may prove more fruitful than employing statistical tests of significance.

The discussion covers statistical measures of association commonly used to characterize relationships among nominal and ordinal variables in contingency tables. It also includes Kendall's Tau-*A* and Spearman's Rho, two rank order statistics frequently used to characterize bivariate relationships among ordinal variables that have few or no ties in rank. The sections that follow, present first nominal and then ordinal measures of association. Nominal measures presented include, Percentage difference, Chi-square, Contingency coefficient, Phi, Cramer's *V*, Lambda, and Goodman–Kruskal Tau. Ordinal measures include Tau-*A*, Tau-*B*, Tau-*C*, Gamma, Somer's *D*, Wilson's *E*, and Spearman's Rho.

We will discuss each measure in the context of the types of questions it seems most suitable to answer. In addition, we will discuss its null and perfect conditions and will attempt to give readers both a formal basis and a more intuitive feel for interpreting the range of values each measure can assume. The final sections will introduce multivariate considerations, review the main advantages and disadvantages of the measures discussed, and make some suggestions for their application.

25.2 NOMINAL MEASURES OF ASSOCIATION

25.2.1 INTRODUCTION

Nominal variables are divided into mutually exclusive and exhaustive categories for purposes of measurement. The categories have no natural order. A city, for example, can be divided into North, South, East, and West sides, and every residence in the city can be reliably placed in one and only one of the four categories. But absent some theory or hypothesis that imposes a direction: e.g., the West and South sides have larger proportions of owner-occupied residences than do the North and East sides; the order in which the four categories are presented makes no difference.

It also follows that the magnitude of any desirable nominal measure of association will be unaffected by the way the categories are ordered. Indeed, as we shall demonstrate, when a theory or hypothesis imposes order or direction on nominal variables, it is usually more appropriate to use ordinal rather than nominal measures of association to characterize their association.

The measures discussed below are used to examine bivariate associations. By examining bivariate relationships within categories of control variables, however, they can also be used to characterize multivariate relationships.

25.2.2 PERCENTAGE DIFFERENCE

There are many ways to describe data. A good general rule is to start simply. For any variable of interest, answering the question, "What have we here?" should normally precede examining the relationship of that variable with any other variables. (See Kaplan, 1964; also see Chapters of this volume for a discussion of levels of measurement and univariate descriptive measures.) After researchers have familiarized themselves with the univariate distributions of nominal or ordinal variables of interest, they normally begin analyzing the data by comparing the proportions (percentages) of observations that fall into various categories.

There are also many ways to display data. Although we will focus on bivariate tables here, standard statistical programs, such as SPSS and Excel, feature excellent graphics that can be used to display bivariate relationships among nominal and ordinal variables (see Pollock, 2005, chapters 3 and 5; Ritchey, 2000, chapter 3). However, researchers decide to display their data on the relationships among two or more nominal or ordinal variables, they should first consider the nature of the underlying hypothesized relationship.

For bivariate relationships, a primary consideration is whether one or more variables are hypothesized as independent (possible causes) and one or more as dependent variables (possible

TABLE 25.1
Type of Residence by Side of Town (Factitious Raw Data)

	West	East	North	South	Total
Owner-occupied	142	73	145	150	510
Rental	68	147	120	55	390
Institution	15	30	35	20	100
Total	225	250	300	225	1000

consequences) or whether the variables are simply expected to have an association of an (as yet) unspecified causal nature. When the former condition holds, it normally makes the most sense to display and then compare percentages across the categories of the independent variable. When the latter condition holds, analysts may choose to display and compare percentages across the categories of either or both row and column variables or to display and compare categories as proportions of the entire number of cases in the set of data.

Consider, for instance, the West-East-North-South side variable mentioned above. Suppose we took a random sample of 1000 residences stratified to replicate the proportion of residences on each side of town and that we interviewed a knowledgeable adult at each residence. If we asked interviewees whether the dwelling unit was owner-occupied, rented, or an institutional residence, such as a halfway house, senior citizen home, or residential treatment center, a simple cross-tabulation of the responses by side of town might produce the results shown in Table 25.1.

We hypothesized that the West and South sides would have larger proportions of owner-occupied residences than would the North and East sides. The univariate marginal (total) distributions show that "owner-occupied" is the modal row category and that the East and North sides have more residences than do the West and South sides. The 73 owner-occupied residences on the East side seem below average, but what about the 145 owner-occupied residences on the North side? The unequal number of cases in the cells and marginal totals hampers direct comparisons. The data in the table may support the hypothesis, but it is difficult to tell just from examining the raw number of cases. If we consider the column variable to be the predictor (independent variable) here, however, then calculating percentages down the columns, the table can be rewritten as Table 25.2.

By comparing the percentages of owner-occupied residences on the West and South sides against those on the East and North it becomes abundantly clear that the data do indeed indicate that the former have greater proportions of owner-occupied residences than do the latter. Moreover, by taking

TABLE 25.2
Type of Residence by Side of Town (Percentages)[a]

	West	East	North	South	Total (Percentage)
Owner-occupied (percentage)	63.1	29.2	48.3	66.7	51.0
Rental	30.2	58.8	40.0	24.4	39.0
Institution	6.7	12.0	11.7	8.8	10.0
Total percentage (N)	100.0 (225)	100.0 (250)	100.0 (300)	99.9 (225)	100.0 (1000)

[a] Figures are presented to tenths of percent for illustrative purposes in the discussion below. Given 95 percent confidence intervals of as much as ±3 percent for estimates of proportions based on a simple random sample of 1000, a researcher would ordinarily round back to whole percentages when presenting the data in a report.

Source: Table 25.1.

TABLE 25.3
Type of Residence by Sides of Town: Combined Percentages

	West and South	North and East	Total Percentage
Owner-occupied (percentage)	64.9	39.6	51.0
Not Owner-occupied (percentage)	35.1	60.4	49.0
Total percentage (N)	100.0 (450)	100.0 (550)	100.0 (1000)

Source: Table 25.2.

the percentage differences across rows, we can make statements like "Approximately two-thirds of South side residences are owner occupied. This proportion (66.7 percent) exceeds the proportion on the East side (29.2 percent) by nearly 38 percentage points." We also observe that not only are rentals the modal residence for East side (58.8 percent), in contrast to all other regions of the city, but that this proportion exceeds the city average (39.0 percent) by nearly 20 percentage points.

Depending upon the principal concerns of our research, we might choose to collapse together some of the rows and columns of the table. For instance, as our original hypothesis suggested that the West and South sides have larger proportions of owner-occupied residences than do the North and East sides we might combine the first and fourth and then the second and third columns of Table 25.2 to produce a table with two columns and three rows that simply contrasts residential patterns on the West and South sides with those on the North and East.[1] And as the hypothesis distinguished only between owner-occupied and other residences, we might further collapse the table by combining the second and third rows as shown in Table 25.3.

The data in Table 25.3 highlights nearly a 25 percent difference between the proportion of owner-occupied dwellings on the West and South sides in comparison to owner-occupied dwellings on the North and East sides. In addition, the West and South sides have 14 percent more owner-occupied dwellings than the average of 51 percent for the city, although the North and East sides have over 11 percent less than the average.

Overall, the data illustrates how the percentage differences appear to support the hypothesis that the West and South sides have proportionately more owner-occupied dwellings than do the North and East sides. The proportions of owner-occupied dwellings seem similar on the West and South sides, and these proportions contrast sharply with those on the North and East sides. The difference between the proportion of owners on the West and South sides (64.9 percent combined) from the East side alone (29.2 percent) seems especially stark: over 35 percentage points. Indeed, the proportion of owner-occupied dwellings on the North side (48.3 percent) is most likely closer to the proportions on the West and South sides than it is to the proportion on East side.

25.2.3 NOMINAL MEASURES BASED ON CHI-SQUARE

Even though analysts can make good use of percentage differences to highlight or otherwise contrast patterns of relationships among two (or more) nominal variables in a contingency table, the descriptions can become prolix. This becomes more apparent as the number of cells in a table or the number of variables under consideration increases. A two by two table has six possible percentage comparisons that can be made among its cells (though some will be redundant) plus up to eight additional comparisons that can be made between cells and their row or column marginal totals. For a three by three table the number of cell comparisons jumps to 36 and 18, respectively. Introducing a third (control) variable increases the number of percentage difference comparisons as many times as the control variable has categories. For example, splitting the data in Table 25.3 to control for dwelling units with above and below the town's median household income would double the number of possible percentage differences; controlling the same data for number of children in household—none, one or two, more than two—would treble the number of possible percentage difference comparisons. Clearly, meaningful statistics that summarize patterns of data in a table would save analysts and their readers both time and space.

Statistics that summarize patterns among nominal variables in a contingency table conventionally range between 0 and 1. Zero represents a null relationship (no association) and one represents a perfect one. The most common null condition for "no association" between two variables is statistical independence. Under this condition, we can determine the expected values for each cell (i,j):

$$\text{Expected}(i,j) = [\text{total for row}(i) \times \text{total for column}(j)]/N \qquad (25.1)$$

where N is the total number of cases in the table.

The familiar chi-square statistic for testing the null hypothesis of statistical independence is based upon the comparison of the expected number of cases in each cell of an r by k table with the actual number observed. Specifically,

$$\text{Chi-square} = \sum [\text{observed}(i,j) - \text{expected}(i,j)]^2/\text{expected}(i,j) \quad \text{for } i = 1 \text{ to } r; j = 1 \text{ to } k.$$
$$(25.2)$$

where
   r is the number of rows
   k is the number of columns

As this statistic's distribution approximates the chi-square distribution when the row and column variables are independent, values for chi-square that indicate a significant deviation from that distribution allow us to reject the null hypothesis of no association. Although a chi-square of 0 indicates that the data support the null hypothesis of statistical independence, the chi-square statistic itself can range to large positive numbers. Thus, it fails to satisfy the conventional criterion of having 1 stand for a perfect relationship between two variables in a contingency table. Chi-square indicates the presence of a relationship, but not its strength. Indeed, if one doubles the cases in each cell of a table, the chi-square statistic will double, even though the proportion of cases in each cell, and hence the percentage differences among cells, will not change at all.

Statisticians have developed several measures of association that adjust for these deficiencies but still retain the familiar chi-square formula. These include[2]

$$\text{Phi} = \sqrt{\text{Chi-square}/N} \qquad (25.3)$$

Pearson's contingency coefficient:

$$C = \sqrt{\text{Chi-square}/(\text{Chi-square} + N)} \qquad (25.4)$$

$$\text{and Cramer's V} = \sqrt{\text{Phi}^2/(\text{min} - 1)} \qquad (25.5)$$

where $\text{min} = r$ or k, whichever is smaller.[3]

Each of these statistics, like chi-square itself, has a value of 0 when the two variables it describes are statistically independent. Using the formulas given above readers can verify that Tables 25.1 through 25.3 generate the statistics shown in Table 25.4.

The statistics show several desirable characteristics. They normally vary between 0 and 1, and as each is based on chi-square, the probability that its value is different from 0 has the same level of statistical significance as chi-square. Their magnitudes remain relatively stable when data presented in a larger table (e.g., four by three) is compressed into a smaller (e.g., two by two) table. Moreover, they are unaffected by proportionate increases or diminution of the number of

TABLE 25.4

Comparing Statistical Measures

	Tables 25.1 and 25.2	Table 25.3
Chi-square	87.5[a]	63.2[a]
Phi	0.296	0.251
Pearson's C	0.284	0.244
Cramer's V	0.209	0.251

[a] $p < 0.001$.

cases in the cells of the table. If we double the cases in the cells of Tables 25.1 through 25.3, only the chi-squares double to 175.0 and 126.4, respectively. The other statistics remain unchanged. Finally, as we would expect of nominal level measures, changing the order of the rows or columns does not affect their values.

Unfortunately, these chi-square-based statistics also have some undesirable characteristics. In tables with more than two rows or columns the value of Phi can exceed 1 for strong relationships. Conversely, regardless of the strength of relationship between any two variables, C can never reach a maximum value of 1. Its maximum value changes from 0.707 for a two by two table to values that approach (but never reach) 1 as the number of rows and columns increases. Only V always remains within the 0–1 range and can attain a value of 1 for tables where $r \neq k$. But for all the statistics, including V, no simple interpretations exist for most magnitudes in their ranges.

In short, the most that can be said about the data in Tables 25.1 through 25.3 is that owner-occupied dwelling units are not distributed proportionately across town. The West and South sides have disproportionately more units, the North has just under the expected average and the East side has disproportionately fewer units. The probability that a full census of housing would reveal no relationship between side of town and owner-occupation of dwelling units is less than one in a thousand. The strength of association between the types of dwelling units occupied and side of town is shows a range of 0.209–0.251 as measured by Cramer's V. Although this is low in the possible range of values $0 \leq V \leq 1$, its strength must be compared relative to the strength of other nominal relationships.[4] Finally, one can compare the expected to the actual values to discern the substantive content of the cells that make the largest contributions to the statistics. For example, in Table 25.5, West, East, and South Owner-occupied, and East and South Rental, show the largest deviations from expected values.

25.2.4 NOMINAL MEASURES OF PROPORTION REDUCTION OF ERROR

Because of the difficulty of interpreting the magnitude of chi-square-based measures, some analysts recommend using statistical measures of association that indicate proportion reduction of error (PRE).

TABLE 25.5

Type of Residence by Side of Town (Raw Data and Expected Values)

	West	East	North	South	Total
Owner-occupied	142	73	145	150	510
(Expected)	(114.75)	(127.5)	(153)	(114.75)	
Rental	68	147	120	55	390
(Expected)	(87.75)	(97.5)	(117)	(87.75)	
Institution	15	30	35	20	100
(Expected)	(22.5)	(25)	(30)	(22.5)	
Total	225	250	300	225	1000

For strength of association among nominal variables these measures again run between 0 and 1, but in this case, their magnitude indicates an easily interpretable improvement in predicting a case's category on a dependent variable based on new information about the case's category for an independent variable.

Two of the most common PRE measures for nominal variables are Lambda and Goodman–Kruskal Tau. Unlike the chi-square measures, each has a symmetric and asymmetric form, the latter in each case being the more easily interpretable. Each of the asymmetric measures has a guessing rule based on the univariate distribution of the dependent variable. The measure's value represents the improvement or proportion reduction of error in making new guesses when information about the case's value on the independent variable is made known. Both Lambda and Tau usually take on different values depending upon which of the two variables under consideration is dependent. When no choice can be made regarding the causal order of the variables, the symmetric forms of the measures are used. The symmetric forms can be interpreted as a weighted average of the asymmetric measures.

Lambda's asymmetric forms are conceptually the simplest. They begin by counting up the number of errors we make if we guess the modal category on the dependent variable. We then compare these errors with the number of errors we make using information about the category (column or row) of the independent variable into which each case falls. The statistical value represents the improvement $0 \leq \text{Lambda} \leq 1$ (proportion reduction of error) of the second set of predictions over the first. The formulas are

$$\text{Lambda for columns independent} = 1 - [N - \sum \text{largest cell in column}(j)] / [N - (\text{number of cases in largest row})] \quad (25.6)$$

where

$r = $ number of rows
$k = $ number of columns
$N = $ number of cases in the table
$j = 1, 2, \ldots, k$

$$\text{Lambda for rows independent} = 1 - [N - \sum \text{largest cell in row}(i)] / [N - (\text{number of cases in largest column}] \quad (25.7)$$

where

$r = $ number of rows
$k = $ number of columns
$N = $ number of cases in the table
$i = 1, 2, \ldots, r$

Consider again the data in Table 25.1. If we choose "Side of Town" as the independent variable, then "Owner-occupied" becomes the modal category on the dependent variable, "Type of Residence." If we guess this category every time for the dependent variable, we will make 510 correct predictions and 490 errors. The 490 errors equal $[N - 510]$, i.e., $[N - $ number of cases in largest row] in Equation 25.6.

Now suppose someone tells us the side of town of each dwelling unit before we guess. For West, North, and South we will still guess "Owner-occupied," the modal cell category for each of these columns. We will make $(142 + 145 + 150) = 437$ correct predictions and $(68 + 15) + (120 + 35) + (55 + 20) = 313$ errors. For the East side, however, we will guess "Rental." This will result in an additional 147 correct predictions and $(73 + 30) = 103$ errors. The new total correct is $(437 + 147) = 584$ with $(313 + 103) = 416$ errors. This is $[N - \Sigma \text{largest cell in column } (j)]$ in Equation 25.6.

Plugging these values into the formula we get Lambda for columns independent $= 1 - [(1000 - 584)/(1000 - 510)] = 1 - (416/490) = 1 - 0.849 = 0.151$, or approximately a 15 percent reduction in errors.[5]

If we chose "Type of Residence" (rows) as the independent variable, our guessing rule would be the same. We would guess that every residence, regardless of its type, was on the North Side. We would make 700 errors. If we knew the residence type, however, we would now guess that "Owner-occupied" was on the South side, Rental on the East side and "Institution" was on the North. We would now make 668 errors. Plugging these values into Equation 25.7 we get Lambda for rows independent $= 1 - (668/700) = 0.046$, or about a 4.5 percent reduction in errors.

It is conceivable, however, that we might have no basis for arguing that one of the other of our variables was independent. For instance, we might theorize that type of housing is really a function of some third variable, such as income. In this case, we would employ Lambda symmetric to characterize the association between the variables. Its formula is

$$\text{Lambda symmetric} = 1 - [2 \times N - \sum \text{largest cell in column}(j) - \sum \text{largest cell in row}(i)]/$$
$$[2 \times N - (\text{number of cases in largest row}) - (\text{number of cases in largest column})] \qquad (25.8)$$

where r, k, N, i, and j are defined as in Equations 25.6 and 25.7.

Applying this formula to the data in Table 25.1 results in a Lambda symmetric of 0.089. This value is essentially a weighted average of the two asymmetric Lambdas. Its magnitude is always less than one of the asymmetric Lambdas and greater than the other (except when all three Lambdas are equal).

In addition to their simplicity of interpretation, the Lambdas are relatively easy to calculate even by hand. Moreover, unlike some of the chi-square-based statistics, none can ever exceed 1. Nor can a "perfect" relationship—one that has no errors of prediction—fail to equal 1.

Lambda does have a major drawback, however. It is insensitive to percentage differences in tables where the modal category on the dependent variable is sufficiently large to dominate all other categories even when information about the category on the independent variable is available. For example, consider the race of the 300 informants who gave us information about the types of residence on the North side displayed in Table 25.1. Suppose there were 50 blacks and 250 whites who identified themselves politically as shown in Table 25.6.

Examining the percentage differences suggests that blacks are more likely than whites to declare affiliation with the Democratic Party. Indeed, chi-square $= 7.67$ $(p < .05)$; $V = \text{Phi} = 0.160$; and $C = 0.158$. But because there are so many more whites than blacks and so many more Democrats than others, "White" and "Democrat" remain the modal categories even when new information about party affiliation or race is given. As a result, Lambda row independent $=$ Lambda column independent $=$ Lambda symmetric $= 0$. This illustrates that unlike the chi-square-based measures, statistical independence is not the null condition for Lambda. In short, because the Lambdas focus

TABLE 25.6
Race by Party Affiliation (Factitious Data: North Side)

	Republican (Percentage)	(N)	Independent (Percentage)	(N)	Democrat (Percentage)	(N)	Total
Black	20	(10)	10	(5)	70	(35)	50
White	40	(100)	10	(25)	50	(125)	250
Total	36.7	(110)	10	(30)	53.3	(160)	300

on modal categories they can fail to show relationships that other more sensitive measures will pick up and even find statistically significant at the commonly used $p \leq .05$ level.[6]

The Goodman–Kruskal Taus are PRE measures that are more sensitive to percentage differences than are the Lambdas. The logic of the Taus is similar to that of the Lambdas, but the Taus are more complex and more tedious to calculate by hand. Nonetheless, Goodman–Kruskal Taus can provide summaries of cross-tabulated data that are more sensitive to some percentage differences than are the Lambdas. And with the advent of computerized routines, the tediousness of the calculations is no longer a serious problem.[7]

The formulas for the asymmetric Taus are

Goodman–Kruskal Tau for columns independent =[(expected mistakes based on row totals)

– (mistakes made knowing cell values by column)]/(expected mistakes based on row totals)

(25.9)

where expected mistakes $= \Sigma$ Rowtotal$(i) \times [(N - \text{Rowtotal}(i))/N]$, for $i = 1$ to r; and mistakes knowing cell values by column $= [\Sigma$ [Cell value$(i, j)] \times [\text{Coltotal}(j) - \text{Cell value}(i,j)]/\text{Coltotal}(j)]$, for $i = 1$ to r; $j = 1$ to k.

Goodman–Kruskal Tau for rows independent =[(expected mistakes based on column totals)

– (mistakes made knowing cell values by row)]/(expected mistakes based on column totals)

(25.10)

where expected mistakes $= \Sigma$ Coltotal$(j) \times [(N - \text{Coltotal}(j))/N]$, for $j = 1$ to k; and mistakes knowing cell values by row $= [\Sigma$ [Cell value$(i, j)] \times [\text{Rowtotal}(i) - \text{Cell value}(i,j)]/\text{Rowtotal}(i)]$, for $i = 1$ to r; $j = 1$ to k, and where r, k, N, i, and j are defined as in Equations 25.6 and 25.7.

Essentially, the asymmetric Goodman–Kruskal Taus differ from the asymmetric Lambdas only by the application of their more complex guessing rule. Instead of choosing the modal category of the dependent variable as the first guess, we make our guesses in proportion to the distribution of categories on the dependent variable. This leads to more errors than does the guessing rule for asymmetric Lambdas. Similarly, instead of guessing the modal cell category on the dependent variable when we are told the category on the independent variable, we now guess in proportion to the cases in each cell category on the dependent variable.

To illustrate, consider once again the data in Table 25.1 with "Side of Town" as the independent variable. We begin by making 510 guesses of "Owner-Occupied," 390 guesses of "Rental," and 100 guesses of "Institution." Although it is possible that all these guesses could be right, the number of erroneous guesses expected by chance is $[510 \times (490/1000)] + [390 \times (610/1000)] + 100 \times [900/1000] = 249.9 + 237.9 + 90 = 577.8$. We note that this guessing rule generates 87.8 more errors than the guessing rule used for the corresponding asymmetric Lambda.

Once we are told the column from which our case is drawn, we begin to guess in proportion to numbers of cases in each cell of that column. Thus, for West side we guess 142 owner-occupied, 68 rental, and 15 institution. We make $[142 \times (83/225)] + [68 \times (157/225] + [15 \times (210/225)] = 113.83$ errors. Continuing across the columns we make an additional $136.65 + 177.83 + 109.77 = 424.25$ errors for a total of 538.08. Substituting in Equation 25.9, the formula reduces to $1 - (538.08/577.8) = 0.069$. This makes Goodman–Kruskal Tau for columns independent smaller than any of the other nominal measures of association for these data. Similarly, Goodman–Kruskal Tau for rows independent comes out to be only about 0.028, again smaller than any of the previous measures.

Nevertheless, because the asymmetric Taus have statistical independence as their null condition, they will detect an association—albeit a weak one—for the data in Table 25.6. Tau for columns independent equals 0.026 and Tau for rows independent equals 0.019.

The symmetric form of Goodman–Kruskal Tau, like the symmetric form of Lambda, can be thought of as a weighted average of the asymmetric measures. Its formula is

Goodman–Kruskal Tau symmetric = [(expected mistakes based on row totals)

+ (expected mistakes based on column totals)] − [(mistakes made knowing cell

values by column) + (mistakes knowing cell values by row)]/[(expected mistakes based

on row totals) + (expected mistakes based on column totals)]   (25.11)

where expected mistakes are calculated as in Equations 25.9 and 25.10.

Inserting data from Tables 25.1 and 25.6 into this formula yields symmetric Taus of 0.044 and 0.021, respectively. As was the case with asymmetric forms, Tau is less than Lambda for Table 25.1 but greater than Lambda for Table 25.6.

At this stage it should be apparent that no single nominal statistic among those we have reviewed is superior to the others in all desired aspects. The chi-square-based statistics are sensitive to percentage differences, but they are difficult to interpret and some of their ranges can exceed 1. The PRE measures are easier to interpret, but Lambda is insensitive to certain percentage differences. Goodman–Kruskal Tau, although more sensitive to weak relationships than Lambda, uses a PRE guessing rule that tends to generate measures of association whose magnitudes are smaller than all the others for tables where no category of a row or column variable is so large that it dominates the overall distribution of cases.

The choice of which statistics to use to characterize a relationship will depend upon the questions a policy analyst or researcher has in mind. We shall have more to say about this matter after we have discussed common ordinal statistics.

25.3 ORDINAL MEASURES OF ASSOCIATION

25.3.1 INTRODUCTION

Ordinal variables, like nominal variables, are divided into mutually exclusive and exhaustive categories for purposes of measurement. The difference is that the categories have a natural or a theoretical order. Places in the finish of a horse race, for instance, can be thought of as having a natural order. Place of finish, therefore, would be an ordinal variable: it runs from first through last, but it says nothing about the distance between any two places in the order.

To continue with our example of sides of town, we could impose a theoretical order on sides of city. Suppose we developed a scale that averaged the z scores for annual family income, per capita years of formal education of adult residents, and school taxes paid per capita. We could then order "Side of Town" on this variable from highest to lowest scale score and investigate the extent to which this order is associated with the pattern of owner-occupation of residential dwellings.[8]

In contrast to nominal measures of association, the magnitudes of desirable ordinal measures of association should be sensitive to the order of the categories of variables in a cross-tabulation. Once again, we would like to standardize our measures so that "0" represents no relationship between the variables and "1" represents a perfect relationship. We can add an additional piece of information to characterize ordinal relationships, however. We can use a negative sign to indicate that when a case falls into the higher ordinal categories on one variable, it tends to fall into the lower ordinal categories on the other; and vice versa: lower categories on the first variable are associated with higher categories on the second. A positive sign would denote that the order of categories would tend to vary in the same direction: higher categories on one variable associated with higher on a second; and similarly, lower categories on one variable associated with lower values on a second.

25.3.2 KENDALL'S TAU-*A*, TAU-*B*, AND TAU-*C*

Table 25.7 contains data on the rank order of the dates of the Democratic presidential primaries or caucuses of selected states and the District of Columbia in 2000 and 2004. Low numbers indicate early dates; high numbers indicate late ones. Since 1996, states that traditionally scheduled their primaries or caucuses in March or April have tried to enhance their influence on the selection of the presidential nominee by moving their dates forward, emulating Iowa and New Hampshire, whose early caucuses and primaries garner national attention disproportionate to their populations and healthy boosts to their economies from campaign expenditures including those of the accompanying the news media. The data in Table 25.7 suggests a continuing trend toward "frontloading" the delegate selection process among the selected states. We can estimate the extent these moves changed the order in which delegates to the Democratic National Convention were selected between 2000 and 2004.

Kendall's Tau-*A* is a statistic that can be used to help answer this question. It consists of the ratio of concordant minus discordant paired comparisons between the ranks of all cases on two variables, to the total number of possible paired comparisons. Specifically,

$$\text{Tau-}A = 2 \times (C - D)/(N^2 - N) \tag{25.12}$$

TABLE 25.7
Democratic Party Delegate Selection Schedules for 15 States, 2000 and 2004

State or District	2000 Rank (Date)	2004 Rank (Date)	d^{a}
Iowa	1 (1/24)	1 (1/19)	0
New Hampshire	2 (2/01)	2 (1/27)	0
Missouri	4.5[b] (3/07)	4.5 (2/03)	0
Washington	4.5 (3/07)	7.5[b] (2/07)	−3
California	4.5 (3/07)	13.5[b] (3/02)	−9
Connecticut	4.5 (3/07)	13.5 (3/02)	−9
South Carolina	7 (3/09)	4.5 (2/03)	2.5
Utah	8.5 (3/10)	12 (2/24)	−3.5
Colorado	8.5 (3/10)	15 (4/13)	−6.5
Arizona	10.5[b] (3/11)	4.5 (2/03)	6
Michigan	10.5 (3/11)	7.5 (2/07)	3
Oklahoma	12.5[b] (3/14)	4.5 (2/03)	8
Tennessee	12.5 (3/14)	9.5[b] (2/10)	3
Wisconsin	14 (4/04)	11 (2/17)	3
Virginia	15 (4/15)	9.5 (2/10)	5.5

[a] d is the difference in ranks between 2000 and 2004. The square of d is used in calculating Spearman's Rho, a rank order statistic that we will discuss later in this chapter.

[b] If more than one state has the same date (has a tied ranking) each is given the midpoint of the ranks. E.g., Missouri, Washington, California, and Connecticut are tied for ranks 4 through 7 in 2000 and the last two are tied for ranks 13 and 14 in 2004.

Source: Applebaum (2000–2007), http://www.gwu.edu/~action/chrnothp.html#02 (2000); http://www.gwu.edu/~action/2004/cands/cal0104.html (2004).

---

where C and D are the total number of concordant and discordant paired comparisons, respectively and N is the total number of cases:

$C = \Sigma$ [Celltotal $(i,j) \times [\Sigma$ Celltotal $(m,n)]$] for $i = 1 \ldots r - 1; j = 2 \ldots k$ and $m > i$ and $n > j$;

$D = \Sigma$ [Celltotal $(i,j) \times [\Sigma$ Celltotal $(m,n)]$] for $i = 1 \ldots r - 1; j = 2 \ldots k$ and $m < i$ and $n > j$.

Essentially, Tau-A looks at the order of rankings of two cases or observations on the first variable and compares it to the order of rankings on the same two cases or observations on the second variable. For clarity and simplicity of calculation the first variable is ranked in as perfect order as possible. If the rankings run in the same direction on both variables, the pairs of observations are considered concordant. If they run in opposite directions, they are considered discordant. If the rankings are tied on either variable, no decision as to concordant or discordant pairs can be made.[9] The paired comparisons for New Hampshire and Washington (rank 2 versus 4.5 for 2000, and rank 2 versus 7.5 for 2004) are concordant whereas the paired comparisons for California and South Carolina (rank 4.5 versus 7 for 2000, and rank 13.5 versus 4.5 for 2004) are discordant. Arizona and Michigan are tied at rank 10.5 for 2000, so no paired comparison can be made against their rankings for 2004. Similarly, Arizona and Oklahoma and Missouri and South Carolina are all tied at rank 4.5 for 2004, so none of the six possible paired comparisons can be made among these states.

There are 63 concordant pairs and 33 pairs that are discordant in Table 25.7. $C - D = 63 - 33 = 30$. Dividing by 105 (all possible paired comparisons $= (N)(N - 1)/2 = (15 \times 14)/2 = 105$), we get $30/105 = 0.286$ as Tau-A from Equation 25.12. For the set of states chosen, this indicates only a modest consistency in the order of delegate selection dates between 2000 and 2004. Indeed, the changes indicate considerable shuffling in the order as state Democratic parties "frontloaded" the delegate selection process.

Tau-A has a straightforward interpretation and a range of $-1 \leq$ Tau-A ≤ 1. It is most useful for describing relationships between two ordinal variables with many ranks and relatively few ties. Its major drawback comes when there are a substantial number of ties in the order of cases on one or both of the variables being compared. By maintaining all possible comparisons in the denominator, Tau-A cannot reach 1 (or -1) if there are any ties. Indeed, because tied comparisons are excluded from both C and D, the numerator is diminished relative to the denominator, and Tau-A effectively counts ties as weakening the relationship.

As most cross-tabulations have many cases in each cell, it follows that there are many ties on one or both of the variables. This makes Tau-A impractical as a measure of association for variables in most cross-tabulations. The current versions of SPSS have dropped Tau-A from their crosstabs output.

Kendall's Tau-B and Tau-C are more forgiving regarding ties. Both maintain $C - D$ in their numerators. The former diminishes the denominator to adjust for ties. The latter is an estimator of Tau-B that adjusts for unequal numbers of rows and columns (Liebetrau, 1983, pp. 72–74). The formulas are

$$\text{Tau-}B = (C - D)/\sqrt{\text{Denomsq}} \qquad (25.13)$$

where Denomsq $= (1/2 \times (N^2 - N) - \text{TieRow}) \times (1/2 \times (N^2 - N) - \text{TieCol})$; TieRow $= \Sigma\{(1/2) \times [\text{Rowtotal}N(i)]2 - \text{Rowtotal}N(i)\}$ for $i = 1 \ldots r$; TieCol $= \Sigma\{(1/2) \times [\text{Coltotal}N(j)]2 - \text{Coltotal}N(j)\}$ for $j = 1 \ldots k$; and Rowtotal$N(i)$ and Coltotal$N(j)$ are the number of cases in the ith row and jth column, respectively, and $N = $ total number of cases.

$$\text{Tau-}C = (2 \times \min \times(C - D))/(N^2 \times (\min -1)) \qquad (25.14)$$

where $\min = r$ or k, whichever is smaller, as in Equation 25.5.

Tau-B and Tau-C also range from -1 to $+1$ with 0 as a null relationship. Tau-B can reach its maximum and minimum values, however, only when $r = k$. Tau-C, like Cramer's V, can reach or -1

TABLE 25.8
Type of Residence by Side of Town Ordered by z-Score Scale
Higher < -----------Scale Scores------- > Lower

	South	West	North	East	Total
Owner-occupied (percentage)	66.7	63.1	48.3	29.2	51.0
Rental	24.4	30.2	40.0	58.8	39.0
Institution	8.8	6.7	11.7	12.0	10.0
Total percentage (N)	100.0 (225)	100.0 (225)	100.0 (300)	99.9 (250)	100.0 (1000)

for a nonsquare table. As it is an estimator of Tau-B, however, Tau-C generally will be close to Tau-B. Lastly, for all cross-tabulations and rank orderings, Tau-B and Tau-C will be greater than or equal to Tau-A.

Returning to the data in Tables 25.1 and 25.2, we would like to use the Kendall's Tau statistics to measure the strength of any underlying ordinal relationship between the variables. We can calculate the Tau values for the data as presented, but it would make little sense to do so, for there is no natural order to the sides of the town. Consider once again, however, the hypothetical z-score scale discussed in the opening paragraph of this section. If we hypothesized that higher scores on the z-score scale were associated with greater likelihood of owner-occupied housing and lesser likelihood of institutional housing, with rentals in-between, then we could reorder the columns from highest to lowest on average scale scores as shown in Table 25.8.

For these data, the Tau-$C = 0.226$, Tau-$B = 0.229$, and Tau-$A = 0.151$. The nominal statistics of course are unaffected by changing the order of the columns. The chi-square-based statistics remain the same as listed in Table 25.4, and the Lambdas and the Goodman–Kruskal Taus remain steady also. The ordinal measures indicate a positive association of modest size, comparable in magnitude to the nominal association, but they also give information about the direction of association.[10]

25.3.3   GAMMA AND WILSON'S E

Tau-B and Tau-C are bracketed by two additional ordinal measures of association which maintain Concordant minus Discordant pairs in their numerator: Gamma and Wilson's E. Gamma is the most forgiving regarding ties: it ignores rather than counts them in its denominator. Wilson's E, a less frequently used statistic, forgives ties only when a case is tied on both the x and y variables. The formulas for these statistics are

$$\text{Gamma} = (C - D)/(C + D) \tag{25.15}$$

$$\text{Wilson's } E = 2 \times (C - D)/(N^2 - N - \text{Tieboth}) \tag{25.16}$$

where $\text{Tieboth} = \Sigma(1/2) \times ([\text{Celltotal}(i,j)]^2 - \text{Celltotal}(i,j)$, for $i = 1$ to r and $j = 1$ to k.

Returning to Table 25.8, Gamma $= 0.342$ and $E = 0.171$. Reviewing the magnitudes of the ordinal measures discussed so far, Tau-$A \leq$ Wilson's $E \leq$ Tau-C and Tau-$B \leq$ Gamma. Each of these measures is symmetrical. None presumes that the x or y variable is independent. The choice of which to use depends on the questions researchers ask.

We shall have more to say about this later.

25.3.4   SOMER'S Ds

Somer's D_{yx} and D_{xy}, in contrast to ordinal statistics presented above, presume that either the x or y variable, respectively, has been hypothesized as independent. The statistics once again have $C - D$

in their numerator, but they are asymmetric. They forgive ties on the independent variable, leaving in the denominator only those cases that cannot be distinguished on the dependent variable. Somer's Ds produce values that bracket Tau-B. One value is greater than (or equal to) Tau-B; the other is less than (or equal to) Tau-B. The formulas are

$$\text{Somer's } Dyx \text{ (for rows independent)} = (C - D)/\text{RowDenom}; \qquad (25.17)$$

where $\text{RowDenom} = (1/2 \times (N^2 - N) - \text{TieRow})$ and x is the row variable and y is the column variable.

$$\text{Somer's } Dxy \text{ (for columns independent)} = (C - D)/\text{ColDenom}; \qquad (25.18)$$

where $\text{ColDenom} = (1/2 \times (N^2 - N) - \text{TieCol})$ and x is the row variable and y is the column variable.

The Somer's Dyx and Dxy for Table 25.8 are 0.260 and 0.202, respectively.[11] Comparing the formulas, readers may also verify that $Dyx \times Dxy = (\text{Tau-}B)^2$.

We have seen that changing the order of the categories affects the magnitudes of ordinal measures of association. Collapsing the categories also affects these magnitudes. Table 25.9 summarizes the values of the measures of association for the data in Tables 25.1 (and 25.2), Table 25.8, and the collapsed categories presented in Table 25.3.

It should be clear that because the columns of Tables 25.1 and 25.2 have no natural or theoretical order, the negative values in the first column represent inappropriate applications of the ordinal measures. They are essentially meaningless; only nominal measures like those in column 1 of Table 25.4 should be applied.

Once we set the columns in an appropriate theoretical order, however, as done in Table 25.8, the measures do yield some useful information. If we hypothesize that higher z-score ratings are associated with greater proportions of owner-occupied dwelling units and lesser proportions of rental and institutional units, the measures indicate that the relationship is positive though not particularly strong. Collapsing the rows and columns as we did in Table 25.3 increases the numbers of observations tied within the categories of each variable. Tau-A, which is unforgiving of ties decreases in magnitude. All the other symmetric measures forgive ties to a greater or lesser degree. Gamma, which essentially ignores ties, shows the greatest increase. Wilson's E shows the least. Tau-B and Tau-C show modest increases. The product of the asymmetric Somer's Ds increases though Dyx decreases slightly due to the increased ties on the y variable. Somer's D is forgiving of ties on the independent variable, and this same increase in tied observations on y, therefore, increases rather than decreases the magnitude of Dxy.

TABLE 25.9
Magnitudes of Ordinal Measures of Association

	Tables 25.1 and 25.2	Table 25.8	Table 25.3
Tau-A	−0.033	0.151	0.125
Tau-B	−0.050	0.229	0.251
Tau-C	−0.049	0.226	0.250
Gamma	−0.074	0.342	0.476
Wilson's E	−0.037	0.170	0.171
Somer's Dyx	−0.056	0.260	0.250
Somer's Dxy	−0.044	0.202	0.253

25.3.5 SPEARMAN'S RHO

Spearman's Rho is a popular symmetric rank order statistic, most commonly applied when variables being compared have few or no tied ranks. The logic of its derivation is such that Rho would equal Pearson's product-moment correlation (r), were the rankings actually interval level measures. Thus, Rho can be defined as (Liebetrau, 1983, pp. 48, 56–58)

$$\text{Rho} = \left(\sum [R_i - \overline{R}] \times [S_i - \overline{S}] \right) \Big/ \sqrt{\left(\sum [R_i - \overline{R}]^2 \times \sum [S_i - \overline{S}]^2 \right)} \qquad (25.19)$$

where

R_i is the rank of X variable
S_i is the rank on the Y variable
$i = 1$ to N for a sample of N paired observations (X_i, Y_i) on each variable
$\overline{R}$ and $\overline{S}$ are the mean ranks on X and Y

It can be shown that this reduces to the calculation formula (Gibbons, 1993, pp. 3–5):

$$\text{Rho} = 1 - \left\{ \left(6 \sum d_i^2 \right) / (N^3 - N) \right\} \qquad (25.20)$$

where d is the difference in ranks between the paired observations, X_i and Y_i.

Rho ranges between -1 (perfect negative relationship) and 1 (perfect positive relationship) with 0 representing no relationship. As in Table 25.7, when ties occur, the tied observations are assigned the mean of the set of ranks that they would otherwise have occupied. The calculation formula yields perfect relationships only when there are no ties. To account for ties, the calculation formula can be modified to:

$$\text{Rho} = \left\{ N^3 - N - 6 \sum d_i^2 - 6(t' + u') \right\} \Big/ \left\{ \sqrt{(N^3 - N - 12t')} \right.$$
$$\left. \times \sqrt{(N^3 - N - 12u')} \right\} \qquad (25.21)$$

where
$t' = (\Sigma t i^3 - \Sigma t i)/12$
$u' = (\Sigma u_i^3 - \Sigma u i)/12$
t_i and u_i are the number of ties at any given rank i

Spearman's Rho is most commonly used when relatively few cases share the same rank on the variables whose rank orders are being compared. When there are many such ties relative to the ranks, we ordinarily produce a cross-tabulation and use the ordinal measures of associations introduced in the previous section to indicate the strength of the relationship.

To calculate Spearman's Rho from the data in Table 25.7, we take the d values and apply Equation 25.20 we find four sets of ties in 2000 and also in 2004. For each year, three of the sets have two observations that share the same rank. For 2000 the fourth set consists of four states tied at rank 4.5; for 2004 the fourth set has three states tied at rank 4.5. Therefore, $t' = 3 \times [(\Sigma 2_i^3 - \Sigma 2_i)/ 12] = 3 \times (8 - 2)/12 = 1.5$ for the three sets of 2, plus $(\Sigma 4_i^3 - \Sigma 4_i)/12 = (64 - 4)/12 = 5$, for a total of 6.5. Similarly, $u' = 3 \times (\Sigma 2_i^3 - \Sigma 2_i)/12 = 1.5$ plus $(\Sigma 3_i^3 - \Sigma 3)/12 = 2$ for a total of 3.5. Plugging these values into Equation 25.20, we get Rho $= 0.289$. This compares to a Rho of 0.305 if we use Equation 25.19, and the Tau-A of 0.286 that we calculated earlier. Generally, when there are relatively few ties among the ranks, the unadjusted Rho calculated from Equation 25.20 will not differ significantly from the adjusted Rho. Nevertheless, computer packages, such as SAS and SPSS, will calculate Rho for any cross-tabulation, even when there are many ties relative to ranks. Before the advent of computerized routines removed the tediousness of applying Equation 25.21, adjustments for ties were often ignored when calculating Rho for data presented as rank orders, such as that in Table 25.7, but the statistic was not commonly used as a measure of strength for data presented as cross-tabulations (Kerlinger, 1964, pp. 260–261; Ritchey, 2000, pp. 530–533).

25.4 MULTIVARIATE ANALYSIS

25.4.1 CONTROL VARIABLES

The measures of association we have discussed throughout this chapter characterize the strength of relationships between two variables. Although these bivariate relationships can be interpreted and their strengths can be compared with one another, researchers and practitioners often are interested in theories or problems that require consideration of more than two variables.

The most straightforward method of carrying out multivariate analysis involving nominal and ordinal variables is to introduce "control" variables. Essentially, for each category (or relevant categories) of the control variables, we examine the bivariate relationships that had been originally measured to determine the extent to which the relationships remain unchanged.

We know, for example, that a greater proportion of women than men voted to re-elect President Bill Clinton in November 1996. We might hypothesize that differences in men's and women's opinions toward the federal government's proper involvement in resolving social problems could explain this particular "gender gap." We could test this hypothesis by comparing the proportions of men and women who voted for Senator Dole or President Clinton within separate categories of a survey variable that measured how much involvement the respondents wanted the federal government to have regarding social problems. If the control variable had three substantive categories regarding such involvement: (1) more, (2) same as now, and (3) less, we would generate three tables, one for each category. If the strength of association between sex and presidential vote dropped to nearly zero for each table, the analysis would affirm (though not prove) our hypothesis. This result would occur if the percentage differences in presidential voting between men and women in each table were small, but that women tended to cluster in the table for category (1) while the men tended to cluster in the table for category (3).

An advantage of this method of control is that the resultant measures of association provide estimates of the strength of the bivariate relationship under three separate circumstances. It is conceivable that the same measures could be different from one another under these separate circumstances. For instance, we might discover that differences between the sexes disappeared within the table for category (1) but that women voted disproportionately for Clinton in the tables for categories (2) and (3). This would suggest that men and women differed in their choices of presidential candidates even when they agreed over the role the federal government should play in resolving social problems, except among those who favored a greater role for the federal government.

We could further extend the multivariate analysis by separating the cases in the tables by race. Such a separation would allow us to check the circumstances (if any) under which a gender gap existed among blacks, who otherwise gave overwhelming support to Clinton over Dole. We would now obtain six separate measures of the association between sex and presidential choice: two comparisons of the sexes—(1) blacks and (2) whites—within each of the three categories regarding role of the federal government.

The disadvantages of this method of analysis stem from two factors. First, as control categories multiply, the presentation and descriptions of the tables and their respective measures of association can become complicated and prolix. This can be thought of as analogous to the problem of always using percentage differences to describe the relationships among variables. Second, as the numbers of tables increase, the cases upon which they are based decrease, and the estimates of strength of association thereby become less reliable. Blacks comprised approximately 10 percent of the voters in 1996 presidential election. As we compare presidential voting choices of men and women, controlling for race and opinion on the federal government's role in the example above, we would expect to find only about 75 black men and 75 black women in a sample of 1500 who actually voted. When we sort these men and women into categories according to their opinions on the degree of involvement in social problems they prefer for the federal government, the numbers of black men and women included in the relevant tables could fall to fewer than 30 cases each. This sparsity of cases would be hardly conducive for making reliable estimates of measures of association, but researchers could view the results as exploratory or preliminary, despite their unreliability. To achieve sufficient cases to make reliable estimates, new data then could be collected or perhaps found in other independent surveys.

25.4.2 PARTIAL CORRELATION

An approach that attempts to overcome the above described disadvantages for ordinal variables employs ordinal measures analogous to those used in calculating partial correlations for interval level data (Garson, 1976, pp. 361–363; Gibbons, 1993, chapter 5). Although this method avoids the problems of small numbers of cases and can facilitate shorter, less complicated explanations, it still lacks the richness of using partial correlations in conjunction with ordinary least squares (OLS) regression models. A single partial ordinal correlation coefficient allows the researcher to comment on the strength of the bivariate relationship under the designated controls without worrying about the paucity of cases in the cells of particular combinations of variables. There is no related regression equation, however, that can be used to provide an estimate of the impact that a unit change in the independent variable has on the dependent variable.

Additional problems arise. When more than one control variable is introduced, the sampling distributions of the partial ordinal correlation coefficients are generally unknown (Gibbons, 1993, p. 50). And when only one control variable is used, examining the bivariate relationship in separate categories often yields a richer analysis, for the table associated with each category of the control variable provides separate measures of association that are unique to that category. Moreover, when only one control variable with a limited number of categories is used, problems that arise from having small numbers of cases are unlikely to arise.

An argument can be made, therefore, that if we really want to employ partial correlations to examine the relationships among ordinal variables, we might do better to presume that a known distribution underlies the observations and that the variables themselves can be treated as interval rather than ordinal (Weisberg, Krosnick, and Bowen, 1996, pp. 182–183, 313–315).

25.5 SUMMARY AND CONCLUSIONS

This chapter has reviewed a number of common nominal and ordinal measures of association that public administrators and policy analysts may find useful for describing relationships among two or more variables of interest. The nominal measures covered included Percentage difference, Chi-square, Contingency coefficient, Phi, Cramer's V, Lambda, and Goodman–Kruskal Tau. Ordinal measures included Tau-A, Tau-B, Tau-C, Gamma, Somer's D, Wilson's E, and Spearman's Rho. Besides presenting the formulas for these measures, the chapter has discussed their relation to one another and has given some examples of the research or policy problems to which they can be applied.

Although these measures have known distributions (Gibbons, 1993, Appendix A), the discussion has focused mostly on their substantive rather than statistical significance. Even though computerized data analysis programs normally produce the statistical significance of these measures, their magnitudes—or substantive significance, if you will—for a table or graph are often of more interest to a policy analyst or administrator than are their levels of statistical significance. If the magnitude of an association is sufficiently large and the question of concern is sufficiently important, then, regardless of the level of statistical significance, a good argument can be made for collecting new data or for seeking new evidence from data collected independently by others. Weak relationships, characterized by low magnitudes of association, however, may achieve statistical significance, even when their substantive importance is dubious. The gender gap in presidential voting, which varied in magnitude between four and seven percent in the four preceding elections before to jumping to 11 percent in 1996, can serve as an example. Although the gap had been of statistical significance since the 1980 election, not until 1996 did majorities of men and women who voted choose presidential candidates of different parties (Connelly, 1996).[12]

The discussion has suggested imposing a theoretical order that permits movement from nominal to ordinal (and possibly from ordinal to interval) levels of measurement is often a reasonable research strategy. Ordinal and interval measures of association generally allow for richer, more meaningful interpretations of relationships among variables than do nominal measures. If a set of data has a sufficient number of cases, however, successive examination of the separate measures of bivariate association within the categories of the control variables can yield insights that the single value produced by an ordinal (or interval) partial correlation or each single partial regression coefficient of an OLS multiple regression equation may not reveal.

In the end, there is no single measure of association that can be applied uniformly to characterize the relationship among two or more nominal or ordinal variables. The choice depends upon the problems or questions the policy analyst or administrator has in mind. Which variables are independent and which are dependent? Or does the theory or hypothesis under investigation provide no definitive guidance as to the possible causal relationships among the variables? To what extent are the bivariate relationships uncovered expected to hold across various categories of control variables? Is the null condition independence, or does the theory require a stronger condition before the relationship under investigation assumes substantive significance?

The discussion has attempted to illustrate how the measures relate to one another and how their magnitudes are affected by marginal distributions of the data and by the presence of tied rankings of cases within the categories of ordinal variables. It is hoped that this discussion will provide the basis for making informed and defensible choices of measures of association suitable to the particular problems or questions of concern.

ENDNOTES

1. Given the 19 percent difference between the proportion of owner-occupied dwellings on the North and East sides, a researcher might choose to combine only the West and South columns.
2. Tshchuprow's $T = \sqrt{(\text{phi}^2/\sqrt{[(r-1) \times (c-1)]})}$, found in some textbooks, is equal to Cramer's V when $r = k$ (Blalock, 1972; Liebetrau, 1983). Cramer's V can equal 1 when $r \neq k$, however, and T cannot. Finally, V, Phi, and C are found in statistical routines such as SPSS crosstabs, but T is not.
3. Note that $V = $ Phi for a two by two table.
4. V directly adjusts for the number of rows and columns in a table, but Phi and C do not. It is generally advisable, therefore, to use Cramer's V for comparing the strengths of relationships in tables among which the rows and columns differ and to reserve Phi or C only for comparing such relationships in tables (1 to N) that have the same numbers of rows and columns, i.e., where $r_1 = r_2 = \cdots = r_N$ and $k_1 = k_2 = \cdots = k_N$.
5. Routines that calculate Lambda and Goodman–Kruskal Tau automatically are built into social science statistical packages, such as SPSS.
6. See Weisberg, 1974 and Bruner, 1976 for more elaborate discussions of the sensitivities of measures in detecting relationships and the effects of the proportions of cases in marginal categories on the magnitudes of the relationships detected.
7. Whenever users select Lambdas for a cross-tabulation, SPSS Versions 13 (MAC) and 14 (PC) also generate Goodman–Kruskal Taus.
8. We are ignoring here the "distance" measured by the z scores.
9. There are $N(N-1)/2$ possible comparisons that can be made taking combinations of N observations two at a time. Using simple algebra to expand this expression leads to $(N^2 - N)/2$, which is divided into $(C - D)$ in Equation 25.12.

10. See Gibbons, 1993 for tests of significance for Kendall's Taus.
11. SPSS also produces a Somer's *D* symmetric, which differs little from Tau-B. It is essentially a weighted average of the asymmetric *D*'s, whereas Tau-*B* is the geometric mean of the two (Garson, 1976, p. 295).
12. Reagan and Bush were the popular choice of both men and women in the presidential elections of the 1980s, as was Clinton in 1992. The Republicans, so to speak, simply were even more popular among men than women, and the opposite was true for Clinton in 1992.

REFERENCES

Applebaum, E.M. 2000–2007. Democracy in action (accessed 09/03/07).
   http://www.gwu.edu/~action/chrnothp.html#02
   http://www.gwu.edu/~action/2004/cands/cal0104.html
   http://www.gwu.edu/~action/2008/chrnothp08.html

Blalock, H.M., Jr. 1972. *Social Statistics* (2nd ed.). New York: McGraw-Hill.

Bruner, J. 1976. What's the question to that answer? Measures and marginals in crosstabulation. *American Journal of Political Science*, XX (November), 781–804.

Connelly, M. 1996. Portrait of the electorate, *New York Times* (National Edition). November 10, p. 16.

Garson, G.D. 1976. *Political Science Methods*. Boston, Massachussetts: Holbrook Press.

Gibbons, J.D. 1993. *Nonparametric Measures of Association*. Newbury Park, California: Sage Publications (Quantitative Applications in the Social Sciences, V. 91).

Kaplan, A. 1964. *The Conduct of Inquiry: Methodology for Behavioral Science*. San Francisco: Chandler Publishing Company.

Kerlinger, F. 1964. *Foundations of Behavioral Research: Educational and Psychological Inquiry*. New York: Holt, Rinehart and Winston, Inc.

Liebetrau, A.M. 1983. *Measures of Association*. Beverly Hills, California: Sage Publications (Quantitative Applications in the Social Sciences, V. 32).

Pollock, P.H. 2005. *An SPSS Companion to Political Analysis* (2nd ed.). Washington, DC: CQ Press.

Ritchey, F.J. 2000. *The Statistical Imagination*. Boston, Massachusetts: McGraw-Hill.

Weisberg, H. 1974. Models of statistical relationship. *American Political Science Review,* LXVIII (December), 1638–1655.

Weisberg, H.F., Krosnick, J.A., and Bowen, B.D. 1996. *An Introduction to Survey Research, Polling and Data Analysis* (3rd ed.). Thousand Oaks, California: Sage Publications.

26 Analysis of Variance

Carmen Cirincione

CONTENTS

26.1 INTRODUCTION

26.1.1 WHAT IS ANOVA?

ANalysis Of VAriance (ANOVA) is a set of statistical methods used to assess the mean differences across two or more groups. As others (Iverson and Norpoth, 1987) have said, a more appropriate name might be "analysis of means," but the name refers to the fact that ANOVA evaluates mean differences across groups by partitioning sources of variance in the dependent variable. In its simplest form, the variance is isolated into two distinct sources, that due to group membership and that due to chance; sometimes the latter is called error, residual, or within group variance. For example, a researcher may be interested in the importance of monetary rewards for mid-level managers serving in three different sectors: public, private, and a hybrid (Wittmer, 1991). ANOVA could be used to determine whether the differences in attitudes among managers across sectors are simply due to chance.

26.1.2 APPLICATIONS

Public administration and policy scholars have applied ANOVA methods to issues of public management, public finance, and public policy. In the realm of public management, Brown and Harris (1993) investigated the influence of workforce diversity in the U.S. Forest Service. They examined attitude differences based on gender while controlling for age, years of experience, education, and professional identification. Edwards, Nalbandian, and Wedel (1981) examined the espoused values of students and alumni from four graduate programs at the University of Kansas: public administration, business administration, law, and social welfare. The purpose of the study was to assess differences in attitude based on program affiliation. Emmert and Crow (1988) attempted to identify characteristics that would distinguish four types of organizations: public-governmental, private-industrial, cooperative, and mixed. Herman and Heimovics (1990) compared the leadership skills of chief executive officers of nonprofit organizations who had been prejudged as effective with those of chief executives of nonprofit organizations who had been prejudged to be less effective. Newell and Ammons (1987) surveyed 527 city managers, mayors, mayoral assistants, and assistant city managers, and found that respondents in each position differed with regard to the perceived emphasis on the management, policy, and political roles played by people in their positions.

Applications of ANOVA also can be found in public budgeting research. For example, Frank (1990) and Gianakis and Frank (1993) used ANOVA to assess the accuracy of various revenue forecasting methods. Klammer and Reed (1990) conducted an experiment to determine the effects of different formats of cash flow reports on decision making. They found that bank analysts were much more consistent when a direct method was used than when an indirect method was employed.

Similarly, ANOVA is used in public policy research in a number of substantive areas. In studies of the criminal justice system, Nunn (1994) assessed the effects of installing mobile digital terminals in police cars on vehicle theft recovery in Texas. Wells, Layne, and Allen (1991) investigated whether learning styles differed for supervisory, middle, upper middle, upper, and executive managers in the Georgia Department of Corrections. In mental health research, Warner and colleagues (1983) compared the efficacy of three client follow-up methods, and found that face-to-face interviews were more effective than either telephone or mail interviews.

ANOVA is one of the many statistical methods used by scholars in testing their theories with regard to public administration. The goals of this chapter are to introduce the reader to the fundamental principles underlying ANOVA, to illustrate the computational steps required to conduct an ANOVA, and to illustrate the links between ANOVA and other commonly used methods, such as t-tests of mean differences and multiple regression analysis.

26.2 APPROACHES TO ANOVA

There are many methods of employing ANOVA, but the fixed effects completely randomized design is most familiar to researchers. This design involves one dependent variable, Y, and one or more independent variables, also called factors. If the analysis involves only one independent variable, X, it is typically called a one-way ANOVA; if it involves multiple independent variables, it is known as a factorial design analysis of variance. The independent variables identify discrete groups of presumably homogenous subjects. They may be qualitative (e.g., participate in a job training program or not) or quantitative (e.g., amount of time in job training program; one month, two months, or three months). Qualitative independent variables measure differences in type or kind; quantitative independent variables measure variations in amount or degree. When analyzing qualitative variables, a researcher wishes to uncover differences in the dependent variable associated with the various groups or kinds. The researcher attempts to determine the nature of the relationship between the dependent and quantitative independent variables. For example, is this relationship best characterized by a linear, a quadratic, or some other, higher-order polynomial function? Qualitative factors are used much more frequently than quantitative factors in ANOVA and therefore are the focus of this chapter.

The choice of the groups, also called levels or treatment conditions, determines whether a fixed or a random factors model is chosen. Some authors refer to the former as a Model I and the latter as a Model II (Hays, 1994). In a fixed factor model, the levels of the independent variable represent the comparisons of interest. In a random effects model, the levels have been sampled from a large pool of potential levels, and the researcher wishes to generalize to the population of levels. Examples will clarify this distinction.

First, assume that a researcher is interested in the efficacy of a proposed job training program as compared with the current program. The researcher could design a study containing one independent variable—program type—in which the two levels represent the precise question to be addressed. This variable would be considered fixed. If another researcher were to replicate the original investigator's work, he or she would use the same two groupings. Second, assume that a researcher is interested in the impact of trainers in a job training program. Further assume that 50 individuals conduct the training sessions and that the researcher cannot include all of the trainers in the study. Instead she takes a random sample of 10 trainers and then conducts an analysis of the impact of trainers. This investigator wishes to draw inferences about the impact of the trainers not included in the study because the theoretical construct is the overall impact of trainers. If other researchers replicated this study, they would likely choose a different set of trainers. The trainer effect would be termed a random factor or effect; a random-effects model should be used for the analysis.

In fixed-effects models, inferences are limited to the specific levels chosen for the study; in random effects models, inferences go beyond the included levels. The method of analysis can differ, and different types of inferences can be drawn in the two situations. Mixed models include more than one independent variable; at least one is a fixed effect and at least one is a random effect. Because of space limitations, this chapter addresses only the most commonly used approach, the fixed-effects model.

A completely randomized design is one in which subjects are assigned randomly to one and only one treatment level in the case of one independent variable. If two or more independent variables are involved, subjects are assigned randomly to one of the treatment combinations. Random assignment is a method of eliminating systematic effects other than the independent variables of interest. It does so by converting systematic sources of variability into random sources. Random assignment is not essential to the use of ANOVA, but it influences the interpretation of the results. Throughout the chapter, assume that random assignment has been used and that the design is balanced; that is, the number of subjects is the same in each treatment condition.

Among completely randomized fixed-effect designs, several models are possible. Those discussed here are one-way ANOVA, multiple comparison tests, and completely crossed factorial designs.

26.3 ONE-WAY ANOVA

26.3.1 TWO GROUPS

We begin with a completely randomized fixed-effects model in which the investigator wishes to determine whether there is a difference between two groups. For instance, assume that a team of researchers wishes to determine the efficacy of a new job training program relative to the one currently in use. Five subjects are assigned randomly to a demonstration program of the new approach and five are assigned randomly to the current program. Upon completion of the program, the research team records the hourly wage rate for the first job placement. Let Y_{ij} represent the starting hourly wage rate for the ith person in the jth group, where i ranges from 1 to 5 and j ranges from 1 (demonstration program) to 2 (current job training program). Let J represent the total number (2) of groups, and n_j represent the number of subjects in the jth group. The total

TABLE 26.1

Starting Hourly Wage: Two Group Case

Program	Hourly Wage
Demonstration	$Y_{11} = 12.00$
	$Y_{21} = 11.00$
	$Y_{31} = 10.00$
	$Y_{41} = 13.00$
	$Y_{51} = 11.00$
Current	$Y_{12} = 7.00$
	$Y_{22} = 8.50$
	$Y_{32} = 5.50$
	$Y_{42} = 8.25$
	$Y_{52} = 8.50$

number of subjects, n, in the study is 10. The sample mean for the first group is denoted by $\bar{Y}_1$, that for the second by $\bar{Y}_2$. The sample variances for two groups are denoted by s_1^2 and s_2^2. In the entire sample of 10 persons, the grand mean and the variance are denoted by $\bar{Y}$ and s^2 respectively. Table 26.1 displays the starting hourly wages for all 10 subjects.

Thus far the problem sounds like an example of an independent sample t-test. The null hypothesis in such a t-test is that the population means for the two groups are equal; the alternative is that they are not. To assess the significance of the sample means, one computes the average for each of the two groups and then the difference between these two averages. The ratio of the difference between the means to the standard error is distributed as t (see Equation 26.1). One then can determine the statistical significance of the sample result.

$$t = \frac{\bar{Y}_1 - \bar{Y}_2}{\sqrt{\dfrac{(n_1 - 1)s_1^2 + (n_2 - 1)s_2^2}{n_1 + n_2 - 2}\left(\dfrac{1}{n_1} + \dfrac{1}{n_2}\right)}} \tag{26.1}$$

Table 26.2 displays the results for the sample statistics of both groups and for the t-value. The results are statistically significant; therefore the null hypothesis of equal means is rejected. The hourly wages for participants who completed the demonstration program are $3.95 higher on average than for people trained in the current program. This approach to testing for mean differences should be familiar to all social scientists. We now recast the problem as an ANOVA.

The null and alternative hypotheses are identical to those for the independent sample t-test, but ANOVA focuses on the partitioning of the variance of the dependent variable. To observe this emphasis, let us first calculate the sample mean and variance for the 10 subjects. Equation 26.2 is used to calculate the grand mean:

TABLE 26.2

Sample Statistics and t-Value for Job Training Example

Sample Statistics for the Demonstration Program	Sample Statistics for the Current Program	t-Value	p-Value
$\bar{Y}_1 = 11.50$	$\bar{Y}_2 = 7.55$	4.76	.001
$s_1^2 = 1.75$	$s_2^2 = 1.70$		

$$\bar{Y} = \frac{\sum\limits_{j=1}^{j}\sum\limits_{i=1}^{n_j} Y_{ij}}{\sum\limits_{j=1}^{j} n_j} \tag{26.2}$$

The first step in computing the variance for the set of 10 wages is to subtract the average wage from each of the values and to square these differences. The results are summed over all subjects. The result is termed the total sum of squares (TSS) and is represented in the following equation:

$$\text{TSS} = \sum\limits_{j=1}^{j}\sum\limits_{i=1}^{n_j} \left(Y_{ij} - \bar{Y}\right)^2 \tag{26.3}$$

The variance of Y thus becomes

$$s^2 = \frac{\sum\limits_{j=1}^{J}\sum\limits_{i=1}^{n_j} \left(Y_{ij} - \bar{Y}\right)^2}{n - 1} \tag{26.4}$$

ANOVA partitions this variability into two sources: that due to the differences among the means and that due to the variability within each group. The latter reflects the dispersion of the values in a group around that group mean.

$$\sum\limits_{j=1}^{J}\sum\limits_{i=1}^{n_j} \left(Y_{ij} - \bar{Y}\right)^2 = \sum\limits_{j=1}^{J}\sum\limits_{i=1}^{n_j} \left(Y_{ij} - \bar{Y}\right)^2 + \sum\limits_{j=1}^{J} n_j(\bar{Y})^2 \tag{26.5}$$

The TSS equals the error sum of squares plus the between groups sum of squares.

$$\text{TSS} = \text{ESS} + \text{BSS} \tag{26.6}$$

Each term then can be transformed into a mean square, a variance, by dividing by the appropriate degrees of freedom.

$$\frac{\sum\limits_{j=1}^{J}\sum\limits_{i=1}^{n_j} \left(Y_{ij} - \bar{Y}\right)^2}{n - 1} = \frac{\sum\limits_{j=1}^{J}\sum\limits_{i=1}^{n_j} \left(Y_{ij} - \bar{Y}_j\right)^2}{n - J} + \frac{\sum\limits_{j=1}^{J} n_j(\bar{Y}_j - \bar{Y})^2}{J - 1} \tag{26.7}$$

$$\frac{\text{TSS}}{n - 1} = \frac{\text{ESS}}{n - J} + \frac{\text{BSS}}{J - 1} \tag{26.8}$$

To test the null hypothesis of equal means, one calculates the ratio of the mean square between groups to the mean squared error. This ratio follows an F distribution with $J - 1$ and $n - J$ degrees of freedom. Table 26.3 is an ANOVA table that displays the sources of variation and the results of the F-test for the job training example. As with the t-test, one would reject the null of equality of means. The p-value is the same for both tests because the two tests are equivalent, F equals t^2.

The computational steps for a one-way completely randomized fixed factor (also called fixed effects) ANOVA are straightforward. First, calculate the between groups sum of squares. Second, calculate the error sum of squares. Third, divide each sum of squares by the appropriate degrees of freedom to calculate the mean squares. Fourth, divide the mean squared between groups by the mean squared error to calculate F. Then determine the significance of the result. Table 26.4

TABLE 26.3
One-Way ANOVA for Job Training Example

Source	df	Sum of Squares	Mean Square	F	p-Value
Between	1	39.01	39.01	22.611	.001
Error	8	13.80	1.72		
Total	9	52.81			

displays the equations for calculating the sums of squares and the mean squares in the format of an ANOVA table.

26.3.2 More than Two Groups

Thus far the coverage of one-way completely randomized fixed-effects ANOVA has addressed only cases in which the independent variable consists of two groups. In such cases, the independent sample t-test and ANOVA are equivalent, but what if the number of groups, J, is greater than 2? Let us build on the job training example. In addition to the demonstration program and the current program, assume that people also are assigned randomly to a third category in which they receive no job training. The data is displayed in Table 26.5.

In this case, the omnibus or overall F-test in the one-way ANOVA assesses the null hypothesis that all group means are the same. The alternative implies that the mean for at least one group is different from the mean for at least one other group or combination of groups. The partitioning of the sums of squares and the steps taken in conducting the F-test are identical whether the number of groups is 2 or more than 2. The computational equations in Table 26.4 still apply. In this specific example, J becomes 3 and n equals 15.

Table 26.6 presents the summary statistics for the sample; Table 26.7 displays the results of the ANOVA. The between groups sum of squares represents the squared differences of all three group means from the grand mean, and the sum of squared error now adds the variability within the third group to the sum of the other two groups. The value of F is 20.55, and this result is statistically significant: the starting hourly wage differs across the groups. The example could readily be extended to independent variables containing even more groups.

26.3.3 Assumptions

Inferences based on the omnibus F-test in a fixed-effects ANOVA rely on three assumptions: (1) the residuals are distributed normally, (2) the variances of the errors are the same for all groups,

TABLE 26.4
ANOVA Formulae

Source	df	Sum of Squares	Mean Square	F
Between	$J-1$	$\sum_{j=1}^{J} n_j(\bar{Y}_j - \bar{Y})^2$	$\dfrac{\sum_{j=1}^{J} n_j(\bar{Y}_j - \bar{Y})^2}{J-1}$	$\dfrac{\dfrac{\sum_{j=1}^{J} n_j(\bar{Y}_j - \bar{Y})^2}{J-1}}{\dfrac{\sum_{j=1}^{J}\sum_{i=1}^{n_j}(Y_{ij} - \bar{Y})^2}{n-J}}$
Error	$n-J$	$\sum_{j=1}^{J}\sum_{i=1}^{n_j}(Y_{ij} - \bar{Y})^2$	$\dfrac{\sum_{j=1}^{J}\sum_{i=1}^{n_j}(Y_{ij} - \bar{Y})^2}{n-J}$	
Total	$n-1$	$\sum_{j=1}^{J}\sum_{i=1}^{n_j}(Y_{ij} - \bar{Y})^2$		

TABLE 26.5

Starting Hourly Wage: Three Group Case

Program	Hourly Wage
Demonstration	$Y_{11} = 12.00$
	$Y_{21} = 11.00$
	$Y_{31} = 10.00$
	$Y_{41} = 13.50$
	$Y_{51} = 11.00$
Current	$Y_{12} = 7.00$
	$Y_{22} = 8.50$
	$Y_{32} = 5.50$
	$Y_{42} = 8.25$
	$Y_{52} = 8.50$
None	$Y_{13} = 6.00$
	$Y_{23} = 6.00$
	$Y_{33} = 8.50$
	$Y_{43} = 5.00$
	$Y_{53} = 7.00$

and (3) the residuals are independent of one another. The omnibus F-test in a one-way fixed factor ANOVA is robust to violations of the normality assumption. In other words, the true Type I and Type II error rates are insensitive to such violations. The omnibus F-test in a fixed factor ANOVA is also robust to violations of the homogeneity of variance assumption when the design is balanced and the samples are not small (Maxwell and Delaney, 1990).

In the case of unbalanced designs, the conclusions are quite different: even small departures from homogeneity can have a large impact on the Type I error rate. Hays (1994) also concludes that the F-test is not robust to simultaneous violations of the normality and the homogeneity of variance assumptions. The effects of the two violations appear to be additive (Glass and Hopkins, 1984); thus it is possible for one violation to cancel out the other. Prior work indicates that the omnibus F-test in a fixed-effects ANOVA is sensitive to violations of the independence assumption. That conclusion appears unanimous. Hays (1994) finds that violations of this assumption can lead to true Type I error rates substantially different from the nominal 0.05 level. Maxwell and Delaney (1990) state that the difference can be dramatic.

A number of solutions may be adopted when one or more of these assumptions have been violated. For violations of the normality or homogeneity of variance assumptions, one might transform the data for the dependent variable to a more "normal" or at least symmetric distribution with stable variances. A transformation is a re-expression of each data value. This re-expression is achieved by exponentiating each data value to some power, P, which ranges from positive infinity to negative infinity. This sequencing of P is known as the ladder of power. In this context, the value of 0 requires taking the natural logarithm of the values. The farther P deviates from 1, the greater the effect of the transformation on the distribution of the values (Velleman and Hoaglin, 1981).

TABLE 26.6

Sample Statistics for Job Training Example

Demonstration Program	Current Program	No Job Training	Whole Sample
$\bar{Y}_1 = 11.5$	$\bar{Y}_2 = 7.55$	$\bar{Y}_3 = 6.50$	$\bar{Y} = 8.52$
$s_1^2 = 1.75$	$s_2^2 = 1.70$	$s_3^2 = 1.75$	$s^2 = 6.45$

TABLE 26.7
ANOVA Table for Job Training Example

Source	df	Sum of Squares	Mean Square	F	p-Value
Between	2	69.51	34.75	20.05	0.0001
Error	12	20.80	1.73		
Total	14	90.31			

Although the use of transformations is quite common, the appropriateness of the approach is disputed. Interpretation of the results is a fundamental issue, and the equality of means in one metric does not guarantee equality in another. Maxwell and Delaney (1990) discuss these issues and cite studies that have contributed to the debate.

Another alternative is the use of nonparametric statistical procedures; these tests do not rely on normality assumptions. A nonparametric procedure that may be used in place of a one-way fixed factor ANOVA is the Kruskall–Wallis one-way analysis of ranks test which assesses the equality of medians across groups. First the data on the dependent variable are ranked and then analysis is performed on the ranked data. For the computational procedures, see *Nonparametric Statistics for the Behavioral Sciences*, by Siegel and Castellan (1988).

Cirincione et al. (1994) used the Kruskall–Wallis test to assess differences in arrest rates among four groups: prison inmates with no prior mental health history, prison inmates with prior mental health history, mental health patients with prior arrest history, and mental health patients with no prior arrest history. The dependent variable was the arrest rate—number of arrests per year at risk—following release into the community. The distributions of arrest rates for the four groups were highly skewed. The rates were extremely low for most of the subjects, but were high in some cases. The sample sizes were not the same across groups: the smallest sample size was 50 and the largest was 315. As a result of these properties, confidence in the validity of the omnibus *F*-test for a fixed factor ANOVA was quite low and the Kruskall–Wallis procedure was employed. Although nonparametric tests are a potential alternative to a fixed-effects ANOVA, their primary drawback is their lack of power.

Another alternative to fixed factor ANOVA is the use of robust procedures such as the Brown and Forsythe test (Maxwell and Delaney, 1990). This procedure relies on an estimate of the mean squared error that accounts for different within group variances. The equation for *F* becomes

$$F* = \frac{\sum_{j=1}^{J} n_j (\bar{Y}_j - \bar{Y})^2}{\sum_{j=1}^{J} \left(1 - \left(\frac{n_j}{n}\right)\right) s_j^2} \tag{26.9}$$

where s_j^2 is the error variance for the *j*th group. Other robust procedures are available as well. These methods have not been applied widely because they were developed recently (Maxwell and Delaney, 1990).

26.4 MULTIPLE COMPARISON TESTS

26.4.1 OVERVIEW

The omnibus *F*-test for a one-way ANOVA evaluates the claim that the population means for all groups are equal. Rejection of the null hypothesis implies that they are not all equal, but does not locate differences. An investigator, having determined that at least one difference exists, might wish to locate the significant difference or differences. Concurrently, when designing a study, a researcher might have theoretical reasons for focusing on particular differences rather than on all possible differences. In the job training example cited above, which involves the demonstration program, the current program, and no job training, the researcher might be concerned with two questions: (1) Are the hourly wages for people participating in a job training program (either the demonstration or the current program) significantly different from the wages for people who receive no job training? (2) are the hourly wages for people participating in the demonstration program significantly different from the wages for people in the current program?

In either case, the researcher would wish to test for hypotheses regarding differences between specific subsets of means. These tests of subsets of groups are commonly termed comparisons or contrasts. Simple contrasts refer to pair-wise comparisons in which one group is tested against another. The number of possible pair-wise comparisons equals $J(J-1)/2$, where J refers to the total number of groups. The comparison between the demonstration program and the current program is an example. The null hypothesis is

$$\mu_1 - \mu_2 = 0 \tag{26.10}$$

General or complex contrasts involve more than two means. For example, a researcher might wish to compare the wages of people who receive no job training (group 3) with the wages of those in a job training program (groups 1 and 2). In this example, one group is compared to a combination or an average of two groups. The null hypothesis is

$$\frac{\mu_1 + \mu_2}{2} - \mu_3 = 0 \tag{26.11}$$

The symbol designated to represent the ith contrast is ψ_i. Each ψ_i addresses a research question. In the job training example, two comparisons are identified:

$$\psi_1 = \mu_1 - \mu_2 = 0 \tag{26.12}$$

and

$$\psi_2 = \frac{\mu_1 + \mu_2}{2} - \mu_3 = 0 \tag{26.13}$$

One also should view each contrast as a linear combination of group means. Equations 26.12 and 26.13 can be rewritten as

$$\psi_1 = (1)\mu_1 + (-1)\mu_2 + (0)\mu_3 = 0 \tag{26.14}$$

and

$$\psi_2 = (1/2)\mu_1 + (1/2)\mu_2 - (1)\mu_3 = 0 \tag{26.15}$$

Both equations can be written as

$$\psi_i = \sum_{j=1}^{J} c_j \mu_j \tag{26.16}$$

A coefficient, c_j, is associated with the population mean of a given group, j. The coefficients sum to 0 and not all coefficients are 0.

$$\psi_1 = 1 - 1 + 0 = 0 \tag{26.17}$$

and

$$\psi_2 = 1/2 + 1/2 - 1 = 0 \tag{26.18}$$

Therefore

$$\sum_{j=1}^{J} c_j = 0 \tag{26.19}$$

Researchers have a wide selection of approaches for testing these contrasts. The choice depends primarily on three factors:

- Type of control over Type 1 error desired
- Planned versus post hoc comparisons
- Orthogonal versus nonorthogonal sets of contrasts

Researchers must determine an acceptable approach to control the probability of committing a Type I error. For example, one could conduct a series of t-tests and set ALPHA to 0.05. This would be the per comparison Type I error rate, for which the symbol is $ALPHA_{PC}$. The experiment-wise error rate, $ALPHA_{EW}$, is the probability of committing at least one Type I error. If one were to test a number of contrasts, the Type I error rate for a given test would be 0.05 but the probability of making at least one Type I error would be higher. The experiment-wise error rate is a function of the number of contrasts to be tested and the per comparison error rate chosen. If the K contrasts are independent of one another, it can be shown that

$$ALPHA_{EW} = 1 - (1 - ALPHA_{PC})^K \tag{26.20}$$

The experiment-wise Type I error rate rises quickly with an increase in the number of independent comparisons. Assuming a per comparison Type I error rate of 0.05, the experiment-wise Type I error rate for 3, 10, and 20 independent contrasts would be 0.14, 0.40, and 0.64, respectively.

In conducting an ANOVA and investigating a set of specific comparisons, researchers must choose an $ALPHA_{PC}$, which in turn determines $ALPHA_{EW}$. The choice is based on the determination of the appropriate balance between Type I and Type II errors. If a low $ALPHA_{PC}$ is chosen to produce a low $ALPHA_{EW}$, then the probability of at least one Type II error—incorrectly failing to reject a null hypothesis—increases. The various statistical approaches for assessing multiple contrasts address this trade off differently; researchers must be aware of these differences in choosing a method.

Multiple comparison approaches also can be characterized as either planned or post hoc. Planned or a priori comparisons are made when researchers wish to test specific contrasts—research questions—before conducting the analysis. The planned tests should be essential to the study design and the purpose of the study. Planned comparisons usually are performed instead of the omnibus F-test in the ANOVA. Post hoc, a posteriori, or incidental methods for assessing multiple are conducted after rejection of the null of equal population means by the overall F-test. The post hoc approaches usually assess all or a large number of possible contrasts.

An advantage of the planned comparison approach is that researchers are less likely to capitalize on chance. They conduct only a small number of tests rather than searching for differences wherever they might be. In the comparisons between planned and post hoc procedures that are governed by the data, planned comparisons offer greater control over experiment-wise Type I error rates. Researchers sometimes allow the data to suggest the comparison to be tested. In these data-driven cases, they are likely to focus on the groups with the greatest observed mean difference. This approach is not appropriate, however, because the sampling distribution of the difference between the highest and the lowest group means is not the same as the sampling distribution for any two groups, for example, groups 1 and 2.

Sets of contrasts can be orthogonal or non-orthogonal. If the normality and homogeneity of variance assumptions hold, orthogonality means independence (Hays, 1994). If two contrasts are independent, the conclusion of rejection or failure to reject the null hypothesis in one contrast is not related to the conclusion reached in the other. Orthogonal contrasts offer greater control over the number of Type I errors one may make. In a set of orthogonal contrasts in which a Type I error has been made for a given contrast, the chances of making another Type I error are unchanged. In the case of non-orthogonal contrasts, multiple Type I errors are likely if at least one such error has been made.

In choosing between orthogonal and non-orthogonal sets of contrasts, researchers must weigh statistical and substantive concerns. Although orthogonal comparisons offer control over the number of Type I errors and although interpretation may thus be enhanced, the research questions of interest may not be orthogonal. These questions should determine the analysis.

26.4.2 MULTIPLE COMPARISON METHODS

Researchers may use a number of methods in assessing the contrasts of interest, such as planned contrasts, Dunn's test, Fisher's least significant difference (LSD), and the Scheffe test.

26.4.2.1 Planned Contrasts

When researchers wish to test a small number of contrasts of theoretical interest, they should employ planned contrasts. Planned contrasts are performed instead of the omnibus F-test. In the example of the job training programs, assume that the researcher wishes to test two research questions: "Are hourly wages for people in the demonstration program the same as the wages for people in the current program?" and "Are hourly wages for people in a job training program, either the demonstration or the current program, the same as those for people who receive no job training?" The two null hypotheses to be tested are

$$H_0\colon \psi_1 = 1\mu_1 - 1\mu_2 + 0\mu_3 = 0 \qquad (26.21)$$

and

$$H_0\colon \psi_2 = 1/2\mu_1 + 1/2\mu_2 - 1\mu_3 = 0 \qquad (26.22)$$

Testing each hypothesis requires estimation of the contrast values, $\hat{\psi}_1$ and $\hat{\psi}_2$. The test statistic used follows a t-distribution with $n - J$ degrees of freedom. The equation is

$$t = \frac{\hat{\psi} - \psi}{\sqrt{\mathrm{MS_e} \sum_{j=i}^{J} \frac{c_j^2}{n_j}}} \qquad (26.23)$$

where
   $\hat{\psi}$ is the value of the contract estimated in the sample
   ψ is the value hypothesized in the null
   $\mathrm{MS_e}$ is the coefficient for the jth group
   c_j is the coefficient for the jth group
   n_j is the sample size for the jth group

On the basis of the job training example, the resulting t-values for the two contrasts are 4.74 and 4.20, respectively. Both contrasts are statistically significant. From the first contrast, one may conclude that wages on average are \$3.95 per hour more for people in the demonstration program than for people in the current program. From the second contrast, one may conclude that wages for people in a job training program, either the demonstration or the current program, are on average \$3.02 per hour higher than for those who received no job training.

26.4.2.2 Dunn's Test

Dunn's test, also known as a Bonferroni test, requires researchers first to specify the desired experiment-wise error rate—say, 0.05. One then distributes this error rate evenly across the comparisons:

$$\frac{ALPHA_{EW}}{K} = ALPHA_{PC} \tag{26.24}$$

The job training example involves two contrasts. In the Dunn test, one would set the per comparison Type I error rate to 0.025 rather than 0.05. The critical values of the t-statistics also would change. With this adjustment, the Dunn test would set a 0.05 limit to the experiment-wise error rate.

On the basis of the results of the planned contrasts for the job training example, the researcher still would reject both null hypotheses because both p-values are less than 0.025. The Dunn test is a commonly used post hoc procedure. If the number of contrasts is large, however, the Dunn test is quite conservative. For example, if a researcher wished to test 10 contrasts with an experiment-wise error rate of 0.05, the per comparison rate would be 0.005. This multiple comparison test is less powerful than other multiple comparison approaches.

To address the conservatism of the Dunn test, modifications to the procedure have been developed (Keppel, 1982; Toothaker, 1991). One approach is to arrange the contrasts on the basis of p-values. The test of the contrast with the lowest p-value is the same equation as used in the unmodified Dunn test. If the null is rejected, one then moves to the contrast with the next smallest p-value. The second test is based on the equation

$$\frac{ALPHA_{EW}}{K-1} = ALPHA_{PC} \tag{26.25}$$

The cutoff for this test is less stringent than for the first. If the result is significant, one proceeds to the contrast with the next smallest p-value and uses

$$\frac{ALPHA_{EW}}{K-2} = ALPHA_{PC} \tag{26.26}$$

If the result is significant, one continues in this way until the full set of contrasts has been tested or until the null has not been rejected. Other modifications to the Dunn test are possible as well (Keppel, 1982; Toothaker, 1991); each is based on partitioning $ALPHA_{EW}$ in some way other than evenly across the full set of contrasts.

26.4.2.3 Fisher's LSD Test

Fisher's least significant difference (LSD) test, also known as a protected t-test, requires researchers to first test the null of equal population means with the overall omnibus F-test. If the results are not significant, testing stops. If the results are significant, further post hoc tests are conducted. To test all pair-wise comparisons, one simply conducts the necessary number of t-tests using Equation 26.23. $ALPHA_{PC}$ is set to the desired level—say, 0.05—for each test.

The logic of the test is that the use of the overall F-test is a control for experiment-wise Type I error. In other words, the procedure contains a set of "protected t-tests." Carmer and Swanson (1973) conclude that the procedure provides a balance between Type I and Type II error rates. Maxwell and Delaney (1990) disagree, however; they argue that the procedure provides no control over Type I error in the second stage and thus the method should not be used.

26.4.2.4   The Scheffe Test

The Scheffe test is an exploratory approach that may be used to test both simple and complex contrasts. It controls the experiment-wise error rate by adjusting the critical value for the hypothesis test. The t-test for a contrast is shown in Equation 26.23. In a typical t-test, one then would refer to the t-distribution with $n - J$ degrees of freedom to determine the cut-off or critical value of t. As discussed earlier, the relationship between the t-distribution and the F-distribution is such that t, with v degrees of freedom, equals the square root of F with $(1, v)$ degrees of freedom. Therefore, in the usual t-test, one rejects the null hypothesis if $t_{n-J} > \sqrt{F_{1,n-J}}$. In the Scheffe test, however, the critical value of F is adjusted to reflect the number of means tested. The appropriate decision rule is to reject null if the sample based value of t exceeds the adjusted critical value of F, as given in the following equation:

$$t > \sqrt{(J - 1)F_{J-1,n-J}} \qquad (26.27)$$

In the job training example, the number of groups is 3 and the critical value of F is 3.89. The appropriate critical value of t is the square root of 7.78, or 2.79. One then would conduct the various t-tests.

In general, the Scheffe test is the most conservative approach for pair-wise comparisons. Hays (1994) states that this test is insensitive to departures from normality, but Maxwell and Delaney (1990) conclude that it is not robust to violations of the homogeneity of variance assumption. In such cases, the procedure may be modified.

26.5   FACTORIAL DESIGNS

26.5.1   INTRODUCTION

ANOVA is not limited to studies involving only one independent variable. When the study is based on two or more independent variables, a factorial design ANOVA can be used. If there are two independent variables, the researcher conducts a two-factor or two-way ANOVA, whereas a z-factor or z-way ANOVA involves z-independent variables. Factorial designs also are referenced by the patterns of groups or levels contained in the factors. For example, a 2×3 (read "2 by 3") factorial design includes two factors; the first has two groups and the second has three. In a completely randomized fixed-effects factorial design, all independent variables are fixed and all subjects are assigned randomly to one and only one treatment combination. Although designs exist to handle studies in which each treatment combination contains only one subject, each treatment combination usually contains at least two subjects.* The independent variables are completely crossed; all possible combinations of groups or treatments exist for all independent variables. If each treatment combination contains an equal number of subjects, the design is said to be balanced.

26.5.2   TWO-FACTOR ANOVA

The discussion of factorial design begins with the simplest case, a two-factor ANOVA. Table 26.8 displays the factorial layout of a 2×3 completely crossed and randomized fixed-effects factorial

---

* Readers interested in single subject designs may consult Iverson and Norpoth (1987) and Montgomery (1991).

TABLE 26.8

Data Layout and Means for Factorial Design ANOVA

		Group 1				Group 2				Group 3			Total
Factor 1 — Group 1	Y_{111}	Y_{711}	Y_{1311}	Y_{1811}	Y_{112}	Y_{712}	Y_{1312}	Y_{1812}	Y_{113}	Y_{713}	Y_{1313}	Y_{1813}	$\bar{Y}_1$
	Y_{211}	Y_{811}	Y_{1411}	Y_{1911}	Y_{212}	Y_{812}	Y_{1412}	Y_{1912}	Y_{213}	Y_{813}	Y_{1413}	Y_{1913}	
	Y_{311}	Y_{911}	Y_{1511}	Y_{2011}	Y_{312}	Y_{912}	Y_{1512}	Y_{2012}	Y_{313}	Y_{913}	Y_{1513}	Y_{2013}	
	Y_{411}	Y_{1011}	Y_{1611}	Y_{2111}	Y_{412}	Y_{1012}	Y_{1612}	Y_{2112}	Y_{413}	Y_{1013}	Y_{1613}	Y_{2113}	
	Y_{511}	Y_{1111}	Y_{1711}	Y_{2211}	Y_{512}	Y_{1112}	Y_{1712}	Y_{2212}	Y_{513}	Y_{1113}	Y_{1713}	Y_{2213}	
	Y_{611}	Y_{1211}			Y_{612}	Y_{1212}			Y_{613}	Y_{1213}			
		$\bar{Y}_{11}$				$\bar{Y}_{12}$				$\bar{Y}_{13}$			
Factor 1 — Group 2	Y_{121}	Y_{721}	Y_{1321}	Y_{1821}	Y_{122}	Y_{722}	Y_{1322}	Y_{1822}	Y_{123}	Y_{723}	Y_{1323}	Y_{1823}	$\bar{Y}_2$
	Y_{221}	Y_{821}	Y_{1421}	Y_{1921}	Y_{222}	Y_{822}	Y_{1422}	Y_{1922}	Y_{223}	Y_{823}	Y_{1423}	Y_{1923}	
	Y_{321}	Y_{921}	Y_{1521}	Y_{2021}	Y_{322}	Y_{922}	Y_{1522}	Y_{2022}	Y_{323}	Y_{923}	Y_{1523}	Y_{2023}	
	Y_{421}	Y_{1021}	Y_{1621}	Y_{2121}	Y_{422}	Y_{1022}	Y_{1622}	Y_{2122}	Y_{423}	Y_{1023}	Y_{1623}	Y_{2123}	
	Y_{521}	Y_{1121}	Y_{1721}	Y_{2221}	Y_{522}	Y_{1122}	Y_{1722}	Y_{2222}	Y_{523}	Y_{1123}	Y_{1723}	Y_{2223}	
	Y_{621}	Y_{1221}			Y_{622}	Y_{1222}			Y_{623}	Y_{1223}			
		$\bar{Y}_{21}$				$\bar{Y}_{22}$				$\bar{Y}_{23}$			
Total		$\bar{Y}_1$				$\bar{Y}_2$				$\bar{Y}_3$			$\bar{Y}$

design ANOVA. Each of the two rows refers to a group or level of the first independent variable, factor 1; each of the three columns refers to a level of factor 2. Each cell or box represents a treatment or group combination. For example, the cell in the upper left hand corner refers to subjects in group 1 of factor 1 and group 1 of factor 2. Each level of factor 1 occurs in each level of factor 2, and vice versa. That is the design is completely crossed. The researcher randomly assigns 132 subjects such that each treatment combination contains 22 subjects. The value of the dependent variable for the ith person in the jth group of factor 1 and in the kth group of factor 2 is represented by Y_{ijk}.

The goal of factorial design ANOVA is to test the effect of the independent variables, both individually and taken together. The ANOVA decomposes the variability in the dependent variable into four sources: (a) the effect of factor 1 alone, (b) the effect of factor 2 alone, (c) the interaction effect of factor 1 and factor 2 taken together, and (d) error variance.

The main effect for a factor is the effect of membership in a level or group of that factor. The main effect of factor 1 in Table 26.8, for example, can be regarded as a row effect while the main effect of factor 2 can be considered as a column effect. An interaction effect is present when the impact of one factor depends on the level of the other factor. In other words, the effect of one factor is not the same for all levels of the second factor. The interaction is the effect of belonging to the j, kth group combination over and above the effect of being situated in the jth row and the kth column.

One can think of interaction effects as nonadditive or contingent. For example, one can modify the job training example used in the discussion of one-way ANOVA to be a 2×3 factorial design. Assume that factor 1 is job training program (demonstration or current) and factor 2 is length of time in training (one, two, or three months). One might find that the effect of time in training depends on the program. For the demonstration program, higher wages might be associated with longer periods of training. For the current program, the average wage might be the same regardless of the number of months in training.

In two-way ANOVA, one typically tests three null hypotheses: one for each of the two main effects and one for the interaction effect. One must partition the variability of the dependent variable

TABLE 26.9

Equations for Two-Way, Fixed Effects ANOVA

Source	df	Sum of Squares[a]	Mean Square	F
Main effect Factor 1	$J - 1$	$nK \sum_{j=1}^{J} (\bar{Y}_j - \bar{Y})^2$	$\dfrac{SS_1}{J - 1}$	$\dfrac{MS_1}{MS_e}$
Main effect Factor 2	$K - 1$	$nJ \sum_{k=1}^{K} (\bar{Y}_k - \bar{Y})^2$	$\dfrac{SS_2}{K - 1}$	$\dfrac{MS_2}{MS_e}$
Interaction effect	$(J - 1)(K - 1)$	$n \sum_{k=1}^{K} \sum_{j=1}^{J} [\bar{Y}_{jk} - \bar{Y}_j - \bar{Y}_K + \bar{Y}]^2$	$\dfrac{SS_{1 \times 2}}{(J - 1)(K - 1)}$	$\dfrac{MS_{1 \times 2}}{MS_e}$
Error	$JK(n - 1)$	$\sum_{k=1}^{K} \sum_{j=1}^{J} \sum_{i=1}^{n_{jk}} (Y_{ijk} - \bar{Y}_{jk})^2$	$\dfrac{SS_e}{JK(n - 1)}$	
Total	$n - 1$	$\sum_{k=1}^{K} \sum_{j=1}^{J} \sum_{i=1}^{n_{jk}} (Y_{ijk} - \bar{Y}_{jk})^2$		

[a] n refers to the number of subjects in each cell in the factorial design. A balanced design is assumed.

to test these hypotheses. Table 26.9 displays the equations necessary to compute the various sums of squares, mean squares, and F-ratios.

The main effect of factor 1 is based on the differences between the row means and the grand mean, whereas the main effect of factor 2 is based on the differences between the column means and the grand mean. Derivation of the sum of squares for the interaction is less intuitive: one starts with the concept of a cell effect, which is based on the difference between the each cell mean and the grand mean weighted by the number of subjects in each cell. The cell effect represents the combined or composite effects (the two main effects and the interaction effect taken together) of the factors. To isolate the interaction effect, one must remove the influence of the two main effects by subtracting them from the composite effect. The F-test for each of the three hypotheses then is based on a ratio of the mean square due to the effect of interest to the mean squared error.

An example will clarify the use of two-way ANOVA; this is an adaptation of an experiment conducted by Cirincione (1992). Assume that a research team wishes to conduct a needs assessment for treatment of drinking problems. The assessment is made for U.S. counties, and the methodology rests on the construction of a model based on expert judgment. To construct the model, experts first identify the important need indicators, namely a county's alcohol-related death rate and annual sales of alcoholic beverages per capita (to persons age 21 and over). The research team then wishes to determine the relative importance of each indicator in predicting need for treatment. To make this determination, each expert judges vignettes that describe hypothetical counties. Each description includes the per capita consumption rate and the alcohol-related death rate for the county. The research team next asks the experts to evaluate the need for treatment for the county in each vignette, and then statistically estimates the relative importance of the two indicators.

The research team is concerned with the potential impact of the way in which information is presented in the vignettes and with the response scale used by the experts. Accordingly, the researchers conduct an experiment that tests these two factors. The first factor, definition of indicators, consists of the use of two different definitions for an alcohol-related death rates. For half of the experts, this cue is defined as the number of alcohol-related deaths (including cirrhosis, alcohol psychosis, alcohol-related homicide or suicide, and alcohol-related vehicular fatalities) per 100,000 persons in a county; the values range from 15 to 75. For the other half of the experts, the alcohol-related death rate is defined on a Likert scale with 1 representing a very low rate and 7 representing a very high rate. For all vignettes, alcoholic beverage sales are measured in dollars; the values range from $50 to $250 per resident age 21 and older.

The second factor tested by the research team is response scale. The research team assigns the experts randomly to one of the three response scale conditions: 1–25 anchored (group 1),

TABLE 26.10

Sample Means for Relative Importance of Alcohol-Related Death Rates in Needs Assessment

		Response Scale 1–25 Anchored	1–25 Unanchored	1–25 Percent	Totals
Definition of death rate	Rates	43.909	54.182	47.045	48.379
	Likert	54.318	60.409	51.500	55.405
	Totals	49.114	57.295	49.273	51.894

1–25 unanchored (group 2), and 1–25 percent (group 3). For the first response scale, the subjects are asked to evaluate the need for treatment on a scale of 1–25: for the set of vignettes they are to judge, they must assign a 1 to the county they believe has the lowest need and a 25 to the county they believe has the highest need. The second response scale is a 25 point Likert scale with no anchor requirement. The third response scale is based on the estimated percentage of each county's population (21 and over) in need of treatment of drinking problems. Estimates of the relative importance of alcohol-related death rates are derived from these judgments.* A total of 132 experts participated, with 22 assigned to each of the six combinations in the 2×3 factorial design. Table 26.10 displays the sample statistics; Table 26.11 contains the results for the ANOVA.

Both main effects are significant. When the description is rendered on a Likert scale, the relative importance of alcohol-related death rates is 7.026 point higher on average than when it is presented on a ratio scale. Concurrently, the average relative weight of alcohol-related death rates is 8.102 points higher when the 1–25 unanchored scale is used. The interaction effect is not significant; the impact of indicator definition does not depend on the response scale used, and vice versa. The ANOVA results suggest that when information is presented and elicited in a format that may not be solidly anchored or well-grounded, the importance of alcohol-related death rates relative to alcoholic beverage sales increases. The findings suggest that in tasks involving somewhat ambiguous information researchers should use multiple methods, provide feedback to the experts, and resolve any differences that arise before employing models developed in this manner for needs assessment. Otherwise the conclusions may be an artifact of the method of presentation or of elicitation.

26.5.3 MULTIPLE COMPARISONS

As with one-way ANOVA, an investigator may wish to test a subset of specific comparisons when the study includes more than one independent variable. As in the one factor case, control of Type I

TABLE 26.11

Two-Way ANOVA Table for Needs Assessment Study

Source	df	SS	MS	F	p-Value
Indicator definition	1	1631.03	1631.030	5.587	.020
Response scale	2	1926.20	963.098	3.299	.040
Interaction	2	205.65	102.826	0.352	.704
Error	126	36783.64	291.934		

* In the case of only two indicators, researchers need derive the relative importance of only one indicator to fully identify the system of relative weights.

error rate is a concern, but a different method is typically used to handle the problem. In the one-way ANOVA, the two types of error rates are the probability of making a Type I error for a given comparison, ALPHA$_{PC}$ (the per comparison error rate), and the probability of making at least one Type I error across all hypothesis tests in the study, ALPHA$_{EW}$ (the experiment-wise error rate).

In a two factor ANOVA, three hypotheses usually are tested with F-tests. Each of the main effects and the interaction effect can be regarded as a representation of a "family" of comparisons. In the needs assessment example, only one comparison-rate versus Liken scale exists for factor 1 because there are only two groups. Factor 2 offers three possible pair-wise comparisons and three complex comparisons. The interaction effects can be tested through several contrasts. In factorial design ANOVA, researchers usually control Type I error rates based on families of tests, ALPHA$_{FW}$ (the family-wise error rate), rather than on an experiment-wise basis. This approach results in an upper limit of ALPHA$_{EW}$ equal to αE where E is the number of families in the ANOVA.

Each of the multiple comparison methods discussed in the connection with one-way ANOVA can be extended to factorial design ANOVA. Tests for the main effects are straightforward. One may treat them as if the experiment were broken down into a series of one-way ANOVAs with each series representing a family. To test interaction effects, the investigator can assess the consistency of the effect of one given factor for two or more levels of the second factor.

26.5.4 Factorial Designs: Assumptions and Unequal Cell Sizes

The assumptions regarding the residuals for the two-factor ANOVA, as well as for higher-order factorial designs, are the same as those for the one-way ANOVA. The errors must be distributed normally with a mean of zero and a constant variance. Furthermore, the error term in any given treatment combination must be unrelated to all other residuals in that treatment combination and to the residuals in other treatment combinations.

This discussion has been limited to studies employing balanced factorial design; that is, each treatment combination contains the same number of cases. Balanced designs guarantee that the main and interaction effects are orthogonal. If they are not orthogonal, the effects are correlated. The formal model for the unbalanced factorial design is the same for as balanced designs, but it is not possible to assess each effect separately from the others. To address this problem, a number of alternative approaches (types of sums of squares) are possible.

26.5.5 Higher-Order Factorial Designs

Factorial design ANOVA is not limited to two independent variables. The addition of each new factor significantly increases the complexity of the design and the number of hypotheses to be tested. Three factors entail three main effects (factor 1, factor 2, and factor 3), three two-way interactions (factor 1 × factor 2, factor 1 × factor 3, and factor 2 × factor 3), and one three-way interaction (factor 1 × factor 2 × factor 3). A four-factor ANOVA involves four main effects, six two-way interactions, four three-way interactions, and one four-way interaction. This pattern continues for each additional factor. The computational procedures are not much more complicated than in the case of two factors. The ease of interpretation however, is often lost, and the required sample sizes are much greater.

26.6 ANOVA AND MULTIPLE REGRESSION

Here we examine briefly the parallels between ANOVA and ordinary least-squares linear regression. In investigating the relationship between a dependent variable and one or more independent variables, researchers must develop a theory of this relationship. The general linear model is a mathematical expression positing that the value of the dependent variable is a linear combination of the independent variables and random error. Equations 26.28 and 26.29 display a typical layout of this model.

$$Y_i = \alpha + \beta_1 X_{i1} + \beta_1 X_{i2} + \cdots + \beta_J X_{iJ} + \varepsilon_i \tag{26.28}$$

and

$$= \alpha + \sum_{j=1}^{J} \beta_j X_{ij} + \varepsilon_i \tag{26.29}$$

where
  Y_i is the observed value of the dependent variable for the ith person in the study
  α is a constant representing the y-intercept. It can be viewed as the effect of independent variables held constant in the study
  β_j is the slope associated with the jth independent variable. It represents the expected change in the dependent variable for a one unit change in the value of X_j holding all other independent variables constant
  X_{ij} is the value for the ith person on the jth independent variable
  ε_i is the error or residual for the ith person

One can use ordinary least squares to estimate the equation.

The reader should recognize Equation 26.29 as the regression model. Using the linear regression model to conduct an ANOVA requires appropriate coding of the variables and appropriate calculation of the F-ratios for the test statistic.

An example will clarify this parallel. Suppose a researcher is interested in comparing attitudes about the importance of monetary rewards across three sectors of the economy: public, private, and nonprofit.* She collects a random sample of six public sector, six private sector, and six nonprofit sector supervisors, and then conducts a one-way ANOVA to assess group differences. The grand mean is 33.3; the means for the public, private, and nonprofit sector supervisors are 33.0, 43.0, and 24.0, respectively. The value of the omnibus F-test is 3.8937, which is statistically significant. Thus the importance of monetary rewards is not the same across the three sectors.

To conduct the same test using a regression model, one must determine how to represent the factor levels as independent variables. In regression models that include an intercept, the number of independent variables needed to represent a factor with J levels is $J - 1$. Thus, in this example, two independent variables are required. Also one must choose a mathematical coding scheme for the variables. Many such schemes exist, but the most commonly used is dummy variable coding. Table 26.12 displays an example of this approach.

Dummy variable coding, also known as indicator variable coding, requires the investigator to represent $J - 1$ of the groups as independent variables, each based on a 0/1 coding. The group not represented by an independent variable is called the omitted or reference group. The value 1 indicates that the subject is a member of the level represented by a given independent variable; the value 0 indicates that the subject is not a member of that group. The cases in the omitted group are coded 0 for all $J - 1$ independent variables. All other cases are coded 1 for one and only one independent variable. Any of the three groups can be chosen to be the omitted category; in this example, the nonprofit sector is omitted. The variable X_1 represents public sector supervisors; the variable X_2 represents private sector supervisors.

Table 26.13 displays the results of the ordinary least squares regression model. The overall test in multiple regression is a test of whether the coefficient of determination, R^2, is equal to 0. In this case, it determines whether a relationship exists between sector of employment and the importance of monetary rewards. The relationship is captured by a linear combination of the $J - 1$ independent variables. In this case, sector of employment can predict 34.2 percent of the variability in the

---

* This example is based on two studies (Edwards et al., 1981; Emmett and Crow, 1988).

TABLE 26.12
Dummy Coding for Single Factor

		Dummy Coding	
Y	Sector	X_1	X_2
48	Public	1	0
42	Public	1	0
36	Public	1	0
30	Public	1	0
21	Public	1	0
21	Public	1	0
61	Private	0	1
49	Private	0	1
52	Private	0	1
40	Private	0	1
31	Private	0	1
25	Private	0	1
30	Nonprofit	0	0
42	Nonprofit	0	0
21	Nonprofit	0	0
21	Nonprofit	0	0
18	Nonprofit	0	0
12	Nonprofit	0	0

dependent variable. Testing the null "no relationship" results in an F-ratio of 3.89 and a p-value of .04. These results are identical to those for the omnibus test in the ANOVA model, because the two tests are the same.

One can use the equation to estimate the group means. For instance,
Public sector:
$9.00(1.0) + 19.00(0.0) + 24.00 = 33.00$
Private sector:
$9.00(0.0) + 19.00(1.0) + 24.00 = 43.00$
Nonprofit sector:
$9.00(0.0) + 19.00(0.0) + 24.00 = 24.00$

From these results, one can see that the y-intercept represents the average value of the omitted group and that each regression weight represents the average difference between the group identified by the independent variable and the omitted group. The tests of the regression weights are pair-wise

TABLE 26.13
Regression Results

	β_j	p-Value
X_1	9.00	.2062
X_2	19.00	.0138
Constant	24.00	.0002
R^2	0.342	
F-ratio	3.89	
p-value	.04	

multiple comparison tests of each group against the omitted group. In this case, we find no statistically significant difference between supervisors in the public and the nonprofit sectors. The difference between the private and the nonprofit sectors, however, is statistically significant.

This presentation of the use of regression analysis to perform a one-way ANOVA assumes a balanced design. As in the case of one-way ANOVA, balanced designs lead to more robust regression models. Among unbalanced designs, unless the lack of balance is due to some extraneous variables not addressed by the investigator, the internal validity of the study is not affected. Unequal sample sizes that result from random sampling and that represent the population proportions of group membership indeed may be preferable. As Pedhazur (1982) argues, such designs are better suited to measure the magnitude of the relationship between the dependent variable and the factor. If one wishes to compare groups, the balanced design is preferable. In either case, the statistical procedures are the same.

Regression analysis also can be used to assess factorial designs. Because main effects and interaction effects are represented by multiple independent variables, one cannot readily assess the significance of the effects according to the significance of the regression weights. Instead, a model comparison approach can be used.*

The logic of model comparison is straightforward. First run the regression model with all the independent variables included, and calculate the coefficient of determination, R_j^2. Then run a second model with the following restriction: do not include in the model the independent variables associated with the effect being tested, and calculate the coefficient of determination, R_j^2. The test of the effect is a test of the change in the coefficient of determination due to the effect and the test statistic is

$$F = \frac{\left(R_f^2 - R_r^2\right)}{\left(1 - R_f^2\right)} \times \frac{n - p_f - 1}{p_f - p_r} \tag{26.30}$$

where
R_f^2 is the coefficient of the determination for the full model
R_r^2 is the coefficient of the determination for the restricted model
n is the total number of subject in the model
p_f is the number of independent variables in the full model
p_r is the number of independent variables in the restricted model

This brief discussion should demonstrate that ANOVA and regression models, when coded properly, can be used to test many of the same research questions.

26.7 CONCLUSIONS

The proper use of ANOVA forces researchers to grapple with several issues when designing studies. The limitations regarding the internal validity of correlation-based conclusions from observational studies are much greater than those for conclusions drawn from experimental research. Although the procedures and statistics in ANOVA are the same in each case, the conclusions that one may properly draw depend on the research design. ANOVA also highlights the issues of Type I error, Type II error, and statistical power; it was developed as a means of dealing with inflated Type I error rates due to multiple t-tests. These issues must be addressed whenever a researcher tests multiple null hypotheses, not only when an ANOVA procedure is used.

---

* In factorial designs that account for interaction effects, coding schemes (e.g., effect and contrast coding) other than dummy variable coding are preferable. Dummy variable coding leads to artificial correlations between main and interaction effects.

Knowledge of ANOVA methods also should improve one's comprehension of regression analysis. The use of categorical independent variables and the proper coding of such variables can be understood in the ANOVA framework. The overall test of fit of the regression model is the same as the test of the composite effects in the ANOVA model. The tests of the regression weights are the same as multiple comparison tests.

Although public administration and public policy scholars use ANOVA less often than some other statistical methods, they would be well served by knowledge in ANOVA methods. If public administration research is to move toward theory testing and more rigorous work, the principle of ANOVA methods and designs must be understood.

REFERENCES

Brown, G. and Harris, C.C. 1993. The implications of work force diversification in the U.S. Forest Service, *Administration and Society*, 25(1): 85–113.

Carmer, S.G. and Swanson, M.R. 1973. An evaluation of ten multiple comparison procedures by Monte Carlo methods, *Journal of the American Statistical Association*, 68: 66–74.

Cirincione, C. 1992. The integrated contingency model: Range-sensitive decision models, Unpublished Doctoral Dissertation, State University of New York at Albany, Albany.

Cirincione, C., Steadman, H.J., Robbins, P.C., and Monahan, J. 1994. Mental illness as a factor in criminality: A study of prisoners and mental patients, *Journal of Criminal Behavior and Mental Health, 4*(1): 33–47.

Edwards, J.T., Nalbandian, J., and Wedel, K.R. 1981. Individual values and professional education: Implications for practice and education, *Administration and Society, 13*(2): 123–143.

Emmert, M.A. and Crow, M.M. 1988. Public, private and hybrid organizations: An empirical examination of the role of publicness, *Administration and Society*, 20(2): 216–244.

Frank, H. 1990. Municipal revenue forecasting with time series models: A Florida case study, *American Review of Public Administration*, 20(1): 45–57.

Gianakis, G.A. and Frank, H.A. 1993. Implementing time series forecasting models: Considerations for local governments, *State and Local Government Review*, 25(2): 130–144.

Glass, G.V. and Hopkins, K.D. 1984. *Statistical Methods in Education and Psychology*, Second Edition, Englewood Cliffs: Prentice-Hall, Inc.

Hays, W.L. 1994. *Statistics*, Fifth Edition, Fort Worth: Harcourt Brace College Publishers.

Herman, R.D. and Heimovics, R.D. 1990. An investigation of leadership skill differences in chief executives of nonprofit organizations, *American Review of Public Administration*, 20(2): 107–124.

Iverson, G.R. and Norpoth, H. 1987. *Analysis of Variance*, Vol. 1, Newbury Park: Sage Publications.

Keppel, G. (1982). *Design & Analysis: A Researcher's Handbook*, Second Edition, Englewood Cliffs: Prentice-Hall.

Klammer, T.P. and Reed, S.A. 1990. Operating cash flow formats: Does format influence decisions? *Journal of Accounting and Public Policy*, 9: 217–235.

Maxwell, S.E. and Delaney, H.D. 1990. *Designing Experiments and Analyzing Data: A Model Comparison Approach*, Belmont: Wadsworth Publishing Company.

Montgomery, D.C. 1991. *Design and Analysis of Experiments*, Third Edition, New York: John Wiley & Sons.

Newell, C. and Ammons, D.N. 1987. Role emphasis of city managers and other municipal executives, *Public Administration Review*, 47(3): 246–253.

Nunn, S. 1994. How capital technologies affect municipal service outcomes: The case of police mobile digital terminals and stolen vehicle recoveries, *Journal of Policy Analysis and Management*, 13(3): 539–559.

Pedhazur, E.J. 1982. *Multiple Regression in Behavioral Research: Explanation and Prediction*, Second Edition, New York: Holt, Rinehart, and Winston.

Siegel, S. and Castellan, J.N.J. 1988. *Nonparametric Statistics for the Behavioral Sciences*, Second Edition, New York: McGraw-Hill.

Toothaker, L.E. 1991. *Multiple Comparisons for Researchers*, Newbury Park: Sage Publications.

Velleman, P.F. and Hoaglin, D.C. 1981. *Applications, Basics, and Computing of Exploratory Data Analysis*, Boston: Duxbury Press.

Warner, J.L., Berman, J.J., Weyant, J.M., and Ciarlo, J.A. 1983. Assessing mental health program effectiveness: A comparison of three client follow-up methods, *Evaluation Review*, 7(5): 635–658.

Wells, J.B., Layne, B.H., and Allen, D. 1991. Management development training and learning styles, *Public Productivity and Management Review, 14*(4): 415–428.

Wittmer, D. 1991. Serving people or serving for pay: Reward Preferences among government, hybrid sector, and business managers, *Public Productivity and Management Review, 4*(4): 369–383.

27 Linear Correlation and Regression

Leslie R. Alm and Susan G. Mason

CONTENTS

27.1 INTRODUCTION

The primary emphasis of social science research, including public administration, is to evaluate relationships between variables in search of causation. As researchers, we want to know how variables are related to each other; that is, we want to know which variable is influencing (causing) the other. For instance, public administrators may want to know if campaign spending is linked to people splitting their ballots between Republicans and Democrats when voting, or if the percentage of African Americans affects the amount of money spent by cities on contracts for businesses run by minorities, or if a focus on results is related to managerial authority. To be sure, establishing that one variable is having a causal effect on another variable requires meeting a rigorous set of standards. Specifically, this includes showing that there is a strong theoretical reason for believing that one variable is the cause of the other, that the relationship between the two variables is not the result of another variable that is related to both variables, that one of the variables precedes the other in time, and that the two variables covary; i.e., move or change in relation to each other (Meier et al., 2006).

Linear correlation and regression analysis are two widely accepted statistical techniques designed to help the researcher establish these criteria for causal linkages by providing an estimation of the way variables are related to each other. Both of these statistical techniques are used early in the research process to check possible linkages and to set the foundation for further, more complex statistical analyses. Correlation analysis produces a measure of association that not only indicates the strength and direction of the relationship, but also provides a measure of how accurate the regression equation is in predicting the relationship. Simple regression analysis provides an equation that describes the numerical relationship between two interval-level variables and is used to predict the value of one variable based on the value of the other.

It is important to note that although these two statistical techniques are most powerful when used in multivariate analysis (analysis involving more than two variables), the purpose of this chapter is to illustrate and explain correlation and regression as they apply to the linear relationship between two variables at the interval or ratio level of measurement. It is common in the social sciences to describe correlation and regression between two variables as linear correlation and simple regression.

Linear correlation and simple regression provide the foundation for multivariate regression (the subject of Chapter 28) in that the logic and principles that underlie their understanding are identical to the logic and principles that underlie the more complex multivariate techniques. The path we take to understanding linear correlation and regression begins with the idea that variables are related to each other in some linear fashion. In fact, the definition, calculation, and interpretation of both correlation and regression coefficients are directly tied to the concept of linearity. If one is to understand linear regression and correlation, one must first come to terms with linearity.

27.2   VARIABLES, RELATIONSHIPS, AND LINEARITY

The concept of linearity is framed within a discussion of variables and how these variables are related to each other. Typically, the researcher wants to know if one variable is influencing another variable. For example, a researcher might want to know if higher levels of education lead to higher income. The variables of concern would be education and income. As researchers, we could illustrate this relationship in terms of independent and dependent variables where the independent variable is the one that provides the influence and the dependent variable is the one that receives the influence. This general relationship would be portrayed by the symbols

$$X \rightarrow Y$$

where X represents the independent variable and Y represents the dependent variable. The arrow points from X to Y indicating that X is influencing Y. The direction of the arrow is chosen by the researcher based on theoretical considerations, good judgment, and past research (Lewis-Beck, 1980). For our example involving education and income, the relationship would be illustrated as follows:

$$Education \rightarrow Income$$

where education would be the independent variable and income would be the dependent variable.

Linear correlation and regression are tools that are used with interval levels of measurement and are based on the assumption of linearity.[1] The level of measurement requirement means that to effectively use linear correlation and regression, our variables must be measured such that they permit either comparisons of quantitative differences among cases on a scale; e.g., time: 1950, 1990, or in absolute distances between cases; e.g., money: \$10, \$20 (Hoover and Donovan, 2004). The assumption of linearity—that our relationship follows the path of a straight line—is justified on the grounds that it is generally considered the most parsimonious alternative and it provides a starting point when theory is weak and inspection of the data themselves fails to provide a clear alternative. Furthermore, in the "real" world, numerous relationships have been found to be empirically linear (Lewis-Beck, 1980).

27.3 RESEARCH SETTING

Research typically begins with a research hypothesis of the form "as one variable (X) increases (decreases) in value, the other variable (Y) increases (decreases) in value." Researchers want to know two things about the relationship of these two variables—the direction and strength. Direction is either positive, when the variables change in the same direction; or negative, when the variables change in the opposite direction. Strength shows how closely the variables covary. For linear correlation and simple regression, strength is determined by how close the relationship comes to being a straight line.

A good way to view relationships between two variables and also check for linearity is through the use of scatter plots. Scatter plots show the distribution of the data points (ordered pairs of values associated with each of the variables) along an X–Y continuum in such a way that one can visualize the way variables change together. Furthermore, scatter plots provide an excellent means of conceptualizing the ideas of strength and direction of relationships.

To get a general feel for scatter plots and how they can help us grasp the concepts of strength and direction, look at Figures 27.1 through 27.4. There does not appear to be a discernable relationship in Figure 27.1, whereas Figure 27.2 appears to be curvilinear (nonlinear) in nature. For now, we will not concern ourselves with nonlinear relationships, but will focus on Figures 27.3 and 27.4, which appear to be linear in nature even though they exhibit different characteristics. For instance, the scatter points in Figure 27.4 appear to be more closely grouped together than the scatter points in Figure 27.3. In fact, this grouping of variables signifies the strength of the relationship— the closer the scatter points come to being grouped (about an imaginary line), the stronger the association between the variables. In this case, the stronger association would be represented by Figure 27.4 and the weaker by Figure 27.3.

Something else that is noticeable about the scatter plots in Figures 27.3 and 27.4 is that each of the plots has a different slant; that is, the scatter points in Figure 27.4 appear to be much flatter than those in Figure 27.3. In addition, the scatter points in Figure 27.3 appear to move upward as one moves right along the X-axis (the horizontal axis), whereas the scatter points in Figure 27.4 appear to move slightly downward. In fact, those characteristics signify both the direction and the nature

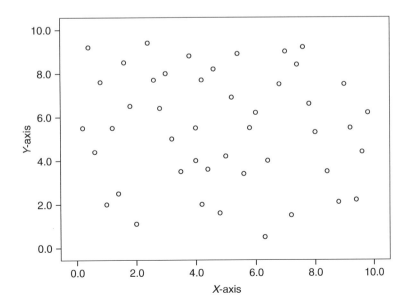

FIGURE 27.1 Scatter plot indicating no linear relationship.

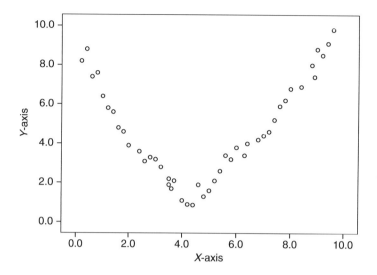

FIGURE 27.2 Scatter plot indicating nonlinear relationship.

of the relationship. We would say that the scatter points in Figure 27.3 would be positive in nature (as *X* increases, *Y* increases) and that the scatter points in Figure 27.4 would be negative in nature (as *X* increases, *Y* decreases). Furthermore, we could also make a distinction between the relationships shown in Figures 27.3 and 27.4 in that the scatter points in Figure 27.3 change at a much higher rate than do the scatter points in Figure 27.4; that is, for Figure 27.3, as we move along the *X*-axis, *Y* changes at a much greater rate than it does in Figure 27.4. This change in *Y*

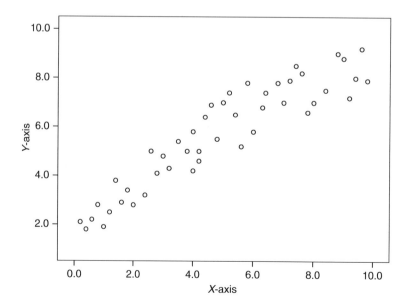

FIGURE 27.3 Scatter plot indicating positive linear relationship.

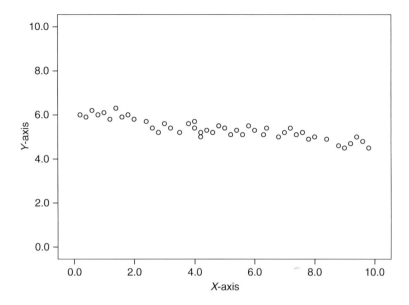

FIGURE 27.4 Scatter plot indicating strong, negative linear relationship.

against the change in X is known as the slope of the line and is formally defined as the change in Y for a one-unit change in X.

One thing that is important to note right away is that the measure of direction and strength is distinct in nature. One measure has to do with whether the variables change in a direct or inverse manner (reflecting the direction of the relationship), whereas the other measure has to do with how closely the scatter points come to forming a line (reflecting the strength of the relationship). Moreover, we have two distinct ways of approaching an explanation and analysis of these relationships. To determine the direction and nature of the relationship we use regression analysis and to determine how strong the relationship is we use correlation analysis.

27.4 LINEAR CORRELATION

The correlation coefficient is the statistical indicator that provides a measure of how closely the relationship between two variables comes to being linear. The most commonly used measure of linear correlation is Pearson's correlation coefficient, often referred to as Pearson's r. As a measure of linear association, Pearson's r varies from -1 to $+1$ in value, with a value of zero meaning that no linear association exists between the variables (Salkind, 2006). The sign provides the direction of the association, while the actual value provides the indication of strength. As the value of Pearson's r moves from 0 to $+1$, it indicates a stronger positive association, with $+1$ indicating a perfect positive linear association. As the value of Pearson's r moves from 0 to -1, it indicates a stronger negative association, with -1 indicating a perfect negative association. Generally, in the real world we do not find perfect associations between variables; hence the values for Pearson's r will fall somewhere between -1 and $+1$.

Using an example depicting the relationship between percent of people with a college education and per capita income in Idaho counties, we use a mathematical process known as the method of least squares to estimate the value of Pearson's r.[2] Fortunately for today's researchers, there are many statistical packages available to calculate this value. However, if the reader is interested, an overview of the hand calculations for Pearson's r is presented in Procedure 1 of the Appendix.

For our example, Pearson's r equals 0.65 and would be interpreted as follows: there is a fairly strong, positive, linear association between percent of people with a college education and per capita income in Idaho counties. We must also test for the statistical significance of Pearson's r. We find that the calculated value for Pearson's r is statistically significant (see Procedure 3 in the Appendix), allowing us to reject the null hypothesis that Pearson's r is equal to zero and accept the fact that for our data, the value of the correlation coefficient equals 0.65.

Before we go too much further, there are several important points that should be made. First, when completing bivariate analysis, the direction of the correlation and regression coefficients will be the same. This is not necessarily true when completing multivariate analysis (which controls for many factors), where it is possible to have different directions for the bivariate correlation coefficient and the regression coefficient. Second, one must always remember that the correlation coefficient and the regression coefficient are two distinct measures of association. Pearson's r is a measure of association and does not distinguish which of the variables is affecting the other. It only shows how strong the association is between the variables, disregarding which direction the arrow of influence is pointing. The regression coefficient specifies the causal direction; that is, the researcher must choose which variable is the independent variable and which the dependent variable. As specified earlier in the chapter, the researcher—based on her reading of the relationship—makes this choice. It does not come from the application of statistical techniques; it comes from the imagination and thought of the researcher.

Third, an interesting and valuable extension of Pearson's r provides the researcher with another very straightforward interpretation of the explanatory power of the regression equation. R^2 (commonly called the coefficient of determination) records the proportion of the variation in the dependent variable "explained" or "accounted for" by the independent variable (Lewis-Beck, 1980). Recall that we began our discussion of bivariate relationships by saying that the researcher was investigating the effect of one variable on another variable. Essentially, one of the things the researcher wants to know is how much of the change (variance) in the dependent variable is "caused" by the change in the independent variable. The coefficient of determination provides us with the answer. Since r varies between -1 and $+1$, R^2 will vary between 0 and $+1$. However, the interpretation of R^2 is one of percent—in practical terms, R^2 gives us the percent of variation in the dependent variable explained by the independent variable. If $R^2 = 0$, then the independent variable explains none of the variance in the dependent variable. If $R^2 = 1$, then the independent variable explains all of the variance in the dependent variable. Of course, in the real world, we will seldom get an R^2 equal to any of these perfect values. Instead we get values between 0 and 1.

From our example, Pearson's $r = 0.65$. Squaring this gives us an $R^2 = 0.42$. The interpretation would then be that the percent of people with a college education in Idaho counties explains 42 percent of the variance (change) in per capita income in Idaho counties. This interpretation of R^2 is also commonly referred to as "the goodness of fit" of the regression line, as it is a function of how closely the data points are to being perfectly linear. In practical terms, however, the coefficient of determination (R^2) indicates to the researcher how much variance in the dependent variable can be explained by knowing the independent variable.

27.5 LINEAR REGRESSION ANALYSIS

As mentioned earlier, as researchers we are often interested in the relationship of one variable to another, usually viewed in the format: $X \rightarrow Y$. However, to determine the exact linear nature of the relationship, we express the relationship in the format of a simple regression equation,

$$Y = a + bX$$

where Y represents the dependent variable, a represents the Y-intercept of the line (the point where the line crosses the Y-axis), b represents the slope of the line, and X represents the independent variable.

The idea of linear regression analysis is to identify the fit of our research data (as represented by a scatter plot) to a straight line and then use the equation of that line to predict the nature of the relationship between the two variables. Returning to our earlier example, suppose a researcher chose all counties in Idaho ($n = 44$) as the unit of analysis for a study investigating the relationship between the percentage of people in a county over the age of 25 with a college degree and the average per capita income of the county.[3] Previous research in Idaho suggests that the educational level of counties is linked to income (Alm and Witt, 1997). Hence, the researcher suspects that the higher the percentage of people with a college education, the higher the per capita income in the county. After she gathers her data (see Table 27.1), the first thing the researcher should do is produce a scatter plot relating the percentage of people in a county over the age of 25 with a college degree and the average per capita income. The scatter plot is shown in Figure 27.5. A glance at the scatter plot suggests to the researcher that the relationship between these two interval-level variables may indeed be linear. Note that the scatter plot is not entirely satisfactory. In fact, it appears quite "messy." That is, the data points do not necessarily flow neatly along a straight line or indicate a clear-cut linear relationship. This is something researchers must deal with on a regular basis as they study relationships that appear in the "real" world. One learns to follow the relationships through all the research (and statistical) procedures before making a final determination concerning strength, direction, and linearity.

We employ the same mathematical principles we used in calculating Pearson's r to calculate the slope (b) and the Y-intercept (a) for the equation of the line that best represents the scatter points as

TABLE 27.1
Variables for Idaho Study

ID	County	Per Capita Income, 2000	Percentage of Population over 25 with Bachelor's Degree, 2000
1	Ada	31,420	21.71
2	Adams	18,212	10.09
3	Bannock	20,252	16.42
4	Bear Lake	15,647	8.73
5	Benewah	19,064	8.30
6	Bingham	17,621	10.66
7	Blaine	41,259	30.21
8	Boise	21,492	13.06
9	Bonner	18,955	11.36
10	Bonnevillle	22,408	17.28
11	Boundary	17,410	9.03
12	Butte	19,376	9.18
13	Camas	21,585	17.33
14	Canyon	18,271	10.31
15	Caribou	20,068	12.41
16	Cassia	21,170	9.10
17	Clark	22,022	9.48
18	Clearwater	18,429	9.10
19	Custer	23,087	12.88
20	Elmore	21,907	11.52
21	Franklin	15,451	10.31
22	Fremont	15,670	9.28

(*continued*)

TABLE 27.1 (*continued*)
Variables for Idaho Study

ID	County	Per Capita Income, 2000	Percentage of Population over 25 with Bachelor's Degree, 2000
23	Gem	18,078	8.62
24	Gooding	25,240	8.48
25	Idaho	17,690	10.65
26	Jefferson	16,947	11.55
27	Jerome	23,434	9.89
28	Kootenai	22,527	13.05
29	Latah	21,391	22.74
30	Lemhi	18,886	12.28
31	Lewis	19,074	11.13
32	Lincoln	19,877	9.52
33	Madison	14,861	14.43
34	Minidoka	16,955	7.04
35	Nez Perce	17,066	13.70
36	Oneida	15,412	12.11
37	Owyhee	16,504	7.61
38	Payette	18,128	7.74
39	Power	18,027	10.80
40	Shoshone	19,426	7.10
41	Teton	15,020	19.95
42	Twin Falls	21,322	10.77
43	Valley	24,390	18.48
44	Washington	16,075	9.77

Source: County Profiles of Idaho, Idaho Department of Commerce Boise, 2000 and Geolytics Census CD + Maps, 2000.

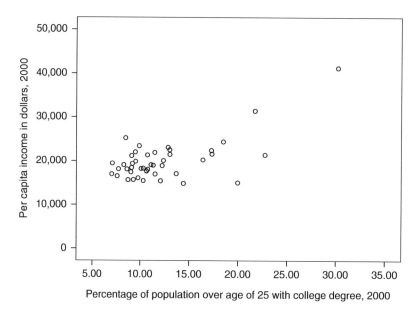

FIGURE 27.5 Scatter plot of education against per capita income.

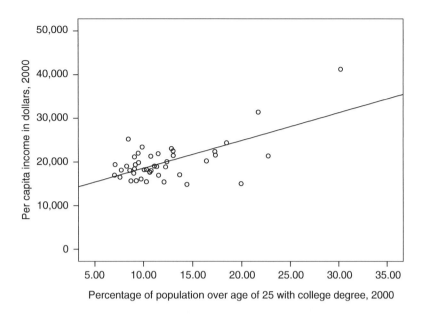

FIGURE 27.6 Scatter plot of education against per capita income.

displayed in Figure 27.5. The calculations for these values are provided in Procedure 1 of the Appendix. Most often, however, these calculations are left to computers and advanced statistical programs readily available to today's researchers.

For this particular example, the researcher ends up with a value for the slope (b) equal to 635.51 and a value for the intercept (a) equal to 12,206.43. The equation of the line $Y = a + bX$ becomes
per capita income $= 12,206.43 + 635.51$ (percent of people with college education).
The actual depiction of this line can be viewed in Figure 27.6. What is important to the researcher is the interpretation of this equation; that is, within the framework of the research project, how do the calculated values of the slope and intercept help to define the relationship between percent of people with a college education and per capita income within Idaho counties.

As shown above, the two primary statistics generated by regression analysis are a and b. The statistic that takes on the value of a is the intercept, often labeled as the constant. The more important of the two statistics is b, which is known as the unstandardized regression coefficient and represents not only the slope of the line, but tells us the specific relationship (on average) between percent of people with a college education and per capita income in Idaho counties. The interpretation of the unstandardized regression coefficient is fairly straightforward. In general, the value for b indicates the average change in the dependent variable (Y) associated with a unit change in the independent variable (X). In this case, the coefficient $b = 635.51$ would be interpreted as follows: for a one percent increase in percent of people with a college education, on average, there would be a corresponding increase of $635.51 in per capita income for Idaho counties.

Several things are important to notice here. First, it is paramount that the researcher operationalizes each of the variables in a manner that is conducive to interpretation. Straightforward and concrete measures serve this purpose well. Although there may be instances when the researcher has no choice in the type of units used, it is important that the researcher puts a good amount of thought and consideration into how he or she will measure variables before the actual data is gathered. Second, the sign in front of the slope indicates the direction of the relationship. If the sign is positive (+), then the dependent variable increases as the independent variable increases. If the sign is negative (−), then the dependent variable decreases as the independent variable increases. For this example, the sign was positive, so as the percent of people with a college education increases, per capita income increases. Third, we are talking about average change; that is, on average, for a one-unit change in the independent variable, the dependent variable changes by a certain amount. For this example, the researcher would not make the claim that in every single instance, a one percent increase in people with a college education leads exactly to an increase of $635.51 in per capita income for a specific county. Rather, the value of the unstandardized regression coefficient represents the average increase in per capita income expected over all of the counties in the study.

The interpretation of the intercept (a) is also quite straightforward. It simply estimates the value of the dependent variable (Y), when the independent variable (X) equals zero. In this example, with $a = 12,206.43$, the interpretation would be that for a county that has zero percent of people with a college education, the per capita income would be $12,206.43. However, there are two major problems that can occur which make the interpretation of the intercept unusable (Lewis-Beck, 1980). First, if the range of values for the dependent (Y) and independent variable (X) does not include the intercept, making generalizations about its meaning is quite risky. For example, if the actual minimum value of the dependent variable was $16,955 and the actual range of the independent variable in our study was from 60 to 90 percent of people with a college education, our calculated value of a (equal to $12,206. 43) would not be very representative of our actual values. Subsequently, it would be risky to put much faith in its meaning.

Second, if the intercept turns out to be a negative value, the meaning would not make sense. For instance, if we had a negative value for a in our example—that would mean for a value of zero percent of people with a college degree in a county, per capita income would be negative, which we know is not possible. Because of these factors, researchers generally ignore the interpretation of the intercept.

As in calculating all statistics, the researcher must ensure that the unstandardized regression coefficient (b) is statistically significant. Simply put, statistical significance tells the researcher whether he or she can have faith that the calculated value for b is representative of a relationship that exists in the population from which the sample was taken. In practical terms, the calculated value for the unstandardized regression coefficient is only descriptive in nature; that is, it merely describes the set of data from which it was computed. In actuality, we want to test this relationship (the value for b) to ensure that it could plausibly exist in the real world (population of study) and was not derived simply by chance. To complete this test, we use a procedure for testing of null hypotheses. (This procedure is described elsewhere in this book (Chapter 26).) The actual calculations are presented in Procedure 2 of the Appendix.

For our example, the value of the unstandardized regression coefficient is statistically significant; hence, the researcher can have confidence that the value for the unstandardized regression coefficient could exist in the "real world" and that the calculated value for b (635.51) is representative of what it would be in the population from which it came. As with the calculations of the coefficients, statistical significance can be easily calculated today by using any number of statistical packages designed to do exactly that.

27.6 A RESEARCH EXAMPLE WITH COMPUTER OUTPUT

Let us take a closer look at the research example presented above through an analysis of the computer output used to estimate the relationship between two variables in the context of linear correlation and regression. The hypothesis with which we began our investigation was: as the percent of people with a college education in Idaho counties increases, per capita income increases. Using SPSS for Windows (SPSS Inc., 2006), the computer output for correlation and simple regression was derived as presented in Tables 27.2 and 27.3.[4]

The researcher would first turn to the correlation table (see Table 27.2) and observe that there is a fairly strong positive linear association between the two variables. The researcher comes to this conclusion because Pearson's correlation coefficient equals 0.65. The positive sign indicates that as the percent of people with a college education in each county increases, per capita income increases.

TABLE 27.2

SPSS Results for Pearson's Correlation Coefficient

	Per Capita Income, 2000	Percentage of Population over 25 with Bachelor's Degree, 2000
Per Capita Income, 2000	1	0.65*
Percentage of Population over 25 with Bachelor's degree, 2000	0.65*	1

$* \ p < .01$, two-tailed t-test.

The value of 0.65 places this correlation coefficient just past the midway point between 0 and $+1$ (see Figure 27.7) on the standardized continuum indicating strength of a measure.

Furthermore, this association is statistically significant. The researcher comes to this conclusion by interpreting the meaning of the * following the value of 0.65 and the notation $*p < .01$. This means that the value for Pearson's correlation coefficient (0.65) is statistically significant to the .01 level. That the value for our correlation coefficient is statistically significant is an extremely important concept. It means that we can be confident that the value we obtained from our sample is representative of the value in the population. In other words, because our obtained significance value is so small (less than 0.01), we are reasonably certain that the association we observed is not due to chance, but exists in the "real" world. Simply put, researchers use correlation coefficients that do not reach statistical significance to provide support for (or against) their hypotheses with extreme caution.

In our example, we did find a statistically significant association between our variables of interest, allowing us to be confident that a fairly strong positive association exists between percent of people with a college education and per capita income in Idaho counties. The researcher then would turn to analysis of the regression equation. From Table 27.3, the researcher first notes the

TABLE 27.3

SPSS Results for Bivariate Regression of Education Level on Per Capita Income

Variable	Estimate (t-score)
Education level	635.57*
	(5.54)
Constant	12,203.35*
	(8.16)
Standard error	3,535.09
N	44
R	0.65
R^2	0.42
Adjusted R^2	0.41
Durbin–Watson d	2.105
$F \ (1, 42)$	30.64*

$* \ p < .001$, two-tailed t-test.

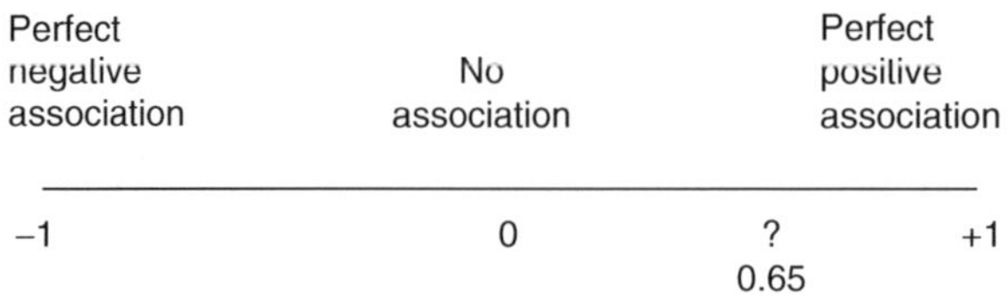

FIGURE 27.7 Correlation continuum for per capita income and educational level.

Adjusted R-square (R^2) of 0.41. In this case, the researcher chooses Adjusted R^2 (instead of R^2) because it provides a better measure of "goodness of fit"—Adjusted R^2 adjusts the value of R^2 to take into account the fact that a regression model always fits the particular data on which it was developed better than it fits the population data (Green and Salkind, 2005). In essence, Adjusted R^2 provides the researcher with a more accurate measurement of explained variance.

The interpretation of Adjusted R^2 is fairly straightforward. In this instance, an Adjusted $R^2 = 0.41$ means that approximately 41 percent of the variation in our dependent variable (per capita income) can be explained by the independent variable (percent of people with a college education). It also tells us that almost 59 percent of the variance is left unexplained, meaning that there are other factors besides percent of college educated people that are affecting the variance in per capita income. For the researcher, this means other variables must be added to the model for a fuller explanation. This would be accomplished through a multiple regression equation (Chapter 28).

Still, the primary statistic of interest in regression analysis is the regression coefficient (b). As noted earlier, the first thing the researcher would do is check the significance of the regression coefficient. The output shows statistical significance at the .001 level ($*p < .001$); hence, the value for b (635.57) is statistically significant and the researcher can feel confident that this value could plausibly exist in the "real" world and the researcher could be confident that this result is representative of the studied population. The interpretation of the regression coefficient is also straightforward. For $b = 635.57$, it means that for a one percent increase in percent of people with a college education in a county, the average per capita income increases by \$635.57. The standard error and the t-score are measures used to determine the statistical significance of b as illustrated in Procedure 2 of the Appendix.

In the final analysis, using linear correlation and simple regression, the researcher would be quite confident that a relationship exists in Idaho counties between the percent of people with a college education in the county and per capita income. It appears that the association is positive (signs of both the correlation coefficient and the regression coefficient are positive), fairly strong ($r = 0.65$), and on average, for a one percent increase in college-educated people in Idaho counties, per capita income increases by \$635.57.

Observe that the simple regression equation would be the same as the one developed earlier from the hand calculations:

per capita income = 12,203.35 + 635.57 (percent of people with college education)

with the value of the intercept ($a = 12,203.35$) obtained from Table 27.3 (the value of the "constant") and being equal to the predicted per capita income when percent of people with a college education is zero.

27.7 ASSUMPTIONS AND RESIDUALS

In order for the researcher to accurately infer that the measures estimated through simple regression are representative of the population values, certain assumptions must be met (Lewis-Beck, 1980; Meier et al., 2006; Norusis, 2000). Among these are: the relationship is linear; the dependent variable is normally distributed for each value of the independent variable; the variance in the dependent variable is constant for all values of the independent variable; and that all observations (cases) in the study are selected independently. These assumptions also apply to multivariate regression as well as simple regression analysis.

The way that researchers check whether these assumptions are being met is through analysis of the error terms, commonly referred to as residuals. Residuals are simply the difference between the observed and predicted values of the dependent variable. For instance, our prediction model for the relationship between percent of people with a college education and per capita income is

per capita income = 12,203.35 + 635.57 (percent of people with a college degree).

The predicted value of per capita income for a county with 21.71 percent of its people with a college degree would be

$$\text{per capita income} = 12{,}203.35 + 635.57(21.71)$$
$$= 12{,}203.35 + 13{,}798.22$$
$$= 26{,}001.57$$

The actual observed value of per capita income (from our data set—see Table 27.1, Ada County) for a county with 21.71 percent of its people with a college degree is 31,420. Hence, the observed value minus the predicted value would be $31{,}420 - 26{,}002 = 5{,}418$. The value of $+5{,}418$ is called the residual and, in this case, it would mean that our observed value for per capita income is larger than the predicted value by 5,418. By analyzing the scatter plots of the residuals, the researcher can check to see if each of the regression assumptions is being met.

The easiest way to check for linearity is to inspect the scatter plot of the dependent variable plotted against the independent variable. In fact, we started the investigation of the relationship between percent of people with a college degree and per capita income by doing exactly that. The results of that scatter plot can be viewed in Figures 27.5 and 27.6. Initial inspection of this scatter plot indicated that a linear regression model may be appropriate, as the points appear to cluster around a positive sloping straight line.

A second way to check for linearity is to inspect the plots of the studentized residuals against the predicted values.[5] For our example, these plots are represented in Figure 27.8. If a nonlinear

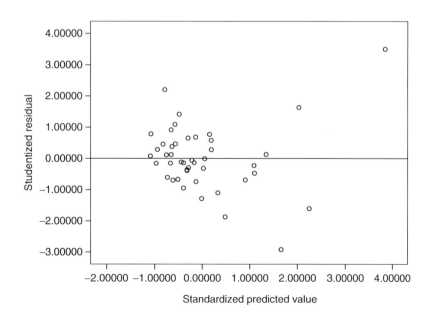

FIGURE 27.8 Scatter plot of residuals for simple regression.

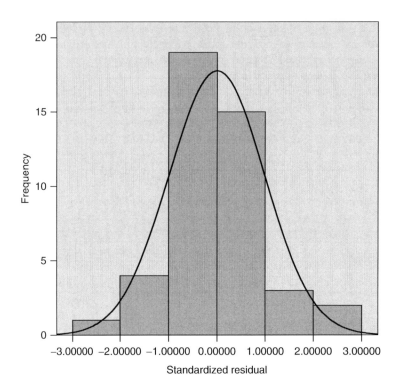

FIGURE 27.9 Histogram of dependent variable.

relationship existed, one would expect to see some type of curvilinear pattern among the residuals. Because the scatter plot of our residuals does not show a particularly curvilinear pattern of plots along a horizontal continuum, we can be reasonably certain that our relationship is linear.

To check the normality assumption that each value of the dependent variable is normally distributed, the researcher would use the computer to plot a histogram displaying the distribution of residuals. The histogram for our example is presented in Figure 27.9. If the dependent variable is normally distributed, for each value of the independent variable, the distribution of residuals should approach normality; that is, the distribution should look like the superimposed normal curve depicted in Figure 27.9. Inspection of our histogram shows a rather symmetrical distribution with a peak more or less in the middle and hence, we could be fairly confident that the residuals meet the normality assumption.

The researcher should also check to ensure that the variance in the dependent variable is constant for all values of the independent variable. In statistical terms, this is known as homoscedasticity. To ensure that we have homoscedasticity for our example, we would inspect the same residual plots that we used to check for linearity (see Figure 27.8). If homoscedasticity were present we would expect to find a balanced scatter plot with an equal distribution of points above and below the zero line, with no discernible funnel pattern. If heteroscedesticity (nonconstant variance) exists, we would expect to find a pattern of increasing or decreasing values for the residuals across the horizontal axis (predicted values) in what is commonly referred to as a funnel effect. In our example (see Figure 27.8) we do see what appears to be funnel-type pattern that is especially prominent in the bottom portion of the plot. As we move across the scatter plot from left to right, residuals increase in value such that they move further and further from the horizontal line representing the zero mark, forming a funnel opening up to the right. This is a clear indication that heteroscedasticity may be present and may pose problems for our analysis and interpretations.

The final assumption that researchers need to check is that all observations (cases) selected are independent from each other. If the observations are not independent, autocorrelation is present. Because autocorrelation is so closely aligned with trend (or time series) analysis, the discussion on its effects and the remedies are left to the relevant chapter (Chapter 33).

For the researcher, the question surely arises of what to do if these assumptions are not met. There are no easy answers to this question. Because of the complexity that may exist in your research, it may be quite likely that you may have to consult with someone who has special expertise in statistical methods. However, there do exist guidelines for the researcher to follow.

If the relationship between the variables is not linear, then you may want to complete a transformation of your data to fit a curvilinear model. The mathematical model that best fits what your scatter plot looks like would determine the choice of the transformation. This determination would be made by a careful inspection of the scatter plot by the researcher. Common transformations include logarithmic, inverse, quadratic, cubic, power, compound, S-curve, logistic, growth, and exponential (Meier et al., 2006; Norusis, 2000; SPSS, 2006). Such transformations are relatively easy to make with the use of a computer, but it must be remembered that the transformation process changes the interpretation of the correlation and regression coefficients. In reality, the researcher should go where the data and theory lead and not attempt to fashion a linear relationship from one that is clearly not linear.

The calculus and the central limit theorem prescribe that if the sample size is large enough (in general, sample sizes are considered small if they are less than 30), then the distributions that are required to estimate our coefficients do approach normality, regardless of the actual distribution in the population (Caldwell, 2006). Essentially, what this means to the researcher is that as long as the researcher has an adequate sample size, the assumption of normality is met.

If the homoscedasticity assumption is violated, one recommended solution is a weighted least squares procedure (Lewis-Beck, 1980). Again, the advent of the computer allows for a fairly straightforward use of this procedure. If the researcher finds autocorrelation or is performing time series analysis, the researcher should consult with someone familiar with the use of these more sophisticated techniques.

One special problem that the researcher may have to deal with is the existence of outliers. An outlier is a case (observation) with an extremely large residual (greater than 2 standard deviations would be considered an outlier and greater than 3 standard deviations would be considered an extreme outlier) that does not "fit" the linear model as well as the other observations. For our example (see Table 27.4), Case Number 7 (Studentized Residual = 3.50) is an extreme outlier and

TABLE 27.4
SPSS Results Indicating Outliers

Rank	Variable ID	Studentized Residual Value
Highest 1	7	3.50
2	24	2.20
3	1	1.63
4	27	1.42
5	17	1.09
Lowest 1	41	−2.92
2	33	−1.87
3	29	−1.61
4	36	−1.28
5	35	−1.10

Case Numbers 24 and 41 (Studentized Residuals 2.20 and −2.92) are outliers. A thorough discussion of outliers is provided in another chapter of this book (Chapter 22).

27.8 CORRELATION MATRIX

The most common use of linear correlation and simple regression in public administration research is to establish the existence of relationships between the independent variable and the dependent variable at the beginning of a research project. Although complex models that represent the world around us inevitably require multivariate analysis, the bivariate nature of linear correlation and simple regression provides the initial clues about which relationships are important. Let us look at an example of how this process works.

Normally, a researcher decides on a dependent variable and selects several independent variables that are suspected of having an important influence. For each independent variable the researcher would follow the process delineated in the earlier sections of this chapter. She would plot the independent variable against the dependent variable, compute simple regression and correlation coefficients, and use the residuals to check the assumptions. The next step in moving toward a multivariate analysis would be for the researcher to create a correlation matrix depicting the correlation coefficients of all of the independent variables of interest with the dependent variable and with each other.

For an example illustrating how correlation analysis might work, let us turn our attention to a researcher who was interested in the political culture and ideology of the Mountain West region of the United States.[6] The researchers surmise that county elected officials in the state of Idaho will be more or less politically conservative based on such factors as: whether their county is predominantly urban or rural, the political party that dominates their county, gender, and the economic well-being of the residents of their county. For this particular study, the unit of analysis is the 44 counties of Idaho. The authors used a survey questionnaire that consisted of 18 questions that were coded as liberal or conservative to create a conservative rating for each county.[7] The average conservative rating for each county (calculated as a percent) then served as the dependent variable for the study.

The four independent variables mentioned above were operationalized for each county as follows: the percent of the population in the county that resides in an urban area, the percent vote for Bush in the 2000 election, the percent of country elected officials who are women, and the welfare payments per capita in dollars.

The correlation matrix for this study is presented in Table 27.5. Before evaluating the actual values for the correlation coefficients, several points should be made. First, note that the dependent variable appears in the first row and the first column. This was intentionally done so that the researcher can quickly glance at the matrix and delineate the correlation of each of the independent variables with the dependent variable. Inspecting Table 27.5 shows that the first row and the first column mirror each other. Second, there is a diagonal of 1 values that go from the upper left entry to the lower right entry. This diagonal divides the matrix into two symmetrical parts allowing the researcher to focus on just one side of the matrix. (The values of 1 make sense because each variable is perfectly correlated with itself.)

The first thing a researcher would do is inspect the first row (or column) to quickly gain a feel for how each of the independent variables is related to the dependent variable. The researcher initially checks to see which of the correlations are statistically significant. This is accomplished by observing which of the correlation coefficients have an observed significance level that meets the chosen standards. In this instance, the researcher would note that two of the correlation coefficients are statistically significant: one at the .01 level (percent vote for Bush in 2000) and one at the .05 level (percent urban). Because the correlations for percent of county elected officials who are women and welfare payments per capita are not statistically significant, the researcher would not be confident that these associations were not due to chance, and hence would not be able to

TABLE 27.5
Correlation Matrix

	Average Conservative Rating of Counties	Urban (Percentage)	Vote for Bush in 2000 (Percentage)	Percentage of County Elected Officials Who Are Women	Welfare Payments per Capita, 1998
Average conservative rating of counties	1	−37*	0.47**	−14	0.09
% Urban	−37*	1	−14	−0.39**	0.06
% Vote for Bush in 2000	0.47**	−14	1	0.01	−0.05
% Of county elected officials who are women	−14	−0.39**	0.01	1	0.11
Welfare payments per capita, 1998	0.09	0.06	−0.05	0.11	1

Source: County Profiles of Idaho, Idaho Department of Commerce Boise, 1998, 2000 and Idaho Secretary of State, 2000.

* $p < .05$.
** $p < .01$, two-tailed t-test.

accurately describe their strength. On the other hand, the researcher can be confident in the correlation measures of percent urban and percent vote for Bush and would evaluate their strengths (and directions). For percent urban, the association is in the direction hypothesized (as a county's percent of people living in an urban area increases, the conservative rating for the county decreases) and is moderately strong at −0.37. The association for percent vote for Bush is also in the hypothesized direction (as the percent vote for Bush increases, the conservative rating increases) and is also moderately strong at 0.47.

Because these two independent variables have both a statistically significant and substantial correlation to the dependent variable, they would be considered strong candidates to include in a multivariate regression equation. The same cannot be said for percent of county elected officials who are women and welfare payments per capita. However, it should be mentioned that just because these independent variables do not reach statistical significance as a bivariate correlation does not mean that they cannot (and should not) be carried forward into a multivariate analysis. First, they could be carried forward as a control variable. Second, and more important, relationships often change when going from a bivariate to a multivariate analysis and this cannot be discovered unless that relationship is tested under those circumstances. In this study, each of these independent variables was carried forward and both reached statistical significance in a multiple regression analysis (Alm et al., 2004).

The second major use of the correlation matrix is as a first-line indicator of multicollinearity within a multiple regression model, a problem whose presence makes interpretation of the regression coefficients highly suspect. Multicollinearity occurs in multivariate analysis when independent variables are highly correlated to each other. The general rule for inspecting a correlation matrix for the presence of multicollinearity is to check each of the correlations (independent variable against independent variable) for high values (usually larger that 0.7). Inspecting Table 27.5 shows that only one association between the independent variables is statistically significant (percent urban with percent of county elected officials who are women, at the .01 level) and because its value (−0.39) is much less than 0.7, multicollinearity does not appear to be a problem. (Remember, the negative sign is used only for determining direction and is not a measure of strength.)

There exist many other tests for multicollinearity that the researcher may use. If multicollinearity does exist, the researcher must then decide how to deal with it. Both the more sophisticated tests and the "causes" for multicollinearity are beyond the scope of this chapter. Readers should refer to the chapter on multivariate regression (Chapter 28) for a more in-depth discussion of these issues.

27.9 RESEARCH EXAMPLES

27.9.1 LINEAR CORRELATION

The most common use of linear correlation and simple regression in public administration research is as a first step leading to multivariate regression analysis. Linear correlation is especially helpful in establishing the existence of bivariate relationships, including the strength and direction of these relationships. In this context, several published research reports will be showcased.

Lenahan O'Connell (2005) recently completed a research project applying the concepts of organizational field and accountability environment to a government funded program—social service transportation in Kentucky. He argues that the formula for accountability inspired by agency theory is frequently impossible to apply. His study used before-and-after statistics on costs and ridership as well as surveys of transportation users and providers to measure and operationalize the variables used in his model, including the ability to group trips, number of second passengers, Medicaid revenues, and fairness of brokers' methods for allocating riders to providers.

A listing of O'Connell's correlation matrix is displayed in Table 27.6. Interpretation of some of his results shows how a correlation table can be used to evaluate relationships between variables. For example, from the bivariate correlations (Pearson's r) listed in Table 27.6, O'Connell concluded that transit providers reporting more second passengers per vehicle have a greater likelihood of reporting that they are receiving more revenues from Medicaid. He based this conclusion on the fact that Pearson's correlation coefficient for "revenue change" and "more second riders" was statistically significant to the .01 level and equal to 0.37. O'Connell also reported that there was a positive association between providers that were able to effectively group trips and Medicaid revenues. He based this assertion on the fact that Pearson's correlation coefficient for "revenue change" and "able to group trips effectively" was statistically significant to the .01 level and equal to 0.45.

TABLE 27.6
Pearson Correlation Coefficients

	1	2	3	4	5	6	7
1. Revenue change							
2. More second riders	0.37**						
3. Able to group trips effectively	0.45**	0.37**					
4. Percent of trips are Medicaid	−0.10	−0.21*	−0.28*				
5. Quality improved	0.43**	0.22*	0.58**	−0.35**			
6. Small taxi companies and no vans and buses	0.15	−0.34**	−0.28**	0.20*	−0.04		
7. Companies with vans and buses	0.18	0.39**	0.28	−0.25	0.17	−0.38**	
8. Brokers are fair	0.36	0.40**	0.65**	−0.32**	0.55**	−0.27**	0.36**

Source: O'Connell, L., *Public Adm. Rev.*, 65, 85, 2005. With permission of Blackwell Publishing.

* $p < .05$,
** $p < .01$.

TABLE 27.7

Correlation between Focus on Results and Measures of Managerial Authority

	Focus on Results
Human resource managerial authority	0.073
Financial management managerial authority	
Program reallocation	−0.055
Object classification reallocation	0.279*
Line-item reallocation	0.252
Carryover power	0.136
Weighted average index	0.265

Source: Moynihan, D.P., *Public Adm. Rev.*, 66, 77, 2006. With permission of
             Blackwell Publishing.

* Significant at .05 level, two-tailed test.

A reader can see that the association between the grouping variable and Medicaid revenue was slightly stronger than the association between the second passenger variable and Medicaid revenue (0.45 – 0.37). Along these lines, a reader can also determine that the strongest association between all the variables listed in the correlation matrix was between providers who thought broker's procedures for allocating trips were fair and being able to group trips effectively. This information is gleaned from the table by assessing the statistically significant Pearson's correlation coefficient of 0.65 (to the .01 level). In the end, O'Connell goes on to use multiple regression analysis to enhance his study of revenue change, especially as it applies to the statistically significant bivariate associations he found by computing his correlation matrix.

Donald P. Moynihan (2006) recently published a study that evaluates the recent trend of state governments to embrace the idea of managing for results. In completing his study, Moynihan uses linear correlation to identify associations between measures of managerial authority and a focus on results. His results are portrayed in Table 27.7. Moynihan measures managerial authority using a scale of 1–6, where 6 is complete managerial control. His measures focus on results based on content analysis of a range of performance information in states managing results documents. What he finds is that there is a low correlation (.073) between human resource managerial authority and focus on results. In fact, as the reader can see from Table 27.7, this association does not reach statistical significance at the author's chosen .05 significance level. Note that authors are free to choose different levels of statistical significance. It is quite common and acceptable in public administration research to use any of the following levels of significance (.10, .05, .01, and .001) as a cut-off for making decisions on statistical significance.

In fact, Moynihan only finds a single statistically significant association at his chosen level of significance (.05), and that is one between object classification reallocation and focus on results. At 0.279, this indicates a weak positive association. Based on these findings, Moynihan concludes "there is no relationship between the more substantive program measures of reallocation discretion and focus on results" (2006, p. 83).

27.9.2   SIMPLE REGRESSION

A published work that uses both linear correlation and simple regression to explore possible relationships between interval-level variables is contained in the *American Political Science Review*. Burden and Kimball (1998) use these statistical techniques to highlight the relationship between campaign spending and split-ticket voting. Burden and Kimball start by producing a scatter plot of

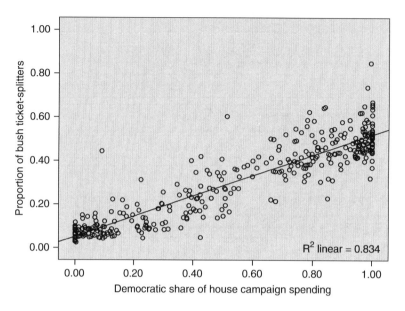

FIGURE 27.10 Split-ticket voting by house campaign spending.

this relationship (see Figure 27.10). Burden and Kimball mention that they are using the simple scatter plot to "illustrate the critical role of spending" in their analysis of this specific relationship (1998, p. 542). One can see from the figure that there does appear to be a linear relationship between democrat's share of campaign spending (operationalized as the democratic candidate's spending as a fraction of total spending in the congressional contest) and proportion of Bush ticket-splitters (operationalized as the proportion of people that voted for Bush for president as well as a Democrat for a congressional seat).

Burden and Kimball calculate and present Pearson's correlation coefficient ($r = 0.91$, statistically significant to the .001 level) to demonstrate that the relationship depicted in Figure 27.10 "is clearly linear, positive, and strong" (1998, p. 542). The authors superimposed the least-squares regression line on the scatter plot. Although they did not present the results of calculating the unstandardized regression coefficient (b) of this relationship, we took the liberty of making that calculation based on the data, which is included in your packet. The unstandardized regression coefficient for the relationship between democrat's share of campaign spending and proportion of Bush ticket-splitters is 0.47 (statistically significant to the .001 level). Interpretation of this measure would mean that, on average, for a one percent increase in the Democratic candidate's spending as a fraction of total spending in the congressional contest, the percent of Bush ticket-splitters would increase by 0.47 percent, all other things being equal. Both the Pearson's correlation coefficient and the unstandardized regression coefficient are statistically significant to the .001 level, meaning that the authors can be confident that these results are representative of the population they are studying.

Another published study illustrates the use of simple regression in public administration research. James D. Ward (1994) studied the impact of the *City of Richmond v. J.A. Croson Co.* court decision on minority set-aside programs in terms of dollars spent before and after the decision was handed down. His findings suggest that the percentage of African American (black) population is the only variable in his model that comes close to explaining the variance in dollars spent. Ward uses a simple regression to support his finding. His results are shown in Table 27.8.

On the basis of the analysis of these results, the author states that the bivariate R^2 value between "percent Blacks in city" and the dependent variable revealed that 20.5 percent of the variance in

---

TABLE 27.8
Regression Analysis of Dollars Spent versus Percent African Americans in City

Year	1988	1990
Pearson's r	.45*	.43*
Multiple R	.45331	.43124
R^2	.20549	.18597
Adjusted R^2	.14437	.12783

Source: Ward, J.D., *Public Adm. Rev.*, 54, 483, 1994. With permission of Blackwell Publishing.

* Significance less than .10.

---

dollars spent on minority business enterprises (MBEs) in 1988. Eighteen and six tenths of a percent of the variance in 1990 could be explained by knowing the percent blacks in the city, regardless of region (Ward, 1994). Essentially, Ward is making the argument—based on his simple regression analysis—that the one factor that he could find that explains spending on MBEs is the percentage of African American population living in the relevant cities. It is also important to observe that in this case, the author chose not to use/interpret the unstandardized regression coefficient as a means of analysis, but instead focuses upon the association (r) and the explanatory power (R^2) of the percent blacks. The author also chooses to highlight R^2 instead of adjusted R^2 while offering the caveat that the model's low adjusted R^2 value diminishes its explanatory power. In this case, the author presents the reader with both values, allowing the reader to make his or her own determination.

27.10 CONCLUSION

When public administration researchers seek to determine the relationship between two variables that are measured at the interval or ratio level of measurement, they turn to linear correlation and simple regression analysis to provide an initial indication of that relationship. Specifically, linear correlation and simple regression analyses help describe the exact nature of the relationship between two variables, allowing the researcher to predict the value of one variable based on the value of the other. Furthermore, these two statistical procedures allow the researcher to estimate both the direction and strength of the association between the variables. In the end, linear correlation and simple regression provide an indication that two variables may be causally connected, and in so doing, also provide the foundation from which to begin multivariate analysis.

PROBLEMS

For the following exercises, use the idaho.sav data set provided by your instructor.

1. There is some literature in political science that suggests that Democrats receive more votes in urbanized areas and Republicans win a greater percentage of votes in rural areas. You may have also heard that people with more formal education tend to be more liberal. Before testing the relationship between any of these variables you decide to see if there is an association between the following variables: percentage vote for Bush in 2004, urbanization, and education.

a. A visual display is often helpful in understanding the relationship. Create a scatter plot of the data using urban on percentage vote for Bush in 2004. Draw a line by hand on the scatter plot. Describe the relationship between the variables given the visual display in your scatter plot.

b. Create another scatter plot of the data using education on percentage vote for Bush 2004. Draw a line by hand on the scatter plot. Describe the relationship presented in this scatter plot.

c. Obtain Pearson's r correlation coefficients for the variables vote for Bush in 2004, urban, and education. Using the table format illustrated in this chapter, create a correlation table and then in your own words describe the strength and direction of the relationship for each correlation coefficient. Indicate if the relationship between the variables is statistically significant.

d. Collect data on all of the counties in your state and repeat steps a), b) and c) using the data you collected. Provide at least one explanation as to why you think the outcomes in your state are similar to or different from those for the Idaho counties.

2. Previously in the chapter we discussed the linear relationship between education and income in Idaho counties. You have reason to believe that more urbanized areas will have more jobs and therefore more income. As such, you hypothesize that there is a positive relationship between the counties that are more urbanized and the amount of the county income. Using the data in the idaho.sav dataset, test your hypothesis on the linear relationship between urbanization (urban) and income in the Idaho counties.

a. Run a linear regression to test the relationship between urban and income. Create a table with your results using the table format for simple regression illustrated in this chapter.

b. If the intercept or coefficient for the dependent variable is statistically significant, interpret their meaning.

c. Fit the regression line to the scatter plot for these two variables either by hand or using your computer software.

d. Interpret adjusted R^2. After examining the scatter plot with the regression line and adjusted R^2, describe how well urbanization predicts per capita income for the counties in Idaho.

e. Run another linear bivariate regression on income using the number of people per square mile (density). Repeat the steps listed in 2 (a), (b), (c) and (d) using the variable density. Is density a better predictor of income than urban in Idaho counties? Why or why not?

ENDNOTES

1. There exist several levels of measurement. Nominal refers to the classification of cases into groups. Ordinal classifies cases into groups and allows ordering of those groups. Interval not only allows classification and ordering but also indicates how far each case is from each other case. Ratio is an extension of the interval level (it establishes a true zero value whereas an interval level allows for an arbitrary zero value) and as such is often treated identically to an interval-level measure. For a more comprehensive discussion of levels of measurement see Neuman (2004).

2. For an explanation of how the method of least squares works, see Kachigan (1991).

3. The measure using the percentage of people in the county over the age of 25 with a college degree is the standard measurement used by the Census Bureau.

4. The reader will observe that the values from the computer output are slightly different than the values from the hand calculations. These differences are simply due to rounding.

5. Standardized residuals are used because it makes it easier for the researcher to determine relative magnitudes of residuals and hence, makes residuals easier to compare. Studentized residuals take into account the fact that the variability of the predicted values changes depending on the value of the dependent variables. Standardized and studentized values allow for more accurate comparisons and analysis. For a detailed discussion of standardized and studentized residuals, see Norusis (2000).

6. The results of this specific research case were published in "Political Culture and Ideology in the Mountain West: Regionalism in the State of Idaho" (Alm et al., 2004).

7. A conservative rating was calculated for each elected county official and was used to formulate an average conservative rating for the county. The resulting conservative measurement was given as a percent with 0 representing perfect liberalism and 100 representing perfect conservatism. For a more detailed description of this research project see the reference listed in Note 6 (above).

REFERENCES

Alm, L.R. and Witt, S. 1997. The rural–urban linkage to environmental policy making in the American West: A focus on Idaho. *Social Science Journal*, 34, 271–284.

Alm, L.R., Burkhart, R.E., Patton, W.D., and Weatherby, J.B. 2004. Political culture in the Mountain West: Regionalism in the state of Idaho. *Social Science Journal*, 41, 163–178.

Burden, B.C. and Kimball, D.C. 1998. A new approach to the study of ticket splitting. *American Political Science Review*, 92, 533–544.

Caldwell, S. 2006. *Statistics Unplugged*. Belmont, California: Thomson/Wadsworth.

Green, S.B. and Salkind, N.J. 2005. *Using SPSS for Windows and Macintosh: Analyzing and Understanding Data*, Fourth Edition. Upper Saddle River, New Jersey: Pearson/Prentice Hall.

Hoover, K. and Donovan, T. 2004. *The Elements of Social Science Thinking*, Eighth Edition. Belmont, California: Thomson/Wadsworth.

Kachigan, S.K. 1991. *Multivariate Statistical Analysis: A Conceptual Introduction*, Second Edition. New York: Radius Press.

Lewis-Beck, M.S. 1980. *Applied Regression: An Introduction*. Beverly Hills, California: Sage Publications.

Matlack, W.F. 1993. *Statistics For Public Managers*. Itasca, Illinois: P.E. Peacock Publishers.

Meier, K.J., Brudney, J.L., and Bohte, J. 2006. *Applied Statistics for Public and Nonprofit Administration*, Sixth Edition. Belmont, California: Thomson/Wadsworth.

Moynihan, D.P. 2006. Managing for results in state government: Evaluating a decade of reform. *Public Administration Review*, 66, 77–89.

Neuman, W.L. 2004. *Basics of Social Research: Qualitative and Quantitative Approaches*. Boston: Pearson, Allyn and Bacon.

Norusis, M.J. 2000. *SPSS 10.0 Guide to Data Analysis*. Upper Saddle River, New Jersey: Prentice Hall.

O'Connell, L. 2005. Program accountability as an emergent property: The role of stakeholders in a program's field. *Public Administration Review*, 65, 85–93.

Salkind, N. 2006. *Exploring Research*, Sixth Edition. Upper Saddle River, New Jersey: Pearson/Prentice Hall.

SPSS, Inc. 2006. Chicago, Illinois.

Ward, J.D. 1994. Responses to Croson. *Public Administration Review*, 54, 483–485.

BIBLIOGRAPHY

Geolytics, Inc. 2000. Census CD and Maps [Computer Software] New Jersey.

Gujarati, D.N. 1995. *Basic Economics*, Third Edition. New York: McGraw Hill.

Pollock III, P.H. 2005. *An SPSS Companion to Political Analysis*, Second Edition. Washington, DC: CQ Press.

Welch, S. and Comer, J. 2001. *Quantitative Methods for Public Administration*: *Techniques and Applications*, Third Edition. Fort Worth, Texas: Harcourt College Publishers.

Appendix

PROCEDURE 1
Calculation of Regression and Correlation Coefficients

County	x	y	$x - \bar{x}$	$y - \bar{y}$	$(x - \bar{x})(y - \bar{y})$	$(x - \bar{x})^2$	$(y - \bar{y})^2$
Ada	21.71	31420	9.55	1485.77	109657.77	91.15	131922975.21
Adams	10.09	18212	−2.07	−1722.23	3569.71	4.30	2966066.77
Bannock	16.42	20252	4.26	317.77	1352.84	18.12	100979.51
Bear Lake	8.73	15647	−3.43	−4287.23	14716.89	11.78	18380317.66
Benewah	8.3	19064	−3.86	−870.23	3361.45	14.92	757295.50
Bingham	10.66	17621	−1.50	−2313.23	3476.16	2.26	5351020.40
Blaine	30.21	41259	18.05	21324.77	384853.93	325.70	454745931.99
Boise	13.06	21492	0.90	1557.77	1397.74	0.81	2426655.88
Bonner	11.36	18955	−0.80	−979.23	786.06	0.64	958886.05
Bonnevillle	17.28	22408	5.12	2473.77	12658.96	26.19	6119551.52
Boundary	9.03	17410	−3.13	−2524.23	7907.72	9.81	6371723.31
Butte	9.18	19376	−2.98	−558.23	1665.04	8.90	311617.68
Camas	17.33	21585	5.17	1650.77	8529.99	26.70	2725050.61
Canyon	10.31	18271	−1.85	−1663.23	3081.51	3.43	2766324.95
Caribou	12.41	20068	0.25	133.77	33.08	0.06	17895.14
Cassia	9.1	21170	−3.06	1235.77	−3784.84	9.38	1527134.24
Clark	9.48	22022	−2.68	2087.77	−5600.93	7.20	4358794.97
Clearwater	9.1	18429	−3.06	−1505.23	4610.10	9.38	2265709.13
Custer	12.88	23087	0.72	3152.77	2261.39	0.51	9939975.89
Elmore	11.52	21907	−0.64	1972.77	−1267.96	0.41	3891832.24
Franklin	10.31	15451	−1.85	−4483.23	8306.21	3.43	20099326.75
Fremont	9.28	15670	−2.88	−4264.23	12292.62	8.31	18183634.21
Gem	8.62	18078	−3.54	−1856.23	6576.11	12.55	3445579.68
Gooding	8.48	25240	−3.68	5305.77	−19539.73	13.56	28151224.26
Idaho	10.65	17690	−1.51	−2244.23	3394.91	2.29	5036556.04
Jefferson	11.55	16947	−0.61	−2987.23	1830.36	0.38	8923526.76
Jerome	9.89	23434	−2.27	3499.77	−7954.04	5.17	12248409.16
Kootenai	13.05	22527	0.89	2592.77	2300.49	0.79	6722470.43
Latah	22.74	21391	10.58	1456.77	15408.68	111.88	2122186.79
Lemhi	12.28	18886	0.12	−1048.23	−122.93	0.01	1098780.41
Lewis	11.13	19074	−1.03	−860.23	888.38	1.07	739990.96
Lincoln	9.52	19877	−2.64	−57.23	151.24	6.98	3274.96
Madison	14.43	14861	2.27	−5073.23	−11502.38	5.14	25737634.93
Minidoka	7.04	16955	−5.12	−2979.23	15261.78	26.24	8875795.13
Nez Perce	13.70	17066	1.54	−2868.23	−4409.24	2.36	8226727.67
Oneida	12.11	15412	−0.05	−4522.23	238.46	0.00	20450539.48
Owyhee	7.61	16504	−4.55	−3430.23	15616.90	20.73	11766459.12
Payette	7.74	18128	−4.42	−1806.23	7988.46	19.56	3262456.95
Power	10.8	18027	−1.36	−1907.23	2599.04	1.86	3637515.86
Shoshone	7.1	19426	−5.06	−508.23	2573.02	25.63	258294.96

PROCEDURE 1 (*Continued*)
Calculation of Regression and Correlation Coefficients

County	x	y	$x - \bar{x}$	$y - \bar{y}$	$(x - \bar{x})(y - \bar{y})$	$(x - \bar{x})^2$	$(y - \bar{y})^2$
Teton	19.95	15020	7.79	−4914.23	−38268.41	60.64	24149629.66
Twin Falls	10.77	21322	−1.39	1387.77	−1932.79	1.94	1925913.15
Valley	18.48	24390	6.32	4455.77	28148.32	39.91	19853910.62
Washington	9.77	16075	−2.39	−3859.23	9234.09	5.73	14893635.12
	535.16	877,106	0.00	0.00	602,346.16	947.82	907,719,211.73

PROCEDURE 1 (*Continued*)

$$\bar{x} = \frac{\sum x}{n} = \frac{535.16}{44} = 12.16 \quad \bar{y} = \frac{\sum y}{n} = \frac{877,106}{44} = 19,934.23$$

$$b = \frac{\sum (x - \bar{x})(y - \bar{y})}{\sum (x - \bar{x})^2} = \frac{602,346.16}{947.82} = 635.51$$

$$a = \bar{y} - b\bar{x} = 19,934.23 - (635.51)(12.16) = 19,934.23 - 7,727.80 = 12,206.43$$

$$r = \frac{\sum (x - x)(y - y)}{\sqrt{\sum (x - x)^2 \sum (y - y)^2}} = \frac{602,346.16}{\sqrt{(947.82)(907,719,211.73)}} = 0.65$$

PROCEDURE 2
Hypothesis Test for the Regression Coefficient

County	x	y	y_{pred}	$(y - y_{pred})$	$(y - y_{pred})^2$
Ada	21.71	31420	26001.60	5418.40	29359096.39
Adams	10.09	18212	18616.99	−404.99	164020.72
Bannock	16.42	20252	22639.76	−2387.76	5701396.47
Bear Lake	8.73	15647	17752.70	−2105.70	4433989.20
Benewah	8.3	19064	17479.44	1584.56	2510844.43
Bingham	10.66	17621	18979.23	−1358.23	1844800.18
Blaine	30.21	41259	31403.41	9855.59	97132582.12
Boise	13.06	21492	20504.45	987.55	975248.73
Bonner	11.36	18955	19424.09	−469.09	220045.19
Bonnevillle	17.28	22408	23186.30	−778.30	605745.46
Boundary	9.03	17410	17943.36	−533.36	284468.98
Butte	9.18	19376	18038.68	1337.32	1788418.04
Camas	17.33	21585	23218.07	−1633.07	2666923.85
Canyon	10.31	18271	18756.81	−485.81	236007.91
Caribou	12.41	20068	20091.37	−23.37	546.30
Cassia	9.1	21170	17987.84	3182.16	10126130.24
Clark	9.48	22022	18229.33	3792.67	14384308.62
Clearwater	9.1	18429	17987.84	441.16	194620.48
Custer	12.88	23087	20390.06	2696.94	7273475.91
Elmore	11.52	21907	19525.77	2381.23	5670251.51
Franklin	10.31	15451	18756.81	−3305.81	10928356.28

(*continued*)

PROCEDURE 2   (*Continued*)
Hypothesis Test for the Regression Coefficient

County	x	y	y_{pred}	$(y - y_{pred})$	$(y - y_{pred})^2$
Fremont	9.28	15670	18102.23	−2432.23	5915758.88
Gem	8.62	18078	17682.80	395.20	156184.54
Gooding	8.48	25240	17593.83	7646.17	58463961.67
Idaho	10.65	17690	18972.88	−1282.88	1645778.88
Jefferson	11.55	16947	19544.84	−2597.84	6748753.16
Jerome	9.89	23434	18489.89	4944.11	24444192.73
Kootenai	13.05	22527	20498.10	2028.90	4116442.94
Latah	22.74	21391	26656.17	−5265.17	27722011.40
Lemhi	12.28	18886	20008.76	−1122.76	1260583.31
Lewis	11.13	19074	19277.92	−203.92	41584.56
Lincoln	9.52	19877	18254.76	1622.24	2631678.17
Madison	14.43	14861	21375.10	−6514.10	42433485.74
Minidoka	7.04	16955	16678.70	276.30	76344.11
Nez Perce	13.7	17066	20911.18	−3845.18	14785395.62
Oneida	12.11	15412	19900.72	−4488.72	20148613.24
Owyhee	7.61	16504	17040.94	−536.94	288299.32
Payette	7.74	18128	17123.55	1004.45	1008917.50
Power	10.8	18027	19068.21	−1041.21	1084108.52
Shoshone	7.1	19426	16716.83	2709.17	7339623.27
Teton	19.95	15020	24883.10	−9863.10	97280793.00
Twin Falls	10.77	21322	19049.14	2272.86	5165892.20
Valley	18.48	24390	23948.91	441.09	194563.92
Washington	9.77	16075	18413.63	−2338.63	5469200.49
				−0.09	524,923,444.2

PROCEDURE 2   (*Continued*)

From Procedure 1, $\sum (x - \bar{x})^2 = 947.82$; $a = 12{,}206.43$; $b = 635.51$

$$y_{pred} = a + bX = 12{,}206.43 - 635.51(X)$$

$$s_{yx} = \sqrt{\frac{\sum (y - y_{pred})^2}{n - 2}} = \sqrt{\frac{524{,}923{,}444.2}{42}} = \sqrt{12{,}498{,}177.24} = 3{,}535.28$$

$$= s_b \frac{s_{yx}}{\sqrt{\sum (x - \bar{x})^2}} = \frac{3{,}535.28}{\sqrt{947.82}} = \frac{3{,}535.28}{30.79} = 114.93$$

$$t_{calc} = \frac{b - \beta}{s_b} = \frac{635.51 - 0}{114.93} = 5.53$$

From a *t*-table for two-tail significance equal to .05 and degrees of freedom equal to 42, read t_{table} equals 2.021 for 40 degrees of freedom. Because t_{calc} is greater than t_{table} at the more conservative level of 40 degrees (42 degrees is typically not reported in tables) reject the null hypothesis that the regression coefficient equals zero and accept the hypothesis that for this set of data, the regression coefficient equals 635.51.

Note: Remember that you may disregard the sign for the calculated value for t in making this interpretation as it does not affect magnitude; it only refers to direction (positive or negative).

Source: Matlack W.F., in *Statistics For Public Managers*, F.E. Peacock Publishers, Itasca, Illinois, 1993, 219–221.

PROCEDURE 3   HYPOTHESIS TEST FOR THE CORRELATION COEFFICIENT

From Procedure 1, $r = 0.65$

$$t_{\text{calc}} = \frac{r\sqrt{n-2}}{\sqrt{1-r^2}} = \frac{.65\sqrt{44-2}}{\sqrt{1-(.65)^2}} = \frac{4.21}{.76} = 5.54$$

From a t-table for two-tail significance equal to .05 and degrees of freedom equal to 42, read t_{table} equals 2.021 for 40 degrees of freedom. Because t_{calc} is greater than t_{table} at the more conservative level of 40 degrees (42 degrees is typically not reported in tables) reject the null hypothesis that the correlation coefficient equals zero and accept the hypothesis that for this set of data, the correlation coefficient equals 0.65.

Note: Remember that you may disregard the sign for the calculated value of t in making this interpretation as it does not affect magnitude; it only refers to direction (positive or negative).

Source: Matlack W.F., in *Statistics For Public Managers*, F.E. Peacock Publishers, Itasca, Illinois, 1993, 227.

Part VI

Advanced Quantitative Analysis

28 Multivariate Regression Analysis

Elizabeth A. Graddy and Lili Wang

CONTENTS

28.1 INTRODUCTION

Multiple regression offers analysts one of the most powerful and useful tools for quantitative analysis. With the exception of descriptive statistics, it is the most widely used quantitative method. There are three primary reasons for its popularity. First, it is accessible. Regression analysis is relatively easy to use and understand, and estimation software is widely available. Second, the multivariate linear specification is robust. Many relationships have been found empirically to be linear. The linear specification is the simplest, and thus always appropriate as a first approximation of a causal relationship. Moreover, we often do not know enough about the relationship under study to justify an alternative (nonlinear) specification. Third, the results of regression analysis have proven to be very useful, both for predicting or forecasting and for explanation (i.e., determining the causes of a phenomenon). It is the ability of multivariate regression to control for confounding influences on the relationship under study that makes it a particularly powerful tool for explanation.

Multiple regression has been used to explore a wide range of phenomena in public administration and public policy. Examples include work on organizational structure (Graddy and Nichol, 1990) and organizational behavior (Robertson, 1995); local service delivery (Clingermayer and Feiock, 1997; Graddy and Chen, 2006); volunteering (Sundeen, 1990) and nonprofit fund-raising (Thornton, 2006); evaluations of programs (Devaney et al., 1992) and laws (Graddy, 1994); government reform (Kearney et al., 2000); and a variety of issues focused on specific policy areas, e.g., health policy (Mann et al., 1995) and public school financing (Johnston and Duncombe, 1998).

Given its power and usefulness as a methodology and the broad range of public sector issues about which it has provided insight, consider what regression analysis is and how one can effectively use it. Assume we want to quantitatively analyze a relationship between two or more variables. We need a set of observations for each variable, and a hypothesis setting forth the explicit form of the relationship. The set of observations, a sample, is chosen from the population of interest. The variable we wish to explore is called the dependent variable (denoted Y). The variables that are believed to cause or influence Y are called independent variables (denoted as Xs).

The model we will explore in this chapter is a multivariate linear relationship between X and Y, or:

$$Y_i = \beta_0 + \beta_1 X_{1i} + \beta_2 X_{2i} + \cdots + \beta_k X_{ki} + \varepsilon_i \qquad (28.1)$$

where
   Y denotes the dependent variable*
   X_j denote the independent variables, $j = 1, 2, \ldots, k$
   β denote the coefficients that measure the effect of the independent variables on the dependent variable
   ε denotes the error term, which represents stochastic, or random, influences on the dependent variable

Consider a simple example involving the determinants of crime. Assume first that we believe that crime increases in poor areas; in other words, the crime rate depends on the poverty rate. Specified as a bivariate linear relationship, this becomes:

---

* Throughout this chapter, observations are denoted with the subscript i and range from 1 to n, while variables are denoted with the subscript j and range from 1 to k. The observation subscript, however, will usually be suppressed for ease of exposition.

$$Y = \beta_0 + \beta_1 X + \varepsilon \qquad (28.2)$$

where

    Y is the crime rate

    X is the poverty rate

    β_1 is the average change in the crime rate associated with a unit change in the poverty rate

    β_0 is the average crime rate when the independent variable is zero

We need to include an error term (ε) in our specification even if we believe that poverty rate is the sole determinant of crime, because there may be minor random influences on Y other than X, and there may be random measurement error. ε represents the difference in the observed Y (the data) and the expected Y, $E(Y)$, in the population, which is based on the model.

Estimating Equation 28.2 using 2000 data on crime and poverty rates for 58 California counties* reveals that the estimated β_0 is 2019 and the estimated β_1 is 93.1. Therefore, the estimated value of Y for a given X is: $2019 + 93.1X$. The interpretation of the estimated equation is

- Crime rate (the number of serious crimes known to police per 100,000 population) increases by 93.1 (the estimated value of β_1) on average for each unit increase in the percentage of the population with income below the poverty level.
- Expected crime rate when the poverty rate is approximately zero is 2019 (the estimated value of β_0).

The estimated line represents the average crime rate for a given poverty rate, and is plotted in Figure 28.1.

Obviously, factors other than poverty rate can affect the crime rate. Consider a slightly more complex model in which crime also depends on population density and the high school dropout rate. Our model becomes

$$Y = \beta_0 + \beta_1 X_1 + \beta_2 X_2 + \beta_3 X_3 + \varepsilon \qquad (28.3)$$

where

    $X_2 =$ population density

    $X_3 =$ the high school dropout rate

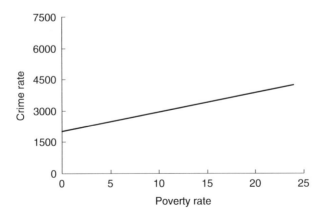

FIGURE 28.1 Estimated line.

---

* Data sources: Crime rate and poverty rate from U.S. Counties, U.S. Census Bureau (2000), dropout rate from the Educational Demographics Unit, California Department of Education (2000), and other data from the California Statistical Abstract (2000), California Department of Finance.

TABLE 28.1
List of Symbols

Population Parameters (Unobserved)		Estimated Parameters (from Sample)	
Name	Symbol	Name	Symbol
Regression coefficient	β	Estimated coefficient	$\hat{\beta}$
Variance of estimated coefficient	$\sigma_{\hat{\beta}}^2$ or $\mathrm{VAR}(\hat{\beta})$	Estimated variance of estimated coefficient	$S_{\hat{\beta}}^2$
Standard deviation of the estimated coefficient	$\sigma_{\hat{\beta}}$	Standard error of the estimated coefficient	$S_{\hat{\beta}}$
Error term	ε	Residual	e
Variance of the error term	σ_ε^2 or $\mathrm{VAR}(\varepsilon)$	Estimated variance of the error term	s^2
Standard deviation of the error term	$\sigma\varepsilon$	Standard error of the error term	s
Expectation operator	$E(\cdot)$		

The interpretation of the coefficients in this multivariate regression equation changes in a subtle, but important, way from the interpretation in the simple regression model. The coefficients now provide the average change in the crime rate associated with a unit change in their respective variables holding the other independent variables constant. For example, β_1 is the average change in the crime rate associated with a unit change in the poverty rate (X_1) with both population density and the dropout rate held constant. β_0 provides the average crime rate when all the independent variables equal zero.

Estimating Equation 28.3 using the California data generates the following parameter estimates: $Y = 1440 + 51.5X_1 + 0.37X_2 + 355.7X_3$. Thus, by including other determinants of the crime rate, we find that the impact of poverty is reduced. With the dropout rate and population density held constant, a unit increase in the poverty rate raises the crime rate by only 51.5.

In general, for the multiple regression model described by Equation 28.1, β_j provides the average change in the dependent variable associated with a unit change in X_j with the other independent variables held constant. This means that we can estimate the effect of X_j alone on Y. Multiple regression thus allows for the statistical control of confounding variables, and this is one of its most powerful characteristics.

This ability is particularly important when the relationship of interest cannot be easily separated from other effects without using statistical techniques. For example, assume we want to estimate the effects of gender discrimination on salaries in an organization, but we know that many of the higher paid males have been in the organization longer than their female colleagues. We can estimate this relationship using multivariate regression analysis by including seniority (and other determinants of income) as independent variables in the model. The parameter estimate on gender will isolate the effects, if any, of gender discrimination.

The effective use of multivariate regression analysis requires an understanding of how to estimate the regression model and interpret the results, and an understanding of the assumptions that underlie the model and their implications for the credibility of the results. The remainder of the chapter is devoted to these topics. Section 28.2 explains the intuition behind estimation. Section 28.3 explains how to evaluate estimation results. Section 28.4 presents the assumptions that underlie the use of regression analysis for statistical inference, and Sections 28.5 through 28.8 addresses how assumption violations are identified and their implications. Section 28.9 concludes the chapter. Table 28.1 provides a list of the symbols that will be used in this chapter.

28.2 ESTIMATION

The correct use of regression analysis requires at least an intuitive understanding of how the multivariate regression model is estimated. We will develop this understanding using a simple regression model.

Recall our first model of the crime rate as a function of only the poverty rate. Assume we believe this model, $Y = \beta_0 + \beta_1 X + \varepsilon$, to be true. Note, that we cannot observe the value of the parameters (β_0 and β_1), but we can observe Y and X (in this case, the crime rates associated with different poverty rates). We would like to use the information we have (a set of n observations on Y and X)*, to estimate β_0 and β_1, because these parameter estimates will provide a quantitative description of the relationship between X and Y.

More precisely, the parameter estimates will provide an estimated value of Y for a given value of X. In this example, the estimated β_0 is 2019 and the estimated β_1 is 93.1, therefore the estimated value of Y is $2019 + 93.1X$. Estimated values will be denoted with a hat, so $\hat{Y} = \hat{\beta}_0 + \hat{\beta}_1 X$ is the estimated version of our model.

The estimated value of Y associated with a particular value of X will usually not be the same as the observed value of Y associated with the same value of X. For example, our estimated equation predicts a crime rate of 2950 for areas with a poverty rate of 10. One of the observations, however, is a county with a poverty rate of 10 and a crime rate of 2807. This difference of 143 between the estimated and observed crime rate is called the residual.

Residuals are denoted e, so the residual associated with a particular observation i is e_i (for each sample observation, $i = 1, 2, \ldots, n$). It is useful to distinguish the residual e from the error term ε:

$$e = Y_i - \hat{Y}_i \tag{28.4}$$

represents the deviation of the observed Y from the estimated line. e is an observable variable.

$$\varepsilon = Y_i - E(Y_i) \tag{28.5}$$

represents the deviation of the observed Y from the expected line. ε is a conceptual variable, because the expected relationship is not observable.

Given that we want to estimate β, how do we do it? Consider our data on crime and poverty, which are plotted in Figure 28.2.

If we draw a line through these data points, we are in effect estimating β. The values of β associated with this particular line (e.g., $\breve{Y} = \breve{\beta}_0 + \breve{\beta}_1 X$) can be read off the axis using any two points on the line. The line, of course, does not perfectly fit the data; no line will unless Y and X have an

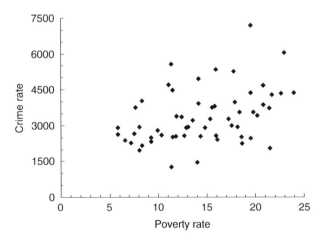

FIGURE 28.2 Scatter plot.

---

* These observations can be either cross-sectional data (data collected on different units—e.g., firms, families, cities—at a single point in time) or time-series data (data collected on the same unit over time).

exact linear relationship. These differences between the points on the line (the predicted value of crime rate) and its observed value (the data point) are the residuals (*e*).

Notice that we could draw many other lines through these same data points, and each line would estimate a different β and produce a different set of residuals. How do we know the correct line to draw? i.e., what are the best estimates of β that can be derived from these data?

Obviously, we would like the predicted values of the dependent variable to be as close as possible to its actual values. In other words, we would like to minimize the difference between Y_i and $\hat{Y}_i$ for all observations of Y, or min $\sum_{i=1}^{n}(Y_i - \hat{Y}_i)$. This criterion, however, will not yield a unique line. Moreover, it has the disadvantage of allowing large positive errors to cancel large negative errors, so some lines satisfying this criterion could have very large residuals.

This problem could be avoided by either minimizing the absolute value of the residuals, or the squared residuals. Large residuals would then be penalized regardless of their sign. Minimizing the squared residuals has the added advantage of penalizing large outliers much more proportionally than small ones. Moreover, the squared term is easier to manipulate mathematically than the absolute value term.

The criterion of minimizing the sum of the squared residuals to obtain the best line through a set of data, or more precisely min $\sum_{i=1}^{n}(Y_i - \hat{Y}_i)^2$, is called ordinary least-squares estimation (or OLS). This is the method used in regression analysis, and the criterion can be shown to yield the following unique estimates of β:

$$\hat{\beta}_i = \frac{\sum_{i=1}^{n}(X_i - \overline{X})(Y_i - \overline{Y})}{\sum_{i=1}^{n}(X_i - \overline{X})^2} \tag{28.6}$$

$$\hat{\beta}_0 = \overline{Y} - \hat{\beta}_1\overline{X} \tag{28.7}$$

Equations 28.6 and 28.7 are the OLS formula for the parameters in the simple two-variable regression model.

Parameter estimation in the multivariate regression model is analogous to the simple case, but considerably more laborious. Estimation requires the simultaneous solution of a system of linear equations. More precisely, for a model with k independent variables, the OLS estimates of β_0 through β_k are determined by the following set of equations:

$$\hat{\beta}_0 = \overline{Y} - \hat{\beta}_1\overline{X}_1 - \hat{\beta}_2\overline{X}_2 - \cdots - \hat{\beta}_k\overline{X}_k \tag{28.8}$$

$$\sum_{i=1}^{n}y_i x_{1i} = \sum_{i=1}^{n}x_{1i}^2\hat{\beta}_1 + \sum_{i=1}^{n}x_{1i}x_{2i}\hat{\beta}_2 + \cdots + \sum_{i=1}^{n}x_{1i}x_{ki}\hat{\beta}_k \tag{28.9}$$

$$\sum_{i=1}^{n}y_i x_{2i} = \sum_{i=1}^{n}x_{1i}x_{2i}\hat{\beta}_1 + \sum_{i=1}^{n}x_{2i}^2\hat{\beta}_2 + \cdots + \sum_{i=1}^{n}x_{2i}x_{ki}\hat{\beta}_k \tag{28.10}$$

$$\sum_{i=1}^{n}y_i x_{ki} = \sum_{i=1}^{n}x_{1i}x_{ki}\hat{\beta}_1 + \sum_{i=1}^{n}x_{2i}x_{ki}\hat{\beta}_2 + \cdots + \sum_{i=1}^{n}x_{ki}^2\hat{\beta}_k \tag{28.11}$$

where $y_i = Y_i - \overline{Y}$ and $x_{ki} = X_{ki} - \overline{X}_k$.

The most important function of a regression software package is to solve this system of equations for $\hat{\beta}_0$ through $\hat{\beta}_k$.

TABLE 28.2

Estimation Output for Crime Rate

Variable	Unstandarized Coefficient		Standardized Coefficient	t	Prob. $\|t\| \geq X$
	B	Standard Error			
Constant	1440.4	393.5		3.66	0.001
Poverty rate	51.5	29.7	0.22	1.74	0.088
Population density	0.37	0.185	0.22	1.99	0.051
Dropout rate	355.7	90.7	0.49	3.92	0.000

To estimate a multivariate regression model using one of the many available software packages (e.g., SAS, SPSS), one needs only input the data and the model statement (formatted as required by the software). The output will include a variety of summary statistics on the dependent variable (e.g., mean and standard deviation) and the estimated model (e.g., R^2, n), followed by the estimates of the coefficients and their associated standard errors and t-statistics.

For example, the multivariate model of crime rates discussed in Section 28.1 was estimated using the software package SPSS 14.0. To run multiple regression analysis in SPSS, select Analyze, Regression, Linear, choose Dependent variable and Independent variables, and click OK. The portion of the output that contains the parameter estimates is presented in Table 28.2. The second column provides the estimated coefficients that were discussed in Section 28.1. The third column provides the standard errors, estimates of the standard deviations associated with the estimated coefficients. The interpretation of the other information and how one evaluates an estimated model is discussed in the next section.

28.3   EVALUATION

Once we obtain estimates of our regression model coefficients, we must evaluate the results. There are two aspects to the evaluation: how well does the regression model fit the data, and how well do the estimated coefficients conform to our a priori expectations?

28.3.1   GOODNESS-OF-FIT

After obtaining coefficient estimates, the obvious question to ask is: how well does the model fit the data, or, equivalently, how well does the regression model explain variations in the dependent variable?

Let us begin by considering the general problem of predicting some variable, Y. If we only have observations on Y, then the best predictor of Y is the sample mean. For example, if we want to predict an individual's weight and the only information available is the weight of a representative sample of individuals, then the sample mean is the best predictor of the individual's weight. However, what if we believe that height is related to weight? Then, knowing an individual's height (X) should improve our predictions of weight (Y).

Consider a particular observation, Y_i. Without knowing X_i, the best guess for Y_i would be the sample mean, $\overline{Y}$, and the error in this guess is $Y_i - \overline{Y}$. By using knowledge of the relationship between X and Y, we can improve that prediction, knowing X_i leads to the prediction of $\hat{Y}_i$. So we have "explained" part of the difference between the observed value of Y_i and its mean. Specifically, we have explained $\hat{Y}_i - \overline{Y}$. But, $Y_i - \hat{Y}_i$ is still unexplained. To summarize

$$Y_i - \overline{Y} = \text{the total deviation of the observed } Y_i \text{ from } \overline{Y}$$

$$\hat{Y}_i - \overline{Y} = \text{the portion of the total deviation explained by the regression model}$$

$$Y_i - \hat{Y}_i = \text{the unexplained deviation of } Y_i \text{ from } \overline{Y}$$

We can calculate these deviations for each observation. If we square them (to avoid cancellation of deviations with opposite signs), we can calculate the total deviation and the explained and unexplained portions for all observations. Specifically, the sum-of-squared deviations are

$$\sum_{i=1}^{n} \left(Y_i - \overline{Y} \right)^2 = \text{total deviation} \tag{28.12}$$

$$\sum_{i=1}^{n} \left(\hat{Y}_i - \overline{Y} \right)^2 = \text{explained deviation} \tag{28.13}$$

$$\sum_{i=1}^{n} \left(Y_i - \hat{Y} \right)^2 = \text{unexplained deviation} \tag{28.14}$$

Our goal in predicting Y is to explain the deviation of the observed values from the sample mean. Note that the unexplained portion of these deviations is the quantity that OLS estimation minimizes. Therefore, one measure of how well the regression model explains the variation in the dependent variable is the ratio of explained to total deviation. This measure is called the coefficient of determination or R^2. Specifically,

$$R^2 = \frac{\text{explained deviation}}{\text{total deviation}} = \frac{\sum\limits_{i=1}^{n} \left(\hat{Y}_i - \overline{Y} \right)^2}{\sum\limits_{i=1}^{n} \left(Y_i - \overline{Y} \right)^2} \tag{28.15}$$

R^2 is the proportion of the variance in the dependent variable explained by all the independent variables. In the crime rate example, R^2 equals 0.447, which means that 44.7 percent of the variance in crime rate is explained by the poverty rate, population density, and the school drop out rate. A high R^2 implies a good overall fit of the estimated regression line to the sample data. As $0 \leq R^2 \leq 1$, an R^2 close to 1 indicates a very good linear fit (most of the variance in Y is explained by X), although an R^2 near 0 indicates that X does not explain Y any better than its sample mean. R^2 is thus an easy to understand, and almost universally used, measure of the goodness-of-fit of the regression model.

Obviously, when we estimate a regression model we would like a high R^2, because we want to explain as much of the variation in Y as we can. We must be careful, however, not to blindly pursue the goal of a high R^2. There are three issues to consider in an evaluation of an R^2.

First, a high R^2 does not necessarily mean a causal explanation, merely a statistical one. For example, consider the following model of the amount of household consumption in year t:

$$Y_t = \beta_0 + \beta_1 Y_{t-1} \tag{28.16}$$

This model is likely to have a very high R^2, but last year's consumption (Y_{t-1}) does not cause this year's consumption. The two are merely highly correlated because the key causal variable (income) is likely to be similar over the two years.

Second, a low R^2 may simply indicate that the relationship is not linear. For example, if one attempts to fit a line to the relationship $Y = X^2$ for X ranging from -100 to 100, as illustrated in Figure 28.3, the R^2 for the OLS estimated line will be 0 even though the relationship between X and Y is an exact nonlinear one.

Finally, if a high R^2 is the only goal, it can be achieved by adding independent variables to the regression model. Additional independent variables cannot lower R^2. In fact, if there are $n - 1$

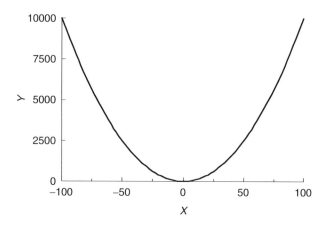

FIGURE 28.3 $3Y = X^2$.

independent variables (where n is the number of observations), then $R^2 = 1$ regardless of the independent variables. For example, if there are only two observations and a model with one independent variable, then the line will fit the data perfectly regardless of which independent variable is used. Adding a third observation will destroy the perfect fit, but the fit will still be good simply because there is only one observation to "explain". This difference between the number of observations (n) and the number of independent variables (k) is called the degrees of freedom (df). Specifically,

$$\text{df} = n - k - 1$$

The greater the degrees of freedom, the more reliable or accurate the estimates are likely to be.

A second measure of the goodness-of-fit of an estimated model is the F-test. The F statistic is the ratio of the explained deviation to the unexplained deviation, adjusted for the degrees of freedom, or

$$F = \frac{(\text{explained deviation})/k}{(\text{unexplained deviation})/(n - k - 1)} \tag{28.17}$$

This statistic is used to conduct a significance test for the overall fit of the estimated equation. A "high" F value indicates it is unlikely that we would have observed the estimated parameters if all the true parameters are zero. Intuitively, the set of independent variables has little explanatory power if the explained variation is small relative to the unexplained variation.

Most software packages provide the results of the F-test by default when we run the regression analysis. In the crime rate example, the F-test result is 14.57 ($p < .0001$). But, note that F-test is a relatively weak test. R^2 provides more information, and is thus the more common measure of model goodness-of-fit.

28.3.2 COEFFICIENT EXPECTATIONS

Determining the extent to which coefficient estimates conform to our a priori expectations has two elements—statistical significance, and expectations about signs and magnitudes.

28.3.2.1 Statistical Significance

The first assessment of a coefficient estimate should be to determine if it is statistically different from zero, for this reveals whether a relationship was found in the sample data. Statistical significance is assessed using tests of whether the observed sample estimate is likely to have occurred even if the population value is zero. The appropriate significance test for individual coefficients in a regression analysis is the *t*-test. The *t*-test is based on the *t*-statistic, which is computed as

$$t_j = \frac{\hat{\beta}_j - \beta_j}{s_{\hat{\beta}_j}}, \quad j = 1, 2, \dots, k \tag{28.18}$$

where s is the standard error of the estimated coefficient, $\hat{\beta}_j$

The *t*-statistic associated with the null hypothesis of β equal to zero is routinely reported with the regression results in most regression software packages (see, for example, Table 28.2, column 5). If not, it is easily calculated by dividing the parameter estimate by its standard error.

A high absolute value of t_j indicates that it is unlikely that we would have observed the sample estimate if $\beta_j = 0$ in the underlying population. If one obtains a high t value, the inference is that $\beta_j \neq 0$. The magnitude of t considered to be "high" depends on the degrees of freedom and the selected probability level (the level of significance). These critical *t*-statistic values can be found in collections of statistical tables or econometric textbooks, but increasingly the probability level associated with the t value is generated by the regression software and included as a standard part of the regression results (e.g., see Table 28.2, column 6).

Selecting the probability level that denotes statistical significance is a subjective decision. A widely used value is five percent. If one obtains a *t*-statistic larger than the critical value for the five percent level (larger than an absolute value of 2.0 for most samples), the interpretation is that only five percent of the time would we expect to observe this particular value of the coefficient estimate if the true coefficient is zero. The implication then is that $\beta \neq 0$. If one prefers more certainty before making this inference, then a lower probability level (e.g., one percent) can be selected. If one is comfortable with a larger potential error, then a higher probability level (e.g., ten percent) can be selected.

Finally, note that it is certainly not necessary that all coefficients pass a *t*-test. Failure means that the hypothesized relationship was not observed in this particular sample, not that there isn't a relationship in the population under study. Such negative information is, in fact, quite useful. If researchers repeatedly find no effect across different samples, this becomes persuasive evidence that the hypothesis, and its underlying theory, need to be reconsidered.

28.3.2.2 Signs and Magnitudes

Once the statistically significant coefficients have been identified, their sign and magnitude should be checked against a priori expectations. In most cases, we will have a specific expectation with respect to the sign of the coefficient, because sign expectations derive directly from our hypotheses. For example, if we expect increasing poverty to increase criminal activities, we expect a positive coefficient on poverty rate; if we expect crime to decrease with an increased police presence, we expect a negative coefficient on our measure of police presence. If the estimated coefficient sign differs from the expected one, it indicates a problem with the underlying theory, variable measurement, or the sample.

We are less likely to have strong expectations about magnitude. Our understanding of most public sector processes is not so well developed that we can identify the magnitude of impacts a priori. Nevertheless, an examination of magnitudes can offer important information about the expected impact of interventions, as well as their cost effectiveness, e.g., the reduction in teenage pregnancies expected to result from an additional $100 K spent on a prevention program. We may also care about relative magnitudes—how the magnitude on one regression coefficient compares to another. These are considered next.

28.3.3 Relative Importance of Independent Variables

Sometimes, we want to make statements about the relative importance of the independent variables in a multiple regression model. For example, recall our multivariate model of crime as a function of poverty rate, the population density, and the high school dropout rate (Equation 28.3). If $\hat{\beta}_1$ is larger than $\hat{\beta}_2$, does this imply that the poverty rate (X_1) is more important than population density (X_2) in determining the crime rate? It does not; one cannot directly compare the magnitudes of estimated regression coefficients, because the variables are measured in different units. The absolute value of a coefficient is easily changed simply by changing the measurement scale of the variable.

To compare the impact of different independent variables on the dependent variable, we must calculate standardized coefficients (sometimes called beta coefficients). These are produced by standardizing each variable (by subtracting its mean and dividing by its estimated standard deviation), and then estimating the model using the standardized values.

$$(Y_i - \overline{Y})/s_Y = \alpha_1(X_{1i} - \overline{X}_1)/s_{X_1} + \cdots + \alpha_k(X_{ki} - \overline{X}_k)/s_{X_k} + \varepsilon_i \qquad (28.19)$$

As all the variables are now measured in the same units (all standardized variables have a mean of zero and a variance of one), their coefficients can be directly compared. If the magnitude of $\hat{\alpha}_1$ exceeds $\hat{\alpha}_2$ then one can state that X_1 has a greater influence on Y than X_2.

Standardizing the variables in our crime model and estimating a model analogous to Equation 28.19 yields the following estimates of $\hat{\alpha}$: $\hat{\alpha}_1 = 0.22$, $\hat{\alpha}_2 = 0.22$, and $\hat{\alpha}_3 = 0.49$. Thus, we can now say that, in this sample, the influence of the dropout rate on crime is more than double that of either the poverty rate or population density. In practice, one rarely has to run a separate standardized estimation because most regression packages will provide standardized coefficients with the regression coefficients, either by default (as in SPSS, see Table 28.2, column 4) or upon request (as in SAS, include/stb option in PROC REG procedure).

The interpretation of a standardized coefficient is in standard deviation terms; it provides the average standard deviation change in the dependent variable resulting from a unit standard deviation change in the independent variable. For example, the standardized coefficient $\hat{\alpha}_1$ is interpreted to mean that the standard deviation change of 1 in the poverty rate will lead to a 0.22 standard deviation change in the crime rate.

Recall that the regression coefficient provides the average change in the dependent variable resulting from a unit change in the independent variable, and is thus in the dependent variable's unit of measurement. The relatively awkward interpretation of standardized coefficients has limited their use. Nevertheless, standardized regressions are common in some fields, like psychology, where the variables may not have a "natural" unit of measurement.

28.4 CLASSICAL ASSUMPTIONS

The use of Ordinary Least Squares (OLS) as the best estimation method for regression models is based on the regression model satisfying a set of assumptions. If these assumptions are not satisfied, we may have to consider an alternative estimating technique. These assumptions are called the "classical assumptions". For convenience, we have grouped them into four assumptions. First, we simply state the assumptions, then for each, we discuss how to identify assumption violations, their effects, and available remedies.

   I Dependent variable, Y, is a linear function of a specific set of independent variables, X, plus an error term, i.e., $Y_i = \beta_0 + \beta_1 X_{1i} + \beta_2 X_{2i} + \cdots + \beta_k X_{ki} + \varepsilon_i$. This assumption implies that:
- the relationship between Y and X is linear,
- no relevant independent variables have been excluded, and
- no irrelevant independent variables have been included.

  II Observations on the independent variables can be considered fixed in repeated sampling.

This assumption implies that the observed values of the Xs are determined outside the model and thus independently of the values of the error term, i.e., the Xs and the εs are uncorrelated, or COV $(X\varepsilon) = 0$.

  III Error term, the random variable ε, is assumed to satisfy the following four conditions:

     a Error term has a zero population mean, or $E(\varepsilon_i) = 0$. A violation of this assumption yields a biased intercept.

     b Error term has constant variance for all observations, or $\text{VAR}(\varepsilon_i) = \sigma^2$ for all observations i. Such an error term is called homoskedastic. If, alternatively, its variance is changing across observations, the error term is said to be heteroskedastic.

     c Error term for one observation (ε_i) is not systematically correlated with the error term for another observation (ε_m), or $\text{COV}\,(\varepsilon_i \varepsilon_m) = 0$ for all observations $i \neq m$. In other words, a random shock to one observation does not affect the error term in another observation. The violation of this assumption is called autocorrelation.

     d Error term is normally distributed.

  IV Number of observations exceeds the number of independent variables, and there are no exact linear relationships among the independent variables. The latter condition, perfect collinearity, occurs if two variables are the same except for a scale factor or the addition of a constant, e.g., $X_1 = aX_2 + b$. In this case, the effects on the dependent variable of movements in one variable cannot be differentiated from movements in the other.

Assumptions I through IV are the classical assumptions. Their importance derives from the Gauss–Markov theorem, which states that if all the above assumptions hold,* then the OLS estimates of β are the best linear unbiased estimators of β. Consider what this means.

The processes of sampling and estimation are used to gain information about a population by estimating its parameters from sample data. These sample estimators have characteristics with respect to the population parameters. Two of the most important are bias and the extent of dispersion.

If the sample estimator has an expected value equal to the population parameter it is estimating, it is said to be unbiased, e.g., $E(\hat{\beta}) = \beta$. This means that if we draw repeated samples from the population and calculate the sample estimator, their average will be equal to the true population parameter. Obviously, we would like our estimator to have this characteristic.

Another important characteristic is the extent of dispersion of the sample estimator around the population parameter. The larger the variance, the more likely it is that a given sample will produce a value for the sample estimator that is very different from the population parameter. Consequently, we would like to minimize this dispersion.

When a sample estimator is unbiased and has the smallest variance among the set of unbiased estimators, it is said to be efficient. The Gauss–Markov theorem assures us that if the classical assumptions hold, the OLS estimator is efficient and thus the best estimator of the population parameters, i.e., the best measure of the relationship between the independent and dependent variables of interest to us.

Therefore, the first step in estimating a regression model is to determine if the classical assumptions are satisfied, and thus whether or not OLS is the appropriate estimating method. The implications of and solutions for assumption violations vary according to the violation, so we discuss each separately in Sections 28.5 through 28.8.

28.5 MODEL SPECIFICATION

Assumption I states that the dependent variable can be expressed as a linear function of a specific set of independent variables, plus an error term. This assumption is critical. The theoretical model must be correct, otherwise credible inferences cannot be made.

---

* Assumption IIId is not necessary for the Gauss–Markov result, but is important for the use of significance tests.

The theory that underlies our understanding of the dependent variable should determine both the nature of the relationship (e.g., linear or not) and the selection of explanatory variables. As noted earlier, the linear specification has proven to be very robust in specifying a broad range of phenomena of interest to public sector scholars and practitioners. We will thus focus our attention on the set of independent variables. We begin by considering the consequences of selecting the wrong set of independent variables—by excluding relevant variables, or by including irrelevant variables, followed by an evaluation of a frequently used selection method—stepwise regression. We then consider two other specification issues—the measurement level of the variables, and nonlinear relationships that can be handled within the regression framework.

28.5.1 EXCLUDED RELEVANT VARIABLES

Consider first the case where a variable we expect to influence the dependent variable cannot be included in the regression model (e.g., data is unavailable). What are the implications for the regression model? More precisely, assume the model we want to estimate (ignoring the intercept) is

$$Y = \beta_1 X_1 + \beta_2 X_2 + \varepsilon \qquad (28.20)$$

Instead, X_2 is omitted from the model and we estimate the following model (where μ is an error term):

$$Y = \beta_1 X_1 + \mu \qquad (28.21)$$

Obviously the latter model will explain less of the variation in Y, but what about the information we obtain? Is the estimate of β_1 affected?

Recall that β_j represents the change in the expected value of the dependent variable given a unit change in X_j holding other independent variables constant. If a relevant independent variable is not included in the model, it is not being held constant for the interpretation of β_j—thus the estimate of β_j may be biased.

Whether or not $\hat{\beta}_j$ is biased depends on whether the omitted variable is correlated with the set of included independent variables. More precisely, in our example, the expected value of $\hat{\beta}_1$ can be shown to be

$$E(\hat{\beta}_1) = \beta_1 + \beta_2 \, \text{COV}(X_1 X_2)/\text{VAR}(X_1) \qquad (28.22)$$

In order for $\hat{\beta}_1$ to be unbiased, i.e., for $E(\hat{\beta}_1)$ to equal β_1, it must be the case that either $\beta_2 = 0$ (X_2 is not a relevant variable) or COV $(X_1 X_2) = 0$ (X_1 and X_2 are uncorrelated). Otherwise, the second term on the left side of Equation 28.22 is not zero, and the estimate of β_1 will be biased.

Intuitively, when X_1 and X_2 are correlated and X_2 is not included in the estimation, $\hat{\beta}_1$ will pick up the effect of X_2 on Y as well as the effect of X_1 on Y, hence the bias. If X_1 and X_2 are uncorrelated, $\hat{\beta}_1$ doesn't incorporate the impact of X_2 (it would be reflected in the error term) and no bias is introduced. For example, assume we believe that salary differences in an organization can be explained by experience, education, and motivation. Unfortunately, we have no measure of motivation. If we estimate the model without motivation and motivation is unrelated to experience and education, then the sample estimates of β will be good indicators of the extent to which education and experience explain salary differences. If, however, highly motivated individuals are, for example, likely to be more educated (or more educated individuals are more motivated) then the effect of education on salaries will be overestimated, as it will include both the effect of education and the effect of motivation on salaries.

Unfortunately, for many public policy and administration applications, it is unlikely that two determinants of a variable are completely uncorrelated, so bias must always be considered when one excludes a relevant variable. Moreover, the probable presence of bias with an omitted relevant variable makes t-tests invalid. The use of t-tests requires that the parameter estimate be unbiased.

In summary, excluding a relevant variable from a regression model is quite serious. It is likely to yield biased parameter estimates (if the excluded variable is correlated with included independent variables) and invalid t-tests. Given this undesirable outcome, researchers may be tempted to include any variables that might be relevant. Consider then what happens if one includes irrelevant variables.

28.5.2 INCLUDED IRRELEVANT VARIABLES

Assume that the dependent variable of interest is only determined by X_1, i.e., the true model (ignoring the intercept and with μ as the error term) is

$$Y = \beta_1 X_1 + \mu \tag{28.23}$$

We, however, include X_2 in the model in error and estimate

$$Y = \beta_1 X_1 + \beta_2 X_2 + \varepsilon \tag{28.24}$$

According to Equation 28.22, $E(\hat{\beta}_1) = \beta_1$ because $\beta_2 = 0$. Therefore, the parameter estimate of the relevant variable is unbiased, even if one includes an irrelevant variable in the model.

The variance of $\hat{\beta}_1$, however, increases unless $\text{COV}(X_1 X_2) = 0$. To see this, consider the variance of $\hat{\beta}_1$ for the estimated model (Equation 28.24):

$$\text{VAR}(\hat{\beta}_1) = \frac{\sigma_\varepsilon^2}{\sum_{i=1}^{n}(X_{1i} - \overline{X})^2(1 - r_{12}^2)} \tag{28.25}$$

r_{12} is the Pearson correlation coefficient between X_1 and X_2, and captures the covariation between the two variables. According to Equation 28.25, if $r_{12} \neq 0$, $\text{VAR}(\hat{\beta})$ increases, which means that the OLS estimates no longer have the smallest variance. In addition, the increased variance means that the t-statistic associated with X_1 is lowered (s_β is its denominator), making it harder to reject the null hypothesis.

So, how do we determine the variables to be included in a regression model? A well-developed theory of the determinants of the dependent variable is required. If theory is uncertain, or data is not available on some variables, there are important costs. To summarize them:

- Excluding a relevant variable usually leads to biased parameter estimates, which means that the parameter estimate may be substantially incorrect in both sign and magnitude, and t-tests are invalid.
- Including an irrelevant variable yields inefficient parameter estimates, and underestimates the value of t, making it harder to pass a significance test.

If one is uncertain about whether or not a measurable variable should be included in a model, it is usually better to include it because the consequences of excluding a relevant variable are direr than those of including an irrelevant one.

28.5.3 STEPWISE REGRESSION

Consider a common and problematic strategy for selecting variables for inclusion in the estimating equation, stepwise regression. This procedure adds explanatory variables to a model based on their marginal contribution to R^2 or based on their t-statistic value. There are four problems with this approach:

1. Invalid population inferences: Stepwise regression ignores the theoretical aspects of estimation, which can lead one to make incorrect population inferences from the sample characteristics. For example, the sample may contain characteristics that are not important in the population (or vice versa).
2. Invalid t- (or F-) statistics: In stepwise regression, t- (or F-) statistics are maximized at each step. Therefore, t- (or F-) statistics no longer have the t- (or F-) distribution. The calculated p values become optimistic (Rencher, 2002).
3. Arbitrary model: The final equation is arbitrary if there is correlation among the independent variables because the order in which they are considered will affect whether or not a variable is included in the model.
4. Biased parameter estimates: Parameter estimates may be biased because the procedure makes it is easy to exclude relevant variables.

One should thus not rely on this technique to select independent variables for a regression analysis. Rather, one should rely on the prevailing understanding of the phenomenon under study.

There is, however, a legitimate use for stepwise regression. If there are no existing theories that explain the phenomenon of interest, then a stepwise technique could be used for hypothesis generation. Identifying the variables that have a large impact on the dependent variable in a particular sample may suggest possible hypotheses that can be explored using another data set. To conduct stepwise regression analysis in SPSS 14.0, select Analyze, Regression, Linear, choose Dependent and Independent variables, then choose "Stepwise" as the method, and click OK.

28.5.4 MEASUREMENT LEVEL OF VARIABLES

Regression analysis requires the use of interval data, variables with values that are ordered and scaled, e.g., income. Many variables of interest to public administration, however, are noninterval. There are two types of noninterval variables—nominal and ordinal. Ordinal variables can be ordered, but the distance between the values cannot be measured. For example, political interest can be categorized as "not interested", "somewhat interested", or "very interested". The order of the values is clear; on a scale of political interest, "very interested" is greater than "somewhat interested" and "somewhat interested" is greater than "not interested". The distance between the values, however, is not quantified. One cannot say, for example, how much more political interest is represented by "very interested" as compared to "somewhat interested." Nominal variables cannot be ordered, e.g., religious affiliation, gender. Values are grouped into named categories, but there is no order to the groupings.

Whether one should use regression analysis with noninterval data depends on which variables are noninterval. If the dependent variable is noninterval, one should use a qualitative dependent variable model (like logit or probit), not regression analysis. Noninterval independent variables, however, can be included in a regression model through the use of dummy variables.

28.5.4.1 Dummy Variables

Dummy variables are variables that take on only two values, for example, $X = 1$ if an individual is a male, and 0 if a female. A dummy variable can be included in a regression model as an independent variable and the OLS estimate of the coefficient remains efficient. The interpretation of the coefficient, however, changes.

Consider an example of a simple regression model of income as a function of gender:

$$Y = \beta_0 + \beta_1 X + \varepsilon \qquad (28.26)$$

where
    Y = income
    X = 1 if male, and 0 if female

Note that for women, the expected value of Y is β_0 ($X = 0$ and $E(\varepsilon) = 0$). β_0 is thus the average level of income for women. Similarly, for men, the expected value of Y is $\beta_0 + \beta_1$ ($X = 1$ and $E(\varepsilon) = 0$). So, $\beta_0 + \beta_1$ is the average level of income for men.

The coefficient on the dummy variable, β_1, is thus interpreted as the average change in income resulting from being male rather than female. Within a more complete model of income determination that includes the key determinants of income differences, this parameter estimate would provide a measure of the average income differences that result from gender discrimination. Note how this interpretation compares to that of an interval variable, where the coefficient represents the average change in the dependent variable resulting from a unit change in the independent variable.

Noninterval independent variables with more than two categories can also be included in the regression model using dummy variables. As an example, consider Graddy and Nichol's (1990) study of the effects of different organizational structures on the rate of disciplinary actions by occupational licensing boards.

They modeled disciplinary actions per licensee as a function of several board and profession-specific variables, as well as the degree to which the board functions as an independent agency. Organizational structure was defined as an ordinal variable, with boards categorized as either independent, sharing power with a centralized agency, or subsumed within a centralized agency. This qualitative indicator of organizational structure can be used in a regression model by creating the following three dummy variables:

    I = 1 if the board is independent, and 0 otherwise
    S = 1 if the board shares power, and 0 otherwise
    C = 1 if the board is controlled by a centralized agency, and 0 otherwise

The estimated model can only include two of these dummy variables. Including all three would create perfect collinearity (as $I + S + C = 1$ for all observations) and the model could not be estimated.* Therefore, estimation requires that one category be omitted.[†] The omitted category serves as a base group with which to compare the others. For example, consider the independent boards as the base case. The model to be estimated is

$$Y = \beta_1 S + \beta_2 C + \beta X + \varepsilon \qquad (28.27)$$

where
    Y is the rate of disciplinary actions
    X denotes all other included determinants of disciplinary actions

β_1 represents the difference in the average number of disciplinary actions of boards that share power compared to independent boards. β_2 represents the difference in the average number of disciplinary actions of centralized boards compared to independent boards.

Estimation of this model revealed negative and significant coefficients on both S and C. This implies that both boards that share power with a centralized agency and those which are controlled

---

* This is a violation of Assumption IV and will be discussed in Section 28.8.
[†] In general, if a noninterval variable has g mutually exclusive and exhaustive categories, then g-1 dummy variables can be used to represent it in the regression model.

completely by a centralized agency produce fewer disciplinary actions than independent licensing boards. Note that these results are always interpreted relative to the base (omitted) category.

What if we want to compare the performance of centralized and shared-power boards? This requires that we re-estimate the model with centralized boards as the omitted category. In this estimation, the coefficient on S was not significantly different from zero, which implies there is no significant difference between the disciplinary performance of boards that share power and those that are fully centralized.

Finally, some researchers, to conserve on degrees of freedom, convert nominal variables to ordinal variables. For example, we could view the organizational structure of licensing boards in terms of their degree of centralization, and construct a variable Z that equals 1 if the board is independent; 2 if the board shares power; and 3 if the board is centralized.

Estimation of Equation 28.27 with Z substituted for S and C produced a negative and significant coefficient. The coefficient on an ordinal variable should be interpreted as one would an interval variable, e.g., the average decrease in disciplinary actions associated with a unit increase in centralization.

There is nothing wrong with this approach if the underlying scale (e.g., centralization) makes sense. But, this estimation strategy yields less precise information. In this case, for example, the estimations using dummy variables revealed that shared-power boards and centralized boards behave about the same with respect to disciplinary actions, but significantly different from independent boards. The estimation using the ordinal variable suggested that centralized boards produce fewer disciplinary actions than those that share power—which is not the case. In SPSS, to recode a variable into dummy variables, select Transform, Recode, Into Different Variables, choose Input Variable, define Output Variable, and Click OK.

28.5.5 ALTERNATIVE FUNCTIONAL FORMS

Thus far we have specified a linear relationship between the dependent and independent variables, but the regression model actually allows more latitude. The regression model in fact requires only that the model be linear in its parameters, which means that some nonlinear relationships can be used. Several specifications that capture nonlinear relationships within the regression framework can be found in the literature. We consider here two of the more common—interaction effects and quadratic relationships.

28.5.5.1 Interaction Effects

What if the expected effect of an independent variable depends on the level of another variable? Consider, for example, the determinants of volunteering. According to Sundeen (1990), marital status and family size are important determinants of volunteering activity. In particular, he argues that it is unlikely that single parents have the time to volunteer, although single individuals without children may. This suggests the need for an interaction term. Consider, for example, the model

$$Y = \beta_1(X_1 X_2) + \beta X + \varepsilon \qquad (28.28)$$

where
  $Y =$ the number of hours volunteered
  $X_1 = 1$ if an individual is single, 0 otherwise
  $X_2 =$ the number of children
  X denotes other determinants of volunteering

The interaction variable is the product of 'singleness' and the number of children. If one is not single or has no children this variable becomes zero and drops out of the model. The interaction variable will thus capture the impact of being a single parent on volunteering behavior. The estimate of β_1 is expected to be negative.

Note, that if theory supports it, we may also include one or both variables separately in the equation. For example, if we believe that more children limit volunteering time for married individuals as well as single parents, we could add X_2 to the model as a separate variable. One would then interpret the impact of an additional child on volunteering as β_1 for single individuals and β_1 plus the coefficient on X_2 for married individuals.

When individual predictors and the interaction terms are both included in the equation, it may cause multicollinearity. A common solution to this problem is to center continuous independent variables on their means and then compute the interaction term and estimate the model.* In SPSS, to create an interaction term or center variables on their means, select Transform, Compute, choose Target Variable, define Numeric Expression, then click OK.

28.5.5.2 Quadratic Relationships

Ferris and Graddy (1988) argue that the relationship between the contracting decision of cities and their size is not linear. Small cities may want to contract out services to gain the advantages of scale economies, but large cities may contract out more than smaller cities because they have a wider selection of available suppliers. This suggests the u-shaped relationship between the probability of contracting and city size. This u-shape represents a quadratic relationship, which can be captured in a regression model for a variable X by including the following specification in the model: $\beta_1 X + \beta_2 X^2$. For the contracting example, the model is

$$Y = \beta_1 X_1 + \beta_2 X_1^2 + \beta X + \varepsilon \tag{28.29}$$

where

Y denotes the incidence of contracting
X_1 denotes city size
X denotes other determinants of contracting

The interpretation of the coefficients depends on the signs of $\hat{\beta}_1$ and $\hat{\beta}_2$. If $\hat{\beta}_1$ is negative and significant this supports the economies-of-scale hypothesis; contracting decreases with increasing city size. If $\hat{\beta}_2$ is positive and significant, this supports the importance of available suppliers; after some size, contracting increases with increasing city size. The u-shaped quadratic hypothesis is only supported if both $\hat{\beta}_1$ and $\hat{\beta}_2$ are statistically significant and the appropriate sign. One can, of course, hypothesize an inverted u-shaped relationship between variables with the sign expectation on the coefficient estimates being reversed.

28.6 ASSUMPTION II VIOLATIONS

According to Assumption II, in order for OLS to provide the best estimates of β, it must be the case that the independent variables are uncorrelated with the error term. To see the rationale for this assumption, consider (ignoring the intercept) the simple regression model: $Y_i = \beta X_i + \varepsilon_i$. It can be shown that[†]

$$E(\hat{\beta}) = \beta + \frac{\sum\limits_{i=1}^{n} \left(X_i - \overline{X} \right) (\varepsilon_i - \overline{\varepsilon})}{\sum\limits_{i=1}^{n} \left(X_i - \overline{X} \right)^2} \tag{28.30}$$

---

* Additional reference on centering is available in chapter 7 of Cohen et al. (2003).
[†] For an accessible derivation, see Johnson et al. (1987), chapter 15.

If, as is stated in Assumption II, the Xs are fixed in repeated samples, then the correlation between X and ε (the numerator of the second term) is zero, and $\hat{\beta}$ is unbiased. If, however, X and ε are correlated, the second term is not zero, and the expected value of $\hat{\beta}$ will not be β, i.e., $\hat{\beta}$ will be a biased estimator.

There are two common situations that violate Assumption II—an independent variable measured with error; and an independent variable determined in part by the dependent variable. The former situation is called "errors in variables", the latter 'simultaneous causality'. We consider each in turn.

28.6.1 ERRORS IN VARIABLES

We have thus far assumed that all variables used in regression analysis are measured without error. In practice, there is often measurement error. What then are the implications for our coefficient estimates? Consider two cases—the dependent variable measured with error, and an independent variable measured with error.

28.6.1.1 Dependent Variable Measured with Error

Assume the true dependent variable is Y, but its measured value is Y^*. The measurement error can be specified as

$$Y^* = Y + w \tag{28.31}$$

where w is an error term that satisfies Assumption III.

The true model (ignoring the intercept) is: $Y = \beta X + \varepsilon$. According to Equation 28.31, $Y = Y^* - w$, so the estimated equation is

$$Y^* = \beta X + \varepsilon + w \tag{28.32}$$

The error term in this regression of Y^* on X is $\varepsilon + w$. As long as X is uncorrelated with this error term (and there is no reason to assume otherwise), then the parameter estimates are unbiased.

The only effect of measurement error in the dependent variable is increased error variance. The measurement error will be reflected in the residuals, increasing them and the estimated error variance,* which in turn inflates the coefficient variance. The practical implication of the increased coefficient variance is a lower t value (recall the related discussion in Section 28.5.2), making it more difficult to pass a significance test.

28.6.1.2 Independent Variable Measured with Error

Let X be the true independent variable and X^* be the measured variable, then measurement error can be represented as

$$X^* = X + v \tag{28.33}$$

where v is an error term that satisfies Assumption III.

The true model (ignoring the intercept) is: $Y = \beta X + \varepsilon$. According to Equation 28.33, $X = X^* - v$. Thus, the estimated equation is

$$Y = \beta X^* + \varepsilon - \beta v \tag{28.34}$$

The error term in a regression of Y on X^* is $\varepsilon - \beta v$. But, according to Equation 28.33, v and X^* are correlated. Thus, the independent variable in Equation 28.34 is correlated with the error term,

---

* The estimated error variance, s^2, equals $\sum e_i^2/(n - k - 1)$.

violating Assumption II. In this situation, OLS will produce biased estimates of β. Moreover, the t-statistic is biased and significance tests are invalid.

Thus, measurement error in independent variables can be quite problematic. Such measurement error can be ignored if it is assumed to be too small and random to affect the parameter estimates. If, however, one cannot make that assumption, then an alternative estimation strategy, instrumental-variable estimation, is needed.*

28.6.2 Simultaneous Causality

In some situations, the dependent variable being modeled influences one or more of the independent variables. The process is thus characterized by simultaneous causality. For example, consider the following simple model of national income determination:

$$C_t = \beta \, N_t + \varepsilon_t \; (\beta > 0) \tag{28.35}$$

where

    C denotes aggregate consumption
    N denotes national income in year t.

Assume, in addition, that national income itself is just the sum of consumption, investment, and government spending, or

$$N_t = C_t + I_t + G_t \tag{28.36}$$

where

    I denotes aggregate investment
    G denotes government spending in year t

Consider a random shock that increases ε. According to Equation 28.35, an increase in ε implies that C goes up, and an increase in C, according to Equation 28.36, will cause an increase in N. But, N is also in Equation 28.35, and if N goes up then C increases too.

If only Equation 28.35 is estimated, OLS attributes both of the increases in consumption to the increase in income, not just the latter (because ε and N are correlated). Therefore, the OLS estimate of β is biased—in this case overestimated. More precisely, recall Equation 28.30, reproduced here with national income (N) as the independent variable:

$$\hat{\beta} = \beta + \frac{\sum\limits_{t=1}^{n} \left(N_t - \overline{N}\right)\left(\varepsilon_t - \overline{\varepsilon}\right)}{\sum\limits_{t=1}^{n} \left(N_t - \overline{N}\right)^2} \tag{28.37}$$

N and ε are correlated because N is a function of C (see Equation 28.36) and C is a function of ε (see Equation 28.35). The amount of the bias is the second term in Equation 28.37.

In general, whenever an independent variable is a function of the dependent variable, OLS will produce biased parameter estimates. The problem is usually identified by theory, in that one must recognize that the relationship is simultaneous. There are two alternative estimation procedures.

---

* Instrumental-variable estimation is a general estimation procedure applicable to situations in which the independent variable is not independent of the error term. The procedure involves finding an "instrument" to replace X that is both uncorrelated with the error term and highly correlated with X. A discussion of this procedure is beyond the scope of this chapter, but can be found in many econometrics textbooks (e.g., Maddala, 1992, chapter 11).

One involves estimating the single equation of interest using a special case of instrumental-variable estimation, two-stage least squares. The second requires estimation of all the equations—multi-equation estimation. Both approaches are beyond the scope of this chapter.*

28.7 ERROR TERM ASSUMPTIONS

Assumption III refers to the assumed distribution of the error term. Specifically, ε is assumed to be normally distributed with a zero population mean, constant variance, and no correlation in the error terms across observations. Each aspect of this assumption has implications for estimation.

28.7.1 BIASED INTERCEPT

Assumption IIIa states that the error term has a population mean of zero. This means that we believe we have included all important nonrandom determinants of the dependent variable in our model. However, even if our model is correct, it is possible for this assumption to be violated. There could, for example, be systematic positive or negative measurement errors in calculating the dependent variable. The consequences are serious. If $E(\varepsilon) \neq 0$, OLS estimation yields biased parameter estimates, i.e., $E(\hat{\beta}) \neq \beta$.

The problem is most easily addressed by forcing the error term to have a zero mean by adding or subtracting the sample error mean to the intercept. For example, if the error term mean for a particular sample is some number d, one could subtract d from ε and add d to $\hat{\beta}_0$:

$$Y = \beta_0 + \beta_1 X + \varepsilon \qquad (28.38)$$

$$Y = \beta_0 + d + \beta_1 X + \varepsilon - d \qquad (28.39)$$

The two equations are equal as only a constant is added and subtracted, but the latter error term $(\varepsilon - d)$ has a zero mean. This transformation is exactly how the OLS procedure corrects a nonzero sample error mean. If an intercept (β_0) is included in the estimation, OLS will force the mean of the error term for the sample to be zero in its estimation of the intercept. For example, for the simple regression model, $Y = \beta_0 + \beta_1 X + \varepsilon$, OLS estimates β_0 as $Y - \beta_1 X$.

This approach assures that Assumption IIIa is satisfied, and that the estimates of the slope parameters (β_1 through β_k) are unaffected. The estimate of the intercept, however, is affected. The OLS correction produces an unbiased estimate of the new intercept ($\beta_0 + d$), but a biased estimate of the original intercept (β_0) (if the sample error term mean is in fact nonzero). Thus, we sacrifice a biased intercept estimate for unbiased slope estimates—a trade we are usually quite willing to make as the intercept estimate is usually unimportant theoretically.

The correction has two implications for estimation. First, we cannot rely on the estimate of β_0. In fact, the constant (intercept) can usefully be thought of as a "garbage-can" term, as it will contain any systematic sample anomalies. Second, we should always include a constant in a regression model. If it is omitted and there is a nonzero error mean in the sample, then all the parameter estimates will be biased. Nonzero sample error means are particularly likely in small samples.

28.7.2 AUTOCORRELATION

Autocorrelation, a violation of Assumption IIIc, occurs when the error terms associated with two or more observations are correlated. This is a common problem in time-series models. Consider, for example, a model of the size of Southern California's economy in year $t(E_t)$:

$$E_t = \beta X_t + \varepsilon_t \qquad (28.40)$$

---

* The interested reader is referred to Pindyck and Rubinfeld (1991), who do a good job of developing both.

The Northridge earthquake was a random shock that caused ε_{94} to be negative. Some of this negative effect carried over and affected ε_{95} and beyond. This phenomenon of a random shock to one period that carries over into future periods is called autocorrelation.

Observed autocorrelation can result from two sources—a random shock or a missing relevant variable. The former, the type described above, is called pure autocorrelation. A missing relevant variable can also generate systematic patterns in the error term over time. Autocorrelation resulting from this source is really a specification error and can be corrected by including the relevant variable in the model.

Pure autocorrelation is much less likely with cross-sectional data as the effects of random shocks to one family, firm, etc. do not normally carry over to another. Therefore, in this section we consider only time-series models.

28.7.2.1 Consequences

What effect does autocorrelation have on OLS estimation? Applying OLS to a model that satisfies all the classical assumptions except the absence of autocorrelation yields:

- Unbiased parameter estimates: The expected value of the parameter estimate is the true β if the independent variables do not include a lagged dependent variable (i.e., Y_t does not depend on Y_{t-1}).
- Inefficient parameter estimates: The variance of the parameter estimates is inflated, making it less likely that a particular estimate obtained in practice will be close to the true β (Studenmund, 2005).
- Invalid t-tests: The t-statistic is incorrect; thus hypothesis testing is invalid. With auto-correlation, s^2 is no longer an unbiased estimator of $\mathrm{VAR}(\varepsilon)$, which leads to bias in $S_{\hat{\beta}}^2$ as an estimator of $\mathrm{VAR}(\hat{\beta})$. Therefore, the denominator of the t-statistic, $S_{\hat{\beta}}^2$, is biased. The direction of the bias typically overestimates the t-statistics, thus increasing the likelihood of a Type I error (Studenmund, 2005).

Autocorrelation is sufficiently common and these problems are sufficiently serious that a solution is needed. The usual approach is to use an alternative estimation strategy, generalized least squares (GLS).

28.7.2.2 Generalized Least Squares

GLS is an estimation procedure that allows a general variance–covariance structure, i.e., one that does not require constant variance and the absence of covariation across error terms. To use GLS to correct for autocorrelation, we must specify the nature of the correlation among the error terms.

The most common specification, first-order autocorrelation, assumes the error term depends on last period's error term as follows:

$$\varepsilon_t = \rho\varepsilon_{t-1} + v_t$$

where
ρ(rho) = coefficient of autocorrelation $(-1 < \rho < 1)$
v is an error term that satisfies Assumption III

The degree and type of autocorrelation is indicated by the magnitude and sign of ρ:

$\rho = 0$ indicates that $\varepsilon_t = v_t$ and the absence of autocorrelation.
$\rho > 0$ indicates positive autocorrelation and is consistent with pure autocorrelation.
$\rho < 0$ indicates negative autocorrelation and suggests a specification error, as an error term switching signs in subsequent observations is inconsistent with pure autocorrelation.

Given this specification of the autocorrelation process, GLS estimation is straightforward. The logic behind the procedure can be revealed by manipulating the following simple regression model with first-order autocorrelation:

$$Y_t = \beta X_t + \varepsilon_t \text{ with } \varepsilon_t = \rho \varepsilon_{t-1} + v_t \tag{28.41}$$

Recall, we can always multiply both sides of an equation by a constant without changing the equality. Multiplying Equation 28.41 by $-\rho$ and rewriting it for period $t-1$ yields

$$-\rho y_{t-1} = -\beta \rho x_{t-1} - \rho \varepsilon_{t-1} \tag{28.42}$$

Adding Equations 28.41 and 28.42 yields

$$y_t - \rho y_{t-1} = \beta x_t - \beta \rho x_{t-1} + \varepsilon_t - \rho \varepsilon_{t-1} \tag{28.43}$$

Substituting $\rho \varepsilon_{t-1} + v_t$ for ε_t (from Equation 28.41) yields

$$y_t - \rho y_{t-1} = \beta [x_t - \rho x_{t-1}] + v_t \tag{28.44}$$

If we know the value of ρ, then we can create two new variables: $y_t^* = y_t - \rho y_{t-1}$ and $x_t^* = x_t - \rho x_{t-1}$. Substituting these new variables into Equation 28.43 yields

$$y_t^* = \beta x_t^* + v_t \tag{28.45}$$

As v_t satisfies Assumption III and β is the same coefficient as in our original model (Equation 28.41), OLS estimation of Equation 28.45 yields unbiased, minimum-variance estimates of β.

If, as is far more likely, we do not know rho, then we must estimate it. This is GLS estimation. In practice, if we request a first-order autocorrelation correction from a regression software package, the software will estimate ρ, and then use this estimate to create y_t^* and x_t^* and estimate β from the equivalent of Equation 28.45. For large samples, the GLS estimates of β (based on an estimated ρ) are unbiased, and have lower variance than the original OLS estimates.

28.7.2.3 Testing for Autocorrelation

Autocorrelation is so common in time-series models that one should always test for it. The most widely used test is the Durbin–Watson test. It relies on the following DW statistic, which is computed by most regression packages:

$$DW \approx 2(1 - r_e) \tag{28.46}$$

where r_e is the correlation coefficient between e_t and e_{t-1}.

The value of DW indicates the presence and probable source of any sample autocorrelation as follows:

- If $r_e = 0$, e_t is not correlated with e_{t-1} (presumably because ε_t is uncorrelated with ε_{t-1}), then DW $= 2$. Therefore, a DW value of approximately 2 indicates the absence of autocorrelation.
- If $r_e > 0$, which is most likely with positive autocorrelation, then DW is less than 2. Therefore, a DW value between 0 (its minimum value) and 2 may indicate positive autocorrelation.
- If $r_e < 0$, which is most likely with negative autocorrelation, then DW is greater than 2. Therefore, a DW value between 2 and 4 (its maximum) may indicate negative autocorrelation.

As negative autocorrelation usually indicates a specification error, we test for positive autocorrelation. The decision rule involves two critical statistics, d_L and d_U, which are found in collections of statistical tables and all econometrics textbooks. These numbers vary with the number of independent variables, the number of observations, and the level of significance. The decision rule is

> If DW $< d_L$, positive autocorrelation is indicated ($\rho > 0$).
> If DW $> d_U$, positive autocorrelation is not indicated ($\rho \leq 0$).
> If $d_L \leq$ DW $\leq d_U$, the test is inconclusive.

Consider an example. Assume we have a time-series model with three independent variables and 25 observations. A Durbin–Watson table reveals that for these values, $d_L = 1.12$ and $d_U = 1.66$. If the computed DW (from a regression package) is

- less than 1.12, assume that positive autocorrelation exists,
- greater than 1.66, assume there is no positive autocorrelation, and
- between 1.12 and 1.66, the test is inconclusive.

The weakness of the Durbin–Watson test is this inconclusive range. There is disagreement about how to treat this result. Some investigators choose to treat this as a support for the absence of autocorrelation. But, given that we do not know how to interpret this information, it seems more appropriate to assume that we may have positive autocorrelation if we are in the inconclusive range.

When the Durbin–Watson test indicates positive autocorrelation, one should apply the GLS correction discussed earlier. Finally, note that a simple correction for some autocorrelation is, if possible, to increase the time unit of the data. Obviously, it is more likely for random shocks to extend to future periods with daily, weekly, or monthly data, than with annual data. In SPSS 14.0, to conduct the Durbin–Watson test, select Analyze, Regression, Linear; click Statistics; check Durbin–Watson.

28.7.3 HETEROSKEDASTICITY

Heteroskedasticity occurs when the variance of the error term is not constant over all observations ($E(\varepsilon_i^2) \neq \sigma^2$ over all i), and is a violation of Assumption IIIb. The concept is best understood with an example. Consider a model of family food expenditures as a function of family income. Homoskedasticity implies that the variation in food expenditures is the same at different income levels; but, we expect less variation in consumption for low-income families than for high-income families. At low-income levels, average consumption is low with little variation. Food expenditures can't be much below average, or the family may starve; expenditures can't be much above average due to income restrictions. High-income families, on the other hand, have fewer restrictions, and thus can have more variation. Heteroskedasticity is indicated a priori.

Heteroskedasticity is much more likely to appear with cross-sectional data than with time-series data because the range in values of the variables is usually much larger in cross-sectional data—e.g., the range in food expenditures or city size.* Thus, heteroskedasticity is discussed in the context of cross-sectional data.

With OLS estimation, the consequences of heteroscedasticity are the same as with autocorrelation—coefficient estimates are unbiased, but their variance is inflated, and t-tests are invalid. The correction is also similar. But first, consider how we detect heteroskedasticity.

28.7.3.1 Testing for Heteroskedasticity

The most common test for heteroskedasticity is a visual inspection of the residuals. The residuals $(Y_i - \hat{Y}_i)$ are plotted on a graph against the independent variable that is suspected of causing

---

* With time-series data, changes in the variables over time are likely to be similar orders of magnitudes.

heteroskedasticity. If the absolute magnitude of the residuals appears on average to be the same regardless of the value of the independent variable, then there probably is no heteroskedasticity. If their magnitude seems related to the value of the independent variable, then a more formal test is indicated. For example, a residual plot of our food expenditure example should indicate more widely scattered residuals at high-income levels than at low-income levels. Most regression software packages will provide residual plots upon request against any variable selected by the user. In SPSS 14.0, to test for heteroskedasticity, select Analyze, Regression, Linear; click Plots; choose ZPRED—the standardized predicted dependent variable, and ZRESID—standardized residual, as X and Y, respectively, and then click Continue and OK. If ZPRED and ZRESID have been saved, one can also use Graphs, Scatterplot.

There is obviously a fair amount of subjectivity in interpreting residual patterns; unfortunately subjectivity is a characteristic of the more formal tests as well. Unlike the widely accepted use of the Durbin–Watson test to detect autocorrelation, there are several competing tests for heteroskedasticity (e.g., the Goldfeld–Quandt, Breusch and Pagan, Modified Levene, and White tests).* Here, we briefly discuss the White test.

White (1980) proposes that we regress the squared residuals against all the explanatory variables suspected on causing heteroskedasticity and their squares and cross products. For example, if two variables X_1 and X_2 are suspected, then one would run the following regression:

$$(Y - \hat{Y})^2 = \alpha_0 + \alpha_1 X_1 + \alpha_2 X_2 + \alpha_3 X_1^2 + \alpha_4 X_2^2 + \alpha_5 X_1 X_2 + \mu \quad (28.47)$$

The R^2 associated with this regression provides a test for heteroskedasticity. If the error term is homoskedastic, then nR^2 is distributed as a chi-square with $k(k+1)/2$ degrees of freedom. If this hypothesis is rejected, either heteroskedasticity or a misspecification is indicated.

28.7.3.2 Correction

As with autocorrelation, a GLS correction is possible for heteroskedasticity if one can specify the error variance.[†] For example, consider the following simple regression model with a heteroscedastic error term:

$$Y_i = \beta X_i + \varepsilon_i \text{ with VAR}(\varepsilon_i) = Z_i^2 \sigma^2 \quad (28.48)$$

where Z_i denotes an exogenous variable that varies across observations (if Z_i is a constant then ε is homoscedastic).

The GLS approach in this case is to transform the original equation into one that meets the homoskedastic assumption. For example, dividing both sides of Equation 28.48 by Z_i yields:

$$Y_i/Z_i = \beta X_i/Z_i + \varepsilon_i/Z_i \quad (28.49)$$

The variance of the new error term (ε_i/Z_i) can be shown to equal σ^2. Thus, the transformed equation has a homoscedastic error.

We need only create three new variables: $Y^* = Y/Z$, $X^* = X/Z$, and $\varepsilon^* = \varepsilon/Z$, and substitute them into Equation 28.49, which yields

$$Y^* = \beta X^* + \varepsilon^* \quad (28.50)$$

Estimating Equation 28.50 using OLS produces unbiased and minimum-variance estimates of β.

---

* For more on the comparison of different test methods, see Cohen et al. (2003), p.133.
[†] The weighted least squares (WLS), a commonly used remedy for heteroscedasticity, is a version of GLS (Abdi, 2003). For more on WLS, see Neter et al. (1996) and Cohen et al. (2003).

The problem, of course, is the specification of Z. It is unusual to know the specification of the error variance. The most common approach is to specify Z as a function of the independent variable suspected of causing the heteroskedasticity problem (e.g., $1/X$). If, however, the specification of Z is arbitrary, then it is uncertain whether GLS estimates are better or worse than the OLS estimates of the original equation.

A more direct solution to heteroskedasticity is to redefine the variable in question—if it makes sense theoretically. For example, assume we want to explain city expenditures for services (E) as a function of the income of its citizens (I), i.e.

$$E = \beta_0 + \beta_1 I + e$$

Obviously, large cities have more income, more expenditures, and presumably more variation in those expenditures, than small cities, which suggests heteroskedasticity. But, the model may in fact be misspecified. Is the relationship of interest between levels of expenditure and income or between per capita expenditures and income? Reformulating the model in per capita terms ($PE = \beta_0 + \beta_1 PI$) removes size and its spurious effect and thus eliminates the heteroskedasticity.

Heteroskedasticity may thus indicate a specification problem, either from an incorrect formulation or from an omitted variable. In these cases the solution is straight-forward—reformulation or inclusion of the omitted variable. In general, one is less likely to apply GLS to correct heteroskedasticity than to correct autocorrelation—because, with heteroskedasticity, we have less confidence in the validity of the GLS specification of the error term.

28.7.4 NORMALITY

Assumption IIId states that the error term is normally distributed. Although the error term need not be distributed according to a normal distribution in order for OLS estimates to be efficient, the use of significance tests requires it. Calculation of confidence interval and significance tests for coefficients are based on the assumptions of normally distributed errors. If the error distribution is significantly non-normal, the confidence interval may be too wide or too narrow.

In most cases, we just assume that the error term has a normal distribution. The Central Limit Theorem states that the distribution of the sum of independent variables (e.g., the error term) approaches the normal distribution as the sample size increases, regardless of the individual distributions of these random variables. Therefore, with large samples, the Central Limit Theorem assures us that the error term is normally distributed. With small samples, we are less confident. Cassidy (1981) demonstrates that the tendency toward a normal distribution occurs at sample sizes as small as ten observations. Nevertheless, one should be skeptical about the reliability of significance tests with very small samples.

Two graphic diagnostic tests for normality are the histogram and the normal probability plot of the standardized residuals. If the error terms are normally distributed, the histogram should show a roughly normal curve or the points on the normal probability plot should fall close to the diagonal line (as in Figure 28.4). Figure 28.4 shows the histogram and the normal probability plot of the crime rate example using SPSS 14,0 (check Histogram and Normal probability plot under Plots option of the regression analysis). If the residuals have excessive skewness (i.e., too many large errors in the same direction), the points will show a bow-shaped pattern of deviation from the diagonal. If the residuals have excessive kurtosis (i.e., there are either too many or too few large errors in both directions), the points will show an S-shaped pattern of deviations.

Other formal statistical tests of normality include the Shapiro–Wilk test for small to medium samples, the Kolmogorov–Smirnov test for large samples, Looney-Gulledge, and Lilliefors test. In SPSS, Shapiro–Wilks test and the Kolmogorov–Smirnov test can be found under Analyze, Descriptive Statistics, Explore; select Both or Plots in the Display group; click Plots and select at least one plot.

Violations of normality may occur because the linearity assumption is violated. In such cases, a nonlinear transformation of variables might solve the problem. In some cases, the problem is mainly

Histogram

Dependent variable: Crime rate

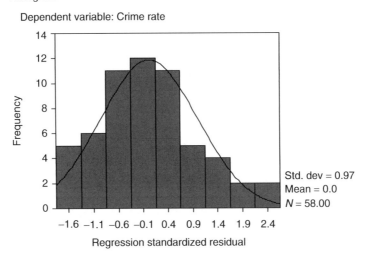

Std. dev = 0.97
Mean = 0.0
N = 58.00

Normal P–P plot of

Regression standardized residual

Dependent variable: Crime rate

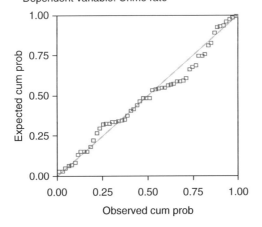

FIGURE 28.4 Histogram and normal probability plot of regression standardized residual.

due to one or two very large errors. If they are merely errors or if they are not likely to be repeated, then they can be removed from analysis.

28.8 MULTICOLLINEARITY

Assumption IV states that there are at least as many observations as independent variables, and that there are no exact linear relationships between the independent variables. This assumption (unlike the others) can easily be checked for any specific model. In fact, if either part of this assumption is violated, it is impossible to compute OLS estimates.

The first part of Assumption IV refers to the need to have more than k pieces of information (observations) to estimate k parameters. It requires only that the sample size be larger than the number of parameters to be estimated—the number of independent variables plus one. In fact, researchers usually seek the largest available and cost effective sample, because increasing the degrees of freedom (the number of observations minus the number of parameters to be estimated) reduces the variance in the estimates. Numerous studies have provided recommendations on adequate sample size for multiple regression analysis (Hair et al., 1998, Chapter 4; Maxwell, 2000; Tabachnick and Fidell, 2007, Chapter 5). However, there are tremendous disparities in these recommendations. The most common rule is that the ratio of observations to predictors be at least 10:1.

The second part of Assumption IV, the absence of an exact linear relationship among the independent variables, is unlikely to be an issue in naturally occurring data. It can, however, occur in data that have been constructed by the researcher. The problems created are easily illustrated. Assume that we want to estimate the following model:

$$Y = \alpha_0 + \alpha_1 X_1 + \alpha_2 X_2 + \varepsilon \qquad (28.51)$$

But,

$$X_2 = 5 + 2X_1 \qquad (28.52)$$

Substituting Equation 28.52 into Equation 28.51 and then rearranging yields:

$$\begin{aligned} Y &= \alpha_0 + \alpha_1 X_1 + \alpha_2(5 + 2_{x1}) + \varepsilon \\ Y &= \alpha_0 + 5\alpha_2 + X_1(\alpha_1 + 2\alpha_2) + \varepsilon \end{aligned} \qquad (28.53)$$

If we could run OLS on this last equation, the parameter estimates would be

$$\begin{aligned} a_0 &= \alpha_0 + 5\alpha_2 \\ a_1 &= \alpha_1 + 2\alpha_2 \end{aligned} \qquad (28.54)$$

But, we have two equations and three unknowns (α_0, α_1, α_2), and therefore cannot recover the model parameters.

As the computer software will reject the regression run, it is easy to detect perfect collinearity. The error is usually one of variable construction, and can be avoided by exercising care. It is quite possible, however, to have an approximate linear relationship among independent variables. The phenomenon of two or more variables that are highly, but not perfectly, correlated is called multicollinearity. High multicollinearity implies that, with a given change in one variable, the observations on the variable with which it is highly correlated are likely to change predictably. Unfortunately, such relationships are relatively common among social science variables.

28.8.1 CONSEQUENCES

Multicollinearity causes problems similar to autocorrelation and heteroskedasticity. OLS parameter estimates are unbiased, but their variance is affected, yielding two undesirable consequences:

Large parameter variances: The variances of the parameter estimates of collinear variables are very large. Intuitively, one doesn't have enough unique information on a collinear variable to produce precise estimates of its effect on the dependent variable. To see this, consider the variance of $\hat{\beta}_1$ in the two-regressor model, $Y = \beta_0 + \beta_1 X_1 + \beta_2 X_2 + \varepsilon$:

$$\mathrm{VAR}(\hat{\beta}_1) = \frac{\sigma_\varepsilon^2}{\sum_{i=1}^{n} (X_{1i} - \overline{X}_1)^2 (1 - r_{12}^2)} \qquad (28.55)$$

r_{12}, the correlation coefficient between X_1 and X_2, captures the collinearity between X_1 and X_2. As r increases, the variance of the estimates of both β_1 and β_2 increase.

Biased t-*statistics*: The denominator of a *t*-statistic, the estimated standard deviation of the parameter estimate (s_{β}^2), reflects the same dependence on the collinearity between the independent variables as the true variances.

$$s_{\beta_1}^2 = \frac{s^2}{\sum_{i=1}^{n} (X_{1i} - \overline{X}_1)^2 (1 - r_{12}^2)} \tag{28.56}$$

where s^2 is an unbiased estimator of the unobserved variance of the error term, σ_{ε}^2.*

As r increases, s_{β}^2 increases, which decreases the associated *t*-statistic. Multicollinearity thus causes *t*-statistics to be biased downward, making it more difficult to achieve statistical significance.

28.8.2 DIAGNOSIS

Although multicollinearity is often suspected a priori, there are estimation results that indicate a problem. Two phenomena are particularly indicative of high multicollinearity. First, what if the estimation reveals a high R^2, but most of the parameter estimates are statistically insignificant? These are inconsistent results, the high R^2 indicates that the model has good explanatory power; the lack of significant variables indicates that most of the independent variables have no effect on the dependent variable. What then is explaining the variance in the dependent variable? One explanation is that something is deflating the *t*-statistics, e.g., high multicollinearity.

Second, what if the parameter estimates in the model change greatly in value when an independent variable is added or dropped from the equation? For example, we are uncertain about whether to include a particular independent variable and estimate the model twice, omitting the variable in question the second time. We find that the parameter estimates associated with one or more of the other independent variables change significantly. This indicates a high correlation with the omitted variable.

These symptoms indicate a potential multicollinearity problem; diagnosis requires examining the intercorrelation among the independent variables using auxiliary regressions. Auxiliary Regressions are descriptive regressions of each independent variable as a function of all the other independent variables. For example, for the model $Y = \beta_0 + \beta_1 X_1 + \beta_2 X_2 + \beta_3 X_3 + \varepsilon$, the associated auxiliary regressions are

$$X_1 = a_0 + a_1 X_2 + a_2 X_3 + \mu_1$$
$$X_2 = b_0 + b_1 X_1 + b_2 X_3 + \mu_2$$
$$X_3 = c_0 + c_1 X_1 + c_2 X_2 + \mu_3$$

If multicollinearity is suspected, one should run the auxiliary regressions and examine the R^2 associated with each. If any are close to 1 in value, indicating that most of the variance in one of the independent variables is explained by the other independent variables, there is high multicollinearity.

Other common diagnostics offered by most software packages include the tolerance and the Variance Inflation Factor (VIF) methods. Tolerance is defined as $1 - R^2$, where R^2 is the multiple R of a given independent variable regressed on all other independent variables. VIF is the reciprocal of tolerance. A commonly used rule of thumb is that any tolerance of 0.10 or less or VIF of 10 or more suggests serious multicollinearity (Hair et al., 1998; Cohen et al., 2003). In SPSS 14.0, select Analyze, Regression, Linear, click Statistics, and check Collinearity diagnostics to get the tolerance and VIF.

---

* The positive square root of s^2 is called the standard error of the equation.

28.8.3 Solutions

The appropriate solution to multicollinearity depends on whether the espoused model is in fact valid. Sometimes the presence of multicollinearity alerts us to a specification error. For example, two measures of the same phenomenon could have been included in the model. In that case, only the measure of the independent variable that most closely captures the theoretical concept should be retained.

If, however, the model is correct, then multicollinearity indicates a sample problem—two or more independent variables that have separate theoretical influences cannot be distinguished due to covariation in the sample. The most straight-forward solution is to increase the sample size. A richer data set may resolve the problem.

Unfortunately, one cannot always obtain more data. This creates a more serious situation. One solution, if it makes sense, is to combine the collinear independent variables. For example, consider a model that explains voting behavior as a function of socioeconomic variables, like income and race, and indicators of media exposure, like the number of hours spent watching television and the number of hours spent reading newspapers. If the two media variables are highly collinear in the sample, they could be combined into a single measure or index of media exposure. Note that the resulting parameter estimate will not allow us to differentiate the effects of different media sources, i.e., the role of television compared to newspapers. But, we will have information on the role of the media compared to the other independent variables.

Another way to combine variables is using the principle components analysis or factor analysis to generate a single measure of those correlated variables. For example, education and income are often highly correlated. In *Participation in American*, Verba and Nie (1987) showed that participation of all forms is more common among individuals of higher socioeconomic status, which they measured with an index combining education, income, and occupation.*

If the highly collinear variables cannot be combined, OLS cannot separate the effects of the individual collinear variables. The model can still be used for prediction (i.e., one can predict Y given all the Xs), but the separate effects of the collinear Xs on Y cannot be identified.

Finally, note that it is not a good idea to just discard the offending variable. If the original model is in fact correct, one is trading the consequences of multicollinearity for the more serious consequences of excluding a relevant variable. Consider, for example, the following two-variable model: $Y = \beta_0 + \beta_1 X_1 + \beta_2 X_2 + \varepsilon$. Unfortunately, X_1 and X_2 are highly correlated, so we drop X_2 and estimate: $Y = \beta_0 + \beta_1 X_1 + \mu$. If X_2 in fact affects Y, the parameter estimate of β_1 will be biased. The estimate will incorporate the effect of X_2, as it does the effect of any omitted relevant variable with which it is correlated.

If multicollinearity is present and all the independent variables should still be included in the model, rigid regression is an alternative estimation method that may be used. A discussion of the rigid regression method is beyond the scope of this chapter. For more information, including the discussion of its strength and weakness, see Draper and Smith (1998, Chapter 17) and Cohen et al. (2003, Chapter 10).

28.9 CONCLUSION

Regression analysis is an extremely powerful methodology. It offers public sector scholars and practitioners an easy to use and readily understandable way to summarize multivariate relationships. Its ease of use, however, makes it vulnerable to misuse and its results to misinterpretation. The legitimate use of regression analysis requires an understanding of the assumptions that underlie its use as a tool of inferential statistics. Understanding the implications of these assumptions will enable the user to either appropriately qualify his or her conclusions or to select a more appropriate estimation strategy.

---

* For more information on the principle components analysis or factor analysis, see Cohen, et al. (2003, Chapter 10).

To conclude our discussion of regression analysis, let's recap the general issues involved with determining an appropriate estimation strategy. It is useful to view estimation strategy in a decision analytic framework. The first decision level considers the nature of the dependent variable. The second level considers the classical assumptions.

I Is the dependent variable an interval-level variable?
   - If yes, then regression analysis is appropriate.
   - If no, a qualitative dependent variable model is indicated.
     Within the Regression Model context, the Gauss–Markov theorem tells us that if the classical assumptions are satisfied, then ordinary least squares (OLS) estimation yields the best linear unbiased estimates of the underlying parameters, β. Thus we need only consider an alternative technique if one of these assumptions is violated.

IIa Is the model correctly specified?
   - If yes, consider the next assumption.
   - If no, there is a specification error. Excluding relevant variables usually yields biased parameter estimates and invalid t-tests. Including irrelevant variables yields inefficient parameter estimates and lowered t-statistics. The solution is to correctly specify the model.

IIb Are the observations of the independent variables determined outside the model and thus independently of the error term?
   - If yes, then OLS estimation is appropriate.
   - If no, OLS parameter estimates are biased. The preferred estimation strategy is Instrumental-Variable Estimation.

IIc Do the random components of the model (the error terms) have a constant variance and are they uncorrelated across observations?
   - If yes, then OLS estimation is appropriate.
   - If no, OLS parameter estimates are not efficient, and t-tests are invalid. Generalized Least Squares (GLS) estimation or a respecification of the model should be considered.

IId Does the number of observations exceed the number of parameters to be estimated, and are there no exact linear relationships among the independent variables?
   - If yes, regression analysis is appropriate.
   - If no, the regression equation cannot be estimated. If high, rather than perfect, multicollinearity exists, OLS parameter estimates are inefficient and t-tests are biased; additional data or a new specification is needed.

REFERENCES

Abdi, H. 2003. Least squares. In M.S. Lewis-Beck, A.E. Bryman, and F. Liao (Eds.), *Encyclopedia of Social Science Research*. Thousand Oaks, California: Sage Publications.

Cassidy, H.J. 1981. *Using Econometrics: A Beginner's Guide*. Reston, Virginia: Reston Publishing.

Clingermayer, J.C. and Feiock, R.C. 1997. Leadership turnover, transaction costs, and external city service delivery. *Public Administration Review, 57*, 231–239.

Cohen, J., Cohen, P., West, S.G., and Aiken, L.S. 2003. *Applied Multiple Regression/Correlation Analysis for the Behavioral Sciences*. 3rd ed. Mahwah, New Jersey: Lawrence Erlbaum Association.

Devaney, B., Bilheimer, L., and Schore, J. 1992. Medicaid costs and birth outcomes: The effects of prenatal WIC participation and the use of prenatal care. *Journal of Policy Analysis and Management, 11*, 573–592.

Draper, N.R. and Smith, H. 1998. *Applied Regression Analysis*. 3rd ed. New York: Wiley.

Ferris, J. and Graddy, E. 1988. Production choices for local government services. *Journal of Urban Affairs, 10*, 273–289.

Graddy, E. 1994. Tort reform and manufacturer payout—An early look at the California experience. *Law & Policy, 16*, 49–61.

Graddy, E. and Chen, B. 2006. Influences on the size and scope of networks for social service delivery. *Journal of Public Administration Research and Theory, 16*, 533–552.

Graddy, E. and Nichol, M. 1990. Structural reforms and licensing board performance. *American Politics Quarterly, 18*, 376–400.

Hair, J.F., Anderson, R.E., Tatham, R.L., and Black, W.C. 1998. *Multivariate Data Analysis*. 4th ed. Upper Saddle River, New Jersey: Prentice Hall.

Johnson, A.C., Jr., Johnson, M.B., and Buse, R.C. 1987. *Econometrics: Basic and Applied*. New York: MacMillan Publishing.

Johnston, J.M. and Duncombe, W. 1998. Balancing conflicting policy objectives: The case of school finance reform. *Public Administration Review, 58*, 145–158.

Kearney, R.C., Feldman, B.M., and Scavo, C.P.F. 2000. Reinventing government: City manager attitudes and actions. *Public Administration Review, 60*, 535–548.

Maddala, G.S. 1992. *Introduction to Econometrics*. 2nd ed. New York: MacMillan Publishing.

Mann, J., Melnick, G., Bamezai, A., and Zwanziger, J. 1995. Managing the safety net: Hospital provision of uncompensated care in response to managed care. In R.M. Scheffler and L.F. Rossiter (Eds.), *Advances in Health Economics and Health Service Research, Vol. 15*. Greenwich, Connecticut: JAI Press, Inc, pp. 49–77.

Maxwell, S.E. 2000. Sample size and multiple regression analysis. *Psychological Methods, 5*, 434–458.

Neter, J., Wasserman, W., and Kutner, M.H. 1996. *Applied Linear Statistical Models*. 4th ed. Chicago, Illinois: Irwin.

Pindyck, R.S. and Rubinfeld, D.L. 1991. *Econometric Models and Economic Forecasts*. 3rd ed. New York: McGraw-Hill.

Rencher, A.C. 2002. *Methods of Multivariate Analysis*. 2nd ed. New York: John Wiley & Sons.

Robertson, P.J. 1995. Involvement in boundary-spanning activity: Mitigating the relationship between work setting and behavior. *Journal of Public Administration Research and Theory, 5*, 73–98.

Studenmund, A.H. 2005. *Using Econometrics: A Practical Guide*. 5th ed. Upper Saddle River, New York: Addison-Wesley.

Sundeen, R.A. 1990. Family life course status and volunteer behavior. *Sociological Perspectives, 33*, 483–500.

Tabachnick, B.G. and Fidell, L.S. 2007. *Using Multivariate Statistics*. 5th ed. Boston, Massachusetts: Allyn and Bacon.

Thornton, J. 2006. Nonprofit fund-raising in competitive donor markets. *Nonprofit and Voluntary Sector Quarterly, 35*, 204–224.

Verba, S. and Nie, N.H. 1987 *Participation in America: Political Democracy and Social Equality*, Chicago, Illinois: University of Chicago Press.

White, H. 1980. A heteroskedasticity-consistent covariance matrix estimator and a direct test for heteroskedasticity. *Econometrica, 48*, 817–838.

29 Multivariate Techniques for Dichotomous Dependent Variables: An Application to Public Policy

Mack C. Shelley, II

CONTENTS

29.1 INTRODUCTION: WHY DICHOTOMIZE?

Research applications in public administration, as in social science research more broadly, have been influenced heavily by the increasing application of statistical methods to handle situations in which the outcomes of interest fall into two discrete possible categories. Dichotomous outcomes arise commonly. For example, you might want to determine what explains whether a city government is run by a strong mayor system or by some other form of government, whether students who participate in learning communities are more likely than those not in learning communities to persist and graduate, the variables that account for why some cities gain and other cities lose population, or whether a local bond referendum will pass or fail.

The National Education Longitudinal Study of 1988 (NELS: 88)

During the spring term of the 1987–1988 school year the National Center for Education Statistics (NCES) initiated a national longitudinal study of 8th grade students attending 1052 high schools across the United States. A total of 24,599 8th graders were surveyed in the base year of NELS: 88. Many of these same students were resurveyed in 1990, 1992, 1994, and 2000. Depending on the year, data also was collected from parents, schools, and teachers, and from high school and postsecondary transcripts. In addition, cognitive tests were administered during the first three data collection waves in the 8th, 10th, and 12th grades. Variables were measured on: junior, high, or middle school and high school student data; dropout data; posthigh school data collected after scheduled high school graduation; school administrator data; teacher data; parent data; high school transcript data; and postsecondary transcript data (National Center for Education Statistics, n.d.).

29.1.1 A Bit of Background: TRIO (Upward Bound, Talent Search, GEAR UP) and NELS

Federal TRIO programs (including Upward Bound, Talent Search, and, more recently, GEAR UP) were created in the 1960s to identify low-income, underachieving students and help them prepare for college as part of a larger strategy, paired with need-based financial aid, to eliminate poverty through education (Groutt, 2003). Upward Bound provides fundamental support to participants in their preparation for college entrance. The program provides opportunities for participants to succeed in precollege performance and ultimately in higher education pursuits. Currently, Upward Bound programs serve "high school students from low-income families, high school students from families in which neither parent holds a bachelor's degree, and low-income, first-generation military veterans who are preparing to enter postsecondary education" (http://www.ed.gov/programs/trioupbound/index.html.). Talent Search is targeted more broadly to identifying and assisting "individuals from disadvantaged backgrounds who have the potential to succeed in higher education," including students who had dropped out of high school (Jaschik, 2006; http://www.ed.gov/programs/triotalent/index.html.), and to providing academic, career, and financial counseling to its participants and encouraging them to graduate from high school and continue on to the postsecondary school of their choice. The goal of Talent Search is to increase the number of youth from disadvantaged backgrounds who complete high school and enroll in the postsecondary education institution of their choice. Both programs provide academic enrichment and guidance with the college application process, and often other services such as tutoring, mentoring, and family involvement. Talent Search Programs can also serve sixth to eighth grade students in addition to high school students and adults. Upward Bound and Talent Search are the primary federally funded postsecondary encouragement initiatives, along with the newer GEAR UP (Gaining Early Awareness and Readiness for Undergraduate Program) program. The GEAR UP program is a discretionary grant program designed to increase the number of low-income students who are prepared to enter and succeed in postsecondary education by providing six-year grants to states and partnerships to provide services at high-poverty middle schools and high schools. GEAR UP grants serve an entire cohort of students beginning no later than the seventh grade and follow the cohort through high school. GEAR UP funds are also used to provide college scholarships to low-income students.

Continued federal funding for these programs is far from assured. Recently, eliminating funding for all three programs was proposed (Jaschik, 2006), to be able to redirect funding to serve 9th graders with grade point averages of 2.5 or below or who were not testing at proficient levels under the Department of Education's No Child Left Behind program (Walters, 2006). At the same time, a commission on the future of higher education convened by the Secretary of Education released its draft report specifying low-income students' and adults' access to college as higher education's highest priority (Field, 2006). The commission's report was scheduled to be completed August 1, the same time that public comments on the proposed budget allocations were due (Field, 2006; Walters, 2006) as well as the final commission report.

A number of efforts had been undertaken to document the outcomes of students' participation in postsecondary encouragement programs. The majority of such studies have focused on Upward Bound participants, many are studies of single-site programs, and the results show a mixed picture of outcomes. For example, program participants tended to score higher in language-related areas (Laws, 1999; Young and Exum, 1982) and in one of these studies in quantitative areas as well (Young and Exum, 1982), yet no grade point average differences were found between participants and nonparticipants (Laws, 1999; "The national evaluation," 1997). A national study involving students in multiple Upward Bound programs showed significantly higher high school graduation rates for participants as compared to the randomly assigned group of nonparticipants, and particularly large differences were noted for boys and program participants with initially lower educational expectations and higher atrisk factors (Myers and Schirm, 1999). Smaller but statistically significant differences were found in participants' greater accumulation of total high school credits. Program-related outcomes among prospective first-generation college students were negligible (Myers and Schirm, 1999). The follow-up study echoed program impacts on students with lower initial educational expectations and noted that participants accumulated only slightly more high school math coursework (http://www.ed.gov/rschstat/eval/highered/upward/upward-3rd-report.html).

29.1.2 OKAY, BUT WHAT ABOUT THE DATA?

To explicate the statistical methods—cross-tabulation tables, logistic regression, and discriminant analysis—we talk about in this chapter, we use data from the base year (1988, or 8th grade) and the second follow up (1992, or 12th grade) of the National Educational Longitudinal Study of 1988 (NELS:88) (National Center for Education Statistics, 1996). In-school respondents who had participated in Upward Bound, Talent Search, or a similar program sometime during their 8th through 12th grade years were identified (GEAR UP then did not yet exist). A comparison group was identified of respondents who were similar to the participating group on family socioeconomic status and parents' education. The 697 respondents who were identified as participating in Upward Bound or Talent Search were compared to a sample of 697 non-UBTS participants from the NELS data matched on parents' highest level of educational attainment and parents' composite socioeconomic status quartile.

The following NELS: 88 variables are used in the examples of data analysis presented in this chapter:

BYS45—the respondent's eighth grade year expectations for postsecondary degree attainment, coded as the following answers to the question "How far in school do you think you will get?":

1. Will not finish high school
2. Will finish high school
3. Vocational, trade, or business school after high school
4. Will attend college
5. Will finish college
6. Higher schooling after college

TSUB or not—indicates whether the respondent is in the Talent Search and Upward Bound program group or not, coded:

1. In Talent Search or Upward Bound (TSUB)
2. Comparison group (not in Talent Search or Upward Bound)

G8LUNCH—a continuous variable, measuring the percentage of students on federal free or reduced price lunch in the eighth grade at school (this variable is used commonly in policy research as a surrogate for poverty-level households, which otherwise is a difficult characteristic to measure in surveys).

29.1.3 So, How, Exactly, Do You Predict a Dichotomous Dependent Variable?

For the examples above, and really any time you have a dependent variable in two categories, we are faced with a very different analytical problem than what can be handled with traditional least-squares tools such as multiple regression, multiple and partial correlation, analysis of variance, analysis of covariance, and related methods. For least-squares-based methods to "work," both so they can provide practical interpretations drawn from their results and to satisfy the statistical properties that are required under what frequently is referred to as "normal theory" (a bit more formally, also known as the Central Limit Theorem), at least these three things must be true:

a. Dependent variable must be distributed following a "normal distribution," that is, a bell-shaped curve with specific proportions of observations occurring within specified standard deviation intervals below and above the mean of the variable;
b. Dependent variable has a constant variance over all values of the independent variables (this is called homoskedasticity); and
c. Observations from which the data was gathered are mutually independent (which is accomplished best by selecting the data as a random sample).

In addition, we usually assume that the values of the independent variables (the X's, in the standard notation) are fixed in repeated samples, and that what we happen to observe in our single sample is a random realization of all such possible samples that could be selected at different times or for different sets of observations. Furthermore, least-squares analysis usually is accompanied by the assumption that all the data was collected from a simple random sample, which means that all samples were equally likely to be chosen and that each individual observation (a city, a student, a state, a voter, for example) has a known and possibly equal chance of having been selected. We also prefer that the independent variables are not too highly correlated with each other—that is, that the condition of multicollinearity does not exist, or at least is not serious, as measured by a Variance Inflation Factor less than 10 or a Tolerance value greater than 0.1.

Pretty much by the very definition of a dependent variable as dichotomous, there is no realistic way to believe that a normal distribution could exist for that variable. For much the same reason, constant error variance is unreasonable; in fact, we are virtually guaranteed to introduce a possibly severe case of heteroskedasticity (nonconstant error variance) because there are only two possible outcome values that can be "predicted." So, assumptions (a) and (b) pretty much automatically go by the board when we consider how to deal with dichotomous dependent variables that are of interest for a research project. However, assumption (c), of independence, still may be true, although whether that assumption is correct also would need to be investigated by thinking through how the data was measured and how the particular observations we have were selected.

29.2 A STARTING POINT: TWO-WAY CROSS-TABULATION FREQUENCY TABLES

Two-way frequency tables are used to assess the relationship between discrete variables, particularly those measured at a nominal or ordinal level with a relatively small number of categories. A large family of nonparametric measures of general association and correlation coefficients are used to measure the relationships between these cross-classified variables. These analyses can be extended to include three or more categorical variables, although doing so requires a large dataset because the analysis divides the total number of observations into "cells" at the intersection of all of the variables' categories.

The simplest, but still effective, method for analyzing dichotomous dependent variables is to formulate the analysis as a two-way cross-tabulation, in which the "predictor" variable also is a dichotomy or polytomy. In this configuration, the information of interest is whether the proportion of observations on the dependent dichotomy varies across the categories of the "predictor" variable.

As an example of what is entailed in this mode of analysis for dichotomous variables, the following SPSS computer syntax code was used to conduct a cross-tabulation analysis of the relationship between students' expectations for further education beyond eighth grade (BYS45) and whether the student participates in Talent Search or Upward Bound (TSUB or not):

```
CROSSTABS
/TABLES = BYS45 BY TSUB or not
/FORMAT = AVALUE TABLES
/STATISTIC = CHISQ CC PHI LAMBDA UC ETA CORR GAMMA D BTAU CTAU
   KAPPA MCNEMAR
/CELLS = COUNT ROW COLUMN ASRESID
/COUNT ROUND CELL
/BARCHART
```

Table 29.1 summarizes the results from the two-way cross-tabulation that relates how far the student expects to get in school to whether he or she participates in Talent Search or Upward Bound. The individual cells within the table contain information on: "Count," or how many students fall into each combination of categories (for example, of the total of 18 students who in 8th grade felt that they would not finish high school, 11 were non-TSUB students and the other 7 were in TSUB), "Percentage within HOW FAR IN SCHOOL DO YOU THINK YOU WILL GET" (61.1 percent—that is, 11 of the 18 students who responded "WON'T FINISH H.S"—of those who expected not to finish high school were non-TSUB and the other 38.9 percent—that is, 7 of 18—were in TSUB), "Percentage within TSUB or not" (1.9 percent—11 of the total of 579 non-TSUB students—did not expect to finish high school, compared to 1.2 percent—7 of the total of 575 TSUB students), and a value larger than 3 in absolute value for "adjusted residual" indicates statistically meaningful differences between TSUB and non-TSUB results for any given row (i.e., how far school students think they may go). A quick examination of the adjusted residual values in the table indicates that non-TSUB students are statistically more likely than TSUB participants to expect to finish high school, but TSUB participants are more likely than non-TSUB students to expect to go on to education beyond the Bachelor's degree.

The question here is whether there is an appreciable difference between the two groups of students. The conclusions that can be drawn from the above data are important for the study of public policy and public administration, because they can inform policymakers and others about whether TSUB participation is affected by student expectations. Whether there is a statistically significant difference overall between the distribution of responses for TSUB and non-TSUB students may be determined by the use of different versions of the chi-square test statistic and other measures based on chi-square that serve as correlation coefficients. Here, we only scratch the surface of what turns out to be a very large and diverse family of nonparametric measures of association. Readers interested in further information on other measures for relationships involving discrete data are referred to Garson (1971) and to Bishop, Fienberg, and Holland (1975). Our interest here is focused on the family of measures based on the chi-square statistic.

The first thing to be noted from Table 29.2 is that several different versions of chi-square are presented. The "Pearson chi-square" is named for Karl Pearson, who invented and popularized much of what we do today in statistical applications. This statistic is appropriate for all variables and

TABLE 29.1

Two-Way Cross-Tabulation of How Far the Student Expects to Get in School (BYS45) with TSUB Participation (TSUB or Not)

Cross-Tab			TSUB or Not		
			0	1	Total
How far in school do you think you will get?	Won't finish high school	Count	11	7	18
		Percentage within how far in school do you think you will get	61.1	38.9	100.0
		Percentage within TSUB or not	1.9	1.2	1.6
		Adjusted residual	0.9	−0.9	
	Will finish high school	Count	86	34	120
		Percentage within how far in school do you think you will get	71.7	28.3	100.0
		Percentage within TSUB or not	14.9	5.9	10.4
		Adjusted residual	5.0	−5.0	
	VOC, TRD, BUS After H.S	Count	59	52	111
		Percentage within how far in school do you think you will get	53.2	46.8	100.0
		Percentage within TSUB or not	10.2	9.0	9.6
		Adjusted residual	0.7	−0.7	
	Will attend college	Count	70	70	140
		Percentage within how far in school do you think you will get	50.0	50.0	100.0
		Percentage within TSUB or not	12.1	12.2	12.1
		Adjusted residual	0.0	0.0	
	Will finish college	Count	230	233	463
		Percentage within how far in school do you think you will get	49.7	50.3	100.0
		Percentage within TSUB or not	39.7	40.5	40.1
		Adjusted residual	−0.3	0.3	
	Higher school after coll.	Count	123	179	302
		Percentage within how far in school do you think you will get	40.7	59.3	100.0
		Percentage within TSUB or not	21.2	31.1	26.2
		Adjusted residual	−3.8	3.8	
Total		Count	579	575	1154
		Percentage within how far in school do you think you will get	50.2	49.8	100.0
		Percentage within TSUB or not	100.0	100.0	100.0

can detect any kind of association, but is less powerful for detecting a linear association because its power is dispersed over a greater number of degrees of freedom than is the "linear-by-linear association" (also known as the "Mantel–Haenszel" version of chi-square). The linear-by-linear association chi-square statistic requires an ordinal scale for both variables, and is designed to detect a linear association. However, the Pearson chi-square has less statistical power than the linear-by-linear association measure, because it requires a larger number of degrees of freedom unless the cross-tabulation table has two rows and two columns (when the Pearson chi-square has one degree of freedom).

Here are the formulas for each of these statistics, and some explanation of what each one does. For a cross-tabulation table with rows labeled by the values X_i, $i = 1, 2, \ldots, r$ and with columns

TABLE 29.2

Chi-Square Summary Statistics for Relating How Far the Student Expects to Get in School (BYS45) with TSUB Participation (TSUB or Not)

Chi-Square Tests	Value	df	Asymp. Sig. (Two-Sided)
Pearson chi-square	34.254[a]	5	.000
Likelihood ratio	35.086	5	.000
Linear-by-linear association	28.222	1	.000
McNemar–bowker test	.	.	[b]
Number of valid cases	1154		

[a] 0 cells (.0 percent) have expected count less than 5. The minimum expected count is 8.97.

[b] Computed only for a P×P table, where P must be greater than 1.

labeled by the values Y_j, $j = 1, 2, \ldots, c$, the cross-tabulation table has the number of degrees of freedom equal to $(r - 1) \times (c - 1)$. The Pearson chi-square (χ_p^2) is defined in Equation 29.1 by

$$\chi_p^2 = \sum_i \sum_j (n_{ij} - m_{ij})^2 / m_{ij} \qquad (29.1)$$

where

n_{ij} is the observed frequency for each cell

m_{ij} is the frequency within each cell that is expected if the two variables are independent

The "likelihood ratio" chi-square statistic, also known as the G^2 statistic (Equation 29.2), is computed by ratios between the observed and expected frequencies, with the alternative hypothesis being that there is general association between the two variables. With $(r - 1) \times (c - 1)$ degrees of freedom

$$G^2 = -2 \sum_i \sum_j n_{ij} \ \ln(n_{ij}/m_{ij}) \qquad (29.2)$$

The linear-by-linear association, or Mantel–Haenszel chi square statistic (Equation 29.3), provides a test of whether there is a linear association between the row and column variables, with one degree of freedom:

$$\chi_{MH}^2 = (n - 1)r^2 \qquad (29.3)$$

where r is the value of the Pearson product–moment correlation between the two variables. This calculation is valid only if both variables are measured on ordinal scales, which is true for BYS45 (how far the student expects to get in school) but not for TSUB or not although that variable does have an implicit ordering of the presence or absence of participation in Talent Search or Upward Bound.

The McNemar–Bowker test is a nonparametric test for relationship between two dichotomous variables. It tests for changes in responses using the chi-square distribution and is useful particularly for detecting changes in responses due to experimental intervention in "before-and-after" designs, but is reported only for square tables (with equal numbers of rows and columns).

Of these chi-square statistics, the most useful for our purposes is the Likelihood Ratio chi-square, because this is closely related to comparable statistics used in more advanced methods for analyzing dichotomous dependent variables. Here, the estimated Likelihood Ratio chi-square value of 35.086 would be compared against an appropriate critical value of chi-square (Equation 29.4) with five degrees of freedom (shown below for Type I error levels of $\alpha = .05$ and $\alpha = .01$):

$$\chi^2_{2,.05} = 11.07; \chi^2_{2,.01} = 15.09 \tag{29.4}$$

The computed Likelihood Ratio chi-square value of 35.086 exceeds these critical values, and the attained level of significance (that is, the area in the right-hand tail of the chi-square distribution that is beyond 35.086) for a chi-square statistic with five degrees of freedom is less than .001, although the SPSS default output shows this value inaccurately as .000 (the actual p-value is much smaller than .001).

A large number of additional measures of association between the dichotomous variable TSUB or not and the ordinal variable BYS45 are summarized in Table 29.3. Details of most of these are beyond the scope of this chapter, but the reader is referred to standard discussions of these nonparametric "symmetric measures" and "directional measures" in sources such as Agresti and Finlay (1997), Hinkle, Wiersma, and Jurs (2003), and Howell (2002). Of this plethora of nonparametric measures, the three listed as "nominal by nominal" symmetric measures are of interest here, because they are functions of the Pearson chi-square value (χ^2_p). Except when the cross-tabulation table has just two rows and two columns, each of these measures is always non-negative (although the Phi coefficient can be negative for a cross-tabulation table with two rows and two columns) and are structured such that larger values (closer to the maximum of 1) imply a stronger relationship between the row and column variables, and smaller values (closer to 0) imply a weaker correlation.

The Phi coefficient (Φ) is calculated by (Equation 29.5)

$$\Phi = [\chi^2_p/n]0.5 = [34.254/1154]^{0.5} = 0.172 \tag{29.5}$$

TABLE 29.3

Nonparametric Correlation Symmetric Measures and Directional Measures of the Relationship between How Far the Student Expects to Get in School (BYS45) and Talent Search or Upward Bound Participation (TSUB or Not)

Symmetric Measures		Value	Asymp. Std. Error[a]	Approx. T[b]	Approx. Sig.
Nominal by nominal	Phi	.172			.000
	Cramer's V	.172			.000
	Contingency coefficient	.170			.000
Ordinal by ordinal	Kendall's tau-b	.136	.026	5.171	.000
	Kendall's tau-c	.165	.032	5.171	.000
	Gamma	.223	.042	5.171	.000
	Spearman correlation	.149	.029	5.128	.000[c]
Interval by interval	Pearson's R	.156	.029	5.376	.000[c]
Measure of agreement	Kappa[d]				
N of valid cases		1154			

[a] Not assuming the null hypothesis.

[b] Using the asymptotic standard error assuming the null hypothesis.

[c] Based on normal approximation.

[d] Kappa statistics cannot be computed. They require a symmetric two-way table in which the values of the first variable match the values of the second variable.

TABLE 29.3 (*Continued*)

Nonparametric Correlation Symmetric Measures and Directional Measures of the Relationship between How Far the Student Expects to Get in School (BYS45) and Talent Search or Upward Bound Participation (TSUB or Not)

Directional Measures			Value	Asymp. Std. Error[a]	Approx. T[b]	Approx. Sig.
Nominal by nominal	Lambda	Symmetric	.047	.021	2.137	.033
		How far in school do you think you will get dependent?	.000	.000	.[c]	.[c]
		TSUB or not dependent	.103	.046	2.137	.033
	Goodman and Kruskal tau	How far in school do you think you will get dependent?	.006	.002		.000[d]
		TSUB or not dependent	.030	.009		.000[d]
	Uncertainty coefficient	Symmetric	.014	.005	3.029	.000[e]
		How far in school do you think you will get dependent?	.010	.003	3.029	.000[e]
		TSUB or not dependent	.022	.007	3.029	.000[e]
Ordinal by ordinal	Somers'd	Symmetric	.133	.026	5.171	.000
		How far in school do you think you will get dependent?	.165	.032	5.171	.000
		TSUB or not dependent	.112	.022	5.171	.000
Nominal by interval	Eta	How far in school do you think you will get dependent?	.156			
		TSUB or not dependent	.172			

[a] Not assuming the null hypothesis.
[b] Using the asymptotic standard error assuming the null hypothesis.
[c] Cannot be computed because the asymptotic standard error equals zero.
[d] Based on chi-square approximation.
[e] Likelihood Ratio chi-square probability.

which is the square root of the Pearson chi-square value (34.254) divided by the total number of nonmissing observations in the cross-tabulation table (1154). The Phi coefficient ranges in value between 0 and 1 (although the upper limit actually may be less than one, depending on the distribution of the marginal values).

The upper bound of Cramer's V, also based on the Pearson chi-square statistic, always equals 1, unlike Phi and the Contingency Coefficient. Cramer's V is defined as (Equation 29.6)

$$V = [(\chi_p^2/n)/\min(r-1, c-1)]^{0.5} = (34.254/1154)/1]^{0.5} = 0.172 \qquad (29.6)$$

which is equal to the Φ coefficient here because one of the dimensions of the cross-tabulation table equals two (which always is the case, of course, for a dichotomous variable, which here is TSUB or not).

The Contingency Coefficient also falls within the range of 0 and 1, although, like Phi, the maximum possible value that it can attain may be less than 1, depending on the marginal distribution. The Contingency Coefficient is calculated by (Equation 29.7)

$$CC = [\chi_p^2/(\chi_p^2 + n)]^{0.5} = [34.254/(34.254 + 1154)] = 0.170 \qquad (29.7)$$

which is an adjusted version of Φ that controls for the magnitude of the Pearson chi-square statistic, which otherwise increases in size with the number of cells in the cross-tabulation table. The Contingency Coefficient is a more conservative statistic than Φ; it must be smaller than Φ because the denominator is larger by the value of χ_p^2.

29.3   THE MAXIMUM LIKELIHOOD APPROACH: LOGISTIC REGRESSION

Logistic regression is used to produce models that correctly classify outcomes for a categorical dependent variable. Unlike cross-tabulation analysis, logistic regression produces prediction models that are based on attempting to classify individual observation outcomes of the dichotomous dependent variable, rather than the less informative aggregated categories that are used in cross-tabular methods. In addition, logistic regression is more flexible than other procedures, such as discriminant analysis (which we will study later), that are designed to classify dichotomous dependent variable outcomes for two reasons: (a) it is more appropriate when there is a combination of continuous (e.g., percentage of a school's students who receive free or reduced lunch) and categorical (e.g., how far does the student expect to get in school) predictor variables, and (b) the validity of logistic regression results is less dependent on the assumption of multivariate normality, which is not true in most datasets.

29.3.1   What's So Different about Logistic Regression?

Logistic regression is an application of a broader class of nonlinear regression models, defined (Equation 29.8) by the implicit form

$$Y_i = f(X_i, \gamma) + \varepsilon_i \qquad (29.8)$$

where each observation Y_i of the dependent, or response, variable Y is the sum of a mean response $f(X_i, \gamma)$, which is determined by the nonlinear response function and the error term ε_i. There are one or more (q, in general) X variables, and one or more (p, in general) regression coefficients; so, X in Equation 29.8 really represents a $qx1$ vector and γ is a $px1$ vector. Although we will treat nonlinear regression as involving a completely different approach than the more familiar approach of linear regression, both nonlinear and linear models may be thought of as belonging to the family of generalized linear models (McCullagh and Nelder, 1989).

Logistic regression analysis usually proceeds under the assumptions that the errors are distributed identically and independent of each other (i.e., that they are iid), following a normal distribution with mean zero and constant variance (Equation 29.9)

$$\varepsilon \sim N(0, \sigma^2 I) \qquad (29.9)$$

where
$$E(\varepsilon) = 0$$
$$E([\varepsilon - E(\varepsilon)^2]) = \sigma^2 I$$
$$E(\varepsilon_i, \varepsilon_j) = 0$$

The logistic regression model, assuming its simplest version of a single predictor variable and normally distributed errors, is (Equation 29.10)

$$Y_i = \gamma_0/[1 + \gamma_1 \exp(\gamma_2 X)] + \varepsilon_i \qquad (29.10)$$

and the fitted, or response, function is given by (Equation 29.11)

$$f(X_i, \gamma) = \gamma_0/[1 + \gamma_1 \exp(\gamma_2 X)] \qquad (29.11)$$

Like linear regression models, parameter estimation for nonlinear regression models, such as logistic regression, may be obtained by either least-squares or maximum likelihood methods. Again just as with linear regression, least-squares and maximum likelihood methods produce identical parameter estimates when the error terms for the nonlinear regression model are mutually independent, normally distributed, and have constant variance.

However, there are a number of important differences between estimation approaches in linear regression and in logistic regression. First, it is crucial to note that the parameters of the logistic response function for the simple model—γ_0, γ_1, and γ_2—are not linear, which means that their interpretations will have to be undertaken with different goals in mind than what we are used to for regular regression models. Also, the number of predictor X variables in the nonlinear regression model (q) is not necessarily the same as the number of regression parameters in the response function (p), unlike ordinary least-squares regression. Another difference from linear regression is that with nonlinear regression methods such as logistic regression, usually it is not possible to derive analytical expressions for the least-squares or maximum likelihood estimators. Instead, numerical search procedures that frequently require considerably greater amounts of computational time must be used for either least-squares or maximum likelihood estimation, using appropriate computer software. This is in contrast to linear regression, where hand calculations may be done rather easily to derive the relevant estimators.

29.3.2 What Does the Response Function Mean When the Outcome is Binary?

It would be possible to estimate the simple linear regression model (Equation 29.12)

$$Y_i = \beta_0 + \beta_1 X_i + \varepsilon_i \qquad (29.12)$$

where the dependent variable Y takes on the binary values of either 0 or 1. In this case, the expected response is (Equation 29.13)

$$Y_i = \beta_0 + \beta_1 X_i = \pi_i \qquad (29.13)$$

where π_i is the probability that $Y_i = 1$ when the level of the predictor variable is X_i, because $E(\varepsilon_i) = 0$. When the dependent variable is a binary 0, 1 indicator variable, the mean response always estimates the probability that $Y = 1$ for the given levels of the predictor variables.

29.3.3 Does This Create a Problem?

Well, yes. Actually there are three particular problems that arise with binary dependent variables in linear regression models. Each of these makes the use of linear regression inappropriate and signifies the need for an alternative approach. The discussion that follows emphasizes the central argument surrounding the use of logistic regression.

1. The first problem is that the error terms cannot be distributed normally. This happens because each error term can assume only two possible values. Consequently, the assumption of normally distributed errors cannot be appropriate.
2. Second, the error terms do not have equal variances when the response variable is an indicator variable taking on values of 0 and 1. This happens because the variance of Y_i

depends on the value of X_i; consequently, the error variances are different for different levels of X. As a result, ordinary least squares is no longer optimal.

3. Finally, the response function represents the set of probabilities when the outcome variable is equal to either 0 or 1. The mean responses from the response function thus are constrained within the limits of 0 and 1, because $0 < E(Y) = \pi < 1$.

Consequently, linear response functions would not be appropriate because they may very well produce predicted values that are either negative or greater than 1; also, it would be unduly constraining in the linear case for all outcomes to have either 0 or 1 probabilities when in fact most outcomes will fall between those two extremes. What we need instead is for these extremes to be approached slowly—that is, asymptotically—as values of X become either very small or very large, and probabilities should decrease or increase toward those extremes nonlinearly. This brings us to discuss the simple logistic response function.

29.3.4 THE SIMPLE LOGISTIC RESPONSE FUNCTION

Thus, for binary response variables the response function typically will be curvilinear, following an S-shaped pattern that fits the previously discussed constraints that are imposed on $E(Y)$ when the outcome variable is binary. This curvilinear relationship may follow either of two general forms: (a) monotonically increasing at a varying rate from an asymptotic expected value for Y of 0 for smaller values of X, toward an asymptotic expected value for Y of 1 for larger values of X, when $\beta_1 > 0$; or (b) monotonically decreasing at a varying rate from an asymptotic expected value for Y of 1 for smaller values of X, toward an asymptotic expected value for Y of 0 for larger values of X, when $\beta_1 < 0$. In either version, it is useful to note that the middle part of the logistic curve is more or less linear, between values for $E(Y)$ of about 0.2 and 0.8, and that only the ends vary dramatically from that pattern.

The fact that this logistic representation is not completely disconnected from linear regression logic is demonstrated by the ability to transform the logistic response function back into linear form. This is done rather easily by performing a logit transformation of $E(Y)$ (Equation 29.14) as the logarithm of the ratio of the probability of a success (say, a student being in Talent Search or Upward Bound), defined here as π, and the probability of a failure (a student not being in Talent Search or Upward Bound), defined here as $(1 - \pi)$

$$\pi' = \log_e[\pi/(1 - \pi)] \tag{29.14}$$

which becomes (Equation 29.15)

$$\pi' = \beta_0 + \beta_1 X \tag{29.15}$$

The ratio of probabilities, $\pi/(1 - \pi)$, is known as the odds ratio. The transformed response function, $\pi' = \beta_0 + \beta_1 X$, is called the logit response function, which is the logarithm of the odds ratio. The value of π' is referred to as the logit mean response, which can vary from $-\infty$ to $+\infty$ as X varies over the same range.

29.3.5 THE SIMPLE LOGISTIC REGRESSION MODEL

When the response variable takes on values of only 1 (with probability π) and 0 (with probability $1 - \pi$), the simple logistic regression model takes the form (Equation 29.16)

$$Y_i = E(Y) + \varepsilon_i \tag{29.16}$$

where the error term ε_i follows the binomial (Bernoulli) distribution of Y_i with expected value $E(Y_i) = \pi_i$.

The likelihood function of the parameters to be estimated in the logistic regression model, given the sample observations, is expressed as $\log_e L(\beta_0, \beta_1)$, which is the logarithm of the likelihood function (or the log-likelihood function). The maximum likelihood estimates of β_0 and β_1 are the values of those parameters that maximize the log-likelihood function, which are found by computer algorithms using search procedures that converge on the estimated values. After these values have been found, they are substituted into the response function to generate the fitted, or estimated, logistic response function (Equation 29.17)

$$\hat{\pi}_i = \exp(b_0 + b_1 X)/[1 + \exp(b_0 + b_1 X)] \tag{29.17}$$

In simple logistic regression, the interpretation of b_1, the estimate of the slope parameter, β_1, differs from the usual interpretation of the corresponding parameter estimate in ordinary least-squares models. This difference comes about because the measured effect of a one-unit increase in the predictor variable, X, is different in a simple logistic model depending on the location of the starting point on the scale of the X variable. In contrast, in ordinary least-squares simple linear regression, the slope parameter represents a constant value at all points on the regression line. So, our interpretation of the effect on Y of a one-unit change in X will need to be expressed in terms of the value of b_1, which measures the proportional relative percentage change in Y in response to a one-unit change in X.

29.3.6 MULTIPLE LOGISTIC REGRESSION

A direct extension of the simple logistic regression model to handle more than one independent variable results in the expression (Equation 29.18)

$$E(Y) = \beta_0 + \beta_1 X_1 + \cdots + \beta_{p-1} X_{p-1} \tag{29.18}$$

The predictor variables may include the full range of options for regression models, including higher-order (quadratic or beyond) polynomials, interaction effects, continuous quantitative variables, or qualitative (indicator) variables. For the special case of a multiple logistic regression model that contains only qualitative variables, this specification often is referred to as a log-linear model.

Then, the multiple logistic response function is (Equation 29.19)

$$E(Y) = \exp(\beta' X)/[1 + \exp(\beta' X)] = [1 + \exp(-\beta' X)]^{-1} \tag{29.19}$$

where
β is a vector containing the p model parameters
X is the matrix of data values for the predictor variables

Just as with linear regression models, it often is the case that not all predictor variables contribute equally well to explaining variation in the dependent variable. In such circumstances, it may be beneficial to attempt to find an optimal subset of predictors that contains only the most important independent variables. However, unlike linear regression approaches that may be used to generate all possible models, the heavy computational demands required to estimate maximum likelihood solutions to logistic regression models generally require an alternative approach— stepwise logistic regression—that is very close to the stepwise methods used with linear regression.

Backward elimination logistic regression model building proceeds for a full-model containing all relevant predictor variables, and then eliminates one at a time at each successive step the predictor variable that is the least helpful for classifying the dichotomous outcomes correctly. Forward selection logistic regression begins by generating a simple logistic model using the single predictor variable that is the most helpful for correct classification of the response variable, and then proceeds by adding more predictor variables that add progressively smaller increments to correct classifications. Both processes cease according to stopping rules, defined by relative changes in significance level, in proportion of correctly classified outcome values, or in other measures of model adequacy.

29.3.7 Logistic Regression: An Example with a Categorical Predictor Variable

Logistic regression constitutes a research method for data analysis, model estimation through maximum likelihood methods, and statistical inference that has found broad applications beyond its initial extensive use in medical and epidemiological studies to social science research in political science, public administration, sociology, economics, education, business, and other related areas of investigation. One of the primary advantages of logistic regression is that the estimated parameters of the model may be interpreted as the ratio of the odds of one outcome occurring relative to the odds of the other outcome occurring. These odds ratios are functions directly of the parameters of the logistic model. This situation is in sharp distinction to least-squares regression models, in which the parameter estimates are expressed in terms of the mean of the continuous dependent variable relative to the mean of continuous predictor variables or relative to different means for the dependent variable across categories of a discrete main effect (as in analysis of variance or analysis of covariance).

An example of logistic regression is provided by the results of the following SPSS syntax, which estimates a model to predict which students in our dataset are in Talent Search or Upward Bound (TSUB or not) given their expectations of how far they will go in school (BYS45):

```
LOGISTIC REGRESSION TSUB or not
/METHOD = ENTER BYS45
/CONTRAST (BYS45) = Indicator
/CLASSPLOT /CASEWISE OUTLIER(2)
/PRINT = GOODFIT
/CRITERIA = PIN(.05) POUT(.10) ITERATE(20) CUT(.5).
```

The output from this syntax is presented in Table 29.4. The Omnibus Tests of Model Coefficients information shows that the $k = 6$ categories of the BYS45 independent variable (hence, $k - 1 = 5$ degrees of freedom) explains 35.086 chi-square units of the variation in TSUB or not, and is a statistically significant ($p < .001$) predictor.

The Model Summary shows that the TSUB or not dependent variable has a total of 1564.684 units of variation, measured by the value of "-2 log likelihood" (Equation 29.20):

$$-2 \log \text{likelihood} = -2 \sum_j w_j \log(\hat{\pi}_j) \qquad (29.20)$$

TABLE 29.4

Simple Logistic Regression Results for Predicting Student Participation in Talent Search or Upward Bound (TSUB or Not) by How Far the Student Expects to Get in School (BYS45)

Omnibus Tests of Model Coefficients

		Chi-Square	df	Sig.
Step 1	Step	35.086	5	.000
	Block	35.086	5	.000
	Model	35.086	5	.000

Model Summary

Step	−2 Log Likelihood	Cox & Snell R Square	Nagelkerke R Square
1	1564.684[a]	.030	.040

[a] Estimation terminated at iteration number 3 because parameter estimates changed by less than .001.

TABLE 29.4 (Continued)

Simple Logistic Regression Results for Predicting Student Participation in Talent Search or Upward Bound (TSUB or Not) by How Far the Student Expects to Get in School (BYS45)

Hosmer and Lemeshow Test

Step	Chi-Square	df	Sig.
1	.000	3	1.000

Contingency Table for Hosmer and Lemeshow Test

		TSUB or Not = 0		TSUB or Not = 1		
		Observed	Expected	Observed	Expected	Total
Step 1	1	86	86.000	34	34.000	120
	2	70	70.000	59	59.000	129
	3	70	70.000	70	70.000	140
	4	230	230.000	233	233.000	463
	5	123	123.000	179	179.000	302

Classification Table[a]

			Predicted		
			TSUB or Not		
Observed			0	1	Percentage Correct
Step 1	TSUB or not	0	156	423	26.9
		1	93	482	83.8
	Overall Percentage				55.3

[a] The cut value is .500.

Variables in the Equation

		B	S.E.	Wald	df	Sig.	Exp(B)
Step 1[a]	BYS45			32.579	5	.000	
	BYS45(1)	−0.827	0.497	2.765	1	.096	0.437
	BYS45(2)	−1.303	0.234	31.016	1	.000	0.272
	BYS45(3)	−0.501	0.223	5.040	1	.025	0.606
	BYS45(4)	−0.375	0.206	3.329	1	.068	0.687
	BYS45(5)	−0.362	0.150	5.869	1	.015	0.696
	Constant	0.375	0.117	10.263	1	.001	1.455

[a] Variables entered on step 1: BYS45.

where w_j is the weight of the jth observation. The Cox & Snell (.030) and Nagelkerke (.040) pseudo R^2 values (Equations 29.21 and 29.22) indicate that the BYS45 independent variable explains a rather modest portion of variation in TSUB or not. The Cox & Snell R^2 and Nagelkerke R^2 are alternative logistic regression analogies to the use of R^2 in ordinary least-squares regression. The Cox & Snell statistic does not have the same limits of 0 and 1 as the least squares R^2, but the Nagelkerke version adjusts the Cox & Snell statistic so that it does vary from 0 to 1.

$$\text{Cox \& Snell pseudo } R^2 = 1 - [\hat{L}(0)/L(\Theta)]^{2/n} \qquad (29.21)$$

where

L(0) is the likelihood of the intercept-only model (without any independent variables)

$\hat{L}(\Theta)$ is the likelihood of the specified model

n is the sample size; and

$$\text{Nagelkerke pseudo } R^2 = R^2_{\text{CS}}/R^2_{\text{max}} \qquad (29.22)$$

where $R^2_{\text{max}} = 1 - [L(0)]^{2/n}$

The Hosmer and Lemeshow test of goodness-of-fit statistic is more robust than the traditional goodness-of-fit statistic used in logistic regression, particularly for models with continuous covariates and studies with small sample sizes. It is based on grouping cases into a number of categories of risk and comparing the observed probability with the expected probability within each category, and then computing a chi-square statistic from the resulting observed and expected frequencies within each category. The p-value = 1.000 here indicates that the logistic regression model provides an extremely good fit to the values of the dependent variable. If the Hosmer and Lemeshow goodness-of-fit test statistic has a p-value of .05 or less, the null hypothesis that there is no difference between the observed and predicted values of the dependent variable is rejected; if $p > .05$, we fail to reject the null hypothesis of no difference, and conclude that the model estimates the data acceptably.

The Classification Table shows the number of observations in each of the categories of the dependent variable that are predicted (classified) correctly into that category and the number that are classified incorrectly. The columns in the Classification Table are the two predicted values of the dependent variable, and the rows contain the two observed (actual) values of the dependent variable. If every observation is predicted or classified correctly, all the observations will fall on the main diagonal from upper left to lower right. These results show that how far the student expects to get in school does a much better job of predicting which students will be in Talent Search or Upward Bound (TSUB or not = 1), 83.8 percent (482 of 482 + 93 = 575) of whom are classified correctly, than of predicting the students not in those programs (TSUB or not = 0), of whom just 26.9 percent (156 of 156 + 423 = 579) are classified correctly. Overall, 55.3 percent ([156 + 482]/[156 + 423 + 93 + 482]) of all cases are classified correctly as either Talent Search or Upward Bound or neither, but it is clear that we have a much better idea of how to predict the Talent Search or Upward Bound participants than nonparticipants.

The variables in the equation information present a test of the statistical significance of the overall main effect of a categorical predictor variable, using the Wald chi-square statistic—the square of the ratio of the parameter estimate to its standard error (Equation 29.23)—and its associated p-value (here, $p < .001$).

$$\chi^2_{\text{w}} = [b_i/s(b_i)]^2 \qquad (29.23)$$

The Wald chi-square test statistic is analogous to a squared t-statistic, or a partial F-test, in ordinary least-squares regression terms.

The variables in the equation information also show the results of testing for the statistical significance of each of the $(k - 1)$ regression coefficients that constitute the degrees of freedom of the main effect. Here, the results show that BYS45(2), BYS45(3), and BYS45(5) are significant ($p < .05$). The Exp(B) column is the antilogarithm of the regression parameter estimates (B) and provides an interpretation of the meaning of the components of the logistic regression model in terms of the odds ratio (as opposed to the B values, which are expressed in terms of the logarithms of the odds ratio). Exp(B) is interpreted as the predicted change in odds for a one-unit increase in the corresponding independent variable. Odds ratios less than 1 translate to decreases, and odds ratios greater than 1.0 correspond to increases, in odds; odds ratios close to 1.0 indicate that one-unit increases in the independent variable do not affect the dependent variable. For example, the value of Exp(B) = .696 for BYS45(5) means that students who respond BYS45(5) (will finish college) are only about 69.6 percent as likely to participate in Talent Search or Upward Bound compared to students who respond BYS45(6) (higher schooling after college), which is the omitted, or comparison, category.

A word of caution is in order here. Using the same data to test the predictive adequacy of the model that were employed to estimate the model in the first place imparts a bias to the results of prediction and classification efforts. There are two standard ways around this difficulty: (1) One could use a new set of observations to test the predictive validity of the model. However, the practical difficulties associated with having only a single sample available in most application situations makes it unlikely that more than one dataset will be sitting around to be evaluated; instead, it is common to split the sample, estimating the model with one half and then evaluating predictive validity with the other half. This assumes, of course, that there are enough observations in the sample for this to be feasible. (2) Alternatively, a jackknife procedure could be employed, in which a single unified sample is used. With jackknifing, one observation is omitted each time, and that observation then is classified into either of the two dichotomous outcomes based on the model that has been estimated without the observation that is being classified.

29.3.8 MULTIPLE LOGISTIC REGRESSION WITH A CONTINUOUS COVARIATE AND A MAIN EFFECT: WHAT DIFFERENCE DOES LUNCH MAKE?

A step upward in complexity with logistic regression is to add a covariate (defined here as a continuous independent variable) to a model containing a categorical main effect. With the model above predicting student participation in Talent Search or Upward Bound (TSUB or not) by how far the student expects to get in school (BYS45), let's see what happens when we add the percent of students in the survey respondents' schools who receive free and reduced lunch (G8LUNCH). Why does this make sense? Well, from the perspective of public administration and public policy analysis, it is important to realize the importance of proper nutrition for student learning—and it is even more important to realize that a student who qualifies to receive a free or reduced lunch by definition comes from a low-income family. A regular finding in education policy research is that lower-income students generally have more difficulty performing well academically and consequently are targeted for participation in programs such as Talent Search and Upward Bound that are designed to help overcome the deleterious effects of living in a relatively impoverished household. That is, we are addressing important public administration and public policy issues about the effectiveness of government programs and expenditures on those programs.

The following SPSS syntax estimates a multiple logistic regression model with one categorical (BYS45) and one continuous (G8LUNCH) independent variable predicting the dependent variable of Talent Search or Upward Bound participation (Table 29.5).

```
LOGISTIC REGRESSION TSUB or not
/METHOD = ENTER BYS45 G8LUNCH
/CONTRAST (BYS45) = Indicator
/CLASSPLOT /CASEWISE OUTLIER(2)
/PRINT = GOODFIT
/CRITERIA = PIN(.05) POUT(.10) ITERATE(20) CUT(.5)
```

The Omnibus Tests of Model Coefficients information shows that these predictors together account for 60.784 chi-square units of variation in Talent Search or Upward Bound participation, which is much more than the amount accounted for by BYS45 alone (35.086) with the addition of one degree of freedom for the continuous covariate.

The Model Summary presents the total units of variation (-2 Log likelihood $= 1498.690$), which is slightly different from the result for the model with BYS45 as the only predictor variable. As fewer observations are available for the multiple logistic regression model because of missing data on the added variable (G8LUNCH), the values of the Cox & Snell R^2 (0.053) and Nagelkerke

R^2 (0.070) pseudo-R^2 measures of goodness of fit are not overwhelmingly strong, but still are about twice as large as for the model containing only BYS45 as a predictor.

The Hosmer and Lemeshow Test result is nonsignificant ($p = 0.400$), which demonstrates that the number of observations predicted to be in each segment of the data closely track the actual number of observations. The Contingency Table for Hosmer and Lemeshow Test information demonstrates the closeness of the fit between observed and expected frequencies within the groups of both nonparticipants (TSUB or not $= 0$) and participants (TSUB or not $= 1$) in Talent Search or Upward Bound.

The Classification Table shows a substantial improvement in Overall Percentage of correctly classified cases (59.8 percent). However, that overall improvement masks two very different trends associated with introducing free and reduced lunch into the model. The new independent variable increases dramatically (to 55.5 percent) the rate at which nonparticipants in Talent Search or Upward Bound are classified correctly, but at the cost of a substantial reduction (to 64.3 percent) in the correct classification rate for students participating in Talent Search or Upward Bound.

The variables in the equation information show that the effect in the model of G8LUNCH is significant and positive; the odds ratio of 1.161 indicates that each one-unit (i.e., one percentage point) increase in the percentage of students in a respondent's school who receive free or reduced lunch results in about a 16.1 percent increase in the probability of a student being in Talent Search or Upward Bound compared to the odds of being a nonparticipant in those programs. It is important, too, to notice that the effects of BYS45 (how far the student expects to go in school) are changed by including the continuous covariate of schoolwide percentage of students receiving free and reduced lunch. In this multiple logistic regression model, the effects of BYS45(2), BYS45(3), BYS45(4), and BYS45(5) are significantly ($p < .05$) negative, with parameter estimates all less than 0 and odds ratios all less than 1, meaning that, compared to the omitted category of BYS45(6)—higher schooling after college—students with these lesser educational aspirations (BYS45(2) = will finish high school; BYS45(3) = vocational, trade, or business school after high school; BYS45(4) = will attend college; and BYS45(5) = will finish college) are significantly less likely than those aspiring to postgraduate education to be in Talent Search or Upward Bound.

29.4   THE LEAST-SQUARES APPROACH: TWO-GROUP DISCRIMINANT ANALYSIS

Discriminant analysis has three fundamental goals:

1. It is designed to determine which variables do the best job of differentiating between observations that belong in one group and those that belong in the other group.
2. Variables that are thus identified as optimal discriminators then are used to develop a parsimonious prediction equation that will boil down the set of potential discriminators to those that are the most effective ones for distinguishing one possible outcome from the other. The objective is to separate the means of the two groups as far from each other as possible, that is, to maximize the between (or explained) sum of squares, and to produce groups that are as homogeneous internally as possible, which is equivalent to minimizing the within-group (the error, or unexplained) sum of squares. Another way to express this second objective is to say that discriminant analysis is designed to maximize the ratio of between-group sum of squares to within-group sum of squares, to provide the maximum possible separation, or discrimination, between the two groups.
3. Models that provide the best results then are used to classify future observations into one or the other of the two groups, and may be used to inform decision makers about policy choices among alternative outcomes. Although the classification operation is not necessarily related to discriminant analysis proper, usually it is a goal that is facilitated and

informed usefully by the method of discriminant analysis. The linear combination of predictor variables that maximize the ratio of between to within sum of squares is known as the linear discriminant function. The values of the new variable (Z) that is formed from the linear discriminant function to provide this optimal degree of group separation are referred to as discriminant scores, and these scores are used to classify future observations. Classification occurs based on a cutoff value that minimizes the number of errors of misclassification or minimizes the costs of misclassification of observations into two mutually exclusive and collectively exhaustive regions. Various forms of such misclassification costs can be investigated.

Two-group discriminant models can be extended rather easily to cases of more than two response categories.

29.4.1 THE LINEAR DISCRIMINANT MODEL

Fisher's linear discriminant function, or the linear combination of predictor variables that forms the new variable Z, is defined as (Equation 29.24)

$$Z = w_1X_1 + w_2X_2 + \cdots + w_{p-1}X_{p-1} = \beta'X \tag{29.24}$$

where
    Z is the discriminant function defining the dependent variable
    the X's represent the independent, or classification, variables
    w_1 and w_2 are the weights of the discriminant function that maximize the value of

$\lambda =$ between-group sum of squares/within-group sum of squares.

In the discriminant analysis model, the significance of each discriminating variable is determined by the outcome of testing the null hypothesis that the two groups have the same mean

$$H_0: \mu_1 = \mu_2$$

Against the alternative hypothesis that the group means are not different (which is the same as asserting that the discriminating variables do not help distinguish one group from the other)

$$H_a: \mu_1 \neq \mu_2$$

This test can be conducted using an independent two-sample t-statistic, but it is more common in applications of discriminant analysis methods to employ Wilks' lambda for this purpose (Equation 29.25):

$$\Lambda = (SS_w/SS_t) \tag{29.25}$$

where SS_w is the sum of squares within and SS_t is the total sum of squares. The smaller the value of Λ, the greater the probability that the null hypothesis will be rejected and the greater is the evidence that the discriminating function contributes to separating the two groups successfully.

It is essential to note that the use of discriminant analysis is not an indiscriminate process. Among the crucial distinctions that must be made correctly for the results of a discriminant analysis to be valid is whether the groups are being compared on an equal footing. The nature of this comparability is evaluated using a chi-squared test for homogeneity of the within-group covariance matrices. The pooled covariance matrix is used unless the test statistic is significant, in which case a different variation of discriminant modeling must be followed. A conclusion of equal covariance matrices leads to the use of Fisher's linear discriminant function, which operates off the assumption that patterns of covariation among the relevant predictor variables are the same in both groups.

Alternatively, if a significant chi-square statistic is found, the assumption of equal covariation within groups is rejected, and a quadratic discriminant function is estimated instead.

It also is important to note that conventional forms of discriminant analysis assume that the variables within each group follow a multivariate normal distribution. When multivariate normality is a reasonable assumption, the discriminant function (also known as the classification criterion) is a function of generalized squared distance (Rao, 1973). Nonparametric alternatives are available, when multivariate normality is not plausible, including kernel methods and the k-nearest-neighbor method (Rosenblatt, 1956; Parzen, 1962).

The probability of observations being classified by the vector of their values of the predictor variables (x) into group t is determined by Bayes' theorem (Equation 29.26) as

$$p(t|x) = q_t f_t(x)/f(x) \qquad (29.26)$$

where $p(t|x)$ is the posterior probability of an observation x belonging to group t, q_t is the prior probability of membership in group t, $f_t(x)$ is the group-specific density estimate at x from group t, and $f(x) = \Sigma_t q_t f_t(x)$ is the estimated unconditional density at x. The discriminant analysis partitions a vector space containing p dimensions, where p is the number of predictor variables that divides the data values into regions, R_t, which is the subspace containing all p-dimensional vectors γ that maximize $p(t|\gamma)$ among all groups. Any observation that lies in region R_t is classified as coming from group t, on grounds that it has the smallest generalized squared distance.

The squared distance from x to group t is (Equation 29.27)

$$d_t^2(x) = (x - m_t)'V_t^{-1}(x - m_t) \qquad (29.27)$$

where $V_t = S_t$ (the covariance matrix within group t) if the within-group covariance matrices are used, or $V_t = S$ (the pooled covariance matrix) if the pooled covariance matrix is used, m_t is the p-dimensional vector containing the means of the independent variables in group t. Then, the generalized squared distance from x to group t, which is used to classify each observation, is (Equation 29.28)

$$D_t^2 = d_t^2(x) + g_1(t) + g_2(t) \qquad (29.28)$$

where $g_1(t)$ equals either $log_e|S_t|$ if the within-group covariance matrices are used, or 0 if the pooled covariance matrix is used, and $g_2(t)$ equals either $-2log_e(q_t)$ if the prior probabilities are not all equal, or 0 if the prior probabilities are all equal.

The posterior probability of a single observation, x, belonging to group t then equals (Equation 29.29)

$$p(t|x) = [\exp(-0.5D_t^2(x))]\Big/ \Big[\sum_{ij} \exp(-0.5D_{ij}^2(x))\Big] \qquad (29.29)$$

An observation then is classified into a particular group, u, if setting $t = u$ produces the largest value of $p(t|x)$ or the smallest value of $D_t^2(x)$. Different thresholds can be specified to define the cutoff probability that must be attained before an observation is classified.

29.4.2 AN EXAMPLE OF TWO-GROUP DISCRIMINANT ANALYSIS

Table 29.6 presents the key results of a two-group discriminant analysis for attempting to classify student participation in Talent Search or Upward Bound (TSUB or not) by how far the student expects to get in school (BYS45) and percent of students in the respondent's school who are receiving free and reduced lunch (G8LUNCH). In many respects these results resemble those of the parallel multiple logistic model results that we just saw in Table 29.5. However, differences between the discriminant analysis and logistic regression approaches and results will be apparent, too.

TABLE 29.5

Multiple Logistic Regression Results for Predicting Student Participation in Talent Search or Upward Bound (TSUB or Not) by How Far the Student Expects to Get in School (BYS45) and Percent of Students in School Receiving Free and Reduced Lunch (G8LUNCH)

Omnibus Tests of Model Coefficients

		Chi-Square	df	Sig.
Step 1	Step	60.784	6	0.000
	Block	60.784	6	0.000
	Model	60.784	6	0.000

Model Summary

Step	-2 Log Likelihood	Cox & Snell R Square	Negelkerke R Square
1	1498.690[a]	0.053	0.070

[a] Estimation terminated at iteration number 4 because parameter estimates changed by less than .001.

Hosmer and Lemeshow Test

Step	Chi-Square	df	Sig.
1	7.286	7	0.400

Contingency Table for Hosmer and Lemeshow Test

		TSUB or Not = 0		TSUB or Not = 1		
		Observed	Expected	Observed	Expected	Total
Step 1	1	85	87.649	36	33.351	121
	2	78	83.044	55	49.956	133
	3	78	66.242	40	51.758	118
	4	59	56.023	47	49.977	106
	5	68	69.359	72	70.641	140
	6	75	72.497	83	85.503	158
	7	59	61.509	87	84.491	146
	8	34	36.798	62	59.202	96
	9	32	34.877	75	72.123	107

Classification Table[a]

			Predicted		
			TSUB or Not		
Observed			0	1	Percentage Correct
Step 1	TSUB or not	0	315	253	55.5
		1	199	358	64.3
	Overall Percentage				59.8

[a] The cut value is .500

(continued)

TABLE 29.5 (*Continued*)

Multiple Logistic Regression Results for Predicting Student Participation in Talent Search or Upward Bound (TSUB or not) by How Far the Student Expects to Get in School (BYS45) and Percent of Students in School Receiving Free and Reduced Lunch (G8LUNCH)

Variables in the Equation

		B	S.E.	Wald	df	Sig.	Exp(B)
Step 1[a]	BYS45			38.372	5	.000	
	BYS45(1)	−0.985	.526	3.505	1	.061	0.373
	BYS45(2)	−1.437	.241	35.556	1	.000	0.238
	BYS45(3)	−0.669	.233	8.242	1	.004	0.512
	BYS45(4)	−0.500	.212	5.560	1	.018	0.607
	BYS45(5)	−0.447	.155	8.350	1	.004	0.640
	G8Lunch	0.149	.030	24.397	1	.000	1.161
	Constant	−0.114	.156	0.541	1	.462	0.892

[a] Variables entered on step 1: BYS45, G8LUNCH.

The results shown in Table 29.6 were produced by the following SPSS syntax:

```
DISCRIMINANT
/GROUPS = TSUB or not(0 1)
/VARIABLES = BYS45 G8LUNCH
/ANALYSIS ALL
/PRIORS SIZE
/STATISTICS = MEAN STDDEV UNIVF BOXM COEFF CORR COV GCOV TCOV
    TABLE CROSSVALID
/PLOT = COMBINED SEPARATE MAP
/PLOT = CASES
/CLASSIFY = NONMISSING POOLED
```

TABLE 29.6

Two-Group Discriminant Analysis Results for Classifying Student Participation in Talent Search or Upward Bound (TSUB or not) by How Far the Student Expects to Get in School (BYS45) and Percent of Students in School Receiving Free and Reduced Lunch (G8LUNCH)

Group Statistics

TSUB or Not		Mean	Std. Deviation	Valid N (List Wise) Unweighted	Weighted
0	How far in school do you think you will get?	4.36	1.407	568	568.000
	Percent free lunch in school	3.49	2.014	568	568.000
1	How far in school do you think you will get?	4.79	1.203	557	557.000
	Percent free lunch in school	4.03	2.092	557	557.000
Total	How far in school do you think you will get?	4.57	1.327	1125	1125.000
	Percent free lunch in school	3.76	2.070	1125	1125.000

TABLE 29.6 (*Continued*)

Analysis 1

Box's Test of Equality of Covariance Matrices

Test Results

Box's M		**17.214**
F	Approx.	5.727
	df1	3
	df2	2E+008
	Sig.	.006

Tests null hypothesis of equal population covariance matrices.

Wilks' Lambda

Test of Functions	Wilks' Lambda	Chi-Square	df	Sig.
1	.952	54.933	2	.000

Standardized Canonical Discriminant Function Coefficients

	Function 1
How far in school do you think you will get?	0.814
Percent free lunch in school	0.687

Classification Statistics

Classification Results[a,b]

		TSUB or Not	Predicted Group Membership		Total
			0	1	
Original	Count	0	349	219	568
		1	226	331	557
	Percentage	0	61.4	38.6	100.0
		1	40.6	59.4	100.0
Cross validated[c]	Count	0	349	219	568
		1	226	331	557
	Percent	0	61.4	38.6	100.0
		1	40.6	59.4	100.0

[a] 60.4 percent of original grouped cases correctly classified.

[b] 60.4 percent of cross validated grouped cases correctly classified.

[c] Cross validation is done only for those cases in the analysis. In cross validation, each case is classified by the functions derived from all cases other than that case.

The Group Statistics show higher means for the Talent Search or Upward Bound participants than for nonparticipants both on how far the student thinks she or he will get in school and the percent of students at each respondent's eighth grade school receiving free or reduced lunch. So, Talent Search or Upward Bound participants overall tend to have higher aspirations for further education and come from economically less privileged families and neighborhoods. The result for Box's Test of Equality of Covariance Matrices shows that they are unequal; hence, a quadratic discriminant function should be employed using separate covariance matrices.

Wilks' lambda chi-square-based multivariate F-test shows that the discriminant model as a whole is significant. This means that we should proceed with further assessment of model fit. The Standardized Canonical Discriminant Function Coefficients show that both predictor variables load highly on this linear combination that maximizes differences between the values of the dependent variable. (There is only one discriminant function with two groups.) The Classification Results summarize the ability of the model to classify observations correctly, much as in logistic regression; however, here the classifications are achieved through a hold-out method by which each observation's classification probabilities are calculated using all data values except that one, to minimize bias. The classification results show that 61.4 percent of the nonparticipants in Talent Search and Upward Bound are identified correctly, with only slightly weaker results for classifying program participants (59.4 percent). From the values in Table 29.6, we also can calculate that $(349 + 331)/(568 + 557) = 680/1125 = 60.4$ percent of all students in our dataset are classified correctly. This compares closely with the successful classification percentages attained by logistic regression.

29.5 CONCLUSIONS

This chapter has only scratched the proverbial surface of the analysis that can be conducted on dichotomous dependent variables. A large family of nonparametric correlational statistics for cross-tabulation tables have been glossed over. More general classes of loglinear models also could be applied to such research problems. LISREL-type structural equation models also have not been covered here, largely because of a host of complexities that place such models beyond our ability to address adequately without the development of much more elaborate statistical and mathematical machinery. The interested reader is invited to investigate these and other related methods for dealing with dichotomous dependent variables in sources such as Neter, Kutner, Nachtsheim, and Wasserman, (1996); Sharma (1996); Johnson and Wichern (1991); Flury and Riedwyl (1988); Tabachnick and Fidell (2001); and Agresti (1990).

ACKNOWLEDGMENTS

The author wishes to express his sincere thanks to Flo Hamrick, his colleague and Associate Professor in the Department of Educational Leadership and Policy Studies at Iowa State University, who proposed the TRIO policy thrust and conducted initial analysis of the NELS data.

REFERENCES

Agresti, A. 1990. *Categorical Data Analysis*. New York: Wiley.

Agresti, A. and Finlay, B. 1997. *Statistical Methods for the Social Sciences* (3rd ed.). Upper Saddle River, New Jersey: Prentice Hall.

Bishop, Y., Fienberg, S.E., and Holland, P.W. 1975. *Discrete Multivariate Analysis: Theory and Practice*. Cambridge, Massachusetts: MIT Press.

Field, K. 2006, April 21. Federal commission gears up for the home stretch: The higher-education panel sets its priorities and considers new approaches to accountability and accreditation. Retrieved April 24, 2006, from http://chronicle.com/weekly/v52/i33/33a03202.htm.

Flury, B. and Riedwyl, H. 1988. *Multivariate Statistics: A Practical Approach*. London: Chapman and Hall.

Garson, G.D. 1971. *Handbook of Political Science Methods*. Boston, Massachusetts: Holbrook.

Groutt, J. 2003. *Milestones of TRIO History, Part 1*. Washington, DC: National TRIO Clearinghouse.

Hinkle, D.E., Wiersma, W., and Jurs, S.G. 2003. *Applied Statistics for the Behavioral Sciences* (5th ed.). Boston: Houghton Mifflin.

Howell, D.C. 2002. *Statistical Methods for Psychology* (5th ed.). Pacific Grove, California: Duxbury.

Jaschik, S. 2006, February 7. On the chopping block again. Retrieved February 7, 2006, from http://www.insidehighered.com/news/2006/02/07/trio.

Johnson, N. and Wichern, D. 1991. *Applied Multivariate Statistical Analysis* (3rd ed.). Englewood Cliffs, New Jersey: Prentice-Hall.

Laws, J.E., Jr. 1999. The influence of upward bound on freshman grade point average, dropout rates, mathematics performance, and English performance. *Western Journal of Black Studies, 23*(3), 139–143.

McCullagh, P. and Nelder, J.A. 1989. *Generalized Linear Models* (2nd ed.). New York: Chapman Hall.

Myers, D. and Schirm, A. 1999. The impacts of upward bound: Final report for phase 1 of the national evaluation. Retrieved July 14, 2006, from http://www.ed.gov/offices/OUS/PES/higher/upward.pdf.

National Center for Education Statistics. 1996. *National Educational Longitudinal Study (NELS:88/94) Methodology Report* (NCES No. 96–174). Washington, DC: U.S. Department of Education, Office of Educational Research and Improvement.

National Center for Education Statistics (n.d.). *Quick Guide to Using the NELS:88/2000 Data.* Washington, DC: U.S. Department of Education, Office of Educational Research and Improvement.

Neter, J., Kutner, M.H., Nachtsheim, C.J., and Wasserman, W. 1996. *Applied Linear Statistical Models* (4th ed.). Chicago: Irwin.

Parzen, E. 1962. On estimation of a probability density function and mode. *Annals of Mathematical Statistics, 33,* 1065–1076.

Rao, C.R. 1973. *Linear Statistical Inference and Its Applications* (2nd ed.). New York: Wiley.

Rosenblatt, M. 1956. Remarks on some nonparametric estimates of a density function. *Annals of Mathematical Statistics 27,* 832–837.

Sharma, S. 1996. *Applied Multivariate Techniques.* New York: Wiley.

Tabachnick, B.G. and Fidell, L.S. 2001. *Using Multivariate Statistics* (4th ed.). Boston: Allyn and Bacon.

Talent Search Program: Purpose. (n.d.). Retrieved July 17, 2006, from http://www.ed.gov/programs/triotalent/index.html.

The impacts of regular upward bound: Results from the third follow-up data collection. 2004. Retrieved July 14, 2006, from http://www.ed.gov/rschstat/eval/highered/upward/upward-3rd-report.html.

The national evaluation of upward bound summary of first-year impacts and program operations: Executive summary. 1997. *Journal of Educational Opportunity, 16*(2), 61–68.

Upward bound program. (n.d.). Retrieved July 19, 2006, from http://www.ed.gov/programs/trioupbound/index.html.

Walters, A.K. 2006, July 14. Upward Bound could shift focus. Retrieved July 14, 2006, from http://chronicle.com/weekly/v52/i45/45a02202.htm.

Young, E.D. and Exum, H.A. 1982. Upward bound and academic achievement: A successful intervention. *Journal of College Student Personnel, 23*(4), 291–299.

30 Identifying Dimensions and Types in Public Administration Research: Introduction to Principal Components Analysis, Factor Analysis, and Cluster Analysis

George Julnes

CONTENTS

30.1   INTRODUCTION

This chapter presents three quantitative techniques for identifying patterns of interdependency, generally called dimensions and types, in data. A decade ago these techniques—principal components analysis, factor analysis, and cluster analysis—were used only rarely in public administration research. The situation is quite different today, inspired not only in part by developments in doctoral training in public administration, but also by the increasing recognition of heterogeneity in the key concerns within public administration. The success of efforts to promote citizen participation in government may require understanding differences among public administrators, including a dimension that captures the degree to which public administrators trust citizens (Yang, 2005), and amidst the variation in state approaches to welfare policy, general types can be identified (Meyers, Gornick, and Peck, 2001).

The increased use of principal component, factor, and cluster analyses creates both opportunities and challenges for public administrators. The opportunities come from the ability to make sense of complexities that previously were muddled and best glossed over. The challenges are not only the technical understanding required to use or understand the results of the techniques but also the practical wisdom of when to apply one technique rather than another. This chapter addresses these challenges, beginning with a conceptual scheme to help organize the analytic options available to researchers and then considering, in turn, principal component, factor, and cluster analysis. Each of these three techniques is presented first in terms of its major conceptual foundations and then applied to actual data taken from an evaluation of a public sector program. Following these technique-specific sections, the conclusion section uses the developed conceptual scheme to address the relationships among the three techniques. A commonality worth noting now is that, unlike techniques such as multiple regression and discriminant analysis that seek to establish the dependence of one set of variables on another, the three multivariate techniques discussed in this chapter seek to reveal interdependencies among variables. The goal is to provide an overview for the readers that will allow you to use these techniques and interpret the results.

A fuller understanding of these techniques, however, will require additional readings, and so throughout this chapter recommendations are made regarding particularly useful sources for specific topics. Of general use, however, are many texts on multivariate analysis, with Tabachnick and Fidell (2001) and Harris (2001) being particularly popular. Tinsley and Brown (2000) is another useful resource as an edited book with chapters on specific multivariate techniques. The primary journal outlet for these techniques in public administration is the *Journal of Public Administration Research and Theory*, with some also published elsewhere, such as in the *American Journal of Public Administration* and *Public Administration Review*. Other scholarly journals that emphasize multivariate techniques include *Multivariate Behavioral Research, Biometrika*, and *Sociological Methods and Research*. The remainder of this introductory section is devoted to (1) distinguishing relevant approaches to organizing phenomena, (2) describing the Resource Mothers Program for pregnant teens that will be used to exemplify the implications of using the different techniques, and (3) introducing the computer package used in analyzing the data.

In public administration, we generally talk about, whether as researchers or practitioners to claim that studying public administration can improve public administration—for example, the claims that restructuring government can lead to more efficient service provision, or that examination of best practices can lead to more effective management—is to claim that there are relationships that are sufficiently enduring and reliable as to be useful in guiding action.

30.1.1 CHOICES IN ORGANIZING PHENOMENA

The quantitative techniques presented in this chapter support our understanding of these relationships by helping us organize our worlds in meaningful ways. Choosing a technique that is appropriate for your particular needs requires considering more issues than can be summarized here. We can, however, understand some of the more fundamental distinctions among principal components analysis, factor analysis, and cluster analysis by considering the conceptual framework presented in Table 30.1. Each of the columns represents a basic issue in methodology with some of the alternative positions listed below. We introduce these issues here as choices in organizing phenomena and return to this framework in the concluding section of this chapter.

30.1.1.1 Focus of Analysis: Objects, Attributes, and Occurrences

One of the first decisions faced by a researcher using quantitative methods concerns just what it is that the researcher wants to analyze. This decision is often between efforts to organize different

TABLE 30.1
Choices in Organizing Phenomena

Focus of Analysis	Scale of Measurement	Goal of Analysis
Objects: Identify similarities among people, agencies, or other concrete entities	Categorical: Discrete groupings that rely on nominal measurement	Nominalism: Derived organization of phenomena is convenient fiction
Attributes: Identify similarities among characteristics being measured	Dimensional: Continuous phenomema that can be organized using ordinal, interval or ratio scales	Realism: Natural categories and dimensions that can be approximated through analysis
Occasions: Identify similarities among periods of time being studied		

types of people (types of "objects") or different groupings of variables (types of attributes or characteristics); one may, however, choose instead to analyze different occasions according to their similarity. Recognizing that researchers might be interested in any one or in all three of these emphases, Dillon and Goldstein (1984) note that for multivariate analysis, "the basic input can be visualized in terms of a data cube with entries denoted by X_{ijk}, where i refers to objects, j refers to attributes, and k refers to occasions or time periods" (p. 3).

The concept of a data cube may be new to some and seem complicated, but the basic idea is fairly simple. We can think of measurement in terms of a cube that has three dimensions, objects, attributes, and occasions, but we cannot organize all three of these dimensions at once. Instead, we take "slices" of this three-dimensional cube and organize the information in those slices: (1) relationships among objects, (2) relationships among attributes, or (3) relationships among occasions. If we wish to identify types of managers, then we are interested in classifying people into groups. The managers being classified are examples of individual "objects" other examples of objects might include distinguishing different types of organizations or even classifying office supplies into different budget categories. Alternatively, focusing on "attributes," one might be interested in identifying the performance measures that covary and are associated with different long-term outcomes. This emphasis would lead to classifying the various performance measures into groups of variables. Another example of this approach would be to group measures of fiscal stress into categories (e.g., spending obligations versus fiscal capacity). Finally, if we wished to group different times into categories, we would be analyzing "occasions." With this focus, organizational performance in the public sector might be analyzed by grouping the available information in terms of changes in elected administration. These examples of the three dimensions of the data cube introduce the idea; in the concluding section of this chapter we develop the data cube notion further by depicting some of the slices of this data cube that are particularly relevant in public administration research.

Each of the techniques of this chapter can be used to organize any slice of the data cube described by Dillon and Goldstein (1984). Organizing attributes that are measured across multiple objects, as in organizing personal characteristics of many people, is referred to as R-analysis (e.g., Pandey and Scott, 2002); grouping objects together based on their attributes is referred to as Q-analysis (e.g., Donahue, 2004); and organizing occasions based on multiple attributes of one object is known as O-analysis (for an introduction to these and the three other slices of the data cube, see Rummel, 1970). Although tradition links certain techniques with these different slices of the data cube, and so these techniques are most developed for these slices, it is up to the investigator to understand which facet of the cube is of greatest relevance to the research questions at hand.

30.1.1.2 Scale of Measurement: Categories versus Dimensions

In addition to distinguishing among objects, attributes, and occasions when organizing phenomena, one must also identify the scale of measurement desired for the results. Measurement is often presented in terms of nominal, ordinal, interval, and ratio scales. The first of these scales, nominal, is categorical; the last three, particularly interval and ratio scales, presume dimensions. Although the three techniques to be addressed generally presume interval data as input (though dichotomous and ordinal data can be used for some purposes), the techniques can be differentiated in terms of their output. Cluster analysis provides categorical groupings (nominal scale) as output, while principal components analysis and factor analysis produce interval dimensions as output.

Both categories and dimensions can be useful in organizing the domain of public administration. We employ categories when we claim that the experiences of abused women with the criminal justice system can be grouped into four clusters (Fleury, 2002). Similarly, we might seek to understand the problems of government by first identifying categories to differentiate types of governmental waste (Stanbury and Thompson, 1995). These types, whether viewed as Weberian ideal types or as empirical groupings, represent claims that it is meaningful to classify styles, individuals, and situations into categories (Bailey, 1994).

As an example of ordering administrative phenomena along dimensions, one might talk of a dimension of "publicness" and claim that, rather than distinguish public and private organizations as representing two discrete categories, organizations can be ordered along a continuous dimension on which most organizations are more "public" than some but less than others (Coursey and Bozeman, 1990). Similarly, one could claim that innovation in support of state economic development is driven by the capacity for innovation and that this capacity is better understood in terms of two components, human capacity and financial capacity (Hall, 2006). Both of these examples of dimensions are presented as if there were reasonably continuous underlying phenomena that are represented best by a continuous variables. Note that dimensions contain more information than simple classification into one of two groups and so may predict outcomes better (see McKernan, Bernstein, and Fender, 2005).

30.1.1.3 Goal of Analysis: Realism versus Nominalism

A final issue of analysis to be considered here concerns the beliefs one has about the proper interpretation of observed interdependence. On the one hand are those who believe that the categories and dimensions used in analysis refer to the real structure of the world (see Julnes and Mark, 1998); on the other hand are those who believe that the identified categories and dimensions are simply "useful fictions" that facilitate discussions and simplify decisions but do not refer to anything real about the world. Those in the former group, the realists, believe, for example, that there really are consistent differences among leaders (whether as different types or in terms of different characteristics that vary along meaningful dimensions) that can be captured more or less effectively by the analysis (e.g., Simonton, 1986). Those in the second camp, the nominalists, might accept that leaders differ in important ways but would not believe that these differences are in any sense systematic.

As we will see below, factor analysis presumes that there are underlying factors that are responsible for observed regularities. Principal components analysis takes no stance on this issue and so can be used even by those who take a nominalist view of the world. Cluster analysis can be differentiated into two types in terms of this dimension, with most varieties presuming underlying groupings that are to be revealed by analysis but also some that view the categories produced by the analyses as merely useful and nothing more (Bailey, 1994).

The point to be made in thinking about these issues is that using the techniques presented below requires, and presumes, prior decisions reflecting beliefs and intentions that are to guide the analysis—a computer can analyze data for each of these possible choices. In the remainder of this introduction we first describe the Resource Mothers Program that serves as a backdrop for this discussion of multivariate techniques and the computer program being used for analysis.

30.1.2 CASE EXAMPLE FOR ANALYSIS: RESOURCE MOTHERS PROGRAM

The Resource Mothers Program is a lay home visiting program that emerged from the Southern Governor's Task Force on Infant Mortality. In Virginia, the Resource Mothers Program began in 1985 in three metropolitan areas and by 1996 had grown to 20 programs throughout the Commonwealth. Focusing on unacceptably high rates of infant deaths, one of the goals of the program has been to reach out to women who are at-risk for negative birth outcomes and who are not reached by traditional prenatal programs (Julnes, Konefal, Pindur, and Kim, 1994). The primary program activities involve the lay home visitor, a woman referred to as a Resource Mother, meeting with the client, usually an at-risk pregnant adolescent, and arranging prenatal medical visits, monitoring and advising on nutrition, and acting as a liaison between the client and other agencies.

In an effort to understand the impact of the program, the March of Dimes Birth Defect Foundation sponsored a two-year, multisite evaluation in Virginia. Although much of the evaluation

TABLE 30.2
Selected Variables from Resource Mothers Program

Birthorder	0 for no prior births, 1 for one prior birth, 2 for two prior births, etc.
Ethnicity	1 for African-Americans, 0 for other.
Marital status	0 for single, 1 for married.
Months of prenatal care	Months of prenatal medical care before delivery, Ranged from 0 to 9.
Mother's age	Age in years at last birthday before current birth.
Mother's education	0–12 for elementary school through high school, 13–16 for one through four years of college, 17 for more than college degree.
Source of prenatal medical care	1 for private physician, 0 for other sources of Primary prenatal care.
Medical prenatal visits	Number of visits for medical prenatal care.
Weight gain	Increase in weight, in pounds, during pregnancy (weight loss coded as 0).
Gestational age	Physician estimate of weeks of pregnancy before giving birth.
Birthweight	Baby's weight, in grams, at birth.

involved qualitative case studies and comparisons of five project sites, quantitative analysis was used to estimate program impact (e.g., logistic regression allowed estimation of the reduction in low birthweight deliveries due to the program) and, using information on program costs and estimated benefits, net economic value. These analyses were based on birth certificate data from 34,104 births, including births from 196 program clients. Table 30.2 presents some of the variables used in the quantitative analysis.

For the purposes of this discussion, we will focus on the characteristics of the 196 clients. With this focus, the three techniques described in this chapter—principal components analysis, factor analysis, and cluster analysis—will be examined in terms of their ability to address the relationships to be found in 196 observations measured on some combination of the eleven variables. For each technique we will provide a short introduction to the essential concepts of the technique and then use the results of the analysis of the Resource Mothers Program client birth data to introduce the other important points.

30.1.3 COMPUTER ANALYSIS OF INTERDEPENDENCIES AMONG VARIABLES

As mentioned above, the goal of this chapter is to present quantitative techniques that support scholars and practitioners in public administration in their efforts to make sense of the complex realities that they face. In order for the techniques discussed to be useful, we need to make sure that they are accessible to those with the appropriate computer resources available. Although there are several highly regarded computer programs available for specific multivariate techniques, most common among scholars and researchers in public administration are SPSS and SAS. For the purpose of this chapter, we will use the SAS computer program (O'Rourke, Hatcher, and Stepanski, 2005). This program provides a wide array of multivariate analysis techniques and is available for both mainframe computers and for personal computers. The program can be run either interactively or as a batch program (series of commands run together); for simplicity in presentation without the use of computer screens, we will limit ourselves to discussing the batch commands.

When used in the batch mode, a SAS program can be viewed as consisting of two steps. First is the DATA step of the program in which the data to be analyzed is identified and read as observations on specified variables. Also in the DATA step are operations that change the data before they are analyzed. For example, the researcher might wish to transform the data or even create new variables based on the inputted data. The second step is the PROC step in which the data is analyzed using SAS procedure statements. It is these procedure statements, referred to as PROC statements, and the associated supplemental statements that control the data analysis, that constitute the focus of the computer programming statements made in this chapter. For each of the quantitative techniques discussed we will present the SAS commands for the statistical procedure in a table and discuss them in the text. The reader wishing to learn more about the programming options available in SAS is directed to the SAS manuals (see www.SAS.com) but also to user-friendly books on such topics as social science inquiry (Spector, 1993), multivariate and univariate analysis (O'Rourke et al., 2005), and factor analysis and principal components analysis (Hatcher, 1994).

30.1.4 PRINCIPAL COMPONENTS ANALYSIS

Principal components analysis is a type of factor analysis that emerged from the work of Pearson (1901) and Hotelling (1933). As a result of this early development, principal components analysis has its roots among the earliest attempts to classify phenomena using quantitative methods. "Its goal is to reduce the dimensionality of the original data set. A small set of uncorrelated variables is much easier to understand and use in further analyses than a larger set of correlated variables" (Dunteman, 1989, p. 7). The analysis that follows makes use of several standard books (Rummel, 1970; Jolliffe, 1986; Dunteman, 1989).

30.1.5 CONCEPTUAL FOUNDATION

30.1.5.1 Underlying Logic: Data Reduction

The basic logic of principal component analysis is straightforward, and its purpose can be summed up in a word—parsimony. The idea is to account for the information provided by many variables (or observations) by using a more limited set of constructed dimensions that are effective substitutes for the variables (Tabachnick and Fidell, 2001). The only way to achieve this goal is to create composites of the many variables that retain much of the information contained in the original variables. For example, if one had 200 organizations measured on 100 variables addressing organizational characteristics, it would help in making sense of the organizations if one could reduce, without losing important information, the 100 variables to something like a dozen or fewer composite variables. Not only would such a reduced set of variables allow clearer informal comparisons across organizations, it also would improve many of the subsequent statistical analyses used to establish relationships between organizational characteristics and various outcome measures.

30.1.5.2 Quantitative Model

"Principal components analysis searches for a few uncorrelated linear combinations of the original variables that capture most of the information in the original variables" (Dunteman, 1989, p. 10). By "capturing the most information" we mean creating a new variable that accounts for the maximal amount of variance of the original variables. Principal components analysis attempts this task of reduction by calculating a linear combination of the original variables as indicated in Formula 1. This formula is presented to emphasize that the principal components (PCs) are viewed as linear combinations, with weights represented as $w_{(i)}$, of the original variables, Xp. The first principal component derived is, as indicated, the one that accounts for the greatest total variance for all variables being analyzed.

Once the first principal component is calculated in this way, the second principal component is calculated to maximize the remaining variance (that not accounted for by the first component) with the constraint that it be orthogonal to the first component. By "orthogonal" we mean statistically independent such that variation on one principal component is not related to variation on any other principal component (Tabachnick and Fidell, 2001). The correlation between orthogonal dimensions is, therefore, zero. This procedure of finding orthogonal dimensions could be continued to generate as many principal components as there are variables; doing so will provide a progressive accounting of the total variance contained in the variables. In interest of parsimony, however, far fewer principal components are typically used.

30.1.5.3 Graphic Representation

The logic and quantitative model described above can be given geometric form and thus displayed graphically. Figure 30.1 presents the simplest case in which there are two standardized variables—height and weight—and one principal component being used to account for the information of the two variables. Note that in this case the scatterplot is narrow and tightly delimited, indicating a high correlation between the two variables. As a result, it is possible to establish a dimension, the first principal component, which accounts for almost all of the information provided by the two variables. Therefore, knowing the position on the first principal component would allow effective prediction of values on both of the original variables. In this case, therefore, the two original variables of height and weight can be replaced by a single "size" factor with little loss of information.

In contrast, Figure 30.2 depicts two variables, "years of training" and "job satisfaction" that are only moderately correlated. As before, principal components analysis will generate a dimension that accounts for the most variance in the data, but this time the first principal component leaves considerable variation unexplained.

A third point to be made from looking at Figures 30.1 and 30.2 refers to the different balance of dimensions represented in the two figures. Whereas the principal component represented in Figure 30.1 is drawn to indicate an equal weighting of the height and weight variables (allowing for the scaling of the figure axes), the line drawn in Figure 30.2 is angled to be much closer to the axis representing "years of training." The reason for this is that the variables in Figure 30.1 are standardized and so have the same variance. In contrast, the variables represented in Figure 30.2 are not standardized—the greater variance of the "years of training" variable (assuming for the sake of illustration that measured job satisfaction varies little in this case) results in the principal component being weighted to account for this greater variance.

The differences in results due to standardizing the variables can be substantial, but there is no definitive answer to the question of whether or not it is better to standardize variables. In some cases you may want certain variables to carry stronger weight in accordance with their variance; other times it will seem preferable to allow the implicit weighting that results from standardization to replace the variance-based weighting. We will rely below on standardized variables, but the point is that each researcher must make this decision based on the situation being confronted by the analysis.

30.1.6 APPLICATION TO RESOURCE MOTHERS PROGRAM

We have presented the basic concepts of principal components analysis and have introduced its quantitative model. We can now use our example of the Resource Mothers Program to address

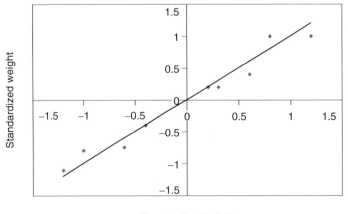

FIGURE 30.1 Principal components analysis with correlated variables.

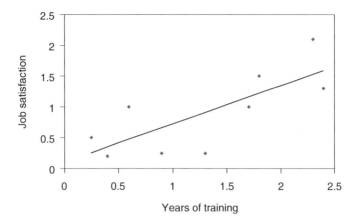

FIGURE 30.2 Principal components analysis with moderate correlation.

additional issues that need to be considered by users. The first issue to address involves choosing the number of principal component dimensions to be included in one's analysis; a second point concerns the possible interpretation of the derived dimensions; and a third issue is the use of the results of principal components analysis as new variables used in subsequent analyses.

The results reported below were produced by using the PRINCOMP procedure in SAS as presented in the left side of Table 30.3 (note, in batch mode it is essential to end commands with a semicolon). As indicated in the right side of Table 30.3, the commands direct the program to perform a principal components analysis that yields, at most, a two-component solution ($N = 2$) using the variables listed in the variable statement (VAR).

30.1.6.1 Determining the Number of Principal Components

Choosing the number of principal components to include in the analysis is not objective and represents a tension between parsimony and retention of the information contained in the original variables. The two examples graphed above make clear that only one principal component is needed in Figure 30.1 whereas two appear more adequate for the data in Figure 30.2. Many situations, however, are not that clear, and so more formal procedures have been developed as guides.

To understand these procedures we must first introduce the concept of the eigenvalue, also called the latent root or characteristic root. We mentioned above that principal components are selected to account for the maximal variance of all analyzed variables; the first component will account for the greatest amount of variance, with the second, third, and subsequent components accounting for progressively less variance. The amount of variance captured by a component is conveyed by its eigenvalue (a value defined in terms of matrix algebra and discussed in greater detail when discussing factor analysis), and, taken together, the eigenvalues for the components support several approaches to guide the decision of how many principal components should be retained for subsequent analyses.

TABLE 30.3

SAS Computer Commands for Principal Components Analysis

Computer Commands	Function of Commands
PROC PRINCOMP N = 2;	N = 2 specifies retaining two components
VAR (variables);	Specifies the variables to be analyzed

In cases where one is using unstandardized data such as raw responses, the number of principal components can be assessed by testing whether the eigenvalues for subsequent principal components are significantly different from each other. The logic of this analysis, based on Bartlett's approximate chi-square statistic, is that the eigenvalues for the meaningful components drop off progressively but then plateau for the subsequent less meaningful principal components (Tabachnick and Fidell, 2001). One difficulty with this test is that it typically results in retaining more principal components than researchers would want when pursuing the goal of parsimony. Further, as illustrated above in Figure 30.2, use of unstandardized variables results in a greater influence of the variables with the greatest variance, a property that means that those variables will be better represented by the derived principal components than will the variables with less variance. In that this influence on the outcomes is generally undesirable, we will focus more attention on determining the number of components when using standardized variables.

In considering standardized variables, recall that the variance of these variables typically is set to equal 1.0. As such, principal components with eigenvalues greater than 1.0 are accounting for more variance than any of the original variables. With this in mind, Kaiser (1958) advocated retaining only those principal components with eigenvalues greater than 1.0. The logic of this procedure being that principal components with eigenvalues less than 1.0 are not contributing to the goal of parsimony. Applying this logic to the analysis of the Resource Mothers Program, we see in Table 30.4 that three principal components have eigenvalues greater than 1.0.

As an alternative to strict quantitative determination, Cattell (1966) developed the scree test to identify qualitative changes in the ability of principal components to account for variance. The name of the scree test comes from the shape of a cliff or mountainside. At the base of a steep cliff is likely to be considerable rubble of fallen stones, a rubble referred to as scree. This accumulated rubble will slope downward away from the cliff but at a different slope than the cliff itself. Using this analogy, the slope of the meaningful principal components as measured by change in eigenvalues can be differentiated from the slope of the noise factors that might otherwise be retained as principal components. The intent is to be guided by the changes in the eigenvalues rather than their actual values. Figure 30.3 illustrates this logic by showing that the slope between the first and second components is steep compared to the slopes between subsequent components. Indeed, the slopes are so similar from the second to the fifth principal components that they can be said to define a straight line. This would suggest that the second component and those higher represent the scree at the base of the real structure.

Unfortunately, the scree test often is an ambiguous guide for several reasons. First, Cattell himself had mixed thoughts on the proper interpretation. In the context of factor analysis, "Cattell originally suggested taking the first factor on the straight line as the number of factors to be sure that sufficient factors were extracted; he has since (Cattell and Jaspers, 1967) suggested that the number

TABLE 30.4
Eigenvalues and Variance Accounted for by Principal Components

Principal Component	Eigenvalues	Proportion of Variance	Cumulative Variance
1	2.148	0.358	0.358
2	1.336	0.223	0.581
3	1.021	0.170	0.751
4	0.744	0.124	0.875
5	0.465	0.077	0.952
6	0.286	0.048	1.000

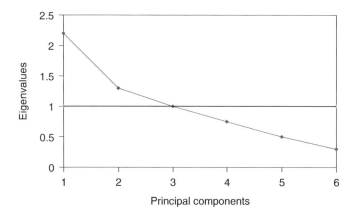

FIGURE 30.3 Scree test for determining number of components retained.

of factors be taken as the number immediately before the straight line begins" (Gorsuch, 1983, p. 167). In the present case, the first component on the straight line would be the second component, the one immediately before the straight line would be the first principal component. The logic of Cattell's revised interpretation is the desire to maximize the ratio of variance accounted for over the number of components.

A second source of ambiguity for the scree test is the lack of objective standards in what constitutes a break in the straight line of the scree. As a result, small changes in eigenvalues for the principal components (e.g., the eigenvalue for the second principal component being only slightly higher) could change perceptions of where the straight line in Figure 30.3 had begun. Cattell and Vogelmann (1977) provide greater elaboration for those wishing to use the scree test in accordance with Cattell's intended logic.

Concerns about the scree test, however, go beyond the issue of ambiguity. In particular, as reasonable as the scree test appears as a guide to avoid interpretation of trivial principal components, it does not necessarily serve the needs of particular research situations. Hatcher (1994) describes two other criteria for determining the number of principal components to retain in the analysis. Returning to quantitative assessment, one option is to focus directly on the proportion of the variance accounted for by the principal components, either individually, in which one might choose to retain any component that accounts for at least 10 percent of the variance of the variables, or cumulatively, in which one might retain enough principal components to account for at least 70 percent, or perhaps 80 percent, of the variance of the variables. In the present example, these criteria would argue for retaining three or four principal components (refer back to Table 30.4). As such, it may be that a two-dimensional solution does not account adequately for one or more of the variables and so a three-dimensional or higher solution might be preferred.

The second option proposed by Hatcher (1994), a more qualitative one, is to determine the number of principal components to retain by using the criterion of interpretability. Analyses with a given number of principal components might yield results that are particularly consistent with the results reported by previous scholars. For the sake of illustration and for comparison with factor analysis, we will present our results in terms of a two-dimensional solution to the principal components analysis. This decision to retain two principal components is seen in the $N = 2$ option included in the PROC PRINCOMP statement provided in Table 30.3.

30.1.6.2 Component Interpretation

Having reduced the six variables to two principal components, it is natural to attempt interpretation of these dimensions. In approaching this task, the variables with the strongest relationships with the

TABLE 30.5
Correlations between Variables and Components

	First Principal Component	Second Prinicipal Component	Variable Variance Accounted for (Percent)
Months of care	0.32	0.52	37
Prenatal visits	0.28	0.68	53
Weight gain	0.14	0.27	9
Age of mother	0.58	−0.26	40
Mother's education	0.53	−0.31	38
Marital status	0.43	−0.18	22
Component explained	1.00	1.00	

principal components are important in defining a principal component. Table 30.5 presents the correlations between the six variables and the two principal components. By looking at each variable row, we can identify the highest correlations (in absolute terms) for each variable. For example, Months of Care is more closely related to the second principal component ($r = 0.52$) than to the first ($r = 0.32$), although Age of Mother is more closely related to the first principal component ($r = 0.58$) than to the second ($r = −0.26$).

Repeating this examination for each variable, we pay particular attention to those coefficients that are large. No set definition exists for what constitutes "large," but many researchers require interpretable loadings to have correlation coefficients of at least 0.35 or 0.40 (absolute value). Thus, we can see that the "large" correlations for the first principal component are 0.58 for Age of Mother, 0.53 for Mother's Education, and 0.43 for Marital Status. In that each of these three variables increases with age, this component is concerned with the personal maturation that is associated with increasing age. The second principal component has its highest correlations with the number of Prenatal Visits (0.68) and Months of Medical Care (0.52), suggesting a dimension of health activities. Note that the variable measuring the weight gained during pregnancy loads highest on the health activity component but does not have a large loading on either of the two principal components. As a result, the variance of Weight Gain accounted for by the two factors is low, only 9 percent (as will be pointed out below, this lack of fit for Weight Gained and, to a lesser extent, Marital Status will help differentiate principal components analysis from factor analysis).

Finally, at the bottom of Table 30.5 there is a row labeled "component explained." This row is not provided when principal components are reported but is presented here to highlight the logic of principal components analysis: if you square each of the six correlations reported for each component and sum them, you get 1.0. This is another way of saying that all of the variance of the principal components is accounted for by the six variables, something that we know by definition in that a principal component is nothing other than a linear combination of the variables being analyzed.

If one wishes to confirm the interpretations suggested by the high loadings, one can explore the relationships between these derived principal components and other variables not used in the original analysis. To the extent that these subsequent analyses produce results consistent with the interpretations given to the principal components, these interpretations are supported. It should be noted, however, that if the goal of analysis is simply parsimony, interpretation of the derived dimensions may not be as important for principal component analysis as we will see it to be for factor analysis.

30.1.6.3 Use of Component Scores

Once the computer has solved for the weights for Formula 1, we can use that formula to calculate the appropriate scores for each observation on the principal components. Doing so allows us to use the derived principal components to predict the birthweights of the babies born to the teen mothers. It turns out that the two principal components as independent variables account for only half of the variation in birthweight that is accounted for by the six original variables, but, because of the fewer explanatory variables in the analysis, the value of the F-test statistic for the overall regression model is higher. Of particular note, the use of the two orthogonal principal components as predictors clarifies the greater impact of the health activity dimension on birthweight than was found for the personal maturation dimension, something that the multicollinearity (the high level of multiple correlation among the explanatory variables) of the original variables obscured when they were used as independent variables.

30.1.7 SUMMARY ASSESSMENT OF PRINCIPAL COMPONENTS ANALYSIS

We have presented the conceptual foundations of principal components analysis and demonstrated its use with data from the Resource Mothers Project. We now need to offer a summary assessment of its key features. First, using the choices in organizing phenomena that were presented at the beginning of this chapter, principal components analysis is traditionally used to identify dimensions that capture the information contained in variables. That is, the focus is on organizing information about attributes (the variables), measured across objects (such as people), into new continuous dimensions. Although such dimensions might refer to the underlying structures posited by realism, principal components analysis makes no such requirement.

30.1.7.1 Strengths

The strengths of principal components analysis follow from the simplicity of the way that it seeks parsimony. By definition, the derived principal components account for a maximal amount of variance in the variables measured using orthogonal dimensions. As mentioned above, the emphasis on accounting for maximal variance is important when attempting to reduce many explanatory variables to a few explanatory factors. This reduction helps avoid the problem of capitalizing on chance associations when using many explanatory variables. A related virtue of simplicity is that principal components analysis does not require the data to have a particular distribution.

The fact that the technique produces orthogonal principal components is valuable in avoiding multicollinearity in subsequent analyses. This strategy for reducing variables and thus minimizing multicollinearity is particularly useful when your explanatory model includes interaction terms based on multiplying the explanatory variables together. An example of this might be when we are interested in how the impact of health activities varies across different client characteristics, such as client age; the interaction variables are almost certainly related to the variables that were multiplied to create them. Principal components analysis does not result in the interaction terms being orthogonal to the principal components, but if the original variables are highly correlated themselves, the problem of multicollinearity with interactions becomes substantially worse.

This use of principal components analysis to generate weighted composite variables for use in subsequent analyses highlights an additional strength of the approach. In contrast to factor analysis as described below, principal components analysis provides an objective rationale for calculating scores based on the original variables. The dimensions that account for the most variance are derived and the weights for the variables appropriate to support these dimensions are used to calculate the scores for each observation.

30.1.7.2 Concerns

The source of the strength of principal components analysis is also the cause for concern in its use. Principal components analysis provides a vehicle for accounting for the total variance of a set of variables. Part of its simplicity is that it takes the variance as it is defined by the inputted data, without performing any transformation of the variance. As such, one concern with principal components analysis is that it is not invariant with regard to scaling decisions involved in measuring the variables to be analyzed. The greater the variance of one variable relative to the others, the more influence it will have on the direction of the principal component. Thus, when using unstandardized data, one could use scaling decisions to influence the results of the analysis.

A second, and more serious, implication of this focus on total variance is that the method does not differentiate between meaningful variance and variance that may be the result of measurement error. This lack of differentiation is appropriate for the goal of principal components analysis but represents a limitation if one wishes the derived principal components to correspond to real phenomena. As we will see when discussing factor analysis, it is the covariance, rather than the variance, that is of interest when we believe that there are underlying factors that are responsible for the patterns observed in the measured variables.

30.2 FACTOR ANALYSIS

Factor analysis, sometimes more precisely referred to as common factor analysis, or as exploratory factor analysis to contrast it from confirmatory factor analysis, was developed by Spearman (1904) in the context of investigating general and specific intellectual abilities and later elaborated by Thurstone (1935). As such, factor analysis emerged at about the same time as principal components analysis and shares with it many features. Nonetheless, factor analysis differs from principal components analysis in fundamental ways that need to be appreciated by those who use either technique. Numerous books address factor analysis, both in terms of the mathematical foundations (e.g., Morrison, 1990) and in terms of an appreciation of the logic underlying this method (see Gorsuch, 1983; Kim and Mueller, 1978a; Thompson, 2004). We develop this appreciation by examining the conceptual foundations of the technique and then by exploring a hypothetical two-factor model. Once these conceptual issues are established, we develop the concepts of factor analysis further by applying them to the study of the Resource Mothers Program.

30.2.1 CONCEPTUAL FOUNDATION: UNDERLYING FACTORS

The primary difference between factor analysis and principal components analysis concerns the meaning of the dimensions, whereas the goal of principal components analysis is parsimony; factor analysis is concerned in addition with what is referred to as underlying structure (Rummel, 1970). "Factor analysis is based on the fundamental assumption that some underlying factors, which are smaller in number than the number of observed variables, are responsible for the covariation among the observed variables" (Kim and Mueller, 1978a, 12). This emphasis on underlying factors follows from a basic philosophical belief that there are real qualities in the world, such as self-esteem (Shevlin, Bunting, and Lewis, 1995), group cohesion (Cota, Evans, Longmen, Dion, and Kilik, 1995), aggression (Harris, 1995), personality (Digman and Takemoto-Chock, 1981), and life satisfaction (Shevlin and Bunting, 1994).

The need for factor analysis comes from the belief that these qualities are not directly measurable but can be revealed through the covariation of related variables. This focus on identifying underlying factors, or constructs, has been used in public administration to study the degree to which public officials *trust* citizens (Yang, 2005), to understand what we mean by *red tape* as an obstructing factor in bureaucracies (Pandey and Scott, 2002), and to distinguish different aspects of previously undifferentiated constructs, as when distinguishing capacity for innovation into human capacity and financial capacity (Hall, 2006) or distinguishing support for regional councils by local officials into political support and fiscal support (Julnes, Atkins, and Pindur, 2002). For more background on the use of factor analysis in revealing underlying constructs, see Thompson and Daniel (1996). In this section we use a simplified model of leadership ability to examine the implications of this focus on underlying factors for the conduct and interpretation of factor analysis.

30.2.1.1 Basic Logic: Factor Identification

Beginning with the observation that some people are better than others at leading organizations, we can accept for illustration the otherwise controversial notion that there is something that we can call "leadership ability." Given our common sense notion of leadership, we might hypothesize that the greater one's leadership ability, the more effective that one might be in improving the quality of services provided by one's subordinates. We recognize, however, that the quality of workgroup performance is the result of many factors, only a subset of which involves the leadership abilities of those in positions of responsibility. As such, we might use a variety of other measures to assess an individual's leadership ability.

Figure 30.4 illustrates the posited leadership ability manifesting itself in three measurement modalities: (1) ratings by subordinates, (2) performance of natural workgroups, and (3) performance in an assessment center that focuses on leadership tasks. The logic of factor analysis is this: If these measures truly reflect an underlying leadership ability, then individuals with high leadership ability should tend to have high scores on each of these measures. Similarly, those with low leadership ability should tend to have low scores on all of the measures. In other words, if the scores on these measures are caused in part by an underlying common factor, the scores will covary, meaning that they will vary together across individuals. This arrangement is depicted in Figure 30.4; each of these measures of leadership is influenced to some extent by "unique factors" that are essentially unrelated to leadership (e.g., leadership ratings by subordinates may be affected also by work conditions and even by salaries) and unrelated to each other (there are no arrows between the unique factors), but each is also a function of the common leadership factor.

Because factor analysis is intended to reveal underlying factors, the technique can be contrasted with principal components analysis in terms of the variation of interest. Whereas principal components analysis lumps all variation in the variables into one category, factor analysis "assumes that data on a variable consists of common and unique parts.... The object of common factor analysis is to define the dimensions of this common vector space" (Rummel, 1970, p. 104). This means that factor analysis begins by determining the extent to which the variables being examined covary with each other. Only the covariance of the variables is used to determine the underlying dimensions; all other variation among the variables is partitioned out as unique variance. Although not illustrated in Figure 30.4, the unique variance can itself be partitioned into two components, the specific factors (unique underlying factors) and random error.

The concern for factor analysis, therefore, is to find successive factors that account for the covariance of the variables being considered. Parallel to principal components analysis of variance, factor analysis begins by identifying the factor that accounts the greatest amount of covariance and

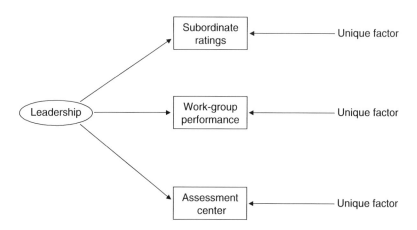

FIGURE 30.4 Measures of underlying leadership factor.

continues by finding additional factors that account for the greatest remaining covariance although subject to the constraint of being orthogonal to the factors already identified. We recall from above that "orthogonal" means that the dimensions are unrelated such that the correlation between any two is zero. If one generates as many factors as there are variables, all of the covariance of the variables will be accounted for by the factors. Typically, however, as with principal components analysis, the number of factors solved for and retained is small relative to the number of variables.

30.2.1.2   Quantitative Model

We stated above that the goal of factor analysis is, in addition to achieving parsimony, to reveal the underlying factors that produced the patterns observed among the variables. Differentiating between common and unique factors, factor analysis, therefore, seeks a solution to Formula 2, wherein the observed variable, X_j, is a function of both common factors, $CF_{(i)}$, and unique influences, e_j. Formula 3 provides the same information using the symbols of matrix algebra.

Notice the difference between Formula 2 and Formula 1; this difference captures much of the contrast between the two techniques. Whereas Formula 1 presented the principal components as functions of the measured variables, Formula 2 highlights the manner in which the observed variables are conceived as functions of underlying factors. Thus, principal components analysis creates a scale based on observed variables; factor analysis estimates factors responsible for observed variables.

The weights in Formula 2 ($v_{j(i)}$) and Formula 3 (Λ) are referred to as factor loadings. Those familiar with multiple regression analysis will recognize the form of these two formulas, and, indeed, it is the case that the factor loadings in Formulas 2 and 3 correspond to regression coefficients. "If all the variables (both hypothetical and observed) are standardized to have unit variance, the linear weights are known as *standardized regression coefficients* (in regression analysis), path coefficients (in causal analysis), or factor loadings (in factor analysis)" (Kim and Mueller, 1978a, p. 21; emphasis in original).

30.2.1.3   Graphic Representation

As with regression coefficients in traditional multiple regression, factor loadings represent the influence of the common factors on the variables. When the factors are orthogonal (as they are in at least the preliminary stages of factor analysis and principal components analysis), they are independent and the factor loadings are equivalent also to the correlations between the variables and the hypothesized common factors. As correlation coefficients, the factor loadings can be squared to equal r^2 (single variable version of R^2) and thus represent the variance of the observed variable that is accounted for by the hypothesized factor. We can illustrate these relationships by assigning values to the paths depicted in Figure 30.4.

Using the loadings provided in Figure 30.5, we can conclude that the ratings by subordinates, the top measure in the figure, have 25 percent (0.50 squared being equal to 0.25) of its variance explained by the common leadership factor and the remaining 75 percent (0.87 squared equaling 0.75) explained by unique factors. In contrast, the variable for work-group performance, the middle variable in Figure 30.5, is shown to have 64 percent (0.80 squared) of its variance accounted for by the leadership factor with the remaining 36 percent (0.60 squared) of the variance left to be explained by unique factors. Performance in an assessment center is presented as intermediate between the other two measures in terms of explanation by the common factor, with an equal percent of its variance accounted for by the leadership factor as by unique factors (50 percent for each, as 0.71 times 0.71 is approximately 50 percent).

30.2.1.4   Extension to Multiple Factors

Extending this analysis to two underlying factors, we can now develop the concepts of factor analysis in the context of a hypothetical two-factor leadership model. In this model we go beyond

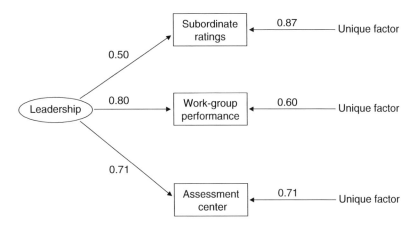

FIGURE 30.5 Correlations between leadership factor and measures.

the view that leadership is a unidimensional capacity and instead elaborate our factor analysis model by using the results of some of the early research on leadership (see Stogdill, 1974) that identified two distinct leadership abilities: (1) task orientation (referred to by Stogdill as "initiating structure") and (2) people orientation (or "consideration"). Figure 30.6 presents this elaborated model, with the three leadership measures conceived now as functions of two common factors. The numbers on the arrows from the two common and the three unique factors are factor loadings and so, as before, when squared they represent the degree to which each of the measures is determined by the underlying factors. We see that the task orientation factor has its greatest influence on the results of the assessment center exercise ($r = 0.80$) and least on the ratings by subordinates ($r = 0.10$). The people orientation factor, on the other hand, has its greatest influence ($r = 0.70$) on the ratings by subordinates and least influence ($r = 0.20$) on assessment center performance (these relationships are for illustration only; research on these two leadership factors has provided little evidence that they influence outcomes in any consistent manner).

The factor loadings displayed in Figure 30.6 can be presented as the factor pattern matrix presented in Table 30.6. In addition to summarizing the relationships between factors and variables that were displayed in Figure 30.6, Table 30.6 has a column labeled "communality" and a row that

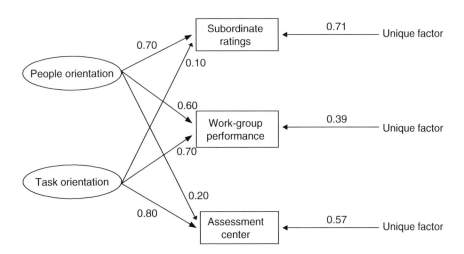

FIGURE 30.6 Two-factor model of leadership.

TABLE 30.6
Factor Pattern for Two-Factor Solution

	Task Orientation	People Orientation	Communality
Assessment center	0.80	0.20	0.68
Workgroup performance	0.70	0.60	0.85
Subordinate ratings	0.10	0.70	0.50
Eigenvalues	1.14	0.89	

refers to "eigenvalues." Communality is defined as the proportion of the variance of a variable that is accounted for by the identified common factors (Gorsuch, 1983, p. 29). An extension of the single-factor calculations described above, the communality measure is calculated by squaring and summing the factor loadings for a particular variable, with the result ranging from 0.0, meaning that the factors explain none of the variance of a variable, to 1.0, which indicates that all of the variance of a variable is in common with the other variables and is accounted for completely by the derived factors (Dillon and Goldstein, 1984, p. 67). In this example with two orthogonal factors, we see that 68 percent of the variance in assessment center performance, 85 percent of the variance of the performance of natural workgroups, and 50 percent of the variance in ratings by subordinates are accounted for by two leadership factors.

Whereas communality refers to the variance of a particular variable explained by all common factors, eigenvalues, introduced above under principal components analysis, represent the complementary concept of the total standardized variance of all variables that is accounted for by a particular factor. As with communalities, eigenvalues can be calculated by squaring the factor loadings, but for this purpose the squared loadings are summed for each factor. The standardized variance of a variable is 1.0, and so, in this example, with three standardized variables, the total variance to be explained is 3.0. Table 30.6 indicates that the first factor, task orientation, accounts for 1.14 of the 3.0 total, or 38 percent of variance of the three variables; the second factor accounts for 0.89 of the 3.0 total, or 27.7 percent of the variance.

In summary, we have presented the logic of factor analysis and have discussed the quantitative model, stressing the similarity between factor loadings and the regression coefficients and correlation coefficients that many in public administration are familiar with through their use of multiple regression analysis and correlation analysis. There are, however, additional concepts that need to be addressed in applying factor analysis to the example of the Resource Mothers Program. We will see that one important concept to be discussed is factor rotation. The issue of rotation arises because, unlike the independent variables in regression analysis, the predictor variables in Formula 2 are hypothetical common factors which must be estimated as well as the regression coefficients. This need to estimate the common factors will mean that the factors derived by the analysis will not be uniquely suitable, that there will be an inevitable indeterminancy as to the nature of the underlying structure. One consequence of this need for estimation is that the factor scores, values for the factors that are parallel to the composite variables produced by principal components analysis, are likely to have nonzero correlations despite the true factors being orthogonal.

30.2.2 APPLICATION TO RESOURCE MOTHERS PROGRAM

The above sections presented the basic concepts of factor analysis, many of which require users to make a variety of choices when applying the technique to their data. This section will address some of these choices and their implications in the context of the Resource Mothers Program. The analyses reported below were conducted using the FACTOR procedure in the SAS statistical package; the actual commands used are displayed in the left side of Table 30.7. Following the

TABLE 30.7

SAS Computer Commands for Factor Analysis

Computer Commands	Function of Commands
PROC FACTOR M = PRIN PRIORS = SMC R = PROMAX N = 2;	M = principal components method; setting PRIORS to SMC means that the squared multiple correlations will be used to estimate the communalities of the variables; F = PROMAX specifies a particular oblique rotation; N = 2 specifies the maximum number of factors
VAR (variables);	Specifies the variables to be analyzed

PROC FACTOR command we see listed M = PRIN. The M refers to "method" and indicates that we will be using what will be described as the principal components method for deriving factors. An alternative is to specify M = ML, which directs the computer to use the maximum likelihood solution for deriving the factors. After the Method option is the command that controls how we are estimating the communalities that will be used to produce the reduced correlation matrix used in factor analysis. By specifying PRIORS = SMC, we are guiding the analysis by estimating the communalities based on the squared multiple correlation of the variables, defined and calculated as the proportion of variance of each variable that can be accounted for by the variance of all other variables. On the following line (moving to the next line is of no consequence in SAS), the command R = PROMAX refers to a variation of what are described below as rotations that are performed on the original results to support more meaningful interpretations. And, finally, N = 2 specifies the maximum number of factors to be retained.

30.2.2.1 Determining the Number of Factors

We will see that there are a variety of available quantitative solutions that can be used to derive underlying factors. Before considering these options, however, we will first address the question of the number of factors to be retained in our analysis. Many of the relevant issues were introduced above when considering this question for principal components analysis and so will be mentioned only briefly here. For example, as with principal components analysis, we can use scree tests to decide on the number of factors. In an attempt to improve on the scree test as presented above, Zoski and Jurs (1996) discuss the use of standard errors to provide a more objective scree test. Also noted under principal components analysis, one can decide on the appropriate number of factors through use of criteria such as the proportion of variance of the variables that are accounted by the total set of factors and the proportion of variance accounted for by each additional factor.

Some aspects of factor analysis, however, require a different understanding from what applied for principal components analysis when choosing the number of dimensions to retain. First, because factor analysis attempts to address only the common variance of the variables, there is less variation to be accounted for by the factors and so fewer factors may be required. Second, because factor analysis is explicitly concerned with identifying underlying structure, it is even more important than with principal components analysis that the number of factors to be retained be decided in the context of the relationships between the derived factors and the constructs that are supported by previous experience. The factor pattern that results should have high loadings on factors from variables that are expected to covary. Third, because factor analysis attempts to partition covariance into distinct groups of reliable variation and error variation, it is important that the number of factors retained be such that we can reduce the error variation included in the interpreted factors. The point of this last concern is to minimize the bias in the factors that result from analysis.

Because of these reasons, we have to be particularly concerned with the relative dangers of overinclusion (retaining too many factors) and underinclusion (too few factors). Recall from above when this issue was addressed for principal components analysis that Cattell's use of the scree test had evolved to signify fewer factors than when he began using the test. Nonetheless, "Thurstone (1947) and Cattell (1978) held that overextraction [too many factors] produces less distortion in factor analytic solutions than underextraction and is therefore to be preferred" (Wood, Tataryn, and Gorsuch, 1996, p. 154).

Based on their study of principal axis factor analysis and varimax rotation, Wood et al. (1996) conclude, "When underextraction occurs [too few factors retained], the estimated factors are likely to contain considerable error.... When overextraction occurs, the estimated loadings for true (i.e., 'core') factors generally contain less error than in the case of underextraction" (p. 359). The implications of their study are that, first, it is important to retain the correct number of factors but that, second, retaining too many factors produces less bias than too few. If one wants to reduce the bias in the core factors (the first several or so that seem strongly supported by high loadings for related variables), one might choose to extract additional factors, recognizing that the additional factors may be false factors that are not to be interpreted. Thus, there may be circumstances in which the users of factor analysis may direct the computer to retain more factors than they intend to use in their subsequent analyses and interpretation.

30.2.2.2　Solutions

There are numerous ways to estimate factors in an attempt to fulfill the basic goal of identifying underlying structure. For more information on the options for deriving the initial estimates for factor analysis, see Buley (1995). In brief, early applications used heuristic strategies to develop estimates of the factors (Gorsuch, 1983). More recently the availability of computers has resulted in the use of iterative solutions in which initial estimates allow calculations that result in more refined estimates and, hence, further calculations. We will begin by considering the basic principal factor method and then the maximum likelihood method, one that makes particular use of iterative estimation.

30.2.2.2.1　Principal Factor Method

Though different in concept, this method is identical in calculations to the factor extraction method described above for principal components analysis. One begins by calculating a correlation matrix for the variables to be factor analyzed. This matrix is modified, however, by replacing the diagonal entries (1.0 for the correlation of each variable with itself) with the estimated communalities of the variables. These communalities are estimated in our analysis by squaring the multiple correlation of each variable with all other variables (indicated by the PRIORS = SMC statement in Table 30.7). This replacement effects the change from an analysis of variance—appropriate for principal components analysis—to an analysis of covariance. This new matrix, with estimated communalities along the diagonal, is referred to as a reduced correlation matrix. Factor analysis then operates on this reduced matrix to reveal its dimensions.

Had we not specified PRIORS = SMC, the SAS program would have, as its default option, used PRIORS = ONE. This default option would have left the 1's along the diagonal of the matrix being analyzed. By putting 1's along the diagonal of the matrix, we are returned to the original, unreduced, correlation matrix and would, therefore, be performing principal components analysis. Thus, we see that we could also perform principal components analysis using the FACTOR procedure in SAS, with METHOD set to be PRINCIPAL and PRIORS set to ONE. This is important to emphasize in that some users might believe that they are performing factor analysis (i.e., common factor analysis) when using the PROC FACTOR program in SAS but, in not changing the default setting of 1.0 for prior communality estimates, are really conducting principal components analysis.

Having raised this concern about possible misuse of principal components analysis as factor analysis, let us also recognize that often it may not matter. That is, if the reduced correlation matrix (with communality estimates along the diagonal) is similar to the original correlation matrix,

TABLE 30.8
Factor Pattern for Principal Components Method

	First Factor	Second Factor	Communality (Percent)
Months of care	0.34	0.45	31
Prenatal visits	0.28	0.56	39
Weight gain	0.13	0.16	4
Age of Mother	0.80	−0.18	66
Mother's education	0.71	−0.22	55
Marital status	0.48	−0.06	23
Eigenvalues	1.57	0.62	

then principal components analysis and factor analysis will yield similar results. One of the ways in which the two matrices will be similar is if the communality estimates of the reduced matrix are all close to 1.0 (in practical terms, if the communalities are all above 0.70). This is why our Resource Mothers Program example deliberately includes two variables with somewhat low communalities; only by including these lower communalities do we have the opportunity to notice some differences between principal components analysis and the principal factor method of factor analysis. The other way in which the reduced and original correlation matrices become similar is if the number of variables is large. If there are, say, 20 variables being analyzed, the 20 entries along the diagonal are only a small part of the correlation matrix (190 other cells in the resulting half matrix), and so the reduced and original matrices, alike in every nondiagonal entry, become essentially the same.

Table 30.8 presents the results of the principal factor method when applied to the data from the Resource Mothers Project. The numbers in the table are factor loadings and so represent the correlations between the variables and the derived factors. As with principal components analysis, these numbers can be used to interpret the meaning of the derived factors. The first three variables have their highest loadings on the second factor, the last three variables load highest on the first factor. From this pattern of loadings we see that each factor is defined primarily by two variables. The largest loadings on Factor 1 are for Age of Mother (0.80) and Mother's Education (0.71). Factor 2 has the highest correlations (absolute value) with the number of Prenatal Visits (0.56) and with the Months of Care (0.49).

We also note in Table 30.8 that the communalities are fairly low. The highest communalities are only 66 percent of the variance of Age of Mother and 55 percent of Mother's Education being accounted for by the two factors. The lowest communalities are 23 percent of Marital Status and only 4 percent of Weight Gain explained in this way. Further, we see from the eigenvalues that although the first factor explains a sufficient amount of variance (1.57 out of a possible 6.0), the second factor explains comparatively little (0.62).

In addition to placing the results in a table, it is possible to depict them graphically, as is done in Figure 30.7. In this figure, the correlations between each of the variables and the two common factors (presented in Table 30.8) are plotted, with positive correlations being placed above and in front of the axes defined by the two factors, negative correlations being below and behind the axes.

Comparing the factor loadings to the results of the principal components analysis, the most immediate impression is of the similarity of the results—in both approaches the rank ordering of variables in terms of their correlations with the derived dimensions is the same. Looking closer, we can see some meaningful differences in the two sets of results. For example, Factor 1 has higher correlations with its primary variables (age of mother, mother's education, and marital status) than does the first principal component. In contrast, Factor 2 is less distinguished in its associations than the second principal component, with lower positive correlations with its primary variables (number of prenatal visits and months of care) and less negative correlations (closer to zero) with the

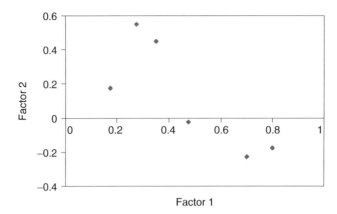

FIGURE 30.7 Factor analysis with principal components method.

other three variables. These differences aside, the relative sizes of the loading on the factors are remarkably consistent; even with few variables and some relatively low communalities, principal components analysis and factor analysis would in this example lead to the same substantive conclusions.

30.2.2.2.2 Maximum Likelihood Solution
A more recent approach to estimating factors uses maximum likelihood analysis to solve for the factors. Although this approach is more demanding of computer resources, it is also more consistent with the intended logic of factor analysis. "What values for the population parameters make the sample observations have the greatest joint likelihood? When we answer this question, we will take such values to be *maximum likelihood estimators* of the population parameters" (Mulaik, 1972, cited by Dillon and Goldstein, 1984, pp. 80–81).

As indicated in the above quote, the maximum likelihood approach offers an appealing strategy for estimating the factors that produced the observed data. This approach, however, does make additional data requirements over the earlier principal components solution. For a more adequate explanation of these added assumptions, the reader is referred to Dillon and Goldstein (1984) or Morrison (1990). We mention here, however, two areas of potential concern if using the maximum likelihood approach. First, the maximum likelihood solution requires that the variables being analyzed are not linearly dependent on each other (i.e., the matrix is nonsingular). Second, the distribution of the variables is presumed to be multivariate normal, an assumption that is violated in the typical case of responses on survey scales. These assumptions can restrict the use of the maximum likelihood solution, but Fuller and Hemmerle (1966) found that most violations of the normal distribution assumption do not distort the results beyond usefulness, at least not when working with large sample sizes ($n = 200$ in their study).

Applying the maximum likelihood solution to the data from the Resource Mothers Project yields first an assessment of the number of factors needed for an adequate solution and then an interpretation of the derived factors. Table 30.9 presents the series of hypothesis tests (these tests presume multinormal distributions and are likely more sensitive to violations of this assumption than are the factor loading results mentioned in the previous paragraph; see Gorsuch, 1983, p. 148), based on the chi-squared distribution, that is provided by the maximum likelihood solution. Interpreting Table 30.9, note that the first null hypothesis, that there are no common factors underlying the three measures, would be rejected based on the relatively large chi-square value and associated low probability ($p < .0001$). Similarly, the second null hypothesis contends that no more than one common factor is needed, and, due to the large chi-square score, is also rejected ($p < .0001$). In contrast, the third null hypothesis, that no more than two common factors are

TABLE 30.9

Chi-Squared Tests for Number of Factors Using Maximum Likelihood Method

Null Hypothesis	Chi-Squared	Probability	Decision
No common factors	375.33	.0001	Reject null
One factor sufficient	60.68	.0001	Reject null
Two factors sufficient	7.05	.133	Fail to reject

required, cannot be rejected at traditional levels of significance ($p = .133$), suggesting, therefore, that two factors may be adequate.

This statistical evidence of the appropriateness of a two-factor solution is consistent with our expectations, but we reiterate that this use of the chi-squared test is recognized as often suggesting more factors than researchers are willing to accept. Although as argued above, overinclusion is to be preferred to underinclusion, this tendency towards overinclusion of factors leads authors such as Kim and Mueller (1978a) to emphasize the importance of the substantive significance of the factors over and above their statistical significance.

As to the interpretation of the two factors, we see in Table 30.10 that the rank ordering of the largest correlations again remains consistent with the previous two analyses of these six variables. To the extent that there are meaningful differences in the results for the maximum likelihood solution and the principal components solution, it is that the maximum likelihood solution is inclined to orient the results to emphasize individual variables. This consistency across methods is reassuring for both the reliability and validity of the approach, particularly as the nature of this example works against this consistency. First, as noted earlier, our example has two variables with relatively low communalities. The results of the maximum likelihood method converge with the results of principal factor method as all of the communalities approach 1.0 (Gorsuch, 1983, p. 121). Second, we have used only six variables. *"As the number of variables increase, communality estimates and the method by which exploratory factors are extracted both become less important"* (Gorsuch, 1983, p. 123; emphasis in original).

30.2.2.3 Factor Rotation

We have described the goal of factor analysis in terms of identifying underlying structure. The methodology of factor analysis presumes that this identification is most effective when the results are relatively easy to interpret. However, several features of the original factor solution work against meaningful interpretation. In particular, because the various solutions begin with the best-fitting

TABLE 30.10

Factor Pattern for Maximum Likelihood Method

	First Factor	Second Factor	Communality (Percent)
Months of care	0.17	0.45	23
Prenatal visits	0.00	1.00	100
Weight gain	0.09	0.22	6
Age of Mother	0.99	0.10	100
Mother's education	0.69	0.05	48
Marital status	0.43	0.14	21
Eigenvalues	1.69	1.28	

factor and continue by identifying progressively less adequate factors, the first factor tends to be a general one with relatively strong relationships with all of the variables. The remaining factors tend to have complicated and potentially confusing relationships with many of the variables. We attempt to counter this potential confusion and achieve the desired interpretable factors by what is called factor rotation.

To understand the logic of rotation, remember that the particular dimensions that result from factor analysis are not uniquely capable of representing the interdependence of the variables analyzed. Rather, the derived factors provide a grid to aid interpretation in much the same way as geographic lines of longitude and latitude provide a grid for representing geographical relationships. Whereas we have conventions for the fixed directions of north, south, east, and west, we might find it more meaningful to rotate the grid placed on a specific geographic area so that the horizontal and vertical dimensions highlighted significant variation (e.g., elevation above sea level or political ideology of residents) that we wished to interpret. Similarly, we rotate the grid for the factors so that the results might be more meaningful and more easily interpretable.

One way in which results are easy to interpret is when they suggest factors that are consistent with our prior expectations. Results are also interpretable if groups of variables cluster together around distinct factors, an outcome referred to as "simple structure." With this simple structure as a goal, rotation is judged successful when

1. Each variable is identified with one or a small proportion of the factors....
2. The number of variables correlated with (loaded on) a factor is minimized....
3. The variance accounted for by the major unrotated factors is spread across all the rotated factors....
4. Each rotated factor is now more or less identified with a distinct cluster of interrelated variances. (Rummel, 1970, pp. 380–381)

The basic idea of simple structure is described in this quote by Rummel as requiring each factor to have its own small set of variables with significant loadings on it. "Significant" in this context refers not necessarily to statistical significance but to loadings that are moderately large. Recognizing that factor analysis, with its goal of accounting only for common variance, is expected to account for less total variance than principal components analysis, as a rule of thumb one can think of loadings of 0.30 or larger as being significant in factor analysis (Dillon and Goldstein, 1984, p. 69).

Researchers have accepted that the primary goal of rotations is to achieve simple structure. "Unfortunately, the concept of simplicity itself is not so straightforward as to allow for a formal and undisputed criterion" (Kim and Mueller, 1978b, p. 30). Given this lack of a straightforward criterion, there are a variety of options. The primary distinction that differentiates types of rotation is between orthogonal and oblique rotations. Orthogonal rotations maintain the constraint that the factors be orthogonal or independent; oblique rotations relax this constraint and allow the factors to be correlated.

Looking first at the orthogonal rotations, each approach is based on a different notion of what constitutes simple structure. Quartimax is the name given to rotation that emphasizes having each variable load on a minimum number of factors; the goal is to avoid having variables load on more than one factor. Varimax rotation emphasizes the other aspect of simplicity, that each factor should have only a few variables loading on it; the goal is to avoid general factors that are associated with many of the variables. Equimax rotation, as its name suggests, takes an intermediate, or equidistant, stance between these two criteria.

Table 30.11 displays the results of a varimax rotation when applied to the principal components solution for factor analysis presented in Table 30.8 (varimax is the initial rotation that SAS uses to prepare the factors for the oblique promax rotation and so is reported when R = promax is specified). We apply the rotation to the principal components solution rather than to the maximum likelihood solution because the results provide clearer illustration of desired effects of rotation.

TABLE 30.11
Factor Pattern for Orthogonal Rotation (Varimax)

	First Factor	Second Factor	Communality (Percent)
Months of care	0.13	0.54	31
Prenatal visits	0.04	0.62	39
Weight gain	0.06	0.20	4
Age of Mother	0.80	0.15	66
Mother's education	0.74	0.08	55
Marital status	0.46	0.14	23
Eigenvalues	1.42	0.77	

Compared with the unrotated results in Table 30.8, we note that the varimax rotation balanced somewhat the variance explained by the two factors, increasing the variance explained by the second factor and decreasing the variance explained by the first. This balancing fulfills the primary objective of the varimax rotation, avoiding a general factor with many variables. Also, the structure is simpler in having variables load on only one factor. For example, whereas the variable Months of Care previously loaded on both the first and second factors, after the varimax rotation it loads on only the second factor. Note, however, that, comparing the results with those in Table 30.8, the communalities do not change; the amount of variance accounted for by the factors does not change because of rotation (the reader is invited to square and sum the loadings to confirm this). Figure 30.8 presents a graphic depiction of this simpler structure wherein the variables are closer to the factor axes than they were in Figure 30.7.

Oblique rotation is similar to orthogonal rotation in that the goal is simple structure with easily interpretable factors; the difference is that with oblique rotation the factors are no longer required to be statistically independent. Graphically this means that the factors are no longer required to be at right angles with each other. As an example of one of the more recent approaches, promax rotation begins with an orthogonal rotation and then modifies the factors using what is called a target matrix as a guide.

The rationale behind the promax rotation is that the orthogonal solutions are usually close to the oblique solution, and by reducing the smaller loadings to near-zero loadings, one can obtain a reasonably good simple structure target matrix. Then by finding the best fitting oblique factors for this target matrix, one obtains the desired oblique solution (Kim and Mueller, 1978b, p. 40).

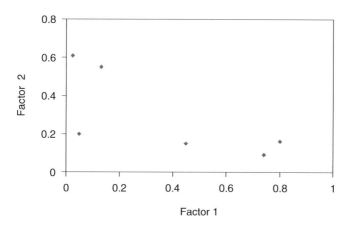

FIGURE 30.8 Varimax orthogonal rotation.

TABLE 30.12

Factor Pattern for Oblique Rotation (Promax)
Standardized Regression Coefficients; Inter-Factor
Correlation = 0.27

	First Factor	Second Factor
Months of care	0.07	0.54
Prenatal visits	−0.04	0.63
Weight gain	0.03	0.19
Age of Mother	0.81	0.03
Mother's education	0.75	−0.04
Marital status	0.46	0.07
Variance accounted for (controlling for other factors)	1.44	0.73

Table 30.12 reports the results of the promax rotation, and, as intended, the smaller loadings are generally closer to zero than with the orthogonal varimax rotation. These smaller loadings represent what has been described as simple structure and provide some rational foundation for the oblique rotation. Changes in the first factor are minor (with, for example, Months of Care decreasing from 0.13 to 0.07), but the decreased loadings for the last three variables on the second factor result in the factor being more clearly associated with only the first three variables. The communalities for the variables remain the same as for the unrotated and varimax solutions but are not reported in this table because, with the factors correlated, they can no longer be calculated by squaring the loadings for each variable.

One virtue of oblique rotations is that they reveal the degree to which the identified factors are correlated. If the results indicate that the rotated factors are essentially not correlated, despite the relaxing of that requirement, then you can be more confident that the real world factors are independent and can use the orthogonal solution. If, on the other hand, the resulting factors are strongly correlated, then you can compare this result with your understanding of the real world relationships among the constructs that you believe that you identified. Often we expect factors to be related and so want our quantitative methods to allow for this. In our example, Factor 1 has a correlation of 0.27 with Factor 2. This is a moderately high correlation that suggests that the construct addressed by Factor 1 is meaningfully related to the construct for Factor 2. This correlation can be displayed graphically as in Figure 30.9.

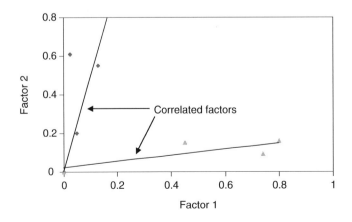

FIGURE 30.9 Promax oblique rotation.

TABLE 30.13

Factor Pattern for Oblique Rotation (Promax) Correlation Coefficients; Inter-Factor Correlation = 0.27

	Age of Mother	Health Behaviors
Months of care	0.21	0.56
Prenatal visits	0.13	0.62
Weight gain	0.09	0.20
Age of Mother	0.81	0.24
Mother's education	0.74	0.16
Marital status	0.48	0.19
Variance accounted for	1.51	0.86

We see that the oblique factors are no longer at right angles (instead, they are at the angle that corresponds to a correlation of 0.27) and that the new factors are more closely associated with distinct clusters of variables.

The primary disadvantage of oblique rotations is that they complicate matters. In particular, the relationships between variables and factors are open to contrasting interpretations. For the unrotated and the orthogonal rotations we presented the factor loadings both as correlations between the variables and the factors and as standardized regression coefficients relating the factors to the variables. As long as the dimensions are orthogonal, these two interpretations involve the same numbers. With oblique factors, however, the regression and correlation coefficients represent different relationships, and the tables that report the regression and correlation coefficients are given different names. The regression coefficients reported in Table 30.12 retain the label "factor pattern" that we used for the orthogonal loadings. The table of correlation coefficients is referred to instead as a table of "factor structure." Thus, to provide a complete account of the oblique promax rotation we need to present the correlations between the variables and factors in Table 30.13. The main thing to note about Table 30.13 is that the significant correlations tend to be about the same size as the corresponding regression coefficients in Table 30.12, although the near-zero loadings in Table 30.12 are noticeably larger in Table 30.13. For example, the small loading for Months of Care on the first factor, 0.07, increases to a correlation of 0.21 on the first factor in Table 30.13. The correlation of 0.21 is the overall relationship between the variable and the first factor; the loading of 0.07 is the relationship when the effect of the correlated factor is controlled (partial relationship).

Gorsuch (1983, pp. 206–208) describes the complementary contributions of these two matrices (and also the matrix of reference vectors) but also explains why the factor structure is typically more central to interpretation of factors. A major advantage of interpreting the factor structure is that the loadings are conceptually independent of the other factors derived in the analysis, a property particularly important when comparing the results of different studies. "Regardless of what other factors occur in the next study, the variables should correlate at the same level with a particular factor" (Gorsuch, 1983, p. 207). Thus, the correlation between Months of Care and the first factor would be expected to remain at approximately 0.21 in future studies whereas the loading of 0.07 is dependent on having variables that produce a factor similar to the second factor in Table 30.12.

In summary, because of the emphasis on underlying structure in factor analysis, it is more important with this technique than with principal components analysis that the resulting factors suggest meaningful interpretations. Thus, although rotations can be valuable for principal components analysis, they are more central for factor analysis. Choices among the various rotations can be daunting as the approach chosen might be expected to influence the eventual interpretation of one's results. The available texts provide further guidance in this matter (see Gorsuch, 1983, pp. 175–238; Kim and Mueller, 1978b, pp. 29–41; or Rummel, 1970, pp. 368–422), but we can offer some crude conclusions.

First, the use of rotations to achieve simple structure presumes that simple structure is desirable. Keep in mind that "simple structure is a mathematically arbitrary criterion concept that will hopefully lead to greater invariance, greater psychological meaningfulness, and greater parsimony than would leave the factors unrotated" (Gorsuch, 1983, p. 231). You may confront situations in which simple structure is not desirable. For example, if you expect to find a general factor that underlies all of your measured variables (as some expect to find a general factor of intelligence underlying a variety of measures or a general leadership factor underlying the range of specific measures), then a varimax rotation would be inappropriate as it would attempt to separate the variables away from this general factor.

As a second point, if you have reason to believe that simple structure is an accurate reflection of the relationships in your data, then many of the available rotations may be adequate: "If the simple structure is clear, any of the more popular procedures can be expected to lead to the same interpretations. Rotating to the varimax and promax or Harris–Kaiser criteria is currently a recommended procedure" (Gorsuch, 1983, p. 205). One advantage of this two-step varimax–promax procedure as performed by SAS is that, as explained above, it allows one to decide whether the orthogonal varimax rotation is adequate or whether the oblique promax rotation is necessary. If the factor correlations are negligible in the oblique solution, you have an important argument for sticking with the orthogonal approach. On the other hand, significant inter-factor correlations argue for an oblique approach.

30.2.3 Summary Assessment of Factor Analysis

We have discussed factor analysis in terms of its goal of revealing underlying structure. This goal suggests the position of factor analysis on the three distinctions in organizing phenomena as described above. First, factor analysis can be used with equal facility to organize attributes (in particular, R-analysis in which one creates dimensions that account for variables, as we have done here), objects (Q-factor analysis), and occasions (O-analysis when one object has many variables measured at different time periods, or T-analysis, where many objects are measured on one variable at different times). Second, these underlying structures are presumed to be represented better using continuous dimensions rather than discrete categories. And, third, factor analysis is based on a realist viewpoint in which underlying structures are presumed to exist and to be important to understand.

30.2.3.1 Strengths

As with principal components analysis, the strengths of factor analysis need to be understood in the way that the approach pursues its goals. In addition to contributing to parsimony in organizing information, factor analysis does operate on common variance and so does provide a technique for exploring the possibility that underlying factors are responsible for covariation among observed variables. That is, unlike principal components analysis, factor analysis does focus on covariance and so does presume a measurement model wherein some of the variance of a variable is understood as being due to unique factors and to measurement error. Because the technique does analyze covariance rather than variance, to the extent that there are underlying influences that have common effects on variables, factor analysis should find it.

30.2.3.2 Concerns

The main concerns in using factor analysis follow from what is said above but can be summarized in terms of (1) indeterminancy, (2) instability across methods, and (3) instability from small changes in the data. The problem of indeterminancy is that factor analysis, unlike principal components analysis, requires estimating unobservable factors. The indeterminacy arises because there will always be alternative conceivable factors that would produce the same observed covariation among the variables measured. Although this presumption of unobservable factors, including their unobservable relationships to the variables measured, is responsible for much of the usefulness of factor analysis, it also creates concern that the results of analysis may be misleading. For example, some consider the problem of correctly estimating the communalities for the variables to be so problematic as to argue for the adoption of principal components analysis rather than factor analysis (e.g., Nunnally, 1972).

Adding to the lack of faith that some have in factor analysis, are the differences that we saw above when comparing the results of different methods of estimating factors (principal components method versus the maximum likelihood method). Although the rank ordering of the relationships between variables and factors remained the same for our two methods, the sizes of loadings changed dramatically, changes that could lead to differing interpretations. In addition to the instability of results across methods is the instability that results from small changes in the data. If a large data set is divided randomly into two parts, analyses of the two separate parts often yield different factor patterns. Similarly, if different samples of a population are taken or data is collected at two points in time, the resulting estimated factors can differ markedly. All of this argues for caution in interpreting the results of factor analysis.

Because of this desire to avoid overinterpretation, some researchers choose, under certain circumstances, to use factor-based scores rather than factor scores in subsequent analyses (see Kim and Mueller, 1978b, pp. 70–72). This means that rather than use the estimated values for factor scores that are based on derived weights provided by computer packages such as SAS, some prefer to use factor analysis to indicate which variables have similar high loadings on a factor (e.g., Months of Care and Prenatal Visits in the promax factor structure of Table 30.13), and simply take the average of those variables as an equal-weighting scale that is comparable to a factor score.

30.3 CLUSTER ANALYSIS

Cluster analysis refers to a quantitative approach to classification that was developed during the 1930s in social science (e.g., Tyron, 1939) and elaborated in the 1960s in biology (Sokal and Sneath, 1963). By classification, we mean "the ordering of entities into groups or classes on the basis of their similarity" (Bailey, 1994, p. 1). As with factor analysis and principal components analysis, the development and use of cluster analysis accelerated considerably after modern computers became available to researchers. We address the major issues in cluster analysis by first presenting the conceptual foundation of the approach and then addressing the practical concerns by applying cluster analysis to the example of the Resource Mothers Program. More information on cluster analysis can be found in general multivariate texts (e.g., Tabachnick and Fidell, 2001) and in books that focus on cluster analysis (Aldenderfer and Blashfield, 1984; Bailey, 1994; Gordon, 1999).

30.3.1 CONCEPTUAL FOUNDATION

Cluster analysis, as an empirical approach to classification, seeks to identify not continuous dimensions along which phenomena vary (the focus of principal components analysis and factor analysis), but categories into which phenomena can be placed. The foundation for cluster analysis is based on prior work on conceptual classification schemas (Bailey, 1994). Examples of particular relevance to administrators include the classification of organizations into mechanistic and organic types (Burns and Stalker, 1961). Scott (1981) used two dimensions, natural versus rational systems and open versus closed systems, to distinguish four variants of organization theory. Daft and Weick (1984), also proposing a two-dimensional model, relate their dimensions to four types of organizations.

Conceptual typologies such as those cited above generally distinguish pure types that define categories, categories into which actual phenomena, such as existing organizations for Daft and Weick (1984), fit to a greater or lesser degree. Cluster analysis, in contrast, is an empirical technique that begins with actual entities, such as individual employees, and then groups them into categories based on measured similarity. For example, Fleury (2002) used cluster analysis to distinguish four groups of abused women victims based on their reported satisfaction with various aspects of the criminal legal system in addressing their needs. Similarly, Julnes, Hayashi, and Anderson (2001) used cluster analysis to distinguish three groups of welfare leavers (those who were fairly successful after having their TANF cases closed, struggling, or intermediate between these two) based on self-reported hardships, satisfaction with life, and comparisons with life while receiving TANF assistance. In order to provide a conceptual foundation for applications of cluster analysis such as these examples, we present below the logic of this similarity grouping, the quantitative model used to assess similarity, and a graphical representation of a cluster model.

30.3.1.1 Underlying Logic: Grouping by Similarity

Although the term "cluster" is not easily defined for quantitative analysis, the goal of cluster analysis is to establish a taxonomy that is comprised of meaningful categories for classifying the phenomena of interest to investigators. Meaningful categories often are presumed to be those that involve "clusters of objects that display small *within-cluster* variation relative to the *between-cluster* variation" (Dillon and Goldstein, 1984, pp. 157–158). Identifying clusters with desired within-cluster and between-cluster variation requires being able to generate overall measures of similarity, or distance as a measure of dissimilarity, for pairs of entities being analyzed.

The logic of cluster analysis is based on the belief that the resulting numerical taxonomies assist researchers and practitioners in describing the phenomena of interest and the relationships among them. This assistance depends, as in the case of principal components analysis and factor analysis, on the value achieved in reducing the complexity of the real world down to more manageable categories. To the extent that the categories derived refer to real distinctions between entities, cluster analysis offers the promise of highlighting real similarities among subsets of phenomena along with real differences between subsets (Bailey, 1994).

The logic as presented so far has been described in terms of developing clusters of objects such as types of organizations or types of leaders, and this is indeed the primary use of cluster analysis (in contrast to the standard use of factor analysis to explicate relationships among variables). The objects for this type of analysis (which we have referred to as Q-analysis) are sometimes called entities, and they are differentiated by virtue of differing characteristics, as measured by variables. Recall, however, that measures can be constructed using other slices of the data cube that was introduced at the beginning of this chapter (Dillon and Goldstein, 1984). For example, variables can be clustered together by using the values of objects on those variables as characteristics of the variables (R-analysis). Similarly, one might cluster occasions together by measuring many characteristics of an entity on multiple occasions (O-analysis).

30.3.1.2 Quantitative Model

The effort to identify meaningful categories based on some notion of similarity assessment requires a quantitative framework that can operationalize similarity judgments and use this sense of overall similarity assessment to make classification decisions. In what follows, we discuss two ways to make similarity judgments and describe a procedure to combine these judgments into an overall schema of classification.

30.3.1.2.1 Operationalizing Similarity
The first task of cluster analysis is to characterize the similarity of the entities being studied. Most approaches to this task depend on calculating a measure of the similarity of each entity to every other entity being studied. This results in a similarity score for each of the possible pairings of entities within the particular population being studied. The two most common approaches to generating these similarity scores are based on distance measures and correlation coefficients.

Distance measures take many forms, but the main points can be made using Euclidean distance as a measure of similarity. In this approach, the differences between two entities on all of the variables measured are combined in the same way that, recalling Pythagorean's theorem, the length of a hypotenuse of a right triangle can be calculated by combining the lengths of the orthogonal legs. Once the differences between the two entities on each of the variables are squared and then summed, the square root is taken to yield the Euclidean distance between the two. Those entities separated by the least Euclidean distance are defined as being most similar. Another type of distance is referred to as city-block distance, represented by the sum of all of the differences between two entities.

Correlation coefficients provide an alternative measure of similarity. When clustering objects, however, the correlation is calculated not between variables measured across objects, as typically done, but between the objects themselves. This may seem counter-intuitive to some, but, as Aldenderfer and Blashfield (1984) point out, it uses the same data matrix as regular correlations; the matrix is simply inverted so that the rows become columns and columns become rows. This inversion of the matrix highlights an important concern for the use of cluster analysis in clustering objects. Just as one would want to have many more observations than variables in traditional factor analysis (R-analysis), so it is reversed in cluster analysis of objects—the desired ratio reverses and one wants many more variables than observations in clustering objects (Bailey, 1994).

Other similarity measures have been developed, such as association measures for dichotomous data; interested readers are encouraged to consult texts (e.g., Gordon, 1999) or the more specific works by Sneath and Sokal (1973) and Clifford and Stephenson (1975). The main reason to consult these other works and to think carefully about your measure of similarity is that the different measures can produce quite different results, a point that will be made again below (Aldenderfer and Blashfield, 1984, pp. 26–28).

30.3.1.2.2 Defining Clusters

Once the chosen similarity measure is calculated for all pairs of the entities being considered, we need a method of using those measures to create categories. Three such methods will be described below, but we can introduce the quantitative methods involved by describing one of the simpler procedures, the single linkage method, as it is applied in one of the more common approaches, hierarchical agglomerative clustering. This method begins by identifying the two entities that are most similar (least distant) based on the variables used. These two entities are grouped together as a cluster. Then the pair of entities with the next highest similarity are grouped together as a cluster. If one of these second most-similar entities is part of the first cluster, then the first cluster incorporates also the other similar entity. Otherwise a second cluster of the two similar entities is formed. This process continues, with new clusters being formed and entities and clusters being incorporated in a hierarchical manner into other clusters, until at the last stage all entities are part of a single, completely inclusive cluster.

This process of forming clusters is fairly straightforward, but there are important decisions that affect the nature of the clusters that result. For example, as with principal components analysis, one has to decide whether or not to standardize the variables before analysis. The argument for standardization is that it allows each variable a somewhat equal opportunity to influence the results; without standardization the variables with the greatest variance will dominate the results. The argument against standardization begins by noting that you may wish variables with the greatest variance to have the greatest impacts on the resulting clusters, the logic being that you want the clustering to reflect the meaningful variation found in those variables (Hartigan, 1975). Related, standardization, although providing some equalization among variables, is not neutral but rather represents a particular weighting scheme that highlights the effect of some variables and diminishes others.

30.3.1.3 Graphic Representation

The successive, hierarchical results of the quantitative model described above can be illustrated in Figure 30.10. In this figure, depicting a fairly simple example, individuals 1 and 2 are rated as most similar based on measured variables and so form the first cluster. In the second stage individual 3 is added to the first cluster, but in the third stage individuals 4 and 5 form a new cluster. In the fourth

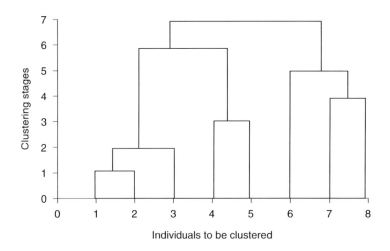

FIGURE 30.10 Dendrogram for hierarchical clustering.

stage, individuals 7 and 8 form a cluster, with individual 6 added to this cluster in the fifth stage. In the sixth stage, the first cluster (1, 2, and 3) is combined with the second (4 and 5), and in the final stage the third cluster (6, 7, and 8) is added to form an all-inclusive cluster.

If we could agree that the observations displayed in Figure 30.10 constitute two clusters and could then display the two clusters in a two-dimensional frame (discriminant analysis provides such a frame), then we might find that the clusters differ from each other in potentially meaningful ways. The depiction in Figure 30.11 of two clusters calls attention to several concepts used to differentiate the appearance of clusters formed by cluster analysis (Aldenderfer and Blashfield, 1984). First, the *density* of clusters refers to the degree to which the members of a cluster are closely grouped. Second, *variance* is the complementary concept of density, referring to the dispersion of members away from the center of a cluster. Third, clusters differ with regard to *shape*.

Using these definitions, cluster 1 in Figure 30.11, as a cluster of five variables, displays greater overall variation than cluster 2, which in turn is characterized by greater overall density. As for shape, the shape of a cluster is often spherical, as depicted by cluster 2 in Figure 30.11 (referred to as hyperspherical if the space in which the clusters are presented involves more than three dimensions;

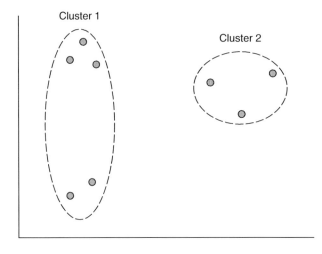

FIGURE 30.11 Illustration of cluster properties.

Ward's method, described below, tends to yield spherical clusters). Other common shapes include cylindrical clusters, as depicted for cluster 1 in Figure 30.11 (these elongated clusters tend to result from the single-linkage approach described in our example).

30.3.1.4 Clustering Solutions

The example above used one particular solution for defining clusters. Without intending to provide a full explanation of all alternatives, we need to introduce other methods of operationalizing our goal of categorizing entities into most appropriate clusters. Addressing the alternative solutions is important for two reasons: (1) none of the available solutions can claim an objective foundation and (2) none of the available solutions appears appropriate for all circumstances. With regard to the first of these reasons, Milligan (1981, p. 380) points out that "None of the clustering methods currently in use offer any theoretical proof which ensures that the algorithm will recover the correct structure." The second reason follows from Monte Carlo simulations that yield conclusions that conflict with other, similar simulations. Milligan (1981) summarizes these sometimes conflicting results, but as examples of his findings, Ward's solution, mentioned below as a hierarchical model, appears to be particularly appropriate when the number of entities per cluster is approximately equal and the clusters overlap with each other.

Given this context of the importance of using solutions that are appropriate for the circumstances, below we describe three of the major approaches to defining clusters: (1) hierarchical methods, (2) iterative partitioning methods, and (3) factor analytic methods. Other methods, such as density searching and graphical methods, are described in Aldenderfer and Blashfield (1984), Dillon and Goldstein (1984), and Gordon (1999).

(1) Hierarchical methods, as illustrated above in Figure 30.10, create a hierarchy of categories such that entities belong to clusters which, in turn, belong to higher-order clusters. These hierarchies can be created either by (a) agglomerative methods which begin with the separate entities and form clusters by joining at successive steps the entities most similar or by (b) divisive methods that begin with an all-inclusive cluster and successively divide the cluster into distinct sub-clusters and eventually into individual entities. Divisive methods require substantially more computer resources as the sample size increases and so are used less frequently (Rapkin and Luke, 1993).

Among the agglomerative hierarchical models, the simplest criterion for joining entities and clusters together is the single linkage rule implicitly displayed in Figure 30.11. Under the single linkage rule, an entity is joined with an existing cluster if the entity is sufficiently similar to any of the cluster members. In contrast, the complete linkage rule "states that any candidate for inclusion into an existing cluster must be within a certain level of similarity to all members of that cluster" (Aldenderfer and Blashfield, 1984, p. 40). Intermediate to these two inclusion rules, average linkage joins entities with clusters if the average of the similarities of the entity with the cluster members is sufficiently high. Ward's method produces hierarchical categories by creating clusters that minimize the within-cluster variation for the set of clusters, an approach in line with the definition of meaningful categories that was presented above when discussing the logic of cluster analysis (Dillon and Goldstein, 1984).

(2) Iterative partitioning methods, often referred to as k-means clustering, begin with an initial set of clusters, calculate the multidimensional centers of the clusters (the centroids), and then iteratively reassign entities to clusters so that all entities belong to the cluster whose center is nearest to them. The strength of the iterative partitioning methods is that they allow entities to be reassigned as the analysis proceeds. The disadvantage to this approach, as with most iterative quantitative methods, is that the iterations may lead to convergence on only a local optimum, making the method overly sensitive to the initial set of clusters that is chosen. In the SAS system, FASTCLUS is the procedure that applies the k-means method to clustering objects based on the characteristics measured by the variables.

(3) Factor analytic methods are in effect categorical versions of factor analysis. The goal of this method is to group things on the basis of dimensions that account for maximal variance. When attempting to group variables, this approach is parallel to using factor-based scores in which one uses factor analysis to identify the variables that load together and then considers each of related variables as equal members of a cluster of variables. In the SAS computer system, the VARCLUS procedure is a factor analytic technique that clusters variables.

This overview of available solutions is sufficient to introduce the techniques; we can elaborate on these concepts by illustrating their application in the context of the Resource Mothers Program. By following the guidance offered here, readers will be able to use cluster analysis in a meaningful way with their own data, but the nature of the data to be clustered has important consequences on the relative usefulness of the various options available. Those wishing to make more informed decisions about which of the various computer options are desirable for their specific requirements need to consult the texts and articles cited above.

30.3.2 APPLICATION OF CLUSTER ANALYSIS TO THE RESOURCE MOTHERS PROGRAM

We provided a graphical example of the hierarchical solution in Figure 30.10. In what follows we apply the other two described approaches, iterative k-means and factor analysis approaches, to the data from the evaluation of the Resource Mothers Program. The SAS computer commands for the iterative and factor analytic variants are listed in Table 30.14. The command PROC FASTCLUS is for k-means clustering of observations, and the PROC VARCLUS command is for the factor analytic approach to clustering variables. The N = 4 statement limits the number of clusters to a maximum of four. The ITER = 10 specifies a maximum of ten iterative passes in search of a solution that converges on what is at least a local optimal solution.

30.3.2.1 Types of Clients

One of the most important questions for a program such as the Resource Mothers Program is whether it is being used effectively and ethically for all clients. One way to address this question is first to identify empirical clusters of clients so that one might then understand the differing needs of these identified groups and evaluate the program effect on them. Recall that grouping objects, people in this case, based on variables is the reverse of the traditional factor analysis problem of grouping variables based on objects. This reversal raises the question of the number of variables to include in a cluster analysis. For example, some scholars have been concerned with having too many variables included in the analysis, particularly when the variables are highly correlated, and

TABLE 30.14
SAS Computer Commands for Cluster Analysis (FASTCLUS for Clustering Objects; VARCLUS for Clustering Variables)

Computer Commands	Function of Commands
PROC FASTCLUS N = 2 ITER = 10	FASTCLUS clusters objects; N = 4 specifies the number of clusters of objects to be retained; ITER = 10 refers to the maximum number of iterations to be used
VAR (variables);	Specifies the variables to be analyzed
PROC VARCLUS N = 4 ITER = 10	VARCLUS instructs the computer to cluster variables rather than objects. N = 4 and ITER = 10 are as with FASTCLUS
VAR (variables);	Specifies the variables to be analyzed

have noted the use of principal components analysis prior to cluster analysis as a way to reduce the number of variables and to make sure that the resulting factors are uncorrelated (see Rapkin and Luke, 1993). Others, however, have emphasized that variables assume the role of observations when clustering objects (Bailey, 1994). Because of this use of variables in the role of observations, we would like in this variant of cluster analysis to have many more variables than objects observed. Not having enough variables available in this example, we move in that direction by using all of the 11 variables presented in Table 30.2.

Using the iterative k-means approach with this expanded set of variables, we can identify any number of nonhierarchical groups of clients. Decisions on the appropriate number of clusters parallel decisions regarding the number of factors or principal components to retain. Rapkin and Luke (1993) outline the primary methods used in supporting this decision. For example, Lathrop and Williams (1990) discuss the use of inverse scree tests. Alternatively, believing that clusters should represent distinct categories of entities, ANOVA could be used to confirm that clusters do entail significant differences on key variables (Rapkin and Luke, 1993). If the differences were not significant, one would try solutions with more clusters.

The SAS program produces several quantitative indicators to aid in this decision. One of the indicators is an estimate of variance accounted for (the R-squared) by the cluster solution, ranging from 0.0 to 1.0. Two other indicators, pseudo F statistic and cubic clustering criterion, use the information on variance accounted for and the number of clusters to provide information on the relative adequacy of the cluster solution. These two criteria are used by selecting the number of clusters that maximize the values of these statistics. Milligan and Cooper (1985) found that the cubic clustering criterion, developed for SAS, was the sixth best of the 30 criteria that they tested for accuracy in replicating a known cluster structure with well-defined clusters. In addition to these quantitative methods, however, it remains important to consider, as we did with factor analysis, the interpretability of the clusters: the clusters derived by quantitative analysis should correspond to some sense that we have about the natural distinctions among the phenomena being studied.

Having tried different numbers of clusters, a four-cluster solution was chosen for our data from the Resource Mothers Program. It turned out that the three-cluster solution maximized the pseudo F and cubic clustering criteria that we just described (with the four-cluster solution being second best), but the four-cluster solution was better at producing recognizable groups with significant differences. Before describing the resulting four clusters, Table 30.15 presents the iterations of the cluster analysis, demonstrating the logic of reassigning individuals to the groups with the closest center until the solution converges and minimal reassignments that no longer influence the group centers.

TABLE 30.15
Iterative Convergence for k-Means Cluster Analysis
(Criterion = 0.02)

| Iteration | Relative Change in Cluster Seeds | | | |
	Cluster 1	Cluster 2	Cluster 3	Cluster 4
1	0.664	0.462	0.584	0.613
2	0.067	0.098	0.079	0.047
3	0.045	0.052	0.027	0.046
4	0.019	0.019	0.000	0.026
5	0.016	0.000	0.010	0.023
6	0.003	0.000	0.021	0.011
7	0.010	0.000	0.000	0.024
8	0.011	0.018	0.000	0.014

The numbers in Table 30.15 represent the changes in the cluster means that result from each round of the iteration process: after individuals are assigned to clusters, the means of the clusters change, resulting in some individuals being reassigned among these adjusted clusters, resulting in additional changes in cluster means, then resulting in additional reassignments of individuals, etc. For example, in the second row of Table 30.15 we see that the mean of cluster 1 changed by 0.067 as a result of the reassignments of people to clusters during the second iteration; the mean of cluster 2 changed by 0.098 during this iteration, cluster 3 by 0.079, and cluster 4 by 0.047. Note that each of these changes is larger than 0.02, the default criterion of an insignificant change. In contrast, during the fourth iteration only one of the cluster means change by as much as 0.02 (the change of 0.026 for cluster 4). Iterations continue until all of changes in the cluster means are below 0.02 (or whatever criterion is chosen). Because none of the changes is as large as 0.02 during the eighth iteration (the largest being 0.018 for cluster 2), the analysis is said to have converged on a stable solution (we set the maximum number of iterations at 10 in the computer program displayed in Table 30.14, but this could have been increased easily had more iterations been required for convergence). These recalculations of cluster means and reassignments can occur in two ways. The default option is to enact these adjustments after each iteration (the option used here for illustration); the alternative in SAS is to make the necessary adjustments after each member is assigned to a cluster, specified in SAS by adding DRIFT after the PROC FASTCLUS command.

Once it is confirmed that the model converges properly, we can go about interpreting the attributes that define the identified groups. Table 30.16 presents the means of the eleven variables for the four clusters produced by the analysis of the 196 clients (a more thorough examination would require including also the standard deviations of the variables). Looking for attributes that distinguish the four groups, cluster 1 has the most members (89 clients in this group) and seems to reflect a fairly typical program client: 80 percent African-American, with somewhat average scores on variables measuring the age of the mother, prenatal weight gain of mother, gestational age, and birthweight. Most distinguishing about this group is that it has the highest percentage of mothers giving birth to their first child (only 13 percent of the mothers having had prior births). Cluster 2, on the other hand, consists of 27 clients who are distinguishable as primarily the older clients who were seen at one of the program sites. This site, prosperous and suburban, had the lowest percent of

TABLE 30.16
Variable Means for Identified Clusters

	Cluster 1: Average Clients	Cluster 2: Older Clients	Cluster 3: Younger Clients	Cluster 4: Prior Births
Months of prenatal care	7.3 months	7.4 months	6.8 months	4.8 months
Age of mother	17.2 years	24.1 years	16.9 years	17.9 years
Ethnicity (percent)	80 (African-American)	22 (African-American)	93 (African-American)	85 (African-American)
Birth order (percent)	13 (prior births)	66 (prior)	57 (prior)	73 (prior)
Weight gain (pounds)	28.9	29.3	17.9	22.1
Education of mother (years)	10.11	12.4	9.7	10.5
Medical prenatal visits	10.1	12.1	7.9	5.6
Marital status (percent)	100 (single)	18 (single)	93 (single)	90 (single)
Source of prenatal care (percent)	24 (private)	63 (private)	36 (private)	29 (private)
Birthweight (grams)	3384	3388	2376	3110
Gestational age (weeks)	39.7	39.6	36.2	36.2
Cluster size (number of clients)	89	27	26	52

African-American clients and the highest percent of clients receiving prenatal care from private physicians and other specialists. Associated with their increased age, this grouping is distinguished also by the related attributes of more education and more likely married.

Cluster 3 represents the group of greatest concern. This group, with 26 clients, is the youngest (average age under 17) and has somewhat low averages on health activities such as number of prenatal visits (7.86) and months of prenatal care (6.82). But most disturbing is the relatively low average gestational age of this group (36.18 weeks) and the low average birthweight (2376 grams; babies less than 2500 grams are classified as "low birthweight" deliveries). Cluster 4, the second largest cluster with 52 clients, also raises concerns, but different concerns from those of the third cluster. Gestational age is average for program participants and average birthweight is higher than the third cluster, but this fourth cluster is distinguished by the lowest averages on the two health activities, only 4.85 months of care and 5.56 medical visits prenatal visits. Associated with this poor attention to the health needs of the developing baby is not a lack of experience but rather the prior experience of motherhood—73 percent of the clients in this cluster have had previous babies, the highest percent of all four clusters. It appears that, consistent with previous research, second-time mothers (and third-time, etc.) in this at-risk population are less concerned than first-time mothers about obtaining proper prenatal care (perhaps because their prior births were fairly successful with minimal effort) and so have the weakest statistics for the health activities being monitored.

Because we wanted to use more variables than was used above for factor analysis and because we were interested in clusters that emphasized the groups with the greatest needs, we clustered together the demographic variables with the birth outcome variables of birthweight and gestational age. Alternatively, one could cluster the variables that would typically be used in regression analysis to predict outcomes, in this case the demographic variables, and relate the resulting clusters to the outcomes, in this case the birth outcomes (Rapkin and Luke, 1993).

30.3.2.2 Clusters of Variables

Just as types of clients can be identified, we may also group together variables into clusters. As described above, this approach is most similar to the use of principal components analysis and factor analysis in organizing variables. The procedure used for this clustering purpose, VARCLUS in SAS, uses an R-squared analysis to group variables with other variables and clusters of variables. Beginning with a single grouping of all variables, VARCLUS successively separates those variables that fit least with the existing clusters.

Table 30.17 displays the R-squared information for the solutions involving one, two, three, and four cluster solutions. We see that the one-cluster solution accounts for 36 percent of the variable variance (2.15 explained out of a total variance of 6.0), with 58 percent explained by the two-cluster solution (3.47 out of 6.0), 74 percent for the three-factor solution (4.43 out of 6.0), and 86 percent for the four-cluster solution (5.13 out of 6.0). As with the other techniques reviewed in this chapter, this approach to cluster analysis requires us to choose the appropriate balance between parsimony (few clusters in this case) and fidelity to complexity (many clusters). If parsimony were paramount

---

TABLE 30.17
Determining the Number of Clusters

	Number of Variables in Each Cluster	Total Variation Explained	Percent Explained
One cluster	6 variables	2.15	36
Two clusters	3 and 3 variables	3.47	58
Three cluster	3, 2, and 1 variables	4.43	74
Four clusters	2, 2, 1, and 1 variables	5.13	86

TABLE 30.18

Two-Cluster Solution for Factor Analytic Clustering

Cluster and Variables	R-Squared with Own Cluster	R-Squared with Next Closest Cluster
Cluster 1		
Age of mother	0.81	0.04
Education of mother	0.72	0.02
Marital status of mother	0.46	0.02
Cluster 2		
Months of prenatal care	0.60	0.04
Medical prenatal visits	0.76	0.01
Weight gain	0.13	0.01

and we were satisfied with explaining less than 60 percent of the variance, we might choose the two-cluster solution displayed in Table 30.18. Note from the table that this analysis results in two groups of variables, groups that correspond to the results of principal components and factor analysis. Just as factor analysis differentiated variables that related to the age and maturation of the client (mother's age, mother's education, and marital status) from those that involved client health behaviors (the month care began, number of medical prenatal visits, and weight gain during pregnancy), so, too, does cluster analysis.

Table 30.19 presents the results of the four-cluster solution. We saw in Table 30.17 that R-squared for the clusters increases to over 85 percent when the four-cluster solution isolates into new clusters the two variables that least fit the previous two clusters. As such, the four-cluster solution accounts for considerable variance but at a cost of parsimony. Looking more carefully, we see that the four clusters also correspond to the results of the principal components and factor analyses. In both of those dimensional analyses of the six variables, two variables formed the core of each of the two derived dimensions with each dimension associated with a third, less closely related, variable. The four-cluster solution replicates this pattern with the core variables forming two-variable clusters and the two less-related variables forming one-variable clusters. In this sense the two-cluster and four-cluster solutions support the reliability of each other, and of the principal components and factor analyses, by yielding corresponding structures.

TABLE 30.19

Four-Cluster Solution for Factor Analytic Clustering

Cluster and Variables	R-Squared with Own Cluster	R-Squared with Next Closest Cluster
Cluster 1		
Age of mother	0.85	0.20
Education of mother	0.85	0.10
Cluster 2		
Months of prenatal care	0.72	0.04
Medical prenatal visits	0.72	0.05
Cluster 3		
Weight gain	1.00	0.01
Cluster 4		
Marital status	1.00	0.20

30.3.3 Summary Assessment of Cluster Analysis

We have presented cluster analysis as a flexible technique for identifying groups within data. As with principal components analysis and factor analysis, we now want to provide a summary that reiterates the stances taken by cluster analysis in organizing phenomena and reviews its strengths and areas of concern.

The most obvious contrast between cluster analysis and the other two methods in this chapter is that it results in categories rather than dimensions. This is an important distinction in that it reflects a belief that discrete categories are at least as useful as continuous dimensions in making sense of a particular domain (one can, however, subsequently use discriminant analysis to derive dimensions that serve to differentiate the clusters).

With regard to the goal of analysis, cluster analysis is somewhat intermediate to principal components analysis and factor analysis in its stance on realism. Most approaches to cluster analysis are based on realism and the associated beliefs that there are real categories among the phenomena of interest and it is, therefore, the task of cluster analysis to reveal those real categories. Bailey (1994), however, notes that this realist stance is not universal and that some approaches attempt only to yield clusters that simplify variations among phenomena.

Finally, cluster analysis is similar to the other two methods in that it can be used to organize phenomena in terms of any of the three dimensions of the data cube—entities, attributes, or occurrences (though typically employed for clustering entities). We illustrated clustering people and variables, and clustering occurrences can be approached in the same way (e.g., a particular Resource Mothers Program could be assessed on a number of variables that were measured quarterly over a period of ten years).

30.3.3.1 Strengths

One of the primary strengths of cluster analysis is that it is simple. This simplicity is of value not only because it requires less computational time (of less concern these days) but also because it requires few assumptions. Not only is the assumption of a multinormal distribution not necessary, one need not even presume a specific measurement model. A second strength of cluster analysis is that it will find a structure for a data set. This is to say that to the extent that there are clusters of variables or of entities, cluster analysis will likely detect it. A third strength of cluster analysis is its diversity. We have seen that there are a variety of approaches, each designed to fulfill a somewhat different purpose. As such, there are variations of cluster analysis available for different disciplines and that are appropriate for different presumptions about the underlying clusters that are being estimated.

To appreciate this variety of approaches to cluster analysis, more reading is required. A particularly useful overview is the monograph on classification by Bailey (1994) that we have cited repeatedly. This resource is written in a nonmathematical manner but is analytical in the sense of providing frameworks for understanding the many choices required in choosing an approach to cluster analysis. For example, Bailey (1994) presents 15 criteria, several of which are addressed above but many are not, to consider in selecting a clustering technique (pp. 40–48) and a typology of clustering techniques (pp. 48–50).

30.3.3.2 Concerns

We have seen in each of the earlier techniques that the strengths of the method tend to entail particular weaknesses, and so it is also with cluster analysis. One of the main concerns about cluster analysis, following from a strength, is that most of the available approaches "are relatively simple procedures that in most cases, are not supported by an extensive body of statistical reasoning" (Aldenderfer and Blashfield, 1984, p. 14). Thus, we cannot rely on formal theory to ensure that our choices in using the available techniques are warranted. A second concern with cluster analysis is that its intended logic is more structure-seeking than structure-imposing, but its quantitative implementation tends to be more structure-imposing. This means that cluster analysis will result in clusters whether there is any real basis for the derived clusters or not.

A third concern is that, as with factor analysis, the diversity of the approach means that some of the techniques are quite different and will result in quite different notions of the appropriate clusters to be derived from the data. For example, had we reported the results of an analysis of the Resource Mothers Program data with the DRIFT option of the SAS FASTCLUS procedure (recall that this results in recalculating cluster means after each individual is assigned to a cluster), we would have seen different clusters. In part these differences across methods result from the different disciplines that came together to form the domain of cluster analysis: (1) biology for the hierarchical interventions and (2) social sciences for the k-means and iterative approaches. But even within the social sciences there are conceptual barriers such that developers of alternative techniques and their followers rarely cite those outside their group (Blashfield, 1980).

These concerns—lack of a foundational theory of cluster analysis, possibility of imposing artificial structure, and observed differences in the results produced by the available methods—make it essential that some effort is made to validate the clusters that result from one's analysis. We have presented some evidence of validation, but more could have presented that would call into question the validity of the clusters. Not having devoted the pages necessary to illustrate the variations in results that follow from method choices, it is important to outline what can be done to strengthen our confidence in the proper use of cluster analysis.

Most of the texts on cluster analysis describe validation procedures (e.g., Aldenderfer and Blashfield, 1984), but Humphreys and Rosenheck (1995) provide a particularly sophisticated example of cluster validation. In their approach, which they refer to as sequential validation, one first assesses replicability with subsets of your data, "If the same clustering procedure generates completely different structures on random subsamples of the data, this may be an indication that no 'real' subgroups exist in the sample" (Humphreys and Rosenheck, 1995, p. 79).

If replications are consistent, one can have some faith in reliability and begin assessing validity by comparing clusters on external variables, variables not used in the clustering but on which the clusters should differ. Once it is established that the clusters differ on external variables, the generalizability or external validity of the structure is then assessed by applying cluster analysis to samples of other populations. The logic of sequential validation is that this sequence of assessing reliability and validity is repeated for several of the major options in cluster analysis, with the method that provides the best results being used for the final analysis.

30.4 CONCLUSIONS

We have described three techniques for organizing phenomena: principal components analysis, factor analysis, and cluster analysis. One of the central themes of our analysis is that the three techniques were developed to serve distinct needs. We want to emphasize, therefore, a framework that will help users choose the techniques best suited to addressing their needs. Figure 30.12 presents the three techniques in terms of the three choices in organizing phenomena that were discussed at the beginning of this chapter. These broad choices do not address the many operational decisions that must be made when using any of the quantitative techniques, but the set of choices is presented as framework that can orient those becoming acquainted with these methods. We turn now to discuss these three choices, not in a formal order that represents a sequential logic of research but rather in an order that simplifies presentation of some key distinctions among principal components analysis, factor analysis, and cluster analysis.

30.4.1 Measurement Scale: Dimensional versus Categorical Analysis

Whether or not it is the first decision confronting those interested in using these quantitative techniques, the most obvious distinction among the three procedures discussed in this chapter is

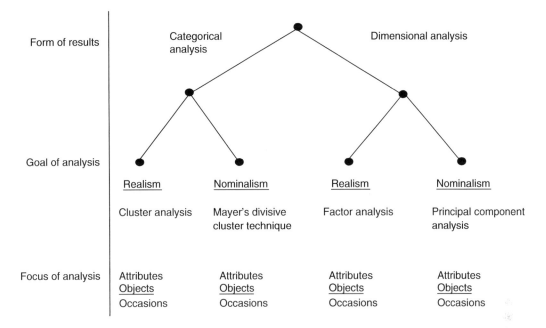

FIGURE 30.12 Choices in organizing phenomena.

the difference between techniques that yield categories or groups and techniques that yield dimensions. Both principal components analysis and factor analysis produce dimensions that order phenomena; cluster analysis groups phenomena into categories. In choosing between categorical and dimensional organizations, two major considerations should influence the decision: (1) your view of the nature of the phenomena of interest and (2) your view of the value of simplicity in your analyses.

The debate between those who see the world in terms of categories and those who see the world as varying along continuous dimensions is persistent and pervasive. In psychology, one form of the debate was between those who studied *personality types* (e.g., "Type A personality") and those who identified *personality dimensions* along which people differ (Digman and Takemoto-Chock, 1981). An example of the debate in public administration is the research cited earlier by Coursey and Bozeman (1990). Rather than accept a categorical notion of "public organization" as a discrete type, they proposed a continuous dimension of "publicness" along which organizations differ (based on a more contextual assessment of organizational attributes).

Some may contend that dimensional analyses in public administration are always superior to categorical ones, based on the belief that our social reality is fundamentally noncategorical (others may argue that categorical analyses are to be preferred for other reasons). A more realistic alternative, however, would seem to be to respect the two traditions, categorical and dimensional, as having emerged in response to particular needs of analysis, each being more appropriate for certain circumstances. Indeed, many call for hybrid approaches that combine the strengths of each stance (Skinner, 1979). This pragmatic perspective places upon you, as the person directing the inquiry, the responsibility of understanding the nature of the phenomena in public administration that you wish to understand. The point of the decision depicted in Figure 30.12 is that you have a choice in any analysis that you conduct as to whether a categorical or dimensional approach is more appropriate and, therefore, should choose accordingly between cluster analysis and its dimensional alternatives of principal components analysis and factor analysis.

Complicating the categorical-dimensional decision is the value you place on the simplicity of the analyses. That is, you might believe that your phenomena of interest is better described by continuous concepts than categorical ones and still choose a categorical analysis because the greater simplicity compensates for the decreased fidelity. The assumptions of cluster analysis are simpler than those of factor analysis and many find interpretation of clusters easier than interpretation of factors. As such, your decision to use categorical or dimensional techniques can be influenced by your assessment of whether the added information in dimensional analyses is justified given the decreased simplicity. For example, Bailey (1994) points out that some people use factor analysis to identify variables that covary and then group the variables together to form a category. In such uses, little information is gained to justify the added complications of factor analysis.

30.4.2 Goal of Analysis: Nominalism versus Realism

Even more fundamental a decision, though less often addressed explicitly, is the choice between nominalism and realism. Realism refers to the position that there are underlying constructs, such as intelligence, leadership ability, and job satisfaction, that exist in some meaningful way but cannot be measured directly (see Julnes and Mark, 1998). Nominalism, in contrast, resists what is seen as reification; what are constructs for the realist are for the nominalist merely convenient labels. As with the prior choice, there are two major considerations that should influence whether one chooses to use a quantitative technique that seeks to identify underlying patterns: (1) one's view of the nature of the phenomena and (2) the value one places on simplicity of analysis.

As for the nature of phenomena (in the sense of our experience of the world), the controversy involved is longstanding. During the middle of the twentieth century "empiricism" was understood by some to mean that we should rely on direct observation and not presume unobservable constructs. This interpretation led to a nominalist view of the categories and dimensions that we use to organize phenomena—that it is useful, for example, to talk of "leadership ability," but all we really see are a variety of behaviors performed by persons in leadership positions, the "ability" construct being just our way of creating parsimony out of chaos.

This view of empiricism was gradually abandoned as it became clear even to proponents that direct observation, not mediated by constructs, was a mythical ideal and, further, was insufficient for making sense of our world in a meaningful way (Meehl, 1986). As a result, construct validity, the extent to which a measure in some way reflects the underlying, unobservable construct that it is intended to measure, became an established part of social inquiry. As a result, most research methods texts with a quantitative orientation include a section on measurement theory and the role of construct validity (including coverage of Cronbach's alpha for scale construction). In recent years, however, some have again questioned the meaningfulness of measures of underlying constructs, believing that the constructs that we choose to use in organizing phenomena are fundamentally arbitrary and reflect only our projection upon the world (Goodman, 1996).

Choosing a position in this controversy leads to choices in methods. One way to frame this decision is to ask whether you want your quantitative methods to identify underlying patterns that are not directly observable. If you opt for the nominalist stance, you will want your quantitative methods to analyze observed variation, believing that to provide the most faithful information about the world. If, on the other hand, you view constructs such as "fiscal stress" and "organizational commitment" as meaningful in making sense of the world, then you will choose quantitative methods that presume that there are natural patterns in the social world and attempt to reveal them. Factor analysis supports the realist stance by distinguishing between common variation, and unique variation, as a result focusing on covariance rather variance. In contrast, the lack of realist presumptions is characteristic of principal components analysis, a technique that can be consistent with a nominal world.

As indicated in Figure 30.12, factor analysis and most variations of cluster analysis presume, in their own way, an underlying structure that is to be revealed. In contrast, principal components analysis makes no assumption of real, underlying patterns. The case of cluster analysis, mostly realist-based, can be addressed with the distinction Bailey (1994) makes between natural (realist) and artificial (nominalist) clustering.

	Nominalism	Realism
Categorical analysis	Mayer's divisive clustering	Cluster analysis
Dimensional analysis	Principal components analysis	Factor analysis

FIGURE 30.13 Two-dimensional model of organizing choices.

Virtually all agglomerative and most divisive methods have the goal of seeking natural, under-lying clusters. Few numerical taxonomists would claim that they are seeking artificial clusters. One salient exception is Mayer's (1971) divisive method designed to create artificial clusters (Bailey, 1994, p. 41).

Mayer's view is that the value of cluster analysis does not depend on it being applied to real clusters, even if identifying real clusters remains a valued goal. "The goal is to create a taxonomy although it may be clear that no obvious natural clustering exists. If an obvious natural clustering does appear then, of course, the researcher is advised to use that clustering" (Mayer, 1971, p. 146).

The second consideration, as before, is about simplicity. Related to our first consideration but more of a tactical rather than strategic issue in research methods, one might believe that there are underlying patterns that we wish to understand but have concerns about the assumptions required in factor analysis and so prefer to use principal components analysis. The logic of this reluctance is that the assumptions required for the realist project of factor analysis might introduce so much ill-considered bias that the realist goal becomes less attainable than it would be with principal components analysis and its more neutral assumptions. In support of this position, we noted that Nunnally (1972) preferred principal components analysis over factor analysis because he was skeptical about such things as the communality estimates that are required as initial assumptions in factor analysis.

Combining the nominalism–realism decision with the categorical–dimensional decision results in the 2×2 matrix depicted in Figure 30.13. We see that each of the three techniques is appropriate for different positions in the matrix. As discussed when addressing these two dimensions, you have the opportunity and responsibility as someone familiar with the phenomena that you are studying to make the necessary decisions when choosing the quantitative techniques that are most appropriate for your particular tasks.

30.4.3 PHENOMENA OF INTEREST: ATTRIBUTES, OBJECTS, AND OCCURRENCES

The last decision depicted in Figure 30.12 relates to the type of administrative phenomena that are of greatest interest for those designing the studies. We introduced this topic at the beginning of this chapter in terms of a data cube comprised of three dimensions: attributes, objects, and occurrences. We now consider the relationships between these three potential dimensions of data and the three techniques of principal components analysis, factor analysis, and cluster analysis. The simple answer to the question about relationships is that each of the techniques can be used to study objects, attributes, and occasions. A longer answer is that there is greater use of some techniques for particular uses and that these differences reveal our inclinations in organizing phenomena. In the context of the Resource Mothers Program, we can think of the data cube in terms of three dimensions composed of (1) selected demographic and health variables (attributes or characteristics) measured for (2) numerous program clients (objects) at (3) specified intervals (occasions; assuming for now that the Resource Mothers Program was studied over many years). Each of these three dimensions can be the focus of analysis in one of two ways. The two alternate approaches for each of the three dimensions yield six possible types of analysis (labeled R-analysis, Q-analysis, O-analysis, P-analysis, S-analysis, and T-analysis by Cattell, 1952). Below, beginning with the attribute dimension, we illustrate one of these alternate analyses for each of the dimensions of the data cube.

30.4.3.1 Attributes

The predominant way in which attributes, or characteristics, have been studied is in terms of the data matrix presented in Table 30.20. This table represents the way that most people code data for computer analysis, with columns representing different variables measured for the rows of individuals in the matrix. Here the matrix is presented as 196 program clients measured on six demographic variables. Each of the techniques discussed is capable of using this data set to identify relationships among the variables. Principal components analysis and factor analysis use the variables measured to create a new variable, a linear composite for one and a measurement of a construct in the other. This type of analysis, organizing the attributes of individuals into clusters or dimensions, is referred to as R-analysis. Although we will not discuss it here, the other approach to organizing attributes, referred to as P-analysis, is to measure the attributes for one organization on many time occasions.

We discussed at length the use of factor analysis in service of R-analysis; less was said about R-analysis for cluster analysis, limiting ourselves to describing the use of the VARCLUS procedure in SAS for grouping variables into either two or four clusters. The reason for this is that cluster analysis is used less often in relating variables, perhaps because we are less inclined to presume "types" of variables. The issue here is the categorical–dimensional distinction and the value we place on the information provided by the two approaches. Although the SAS VARCLUS computer output reports the *R*-squared between each variable and its assigned cluster, this information is lost if one considers only the category assignment as the final result (for an exception to the idea of discrete categories, see Bailey, 1994, p. 42).

In contrast, a major theme of the construct validity concept in measurement is based on the view that different measures differ in their adequacy in reflecting the construct and need to be treated accordingly. This additional information provided by factor analysis is valuable, however, only if we use it. To the extent that factor analysis is used to group variables into what are viewed as homogenous categories, factor analysis will offer little information beyond cluster analysis and, so, cluster analysis will be equally appropriate.

TABLE 30.20
R-Analysis: Organizing Attributes Using Multiple Individuals

	Prenatal Visits	Months of Care	Weight Gained (Pb)	Mother's Age	Mother's Education	Marital Status
Client 1	6	4	19	16	10	0
Client 2	12	7	27	19	12	1
Client 3	8	6	33	17	11	0
Other clients	...	...	...	...	...	...
	...	...	...	...	...	...
Client	9	7	25	16	10	0

TABLE 30.21

Q-Analysis: Organizing Individuals Using Multiple Attributes

	Client 1	Client 2	Client 3	Other Clients	Client 196
Prenatal visits	6	12	8	...	9
Months of care	4	7	6	...	7
Weight gained (Pb)	19	27	33	...	25
Mother's age	16	19	17	...	16
Mother's education	10	12	11	...	10
Other attributes	...	...	...	...	...
...	...	...	...	...	...
Gestational age (weeks)	36	40	39	...	39
Birthweight (g)	2580	3650	3325	...	3460

Thus, although the factor analysis may yield more information, many times users in effect throw away this extra information and attempt to get their cases or variables to have principal loadings on only a single factor, thus in effect transforming them into a sort of de facto cluster analysis (Bailey, 1994, p. 70).

30.4.3.2   Objects

The typical data matrix for analyzing relationships among objects is as represented in Table 30.21. In this table, the 196 program clients are arranged as columns with the 11 measured characteristics of the clients presented as rows. The task with this arrangement of the data cube is to identify patterns of clients that share some inherent similarities, an analysis that is referred to as Q-analysis.

In that the matrix associated with Q-analysis is the simple inverse, or transpose, of the matrix presented in Table 30.20, we mentioned above that Q-analysis reverses the data requirements that we commonly associate with quantitative analysis. Though this leads to the natural conclusion that we need many measures of attributes to conduct Q-analysis, training in research methods can produce the dogma that it is always better to have large samples of people (or other objects) for our analyses, a dogma sufficiently ingrained as to warrant a countering quotation: "Here [Q-analysis], one should have several times as many variables as objects. Thus, we might wish to have a sample of 100 persons, each measured on 400 variables" (Bailey, 1994, p. 70). As Bailey notes, social scientists rarely have this many variables available and so regularly perform Q-analysis with data sets more appropriate for R-analysis, as was done in this chapter with only 11 variables relevant for the Resource Mothers Program.

The last point to be made about organizing objects is to reiterate that the focus of analysis is a separate choice from the choice of categorical or dimensional output. Because cluster analysis has been used primarily for Q-analysis, some might equate the two and think first of cluster analysis whenever they want to organize objects. This would be unfortunate as it would limit the organization of objects to categorical groupings. For circumstances where continuous organization of objects is preferable, Q-technique factor analysis is an established approach and is described in Chapter 37 of this volume.

30.4.3.3   Occasions

Whether or not it represents a natural bias, much less work in public administration and in other areas has focused on relationships among occasions. This neglect is understandable (it does, after all, often take many years to gather the required data), but many of the issues confronting public administrators make more sense when we recognize the time-based patterns of the profession, be

TABLE 30.22

O-Analysis: Organizing Occasions (Years) Using Multiple Attributes of One Entity

	2002	2003	2004	2005	2006	2007
Average prenatal visits	7.7	10.7	11.5	12.3	10.5	10.7
Average months of care	5.4	6.5	7.3	7.4	6.7	6.5
Average weight gained (Pb)	23.7	24.4	26.3	27.2	25.0	24.6
Other attributes	...	...	...	...	...	...
	...	...	...	...	...	...
Average birthweight (g)	3130	3250	3380	3390	3270	3240

they yearly budgeting cycles or longer trends in the changing nature of federalism. In addition, we are increasingly aware of the importance of a "process" orientation in administration. Not only are managers expected to guide the processes of their organizations for such things as continuous quality improvement, they are also expected to support a training process that prepares their subordinates to guide the organization (Julnes, Pang, Takemoto-Chock, Speidel, and Tharp, 1987). It turns out that focusing on process is supported when we emphasize research that organizes changes over time. For example, we might want to understand a natural inquiry process where the evaluation methods most useful for assessing public policies change in a regular developmental pattern over the administrative life of the policy (Julnes and Rog, 2007). The two relevant alternatives from the data cube are to organize occasions using multiple measures of one entity, O-analysis, or to organize occasions by measuring one attribute of many entities, T-analysis.

Table 30.22 presents the data matrix for O-analysis, in which the rows are the average characteristics of the clients of the Resource Mothers Programs and the columns are periodic occasions of measurement. The result of organizing occasions in this way would be clusters or dimensions of time periods with different profiles on the measured variables (e.g., periods in which healthy activities and birth outcomes predominate and other periods with unhealthy activities and outcomes). Another example for public administration might be an examination of patterns of urban development and change over the past century (with various measures of urban characteristics); an O-analysis could produce categories of periods in U.S. history with different profiles of urbanization.

30.4.4 SUMMARY

This chapter provides an introduction to three quantitative techniques with examples of use and interpretation. These three techniques were described as important for public administrators because of the complexity that we confront in this field and the resultant necessity to organize the complexity in a meaningful way. This last section of the chapter has attempted to provide a framework to help users select the technique that is appropriate for their particular needs. Underlying this framework is the belief that people tend to use the quantitative techniques with which they are most familiar, even if other techniques are better suited to the task at hand (as the old saying goes, "for someone who has only a hammer, all the world's a nail"; for a context-sensitive approach to method choice, see Mark, Henry, and Julnes, 2000). Asking questions about the three sets of choices described in this chapter (categorical versus dimensional output, realism versus nominalism, and attributes, objects, and occasions), may seem secondary when one has a data set that needs to be analyzed, but differing positions on these issues have real implications for the proper selection of quantitative techniques (implications preferably considered before data is collected). Fortunately, as we have tried to convey, there is a sufficient variety of techniques available to serve most needs.

REFERENCES

Aldenderfer, M.E. and Blashfield, R.K. 1984. Cluster analysis. *Sage University Paper Series on Quantitative Applications in the Social Sciences*. Newbury Park, California: Sage Publications, pp. 7–044.

Bailey, K.D. 1994. Typologies and taxonomies: An introduction to classification techniques. *Sage University Paper Series on Quantitative Applications in the Social Sciences*. Thousand Oaks, California: Sage Publications, pp. 7–102.

Blashfield, R.K. 1980. The growth of cluster analysis: Tryon, Ward, and Johnson. *Multivariate Behavioral Research*, 15, 439–458.

Buley, J.L. 1995. Evaluating exploratory factor analysis: Which initial-extraction techniques provide the best factor fidelity? *Human Communication Research*, 21, 478–494.

Burns, T. and Stalker, G.M. 1961. *The Management of Innovation*. London: Tavistock.

Cattell, R.B. 1952. *Factor Analysis: An Introduction and Manual for the Psychologist and Social Scientist*. New York: Harper and Row.

Cattell, R.B. 1966. The scree test for the number of factors. *Multivariate Behavioral Research*, 1, 140–161.

Cattell, R.B. 1978. *The Scientific Use of Factor Analysis in Behavioral and Life Sciences*. New York: Plenum Press.

Cattell, R.B. and Jaspers, J. 1967. A general plamode (No. 30-10-5-2) for factor analytic exercises and research. *Multivariate Behavioral Research Monographs*, 67–3, 1–212.

Cattell, R.B. and Vogelmann, S. 1977. A comprehensive trial of the scree and KG criteria for determining the number of clusters. *Multivariate Behavioral Research*, 12, 289–325.

Clifford, H. and Stephenson, W. 1975. *An Introduction to Numerical Taxonomy*. New York: Academic Press.

Cota, A.A., Evans, C.R., Longman, R.S., Dion, K.L., and Kilik, L. 1995. Using and misusing factor analysis to explore group cohesion. *Journal of Clinical Psychology*, 51, 308–317.

Coursey, D. and Bozeman, B. 1990. Decision making in public and private organizations: A test of alternative concepts of "publicness". *Public Administration Review*, 50, 525–535.

Daft, R.L. and Weick, K.E. 1984. Toward a model of organizations as interpretative systems. *Academy of Management Review*, 9, 284–295.

Digman, J. and Takemoto-Chock, N. 1981. Factors in the natural language of personality: Reanalysis, comparison, and interpretation of six major studies. *Multivariate Behavioral Research*, 16, 149–170.

Dillon, W.R. and Goldstein, M. 1984. *Multivariate Analysis: Methods and Applications*. New York: Wiley.

Donahue, A.K. 2004. Managerial perceptions and the production of fire protection. *Administration and Society*, 35(6), 717–746.

Dunteman, G.H. 1989. Principal components analysis. *Sage University Paper Series on Quantitative Applications in the Social Sciences*. Newbury Park, California: Sage Publications, pp. 7–069.

Fleury, R.E. 2002. Missing voices: Patterns of battered women's satisfaction with the criminal legal system. *Violence Against Women*, 8(2), 181–205.

Fuller, E.L. Jr. and Hemmerle, W.J. 1966. Robustness of the maximum likelihood estimation procedure in factor analysis. *Psychometrika*, 31, 255–266.

Goodman, N. 1996. Words, works, worlds. In P.J. McCormick (Ed.), *Starmaking: Realism, Anti-Realism, and Irrealism*. Cambridge, Massachusetts: MIT Press.

Gordon, A.D. 1999. *Classification* (2nd ed.). Boca Raton, Florida: Chapman and Hall.

Gorsuch, R.L. 1983. *Factor Analysis*. Hillsdale, New Jersey: Lawrence Erlbaum Associates.

Hall, J.L. 2006. Disentangling components of innovation capacity and innovation outcomes in Economic growth and development in the U.S. *States Dissertation Abstracts International, A: The Humanities and Social Sciences*, 66(8), 3088-A–3089-A.

Harris, J.A. 1995. Confirmatory factor analysis of the aggression questionnaire. *Behaviour Research and Therapy*, 33, 991–994.

Harris, R.J. 2001. *A Primer of Multivariate Statistics* (3rd ed.). Mahwah, New Jersey: Lawrence Erlbaum.

Hartigan, J.A. 1975. *Clustering Algorithms*. New York: John Wiley and Sons.

Hatcher, L. 1994. *A Step-by-Step Approach to Using the SAS System for Factor Analysis and Structural Equation Modeling*. Cary, North Carolina: SAS Institute.

Hotelling, H. 1933. Analysis of a complex of statistical variables into principal components. *Journal of Education Psychology*, 24, 417–441, 498–520.

Humphreys, K. and Rosenheck, R. 1995. Sequential validation of cluster analytic subtypes of homeless veterans. *American Journal of Community Psychology*, 23, 75–98.

Jolliffe, I.T. 1986. *Principal Component Analysis*. New York: Springer-Verlag.

Julnes, G. and Mark, M. 1998. Evaluation as sensemaking: Knowledge construction in a realist world. In G. Henry, G. Julnes, and M. Mark, (Eds.), *Realist Evaluation: An Emerging Theory in Support of Practice*. New Directions for Evaluation, Vol. 78. San Francisco: Jossey-Bass, pp. 33–52.

Julnes, G., Pang, D., Takemoto-Chock, N., Speidel, G., and Tharp, R. 1987. The process in training in processes. *Journal of Community Psychology*, 15, 387–396.

Julnes, G., Konefal, M., Pindur, W., and Kim, P. 1994. Community-based perinatal care for disadvantaged adolescents: Evaluation of the Resource Mothers Program. *Journal of Community Health*, 19, 41–53.

Julnes, G., Atkins, P., and Pindur, W. 2002. Challange of strengthening fiscal and political support of regional councils: Impact of council activities on support by local officials. *Journal of Global Awareness*, 3(1), 129–148.

Julnes, G., Hayashi, K., and Anderson, S. 2001. Acknowledging different needs: Developing a taxonomy of welfare leavers. In G. Julnes, and E.M. Foster (Eds.), *Outcomes of Welfare Reform for Families Who Leave TANF*. New Directions for Evaluation, Vol. 91. San Francisco: Jossey-Bass, pp. 73–85.

Julnes, G. and Rog, D.J. 2007. Pragmatic support for policies on methodology. In G. Julnes and D.J. Rog (Eds.). *Informing Federal Policies on Evaluation Methodology: Building the Evidence Base for Method Choice in Government Sponsored Evaluation*, New Directions for Evaluation, San Francisco: Jossey-Bass, pp. 129–147.

Kaiser, H.F. 1958. The varimax criterion for analytic rotation in factor analysis. *Psychometrika*, 23, 187–200.

Kim, J. and Mueller, C.W. 1978a. Introduction to factor analysis: What it is and how to do it. *Sage University Paper Series on Quantitative Applications in the Social Sciences*. Newbury Park, California: Sage Publications, pp. 7–013.

Kim, J. and Mueller, C.W. 1978b. Factor analysis: Statistical methods and practical issues. *Sage University Paper Series on Quantitative Applications in the Social Sciences*. Newbury Park, California: Sage Publications, pp. 7–014.

Lathrop, R.G. and Williams, J.E. 1990. The reliability of inverse scree tests for cluster analysis. *Educational and Psychological Measurement*, 47, 952–959.

Mark, M.M., Henry, G.T., and Julnes, G. 2000. *Evaluation: An Integrated Framework for Understanding, Guiding, and Improving Policies and Programs*. San Francisco: Jossey-Bass.

Mayer, L.S. 1971. A theory of cluster analysis when there exist multiple indicators of a theoretic concept. *Biometrics*, 27, 143–155.

McKernan, S.M., Bernstein, J., and Fender, L. 2005. Taming the beast: Categorizing state welfare policies. *Journal of Policy Analysis and Management*, 24(2), 443–460.

Meehl, P. 1986. What social scientists don't understand. In D.W. Fiske and R.A. Schweder (Eds.), *Metatheory in Social Science: Pluralisms and Subjectivities*. Chicago: University of Chicago Press.

Meyers, M.K., Gornick, J.C., and Peck, L.R. 2001. Packaging support for low-income families: Policy variation across the United States. *Journal of Policy Analysis and Management*, 20(3), 457–483.

Milligan, G.W. 1981. A review of Monte Carlo tests of cluster analysis. *Multivariate Behavioral Research*, 16, 379–407.

Milligan, G.W. and Cooper, M.C. 1985. An examination of procedures for determining the number of clusters in a data set. *Psychometrika*, 50, 159–179.

Morrison, D.F. 1990. *Multivariate Statistical Methods*. New York: McGraw-Hill.

Mulaik, S.A. 1972. *The Foundations of Factor Analysis*. New York: McGraw-Hill.

Nunnally, J.M. 1972. *Educational Measurement and Evaluation* (2nd ed.). New York: McGraw-Hill.

O'Rourke, N., Hatcher, L., and Stepanski, E.J. 2005. *A Step-by-Step Approach to Using SAS for Univariate and Multivariate Statistics (2nd ed.)*. Cary, North Carolina: SAS Institute.

Pandey, S.K. and Scott, P.G. 2002. Red tape: A review and assessment of concepts and measures. *Journal of Public Administration Research and Theory*, 12(4), 553–580.

Pearson, K. 1901. On lines and planes of closest fit to systems of points in space. *Philosophical Magazine*, 2, 559–572.

Rapkin, B.D. and Luke, D.A. 1993. Cluster analysis in community research: Epistemology and practice. *American Journal of Community Psychology*, 21, 247–277.

Rummel, R.J. 1970. *Applied Factor Analysis*. Evanston: Northwestern University Press.

SAS Institute, Inc. 1988. *SAS/STAT User's Guide: Version 6.03 edition*. Cary, North Carolina: Author.

Scott, W.R. 1981. *Organizations: Rational, Natural, and Open Systems*. Englewood Cliffs, New Jersey: Prentice-Hall.

Shevlin, M.E. and Bunting, B.P. 1994. Confirmatory factor analysis of the satisfaction with life scale. *Perceptual and Motor Skills*, 79, 1316–1318.

Shevlin, M.E., Bunting, B.P., and Lewis, C.A. 1995. Confirmatory analysis of the Rosenberg self-esteem scale. *Psychological Reports*, 76, 707–711.

Simonton, D.K. 1986. Presidential greatness: The historical consensus and its psychological significance. *Political Psychology*, 7(2), 259–284.

Skinner, H.A. 1979. Dimensions and clusters: A hybrid approach to classification. *Applied Psychological Measurement*, 3, 327–341.

Sneath, P.H.A. and Sokal, R.R. 1973. *Numerical Taxonomy*. San Francisco: Freeman.

Sokal, R.R. and Sneath, P.H.A. 1963. *Principles of Numerical Taxonomy*. San Francisco: Freeman.

Spearman. C. 1904. "General intelligence" objectively determined and measured. *American Journal of Psychology*, 15, 201–293.

Spector, P.E. 1993. *SAS Programming for Researchers and Social Scientists*. Newbury Park, California: Sage Publications.

Stanbury, W. and Thompson, F. 1995. Toward a political economy of government waste: First step, definitions. *Public Administration Review*, 55, 418–427.

Stogdill, R.M. 1974. *Handbook of Leadership*. New York: Free Press.

Tabachnick, B.G. and Fidell, L.S. 2001. *Using Multivariate Statistics (4th ed.)*. Boston, Massachusetts: Allyn and Bacon.

Thompson, B. 2004. *Exploratory and Confirmatory Factor Analysis: Understanding Concepts and Applications*. Washington, DC: American Psychological Association.

Thompson, B. and Daniel, L.G. 1996. Factor analytic evidence for the construct validity of scores: A historical overview and some guidelines. *Educational and Psychological Measurement*, 56, 197–109.

Thurstone, L.L. 1935. *The Vectors of Mind*. Chicago: University of Chicago Press.

Thurstone, L.L. 1947. *Multiple Factor Analysis*. Chicago: University of Chicago Press.

Tinsley, H.E.A. and Brown, S.D. 2000. *Handbook of Applied Multivariate Statistics and Mathematical Modeling*. San Diego, California: Academic Press.

Tyron, R.C. 1939. *Cluster Analysis: Correlation Profile and Orthometric (Factor) Analysis for the Isolation of Unities in Mind and Personality*. Ann Arbor, Michigan: Edwards Brothers.

Wood, J.M., Tataryn, D.J., and Gorsuch, R.L. 1996. Effects of under- and overextraction on principal axis factor analysis with varimax rotation. *Psychological Methods*, 1, 354–365.

Yang, K. 2005. Public administrators' trust in citizens: A missing link in citizen involvement efforts. *Public Administration Review*, 65(3), 273–285.

Zoski, K.W. and Jurs, S. 1996. An objective counterpart to the visual scree test for factor analysis. *Educational and Psychological Measurement*, 56, 443–452.

31 Confirmatory Factor Analysis: A Practical Introduction

David H. Coursey

CONTENTS

ABSTRACT

Confirmatory factor analysis (CFA) is a powerful technique for formal evaluation of measurement models. As a subset of structural equation models (SEM), CFA is underutilized in public administration where formal testing of presumed indicators of complex constructs, such as job satisfaction, is direly wanting. This chapter overviews CFA applications, measures and their interpretations, and special statistical issues toward practical application over theoretical discussion.

31.1 CONFIRMATORY FACTOR ANALYSIS: A PRACTICAL INTRODUCTION

Over the last decade, there has been a surge in the use of structural equation models (SEM) in the business (especially marketing and information technology) and social science literatures. Such models are less common in public administration though there is a noticeable growth in the last few years as well. Like all new techniques to a field, there is considerable divergence in the quality of their application as researchers discover uses and limitations. The advent of graphical interfaces for common programs for SEM estimation, like LISREL, has significantly lessened the technical barriers but at the expense of manuscript quality. This chapter is a practical introduction to the use of confirmatory factor analysis (CFA) or models. The purpose is to familiarize the beginner, and perhaps some journeymen, on the uses, terminology, and statistical issues. The reader is presumed to be familiar with common factor and principal component analyses.

First, we overview SEM and CFA applications and compare CFA to traditional factor analysis (normally called exploratory factor analysis by SEM researchers). Next, the parameters of the model are outlined and defined along with measures of model fit. Third, CFA models usually are repeatedly estimated, with modifications made based on key results and approaches. With this background, we then examine a real-life research example from the public service motivation (PSM) literature, briefly discussed and detailed on the book Web site. Finally, special limitations and statistical issues are reviewed and resources for additional study suggested.

31.2   WHY SEM AND CFA? PURPOSES BEHIND THE MATH

SEM and its subarea CFA have several attractive research uses. SEM allows testing of far more complex models than traditional multiple regression or path models. SEM/CFA presumes there are latent, usually unobserved constructs (or factors) that are represented by observed indicators (or measures). Relationships are hypothesized between the various latent variables as well as the indicators to their respective factors.

For example, you may want to test for relationships between latent factors of formalization, job satisfaction, and employee productivity with their own set of measures (Figure 31.1). Traditionally, you could create an index or scale for the three latent variables, verifying them with Cronbach's Alpha, and then run a path analysis regression model.

SEM, however, is highly advantageous. First, it allows for simultaneous estimates of all model parameters unlike traditional path analysis. Second, it allows for direct model representation of measurement error. Where in regression-based path analysis the factors are produced and then the reliabilities essentially discarded, SEM/CFA can directly consider those in the path estimations. For example, a well-established index (such as those for "job satisfaction") may have a known reliability. This can be used instead of a sample estimate for a more generalizable finding.

SEM and CFA handle complex latent variable relationships. They stress estimation and inclusion of measurement error. But, such precision carries a price. Researchers need strong theory to justify tested relationships. Too often, researchers run multiple regressions and no one really thinks about the implied, often tenuous, assumptions that all the independent variables are exogenous, do not relate to each other, and have only direct effects on the dependent variable. SEM forces a researcher to lay bare their theory at a more complex level but hence the problem. Too often, beginning researchers simply throw several variables into a model that has at best weak theoretical justification. The old adage "garbage in, garbage out" applies. As a field, public administration theory in many areas has not progressed to such defined, complex relationships. Areas that cut across economics, information technology, and psychology where richer models dominate are more appropriate. This is not to suggest SEM should not be used in other cases. SEM and CFA force us to begin considering more complex theory with closer connections to empirical testing, as long as theoretical limitations are realized.

There are three general forms of SEM/CFA models: (1) observed latent, (2) latent variable, and (3) measurement. In an observed latent model, all the latent variables are self-defined; there are no

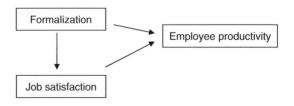

FIGURE 31.1 A typical path model.

indicators. Latent models include both the indicators and the latent variables with their hypothesized associations. Indeed, this is considered one of the strengths of SEM: such simultaneous testing of the measurement and prediction models arguably reduces contamination of the prediction model by measurement error. Measurement models, such as CFA, focus on just the relationships between indicators and their latent variables. As such, they substitute for traditional measurement testing such as exploratory factor analysis and item response theory (IRT).

Why choose CFA over traditional, exploratory factor analysis (EFA)? First, and most importantly, it allows for actual hypothesis testing. EFA has no mechanism to directly test that indicators fall on separate dimensions/factors (divergent validity) or represent their presumed factor well (convergent validity). Second, CFA has far more varied and powerful measures of overall model fit. Like its parent SEM, CFA forces structural testing. The number of indicators per latent variable/factor, their relationships to each other, and presumed error are included. As such, EFA is still very useful for initial measurement model development but CFA is far superior for testing the reliability and validity of a scale or index. There are other CFA advantages and differences related to error estimation and more complex mathematical concerns (Brown, 2006, chapter 3) but hypothesis testing and model fit are the primary, practical distinctive advantages.

Although public administration has begun embracing SEM, CFA is far less common. The social reality of public administration is such research can be seen as relatively boring, "just" measurement, and in some cases even viewed as trivial. Such attitudes could not be less informed. The lack of clearly defined latent constructs and their measurement is an historically noted problem (e.g., Simon, 1946). If theory is to progress, there has to be at least evidence that measures of complex latent variables are validly and reliably measured. Public administration tends to fail this test. Frequently, a researcher defines a construct, writes a few indicators from scratch with at best face validity, perhaps run a Cronbach Alpha on them, and finding the reliability reasonable combines them as a summated scale or index. Even constructs with well-known, psychometrically verified measurement sets like job satisfaction see significant variance in the use of measures across studies. Such variance seriously complicates generalization and comparisons across studies. If findings vary, and they do, is it the measures or the actual latent concepts in question? In short, public administration is hampered by prediction models that have little, if any, validation of their percussive measurement models. It does not matter how well your concepts relate if you cannot even be somewhat confident the measurement model is valid and reliable.

31.3 CFA: PARAMETERS

The first time someone sees a typical SEM/CFA printout, mild panic can ensue. Programs such as LISREL generate an enormous amount of data relevant to model evaluation. Almost everything is referred to by Greek letters and "matrices" and can be quite confusing at first. Here, we outline the key parameters in standard CFA (lambdas, theta-deltas, and phis) and their meanings along with gauges of model fit. There are many other matrices than the ones we review dependent on SEM model complexity.

For our example, consider a CFA on work motivation divided between extrinsic and intrinsic dimensions or latent factors (Figure 31.2). Unobserved or latent variables (intrinsic and extrinsic motivation subdimensions) are generally represented as ovals. Observed indicators are in rectangles. Each has a series of indicators (A–F). Notice that the model shows the paths going from the subdimensions to the indicators.

This is because in CFA and SEM indicators are expected to reflect the variance in the latent variable. They do not "cause" it. These are often referred to as reflective models. There are less common models where the indicators cause the latent variables (called formative models). These are appropriate when there is no inherit reason to believe the indicators are correlated or they combine to form the latent variable. For example, job satisfaction is often conceptualized as a formative construct. Job satisfaction may consist of satisfaction with pay, managers, work

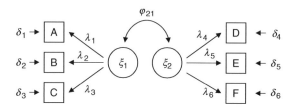

FIGURE 31.2 A reflective confirmatory factor analysis model for work motivation with two latent subdimensions.

environment, and coworkers. Although higher values on all of these mean greater job satisfaction, there is no reason to believe any of these must be correlated and indeed may not be.

Notice also the curved double-headed arrow between extrinsic and intrinsic. This means that the two are free to covary. This is similar to an oblique assumption in exploratory factor analysis. It is possible to "fix" the covariance to zero where it is theoretically presumed the dimensions are completely independent. The arrows to each indicator represent the error variances. Typically, they are not assumed to covary (in a reflective model) and are estimated from the sample. If, however, the error variance is well established, it is usually more appropriate to manually set it in the model. All of these paths are defined by Greek letters (or the combination thereof).

31.4 LAMBDA: THE VALIDITY PATH COEFFICIENT

The value of the paths between each indicator and its latent construct is referred to as a lambda (λ) coefficient. This is essentially like factor loadings in EFA and is thought of as a measure of validity. The typical CFA printout provides a lambda for each path along with its standard error. Lambdas at least double their standard error magnitude are judged statistically significant ($p < .05$).

Lambdas are normally derived from the variance–covariance matrix (preferred) and not the correlation matrix (for a discussion of why, see Kelloway, 1998; Brown, 2006). Unlike EFA, however, the factor loadings can be expressed several, often confusing, ways. EFA presumes a completely standardized set of indicators and the latent variables. CFA usually applies unstandardized indicators and standardized latent variables, referred to as the standardized solution. Significance testing and standard error evaluation are based on the latter though the completely standardized solution is usually presented in publication. It is critical in writing up SEM/CFA results that the researcher indicates which are used. There is debate, however, about which really should be reported. Probably the best rule is that if the indicators all come from a similar metric, such as all four-point Likert variables, the standardized solution is preferable to compare across studies. The reason is in such cases the variation in the indicators may be better presumed reflective of latent variance and not partly due to different metrics. For example, indicators where one is income, one a four-point Likert item, and one a "0–100" temperature scale should be completely standardized given vastly different metrics.

31.5 THETA-DELTA: INDICATOR RELIABILITIES

The values of paths to the indicators represent the residuals, or theta-deltas (δ). When expressed in a completely standardized solution, they are used to judge how well the indicator's variance is accounted for by model. For example, a theta-delta of 0.65 in such a solution means that 65 percent of the variance in that indicator is unaccounted for by the model. Programs such as LISREL by default also provide the squared multiple correlations for each indicator which is just 1-theta-delta and can be referred to as a reliability.

31.6   PHI: INTERDIMENSION CORRELATIONS

The paths between the latent dimensions are the phi (ϕ) coefficients. These represent the correlations between dimensions. Generally you expect these to be statistically significant (at least double their standard errors). After all, if both dimensions reflect a higher order latent variable (work motivation), they must be correlated to some degree. In the case of formative models, however, this does not necessarily hold.

For those used to EFA, the idea of correlated factors being desirable is unusual as most measurement work uses orthogonal rotations where the indicators are loaded on factors set to zero intercorrelations. CFA is analogous to oblique rotation where the factors may be correlated. Indeed, they should be in a reflective model. The reason, in part, is that most EFA measurement work is quite concerned with divergent validity of indicators across dimensions or latent constructs whereas CFA is more attuned to actual model testing.

31.7   ASSESSING MODEL FIT: MULTIPLE DEFINITIONS, MULTIPLE MEASURES

In multiple regression, the coefficient of multiple determination, or R^2, is cited as a measure of how well the model fits or "accounts for" the variance in the dependent variable. Alas, there is no such single, summary measure of model fit in CFA/SEM. Partly this is due to the complexity of the models but also because there are varied ideas of what model fit means: absolute, comparative, and parsimonious. Within each type of fit, there are multiple measures, typically with varied strengths and weaknesses such that published CFA work almost always provides several model fit tests. Here, we define each type of model fit and describe major measures and their relative strengths and weaknesses.

31.8   ABSOLUTE FIT

Absolute fit concerns how well the model reproduces the variance–covariance matrix. Sometimes researchers will provide a "model R^2" for CFA/SEM, likely because it is more familiar. However, R^2 does not measure how well the model fits the data but rather how much variance is accounted for in the endogenous variables. It is quite possible to have a well-fitting model with a small R^2. More holistic model fit measures considering all the presumed model paths are needed.

The oldest absolute fit measure is chi-square, χ^2 (Blalock, 1964). It measures how far the model deviates from the variance–covariance matrix. A significant χ^2 indicates the model does not fit (the opposite of normal hypothesis testing). The test is problematic, however, for its statistical properties. It only becomes really useful around a sample of 200 and then it is likely to reject model fit for only slight differences which really, arguably, are not substantive. Hence, although χ^2 is almost always reported, its rejection is usually not very damaging by itself. Rather, if it is not significant, it is considered very strong support for absolute fit given its sensitivity.

LISREL provides four χ^2 measures: the minimum fit function, the normal theory weighted least squares, Satorra–Bentler, and corrected for non-normality (Jöreskog, 2001). Which ones you get vary by whether an asymptotic covariance matrix is provided and the estimation method used (e.g., maximum likelihood, weighted least squares, etc.). In the case of interval data, the minimum fit function is normally applied. In non-normal situations, the normal theory WLS or corrected for non-normality are preferred. For various small samples and non-normality, the Satorra-Bentler is best, especially in cases of ordinal data. These measures are being subjected to simulations of their distributions under a variety of measurement conditions (e.g., Yuan and Bentler, 1997).

There are several alternatives to the sensitive χ^2. The goodness-of-fit index (GFI) and adjusted goodness-of-fit index (AGFI) center on the discrepancies to the observed variances. Both range from 0 to 1 (higher is better) with AGFI an adjustment for degrees of freedom. Values above 0.90 are generally considered evidence of good model fit. However, these tests have no known sampling distribution and hence there are no hard rules about judging fit or statistical tests.

Of all the absolute fit tests, the root mean squared error of approximation (RMSEA) is really the best (Steiger, 1990). Focusing on the analysis of residuals, it has a known sampling distribution and ranges between 0 and 1 regardless of sample size. There are varied interpretations of what a "good" RMSEA is but generally 0.10 is the borderline for a good fit with lower values indicating better fit. RMSEA also has a statistical test and confidence intervals. Typically a 90 percent confidence interval is applied to see if RMSEA goes beyond the 0.10 cutoff.

31.9   COMPARATIVE FIT

Comparative fit tests ask how well does the model fit compared to others. This almost always involves a comparison to the null model, a model assuming no relationships whatsoever. Not surprisingly, such a test is hardly challenging and almost always succeeds. More useful are comparisons between competing models.

The normed fit index (NFI) considers a ratio of the model chi-squares, ranging from 0 to 1 with 0.9 the usual border for a good fit (higher is better). A variant, the non-normed fit index (NNFI) adjusts for degrees of freedom as the NFI is known to underestimate the fit improvement in small samples. However, this adjustment can result in values outside 0 and 1. The incremental fit index (IFI) rescales the NNFI to the 0 and 1 boundaries. The comparative fit index (CFI) and relative fit index (RFI) also range between 0 and 1 though they use varying ways to compare the mode chi-squares. For all of these, 0.90 is usually considered the borderline for a good fit, with higher scores being better.

31.10   PARSIMONIOUS FIT

Parsimonious fit asks if the model is concise. Like comparing the R^2 and adjusted R^2, the balance between degrees of freedom and fit is evaluated. The parsimonious normed fit index (PNFI) and parsimonious goodness-of-fit index (PGFI) adjust the NFI for degrees of freedom with the later for the GFI. Neither is likely to reach 0.90 and generally they are used more to compare parsimony across models.

The Akaike Information Criterion (AIC) and Consistent Akaike Information Criterion (CAIC) use a combination of model fit and the number of parameters. Smaller values are more parsimonious (range is 0–1) but there are no standards as to what a good parsimonious fit is.

31.11   MODEL RESPECIFICATION: TESTING ALTERNATIVE FORMS

Few scales or indexes are ever final. Even with fairly well-established measurements, researchers may experiment with new indicators or latent subdimensions. Within SEM, the elaborate theoretical relationships can be subjected to robustness tests for reasonable, alternative path specifications. This is especially advisable in nascent theoretical areas.

Many CFA/SEM studies not only report their initial model but also alternative models suggested from various tests associated with the initial model. In CFA work, this is a critical task toward measurement development. For example, in the public service motivation literature, Perry (1996) developed a reduced set of latent subdimensions based on initial CFA model results.

In respecification, paths between latent variables and their indicators are added or deleted toward improved model fit and parsimony. Such follow-up exploratory work is valuable as long as it is viewed within its limitations. Such respecification should always be theory guided. Researchers should not simply add or delete paths due to the mathematical results. Paths across dimensions and latent variables, for example, need careful theoretical justification as well as consideration of divergent validity issues.

To the many disdainful of stepwise regression, which appears similar at first glance in concept, such alternative models may seem capitalizing on the sample data and "data-driven" theory.

CFA/SEM researchers have a different view of such modifications that are often misunderstood by those unfamiliar with the techniques. First, such modifications are based on far more than just that, say, maximizing an adjusted R^2. Second, CFA/SEM researchers always couch their sample-modified models as exploratory toward model improvement for future research. If the researcher uses split-samples, the sample dependence issues are arguably attenuated. For example, some researchers randomly split their samples into halves (sometimes 25/75 percent), test their initial model, and then formally test the revised model on the second half of their data. Of course, this requires a fairly large sample size for reasonable statistical power (rarely less than 300–400 even in the simplest models). CFA/SEM research does not pretend theoretical closure and many researchers view such modifications as critical to guiding future research.

Respecification is divided between theory-trimming (deleting paths or "fixing" parameters to zero) and theory-building (adding paths or "freeing" the parameters for estimation). Theory-trimming is considered by examining the lambdas: their magnitude, statistical significance, and reliabilities. Theory-building is performed through lagrange multiplier tests which LISREL and some other SEM programs refer to as modification indices. These provide how much the model χ^2 would change if a path was estimated (freed) and usually researchers focus on the paths between indicators and latent variables. Lower χ^2 values imply better fit so LISREL reports reductions as positive values.

Exactly what modification index value warrants consideration for adding a path is rather debatable. Some use as low as 5.0 (Kelloway, 1998) but more realistically values should be considered in the context of the initial model χ^2. For example, a reduction of ten is far less meaningful when the initial model χ^2 is 300 as opposed to 150. Researchers must ask if the improved model fit has any real substantive meaning and balances this with theoretical issues. Additionally, paths should be added singularly for each model respecification. This is because any newly freed (or fixed) parameter will likely change the other modification values and estimated parameters. The approach is similar to handling outliers in multiple regression where one first deletes the most extreme, theoretically or practically (e.g., bad data entry) justifiable case and then reestimates.

31.12   AN EXAMPLE: PUBLIC SERVICE MOTIVATION

Between the various parameters and model fit tests, CFA has a lot to evaluate. Typically researchers want to see a good RMSEA as well as alternative, comparative modified models first. Next, the magnitude and significance of the lambdas and theta-delta values are used to judge validity and reliability. It does get more complex, but in a nutshell CFA assessment centers on these values.

Public service motivation (PSM), work motivations grounded in public service, is probably the most intensively CFA evaluated construct. Beginning with Perry and Wise's initial conceptualization (1990) and Perry's (1996) confirmatory and exploratory work, latent subdimensions and their indicators have been tested in a variety of samples and specifications (e.g., Perry et al., forthcoming; Coursey et al., forthcoming; Houston, 2000; Scott and Pandey, 2005).

As an example, consider a CFA testing three latent PSM subdimensions: self-sacrifice, compassion, and commitment. Coursey and Colleagues (forthcoming) use a CFA via LISREL to evaluate this model. The analysis also covers special issues of ordinal data. The book Web site provides printout copies as well as a walk-through of interpreting the output and writing the results for publication.

31.13   STATISTICAL AND ESTIMATION ISSUES IN CFA

Like all techniques, SEM/CFA makes important data assumptions and if improperly used, produces inefficient, biased, misleading results. Discussion of these issues can become highly theoretical and are treated here in a more practical, introductory fashion. Some good books that discuss these issues in more detail include Kline (2005), Brown (2006), and Bollen (1989) as well as the LISREL program guides and supporting Web site (http://www.ssicentral.com). Some issues are common, though in varied forms, to multiple regression such as missing data and statistical power. Here, we overview two major issues rather specific to SEM/CFA: identification and non-normal/discrete data.

31.14 IDENTIFICATION

CFA and SEM involve estimating unknown parameters from known, observed covariances. Researchers must be careful that the number of paths/equations is greater than the number of unknowns. This is called an overidentified model. Under such conditions, there are several unique solutions and the model can be estimated such that it provides the best fit among these. Two other possibilities make the model unusable. A just identified or saturated model has an equal number of equations and unknowns such there is only one unique solution. The model fit will always be perfect under such conditions and it is of no value in testing. The underidentified model has more unknowns than equations and there are no unique solutions. LISREL and other SEM programs typically warn you of these two bad conditions.

How do you achieve overidentification? There is no easy answer but there are some general guidelines that if followed, will produce an overidentified model. Bollen (1989) proposed that a CFA will be identified if (1) there are at least three indicators to each latent variable or (2) there are at least two indicators of each latent factor and they are allowed to covary/correlate. Sample size also appears a factor with samples above 200 less susceptible and it is possible, at times, to use just two indicators (i.e., Kelloway, 1998). In SEM models, limiting your paths to one-way casual flow and perhaps setting some parameters to fixed, unestimated values helps. The latter is especially important in formative CFA models where the observed indicators are causal and exogenous and hence normally free to covary. This drastically increases the number of estimated parameters and is a serious limitation of such models.

31.15 NON-NORMAL AND DISCRETE DATA

In regression, the researchers will often deploy ordinal dependent variables, arguing for the model's robustness, especially with larger sample sizes and ordinal items with ranges above 10–15. This attitude tends to pervade among SEM/CFA beginners.* However, SEM/CFA as standardly applied to interval data is far more troubling than in standard regression and its' ordinary least squares (OLS) estimators. Simply put, researchers should never deploy default, interval, normal-data-based procedures to non-normal and discrete data. Unfortunately, most published SEM/CFA articles within public administration make this all too common mistake.

Standard maximum likelihood estimation (MLE) in CFA assumes a sample covariance matrix from a multivariate normal distribution. Discrete, noncontinuous distributions are not appropriate (Jöreskog, 2001). MLE is just not as robust to non-normality under SEM/CFA as OLS in regression. Simulations demonstrate standard MLE yields significant estimation problems including inflated chi-square fit statistics and biased, underestimation of parameters and standard errors (e.g., Muthen and Kaplan, 1985; Hutchinson and Olmos, 1998; Flora and Curran, 2004).

What can be done? One approach is applying polychoric correlations with weighted least squares (WLS, or sometimes called asymptotic distribution free, ADF) to their inverted asymptotic covariance matrix (i.e., Jöreskog, 1994). But, this is demanding on sample size though exactly what sample size is needed is still debated as it varies by model degrees of freedom and other issues (cf. Jöreskog, 1994, 2001). Research has documented unstable estimates until sample sizes approach

---

* The following discussion relies heavily on Coursey and Pandey (forthcoming).

1000 (Potthast, 1993). Minimum sample size varies by the number of categories on each indicator, the number of observations per item and dimension, how many resulting zero cells are produced in the contingency tables, among other concerns.

Given WLS sample size issues, what else can be done? One possibility is deploying MLE with the asymptotic covariance matrix such that the standard error and resulting statistics are corrected for non-normality. This avoids the data-intensive inverted matrix in WLS (Joreskog, 1990, 2001). Kelloway (1998), in reviewing several authors' recommendations, suggests 200 observations for a latent variable (e.g., CFA) model using this form of MLE. In cases where the indicators are all on the same measurement scale, the matrix is derived from the covariance and not the polychoric correlation matrix.

A more recently suggested and tested approach is to use diagonally weighted least squares (D-WLS), or sometimes called "robust" WLS/ADFS. A recent simulation study (Flora and Curran, 2004) documented that D-WLS performs well compared to WLS/ADF and MLE for ordinal measures especially in smaller samples and a variety of conditions. Coursey and Colleagues (forthcoming) use D-WLS in their CFA for Perry's PSM scale. For more coverage of these issues, see Brown (2006, chapter 9).

31.16 SUGGESTED STUDY RESOURCES

This chapter serves as a basic introduction to CFA and somewhat SEM. Researchers are advised to explore these techniques in more detail toward their actual research. There are quite a few SEM books now, unfortunately many highly technical and not very approachable. Many of the books referenced in this chapter are solid introductions that do not require extensive mathematical backgrounds.

Kelloway (1998) is a short (147 pages), easily read, nontechnical guide using LISREL examples (though in the raw code and not the graphical interface) and is highly recommended as an immediate follow-up to this chapter. Brown (2006) focuses exclusively on CFA. It is a bit more theoretical than Kelloway (1998) but has solid introductions to advanced CFA models (like higher-order and formative specifications) and various data issues such as categorical data. Kline's (2005) SEM book is a good beginner's guide to the various models including CFA though a bit more technical. It includes good chapters on nonrecursive and latent growth models as well as a nice overview of typical ways to misuse SEM. For those wanting a very theoretical treatment, the Bollen (1989) is a classic.

The LISREL program books and their associated company Web site (http://www.ssicentral.com/lisrel) are wonderful resources. The journal Structural Equation Modeling covers cutting-edge research in SEM/CFA applications (often technical) and the listserv, SEMNET (http://www2.gsu.edu/~mkteer/semnet.html) is a great community resource. The list is very active and many famed SEM researchers gladly address even beginner's questions.

Within public administration, most of the best examples of CFA are within public service motivation. There are not many specific to CFA. Perry's (1996) is a good early work with a nice example of respecification analysis. Coursey and Pandey (forthcoming) and Coursey and colleagues (forthcoming) offer solid reviews of many overlooked technical issues in CFA, including indicator variance assumptions, in their assessment of Perry's scale. For an example of testing formative versus reflective specifications and the associated issues, see Coursey and Pandey's (forthcoming) work on red tape measurement.

DISCUSSION QUESTIONS

1. Identify what some of the major uses of SEM and CFA. Why would one use these over multiple regression, path analysis, or exploratory factor analysis?
2. Explain the differences between the three major forms of model fit in CFA and give at least one example of an associated measure.

3. Argue pro and con for respecification analysis in CFA.
4. Search public administration journals for an example of a piece with clearly noted latent variables and indicators using simple summated indices. Explain how you might improve the piece with CFA and draw the theoretical model.

REFERENCES

Blalock, H. 1964. *Causal Inference in Non-Experimental Research.* Chapel Hill: University of North Carolina Press.
Bollen, K. 1989. *Structural Equations with Latent Variables.* New York: John Wiley and Sons.
Brown, T. 2006. *Confirmatory Factor Analysis for Applied Research.* New York: Guilford Press.
Coursey, D. and Pandey, S. (forthcoming). Public service motivation: Testing a shortened version of Perry's scale, *Administration and Society.*
Coursey, D. and Pandey, S. (forthcoming). Content domain, measurement, and validity of the red tape concept, *American Review of Public Administration.*
Coursey, D., Perry, J., Brudney, J., and Littlepage, L. 2007. Psychometric verification of Perry's public service motivation instrument: Results for volunteer exemplars, *Review of Public Personnel Administration (ROPPA).* (Forthcoming, December 2007, 27(4)).
Flora, D. and Curran, P. 2004. An empirical evaluation of alternative methods of estimation for confirmatory factor analysis with ordinal data, *Psychological Methods,* 9, 466–491.
Houston, D. 2000. Public-service motivation: A multivariate test, *Journal of Public Administration Research and Theory,* 10(4), 713–727.
Hutchinson, S. and Olmos, A. 1998. Behavior of descriptive fit indexes in confirmatory factor analysis using ordered categorical data, *Structural Equation Modeling,* 5, 344–364.
Jöreskog, K. 1990. New developments in LISREL: Analysis of ordinal variables using polychoric correlations and weighted least squares, *Quality and Quantity,* 24, 387–404.
Jöreskog, K. 1994. On the estimation of polychoric correlations and their asymptotic covariance matrix, *Psychometrika,* 59, 381–389.
Jöreskog, K. 2001. *Analysis of Ordinal Variables 2: Cross-Sectional Data.* Unpublished manuscript.
Kline, R. 2005. *Principles and Practice of Structural Equation Modeling.* New York: Guilford Press.
Kelloway, E. 1998. *Using LISREL for Structural Equation Modeling: A Researcher's Guide.* London: Sage Publications.
Muthen, B. and Kaplan, D. 1985. A comparison of some methodologies for the factor-analysis of non-normal Likert variables, *British Journal of Mathematical and Statistical Psychology,* 38, 171–180.
Perry, J. 1996. Measuring public service motivation: An assessment of construct validity, *Journal of Public Administration Research and Theory,* 6, 5–22.
Perry, J. and Wise, L. 1990. The motivational bases of public service, *Public Administration Review,* 50, 367–373.
Perry, J., Brudney, J., Coursey, D., and Littlepage, L. (forthcoming). What drives morally committed citizens? A study of the antecedents of public service motivation, *Public Administration Review.*
Potthast, M. 1993. Confirmatory factor analysis of ordered categorical variables with large models, *British Journal of Mathematical and Statistical Psychology,* 46, 273–286.
Scott, P.G. and Pandey, S. 2005. Red tape and public service motivation: Findings from a national survey of managers in state health and human services agencies, *Review of Public Personnel Administration,* 25(2), 155–180.
Simon, H. 1946. The proverbs of administration, *Public Administration Review,* 6(1), 53–67.
Steiger, J. 1990. Structural model evaluation and modification: An interval estimation approach, *Multivariate Behavioral Research,* 25, 173–180.
Yuan, K. and Bentler, P. 1997. Mean and covariance structure analysis: Theoretical and practical improvements, *Journal of the American Statistical Association,* 92, 767–774.

32 Introduction to Panel Data Analysis: Concepts and Practices

Tae Ho Eom, Sock Hwan Lee, and Hua Xu

CONTENTS

32.1 INTRODUCTION

Panel data analysis enables researchers to generate relatively higher level of statistical validity in policy analysis and program evaluation using more sophisticated research design than statistical techniques using cross-sectional data. Due to such advantages, panel data analysis has been used in various research papers and journal articles in social science and it becomes increasingly popular to researchers over the recent years.* In fact, it has been one of the key components in quantitative methods or one of the core statistical or econometrics courses for graduate programs in public policy and public administration as well as political science, economics, finance, sociology, and many other fields of social science. Accordingly, textbooks dealing with this topic are burgeoning: some are titled panel data analysis and others include only chapters for panel data analysis while dealing

---

* For some recent examples, see Frumkin and Kim (2001), Sapat (2004), Hou (2004), Marlowe (2005), Hill (2005), and Eom and Rubenstein (2006).

with a broad range of statistics analysis techniques.* For students who want to gain an introductory level understanding of panel data analysis without using matrix algebra, Wooldridge's *Introductory Econometrics* (2006) is recommendable. The book provides essential components of basic models with a number of good examples and exercises without using complicated proofs with matrix algebra. For advanced students and researchers who have good knowledge of matrix algebra and calculus, books by Wooldridge (2002), Baltalgi (2001), Hsiao (2003), and Greene (2003) are among most useful ones.

32.2 WHAT IS PANEL DATA?

32.2.1 DEFINITION AND STRUCTURE

A panel dataset, as defined, is a cross-sectional time-series dataset, which, ideally, provides repeated measurements of a certain number of variables over a period of time on observed units, such as individuals, households, firms, cities, and states.† A cross-sectional dataset consists of observations on a certain number of variables at certain point of time whereas a time-series dataset consists of a variable or several variables of observations over a number of periods. In a panel dataset, the number of repeated measurements on the same variables on the same population or sample can be as small as two. This is particularly the case for "one-shot" experiments (Campbell and Stanley, 1966). A panel data is easily conceptualized as a three-dimensional structure for each variable: the vertical dimension as time and the horizontal dimension as multiple observations for each variable. In general, observations in the samples are the same across all periods, while in some cases, particularly in random surveys, the observations in the samples from one period are not identical to those from another. The former is termed as a *balanced panel dataset* whereas the latter is termed an *unbalanced panel dataset.* In general, an unbalanced panel dataset results from missing observations for some variables for a certain number of periods of time in the process of data collection. There exist various reasons for the missing values such as "attrition" and "selection bias." So it is critical to know what implications they have on the estimation results. The differences in data structure and treatment of missing values have practical implications for choosing appropriate econometric models. Statistical remedies for missing values and assumptions used for securing valid statistical power are left to more advanced topics.

To understand the structure of a panel dataset, we examine a school dataset below. We begin with a cross-sectional dataset and move to a panel dataset by appending multiple cross-sectional datasets. Assume that we are interested in finding the relationship between the student performance of a school and school expenditure, organizational form of the school, and other variables such as parents' educational attainment by examining the cross-sectional data in 2005 school year.

Table 32.1 shows a typical cross-sectional dataset, which includes N number of observations on four variables. This cross-sectional dataset only captures the "snap shot" of the observations for a particular year. So, we are not able to identify dynamic variations of school performance over time. A time-series dataset, as shown in Table 32.2, in contrast, provides the variations of observations over time. It measures the same four variables on School 1 for 10 years between 1996 and 2005, and thereby now we can identify how the variables change over the past ten years. The cost of excluding other schools other than School 1 is not trivial. The story of a single or several schools is not convincing at all. And we have very little to tell about the relationship between the three independent variables and student performance, which is our primary purpose of the analysis.

---

* For the textbooks especially designed for panel data analysis, see Hsiao (1986), Baltagi (2001), and Wooldridge (2002); for chapters in textbooks, see Wooldridge (2006), Greene (2003), Pindyck and Rubinfeld (1998), Griffiths, Hill, and Judge (1993), Kennedy (2003), and Gujarati (2003).
† Panel data is also termed as longitudinal data (for instance, see Burbridge, 1999).

TABLE 32.1
An Example of Cross-Sectional Data

Observations	Average SAT Scores	Organizational Form of Schools	Average Parents' Years of Education	Per Student Expenditure ($)
School 1	540	Hierarchical	16	3500
School 2	519	Flat	18	4000
School 3	507	Hybrid	14	1800
School 4	499	Hierarchical	14	1890
---	---	---	---	---
School 50	557	Flat	15	2900

To make a panel dataset, now we simply "stack up" the cross-sectional dataset each year or append the time-series datasets for all schools.* Table 32.3 shows a panel dataset that combines information from Tables 32.1 and 32.2. Notice that each observation, i.e., 50 schools in this example, repeats for ten years from 1996 to 2005 with the values of four variables. This implies that a panel dataset brings in much more useful information than does a single cross-sectional or time-series dataset. For example, in case that the organizational forms of some schools have changed in 2000 school year, we are able to examine how the changes have affected student performance thereafter. As such, a panel dataset provides both cross-sectional relationship between the dependent and independent variables and the time variations of variables at the same time.

32.2.2 Panel Data and Its Relations to Social Experimental Designs

Social experimental research design provides a high level of validity for the causal link between the policy interventions such as education reform, and the social outcomes such as student performance. However, social experimental design by nature is far more complex than for natural experiments because of the factors that practically cannot be controlled by researchers (Maxim, 1999). As found in many policy experiments, the difficulties in social experiments, among many others, include nonrandom assignments, ethics, and the length of the interventions.[†] Whereas in natural experiments, researchers are able to randomly assign control and treatment groups, and

TABLE 32.2
An Example of Time-Series Data

Year	Student Performance (SAT)	Organizational Form of Schools	Average Parents' Years of Education	Per Student Expenditure ($)
1996	532	Hierarchical	16	2507
1997	543	Hierarchical	16	2790
---	---	---	---	---
2004	551	Hierarchical	16	3380
2005	540	Hierarchical	16	3500

* Table 32.3 is sorted by observations and year. After constructing a panel dataset, we must designate observational and time variables so that statistics packages, such as SAS and STATA, treat it as a panel dataset. In this example, the observational variable is "schools" and the time variable is "year."
[†] See Burtless (1995) for more comprehensive summaries and critique on social experiments; also see Rosenzweig and Wolpin (2000).

TABLE 32.3

An Example of Panel Data

Observations	Year	Student Performance (SAT)	Organization Form of Schools	Average Parents' Years of Education	Per student Expenditure ($)
School 1	1996	532	Hierarchical	16	2507
School 1	1997	543	Hierarchical	16	2790
School 1	—	—	—	—	—
School 1	2004	551	Hierarchical	16	3380
School 1	2005	540	Hierarchical	16	3500
School 2	1996	501	Flat	18	3590
School 2	1997	523	Flat	18	3790
School 2	—	—	—	—	—
School 2	2004	514	Flat	18	3899
School 2	2005	519	Flat	18	4000
—	—	—	—	—	—
—	—	—	—	—	—
School 50	1996	534	Flat	15	2601
School 50	1997	511	Flat	15	2780
School 50	—	—	—	—	—
School 50	2004	537	Flat	15	2870
School 50	2005	557	Flat	15	2900

control environment effectively, in the most of large-scale social-experiments, the random assignment is ethically and practically impossible. Therefore, in many cases, social experiments become quasi-experiments. (Campbell and Stanley, 1966; Heckman, 1991; Trochim, 2001) For instance, in the Negative Income Tax Programs (1968–1978) and the job training program under the National Job Training Act (1986–1994), the selection of the participating households during the process of the experiments is not strictly random.* Attritions of the program participants also posed practical challenges to the researchers because the participants who exited the program are more likely to have systematic differences from those who remained in the program. In spite of such inherent difficulties, panel data generated by social experiments provides exceptionally high quality information compared with cross-sectional data. Econometricians, in fact, have developed some useful techniques to overcome the shortcomings of social experiments. For instance, Heckman (1991, 2000, 2001) developed a so-called sample selection model to address the sample selection bias.

Policy analysis using quasi-experimental data can be effectively done by a group of panel data analysis techniques introduced in this chapter. In Heckman's words, these are "nonexperimental" or "econometric" approach to policy evaluation with self-selection bias and endogeneity problems (Heckman and Smith, 1995). The dependent variable can be regarded as the effect of treatment or interventions by policies or programs, and the independent variables include the treatment and the control variables. Putting aside the selection bias and endogeneity issues for the advanced readers, it implies that having panel data before and after the policy interventions is extremely useful in examining the impacts of the interventions.

Conducting surveys is another important way to gather panel data. Data collected from survey are also called "observational" or nonexperimental data. Some panel data obtained through surveys

---

* For a more detail discussion on the negative income tax experiments, see Orcutt and Orcutt (1968).

include Panel Study in Income Dynamics (PSID), Current Population Survey (CPS), National Longitudinal Survey (NLS), National Longitudinal Surveys of Youth (NLSY), and the World Bank's Living Standards Measurement Study (LSMS) (Cameron and Trivedi, 2005).

32.3 ADVANTAGES OF USING PANEL DATA

The advantages of using panel data are discussed in full length in Balgati (2001) and Hsiao (1986). Here, we focus on several points useful for readers without in-depth econometrics knowledge, in comparison with cross-sectional data analysis.

One of the advantages of using panel data is to increase the number of observations for the analysis. This is especially true for the pooled OLS model. Technically speaking, by having observations repeating over time, we have lower standard errors compared with those estimated by cross-sectional data analysis. This implies that larger number of observation due to the stacking up cross-sectional data increases the efficiency of estimation, and thereby we have higher possibility of statistically significant estimates. The fundamental advantage of using panel data, however, lies in its efficacy allowing researchers to examine the cause-and-effect relationship using before-and-after observations. Although analysis with cross-sectional data is still effective in examining causal relationship based on theoretical research models, strictly speaking, it is hard to identify which variable "affects" others because it lacks the time dimension that is one of the essential components for causal relationship. In the same vein, the stability of the relationship between the dependent and independent variables can be examined. The cross-sectional analysis only examines the relationships at a single point of time, whereas with panel data, we are able to explore the dynamic variations of the relationships.[*]

Another important motivation for panel data analysis is to reduce the omitted variable bias (Wooldridge, 2006). This is especially true for so-called error component models that will be addressed in the subsequent sections in details. For instance, using fixed effects model, we are able to eliminate time-invariance unobserved errors that are specific to each observation. As a result, we have more statistically robust estimation results.

32.4 ESTIMATION METHODS

In this section, we explain panel data analysis models that are used most frequently in the literature. As we reviewed, panel data contains information of temporal and spatial dimensions. The temporal dimension is the period in which repeated measurements are made such as month, quarter, and year and the spatial dimension is the unit of observations such as people, firms, and states.

The general regression model of panel data can be expressed as follows:

$$y_{it} = \beta_0 + \beta_1 x_{it,1} + \beta_2 x_{it,2} + \cdots + \beta_k x_{it,k} + v_{it}, \ i = 1, \ldots, N; \ t = 1, \ldots, T; \ k = 1, \ldots, K \quad (32.1)$$

where
  i is the unit of observation
  t is the period of time
  k indicates the kth explanatory variable
  β_0 is the intercept
  β_k is the coefficient of each explanatory variable
  v_{it} is the error term[†]

---

[*] Concrete examples are given in pp. 2–5 in Hsaio (1995) and pp. 6–7 in Balgati (2001).
[†] This notation scheme is used through this chapter.

The so-called composite error term, v_{it}, in Equation 32.1 can be decomposed into two components: a cross-sectional unit-specific error,[*] a_i, and an idiosyncratic error, u_{it}.[†]

$$v_{it} = a_i + u_{it} \tag{32.2}$$

The cross-sectional unit-specific error, a_i, does not change over time and the idiosyncratic error, u_{it}, varies over the cross-sectional units and time (Baltagi, 2001; Greene, 2003; Griffiths et al., 1993; Gujarati, 2003; Maddala, 2001; Wooldridge, 2006). The motivation and benefits of decomposing the error terms into two parts are that if we could eliminate some part of them using panel data, we would be better off in terms of minimizing concerns for omitted variable bias caused by unmeasured unit-specific factors.

By incorporating Equation 32.2 into Equation 32.1, we can get the following equation:

$$y_{it} = \beta_0 + \beta_1 x_{it,1} + \beta_2 x_{it,2} + \cdots + \beta_k x_{it,k} + a_i + u_{it} \tag{32.3}$$

Equation 32.3 is called as an error component model. The time-constant and unit-specific error, a_i, are unobserved factors. Examples include individual's ability when the unit of observation is individuals and states' unique culture and institutions in case that the unit of observation of states. Such factors can be regarded as time-invariant and at the same time it is extremely hard to measure them. The estimation methods of error component models are classified by how to treat the error term, a_i. The pooled OLS model does not distinguish it from other types of errors, whereas the fixed effects model regards it as coefficients to be estimated, and the random effects model treats it as random variables (Baltagi, 2001; Greene, 2003; Maddala, 2001; Wooldridge, 2006). In the following, we will introduce these three models and additionally, difference-in-difference (DID) model which is commonly used in examining the effect of policies, programs, and social events.[‡]

We discuss each panel data estimation approach using examples of cost function for New Jersey school districts. Based on the cost function approach, a school district's per pupil spending is determined by student outcome, input prices, and environmental factors over which school districts cannot control such as characteristics of student body measured by percent of students receiving free lunch (Duncombe and Yinger, 1999, 2000). To estimate the cost function for New Jersey school districts, we specify the following equation:

$$\ln(\text{TE}_{it}) = \beta_0 + \beta_1 \text{SP4}_{it} + \beta_2 \ln(\text{FS}_{it}) + \beta_3 \ln(\text{RE}_{it}) + \beta_4 \text{FL}_{it} + \beta_5 \text{PR}_i + \beta_6 \text{BL}_{it} + v_{it} \tag{32.4}$$

where
   $\ln(\text{TE}_{it})$ is the natural log of per pupil total expenditure
   SP4_{it} is the statewide standardized test for students in fourth grade
   $\ln(\text{FS}_{it})$ is the natural log of faculty median salary
   $\ln(\text{RE}_{it})$ is the natural log of the number of resident enrollment
   FL_{it} is the percent of students who receive free lunch
   PR_i is the child poverty rate[§]
   BL_{it} is the percent of black students

---

[*] It is also referred to as unobserved effect, unobserved heterogeneity, and fixed effects in the literature.

[†] The error term can be further decomposed into three components: time-constant and unit-specific error (a_i), time-varying and unit-constant error (λ_t), and idiosyncratic error (u_{it}). The model correcting the time-constant error and time-varying error is called two-way error component model. This chapter focuses on only the one-way model. For more details on two-way models, see chapter 3 in Baltagi (2001), pp. 291–292 in Greene (2003), p. 644 in Gujarati (2003), and p. 625 in Kmenta (1997).

[‡] For more topics on panel data estimation methods such as dynamic model, random coefficient model, panel data with limited dependent variable, censored panel data, unbalanced panel data, see Baltagi (2001), chapter 13 in Greene (2003), pp. 616–635 in Kmenta (1997), and Wooldridge (2002).

[§] The subscript t of PR is dropped because it is constant over the time period.

The primary purpose of the examples is to show the mechanism of panel data estimation methods and the interpretation of the results. Therefore, we disregard the estimation issues of cost function such as endogeneity, simultaneity, and model specification.

We use panel data for school districts in the state of New Jersey to estimate cost functions. The panel data comes from the New Jersey Legislative District Data Book, New Jersey Department of Education, the U.S. Census Bureau, and the National Center for Education Statistics. The data contains statewide standardized test scores, demographics, teachers, and other characteristics of school districts. We use a three-year panel of data from 2001 to 2003 on 405 school districts. There are 596 school districts in New Jersey. However, we exclude vocational school districts, special service school districts, and some school districts with missing data.

32.4.1 THE DIFFERENCE-IN-DIFFERENCE MODEL

In case that some external events are hypothesized to affect social outcomes of interest, we should have data at least for two time periods to examine the changes made to the dependent variable. "External" in this context means that the events are not determined by the observed units' own decision. For instance, suppose that a state government designed and implemented a new state aid formula for school districts with which low-wealth districts became receiving substantially more state aid from the state than in previous year. Research questions of interest include whether it has impacts on districts' spending decisions and student performance. In this case, the state aid formula changes are "external events" to the school districts because the decision was made by the state. As such, government policy changes and implementation of new programs provide a natural experiment or a quasi-experiment setting for researchers. One of the simplest and powerful tools in analyzing the effect of such a natural experiment is the difference-in-difference (DID) estimation. The DID is classified as a special case of first-difference estimation method (Halaby, 2004) and very useful especially when the panel data has only two time period and the treatment group that is affected by the event can easily be distinguished from the control groups.

The logic of DID estimation fits well with the experimental design. The DID estimator is produced by calculating the changes in outcome measures over time for both the treatment and control groups and then comparing the difference between the groups (Wooldridge, 2006). For example, let's assume that New Jersey introduced a new education policy in 2002 and now we are trying to evaluate the effect of the policy using DID estimation. The DID estimator can be expressed by the following formula:

$$\text{DID} = (y_{\text{TA}} - y_{\text{TB}}) - (y_{\text{CA}} - y_{\text{CB}}) = (y_{\text{TA}} - y_{\text{CA}}) - (y_{\text{TB}} - y_{\text{CB}}) \tag{32.5}$$

where
  y is the outcome of the policy
  T represents treatment group
  C represents control group
  A denotes after the policy
  B denotes before the policy

We can easily incorporate the above DID logic in the regression model by using dummy variables. The regression form of DID model is specified as follows:

$$y_{it} = \beta_0 + \beta_1 \, \text{AP} + \beta_2 \, \text{TG} + \beta_3 \, \text{AP} \times \text{TG} + X_{it}\, \theta + v_{it} \tag{32.6}$$

where
  y_{it} is the policy outcome
  AP is a dummy variable for after the policy
  TG is a dummy variable for treatment group
  AP $\times$ TG is the interaction term between after policy time period and treatment group

In Equation 32.6, β_3 measures the effect of the policy. The DID estimation ensures that any unobserved time-constant variables that are correlated with the selection decision and the outcome variable will be eliminated. Thus, the DID estimator is unbiased and consistent (Halaby, 2004).

EXAMPLE 1. THE DID MODEL

To estimate DID model with New Jersey school district data, let's assume that in 2002, New Jersey state government introduced a new education finance policy to increase education spending in low-wealth school districts. The 98 school districts to be received state aid are selected based on per pupil expenditure in 2001. We are interested in examining the impact of this policy change on the total per pupil spending of New Jersey school districts so we specify the following equation:

$$\ln(\text{TE}_{it}) = \beta_0 + \beta_1 \text{SP4}_{it} + \beta_2 \ln(\text{FS}_{it}) + \beta_3 \ln(\text{RE}_{it}) + \beta_4 \text{FL}_{it} + \beta_5 \text{PR}_i$$
$$+ \beta_6 \text{BL}_{it} + \beta_7 \text{AP}_t + \beta_8 \text{TG}_i + \beta_9 \text{AP}_t \times \text{TG}_i + v_{it} \qquad (32.7)$$

where
   AP_t is a dummy for after the policy (year 2003)
   TG_i is a dummy for selected 98 school districts (treatment group)
   $\text{AP}_t \times \text{TG}_i$ is an interaction term between after policy and treatment group

The coefficient of interest for the study is β_8 and β_9. The coefficient β_8 captures the expenditure gap between control and treatment groups before the policy (year 2001) and β_9 measures the change in the expenditure gap between before and after the policy. The following is the regression results of Equation 32.7.* The standard errors of estimates are in the parenthesis.

$$\ln(\text{TE}_{it}) = 7.525 + 1.184\text{SP4}_{it} + 0.116 \ln(\text{FS}_{it}) - 0.038 \ln(\text{RE}_{it}) + 0.262\text{FL}_{it}$$
$$\quad (0.513) \quad (0.307) \qquad (0.045) \qquad\quad (0.007) \qquad\quad (0.093)$$
$$+ 1.399\text{PR}_i + 0.120\text{BL}_{it} + 0.139\text{AP}_t - 0.262\text{TG}_i + 0.138\text{AP}_t \times \text{TG}_t$$
$$\quad (0.644) \qquad (0.058) \qquad (0.017) \qquad (0.022) \qquad (0.030) \qquad\qquad (32.8)$$

$$R^2 = 0.3499, \; N = 810.$$

The coefficient on TG_i (β_8) indicates that before the New Jersey education policy of 2002, the 98 wealth poor school districts spend less by 26.2 percent than the other school districts do. The results show that the New Jersey education policy has a positive effect on the per pupil total expenditure. The coefficient on interaction term between TG_i and AP_t indicates that the New Jersey education policy reduces the per pupil total expenditure gap by 13.8 percent.

Examples of DID approach in journals include Holzer and Neumark (2000), who examine the impacts of Affirmative Action on hiring practices, personnel policies, and employment outcomes with a panel dataset from the survey of employers between 1992 and 1994; Arulampalam, Booth, and Bryan (2004) examine the impact of the U.K. National Minimum Wage (NMW) of 1999 on the work-related training of low-wage workers using the 1998 and 2000 British Household Panel Survey; Kirby and Riley (2004) examine the effect of compulsory work-focused interviews on the probability of leaving social security benefit for lone parents and the sick or disabled; Stewart (2004) examines the impact of the introduction of the U.K. NMW of 1999 on the probability of subsequent employment of the NMW's target workers with three different panel survey; and Robinson (2005) analyzes the impact of the U.K. NMW on gender pay gaps using a panel data before and after the NMW of 1999.

---

* We dropped the 2002 data.

32.4.2 THE POOLED OLS MODEL

One most basic and simplest method to estimate Equation 32.1 is just to pool the data and apply OLS. To estimate Equation 32.1 using pooled OLS, it is required to assume that the composite error term v_{it} is not correlated with the explanatory variable x_{itk} (Greene, 2003; Gujarati, 2003; Wooldridge, 2006). This means that only when there are neither cross-sectional nor temporal effects, we can pool the data and run OLS regression models. The pooled OLS version of Equation 32.1 can be expressed as follows:

$$y = \beta_0 + \beta_1 x_1 + \beta_2 x_2 + \cdots + \beta_k x_k + v \qquad (32.9)$$

In Equation 32.9, subscripts i and t disappear because of the above assumption. There are some drawbacks of pooled OLS method. Panel data contains the information of time and cross-sectional dimensions. Pooled OLS, however, disregards this information of panel data. In addition, the assumption of pooled OLS is not realistic because it is not possible to measure all time-constant and unit-specific effects, a_i, and include them in the model. Thus, when we use OLS in analyzing panel data, the assumption is usually violated. In this case, the pooled OLS estimator is biased and inconsistent (Gujarati, 2003; Wooldridge, 2006). Despite such drawbacks, the pooled OLS models is frequently used in the public administration literature because pooling cross-sectional data increases the number of observations substantially and in many cases, secure more variations of the key independent variables, thereby producing significant estimates.

EXAMPLE 2. THE POOLED OLS MODEL

We estimate the cost function for New Jersey school districts, Equation 32.4, using the pooled OLS method. The following shows the estimation results:

$$\ln(\text{TE}) = 7.025 + 0.115\,\text{SP4} + 0.239\ln(\text{FS}) - 0.036\ln(\text{RE}) + 0.197\,\text{FL} + 1.092\,\text{PR}$$
$$(0.458)\quad(0.253)\qquad(0.041)\qquad\quad(0.006)\qquad\quad(0.087)\qquad(0.608)$$
$$+\ 0.141\text{BL}$$
$$(0.054) \qquad\qquad\qquad\qquad\qquad\qquad\qquad\qquad\qquad (32.10)$$

$$R^2 = 0.0987,\ N = 1215.$$

The results show that four environmental factors have significant effects on per pupil expenditure except child poverty rate. One percent increase in the percent of students receiving free lunch and black students raises per pupil expenditure by 19.7 percent and 14.1 percent, respectively. One percent increase in resident enrollment decreases per pupil expenditure by 0.036 percent. The educational outcome measured by test score is not significant, whereas the cost of input measured by the median faculty salary is significant and positive effect. The coefficient on median faculty salary indicates that one percent increase in the median faculty salary leads to a 0.24 percent increase in per pupil expenditure. As mentioned, however, the OLS results may be biased because other unobserved characteristics of students are not controlled. In the end of this section, we compare the OLS results to those of other panel data estimation methods.

The empirical examples of pooled OLS include Smith (1997), who studies the impact of competing crime policies on homicide rates with a panel dataset on 50 states in United States from 1975 to 1990; Waldfogel (1997) examines the effect of children on women's wages with panel data from the 1968–1988 National Longitudinal Survey of Young Women;* Bauer (2002) analyzes the wage effects of inadequate schooling using a German panel dataset for the period 1984–1998;[†] Meier and Bohte (2003) examine the hypothesis that the span of control has an effect on

---

* Waldfogel (1997) also uses first-difference and fixed effects models.
[†] Bauer (2002) also estimates his model with fixed effects and random effects models.

organizational performance using Texas school districts panel data from 1994 to 1997; Bevan and Danbolt (2004) analyze the determinants of the capital structure of 1054 U.K. companies from 1991 to 1997; and Evans and Kelley (2004) examine the effect of family structure on life satisfaction.

32.4.3   THE FIXED EFFECTS MODEL

The fixed effects model is widely used when we want to control for omitted variables that are constant over the period of time and vary across the units that is called unobserved heterogeneity or fixed effects, a_i. When we estimate Equation 32.3 using the fixed effects model, it is assumed that the unobserved heterogeneity (a_i) is correlated with the explanatory variable (x_{itk}). Another important assumption is that the idiosyncratic error (u_{it}) is independent of the explanatory variable (x_{itk}) (Baltagi, 2001; Kmenta, 1997; Wooldridge, 2006). By eliminating the unobserved effect a_i, which implies reducing omitted variables biases, we can have more robust estimates. There are three widely used methods for eliminating the unobserved effect a_i in panel data analysis. They are the first-difference model, the least squares dummy variables (LSDV) model, and the time-demeaning model. These methods are called as a more general term, the fixed effects model.*

32.4.3.1   The First-Difference Method

One method for eliminating the unobserved heterogeneity (a_i) is to difference the data across the two time periods. The first difference is the change from one period of time to the next. If y_t denotes the value of y at period t, then the first difference of y at period t is equal to $y_t - y_{t-1}$. Therefore, if we subtract Equation 32.3 at the period of time 1 from Equation 32.3 at the period of time 2, we get the following equation:

$$(y_{i2} - y_{i1}) = \beta_1(x_{i2,1} - x_{i1,1}) + \cdots \beta_k(x_{i2,k} - x_{i1,k}) + (u_{i2} - u_{i1}), \text{ or } \Delta y_i = \beta_k \Delta x_{i,k} + \Delta u_i \quad (32.11)$$

where Δ is the change from $t = 1$ to $t = 2$. In Equation 32.11, the unobserved heterogeneity (a_i) disappears. This is a simple cross-sectional regression equation in differences. Therefore, the coefficients on β_k are estimated by OLS, assuming Δu_i is uncorrelated with Δx_{it}.[†]

EXAMPLE 3. THE FIRST-DIFFERENCE METHOD
The first-difference version of Equation 32.4 can be expressed as follows:

$$\Delta \ln(TE_i) = \beta_1 \Delta SP4_i + \beta_2 \Delta \ln(FS_i) + \beta_3 \Delta \ln(RE_i) + \beta_4 \Delta FL_i + \beta_6 \Delta BL_i + \Delta u_i \quad (32.12)$$

where Δ denotes the change from year t to year $t+1$. In Equation 32.12, one explanatory variable, PR_i, disappears in the equation because it is time-constant.[‡] The first-difference estimation results of Equation 32.12 are as follows:

$$\Delta \ln(TE_i) = 1.516 \Delta SP4_i + 0.218 \Delta \ln(FS_i) - 0.361 \Delta \ln(RE_i) - 0.138 \Delta FL_i + 0.351 \Delta BL_i$$
$$\quad\quad (0.284) \quad\quad\quad (0.103) \quad\quad\quad\quad (0.168) \quad\quad\quad\quad (0.273) \quad\quad\quad (0.465) \quad\quad (32.13)$$

$$R^2 = 0.0437, N = 810.$$

---

* The fixed models focus on and try to eliminate the time-invariant unit-specific fixed effects. In case that unobserved effects are important and must be tested for theories and evaluating policies, we should use dynamic unobserved effects models (Wooldridge, 2002).

[†] For differencing more than two time periods, see pp. 472–473 in Wooldridge (2006).

[‡] This does not mean that child poverty rates have not changed over the time. Rather, it is due to the data availability; since we obtain child poverty rates from the Census, no annual data are available.

The number of observation is reduced by 405 because of the first difference. The results of the first difference are somewhat different from those of pooled OLS. Among the environmental factors, only the resident enrollment has the significant effect. One percent increase in resident enrollment leads to a 0.36 percent decrease in per pupil expenditure. Both student performance and faculty median salary have significant and positive effects. The results indicate that one unit increase in student performance raises the per pupil expenditure by 152 percent and one percent increase in faculty median salary leads to 0.2 percent increase in per pupil expenditure.

For empirical examples of first-difference estimation method, see Loeb and Corcoran (2001), who estimate the difference in wage growth between Aid to Families with Dependent Children (AFDC) recipients and nonrecipients using panel data from the National Longitudinal Survey of Youth; Eichler and Lechner (2002), who estimate the effects of participants in public employment programs in the East German States with six waves of surveys from 1992 to 1997; Noonan and Heflin (2005), who examine the effects of welfare participation and employment on women's wages with longitudinal data from the 1996 Survey of Income and Program Participation; Kawaguchi (2006), who analyze the determinants of Japanese woman workers' participation in firm-initiated training and the effect of the training participation on earnings using the two wave of Japan Panel Survey of Consumers between 1994 and 1998;* and Kuziemko (2006), who examines the effect of school enrollment size on student achievement with a school-level panel data of Indiana.

32.4.3.2 The Time-Demeaning Method

One way other than first-differencing to eliminate the time-constant and unit-specific error (a_i) is the time-demeaning. The time-demeaning is the procedure to transform the original variables into the deviations from the group means of each variable. Specifically, we get the average values of the original variables over time (t) and then subtract the average values from the values of the original variables. In the equation form, by averaging Equation 32.3 over time, we get

$$\bar{y}_i = \beta_0 + \beta_1 \bar{x}_{i1} + \beta_2 \bar{x}_{i2} + \cdots + \beta_k \bar{x}_{ik} + a_i + \bar{u}_i \tag{32.14}$$

and then by subtracting Equation 32.14 from Equation 32.3

$$(y_{it} - \bar{y}_i) = \beta_1 (x_{it1} - \bar{x}_{i1}) + \beta_2 (x_{it2} - \bar{x}_{i2}) + \cdots + \beta_k (x_{itk} - \bar{x}_{ik}) + (u_i - \bar{u}_i) \tag{32.15}$$

where $(y_{it} - \bar{y}_i)$ is the time-demeaned values of y and the same for $(x_{it} - \bar{x}_i)$ and $(u_{it} - \bar{u}_i)$. The important thing is that the time-constant heterogeneity (a_i) is now eliminated in Equation 32.15 (Baltagi, 2001; Halaby, 2004; Kmenta, 1997; Wooldridge, 2006). It is no longer required that a_i is uncorrelated with x_{it}. Equation 32.15, therefore, can be estimated by OLS. It seems that the time-demeaning transformation is burdensome. However, we do not need to do time-demean transformation manually. Statistical packages such as LIMDEP, SAS, and STATA automatically process the time-demeaning transformation and produce the fixed effects estimator.

One of the prices of using the time-demean transformation is that we cannot include any time-constant explanatory variable for estimation because their transformed values are all zero. Such variables include gender, race, and locations (Baltagi, 2001; Wooldridge, 2006).

As a partial remedy, however, we can include the interaction term between the time-constant variables and time dummy variables to see how the time-constant variables' coefficients change over time (Wooldridge, 2006).

---

* Kawaguchi (2006) also uses pooled OLS to estimate the effect of the participation on wages.

EXAMPLE 4. THE TIME-DEMEANING METHOD

The following equation is the time-demeaning estimate of the cost function for New Jersey school district, Equation 32.4.

$$\ln(\text{TE}_{it}) = 9.738 + 2.353\text{SP4}_{it} + 0.344\ln(\text{FS}_{it}) - 0.302\ln(\text{RE}_{it}) - 0.188\text{FL}_{it}$$
$$\phantom{\ln(\text{TE}_{it}) = } (1.473) \quad (0.291) \qquad (0.103) \qquad\qquad (0.158) \qquad\qquad (0.284)$$
$$+ 0.316\text{BL}_{it}$$
$$ (0.458) \tag{32.16}$$

$$R^2 = 0.0166, N = 1215$$

Like the first-difference model, the explanatory variable, PR_i, is also dropped in the above equation by the time-demeaning transformation. The results of time-demeaning methods show that only the student performance and the faculty median salary have the significant effects on the education costs while the four environmental factors are not significant. The coefficient on student performance indicates that one unit increase in it raises the per pupil expenditure by about 235 percent. The coefficient on faculty median salary indicates that one percent increase in it leads to 0.344 percent increase in per pupil expenditure. It seems that the variation of educational cost is explained by mainly those two factors. As with the percent of students receiving free lunch, for which we expect a positive coefficients, in many cases, the estimated coefficients using the fixed effects models produce unexpected signs frequents. This is partly due to the little variations of those variables over time. Because we only use the time-demeaned values, in case that there are little variations in the value of the variables over time, the measurement errors associated with the variables become extremely critical. So sometimes, it gives an unexpected sign for the variables. This implies that we must check whether the key variables have enough variations over time first to apply the fixed effects model.

For empirical examples of time-demeaning estimation method, see Cornwell and Trumbull (1994), who estimate economic model of crime with a panel dataset of North Carolina counties; Chakraborty, Biswas, and Lewis (2000), who estimate the relationship between the average cost of education and school characteristics with panel data from Utah school districts; Häkkinen et al. (2003), who investigate the effects of changes in school expenditure on changes in student achievement using a sample of students in the senior secondary schools for the years 1990–1998; Hou (2004), who studies the causal relation between the structural features of Budget Stabilization Fund (BSF) and the actual BSF balance levels using a panel dataset on 39 U.S. states from 1979 to 1999; Hill (2005), who analyzes the short- and long-term effects of managerial succession on school district performance in Texas; and Page et al. (2005), who estimate the impact of minimum wage legislation on Aid to Families with Dependent Children (AFDC) caseloads using state-level panel data that span the years from 1983–1996.

32.4.3.3 The Least Squares Dummy Variables Method

An alternative view of the fixed effects model is that the unobserved effect, a_i, is regarded as an unknown parameter to be estimated for each cross-sectional unit i (Greene, 2003). We can produce the estimator for each cross-sectional unit (i) and for each period of time (t) by including a dummy variable for each cross-sectional unit (i) and each period of time (t) (Baltagi, 2001; Greene, 2003; Griffiths et al., 1993; Gujarati, 2003; Kmenta, 1997). This method is the so-called least squares dummy variable (LSDV) regression.

A dummy variable is a binary variable that is coded either 1 or 0. It is commonly used to examine group and time effects in regression. The general LSDV model is

$$y_{it} = \beta_0 + (\delta_1 D_1 + \cdots + \delta_{i-1}D_{i-1}) + (\theta_1 T_1 + \cdots + \theta_{t-1}T_{t-1}) + \beta_1 x_{it1} + \cdots + \beta_k x_{itk} + u_{it} \tag{32.17}$$

where

D_i is dummy variables for each cross-sectional unit except one

T_t is dummy variables for each time period except one*

The null hypothesis of LSDV is that all dummy parameters except one are 0: H_0: $D_1 = \cdots = D_{i-1} = 0$ (or H_0: $T_1 = \cdots = T_{t-1} = 0$). This hypothesis is tested by the F-test. If the null hypothesis is rejected, we may conclude that the fixed effect model is better than the pooled OLS model (Batagi, 2001; Greene, 2003; Griffiths et al., 1993).[†]

The LSDV is commonly used because it is relatively easy to estimate and interpret (Baltagi, 2001), provides the identical estimator to the time-demean estimator and the standard errors, and other major statistics are the same (Wooldridge, 2006). The LSDV works best when the panel data has relatively fewer cases and more time periods, as each dummy variable removes one degree of freedom from the model (Baltagi, 2001). The LSDV, however, becomes problematic when there are many cross-sectional units in the panel data (Baltagi, 2001).

EXAMPLE 5. THE LSDV METHOD

The LSDV method uses dummy variables for each school district instead of time-demeaning to eliminate unobserved district fixed effect. Putting 405 dummy variables in the cost function (4) produces the following LSDV model.

$$\ln(\text{TE}_{it}) = \beta_1 \text{SP4}_{it} + \beta_2 \ln(\text{FS}_{it}) + \beta_3 \ln(\text{RE}_{it}) + \beta_4 \text{FL}_{it} + \beta_6 \text{BL}_{it}$$
$$+ \beta_7 D_1 + \cdots + \beta_{411} D405 + u_{it} \tag{32.18}$$

where $D1, \ldots, D405$ are the dummy variables for each school district. The constant term and the time-constant variable, PR_i, disappear in the LSDV model. The following equation is the results of the LSDV estimation of the cost function:

$$\ln(\text{TE}_{it}) = 2.353 \; \text{SP4}_{it} + 0.344 \ln(\text{FS}_{it}) - 0.302 \ln(\text{RE}_{it}) - 0.188 \; \text{FL}_{it} + 0.316 \; \text{BL}_{it}$$
$$\quad (0.291) \qquad (0.103) \qquad\quad (0.158) \qquad\quad (0.284) \qquad (0.458)$$
$$+ 9.412 D1 + \cdots + 9.721 D405$$
$$\quad (1.712) \qquad\qquad (1.811) \tag{32.19}$$

$$R^2 = 0.9998, N = 1215.$$

The LSDV estimates of coefficients are exactly the same of time-demeaning estimates except constant.

Empirical examples that use LSDV to eliminate the time-constant unobserved heterogeneity are Korpi (1989), who studies social policy development in 18 OECD countries during the time period from 1930 to 1980; Apodaca and Stohl (1999), who examine the relationship between human rights and U.S. bilateral foreign aid with a panel dataset on 140 countries from1976 to1995; Brown (2000), who examines the impact of two tax and expenditure limitation policies (the Gallagher amendment of 1983 and the Taxpayer's Bill of Rights (TABOR) of 1992) using a panel dataset on 255 municipal governments in Colorado from 1975 to 1996; Chao and Buongiorno (2002), who examine the causal relations between exports and domestic production in the pulp and paper industries of the 15 main exporting countries between 1961 and 1995; Mullins (2004), who examines the effects of statewide tax and expenditure limitations on local autonomy in revenues and expenditures of local governments with panel data consist of local governments within 787 metropolitan counties; and Ram (2004), who studies the effect of school expenditure on student performance in terms of SAT scores with a panel dataset consists of states with the time periods from 1986 to 1994.

---

* This model is the so-called two-way fixed effects model.

[†] This hypothesis test is also applied to the time-demeaning fixed effects model.

32.4.4 THE RANDOM EFFECTS MODEL

When we analyze panel data, we use the fixed effects model to eliminate the unobserved hetero-geneity (a_i) because it is assumed to be correlated with any of the explanatory variables (x_{itj}). However, when a_i is independent of each explanatory variable, the fixed effects model to eliminate a_i results in inefficient estimators (Baltagi, 2001; Greene, 2003). The random effects model, also known as the variance components model, regards the unobserved heterogeneity (a_i) as random variables rather than fixed ones (Baltagi, 2001; Greene, 2003; Maddala, 2001). Therefore, the random effects model is appropriate when the cross-sectional units are randomly selected from a large population (Baltagi, 2001).

If a variance structure among groups is known, the random effects model is estimated by the generalized least squares (GLS). On the other hand, if the variance structure is not known, the feasible generalized least squares (FGLS) method is appropriate to estimate the variance structure (Greene, 2003; Kmenta, 1997). The Lagrange multiplier (LM) test for the existence of the random effects is designed by Breusch and Pagan (1980). The null hypothesis of the one-way random group effect model is that variances of groups are zero: H_0: $\sigma_u^2 = 0$. If the null hypothesis is rejected, the random effect model is better than the pooled regression (Greene, 2003).

EXAMPLE 6. THE RANDOM EFFECTS MODEL

We estimate the cost function using the random effects model. The time-constant explanatory variable, PR_i, is included in this model. This is one of the advantages of using the random effects model because sometimes, the effect of time-constant variable is of interest. The results of random effects estimation of Equation 32.4 is as follows:

$$\ln(TE_{it}) = 7.519 + 1.218\ SP4_{it} + 0.287\ \ln(FS_{it}) - 0.032\ \ln(RE_{it}) + 0.006\ FL_{it}$$
$$(0.577)(0.242)(0.052)(0.009)(0.113)$$
$$+\ 1.134\ PR_i + 0.080\ BL_{it}$$
$$(0.832)(0.074)(32.20)$$

$$R^2 = 0.0816,\ N = 1215.$$

The results show that student performance, faculty median salary, and resident enrollment are significant. Although the coefficient on the percent of free lunch student is insignificant in both fixed and random effects models, its sign is opposite. The other coefficients have the same sign as those of fixed effects model but the magnitude is reduced.

The empirical examples of random effects model are Dubin and Kalsow (1996), who examine the structural factors affecting the decision of voters to cast absentee ballots with a dataset on 33 statewide elections in California from 1962 through 1994; Cerniglia (2003), who investigates the extent and evolution of the allocation of expenditure and tax powers in a sample of 17 OECD countries from 1977 to 1994; Ihlanfeldt (2003), who examines transit's impact on neighborhood crime with a panel data of neighborhood crime in Atlanta; Evans-Cowley et al. (2005), who analyze the effect of impact fees on the value of land used in residential development using 43 Texas cities that impose impact fees; Shu and Strassmann (2005), who analyze the contributions of information technology to the productivity of 12 U.S. banks from 1989 to 1997; Yi and Choi (2005), who analyze the effect of the Internet on inflation with a panel data consists of 207 countries with the time period from 1991 to 2000; and Cohn and Johnson (2006), who analyze the effect of class attendance on student performance on examinations with panel data of 347 students from 1997 to 2001.*

---

* Ihlanfeldt (2003) and Cohn and Johnson (2006) also estimate the fixed effects model.

32.5   THE ISSUES IN PANEL DATA ESTIMATION

Between the fixed effects and random effects models, which model we should use is a critical issue. Some econometric textbooks deal with this issue in depth (e.g., Baltagi, 2001). Essentially, the debate lies in how to treat the unobserved heterogeneity and which model is more efficient. The fixed effects model assumes that the unobserved heterogeneity (a_i) is correlated with the explanatory variables (x_{itk}), whereas the random effects model does not. Therefore, the choice between the fixed and the random effects models depends on whether or not the a_i is independent of the x_{itk}. However, it is not easy to examine if the a_i is correlated with the x_{itk}. (Baltagi, 2001; Greene, 2003; Kmenta, 1997; Wooldridge, 2006).

Many researchers estimate both random effects and fixed effects, and then test the statistical significance of the differences in the coefficients on the time-varying explanatory variables (Wooldridge, 2006). The specification test developed by Hausman is generally used to choose one between fixed and random effects model (Greene, 2003). The Hausman test compares the fixed versus random effects under the null hypothesis that the individual effects (a_i) are independent of the other explanatory variables in the model (Baltagi, 2001; Greene, 2003; Maddala, 2001). If the null hypothesis is not rejected, then it is preferred to use random effects because it produces more efficient estimators. On the other hand, if it is rejected, the fixed effects model is better than the random effects. However, the Hausman test is not an absolute standard to select between the two models. It is suggested that more attention should be paid on the model selection than on the statistical test (Baltagi, 2001).

In addition to the Hausman test, it is required to do poolability test when we analyze panel data. The poolability means that whether or not the slope coefficients are the same across cross-sectional units or over time periods. In both of the fixed and the random effect models, the slope coefficients are assumed to be constant and only intercepts and error variances matter. Thus, the null hypothesis of the poolability test is that the slope coefficients are constant $(H_0:\beta_{ik}=\beta_k)$. To conduct the poolability test, it is needed to run OLS regressions by group or by time. If the null hypothesis is rejected, the panel data is not poolable. In this case, you may consider the random coefficient model (Baltagi, 2001).

32.6   CONCLUSION

As noted earlier, one of the most well-known panel data collection efforts is PSDI. It is a type of nonexperimental dataset that has been collected through repeated rounds of surveys.* As such, there have been many efforts to obtain panel data through large-scaled surveys and the availability of such high quality panel data enables scholars in a variety of discipline to perform in-depth empirical analysis. For example, comparative political scientists increasingly perform longitudinal analysis using the data on a large number of social, economical, and political variables for a host of countries.[†] As a result, it provoked in-depth discussions on the methodological issues and promoted the understanding on the strength and limitations of such a method (Beck, 2001). For economists and development scholars alike, the increasingly available consistent mega datasets on economic, human capital and development, social capital, and international trade and finance for countries, such as the data collections sponsored by the United Nations Millennium Development Goals and the International Monetary Fund, provide unique opportunities to examine various theories and models. Similarly, studies on public policy and program evaluation at state and local level can make good use of multiyear data that has been collected and compiled by different levels of governments and institutions such as Census Bureau and National Center for Education Statistics.

---

* See Burbridge (1999) for more detailed introduction on PSID.
[†] For example, see Plumper, Troeger, and Manow (2005).

It should be noted, however, that in spite of methodological advantages of using panel data models, the fundamental limitations of statistical analysis still exist. For example, in economic policy evaluation, ignoring the complex underlying fundamental structure may lead us to believing some erroneous estimator with regard to the parameters (Heckman, 2000; Lucas, 1976).* Despite the fact that methodologically we can resort to various advanced econometrics techniques and models, the violation of strict exogeneity may be a formidable barrier to overcome (Maddala, 2001).

32.7 SHORT BIBLIOGRAPHY OF PEER-REVIEWED PUBLIC ADMINISTRATION PANEL DATA ANALYSIS RESEARCH

In addition to the references provided in the foregone sections, this section introduces some articles using panel data analysis published in public administration journals.

Cornwell, C. and Kellough, J.E. 1994. Women and minorities in federal government agencies: Examining new evidence from panel data, *Public Administration Review*, 54(3): 265–270.

Employment statistics shows that although the share of female and minority in the public sector has grown, women and minorities remain concentrated in lower level job. Cornwell and Kellough (1994) examine the determinants of the differences among public organizations in the share and share changes of female and minorities. They estimate the effects of the occupational distribution and agency's demographic and organizational characteristics using the fixed effects model and panel data on 30 federal agencies for the years 1982, 1984, 1986, and 1988.

Meier, K.J. and Bohte, J. 2003. Span of control and organization performance: Implementing Luther Gulick's research design, *Public Administration Review*, 63(1): 61–70.

Span of control is an important component of an organization because it affects the productivity of the organization. Meier and Bohte (2003) examine the hypothesis that span of control has an effect on organizational performance. The authors estimate the effect of span of control on organizational performance using pooled OLS with year dummy variables to correct for serial correlation. The authors use 678 Texas school districts panel data from 1994 to 1997. The results show that the two measures of span of control, teacher–administrator ratio and school–level administrator–central office administrator ratio, have positive impact on student test scores.

Brown (2000). Constitutional tax and expenditure limitations in Colorado: The impact on municipal governments, *Public Budgeting and Finance*, 20(3): 29–50.

To control the growth of local government, Colorado introduced two tax and expenditure limitation policies: the Gallagher amendment of 1983 and the Taxpayer's Bill of Rights (TABOR) of 1992. Brown (2000) examines the impacts of the two tax and expenditure limitations on revenue and expenditure using a panel dataset on 255 municipal governments in Colorado from 1975 to 1996. The author estimates the effects of Gallagher amendment and TABOR on revenue and expenditure of municipal governments using both a pooled OLS model and a fixed effects model.

Eom, T.H. and Rubenstein, R. (2006). Do state-funded property tax exemptions increase local government efficiency?, An analysis of New York States STAR program, *Public Budgeting and Finance*, 26(1): 66–87.

In 1999, New York introduced a large state-subsidized property tax exemption program, known as school tax relief program (STAR). It is hypothesized that the STAR reduces local government efficiency by lowering the taxpayer's incentive to monitor government efficiency. Eom and Rubenstein (2006) test the hypothesis using a panel dataset on school districts in New York from 1999 to 2002. The authors estimate the impact of STAR on school district efficiency using a cross-sectional and two panel data approaches: a random effect Tobit model and a fixed effects model.

Pitts, D.W. (2005). Diversity, representation, and performance: Evidence about race and ethnicity in public organization, *Journal of Public Administration Research and Theory*, 15(4): 615–631.

---

* See Lucas (1976) for his critique and Heckman's review (2000).

In the Unites States, racial and ethnic minorities have grown and the academic attention on the issue of diversity has grown. Pitts (2005) examines the effects of diversity in race and ethnicity on organizational performance in public education. He estimates the impacts of diversity on three performance measures (student dropout rate, pass rate on the Texas Assessment of Academic Skills test, percentage of students earning above 1110 on the SAT) using pooled OLS with year dummy variables and a panel dataset on school districts in Texas from 1995 to 1999.

32.8 DATA ANALYSIS QUESTIONS

Use the data in New Jersey Education.dta (or New Jersey Education.xls) for exercise.* The file contains panel data on 40 school districts in New Jersey for the years 2001 through 2003. The file consists of following variables: year (starting school year), sdna (school district name), sdid (school district ID code), lte (natural log of per pupil total expenditure), lfs (natural log of faculty median salary), lre (natural log of resident enrollment), fl (percent of free lunch students), pr (child poverty rate), and bl (percent of black students). We estimate various panel data models using Stata 9.

The basic model for estimation is

$$\ln(\text{TE}_{it}) = \beta_0 + \beta_1 \ln(\text{FS}_{it}) + \beta_2 \ln(\text{RE}_{it}) + \beta_3 \text{FL}_{it} + \beta_4 \text{BL}_{it} + v_{it}$$

where

$\ln(\text{TE}_{it})$ is the natural log of per pupil total expenditure
$\ln(\text{FS}_{it})$ is the natural log of faculty median salary
$\ln(\text{RE}_{it})$ is the natural log of the number of resident enrollment
FL_{it} is the percent of students who receiving free lunch
BL_{it} is the percent of black students

1. Estimate the above model by pooled OLS and report the results with number of observation, R^2, and standard errors of estimates in parenthesis.
2. Estimate the above model by fixed effects (time-demeaning method) and report the results with number of observation, R^2, and standard errors of estimates in parenthesis.
3. Estimate the above model by fixed effects and report the results with number of observations, R^2, and standard errors of estimates in parenthesis.
4. Compares the fixed effects and the random effects model using Hausman specification test.

REFERENCES

Apodaca, C. and Stohl, M. 1999. United States human rights policy and foreign assistance, *International Studies Quarterly*, *43*(1): 185–198.

Arulampalam, W., Booth, A.L., and Bryan, M.L. 2004. Training and the new minimum wage, *Economic Journal*, *114*: C87–C94.

Baltagi, B.H. 2001. *Econometric Analysis of Panel Data*, 2nd ed., New York: John Wiley & Sons.

Bauer, T.K. 2002. Educational mismatch and wages: A panel analysis, *Economics of Education Review*, *21*(3): 221–229.

Beck, N. 2001. Time-series-cross-sectional data: What have we learned in the past few years? *Annual Review of Political Science*, *4*(1): 271–293.

Bevan, A.A. and Danbolt, J. 2004. Testing for inconsistencies in the estimation of UK capital structure determinants, *Applied Financial Economics*, *14*(1): 55–66.

Breusch, T.S. and Pagan, A.R. 1980. The lagrange multiplier test and its applications to model specification in econometrics, *Review of Economic Studies*, *47*(1): 239–253.

---

* This dataset is a subset of education data provided by SED, NJ.

Brown, T. 2000. Constitutional tax and expenditure limitation in Colorado: The impact on municipal govern-
    ments, *Public Budgeting and Finance*, 20(3): 29–50.
Burbridge, L. 1999. Cross-sectional, longitudinal and time-series data: Uses and limitations, in *Handbook
    of Research Methods in Public Administration*, G. Miller and M.L. Whicker (Eds.), New York:
    Marcel Dekker.
Burtless, G. 1995. The case for randomized field trials in economic and policy research, *Journal of Economic
    Perspectives*, 9(2): 63–84.
Cameron, A.C. and Trivedi, P.K. 2005. *Microeconometrics: Methods and Applications*, New York:
    Cambridge University Press.
Campbell, D.T. and Stanley, J.C. 1966. *Experiment and Quasi-Experimental Design for Research*, Chicago:
    Rand McNally.
Cerniglia, F. 2003. Decentralization in the public sector: Quantitative aspects in federal and unitary countries,
    Journal of Policy Modeling, 25(8): 749–776.
Chakraborty, K., Biswas, B., and Lewis, W.C. 2000. Economies of scale in public education: An econometric
    analysis, *Contemporary Economic Policy*, 18(2): 238–247.
Chao, W.S. and Buongiorno, J. 2002. Exports and growth: A causality analysis for the pulp and paper
    industries based on international panel data, *Applied Economics*, 34(1): 1–13.
Cohn, E. and Johnson, E. 2006. Class attendance and performance in principles of economics, *Education
    Economics*, 14(2): 211–233.
Cornwell, C. and Kellough, J.E. 1994. Women and minorities in federal government agencies: Examining new
    evidence from panel data, *Public Administration Review*, 54(3): 265–270.
Cornwell, C. and Trumbull, W.N. 1994. Estimating the economic model of crime with panel data, *Review of
    Economics and Statistics*, 76(2): 360–366.
Dubin, J.A. and Kalsow, G.A. 1996. Comparing absentee and precinct voters: A view over time, *Political
    Behavior*, 18(4): 369–392.
Duncombe, W. and Yinger, J. 1999. Performance standards and educational cost indexes: you can't have one
    without the other, in *Equity and Adequacy in Education Finance: Issues and Perspectives*, H.F. Ladd,
    R. Chalk, and J.S. Hansen (Eds.), Washington, DC: National Academy Press.
Duncombe, W. and Yinger, J. 2000. Financing higher student performance standards: The case of New York
    State, *Economics of Education Review*, 19(4): 363–386.
Eichler, M. and Lechner, M. 2002. An evaluation of public employment programmes in the East German State
    of Sachsen-Anhalt, *Labour Economics*, 9(2): 143–186.
Eom, T.H. and Rubenstein, R. 2006. Do state-funded property tax exemptions increase local government
    inefficiency? An analysis of New York State's STAR Program, *Public Budgeting and Finance*, 26(1):
    66–87.
Evans, M.D.R. and Kelley, J. 2004. Effect of family structure on life satisfaction: Australian evidence, *Social
    Indicators Research*, 69(3): 303–349.
Evans-Cowley, J.S., Forgey, F.A., and Rutherford, R.C. 2005. The effect of development impact fees on land
    values, *Growth and Change*, 36(1): 100–112.
Frumkin, P. and Kim, M.T. 2001. Strategic positioning and the financing of nonprofit organizations:
    Is efficiency rewarded in the contributions marketplace? *Public Administration Review*, 61(3): 266–275.
Greene, W.H. 2003. *Econometric Analysis*, 5th ed., Upper Saddle River, New Jersey: Prentice Hall.
Griffiths, W.E., Hill, R.C., and Judge, G.G. 1993. *Learning and Practicing Econometrics*, New York:
    John Wiley & Sons.
Gujarati, D.N. 2003. *Basic Econometrics*, 4th ed., New York: McGraw Hill.
Häkkinen, I., Kirjavainen, T., and Uusitalo, R. 2003. School resources and student achievement revisited:
    New evidence from panel data, *Economics of Education Review*, 22(3): 329–335.
Halaby, C.N. 2004. Panel models in sociological research: Theory into practice, *Annual Review of Sociology*,
    30(1): 507–544.
Heckman, J.J. 1991. Randomization and social policy evaluation, *NBER Technical Working Paper Series
    No. 107*.
Heckman, J.J. 2000. Casual parameters and policy analysis in economics: A twentieth century retrospective,
    The Quarterly Journal of Economics, 115(1): 45–97.
Heckman, J.J. 2001. Micro data, heterogeneity and the evaluation of public policy: Nobel lecture, *Journal
    of Political Economy*, 109(4): 673–748.

Heckman, J.J. and Smith, J. 1995. Assessing the case for social experiments, *Journal of Economic Perspectives*, 9(2): 85–110.

Hill, G.C. 2005. The effects of managerial succession on organizational performance, *Journal of Public Administration Research and Theory*, 15(4): 585–597.

Holzer, H.J. and Neumark, D. 2000. What does affirmative action do? *Industrial and Labor Relations Review*, 53(2): 240–271.

Hou, Y. 2004. Budget stabilization fund: Structural features of the enabling legislation and balance levels, *Public Budgeting and Finance*, 24(3): 38–64.

Hsiao, C. 1986. *Analysis of Panel Data*, New York: Cambridge University Press.

Hsiao, C. 2003. *Analysis of Panel Data*, 2nd edn, Cambridge, U.K.: Cambridge University Press.

Ihlanfeldt, K.R. 2003. Rail transit and neighborhood crime: The case of Atlanta, Georgia, *Southern Economic Journal*, 70(2): 273–294.

Kawguchi, D. 2006. The incidence and effect of job training among Japanese women, *Industrial Relations*, 45(3): 469–477.

Kennedy, P. 2003. *A Guide to Econometrics,* 5th ed., Cambridge, Massachusetts: The MIT Press.

Kirby, S. and Riley, R. 2004. Compulsory work-focused interviews for inactive benefit claimants: An evaluation of the British ONE pilots, *Labour Economics*, 11(4): 415–429.

Kmenta, J. 1997. *Elements of Econometrics*, 2nd ed., Michigan: The University of Michigan Press.

Korpi, W. 1989. Power, politics, and state autonomy in the development of social citizenship: Social rights during sickness in eighteen OECD countries since 1930, *American Sociological Review*, 54(3): 309–328.

Kuziemko, I. 2006. Using shocks to school enrollment to estimate the effect of school size on student achievement, *Economics of Education Review*, 25(1): 63–75.

Loeb, S. and Corcoran, M. 2001. Welfare, work experience, and economic self-sufficiency, *Journal of Policy Analysis and Management*, 20(1): 1–20.

Lucas, R. 1976. Economic policy evaluation: A critique, *Carnegie–Rochester Conference Series on Public Policy*, 1: 19–46.

Maddala, G.S. 2001. *Introduction to Econometrics*, 3rd ed., New York: John Wiley & Sons.

Marlowe, J. 2005. Fiscal slack and counter-cyclical expenditure stabilization: A first look at the local level, *Public Budgeting and Finance*, 25(3): 48–72.

Maxim, P.S. 1999. *Quantitative Research Methods in the Social Sciences*, New York: Oxford University Press.

Meier, K.J. and Bohte, J. 2003. Span of control and organization performance: Implementing Luther Gulick's research design, *Public Administration Review*, 63(1): 61–70.

Mullins, D.R. 2004. Tax and expenditure limitations and the fiscal response of local Government: Asymmetric intra-local fiscal effects, *Public Budgeting and Finance*, 24(4): 111–147.

Noonan, M.C. and Heflin, C.M. 2005. Does welfare participation affect women's wages? *Social Science Quarterly*, 86(5): 1123–1145.

Orcutt, G.H. and Orcutt, A.G. 1968. Incentive and disincentive experimentation for Income Maintenance Policy, *American Economic Review*, 58(4): 754–772.

Page, M.E., Spetz, J., and Millar, J. 2005. Does the minimum wage affect welfare caseloads? *Journal of Policy Analysis and Management*, 24(2): 273–295.

Pindyck, R.S. and Rubinfield, D.L. 1998. *Econometric Models and Economic Forecast*, 4th ed., Boston, Massachusetts: Irwin/McGraw-Hill.

Pitts, D.W. 2005. Diversity, representation, and performance: Evidence about race and ethnicity in public organizations, *Journal of Public Administration Research and Theory*, 15(4): 615–631.

Plumper, T., Troeger, V.E., and Manow, P. 2005. Panel data analysis in comparative politics: Linking method to theory, *European Journal of Political Research,* 44(2): 327–354.

Ram, R. 2004. School expenditures and student achievement: Evidence for the United States, *Education Economics* 12(2): 169–176.

Robinson, H. 2005. Regional evidence on the effect of the national minimum wage on the gender pay gap, *Regional Studies*, 39(7): 855–872.

Rosenzweig, M.R. and Wolpin, K.I. 2000. Natural "natural experiments" in economics, *Journal of Economic Literature*, 38(4): 827–874.

Sapat, A. 2004. Devolution and innovation: The adoption of state environmental policy innovations by administrative agencies, *Public Administration Review, 64*(2): 141–151.

Shu, W. and Strassmann, P.A. 2005. Does information technology provide banks with profit? *Information and Management*, 42(5): 781–787.

Smith, K.B. 1997. Explaining variation in state-level homicide rates: Does crime policy pay? *Journal of Politics*, 59(2): 350–367.

Stewart, M.B. 2004. The impact of the introduction of the U.K. minimum wage on the employment probabilities of low-wage workers, *Journal of the European Economic Association*, 2(1): 67–97.

Trochim, W.M.K. 2001. *The Research Methods Knowledge Base*, 2nd ed., Cincinnati, Ohio: Atomic Dog Publishing.

Waldfogel, J. 1997. The effect of children on women's wages, *American Sociological Review*, 62(2): 209–217.

Wooldridge, J.M. 2002. *Econometric Analysis of Cross Section and Panel Data*, Cambridge, Massachusetts: MIT Press.

Wooldridge, J.M. 2006. *Introductory Econometrics: A Modern Approach*, 3rd ed., Mason, Ohio: Thomson South-Western.

Yi, M.H. and Choi, C. 2005. The effect of the internet on inflation: Panel data evidence, *Journal of Policy Modeling*, 27(7): 885–889.

33 Forecasting Methods for Serial Data

Dan Williams

CONTENTS

33.1   INTRODUCTION

There may be no statistical practice more mysterious than forecasting. One reason for this mystery is that the word "forecasting" is attached to many different practices. These practices involve discovering something unknown, which is, at least in principle, in the future. From a statistical point of view, forecasting breaks a cardinal rule: "do not generalize outside the range of the data." The future is always outside the range of the data, so, forecasters are statistical renegades.

Three ways of predicting the future are (1) Building a mathematical model that simulates the process that generates the variable of interest; assigning known or expected values of all necessary input variables; and computing the formulas. This form of forecasting is sometimes called "input–output modeling." (2) Using causal models, typically regression models (or systems of equations where some variables are "endogenous"), to "explain" data or the phenomena that dataset represents; assigning known or expected values of all input (exogenous) variables; and computing the predicted value of a variable of interest. This method is called "causal modeling." It is assumed that causal modeling is not substantially-discussed in this chapter. (3) Trending data from the past. This method is usually called "time series forecasting."

Input–output forecasting and forecasting with causal models sound a lot alike, but they are actually quite different. Input–output forecasting relies almost entirely on knowing how the system is supposed to work, whereas forecasting with causal models is empirical. Both can produce prediction intervals,* but for input–output forecasting to do so, one must conduct a sensitivity analysis. A sensitivity analysis involves replacing the expected input variable values for the input–output model with a variety of extreme but not impossible values, and cranking the model under each set of values. The result is a range of possible output values under all of these input scenarios. Although this range is not a true prediction interval, it has a similar effect.

To muddy matters further, forecasting with input–output models and with causal models can be mixed with regression equations used to predict input variables for input–output forecasting and

---

* A prediction interval is a range of likely values surrounding the midline forecast.

regression equations used to replace actual process models within input–output forecasting. In effect, systems of equations in forecasting with causal models are the stochastic equivalent of input–output forecasting, particularly when most of the variables are made endogenous. When the reader occasionally hears of hugely complex models used in forecasting, such as in weather forecasting, it may be that there is some merging of input–output models with causal models.

Forecasting with input–output models and with causal models can also be mixed with time series forecasting by, for example, producing a continuous stream of input values, and recomputing the model in input–output forecasting, thereby producing a time series stream of outputs in the variable of interest, or using a time index of an input variable in forecasting with causal models. The one approach that is specifically discouraged in this chapter is the use of a time index as an input variable.

All of the preceding is for the purpose of saying that this chapter is solely about time series forecasting, which uses the history of a data series as the predictor of the future values of that series. This method is often thought to be too simplistic; however, a little thought experiment should correct this impression. Fix in your mind any familiar place, perhaps, if you are not there at the moment, your home. When you return home you can expect certain things. You can expect rooms to be in particular places. Furniture and the like will be arranged in such-and-such a manner. Electrical equipment will be in various states of current or past use. After you get home, certain things will happen: Lights will go on and off at predictable times. Noise will occur in various locations of your home at certain times. Why do you expect all of this? Not because of the reasoning found in input–output modeling or regression modeling, but because the prior states and tendencies of all of these variables provide a comfortable expectation that they will continue to hold pretty much the same or incrementally change values in the future.

Sometimes the variables (location of the furniture, potential states of the equipment, etc.) will not have their normal values. This change might be temporary (vacation) or permanent (redecorating). In forecasting of economic or social data, these are the conditions where we can, in advance, reliably expect the process generating our data to change and have a pretty good idea how it will change. It is sometimes thought that input–output forecasting or causal modeling produce better forecasts because they help with just these sorts of conditions. These are the conditions where knowing a substantial amount about causal factors helps with prediction. However, time series forecasting is not defenseless in the face of these conditions, which is to say it is able to absorb and make use of causal information. This capacity will be discussed in this chapter.*

The main reason people look to forecasting with input–output methods, causal models or particularly mixed versions using systems of equations is, continuing with the analogy, the break-in. The break-in is something like redecorating, except the "redecorator" is uninvited, destroys the place, and makes off with some valuables. But, most importantly, the break-in takes us by surprise. In the macroeconomy, the break-in is the downturn, although upturns are often just as hard to predict. Just like the break-in, the downturn is always a possibility; in fact, under the right circumstances it may be almost certain, although the timing may be hard to predict.

A recent downturn hit during late 2000 and early 2001. At that time, state governments had been engaged in a binge of spending and tax cuts. Despite more than 50 years of recommended budget policy that urges governments not to cut taxes in the upswing of an apparent economic cycle, there is essentially no evidence that governments have gotten the message. In the end of the 1990s, this practice was abetted by the claim that the internet economy was "different." Ignoring hundreds of years of economic cycles (which is, after all, time serial information), high profile experts, who typically are not actual forecasters, suggested that the sky really was the limit, this time: "As he approaches his 10th anniversary as chairman of the Fed on Aug. 11, Alan Greenspan finds himself

---

* To continue this analogy, input–output modeling is the sort of reasoning that applies when, after carefully following a recipe, you expect to find the cake in the oven to look like the picture in the cookbook. Regression modeling is more helpful with predicting how many cars will cut you off on the highway as you return home, depending on the conditions of environment, if you know how to specify them.

in the unlikeliest of positions: The staunch conservative who once personified industrial-era economic thinking has turned into the avant-garde advocate of the New Economy. 'He is very open to the possibility that we have entered a new economic age,' says Judy Shelton, a conservative scholar who meets with the Fed chief several times a year. 'He really believes in the organic nature of the market economy' " (Foust, 1997).

Some people hope that forecasters will somehow provide a hedge against the vicissitudes of uncertainty; however, anecdotal evidence suggests that when such a hedge is provided, it is ignored. For example, those familiar with economic history are quite aware of economic cycles and, in the mid-1990s, they began warning that downward cycling could be expected to begin in 1996. However, because there was no technical estimate of date certain for the downturn, the surprise of 2000 was once again attributed to forecast failure, as it had been in earlier recessions. In some of the following sections, I will very briefly address the reasons for the lack of such technical estimates. However, the essential characteristic of this failure is surprise. In the mid-1970s, this surprise came in the form of variables that had not previously been considered important (the Organization of Oil Exporting Countries, OPEC, flexing its muscles). In the 2000 recession, the surprise might be in the fact that it did not occur earlier.

Forecasters cannot protect against surprises not found in the empirical sources of the forecast. All of these forecasting method, as well as others not mentioned here, are equally helpless against such surprises. The method most likely to hedge against surprises is to know the range of possible scenarios the future might bring and to anticipate how to respond to all of these scenarios.

33.1.1 TECHNICAL FORECASTS

The rest of this chapter provides some guidance for technical forecasts involving time series data. An analyst may want to know the value of future members of a data series; for example, if a public policy is created to reduce the number of teen pregnancies, the analyst may want to know how many pregnancies would occur in future years in the absence of this policy. This chapter discusses techniques for forecasting serial data, that is, numeric data arranged in a meaningful order or series. Serial dataset follows in a particular order because some process generates them in this order. Commonly, this dataset is arranged in chronological order, that is, some process generates data across time and the dataset is recorded beside a time index (such as the dates on which the data is observed). In this chapter, data of this sort is called "serial data," "time serial data," or "time series." The techniques discussed in this chapter are designed for forecasting numeric time series.

33.1.2 SIMPLE TECHNIQUES

The techniques discussed here are relatively simple to understand and use. Although there are more complex techniques, they are frequently constrained by severe criteria that are difficult to meet. For example, to use a regression based time series technique, it is necessary to know the future values of the predictor variables (the x variables in the equation)

$$\hat{y} = \alpha + \beta_1 x_1 + \beta_2 x_2 + \cdots + \beta_n x_n + \varepsilon \tag{33.1}$$

Often with real-world forecasting problems, predictor variables are no better known than the series that is to be forecast (Vollmann et al., 1993). Research over the past 30 years shows that simpler techniques, such as the ones discussed in this chapter, often provide forecasts that are as accurate as those provided by more complex techniques (Makridakis et al., 1982; Ashley, 1983, 1988).*

---

* The reasons for this result are complex, but one is the conservative nature of simple time serial techniques. These techniques are less likely to predict radically different numbers that have occurred in the past. Complex methods more frequently do predict sharply differing future numbers. Although complex methods may sometimes, or even frequently, attain a gain in accuracy through such predictions, their occasional failures are dramatic.

The main constraint for use of techniques discussed here is that there should be no known reason to expect the data generating process to change significantly over the horizon (the future periods) that is to be forecast, or that reasonably good estimates exist for the effect of any anticipated changes.

33.1.3 NOTATION

Forecast literature contains some standard, or nearly standard, notation, and some unsettled notation. Almost universally, time varying dataset is indexed with a time period subscript. Usually, this subscript is symbolized with a lower case t, thus X_t refers to the observation X at time t. There is relatively general agreement that F_t refers to a forecasted value at time period t; X_t refers to the actual dataset at time period t; and e_t (error or deviation at time t) refers to the forecast error in period t, X_t minus F_t. Order is important. In this chapter e_t refers to $X_t - F_t$ and not $F_t - X_t$. Time change is usually shown with such notation as $t-1$, $t+m$, or $t-L$. These and similar notations refer to relative differences in time. Thus, $t-L$ means relative to an observation at period t look for the observation L time units earlier (L is capitalized to avoid confusion with the number one). It is not hard to find articles that violate any or all of these conventions; however, they will be used here. Other terms are defined as they are introduced.

The symbol $\sum_{i=x}^{v}$ is read as "sum i from x to v"; that is, add up the items indexed by i beginning with x and ending with v. This symbol does not stand alone. To follow the instruction there must be a term following it. For example, $\sum_{t=1}^{n}(X_t - F_t)$ instructs the analyst to sum a column of numbers each of which is computed by subtracting F_t from X_t. Further, the numbers to include start with the first observation ($t=1$) and end with the observation indicated by the superscript n, which usually means the last observation.

Greek characters, such as α, β, φ, γ, and others refer to "parameters." Parameters are values that summarize a time series generating process, and are estimated through observation of a sample. In strict statistical practice, the estimates of parameters are "statistics" and would be signified in a different alphabet; however, in forecast practice, the statistical estimates of parameters are typically signified with the same characters as the parameters. When forecasting, a sample is found by observing a segment of a data series. Because a portion of the series is in the future, it is unobservable, so, there are only samples; the universe is beyond observation. As the forecast literature does not reflect standard usage, it is easy to find articles making conflicting use of these terms.

"Forecast" also has a special meaning in forecast literature. It refers to values estimated by forecast models. Most time series models (and many other models) estimate values in the present and past as well as in the future. These are forecasts. Think of them as training forecasts. When the source of training runs out, the future is estimated by using the parameter values set in the training period. With a little thought, we will see that training forecasts will have errors. Our immediate thought is that we want them to be small. However, our statistical training will also urge us to have them unbiased. The techniques in this chapter are about these two characteristics with respect to "one-step-ahead" forecast errors, that is, models that produce forecasts for the next future period.

Forecasters commonly refer to the forecast period of interest as the "horizon." The novice may expect the horizon to begin with the next period after the dataset runs out and continue through, typically, the next year. However, real forecast problems tend to be less convenient. For example, real data will likely take some time to get to the analyst; so, for monthly data, the month during which the forecast is made will already be in progress, possibly almost over. This month is only inconveniently within the horizon. For example, for budget planning purposes, a state may plan its budget in the fall, beginning around September. Its fiscal year may begin the next July and end the June afterward. With the current data having run out in the past month (August), the horizon is 22 months. For states with two year budget cycles, the horizon would be 34 months. As the legislative session nears, the horizon shrinks, but not by much.

33.1.4   A FEW WORDS ON SOPHISTICATED TECHNIQUES

Sophisticated techniques are not substantially discussed in this chapter, although the reader may consider the techniques discussed fairly challenging. There are two types of sophisticated techniques omitted, sophisticated econometric techniques and sophisticated time series techniques. The reason for this is mentioned in Section 33.1; research does not show that these techniques are more effective than simple techniques.

Nevertheless, readers might want to know a little about these more sophisticated techniques. For example, the public often wants to know why forecasters fail to estimate economic downturns, which they often miss. This question is typically about sophisticated techniques because, typically, forecasts of the general economy are made using such techniques.

33.1.4.1   Econometric Forecasts

In fact, forecasts of the general economy are normally made using econometric techniques. Econometric techniques involve regression models such as Equation 33.1, although they are typically more complex. Although such models can be used to make a "forecast," the forecast is actually a secondary use of these models. The primary use of these models is to explain certain characteristics of the economy.

Although these models have a time element, and the predictor variables are earlier in time than the predicted, the time range may not be very distant and the time element may depend on "lagging," which is to drag a variable from one time period to another. In many ways the model has more cross-sectional characteristics than it does time-series characteristics. The dependent variable is cross-sectionally related to independent variables that come one or a few time periods before it. Even so, those predictor time units may be in the future. Thus, the independent variables may also be predicted with other econometric models, with time series models, or with expert opinion. When all those other variables are predicted well, the econometric models tend to perform very well. But, on occasion, if they are not so well predicted then these models may fail sensationally.

In statistical language, use of predicted independent variable values leads to underestimated prediction intervals. Forecast users tend to think only about the most likely estimate, without paying attention to the interval of likely values. (In fact, the computation of forecast prediction intervals can be quite difficult and the math is mostly omitted, as in this chapter.) When the prediction interval is wide, the forecast can be correct and yet the actual value, when it finally arrives, can be dramatically different from the likely value. Regression estimates of prediction intervals assume that the independent values are actual measurements, not estimates. When this assumption is violated, the prediction interval can expand quite dramatically. Thus, the forecast of the most likely estimate may be correct, but the range of other likely values may be quite wide.

The reader will recall that the forecaster is breaking an important rule by generalizing outside the range of the data. The price for this violation is found in the prediction interval, which is the range of possible values for the forecast. In Figure 33.1 we see both a prediction interval and a narrower confidence interval. The confidence interval is the location where we expect the average of many similar series to fall. The prediction interval is where we expect one future series, such as the one we are forecasting, to fall. There is more risk, thus a wider interval, for prediction one series.

Even without a penalty for using estimates instead of observations in the input variables, the forecast prediction interval widens at the end of the historical data series as depicted in Figure 33.1.* The prediction interval is quite wide in the first place, so it does not widen as much when we begin to generalize outside the range of the data. However, when we add more uncertainty with estimated rather than actual values of the predictor variables, the interval widens again. This extra uncertainty is illustrated with the widest interval shown only in the future period, which depicts carrying the

---

* It is assumed that these concepts will be more thoroughly discussed in a chapter on regression.

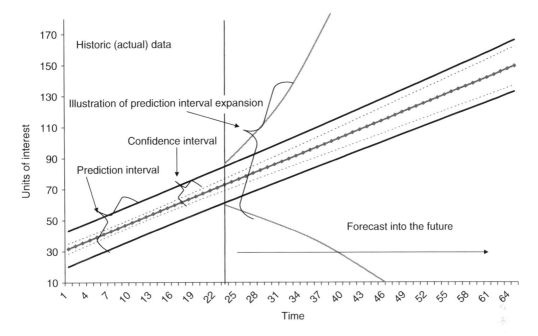

FIGURE 33.1 Confidence and predicition intervals (artificial data).

uncertainty of the input variables through to the prediction interval. It is not hard, under such circumstances, to experience a downturn within the prediction interval of a strong upward trend. Such a result is not so much a forecast failure as a misunderstanding of what a forecast can accomplish.

33.1.4.2 Sophisticated Time Series Techniques

There is a different reason for not discussing sophisticated time series models. These models are sometimes known as ARIMA models, Vector ARIMA models, etc. There are some statistical reasons to be concerned about these models because they implicitly consume large numbers of degrees of freedom, but this is a relatively minor concern. The main reason to be concerned about these models is that they require extraordinary sophistication and effort. Comparative research has not shown that they are superior to simpler models. Thus, it is thought that effort would be better spent getting to know about the data generating process, that is, why the dataset is what it is.

Knowing the data generating process provides a qualitative check on the mathematical results of a forecast. When a forecaster knows more about what is going on to generate the data, he or she has a better opportunity to determine how to interpret unexpected results. Such unexpected results can imply anything from data entry errors to early signals of major changes under way. Knowing the data generating process also provides for an ability to incorporate causal information within a time series model. As compared with committing the same effort to improve forecast fit with ARIMA or other sophisticated models, this author's recommendation is to learn what generates the data and what plans are associated with the data generating activities.

In summarizing this section, one of the advantages of simple techniques is not that they are always right, but that they are often safer than sophisticated techniques. Another is that they allow time to put effort into understanding the actual process that generates the data being forecast.

33.2 PREPARING TO FORECAST

Forecasting begins with data. Usually data must be collected and prepared before it is forecast.

33.2.1 Time Intervals

Usually dataset accumulates over a time interval. If an analyst records the number of cars passing through an intersection each day, the cars do not all pass through the intersection simultaneously. The number accumulates all day. The particular time unit used to refer to that data may be the beginning of that time interval, the end of that time interval, the mid-point of the time interval, a time unit that refers to the whole time interval, or some other rationally selected time unit. No particular reference method is "right"; however, the analyst should know the applications, advantages, and limitations of the method used. Analysts planning to collect data may want to use either the mid-point of the time interval or a unit that refers to the whole time interval to limit confusion about the relationship between the data and the index. However, practical reasons may lead the analyst to prefer a different reference. For example, some Medicaid dataset accumulates over weeks and checks are dated for a day in the next week. For some forecasting purposes the dataset is cumulated over months and recorded beside the month and year, a time unit that refers to the whole period. For other purposes, the date of the check is of interest, so the dataset is recorded beside that date, a time unit that is entirely outside the time period over which the data cumulated. In each case, the index is meaningful considering how the dataset is used. Here are two more considerations for cumulating data:

(1) Use equal or nearly equal time intervals. It would be best to always use equal time intervals, but business practices and the calendar make this hard. Months are not equal in size, and although weeks have the same number of days, they may not have the same number of business days, as some contain holidays. Select a standard time interval (years, quarters, months, weeks, days, hours, minutes, seconds, etc.) and stick with it. Choose the smallest unit of interest. It is far easier to combine dataset that is too detailed (e.g., add days together to get weeks) than to break aggregated data apart (e.g., find data for days from weekly data). It is very unlikely that the smallest unit of interest will be a year, even when you make some summary tables in years. In this chapter, the default unit is a month.

(2) Be consistent. If Fridays' dataset is held over to the next week, it should always be held over to the next week.

33.2.2 Plotting Historical Data

Plot the data to look for recognizable patterns and anomalies. In general practice, forecasters plot data in an XY scatter plot or line plot using the Y axis as the values of the observed data and the X axis as the time index. Older dataset is to the left and more current dataset is to the right as shown in Figure 33.2. We will call Figure 33.2 a time-plot.

When forecasters show the forecast on the same plot, they often demonstrate the break between historical data and future data by drawing a vertical line at the end of the historical data as shown in Figure 33.3.

33.2.3 Data Editing

Once the dataset is arranged in a serial order, make sure that it does not contain mistaken entries. After data entry, plot the data and look for outliers, that is, values that are unusually large or small. In the Figure 33.4, the observation marked by a triangle is an outlier.

The most likely explanation of an outlier will be incorrect data entry. Two common sources of data entry error are reversal of numbers (for example, entering 36 as 63) and decimal error (for example, entering 36.03 as 360.3). Also, when entering several columns of data, the analyst may copy from the wrong column. When an analyst finds an outlier, he or she should look for a data-entry error. However, sometimes the analyst does not have the original data with which to compare, or does not find an error. Does the outlier mean any of the following:

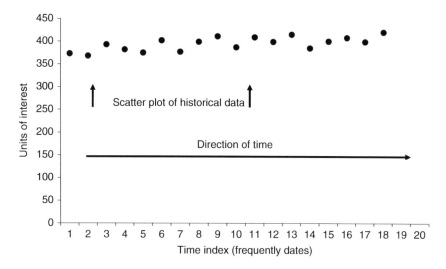

FIGURE 33.2 Example *XY* time-plot of time series (artificial data).

(1) The dataset is subject to occasional large disturbances? If so, leave the data as it is.
(2) There is an undiscoverable recording error? (Make this decision only if the observation is impossible or nearly so, otherwise see option three.) If so, correct the error with the best information available, by substituting a corrected observation for the erroneous one. There are several candidates for corrected observations. First, the analyst might calculate the average of the two surrounding observations. Second, if the dataset is seasonal, the analyst might calculate the average of the two nearest observations that occur at the same point in the seasonal cycle. For example, if the dataset is subject to annual seasonality, calculate the average of the observations from the previous year and the next year. These two approaches may also help solve the problem of missing data.

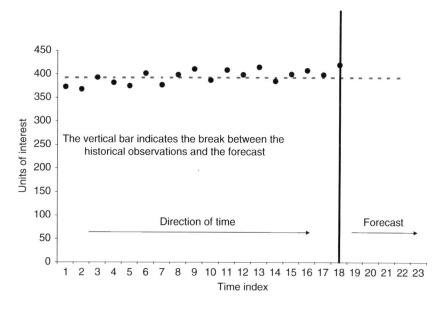

FIGURE 33.3 *XY* plot with forecast (artificial data).

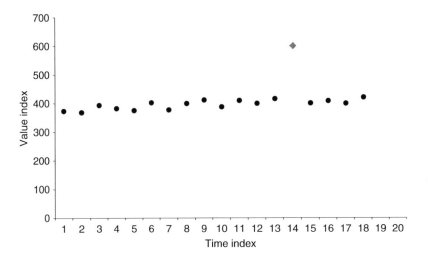

FIGURE 33.4 Example outlier. (Data from Table 33.1.)

(3) In the past, there was an unusual disturbance, but is it unlikely to recur? Or, is it probably a recording error, but it might not be? In this case the analyst may choose to leave the data alone, or he or she might choose to Windsorizing the observation (Armstrong, 1985). This practice consists of reducing the outlier to the most extreme value that is likely to occur. For example, if nearby observations take values from 360 to 420, and the extreme observation is 600, the analyst might choose to reduce the extreme observation to 450. This adjustment is shown in Figure 33.5. Be very cautious with the use of Windsorizing. Do not repeatedly Windsorize the same series.

Suppose that the analyst is not sure what the most extreme likely value is and the dataset is not following a particularly large trend. Then, an option is to calculate the standard deviation (excluding the outlier) of the immediately surrounding data and place the observation at three standard deviations from the average of that data in the direction of the outlier. If the resulting observation

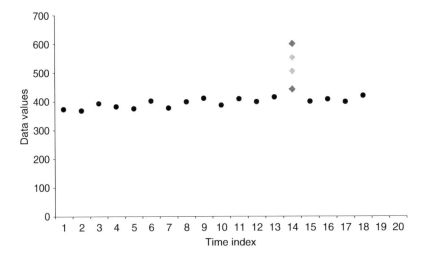

FIGURE 33.5 Reducing the outlier. (Data from Table 33.1.)

TABLE 33.1
Windsorizing Data

Period	Original X	X'	$E = X -$ Average	E Squared	Revised X
1	373	373	−22.1	489.2	373
2	368	368	−27.1	735.4	368
3	393	393	−2.1	4.5	393
4	382	382	−13.1	172.1	382
5	375	375	−20.1	404.7	375
6	402	402	6.9	47.4	402
7	377	377	−18.1	328.2	377
8	399	399	3.9	15.1	399
9	411	411	15.9	252.2	411
10	387	387	−8.1	65.9	387
11	409	409	13.9	192.7	409
12	399	399	3.9	15.1	399
13	415	415	19.9	395.3	415
14	600				442.2
15	400	400	4.9	23.8	400
16	408	408	12.9	166.0	408
17	399	399	3.9	15.1	399
18	420	420	24.9	619.1	420
	Total	6717	SSQ	3941.8	
	Count	17	DF	16	
	μ'	395.1	VAR	246.4	
			σ'	15.7	
			SD* 3	47.1	
			$'+3\,\sigma'$	442.2	

Note: For all tables additions and subtractions may not be exact due to rounding.

is more extreme than the original outlier, the original value should be retained. This technique will not work, however, with rapidly trending data, or dataset that is extremely seasonal. In those cases, the data may be Windsorized using the judgmental estimate of the most extreme likely value.

In Table 33.1, observation 14 is Windsorized by calculating the average plus three standard deviations using the equation

$$O' = \mu' + 3\sigma' \tag{33.2}$$

where O' is the Windsorized observation, and μ' and σ' are the mean and standard deviation of the series excluding the extreme observation.

33.2.4 PATTERNS IN DATA

It is effective to evaluate your data for patterns that show systematic variation, which can be used to simplify the data.

33.2.4.1 Variation along the Time Index

Figures 33.6 and 33.7 demonstrate typical patterns that can be found in data. What gives rise to these patterns is that the phenomena measured are strongly related to recording periods.

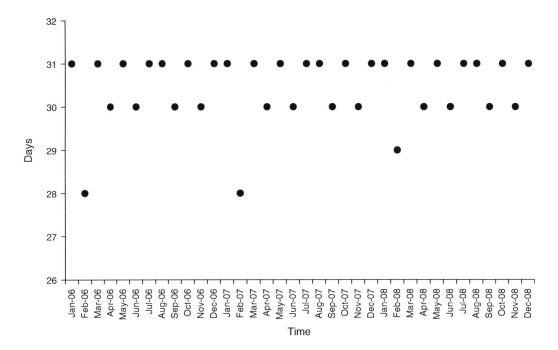

FIGURE 33.6 Days in the month (calendar data).

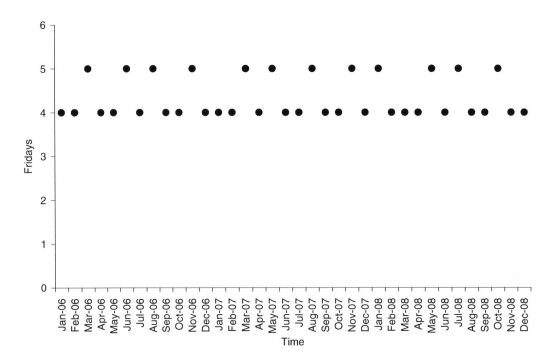

FIGURE 33.7 Fridays (calendar data).

In Figure 33.6, dataset accumulates over the whole recording period. In longer periods more dataset accumulates. For example, during the late 1980s and early 1990s, nursing facilities billed Virginia Medicaid for the number of days of service delivered to their patients over monthly billing periods. Longer months contained more days of service than shorter months.

In Figure 33.7, dataset accumulates over a week but is recorded on one specific day of the week. With the Virginia Medicaid program this pattern occurs when health care providers bill within a few days of delivering the service. The program receives bills all week long every week and pays the bills on Fridays. If the forecaster accumulates the data to months, there will be a natural fluctuation because some months contain four Fridays and others contain five.

In preparing to forecast data that exhibits such patterns, forecasters should first account for this completely predictable variation. For the forecasting techniques discussed here, the best way to account for this predictable phenomenon is to normalize it, that is, divide the data by the factor that causes it to fluctuate. For example, when forecasting the number of days of care delivered in a nursing home from monthly billing data, first divide the data by the number of days in the month over which the data cumulated. Forecast the normalized data series. To complete the forecast, reverse the normalization, that is, multiply the forecast by the future month normalizing factor. For example, if you divide the data by the number of Fridays before forecasting, you should multiply the forecast by the number of Fridays in the future period to get the whole forecast.*

There are many other possibilities. For example, if employees are paid weekly and the payday happens to be the first day of the year, it will also be the last day of the year. That year will contain 53 paychecks, which has the effect of increasing the payroll cost by roughly two percent. By plotting data, analysts can discover patterns, and by examining the process that generates the data, they can determine what the patterns mean. This examination of patterns and data generating process is part of the use of causal information in time series forecasting.

33.2.4.2   Other Complex Phenomena

The procedure of taking sources of variation, such as the days-of-the-month or recording-day-of-the-week, into account is sometimes called decomposition. With decomposition, a complex data series is broken into several component series (Armstrong, 1985). The simpler data series should be easier to forecast and, where relevant, different methods can be used to forecast different component series. In the examples from the last section, the systematic variation (days-of-the-month, etc.) can be known without error; so forecasting it can only introduce error. Once this variation is removed from the data series, the task of the mathematical forecasting model is simpler.

Although plotting data reveals patterns that arise across the time index, it may not help with other complexities. Consider the problem of forecasting teen pregnancy. Two components of this series are the number of female teens and the rate at which they become pregnant. It is ineffective to confuse these issues. Predicting the number of teens over the next few years may be relatively easy, because they are already around as preteens (assuming no important net migration issues). The forecasting challenge involves pregnancy rate. The best way to find these components is to examine the process that generates the series of interest.

Often data can be simplified through such adjustments. Sometimes these adjustments eliminate the need to forecast some of the variation (as with days-in-the-month variation). At other times component forecasts can be obtained from outside sources. At yet other times the chief gain through decomposition is the opportunity to forecast more meaningful homogenous data series.

---

* A more sophisticated approach is to estimate the marginal effect of unit variation with a regression model. Because this variation may interact with the time serial variation, making this determination does not fall within the scope of simple methods.

33.2.4.3 Constant Dollars

An important form of decomposition for public decision making is the removal of inflation from revenues and expenditures (Ammons, 1991, 2002). The impact of inflation can be estimated from indexes known as deflators, which, in the United States, are available from the Bureau of Labor Statistics of the Department of Commerce. There are many deflators depending on the sorts of things a government agency usually purchases. Analysts must choose a deflator that relates to the data forecasted. To apply the deflator, use the following equation:

$$CD_t = ND_t DF_b / DF_t \qquad (33.3)$$

where for year t,
   ND_t = Nominal dollars, funds expressed in dollars before adjusting for inflation
   CD_t = Constant dollars, funds expressed in dollars after adjusting for inflation
   DF_t = Deflator index
   DF_b = Deflator index value for a chosen constant year b

As an example, the analyst may be interested in forecasting sales tax revenue. First, sort out the components of this revenue. If there is no data on total sales within the locality, reason backward from taxes received to tax base. If there is a constant tax rate, simply divide the tax income by the rate. If there is more than one rate, or if the rate changed during the period of time over which there is dataset, divide each amount by its related rate. Reconstructing the base is shown in columns 2 through 4 of Table 33.2 (the revenue dataset is artificial). Choose an index, for sales tax revenue the analyst might choose the consumer price index (CPI) for all urban consumers, and convert nominal dollars to constant dollars using Equation 33.3 as shown in columns 4 through 7 of Table 33.2, using the average CPI for all urban consumers based in 1982–1984 as published at http://www.bls.gov/cpi/home.htm and ftp://ftp.bls.gov/pub/special.requests/cpi/cpiai.txt (accessed August 30, 2005).

Figure 33.8 demonstrates the effect of these calculations. The tax revenue (indexed against the right Y axis) grows faster than the nominal base (left Y axis), because the rate has several incremental increases. More significantly, while the nominal base is growing, the constant base (left Y axis) is shrinking. Forecasting the tax revenue or the nominal tax base without adjusting for these factors could lead to significant error.

33.2.4.4 Aggregated Data

Sometimes, two or more unrelated data series are added together. Figure 33.9 shows the aged, blind, and disabled Virginia Medicaid enrollment from 1986 through 2004. With this dataset we see a sharp enrollment growth beginning around 1990. It may be unrealistic to make a forecast that indefinitely projects the same sort of growth. By breaking the data into separate groups for the two major types of enrollment (Figure 33.10), we observe that the blind and disabled category contributes a smaller amount to the accelerated enrollment growth. The more rapid growth is associated with aged category.

Discovering this difference can lead to an examination why the aged category enrollment began to grow more rapidly in the early 1990s. At that time several federally driven public policies required states to extend Medicare "wrap-around" benefits. These benefits would principally affect people in the aged categories and, thus, lead to enrollment growth for policy, rather than demographic, reasons. Such enrollment growth might be expected to eventually level off. The analyst should become familiar with any policies or intentional behavior that affects the data generating process. This information can be used in the forecast.

TABLE 33.2

Constant Dollars

	Finding the Base			Conversion to Constant Dollars		
Year	Rev R	Tax Rate T	NOM $ ND R ÷ T	CPI (82–84) DF Source: BLS	DF2004 ÷ DF Factor DF_b/DF_t	Const. $ CD Factor*ND
1980	584.9	0.05	11,698	82.4	0.4362	26,817
1981	605.1	0.05	12,102	90.9	0.4812	25,149
1982	605.1	0.05	12,102	96.5	0.5109	23,690
1983	615.2	0.05	12,304	99.6	0.5273	23,336
1984	625.2	0.05	12,504	103.9	0.5500	22,733
1985	698.9	0.055	12,707	107.6	0.5696	22,309
1986	710	0.055	12,909	109.6	0.5802	22,249
1987	732.3	0.055	13,313	113.6	0.6014	22,137
1988	754.3	0.055	13,715	118.3	0.6263	21,899
1989	776.5	0.055	14,118	124	0.6564	21,507
1990	871.3	0.06	14,522	130.7	0.6919	20,988
1991	895.5	0.06	14,925	136.2	0.7210	20,700
1992	919.7	0.06	15,328	140.3	0.7427	20,638
1993	1,035.7	0.065	15,934	144.5	0.7650	20,830
1994	1,048.8	0.065	16,135	148.2	0.7845	20,567
1995	1,101.2	0.065	16,942	152.4	0.8068	20,999
1996	1,195.6	0.0675	17,713	156.9	0.8306	21,325
1997	1,203	0.0675	17,822	160.5	0.8497	20,976
1998	1,213	0.0675	17,970	163	0.8629	20,826
1999	1,223	0.0675	18,119	166.6	0.8819	20,544
2000	1,263.4	0.07	18,049	172.2	0.9116	19,799
2001	1,319.1	0.07	18,844	177.1	0.9375	20,100
2002	1,325	0.07	18,929	179.9	0.9524	19,876
2003	1,363.6	0.07	19,480	184	0.9741	19,999
2004	1,435.5	0.0725	19,800	188.9	1.0000	19,800

Note: The revenue and tax data are artificial; BLS = Bureau of Labor Statistics at www.BLS.gov.;
* = All dollars in thousands.

In the examples of this and the previous sections, the decomposition or disaggregation* is relatively simple, following a few easy steps; however, when working with real world data, analysts may need to go through a series of steps to decompose their data sufficiently to make forecasts. Avoid decomposing your data so far that they have extremely small numbers; it is difficult to forecast a data series that has zero values for some observations or one that has large variation relative to the average observation. As a general guideline, consider this: the Medicaid budget in Virginia accounted for roughly $2 billion in 1995, the state share, $1 billion, was 13 percent of the state general fund revenue. Virginia disaggregated these data into 30 categories of health care service with each category of service further broken into a minimum of two data series and, except for two or three of the most complex categories, a maximum of ten series. So this substantial part of the entire state budget was forecast with roughly 100 to 150 data series.

---

* Decomposition literally means to decompose or break up. For complex dataset that means, break up into its constituent parts. Disaggregation literally means to disaggregate, again break into the constituent parts.

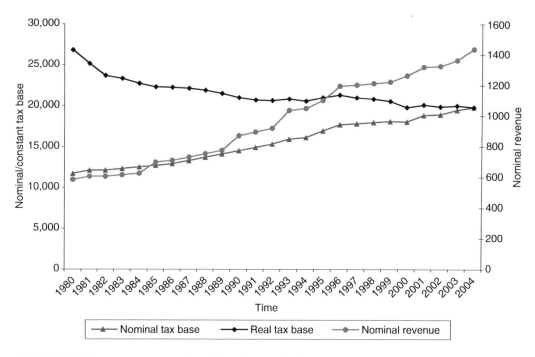

FIGURE 33.8 Compare trends in dollars. (Data from Table 33.2.)

33.2.4.5 Completeness

Another important consideration when breaking up dataset is whether the resulting series are complete. Breaking up the data series provides the opportunity of discovering information left out of the

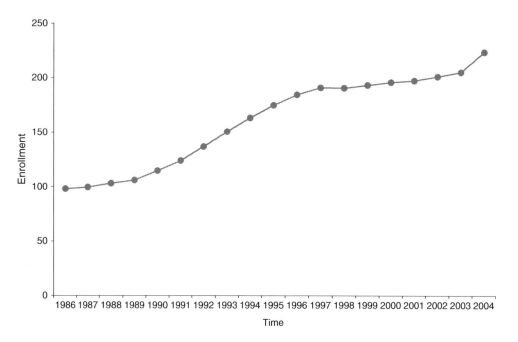

FIGURE 33.9 Virginia medicaid ABD categories enrollment. (Data from http://www.dmas.virginia. gov/ab-2004_stats.htm. Accessed August 24, 2005.)

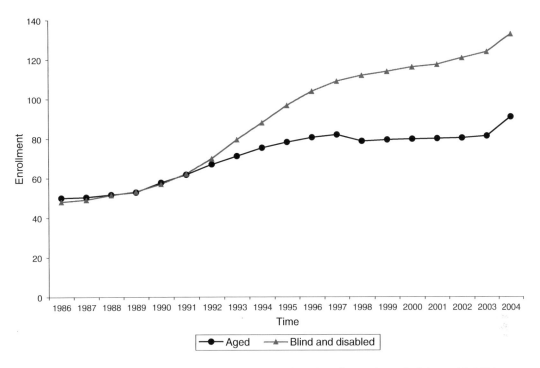

FIGURE 33.10 Components of ABD categories. (Data from http://www.dmas.virginia.gov/ab-2004_stats. htm. Accessed August 24, 2005.)

combined data, but also increases the risk of losing something that is included in the gross data. For example, when forecasting income from licenses, what happens to fines for late applications? Also, if the licensee moves out of the locality, does he or she receive a refund? What source of money pays the refund? When working with financial data, obtain the organization's annual financial reports and reconcile the data sources with these reports. Find out what is missing and assure that it is accounted for. With other data, look for annual reports or other periodic reports with which to reconcile. Imagine how the data could be incomplete and look to see what happens with such data. An excellent forecast of the wrong data can be useless or worse.

When decomposing complex data to make a forecast, decomposition must be reversed to complete the forecast. Combine the data by precisely reversing the steps followed when decomposing them.

33.3 FORECASTING

Some important components of variation in data series are known as level, trend, cycle, seasonality, and randomness (Makridakis et al., 2003). Randomness is the same here as elsewhere in statistical studies. Each of the other components is discussed below. Dataset is forecast by extrapolating these other components.

33.3.1 LEVEL

Level refers to the component of the dataset that determines its location on the Y axis. Although some data series do not exhibit trend, cycle, or seasonality, all data series exhibit a level. Figure 33.11 shows a series that appears to vary around an unknown, but approximately constant, level. It does not particularly increase or decrease over time, nor does it show any other distinguishable pattern.

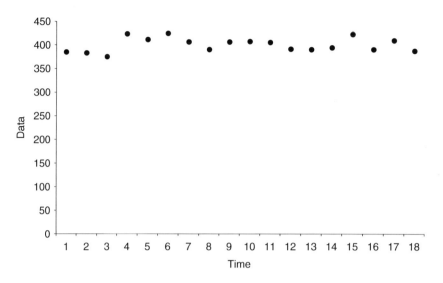

FIGURE 33.11 Variation around a mean (artificial data).

Figure 33.12 shows the same series as a random scatter plot; dataset that varies randomly around a mean will appear as a random scatter plot if the variation is large relative to the mean.

The dataset usually does not keep the same level across the whole series. Consequently, we need a way to talk about the level that is proximate to a particular location on a time index. Here I refer to such a level with a time subscript, so S_t refers to level S at time t. I examine three stages of forecasting techniques for this kind of data.

33.3.1.1 Last Observation

A forecast model is an equation or set of equations (also called expressions) used to generate a projected value. The simplest forecast model of nontrending dataset is to assume that the last observation will be repeated indefinitely into the future. Expressed mathematically, this model is

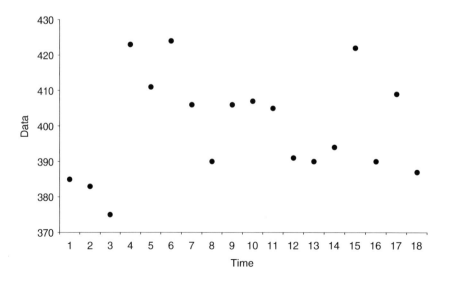

FIGURE 33.12 Random variation (artificial data).

$$F_t = X_{t-1} \tag{33.4}$$

All future periods are forecast with

$$F_{t+m} = F_t \tag{33.5}$$

This model is sometimes called Random Walk or the Naive model (Makridakis et al., 1982; Armstrong, 1985). Although this approach seldom produces the most accurate forecast, it provides a baseline for evaluating other forecast approaches. Any method used should perform at least as well as this approach. If, after repeated use, a method's track record is worse than last observation, stop using it.

33.3.1.2 Improving Last Observation

Last observation is overly influenced by the random component in the data series; although the last observation approaches a number, it misses it because of the noise (random variation) that impacts the particular observation. Rather than moving to the future from the last observation, it would be better to forecast from the central tendency of the data series. The arithmetic mean, more commonly known as the average, fulfills this requirement by "smoothing" the random variation, so

$$F_{t+m} = S_t = \bar{x}_t = \sum_{i=1}^{t} (X_i/t) \tag{33.6}$$

where
   F_{t+m} is the forecast for the mth future period (any future period) at time t
   S_t is the level at time t, $\bar{x}_t$ is the average at time t
   X_i is the vector of time ordered observations ending at time t
   t is the total number of observations at time t

   Table 33.3 demonstrates this calculation.

33.3.1.2.1 Projecting the Past
Table 33.3 forecasts both future and historical periods. The forecast for each historical period is the average of all periods preceding that period, based on the information that would have been available to forecast the specific period. This forecast of the past allows comparison of forecast methods through a "loss function." Loss functions are used to select a forecast model, that is, to

TABLE 33.3

Average as Forecast

	Data	Forecast
Period 1	30	
Period 2	36	30.00
Period 3	31	33.00
Period 4	34	32.33
Period 5	29	32.75
Total	160	32.00
Time periods	5	
Average	32	
Future Periods		32

TABLE 33.4

Loss Functions Used to Compare Forecasts

	Data	Forecast (Average)	Deviation = e	e^2	Forecast (Last Obs)	Deviation = e	e^2
Period 1	30						
Period 2	36	33	3	9	30	6	36
Period 3	31	32.33	−1.33	1.78	36	−5	25
Period 4	34	32.75	1.25	1.56	31	3	9
Period 5	29	32	−3	9	34	−5	25
SSQ				21.34			95
Count				4			4
MSE				5.34			23.75
RMSE				2.31			4.87

choose between different ways to forecast data. A commonly used loss function is the root mean squared error (RMSE) (Armstrong, 1985). Root mean squared error is found by

$$\text{RMSE} = \sqrt{\left(\sum_{i=1}^{t} (X_i - F_i)^2 / t \right)} \qquad (33.7)$$

There is no ideal value for an RMSE because it depends on the size of the data and the amount of variability in the data; however, between any two values of RMSE, the smaller reflects greater accuracy. Table 33.4 compares two forecasts of the same data series as shown in Table 33.3. The first forecast is the average; the second is last observation. The forecasts use only the knowledge the forecaster could have at the time a forecast is made. For period 1 the forecasters had no information, so no forecast is made. Because of the distorting effect, this period is left out of the loss function calculation. For period 2, the forecaster could have known period 1, so the average is the last observation. Beginning with period 3, the two methods produce different forecasts. By forecasting with the average rather than the last observation, the RMSE is reduced from 4.87 to 3.77 or by 23 percent.

33.3.1.3 Better Methods

Although the average accounts for random variation, it treats the data as static. Its use assumes that the level is constant across the whole series. As shown in Figure 33.13, many series exhibit occasional, frequent, or even continual shifts in the level. Two approaches for handling this condition are the moving average and single exponential smoothing.

33.3.1.3.1 Moving Average

Figure 33.14 shows a moving average (Makridakis et al., 2003), which is calculated much like an average except that it is the average of only the most recent observations. As a new observation is included, the oldest observation is discarded. A moving average has some of the advantages of the average, yet it recognizes that the average contains irrelevant dataset that predates the most recent level shift. The number of periods included in the moving average depends on how frequently the level shifts. Because the average is expected to shift, it would be ineffective to include a large number of time periods; however, as the number of observations is reduced, the forecast becomes more and more susceptible to the random variation in the last few observations. The number of

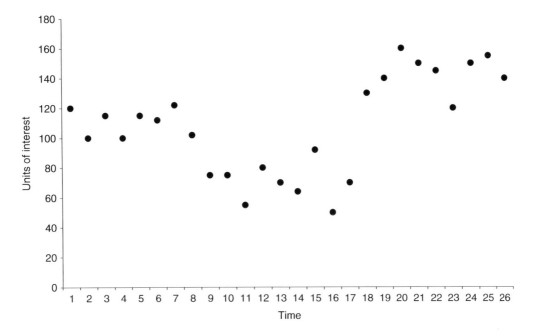

FIGURE 33.13 Shifting data. (Data from Table 33.5.)

observations included in the moving average is a compromise between these considerations. A moving average is calculated using Equation 33.8 as demonstrated in Table 33.5

$$F_{t+1} = \text{MAVG}_t = (X_t + X_{t-1} + \cdots + X_t - (L-1))/L \qquad (33.8)$$

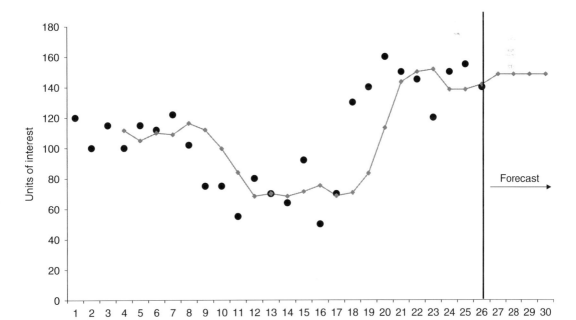

FIGURE 33.14 Moving average. Moving average is three period. (Data from Table 33.5.)

TABLE 33.5

Moving Average

X	Sum 6 6 Obs	L	MA	MA as Forecast	Error = e	Error Sq = e^2	Average as Forecast	Error = e	Error Sq = e^2
120									
100									
115									
100									
115									
112	662	6	110.33						
122	664	6	110.67	110.33	11.67	136.11	110.33	11.67	136.11
102	666	6	111.00	110.67	−8.67	75.11	112.00	−10.00	100.00
75	626	6	104.33	111.00	−36.00	1,296.00	110.75	−35.75	1,278.06
75	601	6	100.17	104.33	−29.33	860.44	106.78	−31.78	1,009.83
55	541	6	90.17	100.17	−45.17	2,040.03	103.60	−48.60	2,361.96
80	509	6	84.83	90.17	−10.17	103.36	99.18	−19.18	367.94
70	457	6	76.17	84.83	−14.83	220.03	97.58	−27.58	760.84
64	419	6	69.83	76.17	−12.17	148.03	95.46	−31.46	989.83
92	436	6	72.67	69.83	22.17	491.36	93.21	−1.21	1.47
50	411	6	68.5	72.67	−22.67	513.78	93.13	−43.13	1,860.48
70	426	6	71.00	68.50	1.50	2.25	90.44	−20.44	417.69
130	476	6	79.33	71.00	59.00	3,481.00	89.24	40.76	1,661.76
140	546	6	91.00	79.33	60.67	3,680.44	91.50	48.50	2,352.25
160	642	6	107.00	91.00	69.00	4,761.00	94.05	65.95	4,349.06
150	700	6	116.67	107.00	43.00	1,849.00	97.35	52.65	2,772.02
145	795	6	132.5	116.67	28.33	802.78	99.86	45.14	2,037.88
120	845	6	140.83	132.50	−12.50	156.25	101.91	18.09	327.28
150	865	6	144.17	140.83	9.17	84.03	102.70	47.30	2,237.70
155	880	6	146.67	144.17	10.83	117.36	104.67	50.33	2,533.44
140	860	6	143.33	146.67	−6.67	44.44	106.68	33.32	1,110.22
Fututre periods				143.33			107.96		
Sum of squares						20,862.81			28,665.84
Count						20			20
MSE						1,043.14			1,433.29
RMSE						32.3			37.86

where
  F = forecast
  X = observed
  t = time index
  L = length (number of periods in the average)

The forecast, F_t, at any particular period is the moving average as of the last previous period. For all future periods, it is the moving average where the historical dataset is exhausted. If the dataset is seasonal, follow the steps for de-seasonalizing it as discussed below before calculating the moving average. The last two columns show the comparative forecast based on the average. The bottom of the table shows that the six-period moving average has an RMSE or 32.3, which is 15 percent lower than the RMSE of 37.9 for the simple average.*

---

* Typically I omit the first few observations in the RMSE calculation to keep these reports comparable, where sometimes I do not initialize.

33.3.1.3.2   Single Exponential Smoothing (SES)

Single exponential smoothing (SES) uses a parameter, α, to choose how much influence the most recent observation has on the forecast (Williams, 1987; Makridakis et al., 2003). If α is 0, the forecast is set at an original value based on very early data, and is never adjusted. It should never be set at zero. As α increases, more weight is placed on the recent observations. If α is 1, the forecast becomes last observation. SES is computed with these equations

$$F_{t+m} = \text{forecast at time } t \text{ of time } t + m = S_t \tag{33.9}$$

$$S_t = \text{level at time } t = F_t + \alpha e_t i = S_{t-1} + \alpha e_t \tag{33.10}$$

$$e_t = \text{error at time t} = X_t - F_t = X_t - S_{t-1} \tag{33.11}$$

where
   $X_t =$ the observation at time t
   $\alpha =$ alpha, a level smoothing parameter subject to $0 \leq \alpha \leq 1$
   $t \ =$ a time index
   $m =$ the number of periods between an observation period and a forecast period

Table 33.6 demonstrates SES using the same data as in Table 33.5. Over the same observations RMSE for SES is 25.3, 22 percent less than the 32.3 RMSE for the six-period moving average and 33 percent lower than the 37.9 RMSE for the average. The forecast made with these equations is shown in Figure 33.15.

33.3.1.3.2.1   Selecting α

The parameter of SES is α, a number which is multiplied times the error (also known as deviation, the distance between observation and forecast, see Equation 33.11) to determine the next forecast. Choosing a particular value of a parameter is called fitting a forecast. In Table 33.6, α is arbitrarily set at 0.5. Common practice requires that α be set between 0 and 1 (formally, inclusive of these limits, but practically, more than 0 and less than 1).* A common method for selecting a specific value for α, that is, to "optimize α" or "optimize the model," is to use a grid of possible α values, such as in the first row of Table 33.7. The analyst calculates a forecast with each α value, determines the value of the loss function, as shown in the second row of Table 33.7 (for the same data as in Table 33.6), and selects the best α value. The best α value is the one with the lowest RMSE value. Using the grid search of Table 33.7, the α value of 0.9 would be selected, with RMSE $= 23.65$, which is 6.8 percent less than the RMSE for $\alpha = 0.5$.

In recent years forecasters using spreadsheets have sometimes used a function labeled "solver" to optimize α, or (for subsequent methods) α and other parameters. Solver is an implementation of a linear programming procedure known as simplex. Solver is not recommended because simplex is known to reach solutions that are suboptimal as a consequence of saddle points. The author has experienced this result. Although the risk of reaching a saddle point may be relatively low with one parameter, as in SES, it greatly expands with multiple parameters that will be discussed in following sections.

---

* Some forecast literature argues that these restrictions are arbitrary; however, the expression of the formulas as shown here provides an intuitive understanding for the reason that α should be limited in this way. Specifically, α is multiplied by the error in the previous forecast. The error itself can be divided into information and noise (the information is that the previous forecast missed because it was wrong, the noise is that the previous forecast missed because the average of the series is mis-estimated or has changed). Alpha divides the error into these two components, selecting the information component to improve the forecast. Since the total error sums to 100 percent (one), it would be odd (although not impossible) that the information portion of the error is more than 100 percent. While the error in one observation might include canceling noise (thus, the information would be more than 100 percent of the error), the presence of a series of such errors would imply that the forecast is biased, and thus, not a good method for forecasting the data.

TABLE 33.6

Single Exponential Smoothing

$\alpha = 0.5$

X	$F = S_{(t-1)} +$ $\alpha e_{(t-1)}$	e	e^2
120		120	
100	60	40	
115	80	35	
100	97.5	2.5	
115	98.8	16.3	
112	106.9	5.1	
122	109.4	12.6	157.8
102	115.7	−13.7	188.2
75	108.9	−33.9	1,146.5
75	91.9	−16.9	286.6
55	83.5	−28.5	810.2
80	69.2	10.8	115.9
70	74.6	−4.6	21.3
64	72.3	−8.3	69.0
92	68.2	23.8	568.6
50	80.1	−30.1	904.6
70	65.0	5.0	24.6
130	67.5	62.5	3,903.8
140	98.8	41.2	1,700.8
160	119.4	40.6	1,650.0
150	139.7	10.3	106.3
145	144.8	0.2	0.0
120	144.9	−24.9	621.1
150	132.5	17.5	307.6
155	141.2	13.8	189.6
140	148.1	−8.1	65.9
Future periods	144.1		
Sum of squares			12,838.6
			20
MSE			641.9
RMSE			25.3

33.3.1.3.2.2   Initializing SES

Initializing is selecting the first value of the SES forecast, the value of S_0 (the period before the period of the first available observation). Initialization is not difficult to accomplish. A likely initial value for SES is the average of the first few observations. Here, we could borrow the average of the first six periods from our earlier consideration of the six-period moving average and initialize our forecast at 110.3.

Initialization can impact the choice of α values. Table 33.8 compares the RMSE for the series {50, 55, 59, 48, 63, 57, 52, 54, 58, 51, 55, 47, 52, 64, 61, 50, 55, 47, 52, 59, 60, 50, 45, 57, 50, 55} first uninitialized and then initialized with 55.3, the average of the first six observations. The RMSE penalty for selecting the lowest α value drops from 26.57 to 5.16 when the series is initialized. More importantly, the optimal parameter value changes from $\alpha = 0.3$, with a forecast beyond the last observation of 53.0, to $\alpha = 0.05$ with a forecast beyond the last observation of 54.2, or about two percent higher. This impact is the particular effect of initialization. Uninitialized SES models use observations at the beginning of the series to initialize themselves. When α is set low, SES uses

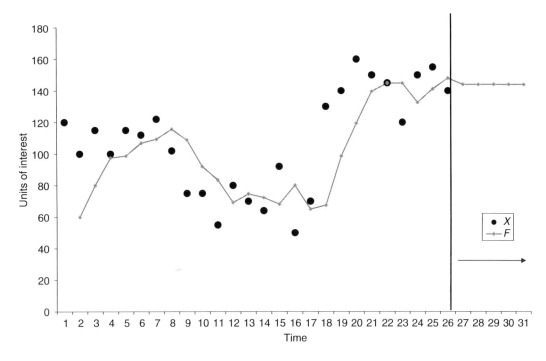

FIGURE 33.15 Single exponential smoothing (SES). (Data from Table 33.6.)

more of the beginning observations to overcome the effects of not being initialized, so the model produces a higher RMSE. This can be seen by comparing the SES model estimate of the first 10 observations of the data for Table 33.8 using $\alpha = 0.05$ and $\alpha = 0.9$ as shown in Figures 33.16 and 33.17. If conditions are such that a low α value is optimal, failure to initialize the SES model may mislead the forecaster into selecting an excessively high α value. Initialization is also very important when there are a limited number of observations, as there is insufficient opportunity for the model to correct for the missing initial value.

33.3.2 TREND-CYCLE

Trend refers to a data series' tendency to grow or shrink over time. On an *XY* plot this tendency can be observed as the slope of the line connecting the observations. Cycle refers to the data series' tendency to curve away from either the constant level or trend location but later to come back and curve away in the other direction. Except in its special seasonal variety, cycle may be treated simply as variation in trend. Thus, trend-cycle is the second component of a data series. It also varies over time so I refer to it as B_t. Figures 33.18 and 33.19 demonstrate trending data.

Trending data can be visualized another way with first differences of the annual period; for monthly data, the annual period is the 12th period. First differences of the annual period are found by

TABLE 33.7
Grid Search for Parameters for SES

α	0.05	0.1	0.2	0.3	0.5	0.7	0.9
RMSE	36.79	35.44	31.74	28.75	25.36	23.96	23.65

TABLE 33.8
Comparing Grid Search, Initialized and Uninitialized

α		0.05	0.1	0.2	0.3	0.5	0.7	0.9
RMSE	(Uninitialized)	26.57	15.00	7.07	5.72	6.06	6.46	6.81
	(Initialized)	5.16	5.23	5.44	5.67	6.09	6.46	6.81

$$D_A = \text{Difference of the annual period} = X_{t+L} - X_t \qquad (33.12)$$

where
  X is an observation
  t is a time index
  L is the number of periods in a year

In Figure 33.20 we see this equation applied. We will call this a trend plot. Because all the values in the trend plot are positive, this dataset exhibits a trend. However, it is noticeable that the values vary sharply in their distance from zero, suggesting that there may be some instability in the trend. If the plot frequently crossed zero, we would expect that there would be no trend in the data.

33.3.2.1 Last Change

If, from frequent experience with a data series, the forecaster knows that the observations usually grow or shrink, it is clear that the last observation is an unlikely value for the data. More likely, the data will continue to grow or shrink. A simple forecast method of this tendency begins with last observation and adds last change. Last change is calculated as last observation minus observation before last

$$B = \text{the change from period 1 to period 2} = X_2 - X_1 \qquad (33.13)$$

$$F_{t+1} = \text{the forecast (next period)} = X_2 + B \qquad (33.14)$$

$$F_{t+m} = \text{forecast at time } t \text{ of the } m\text{th future period} = X_2 + m*B \qquad (33.15)$$

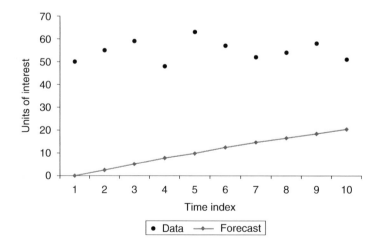

FIGURE 33.16 Uninitialized when $\alpha = 0.05$. (Data related to Table 33.8.)

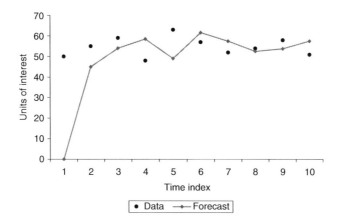

FIGURE 33.17 Uninitialized when $\alpha = 0.9$. (Data related to Table 33.8.)

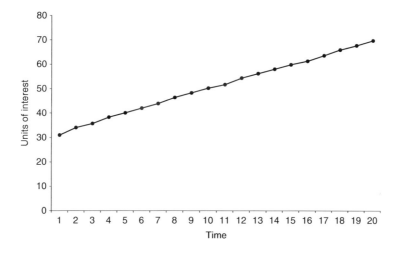

FIGURE 33.18 Increasing trend (artificial data).

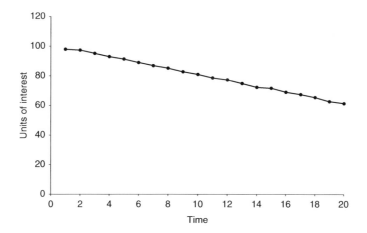

FIGURE 33.19 Decreasing trend (artificial data).

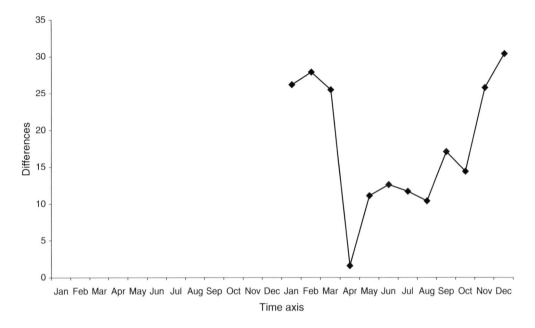

FIGURE 33.20 Trend plot. (Data from Table 33.9.)

where
X_1 = the observed value for the older period
X_2 = the observed values for the more recent period
t = the time index
m = the number of future periods

With dataset that does not trend, the forecast is the same for each future period; however, with trending data, each future period has its own forecast.

Last change includes two undesirable sources of variation: First, the point for beginning calculation of the future dataset is last observation, which is not a good estimate of the time adjusted central tendency of the data. Second, the estimate of change is taken from a single pair of observations, and the change between these two observations is strongly related to the random component of each of these observations. Last change can be improved through the following techniques.

33.3.2.2 First Differences

Differences capture the trending component of a data series. They are calculated using the following equation:

$$D_t = \text{Any difference (period to period change)} = X_t - X_{t-1} \qquad (33.16)$$

These differences, technically "first differences," can be forecast using a moving average or SES. The result is a forecast of the trend component of the series. After forecasting the differences, reconstruct the data series by reversing the differences beginning with the first observation of the data series using these equations

$$F_2' = X_1 + F_1 \qquad (33.17)$$

$$F_3' = F_2' + F_2, \quad F_4' = F_3' + F_3, \text{ etc.} \qquad (33.18)$$

where

X_1 is the first observation of the original (predifferenced) data series
F_t' is the reconstructed data series (forecast)
F_t is the moving average or SES forecast of the differenced data series

This unrolling process is shown in the two right columns of Table 33.9 below (after the discussion of trending exponential smoothing). To reduce the effect of random variation in the first observation, the first two observations are averaged.

33.3.2.3   Trending (Two Parameter) Exponential Smoothing

A technique that is widely used for forecasting trending dataset is two parameter exponential smoothing. A common version of this technique is Holt exponential smoothing or Holt's method. The version shown in and discussed here allows the two parameters to be calculated independently through a minor modification developed by Williams (1987). The forecast is produced through these equations as shown in Table 33.9

$$F_{t+m} = \text{forecast at time } t \text{ of time } t+m = S_t + (B_t m) \tag{33.19}$$

$$S_t = \text{level at time } t = F_t + \alpha e_t \tag{33.20}$$

$$B_t = \text{trend at time } t = B_{t-1} + \beta_{et} \tag{33.21}$$

$$e_t = \text{error at time } t = X_t - F_t \tag{33.22}$$

where

X_t, α, t, and m are as used with SES
β = beta, a trend smoothing parameter subject to $0 \leq \beta \leq 1$

The forecast calculated in Table 33.9 is shown in Figure 33.21. For comparison I show SES of the first differences in the four columns to the right. Because of differences in initialization, the RMSE is calculated ignoring the first four periods. Selection of a forecast model among these two techniques is briefly discussed in Section 33.4. With Holt exponential smoothing both α and β are restricted to values between 0 and 1.

33.3.2.3.1   Initializing Holt
Table 33.9 calculations are not initialized. Because Holt involves estimating both a level and a trend, initialization is more complex than for SES. For monthly data, calculate the initial level, S_0, and the initial trend, B_0, using Equations 33.23 through 33.27, where X refers to monthly observations. The forecaster must make appropriate adjustments to use this with data cumulated over other intervals.

Calculate the average, $\bar{x}_j$ for j = periods 1 and 2 (such as two sequential years) of length L

$$\bar{x}_j = \sum_{i=1}^{L} X_{i,j}/L \tag{33.23}$$

(that is, add the L observations in each of the first two cycles and divide each by L; for monthly data $L = 12$).

Calculate the difference (D) between these two averages

$$D = \bar{x}_2 - \bar{x}_1 \tag{33.24}$$

TABLE 33.9
Holt Exponential Smoothing and SES of First Differences

Month	Data	Holt Exponential Smoothing α F_1	0.9 e	β S	0.05 B	RMSE 5.26	SES of First Differences SES D	α F	0.89 e	F'	e	RMSE 4.987	Combined Average F(Avg)	RMSE 4.923
Jan	65.6	0	65.6	59	3.28									
Feb	66.1	62.3	3.8	65.7	3.47		0.5	0.00	0.5	65.85			64.09	
Mar	68.5	69.2	−0.7	68.6	3.43		2.4	0.44	2.0	66.29			67.74	
Apr	80.6	72.0	8.6	79.7	3.86		12.1	2.17	9.9	68.47			70.24	
May	77.6	83.6	−6.0	78.2	3.56	36.1	−3	10.96	−14.0	79.43	−1.83	3.33	81.52	15.33
June	78.3	81.8	−3.5	78.6	3.39	12.0	0.7	−1.39	2.1	78.03	0.27	0.07	79.90	2.55
July	80	82.0	−2	80.2	3.29	4.2	1.7	0.46	1.2	78.49	1.51	2.28	80.26	0.07
Aug	81.9	83.5	−1.6	82.1	3.21	2.5	1.9	1.56	0.3	80.05	1.85	3.43	81.77	0.02
Sept	80.2	85.3	−5.1	80.7	2.96	25.7	−1.7	1.86	−3.6	81.91	−1.71	2.92	83.59	11.48
Oct	82.7	83.7	−1.0	82.8	2.91	0.9	2.5	−1.29	3.8	80.62	2.08	4.34	82.14	0.31
Nov	78.8	85.7	−6.9	79.5	2.56	47.7	−3.9	2.06	−6.0	82.68	−3.88	15.07	84.19	29.08
Dec	78	82.1	−4.1	78.4	2.36	16.4	−0.8	−3.21	2.4	79.47	−1.47	2.15	80.76	7.62
Jan	91.8	80.8	11.0	90.7	2.91	121.8	13.8	−1.08	14.9	78.39	13.41	179.83	79.58	149.39
Feb	94	93.6	0.4	94.0	2.93	0.2	2.2	12.09	−9.9	90.48	3.52	12.40	92.04	3.83
Mar	94	96.9	−2.9	94.3	2.79	8.4	0	3.34	−3.3	93.82	0.18	0.03	95.35	1.83
Apr	82.2	97.1	−14.9	83.7	2.04	221.3	−12	0.38	−12.2	94.20	−12.00	144.00	95.64	180.58
May	88.7	85.7	3.0	88.4	2.19	8.8	6.5	−10.40	16.9	83.80	4.90	24.00	84.77	15.48
June	90.9	90.6	0.3	90.9	2.21	0.1	2.2	4.56	−2.4	88.36	2.54	6.46	89.48	2.03
July	91.7	93.1	−1.4	91.8	2.14	1.9	0.8	2.47	−1.7	90.83	0.87	0.76	91.95	0.06
Aug	92.3	94.0	−1.7	92.5	2.05	2.8	0.6	0.99	−0.4	91.82	0.48	0.23	92.90	0.36
Sept	97.3	94.5	2.8	97.0	2.19	7.7	5	0.65	4.4	92.47	4.83	23.37	93.49	14.49
Oct	97.1	99.2	−2.1	97.3	2.09	4.5	−0.2	4.5	−4.7	96.97	0.13	0.02	98.09	0.98
Nov	105	99.4	5.2	104.1	2.35	27.1	7.5	0.34	7.2	97.31	7.29	53.21	98.35	39.03
Dec	108	106.4	2.0	108.2	2.45	3.9	3.8	6.68	−2.9	103.98	4.42	19.52	105.20	10.21
Forecast		110.6		110.6	2.45			4.13		108.11			109.38	
		113.1		113.1	2.45			4.13		112.24			112.67	

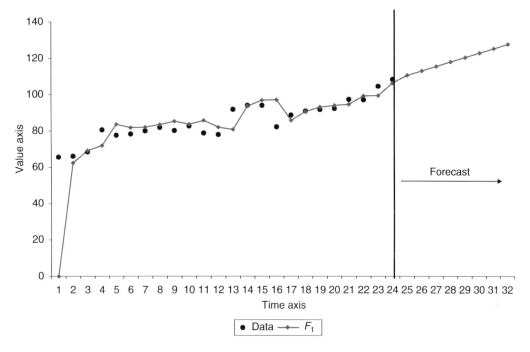

FIGURE 33.21 Holt exponential smoothing. (Data from Table 33.9.)

Divide this difference by L to get an initial trend (B_0):

$$B_0 = D/L \qquad (33.25)$$

Multiply B by $(L+1)/2$ and subtract from $\bar{x}_1$ to get (S_0).

$$S_0 = \bar{x}_1 - B(L+1)/2 \qquad (33.26)$$

For monthly data, $(L+1)/2 = 6.5$. For quarterly data $L = 4$ and $(L+1)/2 = 2.5$. Treat S_0 and B_0 as if they were calculated in the month prior to the month of the first observation, so the forecast value for the first month of actual dataset is

$$F_1 = S_0 + B_0 \qquad (33.27)$$

33.3.2.3.2 Selecting α and β

The parameters for Holt exponential smoothing are selected following the same grid search process as with SES. Table 33.10 shows a typical grid along with the RMSE for each combination for the data shown in the previous example. The initialization with Equations 33.23 through 33.27 results in $S_0 = 66.8$, $B_0 = 1.49$, and $F_1 = 68.3$. With these results, one would select the α, β combination 0.6, 0.05. Failure to initialize results in choosing an inferior model. The optimal RMSE for the initialized model, 4.84 is about two percent lower than the RMSE of 4.92 for the SES of First Differences. The new model is compared with the old in Figure 33.22.

33.3.2.4 Decelerating Trends

Up to here we have examined linear trends, that is, trends that can be approximately modeled using a line. But some trending data curve. In Figures 33.23 and 33.24, the trend is fading over time.

TABLE 33.10
Grid Search for Holt Exponential Smoothing

α, β		BETA (β)					
A	(α)	0.05 RMSE		0.01 RMSE		0.3 RMSE	
L	0.1	0.1, 0.05	5.17	0.1, 0.1	5.60	0.1, 0.3	8.30
P	0.2	0.2, 0.05	5.02	0.2, 0.1	5.32	0.2, 0.3	7.19
H	0.4	0.4, 0.05	4.88	0.4, 0.1	5.10	0.4, 0.3	6.04
A	0.6	0.6, 0.05	**4.84**	0.6, 0.1	5.00	0.6, 0.3	5.66
(α)	0.9	0.9, 0.05	4.94	0.9, 0.1	5.07	0.9, 0.3	5.61

It may be that the data cannot exceed some maximum or minimum. For example, when forecasting the growth in employment in the sector of privatized government activities, there is a natural maximum roughly associated with current government employment. The data in Figure 33.24 might also be thought to be dependent on the magnitude of its level component; this topic is briefly discussed in the next section, which addresses accelerating trends.

When trends have decelerated during the historical period and are not expected to continue decelerating in the future, a well-fit Holt model will produce an adequate forecast. However, sometimes the analyst anticipates that the trend will decelerate or decelerate further in the future. An approach that allows for this adjustment is known as the damped trend method (Gardner and McKenzie, 1985)

$$F_{t+m} = \text{forecast at time } t \text{ of time } t + m = S_t + \sum_{t=1}^{m} (\phi' B_t) \qquad (33.28)$$

$$S_t = \text{level at time } t = F_t + \alpha e_t \qquad (33.29)$$

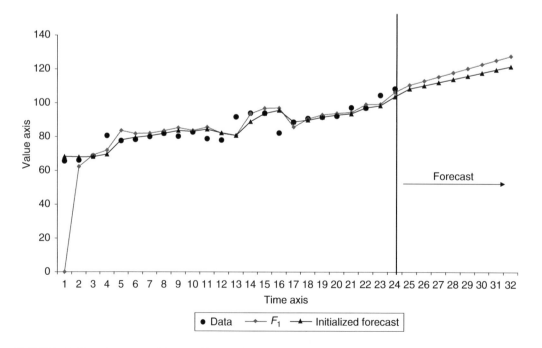

FIGURE 33.22 Holt exponential smoothing: Uninitialized and initialized compared. (Data from Table 33.9.)

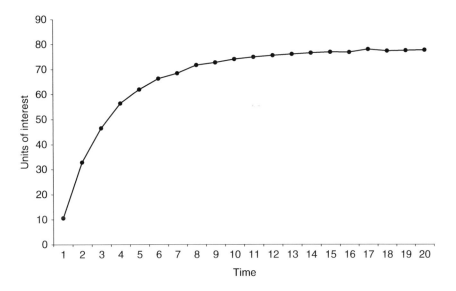

FIGURE 33.23 Decelerating (damped) increase (artificial data).

$$B_t = \text{trend at time } t = \varphi B_{t-1} + \beta e_t \qquad (33.30)$$

$$e_t = \text{error at time } t = X_t - F_t \qquad (33.31)$$

where, X_t, α, β, t, and m are as with Holt exponential smoothing and $\varphi =$ phi, a damping factor subject to $0 \leq \varphi \leq 1$.

These equations are demonstrated in Table 33.11, with an appropriate curving dataset. Table 33.11 looks a lot like Holt exponential smoothing in Table 33.9; however the calculation of B_t differs because of the application of both φ and β. The results are demonstrated in Figure 33.25.

The damped trend is optimized with a three-way grid search as demonstrated with Table 33.12. Gardner recommends considering a full range of values from 0 to 1 for φ (personal communication). However, the analyst should be alert to the implication of low values of φ. In the historic period the

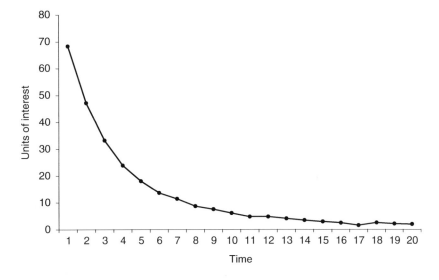

FIGURE 33.24 Decelerating (damped) decrease (artificial data).

TABLE 33.11
Damped Holt Exponential Smoothing

Data	α F_1	0.6 E	β S	0.3 B	RMSE 7.22
28		28.0	16.8	8.4	
52	25.2	26.8	41.2	15.59	
67	56.8	9.7	62.6	16.93	
107	79.6	27.1	95.8	23.37	
129	119.2	9.7	125.0	23.94	93.9
150	149.0	0.6	149.3	21.74	0.4
153	171.1	−18.5	160.0	14.01	342.8
178	174.0	3.9	176.3	13.77	15.0
183	190.1	−7.4	185.6	10.16	55.2
214	195.8	18.5	206.9	14.69	341.4
225	221.6	3.5	223.7	14.29	12.6
233	238.0	−5.0	235.0	11.36	25.1
247	246.3	1.1	247.0	10.55	1.2
262	257.5	4.2	260.1	10.76	17.7
273	270.8	1.8	271.9	10.23	3.4
277	282.1	−4.8	279.3	7.77	23.0
290	287.0	3.1	288.9	7.92	9.7
298	296.8	1.3	297.6	7.52	1.7
301	305.1	−4.6	302.4	5.39	21.0
309	307.8	1.3	308.5	5.23	1.6
319	313.8	5.4	317.0	6.34	29.6
320	323.4	−3.2	321.5	4.76	10.1
332	326.2	6.1	329.9	6.11	37.1
336	336.0	0.4	336.2	5.62	0.2
	341.8		341.8	5.06	

value of B_t is affected by both φ and βe_t. So, with each new observation there is a unique combination of multiplications. However, in the forecast period, βe_t drops out of the equation. So for each future period, φ multiplies again. In other words, the value of

$$B_{t+m} = B_t \times \varphi^m \tag{33.32}$$

where m is the number of periods after the historical data ends. Becasue φ is less than 1, φ^m, gets smaller and smaller as m gets larger. The smaller the initial φ, the faster this happens. To put this in layman's terms, small values of φ will result in a flat (SES) forecast within a very short period of time. If the analyst anticipates a trend in the actual data and if the analyst is interested in a horizon of more than a few periods, φ values below 0.9 should not even be considered.

Another condition arises when the trend has not declined in the past, but some damping is expected in the future. In this case, damping factors may not reflect expectations. Consequently, the analyst may need to set the damping factor by judgment. This should be done with extreme care, keeping the above cautions in mind. Also, there is evidence that judgmentally adjusting a forecast becomes a temptation to fix the forecast to a desired value. If judgment is to be applied, it is best to select the damping factor prior to examining the quantitative results.

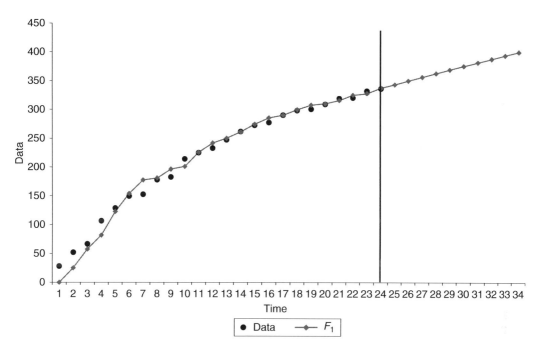

FIGURE 33.25 Damped trend. (Data from Table 33.11.)

33.3.2.5 Accelerating Trends

Figures 33.26 and 33.27 show dataset that has accelerating trends. Accelerating trends are very problematic for forecasting. A moment's reflection will show that no natural process can accelerate without limit. If the limit can be identified, an approach to forecasting this dataset is the use of growth curves.* When dataset has a natural limit, and the use of growth curves is not desired, it is possible to emulate the effect of a growth curve using a damped trend as discussed in the previous section. However, the result will only capture the linear and decelerating components of the trend. It will not capture the accelerating component.

When the rate of acceleration is fairly small, as with population growth or some cases of price inflation, it is possible for acceleration to occur over an extremely long period of time. In such cases, use of ratios might be relevant. These are discussed briefly; however, the reader should be very careful with these techniques. Ratios are appropriate only when the magnitude of the change depends on the magnitude of the level. Thus, the following discussion applies to data that may be similar to Figures 33.24 or 33.26.

Divide each observation by the prior observation

$$R_t = X_t / X_{t-1} \tag{33.33}$$

Then forecast the resulting ratios (R_t) with a moving average or SES. Do not use Holt exponential smoothing or any other trending method for forecasting these ratios. As with first differences, a forecast using ratios is completed by reconstructing a forecast series that originates at the beginning of the data series to avoid adding unnecessary randomness into the forecast. The first two observations should be averaged as the starting value to further reduce the impact of randomness. The ratio

---

* Use of growth curves is a sophisticated regression technique that may sometimes be worthwhile. However, it is outside the scope of this chapter.

TABLE 33.12
Grid Search for Damped Holt Exponential Smoothing

Phi(φ)						1		
α, β, φ					BETA (β)			
A	(α)	0.05 RMSE		0.1 RMSE			0.3 RMSE	
L	0.1	0.1, 0.05, 1	51.98	0.1, 0.1, 1	36.09		0.1, 0.3, 1	25.69
P	0.2	0.2, 0.05, 1	33.02	0.2, 0.1, 1	23.36		0.2, 0.3, 1	17.03
H	0.4	0.4, 0.05, 1	17.86	0.4, 0.1, 1	13.53		0.4, 0.3, 1	10.36
A	0.6	0.6, 0.05, 1	12.42	0.6, 0.1, 1	9.96		0.6, 0.3, 1	8.34
(α)	0.9	0.9, 0.05, 1	9.62	0.9, 0.1, 1	8.30		0.9, 0.3, 1	7.96

Phi(φ)						0.95		
α, β, φ					BETA (β)			
A	(α)	0.05 RMSE		0.1 RMSE			0.3 RMSE	
L	0.1	0.1, 0.05, 0.99	41.27	0.1, 0.1, 0.99	27.71		0.1, 0.3, 0.99	19.73
P	0.2	0.2, 0.05, 0.99	28.11	0.2, 0.1, 0.99	18.78		0.2, 0.3, 0.99	13.70
H	0.4	0.4, 0.05, 0.99	17.05	0.4, 0.1, 0.99	11.56		0.4, 0.3, 0.99	8.81
A	0.6	0.6, 0.05, 0.99	12.73	0.6, 0.1, 0.99	9.13		0.6, 0.3, 0.99	7.43
(α)	0.9	0.9, 0.05, 0.99	10.22	0.9, 0.1, 0.99	8.23		0.9, 0.3, 0.99	7.50

Phi(φ)						0.9		
α, β, φ					BETA (β)			
A	(α)	0.05 RMSE		0.1 RMSE			0.3 RMSE	
L	0.1	0.1, 0.05, 0.95	39.75	0.1, 0.1, 0.95	24.55		0.1, 0.3, 0.95	15.58
P	0.2	0.2, 0.05, 0.95	28.86	0.2, 0.1, 0.95	18.02		0.2, 0.3, 0.95	11.44
H	0.4	0.4, 0.05, 0.95	18.57	0.4, 0.1, 0.95	12.26		0.4, 0.3, 0.95	8.05
A	0.6	0.6, 0.05, 0.95	14.03	0.6, 0.1, 0.95	10.06		0.6, 0.3, 0.95	7.22
(α)	0.9	0.9, 0.05, 0.95	11.05	0.9, 0.1, 0.95	8.98		0.9, 0.3, 0.95	7.55

Phi(φ)						0.99		
α, β, φ					BETA (β)			
A	(α)	0.05 RMSE		0.1 RMSE			0.3 RMSE	
L	0.1	0.1, 0.05, 0.9	48.88	0.1, 0.1, 0.9	33.95		0.1, 0.3, 0.9	24.33
P	0.2	0.2, 0.05, 0.9	31.36	0.2, 0.1, 0.9	22.09		0.2, 0.3, 0.9	16.28
H	0.4	0.4, 0.05, 0.9	17.33	0.4, 0.1, 0.9	12.82		0.4, 0.3, 0.9	9.99
A	0.6	0.6, 0.05, 0.9	12.29	0.6, 0.1, 0.9	9.54		0.6, 0.3, 0.9	8.09
(α)	0.9	0.9, 0.05, 0.9	9.67	0.9, 0.1, 0.9	8.14		0.9, 0.3, 0.9	7.81

Phi(φ)						0.8		
α, β, φ					BETA (β)			
A	(α)	0.05 RMSE		0.1 RMSE			0.3 RMSE	
L	0.1	0.1, 0.05, 0.8	47.24	0.1, 0.1, 0.8	27.79		0.1, 0.3, 0.8	11.81
P	0.2	0.2, 0.05, 0.8	34.63	0.2, 0.1, 0.8	21.95		0.2, 0.3, 0.8	9.95
H	0.4	0.4, 0.05, 0.8	22.09	0.4, 0.1, 0.8	15.64		0.4, 0.3, 0.8	8.39
A	0.6	0.6, 0.05, 0.8	16.30	0.6, 0.1, 0.8	12.58		0.6, 0.3, 0.8	7.99
(α)	0.9	0.9, 0.05, 0.8	12.31	0.9, 0.1, 0.8	10.50		0.9, 0.3, 0.8	8.25

TABLE 33.12 (*Continued*)
Grid Search for Damped Holt Exponential Smoothing

Phi(φ)							0.5	
α, β, φ					BETA (β)			
A	(α)	0.05 RMSE		0.1 RMSE			0.3 RMSE	
L	0.1	0.1, 0.05, 0.5	41.27	0.1, 0.1, 0.5	27.71		0.1, 0.3, 0.5	19.73
P	0.2	0.2, 0.05, 0.5	28.11	0.2, 0.1, 0.5	18.78		0.2, 0.3, 0.5	13.70
H	0.4	0.4, 0.05, 0.5	17.05	0.4, 0.1, 0.5	11.56		0.4, 0.3, 0.5	8.81
A	0.6	0.6, 0.05, 0.5	12.73	0.6, 0.1, 0.5	9.13		0.6, 0.3, 0.5	7.43
(α)	0.9	0.9, 0.05, 0.5	10.22	0.9, 0.1, 0.5	8.23		0.9, 0.3, 0.5	7.50
Phi(φ)							0.2	
α, β, φ					BETA (β)			
A	(α)	0.05 RMSE		0.1 RMSE			0.3 RMSE	
L	0.1	0.1, 0.05, 0.2	41.27	0.1, 0.1, 0.2	27.71		0.1, 0.3, 0.2	19.73
P	0.2	0.2, 0.05, 0.2	28.11	0.2, 0.1, 0.2	18.78		0.2, 0.3, 0.2	13.70
H	0.4	0.4, 0.05, 0.2	17.05	0.4, 0.1, 0.2	11.56		0.4, 0.3, 0.2	8.81
A	0.6	0.6, 0.05, 0.2	12.73	0.6, 0.1, 0.2	9.13		0.6, 0.3, 0.2	7.43
(α)	0.9	0.9, 0.05, 0.2	10.22	0.9, 0.1, 0.2	8.23		0.9, 0.3, 0.2	7.50
Phi(φ)							0.05	
α, β, φ					BETA (β)			
A	(α)	0.05 RMSE		0.1 RMSE			0.3 RMSE	
L	0.1	0.1, 0.05, 0.05	41.27	0.1, 0.1, 0.05	27.71		0.1, 0.3, 0.05	19.73
P	0.2	0.2, 0.05, 0.05	28.11	0.2, 0.1, 0.05	18.78		0.2, 0.3, 0.05	13.70
H	0.4	0.4, 0.05, 0.05	17.05	0.4, 0.1, 0.05	11.56		0.4, 0.3, 0.05	8.81
A	0.6	0.6, 0.05, 0.05	12.73	0.6, 0.1, 0.05	9.13		0.6, 0.3, 0.05	7.43
(α)	0.9	0.9, 0.05, 0.05	10.22	0.9, 0.1, 0.05	8.23		0.9, 0.3, 0.05	7.50

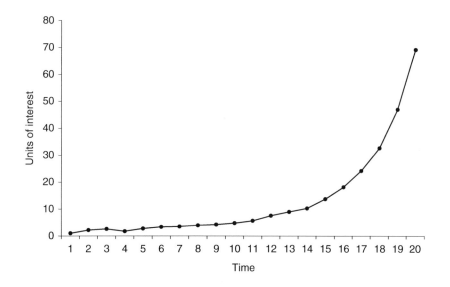

FIGURE 33.26 Exponentiating increase (artificial data).

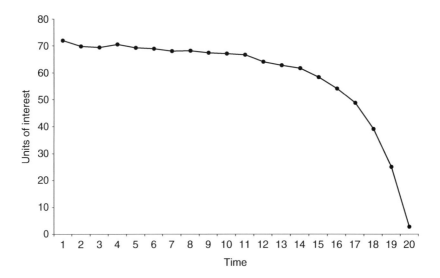

FIGURE 33.27 Exponentiating decrease (artificial data).

approach can also be thought of as forecasting the percentage growth. A percentage (P) is simply a special way of representing a ratio

$$P = (R - 1)100 \tag{33.34}$$

Ratios may be easier to use because the reconstruction of the forecast series is less complex.

Another approach to use with caution is second differences (or second ordered differences), which can be used with accelerating or decelerating trends. First calculate the first differences using Equation 33.16. With accelerating or decelerating data, these differences still exhibit a trend. To eliminate this trend, calculate a second series of differences from the first series; calculate D_3'' (where D_t'' means a second difference ending in time period t) from D_2 and D_3 as follows:

$$D_3'' = D_3 - D_2, \text{ etc.} \tag{33.35}$$

Now the data should not have a trend. With decelerating trends the second differences have the opposite sign of the first differences. Do not continue differencing the data. Forecast the second differences using SES or a moving average, then reverse the differencing process to reconstruct the entire data series. Average the first two observations as the initial value to reduce the impact of randomness on the forecast series.

If data resembles the curve in Figure 33.27, consider these alternatives:

1. Within a few time periods the process generating this data will cease.
2. The rate of accelerating decline is very small, so a linear approximation may provide an adequate forecast (use Holt exponential smoothing, SES of first differences, or a moving average of first differences).
3. The dataset is approaching zero and will not reach zero, so a damped trend is appropriate.
4. The dataset has no natural lower limit, so second differences might be appropriate.

33.3.3 SEASONALITY

A cyclical pattern of special interest is seasonal variation. A data pattern that repeats on a calendar cycle is termed "seasonal." Seasonal patterns repeat over a fixed period of time, usually a year

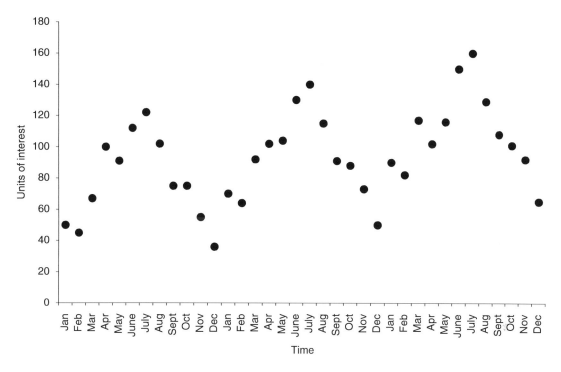

FIGURE 33.28 Seasonal data. (Data from Table 33.13.)

(Makridakis et al., 2003). In Figure 33.28 we observe peaks in July and troughs in December. Seasonality may be easier to observe if the X axis of the plot is limited to the length of the suspected season and sequential cycles are plotted separately as shown in Figure 33.29. Figure 33.29 is called a seasonality plot. Dataset that tends toward the same ups and downs over each segment is seasonal. If the overlapping series have conflicting peaks and troughs, the dataset is not seasonal.

Although seasonality is commonly thought to be an annual phenomenon, it is also possible to have seasonality within other time segments. Figure 33.30 demonstrates seasonality within weeks.

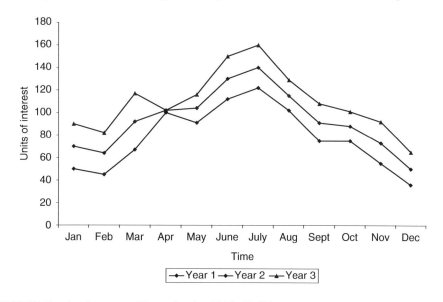

FIGURE 33.29 Overlapping years. (Data related to Table 33.13.)

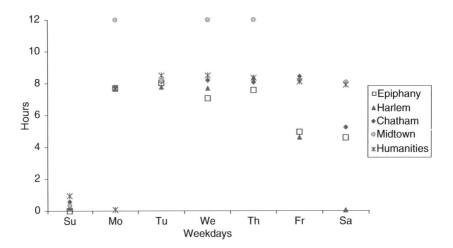

FIGURE 33.30 Seasonality within weeks. Hours of library service at five Manhattan libraries (with jiggle to reveal dots). (Data from various New York City Library Web Sites. Accessed August 24, 2005.)

This dataset reflects hours of operation at branches of the New York Public Library. Traffic may reflect a within week pattern, as well as a within day pattern. Figure 33.31 demonstrates seasonality within quarters.

There are two basic ways to approach seasonality. One is to build seasonality into the forecast model. The other is to take seasonality out of the seasonal data. Both of these approaches have their risks. There are three risks associated with building seasonality into the statistical model, one of which is specific to forecasting, the other two apply to any models:

1. The standard ways of knowing that a statistical model is well fit will be deceived when there is a seasonal model included in the statistical model. The seasonal model may be well fit and everything else in the model may be poorly fit, but novice, journeyman, or sometimes even skilled statistician might get the wrong message. Use of values such as R^2 is essentially meaningless in a seasonal model.

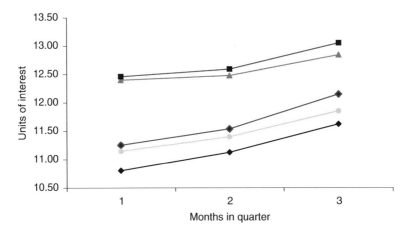

FIGURE 33.31 Within quarter seasonality. (Data from Federal Reserve of St. Louis ARBFLN [selected quarters for illustration] http//:research.stlouisfed.org/fred2/newcategoryzipfileformat. Accessed July 24, 2005.)

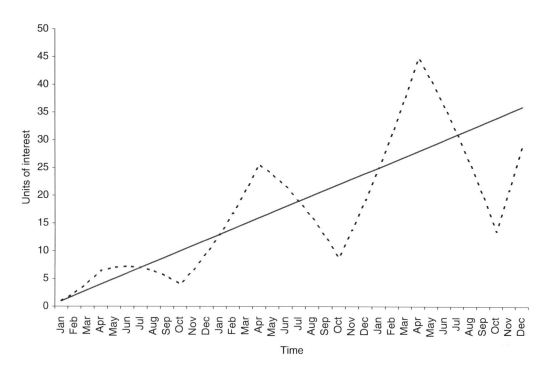

FIGURE 33.32 Multiplicative seasonality (artificial data).

2. Statistical models of seasonality can inappropriately attribute other sources of variation to the seasonal model component.
3. Even if well fit over some length of the data series, forecasters should be particularly concerned that seasonal models may not be well fit for the segment of the series immediately before the period leading into the unknown future.

The other method of treating seasonality is to de-seasonalize the data before forecasting or analyzing them. That is the method recommended here. Seasonal adjustment exhibits some of the same risks as seasonal modeling, particularly risk number 2 above. However, recent work by Miller and Williams (2003, 2004) specifically addresses this risk. Seasonal adjustment does not exhibit risk number 1 and sophisticated methods are designed to overcome risk number 3.

The seasonal adjustment techniques discussed here rest on the assumption that dataset is systematically collected over at least two seasonal cycles, preferably three or more. This chapter only introduces the simplest techniques. Some directions are given for exploring more sophisticated techniques.

Sometimes seasonality depends on the level (current mean) of the series at the time of the season. At other times seasonality is unrelated to the level. Judge this by asking whether the seasonal difference is additive (more like "50 units more in December") or multiplicative (more like "15 percent more in December"). Figure 33.32 shows multiplicative seasonality around linear growth of ten units a month. With larger values of the level, the seasonal peaks and troughs get farther away from the line. Figure 33.33 shows additive seasonality around the same ten units per month growth; in this figure the size of the peaks and troughs is unrelated to level.

33.3.3.1 Calculating a Simple Seasonal Index Using Classical Decomposition

De-seasonalizing is the use of a procedure to remove seasonality from a series. The following shows the calculation of a simple annual seasonal index for monthly data for both multiplicative and

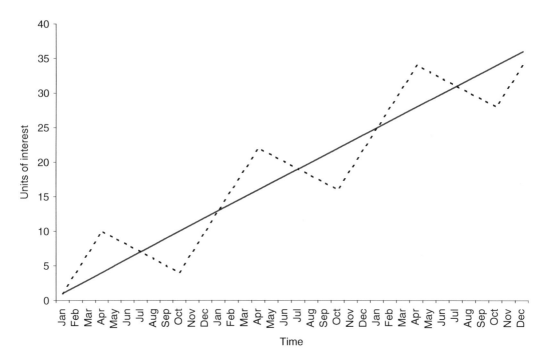

FIGURE 33.33 Additive seasonality (artificial data).

additive techniques. This technique requires a minimum of two seasonal cycles, but works better with three or more seasonal cycles.

1. First, calculate a double moving average as follows:
   a. Calculate a 12 period moving average using Equation 33.8 where $L = 12$.
   b. Still using Equation 33.8, calculate a two period moving average ($L = 2$) of the 12 period moving average. This new moving average is a 12×2 double moving average. For seasonal periods other than monthly, calculate an $L \times 2$ moving average where L is the number of periods for one seasonal cycle. For the rest of this explanation, the 12×2 moving average is labeled S_t.
   c. The center of a moving average is found by the expression

$$(L + 1)/2 \qquad\qquad (33.36)$$

This value should be added to the value of beginning period (0 and 5.5, respectively for our single and double moving averages for 12 monthly periods). The single and double moving averages are centered, respectively, at period 6.5 and period 7. To calculate a seasonal index, enter the result of the S_t in the same row as the actual observation for its centered period (July for years starting in January). There are 12 fewer moving average values than original (raw) values (the six observations at the beginning and the six at the end do not have enough observations for a 12×2 period moving average to be centered beside them).

These calculations produce an estimate of the trend-cycle in the data as shown by the solid line in Figure 33.34.

The seasonal dataset is shown with the scatter plot. The centered trend-cycle estimate extends from the seventh period through the n-6th period (the period that is seven periods before the end).

2. To calculate a multiplicative seasonal index, proceed as follows (you may want to follow along in Table 33.13):

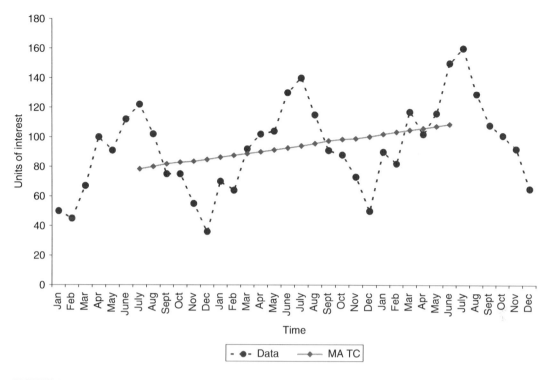

FIGURE 33.34 Trend cycle. (Data from Table 33.13.)

a. Calculate an approximate index (I') by dividing each actual value by the S_t value as described in step a

$$I_7' = X_7/S_7, \ I_8' = X_8/S_8, \ldots, \ I_{n-6}' = X_{n-6}/S_{n-6} \qquad (33.37)$$

b. Average the index estimates for each month to get a smoother index (I'')

$$I_{\mathrm{JUL}}'' = \left(I_7' + I_{19}' + I_{31}' + \ldots\right)/\text{Count of Julys}, \qquad (33.38)$$

$$I_{\mathrm{AUG}}'' = \left(I_8' + I_{20}' + I_{32}' + \ldots\right)/\text{Count of Augusts}, \ldots$$

c. Normalize the index. Sum the 12 seasonal factors. Use this sum as the denominator in a fraction where the numerator is 12. The resulting value is an adjusting value, P, that is multiplied by each value I_t'' to produce an index that sums to 12. When periods are not months, adjust the summing value to reflect the number of periods in the index

$$P = 12 \Big/ \sum_{i=1}^{12} I'' \qquad (33.39)$$

$$I_{\mathrm{JUL}} = I_{\mathrm{JUL}}'' \times P \qquad (33.40)$$

$$I_{\mathrm{AUG}} = I_{\mathrm{AUG}}'' \times P, \text{ etc.}$$

d. Divide the actual data by the index to obtain de-seasonalized data (DESEAS)

$$\mathrm{DESEAS}_t = X_t/I_t \qquad (33.41)$$

TABLE 33.13
Seasonality, Classical Decomposition with Normalization

Month	Data	MA 12	MA 12 × 2	Apx Ind I'	I''	Index I	M Deseas	Apx Fct I'	I''	Factor I	A Deseas
				Multiplicative Seasonal				**Additive Seasonal**			
Jan	50					0.848	59.0			−14.0	64.0
Feb	45				11.979	0.763	59.0		−2.2	−22.3	67.3
Mar	67				12	1.078	62.1		12	7.9	59.1
Apr	100			P = 1.001761		1.050	95.3	P = −0.18056		4.2	95.8
May	91					1.112	81.8			10.9	80.1
June	112					1.394	80.4			39.5	72.5
July	122	77.5	78.3	1.557	1.523	1.525	80.0	43.7	44.8	45.0	77.0
Aug	102	79.2	80.0	1.276	1.239	1.241	82.2	22.0	20.7	20.9	81.1
Sept	75	80.8	81.8	0.917	0.925	0.927	80.9	−6.8	−6.6	−6.4	81.4
Oct	75	82.8	82.9	0.905	0.899	0.901	83.3	−7.9	−9.2	−9.0	84.0
Nov	55	83.0	83.5	0.658	0.698	0.699	78.7	−28.5	−27.3	−27.1	82.1
Dec	36	84.1	84.8	0.424	0.461	0.462	77.9	−48.8	−49.6	−49.4	85.4
Jan	70	85.6	86.3	0.811	0.847	0.848	82.5	−16.3	−14.2	−14.0	84.0
Feb	64	87.1	87.6	0.730	0.762	0.763	83.9	−23.6	−22.5	−22.3	86.3
Mar	92	88.2	88.8	1.036	1.077	1.078	85.3	3.2	7.7	7.9	84.1

Month											
Apr	102	89.5	90.0	1.133	1.048	1.050	97.2	12.0	4.0	4.2	97.8
May	104	90.6	91.3	1.139	1.110	1.112	93.5	12.7	10.7	10.9	93.1
June	130	92.1	92.7	1.403	1.391	1.394	93.3	37.3	39.3	39.5	90.5
July	140	93.3	94.1	1.488		1.525	91.8	45.9		45.0	95.0
Aug	115	94.9	95.7	1.202		1.241	92.7	19.3		20.9	94.1
Sept	91	96.4	97.5	0.934		0.927	98.2	-6.5		-6.4	97.4
Oct	88	98.5	98.5	0.893		0.901	97.7	-10.5		-9.0	97.0
Nov	73	98.5	99.0	0.737		0.699	104.4	-26.0		-27.1	100.1
Dec	50	99.5	100.3	0.498		0.462	108.2	-50.3		-49.4	99.4
Jan	90	101.2	102.0	0.882		0.848	106.1	-12.0		-14.0	104.0
Feb	82	102.8	103.4	0.793		0.763	107.5	-21.4		-22.3	104.3
Mar	117	104.0	104.7	1.117		1.078	108.5	12.3		7.9	109.1
Apr	102	105.4	106.0	0.963		1.050	97.2	-4		4.2	97.8
May	116	106.5	107.3	1.081		1.112	104.3	8.7		10.9	105.1
June	150	108.1	108.7	1.380		1.394	107.6	41.3		39.5	110.5
July	160	109.3				1.525	104.9			45.0	115.0
Aug	129					1.241	103.9			20.9	108.1
Sept	108					0.927	116.25			-6.4	114.4
Oct	101					0.901	112.2			-9.0	110.0
Nov	92					0.699	131.6			-27.1	119.1
Dec	65					0.462	140.6			-49.4	114.4

3. For additive seasonality, follow these steps:
   a. Calculate an approximate factor (I') by subtracting each S_t from the actual observation

$$I'_7 = X_7 - S_7, \quad I'_8 = X_8 - S_8, \ldots, \quad I'_{n-6} = X_{n-6} - S_{n-6} \tag{33.42}$$

If S is greater than X, the approximate factor should be negative.

   b. Average the factor estimates for each month to get a smoother factor (I'')

$$I''_{\text{JUL}} = \left(I'_7 + I'_{19} + I'_{31} + \cdots\right)/\text{Count of Julys}, \tag{33.43}$$

$$I''_{\text{AUG}} = \left(I'_8 + I'_{20} + I'_{32} + \cdots\right)/\text{Count of Augusts}, \ldots$$

   c. Normalize the index. Sum the 12 seasonal factors. Divide this sum by 12. The resulting value is an adjusting value, P, that is subtracted from each value I''_t to produce an index that sums to 0. When periods are not months, adjust the denominator to the number of periods in the index

$$P = \sum_{i=1}^{12} I''/12 \tag{33.44}$$

$$I_{\text{JUL}} = I''_{\text{JUL}} - P \tag{33.45}$$

$$I_{\text{AUG}} = I''_{\text{AUG}} - P, \text{ etc.}$$

   d. Subtract the factor from the actual data to obtain de-seasonalized data (DESEAS)

$$\text{DESEAS}_t = X_t - I_t \tag{33.46}$$

The use of these equations is demonstrated in Table 33.13. In the column labeled Index and the column labeled Factor, the average of I' is calculated in the boxed area, the values shown above and below that area repeat the values from the same months in the calculation area.

Figures 33.35 and 33.36 show the results of multiplicative and additive de-seasonalization. The de-seasonalized series is marked with triangles.

Forecast the de-seasonalized data using a technique such as a moving average, SES, or Holt. To complete the forecast, re-seasonalize the data to know what to expect for various months. Re-seasonalize the multiplicative series by multiplying it by the seasonal factor, or re-seasonalize additive data by adding back the same additive factor.

This discussion has focused on annual seasonality of monthly data with the year beginning in January, but the actual data may begin in any month, be quarterly data, or have seasonality over some period other than a year. If appropriate adjustments are made, this method can be used with data cumulated over any interval and with any seasonal cycle.

33.3.3.2 More Sophisticated Decomposition Methods

The analyst who has fully learned this method will realize that it still has the third limitation mentioned above (the second limitation will be discussed below). That is, the estimated seasonal factors will be static, but actual seasonal factors may change over time. Methods to overcome this limitation are beyond the scope of this chapter. After reaching a level of comfort with this chapter, the student should refer to the software and documentation available at the U.S. Census Bureau at http://www.census.gov/srd/www/x12a/. This website will provide the basic equipment

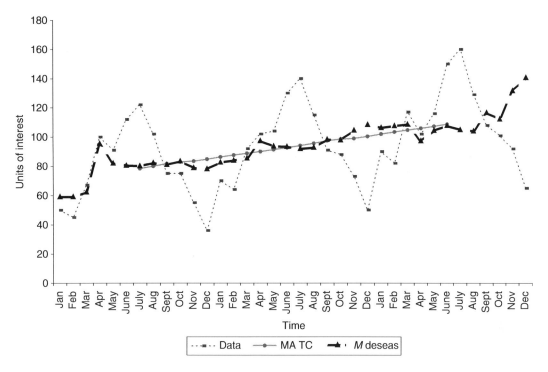

FIGURE 33.35 Multiplicative de-seasonalization. (Data from Table 33.13.)

for using a procedure known as X12, which is a much more sophisticated form of the procedure discussed above, and is likely the most common form of seasonal adjustment in the world. Use of X12 is documented on the website and is also discussed in Makridakis et al. (2003). X12 is a

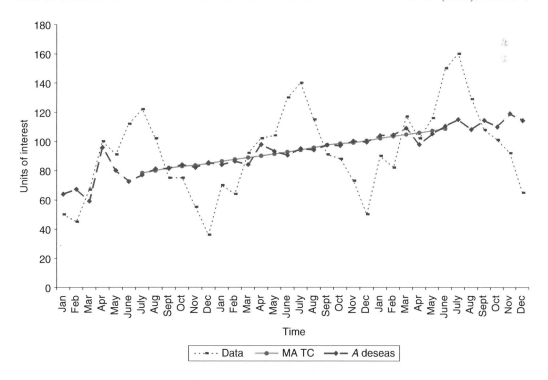

FIGURE 33.36 Additive de-seasonalization. (Data from Table 33.13.)

recently updated version of software long known as X11, and much of the material still refers to the earlier version.

33.3.3.3 Confounding Seasonality

Miller and Williams (2003, 2004) have shown that some typical seasonal methods confound other sources of variation with seasonal factors. Although this demonstration is not made separately for each distinctive method for addressing seasonality, there is no special reason to think any particular method is immune to the confounding effect. The chief focus of these articles is with the confounding of seasonality with random variation. However, other unexplained variations could also be subject to the same confounding effect. Miller and Williams demonstrate techniques for correcting this confounding effect. As with X12, these techniques are more sophisticated than the scope of this chapter. However, once the analyst has become sufficiently comfortable with the techniques demonstrated here, examination of these articles is strongly recommended. Software (spreadsheets) that implement these procedures can be found at http://hops.wharton.upenn.edu/forecast/software.html#Freeware.

33.3.3.4 Aggregating Data

An alternative for working with seasonal dataset is to aggregate them across the season and forecast the aggregated data. For example, if the season is monthly within quarters, cumulate the data to quarters (four observations a year, each accumulated across three months). There are two important restrictions on cumulating data across seasons. First, the forecast must not need to be updated more frequently than allowed by the level of aggregation chosen. For example, a forecast cannot be updated each month if the dataset is aggregated to quarters. Second, the analyst must not need to know about units of data smaller than the aggregated level. If dataset has been aggregated to quarters, the analyst cannot speak about monthly data.

Sometimes analysts aggregate data to the annual level for reporting purposes. This can lead to the temptation to aggregate data to the annual level for forecasting purposes, thereby eliminating seasonal variation. This temptation may be a bad idea. First, there is a serious loss of information at the annual level. What happened over the year may not be what was happening at the end of the year, or during the last half of the year. Bunching up the data into one large chunk loses this information. In addition, annual forecasts cannot be checked against reality until the year is over. This may be too late to take remedial action or plan for shortfalls. This chapter has focused on monthly level data. Where circumstances do not clearly call for other levels of data, this level is likely to be the most meaningful.

33.3.3.5 Differencing

Another alternative to seasonal adjustment prior to forecasting is to calculate the first differences of the seasonal period. Subtract observations that occur at the same point in two sequential seasons. For example, if the data follows annual seasonality, as with the previous discussion, calculate differences across years by taking the observation in January of year 1 and subtracting it from the observation in January of year 2. For year 3, subtract year 2 data from year 3 data, continuing until the dataset runs out. This is an application of Equation 33.12 for annual seasonality. The resulting dataset is no longer seasonal. Observations have been differenced (subtracted one from another) at the same point in the season; between them there was no seasonality. All the new observations are without seasonality. This differenced dataset will also reflect the same impact on trend as occurred when the first differences of the first period (that is, the sequential differences) were calculated. The differenced data can be forecast with SES or a moving average. Then the differencing must be reversed to produce the full forecast. Differencing is the underlying method employed when dealing with seasonal data in the sophisticated forecasting technique known as ARIMA.

33.3.3.6 Winters' Three Parameter Method

A technique developed by Winters (1960) permits seasonality to update within the exponential smoothing model. The problem with this method is that it is unstable, that is, it can produce quite erroneous seasonal factors if a pattern break occurs. Nevertheless, its use is popular among practitioners, hence it is included here. Following is Holt–Winters exponential smoothing as modified by Williams (1987) to allow for independent parameter optimization:

$$F_{t+m} = \text{forecast at time } t \text{ of time } t + m = (S_t + B_t m)I_{t+m-L} \tag{33.47}$$

$$F_t = \text{forecast at time t} = (S_{t-1} + B_{t-1})I_{t-L} \tag{33.48}$$

$$S_t = \text{level at time } t = S_{t-1} + B_{t-1} + \beta e_t / I_{t-L} \tag{33.49}$$

$$B_t = \text{trend at time } t = B_{t-1} + \beta e_t / I_{t-L} \tag{33.50}$$

$$I_t = \text{seasonal index at time } t = \gamma e_t / (S_{t-1} + B_{t-1}) + I_{t-L} \tag{33.51}$$

$$e_t = \text{error at time } t = X_t - F_t \tag{33.52}$$

where
  $X_t, \alpha, \beta, t,$ and m are as with Holt exponential smoothing
  $\gamma =$ gamma, a seasonal smoothing parameter subject to $0 \leq \gamma \leq 1$
  $L =$ the length of the season (number of periods until the season repeats)

As I_t updates the previous I_{t-L}, there are as many updating I factors as there are periods in the seasonal cycle, L. Also, unless otherwise initialized, I must be set at an initial value of 1; the value 0 is invalid. Some forecasters suggest that the I values should be normalized to sum to L, and renormalized with each update. At minimum the forecaster should take care that the factors do not vary radically from this norm.

Table 33.14 demonstrates the calculation of this equation using the seasonal data in Table 33.13. Initial seasonal factors are taken from the multiplicative seasonal index in Table 33.13.

Figure 33.37 shows the results of these calculations.

33.3.3.6.1 Initialization

Trend and level components can be initialized using Equations 33.23 through 33.27. Because each seasonal factor is updated only once each seasonal cycle, the self-initialization of the Winters model is slow, so initialization is strongly recommended. A convenient way to calculate initial seasonal factors is to use the multiplicative seasonal factors from Equations 33.42 through 33.46 as calculated in Table 33.13. Equations 33.42 through 33.46 are more effective when there are at least two seasonal factors for each period (two Januaries, Februaries, Marches, etc.) to average. Because of the $L \times 2$ period moving average, they are available only if there are three seasonal cycles of data (for annual data, three years). If only two cycles of data are available, calculate the S_t values without a moving average (thereby retaining the ability to average two seasonal factors) through these steps. First, calculate the trend and level using Equations 33.23 through 33.27. Then, add B (the trend) back once for each period as shown in Equation 33.53. These values are then used in Equation 33.42

$$S_1 = S_0 + B, \quad S_2 = S_1 + B, \quad S_3 = S_2 + B, \ldots, \quad S_{24} = S_{23} + B \tag{33.53}$$

33.3.3.6.2 Selecting Parameter Values

Parameters can be selected through a grid search using a three-dimensional grid, which can be represented on paper using a series of tables such as Table 33.10, one for each of several γ values.

TABLE 33.14
Multiplicative Holt–Winters

Month	Data	F_1	e	α 0.6 S	β 0.1 B	γ 0.1 I	RMSE = 3.40
Jan	50	65.7	−15.7	54.60	−0.185	0.85	
Feb	45	41.52	3.48	57.15	−0.140	0.76	
Mar	67	61.48	5.52	60.08	−0.089	1.08	
Apr	100	62.97	37.03	81.16	0.264	1.05	
May	91	90.54	0.46	81.68	0.268	1.11	
June	112	114.22	−2.22	80.99	0.252	1.39	4.9
July	122	123.93	−1.93	80.48	0.240	1.53	3.7
Aug	102	100.18	1.82	81.60	0.254	1.24	3.3
Sept	75	75.88	−0.88	81.29	0.245	0.93	0.8
Oct	75	73.42	1.58	82.58	0.262	0.90	2.5
Nov	55	57.92	−2.92	80.34	0.221	0.70	8.5
Dec	36	37.23	−1.23	78.96	0.194	0.46	1.5
Jan	70	67.13	2.87	81.19	0.228	0.85	8.2
Feb	64	62.62	1.38	82.49	0.246	0.769	1.9
Mar	92	89.99	2.01	83.85	0.264	1.088	4.0
Apr	102	92.11	9.89	89.53	0.355	1.095	97.8
May	104	100.00	4.00	92.05	0.391	1.112	16.0
June	130	128.59	1.41	93.05	0.401	1.391	2.0
July	140	142.32	−2.32	92.53	0.386	1.523	5.4
Aug	115	115.52	−0.52	92.67	0.381	1.243	0.3
Sept	91	86.15	4.85	96.19	0.434	0.926	23.5
Oct	88	87.20	0.80	97.16	0.443	0.902	0.6
Nov	73	67.88	5.12	102.02	0.516	0.695	26.2
Dec	50	47.23	2.77	106.15	0.576	0.461	7.7
Jan		90.88		106.72	0.576	0.852	
Feb		82.70		107.30	0.576	0.771	
Mar		117.58		107.88	0.576	1.090	
Apr		119.95		108.45	0.576	1.106	
May		121.76		109.03	0.576	1.117	
June		152.63		109.60	0.576	1.393	

33.3.3.6.3   Four Models in One

The Winters model shown here is a slightly modified version of Holt–Winters exponential smoothing. One of the features of Holt–Winters (or this variant) is that it is four models in one. By setting γ to 0 and initializing all the seasonal factors to 1, the model becomes Holt exponential smoothing. It allows the trend component of the model, but excludes the seasonality variation. By setting β to 0 and initializing B to 0, the model becomes Winters exponential smoothing. It allows seasonal variation, but excludes trend. By setting both factors to these neutral values, the model becomes SES.

33.3.3.7   Winters with Additive Seasonality

When the seasonal pattern is additive, use a Winters' additive exponential smoothing model (Pfeffermann and Allon, 1989). The model shown below approximates Williams' variation of the Winters model with additive seasonality

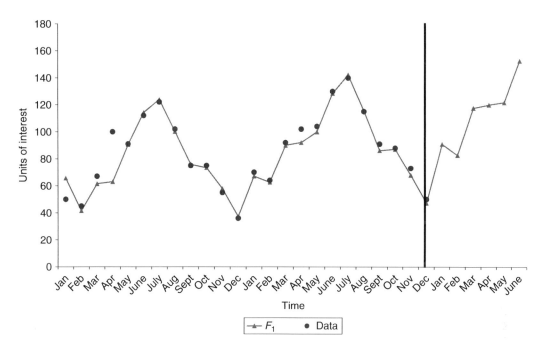

FIGURE 33.37 Multiplicative Holt–Winters exponential smoothing. (From Table 33.14.)

$$F_{t+m} = \text{forecast at time } t \text{ of time } t + m = S_t + B_t m + I_{t+m-L} \qquad (33.54)$$

$$F_t = \text{forecast at time } t = S_{t-1} + B_{t-1} + I_{t-L} \qquad (33.55)$$

$$S_t = \text{level at time } t = S_{t-1} + B_{t-1} + \alpha e_t \qquad (33.56)$$

$$B_t = \text{trend at time } t = B_{t-1} + \beta e_t \qquad (33.57)$$

$$I_t = \text{additive seasonal index at time } t = \gamma e_t + I_{t-L} \qquad (33.58)$$

$$e_t = \text{error at time } t = X_t - F_t \qquad (33.59)$$

where X_t, α, β, γ, t, L, and m are as used with the Holt–Winters multiplicative model.

An example is shown in Table 33.15 using the same data as used with the Table 33.14. The additive factors from Table 33.13 are used as initial additive factors. The RMSE for the additive model is about six percent lower than for the multiplicative data. The forecast is shown in Figure 33.38.

33.3.3.7.1 Initialization

This model should be initialized with 12 prior seasonal factors. Multiplicative initial factors can be calculated using Equations 33.37 through 33.41, or additive factors can be calculated using Equations 33.42 through 33.46. Use Equation 33.53 to calculate S_t values for Equation 33.37 only if necessary. Some discussion indicates that these seasonal factors should be renormalized to sum to zero with each update; at minimum, the forecaster should take care that these factors do not vary radically from this norm. Trend and level can be initialized using Equations 33.23 through 33.27.

33.3.3.7.2 Parameters and Multiple Models

Parameters are selected as with the Holt–Winters multiplicative model, and, as with that model, setting any component to a neutral value eliminates the effect of that component from the model, leaving the other components intact. The neutral value for additive seasonal factors is zero.

TABLE 33.15
Additive Holt–Winters

Month	Data	F_1	e	α 0.5 S	β 0.01 B	γ 0.1 I	RMSE = 3.27
Jan	50	63.51	−13.51	56.76	−0.14	−13.99	
Feb	45	34.28	10.72	61.98	−0.03	−22.34	
Mar	67	69.86	−2.86	60.52	−0.06	7.91	
Apr	100	64.65	35.35	78.14	0.30	4.18	
May	91	89.31	1.69	79.29	0.31	10.87	2.87
June	112	119.09	−7.09	76.05	0.24	39.49	50.3
July	122	121.27	0.73	76.66	0.25	44.97	0.54
Aug	102	97.78	4.22	79.02	0.29	20.87	17.81
Sept	75	72.87	2.13	80.38	0.31	−6.44	4.54
Oct	75	71.67	3.33	82.36	0.35	−9.03	11.12
Nov	55	55.62	−0.62	82.40	0.34	−27.09	0.38
Dec	36	33.34	2.66	84.07	0.37	−49.40	7.09
Jan	70	70.45	−0.45	84.21	0.36	−13.99	0.21
Feb	64	63.31	0.69	84.92	0.37	−21.268	0.48
Mar	92	92.92	−0.92	84.83	0.36	7.623	0.84
Apr	102	92.91	9.09	89.74	0.45	7.716	82.61
May	104	101.23	2.77	91.58	0.48	11.037	7.68
June	130	130.84	−0.84	91.64	0.47	38.784	0.71
July	140	137.15	2.85	93.53	0.50	45.045	8.11
Aug	115	115.32	−0.32	93.87	0.50	21.290	0.10
Sept	91	88.14	2.86	95.80	0.52	−6.231	8.21
Oct	88	87.63	0.37	96.51	0.53	−8.694	0.14
Nov	73	69.89	3.11	98.59	0.56	−27.152	9.70
Dec	50	50.02	−0.02	99.15	0.56	−49.136	0.00
Jan		85.67		99.71	0.56	−14.031	
Feb		79.07		100.26	0.56	−21.199	
Mar		108.36		100.82	0.56	7.532	
Apr		110.01		101.38	0.56	8.625	
May		113.26		101.94	0.56	11.314	
June		141.20		102.50	0.56	38.700	

33.4 OPTIMIZING AND LOSS FUNCTIONS

Optimizing should not be limited to simple minimization of RMSE, or any loss function. Use of RMSE or other techniques has limitations which the forecaster should consider and account for before selecting a forecast model.

33.4.1 LIMITATIONS OF ROOT MEAN SQUARED ERROR

Early in this chapter we began to evaluate the relative accuracy of various forecasting techniques through the interpretation of root mean squared error (RMSE); calculation is shown in Equation 33.7. RMSE is one of several commonly used loss functions whose role is to provide comparative information on forecast accuracy. For a single series RMSE is easily interpreted, a smaller RMSE implies the forecasting model more accurately fits the data, a larger RMSE implies the opposite. However, there are several limitations on using RMSE:

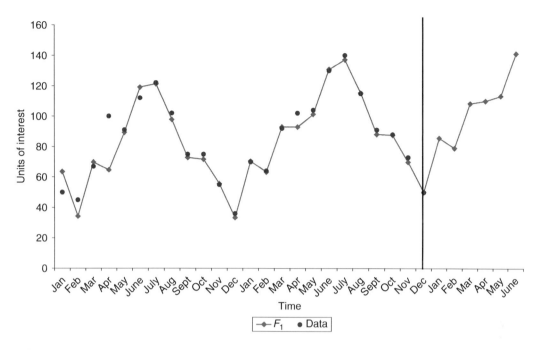

FIGURE 33.38 Additive Holt–Winters exponential smoothing. (From Table 33.15.)

1. Because the magnitude of RMSE depends on the magnitude of the data series, it is not useful for comparing forecast techniques among noncomparable series. Ordinarily this is a problem for forecast researchers, not for forecasters. Nonetheless, a solution is to use a loss function that is independent of data series magnitude. One such loss function is the symmetrical mean absolute percent error, SMAPE (Flores, 1986), which is the average of the symmetrical absolute percent error (SAPE). These are calculated as follows (where F, X, e, t, and n have their usual meanings in this chapter):

$$\text{SAPE}_t = |2e_t/(F_t + X_t)| \tag{33.60}$$

$$\text{SMAPE} = \sum_{t=1}^{n} \text{SAPE}_t/n \tag{33.61}$$

2. Forecasts are vulnerable to two kinds of error: inaccuracy, which is simply getting the wrong future value, and bias, which is systematically getting the wrong future value. RMSE and SMAPE report inaccuracy. An excessive concern for reducing one of these loss functions can increase bias. There are two sorts of systematic wrong future values; first one might tend always to get the wrong value in a particular direction, such as always overestimating the value. A second error is tending always to get the opposite error of the previous error. The presence of either sort of systematic error suggests the forecaster might be able to develop a better forecasting method. The tendency to always get the value wrong in a particular direction is of particular concern. If forecasts are accumulated over multiple periods, such as forecasting monthly data and summing it to annual estimates, these systematic errors augment each other, so the forecast becomes more inaccurate as more periods are added together. Unbiased forecasts should not exhibit this augmenting error.

Two statistics that help evaluate bias are mean error (ME) and the autocorrelation of errors, $\rho(e_t, e_{t-1})$. In an unbiased forecast, both of these statistics will be near zero. Mean error (Flores, 1986) helps evaluate the tendency to get the value wrong in a particular direction

$$\text{ME} - \sum_{t=1}^{n} e_t/n \tag{33.62}$$

Autocorrelation of error (Chatfield, 1978) evaluates any systematic error; $\rho(e_t, e_{t-1})$ can take on values ranging from -1 to 1. Values close to 0 imply no systematic error. Negative values imply alternating errors, which might arise if the trend component of the forecast is over-responsive (β is too high in a Holt model), or if the dataset was inadequately decomposed before forecasting. Positive values imply successive errors with the same sign (the tendency to get the value wrong in a particular direction). This statistic is simply the Pearson's product moment correlation coefficient applied to successive errors, calculate $\rho(e_t, e_{t-1})$ as follows:

$$\bar{e} = \sum_{t=1}^{n} e_t/n \tag{33.63}$$

$$\sigma_{e(t)} = \sqrt{\sum_{t=2}^{n} (e_t - \bar{e})^2/(n-1)}, \quad \sigma_{e(t-1)} = \sqrt{\sum_{t=1}^{n-1} (e_t - \bar{e})^2/(n-1)} \tag{33.64}$$

$$\text{COV}(e_t, e_{t-1}) = \sum_{t=2}^{n} [(e_t - \bar{e})(e_{t-1} - \bar{e})]/(n-1) \tag{33.65}$$

$$\rho(e_t, e_{t-1}) = \text{COV}(e_t, e_{t-1})/\left(\sigma_{e(t)} \times \sigma_{e_{(t-1)}}\right) \tag{33.66}$$

The point of considering more than one loss function is that each loss function may be optimal with a different combination of parameter values. There is no algorithm for resolving this conflict. When different loss functions suggest different optimal parameters, the analyst must choose a set of parameters based on the reasons for considering the various loss functions.

3. RMSE is vulnerable to outliers because it puts more weight on the deviations that are furthest from the forecast estimate (by squaring the deviations). One way to reduce the risk of vulnerability to outliers is to Windsorize the data as discussed early in this chapter. Another way is to use median related loss functions; however, the forecaster may have considerable loss of information when looking at the median error of a time series. A third option is to consider several loss functions, including at least one bias-related loss function.

4. When a loss function is calculated over the whole range of the data, it puts as much weight on accurately estimating the oldest data as it does on accurately estimating the most recent data. However, the forecaster might be more interested in errors near the end of the data series. Also, certain errors may be particularly difficult to evaluate. For example, when an uninitialized exponential smoothing model is used, the early errors tend to overwhelm the later errors, whereas when early observations are used to initialize an exponential smoothing model, the errors associated with these observations may be artificially reduced. Several approaches are available for addressing these issues. First, questionable errors (such as the first few errors in an uninitialized model) should be discarded from calculation of the loss function unless there simply are not enough observations to discard them. Second, the forecaster can concentrate special attention on the most recent errors. Summarize the loss function twice, once for all observations, and a second time for the last two years (assuming monthly data) observations. Excepting with $\rho(e_t, e_{t-1})$, the math for calculating a separate summary for the most recent dataset is quite easy. A third approach is to calculate weighted statistics. Again, the math is not difficult except with $\rho(e_t, e_{t-1})$: the error term (e^2 for RMSE, SAPE for SMAPE, or e for ME) of the most recent observation is assigned a weight of 1, and

each prior error term is assigned some smoothly declining smaller weight. The more rapidly the weights decline, the more the focus of the loss function is shifted to recent observations. To calculate the weighted statistic, multiply the error term by the weight before summing, then divide by the sum of the weights rather than by n to calculate the mean error term. This is illustrated with mean deviation (where ω_t is the weight for the observation at time t)

$$\text{ME} = \sum_{t=1}^{n} (\omega_t \times e_t) \Big/ \sum_{t=1}^{n} \omega_t \qquad (33.67)$$

5. An examination of the use of RMSE shows that it is calculated for the one-period-ahead forecast. The forecast techniques adjust with each new observation; although this improves the forecast, it limits the number of observations that are available for evaluating any particular projection. In fact, only the projection to the next period is available for evaluation, projections into later periods reflect additional updates by the time the actual dataset is available for comparison. So, the loss function evaluates only how well the forecast projects ahead a single period. Projection into subsequent periods is taken on faith. Two options are available to forecasters:

   a. Hold out data from the forecast model for evaluation (Armstrong, 1985). Instead of optimizing the parameters with all data entered into the calculation, hold out the last year's data (or however much dataset is associated with the furthest horizon to be projected) when estimating parameters. Project through the hold out period. Then compare the results with the actual data held out. If the forecast model makes a satisfactory projection of the hold out period, add these data to the calculations without updating the parameters. Then make a new forecast of the future period. Obviously, this approach would be difficult to implement with every forecast update; however, this approach may be appropriate when preparing particularly critical forecasts. It may also be worthwhile to systematically evaluate all forecasts using this approach on an annual schedule.

   b. A second option is to de-emphasize the use of loss functions. In Figure 33.39 we see the SES of the first differences forecast compared with the Holt forecast as previously shown in Table 33.9. The Holt forecast is previously demonstrated in Figure 33.21. The comparative RMSE values for Holt exponential smoothing and SES of the first differences are 5.3 and 5.1, respectively. By implication, the SES model produces the better forecast. However, the SES estimate of the trend ranges from -10.6 to 12.3, whereas the Holt estimate ranges from 2.0 to 3.9 (except following a few upshifts in the data, the Holt model gradually decreases the estimate of trend). The SES model of the differences rapidly responds to variation in the data, but this response leads to one-period-ahead forecast success, hence the slightly lower RMSE.

If the forecaster is interested in projecting only through the next period, he or she should select the SES model based on the RMSE results. However, if the forecaster is interested in a multiple period horizon, he or she can balance the information provided by the loss function with other information. In particular, he or she might notice that the trend estimated through the SES forecast of differences frequently changes by relatively large amounts and ask how he or she can to rely on a forecast that will likely be considerably different with just a few more updates. By balancing such common sense considerations against the one-period-ahead loss function, the forecaster can improve his chances of making a reasonable forecast.

33.4.2 RULES OF THUMB

Although the optimization approach assumes that exponential smoothing parameters should be fit to the historical data, some forecasters argue otherwise. For example, Armstrong argues that there is no

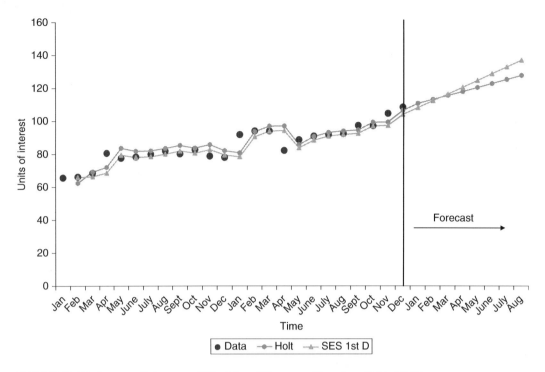

FIGURE 33.39 Compare Holt versus SES of first differences. (Data from Table 33.9.)

evidence that fitting the historical data produces better forecasts. He recommends the forecaster use judgment in selecting parameters. It is likely that the best approach is a balance between optimizing with historical data and use of rules of thumb such as these: (1) Armstrong (1985) recommends high α values when the process that generates the dataset is unstable and low α values when there is a high risk of measurement errors. (2) It is my experience that β values should be extremely low, particularly when using the variant of Holt exponential smoothing shown in this chapter. High β values (even small β values, such as 0.2, are relatively high) lead to unstable forecasts. (3) As discussed above, low values of φ (below 0.9) effectively convert Holt models to SES models in a very short period of time, so they should be used with care.

33.5   COMBINING FORECASTS

There is evidence that forecasts can be improved through the simple averaging of equally reasonable forecasts made with different techniques (Clemen, 1989; Makridakis and Winkler, 1983). Averaging of forecasts is not difficult. It consists of making a forecast through each of several reasonable methods, and then averaging the results. An example of two forecasts made with reasonable methods might be the two forecasts in Table 33.9. The last two columns of Table 33.9 show these two forecasts combined (averaged) and show that the RMSE for the combined forecast, 4.92, is lower than the RMSE for either of the individual forecasts. Figure 33.40 demonstrates the combined forecast.

33.6   PLANNED DISCONTINUITIES

Williams and Miller (1999) describe level adjusted exponential smoothing (LAES), a technique for the situation where the forecaster anticipates a policy intervention within the forecast horizon.

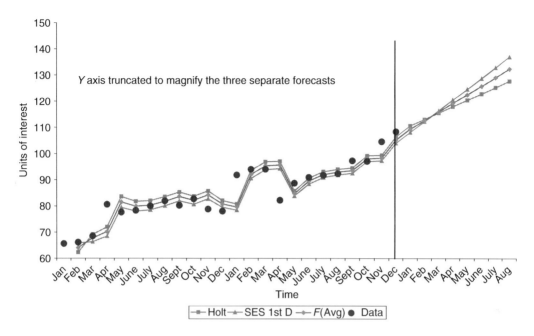

FIGURE 33.40 Combining forecasts. (Data from Table 33.9.)

This technique modifies Holt exponential smoothing to integrate the anticipated policy impacts. The equations for this technique are

$$F_{t+m} = \text{forecast at } t \text{ for } t+m = S_t + mB + (P_{t+m} - P_t) \tag{33.68}$$

$$F_{t+1} = \text{one-step-ahead forecast at } t \text{ for } t+1 = S_t + B_t + A_{t+1} \tag{33.69}$$

where, X_t, e_t, S_t, and B_t are as defined with Holt above and

$$A_t = \text{adjustment factor at time } t = P_t - P_{t-x} \tag{33.70}$$

$$P_t = \text{the cumulative effect of policy through } t \tag{33.71}$$

$$m = \text{any arbitrary number of periods after period } t \tag{33.72}$$

For these equations to be used, one must have a period-by-period estimate of the policy effect on the data series. Preferably this estimate would be a nonseasonal estimate; this is an adjustment to Holt, not to Holt–Winters. Planning documents for the policy are most likely a good place to find the information necessary to begin the period-by-period estimate of the policy effect. Plans may need to be decomposed or disaggregated as described for forecast data above. The analyst should also consider the nature of the change. The change may occur in a single period, which is typically called a step shift. However, often public policies phase in over several or many periods of time. This phase-in would be called a "ramp." Because the policy estimate may not be made with the forecaster's use as a priority, the forecaster may have to make crude estimates to convert the policy expectations into period-by-period forecast expectations.

These equations are demonstrated in Table 33.16 and Figure 33.41. The policy adjustment is a ramp of 30, 10, and 10 for a cumulative P of 50 units. The effect is seen in the right hand (forecast) side of the plot.

TABLE 33.16

Level Adjusted Exponential Smoothing

Data	F_1	P	A	α 0.6 F'	0.6 e	β S	0.05 B	RMSE 4.84
65.6	68.3			68.3	-2.7	66.7	1.4	
66.1	68.0			68.0	-1.9	66.9	1.26	
8.5	68.1			68.1	0.4	68.4	1.28	
80.6	69.6			69.6	11.0	76.2	1.82	
77.6	78.0			78.0	-0.4	77.8	1.80	0.2
78.3	79.6			79.6	-1.3	78.8	1.74	1.6
80	80.5			80.5	-0.5	80.2	1.71	0.3
81.9	81.9			81.9	0.0	81.9	1.71	0.0
80.2	83.6			83.6	-3.4	81.6	1.54	11.7
82.7	83.1			83.1	-0.4	82.9	1.52	0.2
78.8	84.4			84.4	-5.6	81.0	1.24	31.1
78	82.3			82.3	-4.3	79.7	1.03	18.2
91.8	80.7			80.7	11.1	87.4	1.58	122.5
94	89.0			89.0	5.0	92.0	1.83	22.5
94	93.8			93.8	0.2	93.9	1.84	0.0
82.2	95.8			95.8	-13.6	87.6	1.16	184.0
88.7	88.8			88.8	-0.1	88.7	1.16	0.0
90.9	89.9			89.9	1.0	90.5	1.21	1.0
91.7	91.7			91.7	0.0	91.7	1.21	0.0
92.3	92.9			92.9	-0.6	92.5	1.18	0.4
97.3	93.7			93.7	3.6	95.9	1.36	12.8
97.1	97.2			97.2	-0.1	97.1	1.35	0.0
104.6	98.5			98.5	6.1	102.2	1.66	37.2
108.4	103.8			103.8	4.6	106.6	1.88	21.0
	108.5			108.5		108.5	1.88	
	110.3			110.3		110.3	1.88	
	112.2	30	30	142.2		142.2	1.88	
	144.1	40	10	154.1		154.1	1.88	
	156.0	50	10	166.0		166.0	1.88	
	167.9			167.9		167.9	1.88	
	169.8			169.8		169.8	1.88	

Including these step and ramp adjustments changes the meaning of the forecast error once the occasion of the policy arises. In a forecast not adjusted for policies, a large error at the update may mean that the policy has arrived and the forecast will just be difficult to manage for a while. Or it may mean something else has gone wrong, but the forecaster is in the dark. In a forecast adjusted for the policies, a large forecast error signals that the policy is not occurring as expected. The absence of a large forecast error implies that the policy has gone into place roughly as expected, and the model remains manageable. Keeping in mind that rough estimates may be used in converting the policy estimate into the forecast estimates, it is likely that the forecast error will rise somewhat. A small rise should not be cause for concern.

33.7 REALLY SIMPLE TECHNIQUES

Sometimes, it occurs that a forecast is needed when there is no historical data or when the data is spotty and unreliable. There is one very simple forecast technique that can be made as soon as

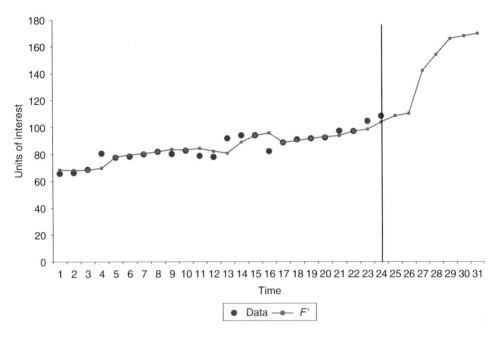

FIGURE 33.41 Level adjusted exponential smoothing. (Data from Table 33.16.)

there is one observation. This technique produces poor forecasts at the beginning, but will cumulatively improve.

33.7.1 SIMPLE METHOD

After the first monthly observation, the forecast for the first year becomes $X_1/0.0833$, after the next month, the forecast becomes $(X_1 + X_2)/0.1667$, after the third observation, the forecast is $(X_1 + X_2 + X_3)/0.25$, and so forth. If the first month is particularly weak, the second month might be substituted for the first month in making the forecast for the first year. By the end of the first year, there will be two kinds of information, seasonality and trend. If there is no evidence of seasonality, a simple Holt or SES model is likely the best forecast for the second year. Initialization may have to be arbitrary, but is critical with such a short series. If there is evidence of a seasonality, which may be hard to judge with just one year of data, the second year can be estimated using the same approach above, but replacing 0.0833 with

$$\left(X_{1,1} / \sum_{i=1}^{12} X_{i,1} \right) \tag{33.73}$$

where the 1 after the comma refers to year 1. For months two, three, etc., the numerator expands to $(X_{1,1} + X_{2,1})$, $(X_{1,1} + X_{2,1} + X_{3,1})$, etc. Although this does not distinguish randomness from seasonality, there is little that can be done about that in the second year. After two years, seasonal adjustment and use of methods described before this section would be preferred.

33.7.2 REALLY SIMPLE METHODS NOT RECOMMENDED

Two methods that are sometimes recommended by and to naïve forecasters are the annual change method and the annual percent change method. The annual change method determines the change from last year to this year and assumes that this will be the change from this year to next year. The annual percent change method takes essentially the same approach, but calculates the change as a multiplier rather than an additive change. These are very crude approaches which have the disadvantages of seeming easy to do and easy to understand, while having some common sense appeal. The full list of shortcomings will not be listed here. The annualization problem was discussed with seasonality above. In addition, they introduce two unnecessary sources of randomness and they confuse short term and long term change. These should be enough reasons to avoid these techniques.

33.8 UPDATING AND MONITORING

So far, I have focused on making an initial forecast. The steps for making such a forecast include collecting data, analyzing, and decomposing it, selecting a model, optimizing the model, making projections, and possibly averaging those projected values. Sometimes a forecaster can then make a report and move on to his next project. However, in many situations, this is only the beginning of a forecasting effort. After completing the initial forecast, the forecaster finds that the data generating process generates more data, which leads to the need for updating and monitoring.

33.8.1 UPDATING

Updating is adding one or more new observations to the historical data to get a new forecast. An advantage of simple forecast techniques is that they allow relatively easy updating. When updating, it is possible, although not implied, to update the forecast parameters, that is, re-optimize the forecast through a new grid search. If the forecast is being managed in a spreadsheet, this re-optimization can be automated with macros. If each update includes re-optimization, it would be wise to keep a record of the parameters. Small variations in the parameters with no special tendencies are probably of little concern. However, systematic change or sharp sudden change should signal the forecaster to take a closer look at what is happening.

Armstrong (1985) says that frequent updating is important for accuracy, but, uncharacteristically, he provides no evidence to support this claim. Nevertheless, this view makes sense. The frequency of the updates depends on several factors. The forecast should be updated at least as frequently as required for users. Also, it cannot be updated more frequently than dataset becomes available. If the process for updating is not labor intensive, it might be best to update as often as possible.

Updating produces a new forecast. However, the new forecast may not differ significantly from the old forecast. Forecasts, like other statistical estimates, are contained in confidence and prediction intervals. For most of these techniques, production of these intervals is complex, and there is evidence they are unreliable (Makridakis et al., 1987). One of the advantages of frequent updating is that it concretely demonstrates the uncertainty of the forecast. Although the most recent forecast update becomes the best estimator of the future values, it is also uncertain. The forecaster should not feel obliged to interject repeated minor changes to forecasts into complex decision making processes, such as legislative sessions. Instead, by demonstrating the history of updating, the forecaster can provide the forecast user with useful information on how certain the forecast is. Once a forecast is used in formal decision making setting, the update might be thought of as part of the monitoring process, useful for asking whether the estimate is so changed as to require interrupting the decision making with new estimates.

33.8.2 MONITORING

Three forms of monitoring are shown here, tracking signals, the wineglass graph, and the outlook graph.

33.8.2.1 Tracking Signals

The simplest method of monitoring a forecast (other than just updating) is to use a tracking signal while updating. A tracking signal is a statistic that alerts the forecaster that the forecast is out of control, that is, that the model fit needs re-evaluation. A typical tracking signal is the smoothed error tracking signal (McClain, 1988)

$$\text{MAD}_t = \delta|e_t| + (1 - \delta)\text{MAD}_{t-1} \tag{33.74}$$

$$\text{ME}_t = \theta e_t + (1 - \theta)\text{ME}_{t-1} \tag{33.75}$$

$$\text{SE}_t = |\text{ME}_t/\text{MAD}_t| \tag{33.76}$$

where
MAD   = mean absolute deviation
MAD_t = a smoothed estimate of MAD for time period t
e = error
ME_t = a smoothed moving estimate of average error at time period t
δ and θ = smoothing constants for MAD_t and ME_t, respectively
SE_t = smoothed error tracking signal at time period t

The values for δ and θ are set arbitrarily, but δ should be set low, such as $\delta = 0.05$. A possible equation for the determination of θ is

$$\theta = 1/(N(1 + 3\alpha)) \tag{33.77}$$

where N is the number of time periods the forecaster is willing to risk overlooking an out-of-control situation and α is the level parameter of an exponential smoothing model. McClain suggests that δ should be higher for highly variable data than for less variable data. The forecaster watches for an increase, particularly a sharp increase, in SE_t which signals a need to fit the forecast model through a new grid search.

The next two methods are powerful tools, but they require sophisticated skills. The user may need substantial experience with forecasting before trying to implement these tools.

33.8.2.2 Wineglass

Suppose that an analyst made a monthly forecast for the current year. The year has now begun and the analyst wants to know how well the forecast is holding up. Wineglass (Wu et al., 1992) is a tracking tool that graphically demonstrates forecast accuracy under such circumstances. It depends on having several types of information: (1) the availability of monthly forecasts for the year and (2) access to the previous year's monthly data series for nonseasonal data, or at least two previous years' information for seasonal data. For nontrending nonseasonal data the wineglass graph can be produced through these equations.

$X_{i,j}$ = the actual monthly observation for month i in year j

$$X_{*,j} = \text{the sum of actual monthly observations in year } j = \sum_{i=1}^{12} X_{i,j} \tag{33.78}$$

$F_{i,j}$ = the forecast for month i in year j. For nontrending nonseasonal data, in historic years estimate

$$F_{i,j} = (1/12)X_{*,j} \tag{33.79}$$

For the forecast year, $F_{i,j}$ should be the actual forecast

$$F_{*,j} = \text{the sum of the monthly forecasts in year } j = \sum_{i=1}^{12} F_{i,j} \tag{33.80}$$

I = a subscript for the Ith month.

$g_{i,j}$ = ratio of total actual to total forecast year to date = for month i in year j

$$\sum_{i=1}^{I} X_{i,j} \Big/ \sum_{i=1}^{I} F_{i,j} \tag{33.81}$$

$$g_{*,j} = X_{*,j}/F_{*,j} \tag{33.82}$$

$$\omega_{*,j}^2 = 1/11 \sum_{i=1}^{12} \left[(X_{i,j} - F_{i,j})^2 \Big/ \left(F_{i,j} F_{*,j} \right) \right] \tag{33.83}$$

$$VW_{I,j+1} = \omega_{*,j}^2 \left(\sum_{i=I+1}^{12} F_i \Big/ \sum_{i=1}^{I} F_i \right) \tag{33.84}$$

ξ = Z value of the normal distribution for $1/2$ the area associated with a confidence interval, e.g., ci = 80 percent, ξ = 1.282, smaller values imply lower tolerance for error

$$\text{Upper}_I, \text{Lower}_I = \text{Bound for the period } I \text{ (upper and lower)} = 1 \pm \xi \sqrt{VW_I} \tag{33.85}$$

The calculation of these equations is shown in Table 33.17 (the forecast is artificial).

As shown in Figure 33.42, the wineglass chart shows the ratio of year-to-date actual-to-forecast (g_i) along with tolerance boundaries that demonstrate whether the forecast is "on track," that is, the likelihood of attaining a cumulative value consistent with the original forecast within the tolerance level. If g_i is outside the tolerance boundaries as in Figure 33.40, the apparent conclusion is that the forecast will not be attained within the tolerance level. There will be more error in the ultimate actual number than the forecast user is willing to tolerate.

Calculation of the wineglass graph as shown here applies only to nontrending nonseasonal data. For other data Equation 33.54 must be replaced with actual historical forecasts and Equation 33.58 must be revised to follow Equation 33.5 (Wu et al., 1992).

33.8.2.3 Outlook

The outlook model revises the current year forecast based on year to date experience and displays the revised forecast and confidence intervals graphically (Wu et al., 1992). Beginning with the wineglass variance and g_i ratios, outlook can be calculated as follows:

ξ = the outlook confidence level

$$F_I^M = g_i F_{*,j} = \text{the medium outlook forecast as of period } I \tag{33.86}$$

$$VO_I = g_i^2 VW_I F_{*,j}^2 \tag{33.87}$$

$$F_I^H = F_I^M + \xi \sqrt{VO_I} = \text{the high outlook as of period } I \tag{33.88}$$

$$F_I^L = F_I^M - \xi \sqrt{VO_I} = \text{the low outlook as of period } I \tag{33.89}$$

Calculations are shown in the Table 33.18. The resulting graph is shown in Figure 33.43.

Above each month on the X axis, the outlook graph reports low, medium, and high estimates of the annual forecast. As the unknown portion of the year diminishes, the range between low and high diminishes. This graph reports not only how confident the forecaster remains in the prior forecast, but also what the current likely forecast would be.

TABLE 33.17
Wineglass

Prior Year	X_i	$X_{*,j}$	F_i	$F_{*,j}$	$(X_i - F_i)$	$(X_i - F_i)^2$	$F_{ij} \times F_{*,j}$	$(X_i - F_j)^2 / F_{ij} \times F_{*,j}$	Sum Last	11	ω^2
Jan 92	1,067		1,089.92		−22.92	525.33	14,255,107	0.00004			
Feb 92	983		1,089.92		−106.92	11,431.89	14,255,107	0.00080			
Mar 92	909		1,089.92		−180.92	32,732.05	14,255,107	0.00230			
Apr 92	931		1,089.92		−158.92	25,255.57	14,255,107	0.00177			
May 92	1,511		1,089.92		421.08	177,308.37	14,255,107	0.01244			
Jun 92	1,197		1,089.92		107.08	11,466.13	14,255,107	0.00080			
Jul 92	1,053		1,089.92		−36.92	1,363.09	14,255,107	0.00010			
Aug 92	1,160		1,089.92		70.08	4,911.21	14,255,107	0.00034			
Sep 92	871		1,089.92		−218.92	47,925.97	14,255,107	0.00336			
Oct 92	1,057.5		1,089.92		−32.42	1,051.06	14,255,107	0.00007			
Nov 92	1,057.5		1,089.92		−32.42	1,051.06	14,255,107	0.00007			
Dec 92	1,282	13,079	1,089.92	13,079.04	192.08	36,894.73	14,255,107	0.00259	0.0247	11	0.0022

The contribution of the preceding calculations is the resulting number $\omega^2 = 0.0022$. Continuing:

Forecast Year	X_i	$\sum = 1X_{i,j}$	F_i	$\sum = 1F_{i,j}$	$g_i = \dfrac{\sum = 1X_{ij}}{\sum = 1F_{i,j}}$	$\sum 1 + 1F_i$	$\sum_1 F_i / \sum = 1F_i$	VW₁ Uses ω^2 (Percent)	$\sqrt{VW_1}$ (Percent)	ξ	Upper	Lower
Jan 93	1,468	1,468	1,450	1,450	1.0124	15,950	11	2.47	15.71	1.282	1.201	0.799
Feb 93	988	2,456	1,450	2,900	0.8469	14,500	5	1.12	10.59		1.136	0.864
Mar 93	950	3,406	1,450	4,350	0.7830	13,050	3	0.67	8.21		1.105	0.895
Apr 93	1,009	4,415	1,450	5,800	0.7612	11,600	2	0.45	6.70		1.086	0.914
May 93	1,484	5,899	1,450	7,250	0.8137	10,150	1.4	0.31	5.61		1.072	0.928
Jun 93	1,042	6,941	1,450	8,700	0.7978	8,700	1	0.22	4.74		1.061	0.939
Jul 93	1,133	8,074	1,450	10,150	0.7955	7,250	0.71	0.16	4.00		1.051	0.949
Aug 93	1,183	9,257	1,450	11,600	0.7980	5,800	0.50	0.11	3.35		1.043	0.957
Sep 93	1,278	10,535	1,450	13,050	0.8073	4,350	0.33	0.07	2.74		1.035	0.965
Oct 93			1,450	14,500		2,900	0.20	0.04	2.12		1.027	0.973
Nov 93			1,450	15,950		1,450	0.09	0.2	1.43		1.018	0.982
Dec 93			1,450	17,400								

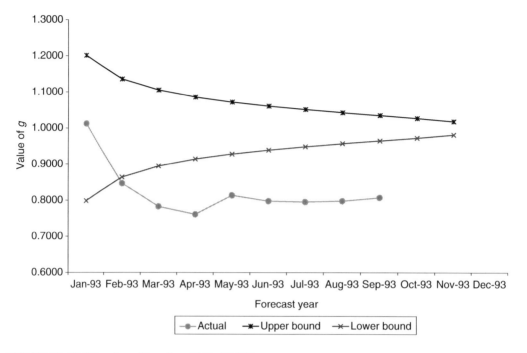

FIGURE 33.42 Wineglass. (Data from Table 33.17.)

These last two graphs have the advantage of communicating complex information graphically such that it is easily interpreted. Disadvantages include that they are complex to establish, the choice of ξ is somewhat arbitrary, and, as designed, they work only with monthly data in forecasts that cumulate to years and only once the year has begun. A reasonable forecast monitoring strategy could be to use frequent updating with a tracking signal as the primary source of monitoring prior to the forecast year, then to supplement this strategy with wineglass and outlook once the forecast year has begun. For other sorts of data, focus forecast monitoring efforts on updating and tracking signals.

TABLE 33.18

Outlook

Forecast Month-Year	g_i	$F_{*,j}^2$	VW_I (Percent)	$VO_I = g_i^2 VW_I F_{*,j}^2$	$\sqrt{VO_I}$	F	ξ	F	F
					17,400				
Jan-93	1.012	17,400	2.47	7,660,967.9	2,767.8	17,616	1.282	14,068	21,164
Feb-93	0.847		1.12	2,436,719.7	1,561.0	14,736		12,735	16,737
Mar-93	0.783		0.67	1,249,703.2	1,117.9	13,624		12,191	15,057
Apr-93	0.761		0.45	787,426.9	887.4	13,245		12,107	14,383
May-93	0.814		0.31	629,772.5	793.6	14,158		13,140	15,175
Jun-93	0.798		0.22	432,494.3	657.6	13,882		13,039	14,725
Jul-93	0.795		0.16	307,108.8	554.2	13,841		13,131	14,552
Aug-93	0.798		0.11	216,356.2	465.1	13,886		13,289	14,482
Sep-93	0.807		0.07	147,605.2	384.2	14,047		13,554	14,539

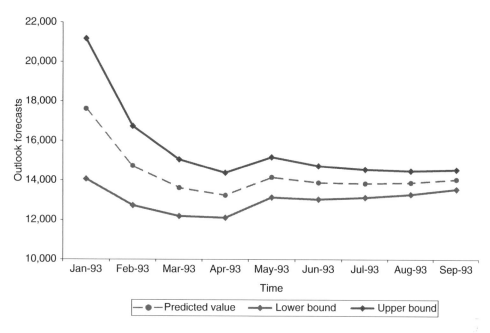

FIGURE 33.43 Outlook. (Data from Table 33.18.)

33.9 SUMMARY

A recurrent theme throughout this chapter is that the forecaster should know his or her data. For example, decomposition depends on forecaster knowledge of the data generating process. Decomposition also takes advantage of any prior knowledge the forecaster has of any component series. Finally, through decomposition, the forecaster comes to better understand both the data generating process and many of the component processes. Preparing the data for forecasting consists of analyzing the data and sorting out its variability, and forecasting consists, primarily, of taking advantage of that knowledge. Finally, updating and monitoring brings the forecaster into constant contact with the data series whereby he or she learns to anticipate how and when it changes. For effective forecasting, this familiarity with the dataset is the most important tool the forecaster can bring to the forecast.

33.10 PROBLEM SETS

33.10.1 THE VIRGINIA STATE GIRL SCOUT COUNCIL STORE

The Virginia State Girl Scout Council store has a retail store. The store manager is responsible for purchasing, inventory, and sales. Budget restrictions are numerous, and every sales department is evaluated on its ability to meet and plan for specific budget criteria. The store manager has the opportunity to order, at a significant discount, large quantities of supplies in June from Girl Scout national headquarters in New York City. However, State Council policy requires that inventory be very low at the end of the fiscal year in December. If fall sales could be forecasted accurately, the store manager could achieve considerable savings by ordering at the June discount level.

However, the store manager has been unable to predict fall sales accurately enough to justify ordering in June, for fear of violating the inventory restrictions. The historical dataset seems to vary unpredictably and by a great amount.

To explore the possibility of developing a more accurate forecasting procedure, a consultant focused on a bell-weather item—girl scout pins. Sales of many other items are related to sales of pins.

TABLE 33.19
Problem 1

	Jan	Feb	Mar	Apr	May	Jun
1989	171	219	263	290	278	238
1990	219	252	280	279	313	353
1991	250	274	347	301	260	174
1992	265	320	342	353	—	—
	Jul	Aug	Sep	Oct	Nov	Dec
1989	125	147	349	449	381	251
1990	102	172	362	491	428	315
1991	152	171	408	562	480	341
1992	—	—	—	—	—	—

Monthly sales of pins were available for January 1989 through April 1992. They are provided in the spreadsheet at the tab "sales FC girl scout pins" and in Table 33.19.

(a) Develop a graphical analysis (time-plot, trend plot, seasonality plot) of "girl scout pins." Describe the pattern of the data.
(b) Using classical decomposition, determine seasonal factors and use them to seasonally adjust the data.
(c) Should you Windsorize any observations? What are the new values?
(d) Based on (a) and (b) above, would you expect sales of pins to be difficult to forecast through December with reasonable accuracy?

33.10.2 YOU HAVE DEVELOPED THREE GRAPHS OF THE GIRL SCOUT DATA

(1) The time-plot of the sales data suggest a seasonal pattern with positive trend.
(2) The trend plot confirms the positive trend in that almost all year-over-year differences are positive. It also suggests that there was either an extremely low sales value around June 1991 or a very large value in June of 1990, or both. Perhaps this contributed to the manager's perplexity.
(3) The seasonality plot reveals the seasonal pattern more clearly.

To prepare for forecasting, you have seasonally adjusted the data by dividing each data value by the corresponding seasonal factor for the given month.

The goal now is to develop a forecast of sales through year-end (December).

(a) Based on the plots, which method do you expect to produce the most realistic forecast?
(b) Using simple exponential smoothing, develop a forecast of de-seasonalized sales through December.
(c) Using either Holt's linear exponential smoothing or damped-trend exponential smoothing, develop another forecast of de-seasonalized sales through December.
(d) Develop a time-series plot of the seasonally adjusted actual sales values and both forecasts. Which forecast looks more plausible?
Choose your preferred forecast.
    Now re-seasonalize your forecast. This is your official forecast.
(e) Develop a time-series plot of (i) the actual sales data and (ii) your re-seasonalized forecast.

EQUATIONS

Regression Forecast   Number
$$\hat{y} = \alpha + \beta_1 x_1 + \beta_2 x_2 + \ldots + \beta_n x_n + \varepsilon \qquad (33.1)$$

Windsorize
$$O' = \mu' + 3\sigma' \qquad (33.2)$$

Constant Dollars
$$CD_t = ND_t \times DF_b / DF_t \qquad (33.3)$$

Random Walk/Last Observation
$$F_t = X_{t-1} \qquad (33.4)$$

$$F_{t+m} = F_t \qquad (33.5)$$

Average as Forecast
$$F_{t+m} = S_t = \bar{x}_t = \sum_{i=1}^{t} (X_i / t) \qquad (33.6)$$

Root Mean Squared Error
$$RMSE = \sqrt{\left(\sum_{i=1}^{t} (X_i - F_i)^2 / t \right)} \qquad (33.7)$$

Moving Average
$$F_{t+1} = MAVG_t = (X_t + X_{t-1} + \ldots + X_{t-(L-1)})/L \qquad (33.8)$$

Simple Exponential Smoothing (SES)
$$F_{t+m} = \text{forecast at time } t \text{ of time } t+m = S_t \qquad (33.9)$$
$$S_t = \text{level at time } t = F_t + \alpha e_t = S_{t-1} + \alpha e_t \qquad (33.10)$$
$$e_t = \text{error at time } t = X_t - F_t = X_t - S_{t-1} \qquad (33.11)$$

Difference of the annual (or any) period
$$D_A = \text{difference of the annual period} = X_{t+L} - X_t \qquad (33.12)$$

Last Change
$$B = \text{the change from period 1 to period 2} = X_2 - X_1 \qquad (33.13)$$
$$F_{t+1} = \text{the forecast (next period)} = X_2 + B \qquad (33.14)$$
$$F_{t+m} = \text{forecast at time } t \text{ of the } m\text{th future period} = X_2 + mB \qquad (33.15)$$

First Difference
$$D_t = \text{any difference (period to period change)} = X_t - X_{t-1} \qquad (33.16)$$

Reversing Differences to Finish Forecasting
$$F_2' = X_1 + F_1 \qquad (33.17)$$
$$F_3' = F_2' + F_2, \ F_4' = F_3' + F_3, \text{ etc.} \qquad (33.18)$$

Holt (Two Parameter Trending) Exponential Smoothing
$$F_{t+m} = \text{forecast at time } t \text{ of time } t+m = S_t + (B_t \times m) \qquad (33.19)$$
$$S_t = \text{level at time } t = F_t + \alpha e_t \qquad (33.20)$$
$$B_t = \text{trend at time } t = B_{t-1} + \beta e_t \qquad (33.21)$$
$$e_t = \text{error at time } t = X_t - F_t \qquad (33.22)$$

Initializing Holt Exponential Smoothing
$$\bar{x}_j = \sum_{i=1}^{L} X_{i,j} / L \qquad (33.23)$$

$$D = \bar{x}_2 - \bar{x}_1 \tag{33.24}$$
$$B_0 = D/L \tag{33.25}$$
$$S_0 = \bar{x}_1 - B \times (L+1)/2 \tag{33.26}$$
$$F_1 = S_0 + B_0 \tag{33.27}$$

Damped Trend Holt Exponential Smoothing
$$F_{t+m} = \text{forecast at time } t \text{ of time } t+m = S_t + \sum_{t=1}^{m}(\phi' B_t) \tag{33.28}$$
$$S_t = \text{level at time } t = F_t + \alpha e_t \tag{33.29}$$
$$B_t = \text{trend at time } t = \varphi B_{t-1} + \beta e_t \tag{33.30}$$
$$e_t = \text{error at time } t = X_t - F_t \tag{33.31}$$
$$B_{t+m} = \text{trend for future periods} = B_t \times \varphi^m \tag{33.32}$$

Ratio and Percentage in Time Series
$$R_t = \text{ratio change} = X_t/X_{t-1} \tag{33.33}$$
$$P = \text{percentage from ratio} = (R-1)100 \tag{33.34}$$

Second Ordered Differences
$$D_3'' = D_3 - D_2, \text{ etc.} \tag{33.35}$$
Center of Moving Average
$$(L+1)/2 \tag{33.36}$$

Classical Decomposition: Multiplicative
$$I_7' = X_7/S_7, \quad I_8' = X_8/S_8, \ldots, \quad I_{n-6}' = X_{n-6}/S_{n-6} \tag{33.37}$$
$$I_{\text{JUL}}'' = (I_7' + I_{19}' + I_{31}' + \ldots)/\text{Count of Julys,} \tag{33.38}$$
$$I_{\text{AUG}}'' = (I_8' + I_{20}' + I_{32}' + \ldots)/\text{Count of Augusts,} \ldots$$
$$P = 12/\sum_{i=1}^{12} I'' \tag{33.39}$$
$$I_{\text{JUL}} = I_{\text{JUL}}'' P \tag{33.40}$$
$$I_{\text{AUG}} = I_{\text{AUG}}'' P, \text{ etc.}$$
$$\text{DESEAS}_t = X_t/I_t \tag{33.41}$$

Classical Decomposition: Additive
$$I_7' = X_7 - S_7, \quad I_8' = X_8 - S_8, \ldots, \quad I_{n-6}' = X_{n-6} - S_{n-6} \tag{33.42}$$
$$I_{\text{JUL}} = (I_7' + I_{19}' + I_{31}' + \ldots)/\text{Count of Julys,} \tag{33.43}$$
$$I_{\text{AUG}} = (I_8' + I_{20}' + I_{32}' + \ldots)/\text{Count of Augusts,} \ldots$$
$$P = \sum_{i=1}^{12} I''/12 \tag{33.44}$$
$$I_{\text{JUL}} = I_{\text{JUL}}'' - P \tag{33.45}$$
$$I_{\text{AUG}} = I_{\text{AUG}}'' - P, \text{ etc.}$$
$$\text{DESEAS}_t = X_t - I_t \tag{33.46}$$

Holt–Winters: Multiplicative
$$F_{t+m} = \text{forecast at time } t \text{ of time } t+m = (S_t + B_t m) \times I_{t+m-L} \tag{33.47}$$
$$F_t = \text{forecast at time } t = (S_{t-1} + B_{t-1})I_{t-L} \tag{33.48}$$
$$S_t = \text{level at time } t = S_{t-1} + B_{t-1} + \alpha e_t/I_{t-L} \tag{33.49}$$
$$B_t = \text{trend at time } t = B_{t-1} + \beta e_t/I_{t-L} \tag{33.50}$$
$$I_t = \text{seasonal index at time } t = \gamma e_t/(S_{t-1} + B_{t-1}) + I_{t-L} \tag{33.51}$$
$$e_t = \text{error at time } t = X_t - F_t \tag{33.52}$$

Trend Estimate with Limited Data
$$S_1 = S_0 + B, \quad S_2 = S_1 + B, \quad S_3 = S_2 + B, \ldots, \quad S_{24} = S_{23} + B \tag{33.53}$$

Holt–Winters: Additive

F_{t+m} = forecast at time t of time $t+m = S_t + B_t m + I_{t+m-L}$ (33.54)

F_t = forecast at time $t = S_{t-1} + B_{t-1} + I_{t-L}$ (33.55)

S_t = level at time $t = S_{t-1} + B_{t-1} + \alpha e_t$ (33.56)

B_t = trend at time $t = B_{t-1} + \beta e_t$ (33.57)

I_t = additive seasonal index at time $t = \gamma e_t + I_{t-L}$ (33.58)

e_t = error at time $t = X_t - F_t$ (33.59)

Symmetrical Absolute Percent Error/Symmetrical Mean Absolute Percent Error

SAPE_t = symmetrical absolute percent error = $|2e_t/(F_t + X_t)|$ (33.60)

$$\text{SMAPE} = \text{symmetrical mean absolute percent error} = \sum_{t=1}^{n} \text{SAPE}_t/n \qquad (33.61)$$

Mean Error

$$\text{ME} = \sum_{t=1}^{n} e_t/n \qquad (33.62)$$

Autocorrelation (Serial Correlation of Errors)

$$\bar{e} = \sum_{t=1}^{n} e_t/n \qquad (33.63)$$

$$\sigma_{e(t)} = \sqrt{\sum_{t=2}^{n} (e_t - \bar{e})^2/(n-1)}, \sigma_{e(t-1)} = \sqrt{\sum_{t=1}^{n-1} (e_t - \bar{e})^2/(n-1)} \qquad (33.64)$$

$$\text{COV}(e_t, e_{t-1}) = \sum_{t=2}^{n} [(e_t - \bar{e})(e_{t-1} - \bar{e})]/(n-1) \qquad (33.65)$$

$$\rho(e_t, e_{t-1}) = \text{COV}(e_t, e_{t-1})/(\sigma_{e(t)}\, \sigma_{e(t-1)}) \qquad (33.66)$$

Weighted Mean Error

$$\text{ME} = \sum_{t=1}^{n} (\omega_t \times e_t) \Big/ \sum_{t=1}^{n} \omega_t \qquad (33.67)$$

Level Adjusted Exponential Smoothing (LAES)

F_{t+m} = forecast at t for $t+m = S_t + mB + (P_{t+m} - P_t)$ (33.68)

F_{t+1} = one-step-ahead forecast at t for $t+1 = S_t + B_t + A_{t+1}$ (33.69)

A_t = adjustment factor at time $t = P_t - P_{t-x}$ (33.70)

P_t = the cumulative effect of policy through t (33.71)

M = any arbitrary number of periods after period t (33.72)

Really Simple Method

$F_{(1,1)} = X_1/0.0833$

$F_{(2,1)} = (X_1 + X_2)/0.1667$ (33.73)

$F_{(3,1)} = (X_1 + X_2 + X_3)/0.25$, etc.

$$F = \left(X_{1,1} \Big/ \sum_{i=1}^{12} X_{i,1} \right)$$

Smoothed Error Tracking Signal

$\text{MAD}_t = \delta|e_t| + (1 - \delta)\, \text{MAD}_{t-1}$ (33.74)

$\text{ME}_t = \theta e_t + (1 - \theta)\, \text{ME}_{t-1}$ (33.75)

$\text{SE}_t = |\text{ME}_t/\text{MAD}_t|$ (33.76)

$\Theta = 1/(N(1+3\alpha))$ (33.77)

Wineglass

$$X_{*,j} = \text{the sum of actual monthly observations in year } j = \sum_{i=1}^{12} X_{i,j} \qquad (33.78)$$

$F_{i,j}$ = the forecast for month i in year j. For nontrending nonseasonal data, in historic

years estimate $F_{i,j} = (1/12)X_{*,j}$ (33.79)

$F_{*,j}$ = the sum of the monthly forecasts in year $j = \sum\limits_{i=1}^{12} F_{i,j}$ (33.80)

$$\sum_{i=1}^{I} X_{i,j} \Big/ \sum_{i=1}^{I} F_{i,j}$$ (33.81)

$$g_{*,j} = X_{*,j}/F_{*j}$$ (33.82)

$$\omega_{*,j}^2 = 1/11 \sum_{i=1}^{12} [(X_{i,j} - F_{i,j})^2/(F_{i,j}F_{*,j})]$$ (33.83)

$$\mathrm{VW}_{I,j+1} = \omega_{*,j}^2 \left(\sum_{i=I+1}^{12} F_i \Big/ \sum_{i=1}^{I} F_i \right)$$ (33.84)

Upper$_I$, Lower$_I$ = bound for the period I (upper and lower) = $1 \pm \xi\sqrt{\mathrm{VW_I}}$ (33.85)

Outlook

$F_I^M = g_i F_{*,j}$ = the medium outlook forecast as of period I (33.86)

$\mathrm{VO}_I = g_i^2 \mathrm{VW}_I F_{*,j}^2$ (33.87)

$F_I^H = F_I^M + \xi\sqrt{\mathrm{VO_I}}$ = the high outlook as of period I (33.88)

$F_I^L = F_I^M - \xi\sqrt{\mathrm{VO_I}}$ = the low outlook as of period I (33.89)

REFERENCES

Ammons, D.N. 1991. *Administrative Analysis for Local Government: Practical Applications of Selected Techniques*, Carl Vinson Institute of Government, Athens, Georgia, pp. 68–73.

Ammons, D.N. 2002. *Tools for Decision Making: A Practical Guide for Local Government*, CQ Press, Washington, DC.

Armstrong, J.S. 1985. *Long-Range Forecasting, From Crystal Ball to Computer*, 2nd ed., John Wiley & Sons, New York.

Ashley, R. 1983. On the usefulness of macroeconomic forecasts as inputs to forecasting models, *Journal of Forecasting 2*: 211–223.

Ashley, R. 1988. On the relative worth of recent macro-economic forecasts, *International Journal of Forecasting 4*: 363–376.

Chatfield, C. 1978. The Holt–Winters forecasting procedure, *Applied Statistics 27*: 264–279.

Clemen, R.T. 1989. Combining forecasts: A review and annotated bibliography, *International Journal of Forecasting 5*: 559–583.

Flores, B.E. 1986. A pragmatic view of accuracy measurement in forecasting, *Omega 14*: 93–98.

Foust, D. 1997. *Business Week*, July 14, Issue 3535, pp. 44–50.

Gardner, Jr., E. and McKenzie, E. 1985. Forecasting trends in time series, *Management Science 31*: 1237–1245.

Makridakis, S. and Winkler, R.L. 1983. Averages of forecasts: Some empirical results, *Management Science 29*: 987–996.

Makridakis, S., Anderson, A., Carbone, R., Fildes, R., Hibon, M., Lewandowski, R., Newton, J., Parzen, E., and Winkler, R. 1982. The accuracy of extrapolation (time series) methods: Results of a forecasting competition, *Journal of Forecasting 1*: 111–153.

Makridakis, S., Hibon, M., Lusk, E., and Belhadjali, M. 1987. Confidence intervals an empirical investigation of the series in the M-competition, *International Journal of Forecasting 3*: 489–508.

Makridakis, S., Wheelwright, S.C., and Hyndman, R.J. 2003. *Forecasting: Methods and Applications*, 3rd ed., John Wiley & Sons, New York.

McClain, J.O. 1988. Dominant tracking signals, *International Journal of Forecasting 4*: 563–572.

Miller, D.M. and Williams, D. 2003. Shrinkage estimators of time series seasonal factors and their effect on forecasting accuracy, *International Journal of Forecasting 19*(4): 669.

Miller, D.M. and Williams, D. 2004. Damping seasonal factors: Shrinkage estimators for the X-12-ARIMA program, *International Journal of Forecasting 20*(4): 529.

Pfeffermann, D. and Allon, J. 1989. Multivariate exponential smoothing: Method and practice, *International Journal of Forecasting 5*: 83–98.

Vollmann, T.E., Berry, W.L., and Whybark, D.C. 1993. *Integrated Production and Inventory Management: Revitalizing the Manufacturing Enterprise*, Business One Irwin, Homewood, Illinois, p. 71.

Williams, D.W. and Miller, D. 1999. Level-adjusted exponential smoothing for modeling planned discontinuities, *International Journal of Forecasting 15*(3): 273.

Williams, T.M. 1987. Adaptive Holt–Winters forecasting, *Journal of the Operational Research Society 38*: 553–560.

Winters, P.R. 1960. Forecasting sales by exponentially weighted moving averages, *Management Science 7*: 324–342.

Wu, L.S.-Y., Hosking, J.R.M. and Doll, J.M. 1992. Business planning under uncertainty, *International Journal of Forecasting 8*: 545–557.

Part VII

Other Techniques

34 Data Envelopment Analysis for Performance Assessment and Decision Making

Patria de Lancer Julnes

CONTENTS

Assessing the performance of government services is an important component of current managing for results strategies. A number of commonly used techniques for measuring performance and informing decision making in the public sector are discussed in this volume. In this chapter we attempt to expand the repertoire of available techniques by providing an introduction to data envelopment analysis (DEA), a powerful linear programming technique for assessing the efficiency of organizations or decision-making units (DMU) providing similar services. One of the advantages of DEA is that in assessing efficiency it also helps to determine the course of action the decision maker should take for improving the performance of inefficient units (Melao, 2005). DEA helps to determine the amount of resource conservation or output increase necessary for a program or unit to achieve managerial efficiency.

Although discussions and applications of DEA are not found as often as other decision-making techniques in mainstream public administration literature, DEA was originally introduced as a "new Management Science tool for technical-efficiency analyses of public sector decision-making units (DMUs)" (Charnes, Cooper, Lewin, and Seiford, 1994, p. 4). The technique is ideal for use in the public sector because, as explained by Charnes, Cooper, and Rhodes (CCR) in their seminal 1978 article, the public sector managers are not free to divert resources to other programs for their profitability or attractiveness. (This is also true for nonprofit organizations.) In addition, DEA does not require that the data being analyzed be weighted by reference to market prices or other economic indicators.

Another characteristic of DEA, which at times may make it more appropriate than other methods for decision making, is that it is a nonparametric approach. Therefore, it does not depend on specific population distributions and does not require samples from normally distributed populations. Indeed, one of the advantages of nonparametric methods is their generalizability. Furthermore, these methods are inherently resistant to outliers and skewness and can use categorical variables, ranks, and frequency (Watson, Billingsley, Croft and Huntsberger, 1993). As long as the assumptions underlying nonparametric methods hold, these methods can be more powerful than other parametric approaches.

Several authors report that since the initial introduction of the technique by Charnes, Cooper, and Rhodes (CCR) (1978), there have been thousands of papers, over 50 books, and about 200 dissertations about DEA or its application (Melao, 2005). Appendix A lists a sample of DEA-related publications. Notwithstanding, the use of DEA in management decision-making in the public sector has been scant. Most of the application of the technique has been by academics. Also, few, if any, decision-making books focused on public administration include a discussion of this technique.

In what follows, readers will be introduced to the technical and theoretical aspects of DEA, including the advantages and limitations of the technique. Using both hypothetical and real data, we illustrate how the technique works. The goal is for readers to gain an intuitive understanding of the technique and an appreciation for its potential to contribute to improved government decision making and performance. It should be noted that this is only an introduction. Those wishing further technical guidance and detail are encouraged to read Cooper, Seiford and Tone (2000), Charnes et al. (1994), Melao (2005), and Sexton (1986).

Finally, in this chapter we will use the term output whether or not a particular indicator can be considered an outcome. This is done to be consistent with DEA literature.

34.1 HOW DATA ENVELOPMENT ANALYSIS WORK

The DEA approach applies linear programming to measure the efficiency of any organization (DMU) as the maximum of a ratio of weighted outputs to weighted inputs. This is subject to the condition that the similar ratios for every organization in the reference group (the set being analyzed) be less than or equal to unity. That is, efficiency rating is relative to some maximum possibility so that always efficiency $(E) > 0$ but $<= 1$. This condition, Pareto efficiency, or as it is also called Pareto–Koopmans Efficiency, implies that in order for an organization to be considered efficient in producing its outputs, no other DMU or a combination of organizations in the reference set can produce more of an output without producing less of any other output and without using more resources (Bessent and Bessent, 1980).

Thus, in a given analysis, an organization is identified as inefficient only after all possible weights have been considered to give that organization or DMU the highest rating possible, consistent with the constraint that no DMU in the data set can be more than 100 percent efficient. As stated in the economic theory of optimization, an organization is considered to be technically inefficient "if it cannot increase the amount of one of its outputs without reducing other outputs or increasing inputs" (Hughes and Edwards, 2000, p. 653). When the concern is output augmentation, a unit is inefficient if some other unit or combination of units use no more of any inputs, and yet produce at least the same amounts of all outputs, or more of at least one output, and accomplish the above with at least the same difficulty in terms of environmental constraints. As highlighted above, DEA measures the "relative efficiency" of DMU's producing similar outputs and using similar inputs. It is called relative efficiency because a hypothetical composite DMU is constructed based on all the DMUs in the reference group. The other DMUs are then evaluated relative to this efficient DMU.

Unlike other commonly used statistical approaches to evaluating performance, data envelopment analysis is an extreme point method, producing a piecewise empirical extremal production surface known in economic terms as the "revealed" best-practice production frontier. This production frontier represents the maximum output that can be obtained empirically from any DMU in a set under study, given its level of inputs. This particular characteristic of DEA makes it susceptible to certain difficulties (explained in Section 34.2). The technique, as described by Seiford and Thrall (1990), focuses on frontiers rather than central tendencies. Therefore, "instead of trying to fit a regression plane through the center of the data," one "floats" a piecewise linear surface to rest on top of the observations. "Because of this unique perspective, DEA proves particularly adept at uncovering relationships that remain hidden for other methodologies" (Seiford and Thrall, 1990, p. 8). Without the analyst having to specify the functional forms between inputs and outputs or having to impose weights, DEA estimates a production frontier derived from the "optimizations of each DMU in a collection of DMUs with similar inputs and outputs" (Huang, Li, and Zhu, 2005).

The mathematical models of DEA as introduced by Charnes, Cooper and Rhodes in 1978 (the CCR models) are presented in Appendix B. This ratio formulation is used to establish a best-practice group of units to determine which units are inefficient compared to the best-practice groups and estimate the magnitude of inefficiencies present. In addition, it tells which units should be able to improve productivity and the amount of resource savings or output augmentation these inefficient units must achieve to meet the level of efficiency of best-practice units.

To conclude, the two dimensions of efficiency in DEA, based on Pareto efficiency can be summarized as follows (Bessent and Bessent, 1980; Nunamaker, 1983):

1. Output orientation. A DMU is not efficient in output production if the level of one or more outputs can be increased without decreasing other outputs and without utilizing more inputs.
2. Input orientation. A DMU is not efficient in converting its inputs to outputs if other DMUs can produce the same level of output by using fewer inputs.

34.1.1 ESTABLISHING THE BEST PRACTICE

As succinctly put by Anderson (1996) "the heart of the analysis lies in finding the 'best' virtual producer for each real producer." If the virtual producer is better than the original producer by either making more output with the same input or making the same output with less input then the original producer is inefficient." To determine this virtual producer one formulates the problem as a linear program where efficiency of each organization in the set is determined by running the same number of linear programming problems. The following simple example, inspired by Anderson's own, will help illustrate the "virtual" organization concept.

Suppose that you are a city manager trying to decide whether to outsource snow removal. You think that there is a possibility that a contractor might do a more efficient job than the city's own employees. You call your colleagues in two other cities and obtain information that allows you to compare your city's performance on snow removal to theirs. You all have a fixed budget of $10,000 and each accomplish the following:

- City A: 40 miles worth of road snow removal, 0 miles worth of snow removal in parking lots and school fields

- City B: 20 miles worth of road snow removal, 5 miles worth of snow removal in parking lots and school fields
- Your City: 10 miles worth of road snow removal, 20 miles worth of snow removal in parking lots and school fields

By inspection alone you are able to determine that no combination of parts of Your City and City B can produce the 40 miles worth of road snow removal with the $10,000 budget that City A has. Therefore, City A is given an efficiency rating of 1.

The next step is to analyze City B. Visual inspection of the data suggests that some combination of City A and Your City might be able to produce the same or more miles of snow removals on roads and in parking lots and school fields than City B. If we combine 50 percent of the outputs of City A with 50 percent of the outputs of Your City, we will find that this combination will lead to a virtual best-practice city that produces more outputs than City B with the same amount of resources. In numerical terms we are saying that

Virtual city = 50 percent of outputs of City A + 50 percent outputs of Your City.

Virtual city = $(0.5 \times 40 + 0.5 \times 10 + 0.5 \times 0 + 0.5 \times 20) = 25$ miles road; 10 miles parking lots and school fields.

Virtual city (25,10) > City B (20, 5).

The analysis suggests that City B is inefficient. The actual efficiency score needs to be calculated using linear programming. However, we would expect it to be below 1.

Next, let us analyze Your City. Visual inspection indicates that no combination of City A and City B can produce the same or greater amount of miles road and parking lots and school fields snow removal. Therefore, Your City is efficiently removing snow given the budget constraint. Likewise, City A is efficient at road snow removal. On the other hand, City B is inefficient. Its performance on snow removal is below what would be expected given the resources and compared to the other two cities. Therefore, DEA would calculate an efficiency score below 1. Thus, the conclusion would be that compared to its peers and given the resource constraint, Your City is doing just as well, if not better, than other cities at snow removal.

When explained in graphical terms, the best-practice organization is a convex combination of other inputs and outputs. This assumption of convexity is equivalent to assuming that if two production possibilities are observed in practice, then any production plan which is a convex weighted combination of the two production possibilities is also achievable. DEA estimates a production frontier, calculated in a piecewise linear fashion, which optimizes each individual observation (performance measure) of each DMU (Charnes, Cooper, and Rhodes, 1978). To illustrate this, we will use another example. However, whereas in the previous example we focused on outputs, this time we will focus on inputs. The goal of the analysis is to determine the extent to which a DMU can reduce the level of resources used without reducing its level of output.

There are five agencies, each using a unique combination of two inputs (X_1 and X_2) to produce 1 unit of output (Y). The input combinations are as follows: Agency 1 (2, 3); Agency 2 (2, 2); Agency 3 (4, 1); Agency 4 (3, 2); and Agency 5 (1, 4). For the purpose of illustration, I have drawn the efficiency frontier. But in reality, the efficiency frontier is determined by the DEA model we use.

Figure 34.1 shows that relative to Agencies 2, 3, and 5, Agencies 1 and 4 are inefficient. Those two agencies are outside the efficiency frontier, the line that connects Agencies 5, 2, and 3. DEA determined that Agencies 1 and 4 could decrease their use of inputs without decreasing the level of output.

As can be observed in Figure 34.1, Agency 1 uses the same amount of input X_1 as Agency 2, but more of input X_2 than Agency 2 to produce the same amount of the output. In order for Agency 1 to become efficient, it would have to reduce its use of both inputs. Thus, the distance between E and Agency 1 is the reduction in input utilization necessary for this agency to become efficient.

The line segments from A5A2 along the efficiency frontier shows the possibilities of "best" practice that can be formed from these two agencies. In other words, it shows the different

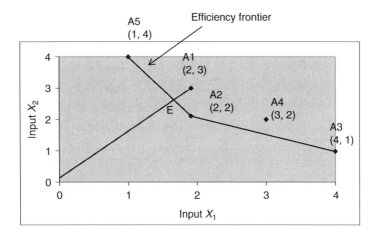

FIGURE 34.1 Graphical representation of DEA.

combinations of inputs that would be needed to produce the same level output. Thus, in that point E lies on the line segment A5A2, its coordinates are a weighted average of the coordinates of points A5 and A2 so that the virtual (best) practice for Agency 1 is a weighted average of A5 and A2. Similar conclusions can be drawn for Agency 4 and the line segment A2A3.

34.1.2 AVAILABLE MODELS AND SOFTWARE

In the decades since its introduction, numerous studies have helped to develop a variety of DEA models and extensions that have greatly enhanced its application. Some of those models are: the Banker, Charnes, and Cooper (BCC) model, which distinguishes between technical and scale inefficiencies; the multiplicative models, which provide a log-linear envelopment surface; the cone-ration model; the free disposal hull (FDH) model; models with nondiscretionary variables; stochastic models; and benchmarking models (Huang, Li, and Zhu, 2005).

The choice of DEA model will depend on the assumptions made by the analyst. For example, if the analyst assumes constant or variable returns to scale (explained below) and whether the focus is on input reduction or output augmentation to achieve efficiency, both the CCR and the BCC models allow for either an output or input orientation in their formulation. In input-oriented models, the primary focus is to "minimize the extent to which inputs can be proportionally reduced" (Charnes, Cooper, Lewin, and Seiford, 1994, p. 71). In output-oriented models, the goal is to "maximize the extent to which outputs can be proportionally augmented" (p. 71). Therefore, one of the main considerations of analysts using DEA is the purpose of the analysis.

DEA analysis can be performed with basic linear programming software. However, there is drawback: the analyst needs to run as many linear programs as there are DMUs in the data set. This drawback can be overcome. Over the last decade a number of software tools that make the use of DEA more practical have become available. These tools, many of which are Microsoft Windows-based, not only make DEA easier to use and interpret, but also take advantage of the different modeling options mentioned above. Some of the software tools are available commercially and others are available free of charge. Barr (2004) provides a very useful assessment of the best commercial and noncommercial DEA software available today. A list of available DEA software is shown in Appendix C.

34.1.3 RETURNS TO SCALE

For the sake of simplicity, we have assumed constant inputs and outputs. However, such assumptions do not allow for increasing or decreasing production based on size. With DEA The analyst may choose between constant return to scale (CRS), in instances when the organization is able to linearly scale the inputs and outputs without increasing or decreasing efficiency, or variable return to scale (VRS), in instances of increasing or decreasing returns to scale.

It is important to note that CRS tends to lower the efficiency scores while VRS tends to raise efficiency scores (Anderson, 1994). The reason for this is that CRS models tend to be less constrained than VRS models and thus the more constrained the model, the less likely it is to be found inefficient. Also, when the production process is designated as CRS, the analyst can determine the cause of the inefficiency as being due to scale efficiency—related to size of the organization and whether it is cost efficient, or purely technical inefficiency—due to waste in the production, regardless of size (Hughes and Edwards, 2000). In the end, the analyst decides which model is more appropriate given the characteristics of the DMUs under consideration.

For example, taking into account economic considerations, when analyzing physician's hospital practice Chilingerian (1994) chose to use a CRS model. The author argued that because physicians take patients with similar diagnosis through the same clinical process, when they decide to treat twice as many patients with a common diagnosis, they are likely to use twice as many resources. Thus, an increase in physicians' caseloads does not affect the productivity of the inputs. Therefore, the assumption of variable returns to scale is not appropriate.

34.2 STRENGTHS AND WEAKNESSES OF DEA COMPARED TO TWO POPULAR TECHNIQUES FOR MEASURING EFFICIENCY

34.2.1 COMPARISON WITH RATIO ANALYSIS

Ratio analysis in efficiency evaluation often takes the form of cost–benefit analysis and cost–effectiveness analysis. These are based on simple ratios or several ratios being compared simultaneously (Tseng, 1990). Ratio analysis requires common measures of inputs and outputs, which could create difficulties because of the need to transform all inputs and outputs into a common measure, or assigning a value to each input and output (Rossi and Freeman, 1982).

If the analyst decides to use totals, the result of the analysis would be biased because the mix of output and inputs cannot be recognized (Sherman, 1984). It might be argued that this deficiency in ratio analysis could be corrected if it was possible to set efficient relative weights or costs. However, the result of the analysis would still be biased because ratio weights would be assigned arbitrarily (Sherman, 1984).

One of the most appealing characteristics of DEA is that it allows for the evaluation of DMUs with multiple outputs and inputs and different units of measurement. (Lewin, Morey, and Cook, 1982). Data envelopment analysis does assign weights to the observations, but these weights are derived empirically from the data. For further reading on ways to overcome the deficiencies of ratio analyses see Stokey and Zeckhauser (1978).

34.2.2 COMPARISON WITH ECONOMETRICS METHODS

Econometric regression techniques are often used to evaluate efficiency by comparing the expected outputs with the actual output assuming that the output level of a DMU is dependent on the level of inputs (Sexton, 1986). Thus, if a DMU in question produces fewer outputs than the regression analysis predicts, it is considered inefficient.

There are some drawbacks to this approach. First, the models do not discriminate between efficient and inefficient units. This, according to Sherman (1984), renders these models weak. Unlike DEA, these models do not identify the inefficient unit. The models only compare the unit to the average DMU rather than to the best performer (de Lancer Julnes, 2000). This is not as useful as DEA because decision makers get little information that can suggest different resource allocations that can help to achieve optimal performance.

Another drawback, explained by Lewin, Morey, and Cook (1982), is that regression models require that the functional form of the production function be specified. Further, because econometrics least square models regress one output at a time against the inputs, they make strong assumptions of independence among the outputs (Charnes, Cooper, and Rhodes, 1981). Thus, without the appropriate modifications, the application of these models may be impractical for organizations with more than one output. Those organizations would need to combine the different outputs into one before running the analysis. For further information on ways to overcome the limitations of regression analysis, see Neter, Kutner, Nachtstheim, and Wasserman (1996).

34.2.3 STRENGTHS

Data envelopment analysis has many appealing characteristics. Many of these have been highlighted throughout this chapter. For example, as inferred earlier, one of the strengths of DEA over other techniques is that it allows the analyst to use multiple outputs and inputs in different units of measures and at different levels of measurement–categorical and continuous data (Banker and Morey, 1986).

Moreover, DEA can be used to obtain the relative measures of efficiency, involving technical and scale efficiency (Lewin, Morey, and Cook, 1982). In identifying the inefficiency units in a data set, DEA also determines the magnitude of their inefficiency (Sherman, 1984).

Perhaps most importantly, DEA allows the analyst to overcome many of the limitations associated with other techniques. The strengths of DEA can be summarized as follows:

- DEA is capable of deriving a single aggregate measure of the relative efficiency of a DMU's utilization of its inputs to produce desired outputs.
- DEA models are able to handle noncommensurate multiple outputs and multiple input factors. These models do not require for all outputs or inputs in the model to have the same unit of measure.
- DEA allows the analysis to adjust for factors outside the control of the unit being evaluated.
- DEA models are not dependent on setting weights a priori or prices for the inputs or the outputs. DEA derives weights empirically, which makes the results more objective.
- DEA is capable of handling qualitative factors. As long as the qualitative factors can be quantified or can be given a nominal value, it is possible to include them in this nonparametric approach.

34.2.4 WEAKNESSES

Several concerns have been raised about the robustness of the DEA models. Sherman (1984) for example, concluded that because DEA only determines relative efficiency, it cannot locate all inefficient DMUs because all DMUs in a data set may be inefficient. Indeed, DEA identifies the best practice among the group under analysis. Thus, for example, in our snow removal illustration above, it is quite possible that all three cities in our example, including Your City and City A are inefficient when compared to other cities not included in the analysis. Nonetheless, the results of our current snow removal analysis can help us decide whether our snow removal goals are being attained compared to previous years or to other cities providing the same services. Also, management attention is directed toward identifying formal structures, processes, or other organizational factors that may account for the observed differences (Charnes, Cooper, Lewin, and Seiford, 1994).

Another concern expressed by Sherman (1984) is that DEA does not identify the factors that cause the inefficiency. In our snow removal analysis DEA did not pinpoint the factors that contributed to the observed inefficiency in City B. As such, DEA only directs a manager's attention to the units where inefficiency exists. But as explained by Bessent and Bessent (1980) this can be useful information because the inputs and outputs that are contributing to this inefficiency are also identified and administrators can decide whether a reallocation of resources is necessary or feasible.

Diewert and Mendoza (1995) identified other limitations of DEA models. One of those is that measurement errors may cause the results of a model to be severely biased because the best or most efficient DMU may be "best" due to the overstatement of outputs or the understatement of an important input. This limitation, however, is also present in index number models. In econometrics models, the presence of such outliers can be detected and the model may be adapted to deal with this situation. This limitation represents one of the types of misspecification problems discussed by Sexton, Silkman, and Hogan (1986). As explained by the authors, all estimation techniques are subject to errors and biases due to misspecification problems. However, because DEA is an extremal method, it is highly sensitive to data errors.

Another type of misspecification identified by Sexton, Silkman, and Hogan (1986) is variable selection. There are no set criteria for selecting the appropriate input and output factors in DEA models (Melao, 2005). The problem with this is that DEA does not identify causal relationships between the input and output variables in the analysis. And, it is not possible to determine the "strengths of different model specifications, because the calculated efficiency frontier perfectly explains the full set of extremal relationships under any specification" (p. 82). Then, how do you know if you are including relevant factors?

A related weakness is that DEA is sensitive to the number of inputs and outputs relative to the number of DMUs being analyzed (Melao, 2005), an issue referred to as discrimination. Specifically, the greater the number of outputs and inputs for a given set of DMUs, the greater the number of DMUs that are going to be classified as efficient (Coates and Lamdin, 2002). DEA is unable to discriminate in analyses where the number of DMUs is small relative to the number of input and output variables. Thus, Coates and Lamdin suggest that DEA models be kept simple and only variables that are truly distinct be included in the analysis.

Another discrimination-related problem in DEA analyses is its inability to provide information on price efficiency—that a particular DMU is producing the "socially optimum (most highly valued) output mix using the least-cost technologies" (Sexton, Silkman, and Hogan, 1986, p. 74). DEA only determines technical efficiency. That is, given its available technology, a DMU cannot reduce its inputs without reducing its outputs. This is an important consideration for governmental entities.

The advent of numerous DEA software packages and the development of models and extensions to the basic DEA model have greatly reduced some of the difficulties and limitations of DEA (see Melao, 2005, for a good discussion of this topic). Furthermore, Sherman (1984) suggested that complementing DEA analysis with other analytical techniques can ameliorate some of the weaknesses of DEA. One of those techniques is econometric-regression analysis. Regression analysis can help to validate DEA models in several ways including factor selection and corroboration of DEA findings (Hughes and Edwards, 2000; Lovell, Walters, and Wood, 1994; Thanassoulis, Dyson, and Foster, 1987; and others). Also, Cluster analysis has been used to address some of the discrimination problems (see for example Golany and Roll, 1994); and sensitivity analysis has been used to improve the robustness of the models (e.g., Charnes et al., 1985).

Finally, a different type of limitation has been highlighted by scholars in the field of public productivity. They argue that the technique is too technical, making it too difficult for the average person to interpret and understand the analysis (Hatry and Fisk, 1992). As a result, it requires a solid knowledge about linear programming (Nyhan and Marlowe, 1995). Although these criticisms have merit, they might be overstated. Indeed, all analytical approaches require knowledge about the formulation of the problem, choice of variables, data representation, interpretation of results, and limitations of the approach (Charnes, Cooper, Lewin, and Seiford, 1994). For example, using and interpreting econometric models requires a certain level of skill. The analyst needs to understand the concept of slope of a line, R-squares, betas, significance levels, etc.

34.3 EXAMPLES OF DEA APPLICATIONS

In this section we develop two examples of DEA using different software packages. Data envelopment analysis is applied to evaluating the performance of employees and high schools in a school district. A point of clarification is in order here. Although most of this chapter, and the literature in general, contains examples of performance assessment of individual entities (e.g., schools, hospitals, cities, baseball players, etc.), as demonstrated by Ellis (2006) DEA can also be applied to track the efficiency of one single unit over time. In such analyses, the DMUs are the years of observation.

An excellent free source of data for use with DEA is the DEA Dataset Repository of Portland State University and the University of Auckland at: http://www.etm.pdx.edu/dea/dataset/default. htm. The only requirement is that users login each time they use it. Creating an account is free of charge. Another source is Dr. Ali Emrouznejad's DEA web page (http://www.deazone. com/datasets/FILE1/index.asp). No account is required.

34.3.1 EVALUATING THE PERFORMANCE OF EMPLOYEES

The following example will illustrate the application of data envelopment analysis using a standard linear programming software (LINDO). We will assess the overall performance of DMUs using multiple inputs and delivering multiple outputs. The example consists of five employees in a hypothetical nonprofit agency offering social services. The outputs are number of visits and number of applications processed per day. The employees use five distinctive combinations of inputs, hours worked per week, and cost of supplies used. Table 34.1 summarizes the combination of outputs and inputs for each employee.

As mentioned earlier, to find the efficiency rating for each one of the employees using a standard linear programming package separate linear programming models have to be run. The model to be developed here will evaluate the relative efficiency of employee number 1 (EMP1). For this example we will use Model 2 shown in Appendix B. The goal is to maximize the outputs of the employees. Before going further with the example, here are some key linear programming terms that will allow us to better interpret the program formulation and results:

(a) Objective function: required to solve any linear programming model. In the present example the objective is to maximize outputs.
(b) Value: provides the values of the decision variables at the optimal solution. In our example, it shows the weights to be assigned to each input and output.
(c) Constraints: rule out possible combination of decision variables as feasible solutions.
(d) Feasible solution: a solution that satisfies all the constraints.
(e) Reduced cost: indicates how much the objective function coefficient of each decision variable would have to improve before it would be possible for the variable to assume a positive value in the optimal solution. For a maximization problem "improve" means get bigger; for a minimization problem it means get smaller.

TABLE 34.1

Input and Outputs of Employees

DMU	Emp1	Emp2	Emp3	Emp4	Emp5
Outputs					
Visits	25	35	45	25	25
Applications	10	10	15	10	15
Inputs					
Hours	40	35	40	35	40
Supplies	105	140	135	125	120

(f) Slack or surplus: in a problem having less-than or equal constraints it is the amount of unused resources. It is added to the left-hand side of a less-than-or-equal-to constraint to convert the constraint into an inequality.

(g) Dual prices: this is associated with a constraint and represents the improvement in the optimal value of the objective function per unit increase in the right-hand side of the constraint. In Model 2 of the DEA formulation it represents the proportion of the input/output levels of the peer employee going into the composite set.

Consistent with Model 2, our formulation for this problem is follows. The computer program will ask for the objective function. That is the first line of the problem formulation. Then, we are asked to enter the constraints.

Max 25 ua + 10 ub
Constrains:

1) 25 ua + 10 ub − 40 va − 105 vb <= 0
2) 35 ua + 10 ub − 35 va − 140 vb <= 0
3) 45 ua + 15 ub − 40 va − 135 vb <= 0
4) 25 ua + 10 ub − 35 va − 125 vb <= 0
5) 25 ua + 15 ub − 40 va − 120 vb <= 0
6) 40 va + 105 vb = 1
7) ua, ub, va, vb >= 0

where
  va = weight of input hours worked
  vb = weight of input cost of supplies
  ua = weight of output number of visits
  ub = weight of output applications processed

As mentioned above, the first line of the formulation is the objective function. Here the goal is to maximize the weighted sum of the outputs. The weights will be assigned by the program. Because the evaluation is for employee 1, the coefficients of the variables in the objective function are those of employee 1. Then, under the heading "Constraints," there are several constraint or condition. By specifying those conditions, DEA allows each DMU (employees) to select any possible set of weights that will present its efficiency in the best possible light (Tankersley, 1990). The specified conditions are

1. No weight can be negative
2. Each DMU must be allowed to use the same set of weights to evaluate its efficiency
3. ratios resulting from each of these separate evaluations must not exceed one

In this example DEA asks the employee under analysis to maximize efficiency subject to the set conditions. The efficiency ratio for this employee is forced into comparison with the efficiency ratio for each one of the other employees using the chosen input and output weights. It is in this manner that the relative efficiency of the unit under analysis is calculated. The solution of this DEA model is shown in Table 34.2. To confirm the solution, the analysis was also conducted using EMS, a noncommercial DEA software (see Appendix C).

34.3.1.1 Efficiency Rating

The efficiency rating is the proportion of inputs that a unit (employees, in this case) should use to achieve its output level and remain efficient as it is compared with other units. The efficiency rating

---

TABLE 34.2

Computer Solution of the Data Envelopment Analysis Employee 1 Model (Using LINDO)

Objective Function Value

0.8214286

Variable	Value	Reduced Cost
Visits	0.007143	0.000000
Processed	0.064286	0.000000
Hours	0.000000	6.190476
Supplies	0.009524	0.000000

Row	Slack or Surplus	Dual Prices
1	0.178571	0.000000
2	0.440476	0.000000
3	0.000000	0.416667
4	0.369048	0.000000
5	0.000000	0.250000
6	0.000000	0.000000
7	0.000000	0.000000

---

is printed as the value for the objective function. The objective function specifies the maximization of outputs. The DEA analysis of the efficiency of employee shows that he is only 82 percent efficient (0.8214286×100). That is, given his output level (25 hours of visits processed and 10 applications processed) he should only be using 82 percent of the amount of his available inputs (40 hours and $105 worth of supplies).

34.3.1.2 Weight/Value

The value of the weights assigned to each input and output by DEA is shown under the column marked Value. As can the observed, the weight for the output variable Visits is 0.007 and for the variable Applications be weight is 0.064286. If we substitute these weights into the objective function, the resulting value is approximately 0.82. For the input variables the weights are 0.00 for "hours" and 0.009524 for "applications."

34.3.1.3 Reduced Cost

Consistent with the definition of reduced cost provided earlier, in order for the variable Hours to have a positive value, its corresponding coefficient must be reduced by approximately 6.2 units. That is, the amount of hours used must be reduced by at least 6.2 hours before this variable can obtain a positive weight which would result in an improved objective function or higher efficiency rating.

34.3.1.4 Slack or Surplus

In this column DEA shows the percent of inputs that can be considered a surplus. That is, given his output level, the worker uses approximately 18 percent more inputs than he should. Notice that this percentage is the difference between 100 percent and the calculated efficiency rating for the DMU in question ($100 - 82 = 18$).

34.3.1.5 Dual Prices

This shows the efficient reference set or peer against which the particular employee is being compared. This simply means that DEA has identified a combination or composite employee which can obtain the same level of outputs with only a proportion of the inputs available to the employee under evaluation. The numbers under the dual price column represent the proportion of the input/output levels of the peer employee going into the virtual or best-practice DMU.

Thus, the composite employee derived by the model is made out of 41.7 percent of the input level used by employee number 3 and 25 percent of the input level used by employee number 5. Thus the composite employee uses 26.7 hours [(0.417 × 40 + (0.25 × 40)]; and $86.3 worth of supplies [(0.417 × 135) + (0.25 × 120)] to achieve the same level of outputs achieved by employee 1. The supervisor could use these numbers as performance targets for employee 1.

If specified, the computer solution will also print a sensitivity analysis. This would allow us to determine the amount by which the coefficients of the objective function could increase/decrease without changing the solution. It also provides ranges for the right-hand side of each of the constraints which would not change the solution.

34.3.2 EVALUATING THE PERFORMANCE OF SCHOOLS

This example is an analysis of the 1996 high school report cards of a school district in New Jersey (The *New York Times*, 1996). The analysis is only applicable to high schools within the particular district. For purpose of illustration, the analysis in this example was conducted by means of the commercially available Warwick-DEA software (now, Performance Improvement Management Software, http://www.deasoftware.co.uk/). A summary of the data used for this example is presented in Table 34.3 along with the efficiency scores and peer groups against which DEA compares each school. Only two inputs and two outputs were selected for inclusion in the analysis.

The input variables are

1. Student/faculty ratio (S/F RATIO)
2. Spending per pupil (SPENDING)

The output variables are:

1. High school proficiency test (HSPT)
2. Graduation rate (GRAD)

where
S/F RATIO is the ratio of students to full-time faculty members.
SPENDING is total school spending divided by the average daily enrollment.

TABLE 34.3
Data for Analysis of High Schools, Efficiency Ratings (EFF) and Peer Reference Set (PEER)

DMU	S/F RATIO	SPENDING	HSPT	GRAD	EFF (%)	PEER
HS1	13.5	8489	47.1	111.0	99.22	HS3
HS2	13.9	7493	65.6	97.1	98.33	HS3
HS3	9.8	7603	81.7	100.2	100	HS3
HS4	10.9	12256	73.8	99.7	89.46	HS3
HS5	10.1	12256	68.0	96.0	92.96	HS3
HS6	11.0	8255	83.1	98.1	93.68	HS3
HS7	10.4	10736	91.6	100.0	100	HS7
HS8	12.4	8730	44.2	101.2	87.23	HS3

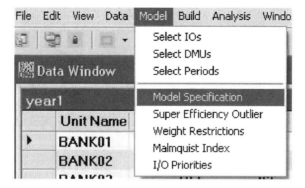

FIGURE 34.2 Sample screenshot of the performance improvement management DEA software. (From http://www. deasoftware.co.uk/ screenshots.asp?sc = Sc3_1.jpg.)

HSPT is the percentage of high school juniors who passed all three sections of the high school proficiency test (reading, mathematics and writing).

GRAD is the ratio of high school seniors who graduated by August 1996 to enrollment in October 1995. Because some seniors do not graduate with their original class, percentages may add to more than 100.

This Windows-based software does not require the analyst to elaborate the model as we did above using basic linear programming software. The analyst only has to input the data and use the dropdown window commands to run the analysis. Figure 34.2 is a picture of one of the screens users of the PIM software will see. The results of the analysis of the high school data indicate that of the eight high schools in the district only two high schools (HS3 and HS7) are efficient, with six others underperforming. Not shown in the table are the calculated weights and target performance.

34.4 CONCLUDING REMARKS

In this chapter we attempted to enlarge the repertoire of available techniques for those needing to make allocation decisions in the public sector. To that end, this chapter provided an overview of data envelopment analysis (DEA). The strengths and weaknesses of the technique were discussed in the context of two widely used approaches for decision making in the public sector—ratio analysis and regression analysis.

Under the right circumstances, DEA may be a preferred management tool. DEA analysis allows for the inclusion of multiple outputs and inputs, as well as nondiscretionary factors to derive an overall index of performance (efficiency in DEA jargon). When the models are well-specified, the results of the analysis can help direct managers' attention to inefficient DMUs and provide suggestions as to how best to allocate resources to improve performance.

As discussed here, DEA has several limitations. However, strategies have been developed to assist in overcoming these limitations. Those strategies include model expansions, an extensive availability of software, and showing ways for using DEA in conjunction with other techniques. Nevertheless, the concern about the lack of use of DEA by practitioners in the public sector remains. This lack of use can be blamed on the perceived technical complexity of this approach. Indeed, DEA may be best performed by an analyst trained in decision-making techniques. But the results can be presented in a parsimonious way so that anyone can understand what is going on. As suggested by some, more work needs to be done to continue to expose practitioners to the tremendous potential of the technique, and to teach them how to overcome the perceived technical difficulties (de Lancer Julnes, 2000; Berquist, 1996).

EXERCISES

1. Using a standard linear programming package: (1) calculate the efficiency ratings of all employees in the data set of Example 1 (Section 34.3); (2) determine the reference set (best practice) for each employee in the example.
2. Using any of the available free software (e.g., EMS, http://www.wiso.uni-dortmund.de/lsfg/or/scheel/ems/) answer the following questions regarding High School 1:
   (a) Given its graduation rate and the percentage of juniors who pass the high school, find the input reduction necessary for this DMU to become efficient.
   (b) What level of outputs should this DMU be producing at the given level of input to be considered efficient?

REFERENCES

Anderson, T. (1996). A data envelopment analysis homepage. http://www.etm.pdx.edu/dea/homedea.html.
Banker, R.D. and Morey, R. (1986). The use of categorical variables in data envelopment analysis, *Management Science 32*, 1613–1627.
Barr, R. (2004). DEA software tools and technology: A state-of-the-art survey (2004). In W.W. Cooper, L.M. Seiford, and J. Zhu (Eds.), *Handbook on Data Envelopment Analysis*, pp. 539–566. Boston: Kluwer Academic Publishers. Chapter available on-line at: http://faculty.smu.edu/barr/pubs/tr04–05.pdf.
Berquist, R. (1996). Audit risk analysis: An experiment using data envelopment analysis. *Internal Auditing 12*, 3–12.
Bessent, A.M. and Bessent, E.W. (1980). Determining comparative efficiency of schools through data envelopment analysis. *Educational Administration Quarterly 16*(2), 57–75.
Charnes, A., Cooper, W., and Rhodes, E. (1978). Measuring the efficiency of decision making units. *European Journal of Operational Research 2*, 429–444.
Charnes, A., Cooper, W., and Rhodes, E. (1981). Evaluating program and managerial efficiency: An application of data envelopment analysis to program follow through. *Management Science 27*, 668–697.
Charnes, A., Cooper, W., Lewin, Morey, R., and Rousseau, J. (1985). Sensitivity and Stability Analysis in DEA, *Annals of Operations Research 2*, 139–156.
Charnes, A., Cooper, W., Lewin, A., and Seiford, L. (1994). *Data Envelopment Analysis, Theory, Methodology and Applications*. Boston: Kluwer Academic Publishers.
Chilingerian, J.A. (1994). Exploring why some physician's hospital practices are more efficient: Taking DEA inside the hospital. In A. Charnes, W. Cooper, A.Y. Lewin, and L. Seiford (Eds.), *Data Envelopment Analysis, Theory, Methodology and Applications*, pp. 167–193, Boston: Kluwer Academic Publishers.
Coates, D.C. and Lamdin (2002). School performance evaluation using data envelopment analysis. *Public Finance and Management 2*(4), 566–591.
Cooper, W., Seiford, L., and Tone, K., (2000). *Data Envelopment Analysis: A Comprehensive Text with Models, Applications, References and DEA-Solver Software*. Boston: Kluwer Academic Publishers.
de Lancer Julnes, P. (2000). Decision-making tools for public productivity improvement: A comparison of DEA to cost–benefit and regression analyses. *Journal of Public Budgeting, Accounting & Financial Management 12*(4), 625–648.
Diewert, W. and Mendoza, M. (1995). Data envelopment analysis: A practical alternative? Department of Economics. University of British Columbia. Vancouver. Discussion Paper No: DP 95–30.
Ellis, P.M. (2006). Measuring organizational efficiency with data envelopment analysis: The Horance Mann insurance company. In K.D. Lawrence and R.K. Klimberg (Eds.), *The Applications of Management Science: In Productivity, Finance, and Operations*. New York: JAI Press.
Golany, B. and Roll, Y. (1994). Incorporating standards via data envelopment analysis. In A. Charnes, W. Cooper, A.Y. Lewin, and L. Seiford (Eds.) *Data Envelopment Analysis, Theory, Methodology and Applications*, pp. 313–328, Boston: Kluwer Academic Publishers.
Harry, P. and Fisk, D. (1992). Measuring productivity in the public sector. In M. Holzer (Ed.), *Public Productivity Handbook*, New York: Marcel Dekker, pp. 139–160.

Huang, Z., Li, S., and Zhu, J. (2005). A special issue on data envelopment analysis: Theories and applications. In Honor of William W. Cooper. *International Journal of Information Technology and Decision Making* 4(3), 311–316.

Hughes, P. and Edwards, M. (2000). Leviathan vs. Lilliputian: A Data Envelopment Analysis of Government Efficiency. *Journal of Regional Science* 40(4), 649–669.

Lovell, C.A., Walters, L.C., and Wood, L.L. (1994). Stratified models of education production using modified DEA and regression analysis. In A. Charnes, W. Cooper, A.Y. Lewin, and L. Seiford (Eds.), *Data Envelopment Analysis, Theory, Methodology and Applications*, pp. 329–352, Boston: Kluwer Academic Publishers.

Lewin, A.Y., Morey, R.C., and Cook, T.J. (1982). Evaluating the administrative efficiency of courts. *Omega* 10, 401–411.

Melao, N. (2005). Data envelopment analysis revisited: A neophyte's perspective. *International Journal of Management and Decision Making* 6(2), 158–179.

Neter, J., Kutner, M.H., Nachtsheim, C., and Wasserman, W. (1996). *Applied Linear Statistical Models*, 4th ed. McGraw-Hill/Irwin.

Nyhan, R. and Marlowe, H. (1995). Performance measurement in the public sector, *Public Productivity and Management Review*, *18*, 333–348.

Nunamaker, T. (1983). Measuring Routine Nursing Service Efficiency: A Comparison of Cost Per Patient Day and Data Envelopment Analysis Models. *Health Services Research 18*, 183–205.

Rossi, P.H. and Freeman, H.E. (1982). Evaluation: A systematic approach, CA: SAGE.

Seiford, L. and Thrall, R.M. (1990). Recent developments in DEA: The mathematical programming approach to fronteir analysis, *Journal of Econometrics 46*, 7–38.

Sexton, T.R. (1986). The methodology of data envelopment analysis. In R.H. Silkman (Ed.), *Measuring Efficiency: An Assessment of Data Envelopment Analysis*, pp. 7–29, New Directions for Program Evaluation. Wiley, Inc., San Francisco.

Sexton, T.R., Silkman, R.H, and Hogan, A.J. (1986). Data Envelopment Analysis: Critique And Extensions. In R.H. Silkman (Ed.), *Measuring Efficiency: An Assessment of Data Envelopment Analysis*, pp. 73–105. New Directions for Program Evaluation. Wiley, Inc., San Francisco.

Sherman, H.D. (1984). Hospital efficiency measurement and evaluation. Empirical test of a new technique. *Medical Care 22(10)*, 922–938.

Stokey, E. and Zeckhauser, R. (1978). *A Primer for Policy Analysis*. Norton: New York.

Tankersley, W. (1990). The effects of organizational control structure and process on organizational performance, Ph.D. Dissertation, Florida State University, Tallahassee.

Thanassoulis, E., Dyson, R., and Foster, M. (1987). Relative efficiency assessments using data envelopment analysis: application to data on rates departments. *Journal of the Operational Research Society 38*, 397–411.

The *New York Times*, New Jersey Section (1996). Comparing the districts: The '96 high school report cards, December, 8. pp. 8, 10.

Tseng, M. (1990). Efficiency comparison of nursing homes: An application of data envelopment analysis, Ph.D. Dissertation, University of Alabama: Birmingham.

Watson, C.P. Billingsley, D. Croft., and Huntsberger, D. (1993). *Statistics for Management and Economics*, 5th ed. Allyn and Bacon: Boston.

Appendix A: Examples of Applications of DEA

- For examples of the application of DEA in education see Bessent, A. M., and Bessent, E., supra: Bessent, A.M., Bessent, E., Clark, T.C., and Garrett, A.W. (1987), Managerial efficiency measurement in school administration, *National Forum of Educational Administration Journal*, *3*, 56–66; Desai A. and Schinnar, A.P. (1990), Issues in measuring scholastic improvement due to compensatory education programs, *Economic Planning Sciences*, *24*(2), 143–153.
- For examples using DEA in hospital and physician evaluation see Chilingerian, J.A. (1994). Exploring why some physicians' hospital practices are more efficient: Taking DEA inside the hospital, in Charnes, A., Cooper, W.W., Lewin, A.Y., and Seiford, L.M. (Eds.), *Data Analysis: Theory, Methodology, and Applications*, Boston: Kluwer Academic Publishers; Sherman, H.D. (1988). *Service Organization Productivity*. The Society of Management Accountants of Canada: Hamilton. Ontario.
- In court systems see Lewin, A.Y., Morey, R.C., and Cook, T.J. (1982), Evaluating the Administrative Efficiency of Courts, *Omega 10*, 401–441.
- For analysis of police services see Nyhan, R.C. and Martin, L.L. (Winter 1999), Assessing the performance of municipal police services using data envelopment analysis: An exploratory study, *State and Local Government Review 31*(1), 18–30.
- In nursing services see Chattopadhyay, K. (1991), Economics of nursing home care in Connecticut: Financing, cost and efficiency, Ph.D. dissertation, University of Connecticut: Connecticut.
- For the use of DEA in the evaluation of the efficiency of highway maintenance see the work of Cook, W., Roll, Y., and Kazakov, A. (1990). A DEA Model for Measuring the Relative Efficiency of Highway Maintenance Patrols, *INFOR 28*(2), 113–124; Cook, W., Roll, Y., Seiford, L., and Kazakov, A. (1991). Data Envelopment Approach to Measuring Efficiency: Case Analysis of Highway Maintenance Patrols, *Journal of Socio-Economics 20*(1), 83–103.
- In Banking and other financial applications see Ferrier, G.D. and Lovell, C.A. (1990), Measuring cost efficiency in banking: Econometrics and linear programming evidence, *Journal of Econometrics*, *46*, 229–245; Giokas, D.I. (1991), Bank branch operating efficiency: A comparative application of DEA and the log linear modeal, *Omega, 19*(6): 549–557; and Basso, A. and Funari, S. (2001), A data envelopment analysis approach to measure the mutual fund performance, *European Journal of Operational Research*, *135*(3), 477–492.

Appendix B: Mathematical Models

MODEL 1

$$\max \frac{\sum\limits_{r} u_r y_{r0}}{\sum\limits_{i} v_i x_{i0}}$$

subject to

$$\frac{\sum\limits_{r} u_r y_{rj}}{\sum\limits_{i} v_i x_{i0}} \leq 1 \quad \text{for } j = 0, \cdots, n$$

$$\frac{u_r}{\sum\limits_{i} v_i x_{i0}} \geq e \quad \text{for } r = 1, \ldots, s$$

$$\frac{v_i}{\sum\limits_{i} v_i x_{i0}} \geq 1 \quad \text{for } i = 1, \ldots, m$$

where
u_r = weight for output "r"
v_i = weight for input "i"
$y_{rj'}$ = observed value of output "r" for DMU j'
$X_{ij'}$ = observed value of input "i" for DMU j'
ε = non-Archimedean infinitesimal appears in the primal objective function and as a lower
  bound for the multipliers in the dual. This constants value is often set at 10^{-6}

The next model, model 2, is the equivalent linear programming formulation of the fractional programming problem presented in model 1.

MODEL 2

$$\max_{UV} \omega_0 \sum\limits_{r} u_r y_{r0}$$

subject to

$$\sum\limits_{i} v_i x_{i0} = 1$$

$$\sum_r ur y_{rj} \sum_i v_i x_{ij} \leq 0$$

$$u_r \geq \varepsilon$$

$$y_{rj} \geq \varepsilon$$

The LP dual problem for Model 2 is as follows:

$$\min_{\theta, \lambda, s_r+, s_i-} z = \theta - \varepsilon \sum_r s_r^+ - \sum_i s_i^-$$

subject to

$$\sum_j \lambda_j Y_j - s^+ = Y_0$$

$$\theta X_0 - \sum \lambda_j X_j - s^- = 0$$

$$\lambda_j, s_r^+, s_i \geq 0$$

where

θ = a scalar variable, the proportional reduction applied to all inputs of DMUo (the DMU being evaluated) to improve efficiency

s^+, s^- = slack variables

Appendix C: Available DEA Software

1. Available free of charge or at little cost
   - DEA Excel Solver. Available at: www.deafrontier.com
   - DEAP, Version 2.1. Available at: www.uq.edu.au/economics/cepa/software.htm
   - EMS: Efficiency Measurement System, Version 1.3. Available at: www.wiso.uni-dortmund.de/lsfg/or/scheel/ems
   - PIONEER, Version 2.0. Available at: http://faculty.smu.edu/barr/pioneer/
2. Available for purchase
   - DEA-Solver-Pro,Version 4.0. Available at: http://www.saitech-inc.com/index.asp
   - Frontier Analyst, Version 3.1.5. Available at: www.banxia.com
   - OnFront, Version 2.02. Available at: www.emq.com
   - Performance Improvement Management DEA software. Available at: www.deasoftware.co.uk/index.htm

35 Content Analysis

Chieh-Chen Bowen and William M. Bowen

CONTENTS

35.1 INTRODUCTION

Content analysis is a technique for analyzing a body of text. It treats the elements of the body of text as empirical entities. It establishes and documents aspects of their characteristics and the relationships between them. In doing so, it enables investigators to ask and systematically answer research questions about the manner in which the ideas and information contained in that body are conceived or expressed. The elements may be words, idioms, sentences, paragraphs, articles, papers, or similar units of text comprising a larger body.

Content analysis is based upon an explicit sequence of steps with which to systematically organize elements of text so as to enable an investigator to meaningfully interpret and make inferences about the patterns in the content of the overall body. These steps include identifying the relevant body of text, stipulating a classification schema to use in analyzing that text, classifying individual units of text in terms of the schema, applying consistency tests to ensure that the units are consistently interpreted and assigned to a class within the schema, and finally making inferences about patterns found in the overall body. When these steps are followed and their results carefully documented, they can lead to rationally justified and systematic inferences about the congruence of the classification schema in relation to the message or messages contained in the overall body of text. In the end, the patterns identified in the overall body of text can be used for many purposes including making inferences about antecedents to the content of the text, describing and making inferences about the characteristics of the text, and making inferences about what actions might follow from the messages contained within the text (Holsti, 1969).

A wide variety of different types of questions can be answered with content analysis. For example, it can be used to identify themes in a body of text, or to describe the frequency of terms or to examine the relationship between terms, or to gauge the value orientations behind the documents. One example of using content analysis to describe and make inferences about the characteristics of a body of text can be drawn from one of the authors' experiences. He was hired into a public administration faculty position after having completed a master of public administration degree and a doctorate in regional analysis and planning. Upon accepting the position, he was told that some members of the faculty search committee had initially objected to hiring him into the position because, given that his doctorate was in a field other than public administration, he was probably not sufficiently attuned with the mainstream theoretical and substantive concerns within the field. It was evidently argued that he did not "belong" to the field and therefore should not be hired into the program. Not wanting to remain in a position in which he did not belong, he, therefore, with the cooperation of a similarly situated colleague, did a topical content analysis of a random sample of 50 years worth of articles from *Public Administration Review* (PAR) (Bingham and Bowen, 1994).

The stated purpose of the content analysis of PAR was to identify and characterize the "mainstream" theoretical and substantive concerns in the field. The private purpose was to assess empirically whether he "belonged" to the field. Accordingly, the first step was to stipulate a topical classification schema with which to describe and differentiate between PAR articles in terms of the various subfields of public administration. This schema was inferred from a review of a set of prominent introductory public administration textbooks. It was made up of the following fourteen categories: (1) government and organizational behavior, (2) public management, (3) human resources, (4) budgeting and finance, (5) program evaluation and planning, (6) introspection, (7) testimonials, (8) decision making, (9) intergovernmental relations, (10) ethics, (11) management science and technology, (12) public policy analysis, (13) implementation, and (14) administrative law. The categories were thought to cover the range of scholarship contained in PAR. In other words, having thoroughly reviewed the introduction to public administration texts, both investigators thought that each and every article within PAR could be meaningfully assigned to one of the fourteen categories. Once both investigators agreed upon the overall schema, and upon the characteristic features of the articles that would be assigned to each of the constituent categories, they were ready to read and classify the articles. Each investigator reviewed each of 240 articles randomly selected from 52 volumes of PAR articles and they independently assigned each article to the appropriate category. Once this was done the level of agreement between the investigators in terms of their classifications (inter-rater reliability) was calculated using techniques described below. The inter-rater reliability of the classifications to categories was found to be high enough to ensure that the study would be replicable by other investigators. In other words, the level of intersubjective agreement between investigators was found to be adequate to justify a belief that the inferences made from the analysis were reliable reflections of the intrinsic content of the articles rather than descriptions of any idiosyncratic psychological tendencies of the investigators. Analysis of the distribution of articles across categories clearly showed that introductory public administration textbooks tend to cover a much broader range of topics and to embrace a considerably broader vision of the field of public administration than do the articles published in PAR. Given that the author's research, teaching interests and background fit foursquare within the broader vision, but not the narrower one, it thus became evident that the question as to whether or not the author belongs in public administration depends at least in part upon one's vision of the field.

The conventional treatments and courses on data analysis in public administration do not, in the authors' view, give content analysis enough attention for beginners at empirical investigation to fully grasp the elementary ideas involved, much less the proper applications of these techniques in real world settings. As a consequence there is a widespread lack of appreciation among both scholars and practitioners in public administration with respect to the enormous potential for innovation and practical applications of these empirical data analysis techniques. To help ensure adequate background knowledge, the following sections consider a few basic ideas about the technique. They also stipulate and illustrate step-by-step instructions on how to conduct such analyses and then an actual study is presented at the end of this chapter.

35.2   ELEMENTS OF CONTENT ANALYSIS

Content analysis is a dynamic technique for making inferences about the content of recorded text. Such content is composed of elements that, in the vernacular, are referred to as "sign-vehicles." The term "sign-vehicle" refers to the units of content of the recorded text containing the particular information or signal of interest in the investigation (word, symbol, theme, story, article, or other product of intellectual activity). The technique is dynamic in the sense that the definitions of content analysis have changed over time with technical innovations and application of the tool itself to new problems and types of materials.

A couple of representative definitions are as follows:

> "Content analysis" may be defined as referring to any technique a) for the classification of the sign-vehicles, b) which relies solely upon the judgments (which theoretically may range from perceptual discriminations to sheer guesses) of an analyst or group of analysts as to which sign-vehicles fall into which categories, c) on the basis of explicitly formulated rules, d) provided that the analyst's judgments are regarded as the reports of a scientific observer. (Janis, 1949, p. 55)

> Content analysis is a phase of information-processing in which communication content is transformed, through objective and systematic application of categorization rules, into data that can be summarized and compared (Paisley, 1969).

In the early stages of development, content analysis was considered to be a simple descriptive tool. Later, it was developed into an inferential tool through the creation of techniques that transformed the sign-vehicles into comparable data. In this chapter, content analysis is considered broadly as a scientific data analysis technique which has the following characteristics:

a. Systematic inclusion and exclusion of relevant sign-vehicles regardless of the researcher's personal preferences or psychological tendencies.
b. Each step in the research process is carried out on the basis of explicitly formulated rules.
c. The findings of the content analysis have theoretical or general relevance.*

When an analysis of text exhibits these characteristics, it may be considered to be a content analysis. As such, it may, among other things, be used to generate rationally justified indicators that point to the state of beliefs, values, ideologies, or other aspects of the cultural or linguistic system reflected in the body of text (Weber, 1985).

Content analysis entails reducing data by classifying many words into far fewer categories. The degree of difficulty of this data reduction process depends largely on the content unit chosen by the investigator. It is usually easier to classify smaller content units (i.e., words or phrases) into categories than larger ones (i.e., themes, paragraphs, or articles). This is because larger content units contain more information and greater topical variety. They therefore afford a greater chance of providing conflicting or ambiguous cues. If, for instance, the sign-vehicles are words, there tends to be fewer interpretations (and misinterpretations) of each than if they are sentences, and correspondingly less ways to invoke error or disagreement in assignment. Similarly, there are fewer feasible ways to interpret sentences than paragraphs, and fewer ways to interpret paragraphs than entire papers. Thus, as the size of the sign-vehicle increases, the probability that two or more investigators will independently assign it to the same category is likely to decrease. A clearly defined and precise coding process is thus one of the first steps toward successfully dealing with this difficulty.

---

* This third characteristic implies that the investigator using content analysis to answer a research question does so within the context of a larger research design.

35.2.1 THE REQUIREMENTS OF SYSTEM, OBJECTIVITY, AND GENERALITY

In general, careful attention is required to ensure that a content analysis meets requirements of system, objectivity, and generality. These requirements function to give discipline to and ensure the systematicity of the reasoning processes behind inferences about the characteristics of the body of text. The validity, credibility, and coherence of those inferences depend upon the way reason is systematically used to organize and think through the nexus of relationships between the sign-vehicles, on one hand, and the way the sign-vehicles are classified, organized, and analyzed on the other. Important considerations include the thoroughness with which the information used in the analysis is documented, the soundness of the logic used in the evidential reasoning processes, and the clarity with which the resulting intellectual products are communicated. The requirements of system, objectivity, and generality help enable these aspects of the analysis to be disciplined and systematic. When followed conscientiously, they serve to help guide the inductive reasoning processes beyond simply describing the text, to provide a blueprint from which to determine the appropriate methodology for generalizing beyond the sign-vehicles, and to corroborate the resulting inferences on the basis of abstraction.

35.2.1.1 The Requirement of System

Content analysis requires the investigator to make explicit and to document those aspects of the body of text upon which the validity, credibility, and meaning of the analysis depend. At a minimum, every content analysis should include answers to the following six questions (Krippendorff, 2004):

1. Which data is analyzed? In the previous example of the content analysis of PAR, for instance, the investigators decided to analyze the content of 50 years worth of PAR articles. An example will be given below in which the investigator analyzed personnel advertisements found in two months worth of editions of the three largest newspapers in Taiwan. In that example, the data was the personnel advertisements in those newspapers.
2. How is the data defined? In the PAR example, the elements of the analysis were defined to be individual articles. In the newspaper example below, the elements are individual job advertisements.
3. What is the population from which they are drawn? In the PAR example, the population was made up of scholarly publications within the field of public administration. In the newspaper example below, the population is made up of all job advertisements in Taiwan. Ultimately, the job advertisements were considered to represent aspects of the personnel selection processes in Taiwan.
4. What is the context relative to which they are analyzed? In the PAR example, the context was one of the delineating some boundaries on the field of public administration. In the following newspaper example, the context will be one of the characterizing sexually biased hiring practices in Taiwan.
5. What are the boundaries of the analysis? This is a matter of determining what is irrelevant with respect to the context. Thus, in the PAR example, among other irrelevancies, other academic fields besides public administration were irrelevant. In the newspaper example, other ads were irrelevant.
6. What is the target of the inferences? In the PAR example, the target was to answer the question as to how empirically to define the field of public administration scholarship. In the newspaper example, the target is to provide clear and explicit documentation regarding the sexually biased hiring practices in Taiwan.

When these questions are answered clearly and explicitly, one of the effects is to enhance an investigator's ability to reason systematically through the relationships between the concepts embodied in the research questions, the sign-vehicles within the text of interest, and the answers he or she gives to those questions. It also enhances the investigator's ability to clearly and meaningfully communicate the results of the analysis. These enhancements are achieved partially as a consequence of purging the investigator's internalized and unarticulated beliefs and misguided presuppositions from the thought processes used in answering the research question. They are also achieved partially as a consequence of documenting and making explicit any information and judgments the investigator uses and makes while in the process of doing the analysis. For instance, one of the effects of documenting exactly which sign-vehicles are assigned to which categories is to help establish the possibility that other investigators might independently replicate the analysis and come to the same, or very similar, conclusions. In turn, this makes validation possible and gives credibility to the inferences drawn from the analysis.

The requirement of system stipulates that the answers to the above questions must be given clearly so that the purpose, methods, and limitations on the analysis are explicit. Furthermore, to analyze the text, the elements (sign-vehicles) must be perceived. This perception will inevitably be different in some degree for different observers and even a single observer may perceive it in different ways at different times. Thus, for a content analysis to be meaningful (in the sense that it refers to elements and structures that actually inhere within the text, and not merely to the idiosyncratic psychological characteristics and tendencies projected into it by the observer or observers), the system used to analyze the text must be made explicit and documented. In turn, this implies that the categories within the schema must be clearly defined. The procedures used to assign particular sign-vehicles to categories must be made consistently and in such a manner that enables shared understandings. The language used to support communication about the investigator's evidential reasoning process must be high quality. The language must enable a tight, high-quality connection between the schema, the sign-vehicles, the assignments of sign-vehicles to categories, and the data analysis used by the investigator, on one hand, and the understanding of the whole process by others who evaluate it, on the other. Unless the requirement of system is met, the analysis cannot be meaningfully evaluated, and in turn intercoder agreement upon it cannot possibly be reached. Without meeting this requirement, a content analysis thus cannot be considered scientific.

The requirement of system establishes the possibility to verify the content analysis based on a standard of substantial intersubjective agreement within the relevant scientific community. Intersubjective agreement means that the way one person within the community organizes and understands the relevant sign-vehicles in his or her mind is very similar to, if not identical with, the way others organize and understand them. Note that the standard here is "substantial" agreement rather than "perfect" agreement. Perfect intersubjective agreement upon a content analysis would require that the relationships between all pairs of sign-vehicles in the mind of the investigator would map uniquely into the relationships between all pairs of sign-vehicles in the mind of the reviewer or evaluator of the study.* Because in practice perfect mappings of this sort are not normally feasible, therefore, only "substantial" agreement is expected. The requirement of system is thus fulfilled in proportion to the degree to which the investigator is able to construct and communicate the analysis of the text in such a way as to enable replication of the entire analysis, from start to finish, by competent reviewers. This, in turn, establishes the possibility of the substantial intersubjective agreement upon which scientific validation depends.

In effect, when doing a content analysis, an investigator explicitly specifies the source of his or her content, carefully encodes this body of content, and then categorizes the textual information according to a certain theoretical framework. In turn, the theoretical framework guides the data

---

* Perfect intersubjective agreement would occur if the structure of the sign-vehicles in the mind of one person were to map uniquely into their structure in the mind of another person. Technically, this would occur if groups of sign-vehicles were to map homomorphically from one person's mind to the other. Mathematically, let A_1 and A_2 be groups of sign-vehicles with relations O_1 and O_2, respectively. A mapping K from G_1 to G_2 is a homomorphism if $K(O_1(x,y)) = O_2(K(x),K(y))$ for all x and y in G_1.

analysis and provides a meaningful reading of the content under scrutiny. Accordingly, there is no absolutely "true" content analysis of any given body of text. Many different content analyses of any such body may be feasible. Any one of these may be adequate for answering any given question an investigator might ask about the content of that body. But none of them will be adequate for answering all such questions. The objective of the analysis is thus not to proclaim "the truth" about the text, but rather to answer questions about it in an explicit and systematic way that makes possible substantial agreement about the answers within the scientific community. It is also to provide credibility to the inferences drawn from the analysis, especially in the face of critical scrutiny.

An important aspect of the system requirement has to do with the decisions made regarding inclusion of relevant sign-vehicles and exclusion of irrelevant ones. After the rules have been stipulated for separating the body of text to be analyzed from the rest of the universe, they must be strictly adhered to. This facilitates consistency and communication, and helps protect against bias. This is particularly valuable in an era of information overflow, in which a subjectively biased investigator could, perhaps unwittingly, find enough written materials to conduct a quantitative study to support his or her preconceived beliefs about almost anything.

Content analysis is often based upon sampling rules which, when properly applied, minimize (if not completely eliminate) the possibility that only those sign-vehicles supporting the investigator's predispositions are admitted as evidence. For instance, in the aforementioned topical content analysis of PAR, a random sample of articles was selected. This sort of sampling rule guides the investigator's decisions in the process of delimiting the analysis. Often the first such decision is how to take a potentially tremendous volume of text related to any given topic and reduce it to an analytically manageable one. There are rarely clear and universally applicable normative criteria to systematically identify the most important sources of text in a way that avoids the unconscious, subjective, or other prejudices of the investigator. Failure to recognize and control such prejudices clearly poses a threat to the validity of any inferences drawn from a content analysis. Nevertheless, there are ways to minimize it. For one, sampling rules might prescribe use of pooled experts' judgments about the relevant material. For another, the investigator might use some quantitative criterion to select sources of text such as using three newspapers with largest circulation as sources of classified job ads in Bowen's (2003) content analysis of classified job ads.

35.2.1.2 The Requirement of Objectivity

There are different ways to view the objectivity requirements of content analysis. One view stipulates that objectivity is achieved if the characteristics of the investigators do not determine any of the main features of the analysis. Another (weaker but more easily achievable) view stipulates that objectivity is achieved if the analysis enables substantial intersubjective agreement within the relevant scientific community in terms of the reliability and reproducibility of the analysis. One way or the other, the objectivity requirement in content analysis stipulates that each step in the analytic process must be carried out on the basis of explicitly formulated and replicable rules and procedures. What categories are to be used and what criteria are to be used in evaluating the sufficiency of these categories? What criteria are to be used to evaluate the rules and procedures used to assign sign-vehicles to them? Exactly how, in terms of what explicit and definite characteristics, are sign-vehicles that belong to category A to be distinguished from those that belong to category B? Regardless of how one views objectivity as such, the objectivity requirement implies that these and other decisions made in the course of the analysis must be made as impartially as possible and must be guided by a systematic, clearly stated, and explicit set of rules designed to minimize the possibility that the findings reflect more of the investigator's subjective predispositions than the content of the text under analysis.

The requirement of objectivity stipulates that if the process of doing a content analysis is designed appropriately and conducted well, any inferences regarding the text should refer completely to matters of fact about structures that would be found within sign vehicles in the body of text. They should be highly consistent and would be found by any intelligent investigators who know and understand the method and carefully follow the same procedures. Any skepticism about them should not refer in any substantial way to the thinking of the particular investigators who conducted the particular study under scrutiny. If matters of fact rather than the thinking of the investigators are the only substantial sources of uncertainty, the inferences can be warranted as being valid. Determination of such is a matter of whether or not the investigators, in the process of reasoning about the body of text, make sufficient reference to the appropriate content analytic principles for observation, inference, analysis, and communication so that the inferences are made to reliably represent structures found within the corresponding text.

One important fact to remember is that one of the primary aims of a content analysis is to make intelligible and valid inferences about the body of text. This means that a rational evaluator other than the investigator must be able to recognize and clearly and correctly comprehend the way the analysis was conducted and the structure of the body of text was constructed by the investigator. In turn, this is necessary for purposes of establishing the possibility of replicating the analysis independently. Validation of scientific inferences rests in principle upon the possibility of replication of the investigation independently of the investigator. Thus, unless replication of a content analysis is feasible, it is not possible to validate that content analysis. The possibility of replication is ensured by a host of factors including use of sound sampling procedures, stipulation of clear and explicit analytic rules, training the investigators, use of two or more investigators for coding the sign-vehicles, use of pretests, requiring investigators to work independently on coding the sign-vehicles, and proper computation of levels of intercoder reliability.

Another aim in doing a content analysis is to determine on the basis of replicable observation and independent analysis, the strength of the inferences with respect to the body of text. The question is: do the inferences reflect the sign-vehicles and structures of sign-vehicles that would be found by any careful and conscientious investigator who understands the system (and the language) and who makes an intelligent and careful effort to minimize the effects of any subjective or arbitrary factors on the inferences?*

35.2.1.3 The Requirement of Generality

The requirement of generality stipulates that after the investigator has made inferences from a content analysis, there must be a good answer to the question of "so what?" In other words, for a content analysis to be coherent it must be possible to generalize in some degree from the analysis. The answer to the so what question may be given either in terms of theory or practice. For instance, content analysis may be based upon a theoretical perspective and used to test a theory or to do hypothesis testing. That is, it may be used to test the predictions of a theory. For instance, the purpose of Bowen's (2003) content analysis of personnel classified job ads was to test dual labor market theory by examining the employment opportunities for men in comparison to women. In this case, the answer to the so what question would be given in terms of that theory. But a content analysis need not have explicit theoretical underpinnings. It may be used to foster future research and theory building effort by collecting data on a communication form. Or it may be used simply to help interpret and gain insight into a phenomenon. Content analysis of newspaper articles from a foreign country could, for instance, be used by individuals within the Central Intelligence Agency to gain insight into the prevailing concerns among the public in that country. Such an analysis would have no explicit theoretical underpinnings but could nevertheless meet the requirement of generality. That is, it could have implications not for theory but instead for practice. But regardless of

---

* Note that one's conception of objectivity depends heavily upon the prior assumptions one makes about how to characterize the coupling between the human mind, the environment, and their interactions. Accordingly, in some views, the determination of objectivity cannot be separated from the purpose for which the analysis was designed and used (Dewey, 1958; Quine, 1960). But regardless of one's view, the attainment of objectivity is necessary for scientific validation.

whether the answer to the so what question goes to theory or practice, a coherent content analysis requires a good answer.

The requirement of generality stipulates that a content analysis will only be coherent if it leads to some implications beyond the analysis. Even if the reasoning process used to construct the inferences meets high standards of system and objectivity, unless the inferences have theoretical or general relevance they will not meet the requirement of generality.

Adherence to the requirements of system, objectivity and generality does not guarantee that a content analysis will disclose the reality contained in the text. But then, there are no requirements of any scientific methods that can ever guarantee certainty. Instead, these requirements provide normative guidance for making the content of bodies of text rationally intelligible. If they are strictly adhered to, they help to guarantee that inferences about the text will be the result of well-documented, explicitly rationalized and disciplined, long and deep logical chain of reasoning based upon a replicable method of analysis. In this respect, they help to marshal good reasons for authorizing and justifying inferences about the content of the text. When all is said and done, rational justification for inferences about the content of bodies of text can be of considerable power and usefulness.

35.2.2 NECESSARY STEPS FOR DESIGNING A CODING SCHEMA

A carefully conceptualized and well-designed coding schema is a prerequisite to a successful content analysis. After the investigator has identified the relevant theories, found the important questions, and made the sampling decisions, the next step is to design a coding schema. There are a series of necessary steps for designing a coding schema (Weber, 1985).

First, one defines the coding units. There are six coding units commonly employed:

a. word, simply recording every word,
b. word sense usually referred as a semantic unit such as idioms or proper nouns,
c. sentence, recording meaning of the entire sentence,
d. theme, the definition of a theme as a unit of text has no more than one each of the following elements: the perceiver, the agent of action, the action, the target of the action, and the situation,
e. paragraph, and
f. whole text.

Larger units contain more information or potential conflicting information than smaller units and may require more subjective judgment of the individual coders, so it is usually more difficult to achieve high intercoder reliability when coding larger units than when coding smaller units. There is a trade-off, however. Larger units require less effort in the coding process and make the size of the coding load more manageable. No one single coding unit is necessarily better than another in every case. Rather, the investigator needs to consider the purpose of the study, the available time, and resources to make the most suitable choice of coding units.

Having defined the coding units, the investigator must next define the categories. The most important consideration in defining categories is to make sure that the definitions of the categories are collectively exhaustive and mutually exclusive with respect to the population or target of generalization. In other words, the categories should exhaust the entire range of settings, people, situations, or systems to which the inferences are expected to generalize, should do so in a way that is maximally congruent with the divisions inherent within this range, and each coding unit should be able to be assigned to one and only one category. The choices of category should if at all possible be theory-guided.

One way to create a satisfactory coding schema is to make sure that the investigator is already familiar with results of previous studies, currently sampled materials, and relevant theories when creating the coding schema. The next step is to conduct a pilot test on the coding schema.

This involves selecting a small proportion of the text and carefully going through the coding schema. Pilot testing not only provides a chance to clear any potential ambiguity in the category definitions but it also leads to insights in terms of revising the classification rules.

The pilot test allows the investigator to assess the reliability of the entire coding process before doing any further analysis on the data. It may be found that the coding schema is unreliable, in which case the schema needs to be changed or else the results of content analysis will not be credible. The pilot test also enables the investigator to revise the coding rules as needed. If the reliability of the coding rules is low, then they must be revised. Studies show that clarity on the coding schema increases measurement reliability in content analysis even more than does coder training. In other words, the reliability of untrained coders using clearly defined coding rules is higher than trained coders using ambiguous coding rules. After the revisions are made, the next step for the investigator is to do another pilot test and make further revisions until the coders reach sufficient reliability. Once coder reliability is deemed on the basis of the pilot tests to be adequate, the investigator is ready to code all the text.

After all the text has been coded, the final reliability should be assessed. Clear defined coding rules and coder training do not guarantee a high reliability. Factors such as fatigue, subtle cognitive shifts, mood changes, or simple carelessness of coders may still lead to unreliability. The rule is to never assume high reliability of all coded text until statistical assessment has been performed and sufficient evidence has been gathered. The advance of technology allows computers to replace human coders to do the coding. However, the principles applied to human coders still are applicable to the design of computer procedures before computers can do the coding reliably.

35.2.3 RELIABILITY OF THE CONTENT CODING PROCESS

As is the case with all analyses of data, the accuracy of the results of a content analysis depends upon the reliability and validity of the observations. The coding process, which is to say the process of classifying or assigning specified content units into categories, is therefore critically important to a successful content analysis. A high degree of reliability is a minimum requirement for the coherence and accuracy of a content analysis. Inconsistencies in coding constitute a major potential source of errors, thus reducing the reliability of the data. This is of special concern given that the content coding process usually involves some degree of subjective and idiosyncratic judgment.

In another world, it might be possible to recognize and identify sign-vehicles purely on the basis of the ideas and information contained in a body of text, without any interpretive cognitive processing whatsoever. The process of coding the occurrence of sign-vehicles in a body of text and assigning them to categories would thus require no subjectivity, no interpretation. The investigator would be able to restrict himself or herself to the task of classifying individual units of text without any concern that her own idiosyncratic psychological characteristics might unwittingly infuse her perceptions and interpretations of sign-vehicles with error. However, that world is incongruent with the one in which sentient human beings actually do live. In this world, individuals take an active psychological role in learning about the world around themselves (Bowen, Chang, and Huang, 1996). They cannot recognize and identify sign-vehicles and assign them to categories purely on the basis of their inherent content without involving at least some degree of interpretation and cognitive processing. The process of coding content thus depends at least partially on conditions preexisting in the mind of the investigator. Moreover, this dependence upon subjective factors threatens the replicability, the objectivity, and thus the validity of the inferences and results. How, then, can an investigator, or a reviewer of a content analysis, ensure that the assignments of sign-vehicles to categories are primarily determined by the ideas and information within the text rather than the idiosyncratic psychological characteristics unwittingly or otherwise projected into them by the investigator?

Unless one properly checks the reliability of the coding process, the results of a content analysis will remain, at best, questionable. Appropriately trained coders, clear and well-defined content units, and clear, well-defined, theory-guided categories all tend to increase the consistency of the coding process. Three types of reliabilities are pertinent to evaluating the coding process: stability, reproducibility, and accuracy (Krippendorff, 2004). Among them, stability and reproducibility are used more frequently than accuracy.

Stability refers to the extent to which the results of content classification are consistent over time. This is the most lenient indicator of reliability. It can be calculated when the same content is coded by the same coder at two different times. Because the coder and the content stay the same, this type of reliability contains the fewest possible sources of uncontrolled variation. Such sources include inconsistencies in the written material, ambiguities in the coding rules, emotional changes within the coder, or simple marking errors.

Stability measures the consistency of one person's understanding or interpretation of certain material over time, whereas intercoder reliability measures the consistency of shared understanding or meaning of the text. Intercoder reliability, also called reproducibility, refers to the degree to which two or more coders replicate each other's results. The coding process is said to be replicable if the coders code the same text in the same way. Intercoder reliability is a more objective indication of reliability than stability. Inconsistent codings usually result from ambiguities in the text, cognitive differences among the coders, ambiguous coding rules, or arbitrary recording errors.

Accuracy refers to the extent to which the coding of text corresponds to a standard or norm. However, such a standard or norm seldom exists in the field of public administration. It more often pertains in situations such as for training purposes, when it is used to test the performance of human coders against pre-established standards for coding some text.

The type of reliability appropriate to evaluating an analysis depends on the criterion used to check the consistency of the coding. When the criterion is from the same coder but only at a later time, it is stability. When the criterion is from another coder, it is replicability or intercoder reliability. When the criterion is a previously established standard or norm, it is accuracy.

The calculations of reliability prescribed specifically for nominal data, the most common form of data in content analysis, are available (Cohen, 1960). Content analysis usually involves nominal data. The agreement of nominal data codings between coders may be computed using a kappa coefficient. Its formula is

$$k = \frac{p_o - p_e}{1 - p_e} \tag{35.1}$$

where
$p_o =$ the proportion of units for which the judges agree
$p_e =$ the proportion of units for which agreement is expected at random

When the observed agreement equals the agreement expected at random, $k = 0$. When the observed agreement is less than the agreement expected at random, k becomes a negative value. When there is perfect agreement between two judges, $k = 1$. The calculations are demonstrated in the example below, based upon the previously mentioned study of classified ads.

A kappa coefficient needs to be calculated for every nominal variable coded in a content analysis. For example, in the study of classified ads, two coders, A and B, independently read a random sample of 100 classified job ads. Then, based on the content of the ads in terms of whether gender was stated as a requirement for the job, they classified them into three categories: male only, female only, or either as shown in Table 35.1.

In a situation where there is perfect agreement between two coders, the tally of each category would only show up in the diagonal cells and all other cells would be zeros. Table 35.1 shows less than perfect agreement between two coders. However, perfect agreement is not required for a content analysis. We only need to demonstrate that the intercoder agreement is at a substantial level compared to the agreement that happened by chance. We first calculate the expected coding results

TABLE 35.1

Observed Coding Results from Coders A and B

Coder B's Codings	Coder A's Codings			
	Male Only	Female Only	Either	Total
Male only	28	0	1	29
Female only	0	18	4	22
Either	2	3	44	49
Total	30	21	49	100

based on chance. The expected cell frequency is based on the column total times the row total divided by the grand total. For example, the expected cell frequency for "Coder A Male Only" and "Coder B Male Only" is $30 \times 29/100 = 8.7$. The expected coding result based on chance is shown in Table 35.2.

In this example, p_o, the proportion of units for which the judges agree, is calculated as the sum of diagonal cells in Table 35.1 divided by the grand total, $p_o = (28 + 18 + 44)/100 = 0.90$. And p_e, the proportion of units for which agreement is expected at random, is calculated as the sum of diagonal cells in Table 35.2 divided by the grand total, $p_e = (8.7 + 4.6 + 24)/100 = 0.373$. Then according to the kappa formula, $k = (0.90 - 0.373)/(1 - 0.373) = 0.84$. Such calculation needs to be conducted for every coded nominal variable to test intercoder reliability.

The magnitude of kappa coefficient reflects the level of agreement between two coders. Landis and Koch (1977) provided a rough guideline for interpreting different levels of kappa:

Kappa	Strength of Agreement
≤ 0.00	Poor
0.01–0.20	Slight
0.21–0.40	Fair
0.41–0.60	Moderate
0.61–0.80	Substantial
0.81–1.00	Almost perfect

Therefore, kappa $= 0.84$ in this example reflects an almost perfect agreement between Coder A and Coder B on whether the ad called for male only, female only, or either. Another way to test the significance of a kappa coefficient is to calculate the standard error (SE) of kappa. The formula for

TABLE 35.2

Expected Coding Results from Coders A and B

Coder B's Codings	Coder A's Codings			
	Male Only	Female Only	Either	Total
Male only	8.7	6.1	14.2	29
Female only	6.6	4.6	10.8	22
Either	14.7	10.3	24	49
Total	30	21	49	100

calculating the SE of kappa is complicated and beyond the scope of this chapter. However, SPSS can calculate kappa, the standard error of kappa, and test its significance by using the SPSS manual options in the following sequence: ANALYZE, DESCRIPTIVE STATISTICS, CROSSTABS, STATISTICS, and kappa. For example, the standard error for the kappa in Tables 35.1 and 35.2 is 0.0725, therefore the Z-value for the kappa is $0.84/0.0725 = 11.58$. This kappa coefficient is statistically significant.

The kappa coefficient is only one of the many statistics to calculate intercoder reliability. Other methods of calculating intercoder reliability can be found at PRAM: a program for reliability assessment with multiple coders which could be downloaded free of charge for research purposes from http://www.geocities.com/skymegsoftware/pram.html. The PRAM version 0.4.5 is a program copyrighted and developed by the Skymeg Software, Inc. in 2004. However, users are urged to read the warnings and disclaimer on PRAM's website about possible bugs in the program. Readers who are interested in further investigating the formulas and explanations of these statistics for intercoder reliability might want to consult Neuendorf's (2002) *Content Analysis Guidebook*.

PRAM currently is capable of calculating the following intercoder reliability based on the level of measurement in the variables:

1. Percent agreement (for nominal variables)
2. Scott's pi (for nominal variables)
3. Cohen's kappa (for nominal variables)
4. Spearman rho (for ordinal variables)
5. Pearson correlation (for interval or ratio variables)
6. Lin's concordance (for interval or ratio variables)
7. Holsti's reliability (for nominal variables)

The input file shall be an Excel file, with the following:

1. The first column must contain the coder IDs in numeric form.
2. The second column must contain the unit (case) IDs in numeric form.
3. All other columns may contain numerically coded variables, with variable names on the header line.

In a Windows environment, the PRAM user may select the following for each analysis conducted:

- The ID numbers of the coders to be included
- The variable names of the measures to be assessed
- The statistic to be calculated

35.2.4 ANALYTIC TOOLS FOR THE CODED DATA AND INTERPRETATION OF CONTENT ANALYSIS

Statistical analysis tools for content analysis are similar in many respects to those used for any other type of data. The coded content analysis data is treated as any other type of data. The appropriate criteria for selecting suitable statistical tools for the coded data follow from the purposes for which the analysis is conducted and the measurement properties for the pertinent level of data such as nominal, ordinal, interval, or ratio data. With this in mind, there is always more than one way to approach the analysis. Data does not speak for itself; the investigator must explain its significance in the light of theoretical and substantive concerns. It is incumbent upon the investigator to explain what the data says and how he or she arrives at this understanding. Are there competing interpretations? If so, which interpretation makes the most sense in light of the statistical evidence and whatever theories or other knowledge pertains to the current situations? The answers to these and similar questions all involve some level of idiosyncratic judgment on behalf of the investigator. They ultimately depend upon the investigator's experience, knowledge, and capacity for judgment. Unbiased and credible results from a content analysis may only be achieved if all of the requisite subjective judgments are backed up with statistical evidence. Beyond this point, the decision as to what particular statistical techniques are appropriate to establish this evidence depends largely upon the type of data one is working with.

35.2.5 An Example of Content Analysis

This section gives an overview of Bowen's (2003) content analysis of classified job ads in leading Taiwanese newspapers. It was designed as a test of dual labor market theory. The results of the analysis were compared with other attributes of the documents analyzed, with documents produced by other sources, with characteristics of the persons who produced the documents, and the audience for which they were intended. It started with her repeated observations of blatantly discriminatory classified ads in the Taiwanese newspapers specifying a particular sex as one of the job requirements, such as the one listed below:

LEADING MANUFACTURE & EXPORTER
Merchandise Assistant
We are seeking to employ a foreigner to handle exportation.
* **Female, under age of 35**
* One year experienced in export field (without working experience is available)
* Aggressive personality and team work spirit

    We offer a strong commitment to training & development of our staff and attractive salary packages and benefits are offered to attract the best applicants.
Source: *The China News*, January 1, 1999 (emphasis added)

To achieve the objectivity and requisite replicability of a content analysis, a clearly stated and explicit set of rules for selecting research targets is necessary to minimize the possibility that findings merely reflect the investigator's subjective predispositions rather than the content of the text under analysis. Bowen (2003) stated the following set of rules for selecting the classified ads:

a. The ads were taken from the top three newspapers with highest circulation.
b. The classified ads were taken from Sunday newspaper between January 1 and February 28, 1999.
c. The classified ads were for full-time positions only.

To ensure reliability of the data, the kappa coefficient was conducted on a random sample of 200 ads from the larger data set with two coders coding the ads independently. Randomly selecting a subset of the data to check for intercoder reliability is a good way to test the reliability for the codings without imposing undue burden to the investigators to provide such evidence on the entire data set. Kappa coefficients need to be calculated for every categorical variable. In Bowen's (2003) content analysis, every categorical variable reached substantial to almost perfect agreement between coders.

The coding schema started with identifying the purpose of the content analysis. Bowen (2003) used the content of the classified ads to illustrate sex segregation in the Taiwanese workplace. Therefore, the investigator read over the ads and figured out that most of the classified ads called for "male only," "female only," or "either." Then the first coded variable was created as "specifying particular sex as job requirement" with three option categories: male only, female only, or either. Bowen (2003) also suspected that the preference for male or female applicants varied by jobs. She used the Standard Occupational Classification System of the Republic of China to classify ads

TABLE 35.3
Sex Requirement Listed in Classified Ads by Job Category

	Prof.	Admin.	Clerks	Sales	Service	Production	Total
Male only	931	428	43	218	42	278	1940
Female only	256	38	188	91	92	72	737
Either	1899	824	241	527	183	245	3919
Total	3086	1290	472	836	317	595	6596

Note: Job classification was based on the Standard Occupational Classification System of the Republic of China published by the Directorate-General of Budget, Accounting and Statistics, Executive Yuan at http://www.stat.gov.tw/bs1/english/occu.htm.

Prof. stands for professional jobs and Admin. stands for administrative jobs.

into the following job categories: professional, administrative, clerical, sales, service, or production. As a result, she cross-tabulated the ads into a 3 × 6 table (Table 35.3) with sex requirement listed in classified ads by job categories and then conducted a standard chi-square analysis to test whether the sex requirement in the classified ads was independent of job categories. The chi-square test generated a $\chi^2 = 751.26$, $p < .000$, which meant that classified ads for jobs clearly sent out the message that there were dual labor markets in Taiwan. Upon closer comparisons between the observed frequency and expected frequency in each cell, Bowen (2003) found that male applicants were wanted more in professional, administrative, sales, and production positions. In contrast, female applicants were wanted more in clerical or service jobs.

After arriving at such a strong χ^2, Bowen (2003) searched for other possible explanations which might account for such differential preference for males or females in different jobs. One suspected reason and commonly used excuse would be that "men are better educated." However, upon close examination, Bowen (2003) found that, in Taiwan, female university students outnumbered males in nine out of eleven colleges, and males only outnumbered females in Engineering and Natural Sciences. Female students' enrollment in universities has been steadily on the rise. It increased from 31 percent in 1965 to 50 percent in 1997. Therefore, the differential preference for males at higher ranking positions such as Professional or Administrative could not be logically accounted for by the common but ungrounded speculation that men are better educated. In the end, the truth is that though women in Taiwan are equally as well educated as men, Taiwanese companies still prefer male job applicants for professional or administrative positions. The truth could not have been asserted with such undeniable force without the rational justification provided by this content analysis.

35.3 REVIEW OF THE MAIN POINTS

Before bringing this chapter to its conclusion, it is appropriate to briefly summarize the main points of the discussion. Content analysis is a system for analyzing and making inferences about the empirical content of recorded text. The quality of a content analysis depends on its conformity to the requirements of system, objectivity, and generality. In this respect, the schema used to classify the sign-vehicles is especially important, as is the process through which sign-vehicles are identified and assigned to categories by the investigators. Also in this respect, the clarity of the classification rules which assign each sign-vehicle to its appropriate category is paramount. Assessing intercoder reliability in a pilot study using a subset of the sample allows investigators to get a preliminary measure on intercoder reliability, modify the classification rules, and improve the intercoder reliability. In the end, the technique of content analysis is about marshaling good reasons for authorizing and rationally justifying inferences about the content of the text. High intercoder reliability is a necessary but not sufficient condition for this. When properly conducted, content analysis can be of considerable power and usefulness in application.

35.4 HOMEWORK PROBLEMS

Each student in the class is to gather and bring to class 40 personal ads from a periodical such as a newspaper or an online source. The ads should be gathered so that 10 ads each come from the following four orientation groups: "men seeking women," "women seeking men," "men seeking men," and "women seeking women." After all of the ads have been gathered, students are to pair off into groups of two. Each group of two students will have 80 total ads. The 80 ads will be coded by both students. The content of each ad will represent individuals who exhibit or seek one or more personal characteristics. The personal characteristics are organized into the following categories: physical attributes (e.g., body size, shape, degree of attractiveness); income or social status; education or intelligence; age; attitudes, values, personalities; race; religion; smoking or drinking preferences? Each student is to independently code the 80 ads for his or her group in terms of the personal characteristics sought after in the ad. In other words, each student is to independently code which of these characteristics are stipulated in each ad. Note that each ad will probably state more than one personal characteristic, so each ad can be coded for multiple personal characteristics. After the students have coded the ads, each group is to answer the following questions:

Question 1. What is the reliability coefficient for your coding of your 80 ads? Treat each characteristic perceived by either coder in each ad as a separate sign-vehicle.

Question 2. With respect to the 80 ads for your group, what is the distribution of characteristics sought after by individuals from each of the four orientation groups?

Question 3. Do the personal characteristics sought by any of the four orientation groups differ in any significant way from those sought by individuals from the others? In other words, can any or all of these four orientation groups be distinguished from the others on the basis of the distribution of the sought-for mix of the personal characteristics?

REFERENCES

Bingham, R.D. and Bowen, W.M. 1994. "Mainstream" public administration over time: A topical content analysis of the public administration review. *Public Administration Review, 54,* 204–208.

Bowen, C.C. 2003. Sex discrimination in selection and compensation in Taiwan. *International Journal of Human Resource Management, 14,* 297–315.

Bowen, W.M., Chang, C.C., and Huang, Y.K. 1996. Psychology and global environmental priorities in Taiwan: A psychometric comparison of two learning models. *Journal of Environmental Psychology, 16:* 259–268.

Cohen, J. 1960. A coefficient of agreement for nominal scales. *Educational and Psychological Measurement, 20* (1): 37–46.

Dewey, J. 1958. *Experience and Nature.* New York: Dover Publications.

Glascock, J. and LaRose, R. 1992. A content analysis of 900 numbers: Implications for industry regulation and self regulation. *Telecommunications Policy, 16:* 147–155.

Ho, A. Tat-Kei. 2002. Reinventing local governments and the e-government initiative. *Public Administration Review 62* (4), 434–444.

Holsti, O.R. 1969. *Content Analysis for the Social Sciences and Humanities,* Reading, Massachusetts: Addison-Wesley.

Janis, I.L. 1949. The problem of validating content analysis, in *The Language of Politics, Studies in Quantitative Semantics*, H.D. Lasswell, N. Leites, and R. Fadner, J.M. (Eds.), Cambridge: The MIT Press.

Krippendorff, K. 2004. *Content Analysis: An Introduction to Its Methodology.* Beverly Hills, California: Sage publications.

Landis, J.R. and Koch, G.G. 1977. The measurement of observed agreement for categorical data. *Biometrics, 33*, 159–174.

Neuendorf, K. 2002. *The Content Analysis Guidebook.* Thousand Oaks, California: Sage Publications.

Quine, W.V.O. 1960. *Word and Object.* Cambridge: MIT Press.

Paisley, W.J. 1969. Studying "style" as deviation from encoding norms, in *The Analysis of Communication Content: Developments in Scientific Theories and Computer Techniques*, G. Gerbner, O.R. Holsti, K. Krippendorff, W.J. Paisley, and P.J. Stone (Eds.), New York: John Wiley and Sons.

Weber, R.P. 1985. *Basic Content Analysis.* Beverly Hills, California: Sage Publications.

36 Meta-Analysis

Chieh-Chen Bowen

CONTENTS

36.1 INTRODUCTION

Meta-analysis was defined by the *American Heritage Dictionary of the English Language* (2000) as "the process or technique of synthesizing research results by using various statistical methods to retrieve, select, and combine results from previous separate but related studies." The term meta-analysis was first used by Glass in 1976. Later he and his associate used the method to statistically integrate the results of 375 psychotherapy studies to show the benefits of psychotherapy to patients' mental health (Smith and Glass, 1977).

The basic requirements of a meta-analysis include: (1) conducting a complete, systematic, and unbiased search of previous studies on a clearly specified topic; (2) coding study characteristics from previous studies for analyzing and interpreting the possible heterogeneous results; (3) calculating effect sizes to standardize research findings across studies; (4) identifying moderators to analyze the effect sizes; and (5) interpreting the meta-analysis results. A meta-analysis integrates multiple studies on a clearly specified topic conducted under different situations, different research participants, different times, or different locations. The strength of a meta-analysis is that it provides better generalizations of the research findings than single studies. A meta-analysis also statistically integrates and standardizes research outcomes across studies.

Readers need to be clear on the distinctions between narrative literature reviews and meta-analyses. Narrative literature reviews have been used for a long time; they also generalize results from previous studies. However, narrative literature reviews are subjective. In other words, the review results are heavily influenced by the reviewers' idiosyncratic ideas, beliefs, and values. One researcher may selectively include a limited number of studies (usually between 10 and 20 studies) to support his or her own research agenda while another researcher may simply select a different set of previous studies and come to a completely different conclusion reviewing the same type of studies. This bias is far less likely to occur in a meta-analysis due to the fact that a meta-analysis requires a comprehensive, complete, and systematic search of previous studies on the same topic, which usually generates hundreds of relevant studies. Researchers need to come up with explicit criteria for exclusion and inclusion of studies in the meta-analysis. So other people who are interested in replicating the meta-analytic results will be able to do so by following the explicit criteria. Details regarding step-by-step instructions for conducting a meta-analysis will be presented in the next section.

Many researchers have used the term "meta-analysis" incorrectly and many publications have mislabeled themselves as meta-analyses. The purpose of this chapter is to define meta-analysis clearly, provide step-by-step instructions and an actual example of a meta-analysis. Even if readers cannot conduct a meta-analysis on their own after reading this chapter, at least they will have been properly introduced to it, will be able to identify publications that were mislabeled as meta-analyses, and will have a list of references for further guidance.

36.2 META-ANALYSIS

A meta-analysis statistically combines the numerical results of previous studies on a specific topic which investigates the relationship between two specific variables. Recognizing that statistical research findings are inherently probabilistic (the results of any single study could have occurred by chance), meta-analysis utilizes statistical procedures to integrate a large number of empirical results on a specific topic (Hunter and Schmidt, 1990). The result of a meta-analysis is a more comprehensive and systematic synthesis of previous studies than would be feasible with a narrative review, limited by unaided human cognitive information processing and interpretation. The additional inferential power of a meta-analysis comes from standardizing results from previous empirical studies into "effect sizes" (to be explained below) for further statistical analyses. A meta-analysis, when it is executed correctly, may help draw more precise conclusions about inconsistent findings in a particular area of investigation (Gaugler et al., 1987).

Based on the measurement-scale properties of the two key variables examined by a meta-analysis (i.e., nominal, interval, ordinal, or ratio), there are three different approaches to a meta-analysis: (1) standardized mean differences, (2) correlations, and (3) odds ratio of different probabilities of dichotomous events. These three approaches will be discussed later.

There are eight basic steps involved in conducting a meta-analysis: (1) conceptualize the relationship between two specific variables; (2) gather a set of studies that have tested the specified relationship; (3) design a coding sheet to record the characteristics of the conditions under which each study was conducted; (4) examine each study and, using the coding sheet; record the conditions under which it was conducted; (5) compute the intercoder reliability of the codings; (6) compute the "effect size" for each study; (7) statistically analyze the characteristics and effect sizes for all of the studies; and (8) write a research report. The following sections briefly describe and illustrate the eight steps.

36.2.1 CONCEPTUALIZE THE RELATIONSHIP

The first step is to provide a detailed specification of the relationship to be examined, giving attention to the major theories and methods important in the literature. The investigator must define the X and Y (independent and dependent) variables in both theoretical and operational terms. This definition may set the boundaries of the literature under consideration. Moderator variables, or study characteristics (W), are also important. These are variables that can be expected to change the direction or magnitude of the relationship between X and Y. They should be considered as clearly as possible. The greater the clarity given to X, Y, and W before the literature search begins, the stronger the review is likely to be. An example of this process will be provided later.

36.2.2 GATHER RELEVANT EMPIRICAL STUDIES

Clear definitions of X, Y, and W may be expected to set clear boundaries for the relevant literature. The next step is to locate and retrieve all of or at least as many as possible of the pertinent reports. Not all studies containing the specified relationship between X and Y will be suitable to be included in the meta-analysis. For example, Bowen, Swim, and Jacobs's (2000) meta-analysis compared men's and women's job performance in different organizations. They found, some studies used an atypical group of employees—people with substance abuse records or employees with mental health problems. Such atypical studies are likely to be found in the course of any meta-analysis and it is important for the investigator to spell out the reasons for exclusions. Whenever possible, effort should be made to include unpublished studies such as theses, dissertations, technical reports, and working papers. The investigator should always thoroughly describe his or her methods of locating articles, along with descriptions of the criteria used for study selection and the reasons for rejection of studies. Guidelines one can use to locate and retrieve all of the pertinent studies include (Johnson, 1993):

1. Computer database searches can be used as a starting point to locate references or abstracts that contain keywords relevant to the topic specified by the investigator. A lot of research databases may be used such as Business Source Complete, Dissertation Abstracts, Education Research Information Center (ERIC), Infotrac, IngentaConnect, PsyINFO, Social Science Citation Index, and Social Science Full Text. Identifying appropriate keywords to use in the computer research database search is essential to a successful search. Usually investigators start out by putting the X and Y variables as the keywords. Then other words synonymous with the X or Y variables should also be included in the keywords search. Different labels are often used to refer the same thing in the field of public administration. For example, in Bowen et al.'s (2000) meta-analysis, gender was one of the variables of interest. Therefore, in the computer database search, the keyword for gender actually included gender, sex, men and women, man and woman, males and females. All the terms which may be used interchangeably to refer to the same thing need to be included in the keyword search.
2. The ancestry approach involves examining the reference lists of previous narrative reviews. One can start with the most recent articles and proceed to older articles.
3. The descendance approach involves identifying a critical study in the literature and trying to locate all the studies which cited it. Social Science Citation Index is a good tool for this purpose.
4. Research networks may be contacted. This involves writing letters to other investigators who are known to work on the specified topic and asking whether they know of any other unpublished studies.
5. Manual searches of important journals may be conducted. Although manual searches may be old-fashioned, they may still turn up some articles that are overlooked by other techniques.

It is advisable that the investigator starts a potential meta-analysis with a sizable number of empirical studies to create sufficient sample size for the meta-analysis.

The sample size in a meta-analysis refers to the number of effect sizes generated from previous studies. Based on my own experience, I recommend having a reasonably large sample size, which means $N \geq 30$. When you only have located ten previous studies on the specific topic (i.e., studies that calculated and reported the relationship between specific X and Y variables of interest), then you will be better off to widen your interest, to conduct a few more individual empirical studies, or to wait for a few years to revisit the possibility of conducting a meaningful meta-analysis on the topic. A large sample size allows more options for statistical analysis and is more likely to generate meaningful results.

36.2.3 DESIGN A CODING SHEET

Although each study in the selected set of studies examines a single clearly specified X–Y relationship, the conditions under which the relationship was examined (W) may vary from study to study. These conditions must be considered. The coding sheet is designed to record the characteristics of these conditions. These characteristics may be used later on to explain any inconsistent results of different studies. To properly design a coding sheet, the investigator must be familiar with all the studies included in the meta-analysis, use relevant theory as a guide to generate moderator variables that might influence the strength or direction of the relationship between X and Y, and make sure the coding sheet covers all study characteristics to be coded.

36.2.4 CODE STUDY CHARACTERISTICS

Having gathered the relevant literature, the next step is to record the important characteristics (W) of each study. It is important to record all moderator variables. Since they could alter the direction and/or magnitude of the relationship between X and Y, they become extremely important when the investigator tries to integrate and interpret inconsistent findings of previous studies. Study characteristics may be either continuous or categorical. Categorical characteristics reflect qualitative differences among different values of the relevant variable (such as the type of organization the study was conducted in) while continuous characteristics reflect differences that could be measured with equal units (such as percentage of male raters on the job).

36.2.5 COMPUTE THE INTERCODER RELIABILITY OF THE CODINGS

This step is the same as the intercoder reliability for a content analysis. The coding process, which is to say the process of classifying specified content units into categories, usually involves some degree of subjective and idiosyncratic judgment. Intercoder reliability provides a quantitative way to verify that two different investigators read the same study independently and they are able to extract the same information. Intercoder reliability can be calculated for both categorical and continuous variables. A Kappa Coefficient may be utilized for categorical data (including nominal and ordinal variables) and Pearson Product Moment Correlation may be utilized for continuous data (including interval and ratio variables). These two are the most frequently used statistics for intercoder reliability. Readers who are interested in other ways of calculating inter-coder reliability may refer to the content analysis chapter.

36.2.6 COMPUTE EFFECT SIZES

An effect size computation standardizes the strength of the X–Y relationship in an individual study and expresses the strength in units of standard deviation. The effect sizes may be computed from different statistics provided in the individual studies. The goal of effect size computation is to convert the summary statistics provided in the individual studies into standard deviation units that may be statistically integrated across studies. When the effect sizes are properly computed, they may be used to aggregate or compare the studies for purposes of overall summary description and statistical inference.

As previously mentioned, according to the measurement-scale properties of the two key variables (X and Y) examined by a meta-analysis, there are usually three different approaches to a meta-analysis: (1) standardized mean differences, (2) correlations, and (3) odds ratio of different probabilities of dichotomous events.

When the X variable is dichotomous (i.e., experimental versus control groups) and the Y variable is continuous (i.e., the amount of weight loss during the treatment period), the proper approach for calculating effect size is the standardized mean differences. The effect size may be referred to as "g." The formula for g according to Johnson (1993) is as follows:

$$g = \frac{M_E - M_C}{s_{\text{pooled}}} \tag{36.1}$$

where M_E is the mean for the experimental group, M_C is the mean for the control group. s_{pooled} is the pooled standard deviation for both the experimental and control groups. s_{pooled} is calculated as

$$s_{\text{pooled}} = \{[(n_E - 1)(s_E)^2 + (n_C - 1)(s_C)^2]/[n_E + n_C - 2]\}^{1/2} \tag{36.2}$$

where n_E and n_C are the number of observations in the experimental and control groups, and s_E and s_C are the standard deviations for the experimental and control groups. Bowen et al. (2000) applied the effect size formula to their gender bias and performance appraisal meta-analysis by using

$$g = \frac{M_M - M_F}{s_{\text{pooled}}} \tag{36.3}$$

where M_M was the mean job ratings for men, M_F was the mean job ratings for women. s_{pooled} was the pooled standard deviation for both men and women. s_{pooled} was calculated as

$$s_{\text{pooled}} = \{[(n_M - 1)(s_M)^2 + (n_F - 1)(s_F)^2]/[n_M + n_F - 2]\}^{1/2} \tag{36.4}$$

where n_M and n_F were the number of men and women reported in each study, and s_M and s_F were the standard deviations for men's and women's job ratings. A positive effect size implied that male workers received higher job ratings than their female counterparts and a negative effect size implied that female workers received higher job ratings than their male counterparts.

A specially designed computer software for meta-analysis, DSTAT, allows the following source report summary statistics to be converted to g easily: (a) means and standard deviations; (b) t-tests or F-value from analysis of variance (ANOVA); (c) correlation coefficient, r values; (d) chi-square; (e) proportions or frequencies; (f) exact p-values from univariate statistics. Details of DSTAT will not be discussed in this chapter. Instead, interested readers should refer to Johnson's (1993) DSTAT manual.

When the X and Y variables are both continuous (i.e., employees' conscientiousness and the supervisory ratings of their job performance) the proper approach for calculating effect size is to use correlations. The most commonly used meta-analysis approach when X and Y are both continuous is Hunter and Schmidt's (1990) approach. Conceptually, their approach can be outlined in the following simple steps without getting into the complicated formulas.

1. Calculate the desired descriptive statistics (i.e., correlations between X and Y) for each study available, and calculate a weighted average to give greater weight to large studies than to small studies.
2. Calculate the variance of the statistic across studies.
3. Correct the observed variance by subtracting the amount due to sampling error.

4. Correct the mean and variance for study artifacts other than sampling error, such as unreliability of the measures for the independent and dependent variables as well as restriction of range.

5. Compare the corrected standard deviation to the mean to assess the size of the potential variation in results across studies. If the mean is more than two standard deviations larger than zero, then it is reasonable to conclude that the relationship considered is always positive.

Hunter and Schmidt (1990) argued that artifacts of individual studies were independent across studies. Whenever possible, therefore, they should be corrected to give a more accurate estimate of the true population effect size in that research domain. Here are the ten potentially correctable artifacts:

1. Sampling error
2. Error of measurement in the dependent variable
3. Error of measurement in the independent variable
4. Dichotomization of a continuous dependent variable
5. Dichotomization of a continuous independent variable
6. Restriction of range in the independent variable
7. Restriction of range in the dependent variable
8. Deviation from perfect measurement in the independent variable
9. Deviation from perfect measurement in the dependent variable
10. Variance due to extraneous factors

Hunter and Schmidt (1990) provided a copious list of formulas for such corrections.

For most medical research, the following research design is most likely to be implemented. When X (i.e., experimental versus control groups) and Y variables (success versus failure) are both dichotomous variables, the 2×2 contingency table of frequency of events in each cell is shown as follows:

	Success	**Failure**
Experimental group	A	B
Control group	C	D

$$\text{Odds ratio} = AD/BC \tag{36.5}$$

$$\text{Log odds ratio} = \log (AD/BC) \tag{36.6}$$

$$\text{Log odds variance} = (1/A + 1/B + 1/C + 1/D) \tag{36.7}$$

$$\text{Log odds standard error} = \text{SQRT} (1/A + 1/B + 1/C + 1/D) \tag{36.8}$$

Based on Formulas 36.5 to 36.8, a Z-value can be calculated

$$Z = \log \text{ odds ratio}/\log \text{ odds se} \tag{36.9}$$

and a 95 percent confidence interval for the log odds can be calculated

$$95\% \text{ C.I.} = \log \text{ odds ratio} \pm 1.96 \log \text{ odds se} \tag{36.10}$$

There are many options for calculating the effect sizes with computer programs besides DSTAT. One option is the Effect Size Determination Program developed by David B. Wilson in 2001 with codes written in EXCEL, which is available for free download from http://mason.gmu. edu/~dwilsonb/ma.html and another option is the more elaborate and expensive Comprehensive Meta-Analysis Version 2 developed by Biostat, Inc. in 2006, which is designed toward medical research (but also applicable in other contexts) and detailed information is available at www.meta-analysis.com/index.html. The Comprehensive Meta-Analysis Version 2 program allegedly can convert 100 different data formats into effect sizes.

Some studies may yield more than one effect size. This occurs when the X or Y variables are operationalized in more than one way in a particular study. For example, in Bowen et al.'s (2000) study, the Y variable represented actual performance appraisal. But in several studies the concept of performance appraisal was operationalized in slightly different ways, even within the same study. Some studies operationalized it in terms of both reported objective productivity and subjective supervisory job performance ratings. Some studies gathered job performance data on more than one position. Some used both self-ratings and supervisory ratings. When sufficient data is available, then multiple effect sizes may be calculated from one study. When multiple effect sizes are computed for a study, they may be combined or simply reported as they are. The judgment is based on the nature of multiple effect sizes according to the purpose of the meta-analysis. For example, if one study reported supervisory job ratings on incumbents of five different positions, it would make sense to report them as multiple effect sizes. However, if one study reported supervisory ratings on eight different job dimensions of the regional managers, it would make sense to combine these eight effect sizes into one composite effect size. Combining multiple effect sizes avoids the fallacy of overweighting those studies with multiple effect sizes in the meta-analysis. To combine multiple effect sizes, one may simply average them or, alternatively, compute Rosenthal and Rubin's (1986) "Composite g." The advantage of computing the Composite g is that it corrects the underestimation bias that inheres in simple averaging. Composite g may be computed if the source reports provided sufficient statistical information about the intercorrelations between the multiple Y variables. Details of calculating a Composite g will not be discussed in this chapter. Interested readers should refer to Rosenthal and Rubin (1986).

36.2.7 Analyze the Data

The next step is to analyze effect sizes and determine their overall mean and consistency with respect to all of the source studies. Reference to the study characteristics (W) may provide the required explanations of any inconsistencies noted between studies.

Another common reason for inconsistencies between studies is the fact that different studies contain different sample sizes. Specifically, the results of a study with a large sample size are usually more stable than are the results of one with a small sample size. Therefore, when the source studies contain a large variance in sample size, before conducting any further data analysis, the effect size for each study should be weighted. To accomplish this, the reciprocal of the variance for the Y variable is used as a weight. In the process of combining the effect sizes, this weight is multiplied by the effect size in a particular study to adjust for the various degrees of stability of the results from the various studies. This process tends to give small weights to studies with large variances, and large weights to studies with small variances (Johnson, 1993). The weighted effect size is referred to as "d" in this chapter. Once d is obtained, the investigator is ready to begin the analysis process.

The analysis process begins with the computation of an average effect size for all of the d values. In addition to the average effect size, the investigator also needs to assess the magnitude, direction, 95 percent confidence intervals, and homogeneity of the overall effect sizes in the combined dataset. If all the effect sizes present a homogeneous picture, then the job is done and the investigator may draw conclusions based on the magnitude, direction, and significance of the average effect size across all studies. When the 95 percent confidence interval includes zero, the average effect size is not different from zero. In this situation, it may be concluded that there is no relationship between X and Y across all the studies. When the 95 percent confidence interval does not include zero, it may be concluded that across all the studies, there is a significant relationship between X and Y.

Research usually shows that most effect sizes are heterogeneous across studies. Heterogeneous effect sizes mean that individual study outcomes are quite different from each other in terms of the magnitude or direction of the X–Y relationship. Therefore, one simple average effect size across all studies does not adequately represent the findings of previous studies. More work needs to be done before a reasonable conclusion can be made.

One way to try to attain homogeneity in heterogeneous cases is to identify outliers among the effect sizes and sequentially remove those that reduce the heterogeneity statistics by the largest amount (Hedges and Olkin, 1985). Usually homogeneity can be reached by removing as few as 20 percent of the largest outliers in the combined dataset. However, it is rarely the case that any investigator can afford to lose 20 percent of the data without worrying about the adequacy of the sample size. If homogeneity may be accomplished by removing less than 20 percent of the largest outliers, then the investigator may consider presenting the effect sizes in the following ways: (1) reporting the results with outliers, (2) reporting the results without the outliers, and (3) reporting the results with outliers only. Sometimes, the characteristics of the outliers could be logically separated from the rest of the studies. For example, hypothetically speaking, in a job performance meta-analysis, the outliers were found to be in the military settings with large sample sizes produced effect sizes that were in the opposite direction of the effect sizes found in nonmilitary settings. Then the logical solution would be to report the results separately. First, report the findings with an average effect size across all studies and make a note of its heterogeneity. Second, report an average effect size without the military studies (a homogenous outcome). And third, report an average effect size across only the studies done in the military and contrast the result with the rest of the studies.

Another way to try to attain homogeneity is to do statistical modeling, though this approach is fraught with difficulties when sample size is small. It could not be overemphasized that a sound meta-analysis needs to start with an adequate sample size. In other words, the topic of a meta-analysis is feasible only when there are enough empirical studies done on the topic.

In heterogeneous cases, the study characteristic variables (W) may be used to statistically account for some of the variability. Both categorical and continuous study characteristics may be used for this purpose. With respect to categorical characteristics, statistical analysis such as analysis of variance may show that heterogeneous outcomes are only heterogeneous between the groups established by dividing the studies into different groups based on the study characteristics but studies are homogeneous within each group. Such analysis may be used to estimate both a between-group effect and a test of homogeneity of the effect sizes within each group. With respect to continuous characteristics, on the other hand, linear regression analysis may be used. Ordinary least squares regression is commonly used for this purpose. The goal in such analyses is to use the moderator (W) variables to statistically account for as much as possible of the variation in the effect sizes. Each such linear analysis yields a test of significance of each moderator variable as well as a specification test which evaluates whether significant systematic variation remains unexplained in the analysis. Oftentimes the W variables are not successful in explaining the variation in the effect sizes. For example, Bowen et al. (2000) tested all possible study characteristics in their meta-analysis of gender and performance appraisals. These included stereotype of the measurement, subjectivity of the measurement, number of items in the work performance scale, job stereotype, gender composition of job incumbents, rater training, and familiarity of rater with ratees' performance, publication year, and percentage of male authors. They found only one of them, stereotype of the measurement, to be significantly correlated with effect sizes. Outlier elimination and statistical analysis may be used for each moderator variable in the meta-analysis. Meta-analysis is a trial-and-error process, not an exact and prescriptive science. One clear guiding principle is that it is better to record more study characteristics than needed in the statistical analysis so as to avoid finding that one needs information about certain critical study characteristics but has failed to record them. The best guideline is for the investigator to choose the most parsimonious and convincing possible combination of outlier elimination and statistical analysis.

36.2.8 WRITE THE REPORT

The process of writing a research report to describe the meta-analysis process and results is not different from writing any other report. The primary elements of such a report are (a) abstract, (b) introduction, (c) methods, (d) results, and (e) discussion. A well-written guideline can be found in the *Publication Manual of the American Psychological Association* (2001). One section of such a report requires special attention in a meta-analysis study. The "methods" section should include (a) procedures for locating and retrieving previous studies, (b) criteria for including and excluding studies, (c) coded study characteristics and a measure of the intercoder reliability (similar to one used in content analysis), (d) effect size calculations, and (e) data analysis procedures. A meta-analysis should always include an appendix containing the references of the source studies included in the sample. The list should contain all the studies before the investigator conducts the outlier elimination procedures. Such a list is helpful for future studies and for reviewers to judge the completeness of the sample.

36.3 AN EXAMPLE OF A META-ANALYSIS

There is a lot of misunderstanding about what a meta-analysis is and is not. Many studies that claim to be meta-analytical studies fail to conduct any standardization of previous outcomes, or attempt to explain the heterogeneity of the effect sizes. Those studies are not, properly speaking, meta-analytic studies. I will go through Bowen et al.'s (2000) meta-analysis as an example to show readers how these eight steps are followed in an actual meta-analysis. By showing an actual example of a meta-analysis and showing every step of it, readers will hopefully get a better understanding of what a meta-analysis actually involves.

Gender bias in performance appraisal has been a hot research topic for years. Intrigued and confused by numerous empirical studies on gender bias in performance appraisals in real work settings, Bowen et al. (2000) conducted a meta-analysis on gender and actual job performance in work settings. A meta-analysis is an extremely useful tool to statistically integrate inconsistent results from previous studies. As you might have imagined it is not difficult to find studies showing that men performed better than women in certain jobs. On the other hand, it is also easy to find that women performed better than men in other positions. To make things even more confusing, there are also studies showing that men and women perform equally well on a job. In a situation where plenty of empirical studies on the same topics are available and inconsistent results are generated from different studies, a meta-analysis is the perfect tool to statistically integrate the results and analyze the heterogeneity of the effect sizes.

36.3.1 CONCEPTUALIZE THE RELATIONSHIP

In Bowen et al.'s (2000) review of the relationship between gender bias and performance appraisals in the work settings, the independent variable, X, was defined as the sex of the ratee (i.e., male or female); the dependent variable, Y, was defined as a performance evaluation given to the ratee in a real work setting. Previous studies had shown inconsistent results in terms of the relationship between these two variables. Several moderators (W) were deemed important including gender stereotype of the job, group composition in terms of percentage of men, stereotype of the measurement, purpose of performance appraisal, amount of performance-related information, subjectivity of measurement, rated position, and type of work setting were all coded as W variables. Theoretically based expectations were developed to specify the influence of W on the relationship between X and Y. For example, one of the W variables was the position of the ratee. Among all the positions in an organization, managerial positions usually hold higher prestige than professional, clerical, technical, or blue-collar positions. Moreover, in managerial positions, job tasks are varied, unpredictable and the criteria for performance are relatively subjective. In this situation, nonperformance factors are likely to enter the evaluation. The expectation is that in this sort of a job situation, because of the lack of clear performance-specific criteria, the rating process is likely to be influenced by moderator variables such as the sex-role stereotype of the job. Therefore, males are likely to receive higher performance evaluations.

36.3.2 GATHER RELEVANT EMPIRICAL STUDIES

Once the X variable was defined as the gender of the ratee and the dependent variable was defined as the performance evaluation in a work setting, all the synonyms of both X and Y were included in the computer database searches. Keywords performance appraisal, performance evaluation, job performance paired with gender, sex, man and woman, men and women, male and female, and males and females. Databases searched included Psychological Abstracts (PsycLIT: 1967 to 1998), Educational Resources Information Center (ERIC: 1966 to 1998), Social Sciences Index (SSI: 1974 to 1998), Dissertation Abstract International (DAI: 1861 to 1998), Business Periodicals Index (BPI: 1980 to 1998), Social Sciences Citation Index (SSCI: 1972 to 1998), Current Contents-Behavioral and Social Sciences (BEHA: 1990 to 1998), Management Contents (MGMT: 1984 to 1998) and National Library of Medicine Evaluation Forum (MEDLINE: 1983 to 1998). Reference lists of review articles, chapters, and books as well as the reference lists of all located studies were also searched. The studies included in this meta-analysis were restricted to published sources: books, journals, theses, dissertations, and technical reports written in English (Bowen et al., 2000).

Such computer database searches often generate hundreds of studies with abstracts. Researchers need to read the abstracts carefully and screen out those studies which obviously do not fit the purpose of the meta-analysis. For example, Bowen et al. (2000) generated over 400 promising studies from the computer database search. They used four criteria for study exclusion, to avoid unnecessary repetition of previous meta-analyses and set clear boundaries for the present one. These criteria were

1. Any laboratory study of the written performance of "paper-people" or videotaped recordings of a scripted performance.
2. Any study about leadership style or attributions for success and failures that had been covered by Eagly and Johnson (1990) and Swim and Sanna's (1995) meta-analyses, respectively.
3. Studies that investigated the work performance of atypical subgroups of employees who were alcoholic or drug-users.
4. Field studies that failed to take confounding demographic variables into consideration.

The first three criteria were designed to set the boundary of the meta-analysis and the last criterion was to control the quality of studies included the meta-analysis. The quality of a meta-analysis is limited by the quality of the previous studies. It is a good idea to set up criteria to select only high-quality studies in a meta-analysis.

36.3.3 DESIGN A CODING SHEET

The coding sheet is designed to record the different characteristics of the previous studies. These characteristics may be used later on to explain any inconsistencies in the results of different studies. Before the investigator can properly design a coding sheet, she or he needs to read through all the studies included in the meta-analysis, use relevant theory as a guide to generate moderator variables that might influence the strength and direction of the relationship between X and Y, and make sure the coding sheet covers all study characteristics to be coded. Some study characteristics may be factual information extracted from each study, such as rater status, reliability of performance scale, and type of reported data. Others may be subjective ratings made by the coders who independently read the studies, such as sex stereotype of the job, sex stereotype of the measure (five-point Likert scale), rater training, and rater's familiarity with ratee's performance (low, moderate, or high) in Bowen et al. (2000).

36.3.4 CODE STUDY CHARACTERISTICS

After the investigator properly designs the coding sheet, two coders read the studies independently and use the coding sheet to record the important study characteristics. Completely independent readings and independent coding of the study characteristics are important to assure a high-quality analysis. In Bowen et al.'s (2000) study, the coding sheet included the following variables: publication form, sex of first author, type of work setting, purpose of the performance appraisal, rater's gender, rated position, rating instrument, type of rater, year of publication, percentage of male authors, clarity of the presentation, amount of training on rating scale usage, familiarity of raters with ratees' performance, degree of rater–ratee interdependence, percentage of male incumbents in the organization, sex stereotype of the job, and sex stereotype of the measurement.

36.3.5 COMPUTE THE INTERCODER RELIABILITY OF THE CODINGS

Intercoder reliability provides a quantitative measurement for the quality of the meta-analysis data. Kappa coefficient (see Content Analysis chapter for Kappa formula) can be applied to categorical study characteristics and Pearson Product Moment Correlation can be applied to continuous study characteristics. In Bowen et al. (2000), intercoder reliabilities for factual variables were all 1.00, and the intercoder reliabilities for ratings were between 0.79 and 1.00. The intercoder reliability results showed acceptable consistency for both factual variables and judgmental ratings.

36.3.6 COMPUTE EFFECT SIZES

Different empirical studies might report different statistical results. As a rule of thumb, univariate statistical procedures testing the relationship between the specified X and Y are sufficient to convert into effect sizes. These procedures include (a) means and standard deviations; (b) t-tests or F-value from analysis of variance (ANOVA); (c) correlation coefficient, r values; (d) chi-square; (e) proportions or frequencies; (f) exact p-values from univariate statistics. On the other hand, results from multivariate analyses are less likely to be sufficient because the procedures require taking all variables into consideration at the same time. You could not isolate the other variables to obtain a "clean" relationship between the specified X and Y out of a multivariate analysis result. Also, it is highly unlikely that you would get a large enough number of studies with identical multiple variables specified in the multivariate analysis models to conduct a meta-analysis.

In Table 36.1, I present different univariate statistics results from some of the previous studies that were sufficient to convert into effect sizes. The studies included in the table were arbitrarily selected from the entire set used in the meta-analysis to show how different types of data may be used to compute effect sizes. In every study, the investigator needs not only to calculate the magnitude of the relationship between X and Y but also to note the direction of such a relationship. For example, in Bowen et al.'s (2000) meta-analysis, it was important to note whether men received higher performance ratings or women received higher performance ratings in every study. When the univariate statistics were converted into effect sizes, they would carry the correct positive or negative sign to accurately reflect the direction of the relationship. Positive effect sizes meant men received higher performance ratings than women and negative effect sizes meant women received higher performance ratings than men.

TABLE 36.1

Univariate Statistics Converted into Effect Sizes

Study ID	Data Type	Male Ratees	Female Ratees	Reported Statistics	Direction	Unweighted Effect Size g	Weighted Effect Size d
Study #53	Means, s.d.s	407	239	Male: 0.227, 0.11 Female: 0.187, 0.10	M > F	0.376	0.376
Study #48	t or F values	43	39	$F = 14.15$	M > F	0.832	0.824
Study #51	r Values	53	99	$r = 0.05$	F > M	−0.100	−0.099
Study #71	Chi-square	8885	4846	$\chi^2 = 31.672$	M > F	0.101	0.101
Study #56	Proportions or frequencies	748	156	Male 73 percent, female 87 percent	F > M	−0.328	−0.327
Study #77	p Value	608	427	$p < 0.001$	F > M	−0.206	−0.206

36.3.7 ANALYZE THE DATA

A meta-analysis integrates results from many previous studies on the same topic by treating the results of each as a single piece of data for statistical purposes. Once each study is coded into the coding sheet and reported statistics are converted into effect sizes, you have a dataset where each study is entered as a case along with all the study characteristics and the calculated effect sizes.

An arbitrarily selected subset of the data used in Bowen et al.'s (2000) meta-analysis is shown in Table 36.2 for purposes of illustration. The upper section of Table 36.2 shows the data in EXCEL format which can be easily read into SPSS or SAS for further analysis. The lower section of Table 36.2 shows the data in DSTAT data format. Meta-analysis data needs to be laid out in both formats to complete the necessary analyses.

The EXCEL data format is easy to understand. In Table 36.2, the first row in Section A is variable name. It starts with "study id" to identify the source of the information, "effect size g" to represent the unweighted calculated effect size, "m ratee" to represent number of male ratees, "f ratee" to represent number of female ratees, and 11 study characteristics that may moderate the relationship between sex bias and performance appraisal. Coded study characteristics in the dataset represent mutual agreement between raters on factual variables such as setting of the study, purpose of the performance ratings, percentage of male ratees, and percentage of male raters or compromised average ratings on subjective ratings such as clarity of the writing, sex stereotype of the job, amount of rater training, raters' familiarity of ratees' performance, and sex stereotype of the measure.

The DSTAT data format is unique to this particular software. Follow Session B in Table 36.2 for the following explanations. The first three lines describe the entire data layout. The first line of the data always reads DSTAT INPUT FILE. The second line allows researchers to specify the following: the topic of the meta-analysis, labeling the experimental group, labeling the control group, reporting calculated effect size, number of study characteristics, and specifying a value to represent missing data. The third line of the data represents the study characteristics coded in the dataset and at the end of the third line the file name for the dataset is specified. The actual data starts from the fourth line, and each study takes three lines. The first line of each study indicates the study id with a short description of the study. The second line of the study specifies the research design of the study as either B (Between-Subject design) or W (Within-Subject design), reported calculated effect size, number of male ratees, and number of female ratees. The third line of the study describes the 11 study characteristics coded in the dataset. At the end of the entire dataset, the last line always reads @EOF to signal the end of data file.

According to Johnson (1993), DSTAT's analysis functions include: (a) a calculation of effect size homogeneity and outlier analysis, (b) fitting categorical models to effect sizes, and (c) fitting

TABLE 36.2
A Subset of Data Used in Bowen et al.'s (2000) Meta-analysis in Both EXCEL and DSTAT

A. A Subset of Meta-Analysis Data in EXCEL Format

Study Id	Effect Size g	M Ratee	F Ratee	Clarity	Confound	Setting	Purpose	Training	Familiarity	Percentage M Ratee	jbstr	Rater Sex	Percentage M Rater	Measure
77	−0.37	608	427	6.5	5	1	1	3	3	6	4	3	8	4
81	−0.08	595	97	5.5	5	1	1	3	3	−9	4.5	−9	−9	3
82	−0.22	110	176	6.5	4	1	2	1	2	−9	−9	3	5	2.4
1	0.27	202	34	6	5	6	1	3	3	9	5	4	−9	3.3
2	0.18	254	402	7	3	1	1	3	2	4	2	3	7	3.1
3	−0.17	68	68	6	1	6	1	−9	−9	10	5	4	−9	2.9
4	0.22	76	104	6	3	1	2	1	3	5	3	−9	−9	3.5
6	−0.87	39	31	5	3	2	3	3	2	6	3	−9	−9	3
8	−0.18	94	17	5	5	2	1	3	−9	9	3	−9	−9	2.75
9	−0.58	86	34	6	4	7	1	3	3	−9	4	3	−9	3.5
12	−0.49	66	130	1	5	2	2	2	2	4	2	−9	−9	2.5

B. A Subset of Meta-Analysis in DSTAT Format

```
DSTAT INPUT FILE
SEX BIAS AND PERFORMANCE APPRAISAL, MALE RATEES, FEMALE RATEES, Y, 11 – 9
Clarity, Confound, Setting, Purpose, Training, Familiarity, Percentage M Ratee, jbstr, Ratersex, Percentage M Rater, Measure, Filename
Study #77 Performance Ratings
B, –0.37 608 427
6.5 5 1 1 3 3 6 4 3 8 4
Study #81 Sales Productivity
B, –0.08 595 97
5.5 5 1 1 3 3 –9 4.5 –9 –9 3
Study #82 Work Facilitation
B, –0.22 110 176
6.5 4 1 2 1 2 –9 –9 3 5 2.4
@EOF
```

continuous models to effect sizes by using the output of an SPSS weighted regression analysis. All three types of analyses are recommended in conducting meta-analytical studies. The actual analyses are highly technical and interested readers may investigate further in Johnson (1993) and Hedges and Olkin (1985).

36.3.8 WRITE THE REPORT

Just follow the steps in Section 36.2.8 and clearly document the five subsections in the method session as instructed. There are numerous meta-analytic research reports which can provide excellent examples on presenting meta-analytical results such as Eagly and Johnson (1990), Swim, Borgida, Maruyama and Myers (1989), and Bowen et al. (2000).

36.4 CRITICISMS OF META-ANALYSES

This chapter would not be complete without addressing three major criticisms of meta-analyses: (1) comparing apples with oranges, (2) publication bias, and (3) quality control.

36.4.1 COMPARING APPLES WITH ORANGES

The most common criticism of meta-analysis is that it mixes apples with oranges (Hunter and Schmidt, 1990) especially when a meta-analysis combines studies that are very different and it makes no sense to compare their outcomes. This criticism can be easily avoided when the researchers use the same construct of the independent and dependent variables across all the studies in the meta-analysis. When a meta-analysis contains a large number of individual studies and the constructs of independent variables or dependent variables are defined and measured by very different instruments, then the results of this meta-analysis should be analyzed separately according to the constructs of the variables. It is inappropriate to conduct a meta-analysis with a small number of studies which came with different independent and dependent variables.

36.4.2 PUBLICATION BIAS

Journal reviewers are usually more favorable toward studies with significant findings. Therefore, it is logical to assume that published studies are likely to have larger effect sizes than are the results of unpublished studies, Rosenthal (1979) developed a file drawer analysis to estimate the number of unpublished or "lost" studies with insignificant findings needed to bring the significant level for a meta-analysis result down to the "just significant" level ($p = .05$). If the result of a file drawer analysis indicates that a small number of unpublished studies are likely to alter the outcome of a meta-analysis, then researchers should caution readers about the possibility that the conclusions are attributable to chance. However, when the estimated number of lost studies is large, the probability that so many lost studies exist is small. Thus, if file drawer analysis indicates that, say, 300 additional studies would be needed to significantly alter the conclusions, the researcher could put considerable confidence in them.

File drawer analysis has been criticized for its simplistic approach because it only takes the significance level of individual research outcomes into consideration but ignores the magnitude of the effect sizes. Readers who are interested in more sophisticated techniques designed to address the publication bias may refer to Hedges and Vevea (2005).

36.4.3 QUALITY CONTROL DIFFICULTIES

The quality of a meta-analysis depends on the quality of the previous studies included in the analysis. If there were problems with the measurement reliability and validity from previous studies, such problems will limit the quality of any meta-analysis that includes those problematic measurements.

Although statistical correction formula does exist and claim to be able to correct the unreliability of measurements, researchers are better off solving such measurement issues by implementing a set of quality control screening rules to screen out studies with questionable measurement quality. The quality of research is better insured by high-quality research design and measurement than by fancy statistics. However, evaluating research quality is a highly subjective task. Research quality is, in large degree, in the eyes of the beholder.

36.5 REVIEW OF THE MAIN POINTS

Before bringing this chapter to its conclusion, it is appropriate to briefly review the main points of the discussion. A meta-analysis is a statistical system for numerically estimating parameters of effect size that span across individual studies on a specific topic. The basic requirements for conducting a meta-analysis are as follows:

1. There were a large number of empirical studies conducted on a specific topic where constructs of independent and dependent variables were the same.
2. These empirical studies reported enough summary statistics on the relationship between the independent and the dependent variable to allow the calculation of the effect sizes.

There are eight steps involved in conducting a meta-analysis: (1) conceptualize the relationship between two specific variables; (2) gather a set of studies that have tested the specified relationship; (3) design a coding sheet to record the characteristics of the conditions under which each study was conducted; (4) examine each study and, using the coding sheet, record the conditions under which it was conducted; (5) compute the intercoder reliability of on the codings; (6) compute the effect size for each study; (7) statistically analyze the characteristics and effect sizes for all of the studies; and (8) write a research report. Several computer programs are available for calculating effect sizes and running special analyses. Numerous useful references are provided throughout the chapter for the researcher who wants to use any of these techniques.

Readers also are reminded of three criticisms of meta-analyses: (1) comparing apples with oranges, (2) publication bias, and (3) quality control difficulties. There were many studies that claim to be meta-analytical research but that nevertheless fail to demonstrate all the necessary components of a meta-analysis. It is a hope of this author that after reading this chapter, readers recognize what a meta-analysis involves and can identify those falsely claimed meta-analytical research reports.

36.6 HOMEWORK PROBLEMS

1. What are the distinctive features separating a meta-analysis from a narrative literature review?
2. Identify three meta-analytical articles in the *Public Administration Review* or related journal publications. Use the basic requirements of a meta-analysis you learn in this chapter to evaluate them either as meta-analyses or mislabeled review studies.
3. You are conducting a meta-analysis comparing male and female employees' job performance ratings. Go to http://mason.gmu.edu/~dwilsonb/ma.html and click on es_calculator to convert the following raw statistics from individual studies into effect sizes. When calculating effect sizes for each study, you need to pay attention to the direction of the results in individual studies and make sure the effect sizes' signs (i.e., positive versus negative) are consistent across studies. In question 3, we will make the positive effect sizes represent males' scores were higher than females' and the negative effect sizes represent females' scores were higher than males'.

Study ID	Data Type	Male Ratees	Female Ratees	Reported Status	Direction	Unweighted Effect Size
Study #1	Means, s.d.s	256	239	Male: 2.27, s.d. = 1.2 Female: 1.87, s.d. = 1	M > F	
Study #2	T or F values	43	49	$t = 4.15$	M > F	
Study #3	R values	53	99	$r = 0.15$	F > M	
Study #4	Chi-square	208	248	$\chi^2 = 11.672$	F > M	
Study #5	Proportions or frequencies	135	348	Male 73%, female 87%	F > M	

REFERENCES

American Heritage® *Dictionary of the English Language* 2000. 4th ed. Boston, Massachusetts: Houghton Mifflin Company.

American Psychological Association 2001. *Publication Manual of the American Psychological Association*, 5th ed. Washington, DC: American Psychological Association.

Bowen, C.C., Swim, J.K., and Jacobs, R. 2000. Evaluating gender biases on actual job performance of real people: A meta-analysis. *Journal of Applied Social Psychology, 30*, 2194–2215.

Eagly, A.H. and Johnson, B.T. 1990. Gender and leadership style: A meta-analysis. *Psychological Bulletin, 108*, 233–256.

Gaugler, B.B., Rosenthal, D.B., Thornton, G.C., III, and Bentson, C. 1987. Meta-analysis of assessment center validity, *Journal of Applied Psychology Monograph, 72*(3): 394–511.

Glass, G.V. 1976. Primary, secondary and meta-analysis. *Educational Researcher, 5*, 3–8.

Hedges, L.V. and Olkin, I. 1985. *Statistical Methods for Meta-Analysis*, New York: Academic Press.

Hedges, L.V. and Vevea, J. 2005. Selection model approaches to publication bias. In H. Rothstein, A. Sutton, and M. Borenstein (Eds.) *Publication Bias in Meta-Analysis*. New York: John Wiley.

Hunter, J.E. and Schmidt, F.L. 1990. *Methods of Meta-Analysis: Correcting Error and Bias in Research Findings*, Beverly Hill, California: Sage.

Johnson, B.T. 1993. *DSTAT 1.10: Software for the Meta-Analytic Review of Research Literatures*, New Jersey: Lawrence Erlbaum Associates.

Rosenthal, R. 1979. The "file drawer problem" and tolerance for null results. *Psychological Bulletin, 86*, 638–641.

Rosenthal, R. and Rubin, D.B. 1986. Meta-analysis procedures for combining studies with multiple effect sizes. *Psychological Bulletin, 99*(3): 400–406.

Smith, M.L. and Glass, G.V. 1977. Meta-analysis of psychotherapy outcome studies. *American Psychologist, 32*, 752–760.

Swim, J.K. and Sanna, L.J. 1995. He's skilled, she's lucky: A meta-analysis of observers' attributions for women's and men's success and failures. *Personality and Social Psychology Bulletin, 22*, 507–519.

Swim, J.K., Borgida, E., Maruyama, G., and Myers, D.G. 1989. Joan McKay versus John McKay: Do gender stereotypes bias evaluations? *Psychological Bulletin, 105*, 409–429.

37 Q Methodology

Steven R. Brown, Dan W. Durning, and Sally C. Selden

CONTENTS

37.1 INTRODUCTION

Q methodology resembles in many ways the other public administration research methods described in this book. It requires the collection and manipulation of data, followed by the analysis of this data using sophisticated statistical techniques. And, as with other methods, Q methodology can be used to explore a phenomenon of interest to gain insight into it and to generate and test hypotheses.

Despite these common traits, Q methodology differs from the usual body of statistical techniques employed in public administration research in ways that have profound implications for its use. In fact, the designation of this method as "Q" is intended to differentiate it from "R" methodology, the statistical methods used for "objective" or "scientific" research in the social sciences. The differences between Q and R methods are not simply a matter of technique; they reflect different philosophies of inquiry that encompass competing epistemologies and different understandings of what constitutes sound scientific practice.

Although some researchers are attracted to Q methodology by its philosophical underpinnings, others value it for the insights it provides. The first set of researchers view Q methodology as an alternative to R methods, which they consider to be inadequate tools of a discredited positivism, whereas the second group is drawn for practical reasons: it yields information that often differs from that obtainable through R methods. For these researchers or public administration professionals, Q methodology is a new research or analytic tool to add to their repertoire. It provides them with another lens to investigate an issue or research topic.

Whatever the motivation for its use, Q methodology is both accessible to novice researchers and a challenge to the most experienced. It is an intensive methodology that maps how individuals think about an event, issue, or topic of research interest. Depending on the focus of the study, Q can provide deeper understanding of the opinions, beliefs, perspectives, decision structures, frames, or narratives of individuals on any topic that has a subjective component. In fact, it has been described as "the best-developed paradigm for the investigation of human subjectivity" (Dryzek and Holmes, 2002, p. 20).

This chapter introduces Q methodology to researchers who know little about it but might like to employ it in their work. First we summarize the essentials of conducting Q-methodology research and compare research using Q and R methodologies. The second section provides a short history of Q methodology and its foundations, then illustrates in detail how a Q method study is carried out. In the third section, we review public administration-related studies that have been carried out using Q methodology and suggest future projects.

37.1.1 ESSENTIAL ELEMENTS OF Q METHOD

Q methodology is best understood as a type of research that identifies the operant subjectivity of individuals in regard to a particular subject. The methodology encompasses a broader philosophy of how subjectivity can best be studied, an inherent epistemology, and a method that includes a series of well-defined steps or phases. In this section, we introduce these steps or phases, and then show how they are applied.

The major steps or phases of Q method research include identifying the concourse (what is the flow of communication—that is, what is being said or written—about the topic of interest), creating a sample of the concourse that captures its diversity (the Q sample), selecting the people of interest to carry out the sort (the P sample), administering the sort, conducting a statistical analysis of the completed sorts, and interpreting the Q factors that emerge from the analysis. In carrying out these steps, the researcher's role is manifest and transparent, beginning with the identification of the concourse to the interpretation of the factors. Unlike R methods, which obscure or hide the importance of researcher judgment and a priori choices in the technicalities of technique, Q methodology clearly engages researchers in each step of the research process. These phases are summarized as follows and are elaborated more fully in Section 37.2:

(1) Identifying the concourse: Any topic of interest to people in general or to individuals in specific roles, such as policy maker or bureaucrat, generates conversation about it. This conversation occurs in natural language, and it may appear in discussions or arguments, in e-mails and blogs, in newspapers and magazines, in books, and in other forms of communication. This communication of facts, information, beliefs, opinions, and feelings about a topic comprises a concourse. In the first Q method phase, the researcher identifies—to the extent possible—the communication on the topic of interest. To do so, the researcher may interview people likely to be engaged in communicating about the topic; alternatively, the researcher may collect statements from written sources. Depending on the topic, the researcher will collect dozens to hundreds to thousands of expressions of opinions, assertions, and arguments related to the topic. These expressions—usually in the form of statements—comprise the concourse.

(2) Sampling the concourse: When the concourse has been thoroughly documented, the researcher extracts a representative sample from it. This sample is not randomly drawn from the concourse, but is selected carefully by the researcher with the goal of capturing the diversity and complexity of the different views contained within the concourse. Usually, the researcher is guided in the selection of a sample by a framework that has been formulated to model the important elements of the topic. This framework is practical in that it is designed to insure that the main viewpoints are fully represented in the sample, and it is theoretical in that, instead of being ad hoc, it draws on models explicated in previous research. The sample must include enough statements to fully represent the diversity of the concourse, but must not have so many statements that it cannot be used effectively in the sorts to be administered.

(3) Q sorting: A Q sort results when the researcher asks a selected person to place the statements comprising the Q sample in rank order. The researcher provides (a) a Q sort deck, which consists of all Q-sample statements written on separate cards that have been randomly numbered, (b) instructions on how the cards should be ranked; for example, the sorter may be asked to place the cards along a nine-point continuum (beginning with -4 and ending with $+4$ with 0 as midpoint) following a quasi-normal distribution, and (c) instructions on the conditions governing the sort; for example the sorter may be asked to rank the statements from agree or disagree, placing two statements with which the sorter disagrees the most in the -4 category and the two statements with which the sorter agrees the most in $+4$ category, then to put three of the remaining statements with which the sorter most disagrees in the -3 category and the three that are agreed with the most in the $+3$ category, and so on. If the sort is administered in person, the researcher can observe the sorting process, record comments, and ask questions about the decisions involved in placing certain statements in the extreme categories.

(4) Selecting the sorters (the P sample): Because Q methodology is an intensive methodology, the selection of the people to complete a sort (the P sample) is an important element of the method. The selection depends highly on the topic that is being investigated. If the study focuses on a topic of concern largely to a specific organization, every person of interest can be included. If the study addresses a broader topic affecting a larger group of people and interests, the selection of participants should be designed to make sure that the full range of opinions and positions are represented in the P sample.

(5) Analyzing the Q sorts: After the sorting is complete, the researcher analyzes the completed Q sorts. The statistical analysis begins by correlating the Q sorts, followed by factor analysis of the correlation matrix and factor rotation. This statistical analysis takes into account a distinct feature of the Q sort data: the statements comprising the Q sample are the

observations of the study and the individuals completing the Q sorts are the variables. In other words, in a statistical analysis, the statements are the dependent variables and the sorters are the independent variables. Thus, when factor analysis and factor rotation are completed, the Q factors are made up of groups of sorters who have similar views on the topic of interest.

(6) Interpreting the factors: The final research step is to interpret the factors that have been identified, including how they differ and how they are similar. To carry out this step, the researcher examines the weighted average sort of each factor and compares that sort to the weighted average sorts of the other factors. This type of analysis uses abductive logic, which involves reasoning from observed effects to plausible causes (Brown and Robyn, 2004; Wolf, 2004). From this comparison, the researcher can describe the structure of thought that exists for each factor, and can identify how the factors resemble each other and how they differ.

37.1.2   RESEARCH WITH Q AND R METHODS: A PRACTICAL EXAMPLE

How does Q method work in practice? Suppose a researcher is interested in how managers of public agencies in another country, say Ukraine, view their jobs, specifically the organization of their work; the methods of control and discipline they use; their attitudes toward change; and their relationships with subordinates, superiors, and the public. As part of this study, the researcher would like to investigate whether younger managers have perspectives different from those of older managers. Also, the investigator might wish to compare the attitudes of Ukrainian public managers with those of public managers in the United States.

37.1.2.1   The R Method Approach

The common scientific approach to this type of research would be to formulate hypotheses about the different types of managers, and how the types of managers would vary by location and age. Then, the hypotheses would be tested with data collected from application of a survey instrument that would contain questions or statements with scales allowing the respondents to indicate their degree of agreement or disagreement. The survey instrument would seek to measure the dimensions of the public manager's job addressed in the hypotheses. For example, to test the hypothesis that older managers in Ukraine are more likely than younger managers to have an autocratic managerial style, the researcher would create a set of questions and statements designed to measure how the manager relates to subordinates (e.g., whether the manager gives orders or invites participation in decisions).

This survey might be sent to a random sample of public managers in Ukraine, or perhaps a stratified random sample to insure that both younger and older managers are fully represented. Most likely, however, because of the difficulties in identifying the whole population of public administrators and extracting a random sample, the target population would be the public employees in a particular city or region, and the sample would be drawn from that population. To render it a cross-national comparison, a random sample of public managers in the United States, or more likely, managers in a comparable government, would be selected and sent the survey.

After receiving the completed surveys, the researcher would enter the data into a spreadsheet or statistical program, creating a huge matrix of variable responses by observation. Then, different statistical analyses would be performed. Likely, the responses to different questions or statements would be used to construct dependent variables, which would represent different views of the elements of public management under study (for example, more or less autocratic managerial style). Then, these dependent variables could be included in regression analyses to test hypotheses (for example, with managerial style as the dependent variable, the independent variables might be the age of the respondent, years of experience, educational background, nationality).[1]

37.1.2.2 Using Q Methodology

The researcher could also use Q methodology to investigate this research question and to explore many of the same hypotheses. However, the process of research and the results would look much different and, we would argue, they would more accurately reflect the richness and complexity of the views of the different managers.

The researcher would follow the steps or phases described above, beginning by identifying the communication (what is being said) about the topic of interest, the jobs of public managers. This communication could be identified by interviewing several public managers about their jobs, focusing particularly on the job dimensions of research interest, or it might be done by reading accounts of managers in the two countries about their jobs. From this concourse about the jobs of public managers, a sample would be selected that represented, as far as possible, the diversity of communication in all of its important dimensions. This sample, in the form of 30 to 60 statements, would comprise the Q sort to be administered to managers.

The researcher would then ask selected managers to complete the Q sorts. The selection of managers would be intended to insure that those most likely to have different views would be included. A key goal in selecting managers to complete the Q sorts would be to obtain the largest possible diversity of views. Also, the researcher would purposely select a group of younger and older managers to insure that information would be obtained that would help explore whether the two groups have different views toward their jobs. For a comparative perspective, the sorts would of course be administered to groups of Ukrainian and American public administrators.

The managers would complete the Q sort by placing the statements in a quasi-normal distribution from "most agree" to "most disagree." The sort would be forced, in that the number of cards to be placed in each category—say, from +4 (most agree) to −4 (most disagree)—would be specified. In this case, there would be nine categories, with the largest number of cards to be placed in the 0 category and the fewest to be placed in the +4 and −4 categories. As the sort was being completed, the researcher could engage in a dialogue with the sorter, noting questions that were raised, comments that accompanied the placement of statements, and reactions to certain statements. Then, the sort could be followed up by inquiring into the manager's reasons for placing statements in the most extreme positions.

When all of the Q sorts were completed, they would be analyzed by first correlating them, then using the correlation matrix for factor analysis. However, because the factor analysis would treat the sorters as variables and the statements as observations, the resulting factors would represent the cluster of managers whose views of public management are quite similar. Using information about how the different clusters of managers completed their sorts, the researcher would then identify and discuss the different views about public management among the managers who completed the sorts.

The analysis of the Q sorts would provide insight into how public managers understand their job. These views would not necessarily conform any models that were specified a priori, nor would they be forced into categories based on responses to any particular statements whose meaning was specified in advance by the researcher. In fact, before carrying out the analysis of the sorts, the number of different perspectives and their nature would be unknown. Thus, the managers participating in the Q study would determine the number and nature of the perspectives of public management by revealing through their Q sorts their operant subjectivities.

In some cases, a researcher might want to use the Q sort results to explore the extent to which sorters with specific characteristics are clustered in the same factors or are spread out among different factors. For example, with this study of Ukrainian and American managers it is possible to examine the characteristics (e.g., age, experience, nationality) of the managers in different factors to see if managers with specific characteristics have similar or different understandings of the job of public manager. In this way, it is possible to explore hypotheses, e.g., that older managers will display more autocratic management styles than will younger managers. To the extent that older managers grouped together in a factor that could be characterized as more autocratic, and younger managers clustered together in another factor with a less autocratic orientation, the Q study would provide support for acceptance of the hypothesis. (Of course it is possible that a factor is not systematically associated with any demographic variables; such a factor could therefore never be predicted in advance, yet through Q methodology it could be demonstrated to exist.)

It should be emphasized that researchers must be cautious when using Q sort results to investigate the distribution of (R-type) populations among different factors. This type of investigation should be acknowledged as only suggesting a pattern of common or different viewpoints related to certain demographic characteristics because Q methodology is intended to identify subjectivities that exist, not to determine how those subjectivities are distributed across a population.

37.1.3 SUMMARY: KEY DIFFERENCES IN Q AND R METHODOLOGIES

This comparison of how Q and R methodological studies would be carried out on the same topic provides some insight into the key differences in the methodologies.[2] These include:

- Q methodology seeks to understand how individuals think (i.e., the structure of their thoughts) about the research topic of interest. R methodology identifies the structure of opinion or attitudes in a population. Thus, the results of Q method will identify how an individual, or individuals with common views, understand an issue; the results of R methods describe the characteristics of a population that are associated statistically with opinions, attitudes, or behavior (e.g., voting) being investigated.
- Although R methods are intended for the "objective" analysis of research issues, Q methodology is designed to study subjectivity. R methodology is found on logical positivism in which the researcher is an outside objective observer. In contrast, Q methodology is more closely related to postpositivist ideas (Durning, 1999) that reject the possibility of observer objectivity and question the assumption that the observer's vantage point, if not objective, is in some sense superior to that of any other observer, including the person being observed. Thus, Q methodology is in tune with phenomenological (Taylor et al., 1994), hermeneutic (McKeown, 1990, 1998), and quantum theories (Stephenson, 1983).[3]
- Q methodology is an intensive method that seeks in-depth understanding of how at least one person thinks about the topic of investigation. As an intensive method, Q methodology requires a small number of well-selected subjects to complete the Q sort. R methods are extensive methods designed to extract an understanding of populations through representative samples of them; thus, they require—depending on the population size and sampling techniques—data from a certain percentage of the population of interest.

37.2 UNDERSTANDING AND USING Q METHODOLOGY: A DETAILED EXPLANATION

In this section of the chapter, we discuss in more detail the history and some of the intellectual foundations of Q methodology; then we present a detailed case study of the use of Q methodology. This case study is intended to be a methodological guide for researchers and practitioners who would like to conduct their own Q method research.

37.2.1 HISTORY AND INTELLECTUAL FOUNDATIONS OF Q METHODOLOGY

37.2.1.1 Brief History

William Stephenson, the inventor of Q methodology, was the last graduate assistant to Charles Spearman, who in turn is best remembered as the inventor of factor analysis. Spearman's main interest, however, was in unlocking the creative potential of the mind, and factor analysis was merely his way of mathematically modeling the processes of thinking in which he had interest. Spearman once referred to Stephenson as the most creative statistician in psychology, but like his mentor, Stephenson was likewise interested in the mind's potential, and the mathematics of his Q methodology are to a large extent secondary to that interest.

Stephenson's innovation can be traced to an August 24, 1935 letter to the editor of the British science journal *Nature* (Brown, 1980, pp. 9–10; Good, 1998, 2005a,b) in which he drew attention to the possibility of "inverting" conventional factor analysis. In R factor analysis, as the conventional approach is often called, traits are correlated across a sample of persons, where "trait" is taken to mean any quantitatively measurable characteristic: the factor analysis of the trait correlations points to families of similarly covarying traits. In Q factor analysis, by way of contrast, persons are correlated across a sample of statements which they have rank-ordered, the ranking being called a Q sort: the correlations reflect the degree of similarity in the way the statements have been sorted, and factor analysis of the person correlations points to families of like-minded individuals. A detailed illustration of what is technically involved is presented later in this part of the chapter.

Stephenson's innovation was misunderstood practically from the start and by such eminent University of London colleagues as Sir Cyril Burt, R.B. Cattell, and Hans Eysenck, and at the University of Chicago by L.L. Thurstone, so that even today his name is often associated with a statistical development which was not only not his, but also was one which he strongly opposed. Virtually without exception, texts which address Q and R factor analysis regard the two as simply the transposed equivalents of one another—that R consists of correlating and factoring the columns of a data matrix, and that Q consists of correlating and factoring the rows of the same matrix. In fact, Stephenson's most sustained articulation of Q methodology, his book *The Study of Behavior* (Stephenson, 1953, p. 15), is typically cited in support of this position despite his clear assertion, repeated often, that "there never was a single matrix of scores to which *both* R and Q apply." In this connection, Miller and Friesen (1984, pp. 47–48) are far from alone when, in their factor-analytic studies of organizations, they confidently assert that "Q-technique is merely R-technique using a transposed raw-data matrix. It treats similarities between companies, rather than between variables. ... Discussion of Q-technique in particular can be found in Stephenson. ..." And more recently, Waller and Meehl (1998), with equal confidence, state that "mathematically, there is nothing remarkable about how Q correlations work. They can be computed... by simply transposing a persons × variables matrix into a variables × persons matrix prior to calculating the correlations" (p. 80). And Stephenson, they go on to say, is "one of the developers and most vociferous advocates of this technique" (p. 81), when in fact he was a life-long critic of it.

37.2.1.2 The Quantum Connection

Miller and Friesen's (1984) book is entitled *Organizations: A Quantum View*, which is fortuitous inasmuch as factor analysis and quantum mechanics (as elaborated by Werner Heisenberg and Max Born in particular) are virtually identical mathematically, both relying on matrix algebra and sharing much of the same nomenclature. Originally trained as a physicist, Stephenson was aware of this parallel in the 1930s, as was Burt (1940), who wrote extensively about it in his *The Factors of the Mind*, which is as fundamental for R methodology as Stephenson's book is for Q.

But Burt and Stephenson (1939) parted company over what it was that was to be measured. Burt was locked into the study of variables, such as intelligence, assertiveness, temperament, and the thousands of others with which social and psychological science is familiar. Variables have known properties, but they are largely categorical and owe much to logic and to "operational definitions," hence their quantum character is nothing more than an analogy: Quantum theory is not about variables as such, but about states (of energy). Although they may enter into dynamic relations with other variables, the variables of R methodology are not in themselves dynamic and are typically expressed in a single number, usually an average score across a number of responses.

The situation is quite different in Q methodology. Suppose that a person ranks a set of statements (say, from agree to disagree) to represent the person's own point of view about the organization. The statements do not measure anything a priori, i.e., their meaning is indeterminate; they are simply assertions that have been made about the organization (e.g., that "it is a pleasant place to work"). Meaning and significance are imposed on the statements by the person in the course of Q sorting them, hence the inseparability of measurement and meaning. The process reflects a dynamic state (of mind) in a relationship of complementarity to other states (i.e., to Q sorts by others in the organization). The final product (the completed Q sort) is not an average, nor is it subject to any external norms; rather, it is a dynamic pattern of interrelationships. The self-referentiality of the Q sorter is obviously central to the situation, and the way in which the statements will be understood and scored is solely in the hands of the Q sorter; it can never be known in advance, therefore, how many factors will emerge, nor what their form and content will be. Everything is indeterminate, and the parallel with quantum theory is made the more remarkable by virtue of the fact that it is a function not of analogy, but of the "sovereignty of measurement" (Stephenson, 1989).

In sum, there is considerably more to the difference between R method and Q method than a simple decision whether to analyze the relationships between the columns of a data matrix or the rows of the same data matrix. A much more fundamental difference is between the study of the variables of R methodology, conceived as objective and subject to classical conceptions of cause and effect; and the study of a data matrix of a wholly different kind, one thoroughly saturated with self-referentiality and probabilism.

37.2.1.3 Concourse Theory

As was noted previously, Stephenson, like his mentor Charles Spearman, was interested in the creative potential of the mind. What is the source of creativity and how do we liberate it for the social good—more specifically, for administrative advantage?

In an instructive book on word origins, C.S. Lewis (1960) devotes a chapter to "conscience and conscious," both of which derive from a common Latin antecedent in which the prefix *con* means *with*—hence *conscio* means sharing what one knows with someone, which includes sharing with oneself, as in musings, daydreams, and mulling things over. But there was also a weaker sense in which *conscientia* connoted simply awareness, as in being conscious of something, epitomized in Descartes's awareness of his own thinking (*cogito ergo sum*) and in introspectionism. Needless to say, this weaker sense of *conscientia*, upon which modern cognitive psychology is based, has virtually replaced the stronger sense of knowledge as shared, thereby elevating the individual thinker while removing almost all traces of the social context within which thinking takes place.

Yet most of ordinary life is based on shared knowledge, and it was on this account that Lewis introduced the term *conscircing* (Stephenson, 1980). Administrators and policy makers spend much of their time exchanging views in committee meetings or around the drinking fountain, and in reading and responding to one another's memos and reports. Under more managed conditions, ideas are shared via Delphi or nominal group techniques in which each person's idea-sharing may release new thoughts in others, the total being greater than what could be produced by the same participants working in isolation. The opposite is equally true that a single individual can often produce ideas that elude groups due to the isolate's relative freedom from conformity and the sometimes suffocating effects of collegiality.

Administration in general has been characterized as "the activities of groups cooperating to accomplish common goals" (Simon et al., 1950, p. 3), and as a group assembles and begins to cooperate, a vast array of possibilities begins to appear, typically in linguistic form. We may assume that the impetus for an assemblage is the existence of a task or problem—e.g., how to pare the budget, what to do about a councilman's complaints concerning the streets in his ward, when to mount a campaign for the school levy, determining who would make the best executive director, etc.—and that the fruits of the group's cooperative efforts take the form of proposed solutions. Hence, using the budget as illustrative, we might hear proposals such as "The easiest thing to do is to slash 3.2 percent across the board," or "We can't really cut back further on social services," or "It's been a mild winter so there should be some fat in the street maintenance line," which may prompt the service director's warning that "We haven't even completed all the repairs from last winter's freeze," and so forth.

All such communicability is inherently contestable, infinite in principle, ubiquitous in character, and inescapably subjective. In quantum theoretical terms, it is also unpredictable, paradoxical, and erratic. No one knows in advance what someone else is going to say or suggest, or how what one person says is going to impact on what others say or think. In Q methodology, such communicability is referred to as a concourse (Stephenson, 1978, 1980), a concept traceable to Cicero, but which takes its most modern form in Peirce's (1955) "Law of Mind"—that ideas spread and affect other ideas and eventually combine into a system, or schema. Concourse is therefore at the foundation of a society and provides lubrication for all its parts, and it constitutes the very stuff of which decisions are made and problems solved. And it is concourse that supplies the elements of Q methodology.

Concourse is present in the loftiest of philosophical discourse to the simplest coos and gurgles of the nursery, as almost any random examples will easily show. In a recent posting on an Internet list devoted to quantum theory and consciousness, for instance, the following assertions were made:

The universe is simple at fundamental levels. ... A unified approach requires complementary modes of description. ... Non-locality is firmly established. ... Self-organization and complexity are prevalent at all scales in the universe. ... All human experience is connected to the universe.

Of such things volumes have been written, many by Nobel laureates and others of repute, each idea midwifing yet other ideas in endless profusion. And although supported in part by facts, communicability of this kind is thoroughly subjective and typically goes beyond known facts, with the facts as such colloidally suspended in the subjectivity. Such is the character of concourse.

Or consider Sasson's (1995) study of the way in which citizens construct crime stories, based on the shared communicability found on op-ed pages of newspapers; or Finkel's (1995) study of jurors' common sense understandings of justice; or Roe's (1994) volume, which is brimming with narratives on such diverse social problems as budgets, global warming, animal experimentation, and so forth. With the contemporary move away from government and in the direction of governance, more emphasis is being given to deliberation (Hajer and Wagenaar, 2003) and to actionable political talk (Irwin, 2006), but apart from their narrative richness, the common limitation of efforts such as these is methodological in character—i.e., once Sasson and the others have gathered their mountains of discourse material, they typically end up sorting it into various more-or-less logical categories. What began on a sound footing of naturalism, therefore, ends up being sectioned according to the categorical proclivities of the analyst.

Perhaps of more direct pertinence to decision-making settings of the kind more familiar to administrators is the concourse that emerged from a meeting of an international commission established to assist in encouraging Central American development (Brown, 2006a). The organizing question concerned the commission's role, and the following observations were among those which were added to the concourse as each commissioner stepped to the microphone:

The Commission must attend not only to economic growth, but to social and cultural growth. ... We must begin with those elements which bring us together, and only later address those issues which divide us. ... It is incumbent upon the Commission to recognize the central role of agriculture in the development of the region. ... It must be adopted as an operating principle that the problems to be considered are autonomous to the region, and not reflections of East-West security issues. ... The process which the Commission works out must, through its structure, recommend that aid be conditioned on measurable and swift progress toward genuine democracy.

The commission spent the better part of a day and a half in this vein, which continued during meals, breaks, over drinks, and in walks on the hotel grounds—perhaps even into some members' dreams. Such is the nature of ideational spreading and affectability characteristic of Peirce's Law of Mind.

Concourse proliferates not only around problems, but in terms of the interests of problem solvers: Ask a manager and a worker how best to improve the organization and different suggestions will be offered. This can be seen concretely in the comments obtained from a group of sixth grade students when asked what might be done to improve their school:

> Have more plays or assemblies. ... Show more movies. ... Make the halls more colorful and interesting by decorating them with students' work. ... Have the PTA hold more activities like the carnival. ... Plant more flowers, bushes, and trees around the building.

Aesthetics, desire for pleasurable activities, and something of a communal spirit predominate, as does the kind of dependency upon adults still characteristic of students at this age. When the same question is asked of a group of young eleventh grade policy makers, however, some of the same issues remain at the surface, but private interest and a desire for autonomy are now more prominent:

> Increase the variety and amount of food for lunch. ... Do away with assigned seats in classes. ... Don't assign homework on Friday or the day before a vacation. ... Add vending machines to the cafeteria (such as candy and pop machines), and put a juke box in the cafeteria. ... Add a course for fourth year French and Spanish. (Ad infinitum)

And in equal volume the solutions were proffered by a group with different interests—graduate students and faculty who were queried as to how best to improve their graduate program:

> Establish a rule or procedure whereby faculty are required to specify clearly and precisely the criteria for grading. ... Structure course offerings so that students can choose between quantitative and non-quantitative approaches. ... Increase the minimum grade-point requirement for newly admitted graduates. ... Place more pressure on the faculty to do research and to publish.

Assembling a concourse relative to a particular decisional situation is part of what Simon (1960) designated as the design phase of the process, in which alternative courses of action are collected. Mere archiving is not the goal, of course, but a new starting point from which alternatives are then appraised, developed, and eventually adopted or discarded, and it is at this point in the process that some of the qualitative methods (e.g., narrative, discourse, and ethnographic analysis) often falter and sometimes never fully regain balance. Given a welter of textual material, the qualitative analyst must find some method of categorization so as to bring order to the enterprise, and this almost inevitably means the superimposition onto verbal protocols of a logical scheme of one kind or another. The conscientious analyst will of course exercise as much care as possible in an effort to assure that the categories used are also functional and not logical only, but there is no cure for the nagging doubt that the categories belong to a greater or lesser extent to the observer rather than the observed.

Q methodology alleviates these doubts to a considerable extent by revealing the participants' own categories and establishing these as the basis for meaning and understanding (Brown, 1996, in press; Watts and Stenner, 2005). How this is accomplished is best grasped in the context of a more extended example, which will also serve to illustrate the quantitative procedures that are involved.

37.2.2 PROBLEM CLARIFICATION WITH Q METHODOLOGY: A CASE STUDY

This study, which has been reported in more detail elsewhere (Mattson et al., 2006), focuses on the problem-identification phase of the policy process. In this particular case, a group of stakeholders

concerned with large carnivore conservation in the Northern Rocky Mountains—ranchers, environmentalists, animal activists, government officials, and academics—met for a two-day workshop
to explore one another's perspectives and to search for a common-interest alternative to legal
confrontation. The first day of the workshop was devoted to examining different understandings
of the underlying problems and the second day to proposing possible solutions.

The process began by inviting the approximately two dozen assembled participants silently to
contemplate "what are the various aspects of the problems associated with carnivore conservation?"
Participants anonymously jotted down freely associated ideas on a sheet of paper until it became
apparent that few if any new ideas would be forthcoming, at which point the sheets were placed in
the middle of the table and each participant picked up a sheet containing ideas generated anonymously by some other participant. Exposure to others' ideas typically generated new ideas, which
were added to the sheets. After sheets had been widely circulated, the number of new ideas
gradually dwindled. The facilitator then proceeded to guide the group through a round-robin process
in which one of the solutions was nominated in turn from the sheet in each participant's possession.
Each nominated solution was discussed, modified through group discussion, and finally added to a
list that was taped to the wall for all to see. (Ultimately, second and third round-robin phases assured
that no good ideas were omitted from the final sample of problem elements.) Group members then
copied each item on a $3'' \times 5''$ card that had been provided, using the same wording as on the wall.
The items were numbered serially, and the item numbers were also recorded on each of the cards.
Eventually, the participants collectively generated $N = 51$ problem elements, and each member was
in possession of a pack of 51 cards on which those problems were written.

Before proceeding to technicalities, it is important to note that the participants had been
purposely selected so as to represent the diverse interests associated with large carnivore conservation in the Northern Rocky Mountain region; consequently, the 51 propositions generated were of
wide scope, and there was not a single one among the 51 that all participants did not immediately
understand as a matter of shared knowledge. All of the items are reported in Table 37.6, but a small
sampling will give a sense of the problems confronting the region:

1. Not all citizens have equal say.
4. Some stakeholders have purposely attempted to accentuate the uncertainty in carnivore
   science to forestall land management decisions.
8. Increased anxiety among the general public regarding carnivore attacks.
13. Habitat fragmentation and isolation are reducing management options.

Tributaries into this concourse of communicability obviously emanate from values, political
commitments, specialization expertise, and other social forces, and it is a virtue of Q methodology
that it sharpens and clarifies the form and substance of such forces.

It should be noted in passing that the wording of some of the items may sound odd and lacking
in the niceties of conventional prose, but participants were given ample time in which to offer
editorial amendments and to clarify meaning, and many items underwent alteration before the final
version was collectively approved. However, unusual or ambiguous the phrasings might appear to
an outsider, therefore, there is little reason to doubt that the insiders themselves understood each and
every statement.

The purpose of this initial phase of item generation was, in this instance, to gather as
comprehensive a set of problems as possible, i.e., to render manifest the problems at the top of
each individual's and group's agenda. The next phase involved distinguishing important from
relatively less important problems, and this was accomplished by instructing each participant to
Q sort the 51 items along a scale from +4 (agree) to −4 (disagree), as shown in Table 37.1 for one
of the participants. It was first recommended that participants divide the items into three groups
(agree, unimportant, and disagree) and that from the agreeable items they then select those five
deemed most agreeable: these were placed under the +4 label, with the five next-most agreeable

TABLE 37.1

Q Sort for Person 1

Most Disagree					Most Agree			
−4	**−3**	**−2**	**−1**	**0**	**+1**	**+2**	**+3**	**+4**
12	7	1	6	2	18	15	10	3
19	21	14	8	9	34	17	13	4
22	41	24	11	16	36	30	20	5
26	43	44	37	23	38	31	28	27
33	51	45	46	25	42	32	35	29
		47	50	40	49	39		
				48				

being placed under the +3 label. (The labels were arrayed across the tabletop in front of each participant, to serve as an aid in the sorting.) The participants then examined the stack of problem statements with which they most disagreed and selected the five most disagreeable of all (for −4), and then the five next-most disagreeable (−3). Eventually all 51 items were arrayed in front of the participant, from those most agreeable on the right down to those most disagreeable on the left. The statement numbers were then entered on score sheets so as to preserve the way in which each of the participants prioritized the problems.

It deserves mention in passing that the so-called forced distribution pictured in Table 37.1, although somewhat arbitrary in shape and range, is nevertheless recommended for theoretical and practical reasons. Theoretically, a quasi-normal distribution models the Law of Error and is backed by a hundred years of psychometric research indicating that Q sorting and other quasi-ranking procedures typically result in distributions of this kind (Brown, 1985). From a practical standpoint, a standard symmetrical distribution of this kind constrains responses and forces participants to make decisions they might otherwise conceal (e.g., by placing all statements under +4 and −4), thereby increasing the likelihood that implicit values and priorities will be rendered explicit and open to view. However, because the shape of the sorting distribution has little statistical impact on the subsequent correlation and factor analysis, recalcitrant respondents (who might otherwise refuse to cooperate) can be permitted to follow their own inclinations while being encouraged to adhere as closely as possible to the distribution specified.

Given 51 possible problems to consider, there are literally billions of different ways—in fact, more than a billion billion—in which they could be prioritized, and yet the participants individually work through the complexities involved within just a few minutes, which is testimony to the adaptability and efficiency of the human mind. Each person is guided in this enterprise by the values, interests, and principles that are brought to the task, and what these values and interests are can usually be inferred through inspection of the person's Q sort.

Consider, for instance, the Q sort provided by participant 1 (Table 37.1), who singled out the following problems as most important (score +4):

3. People tend to talk to members of their own group and reinforce their own prejudices.
4. Some stakeholders have purposely attempted to accentuate the uncertainty in carnivore science to forestall land management decisions.
5. Costs of carnivore conservation are disproportionately accrued by local citizens.
27. Lack of trust among participants.
29. Necessary incentives for appropriate behavior by all parties are absent.

To maximize candidness, participants were not required to place names on their score sheets, and so in many instances it was not possible to associate specific responses with particular individuals, although the identities of many of the respondents eventually came to be known. Personal identities are generally unimportant in a study such as this, however, for what is of interest are the subjective views themselves—i.e., the perspectives that exist within the group—and not the associated characteristics of those who espouse them. In this connection, the first participant's choice of important issues indicates no allegiance to any side; rather, a sensitivity in particular to process factors such as trust, reinforcement of prejudices, and lack of incentives on all sides.

The problem elements with which this person most disagrees (score −4) are also illuminating:

12. Recovery zones for carnivores are arbitrary.
19. Worldview of locals does not include the scarcity of large carnivores.
22. People whose livelihoods are hindered by carnivores are clinging to outmoded ways of life.
26. Wolves are reducing hunting opportunity, and therefore hurting the economy.
33. Humans are intolerant of carnivores.

This Q sorter was open about his identity as a Canadian government official whose duties brought him into contact with both environmentalists and ranchers threatened in particular by expanding grizzly populations, and who was therefore aware both that recovery zones are not arbitrary and that the worldviews of local people were not opposed to issues of wildlife scarcity.

The Q sort is part of the technical accouterment of Q methodology, to which it bears a relationship analogous to the telescope to astronomy or the galvanometer to electricity; i.e., it brings into view for direct and sustained inspection those structures of subjectivity and preference that suffuse political and administrative life. The decisional situation facing the participants in this study contains objective realities—e.g., the existence of wolf packs and grizzlies, disconnected habitats, farming and ranching operations, and public lands, as referred to in the statements above—but what is felt to constitute an important as distinguished from an unimportant problem is a phenomenon of another kind: it is the subjective medium within which the facts as known by each participant are suspended, and in terms of which they are given meaning and salience, as rendered manifest by the +4/−4 subjective scale. The concourse of problems that the participants produced is fed from such subjective currents, and yet these sources remain obscure until transformed by the mechanics of Q sorting.

Among the features of Q methodology which distinguish it from many other quantitative procedures is that the elements comprising the Q sort, unlike those in a rating scale, are not constrained by prior meaning; consequently, there can be no correct way to do a Q sort in the same sense as there is a right way to respond to an IQ test or to the Graduate Record Examination. What a particular rancher or environmentalist considers the most important problems facing society is simply that person's judgment, which may or may not be in agreement with others' appraisals. It is this absence of norms—not just in practice, but in principle—that renders the issue of validity of such little concern in Q methodology (Brown, 1992, 1993). Validity aside, however, we can nevertheless proceed to compare subjective appraisals, and to determine the varieties of perspectives in existence and the shape and character of each, and it is at this point that quantification is brought to bear.

Q sorts are conventionally intercorrelated and factor analyzed, and the correlation phase is fairly elementary, as shown in Table 37.2 for the Q sorts provided by participants 1 and 2. The scores in column 1 are the same as those shown in the previous table (for the 51 issues and problems which were sorted), whereas those in column 2 were given during the same sitting by participant no. 2. The numbers in column d^2 are the squared differences in score between the two performances. Were the two participants' views absolutely identical, there would of course be no differences in score between the two for any of the statements, in which case the squared differences would also be zero, as would the sum of squared differences: In this extremely rare and virtually impossible instance,

TABLE 37.2
Correlation between Q Sorts 1 and 2

Item	1	2	d^2
(1)	−2	−2	0
(2)	0	−1	1
(3)	4	−2	36
(4)	4	0	16
(5)	4	−3	49
(6)	−1	4	25
(7)	−3	−4	1
(8)	−1	−1	0
(9)	0	4	16
(10)	3	−1	16
(11)	−1	0	1
(12)	−4	3	49
(13)	3	3	0
(14)	−2	4	36
(15)	2	3	1
(16)	0	4	16
(17)	2	1	1
(18)	1	0	1
(19)	−4	0	16
(20)	3	0	9
(21)	−3	−4	1
(22)	−4	−3	1
(23)	0	−2	4
(24)	−2	−2	0
(25)	0	3	9
(26)	−4	−4	0
(27)	4	0	16
(28)	3	−1	16
(29)	4	−4	64
(30)	2	−3	25
(31)	2	−4	36
(32)	2	2	0
(33)	−4	−1	9
(34)	1	2	1
(35)	3	−2	25
(36)	1	−1	4
(37)	−1	2	9
(38)	1	1	0
(39)	2	1	1
(40)	0	−2	4
(41)	−3	1	16
(42)	1	3	4
(43)	−3	1	16
(44)	−2	−3	1
(45)	−2	4	36
(46)	−1	0	1
(47)	−2	2	16
(48)	0	−3	9

TABLE 37.2 (Continued)
Correlation between Q Sorts 1 and 2

Item	1	2	d^2
(49)	1	2	1
(50)	−1	2	9
(51)	−3	1	16
			$\Sigma d^2 = 640$

$$r_{12} = 1 - \frac{640}{620} = -0.03$$

the correlation would be $r = 1.00$; were the two views diametrically opposite, the correlation would be $r = -1.00$.

In the instant case, there are differences of a greater or lesser extent among the statements, as recorded in column d^2, the sum amounting to 640. When Q sorts follow the same distribution (hence have the same mean and variance), a convenient formula for correlation is as shown in Table 37.2, where 640 is the sum of squared differences and 620 is the combined sum of squares of the scores in the two Q sorts. The correlation between these two Q sorts is therefore $r = -0.03$.

Q-sort correlations are rarely of any interest in and of themselves and typically represent only a phase through which the data passes on the way to being factor analyzed. It is worth noting, however, that the correlation coefficients are subject to standard error formulae. For example, we can assume pro tem that two participants' views are substantially related if they exceed $2.58(1/\sqrt{N}) = 0.37$ (for $N = 51$ Q statements), where $\sigma_{r=0} = 1/\sqrt{N}$ is the standard error of a zero-order coefficient, and $z = 2.58$ is the number of standard errors required to incorporate 99 percent of the area under the normal curve. The above correlation of -0.03 for participants 1 and 2 (which is less than the requisite 0.37) therefore indicates that their respective appraisals of problems associated with carnivore conservation share little in common.

Of the 26 participants originally involved in this problem-clarification process, only seven have been included in the following analysis so as to keep calculations and tabular displays within manageable limits for illustrative purposes. The intercorrelations among the seven participants are displayed in Table 37.3. Note that the correlation between respondents 1 and 2 is $r = -0.03$, as calculated above.

The correlation matrix has a certain dynamic to it, just as did the group from which the Q sorts were taken: hence a rancher may have been concerned about the threat to his herds and pets from wolf packs, and might therefore have been less sympathetic to other participants' expressed concerns about endangered species and habitat fragmentation. Which issues each person places at the top, middle, or bottom of the Q sort can therefore be influenced by myriad considerations, from personal motivation to the climate created by national and local politics, each force being explicitly or sometimes only implicitly weighed by the Q sorter and ultimately having its impact on the final statement arrangement. The correlation matrix is therefore a thick soup of dynamic forces of chaotic proportions that nevertheless summarizes the balance of influences and the way in which the various participants have worked their way to separate conclusions about what are important versus unimportant problems related to carnivore conservation.

Q methodology was conceived in the context of factor analytic developments as they were unfolding in the 1930s, which was late in the heyday of Charles Spearman and the "London School." Stephenson's (1935) psychometric innovation of "correlating persons instead of tests" consisted of applying the mathematics of factor analysis to correlation matrices of the above kind, in which one person responses were correlated with other person responses. The result was typically a typology of response, with one subgroup of similar Q sorts constituting one factor, another group

TABLE 37.3

Correlations among Seven Q Sorts

Ps	1	2	3	4	5	6	7
(1)	—	−03	39	15	19	05	09
(2)		—	36	−59	36	84	22
(3)			—	−30	45	27	50
(4)				—	−10	−42	−33
(5)					—	34	39
(6)						—	32
(7)							—

Note: Decimals to two places omitted.

constituting another factor, and so forth. Q factors therefore have the status of separate attitudes, perspectives, or understandings, or, in the extant case, of problem priorities.

By whatever substantive terminology (attitudes, perspectives, value orientations, problem priorities, etc.), the factors in Q methodology consist of conglomerates of convergent subjectivity as determined by the concrete operations of the persons themselves as they perform the Q sorts—hence the term *operant subjectivity* (Stephenson, 1977). The number and content of the factors, despite their thoroughly subjective character, are therefore emergent and purely empirical features of the thinking and feeling of the persons who provided the Q sorts: Had the group members felt differently about the issues, their Q sorts would have been different, and so would the structural features of the correlation matrix and so, as a consequence, would the factors, which in their turn summarize those structural features. The role of factor analysis in this instance is to document the current state of thinking within this diverse group with respect to the issues at the group's focus of attention.

The technicalities of factor analysis are addressed elsewhere in this volume, and relatively simplified introductions are available for those wishing to achieve a conceptual grasp (e.g., Adcock, 1954; Brown, 1980, pp. 208–247; Kline, 1994); we will therefore bypass the detailed calculations involved in extracting the unrotated loadings for centroid factors (a) through (g), as shown in Table 37.4.

Suffice it to say that from a statistical standpoint, the seven unrotated factors represent a partial decomposition of the previous correlation matrix. This can be illustrated in terms of any two Q sorts (say, 2 and 6), which are correlated in the amount 0.84 (see Table 37.3). The sum of the cross products of the unrotated factor loadings for these two Q sorts is $(0.75)(0.71) + (−0.58)(−0.39) + \cdots + (−0.05)(0.12) = 0.84$, which indicates that all of the original correlation of 0.84 can be composed from these seven factors. (Factor loading cross products rarely sum up to exactly the original correlation, as they did in this instance, due to residual correlations that typically remain after the seven factors have been extracted.) The factor loadings indicate the correlation of each Q sort with the factor; hence, Q sort 2 correlates with the first factor in the amount $f = 0.75$; factor loadings are therefore subject to the same standard error estimates as noted previously for correlation coefficients, i.e., $\sigma_{r=0} = 1/\sqrt{N} = 0.14$, where $N = 51$ statements. Factor loadings in excess of $2.58(0.14) = 0.37$ are significant ($p < .01$), which means that the Q sort of the second person is significantly associated with the first factor.

Had there been only a single viewpoint shared by all participants, then all of the correlations would have been large and positive, only one significant factor would have been in evidence, and there would have been no trace of significant loadings on the other factors. As Table 37.4 shows, however, at least the first two of the unrotated factors contain significant loadings, and some of the loadings on the fifth and sixth factors are also substantial; we would therefore anticipate that there are at least two and perhaps three or four separate points of view within this group of participants.

TABLE 37.4

Unrotated and Rotated Centroid Factor Loadings

Ps	Unrotated Factors							Rotated	
	a	b	c	d	e	f	g	X	Y
(1)	14	**39**	21	16	22	10	04	−14	**39**
(2)	**75**	**−58**	18	30	04	−09	−05	**97**	13
(3)	**72**	**43**	−03	22	26	11	11	22	**82**
(4)	**−46**	31	34	−29	02	15	−15	**−61**	−08
(5)	**55**	22	18	04	−04	05	−15	21	**54**
(6)	**71**	**−39**	28	12	−12	−07	12	**77**	22
(7)	**56**	17	−22	13	−37	**51**	24	25	**67**

Note: Factor loadings in boldface significant ($p < .01$).

Although there are some occasions in which the factor analyst might rest content with the unrotated loadings as these have been extracted from the correlation matrix, in the overwhelming number of cases unrotated loadings do not give the best view of what is transpiring; it is typically the case, therefore, that the unrotated factor loadings are superseded by an alternative set of loadings which give a more focused view. This transformation process from the unrotated to an alternative set of loadings is accomplished through the process of factor rotation.

The most conventional scheme for factor rotation is to rely on the Varimax routine found in all software packages (such as SPSS) containing factor analysis, and it is the statistical goal of Varimax to rotate the factors in such a way that each variable (or Q sort) is maximized on a single factor and minimized on all other factors, a solution referred to as "simple structure." If a researcher is totally in the dark about the topic under examination, as is sometimes the case, then leaving factor rotation to Varimax or some other algorithm may be as good a strategy as any other.

However, it is unlikely that there is a single set of mathematical rules, such as Varimax, which is apt to provide the best solution to problems under any and all conditions. In particular, when an investigator has some knowledge or even vague hunches about a situation, then it is often wise to permit that information to play some role in the experimental setting. It is for situations such as these that room was made in Q methodology for "theoretical rotation," a judgmental procedure that is explicitly built into the PQMethod freeware program (Schmolck and Atkinson, 2002) and into the PCQ Windows-based program (Stricklin and Almeida, 2004).

Space precludes going into great detail concerning theoretical rotation (see Brown and Robyn, 2004; Kramer and Gavina, 2004), but what is essentially at issue can be demonstrated in terms of Figure 37.1, which graphically displays the location of each Q sort in terms of unrotated factors (a) and (b) in Table 37.4. The pairs of loadings for each of the seven Q sorts are duplicated in Figure 37.1 where it is shown that Q sort 1 has a loading on factor (a) in the amount 0.14 and on factor (b) in the amount 0.39, and these two loadings serve to locate Q sort 1 in the two-dimensional space in Figure 37.1. Similarly, Q sort 6 is located 0.71 on factor (a) and −0.39 on (b). The relative proximity of each of the Q sorts is a spatial expression of their degree of similarity with respect to these two factors, the nature of which are undefined at this point.

Seven unrotated factors were originally extracted, which is the default in the PQMethod program. Of these seven, factors (a) and (b) were initially chosen for rotation due to an interest in Q sorts 4 and 6, the former a rancher and the latter an environmental activist, who were expected to be at loggerheads vis-à-vis most of the issues associated with large carnivores. As indicated in Table 37.4, Q sorts 4 and 6 have substantial loadings on factor (a) (−0.46 and 0.71, respectively) and also on (b) (0.31 and −0.39), which means that they are to a considerable extent at opposite poles of both factors.

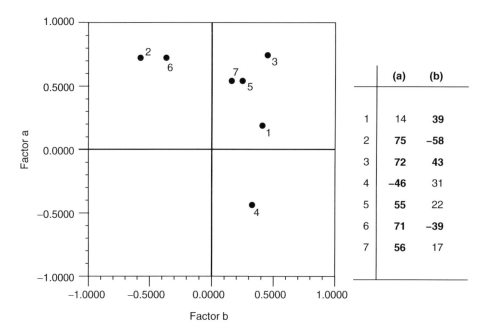

FIGURE 37.1 Location of each Q sort in terms of unrotated factors (a) and (b), illustrating spatially the degree of similarity of the Q sorts with respect to factors (a) and (b). Factor loadings in boldface significant ($p < .01$).

Figure 37.2 displays the relationships among the Q sorts when the original vectors are rotated counterclockwise by 37°. Also shown are the new factor loadings which indicate that Q sort 4 is now saturated on the new factor (a) in the amount -0.56 (up from -0.46) and on (b) at -0.03 (down in magnitude from 0.31). Q sort 6 is likewise more focused on factor (a) to the extent of 0.80.

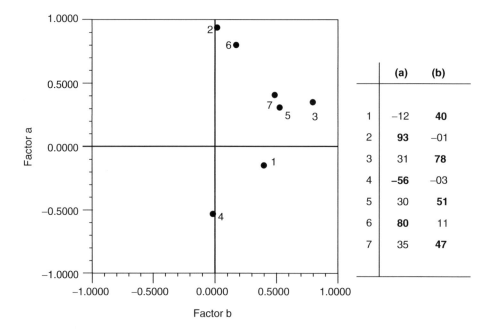

FIGURE 37.2 Displays each Q sort after rotating the original vectors counterclockwise by 37°. Factor loadings in boldface significant ($p < .01$).

These two sets of coefficients, unrotated, and rotated, are mathematically equivalent, as can be seen when the respective loadings are squared and summed, as follows (to four decimal places, for accuracy):

$$\begin{aligned}
\text{Q sort 4} \quad &\text{unrotated: } (-0.4615)^2 + 0.3103^2 &&= 0.3093 \\
&\text{rotated: } (-0.5553)^2 + (-0.0300)^2 &&= 0.3093 \\
\text{Q sort 6} \quad &\text{unrotated: } 0.7051^2 + (-0.3908)^2 &&= 0.6499 \\
&\text{rotated: } 0.7983^2 + 0.1122^2 &&= 0.6499
\end{aligned}$$

These sums are identical in both cases as they would be for any of the infinite number of other rotations. Another method of verification is to examine the cross products of factor loadings for any two Q sorts, e.g., 4 and 6:

$$\begin{aligned}
\text{Unrotated:} \quad &(-0.4615)\,(0.7051) + (0.3103)\,(-0.3908) = -0.4467 \\
\text{Rotated:} \quad &(-0.5553)\,(0.7983) + (-0.0300)\,(0.1122) = -0.4467
\end{aligned}$$

which, again, are identical. The cross product sums of -0.4467 indicate that of the original correlation of -0.42 between Q sorts 4 and 6 (see Table 37.3), factors (a) and (b), both the rotated and unrotated versions, account for 45 percent of that amount.

It is scarcely necessary for an investigator to comprehend the mathematics underlying the rotational phase of a Q study because the PQMethod program (Schmolck and Atkinson, 2002) displays the data configuration pictorially, similar to Figure 37.1: the investigator then simply directs the vectors to a new location based on theoretical considerations, e.g., by specifying that factors (a) and (c) be rotated 37° counterclockwise so as to locate Q sort 4 on a single factor. The selection of any particular Q sort response as the focus for factor rotation can be due to any considerations that might arise in the course of a study—for instance, the person's status (e.g., as an environmental activist, as in the case of participant 4, or as rancher, as in the case of participant 6), something a person said in the course of an interview, others' attitudes toward a specific person or group, and so forth. It is at the stage of factor rotation that an investigator's hunches, guesswork, and hypothetical interests enter into the analysis.

The rotation described above was only the first of several that resulted in the final two-factor solution shown in Table 37.4. Space precludes detailing the thinking that went into these rotations, but the two rotated factors (X and Y) indicate that the participants were, like Gaul, divided three ways in their understanding of the problems associated with large carnivore conservation. The figures show that participants 2 and 6, both environmental activists, define the positive pole of factor X, which means that these two participants share a common view about the problems before them; that participant 4, a rancher, takes a position that is diametrically opposed to participants 2 and 6 (hence tends to score at -4 what the other two score at $+4$, and vice versa); and that participants 1, 3, 5, and 7 define factor Y, which represents a third perspective that is orthogonal to the other two.

As noted previously, the seven Q sorts featured above (in Tables 37.4 and 37.5 and Figures 37.1 and 37.2) were abstracted from a larger group of 26 Q sorts for purposes of demonstrating the mechanics of correlation, factor analysis, and factor rotation. The complete analysis therefore involved a 26×26 correlation matrix that condensed into three factors (A, B, and C), as shown in Table 37.5. (As a technical sidelight, factors X and Y in Table 37.4 were based on a centroid factor analysis with theoretical rotation, whereas factors A, B, and C in Table 37.5 were based on a principal components analysis with Varimax rotation.) Factor A in the larger study represents the same polarity between environmentalists and ranchers that was captured in factor X (Table 37.4), and factor B is equivalent to the previous factor Y and represents the view mainly of academic policy scientists. Factor C is yet a fourth view and one adopted by many participants occupying government positions. This latter set of factors (A, B, and C) provides the basis for factor interpretation, which relies on the arrays of factor scores.

Before moving on to the interpretative phase of Q methodology, it is important to emphasize once again the operant character of these three factors. The Q sample of problems concerning

TABLE 37.5
Rotated Factor Loadings

Ps	A	B	C
(1)	−23	**41**	**61**
(2)	**87**	21	−05
3	**71**	03	**42**
4	26	05	**56**
5	**64**	11	04
6	25	**52**	16
(7)	15	**75**	06
(8)	**−60**	−11	13
9	29	**38**	**40**
10	29	**56**	29
11	**72**	08	15
(12)	23	**71**	−04
13	−28	**66**	34
14	**−53**	33	31
15	−25	**42**	**38**
16	05	**75**	20
17	**−43**	08	**61**
18	**85**	20	02
(19)	**79**	28	00
20	**72**	00	27
21	−15	**63**	−11
(22)	25	**66**	06
23	**41**	02	**66**
24	**−62**	34	20
25	08	−07	**64**
26	−16	32	**53**

Note: Participants (Ps) in parentheses are the same as 1–7, respectively, in Table 37.4. Loadings in boldface significant ($p < .01$); decimals to two places omitted.

carnivore conservation was generated solely by the 26 participants themselves, the Q technique rankings of the problems emanated from their own subjective perspectives, and the three factors are therefore natural categories of thought and sentiment within the group itself; i.e., they are of functional and not merely categorical significance (Brown, 2002, 2006b). This is not to assert methodological individualism, nor is it to deny that the views expressed in the group could have been socially constructed or in other ways a function of forces in the social and economic order. It is simply to acknowledge that the factors are a function of the lived experiences of individuals, and that they are purely inductive in the sense that their number and character have been induced from those individuals who produced them.

Table 37.5 shows that participants 2, 3, 5, 11, 18, 19, and 20 (those in boldface) share a common outlook (i.e., the seven of them have sorted the Q-sample statements in essentially the same pattern), and what is common to their perspective can be approximated by melding their separate responses into one. This is accomplished by calculating factor scores, which are the scores (from +4 to −4) associated with each statement in each of the factors. The seven responses first have to be weighted to take into account that Q sort 2 (with a loading of 0.87) is a closer approximation to factor A than is Q sort 3 (with a loading of 0.71). Weighting proceeds according to the formula $w = f/(1 - f^2)$, where f is the factor loading. The weight of Q sort 2 is therefore $w(2) = 0.87/(1 - 0.87^2) = 3.58$, and by the same calculations $w(3) = 1.43$, hence the former is magnified $3.58/1.43 = 2.50$ times the former when the two responses are merged. The same process is repeated for factors B and C. Computational details are to be found in Brown (1980, pp. 239–247).

The end products of the above calculations, as shown in Table 37.6, are three composite Q sorts (one each for factors A, B, and C), with each factor Q sort being composed of the weighted individual Q sorts which define the factor. (All computations are built into the PQMethod and PCQ

TABLE 37.6
Factor Score Arrays

Factors			
A	B	C	Q-Sample Statements
0	2	−2	1. Not all citizens have equal say.
−1	4	−2	2. Agencies use rigid "planning" that excludes people in genuine problem solving.
−1	4	3	3. People tend to talk to members of their own group and reinforce their own prejudices.
−2	−1	3	4. Some stakeholders have purposely attempted to accentuate the uncertainty in carnivore science to forestall land management decisions.
−2	2	3	5. The costs of carnivore conservation are disproportionately accrued by local citizens.
3	2	1	6. Elected and appointed officials are captured by industry.
−4	−4	−2	7. There are too many grizzly bears on private land.
−1	0	2	8. Increased anxiety among the general public regarding carnivore attacks.
4	−2	−2	9. Carnivore population goals are set politically and not biologically.
−3	−3	0	10. National groups fail to acknowledge local support for conserving carnivores.
1	0	2	11. Over consumption creates demands for gas and oil production in carnivore habitat.
3	−3	−4	12. Recovery zones for carnivores are arbitrary.
4	4	4	13. Habitat fragmentation and isolation are reducing management options.
4	1	1	14. Too few carnivores; not enough carnivore habitat, in quantity and quality.
3	1	1	15. Known trends in human population and development are ignored in management plans.
4	−2	0	16. Carnivore management falls short of what science shows—a need for recovery.
1	3	−1	17. Fragmented efforts and jurisdictions.
0	1	2	18. Participants in carnivore conservation do a poor job of distinguishing facts from values.
0	−2	−1	19. The worldview of locals does not include the scarcity of large carnivores.
0	2	2	20. Communication, especially listening, is poor or insufficient.
−3	3	−3	21. Current federal regulations promote deadlock and conflict more than collaboration.
−2	−4	−4	22. People whose livelihoods are hindered by carnivores are clinging to out-moded ways of life.
−4	−2	−2	23. The listing of the species through litigation only is having a negative impact on conservation.
−3	1	−3	24. The Endangered Species Act doesn't define what recovery is.
3	1	1	25. Public lands are managed to protect business and political interests instead of maintaining biodiversity, including carnivores.
−4	−4	−4	26. Wolves are reducing hunting opportunity, and therefore hurting the economy.
−1	4	4	27. Lack of trust among participants.
−2	3	0	28. Local affected interests are alienated by current processes.
−1	1	2	29. The necessary incentives for appropriate behavior by all parties are absent.
−3	−3	4	30. Economic incentives aren't playing a large enough role in carnivore conservation.

(continued)

TABLE 37.6 (*Continued*)
Factor Score Arrays

Factors			
A	B	C	Q-Sample Statements
−4	−4	1	31. Carnivore conservation is in the context of declining populations when the opposite is happening.
2	2	4	32. Human population growth and consumption patterns contradict large carnivore conservation.
0	0	0	33. Humans are intolerant of carnivores.
2	−1	3	34. The role of carnivores in the ecological system is undervalued and misunderstood.
−3	0	3	35. The human/carnivore interface challenges individual values concerning living with carnivores.
0	−1	4	36. Insufficient funding for conservation, research, and management.
1	−1	−4	37. Federal managers fail to respect and include independent researchers.
2	0	0	38. Past and ongoing forest practices.
2	0	1	39. Too much motorized access.
−2	−2	2	40. Carnivore conservation interferes with economic interests.
2	0	−1	41. Dependence on hunting license revenue compromises the integrity of game and carnivore management.
3	3	−3	42. Critical voices are denied access to the process.
0	−4	−3	43. Inadequate understanding and appreciation of laws directing the conservation of carnivores and their purpose.
−4	−3	−2	44. Too much data is required to implement management actions.
1	2	−3	45. Lack of skill and leadership within the agencies.
−1	4	−1	46. Carnivores are emotionally charged political symbols.
4	−1	0	47. Too many carnivores killed by people.
−2	−1	0	48. A federal compensation program funded by public–private investment does not exist.
2	3	−1	49. Lack of critical thinking about management choices before decisions are made.
1	−3	−1	50. Too much deference is given to paranoia or the implicit threat of violence.
1	−3	−1	51. Lack of good information and education.

software packages; see Schmolck and Atkinson, 2002; Stricklin and Almeida, 2004.) In the case of factor A, for instance (see Table 37.6), the five highest scores (+4) are associated with statements 9, 13, 14, 16, and 47, the five next highest (+3) with statements 6, 12, 15, 25, and 42, and so forth in the same distribution as employed in the original Q sorts (see Table 37.1). What started off as 26 Q sorts is therefore reduced to 3, which subsume the others, and it is these 3 Q sorts that provide the basis for factor interpretation.

In most circumstances, factor interpretation proceeds best by (a) physically laying out the factor Q sort and describing its manifest content, giving special attention to those statements at the positive and negative extremes of the distribution, (b) establishing the underlying theme, which is the glue holding the Q sort together, and (c) comparing and contrasting the factor with whatever other factors have also been revealed. Factor interpretation is as much hermeneutical art as science, and necessarily so, but the interpreter is not given free rein in this respect because an interpretation is constrained by the factor scores from which it cannot stray too far. Interpretation is further complicated by the fact that the statements in a Q sort can assume various meanings depending on their position relative to other statements, and this places Q methodology in the same league with literary theory in the sense that it has to address "the ways in which the form that transmits a text . . . constrains [or facilitates] the production of meaning" (Chartier, 1995, p. 1).

Space again precludes going into detail, but something of what is involved can be seen in reference to a cursory look at factor A, which, as Table 37.6 reveals, gave highly positive scores to the following statements:

Most Positive (+4, + 3): (9) Carnivore population goals are set politically and not biologically. (12) Recovery zones for carnivores are arbitrary. (14) Too few carnivores; not enough carnivore habitat, in quantity and quality. (15) Known trends in human population and development are ignored in management plans. (16) Carnivore management falls short of what science shows—a need for recovery. (25) Public lands are managed to protect business and political interests instead of maintaining biodiversity, including carnivores. (47) Too many carnivores killed by people.

There were other statements receiving high positive scores, but the statements displayed above were selected because they also serve to distinguish factor A from B and C; i.e., the factor scores associated with the above statements in A are significantly higher than the scores for the same statements in factors B and C, as Table 37.6 shows (as a rule of thumb, differences in score of 2 or more are significant, $p < .01$; for details, consult Brown, 1980, pp. 244–246).

The statements given positive emphasis suggest that the persons comprising factor A, many of whom are environmental activists, are prepared to advocate on behalf of carnivores as well as the proconservation clientele groups that many of their agencies serve, consequently they complain about too little habitat, that carnivores still need to be protected, and that decisions concerning control of animal populations are made on the basis of politics rather than science and are designed to protect economic and political interests.

As Figure 37.2 and Table 37.5 show, factor A is bipolar and therefore represents two diametrically opposed points of view. In marked contrast to the environmentalists at the positive pole of factor A, participants 8 and 14 are ranchers who have tended to agree most with those statements with which the environmentalists have disagreed most. Consequently, the ranchers' perspective can be approximated by reversing the signs of the factor A scores in Table 37.6, which reveals the following distinguishing statements:

Most Positive Statements for Factor A-negative (+4, + 3): (7) There are too many grizzly bears on private land. (10) National groups fail to acknowledge local support for conserving carnivores. (23) The listing of the species through litigation only is having a negative impact on conservation. (24) The Endangered Species Act doesn't define what recovery is. (26) Wolves are reducing hunting opportunity, and therefore hurting the economy. (31) Carnivore conservation is in the context of declining populations when the opposite is happening. (44) Too much data is required to implement management actions.

Unlike the environmentalists, therefore, who strongly disagree with the above, the participants involved in ranching think that there are too many large carnivores, that these animal populations are not in decline, and that the listing of endangered species is ambiguous. They also object to national groups characterizing local ranchers as somehow opposed to conservation, and complain about excessive bureaucratic demands (requiring "too much data") associated with management implementation.

The polarity between the environmentalists and agricultural interests as documented in factor A is thrown into sharper relief when it is contrasted with the different commitments of the other two factors. Consider first a few of those statements to which factor B gives high scores and which distinguish B from factors A and C (see scores in Table 37.6):

Distinguishing Statements for Factor B (+4, + 3): (2) Agencies use rigid "planning" that excludes people in genuine problem solving. (17) Fragmented efforts and jurisdictions. (21) Current federal regulations promote deadlock and conflict more than collaboration. (28) Local affected interests are alienated by current processes. (46) Carnivores are emotionally charged political symbols.

Factor B is not partisan in the way in which the polarized groups comprising factor A are; rather, B regards the problems surrounding carnivore conservation (including the factor-A polarization itself) as more a function of jurisdictional complexities that have resulted in fragmented authority and decision making, the exclusion of local participation, and the inadvertent stirring of emotions and conflict. As it turned out, almost all of the participants serving to define factor B—nos. 6, 7, 12, 13, 16, 21, and 22 (see Table 37.5)—were primarily academic policy specialists with substantive interest in conservation biology, and who therefore saw problems more as a consequence of structural defects one level above the fray.

Factor C seemed least well defined of the factors, but of those few Q sorters significantly loaded on that factor only (see Table 37.5), most were state and federal agency employees. As might be expected, therefore, factor C deflects attention from government and points a figure at other problematic (and especially economic) sources:

Distinguishing Statements for Factor C (+4, +3): (4) Some stakeholders have purposely attempted to accentuate the uncertainty in carnivore science to forestall land management decisions. (30) Economic incentives aren't playing a large enough role in carnivore conservation. (32) Human population growth and consumption patterns contradict large carnivore conservation. (35) The human/carnivore interface challenges individual values concerning living with carnivores. (36) Insufficient funding for conservation, research, and management.

In fact, statements that place blame specifically on government officials are among those that factor C rejects to a much greater degree than do factors A and B (see Table 37.6):

Distinguishing Negative Statements (−4, −3): (37) Federal managers fail to respect and include independent researchers. (42) Critical voices are denied access to the process. (45) Lack of skill and leadership within the agencies.

Before concluding, it is important to note that just as there are statements that can serve to distinguish a factor from all others, so are there often statements on which all factors converge as a matter of consensus, and these provide the basis for locating common understandings of the core problems and possible ways out of the conceptual quagmire. In the instant case, there is precious little common ground on which the three factors might stand together, especially given the polarity of factor A, but more detailed inspection of the perspectives at issue reveals several points of virtual consensus, among which are the following (for details, consult Mattson et al., 2006, p. 401):

(3) People tend to talk to members of their own group and reinforce their own prejudices. (13) Habitat fragmentation and isolation are reducing management options. (27) Lack of trust among participants. (32) Human population growth and consumption patterns contradict large carnivore conservation. (36) Insufficient funding for conservation, research, and management.

Despite the distinct and often incompatible views of the four groups, there remains at least mild agreement and no strong disagreement with the perceptions that all parties tend toward intransigence and mistrustfulness, and that habitat fragmentation, human settlement patterns, and insufficient funding are aggravating the situation. The scores for these statements range from +4 to no lower than −1, which gives rise to the possibility that the four factor groupings could begin to cooperate by endeavoring to effect outcomes in the directions in which these statements point. In this regard, Harold Lasswell (1963) once remarked that "a continually redirected flow of events can be progressively subordinated to the goals conceived in central decision structures" (p. 221), and those structures which he conceived are not unlike these factors, which are clearly aimed at directing the flow of events. Whether any one or all three of them can succeed in bending future events to their preferences depends at least in part on the kind of self clarification which Q methodology can provide, as the preceding illustration demonstrates.

37.3 APPLICATIONS OF Q METHODOLOGY IN PUBLIC ADMINISTRATION: A BIBLIOGRAPHICAL GUIDE AND RESEARCH AGENDA

Q methodology is valuable for public administration research, including the investigation of topics related to general public administration and management and to fields such as budgeting, public personnel administration, and public policy. In this section, we review the use of Q methodology for public administration research and summarize some representative studies. Also, we point out other possible avenues for future research using Q. Of course, this section only suggests the potential contribution of Q methodology to the study of public administration and is not exhaustive: the possibilities for the application of Q methodology are boundless wherever subjectivity is implicated.

37.3.1 GENERAL PUBLIC ADMINISTRATION AND PUBLIC MANAGEMENT

Q methodology has been used to explore many larger issues in public administration and public management, including the attitudes and perceptions of bureaucrats, administrative behavior, organizational culture, and leadership. These issues can be divided into three categories: how bureaucrats view different issues affecting their jobs, decisions, and behaviors; how public administrators and other public sector professionals perceive their jobs and their work; and how public organizations function, including their culture and leadership.

37.3.1.1 How Bureaucrats View Issues Affecting Their Jobs and Management Decisions

Q methodology can identify the opinions or viewpoints of individuals on relevant events or issues and is consequently well suited to investigate the viewpoints and attitudes of bureaucrats, which have received much attention in public administration. In fact, researchers have used Q methodology to assist in understanding the views of bureaucrats on issues such as affirmative action programs (Decourville and Hafer, 2001), bureaucratic discretion (Wood, 1983), administrative ethics (Hiruy, 1987), the impact of diversity on government policies (Wolf, 2004), and public service motivation. This latter topic was addressed by Brewer et al. (2000), who examined why people choose to work in the public sector. They administered Q sorts on public sector motivation to 69 public employees and students of public administration in six different states. In their analysis of the Q sorts, they identified four Q factors—labeled Samaritans, Communitarians, Patriots, and Humanitarians—each representing a different motivation for engaging in public service. Among other things, they found that "the desire for economic rewards" was not a defining feature of any of these motivations.

Related studies have ventured into more remote territory. For example, studies by Sun (1992) and Sun and Gargan (1999) examined the opinions of public administration scholars and practitioners regarding the practical use of scholarly research in Taiwan, and Vajirakachorn and Sylvia (1990) investigated the influence of traditional Buddhist culture and modern bureaucracy on Thai administration attitudes. They asked 94 Thai administrative elites in the Ministry of Interior to sort 54 statements,[4] and from this process four administrative types emerged: the first group endorsed modern and bureaucratic values most strongly; the second group was characterized by mixed attitudes and held values that were midway between modern bureaucratic principles and Buddhist traditional ideas; and the third and fourth groups expressed a slight mix in opinion, but in general expressed more agreement with values that correspond to traditional bureaucratic practices, such as planning in management, rationalism and scientific reasoning in making decisions, and merit based civil service. This research illustrates the utility of Q in discerning attitude differences among public administrators.

37.3.1.2 How Public Sector Professionals Understand Their Jobs and Carry Out Their Work?

Q methodology has been applied in research to understand better how different public administrators perceive their work and their roles, including their relationships with superiors, subordinates, colleagues, and the public (Bidwell, 1957; Johnson, 1973; McDale, 1989; Scheb, 1982; Selden et al., 1999; Vroman, 1972). Typically these studies have identified varying perspectives that managers have toward their jobs and work, and they show that managers differ greatly in how they approach and carry out their work.

Although most of these Q studies have focused on American public managers, at least two have included comparisons of American public managers with managers in other countries. Durning and Gajdamaschko (1998, 2000) examined how Ukrainian public managers perceive their jobs and roles in society, and they compared those perspectives to those of a group of American public managers. Gough et al. (1971) compared the managerial perspectives and preferences of American to those of Italian public managers. The Q sorts of Italian administrators were analyzed, and the following administrative types were identified: innovator, mediator, actionist, the moderate, achiever, and the realist. Then, the authors collected Q sorts from 110 American administrators to analyze typological variations among the two cultures. The addition of American public administrators revealed some stylistic variations in perspectives and practices among the two groups of administrators.

The result of the Q sorts showed that American administrators perceived interpersonal relationships and career opportunities to be highly important, whereas Italian administrators were more concerned with job security and structure. In terms of the administrative types identified in the analysis of Italian administrators, American bureaucrats identified more with the mediator role; that is, they perceived themselves as tolerant, modest in demands, and generous in relationships. American administrators were least likely to assume the role of actionist, a manager who is tough minded, decisive, and indifferent to the feelings of subordinates.

In related studies using Q methodology, Yarwood and Nimmo (1975) examined different stakeholders' perceptions of bureaucratic images and how these images differed between academicians and other stakeholders. Also, Yarwood and Nimmo (1976) explored the ways in which administrators, legislators, and citizens orient themselves to bureaucracy and the accuracy of these groups in estimating the attitudes of each other toward the bureaucracy.

37.3.1.3 Public Management Topics Such as Organizational Culture and Leadership

Public management research is closely linked to general public administration and public personnel scholarship. It includes topics related to organization development and leadership, and scholars have employed Q to research both. For example, organization culture has been the focus of studies by Chatman (1989), O'Reilly et al. (1991), and Sheridan (1992), and in Romania by Iliescu (2005, pp. 174–196). Dunlap and Dudley (1965), Thomas and Sigelman (1984), and Wong (1973) have researched topics related to leadership, and Tolymbek (2007) has examined emerging leadership patterns and expectations in Kazakhstan. Beyond these uses of Q methodology, Q could be valuable to explore public management topics such as public–private distinctions. For example, scholars could explore patterns among public and private managers on a wide range of subjects related to organizational tasks, functions, and characteristics. Overtures to this effect from the private side have recently been made by Gauzente (2005).

Another potential application of Q would be to assess the trust of managers, an increasingly important topic in public management. Most of the existing research on trust is based on attitude surveys and personal interviews of public managers (Carnevale, 1995). Alternatively, Q methodology could be used to explore public managers' worldviews toward trust. A concourse of statements could be constructed that captures dimensions that are fundamental in understanding managerial philosophies (Wong, 1973, p. 35). These include

1. Degree to which individuals perceive that people are trustworthy or untrustworthy
2. Degree to which individuals believe that people are altruistic or selfish
3. Degree to which individuals believe that people are independent and self reliant or, alternatively, dependent and conformist
4. Degree to which individuals believe that people are simple versus highly complex

The two dimensions, trust (1 and 2) and control (3 and 4), suggest something about the kinds of management methods, personnel policies, and work procedures to which an individual would respond or elect to use as a manager (Carnevale, 1995). With a good understanding of one's own perceptions and the perceptions of others who work in the organization, a manager could shape agency practices and culture to maximize performance by facilitating views congruent with the mission and goals of the agency.

It is worth noting in passing that many of the tasks that often fall under the management heading have begun to receive independent attention by scholars employing Q methodology, such as conflict management (Dayton, 2003; Wood, 2004), informatics (Gottschalk, 2002; Kendall and Kendall, 1993; Kim, 2002; Morgado et al., 1999; Thomas and Watson, 2001; Valenta and Wigger, 1997), operations (Nelson et al., 2003; Wright and Meehling, 2002), quality assessment (McKeown et al., 1999; Wright et al., 1998), risk management (Karasz, 2006; McKeown et al., 1999; Simmons and Walker, 1999), and strategic planning, which is addressed in more detail below.

37.3.1.4 Potential Topics for Further Research

Beyond the use that has already been made of Q methodology to research general public administration topics, it could be employed to study a myriad of other public administration issues. For example, a Q study of bureaucratic responsibility would provide a new approach for examining an enduring and important issue. Most of the empirical research on bureaucratic responsibility has relied primarily on R methodology and has frequently concentrated on a single method of ensuring bureaucratic responsibility. However, with Q methodology, different conceptions of bureaucratic responsibility could be considered and evaluated simultaneously. In this regard, a useful framework for such a study would be Gilbert's (1959) two-by-two typology of administrative responsibility. The concourse of statements would represent the four categories that emerge from dividing the horizontal axis into internal and external categories of responsibility and splitting the vertical axis into formal and informal means of control. The researcher could specify different conditions for sorting the statements. For example, subjects could be asked to order the statements to reflect to whom the administrator feels most responsible or, alternatively, to indicate to whom the subject perceives that he or she should be responsible. Moreover, bureaucrats' perceptions of responsibility could be compared to other important stakeholders, such as elected officials and the public, to identify the extent to which views of bureaucratic responsibility converge among these groups.

As suggested by research described above, Q methodology has been utilized in the study of administrative roles (e.g., Bidwell, 1957; Van Dusen and Rector, 1963) and could be applied to study other frameworks. For example, a Q study could be based on competing values model of managerial roles of Faerman et al. (1990), which has been used extensively to study public management (see, for example, Giek and Lees, 1993). So far, the empirical research using this model has relied on extensive closed-ended questionnaires that address numerous managerial tasks (Ban, 1995). An alternative approach would be to use Q methodology to allow public managers to define operantly and formally model their perspectives towards the managerial roles set forth in the competing values framework. The competing values model is based on a two-dimensional scheme: the horizontal axis is split into two categories of focus, internal versus external, and the vertical axis is divided into two managerial approaches, control versus flexibility. The quadrants that emerge reflect existing models from the classic management literature: (A) human relations model, (B) open systems model, (C) internal process model, and (D) rational goal model. Each quadrant or model includes two specific roles. Hence, A is identified with (a) facilitator and (b) mentor; B with (c) innovator and (d) broker; C with (e) monitor and (f) coordinator; and D with (g) director and (h) producer. Administrators would be asked to weight the alternative roles and to sort the statements to reflect their role orientations.

37.3.2 Public Administration Fields, Including Personnel Administration

Q methodology has been employed not only to research general issues of public administration and public management, but also to investigate issues in different fields within the discipline, including public personnel administration, budgeting, and evaluation.

37.3.2.1 Researching Public Personnel Administration

Just as Q methodology has provided insights into how public managers view their work, it can also help to identify the personnel-related concerns—such as job satisfaction and motivation—of public sector employees. In fact, some studies have used Q methodology for this purpose (e.g., Chinnis et al., 2001; Gillard et al., 2005). As an illustration, Sylvia and Sylvia (1986) studied job satisfaction and work motivation by collecting 43 Q sorts on these topics from a randomly selected sample of midlevel rehabilitation managers. Analyzing and interpreting the Q sorts, they identified factors representing different viewpoints. The first, "the positive concerned supervisor," identified managers as being concerned for subordinates, with achievement, recognition, and work as sources of satisfaction. The second characterized job satisfaction as stemming from a positive attitude toward advancement, work, and coworkers. Individuals loading on the third factor experienced feelings of job satisfaction for a number of the same reasons as found in the first two factors, as well as from the freedom they were granted to try new ideas and programs.

Job satisfaction is widely studied using R methodology and, as illustrated above, some effort has been made to use Q to study job satisfaction. Despite this research, no coherent framework of factors that determine job satisfaction has surfaced. According, to Rainey (1991, p. 146), this absence of a coherent framework is not surprising "because it is obviously unrealistic to try to generalize about how much any single factor affects satisfaction." Nevertheless, progress might be made toward identifying the relative importance of different factors for job satisfaction through the application of Q methodology, as in the study by Shah (1982), who showed that some administrators' rewards were intrinsic to the job whereas others' were extrinsic. Studies such as this could provide insights into the facets of the job such as supervision, pay, and promotion that contribute to an individual's job satisfaction, which could then be used to shape agency practices, training, and development.

Another personnel-related area of research that has been studied via Q technique is work motivation. Gaines et al. (1984) explored the relationship between perceptions of promotion and motivation in two Connecticut police departments. Specifically, they investigated the need structures of police officers and the extent to which promotion fulfilled those needs.

Applications of Q methodology in the study of work motivation could provide insights into what needs, motives, and values are most important to public sector employees. Exemplary in this regard is the study by Davis (1997), which examined the value structures operable among managers in a Canadian agency involved in research and development funding. Further research of this kind could draw from a number of existing typologies such as Murray's (1938) List of Basic Needs, Maslow's (1954) need hierarchy, Alderfer's (1972) ERG model, Lasswell's (1963) value categories, and Rokeach's (1973) value survey.

In addition, Q could be used to study the types of incentives that induce public sector employees to contribute positively to their agency. The following frameworks are suitable for studying this using Q methodology: Herzberg et al. (1957), Locke (1968), and Lawler (1973).

Another potential application of Q would involve identifying methods and techniques that motivate employees. A concourse could be constructed to represent various methods and techniques employed to facilitate high performance in public organizations, such as performance appraisals, merit pay, pay for performance, bonuses, job redesign, job rotation, flex time, and quality circles. The completed sorts would show how employees would view and value alternative efforts to improve organizational performance.

Q would also be an appropriate technique to use to develop a self-assessment performance tool. Employees would be asked to sort a group of statements pertaining to their performance and the resulting Q sorts would represent the employees' own constructions of their performance strengths and weaknesses. As part of a performance appraisal system, Q could facilitate and structure feedback discussions and suggest employee skills and knowledge that need further development. Also, as suggested by Chatman (1989), Q could be used to assess the extent to which an individual "fits" into a specific public agency setting or job.

37.3.2.2 Q Research in Other Fields of Public Administration

Q methodology could help in the budgeting process to identify spending priorities of decision makers, stakeholders, and others whose opinion is important. However, researchers have made limited use of Q for studies of budgeting. The best example is research by Cooper and Dantico (1990), who used Q methodology to determine if groups of employees in an organization had similar or different perspectives on budget expenditure or taxing priorities. In another brief study, Dick and Edelman (1993) demonstrate how Q technique was used as a way to prioritize journal subscriptions fated for cancellation in light of budget reductions.

As noted previously, Q methodology can also be a valuable tool to aid the process of strategic planning; that is, in exploring different understandings of the organization's past, its present problems, and its paths to the future. For example, Fairweather and Swaffield (1996) employed Q methodology to identify preferences among stakeholders for land use in the Waitaki Basin in New Zealand, and Popovich and Popovich (2002) described how Q methodology assisted the strategic planning process of a hospital. Users of Q methodology have themselves recently engaged in a self-study appraisal designed to clarify past achievements and future threats and opportunities (Hurd and Brown, 2004, 2005).

In using Q methodology to assist with strategic planning, Gargan and Brown (1993) found that Q methodology facilitates clarification of "the perspectives of decision makers" and, in conjunction with other procedures, can ferret out "prudent courses of action" (p. 348). According to them, Q methodology helps overcome the limitations of the mind in dealing with complexity and serves to locate elements of consensus (if they exist) that might otherwise go unnoticed in the emotional turmoil of political debate.

Beyond budgeting and planning, Q methodology has strong potential to be a valuable tool for policy evaluation, both to identify better how different participants and stakeholders perceive the impacts of a program and to measure the effects of a program on individuals. The first use is exemplified by Kim (1991), who studied the design and implementation of community development block grants (CDBG). Kim asked citizens, General Accountability Office (GAO) administrators, and other employees of federal, state, and local agencies to provide their viewpoints through Q sorts. Other evaluations of this type have been carried out by Corr, Phillips, and Capdevila, (2003), Fang (2006), Garrard and Hausman (1986), Meo et al. (2002), and Oring and Plihal (1993).

Examples of the second use—to determine how a program affected individual attitudes—are found in Pelletier et al. (1999) and Nobbie (2003). Both measured the impacts of programs by administering pre- and postintervention Q sorts to persons in the target audience. Pelletier et al. (1999)

examined the effects of two-and-a-half day participatory planning events in six rural counties in northern New York. The researchers were interested in finding out whether participant views of the local food system—the topic of the events—would change following attendance at the events. They found that participation in a participatory planning event may cause some participants to alter their viewpoints in ways that appear contrary to their values and interests as expressed prior to the deliberative event.

Nobbie (2003) measured the effects of a program by the Georgia Development Disabilities Council (GDDC) to "empower people with disabilities and their families to obtain appropriate services, develop leadership potential and influence policy change in this arena." As part of her evaluation, she administered Q sorts to the participants in this program at the beginning of the program and after the eight-month program was completed. The Q sort measured perspectives on advocacy, citizenship, and empowerment. Both the pre- and postprogram sorts were completed by 21 of 34 participants.

Nobbie's analysis of the completed Q sorts showed three Q factors, which were labeled as Beginning/Dependent Advocate, Excluded Advocate, and Unfolding Advocate, the latter most resembling the type of advocate envisioned by the GDDC. Nobbie found that seven participants changed their perspectives after participating in the program. They loaded on the first two factors in the preprogram sort, but were in the third factor in the postprogram sort. Another ten participants had mixed factor loadings in the first sort, but were solidly part of the third factor in the second sort. These changes indicate that the program helped change attitudes of most of the program participants in the direction desired by the GDDC. Combes et al. (2004) provide another illustration of persons with disabilities being involved, via Q methodology, in the evaluation of planning aimed at this particular stakeholder group.

37.3.3 RESEARCHING DECISION MAKING AND PUBLIC POLICY

The use of Q methodology in the study of decision making traces back to an early paper by Stephenson (1963), which was given scant attention, but in the past decade, an increasing number of policy analysts and policy researchers have turned to Q methodology for leverage in understanding decisions within their own policy domains (see Durning and Brown, 2007, for a detailed overview). The various uses of Q methodology can be divided into four major categories, although individual projects may well fit into more than one of the categories. These categories are the use of Q methodology (1) to research influences on decisions that were made in the past, (2) to understand better the perspectives of stakeholders and decision makers on decisions that will be made in the future, (3) to provide a mechanism for marginalized or powerless groups to make their views known, and (4) to facilitate the search for compromise solutions to difficult policy issues.

37.3.3.1 Understanding Influences on Decision Makers

Some researchers have turned to Q methodology to help understand why certain decisions were made by identifying the "decision structures" of the people who made them. Decision structures—a term borrowed from Harold Lasswell (1963) and incorporated into Q methodology by Stephenson (1987)—are the configuration of values, beliefs, interests, and information that influence the position taken by a decision maker (see Durning and Brown, 2007).

Examples of Q-methodology studies designed for this purpose have been conducted by Donahue (2004), who identified the factors affecting the decisions of fire chiefs about the level of fire protection their local fire departments would provide; by Van Exel et al. (2004) and Steg et al. (2001), who examined motivations behind automobile use and other modes of transportation; and by Webler et al. (2001), who explored the question of what factors influenced New England local government officials to participate or refuse to participate in regional collaborative environmental policy making on watershed management planning (see also Webler and Tuler, 2001; Webler et al., 2003).

To carry out their research, Webler et al. (2001) created a sample of 52 statements based on their interviews with 45 local officials on the topic of why they did or did not participate in a watershed management planning process. This Q sort was administered to 39 local government officials in three states (New Hampshire, Massachusetts, and Connecticut) in which these planning processes were active. The authors identified five factors—which they called "coherent narratives"—that reflected the perspectives of the local officials toward the opportunity to participate in a watershed management planning process. The authors described these narratives (or decision structures) as follows: "One centers on strategic calculations of influencing outcomes. A second weighs interest and available time. A third looks at how the community would benefit. A fourth is rooted in one's personal environmental ethics. And a fifth attempts to match skills and experiences with the needs of the policy endeavor" (p. 105). The authors found that local government officials made their decision to participate or not based on three general considerations: "They feel they can help make a positive difference; they see working on the problem as consistent with their environmental ethic; and it is in their community's interest that they participate in the process" (p. 118).

Related to these studies of specific decisions, another Q study explored the attitude climate among legislators and administrators on issues of policy making and policy implementation: Cunningham and Olshfski (1986) focused their investigation on the context of policy decisions rather than on specific decisions. Looked at the other way around, Bedrosian (2004) showed how the decision-making styles of preschool teachers impacted the teaching environment.

37.3.3.2 Identifying the Perspectives (Decision Structures) of Stakeholders

Policy decisions are made within specific contexts; that is, every policy issue is unique in that it is located within a particular policy domain and involves a set of decision makers and stakeholders whose interests and beliefs are engaged. Over time, controversial issues generate narratives that link the issue and proposed solutions to symbols, history, and imagined futures. Q methodology can provide insights into these policy domains and narratives by identifying the competing decision structures and narratives of stakeholders on particular issues, showing the values and beliefs underlying their positions.

In recent years, many researchers have employed Q methodology to clarify competing stakeholder perspectives on particular policy issues or broader issues areas. These studies typically seek to identify and understand the different decision structures (values, beliefs, interests, and knowledge) or narratives that underlie the positions of decision makers, stakeholders, and the public on issues to be decided. Studies of this type have addressed many different issues, including forests (Clarke, 2002; Steelman and Maguire, 1999), coastal zone management (Shilin et al., 2003), nature restoration and sustainability (Addams and Proops, 2000; Barry and Proops, 1999, 2000; Colorado Institute of Public Policy, 2006; Meo et al., 2002; Peritore, 1999; Walton, 2006; Wooley and McGinnis, 2000; Wooley et al., 2000), conservation biology (Byrd, 2002; Mattson et al., 2006; Rutherford and Gibeau, 2006), biotechnology in Mexico (Galve-Peritore and Peritore, 1995), agricultural practices (Brodt et al., 2004; Kramer et al., 2003; Wilkins et al., 2001), health-related issues (Baker, 2006; Baker et al., 2006; Barbosa et al., 1998; Mrtek et al., 1996; Stainton Rogers, 1991; Valenta and Wigger, 1997) land use (Coke and Brown, 1976), city-county consolidation (Durning and Edwards, 1992), institutional development (Lindsey and Rafferty, 2006; Ramlo, 2005), corrections policy (Baker and Meyer, 2002, 2003), school violence (Greene, 1999; Wester and Trepal, 2004), the redevelopment of brown fields (Deitrick, 1998), and the impact of diversity on New Zealand's government (Wolf, 2004).

A good example of these types of studies is Hooker's (2001) research to understand the competing concepts of preservation, conservation, and development that influence individual perspectives on forest policy. Specifically, she was interested in how different stakeholders perceive the relationship of individuals to society and to forests. In her study, Hooker selected 60 statements from approximately 400 taken from literature on forest and natural resource policy, and administered these in a Q sort to a diverse group of 189 participants, including forest landowners, government officials, forest industry representatives, trade association representatives, scientists, leaders of conservation groups, academics, and public interest group representatives. From her analysis of the completed sorts, Hooker identified five factors (labeled New Stewards, New Conservationists, Individualists, Traditional Stewards, and Environmental Activists), each representing a different perspective or decision structure influencing the positions that people take on forestry issues, and each explained in terms of different, but sometimes overlapping, views on policies regarding the use of forests.

Hooker suggested that knowledge of these five different perspectives, especially information on the views they have in common, would be a good starting point for structuring beneficial interactions among factors. She wrote, "Conversations among analysts and members of the public who are interested in forest policy can use the new framework of beliefs identified in this study to redefine a policy agenda as well as commence facilitating dialogue" (p. 174). She also suggested that the results of her study could be used to assist an effort to "structure a more effective public involvement strategy" (p. 174), and argued that citizen participation should be set up so that all of the four perspectives were represented in the discussions. By including people with the four main perspectives in public hearings and advisory groups, policy makers could make sure that all of the competing views are heard.

37.3.3.3 Studying the Marginalized and Less Powerful, and Giving them Voice

Many advocates of Q methodology suggest that it is an excellent research tool to identify the attitudes and perspectives of underrepresented, ignored, marginalized, or less powerful groups on issues that are important to them. Some argue that Q methodology also has a practical value in this regard: it can allow these groups to have a voice—to have their opinions heard—when decisions are being made or their interests are at stake. If used for this purpose, Q methodology can make the decision-making process more democratic by providing a structure to enable the widest range of attitudes and opinions to be heard.

According to Brown (2005, 2006a), Q methodology is perfectly suited for clarifying the perspectives of the marginalized on issues of interest to them, and he identifies different research that has addressed issues of concern to the less powerful—among them, race (Abrams, 2002; Benoit, 2001; Carlson and Trichtinger, 2001; Smith, 2002; Stowell-Smith and McKeown, 1999), gender (e.g., Anderson, 2004; Beaver, 2002; Gallivan, 1994, 1999; Jacobson and Aaltio-Marjosola, 2001; Kitzinger, 1999; Oswald and Harvey, 2003; Snelling, 1999; Wrigley, 2006), the disabled (Combes et al., 2004; Goodman et al., 2002), patients, and clients who pose special difficulties (Jones et al., 2003; Lister and Gardner, 2006), farm workers (Kramer et al., 2003; Warnaars and Pradel, 2007; Züger Cáceres, 2003), and the poor (Brown, 2005).

Peace et al. (2004) turned to Q methodology to investigate the views of two large client groups, the recipients of Sickness Benefits and Invalid Benefits (SB/IB) in New Zealand, about "well being, employment, and interdependence." They administered Q sorts to 20 clients, and their analysis of the sorts identified five different factors, showing that "the client community holds a range of different views about what constitutes well-being in the context of independence and employment." In related research, Combes et al. (2004) employed Q methodology to involve people with intellectual disabilities in the evaluation of a planning process. Both of these studies documented innovative uses of Q methodology to obtain the opinions and perspectives of a less powerful group of people.

Donner (2001) has provided guidelines for using Q methodology as a "participatory exercise" in international development to help clarify views concerning proposed local development projects, and suggests Q methodology as a way to involve a wide range of people and groups in a process to obtain consensus on local development investments. In a worked application, he demonstrates the variety of Q factors that exist among adopters of mobile phones among Rwandan businessmen (Donner, 2005).

37.3.3.4 Facilitating the Search for Compromise Solutions to Difficult Problems

Q methodology is being used by many policy analysts and researchers to do more than attempt to understand why decisions were made or to identify different stakeholder positions. They are using information about stakeholder positions (decision structures) to assist the search for compromise solutions to policy issues. Q methodology can aid the search for compromises because it not only identifies different stakeholder perspectives, but it also shows those statements upon which many or most of the different factors agree. These statements can be the focus of negotiations concerning which actions could be taken that would gather enough support to be adopted.

Good examples of this type of study are Maxwell's (2000) use of Q methodology to solve a conflict within a county government and two studies by Focht (2002) and Maxwell and Brown (1999). Focht (2002) used Q methodology to identify different perceptions of water management problems in the Illinois River Watershed (Oklahoma) and their proposed solutions. He administered two Q sorts to 120 stakeholders representing the diversity of interests at issue, the first gauging the perceptions of the current problems created by the impacts of different activities (e.g., agriculture, tourism) on the river, and the second addressing viewpoints toward different ways to manage negative impacts on the river by different activities. From his analysis of these sorts, Focht discerned major differences in views, but also some areas of agreement that, he concluded, could help formulate a strategy for the management of conflict when writing a policy to regulate use of the river. Based on common views across factors, Focht wrote that for a management plan to have broad support, it should "(1) initially [focus] on the illegal dumping of trash, (2) [commission] unbiased scientific studies of the magnitude and sources of threats to water quality, and (3) [examine] how potential impact management alternatives will impact economic development, land use rights, and traditional lifestyles and freedoms" (p. 1134).

Maxwell and Brown (1999) described the use of Q methodology as a technique that consultants can use to help solve difficult disputes within organizations. Their case concerned a middle school in which faculty members disagreed about how best to deal with increasing levels of student misconduct. The consultants were brought in to help the school manage the conflict and to find solutions that would be widely accepted.

They began by conducting a study to determine how members of the organization understood the problem of student misconduct. They interviewed the teachers, staff members, and administrators in the middle school, and from those interviews they compiled a list of 44 problems. Using these as a Q sort, they asked teachers and staff members to sort them according to their importance (i.e., most important problems to least important). The factor analysis of the sorts showed that most participants loaded on one of two factors, which the consultants labeled as (1) the resentment factor and (2) the differentiating factor. The first factor strongly identified with teachers and staff and complained about students, parents, administrators, and the school board, all of whom were viewed as "placing them in an untenable position" (p. 38). The second factor was more concerned with intragroup relations, and differentiated among students (those needing support as well as those needing discipline) and among teachers (those who punish effectively and those who do not).

The consultants presented the results of this study to the participants, showing them the statements that represented the sources of disagreement about the issue, but also pointing out the statements on which they agreed. They likened this process to "holding a mirror up to the teachers and staff ... so that they might see themselves and co-workers more clearly" (p. 40).

In the second part of the study, the same participants were interviewed to elicit their proposals about how to address the problems that had been identified. The faculty produced a list of 35 potential solutions, which became the Q sort that was completed by 28 faculty and staff members. Analysis revealed three different perspectives, which were described as (1) punishment (solve the discipline problem through harsher punishment), (2) quarantine (use special programs to segregate problem children from others), and (3) coordination (get teachers and staff to work together more effectively through cooperation and coordination).

In addition to these competing approaches to solving the problem, the Q sorts identified actions that all three groups agreed should be implemented or should be avoided: (a) Establish a parental contract regarding the rules of conduct and the consequences for misconduct that would apply to their child and (b) consistently follow rules and regulations already in existence, such as the Student Conduct Code. Based on their findings, the consultants informed school administrators about the differences of opinion concerning the causes of student misconduct and the differing preferences for actions to address the problems, and identified the actions that were agreeable to all three factors as well as options that were unanimously opposed.

Other studies report a similar approach to identifying competing problem definitions and solutions for other policy issues. For example the study by Mattson et al. (2006), which is presented in detail above (see Tables 37.1 and 37.6), describes a two-day workshop that had as its goal "to gain insight into perspectives and narratives of participants in large carnivore conservation, and to identify areas of potential common ground" (p. 393). And Brown et al. (2004) describe a similar workshop designed to identify challenges and potential solutions for efforts to plan for conservation from Yellowstone to the Yukon (Y2Y). At both workshops, stakeholders were asked what problems they perceived, and the list of problems generated was used as a Q sort. After the different perspectives of the problems were identified, the stakeholders were asked how they would address these problems and these potential solutions made up a second Q sort, which was used to identify different perspectives on solutions. From these sorts, it was possible to identify both differences in perspectives and agreements across perspectives on specific statements concerning problems and solutions. These mutually accepted statements can be used to start the effort to find agreements on what should be done concerning the issues being considered.

Two other researchers have demonstrated that Q methodology can be valuable in helping to find solutions to "intractable" policy problems. Dayton (2000) proposed that Q methodology be used to identify the competing frames (models, metaphors, understandings) of elites on major controversial issues. According to Dayton, by understanding the competing frames, it is possible to gain insight into the origins of policy conflicts, the beliefs that underlie the intractability of the issue, and possible ways to build a consensus to address the issue. He used the issue of global warming as an example of how Q methodology could identify frames and focus dialogue on areas of agreement.

Van Eeten (2001) demonstrates the utility of Q methodology in helping to "recast intractable problems" so as to make them more amenable to solution, using as a case study efforts to determine the future policy for expanding Amsterdam's Schipol Airport. A controversial expansion of the airport (building a fifth runway) had been approved in 1995, and future expansion was due to come up again soon for consideration.

Through a Q-methodology study, Van Eeten identified five different perspectives (which he called "policy arguments") of the relevant stakeholders on the proposed expansion and the problem that it would address. He concluded that only two of the five factors were bipolar—these represented the public arguments that were magnified by media accounts—but that the others had overlapping elements. Van Eeten suggested that the search for policy should de-emphasize the two bipolar factors, which had made the issue intractable, and to give more attention to elements of the nonpolar factors, which defined the problem in tractable ways so that a compromise could be found.

37.4 CONCLUSION

In this chapter, we have discussed the motivations for using Q methodology and described in some detail how to carry out Q studies. We have suggested that some researchers and practitioners will use Q methodology pragmatically to answer important research and practical public administration questions from a perspective that differs from the usual R method approach. Other researchers and practitioners may turn to Q methodology in reaction to the shortcomings of R methods, which are founded on a barren positivism, an epistemology increasingly challenged by theorists in all social science disciplines (e.g., Morçöl, 2002).

Whatever the motivation for using Q methodology, public administration researchers and practitioners will find that this method can be valuable for their work. As we have described in the chapter, researchers have used Q method to investigate important issues in general public administration, public personnel administration, public management, and public policy, and this methodology is well suited for exploration of other key issues in these research areas. Q methodology can also be a valuable tool for public managers and policy analysts to identify and understand conflicting values, preferences, and opinions concerning organizational and policy issues. Also it has been used, and should be used further, in policy evaluations. In addition, it can contribute to the democratization of management and policy making by allowing the voices of stakeholders and the interested public to be more fully articulated and understood.

A researcher or practitioner who wishes to conduct a Q-methodology study can do so by following the general procedures described in the case study described in Section 37.2 of this chapter. We believe that the value of Q methodology, both as a pragmatic tool and as a nonpositivist or postpositivist research method, is more than sufficient to reward public administration researchers and practitioners fully for their efforts to master it.

ENDNOTES

1. The procedures for carrying out Q method research are discussed in more detail in Section 37.2. The most useful and complete methodological guides are Brown (1980, 1993) and McKeown and Thomas (1988). After mastering the basics of Q methodology, researchers may want to read Stephenson (1953), *The Study of Behavior,* which laid the foundation for Q methodology as the science of subjectivity (Brown, 1994–1995).
2. See Dryzek (1990), chapters 8 and 9, for an in depth comparison of the use of survey research (an R methodology) and Q methodology to investigate public opinion.
3. We should note that sensible positivists have been aware of the limits of science. For example, Stephenson, the creator of Q methodology and a physicist as well as a psychologist, regarded himself as a positivist, yet would not have taken the extreme position attributed to positivists by some postmodernists. Stephenson's view of science was not defended on the basis of objectivity, but of detachment; that is, trying to establish conditions under which the observer might have reason to believe that what was being observed was independent of the self and its desires. Ironically, it is precisely in terms of detachment that R methodology falters: the measuring device (e.g., an autocratic management scale) carries the observer's undetached meaning along with it; in Q, on the other hand, the respondent's meaning is permitted to reign, as detached from whatever meaning the investigator might have given to the same statements. It is Q, not R, that comes closest to achieving detachment (as opposed to "objectivity"). On the relationship of Q methodology to postpositivist assumptions, consult Durning (1999).
4. Statements about the two main concepts were collected for the following nine issues: source of authority, dominant values in work, decision making patterns, recruitment, placement, transfer and promotion, superior-subordinate relationships, work performance, accountability, and group orientation.

REFERENCES

Abrams, M.E. 2002. Like a tree planted by the water: Black journalism students face the job market, *Negro Educational Review, 53*: 13–29.

Adcock, C.J. 1954. *Factorial Analysis for Non-Mathematicians,* Melbourne University Press, Melbourne.

Addams, H. and Proops, J. (Eds.) 2000. *Social Discourse and Environmental Policy: An Application of Q Methodology,* Edward Elgar, Cheltenham, United Kingdom.

Alderfer, C.P. 1972. *Existence, Relatedness, and Growth: Human Needs in Organizational Settings,* Free Press, New York.

Anderson, D.R. 2004. *The Application of Q Methodology to Understanding the Experiences of Female Executives in Biotechnology Companies in Massachusetts: A Contextual Perspective.* Unpublished Ph.D. dissertation, Regent University.

Baker, R. and Meyer, F. 2002. Women and support for correctional reform. Paper presented at the meeting of the American Political Science Association, Boston, Massachusetts.

Baker, R. and Meyer, F. 2003. A community economic elite and support for correctional reforms. Paper presented at the meeting of the Midwest Political Science Association, Chicago, Illinois.

Baker, R.M. 2006. Economic rationality and health and lifestyle choices for people with diabetes, *Social Science & Medicine, 63*: 2341–2353.

Baker, R.M., Thompson, C., and Mannion, R. 2006. Q Methodology in Health Economics, *Journal of Health Services Research & Policy, 11*: 38–45.

Ban, C. 1995. *How Do Public Managers Manage? Bureaucratic Constraints, Organizational Culture, and the Potential for Reform,* Jossey Bass, San Francisco, California.

Barbosa, J.C., Willoughby, P., Rosenberg, C.A., and Mrtek, R.G. 1998. Statistical methodology: VII. Q-methodology, a structural analytic approach to medical subjectivity, *Academic Emergency Medicine, 5*: 1032–1040.

Barry, J. and Proops, J. 1999. Seeking sustainability discourses with Q methodology, *Ecological Economics, 28*: 337–345.

Barry, J. and Proops, J. 2000. *Citizenship, Sustainability, and Environmental Research: Q Methodology and Local Exchange Trading Systems,* Edward Elgar, Cheltenham, United Kingdom.

Beaver, A.K. 2002. Women leaders alter medical training and practice, *Women in Higher Education, 11*(2): 32–33.

Bedrosian, W.K. 2004. *Teacher Decision Making in the Stage Manager Role: A Q Method Study.* Unpublished Ph.D. dissertation, Kent State University.

Benoit, M.A. 2001. I want to participate in the go girls program because . . . using Q-methodology to assess overweight African-American girls' motivation to participate in a physical activity and nutrition education program. Unpublished M.A. paper, Emory University.

Bidwell, C.E. 1957. Some effects of administrative behavior: A study in role theory, *Administrative Science Quarterly, 2:* 162–181.

Brewer, G.A., Selden, S.C., and Facer, R.L. 2000. Individual conceptions of public service motivation, *Public Administration Review, 60*: 254–264.

Brodt, S., Klonsky, K., Tourte, L., Duncan, R., Hendricks, L., Ohmart, C., and Verdegaal, P. 2004. Influence of farm management style on adoption of biologically integrated farming practices in California, *Renewable Agriculture and Food Systems, 19:* 237–247.

Brown, S.R. 1980. *Political Subjectivity: Applications of Q Methodology in Political Science,* Yale University Press, New Haven, Connecticut.

Brown, S.R. 1985. Comments on "The search for structure," *Political Methodology, 11:* 109–117.

Brown, S.R. 1992–1993. On validity and replicability, *Operant Subjectivity, 16*: 45–51.

Brown, S.R. 1993. A primer on Q methodology, *Operant Subjectivity,* 16: 91–138.

Brown, S.R. 1994–1995. Q methodology as the foundation for a science of subjectivity, *Operant Subjectivity, 18:* 1–16.

Brown, S.R. 1996. Q methodology and qualitative research. *Qualitative Health Research, 6*: 561–567.

Brown, S.R. 2002. Structural and functional information, *Policy Sciences, 35*: 285–304.

Brown, S.R. 2005. Applying Q methodology to empowerment, *Measuring Empowerment: Cross-Disciplinary Perspectives*, D. Narayan (Ed.), The World Bank, Washington, DC, pp. 197–215.

Brown, S.R. 2006a. A match made in heaven: A marginalized methodology for studying the marginalized, *Quality and Quantity, 40*: 361–382.

Brown, S.R. 2006b. Q methodology and naturalistic subjectivity, *Modern Perspectives on J.R. Kantor and Interbehaviorism*, B.D. Midgley and E.K. Morris (Eds.), Context Press, Reno, Nevada, pp. 271–276.

Brown, S.R. (in press). Q methodology. In L.M. Given (Ed.), *The SAGE Encyclopedia of Qualitative Research Methods*. Thousand Oaks, California: Sage.

Brown, S.R., Byrd, K.L., Clark, T.W., Rutherford, M.B., Mattson, D.J., and Robinson, B. 2004. Challenges and strategies in large-scale conservation: The case of the Yellowstone-to-Yukon conservation initiative. Paper presented at the meeting of the Policy Sciences Annual Institute, Yale University School of Law, New Haven, Connecticut.

Brown, S.R. and Robyn, R. 2004. Reserving a key place for reality: Philosophical foundations of theoretical rotation, *Operant Subjectivity, 27*: 104–124.

Burt, C. and Stephenson, W. 1939. Alternative views on correlations between persons, *Psychometrika, 4:* 269–281.

Burt, C. 1940. *The Factors of the Mind,* University of London Press, London.

Byrd, K. 2002. Mirrors and metaphors: Contemporary narratives of the wolf in Minnesota, *Ethics, Place, and Environment, 5:* 50–65.

Carlson, J.M. and Trichtinger, R. 2001. Perspectives on entertainment television's portrayal of a racial incident: An intensive analysis, *Communication Review, 4:* 253–278.

Carnevale, D.G. 1995. *Trustworthy Government,* Jossey Bass, San Francisco, California.

Chartier, R. 1995. *Forms and Meanings,* University of Pennsylvania Press, Philadelphia, Pennsylvania.

Chatman, J.A. 1989. Improving interactional organizational research: A model of person-organization fit, *Academy of Management Review, 14:* 333–349.

Chinnis, A.S., Summers, D.E., Doerr, C., Paulson, D.J., and Davis, S.M. 2001. Q methodology: A new way of assessing employee satisfaction, *Journal of Nursing Administration, 1:* 252–259.

Clarke, A.H. 2002. Understanding sustainable development in the context of other emergent environmental perspectives, *Policy Sciences, 35:* 69–90.

Coke, J.G. and Brown, S.R. 1976. Public attitudes about land use policy and their impact on state policy makers, *Publius, 6:* 97–134.

Colorado Institute of Public Policy 2006. Water in 2025: Beliefs and values as a means for cooperation, Colorado Institute of Public Policy, Fort Collins, Colorado. Available http://www.cipp.colostate.edu/pdf/CIPP_Water_2025_www_Final2.pdf

Combes, H., Hardy, G., and Buchan, L. 2004. Using Q-methodology to involve people with intellectual disability in evaluating person-centred planning, *Journal of Applied Research in Intellectual Disabilities, 17:* 149–159.

Cooper, D.R. and Dantico, M.K. 1990. Priority setting techniques for the budgetary process: An experimental comparison to determine what works, *Experimental Study of Politics, 9*(1): 94–117.

Corr, S., Phillips, C.J., and Capdevila, R. 2003. Using Q methodology to evaluate a day service for younger adult stroke survivors, *Operant Subjectivity, 27:* 1–23.

Cunningham, R. and Olshfski, D. 1986. Interpreting state administrator-legislator relationships, *Western Political Science Quarterly, 39:* 104–117.

Davis, C.H. 1997. Value structures in international development research management: The case of a Canadian R&D funding agency, *Science and Technology in a Developing World,* T. Shinn, J. Spaapen, and V. Krishna (Eds.), Kluwer Academic, Dordrecht, The Netherlands, pp. 263–296.

Dayton, B.C. 2000. Policy frames, policy making and the global climate change discourse, *Social Discourse and Environmental Policy,* H. Addams and J. Proops (Eds.), Edward Elgar, Cheltenham, United Kingdom and Northampton, Massachusetts, pp. 71–99.

Dayton, B.C. 2003. Policy dialogues under conditions of uncertainty: Using Q methodology as an aid to dispute resolution. Paper presented at the meeting of the Western Political Science Association, Long Beach, California.

DeCourville, N.H. and Hafer, C.L. 2001. Attitudes toward affirmative action programs: A Q methodological study, *Operant Subjectivity, 24:* 183–200.

Deitrick, S. 1998. Examining community perceptions of brownfields revitalization in Pittsburgh, Pennsylvania. Paper presented at the meeting of the Association of Collegiate Schools of Planning, Pasadena, California.

Dick, M.J. and Edelman, M. 1993. Consequences of the budget crunch: Using Q-methodology to prioritize subscription cancellations, *Journal of Nursing Education, 32:* 181–182.

Donahue, A.K. 2004. Managerial perceptions and the production of fire protection, *Administration & Society, 35:* 717–746.

Donner, J.C. 2001. Using Q-sorts in participatory processes: An introduction to the methodology, *Social Analysis: Selected Tools and Techniques* (Social Development Papers 36), R.A. Kreuger, M.A. Casey, J. Donner, S. Kirsch, and J.N. Maack (Eds.), Social Development Department, The World Bank, Washington, DC, pp. 24–29. Available http://siteresources.worldbank.org/INTRANETSOCIAL DEVELOPMENT/873467-1111741676294/20502176/SDP-36.pdf

Donner, J. 2005. Microentrepreneurs and mobiles: An exploration of the uses of mobile phones by small business owners in Rwanda, *Information Technologies and International Development, 2:* 1–21.

Dryzek, J.S. 1990. *Discursive Democracy,* Cambridge University Press, Cambridge, United Kingdom.

Dryzek, J.S. and Holmes, L.T. 2002. *Post-Communist Democratization: Political Discourses across Thirteen Countries*, Cambridge University Press, Cambridge, United Kingdom.

Dunlap, M.S. and Dudley, R.L. 1965. Quasi Q-sort methodology in self evaluation of conference leadership skill, *Nursing Research, 14*: 119–125.

Durning, D. 1999. The transition from traditional to postpositivist policy analysis: A role for Q-methodology, *Journal of Policy Analysis and management, 18*: 389–410.

Durning, D.W. and Brown, S.R. 2007. Q methodology and decision making, *Handbook of Decision Making*, G. Morçöl (Ed.), CRC Press (Taylor & Francis Group), New York, pp. 537–563.

Durning, D. and Edwards, D. 1992. The attitudes of consolidation elites: An empirical assessment of their views of city county mergers, *Southeastern Political Review, 20*: 355–383.

Durning, D. and Gajdamaschko, N. 1998. Are the managerial perspectives of Ukrainian public administrators changing? An exploratory study using Q methodology, *Proceedings of the Conference on Organizational Psychology and Transition Processes in Central and Eastern Europe, September 1998*, Dubrovnik, Croatia.

Durning, D. and Gadamaschko, N. 2000. The managerial perspectives of local public administrators in Ukraine, *Proceedings, Public Administration and Local Government in Ukraine: Ways of Reforming*, Uzhhorod, Ukraine, pp. 18–31.

Faerman, S.R., Quinn, R.E., Thompson, M.P., and McGrath, M.R. 1990. *Supervising New York State: A Framework for Excellence*, Governor's Office of Employee Relations, Albany, New York.

Fairweather, J.R. and Swaffield, S. 1996. Preferences for scenarios of land-use change in the Mackenzie/ Waitaki Basin, *New Zealand Forestry, 41*: 17–26.

Fang, K.H. 2006. *Taiwan's Officials' Perceptions of Fiscal Decentralization: An Analysis Using Q Methodology*. Unpublished Ph.D. dissertation, University of Pittsburgh.

Finkel, N. 1995. *Commonsense Justice: Jurors' Notions of the Law*, Harvard University Press, Cambridge, Massachusetts.

Focht, W. 2002. Assessment and management of policy conflict in the Illinois River watershed in Oklahoma: An application of Q methodology, *International Journal of Public Administration, 25*: 1311–1349.

Gaines, L.K., Van Tubergen, N., and Paiva, M.A. 1984. Police officer perceptions of promotion as a source of motivation, *Journal of Criminal Justice, 12*: 265–275.

Gallivan, J. 1994. Subjectivity and the psychology of gender: Q as a feminist methodology, *Women, Girls, and Achievement*, J. Gallivan, S.D. Crozier, and V.M. Lalande (Eds.), Captus University Publications, Toronto, Canada, pp. 29–36.

Gallivan, J. 1999. Gender and humor: What makes a difference? *North American Journal of Psychology, 1*: 307–318.

Galve-Peritore, A.K. and Peritore, N.P. 1995. Mexican biotechnology policy and decision makers' attitudes toward technology policy," *Biotechnology in Latin America: Politics, Impacts, and Risks*, N.P. Peritore and A.K. Galve-Peritore (Eds.), Scholarly Resources, Wilmington, Delaware, pp. 69–95.

Gargan, J.J. and Brown, S.R. 1993. 'What is to be done?' Anticipating the future and mobilizing prudence, *Policy Sciences, 26*: 347–359.

Garrard, J. and Hausman, W. 1986. The priority sort: An empirical approach to program planning and evaluation, *Evaluation Studies Review Annual, 11*: 279–286.

Gauzente, C. 2005. La méthodologie Q et l'étude de la subjectivité (Q Methodology and the Study of Subjectivity), *Management des Ressources Humaines: Méthodes de Recherche en Sciences Humaines et Sociales*, P. Roussel and F. Wacheux (Eds.), De Boeck, Brussels, Belgium, pp. 177–206.

Giek, D.G. and Lees, P.L. 1993. On massive change: Using the competing values framework to organize the educational efforts of the human resource function in New York state government, *Human Resource Management, 32*: 9–28.

Gilbert, C. 1959. The framework of administrative responsibility, *Journal of Politics, 21*: 373–407.

Gillard, L.A., Lewis, V.N., Mrtek, R., and Jarosz, C. 2005. Q methodology to measure physician satisfaction with hospital pathology laboratory services at a midwest academic health center hospital, *Labmedicine, 36*: 361–365.

Good, J.M.M. 1998. William Stephenson and the quest for a science of subjectivity, *Revista de Historia de la Psicología, 19*: 431–439.

Good, J.M.M. 2005a. Stephenson, William (1902–1989), *Dictionary of Modern American Philosophers*, J.R. Shook (Ed.), Thoemmes Press, Bristol, United Kingdom, pp. 2322–2323.

Good, J.M.M. 2005b. Stephenson, William, *Encyclopedia of Statistics in Behavioral Science*, Vol. 4, B.S. Everitt and D.C. Howell (Eds.), John Wiley, Chichester, United Kingdom, pp. 1898–1900.

Goodman, G., Tiene, D., and Luft, P. 2002. Adoption of assistive technology for computer access among college students with disabilities, *Disability and Rehabilitation, 24*: 80–92.

Gottschalk, P. 2002. Key issues in IS management in Norway: An empirical study based on Q methodology, *Advanced Topics in Information Resources Management* (Vol. 1), M. Khosrowpour (Ed.), Idea Group, London, United Kingdom, pp. 127–140.

Gough, H.G., Misiti, R., and Parisi, D. 1971. Contrasting managerial perspectives of American and Italian public administrators, *Journal of Vocational Behavior, 1:* 255–262.

Greene, M.W. 1999. Redefining violence in Boulder Valley, Colorado, *Peacebuilding for Adolescents*, L.R. Forcey and I.M. Harris (Eds.), Peter Lang, New York, pp. 57–88.

Hajer, M.A. and Wagenaar, H. (Eds.) 2003. *Deliberative Policy Analysis: Understanding Governance in the Network Society*, Cambridge University Press, Cambridge, United Kingdom.

Herzberg, F., Mausner, B., Peterson, R.O., and Capwell, D.F. 1957. *Job Attitudes: Review of Research and Opinion,* Psychological Service of Pittsburgh, Pittsburgh, Pennsylvania.

Hiruy, M. 1987. *Exploring the Perspectives of Ethics: The Case of Public Administrators in the United States*. Unpublished Ph.D. dissertation, Kent State University.

Hooker, A.M. 2001. Beliefs regarding society and nature: A framework for listening in forest and environmental policy, *Operant Subjectivity, 24*: 159–182.

Hurd, R.C. and Brown, S.R. 2004–2005. The future of the Q methodology movement, *Operant Subjectivity, 28*: 58–75.

Iliescu, D. 2005. *Metodologia Q*, Comunicare.ro, Bucureşti, României.

Irwin, A. 2006. The politics of talk: Coming to terms with the 'new' scientific governance, *Social Studies of Science, 36*: 299–320.

Jacobson, S.W. and Aaltio-Marjosola, I. 2001. 'Strong' objectivity and the use of Q-methodology in cross-cultural research: Contextualizing the experience of women managers and their scripts of career, *Journal of Management Inquiry, 10*: 228–248.

Johnson, P.E. 1973. *Functional Typologies of Administrators: A Q sort Analysis*. Unpublished Ph.D. dissertation, University of Iowa.

Jones, S., Guy, A., and Ormrod, J.A. 2003. A Q-methodological study of hearing voices: A preliminary exploration of voice hearers' understanding of their experiences, *Psychology and Psychotherapy, 76*: 189–209.

Karasz, H.N. 2006. *Anti-Corporate Collectivists, Capable Individualists, and Relativists: A Q-Methodological Exploration of Audiences for Health Communication about Contaminated Soils*. Unpublished Ph.D. dissertation, University of Washington.

Kendall, J.E. and Kendall, K.E. 1993. Metaphors and methodologies: Living beyond the systems machine, *MIS Quarterly, 17*: 149–171.

Kim, S.E. 1991. *Factors Affecting Implementation Effectiveness: A Study of Community Development Block Grant Implementation*. Unpublished Ph.D. dissertation, Kent State University.

Kim, S.E. 2002. An application of Q-methodology in selecting evaluation criteria for information projects, *Korean Local Government Studies, 5*: 207–226. [Korean]

Kitzinger, C. 1999. Commentary: Researching subjectivity and diversity: Q-methodology in feminist psychology, *Psychology of Women Quarterly, 23*: 267–276.

Kline, P. 1994. *An Easy Guide to Factor Analysis*. London: Routledge.

Kramer, B., de Hegedus, P., and Gravina, V. 2003. Evaluating a dairy herd improvement project in Uruguay: Testing and explaining Q methodology, *Journal of International Agricultural and Extension Education, 10*(2), 41–50.

Kramer, B. and Gravina, V. 2004. Theoretical rotation as a tool for identifying points of leverage in people's perspectives for program improvement, *Operant Subjectivity, 27*: 125–144.

Lasswell, H.D. 1963. *The Future of Political Science,* Atherton, New York.

Lawler, E.E. 1973. *Motivation in Work Organizations,* Brooks/Cole, Pacific Grove, California.

Lewis, C.S. 1960. *Studies in Words,* Cambridge University Press, Cambridge, United Kingdom.

Lindsey, J.L. and Rafferty, T.J. 2006. Organizational change research using the Q method: Developing a doctoral program. Paper presented at the meeting of the Midwest Educational Research Association, Columbus, Ohio.

Lister, M. and Gardner, D. 2006. Engaging hard to engage clients: A Q methodological study involving clinical psychologists, *Psychology and Psychotherapy, 79*: 419–443.

Locke, E.A. 1968. Toward a theory of task motivation and incentives, *Organizational Behavior and Human Performance, 3:* 157–159.

Maslow, A.H. 1954. *Motivations and Personality,* Harper and Row, New York.

Mattson, D.J., Byrd, K.L., Rutherford, M.B., Brown, S.R., and Clark, T.W. (2006). Finding common ground in large carnivore conservation: Mapping contending perspectives, *Environmental Science & Policy, 9*: 392–405.

Maxwell, J.P. 2000. Managing conflict at the county level: The use of Q methodology in dispute resolution and strategic planning, *Public Administration Quarterly, 24*: 338–354.

Maxwell, J.P. and Brown, S.R. 1999. Identifying problems and generating solutions under conditions of conflict, *Operant Subjectivity, 23,* 31–51.

McDale, S.E. 1989. *The Identification of Employee Types through Q Methodology: A Study of Parttime and Seasonal Recreation and Parks Employees.* Unpublished M.A. thesis, Pennsylvania State University.

McKeown, B. 1990. Q methodology, communication, and the behavioral text, *Electronic Journal of Communication, 1.*

McKeown, B. 1998. Circles: Q methodology and hermeneutical science, *Operant Subjectivity, 21*: 112–138.

McKeown, B. and Thomas, D. 1988. *Q Methodology,* Sage Publications, Newbury Park, California.

McKeown, M., Hinks, M., Stowell-Smith, M., Mercer, D., and Forster, J. 1999. Q methodology, risk training and quality management, *International Journal of Health Care Quality Assurance, 12*: 254–266.

Meo, M., Focht, W., Caneday, L., Lynch, R., Moreda, F., Pettus, B., Sankowski, E., Trachtenberg, Z., Vieux, B., and Willett, K. 2002. Negotiating science and values with stakeholders in the Illinois River Basin, *Journal of the American Water Resources Association, 38:* 541–554.

Miller, D. and Friesen, P.H. 1984. *Organizations: A Quantum View,* Prentice Hall, Englewood Cliffs, New Jersey.

Morçöl, G. 2002. *A New Mind for Policy Analysis: Toward a Post-Newtonian and Postpositivist Epistemology and Methodology*, Praeger, Westport, Connecticut.

Morgado, E.M., Reinhard, N., and Watson, R.T. 1999. Adding value to key issues research through Q-sorts and interpretive structured modeling, *Communication of the Association for Information Systems, 1,* art 3.

Mrtek, R.G., Tafesse, E., and Wigger, U. 1996. Q-methodology and subjective research, *Journal of Social and Administrative Pharmacy, 13*(2): 54–64.

Murray, H.A. 1938. *Explorations in Personality,* Oxford University Press, New York.

Nelson, B.D., Simic, S., Beste, L., Vukovic, D., Bjegovic, V., and VanRooyen, M.J. 2003. Multimodal assessment of the primary healthcare system of Serbia: A model for evaluating post-conflict health systems, *Prehospital and Disaster Medicine, 18:* 6–13.

Nobbie, P.D. 2003. Evaluating partners in policymaking: Using Q-sort to assess changes in perception, attitudes, and efficacy in advocacy and empowerment. Paper presented at the meeting of the International Society for the Scientific Study of Subjectivity, Athens, Georgia.

O'Reilly, C.A., Chatman, J.A., and Caldwell, D.F. 1991. People and organizational culture: A profile comparison approach to assessing person-organization fit, *Academy of Management Journal, 34:* 487–516.

Oring, K.E. and Plihal, J. 1993. Using Q-methodology in program evaluation: A case study of student perceptions of actual and ideal dietetics education, *Journal of American Dietetic Association, 93:* 151–157.

Oswald, D.L. and Harvey, R.D. 2003. A Q-methodological study of women's subjective perspectives on mathematics, *Sex Roles, 49*: 133–142.

Peace, R., Wolf, A., Crack, S., Hutchinson, I., and Roorda, M. 2004. Well-being, employment, independence: The views of sickness and invalids' benefit clients. Working paper prepared for the Centre for Social Research and Evaluation, New Zealand Ministry of Social Development, Wellington, New Zealand.

Peirce, C.S. 1955. The law of mind, *Philosophical Writings of Peirce,* J. Buchler (Ed.), Dover, New York, pp. 339–353.

Pelletier, D., Kraak, V., McCullum, C., Uusitalo, U., and Rich, R. 1999. The shaping of collective values through deliberative democracy: An empirical study from New York's north country, *Policy Sciences 32*: 103–131.

Peritore, N.P. 1999. *Third World Environmentalism: Case Studies from the Global South*, University Press of Florida, Gainesville, Florida.

Popovich, H. and Popovich, M. 2002. Use of Q methodology for hospital strategic planning: A case study, *Journal of Health Management, 45*: 405–414.

Rainey, H.G. 1991. *Understanding and Managing Public Organizations,* Jossey Bass, San Francisco, California.

Ramlo, S.E. 2005. An application of Q methodology: Determining college faculty perspectives and consensus regarding the creation of a school of technology, *Journal of Research in Education, 15*: 52–69.

Roe, E. 1994. *Narrative Policy Analysis,* Duke University Press, Durham, North Carolina.

Rokeach, M. 1973. *The Nature of Human Values,* Free Press, New York.

Rutherford, M.B. and Gibeau, M. 2006. Interdisciplinary problem solving for grizzly bear conservation in the Banff-Bow Valley region of Alberta, Canada. Paper presented at a meeting of the Society for Conservation Biology, San Jose, California.

Sasson, T. 1995. *Crime Talk: How Citizens Construct a Social Problem,* Aldine de Gruyter, New York.

Scheb, J.M. 1982. *Merit Selection, Role Orientation and Legal Rationalization: A Q Technique Study of Florida State District Courts.* Unpublished Ph.D. dissertation, University of Florida.

Schmolck, P. and Atkinson, J. 2002. PQMethod (2.11). Computer program, available at http://www.rz.unibw-muenchen.de/~p41bsmk/qmethod/

Selden, S.C., Brewer, G.A., and Brudney, J.L. 1999. Reconciling competing values in public administration: Understanding the administrative role concept, *Administration and Society, 31*: 171–204.

Shah, S.M. 1982. *Work Orientation of Middle-Level Managers from the Public Sector.* Unpublished Ph.D. dissertation, Kent State University.

Sheridan, J.E. 1992. Organizational culture and employee retention, *Academy of Management Journal, 35:* 1036–1056.

Shilin, M.B., Durning, D., and Gajdamaschko, N. 2003. How American ecologists think about coastal zone environments, *Values at Sea: Ethics for the Marine Environment,* D. Dallmeyer (Ed.), University of Georgia Press, Athens, Georgia, pp. 239–259.

Simmons, P. and Walker, G. 1999. Tolerating risk: Policy principles and public perceptions, *Risk Decision and Policy, 4*: 179–190.

Simon, H.A., Smithburg, D.W., and Thompson, V.A. 1950. *Public Administration,* Knopf, New York.

Simon, H.A. 1960. *The New Science of Management Decision*, Harper, New York.

Smith, J. 2002. Fear as a barrier?: African American men's avoidance of counseling services, *Journal of African American Men, 6*(4): 47–60.

Snelling, S.J. 1999. Women's perspectives on feminism: A Q-methodological study, *Psychology of Women Quarterly, 23*: 247–266.

Stainton Rogers, W. 1991. *Explaining Health and Illness,* Harvester Wheatsheaf, London, United Kingdom.

Steelman, T.A. and Maguire, L.A. 1999. Understanding participant perspectives: Q-methodology in national forest management, *Journal of Policy Analysis and Management, 18*: 361–388.

Steg, L., Vlek, C., and Slotegraaf, G. 2001. Instrumental-reasoned and symbolic-affective motives for using a motor car, *Transportation Research, Part F: Psychology and Behaviour, 4*: 151–169.

Stephenson, W. 1935. Correlating persons instead of tests, *Character and Personality, 4*: 17–24.

Stephenson, W. 1953. *The Study of Behavior: Q-Technique and Its Methodology*, University of Chicago Press, Chicago, Illinois.

Stephenson, W. 1963. Applications of communication theory: III. Intelligence and multivalued choice, *Psychological Record, 23*: 17–32.

Stephenson, W. 1977. Factors as operant subjectivity, *Operant Subjectivity, 1*: 3–16.

Stephenson, W. 1978. Concourse theory of communication, *Communication, 3*: 21–40.

Stephenson, W. 1980. Consciring: A general theory for subjective communicability, *Communication Yearbook 4*, D. Nimmo (Ed.), Transaction Books, New Brunswick, New Jersey, pp. 7–36.

Stephenson, W. 1983. Quantum theory and Q-methodology: Fictionalistic and probabilistic theories conjoined, *Psychological Record, 33*: 213–230.

Stephenson, W. 1987. How to make a good cup of tea, *Operant Subjectivity, 10:* 37–57.

Stephenson, W. 1989. Quantum theory of subjectivity, *Integrative Psychiatry, 6*: 180–195.

Stowell-Smith, M. and McKeown, M. 1999. Locating mental health in black and white men: A Q-methodological study, *Journal of Health Psychology, 4*: 209–222.

Stricklin, M. and Almeida, R. 2004. *PCQ for Windows* (academic edition). Computer program, available at http://www.pcqsoft.com/

Sun, T.W. 1992. Indigenization of public administration knowledge in Taiwan, *Asian Thought and Society, 17*: 97–112.

Sun, T.W. and Gargan, J.J. 1999. Public administration scholar-practitioner differences: A Q study of theory-practice connections in Taiwan, *Handbook of Comparative Public Administration in the Asia-Pacific Basin*, H-K. Wong and H.S. Chan (Eds.), Marcel Dekker, New York, pp. 141–161.

Sylvia, R.D. and Sylvia, K.M. 1986. An empirical investigation of the impacts of career plateauing, *International Journal of Public Administration, 8*: 227–241.

Taylor, P., Delprato, D.J., and Knapp, J.R. 1994. Q-methodology in the study of child phenomenology, *Psychological Record, 44*: 171–183.

Thomas, D.B. and Siegelman, L. 1984. Presidential identification and policy leadership: Experimental evidence on the Reagan case, *Policy Studies Journal, 12*: 663–675.

Thomas, D.M. and Watson, R.T. 2001. Q-sorting and MIS research, *CAIS: Communications of the Association for Information Systems, 7*. Available http://cais.isworld.org/articles/8–9/default.asp?View = Journal& x = 46&y = 12

Tolymbek, A. (2007). *Political Leadership Style in Kazakhstan*. Unpublished Ph.D. dissertation, Kent State University.

Vajirakachorn, S. and Sylvia, R.D. 1990. Administrative attitudes of elite officials in a buddhist polity, *Operant Subjectivity, 13*: 163–174.

Valenta, A.L. and Wigger, U. 1997. Q-methodology: Definition and application in health care informatics, *Journal of the American Medical Informatics Association, 4*: 501–510.

Van Dusen, W. and Rector, W. 1963. A Q sort study of the ideal administrator, *Journal of Clinical Psychology, 19*: 244.

Van Eeten, M. 2001. Recasting intractable policy issues: The wider implications of the Netherlands civil aviation controversy, *Journal of Policy Analysis and Management, 20, 391*–414.

Van Exel, N.J.A., de Graaf, G., and Rietveld, P. 2004. Getting from A to B: Operant approaches to travel decision making, *Operant Subjectivity, 27*: 194–216.

Vroman, H. 1972. *Types of Administrators and Some of Their Beliefs—A Q Factor Analysis*. Unpublished Ph. D. dissertation, University of Iowa.

Waller, N.G. and Meehl, P.E. 1998. *Multivariate Taxometric Procedures: Distinguishing Types from Continua* (Advanced Quantitative Techniques in the Social Sciences series, No. 9), Sage Publications, Thousand Oaks, California.

Walton, M.L. (2006). *An Investigation of the Effect of Deliberative Discussion on Environmental Preferences, Using the Coastal Plain of the Arctic National Wildlife Refuge as a Case Study*. Unpublished Ph.D. dissertation, Rensselaer Polytechnic Institute.

Warnaars, M. and Pradel, W. (2007). *The Perceptions of Urban and Rural Farmer Field School Participants in Lima: A Q-Method Approach*, Urban Harvest, Centro Internacional de la Papa, Lima, Peru.

Watts, S. and Stenner, P. 2005. Doing Q methodology: Theory, method, and interpretation, *Qualitative Research in Psychology, 2*: 67–91.

Webler, T. and Tuler, S. 2001. Public participation in watershed management planning: Views on process from people in the field, *Human Ecology Review, 8*(2): 29–39.

Webler, T., Tuler, S., and Krueger, R. 2001. What is a good public participation process? Five perspectives from the public, *Environmental Management, 27*: 435–450.

Webler, T., Tuler, S., Shockey, I., Stern, P., and Beattie, R. 2003. Participation by local governmental officials in watershed management planning, *Society and Natural Resources, 16*: 105–121.

Wester, K.L. and Trepal, H.C. 2004. Youth perceptions of bullying: Thinking outside the box, *Operant Subjectivity, 27*, 68–83.

Wilkins, J.L., Kraak, V., Pelletier, D., McCullum, C., and Uusitalo, U. 2001. Moving from debate to dialogue about genetically engineered foods and crops: Insights from a land grant university, *Journal of Sustainable Agriculture, 18*, 167–201.

Wolf, A. 2004. The bones in a concourse, *Operant Subjectivity, 27*, 145–165.

Wong, H.S. 1973. Utilizing group Q-technique to index leadership behavior in task-oriented small groups, Unpublished M.A. thesis, University of Hawaii.

Wood, J. 2004. Mediation styles: Subjective description of mediators, *Conflict Resolution Quarterly, 21*: 437–450.

Wood, R.A. 1983. *Perspectives on Prosecutorial Discretion: A Q-Methodology Analysis.* Unpublished Ph.D. dissertation, University of Missouri-Columbia.

Woolley, J.T. and McGinnis, M.V. 2000. The conflicting discourses of restoration, *Society & Natural Resources, 13*: 339–357.

Woolley, J.T., McGinnis, M.V., and Herms, W.S. 2000. Survey methodologies for the study of ecosystem restoration and management: The importance of Q-methodology, *Integrated Assessment of Ecosystem Health,* K.M. Scow, G.E. Fogg, D.E. Hinton, and M.L. Johnson (Eds.), Lewis, Boca Raton, Florida, pp. 321–332.

Wright, C.M. and Meehling, G. 2002. The importance of operations management problems in service organizations, *Omega, 30*: 77–87.

Wright, C.M., Riggle, C.G., and Wright, B.G. 1998. Technique for pre-implementation assessment in total quality programs, *International Journal of Quality & Reliability Management, 15*: 414–430.

Wrigley, B.J. 2006. Bumping their heads: A study of how women in public relations and communications management view variables contributing to the glass ceiling, *Journal of Human Subjectivity, 4*(1): 33–47.

Yarwood, D.L. and Nimmo, D.D. 1975. Perspectives for teaching public administration, *Midwest Review of Public Administration, 9*: 28–42.

Yarwood, D.L. and Nimmo, D.D. 1976. Subjective environments of bureaucracy: Accuracies and inaccuracies in role-taking among administrators, legislators, and citizens, *Western Political Quarterly, 29*: 337–352.

Züger Cáceres, R. 2003. Do participatory interventions empower people? Paper presented at the meeting of the International Society for the Scientific Study of Subjectivity, Canton, Ohio.

38 Methods of Network Analysis

Simon A. Andrew and Richard C. Feiock

CONTENTS

Network analysis is a distinct research perspective within the social and behavioral sciences; distinct because network analysis is based on the assumed importance of relationships or interaction among units rather than physical position or personal attributes of units such as race, class, and gender. It emphasizes the importance of relational concepts and processes defined by linkages or ties among multiple units. These relations are a fundamental component of network theories in which actors and their actions are viewed as interdependent rather than independent, autonomous units. The relational ties or linkages between actors are assumed to channel the flow of resources i.e., material or non-materials, and represent a structural environment that can provide opportunities for or constraint on individual actions (Monge and Contractor, 2003; Scott, 2000; Wasserman and Faust, 1998).

In the field of public administration, administrative situations where interpersonal ties among public managers play an important role are wide and varied. For instance, personal contacts play critical roles in obtaining information about task accomplishments (O'Toole, 1997). Meier and O'Toole (2001) found that the frequency of interaction among school superintendents is positively related to school district performance; the greater the number of actors and interaction with whom the superintendents networked, the higher the performance. Network analysis has also been used to explain administrative structures within the American federal system (Agranoff and McGuire, 2001).

Interpersonal ties are crucial to collaborative problem solving. McGuire (2002) outlines network management behaviors to understand how public managers strategically match their behaviors with their surrounding environment. This perspective views public managers as interdependent; they need each others resources to achieve their administrative goals (Agranoff and McGuire, 2001; McGuire, 2002). In an effort to resolve common problems, for example, public managers involved in a project or program jointly reach decisions about directions and operations. Through formal and informal interactions, public managers identify and refine problems and agree about a course of action. They share resources, develop strategies and mechanisms for operation and program implementation, and require a means to determine whether the expected results can be accomplished. Central to this discussion have been questions about how to achieve effective delivery of public goods and services, especially in fragmented systems in which public managers must operate together.

38.1 THREE LEVELS OF NETWORK ANALYSIS

We characterize network analysis as falling into one of the three types depending on whether the units of analysis are (1) entire networks; (2) individuals or members of a network; or (3) ties among network members. There is great diversity in network research conducted at the first level. Some of this work is normative or descriptive or simply treats networks as a metaphor. Although such treatments can be interesting and useful they do not lend themselves to systematic empirical analysis because they focus attention at a meta-theoretical level and thus cannot specify the mechanisms by which people, groups, and organizations forge, maintain, and dissolve network relationships. Some studies in this category, although descriptive, measure network characteristic, based on summary measures of social network structure such as centrality, density, etc.

Thurmaier and Wood (2002) provide an example of analysis at this first level. They described intergovernmental relations in the Kansas City metropolitan area as a web of relations underlining local governments' exchange of goods and services in a noncentralized metropolitan political system. Some scholars in public management have used networks to describe an approach to administration. This approach is based on the idea of "networked government" and the management of relationships between public, private, and semipublic organizations that influence policy (Kamarck, 2004, p. 111), thus supplementing a traditional form of governance by market and bureaucratic structures (Thompson, Frances, Levacic, and Mitchell, 1991).

Summary measures of network structure can be constructed across multiple networks to test hypotheses about the predictors or consequences of network structure (Brass et al., 2004). In practice comparative analysis of entire networks is rare because of the cost and difficulty of constructing network measures for more than a few networks. For example, Provan and Milward (1995) examined interorganizational network structures of mental health delivery networks in four U.S. cities. Their analysis linked network effectiveness to network integration, i.e., networks with a centralized decision-making agency. A larger study was conducted by Schneider, Sholz, Lubell, Mindruta, and Edwardsen (2003). They examined network structure in 22 national estuaries in the United States. By comparing networks in the National Estuary Program to networks in estuaries that are not, they concluded that networks in NEP areas "span more levels of government, integrate more experts into policy discussions, nurture stronger interpersonal ties between stakeholders and create greater faith in the procedural fairness of local policy, thus laying the foundation for a new form of cooperative governance." (Schneider et al., 2003, p. 143). Recently, a network study of Washington politics by Carpenter, Esterling, and Lazer (2004), analyzed 40,000 dyadic relationships among lobbyists, government agencies, and congressional staff and showed that lobbyists disproportionately inform those with similar preferences and were more likely to communicate with another lobbyist if their relationship is brokered by a third party.

One expedient has been to measure the number of links of a single central member of each network as a proxy for the structure of the network. Although it has proven popular, this design is weak because it provides no information on the structure of the relationships in which the member is imbedded, just a count of links to or from the member. For example, several studies of local economic development networks simply measure the frequency with which a city development agency interacts with various actors rather than measuring the structural position of the agency in a network (Agranoff and McGuire, 2003; Feiock and Park, 2005). Although there have been calls for more systematic and analytic treatment of networks in the field of public administration (Berry et al., 2004; Kamensky and Burlin, 2004; Miller, 1994; O'Toole, 1997), most work on collaboration in government falls into this first category of network analysis.

Even for a single network, a large N of cases can be generated by taking the individual members (nodes) of the network as units of analysis. This second type of analysis can take into account the entire network or relationships each member is embedded in. Measurement techniques of social network analysis can be used to operationalize the structural position of each member including ego's centrality, density, and many more. Specialized software and graphical techniques allow users to map the structure of the network and position of each member measured in different ways (see Huisman and van Duijn, 2005 for review on specialized software). Because network members (individuals, organizations, etc.) are the units of analysis, conventional statistical approaches can be applied to test hypotheses about characteristics of members that influence position in the network or the influences of network positions on member outcomes or performance.

Although this second level of network analysis facilitates some sophisticated analytic approaches to understanding networks, it is limited by its focus on members of the network rather than relationships between members. The third type of analysis examines dyadic ties among network members. The units of analysis are thus all of the possible links between network members. This approach is positive and analytical, focusing on the structure of network relations among the actors or units in the network and changes in that structure. It builds more directly upon social network analysis because relationships or ties among individuals or organizations are the unit of analysis (Snijders, 2005).

The third approach allows predictions to be made based on both the structure of ties and the characteristics of members simultaneously. It also allows researchers to examine and test hypotheses about the emergence of ties among members and the evolution of the network over time. Although conventional statistical techniques are often adequate for the first two types of analyses, a unique set of concepts, measures, and analytic techniques are required for analyzing relational linkages in longitudinal dyadic datasets. This approach has recently been applied to environmental resource networks (Berardo and Scholz, 2005), public safety and emergency response networks (Andrew, 2006), and water services in Pinellas County (Shrestha and Feiock, 2006).

This chapter presents the basic concepts of network analysis and then describes procedures to describe, measure, graph, and analyze networks. We start with the basic dimension of network analysis for understanding relational data and the techniques applicable to all three types of network analyses. We then introduce measures and analytic tools relevant to analysis of network members and dyadic network links. Several widely used network concepts for describing and analyzing social networks are presented: three centrality measurements, density, and structural holes. The emphasis here focuses on the calculations of network concepts by using UCINET and the interpretation of UCINET results.

38.2 NETWORK CONCEPTS AND MEASURES

A network is a set of actors connected by a set of ties. The actors, typically represented as nodes, can be persons, teams, organizations, etc. Ties connect pairs of actors typically based upon assigned properties that are believed to be inherent to the relations. Depending on the context, networks of relationships may take different forms. The simplest form is nondirectional ties, where two actors are either connected or not. Nondirectional ties do not specify a direction, representing instead a reciprocal relationship. For instance in a network where links represent collaborative partnerships, the network is naturally a nondirectional network. This is generally true of many social and economic relationships such as partnerships, friendship, alliances, or acquaintances. However, there are other situations that are modeled as directed ties. Directional ties are links that go from one node to another, having an origin and destination. They are directional because they are potentially one-dimensional such as in giving advice to someone. One actor may be connected to a second without the second being connected to the first.

This distinction between directional and nondirectional ties is no mere technicality; it is fundamental to network analysis as the applications and modeling are quite different (Wasserman and Faust, 1998). When links are necessarily reciprocal, joint consent is typically needed to establish or maintain the link. For instance, to form a formal contractual arrangement, both partners need to agree. To maintain the contractual ties such as in maintaining business relations or alliances, the applications fall into reciprocal links or mutual consent. In the case of directional ties, one individual may direct a link to another without the other's consent.

In many situations, relational ties might also have some intensity associated with them, which indicates the strength of the relations. For instance, if city managers have closer relationship with other city managers than with other local government actors, there are consequences for the flow of information. Most network analysis to date has been restricted to the case where the strength of a tie is "dichotomous," i.e., as in being either present or absent. This makes representing networks somewhat easy although restrictive. Another approach is to treat the relations as scaleable "values," as in strength of friendship.

A set of ties of a given type constitutes a binary social relation and each relation defines a different network, i.e., a friendship network is distinct from an advice network, although empirically they can be correlated. Different types of ties are often assumed to function differently. For example, centrality in the "who has conflicts with whom" network has different implications for the actor than centrality in the "who trusts whom" network. When focusing on a single focal actor, we can refer to the actor as "ego" and call the set of nodes that ego has ties with as "alters." The collection of ties representing ego, alters, and all ties among them is called an ego-network.

38.3 MANAGING NETWORK DATA

Following the basic network analysis approach, a network structure can be represented as an $N \times N$ matrix reporting all ties among all N actors. For instance, suppose we have a set of g actors. The set N containing g actors can be denoted by $N = \{n_1, n_2, n_3 \ldots, n_g\}$. For simplicity, a network representing a list of unordered pairs of actors i and j establishes a link indicated by $\{i,j\}$. For instance, if $N = \{A, B, C\}$ and $g = \{AB, BC\}$, then the network is represented by a link between actors A and B, a link between actors B and C, but no link between actors A and C. It is important to note that different networks that connect the same actors may lead to different values. The value of a network is derived from its structure and not the labels of the actors who occupy various positions in the network. For instance, a network $N = \{A, B, C\}$ may have a different value depending on whether it is connected via the network $g = \{AB, BC\}$ or the network $g^N = \{AB, BC, AC\}$. The network g^N is referred to as the "complete" network. Figure 38.1 illustrates graphically these networks.

38.4 MEASURING NETWORK PROPERTIES

In the next section, three concepts and measurements for centralities are presented: degree, closeness, and betweenness. Two widely referred network measures: density and structural holes are also described. The example analyses and graphs in the chapter are generated using UCINET version

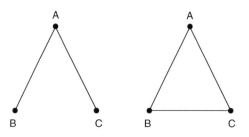

FIGURE 38.1 Different social positions yield different for the study of betweeness.

6.109* to measure the properties of networks and their members. This social network analysis software was developed by Borgatti, Everett, and Freeman (2002) and is widely used because of its graphing capabilities and capability of reading matrices input as Excel spreadsheets.[†]

Suppose that we have a single set of actors, and a single dichotomous nondirectional tie measured in a pair of actors. The information in a sociogram shows "who is connected to whom" and can be represented by a matrix known as the adjacency matrix, in which a given cell $X(i,j)$ contains a value of 1 if nodes i and j are connected, and 0 otherwise. For such data, the ith row of the sociomatrix is identical to the ith column. The sociomatrix can be managed in an Excel spreadsheet and then imported to UCINET as an $N \times N$ matrix of social network data. The data used in the examples presented in this chapter can be found in the Appendix. The network size is $g = 19$ actors, which means that this data represents the relationships of 19 actors in the corresponding sociogram shown in Figure 38.2.

38.4.1 CENTRALITY MEASURES

The most important and widely used network concept for describing and analyzing social networks is centrality. Centrality measures can be used to measure the entire network or, at an individual level, the core or peripheral position of an actor (Borgatti and Everett, 1999). At the individual member or microlevel, it identifies the position of actors in relation to other actors within a network. The most central actor is one that has the most ties to other actors in a network or

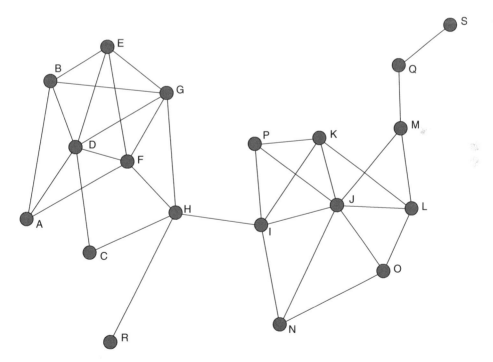

FIGURE 38.2 Sociogram.

---

* UCINET software can be downloaded from http://www.analytictech.com/ucinet.htm.
† An online text by Hanneman and Riddle (2005) provides illustrations and ways to apply network data, analyze, and interpret results using UCINET. A UCINET tutorial by Bob Hanneman is available at http://faculty.ucr.edu/~hanneman/nettext/. A reference book widely used in social network analysis by Wasserman and Faust (1998) reviews and discusses network methodology and applications in the field.

graph. At the network or macrolevel, network centrality examines the variations in centrality positions in a set of individuals within a network. In general, a network is centralized if a few individuals have considerably higher centrality scores than others in the network. A network is decentralized if the individuals in the network have roughly the same centrality scores.

38.4.1.1 Degree Centrality

A very simple and effective way to identify actors' centrality position is their degree centrality score. Freeman's approach is the basic measure of centrality of actors based on their degree and the overall centrality of a network graph. The measure simply counts the number of direct ties for a node. The approach suggests certain actors are more central than others. In Figure 38.2, we can see centrality as an attribute of individual actors given their social position in the network; we can also see inequality in the distribution of centrality of the overall network structure. For example, actor J has the highest degree centrality scores of 7. Actor J might be regarded as the most influential in this network followed by actor D with its 6 degree centrality score.

Conceptually, actors who have more ties to other actors may have alternative ways to satisfy their organizational or personal needs and hence may be less dependent on other actors in the network. Because they have more ties, they may also have more access to information and be able to gain more resources from the network as a whole. They can also act as deal makers in an exchange and benefit from their position as broker. Empirically, degree centrality has been used to measure the size of an actor's relationships with others in a network. For example, Tsai (2001) used degree centrality index to measure individual actor's visibility, information access, and potential communication activities. The author found that when two units are more central in a resource exchange network, they are quicker than others to establish interunit linkages with a newly formed unit. Ahuja (2000) also used degree centrality index to measure a firm's prior embeddedness in an industry, and found that firms that had more interfirm ties generally are more likely to form joint ventures based on new technologies with the same partner. Barley, Freeman, and Hybels (1992) examined factors that explain organization degree centrality in a network of strategic alliances in the commercial biotechnology industry and found a dedicated biotechnology firm and diversified corporation are more involved in the network than other types of organizations.

Formally, as expressed by Wasserman and Faust (1998), the actor degree centrality index can be denoted by $C_D(n_i)$:

$$C_D(n_i) = d(n_i) = x_{i+} = \sum_j x_{ij} = \sum_j x_{ji}$$

Note that the formula for the degree centrality of actor's node, $d(n_i)$ also depends on the group size g; its maximum value is $(g-1)$. To make comparison across networks of different sizes, the degree centrality index is normalized. The process standardizes the measure of degree as the proportion of other actors that are adjacent to ego, n_i. Thus,

$$C_D'(n_i) = \frac{d(n_i)}{g-1}$$

For a network degree centralization index (C_D), Freeman (1979) recommends use of a general index. It measures the variability or dispersion of individual actors' degree centrality indices. That is, how centralized the degree of the set of actors is when compared to the maximum attained value of the same network size. Applying his general formula for network centralization here (Freeman, 1979; Wasserman and Faust, 1998), we find

$$C_D = \frac{\sum_{i=1}^{g} [C_D(n^*) - C_D(n_i)]}{(g-1)(g-2)}$$

The applicability of centrality measures can be illustrated with an example from the information in the Appendix. The centrality of actors in Figure 38.2 can be computed using UCINET 6. The output of UCINET 6 commands *Network>Centrality>Degree* presents several results (Output 1). In the first set of results, the highest degree centrality of actor J is reported as 7 and the degree normalization is 38.88 percent; whereas actor D has the second highest degree centrality score of 6 with the degree normalization 33.33 percent. Based on these results, actors J and D have the greatest degrees and can be regarded as the most influential. The normalization score for actor J, expressed as the percentage of all degree counts of actor J divided by the number of actors in the network, less one (actor J), is $7/18 \times 100 = 38.88$.

The next panel of the UCINET output provides summary statistics on the distribution of the actors' degree centrality scores, which can be interpreted in a manner similar to descriptive statistics. The distribution of the actor's degree centrality score, on average, is 3.7. This is somewhat low given the number of actors in the network is 18. According to Hanneman and Riddle (2005), the range and variability of degree can be important because they describe whether actors in the network are homogeneous or heterogeneous in structural positions. The heterogeneity index is constructed like the coefficient of variation: higher variance implies higher inequality, i.e., actors have different positional advantage in the network.

The final results provide Freeman's graph centralization measure, which describes the centrality score at the network level. Freeman's approach to network centralization scores is based on the comparison of a "star" network that is the most centralized network or the most unequal possible network for any number of actors to the observed network. In other words, Freeman's approach expressed the magnitude of variability of actors' degree centrality in the observed network as a percentage of degree of actors in a star network of the same size. In the example above, the network degree centralization score suggests when compared to a pure star network of similar size, the degree of inequality of the data is only 20.59 percent of the maximum possible.

OUTPUT 1
Freeman's Degree Centrality Measures

	1 Degree	2 NrmDegree	3 Share
10 J	7.000	38.889	0.100
4 D	6.000	33.333	0.086
7 G	5.000	27.778	0.071
6 F	5.000	27.778	0.071
9 I	5.000	27.778	0.071
8 H	5.000	27.778	0.071
12 L	4.000	22.222	0.057
2 B	4.000	22.222	0.057
5 E	4.000	22.222	0.057
11 K	4.000	22.222	0.057
1 A	3.000	16.667	0.043
16 P	3.000	16.667	0.043
13 M	3.000	16.667	0.043
14 N	3.000	16.667	0.043
15 O	3.000	16.667	0.043
3 C	2.000	11.111	0.029
17 Q	2.000	11.111	0.029
18 R	1.000	5.556	0.014
19 S	1.000	5.556	0.014

(continued)

OUTPUT 1 *(Continued)*
Freeman's Degree Centrality Measures

```
DESCRIPTIVE STATISTICS
                         1               2               3
                      Degree         NrmDegree         Share
                   ------------    ------------    ------------

1   Mean               3.684          20.468          0.053
2   Std Dev            1.558           8.654          0.022
3   Sum               70.000         388.889          1.000
4   Variance           2.427          74.895          0.000
5   SSQ              304.000        9382.716          0.062
6   MCSSQ             46.105        1423.002          0.009
7   Euc Norm          17.436          96.864          0.249
8   Minimum            1.000           5.556          0.014
9   Maximum            7.000          38.889          0.100

Network Centralization = 20.59%
Heterogeneity = 6.20%. Normalized = 0.99%
```

38.4.1.2 Closeness Centrality

Closeness centrality measures how quickly an actor can connect to other actors in the network. It emphasizes the distance of an actor to all others in the network. For example, Soh, Mahmood, and Mitchell (2004) used closeness centrality to determine whether a firm with a lower centrality position in an interfirm alliance network increases the firm's R&D investment after it has received new product awards.

The closeness centrality measure is based on a two-stage calculation. The first stage calculates the "farness" of each other from all others. There are several alternative approaches to calculating farness. One approach is based on the sum of the geodesic path distance, i.e., the total number of geodesic paths from actor i to every other actor (Freeman, 1979; Sabidussi, 1966). A geodesic path is the shortest path, in terms of number of ties between a specified pair of actors. The notion has led researchers to equate closeness with minimum distance. The second stage is to transform the farness into "closeness." The idea is that centrality is inversely related to distance. That is, an actor's normalized closeness centrality is one divided by the actor's farness distance to all the other actors. So, as the actor's total farness increases in length, the closeness centrality of the actor would decrease. Intuitively, if the total number of direct and indirect ties to reach all others in the network is kept at a minimum, the greater the actor's closeness centrality and the more easily that actor can interact with all the other members of the network. Closeness centrality measure is meaningful for connected graphs only.

For the actor's closeness centrality measure, the formal definition can be written as follows: Let $d(n_i,n_j)$ be the number of ties in the geodesic path connecting actors i and j. The total distance that actor i is from all other actors is $\sum_{j=1}^{g} d(n_j,n_i)$, where the sum is taken over all $j \neq I$ (Wasserman and Faust, 1998). This is a formal way to express the first stage of calculating actor's closeness centrality index. As per Sabidussi's (1966) index, the closeness centrality, $C_C(n_i)$ is expressed as the inverse of the sum of the distance from actor i to all other actors.

$$C_C(n_i) = \left[\sum_{j=1}^{g} d\left(n_i,n_j\right) \right]^{-1}$$

When actor is adjacent to all other actors, at the maximum, the actor's closeness index equals $(g-1)^{-1}$; and equals 0 when there is no path linking one or more actors from the actor in question.

So, the index depends on the size of a network, g. The normalization of the actor closeness centrality index, $C_C'(n_i)$ is obtained simply by multiplying $C_C(n_i)$ by $(g-1)$.

For the network centrality index, Freeman's general group closeness centrality index is based on the actor closeness centralities. The index of group closeness centrality is expressed as follows:

$$C_C = \frac{\sum_{i=1}^{g} [C_C'(n^*) - C_C'(n_i)]}{[(g-2)(g-1)]/(2g-3)}$$

Note that $C_C'(n^*)$ denotes the largest standardized actor's closeness. For example, the sociomatrix in the Appendix when analyzed using UCINET's *Network>Centrality>Closeness* routine produces Freeman's general group centrality index at the bottom of the output. The largest standardized actor's closeness centrality is actor I with the "nCloseness" score of 47.368. The difference between the largest standardized actor closeness index and each of the individual actor standardized closeness centrality scores, when summed and expressed as a ratio to the numerator $[(g-2)(g-1)/(2g-3)]$ should yield Freeman's group centrality index of 27.69 percent, i.e., $\frac{242.08}{8.743}$. Freeman's general group closeness centrality index can attain its minimum value of 0 when the lengths of geodesics are all equal such as in a complete graph, i.e., when all of the actors are connected to each other. For example in Figure 38.2, the index equals 27.69 percent a relatively small value.

How was an actor's farness from all other actors, or $C_C(n_i)$ calculated? Let us take Actor I's distance from each of the other actors as an example. The length of the shortest path that actor I would need to take to reach each of the actors A, B, D, E, and Q is three steps. Actor I also need two steps to reach each actor C, F, G, L, M, O, and R; one step each to reach each actor H, J, K, N, and P; and four steps to reach actor S. The total number of shortest paths for actor I to reach each of the other actors is 38. Based on the formula of actor closeness centrality index above, $C_C'(n_i)$, this yields 0.47368 as actor I's closeness centrality index, i.e., $\frac{18}{38}$.

OUTPUT 2
Closeness Centrality

Closeness Centrality Measures

	1 Farness	2 nCloseness
9 I	38.000	47.368
8 H	39.000	46.154
10 J	42.000	42.857
11 K	47.000	38.298
7 G	48.000	37.500
6 F	48.000	37.500
14 N	48.000	37.500
16 P	48.000	37.500
3 C	51.000	35.294
13 M	54.000	33.333
12 L	54.000	33.333
18 R	56.000	32.143
15 O	57.000	31.579
4 D	58.000	31.034
2 B	60.000	30.000

(continued)

OUTPUT 2   (*Continued*)
Closeness Centrality

Closeness Centrality Measures

	1 Farness	2 nCloseness
5 E	60.000	30.000
1 A	61.000	29.508
17 Q	69.000	26.087
19 S	86.000	20.930

Statistics

		1 Farness	2 nCloseness
1	Mean	53.895	34.627
2	Std Dev	10.823	6.371
3	Sum	1024.000	657.920
4	Variance	117.147	40.587
5	SSQ	57414.000	23553.174
6	MCSSQ	2225.790	771.153
7	Euc Norm	239.612	153.470
8	Minimum	38.000	20.930
9	Maximum	86.000	47.368

Network Centralization = 27.69%

38.4.1.3 Betweenness Centrality

A third measure often used to analyze centrality is the betweenness centrality index. The betweenness index takes into consideration the actors lying along the shortest path between other actors. Conceptually, ego with the greatest betweenness would have the most influence over what information flows within the network. That is, the more actors in the network depend on ego to make connections with others, the more influence that ego would have. On the other hand, if two alters are connected by more than one geodesic path to others and ego is not on any of the paths, then ego is not influential.

Empirically, Cross and Cummings (2004) used betweenness centrality to assess the effect of ties beyond one remove from a person on individual performance in knowledge-intensive work. They found a positive association betweenness centrality and individual performance among 101 engineers in a petrochemical company and 125 consultants in a strategy-consulting firm. Barley et al. (1992) examined factors that explain the relative betweenness of strategic alliances in the commercial biotechnology industry. They found, on average, that an organization which is a dedicated biotechnology firm, being publicly owned, or being Western European significantly increased its betweenness in the network of strategic alliance. They argued that such organizations are likely to have greater power in the biotechnology community because they are best positioned to control the flow of information and technology.

Ego's betweenness is based on the probability that the shortest paths between any two other actors pass through ego. This probability is then divided by the total number of possible connections involving the other actors. For example, let the betweenness centrality for n_i be the fraction of geodesic paths between other actors that i falls on. That is, we find the shortest path (or paths) between every pair of actors, and ask in what fraction of those paths does actor i lie. Freeman's betweenness centrality index is very useful, but requires some illustrations to appreciate the concept.

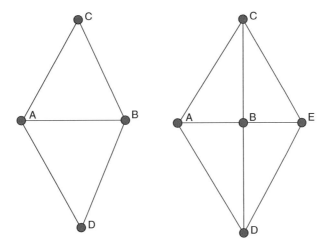

FIGURE 38.3 Two illustrative networks for the study of betweenness.

Two artificial graphs that highlight the differences among actors betweenness positions are presented in Figure 38.3a and b. Inspection of these figures shows that the numbers of actors in the networks are quite different. In Figure 38.3a, for actor C to reach actor D it must go through two possible geodesic paths: it either goes through actor A or B. Then, if any of these routes are likely to be chosen for the path, the probability of the connection using any one of them is $1/g_{jk}$, where g_{jk} is the number of the geodesics connecting the two actors. In our example for Figure 38.3a, the number connecting the two actors is two.

In Figure 38.3a, the number of geodesics linking actors C and D is $1/2$. To calculate the individual actor's betweenness centrality score, let $g_{jk}(n_i)$ be the number of geodesics connecting actors C and D that involved, say actor A. Freeman's betweenness centrality measure then estimates the probability of an actor's betweenness position by $g_{jk}(n_i)/g_{jk}$. So, the betweenness centrality for actor A is 0.500. In Figure 38.3a, both actors A and B have the same betweenness score; whereas for actors C and D, their betweenness score is 0 because actor A can directly connect to actor B without involving them.

To further appreciate the Freeman approach in calculating actor's betweenness, let's illustrate the calculation further using Figure 38.3b as an example. There are two sets of pair of actors indirectly connected through some other actors: The first set of pairs, actors C and D, can be connected by three possible geodesic paths that either involve actors A, B, or E. Each path has an equal probability of $1/3$. The second set of pairs, actors A and E, which also can be connected by three possible geodesic paths, can either be connected via actors B, C, or D. Each path also has an equal probability of $1/3$. Note that actor B is involved twice in connecting both sets of these actors; whereas the others are involved only once. This makes actor B the most central actor in Figure 38.3b. The betweenness index for actor B is 0.667 and may be defined loosely as the sum of both of these estimated probabilities over all pairs of actors in the network. Specifically, the actor's betweenness centrality index is

$$C_B(n_i) = \sum_{j<k} g_{jk}(n_i)/g_{jk}$$

As both of these graphs have shown, the actor's betweenness centrality index depends on g, the size of the network. Because of this, we standardize the measure just like the other actor centrality indices by the maximum number of geodesic paths on which n_i falls. Freeman shows that the maximum possible value is $(g-1)(g-2)/2$. Thus, the normalized actor betweenness centrality is expressed as

$$C_B'(n_i) = C_B(n_i)/[(g-1)(g-2)/2]$$

At a network level, the centralization index can be calculated based on actor betweenness score. This allows researchers to compare networks with respect to heterogeneity of the betweenness of the members across different network structures. Freeman proposes $\sum_{i=1}^{g} [C_B(n^*) - C_B(n_i)]$ as the numerator. Note that Freeman's approach uses $C_B(n^*)$, which is the largest observed actor betweenness index rather than the actor's normalized betweenness index. Freeman shows that the maximum possible value for this sum is $(g-1)^2(g-2)/2$, so that the normalized index of group betweenness score is

$$C_B = \frac{2 \sum_{i=1}^{g} [C_B(n^*) - C_B(n_i)]}{[(g-1)^2(g-2)]}$$

How to analyze a network structure using Freeman's betweenness centrality measures in UCINET? Once again, let us return to the example in Figure 38.2. The UCINET commands *Network>Centrality>Betweenness>Nodes* for the sociomatrix file produce actor betweenness index, a descriptive statistic, and the group centralization index. In Figure 38.2, actor H has the highest betweenness score of 88.00. This means that actor H's presence facilitates the flow of information. If actor H, given his highest score on betweenness centrality, is removed from the network, the speed and certainty of transmission information from one actor to another in the network will be damaged.

The descriptive statistics reported in UCINET's output for each measure are presented. There is substantial variation in actor betweenness scores, ranging from 0 to 88.00. There is also great variation because the standard deviation is larger than the mean. The overall network centralization index of 48.33 percent is also quite large. This makes sense given the unequal distribution of power in this network. There are only a few actors having relatively high betweenness scores. For example, two actors, i.e., actors H and I play an important role in bridging all other actors across the network. In the structural sense, they have the most power in this network.

OUTPUT 3
Freeman Betweenness Centrality

Un-Normalized Centralization: 1331.000

	1 Betweenness	2 nBetweenness
8 H	88.000	57.516
9 I	82.000	53.595
10 J	52.500	34.314
13 M	32.000	20.915
6 F	22.667	14.815
7 G	22.250	14.542
17 Q	17.000	11.111
11 K	5.500	3.595
14 N	5.000	3.268
4 D	4.917	3.214

OUTPUT 3 *(Continued)*
Freeman Betweenness Centrality

```
Un-Normalized Centralization: 1331.000
                        1            2
                   Betweenness   nBetweenness
                   -----------   ------------

       3 C            4.000         2.614
      12 L            3.500         2.288
       2 B            0.667         0.436
      15 O            0.500         0.327
       1 A            0.250         0.163
       5 E            0.250         0.163
      16 P            0.000         0.000
      18 R            0.000         0.000
      19 S            0.000         0.000
```

```
DESCRIPTIVE STATISTICS FOR EACH MEASURE

                        1            2
                   Betweenness   nBetweenness
                   -----------   ------------

  1  Mean            17.947        11.730
  2  Std Dev         26.690        17.444
  3  Sum            341.000       222.876
  4  Variance       712.344       304.303
  5  SSQ          19654.584      8396.165
  6  MCSSQ        13534.530      5781.764
  7  Euc Norm       140.195        91.631
  8  Minimum          0.000         0.000
  9  Maximum         88.000        57.516
```

```
Network Centralization Index = 48.33%
```

38.4.2 DENSITY

Density has been used by scholars to capture the concept of social capital. This conceptualization is based on the premise that resources that are quantitatively unobserved such as social norms, obligations, and trust can signal "something of value" for those actors who have these resources available; and that, the value depends on social organization (Coleman, 1988, p. 101). In line with the work of Putnam (1993), and Coleman (1988), the concept can be understood as dense networks of social relations which are characterized by norms of trust and reciprocity leading to outcomes of mutual benefit. A densely connected set of actors in a network is treated as an instrumental mechanism enabling effective monitoring and sanctioning crucial for cooperative behavior among network members.

Empirically, density has been used by Reagans and Zuckerman (2001) to measure the level of communication between members in a network. In this study, they argue that the higher the density score, the more members in the network are in communication with each other. Teams that have higher average communication generally achieve higher productivity. A recent study by Oh, Chung, and Labianca (2004) uses a group's density to determine group's social capital and effectiveness of 11 South Korean organizations.

In social network analysis, a densely or closely knit network can be quantified using density measurement. At the individual level, the measurement for actor density has been applied by theories of collective action to examine the nature and forms by which actors in a network would behave cooperatively to achieve collective benefits (Ostrom and Ahn, 2003). At the network level of analysis, network density focuses on the favorable or unfavorable conditions for cooperation. Scholars have also examined network density as a potential source of resources such as information and social support (Lin, 2001). For example, network density tests theories that focus on mechanisms conveying values and the importance of norms for integration and social cohesion. A network is structurally cohesive when ties are distributed evenly across the network, implying very few disconnected subgraphs in the underlying structure. When actors are removed the network would still remain connected. Hence, in a dense network structure, according to the theories of collective action, it would be easier for the members to enforce norms of cooperation and foster cooperation without jeopardizing the whole network.

How have empirical studies such as those referenced above measured network density? At the individual level, ego's density score can be calculated as the total number of observed ties in ego's neighborhood divided by the total number of potential pairs of alters connected to ego, times 100 (Borgatti et al., 2002). Thus, an actor density measure can be expressed as

$$\frac{\text{Total number of actual ties in the ego network}}{\text{Total number of pairs of alters in ego network, i.e., potential ties}} \times 100$$

The total number of actual direct ties in the ego network is determined by simply counting all existing ties in ego's immediate neighborhood network. The denominator, the total number of pairs of alters in the ego network, i.e., potential ties, as it turns out, is the maximum number of possible ties. For example, if $g(n_i)$ equals the number of actors connected to actor i, then the potential ties can be calculated by $\frac{g(n_i)[g(n_i)-1]}{2}$ for a nondirectional network; or $g(n_i)[g(n_i) - 1]$ for a directional network.

In the data representing Figure 38.2 above, the UCINET command *Network>Ego networks> Density* calculates a number of indices that describe aspects of the neighborhood of each ego in a dataset. For example, take actor J's density index measurement. The number of actors connected to actor J is 7. Its total number of potential ties is 42. The actual count on the number of ties in ego's network is 16. So, actor J's density score is 38.10. However, actor J does not have the highest actor density score. Actor P has the highest score of 1.00, which means that actor P's alters are highly connected to every other alter in the ego's neighborhood. A density of 0 implies that the actor's alters are not connected to each other.

At the network level, the density is the degree to which the whole network is filled with social ties. A network density is defined as the proportion of possible ties between a set of actors that actually do exist (Borgatti et al., 2002). One way to measure the density of a whole network is by following a method proposed by Watts and Strogatz (1998)—overall network clustering coefficient. The measure captures the probability that ego's alters are also connected to other alters in ego's network. It analyzes the overall graph clustering coefficient as the average of the clustering coefficient of all the actors in a network. That is, actors with larger neighborhoods get more weight in computing the graph's overall average density.

In the UCINET command *Network>Cohesion>Clustering Coefficient*, the overall network clustering coefficient is calculated. In our example (Figure 38.2), the overall network clustering coefficient is 0.497, which means the average of the densities of the neighborhoods of all of the actors is rather high. This makes sense. Virtually in Figure 38.2, we see that all of the actors are surrounded by two local neighborhoods that are fairly dense—such a network structure can be regarded as embedded in dense local neighborhoods.

38.4.3 STRUCTURAL HOLES

Burt (1992) introduced the idea of structural holes to illustrate the notion that entrepreneurs choose with whom they establish, maintain, or break ties to reap selective benefits of networking. A structural hole exists in the social space between closely clustered communities. According to

OUTPUT 4
Ego Networks: Density Measures

		1 Size	2 Ties	3 Pairs	4 Densit	5 AvgDis	6 Diamet	7 nWeakC	8 pWeakC	9 2StepR	10 ReachE	11 Broker	12 nBroke	13 EgoBet	14 nEgoBe
1	A	3.00	4.00	6.00	66.67	1.33	2.00	1.00	33.33	38.89	46.67	1.00	0.17	0.50	16.67
2	B	4.00	8.00	12.00	66.67	1.33	2.00	1.00	25.00	38.89	38.89	2.00	0.17	1.00	16.67
3	C	2.00	0.00	2.00	0.00			2.00	100.00	50.00	81.82	1.00	0.50	1.00	100.00
4	D	6.00	14.00	30.00	46.67	1.17	2.00	2.00	33.33	38.89	30.43	8.00	0.27	5.92	39.44
5	E	4.00	10.00	12.00	83.33	1.60	3.00	1.00	25.00	38.89	35.00	1.00	0.08	0.33	5.56
6	F	5.00	10.00	20.00	50.00	1.60	3.00	1.00	20.00	50.00	39.13	5.00	0.25	3.00	30.00
7	G	5.00	12.00	20.00	60.00	1.50	3.00	1.00	20.00	50.00	37.50	4.00	0.20	2.33	23.33
8	H	5.00	2.00	20.00	10.00			4.00	80.00	72.22	72.22	9.00	0.45	9.00	90.00
9	I	5.00	8.00	20.00	40.00			2.00	40.00	66.67	54.55	6.00	0.30	5.00	50.00
10	J	7.00	16.00	42.00	38.10	1.81	3.00	1.00	14.29	50.00	36.00	13.00	0.31	8.50	40.48
11	K	4.00	8.00	12.00	66.67	1.33	2.00	1.00	25.00	44.44	42.11	2.00	0.17	1.00	16.67
12	L	4.00	6.00	12.00	50.00	1.50	2.00	1.00	25.00	44.44	47.06	3.00	0.25	1.50	25.00
13	M	3.00	2.00	6.00	33.33			2.00	66.67	50.00	69.23	2.00	0.33	2.00	66.67
14	N	3.00	4.00	6.00	66.67	1.33	2.00	1.00	33.33	44.44	53.33	1.00	0.17	0.50	16.67
15	O	3.00	4.00	6.00	66.67	1.33	2.00	1.00	33.33	38.89	50.00	1.00	0.17	0.50	16.67
16	P	3.00	6.00	6.00	100.00	1.00	1.00	1.00	33.33	44.44	50.00	0.00	0.00	0.00	0.00
17	Q	2.00	0.00	2.00	0.00	0.00	0.00	2.00	100.00	22.22	100.00	1.00	0.50	1.00	100.00
18	R	1.00	0.00	0.00		0.00	0.00	1.00	100.00	27.78	100.00	0.00	0.00	0.00	0.00
19	S	1.00	0.00	0.00		0.00	0.00	1.00	100.00	11.11	100.00	0.00	0.00	0.00	0.00

1. Size. Size of ego network.
2. Ties. Number of directed ties.
3. Pairs. Number of ordered pairs.
4. Density. Ties divided by Pairs.
5. AvgDist. Average geodesic distance.
6. Diameter. Longest distance in egonet.
7. nWeakComp. Number of weak components.
8. pWeakComp. NWeakComp divided by Size.
9. 2StepReach. # of nodes within 2 links of ego.
10. ReachEc. 2StepReach divided Size.
11. Broker. # of pairs not directly connected.
12. Normalized Broker. Broker divided by number of pairs.
13. Ego Betweenness. Betweenness of ego in own network.
14. Normalized Ego Betweenness. Betweenness of ego in own network.

OUTPUT 5
Clustering Coefficient

Overall graph clustering coecient: 0.497
Weighted Overall graph clustering coecient: 0.487
Node Clustering Coecients

	1 Clus Coef	2 nPairs
1 A	0.667	3.000
2 B	0.667	6.000
3 C	0.000	1.000
4 D	0.467	15.000
5 E	0.833	6.000
6 F	0.500	10.000
7 G	0.600	10.000
8 H	0.100	10.000
9 I	0.400	10.000
10 J	0.381	21.000
11 K	0.667	6.000
12 L	0.500	6.000
13 M	0.333	3.000
14 N	0.667	3.000
15 O	0.667	3.000
16 P	1.000	3.000
17 Q	0.000	1.000
18 R	0.000	
19 S	0.000	

Burt, an entrepreneur acting as broker gains advantage by bridging such unexplored spaces of opportunities, which he termed "structural holes." The theory argues that actors should aim to form weak ties over strong ties by spanning across communities, as strong ties only lead to redundancy of information. The structural holes theory articulates an actor's advantageous position when the actor is connected to a significant number of powerful, sparsely linked actors with only minimal investment in tie strength.

Structural holes theory has been applied to the concept of social capital (Burt, 1992) and has been empirically tested using Burt's network constraint index C. The concept of network constraint is important in Burt's structural holes argument. For example, in his criticism of densely knitted network structure, he argued that the more constrained networks will span fewer structural holes. A high score on actor's network constraint index C implies less social capital and thus the performance and value of an individual's idea, promotion, and rewards (Burt, 1992) would have a negative association with network constraint.

Some empirical studies have applied Burt's measure of network constraint. Ahuja (2000) applied the network constraint index to determine whether a firm's position in a collaborative network has an association with the firm's innovation output. Using a longitudinal study from the international chemical industry, the author found that an increase in structural holes has a negative effect on innovation output. A study conducted by Soda, Usai, and Zaheer (2004) in Italy on a network of 501 TV productions uses structural hole measurement to determine whether a production team that taps diverse ideas and skills from a range of other projects has a higher project network performance—measured in terms of the size of the audience that watched a show.

OUTPUT 6
Structural Holes

Dyadic Redundancy

	1 A	2 B	3 C	4 D	5 E
	----	----	----	----	----
1 A	0.00	0.50	0.00	0.50	0.00
2 B	0.33	0.00	0.00	0.67	0.33
3 C	0.00	0.00	0.00	0.00	0.00
4 D	0.25	0.50	0.00	0.00	0.25
5 E	0.00	0.50	0.00	0.50	0.00

Dyadic Constraint

	1 A	2 B	3 C	4 D	5 E
	----	----	----	----	----
1 A	0.00	0.39	0.00	0.44	0.00
2 B	0.17	0.00	0.00	0.44	0.17
3 C	0.00	0.00	0.00	1.00	0.00
4 D	0.11	0.25	0.06	0.00	0.11
5 E	0.00	0.39	0.00	0.44	0.00

Structural Hole Measures

	1 ESize	2 Ecie	3 Constra	4 Hierarc
	-------	-------	-------	-------
1 A	1.000	0.500	0.835	0.003
2 B	1.667	0.556	0.792	0.099
3 C	1.000	1.000	1.000	1.000
4 D	3.000	0.750	0.535	0.092
5 E	1.000	0.500	0.835	0.003

Burt's network constraint argument can be measured using Constraint Index C (Burt, 1997, p. 347). The index measures the extent to which "actor i network is directly or indirectly invested in his or her relationship with contact j" (Burt, 1992, pp. 54–55).

$$C_{ij} = (p_{ij} + \sum_q p_{iq}p_{qj})^2, \quad \text{for } P \neq i,j$$

where p_{ij} is the proportion of i's relations invested in actor j. The sum, $\sum_q p_{iq}p_{qj}$ is the extent of i's relations invested in actor q's which in turn are invested in actor j. The total in the parentheses is the proportion of i's relations that are directly or indirectly invested in its connection with actor j. This equation measures constraint based on marginal strength relations, which increases exponentially as network size and density increase together (Burt, 1992, p. 61; 1997, p. 347).

In the UCINET command *Network>Ego Networks>Structural Holes*, Burt's network constraint index C is presented as the last table in Column 3 of the output. The first two sets of output: "Dyadic Redundancy" and "Dyadic Constraint" examine various aspects of the advantages or disadvantages of each of the actors' social positions in their neighborhoods for the presence of structural holes. In our example, actor H has the least constraint.

38.5 CONCLUSIONS

In network analysis, an actor's social position is relational to others in a network. That is, an actor serves as intermediary between groups of people that are not directly connected to other groups. At the individual level, network properties are different from the exogenous attributes of individuals such as age, gender, or organizational affiliations in the sense that individual actors' social position is inherent in the network whereas actors' attributes are independent of the relations. At the dyadic level, a tie between two actors is established to forge exchange for materials or nonmaterial resources. In its most elementary level, individual actor's relations are likely to establish exchange ties when the relations are based on mutual ties or a high degree of reciprocation. Relations can also be examined at the triad level. For example, in a three actor combination, actor A has a tie with actor B and actor B has a tie with a third actor C. Depending on the context of the interactions, such ties may take the form of friendship or formal relations such as the exercise of authority. At the network level of analysis, the property of a whole network structure is taken into account to measure the effect of the configuration of ties. For example, researchers may be interested to determine whether a centralized or decentralized network structure is likely to lead to a particular level of collective benefits.

One of the advantages of using network analysis is that we can calculate the social positions of various actors in a predefined network space. In our example, we have used an undirected matrix to calculate actor's degree centrality, closeness, and betweenness; and we have illustrated how density and constraint measurements have been used by scholars to develop and predict social phenomena. Table 38.1 presents the summary of each measure at the individual level of analysis and a summary of network level calculations. Most of these measurements can be used as independent variables if researchers were interested to run regression models. When such models are used, social position is assumed to have an impact on certain policy outcomes.

TABLE 38.1
Results Summary of Network Analysis

	Degree	Closeness	Betweenness	Density	Constraint
A	16.67	29.51	0.16	66.67	0.54
B	22.22	30.00	0.44	66.67	0.53
C	11.11	35.29	2.61	0.00	0.50
D	33.33	31.03	3.21	46.67	0.42
E	22.22	30.00	0.16	83.33	0.57
F	27.78	37.50	14.81	50.00	0.42
G	27.78	37.50	14.54	60.00	0.46
H	27.78	46.15	57.52	10.00	0.24
I	27.78	47.37	53.59	40.00	0.40
J	38.89	42.86	34.31	38.10	0.39
K	22.22	38.30	3.59	66.67	0.53
L	22.22	33.33	2.29	50.00	0.47
M	16.67	33.33	20.92	33.33	0.43
N	16.67	37.50	3.27	66.67	0.55
O	16.67	31.58	0.33	66.67	0.57
P	16.67	37.50	0.00	100.00	0.65
Q	11.11	26.09	11.11	0.00	0.50
R	5.56	32.14	0.00	—	1.00
S	5.56	20.93	0.00	—	1.00
Overall graph[a]	20.59	27.69	48.33	0.497	—

[a] Overall graph measure for density is using clustering coefficient calculation.

The importance of theory in using network analysis cannot be overemphasized. Social actors having different social position scores, the type, and structure of network relationships can inform causal explanation. For example, an actor might have a low degree centrality score, but if it has direct or indirect connections with all others that have high degree scores, the actor's social position may have important practical implications. An actor who has the highest betweenness score is likely to be the gatekeeper as well as bridging structural holes in the network; whereas the actor with a high closeness centrality score can be interpreted as having access to information or resources directly or indirectly through his network. Structural holes theory, for example, would argue that actor H has less network constraint and therefore acts as a source of information and is more likely to have higher social capital; on the other hand, closure theory would argue that actor P has the highest source of capital through his or her networks and is likely to have higher rewards/output.

Actors purposely create nonrandom links to others. Actors in a network are assumed to use a wide variety of direct and indirect ties to obtain information. That is, social actors are assumed to choose who they think will be best in serving their needs or provide them with the scarce resources best to achieve their goals. Implicit in this argument is an assumption that actors are constrained by limited time and resources so that a nonrandom interaction implies uneven investments in relationships. The idea that interactions are nonrandom has an important implication on theory building and model predictions, i.e., the homophily or preference treatment hypotheses would argue certain groups would yield certain advantages based on their interactions with similar others.

At the level of network structure, the properties and measures also differ. Each measurement implies networks with many linkages are dense or highly clustered. Networks with fewer linkages have been referred to as sparse or thinly connected network structures. For example, the density of clusters, the tightness of cluster boundaries, and the patterns of ties within and between clusters all structure resource flows. Because of structural location, members of a social system differ greatly in their access to these resources. Several metaphors have also been used to describe different configurations of network structures such as "strength of weak ties" (Granovetter, 1973), "dark networks" (Raab and Milward, 2003), "strong ties" (Carpenter, Esterling, and Lazer, 2003), and "small world networks" (Watts and Strogatz, 1998). Sometimes, authors have a specific measure in mind, i.e., a small world network implies a very large network structure with a short average path length but high clustering coefficient. Sometimes, networks are used simply as metaphors to capture the essence of social interactions.

REFERENCES

Agranoff, R. and McGuire, M. (2001). American federalism and the search for models of management. *Public Administration Review*, *61* (November/December): 650–660.

Agranoff, R. and McGuire, M. (2003). Collaborative Public Management. Washington, D.C.: Georgetown University Press.

Ahuja, G. (2000). Collaboration networks, structural holes, and innovation: A longitudinal study. *Administrative Science Quarterly*, *45*, 425–455.

Andrew, S.A. (2006). Institutional Ties, Interlocal Contractual Arrangements, and the Dynamic of Metropolitan Governance, Florida State University. Unpublished dissertation.

Barley, S.R., Freeman, J., and Hybels, R. (1992). Strategic alliances in commercial biotechnology. In: R. Eccles, and N. Norhia (Eds.), *Networks and Organizations*. Boston: Harvard Business School Press.

Berardo, R. and Scholz, J.T. (2005). Micro-incentives and the dynamics of policy networks. Prepared for presentation at the American Political Science Association Annual Meeting, September 1–4, Washington, DC.

Berry, F.S., Brower, R.S., Choi, S.O., Goa, W., Jang, H., Kwon, M., and Word, J. (2004). Three traditions of network research: What the public management research agenda can learn from other research communities. *Public Administration Review*, *64* (5), 539–553.

Borgatti, S.P., and Everett, M.G. (1999). Models of core/periphery structures. *Social Networks 21*, 375–395.

Borgatti, S.P., Everett, M.G., and Freeman, L.C. (2002). Ucinet for Windows: Software for Social Network Analysis. Harvard, Massachusetts: Analytic Technologies.

Brass, D.J., Galaskiewicz, J., Greve, H.R., and Tsai, W. (2004). Taking stock of networks and organizations: A multilevel perspective. *Academy of Management Journal, 47* (6), 795–817.

Burt, R.S. (1992). *Structural Holes: The social structure of competition*. Cambridge: Harvard University Press.

Burt, R.S. (1997). The contingent value of social capital. *Administrative Science Quarterly, 42*, 339–365.

Carpenter, D.P., Esterling, K.M., and Lazer, D.M.J. (2003). The strength of strong ties: A model of contact-making in policy networks with evidence from U.S. health politics. *Rationality and Society, 15* (4), 411–440.

Carpenter, D.P., Esterling, K.M., and Lazer, D.M.J. (2004). Friends, brokers, and transitivity: Who informs whom in Washington politics? *Journal of Politics, 66*, 224–246.

Coleman, J. (1988). Social capital in the creation of human capital. *American Journal of Sociology, 94*, 95–120.

Cross, R. and Cummings, J.N. (2004). Tie and network correlates of individual performance in knowledge-intensive work. *Academy of Management Journal, 47* (6), 928–937.

Feiock, R.C. and Park, H.J. (2005). Institutional collection action and economic development joint ventures, Paper presented at the Public Management Research Association Conference, Los Angeles, California.

Freeman, L.C. (1979). Centrality in social networks: Conceptual clarification. *Social Networks, 1*, 215–239.

Granovetter, M. (1973). The strength of weak tie. *American Journal of Sociology, 78*, 1360–1380.

Hanneman, R.A. and Riddle, M. (2005). *Introduction to Social Network Methods*. Riverside, California: University of California, Riverside.

Huisman, M. and Van Duijn, M.A.J. (2005). Software for social network analysis. In: P.J. Carrington, J. Scott, and S. Wasserman (Eds.), *Models and Methods in Social Network Analysis*. Cambridge: Cambridge University Press, pp. 270–316.

Kamarck, E.C. (2004). Applying 21st-century government to the challenge of homeland security. In: M.J. Kamensky and T.J. Burlin (Eds.), *Collaboration: Using Networks and Partnerships Series*. The IBM Center for the Business of Government, Lanham, Maryland: Rowman & Littlefield Publishers.

Kamensky, J. and Burlin, T. (Eds) (2004). *Collaboration: Using Networks and Partnerships*. The IBM Center for the Business of Government, Lanham, Maryland: Rowman & Littlefield Publishers.

Lin, N. (2001). *Social Capital: A Theory of Social Structure and Action. Series: Structural Analysis in the Social Sciences* (No. 19 Series). New York: Cambridge University Press.

Monge, P. and Contractor, N. (2003). *Theories of Communication Networks*. New York: Oxford University Press.

McGuire, M. (2002). Managing networks: Propositions on what managers do and why they do it. *Public Administration Review, 62* (5), 599–609.

Meier, K.J. and O'Toole, L.J. Jr. (2001). Managerial strategies and behavior in networks: A model with evidence from U.S Public Education. *Journal of Public Administration Research and Theory, 11* (3): 271–294.

Miller, H.T. (1994) Post-progressive public administration: Lessons from policy networks, *Public Administration Review, 54* (4), 378–386.

Oh, H., Chung, M., and Labianca, G. (2004). Group social capital and group effectiveness: The role of informal socializing ties. *Academy of Management Journal, 47* (6), 860–875.

Ostrom, E. and Ahn, T.K. (2003). *Foundations of Social Capital*. London: Edward Elgar.

O'Toole, L.J. (1997). Treating networks seriously: Practical and research-based agendas in public administration. *Public Administration Review, 57*, 45–52.

Provan, K.G. and Milward, H.B. (1995). A preliminary theory of interorganizational network effectiveness: A comparative study of four community mental health systems. *Administrative Science Quarterly, 40*, 1–33.

Putnam, R. (1993). The prosperous community: Social capital and public life. *The American Prospect, 13* (Spring), 35–42.

Raab, J. and Milward, H.B. (2003). Dark networks as problems. *Journal of Public Administration Research and Theory, 13*, 413–439.

Reagans, R.E. and Zuckerman, E.W. (2001). Networks, diversity, and performance: The social capital of corporate R&D Units. *Organization Science, 12*, 502–517.

Sabidussi, G. (1966). The centrality index of a graph. *Psychometrika, 31*, 581–603.

Schneider, M., Sholz, J.T., Lubell, M., Mindruta, D., and Edwardsen, M. (2003). Building consensual institutions: Networks and the national estuary Program. *American Journal of Political Science, 47* (1), 143–158.

Scott, J. (2000). *Social Network Analysis: A Handbook*. London: Sage Publications.

Shrestha, M. and Feiock, R.C. (2006). The network structure of interlocal cooperation for water related services. Paper presented for the Midwest Political Science Association Meeting, Chicago, April 27.

Snijders, T.A.B. (2005). Models for longitudinal network data. In: P.J. Carrington, J. Scott, and S. Wasserman (Eds.), *Models and Methods in Social Network Analysis.* Cambridge: Cambridge University Press, pp. 270–316.

Soda, G., Usai A., and Zaheer, A. (2004). Network memory: The influence of past and current networks on performance. *Academy of Management Journal, 47* (6), 893–906.

Soh, P.H, Mahmood, I., and Mitchell, W. (2004). Dynamic inducements in R&D investment: Market signals and network locations. *Academy of Management Journal, 47* (6): 727–744.

Thompson, G., Frances, J., Levacic, R., and Mitchell, J. (Eds.) (1991). *Market, Hierarchies and Networks—The Coordination of Social Life,* London: Open University: Sage Publications.

Thurmaier, K. and Wood, C. (2002). Interlocal agreements as overlapping social networks: Picket-fence regionalism in metropolitan Kansas City. *Public Administration Review, 62* (5): 585–598.

Tsai, W. (2001). Knowledge transfer in intraorganizational networks: Effects of network position and absorptive capacity on business unit innovation and performance. *Academy of Management Journal, 44*: 996–1004.

Wasserman, S. and Faust, K. (1998). *Social Network Analysis: Methods and Applications.* Cambridge, Massachusetts: Cambridge University Press.

Watts, D. and Strogatz, S. (1998). Collective dynamics of "small-world" networks. *Nature, 393*: 440–442.

Appendix: Sociomatrix

	A	B	C	D	E	F	G	H	I	J	K	L	M	N	O	P	Q	R	S
A	0	1	0	1	0	1	0	0	0	0	0	0	0	0	0	0	0	0	0
B	1	0	0	1	1	0	1	0	0	0	0	0	0	0	0	0	0	0	0
C	0	0	0	1	0	0	0	1	0	0	0	0	0	0	0	0	0	0	0
D	1	1	1	0	1	1	1	0	0	0	0	0	0	0	0	0	0	0	0
E	0	1	0	1	0	1	1	0	0	0	0	0	0	0	0	0	0	0	0
F	1	0	0	1	1	0	1	1	0	0	0	0	0	0	0	0	0	0	0
G	0	1	0	1	1	1	0	1	0	0	0	0	0	0	0	0	0	0	0
H	0	0	1	0	0	1	1	0	1	0	0	0	0	0	0	0	0	1	0
I	0	0	0	0	0	0	0	1	0	1	1	0	0	1	0	1	0	0	0
J	0	0	0	0	0	0	0	0	1	0	1	1	1	1	1	1	0	0	0
K	0	0	0	0	0	0	0	0	1	1	0	1	0	0	0	1	0	0	0
L	0	0	0	0	0	0	0	0	0	1	1	0	1	0	1	0	0	0	0
M	0	0	0	0	0	0	0	0	0	1	0	1	0	0	0	0	1	0	0
N	0	0	0	0	0	0	0	0	1	1	0	0	0	0	1	0	0	0	0
O	0	0	0	0	0	0	0	0	0	1	0	1	0	1	0	0	0	0	0
P	0	0	0	0	0	0	0	0	1	1	1	0	0	0	0	0	0	0	0
Q	0	0	0	0	0	0	0	0	0	0	0	0	1	0	0	0	0	0	1
R	0	0	0	0	0	0	0	1	0	0	0	0	0	0	0	0	0	0	0
S	0	0	0	0	0	0	0	0	0	0	0	0	0	0	0	0	1	0	0

Note: To import a sociomatrix dataset from Excel spreadsheet, from the UCINET command, click on *Data>Import>Excel Matrix*. To double check whether the Excel file has been converted to UCINET file, go to the UCINET spreadsheet icon and search for the file name under the extension .##h or, in this example, "actor_19.##h."

39 Economic Modeling

Ronald John Hy and Jim R. Wollscheid

CONTENTS

39.1   INTRODUCTION

An important component of policy making involves estimating what probably will happen if a policy change is implemented. Decisions, after all, are not made without an idea of what to expect. That is, decisions seldom are made without regard to estimated future consequences. Knowing the possible future effects of policy changes will affect an organization's decisions. As many policy decisions involve fiscal matters, economic modeling is being used increasingly to estimate the future effects of policy changes.

One of the most striking developments in recent decades has been the increased emphasis on the use of statistical models to analyze the economic aspects of public policy issues. The value of these models is predicated not so much whether they hold true as it is in helping policy makers select satisfactory courses of action from among alternatives to increase the chances of attaining desired effects (Quade, 1982, p. 279).

A primary use of economic modeling, therefore, is directed toward improving fiscally based policy decisions. In addition, economic modeling helps identify limits beyond which further actions are not desirable and rates of progress are negligible.

Specifically, economic modeling

* measures the impacts of changes in terms of volume of activity,
* projects possible levels of activity as a bases for making decisions, and
* ascertains the effects of alternative policy changes.

Some forms of economic modeling also measure the impact of policy changes on jobs, personal and corporate income, multipliers, as well as interindustry linkages. (Measuring the impact on jobs is exceedingly important politically, even though it often represents only a portion of the total impact of policy changes.)

The increasing complexities of policy making coupled with its need to address a variety of economic and social problems have led to an expanded interest in economic modeling. As public funds begin to shrink and as the public becomes increasingly sensitive to the way their dollars are spent, policy makers are interested in learning more about the possible effects of changes before they occur.

39.2   WHAT IS ECONOMIC MODELING?

Economic modeling uses quantitative techniques to untangle enormous amounts of available empirical economic data to describe and estimate the future impacts of policy changes before they occur, thus helping policy makers optimize their decisions. Economic modeling, then, is a mathematical system of sectoral allocation equations, each including several interdependent variables (Makridakis and Wheelwright, 1973, p. 21). Relationships and impacts among variables are estimated by developing and computing a variety of rigorously defined equations.

Modeling, which combines data and theory, is a method of analysis that examines relatively stable patterns of the flow of goods and services among elements of an economy "to bring a much more detailed statistical picture of the [economic] system into the range of manipulation by economic theory" (Leontief, 1986, p. 4). The purpose of modeling is to reduce errors in estimates by bringing theory into closer association with data.

Economic theory constantly seeks to explain the operation of an economy in terms of interactions of key variables—namely, supply, demand, wages, and prices. This operation undoubtedly involves complex series of transactions where goods and services are exchanged by people. Consequently, there is a fundamental relationship between the volume of a sector's outputs and the amount of inputs needed to produce those outputs. The interdependence among sectors (industries) also is measured by a set of equations that express the balance between the total input and aggregate output of each good and service produced and used in a given time period (Leontief, 1986, p. 424).

The two most widely used economic models are predictive regression and input/output models. Given the mathematical complexity of these models, it is virtually impossible to discuss their computations in a single chapter. Therefore, the principal objective of this chapter is to focus on comprehension rather than on computational knowledge.

39.3   PREDICTIVE REGRESSION MODELS

Predictive regression models, which are reasonably useful when short-term forecasting is more important than is sectoral planning, are the simplest and most commonly used economic models. These types of models are designed to forecast outcomes based on specified activities.

Translated into its simplest terms, a predictive model is a set of definitions and assumptions that estimate the effect of specific activities (predictive variables) on a public policy issue (dependent variable). These definitions and assumptions are expressed in mathematical terms which state that an impact is a function of activities. For instance, Keynes argued in part that consumption spending is a function of disposable income, or mathematically, Y (f) X where Y is consumption spending and X is disposable income. Simply put, if disposable income increases, consumption spending increases.

A predictive regression model, which is expressed as a set of equations, describes not only the way variables interact, but also the magnitude of that interaction. Such a model, for example would show not only how, but also how much a given tax cut would affect state spending. Consequently, a predictive model generates estimates of magnitude in addition to describing the relationships between and among variables.

The basic idea behind a predictive regression model is quite simple—if a patterned relationship exists between specified activities (predictor variables) and a public policy issue (the dependent variable) and if that pattern continues with virtually no interruptions over a short period of time, the predictor variables can be used to estimate the effect of activities on a policy issue.

A simple example illustrates this basic idea. Assume a predictive regression model is built stating that a state's sales tax (dependent variable) is affected by its personal income and employment (predictor variable). As the state's personal income and employment increases, the state's sales tax collections increase. A predictive model will show how much the state's income tax collections will increase in relation to changes in the state's personal income and employment.

39.4   REVIEW OF REGRESSION MODELS

Essentially, there are two types of regression models—simple and multiple. A simple regression model uses a single predictor variable to estimate the direction and magnitude of a change on the dependent variable. Conversely, a multiple regression model uses two or more predictor variables to estimate the direction and magnitude of a change on the dependent variable.

Each of these two types of regression models, in turn, can use either a linear or nonlinear computational formula, depending on whether the pattern of the relationship is along a straight or curved line. When the pattern of the relationship between the predictor variables and the dependent variables is relatively straight, a linear regression model is appropriate. However, when the pattern of the relationship between the predictor variables and the dependent variables is curved, a nonlinear regression model is apropos. Table 39.1 illustrates the different types of predictive regression models. The appropriate regression model must be used to arrive at the most precise estimates—that is, the estimates with the narrowest range of estimate values.

TABLE 39.1

Types of Variations of Regression Models

	Simple Regression	Multiple Regression
Linear regression	One variable is used to estimate the dependent variable	More than one variable is used to estimate the dependent variable
	Pattern of data fall along a straight plane	Pattern of data fall along a straight plane
Nonlinear regression	One variable is used to estimate the dependent variable	More than one variable is used to estimate the dependent variable
	Pattern of data fall along a curved plane	Pattern of data fall along a curved plane

A simple example describes this point. If a model estimates sales tax revenue for next year to be $1.7 billion, and the range of that estimate to be $0.7 billion, the range of the estimate is between $1 billion and $2.4 billion. On the other hand, if a model estimates sale tax revenue for next year at $1.2 billion and the range of the estimate to be $0.05 billion, the range of the estimate is between $1.15 billion and $1.25 billion, a much more precise estimate. The most appropriate regression model will be the one that yields the most precise estimate.

39.5 DETERMINING THE MOST APPROPRIATE MODEL

Unfortunately, there is no simple way to ascertain the pattern of the relationship between the predictor variables and the dependent variables, especially when more than one predictor variable is used. One way, therefore, to determine the pattern of the relationship is to use the following modified trial and error method:

Calculate various linear and nonlinear regression models and select the one which yields the largest (strongest) coefficient of determination, the least amount of autocorrelation, and an acceptable probability of error.

The coefficient of determination (R^2) is the fraction of variance explained by the model. (As the coefficient of determination was discussed in Chapters 14 and 15, consult these chapters for further explanation.)

The three types of regression models that are generally used are linear, polynomial, and transformative. As simple linear and multiple regression models are discussed in Chapters 14 and 15, the brief discussion presented below will focus on polynomial and transformative models. Listed below are the basic formulas for multiple linear, polynomial, and transformative predictive regression models. In practice, however, most predictive regression models are not linear.

Formulas for multiple, linear, polynomial, and transformative equations linear equation:

$$\ddot{Y} = a + b_1 X_1 + b_2 X_2 + \cdots b_n X_n$$

Second-degree polynomial equation:

$$\ddot{Y} = a + b_1 X_1 + c_1 X_1^2 + b_2 X_2 + c_2 X_2^2 + \cdots + b_n X_n + c_n X_n^2$$

Third-degree polynomial equation:

$$\ddot{Y} = a + b_1 X_1 + c_1 X_1^2 + d_1 X_1^3 + b_2 X_2 + c_2 X_2^2 + d_2 X_2^3 + \cdots b_n X_{2n} + c_n X_n^2 + d_n X_n^3$$

Transformative equations:

- When data pattern turn slightly upward:

$$\sqrt{\bar{Y}} = a + b_1 X_1 + b_2 X_2 + \cdots + b_n X_n$$

- When data pattern turn upward more drastically:

$$\log \ddot{Y} = a + b_1 X_1 + b_2 X_2 + \cdots + b_n X_n$$

- When data pattern turn slightly downward:

$$\ddot{Y} = a + b_1 \sqrt{X_1} + b_2 \sqrt{X_2} + \cdots + b_n \sqrt{X_n}$$

- When data pattern turn downward more drastically:

$$\ddot{Y} = a + b_1 \log X_1 + b_2 \log X_2 + \cdots + b_n \log X_n$$

39.5.1 POLYNOMIAL MODELS

Polynomial models rely on each predictor variable's values and powers to estimate its impact on the dependent variable. Logically, this means that polynomials are used to bend the trend plane until it conforms to the nonlinear pattern of the data. A second-degree polynomial bends the [trend] plane once; a third-degree polynomial bends the plane twice; and so forth. There will always be one less bend than indicated by the degree of the polynomial equation. Solving a polynomial model is straightforward inasmuch as the procedure is identical to solving linear models. The value of each predictor variable (X) and the power of the value for each predictor variable (e.g., X_2) are substituted into the model to estimate the value of the dependent variable.

39.5.2 TRANSFORMATIVE MODELS

Often a transformative regression model is used with data whose patterns are nonlinear. Such a model is one in which either the predictor variables or the dependent variables are transformed mathematically, and those products, rather than the original data, are used to compute a regression model. Such a model rearranges a nonlinear pattern of data in a way that a linear regression model can estimate the value of the dependent variable.

When a transformative regression model is used, data must be transformed before the model is computed, a relatively easy task with the aid of a computer. For instance, when using a transformative model which utilizes the square root of Y ($\sqrt{Y}$), the square root of the Y values is calculated and those transformed values instead of the actual values are used to compute the regression model. When a transformative model which alters the X values is employed, identical mathematical functions are performed on the values of the predictor variables ($\sqrt{Y}$ and $\log X$).

39.6 DIAGNOSTICS

The preceding section of this chapter focused on different types of predictive regression models, each depending on the number of predictor variables as well as the pattern of the relationship between the predictor variables and the dependent variables. The utility of these models, however, depends on a number of regression-base assumptions that are part of regression models. The three primary assumptions that must be discerned and addressed when using predictive regression models are (1) autocorrelation, (2) multicollinearity, and (3) selection of appropriate variables.

39.6.1 Autocorrelation

Recall from Chapter 14 that a correlation between two variables describes statistically what happens to one variable (Y), if there is a change in the other variable (X). The degree of change is measured by a correlation coefficient, which varies between $+1.00$ and -1.00, with a coefficient of zero suggesting that no matter what happens to one variable (X), nothing much will happen to the other variable (Y). Autocorrelation is similar to a correlation coefficient except that it describes statistically a relationship (mutual dependence) among values of the same variable measured at different time intervals. As predictive regression models rely on times series data, which are not made up of a set of randomly selected data points but rather of data points collected at periodic intervals, one of the most troublesome problems frequently encountered when using these models is autocorrelation.

Regression models assume that the residuals are independent of one another; that is, each data point does not have independent error terms. When the residuals are not independent, the model may treat the predictor variable as if it has been omitted. Rather than having the model explain the basic underlying patterns and let the residuals represent random errors, the model's residuals are included as part of the basic pattern (Makridakis and Wheelwright, 1973, p. 111). If this pattern is not eliminated, the regression model will not be so accurate as it would otherwise be.

With an auto correlated series regression, coefficients still will be unbiased, but many of the associated statistics may be invalid. The standard errors of the regression coefficients as well as the estimated variance around the regression may be understated, and the t and F distributions may not be applicable.

Autocorrelation furnishes important information about the pattern of the data. When the autocorrelation is zero, the data points are completely random. When the autocorrelation is close to 1.00, the data points are seasonal or cyclical. Information gained from autocorrelation calculations can be utilized by many of the predictive regression models to arrive at optimal estimates.

39.6.2 Recognition

Standard diagnostics normally are displayed on a computer printout each time a model is fitted to the data. Although many other statistics are available, the Durbin–Watson d statistic and the Ljung-Box Q-statistic—along with the mean and standard deviation—are used most commonly to validate the estimates of a predictive regression model.

The Durbin–Watson d statistic checks for autocorrelation in the first lag of the residual errors. (Recall that autocorrelation describes the association—mutual dependence—among the values of the same variable at different time periods.) When autocorrelation exists, the residuals do not represent random error, as the model would suggest. Thus, the model, which is designed to describe the basic underlying pattern and estimate from that pattern, will not be as accurate as it would otherwise be. Testing for autocorrelation involves establishing a hypothesis stating that the first-lag autocorrelation is zero—that is, there is no autocorrelation.

The Durbin–Watson d statistic is based on the sum of the squared differences of the residuals. The following is a computational formula for the Durbin–Watson d statistic:

$$d = \frac{\sum_{t=2}^{T}(e_t - e_{t-1})^2}{\sum_{t=1}^{T}e_t^2}$$

where
e_t = the residual of a given observation and
e_{t-1} = the residual of the preceding observation

Because of certain statistical difficulties, the regions of certainty for rejection of the hypothesis are uncertain—unlike other significance tests presented in this book. Consequently, there is a region between two bounded limits where one can never be sure that autocorrelation exists. This is because of certain statistical difficulties.

After calculations are made, d is compared to the upper and lower bounds in a Durbin–Watson test bounds table (found in any statistics book) for various significance levels, sample sizes, and independent variables. If d is below the lower bound, autocorrelation exists. If d exceeds the upper bound, autocorrelation does not exist. When d falls in the middle of the two bounds, autocorrelation may or may not exist.

A significant limitation with the Durbin–Watson d statistic is that it is only applicable with regression models that include constant intercepts. Moreover, the statistic is not strictly reliable for models with lagged dependent variables. In such cases the Ljung-Box Q-statistic is a useful tool to determine the existence of an autocorrelation.

The Ljung-Box Q-statistic checks for autocorrelation in the first several lags of the residual errors. The statistic is used to test for overall autocorrelation of fitted errors of a model. The computational formula is as follows:

$$Q = T(T + 2) \sum_{i-1}^{L} \left(r_i^2 / (T - i) \right)$$

where
  $T =$ number of sample points
  $r = i$th autocorrelation coefficient
  $L =$ number of autocorrelation coefficients

As the formula indicates, Ljung-Box Q-statistic is the sum the squared autocorrelation. As such, it is zero only when every autocorrelation is zero. The larger the number of autocorrelations, the larger Q. When the Ljung-Box Q-statistic test is significant, the model needs to be improved. As a rule of thumb, the test is significant, if its probability is greater than 0.99.

At this point, it should be noted that several other diagnostic statistics that are beyond the scope of this book are, and can be, used, depending on the predictive regression model.

39.6.3 SOLUTION

When the autocorrelation is either nonexistent or small, unstandardized regression models are appropriate. However, when the autocorrelation is too large, certain data transformation needs to be applied to the data. The simplest way to correct for an autocorrelation is to use the method of first differences. Essentially, this method creates a new variable by computing the differences for each variable in the model and using this new variable to compute regression coefficients. In other words, $Y_i - Y_{i+1}$. For instance, if a series has values of 6, 9, 7, 5, and 8, the new variable would consist of the values $+3$, -2, -2, and $+3$. For more sophisticated analyses, more complex regression-based models need to be used (e.g., exponential smoothing and Box-Jenkins for simple regression models and dynamic regression for multiple regression models).

39.6.4 MULTICOLLINEARITY

A high level of multicollinearity exists when two or more of the predictor variables are correlated strongly with each other. Multicollinearity does not exist when the predictor variables correlate strongly with the dependent variable. Such a correlation can and should exist. As multicollinearity occurs between or among predictor variables, it occurs only when multiple regression models are used.

Multicollinearity can be a problem because two or more highly correlated predictor variables can make it difficult to determine each of their effects on the dependent variable. (The stronger the correlation, the greater the problem.) When predictor variables are strongly correlated, the regression coefficients tend to vary widely, creating less precise estimates. Consequently, each coefficient may be found not to be statistically significant—even when a relationship between the predictor variables and the dependent variables actually exists. More specifically, multicollinearity results in large variances for the estimators, thus leading one to have skeptical confidence in the estimates because they may be very unreliable.

Stated succinctly, severe multicollinearity leads to

1. Regression coefficients which can be so unreliable that they can be meaningless
2. Impaired predictive accuracy
3. A standard error which is inordinately large (Gustafson, 1974, p. 138)

Predictive regression models are less sensitive to multicollinearity than are explanatory models because the former depend on the overall patterns of the relationships. Caution must be exerted, however, as a predictive model assumes that the patterns among the predictive variables will continue to hold for the future. So long as this happens, multicollinearity is not a major problem. Nevertheless, multicollinearity is a frequent problem in short-term economic forecasting because of the high level of correlation between significant economic factors such as population, personal income, disposable income, taxes, and profits. One should be aware of its existence when collecting data so that the problem can be addressed as well as be aware of the fact that it is less than perfect multicollinearity that causes most of the problems.

39.6.5 Recognition

A certain level of multicollinearity always exists because it is practically impossible to use meaningful predictor variables that are statistically independent of each other. A low level of multicollinearity does not affect the reliability of the regression coefficients, whereas a high level does. As a rule of thumb, "a high level of multicollinearity exists when a coefficient resulting from the correlation of two or more predictor variables is larger than .700." (Reinmuth, 1974, p. 44)

39.6.6 Solution

Fundamentally, there are two ways to alleviate multicollinearity: (1) eliminate all but one of the multicollinear predictive variables and (2) multiply the mulitcollinear variables and use that product as a variable to estimate the change in the dependent variable. Although the first method is easier, the second is methodologically sounder, because it enhances the predictive capability of the regression model (Hy et al., 1983, p. 315).

Eliminating the multicollinear variables: After the multicollinear variables have been identified, all but one of them can be removed from the regression model, because removal of such variables may only slightly decrease the predictive power of the model. This is a useful approach, especially when the multicollinear variables measure the same concept. Selecting which variable to eliminate is a judgment call based on one's knowledge and expertise.

Employing multiplicative transformation: Another method used to eliminate severe multicollinearity is multiplicative transformation, a process which generates a new variable by multiplying the values of the multicollinear variables together. This new variable, in other words, replaces the original variables.

Although a multiplicative variable is artificial, it is quite useful in estimating the values of the dependent variable because such a variable represents the combined effects of two real variables, thus the predictive power of the model is not diminished. When using predictive multiple regression models, one is strongly encouraged to use multiplicative transformation to eliminate the affects of multicollinearity.

39.6.7 SELECTION OF VARIABLES

The variables in a predictive regression model must be selected carefully. Normally the predictor variables are chosen by drawing on a theoretical construct that attempts to explain causality. These theoretical constructs, in other words, specify the predictor variables which best describe and explain the direction and strength of change in the dependent variable.

When using a multiple regression model, two potential errors can occur as the predictor variables are selected. In the first place, an important predictor variable could be omitted from the model. Second, too many predictor variables could be included in the regression model.

Omitting a significant predictor variable implies that the dependent variable (Y) is not affected by the omitted variable (X), even though it actually is. As a result, if Y is a function of X, but X is not included in the regression model, the estimates could be biased and inconsistent, as omitting a significant variable gives undo weight to the other predictor variables. Moreover, in most regression models with several predictor variables, the direction of the bias usually cannot be determined.

A tact sometimes used when developing a predictive regression model is to include all possible predictor variables and see which are the most important. Consequently, a regression model often times is constructed using too many predictor variables, implying that there is nothing to lose by including many variables. This is not the case—costs do occur when using too many predictor variables.

Probably, the most important cost encountered when using too many variables is that the variance of the parameter estimators tends to increase with the number of predictor variables. The more predictor variables included in the model, the larger the variance, the wider the confidence intervals, and the less precise the estimates.

These two potential errors create a dilemma. If significant predictor variables are left out of the model, the results can be biased and inconsistent. However, if too many predictor variables are included in the model, the precision of the estimates is affected negatively. The judgment of those constructing and interpreting a predictive regression model, thus, is crucial. Only predictor variables that are based on theoretical constructs and sound expert judgment need to be selected.

39.7 A PREDICTIVE REGRESSION ILLUSTRATION

In keeping with the principal objective of this chapter, which is to focus on user comprehension rather than computational knowledge, the following illustration exemplifies how a predictive regression equation model can be used to estimate the impact of future sales tax collections.

39.7.1 PROBLEM TO BE ADDRESSED

The State Department of Education is interested in locating a state boarding-type high school somewhere in the state. The state is willing to fund the operating costs of the school, but wants the selected locality to furnish adequate campus-like facilities. The school will operate on the standard school year and will eventually have a total enrollment of 300 junior and senior level high school students. Upon completion of the construction (at the beginning of the 2007–2008 school year), the school will enroll 150 students in their junior year. The following year, another 150 students will begin their junior year at the school.

Bay county proposed a 25-acre site which includes new construction of a 75,135 square feet facility for instructional and administrative support functions and renovation of five existing buildings for dormitories, dining, and multipurpose activities. The county will spend $8 million for new construction, renovations, and equipment purchases. The money will be generated by an additional one-half cent sales tax. The basic question is "how much money will the county generate from a one year one-half cent increase in the sales tax?"

39.7.2 ASSUMPTIONS

The analysis is limited to the two-year period, 2007 and 2008. The tax base will remain unchanged and no substantial economic downturn or upturn will occur before 2008.

Economic theory suggests that personal income is a good predictor of sales tax revenues. In other words, as personal income increases, disposable income increases. As disposable income increases, people spend more on taxable goods and services. Consequently, sales tax revenues increase.

Data Analysis: Both county personal income and sales tax revenues were collected by quarter for the past six years, 2001–2006. In addition, quarterly personal income estimates for 2007 and 2008 were obtained from state and national forecasting organizations.

A dynamic predictive regression model was used to estimate 2007 county revenues. The forecasted personal income figures, then, were inserted into the equation to estimate the amount of sales tax revenues that will be generated. They are as follows:

Forceast of County Sales Taxes for 2007 and 2008 Based on Personal Income

2007		2008	
Quarter	Revenues	Quarter	Revenues
200701	$4,012,526	200801	$4,042,770
200702	$3,795,772	200802	$3,821,894
200703	$4,107,361	200803	$4,133,048
200704	$3,954,431	200804	$4,159,635
TOTAL	$15,870,090		$16,157,347
R SQUARE		0.983	
ADJUSTED R SQUARE		0.978	
DURBIN-WATSON		1.79	

39.7.3 FINDINGS

Taking into account the needed adjustments, as determined by revenue experts, the predictive models shows that in 2007 the county will generate approximately $15.8 million with a one cent sales tax and $7.9 with a one-half cent sales tax. In addition, it is estimated that the county would generate about $8.1 million ($16.2/2) if it kept the sales tax in effect for an additional year. The 2008 estimate indicates that the 2007 estimate is quite consistent with past data.

39.8 INPUT/OUTPUT MODELS

The economic impact of an event on a particular geographic area is dependent upon the interrelationships among various industry sectors. Because any expenditure by one industry sector (the purchaser of goods and services) involves at least one other sector (the seller of the goods and services, there will be some effect upon the economy of an area each time a purchase is made. Input/output modeling is a method of determining the magnitude of the impact based on the identified relationships among industrial sectors in an area.

In input/output modeling, the economy is represented as a variety of industry sectors which purchase goods and services from each other (and from themselves, as well) to produce outputs (e.g., raw materials, semi finished and finished goods, capital equipment, labor, and taxes). Industry sectors can, and are, grouped into economic sectors on the basis of the product made, services rendered, or functions performed (e.g., agriculture, transportation, real estate, and services, including government).

The output produced by each sector or industry is sold and consumed, invested, or exported to either final users (e.g., consumers and government and industrial sectors) or as inputs to other sectors. Leakages of supply and demand from an area's economy are represented by imports and exports in an input/output model. Together these sectoral and consumer purchases represent the final demand for a product. Within this closed economy, therefore, total input must always equal total outputs.

An input/output model describes the transactions among these economic sectors in dollar values. Transactions among economic sectors include:

sales of finished goods and services to meet final user demand, sales of raw materials and partially finished goods to intermediate users, sales to customers outside the economy being modeled, payments of wages and salaries to the labor and management forces (human resources), taxes to government to pay for publicly produced goods and payments for the use of capital, and depreciation allowances to recover the costs of capital goods used in production. The ordinary business sales and purchases transactions of an economy are systematically classified and tabulated so as to readily show the dollar value of trading among all the sectors of the economy. (Grubb, 1974, p. 4)

39.9 HISTORY OF INPUT/OUTPUT MODELING

The initial development of input/output models dates back to the mid-1700s with the publishing of Francios *Quesnay's Tableau Economique of 1758*, a volume that examined the French economy by incorporating the concepts of circular product flows and general equilibrium into an economic analysis. Then, in the 1870s, Leon Walras, building on Quesnay's analyses, developed a general equilibrium model for a national economy. Walras's model, however, remained a theory which was not empirically testable until the mid-1930s.

In 1936, Wassily Leontief simplified Walras's general equilibrium model so that its results could be estimated empirically. Leontief modified Walras's model by simplifying two of its basic assumptions. First, Leontief aggregated the large number of commodities in Walras's model so that the actions occurring in each industry or economic sector was measured by a group of commodities. Second, Leontief parsimoniously reduced the number of equations in the model by omitting both the supply equations for labor and the demand equations for final consumption. Finally, the remaining production equations in Walras's model were incorporated into Leontief's input/output model as linear, rather than nonlinear, equations (Richardson, 1972, p. 7).

By simplifying Walras's general equilibrium model, Leontief artificially reduced the number of equations and unknowns to a manageable number without distorting the major thrust of the model. For instance, a feed plant undoubtedly produces a variety of products. Nevertheless, most of its products are sufficiently similar to be aggregated without distorting either the "things" needed to produce the products (inputs) or the number and types of products produced (outputs). In addition, by assuming that production functions are linear—although some certainly are not—Leontief was able to solve many of the implementation problems associated with Walras's theoretical model so that it could be tested empirically.

Following Leontief's lead, the U.S. Bureau of Labor Statistics published *The Structure of the United States Economy, 1919–1939*—a 96 sector table for the U.S. economy—in 1941 and continued this effort until 1944. (The Bureau of Labor Statistics resumed publishing the table in 1964.) Then, in 1944 the first practical input/output model was developed to estimate the effects of the war's end on unemployment. In 1949, the Bureau of Labor Statistics developed a 200 sector input/output table (Richardson, 1972, p. 9).

Another important development was the incorporation of linear programming as an essential component to input/output modeling (Koopmans, 1951, p. 125). Linear programming and input/output models are closely related as linear programming can convert input/output models into equations.

These two evolvements in the early 1950s led to the development of regional input/output models as it became increasingly possible to derive intersector transaction flow tables for regional gross outputs. A limitation, however, was that the format of the regional tables were almost identical to those of the national tables, even though regional economies are not identical to national economies. The regional input/output models are needed to represent regional production and interregional trade. As a result, this limitation coupled with the lack of available data meant that in the early 1950s the most important work on regional input/output models was conceptual instead of empirical (Isard, 1951, pp. 318–328; Isard and Kuenne, 1953, pp. 289–301; Leontief, 1953, pp. 93–115; Moses, 1955, pp. 803–832).

These conceptual studies, however, led to the rise of economic impact analyses which treated local direct inputs of an expanded output in a sector as an addition to the final demand. This development addressed the previously stated problem that regional production functions differ from nation production functions by abandoning regionally unadjusted national input coefficients in favor of regionally adjusted national coefficients to account for differences in regional production (Moore and Petersen, 1955, pp. 363–383).

Because of this development, regional input/output models demanded that regional coefficients of sales and purchase flows be used instead of assuming that national coefficients could be used as regional coefficients. That is, the sales and purchase flows of sectors at the national level could not be assumed to be similar to the regional level.

Because of the high cost of surveying sales and purchase flows for each major sector in each region of the country, recent efforts have focused on ways to adjust the national coefficients for a region. Some of these methods have become quite precise and are being used with increasing frequency.

It also should be noted that the United States is not the only country involved in developing input/output models. Considerable and substantial work has been and is being done in Great Britain, the Netherlands, Japan, and some former communist countries.

39.9.1 BASIC INPUT/OUTPUT MODEL

The model in Figure 39.1 incorporates five basic relationships, each consisting of a number of equations designed to measure certain functions. In this model, local consumption and demand, along with wages, prices, and profits determine employment. Capital demand depends on the relative cost of capital and labor and on local consumption and demand. Labor supply depends on population

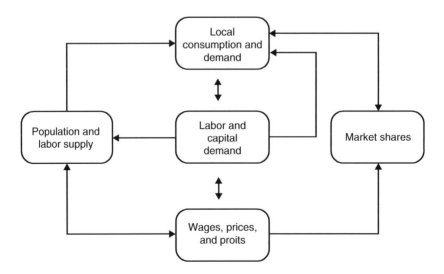

FIGURE 39.1 Basic model relationships. (From Treyz, G.I., *Model Documentation for the REMI EDSF-53 Forecasting and Simulation Model*. Regional Economic Models, Inc., Amherst, Massachusetts, 1995a, pp. 2–3.)

and wages, prices, and profits. Demand and supply interact to determine wages, prices, and profits. Local consumption and demand, together with wages, prices, and profits, determine market shares. Directly, and indirectly, these relationships are interrelated. Thus, estimates derived from the model are the result of satisfying all the equations simultaneously (Treyz, 1995a, pp. 1–9).

These transactions (sales and purchases) are systematically classified and tabulated to show the dollar value of trading among all sectors of the economy. A transaction (input/output) table summarizes the origins of the inputs and the destination of the outputs for all sectors of the economy.

Table 39.2 illustrates a simple transaction table consisting of three sectors—agriculture, manufacturing, and services. For purposes of this illustration each sector produces only one type of output. The three sectors are interdependent because they purchase their inputs from each other and in turn sell their outputs to each other. To produce outputs also requires labor. In this illustration, furthermore, all final goods are consumed and do not re-enter the production process as inputs (Yan, 1969, p. 6).

Row data shows output distributions to other sectors, while column data indicates the sources of inputs needed to produce goods and services. Reading across the row called agriculture, one finds that

- Total output of agricultural goods produced is $400,
- $80 of the agricultural goods produced are "sold" to companies comprising the agricultural sector itself,
- $160 of the agricultural goods produced are "sold" to companies comprising the manufacturing sector,
- None of the agricultural goods produced are "sold" to service sector companies, and
- $160 of the agricultural goods produced are "sold" to final consumers.

Reading down the column called agricultural, one can see that the agricultural sector companies

- Consume $80 of its own products to produce $400 of total output
- Consume $40 of manufactured goods
- Consume nothing from companies in the service sector
- Hire 60 persons to produce their goods

Input/output tables also assume fixed proportions. This concept suggests that when the level of output is changed, the amount of input required to produce this new level changes proportionately. Accepting the concept of fixed proportions allows for the calculation of the amount of input needed to achieve a given level of input and for the development an input/output (transaction) coefficient table.

Table 39.3, a slightly more complex input/output table, illustrates the direct, indirect, and induced transaction coefficients for purchases for each sector. Each row shows the sector to

TABLE 39.2
Simple Input/Output Table

Input from	Output to				
	Agriculture	Manufacturing	Services	Final Demand	Gross Output
Agriculture	$80	$160	$0	$160	$400
Manufacturing	$40	$40	$20	$300	$400
Services	$0	$40	$10	$50	$100
Labor	60	100	80	10	250

Source: From Yan, C.S, in *Introduction to Input–Output Economics*, Holt, Rinehart, and Winston, New York, 1969, 6.

TABLE 39.3
Direct, Indirect, and Induced Requirements

Purchases	Agriculture, Forestry, Fisheries	Mining	Construction	Manufacturing	Transportation	Communications	Utilities	Wholesale Trade	Retail Trade	Finance, Insurance, Real Estate	Education	Services
Agriculture, forestry, and fisheries	1.22537641	0.01381689	0.03913482	0.08463068	0.02569174	0.01647700	0.01478750	0.02213544	0.02648238	0.02071452	0.03308053	0.02548514
Mining	0.07016532	1.13710134	0.07903034	0.16526314	0.05992353	0.03545022	0.42699929	0.04687679	0.05107547	0.04641886	0.07087945	0.05369148
Construction	0.02214800	0.00809733	1.01510726	0.01614288	0.02112891	0.00816496	0.01316231	0.01314784	0.01179763	0.02356364	0.01905686	0.01666937
Manufacturing	0.40302254	0.13944897	0.41883304	1.29278563	0.28294854	0.16573591	0.15496658	0.21266627	0.24872962	0.19809917	0.35017059	0.26202499
Transportation	0.06271180	0.02976966	0.06180456	0.06025327	1.06820127	0.03062685	0.02945890	0.04428404	0.04106694	0.03785431	0.05743343	0.05069589
Communications	0.02582966	0.01406657	0.02289225	0.01743794	0.04207247	1.01819875	0.01674030	0.03550498	0.03292383	0.03294260	0.03246196	0.03521565
Utilities	0.06266197	0.03149213	0.04508049	0.05131108	0.06241122	0.04266059	1.11117052	0.05748948	0.05843207	0.06066301	0.07989930	0.06113856
Wholesale trade	0.13785936	0.05149459	0.07286388	0.06362144	0.09421524	0.05671079	0.05424959	1.08098207	0.08311451	0.07902238	0.10891616	0.09699340
Retail trade	0.27153692	0.12155969	0.18963027	0.12420137	0.19374012	0.14317030	0.12561426	0.20602259	1.20451992	0.19730627	0.26225334	0.21684641
Finance, insurance, and real estate	0.14070990	0.06615776	0.12361917	0.07224301	0.15865321	0.08212784	0.07433749	0.13362397	0.13407484	1.17213070	0.15674982	0.12893004
Education	0.07091660	0.05075866	0.04728889	0.03870723	0.06164289	0.06758011	0.07868178	0.05505502	0.05391564	0.07064601	1.06095950	0.05748923
Services	0.15385003	0.09486036	0.10557406	0.10555053	0.16989998	0.13374446	0.10669647	0.16810162	0.17372667	0.19532198	0.19541226	1.20436117

Source: Grubb, T., *The Input Output Model for the State of Texas, Texas Business Review*, Bureau of Business Research, University of Texas, Austin, 1974.

which payments are made for purchasing inputs. Each cell within each column is the purchasing coefficient, that is, the percentage of $1.00 expenditure for inputs used by each sector listed in the column. For example, of each dollar spent by the manufacturing sector, almost 8.5 cents (8.46) is spent for agricultural related goods and 6 cents is spent for transportation.

These input coefficients are used, in a system of simultaneous linear equations to measure the magnitude of the transactions among the economy (Grubb, 1974, p. 8). The system of equations is as follows:

$$X_i = \sum_{i \text{ and } j=1}^{\pi} a_{ij} X_j + \text{FD}_i$$

where

X_i = total annual dollar value of output of sector i
a_{ij} = dollar value of sales by sector i to sector j per dollar of output of sector j
X_j = annual dollar value of outputs of sector j
FD_i = annual dollar value of sales by sector i to final demand

The total annual outputs of sector i, X_i are accounted for in the ith equation by summing the sales to other processing sectors ($a_{ij}X_j$) and the sales to final demands (FD_i). This set of simultaneous equations allows for the calculation of direct, indirect, and induced effects of the transactions.

The effects of any change in the economy, then, are determined by using matrix computations to ascertain the direct, indirect, and induced impacts of the change in the economy. From these mathematical processes the total economic effects (direct, indirect, and induced) can be computed to measure both the positive and negative impacts of a proposed change in the economy.

39.9.2 TYPES OF ECONOMIC EFFECTS

Basically, input/output models compute three types of economic effects generated by an expenditure change in the economy. The models measure direct, indirect, and induced effects but are static rather than dynamic. Direct effects are changes associated with immediate changes in demands generated by employment, personal and household income, governmental expenditures, and private and public capital investment and formation.

Indirect effects are changes caused by the needs directly affected by businesses and governments. Essentially, they are interindustry impacts. These changes measure the effects on employment, household income, governmental expenditures, and private and public capital investment and formation added from industry purchases of all items needed to furnish a product. For example, construction contractors buy goods and services from other sectors, who in turn purchase goods and services from suppliers, each of whom makes additional purchases from still other suppliers. Indirect effects measure the impacts of these purchases.

Induced effects are changes in spending patterns of households caused by changes in household income—generated by direct and indirect effects. These new expenditures are reintroduced into the economy as a new demand. Thus, the indirect effects are related to sector interaction, whereas the induced effects are related to consumption.

A demand to build a new bridge in a county illustrates these concepts. Building a bridge in a county causes the contractor to purchase various types of building materials from suppliers (direct effect). In turn, suppliers must buy materials from various manufacturers (indirect effect). Finally, this increase in demand for building products leads to income and employment increases that stimulate spending in the economy in general (induced effect). This process, to be sure, also works in reverse, permitting policy analysts to estimate the impact of reductions as well as expansions (Hy et al., 1992, pp. 3–4).

The total impact is the combined effect of the direct, indirect, and induced effects on the economy. The magnitude of each of the types of effects is determined by the size of the multiplier

TABLE 39.4
Types of Multipliers

	Total Multipliers (Direct, Indirect, and Induced)
Employment multipliers	
Construction/renovation	1.935
County spending	1.619
State spending	1.985
Personal income multipliers	
Construction/renovation	2.031
County spending	1.754
State spending	1.845

associated with each sector in a defined area. Based on the production functions generated through an analysis of input/output data from an area, the multipliers for each sector can be calculated to provide a measure of the amount of direct, indirect, induced, and total impact of a given increase in demands of a particular sector. Table 39.4 illustrates typical employment and personal income multipliers provided by an input/output model for a given area.

39.9.3 FOUNDATIONS OF ECONOMIC MODELING

Input/output models are founded on system dynamics. Modeling, in other words, is based on interdependence and circular flows. That is, the models rely on circular, instead of linear, causality and on interdependent, rather than independent, relationships. In effect, such models abandon static, stimulus-response relationships so often used with regression-based models (Richmond, 1993, p. 118).

Systems dynamics assumes that all causal factors are connected in a circular process and affect each other. Analysis, thus, changes focus from linear to circular causality and from independent to interdependent relationships. (Figure 39.1 illustrates this point.) Mathematically, the shift is away from correlation and regression approaches to operational modeling approaches which involve dynamic weighing—meaning that some circular loops dominate at certain periods in the analysis, followed by others, and so forth.

Dynamic models are theoretically conservative. Generally speaking, the estimates generated by these models are based on equilibrium theory, which means that an economy—be it national, state, or local—ultimately exists in a state of balance. When that balance is upset by some change, the economy will eventually correct itself over time, and return to a state of balance. As a result, over time estimates produced by these models tend to be somewhat conservative.

Equilibrium is achieved when the demand for and supply of a good or service is equal to each other and no more adjustments in the price and quantity traded are needed. As sectors are not isolated from each other, a change in the equilibrium of one sector will affect the equilibrium of other sectors. Thus, to examine the effects of a change, the impact of that change on all affected sectors must be examined—a form of system dynamics.

39.9.4 DATA SOURCES

Input/output models are built with data gleaned from various sources. No single data source can be used, however, because a variety of agencies gather, organize, and publish statistics. The Department of Labor is mainly, but not entirely, in charge of employment, wage, and cost of living statistics. Information on railroad and trucking freight is collected by the Interstate Commerce

Commission, and information on air shipments is collected by the Federal Aviation Administration. The Federal Power Commission is the principal collector of data for electric and power companies, whereas the Department of Interior is the primary gatherer of coal and oil output data. Although the Standard Industrial and Commodity Classifications are commonly adhered to, each agency feels free to use its own classification and definition and to determine on its own the frequency and timing of its statistical operations (Leontief, 1986, p. 425).

As a result of these decentralized data gathering sources and processes, input/output models incorporate data collected from a wide variety of sources. The three primary sources are (1) the Bureau of Economic Analysis (BEA), (2) the Bureau of Labor Statistics (BLS), and (3) County Business Patterns (CBP).

The Bureau of Economic Analysis (BEA) has employment, wages, and personal income series data. These series contain data such as employment, personal income, wage and salary disbursements, other forms of labor income, proprietors' income, rental income, dividends, interest, transfer payments, and personal contributions for social insurance.

Another vital source of data used with these models is the Bureau of Labor Statistics (BLS) which furnishes data such as state and county employment, unemployment, and wage and salary figures. Yet another major data source is County Business Patterns (CBP) which, because it has ranges for suppressed data, is customarily used to estimate suppressed information. CBP data also are used to generate Regional Purchasing Coefficients (RPSs) for economic models. (RPCs are measures that show how much one sector purchases from another sector and, as such, are a major component of any economic model.)

These three primary data sources are supplemented frequently with data from other sources. Though not all-inclusive, Table 39.5 lists some of the major types of supplementary data and their sources.

TABLE 39.5
Supplementary Data and Their Sources

Data	Sources
Fuel and energy	State and price expenditure report
	Census of manufacturers
	Census of construction industries
	Census of service industries
	Census of retail trade
	Census of wholesale trade
Tax	Government finance
	Survey of current business
Cost of capital	Quarterly financial report of manufacturing
	Survey of current business
Gross state product	National income and product accounts
	BEA
	BLS
	Survey of current business
Housing prices	Census of housing
	National association of realtors regional and metropolitan growth rates

Source: From Treyz, G.I., in *Model Documentation for the REMl EDSF-53 Forecasting and Simulation Model*. Regional Economic Models, Inc., Amherst, MA, 1995, pp. 4–16, 4–19.

39.9.5 LIMITATIONS

Since the 1930s input/output models have become a widely accepted technique for economic planning and decision making. Despite their popularity, these models must be used with care because they possess certain weaknesses that can be debilitating to some types of economic impact analyses. These weaknesses can be grouped into the two categories—(1) reliance on "historical" data and (2) dependence on linear programming equations.

39.9.5.1 Historical Data

Input/output tables are based on periodically provided chronicled data. The construction and computation of input/output tables are complex and laborious. Immense amounts of data must be gathered, most of which is historical due to the time it takes to accumulate and collect such volumes of information. Consequently, input/output tables must be revised constantly as new data become available.

In addition to gathering and updating data an enormous amount of time is needed to solve a sizable number of simultaneous equations, inasmuch as outputs of each sector are dependent upon inputs of other sectors. The number of equations to be solved generally is two to three times the number of sectors into which the economy is divided, normally between 500 and 600 sectors.

More accurate estimates can be generated when input/output tables are kept up-to-date. Unfortunately, census data is gathered only every ten years, and other survey data is costly to obtain. A promising alternative is to collect representative sample data so that estimates can be generalizable. Instead of gathering data from all sectors, only data from industries representative of a particular sector are collected. Sector input/output coefficients, then, are estimated from the sample data, reducing the time, effort, and cost of data collection and allowing input/output tables to be constructed more frequently. The reliability of the estimates, of course, must be verified.

39.9.5.2 Linear Programming Equations

Linear programming equations provide a solution that can be applied under conditions of certainty. Certainty exists when a course of action definitely leads to a given result, even though the range of that result is unknown before application of the linear programming equations. These equations suggest the most efficient or least inefficient way to solve a problem. Linear programming is a powerful tool that allows one to either maximize an efficient course of action or minimize an inefficient course of action, given constraints (restrictions imposed on the solution of a problem). A typical set of linear programming equations include hundreds and sometimes even thousands of variables and constraints computed in an iterative process.

Linear programming equations are composed of several types of equations. The first, called the objective equation, states the relationship between the objective of the problem (minimizing inefficiency or maximizing efficiency) and the key variables. The other equations, called constraint equations, specify the limitations imposed on the solution. (There is one constraint equation for each constraint.)

Linear programming equations incorporate the following assumptions:

- Problem can be formulated in quantitative terms.
- Relationships among key variables are linear; that is the variables have a constant and reciprocal ratio.
- Relationships among key variables are additive, meaning that the total effect of the variables is equal to the sum of the effects of each variable. Thus, all key variables are included in the equations.

Linearity assumes that all statistical relationships among variables are proportional; that is, the coordinates fall on a straight plane. Thus, the use of large sets of linear equations signals a potential problem because an input/output model is the based on fixed proportional relationships between purchases and sales among sectors. Although linear functions solve various types of empirical problems, the use of them also creates others, the primary one being that production functions may not be linear—especially in the agricultural, service, and trade sectors.

This limitations, however, is not totally insoluble. Various nonlinear programming equations, which are similar to linear programming and which can be used when relationships among variables are assumed to be nonlinear, can be supplemented for linear equations. As Rubinstein (1975, p. 386) stated

> Nonlinear programming problems can be solved by a number of techniques. One technique approximates the nonlinear functions as a combination of linear function segments (piecewise linear functions) and proceeds by and algorithm similar to that of linear programming. Some problems require, however, much more sophisticated techniques. While there is no single efficient solution method for the general nonlinear programming model, many efficient algorithms have been developed for certain classes of models.

Normally, however, the usual somewhat nonlinear economic assumptions of profit maximization, optimal resource allocation, and consume utility maximization are built into an input/output model as if they were linear (Richardson, 1972, p. 9).

39.9.6 SOLUTION

When most recent transactions are not incorporated into the model, care must be exerted when interpreting the estimates. If major changes have or will occur and if they are not taken into account, the estimates furnished by the model can be misleading or incorrect. Customarily, major transactional changes do not occur, and the estimates are relatively accurate. If it can be shown that the effects of the changes are negligible, an input/output model can be quite reliable.

The reliability of an input/output model also depends on the length of the period for which estimates are made. If estimates are projected for too long a period, the results will be unreliable. If, however, estimates are projected for only a couple of years into the future, the estimates may be quite reliable.

39.10 AN INPUT/OUTPUT ILLUSTRATION

In keeping with the principal objective of this chapter, which is to focus on user comprehension rather than computational knowledge, the following illustration exemplifies how an input/output model can be used to estimate the impact of an economic change on a community.

39.10.1 PROBLEM TO BE ADDRESSED

The State Department of Education is interested in locating a state boarding-type high school somewhere in the state. The state is willing to fund the operating costs of the school, but wants the selected locality to furnish adequate campus-like facilities. The school will operate on the standard school year and will eventually have a total enrollment of 300 junior and senior level high school students. Upon completion of the construction (at the beginning of the 2007–2008 school year), the school will enroll 150 students in their junior year. The following year, another 150 students will begin their junior year at the school.

Bay county proposed a 25-acre site which includes new construction of a 75,135 square feet facility for instructional and administrative support functions and renovation of five existing buildings for dormitories, dining, and multipurpose activities. The county will spend $8 million for new construction, renovations, and equipment purchases. The money will be generated by an additional one-half cent sales tax.

Because of the construction and operation expenditures associated with the school, the presence of the school at this site will have a positive impact upon the economy of Bay county. For example, local construction contractors will be hired, local supplies purchased, and many school faculty and staff will likely live within the county. The purpose of this analysis is to determine the potential level of the economic impact felt throughout Bay county. The basic question is "what specifically will the county receive for its $8 million investment?"

39.10.2 ASSUMPTIONS

The analysis is limited to the three-year period of 2007 through 2009. The economic transactions associated with the school during this period have three major components: (1) construction activities for both the new and renovated buildings on the campus, (2) purchase of equipment for the school, and (3) actual operating budget of the school, including salaries and purchases.

Several assumptions—detailed below—underlie the analysis of the economic impact upon Bay county. They are based on information collected from various sources. The expenditure levels assumed to occur are depicted in Figure 39.2.

2007 Expenditure assumptions: The transactions which will occur in 2007 consist of construction costs, operating expenditures, and equipment purchases. Construction costs of $6.5 million for the project were allocated entirely to 2007, and funding is provided by Bay county. These expenditures will not subject to state purchasing rules and regulations. Consequently, these dollars will be spent in Bay county whenever possible (decided by the model's input/output tables). Of the $6.5 million, $3.2 million will be spent on new construction. The remaining $3.3 million for renovation work. As the renovation of the existing facilities will be extensive, renovations have been treated in the analysis as new construction.

During the latter half of 2007, 150 students will be enrolled in the school. Operating expenditures and equipment purchases during 2007 amount to $1.6 million in state funds and $750,000 in county funds for equipment purchases. These equipment purchases will not subject to state purchasing rules and regulations. Therefore, it will be expected that most of these dollars will be spent in Bay county.

The state funds will be subject to state purchasing regulations. However, out of the $ 1.6 million, $508,980 consists of wages and salaries. It was assumed that most of the employees will live in Bay

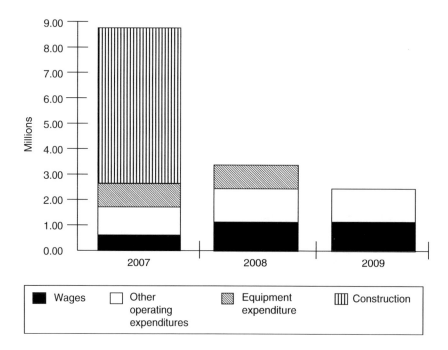

FIGURE 39.2 Expenditure assumptions for 2007–2009 (in $ millions).

county and therefore, most of these dollars will be spent in Bay county. The remaining $1,091,020 is subject to state rules and regulations and programmed into the model accordingly.

2008 Expenditure assumptions: During 2008, 300 students will be enrolled in the school, construction will be completed, and some continuing purchases of equipment will be made. Equipment purchases totaling $750,000 will be made with county funds, under the same 2007 assumption—most of these dollars will be spent in Bay county. The $2.5 million operating budget for the school in 2008 consists of $1,032,000 in wages and salaries, which will be spent primarily in Bay county; and $1,468,000 in operating expenses which will be subject to state purchasing regulations.

2009 Expenditures assumptions: The 2009 scenario is similar to 2008, with the exception that the county will no longer be purchasing equipment for the school. The remaining state expenditures will be broken down in the same manner and amounts as is the case in 2008 (and, it is assumed, will continue for years to come with the possibility of at least increases for inflation).

39.10.3 ADDITIONAL ASSUMPTIONS

The impact analysis does not include any funds generated during summer months. Although it is very likely that some revenue generation will take place during the summer, there are no data currently available upon which to appropriately estimate such an amount. This analysis also is limited to the impact of the expenditures made by the state and county on the school. It does not include the impact of tax dollars generated by the county from additional wages and salaries.

39.10.4 FINDINGS

Using an input/output model, the negative impact of taking $8 million out of the county's economy as well as the positive impact of the investments made to build and operate the high school have been calculated for each of the first three years of the project.

2007 Impact: During 2007, there are two distinct sets of events: the construction of the school and the initial operation of the school with 150 students enrolled.

Effects of construction expenditures: The direct effects of construction activities amount to $6.5 million dollars in final demand, $1.5 million in employee compensation income, and an additional 95 jobs produced. Table 39.6 describes the effects of the construction expenditures on Bay county. (See the glossary at the end of this illustration for a definition of terms.) These amounts are the direct result of expenditures on construction, including all materials purchased and labor supplied to the job site.

The indirect effects trace the impact of purchases of construction materials on other local suppliers. Final demand for these firms amounts to $1.6 million, producing nearly $600,000 in employee compensation from an additional 32 jobs.

The induced effects produced by the construction activities are the result of consumer expenditures generated by the new dollars flowing through the retail economy. This amounts $5.6 million in final demand, producing $1.7 million in employee compensation income from 102 new jobs.

The total impact of construction activities in 2007 are a summation of the direct, indirect, and induced effects and amount to $12.1 million in final demand, $14.8 million in total industry output, $3.9 million in employee compensation income, and 229 new jobs.

Effects of operating expenditures: The school will also generated an impact in 2007 as a result of expenditures including wages, other operating expenses (purchases of equipment and supplies), and county equipment purchases. Table 39.7 traces the impacts of these expenditures on Bay county.

The direct effects of the 2007 operating expenditures amount to $2.5 million dollars in final demand and $890,000 in employee compensation income from an additional 53 jobs produced. These amounts are the direct result of expenditures on staffing, equipping, and supplying the school.

The indirect effects trace the effect of the purchases of equipment and supplies on local suppliers, the vendors. Total industry output for these firms amounts to $1.0 million, producing nearly $200,000 in employee compensation and an additional 10 jobs.

TABLE 39.6
2007 - Estimated Impact of Construction/Renovation Expenditures

Industry	Final Demand ($)	Total Industry Output ($)	Employee Comp Income ($)	Property Income ($)	Total POW Income ($)	Total Value Added ($)	Number of Jobs
Direct effects							
Agriculture, forestry, and fisheries	0	0	0	0	0	0	0
Mining	0	0	0	0	0	0	0
Construction	6,499,956	6,499,956	1,515,780	1,335,184	2,850,963	2,892,794	94.96
Manufacturing	0	0	0	0	0	0	0
Trans., communications, and utilities	0	0	0	0	0	0	0
Wholesale and retail trade	0	0	0	0	0	0	0
Finance, insurance, and real	0	0	0	0	0	0	0
Services	0	0	0	0	0	0	0
Govt. enterprise and special	0	0	0	0	0	0	0
Total—Direct Effects	6,499,956	6,499,956	1,515,780	1,335,184	2,850,963	2,892,794	95
Indirect effects							
Agriculture, forestry, and fisheries	0	19,663	7,640	3,381	11,021	11,773	0.73
Mining	0	1,127	376	250	626	626	0.01
Construction	0	19,537	4,008	4,509	8,642	8,642	0.26
Manufacturing	0	80,028	20,539	5,511	26,551	26,927	0.75
Trans., communications, and utilities	0	143,149	47,215	37,196	84,787	89,171	1.84
Wholesale and retail trade	0	119,479	45,462	19,663	64,874	81,281	1.91
Finance, insurance, and real	0	62,996	14,403	27,052	41,454	46,214	0.83
Services	0	1,182,266	449,862	227,060	677,047	690,949	25.49
Govt. enterprise and special	0	20,539	8,516	501	8,892	8,892	0.28
Total—Indirect Effects	0	1,648,785	598,021	325,123	923,895	964,473	32
Induced effects							
Agriculture, forestry, and fisheries	65,125	167,195	10,144	46,464	56,108	57,986	2.09
Mining	0	0	0	0	0	0	0
Construction	0	126,618	22,543	25,298	47,967	48,969	1.44
Manufacturing	177,841	234,575	46,214	11,773	58,237	59,113	2.12

TABLE 39.6 *(Continued)*
2007 - Estimated Impact of Construction/Renovation Expenditures

Industry	Final Demand ($)	Total Industry Output ($)	Employee Comp Income ($)	Property Income ($)	Total POW Income ($)	Total Value Added ($)	Number of Jobs
Trans., communications, and utilities	399,265	573,474	124,113	146,406	270,518	306,838	4.05
Wholesale and retail trade	1,551,849	1,630,124	609,418	278,409	888,077	1,066,669	29.64
Finance, insurance, and real	1,308,508	1,582,032	182,349	873,799	1,056,274	1,205,936	12.75
Services	1,900,642	2,135,092	664,899	490,064	1,155,589	1,290,974	47.25
Govt. enterprise and special	176,213	234,324	76,146	13,025	89,421	89,421	2.82
Total—Induced effects	5,579,442	6,683,433	1,735,826	1,885,238	3,622,191	4,125,907	102
Total effects[a]							
Agriculture, forestry, and fisheries	65,125	186,858	17,784	49,846	67,129	69,633	2.81
Mining	0	1,127	376	250	626	626	0.01
Construction	6,499,956	6,646,111	1,542,581	1,364,991	2,907,572	2,950,404	96.67
Manufacturing	177,841	314,352	67,379	17,784	84,787	86,416	2.92
Trans., communications, and utilities	399,265	716,373	171,579	183,351	355,181	396,134	5.9
Wholesale and retail trade	1,551,849	1,749,478	654,755	298,196	952,826	1,147,825	31.55
Finance, insurance, and real	1,308,508	1,644,902	196,752	900,977	1,097,603	1,252,275	13.56
Services	1,900,642	3,317,232	1,115,387	717,124	1,832,762	1,982,173	72.74
Govt. enterprise and special	176,213	254,863	84,662	13,776	98,313	98,313	3.1
Total effects	12,079,398	14,831,297	3,851,255	3,546,296	7,396,800	7,983,800	229

[a] Data may not sum to total effects due to rounding.

The induced effects produced by the operating expenditures are the result of consumer expenditures generated by the new wage income dollars flowing through the economy. This amounts $3.2 million in final demand, $3.8 million in total industry output, producing just under $1 million in employee compensation income from 51 new jobs.

The total impact of the wages, other operating expenditures, and county equipment purchases in 2007, amount $5,7 million in total demand, $7.4 million in total industry output, $2.0 million in employee compensation income, and 114 new jobs.

Because both of these events will be occurring within Bay county in 2007, it is appropriate to sum the impacts to judge the full positive impact upon the county. The first section in Table 39.8 is a summation of Table 39.6 and 39.7 and details the results of the total investment in the community.

The total economic impacts on Bay county in 2007 amount to $17.8 million in total final demand, of which $12.1 million is due to construction/renovation expenditures. The additional impact of $5.7 million in total final demand is the result of $1.6 million budget for wages and

TABLE 39.7

2007 - Estimated Impact of Wages, Other Operating Expenditures, and County Equipment Purchases

Industry	Final Demand ($)	Total Industry Output ($)	Employee Comp Income ($)	Property Income ($)	Total POW Income ($)	Total Value Added ($)	Number of Jobs
Direct effects							
Agriculture, forestry, and fisheries	0	0	0	0	0	0	0
Mining	0	0	0	0	0	0	0
Construction	0	0	0	0	0	0	0
Manufacturing	0	0	0	0	0	0	0
Trans., communications and utilities	28,598	28,598	4,961	7,004	11,965	14,299	0.24
Wholesale and retail trade	0	0	0	0	0	0	0
Finance, insurance, and real	0	0	0	0	0	0	0
Services	1,435,025	1,435,025	576,199	97,614	673,812	673,812	36.37
Govt. enterprise and special	1,067,902	1,067,902	308,896	82,601	391,615	391,615	16.18
Total—Direct effects	2,531,526	2,531,526	890,056	187,218	1,077,392	1,079,727	53
Indirect effects							
Agriculture, forestry, and fisheries	0	9,776	2,918	1,897	4,961	5,253	0.24
Mining	0	0	0	0		0	0
Construction	0	391,477	67,848	76,311	144,159	147,223	3.73
Manufacturing	0	20,281	4,961	1,751	7,004	7,296	0.19
Trans., communications and utilities	0	176,405	34,289	51,069	85,357	97,614	0.86
Wholesale and retail trade	0	57,051	21,449	9,484	30,933	38,520	0.81
Finance, insurance, and real	0	166,337	20,136	96,447	116,436	133,508	1.63
Services	0	129,568	30,933	43,335	74,122	79,229	239
Govt. enterprise and special	0	66,175	15,835	5,436	21,271	21,271	0.6
Total—Indirect effects	0	1,017,071	198,368	285,729	484,243	529,913	10
Induced effects							
Agriculture, forestry, and fisheries	37,353	96,301	5,399	27,139	32,684	33,413	1.02
Mining	0	0	0	0	0	0	0
Construction	0	73,101	13,132	14,591	27,723	28,307	0.72
Manufacturing	102,429	135,550	26,702	6,712	33,559	34,435	1.05

TABLE 39.7 *(Continued)*

2007 - Estimated Impact of Wages, Other Operating Expenditures, and County Equipment Purchases

Industry	Final Demand ($)	Total Industry Output ($)	Employee Comp Income ($)	Property Income ($)	Total POW Income ($)	Total Value Added ($)	Number of Jobs
Trans., communications and utilities	230,392	331,216	71,642	84,628	156,270	177,281	1.99
Wholesale and retail trade	896,033	941,411	351,935	161,085	512,874	616,032	14.69
Finance, insurance, and real	755,522	913,543	105,347	504,703	609,904	696,283	632
Services	1,097,681	1,232,794	384,473	282,774	667,246	745,600	23.44
Govt. enterprise and special	82,364	109,662	35,687	6,145	41,832	41,832	1.41
Total—Induced effects	3,201,774	3,833,577	994,316	1,087,776	2,082,092	2,373,182	51
Total effects[a]							
Agriculture, forestry, and fisheries	37,353	106,514	8,317	28,890	37,499	38,520	1.28
Mining	0	146	0	0	0	0	0
Construction	0	464,577	80,980	90,902	171,882	175,530	4.44
Manufacturing	102,429	155,394	32,392	8,463	41,293	41,584	1.28
Trans., communications and utilities	258,844	535,927	110,892	142,554	253,300	288,902	3.11
Wholesale and retail trade	896,033	998,462	373,530	170,569	543,661	654,406	15.5
Finance, insurance, and real	755,522	1,080,026	125,337	601,003	726,486	829,936	7.95
Services	2,532,706	2,797,095	991,313	424,014	1,415,035	1,498,496	62.21
Govt. enterprise and special	1,150,267	1,243,739	360,300	94,300	454,600	454,600	18.18
Total effects	5,733,154	7,381,881	2,083,060	1,560,695	3,643,755	3,981,974	114

[a] Data may not sum to total effects due to rounding.

other operating expenses and $750,000 in additional county purchases of scientific equipment. The total number of jobs created in Bay county is estimated to be 343. Of these, 229 jobs are construction related, while 114 are related to operating expenditures and equipment purchases. Thus, the total first year impact ratio is approximately 2:1 ($2 dollars for every dollar spent). The percentage contribution by the county to the total first year investment is approximately 82 percent.

Total impact: The above mentioned figures, however, do not account for the negative economic impact of taking $8 million out of the county's economy in 2007 via a one-half cent sales tax increase. The second section in Table 39.8 shows these impacts. Total industry output is reduced by $4.6 million and employees compensation income by $1.3 million from the loss of 104 jobs.

Net impact: Despite these losses, the net economic impact is positive, as shown in the last section of Table 39.8. Total industry output will be increased by $17.5 million and employee

TABLE 39.8

2007 - Estimated Tax Effects and Impact of Wages, Other Operating Expenditures, and County Equipment Purchases

Industry	Final Demand ($)	Total Industry Output ($)	Employee Comp Income ($)	Property Income ($)	Total POW Income ($)	Total Value Added ($)	Number of Jobs ($)
Total effects of construction, wages, other operating expenditures, and county equipment purchases							
Agriculture, forestry, and fisheries	102,478	293,372	26,101	78,736	104,628	108,153	4.09
Mining	0	1,273	376	250	626	626	0.01
Construction	6,499,956	7,110,688	1,623,561	1,455,893	3,079,454	3,125,934	101.11
Manufacturing	280,270	469,746	99,771	26,247	126,080	128,000	4.20
Trans., communications and utilities	658,109	1,252,300	282,471	325,905	608,481	685,036	9.01
Wholesale and retail trade	2,447,882	2,747,940	1,028,285	468,765	1,496,487	1,802,231	47.05
Finance, insurance and real	2,064,030	2,724,928	322,089	1,501,980	1,824,089	2,082,211	21.51
Services	4,433,348	6,114,327	2,106,700	1,141,138	3,247,797	3,480,669	134.95
Govt. enterprise and special	1,326,480	1,498,602	444,962	108,076	552,913	552,913	21.28
Total effects	17,812,552	22,213,178	5,934,315	5,106,990	11,040,555	11,965,774	343.00
Tax effects							
Agriculture, forestry, and fisheries	(29,500)	(78,400)	(8,400)	(18,900)	(27,400)	(28,900)	(1.37)
Mining	(2,100)	(3,400)	(300)	(1,600)	(2,000)	(2,600)	(0.03)
Construction	0	(127,900)	(43,500)	(20,800)	(64,200)	(65,000)	(3.21)
Manufacturing	(117,000)	(161,000)	(29,200)	(14,100)	(43,700)	(44,700)	(1.60)
Trans., communications and utilities	(245,700)	(324,400)	(59,100)	(89,300)	(148,300)	(163,100)	(2.69)
Wholesale and retail trade	(1,194,200)	(1,223,600)	(623,800)	(146,600)	(770,400)	(949,500)	(51.26)
Finance, insurance, and real	(1,262,400)	(1,331,500)	(98,500)	(683,200)	(781,500)	(997,300)	(7.32)
Services	(1,033,500)	(1,138,600)	(435,500)	(170,200)	(604,900)	(627,900)	(34.58)
Govt. enterprise and special	(224,000)	(276,700)	(76,600)	(49,000)	(125,600)	(125,700)	(2.39)
Total effects	(4,108,400)	(4,665,500)	(1,374,900)	(1,193,700)	(2,568,000)	(3,004,700)	(104.45)

TABLE 39.8 (*Continued*)

2007 - Estimated Tax Effects and Impact of Wages, Other Operating Expenditures, and County Equipment Purchases

Industry	Final Demand ($)	Total Industry Output ($)	Employee Comp Income ($)	Property Income ($)	Total POW Income ($)	Total Value Added ($)	Number of Jobs ($)
Net effects							
Agriculture, forestry, and fisheries	72,978	214,972	17,701	59,836	77,228	79,253	2.72
Mining	(2,100)	(2,127)	76	(1,350)	(1,374)	(1,974)	(0.02)
Construction	6,499,956	6,982,788	1,580,061	1,435,093	3,015,254	3,060,934	97.90
Manufacturing	163,270	308,746	70,571	12,147	82,380	83,300	2.60
Trans., communications and utilities	412,409	927,900	223,371	236,605	460,181	521,936	6.32
Wholesale and retail trade	1,253,682	1,524,340	404,485	322,165	726,087	852,731	(4.21)
Finance, insurance, and real	801,630	1,393,428	223,589	818,780	1,042,589	1,084,911	14.19
Services	3,399,848	4,975,727	1,671,200	970,938	2,642,897	2,852,769	100.37
Govt. enterprise and special	1,102,480	1,221,902	368,362	59,076	427,313	427,213	18.89
Total effects	13,704,152	17,547,678	4,559,415	3,913,290	8,472,555	8,961,074	238.55

compensation income by $4.5 million from the creation of 238 jobs. The losses occur primarily in wholesale and retail trade, whereas the gains are in the service, construction, and government (including education) sectors of the county's economy.

2008 Impact: The impacts in 2008 will be substantially less than the 2007 impacts, because construction activities will be completed during 2007. Some county equipment purchases will continue, however, and the school's operating budget in 2008 will be increased. In addition, the one-half sales tax levy will expire at the end of 2007, meaning that there will be no negative economic effects generated by a forced reduction in personal consumption spending.

The impact of the total investment in the school in 2008 is detailed in Table 39.9. (As the direct, indirect, and induced effects were discussed during the examination of the 2007 impact, the examination of the 2008 and 2009 impacts will focus only on the total effects.)

Total impact: The total economic effect on Bay county in 2008 amount to $7.9 million in total final demand resulting from $2.5 million budget for wages and other operating expenses, and $750,000 in additional county purchases of scientific equipment. The total number of jobs created in the county is estimated to be 150, all of which are related to operating expenditures and purchases. Thus, the total second year impacts are a ratio of about 2.4:1. The percentage contribution by the county to the total second year investment is reduced from 82 percent to approximately 23 percent, due to the elimination of construction renovation obligations. Although the second year impacts are lower, the contributions from Bay county to the project are also much less.

2009 Impact: In 2009 the total impacts of the school upon the county will again decline, because the county will no longer be investing money into the construction or equipping of the school. The impacts are presented in Table 39.10.

TABLE 39.9

2008 - Estimated Impact of Wages, Other Operating Expenditures, and County Equipment Purchases

Industry	Final Demand ($)	Total Industry Output ($)	Employee Comp Income ($)	Property Income ($)	Total POW Income ($)	Total Value Added ($)	Number of Jobs
Direct effects							
Agriculture, forestry, and fisheries							
Mining	0	0	0	0	0	0	0
Construction	0	0	0	0	0	0	0
Manufacturing	0	0	0	0	0	0	0
Trans., communications and utilities	39,078	39,078	6,717	9,617	16,486	19,539	0.31
Wholesale and retail trade	0	0	0	0	0	0	0
Finance, insurance, and real	0	0	0	0	0	0	0
Services	1,974,986	1,974,986	793,017	134,332	927,349	927,349	47.85
Govt. enterprise and special	1,436,890	1,436,890	415,674	111,202	526,876	526,876	21.19
Total—Direct effects	3,450,955	3,450,955	1,215,407	255,151	1,470,711	1,473,764	69
Indirect effects							
Agriculture, forestry, and fisheries	0	13,281	3,969	2,595	6,564	7,022	0.31
Mining	0	153	0	0	0	0	0
Construction	0	36,717	93,117	104,565	197,529	201,956	4.88
Manufacturing	0	27,172	7,022	2,442	9,770	10,075	0.23
Trans., communications and utilities	0	241,645	46,864	70,219	116,777	134,027	1.12
Wholesale and retail trade	0	78,309	29,614	12,975	42,589	52,664	1.07
Finance, insurance, and real	0	228,822	27,630	132,653	160,283	183,638	2.14
Services	0	177,837	42,437	59,686	102,123	108,534	3.17
Govt. enterprise and special	0	89,229	21,245	7,405	28,650	28,650	0.78
Total—Indirect effects	0	1,393,165	71,896	392,541	664,285	726,566	14
Induced effects							
Agriculture, forestry, and fisheries	51,296	132,653	7,938	36,789	44,726	45,795	1.37
Mining	0	0	0	0	0	0	0
Construction	0	100,444	18,013	20,150	38,010	38,773	0.94

TABLE 39.9 *(Continued)*

2008 - Estimated Impact of Wages, Other Operating Expenditures, and County Equipment Purchases

Industry	Final Demand ($)	Total Industry Output ($)	Employee Comp Income ($)	Property Income ($)	Total POW Income ($)	Total Value Added ($)	Number of Jobs
Manufacturing	141,201	186,386	36,789	9,159	46,253	47,016	1.39
Trans., communications and utilities	316,749	455,050	98,459	115,861	214,473	243,477	2.63
Wholesale and retail trade	1,231,428	1,293,556	483,595	221,037	704,632	846,597	19.3
Finance, insurance, and real	1,038,478	1,255,699	144,712	693,336	538,201	956,963	8.28
Services	1,508,335	1,693,957	527,711	388,952	916,663	1,024,434	30.76
Govt. enterprise and special	111,202	147,865	48,196	8,255	56,330	56,330	1.84
Total—Induced effects	4,398,683	5,265,609	1,365,413	1,493,540	2,859,289	3,259,385	67
Total effects[a]							
Agriculture, forestry, and fisheries	51,290	146,086	11,907	39,536	51,290	53,122	1.69
Mining	0	153	0	0	0	0	0
Construction	0	637,161	110,977	124,562	235,692	240,729	5.83
Manufacturing	141,201	214,015	44,269	12,212	56,481	57,854	1.66
Trans., communications and utilities	355,980	735,926	152,039	195,697	347,889	396,890	4.06
Wholesale and retail trade	1,231,428	1,371,713	513,057	34,318	747,374	898,956	20.37
Finance, insurance, and real	1,038,478	1,484,369	172,495	826,142	998,331	1,140,601	10.43
Services	3,483,320	3,846,933	1,363,317	583,123	1,946,288	2,060,775	81.8
Govt. enterprise and special	1,548,093	1,673,985	485,114	126,863	611,856	611,856	23.81
Total effects	7,849,790	10,110,340	2,853,174	2,142,454	4,995,201	5,460,783	150

[a] Data may not sum to total effects due to rounding.

Total impact: The total economic impacts on Bay county in 2009 amount to $5.6 million in total final demand resulting from continuing state investment of $2.5 million toward the school's operating budget. The total number of jobs created in the county is estimated to be 100, all of which are related to the continuing operating expenditures. Thus, the total third year impact is a ratio of about 2.2:1. By the third year Bay county's financial obligations are negligible. The percentage contribution by the county to the third and succeeding years investment is reduced to zero. In other words, after the third year, all the money will come from outside the county (state money) to inside the county and can be assumed to be "new" money for the county's economy.

TABLE 39.10
2009 - Estimated Impact of Wages, Other Operating Expenditures, and County Equipment Purchases

Industry	Final Demand ($)	Total Industry Output ($)	Employee Comp Income ($)	Property Income ($)	Total POW Income ($)	Total Value Added ($)	Number of Jobs
Direct effects							
Agriculture, forestry, and fisheries	0	0	0	0	0	0	0
Mining	0	0	0	0	0	0	0
Construction	0	0	0	0	0	0	0
Manufacturing	0	0	0	0	0	0	0
Trans., communications and utilities	39,880	39,880	6,859	9,890	16,750	19,940	0.3
Wholesale and retail trade	0	0	0	0	0	0	0
Finance, insurance, and real	0	0	0	0	0	0	0
Services	1,031,935	1,031,935	414,433	70,189	484,622	484,622	23.93
Govt. enterprise and special	1,436,937	1,436,937	415,683	111,215	526,898	526,898	20.63
Total—Direct effects	2,508,752	2,508,752	836,975	191,294	1,028,269	1,031,459	45
Indirect effects							
Agriculture, forestry, and fisheries	0	10,528	3,350	1,914	5,264	5,583	0~5
Mining	0	160	0	0	0	0	0
Construction	0	534,711	92,522	103,848	$196,210	200,517	4.65
Manufacturing	0	20,897	5,105	1,755	7,497	7,497	0.16
Trans., communications and utilities	0	212,481	39,242	62,213	101,295	116,928	0.89
Wholesale and retail trade	0	66,360	25,045	11,007	36,211	44,347	0.89
Finance, insurance, and real	0	131,285	16,590	74,974	91,564	104,645	1.18
Services	0	118,204	27,756	39,720	67,477	72,741	2.02
Govt. enterprise and special	0	79,296	17,455	6,982	24,437	24,437	0.63
Total—Indirect Effects	0	1,173,923	227,064	302,413	529,956	576,696	11
Induced effects							
Agriculture, forestry, and fisheries	35,892	92,362	5,583	26,002	31,266	32,223	0.9
Mining	0	0	0	0	0	0	0
Construction	0	70,029	12,443	14,038	26,640	27,118	0.63

TABLE 39.10 (*Continued*)
2009 - Estimated Impact of Wages, Other Operating Expenditures, and County Equipment Purchases

Industry	Final Demand ($)	Total Industry Output ($)	Employee Comp Income ($)	Property Income ($)	Total POW Income ($)	Total Value Added ($)	Number of Jobs
Manufacturing	98,105	129,530	25,842	6,381	32,542	33,021	0.91
Trans., communications and utilities	221,095	318,083	68,753	80,877	149,789	169,889	1.75
Wholesale and retail trade	860,132	903,521	337,704	154,415	492,119	591,181	12.9
Finance, insurance, and real	725,337	876,881	101,136	484,462	585,119	668,389	5.54
Services	1,053,470	1,183,319	368,491	271,822	640,313	715,128	20.55
Govt. enterprise and special	76,304	101,490	33,040	5,611	38,900	38,900	1.24
Total—Induced Effects	3,070,335	3,675,216	952,992	1,043,607	1,996,689	2,275,849	44
Total effects[a]							
Agriculture, forestry, and fisheries	35,892	103,369	8,933	28,076	37,009	37,966	1.18
Mining	0	160	0	0	0	0	0
Construction	0	604,900	104,964	117,885	222,849	227,635	5.28
Manufacturing	98,105	151,384	31,585	8,614	39,880	40,997	1.12
Trans., communications and utilities	260,815	569,965	114,535	153,139	267,994	306,438	2.93
Wholesale and retail trade	860,132	969,722	362,589	165,422	528,171	635,368	13.78
Finance, insurance, and real	725,337	1,008,166	117,566	559,277	676,843	772,874	6.72
Services	2,085,564	2,333,778	811,478	381,891	1,192,412	1,272,651	46.51
Govt. enterprise and special	1,513,116	1,617,598	466,179	123,932	589,986	589,986	22.5
Total effects	5,578,962	7,359,042	2,017,830	1,538,236	3,555,144	3,883,914	100

[a] Data may not sum to total effects due to rounding.

39.11 SUMMARY

Despite simplistic theoretical assumptions, input/output models have exhibited staying power. Although the degree of interest in using input/output models at the national level is slackening, interest in using input/output models at the regional and substate levels is increasing rapidly, primarily because they can be used when data shortages prevent hardcore empirical analysis. Input/output models can be applied to answer a wide range of regional and substate economic questions. It is possible to reduce the errors of estimates by applying input/output models to a specific and narrow set of questions when alternative methods are either inappropriate or data is unavailable.

The types of information that usually can be gleaned (depending on the model) are:

- Direct and indirect production changes
- Total payroll costs
- Direct and indirect consumer demand
- Household spending patterns
- Industry multipliers
- Wages and salaries
- Total value of production
- Amount added to cost of production
- Disposable income
- Government spending
- Investment spending
- Labor and occupational supply and cost
- Business and tax credits

39.12 USES

Over the years, a variety of local issues have been analyzed with economic models. Though not all-inclusive, some are:

- New plant development
- Facility expansion
- Utility cost increases
- New port development
- Rate changes
- Spending increases
- Tourism increases
- Welfare changes
- Gambling establishment development
- Shopping and entertainment complexes
- Transportation systems
- Changing gasoline prices
- Solid waste management regulations (Treyz, 1995b, p. 14).

39.13 THE NEXT STEP: DYNAMIC MODELS

Although dynamic economic models are beyond the scope of this chapter, a brief mention of them is helpful to understand more fully economic modeling.

Given that input/output models are static and linear, the next logical step in the modeling process is to use dynamic models, which better approximate actual economic behavior. In other words, dynamic models account for more factors and relationships than do input/output models. Dynamic models also incorporate economic responsiveness (feedback) based on economic theory. The inclusion of economic responsiveness allows the models to respond to changes in policy and to embody into the analysis labor and product substitution. Economic responsiveness also incorporates the element of time into dynamic models by recognizing that over the near term supply and demand are fixed, but that large changes to the economic system will affect both supply and demand curves over a longer period of time.

The structure of dynamic models is built by coupling theoretical descriptions of an economy with empirically estimated relationships of that economy. To handle such elaborate processes, dynamic models require more advanced mathematical methods such as linear differential and nonlinear programming equations.

Like input/output models, dynamic models have certain inherent limitations. They are as follows:

- Appropriate data is not always available.
- Data is not always in the form needed to address policy questions.
- Effects of unknowns such as legislative and judicial decision are not incorporated into the models.
- Coefficients derived from historic responses to changes in supply and demand mean that results are only valid over the ranges of past changes, thus making the impact of larger changes much more speculative.

Despite these limitations, dynamic models are widely used, primarily because of all the different types of economic models they correspond most closely to actual economic behavior. This characteristic allows for numerous scenarios to be analyzed with various levels of detail and frequency. In addition, the evolution in the power and capacity of computers has made dynamic economic models more useful and understandable.

A note of caution is in order. When using dynamic models, the subsequent suggestions need to be considered seriously and followed rigorously:

- Make sure all spending and cost accounts are balanced.
- Keep track of all the large numbers—be sure they reconcile.
- Do experiments—use each key variable in a simple setting to confirm that it is acting as expected.
- Always look at both the population and economic results.
- When comparing more than one scenario, use the same methodology.
- Use graphs and an assortment of exhibits (Treyz, 1995b).

39.14 CONCLUSION

Economic modeling has become an important tool for policy analysis because it identifies the economic impact of public policy changes. (It does not, however, incorporate non-fiscal costs and benefits.) As a result, economic modeling provides an excellent way to analyze and simulate policy changes, but it should not be used as the sole criterion for accepting or rejecting changes in public polices. Modeling is not a substitute for decision-making, but it does provide useful information for the decision making process.

Despite some limitations, economic modeling provides an excellent way to analyze and estimate policy impacts before they occur. Modeling indicates what is likely to happen given a set of assumptions or actions. Economic modeling improves public policy analysis by making it more systematic and explicit. Even in its inchoate form, modeling is indispensable for the systematic understanding of the functioning and malfunctioning of an economy as well as for deciding which adjustments should be made to produce corrective actions (Leontief, 1986, p. 425). The implications for policy analysis are exceptional.

PROBLEMS

The data, House.xls or House.sav, provides information concerning the Sales Price of Homes in the past year in Bay County. The predictor variables for the sales price included are the total number of square feet, number of bedrooms, number of bathrooms, total rooms, age of house, and whether the house has a garage. Using this information, solve the following questions:

1. Determine the correlation between the predictor variables (Square feet, Number of Bedrooms, Number of Bathrooms, Total Rooms, Age of House, and whether the house has a Garage). Does any variable combination show correlation greater than 0.700?
2. Find the linear regression coefficients on linear, second-degree, third-degree polynomial equations and the four transformative equations from the chapter using sales price as the dependent variable and the predictor variables from above.
3. Determine from R^2 which predictive regression model best describes the data.
4. Predict the sales price of a house that has 1,750 square feet house with 3 bedrooms, 2 bathrooms, and 8 total rooms. The age of the house is ten years old with a garage.

GLOSSARY

direct effects: The production changes associated with the immediate effects of formal demand changes.

employment: The number of jobs (annual average) in an industry, including self employment.

employee compensation income: Total payroll costs (wages, salaries, and benefits) paid by local industries.

final demand: The demand for goods and services from ultimate consumers, rather than from other producing industries.

indirect effects: the production changes in backward-linked industries caused by the changing input needs of directly effected industries.

induced effects: The changes in regional household spending patterns caused by changes in household income (generated from direct and indirect effects).

multipliers: Type I multipliers are the direct effect (produced by a change in final demand) plus the indirect effect divided by the direct effect. Type III multipliers are the direct effect plus the indirect and induced effects divided by the direct effect.

REFERENCES

Hy, R. et al. 1983, *Research Methods and Statistics,* Cincinnati, Ohio: Anderson Publishing Company.

Hy, R. et al. 1992. *An Assessment of the Economic Impact of Locating the Arkansas Math and Science School,* Little Rock, Ark: UALR

Isard, W. 1951, Interregional and regional input–output analysis: A model of a space economy, *RE & S,* 33.

Isard, W. and Kuenne, R.E. 1953, The impact of steel upon the greater New York—Philadelphia urban industrial region, *RE & S,* 35

Koopmans, T.C. 1951, *Activity Analysis in Production and Allocation,* New York: John Wiley and Sons.

Quade, E.S. 1982, Analysis for public decisions, 2nd ed., North Holland, New York.

Leontief, W.W. 1953. Interregional theory, in W. Leontief, H. Cheney, P. Clark, J. Duesenberry, A. Ferguson, A. Grosse, R. Grosse, M. Holzman, W. Isard, and H. Kistin (Eds.), *Studies in the Structure of the American Economy,* New York: Oxford University Press.

Leontief, W.W. 1986, *Input-Output Economics,* 2nd ed., New York: Oxford University Press.

Makridakis, S. and Wheelwright, S.C. 1973, *Forecasting Methods for Management,* 5th ed., New York: John Wiley and Sons.

Moore, F.T. and Petersen, J.W. 1955, Regional economic reaction paths, *AER,* 45.

Moses, L. 1955, A general equilibrium model of production, interregional trade, and location of industry, *RE & S,* 42.

Reinmuth, J.E. 1974, The use of multivariate statistical methods in assessment analysis, with special emphasis on the problem of multicollinearity, in International Association of Assessing Officers (Ed.), *The Application of Multiple Regression Analysis in Assessment Administration,* Chicago: International Association of Assessing Officers.

Richardson, H.W. 1972, *Input–Output and Regional Economics*, New York: John Wiley and Sons.

Richmond, B. 1993, Systems thinking: Critical thinking skills for the 1990s and beyond. *Systems Dynamics Review* 9. Summer.

Rubinstein, M. 1975, *Patterns of Problem Solving*, Englewood Cliffs, New Jersey: Prentice-Hall.

Grubb, T. 1974. *The Input Output Model for the State of Texas*, Texas Business Review, Austin: Bureau of Business Research, University of Texas.

Treyz, G.I. 1995a, *Model Documentation for the REMl EDSF-53 Forecasting and Simulation Model*. Regional Economic Models, Inc., Amherst, Massachusetts.

Treyz, G.I. 1995b, Policy analysis applications of REMI economic forecasting and simulation models. *International Journal of Public Administration*, 18.

Yan, Chiou-shuang 1969, *Introduction to Input–Output Economics*, New York: Holt, Rinehart, and Winston.

40 Grounded Analysis: Going Beyond Description to Derive Theory from Qualitative Data

Ralph S. Brower and Hong-Sang Jeong

CONTENTS

Grounded analysis is a general methodology for inducing or deriving theory from an analysis of the patterns, themes, and common categories underlying observational data while the analyst holds to a minimum the predisposition to particular theoretical interests (e.g., Creswell, 1998; Strauss, 1987; Strauss and Corbin, 1998). This approach was initially developed by Barney Glaser and Anselm Strauss as part of a field study based on their observations of the ways that hospital staff members handled dying patients. Their pioneering book, *Discovery of Grounded Theory* (1967), laid the foundation for major ideas about grounded analysis used today and became a procedural guide for numerous qualitative researchers claiming the use of the method to legitimate their research. Their collaboration in this project and in devising the method almost defies probability because of the vast differences in their training and orientation. Strauss, trained in sociology at the University of Chicago, was steeped in the traditions of urban ethnography, symbolic interactionism, and pragmatism in the work of scholars such as Everett Hughes, George Herbert Meade, Herbert Blumer, Robert Park, W.I. Thomas, and John Dewey (Strauss, 1987; Strauss and Corbin, 1998). Glaser, on the other hand, was the student of Paul Lazersfeld at Columbia University, a German émigré from The Frankfurt School who is credited with innovating quantitative methods in sociology and introducing the analysis of massive databases of societal data (Strauss, 1987).

Despite these differences their collaboration in the pioneering study combined several powerful ingredients. Strauss's Chicago tradition emphasized the importance of getting out in the field to examine closely what is really going on in people's everyday activities and an appreciation for the importance to the emerging discipline of sociology in the United States to produce theory grounded in data. Glaser, trained in the Columbia tradition, saw a need to make comparisons between data points to induce clear, refined concepts. Both traditions valued research that could be useful to both professional and lay audiences. For this reason, Glaser and Strauss produced, in addition to the treatise on methods, several original monographs about dying (1965, 1968) that were addressed to both sociological colleagues and lay audiences. In recent years their orientations to grounded analysis have moved in somewhat conflicting directions (e.g., Glaser, 1992; Strauss, 1987; Strauss and Corbin, 1998), and we return to these differences later.

We undertake four tasks in this chapter. We begin by clearing up common misunderstandings and misuses of grounded analysis. Next we lay out the basics of the grounded analytic procedure outlined by Strauss and Corbin (1998) in their widely used book, supplementing their presentation with a brief discussion about using qualitative analysis software to accommodate the analytic process. Third, we provide a summary of the conflicting models of grounded analysis proposed by Glaser (1978, 1992), Strauss and Corbin (1998), and a newcomer, Charmaz (2003). Finally, because we believe the grounded approach is eminently flexible, we provide two illustrations about how it can be used with other analytic frameworks.

40.1 MISUNDERSTANDINGS AND MISUSES OF GROUNDED THEORY ANALYSIS

First, it is important to understand that grounded analysis is not a theory in and of itself. Rather, when we refer to grounded theory, we refer to a specific theory developed by the researcher from using grounded analysis in a study of a specific phenomenon. When we talk about grounded theory, therefore, we are referring to theory developed from an inductive analytic process, and the theory thus derived is said to be grounded in the everyday experiences of the individuals who have been interviewed or observed in their natural settings. Typically the theories produced from this process are not "grand theories" (Mills, 1959) about the social world; rather, grounded analysts who have achieved "theoretical saturation" are usually careful to bound the parameters and the implications of their theories.

Second, there is no recipe book for doing grounded analysis. Although the later work by Strauss and Corbin (e.g., 1998) contained more "how to" content than Strauss's earlier work (e.g., 1987) or the foundation work from Glaser and Strauss (1967), we contend that grounded analysis cannot be learned from a book. Good grounded analysis, like all qualitative inductive analysis, needs teaching and coaching. Good grounded analysts need a broad familiarity with inductive research processes and with the interpretive, social constructionist perspective more generally. Hong-Sang, for example, worked for several years under Ralph's guidance, and, in the process, developed not only a comfort for grounded analysis, but nurtured his appreciation of the process into a unique orientation that supported his growing understanding of phenomenology. Ralph learned the craft from Mitch Abolafia at SUNY Albany, who often credits his understanding to sitting at the knee of Gerald Suttles, a University of Chicago sociologist.

The point we make here is not an equation about academic pedigree, but of the importance of working with others who have done it themselves, who have a real understanding of the inductive, interpretive research process. Obviously there are others outside the authors' pedigree line that do good qualitative research, and we wholeheartedly endorse efforts that reach outside public administration faculties to departments of sociology and anthropology. Although this list is hardly exhaustive, we note that departments in nursing, education, communications, and business administration have experienced noteworthy progress in the quality of qualitative research and may therefore contain useful mentors and role models.

Third, grounded analysis is not about hypothesis testing. As obvious as this may seem to most observers, some authors continue to find justification in the established literature for the notion that grounded analysis supports hypothesis testing. Whereas we can debate whether grounded analysis implies a researcher who engages empirical materials totally *tabula rasa*, as though the researcher has no predispositions in examining the data, good grounded analysis is open-ended enough that we do not need to narrow our research endeavors to simple dichotomous questions. As in other types of interpretive research, the grounded analyst typically finds the research question mutating somewhat over the course of study. This is because the open-ended analytic process leads to unexpected results, and this in turn leads the researcher to explore empirical materials and side questions that could not initially have been anticipated. Occasionally we see articles or papers in which an author begins by arguing for a particular theoretical or descriptive account of the world and then reports using grounded analysis to examine whether the theory or description is correct. These authors clearly misuse the grounded analytic approach, because a researcher whose eye is trained on proving or disproving a particular account of the world will miss the rich variability of connections among the empirical materials at hand.

Fourth, grounded analysis is not about identifying variables. As in the question of hypothesis testing, this may seem obvious, but we have encountered students trained presumably by others who were not themselves fully initiated in an interpretive, constructionist perspective, who equate the activities of coding and collapsing and expanding families of codes as essentially an effort to identify variables. We believe this misdirection is a natural result of the overwhelmingly positivist orientation in the research methods courses that we require in most graduate programs. Those who equate grounded analysis with searching for and tabulating variables are misguided in at least two distinct ways. For example, "variables" are consistent with a *nomothetic* orientation in which the researcher seeks to identify variables of interest, rules and parameters for these constructs are stipulated (in the process of creating operational validity) prior to collecting data, and the researcher pursues associations among these constructs by studying variations in the corresponding numbers of cases for each variable. By way of contrast, grounded analysis and other interpretive approaches assume that social causation is *idiographic* in nature. That is, they see causation in everyday, emergent processes of human social interaction and meaning construction. Thus a researcher who focuses on identifying "variables" will get caught up in identifying and counting examples of static abstractions that exist "out there" in the social world while missing the sense of fluidity of meaning that naturally emerges from social interaction in people's everyday lives.

Although some interpretivists might take issue, we depict the interpretive, constructivist perspective as containing at minimum the following assumptions: that human action is both complex and variable; that human actors actively respond to problematic situations in which they find themselves; that individuals act on the basis of meanings in which they are embedded; that meaning is defined and altered through human interaction; and, that the events of human social experience are necessarily emergent and evolving (Strauss and Corbin, 1998, pp. 9–10; see Brower et al., 2000, pp. 364–370, for further explanation). Our assumptions permit a broad range of qualitative researchers to find cover under the tent; we deliberately avoid the ontological assumption – too radical in our view – that reality exists only in the human mind.

In addition, a preoccupation with identifying variables in the data inhibits the latter stages of the grounded analytic process as, for example, when the analyst uses selective coding to refine the underlying theoretical story line emerging from analysis. By focusing on identifying variables it is possible to get so caught up in open coding and collapsing families of codes that the analyst misses the overall picture that the goal is a theory about relationships among groups of codes. We suspect that some of this misplaced activity results from scholars who purchase and bury themselves in qualitative analytic software without first acquiring an understanding of the interpretive, constructivist perspective. We have found that some of these software packages support the grounded analytic process remarkably well, as we discuss below. Unfortunately, in the hands of those who see them as a shortcut to developing their own interpretive orientation these programs can lead to results that are antithetical to the interpretive perspective.

Finally, as with other interpretive approaches, grounded analysis is not well suited to answer "why," "when," "who," "where," or "whether" questions. In making this claim, we offer the proviso that these subquestions may become components of an emergent theory, but that the overall research question does not take these forms. Explaining why certain phenomena occur is by its nature a multivariate problem. That is, "why" questions can rarely be explained by single influences, and thus multivariate quantitative tools are much better suited to assessing the relative influences of various contributing factors. Similarly, questions that test whether certain conditions or explanations hold up under close examination are essentially hypothesis testing propositions, which we addressed previously. Studies that address the when, who, and where as explanations of events are similarly more suited to quantitative analysis or qualitative approaches whose intentions are more descriptive, such as biographies or case studies (see Creswell, 1998 for a comparison of such methods). Grounded analysis is, however, especially well suited to answering "how" and "what" questions. "How" questions imply process and change. Grounded analysis is very good at tracing the processes by which humans accomplish tasks and deal with problematic situations that they encounter. These methods are designed to explore the various sets of conditions and influences that alter how humans interact in social settings and how they make sense of these situations. Grounded analysis is similarly good for exploring "what" questions, that is, for inducing the components of a social phenomenon of human interest or creating typologies of various types of human social action, their implications, and the conditions that create and shape them.

40.2 PREDISPOSITION AND PREPARATION FOR GROUNDED ANALYSIS

40.2.1 PREDISPOSITION

We contend that not everybody is well suited to doing grounded analysis or qualitative inductive research more generally. The best reason for using these methods is that the individual has experimented with them and finds the work enjoyable. Many who use and take pleasure in these methods find that they particularly enjoy the intense engagement with the data – digging to find the deep meaning in the native's view of the world, relishing the ambiguity of multiple interpretations, becoming excited as the hours of hard analytic work begin to yield a more coherent theoretical picture. But because the methods require a tolerance for ambiguity and a willingness to explore ambiguities, students who like clear, concise, and early closure on the meanings of concepts and the boundaries of categories are likely to find that grounded analysis is not their cup of tea. Similarly, turning to grounded analysis simply because one has trouble mastering multivariate quantitative techniques is likely to lead to disappointment as well.

Strauss and Corbin (1998, p. 7) have suggested that, although some of the skills and attitudes can be developed over time, grounded analysts generally need to exhibit the following six attributes:

(a) An ability to step back and critically analyze situations
(b) A knack for identifying one's own biased predispositions and those of others
(c) A propensity for abstract thinking
(d) An ability to be flexible, willing to change course, and to seek criticism and suggestions from others
(e) An aptitude for observing subtlety in words and actions of those under study
(f) A willingness to become absorbed in the analytic process

We submit that, in addition to these qualities, those who want to explore grounded analysis or other interpretive research approaches would do well to expose themselves to the foundations of the social construction perspective (e.g., Berger and Luckmann, 1967) and to enter the grounded analytic project with a well-rounded view of existing theoretical explanations for their phenomenon of interest. Indeed, a modicum of confusion about which of several existing explanations for a phenomenon of interest may be most applicable often sets a tone of creative tension that can lead to a productive grounded analytic study.

40.2.2 GATHERING AND PREPARING DATA

In recent years, particularly with the assistance of qualitative analytic software, researchers have begun to apply grounded procedures to a vast new array of media types and fields of study, including dance, drama, and other body kinesthesia studies; film; audio recordings; musical scores; and, computer–human interfaces, to name a few. We will restrict our discussion here to the more traditional types of empirical materials, those with which we are more familiar: field notes, interview and focus group transcripts, and archival documents. It is not within our scope to review here how to gather and prepare such materials, but we do offer a few general guidelines.

Some dyed-in-the-wool interpretivists cringe at any characterization of "qualitative sampling," but we believe it is necessary to comment briefly about it. Sampling in the interpretive tradition bears little resemblance to sampling procedures that are undertaken in quantitative research to establish generalizability to a population of similar cases. Rather, the goal in qualitative sampling is generalizability to theory. That means we often seek extreme cases rather than typical cases, and we intentionally sample for variability. We do this because we hope to create theoretical saturation, that is, to derive theory that addresses the breadth of conditions and actions for our phenomenon of interest, not merely the relationships between variables for average cases. We typically pursue a sampling scheme that identifies distinctive settings we wish to examine and within those settings, specific individuals or subsettings to examine. Moreover, as we discuss axial and selective coding activities in our analysis, we will describe how sampling for cases continues, not only prior to gathering data, but throughout the analytic process.

Many researchers consider field observation the most fundamental qualitative data source, primarily because through observation we can record what people actually do rather than what they claim to do or to believe. Field observation is also a good starting point for identifying individuals to interview who are likely to be most knowledgeable about the setting or phenomenon under study. To yield coherent results in a grounded analytic study, however, one's field notes need to have been prepared in a thoughtful and disciplined way. We strongly encourage students to familiarize themselves with established methods for field observation and preparing field notes (e.g., Emerson et al., 1995; Sanjek 1990), to practice doing field observation, and to do so under the tutelage of others who are familiar with good field observation technique.

Depth interviews, sometimes referred to as long interviews, are another principal source of data for grounded analysis. Regrettably, in our view, many who conduct such interviews have not been properly trained to do them. The goal of a depth interview is to learn about some aspect or event of the world from the viewpoint of the "native" or interviewee. Untrained interviewers, however, often end up with materials in which the interviewee has been coached more or less unintentionally to mirror back the interviewer's preconceived "reality." This occurs because interviewing is a stressful activity, and, as the person "in charge," the interviewer takes responsibility to relieve the anxiety that both interviewer and interviewee are experiencing. Thus, faced with a silent impasse in which the interviewee is not offering an immediate answer to a question posed by the interviewer, the interviewer unwittingly jumps into the silence by clarifying the previous question, offering potential answers from which to pick, or otherwise "leading the witness." In training students to interview Ralph has them take turns interviewing each other and then playing back to their classmates the tape recordings they have made of their experiences. Nearly always they are unaware of and shocked at the extent to which they have led their interviewees when they hear the tape played back. Good interviewing requires practice and coaching.

A classic in the field is Spradley's (1979) *The Ethnographic Interview*, although some may be put off by the detailed interview process he proposes. The core of his model, however, is to devise an interview that is as nondirective as possible, using the interviewee's own answers to push for further and further clarification of the interviewee's view of things. An often untapped resource for learning to do nondirective interviewing is the campus program that teaches erstwhile counselors how to interview young children. Cultivating relations with these programs has a promising payoff for those who are serious about improving their interviewing skills.

Although there are noteworthy limitations imposed by cost and time, we strongly encourage that interviews be tape-recorded and transcribed. We know from experience that notes taken by the interviewer during an interview lose the nuances of native language, often change the intentions of the interviewee, and distract the interviewer from being able to listen closely to the interviewee's answers.

Regardless of whether the researcher focuses primarily on a single type of empirical material or mixes field notes, interview or focus group transcripts, and archival materials, we submit that good grounded analysis must be based on a substantial quantity and quality of data. As Ralph and his colleagues have noted:

> Many qualitative studies are based on weak, even casual data. Data gathering requires an intense engagement with the people and institutions under study. Researchers must spend time in the field, do numerous interviews, take exhaustive field notes, and sample widely among settings and individuals. (Brower et al., 2000, p. 388)

We offer one final point about the data used in a grounded analytic study: Data gathering often continues until nearly the point at which the final write-up of the study is completed. That is, the grounded analytic process itself leads us to pursue and examine new data as the emerging theory begins to take shape and the unclear or disputed areas of the theory need resolution. This is not to say that data collection does not begin before our sleeves are fully rolled up in the work of analysis, but that the two types of activity cannot be neatly separated from each other.

40.3 EXECUTING GROUNDED ANALYSIS: THREE PHASED CODING ACTIVITIES

At risk of oversimplifying the process, the core of the analytic process presented by Strauss and Corbin (1998) hinges on three successive phases or activities of "coding": open coding, axial coding, and selective coding. Although it is necessary to do open coding before one can commence axial coding and to initiate axial coding before selective coding, the three blend together in a fluid process rather than into neatly separated activities. Part of the reason for this is that the grounded analytic approach is necessarily iterative; that is, the analyst often discovers in latter stages of the process that some element of the emerging theory has been inadequately saturated and that it is necessary to gather additional empirical material and return to open coding and axial coding for those missing components. Moreover, although the overall process is inductive, analysts invariably find themselves iterating between inductive and deductive thinking. For example, the analyst reaches a point where an initial theoretical structure starts to take shape, thus creating a minimal working thesis about relationships among elements in the data. Then, on examining the working thesis more closely, the analyst realizes that some parts of the theory can either not be fully sustained by the data at hand, or that the thesis is incomplete in some respect. The analyst then returns to a more exploratory mode to gather additional data to fill in the missing elements.

40.3.1 OPEN CODING

Open coding, the first of the coding phases, is an open-ended process of discovering ideas or concepts within the data. The purpose of open coding is to "open up the text and expose the thoughts, ideas, and meanings contained there" (Strauss and Corbin, 1998, p. 102). In this early phase we are essentially fragmenting or breaking down the empirical materials. In this process of microanalyzing the data we label these thoughts, ideas, and meanings to begin to identify them with particular concepts. The codes or concepts to be discovered are of two types: native, or in vivo codes, and sociological codes (Strauss, 1987). In vivo codes are expressions used by the "natives" of a setting that are unique to the setting or lexicon of the natives. Grounded researchers typically try to preserve such terms in the analysis if they are important terms that capture a unique notion not easily explained in other everyday language. For example, Ralph, situated in the Philippines as this chapter is being composed, is learning to accommodate himself to a peculiar Philippine public transportation conveyance, the *Jeepney*. The original Jeepneys were modified from military surplus jeeps, with bodies extended somewhat and two parallel bench seats placed along the sides in the rear. The behaviors of drivers and passengers and the system of Jeepney routes constitute a distinctive cultural phenomenon, but there is no practical term to substitute for the word Jeepney in any description we might undertake. The word Jeepney is a distinctively irreducible in vivo code.

Sociological codes are concepts taken from the social science literature or terms that analysts invent to describe the behavioral and social phenomena that they observe. For example, in his grounded analytic dissertation about resistance behaviors in public organizations, Brower (1995) discovered that some resistors find themselves opposed to the goals of the public policies that they are asked to implement, and in other circumstances merely object to the means or procedures that constrain their actions. In his coding activities both public policy and procedure became important sociological codes. For reasons that may seem obvious most analysts find that they identify many more sociological codes than in vivo codes.

Also within the open coding phase we work to begin to group similar concepts, or more precisely, concept labels, into "categories." We have found that grouping codes in this way is a fairly intuitive process. Perhaps in the interest of the intuitively challenged, however, Strauss and Corbin (1998) suggest that analysts attempt to explore and manipulate their emergent categories by grouping together concepts with similar properties (size, shape, contour, mass, etc.) while simultaneously distinguishing among them in terms of dimensions on which they vary. In Ralph's resistance research, for example, he identified rules, supervisory oversight, the visibility of actions, and peer pressure as concepts that he grouped together in a category called "conditions that constrain employee actions." Similarly he noted how employees' resistance behaviors could be seen as distinguished from each other on a variety of dimensions, such as degree of overtness/covertness, severity of supervisory sanction, and degree of peer support and participation.

We have found that it may be useful to make numerous passes over the data, coding in one instance for the sorts of micro-behavioral characteristics that a psychologist might emphasize, a second time for the characteristics of interest to a sociologist, and subsequent times for elements of interest to economists, political scientists, and those in other social science disciplines. Newcomers to the open coding process are often uncertain about the sizes of chunks of data to examine as they begin coding. There is no single answer. It may be reasonable to start coding word-by-word or a line at a time to begin establishing comfort with the process. Later, as the analyst's understanding grows, it may be possible to move to larger chunks of data—to whole sentences, paragraphs, or passages. In addition to the analyst's comfort with handling and coding the data, the research question itself often dictates the size of data chunks that are appropriate for coding.

As the analysis begins to create emergent categories of codes the analyst makes notes about the groupings themselves and their definitions. These notes about definitions are ultimately fluid. Indeed, as we continue to merge concepts into categories, collapse categories into larger or smaller abstract groupings, and outline the dimensional differences among category groupings, our definitions for these groupings will necessarily change. But it is eminently important to commit this process to record; otherwise the analyst ends up going around in circles—"now why did I put those two codes together?" or, "what did I think was the potential relationship between those categories?" In addition, it is at this point that we begin our first efforts at "memoing." Here our first memos are simply an exercise in articulating our thinking about our categories, the dimensions that distinguish them, and the potential theoretical connections among them. These first memos are often open-ended questions, a sort of admission to oneself that our initial groupings are tentative and fluid. We commit our thinking to memos (a) to make it explicit to ourselves and (b) so as not to lose our formative thoughts about our categories and dimensional distinctions. Having committed these thoughts to paper, we can revisit them as often as necessary as the theoretical connections in our data begin to take form. Some memos ultimately prove to be unimportant, whereas others are eventually resolved as the emergent, grounded theory takes shape.

40.3.2 AXIAL CODING

If open coding is about breaking down or fragmenting the data, in axial coding we begin to reassemble the categories and, more importantly, to begin assembling relationships among the categories we have created in open coding. To the extent that we are thinking about our coding categories and writing notes and memos about them in open coding, we are already to some degree engaging in axial coding. In other words, the relationship between these phases or coding activities is ultimately very fluid. Strauss (1987; Strauss and Corbin, 1998) describes axial coding as hinged on a paradigm in which conditions, actions, and consequences are the core components of the emergent, grounded theory.

> The basic components of the paradigm are as follows. There are *conditions*, a conceptual way of grouping answers to the questions why, where, how come, and when. These together form the structure, or set of circumstances or situations, in which phenomena are embedded. There are *actions/interactions*, which are strategic or routine responses made by individuals or groups to issues, problems, happenings, or events that arise under those conditions. Actions/interactions are represented by the questions by whom and how. There are *consequences*, which are outcomes of actions/interactions. Consequences are represented by questions as to what happens as a result of those actions/interactions or the failure of persons or groups to respond to situations by actions/interactions, which constitutes an important finding in and of itself. (Strauss and Corbin, 1998, p. 128; emphasis in original)

In labeling conditions, Strauss (1987) and Strauss and Corbin (1998) distinguish among causal conditions, intervening conditions, and contextual conditions. We are uncomfortable with these distinctions, although we believe it is important to consider conditions across a wide array of direct and indirect influences on social settings and behavioral phenomena. We are concerned, however, that imposing these distinctions as types of conditions actually inhibits the emergent theory formation process by prestructuring the ways that the grounded analyst subsequently arrays conditions in the resultant grounded theory. That is, these conditions imply a theory of action that we would prefer to see emerge from the analytic process rather than be imposed on it. Similarly, we find the distinction between strategic and routine actions/interactions to be useful in thinking creatively about human action in the emergent theory, but we prefer to see grounded analysts induce their own accounts of human action and interaction from their data rather than impose a potentially artificial characterization on their data.

As the axial coding phase unfolds, the analyst creates relational statements about how concepts and categories relate to each other. These statements are, in effect, working "hypotheses." In formulating such statements, however, it is important for the analyst to validate and further elaborate the emergent theory through continuous comparisons to other instances in the data. When new instances in the data appear to contradict the working hypothesis, this does not necessarily mean the working thesis is wrong. Rather, it typically means that the analyst needs to consider how the contradictory evidence implies a further elaboration of the emergent theory or "an extreme dimension or variation of the phenomenon in question" (Strauss and Corbin, 1998, p. 135). In some instances these contradictions may dictate further sampling of data to round out an emergent theory that is capable of explaining variation in the phenomenon of interest.

As in open coding, memoing is a crucial aspect of axial coding activities. That is, the analyst should commit the emergent theory, along with those aspects of it that remain incomplete, to the same sorts of probing questions in the form of memos as in the open coding stages. It may well be that the unresolved questions in memos in the axial coding phase take on a more focused quality, and there may also be more of them. This is a natural result of the process of refining categories and relational statements about the connections between categories of conditions, actions, and consequences. That is, as the boundaries of categories become clearer, so too do the questions that remain to be answered about the category boundaries and relations among categories. In addition to memos about categories and relationships, it often proves helpful to prepare memos of a "journaling" nature as a record of the analytic process as it unfolds. These statements prove useful to the researcher who needs subsequently to explain to an audience how particular conclusions were reached and how troubling analytic dilemmas were resolved.

Strauss and Corbin (1998, p. 142) offer this concluding counsel about the axial coding process: "it is not the notion of conditions, actions/interactions, and consequences that is significant; rather, what is important is discovering the ways that categories relate to each other." We reiterate this point because it addresses our earlier admonition that grounded theory is not principally about identifying variables, it is about building theory that connects the categories to each other.

40.3.3 SELECTIVE CODING

The third coding phase, selective coding, is an extension of axial coding in which the emergent theory is refined and its elements integrated. The dividing line between axial and selective coding is fluid at best, although the title "selective" does imply that the analyst is selective in the elements that are refined and makes careful decisions occasionally to do additional selective data gathering—always with the intent of refining conceptual categories and the emergent theory. Strauss and Corbin (1998) emphasize several steps that help integrate the various elements into a coherent theory.

Perhaps most fundamental to integrating the various elements of a grounded theory are the tasks of identifying the central category and central story line. Uninitiated grounded analysts often find this step perplexing, and the mountain of data they typically have amassed contributes to this sometimes overwhelming dilemma. Several practical remedies may help in getting beyond this hurdle. One option is to brainstorm with a teacher or mentor; sometimes the solution resides clearly in the researcher's head but merely needs a little gentle prodding from an informed person to bring it out into the open. A second technique is to force oneself into a mental exercise of "writing out" the story line. Even a failed attempt at this may raise possibilities to the fore from which the researcher subsequently can move forward with the story line. Using diagrams to capture the central phenomenon and story line is another potential tactic for moving forward with the central story line. This technique can be especially fruitful when executed within a qualitative software program in which elements of the diagram are linked to specific codes, categories, or memos. Still another useful technique is to review and sort through memos. Typically memos move to higher and higher levels of abstraction as the analysis moves forward. Often they prove to be quite informative, and they typically constitute a comprehensive portrait of the researcher's developing theoretical insights. In this tactic the memos are used almost as though they are empirical materials in their own right, although, in fact, they are summaries of empirical insights. One final tactic for breaking through to the central story line is to consult the existing literature for similar explanations. This tactic comes with the proviso that analysts must retain confidence in their own data and analysis rather than attempt to force fit some existing theory onto the data. What an examination of the literature may afford, however, is an opportunity to push off against the existing explanations in the literature and point out on the basis of one's own evidence and analysis what is lacking or slightly in error in the existing theoretical contributions.

Even when the central theoretic story line has been articulated, there is invariably work to be done in refining the theory. We offer an illustration here to illuminate how selective coding works in practice. Grigoriy Pershin, whose grounded analytic dissertation (2006) is discussed below, discovered a central theme (referred to as a "frame" in his analysis) in which various policy makers and policy entrepreneurs in Florida were advocating to offer bachelors degrees selectively at some of Florida's community colleges. From some informants, however, he began to hear variations of the framed story as though there was a conscious effort to modify and soft sell the proposition to stakeholder groups who might be resistant or opposed to offering community college baccalaureates. In his selective coding effort, therefore, Grigoriy began to ferret out the differences in these framed stories, the contexts in which they were presented, and the circumstances of the individuals who were presenting them. What initially appeared to be inconsistencies in the data, therefore, ultimately illuminated what Grigoriy later referred to as primary and secondary frames. That is, his emergent theory was able to accommodate these variations in his theoretical explanation by accounting for why these various informants honed their "frames" or stories for their own particular audiences. In the process of exploring these differences and elaborating these distinctions, Grigoriy intentionally gathered additional interviews and reexplored data passages in his existing interviews to round out his theoretical explanation of the primary and secondary policy frames.

Strauss and Corbin (1998, p. 156) explain that refining the theory "consists of reviewing the scheme for internal consistency and for gaps in logic, filling in poorly developed categories and trimming excess ones, and validating the scheme." One useful exercise for filling in poorly developed categories is to return to the various memos that have been written and deciding whether the uncertainties or dilemmas they pose have been resolved. Pershin (2006) in the study cited above made good use of this technique. In fact, as he proceeded through the analysis of his interview data he found he had accumulated a number of memos describing the inconsistencies in the ways that various actors presented their "frames" or stories that ostensibly justified the community college baccalaureate degrees. As he began to recognize that the conditions they described implied that they were actually attempting to appeal to quite different groups of stakeholders, the importance of the varied "frames" became clearer. As we noted above, it was through this process that he began to see the presence of a primary frame and various secondary frames that the advocates of community college baccalaureates had spun to sell the policy to diverse stakeholder groups. As the theoretical implications became clearer he then returned to the various memos he had accumulated under a title of "frame inconsistencies" and ascertained that he could in fact account for these inconsistencies in his evolving theory. Had he been unable to account for these themes in his earlier memos he would have needed consciously to fill in the theory where these unresolved themes applied.

Sometimes data and memos suggest themes that are simply foreign or tangential to the central story line. In these instances, it is probably best to trim them out while leaving open the option to return to them in subsequent research. At least two tactics lend themselves to validating the theoretical scheme. One is to extract the various cases in the original data and examine whether the central story line can explain them. When some do not fit, the theory may require a modest tweaking or qualifying statement. A second tactic is to present the story line to informants and ask them to respond. Not every nuance of every informant's story will fit the theory, but, in general, respondents should be able to see themselves in the story the researcher tells them.

Finally, although the central story line is the core of a theory successfully grounded in empirical materials the researcher has gathered, it is critical that the final presentation of the theory build in explanatory apparatus for the variations within and between categories. A story line that is overly parsimonious will simply be unsatisfying to the social phenomenon from which the analysis arose and will fail the test of theoretical saturation of the empirical materials.

40.3.4 AIDING THE ANALYTIC PROCESS WITH QUALITATIVE SOFTWARE

We cannot emphasize enough the importance of learning the inductive, grounded analytic process before embarking on the use of qualitative analysis software. We have witnessed the dangers that await those who believe the software is a substitute for learning how to do qualitative analysis. The problem is this: Unlike in quantitative analysis, in which the software is the tool of analysis, the instrument of analysis in qualitative research is the analyst. The software does not do the analysis for the researcher; it merely assists the handling of what are sometimes massive amounts of data and empirical insights. Notwithstanding this caution, qualitative analytic software can greatly ease the handling of data for the analyst.

It seems that new qualitative software products are coming in the market regularly, and although we do not wish to advocate for a particular product over others, we will illustrate one product with which we are most familiar, a German software product developed specifically for grounded analysis, Atlas.ti.* The description that follows is synopsized from the ongoing study of Brower and associates (2006).

At the core of the qualitative software products is a mouse-driven system that plants reference points in original texts of interviews, field notes, or archival documents, etc. These reference points permit the analyst to attach whatever codes, commentaries, or memos that apply to various passages or other empirical details. The system then provides an array of tools for managing, arranging, sorting, and displaying these implanted ideas, codes, comments, memos, and emerging theories. Thus the software's tools facilitate the time-consuming iterative steps of a systematic analytic approach such as grounded analysis. Whereas traditional grounded analysts often recorded their codes, categories of codes, code definitions, and other related comments on index cards, the software eliminates the need for index cards and other hardcopy notes and memos. Moreover, every note, comment, or memo the analyst records is permanently tied to one or more points in the data—field notes, interview transcripts, or archival documents—to which the notation refers. This system permits easy changes and dissolutions and updates of earlier notes and memos while retaining previous work. Whereas grounded analysts traditionally spread out their emergent array of index cards and memos on a tabletop or living-room floor, a software program such as Atlas.ti retains it within a single, colorful file. The time-saving value of these programs is tremendous. In Table 40.1 we illustrate typical tools in Atlas.ti and the steps in grounded analysis to which they correspond.

TABLE 40.1
Grounded Analysis and Corresponding Tools in Atlas.ti

Traditional Approach with Index Cards	Tools within Atlas.ti
Open coding	
Adding content labels	Coding Tools and Coding Manager
Creating groups/categories of labels	(drop down menus, lists of codes, etc.)
Axial coding	
Merging and dividing groups	Coding Manager Quotation Manager
Finding code frequencies and relationships	Memo Manager
Creating memos, reviewing them, relating them to codes, definitions, comments	Coding and Memo Family Managers
	Primary Document Manager
	Network View (Diagram) Manager
Selective coding	
Identifying a central theoretical phenomenon	Query Tool (e.g., working with families of codes)
	Global Memo Function (e.g., relabel memos as global or "macro")
Building a "story line" that connects the categories of codes	Quotation Manager
Iteratively confirming/validating the theory	Network View (Diagram) Manager

* A comprehensive listing of available software packages, complete with prices and contact information can be found at http://www.eval.org/Resources/QDA.htm.

We note several other caveats about using qualitative software for grounded analysis. First, with one or two exceptions, the programs have steep learning curves. In general, the more powerful the software, the steeper the curve. Although this may be a matter of judgment, we suspect it is more difficult to justify learning to use the software when one's project is an article-length study. That is, there is an economy of scale which justifies learning the software for larger projects, but only after the analyst has a good familiarity with the software do article-length projects lend themselves to the software. Finally, the ongoing study of Brower et al. (2006) identified only ten articles out of 243 qualitative studies published in three leading public administration journals between 1996 and 2005 that employed qualitative software. We strongly believe that this reflects not just lack of exposure to the software, but a more general lack of training, familiarity, and cultural expectations within public administration for systematic analytic approaches like grounded analysis (Brower et al. 2000; Lowery and Evans, 2004). The ten articles that used software provided elaborate description and justification for their analytic methods, and this was an atypical trait for most of the other 233 articles.

40.4 TWO VARIANT APPROACHES TO GROUNDED ANALYSIS

40.4.1 Glaser's Constant Comparative Approach

Although Glaser participated with Strauss in the foundational text, *Discovery* (Glaser and Strauss, 1967), he has since written critically of the approach developed by the late Strauss and Corbin. In *Basics of Grounded Analysis: Emergence vs. Forcing* (1992), Glaser finds "Strauss and Corbin to be forcing data and analysis through their preconceptions, analytic questions, hypothesis, and methodological techniques" (Charmaz, 2003, p. 254). According to him, Strauss and Corbin's analytic categories set forth in their axial coding paradigm lock researchers into preconceived analytic categories, divert them from the data, and result in poorly integrated theoretical frameworks (Charmaz, 2003; Creswell, 2002).

For Glaser, the so-called "constant comparative method" (Glaser and Strauss, 1967) is enough strategy to build grounded theory. The constant comparison method is an inductive data analysis that Glaser proposed (with Strauss) in *Discovery* (1967). The overall intent is to "discover" theory from the data of social research (Glaser and Strauss, 1967). The method is a "concept-indicator model" (Strauss, 1987), composed of a series of procedures of "generating and connecting categories by comparing incidents in the data to other incidents, incidents to categories, and categories to other categories" (Creswell, 2002, p. 451). As Creswell (2002) has explained, raw data are formed into indicators—small segments of information that come from different people, different sources, or the same people over time. These indicators are, in turn, grouped into several codes (e.g., Code A, Code B, Code C), and then formed into more abstract categories (e.g., Category I, Category II). Throughout this process, the researcher constantly compares indicators to indicators, codes to codes, and categories to categories. In the process, the researcher lets a theoretical scheme emerge from the data. Once a scheme emerges from the data the analyst "compares the scheme with the raw data to ground the categories in the information collected during the study" (Creswell, 2002, p. 451).

In Glaser's eyes, the analytical method advanced by Strauss and Corbin is already tampered by structural concepts (e.g., causal conditions, context, intervening conditions, strategies, and consequences) that properly belong to theory. In this context, Glaser proposes the constant comparative method as a transparent analytic technique in which the grounded analyst can capture theory fully grounded in the data.

40.4.2 Charmaz's Constructivist Approach

Partially in response to these other two approaches, Charmaz has articulated what she calls the constructivist approach (2003) as an effort to move grounded theory into the realm of interpretive social science. Her critique hinges on the others' realist perspective. According to Charmaz

(2003, p. 255), "[B]oth Glaser and Strauss and Corbin assume an external reality that the researcher can discover and record" that endorses "a realist ontology and positivist epistemology." They are realists in that they claim to pose "the reality of the data" (p. 255) unaltered by the researcher. They are positivists in that they believe that their knowledge of "*the* reality of the data" (p. 255) is derived from and justified by direct observation of the reality, which is unaltered by the subjectivity of the researcher (emphasis in original).

In contrast to the realist and positivist perspective to which she assigns these earlier accounts, Charmaz (2003) proposes a version of grounded theory that does not embrace the assumption of an "objective" researcher that she finds in the work of the earlier proponents: "constructivist grounded theory." Charmaz purports to introduce two data handling techniques that appear to be slight modifications of techniques from Strauss and Corbin (1998): a two-step coding technique, "line-by-line coding" in combination with "focused coding," and, memo writing as an intermediate step between coding and writing the first draft of the final analysis. We find nothing new in these techniques that Strauss (1987) or Strauss and Corbin (1998) have not already proposed. The real distinction between Charmaz and earlier proponents, however, is her insistence that grounded theory is a process in which researchers create "a reality," clothe the data with the created reality, and in doing so take the clothed realty as the "real" reality of the data. That is, she acknowledges in her approach that the analyst creates or constructs the discovered reality rather than apprehending it as a reality "out there."

One limitation of the Charmaz critique, in our view, is that by focusing attention on the analyst's interpretive dilemma, she disregards the audience's equally important interpretive role. Astute audiences recognize that the analyst is an interpreter, a subjective filter who offers a particular representation of that part of the social world that has been observed. Analysts, in turn, recognize this capacity in their audiences. When all parties hold this common realization the distinction as to whether the represented reality was discovered or merely constructed seems to us to be more semantic than substantive. We invite our own audience members to explore these alternative viewpoints and to pursue or create unique grounded analytic styles that suit their own interpretive orientations.

40.5 ON THE FLEXIBILITY OF GROUNDED ANALYSIS: TWO ILLUSTRATIONS

We conclude with two applications of the grounded analytic process that illustrate its flexibility. The first illuminates how the method can accommodate the subject matter itself and the analyst's own a priori theoretical sensitivity. The second demonstrates its use within a broader qualitative design.

40.5.1 SENSEMAKING, PHENOMENOLOGY, AND KOREAN FIRE SERVICE OFFICIALS

The first illustration is from Hong-Sang's (Jeong, 2006) study of the sensemaking processes of Korean street-level fire service officials. His study was grounded in 45 working episodes collected from 36 workers, including fire inspectors, firefighters, members of rescue squads, and EMS (Emergency Medical Services) staff. Interviews were conducted at work sites in Seoul, Cheongju, Kongju, and at the National Fire Academy in Cheonan during the summer of 2004. Interviewees were asked to describe unstructured dilemmas, uncertainties, ambiguities, or other "puzzlements" or troubles they had encountered in real work situations and how they made sense of and worked their way through them. Hong-Sang used an open-ended interview instrument to explore aspects of their sensemaking processes that were not otherwise forthcoming from their stories. He gathered a broad range of sensemaking experiences which, in turn, generated a large amount of nonstandard qualitative data. His study called for an analytic method that made it possible to sustain an intimate relationship with the data while simultaneously providing a rigorous, systematic process. Grounded analysis fit the bill.

His analytic process was complicated by two compelling factors. First, he was already richly steeped in the literature of sensemaking (e.g., Weick, 1979, 1995), Mead's symbolic interactionism,

Husserl's transcendental phenomenology, Heidegger's existential (or hermeneutical) phenomenology, and Schutz's sociological phenomenology. Second, he quickly discovered that he was engaged in attempting to interpret others' interpretive processes. In short, he became captive to a series of reflective and reflexive dilemmas.

He concluded that data analysis in the study could not be a process of examining the episodes as or for themselves. Rather, he found himself paying attention to the sensemaking process exemplified by particular working episodes and in doing so revealed the process to the mind. In disclosing the sensemaking process in the data, he referred to the coding procedures advanced by Strauss and Corbin but avoided imposing their prescriptive and predetermined "coding paradigm," discussed earlier. Rather, he focused on allowing his own theory to emerge through the process of analyzing (coding) the collected data.

The analysis was a process in which he experienced the sensemaking exemplified by the data, and in doing so presented it to his mind in the form of a conceptual scheme. In the sense that his analysis (experience) was grounded in the data, it was an inductive analysis. Yet the analysis was not so purely an inductive inferential process as assumed by Glaser (1978, 1992). He neither entered the analysis *tabula rasa* by completely disengaging himself from prior theoretical commitments, nor was he capable of doing so. Rather, he carried into the analysis his former theoretical understandings of sensemaking, symbolic interactionism, and the several variants of phenomenology.

Each informant brought a distinctive story, but because informants were unattuned to sensemaking as an abstract process their stories contained many elements that were extraneous to Hong-Sang's theoretical interest. His focus during interviews and subsequent analysis, therefore, was not on each story as a whole but on the sensemaking process exemplified in the story. Indeed, one could argue (and we would disagree, as we illustrate below) that sensemaking did not exist within any given episode other than as a theoretical framework that Hong-Sang brought to the episode. Although the theoretical lenses that he carried into the interviews and analysis were speculative his engagement of these theoretical perspectives made it possible for him to direct himself toward, and in doing so to experience (understand) the sensemaking process contained in the data, and as a result to present it as it was experienced (understood). In this respect, "the grounded theory" in the study was not an atheoretical but a theoretically sensitized inductive analysis.

In this process he shared with Charmaz (2003) a viewpoint that data analysis in grounded theory is essentially the process of "interpretive understanding (*Verstehen*)" (Schutz, 1963). Yet, unlike her constructivist approach, his approach to the method of "interpretive understanding" was phenomenological. His analysis in the study was not a process in which he created a sensemaking (reality), imputed it to the data, and understood the data in terms of the imputed sensemaking (reality). Rather, the analysis was a process in which he constantly encountered the sensemaking (reality) as presented (exemplified in cases) through the data, and in doing so continuously clarified his apprehension of the "real" phenomenon. In short, we are confident there is an order (reality) to human cognitive processes in the fire officials' behaviors that underlie the stories from Hong-Sang's informants. We suspect eminent cognitive psychologists such as Piaget and Bandura would have been startled by the prospect that there is no such order to the human cognitive routines to which their lifelong work was devoted. Certainly there is slippage between reality and Hong-Sang's representation that is due to biases in informants' recall and his own subjective limitations. But this slippage is fully consistent with the notion of *Verstehen* offered by Weber (1949) and refined by Schutz (1963) and other disciples. Thus Hong-Sang's analysis assumes the presence of an order (reality) that is prior to his actions in representing what he perceived in his data.

If Charmaz's "interpretive understanding" is the construction of a reality of the data, Hong-Sang's "interpretive understanding" was the construction of knowledge of the reality in the data. As a matter of course, the grounded analysis in his study was not a "method of creating" a reality of the data. His grounded analysis as a method of *Verstehen* was a "method of being aware" of the reality in the data.

The understanding (experience) was not only bound to the reality of which it was the understanding (fire official's experience); it was also united with "I" for which it became understanding

(Hong-Sang's experience). Certainly the possibility of inaccuracy was inherent in the "interpretive understanding" because of its private character, derived from his subjectivity itself. From his vantage point, therefore, it was necessary to bring into question, and consequently to critically inspect "*my* interpretive understanding." In order to do so, he relentlessly distanced himself from "living in interpretive understanding," attended to, and placed in question his lived "interpretive understanding." Through this reflexive procedure, he made his *Verstehen* the explicit object of propositional inspection, and in doing so closely and continuously examined its legitimacy. Through this persistent state of mind it was possible for him ultimately to gain confidence in "*his* understanding of *the* reality in the data" on a more unbiased basis.

Hong-Sang's challenge was compounded by the difficulties of coding and composing in English, while working from data and realities in Korean, and engaging theoretical materials that in many instances were originally written in German and imperfectly translated to English. But challenges of this sort often yield well-deserved rewards. In this instance, we are hopeful that Hong-Sang's efforts will be appreciatively received by Korean audiences for whom both the phenomenological conceptions and grounded analytic methods constitute unique contributions to existing scholarship.

40.5.2 Grounded Analysis for the Microanalytics within a Case Study

Ralph's student and Hong-Sang's student colleague, Grigoriy Pershin, became fascinated with the unlikely public policy initiative that eventually led to several Florida community colleges receiving authority to grant baccalaureate degrees. This particular policy initiative attracted a great deal of attention because it seemed to fly in the face of the traditional role of community colleges, its negotiation and enactment attracted a great deal of resistance from competing interest groups in the state, and it raised a set of difficult questions about accreditation, program approval, and institutional sustainability. At the time of the policy's enactment Florida became one of only a few states to offer community college baccalaureates.

Even though case study methods seemed more appropriate to his needs, his extensive training in grounded analysis led him initially to attempt to manage the data through grounded analytic techniques. Early on in his study he received some timely advice to consider using "frame analysis" as a way to understand the construction of arguments in which the political and administrative actors had been engaged.* Fortunately, Abolafia's (2004) frame analysis of a dramatic change in monetary policy under Paul Volcker's leadership at the Federal Reserve Board offered a useful example in which grounded analysis had been applied to examine the microanalytics in a public policy case study. Frame analysis and grounded analysis proved to be an amiable match for Greg's dissertation research (Pershin, 2006).

In Greg's analysis, as we discussed briefly above, it became clear that a central frame, that of justifying the awarding of baccalaureates at community colleges, was the central story line. But it similarly appeared that other, secondary frames, similar to the main story line in some respects but different in others, were important as well. Greg's comparison of the frames lent itself nicely to grounded analytic methods. This analytic process led Greg to conclude that the frames were distinct because they were constructed by disparate actors attempting to accommodate the distinct structural and cultural circumstances in which they were embedded. That is, the frame that sells the proposed policy to the state legislature is not the same frame that convinces a research university that it need not feel threatened by the efforts of the nearby community college to begin offering baccalaureates.

Meanwhile, following the conventions of case study methodology that suggest triangulating accounts from multiple sources of information, Greg was able to identify the structural and cultural constraints that bounded the distinct frames being constructed by these various principal actors. Among other interesting findings, Greg discovered that those most actively engaged in frame

---

* Dvora Yanow was the source of this helpful advice.

construction were well aware that their frames designed to work with particular audiences often meet opposition when brought to bear with other audiences. Ambiguity proves to be an important lubricant against potential outside sources of friction—"this is just a pilot project"; "this is a stop-gap measure to meet the immediate workforce needs of the community"; "we will limit it to a few case-by-case instances." In the instance of this third delimiter, the implication was that only a limited number of community colleges would be granted this authority, but the advocates who touted this particular line carefully courted the ambiguity of failing to distinguish the guidelines by which the "limited number of community colleges" would be selected.

Each of the distinctive frames, each frame's unique conditions, and the unique actions of the frames' architects contributed to a massive accumulation of codes, categories of codes, code definitions and commentaries, and memos about categories, families of categories, and even memos about groups of memos. Atlas.ti proved to be exceptionally useful in managing this mass of notes, comments, and memos, and the program's drawing tool (the Network Manager) was especially helpful in outlining connections among them all.

Greg's experience and the work from Abolafia (2004) that it mimicked illustrate the compatibility of grounded analytic methods within other qualitative research designs. Although various authors propose distinctions among overall qualitative design types (e.g., Creswell, 1998) —such as case studies, ethnographies, phenomenology, biographies—we submit that grounded analysis, used in part or in whole, is a useful data management approach that is largely compatible with these other designs and that can be made quite flexible in the hands of scholars willing to work within its general framework.

We have completed our initial journey—clearing up common misunderstandings and misuses of grounded analysis, laying out the basics of the grounded analytic procedure, providing a summary of recent discussions about conflicting models of grounded analysis, and illustrating the flexibility of the approach and its compatibility with other qualitative research designs. We would be remiss to suggest that grounded analysis is universally useful, that it will appeal to all erstwhile qualitative researchers, or that the path to learning to use it is smooth and effortless. But in the hands of those ready to learn from others who have used it successfully, who are willing to roll up their sleeves and get their hands dirty, it is an eminently systematic and rigorous approach to qualitative data analysis that leads to results in which mere empirical description has been pushed to defensible theoretical explanation.

REFERENCES

Abolafia, M.Y. 2004. Framing moves: interpretive politics at the federal reserve. *Journal of Public Administration Research and Theory*, 14, 349–370.

Berger, P.L. and Luckmann, T. 1967. *The Social Construction of Reality*. New York: Doubleday.

Brower, R.S. 1995. Everyday forms of bureaucratic resistance: An ethnographic investigation. Dissertation completed at the State University of New York, Albany.

Brower, R.S., Abolafia, M.Y., and Carr, J.B. 2000. On improving qualitative methods in public administration research. *Administration and Society*, 32, 363–397.

Brower, R.S., Ahn, S., Hsieh, C.-W., and Pershin, G. 2006. Using qualitative analysis software in public administration research. Paper presented at the *Southeastern Conference on Public Administration*, Athens, Georgia, September 29, 2006.

Charmaz, K. 2003. Grounded theory: Objectivist and constructivist methods. In. Denzin, N.K. and Lincoln, Y.S. (Eds.), *Handbook of Qualitative Research*. Thousand Oaks, California: Sage.

Creswell, J.W. 1998. *Qualitative Inquiry and Research Design: Choosing Among Five Traditions*. Thousand Oaks, California: Sage.

Creswell, J.W. 2002. *Educational Research: Planning, Conducting, and Evaluating Quantitative and Qualitative Research*. Upper Saddle River, New Jersey: Pearson.

Emerson, R.M., Fretz, R.I., and Shaw, L.L. 1995. *Writing Ethnographic Fieldnotes*. Chicago, Illinois: University of Chicago Press.

Glaser, B. 1978. *Theoretical Sensitivity*. Mill Valley, California: Sociology Press.

Glaser, B. 1992. *Basics of Grounded Theory Analysis: Emergence vs. Forcing*. Mill Valley, California: Sociology Press.

Glaser, B. and Strauss, A. 1965. *Awareness of Dying*. Chicago, Illinois: Aldine.

Glaser, B. and Strauss, A. 1967. *Discovery of Grounded Theory*. Chicago, Illinois: Aldine.

Glaser, B. and Strauss, A. 1968. *Time for Dying*. Chicago, Illinois: Aldine.

Jeong, H.S. 2006. A grounded analysis of the sensemaking process of korean Street-Level fire service officials. Dissertation completed at Florida State University, Tallahassee, Florida.

Lowery, D. and Evans, K.G. 2004. The iron cage of methodology: The vicious circle of means limiting ends limiting means. *Administration and Society*, 36, 306–327.

Mills, C.W. 1959. *The Sociological Imagination*. Middlesex, England: Penguin.

Pershin, G. 2006. Adoption of policies that permit community colleges to grant Bachelor Degrees in Florida: Frame analysis. Dissertation completed at Florida State University, Tallahassee, Florida.

Sanjek, R. 1990. *Fieldnotes: The Making of Anthropology*. Ithaca, New York: Cornell University Press.

Schutz, A. 1963. Concept and theory formation in the social sciences. In Nathanson, M. (Ed.), *Philosophy of the Social Sciences*. New York: Random House.

Spradley, J.P. 1979. *The Ethnographic Interview*. New York: Holt, Rinehart & Winston.

Strauss, A. 1987. *Qualitative Analysis for Social Scientists*. Cambridge, United Kingdom: Cambridge University Press.

Strauss, A. and Corbin, J. 1998. *Basics of Qualitative Research*, 2nd ed. Thousand Oaks, California: Sage.

Weber, M. 1949. *The Methodology of the Social Sciences*. (Shils, E.A. and Finch, H.N., Eds. and Trans.). Glencoe, Illinois: Free Press.

Weick, K.E. 1979. *The Social Psychology of Organizing*, 2nd ed. Reading, Massachusetts: Wesley-Addison.

Weick, K.E. 1995. *Sensemaking in Organizations*. Thousand Oaks, California: Sage.

41 Research Methods Using Geographic Information Systems

Akhlaque Haque

CONTENTS

41.1 INTRODUCTION

Geographic information systems (GIS) are being widely used as decision-support tools to understand the spatial dimension of data and its linkages to nearby phenomenon on Earth. In the information age as consumers demand more from raw data than just numbers and texts, maps can be powerful means by which information about space and people can be communicated to better understand the impact of our decisions about people and places. As an enabler of sorts, GIS makes mapmaking a process by which new information is revealed and explained through computer systems (hard drive, software, and plotter or printer) and spatially referenced data (geographical data) for management and analysis of various tasks. Such interest and focus has been possible with higher computer processing capabilities, surge in the internet usage and its impact on information gathering and dissemination. By adding the spatial dimension to any data (addressing the location of the data), GIS allows far better understanding of the characteristics of the data and how it may be related to other variables that are in proximity to the geo-referenced data* in question. Whereas statistical analysis may reveal nuances between and within variables (quantitative or qualitative) in a model, a map of location-specific data concisely communicates spatial distribution, enabling the viewer to better understand patterns and relationships through scenarios (of maps). Such an understanding of data becomes critical in many management, planning, and policy decisions.

---

* Data that has been linked to locations through geographical referencing, such as latitude and longitude.

Maps can be used as an efficient data storage medium to locate people, places, and objects or to record administrative and other land boundaries. It is also used to demonstrate phenomena or relationships of interest. Fundamentally, GIS adds value to data. For example, the location of crime in a neighborhood can be integrated in a single data set to be portrayed on a map for analyzing public safety response for the neighborhood; at the same time, tax data for the neighborhood can be analyzed to store, identify, and manage tax bases, including tax evasion and tax usage. Crime and tax base may not appear to have direct relationship in the first place but a snapshot of the neighborhood with both the information on a map could reveal new information about the neighborhood and generate hypothesis for solutions to neighborhood problems. Today GIS is recognized as the key information management tool for congressional redistricting, disaster management and mitigation, emergency management, public service delivery and dispatch, distribution of public funds including minimizing frauds, monitor and localize disease outbreaks, transportation planning and modeling, and real estate management. Many find GIS appealing because of its visualization capability—complex phenomenon can be displayed with colorful maps with relative ease and accuracy. To researchers and policy makers, however, in addition to the visual appeal, it is a sound methodological tool to structure problems and identify potential solutions for evaluation. Moreover, unlike statistical applications, GIS is a communication tool, bringing diverse participants to communicate their views through "what if" scenarios presented in maps (Berry, 1993). At the end the definitive goal of GIS is the understanding of spatial information and knowledge formation by revealing the unknown.

The purpose of this chapter is to present GIS as a methodological tool for improving our understanding of spatial data and its implications for decision making in social science. Section 41.2 asks the question why GIS in research and describes what is expected from GIS for conceptualizing problems and helping solve them. Section 41.3 describes the underlying concepts of GIS related to spatial data and visualization. Section 41.6 will be devoted to GIS methods of map visualization with examples of spatial analysis.

41.2 DEFINITION OF GIS

There is almost as much variation in the definition of GIS as its usage in increasing number of disciplines. Initially developed as a mapmaking tool, it has evolved into a decision-support system that enables spatially referenced data to be manipulated to produce user-friendly management and planning tasks. Through a combination of hardware and software geared toward gathering and disseminating information about places on Earth's surface, GIS has helped the understanding of geographic information science—a rapidly growing discipline supported by disciplines of geography, surveying, engineering, cartography, computer science, social and behavioral sciences, health sciences, and the law. The increasing demand of GIS can be deemed in its ability to add value to spatially referenced data. For example, population density of a given jurisdiction can raise enough interest among demographers as would the type of health insurance coverage, among health professionals. Both observations about the population can be brought into GIS with relative ease and presented in a meaningful fashion for decision making. Maps can be a meaningful medium, and GIS as the avenue for participatory research and decision making.

GIS can be defined as a research-evaluation tool that combines disparate data about places into one organized information management system to present the characteristics or activities of that place and evaluates impacts of decisions that are specific to that place. Table 41.1 shows a sample list of industries where GIS has been used.

41.3 GIS: A RESEARCH TOOL

All problems are complex and require a methodical approach in solving them. One way of grasping the complexity of our problems is by simplifying the assumptions of the real world. Parsimony,

TABLE 41.1
Use of GIS by Industry

Industry	Use of GIS
Forestry	Inventory and management of resources
Police	Crime mapping to target resources
Epidemiology	To link clusters of disease to sources
Transport	Monitoring routes
Utilities	Managing pipe networks
Oil	Monitoring ships and managing pipelines
Central and local government	Evidence for funding and policy, e.g., deprivation
Health	Planning services and health impact assessments
Environment agencies	Identifying areas of risk from, e.g., flood
Emergency departments, e.g., ambulance	Planning quickest routes
Retail	Store location
Marketing	Locating target customers
Military	Troop movement, deployment
Mobile phone companies	Locating masts
Land ReGIStry	Recording and managing land and property
Estate agents	Locating properties that match certain criteria
Insurance	Identifying risk, e.g., properties at risk of flooding
Agriculture	Analyzing crop yields

Source: Getting started with GIS. (n.d.). Who uses GIS and why. Retrieved on August 9, 2005, from http://www.gis.rgs.org/10.html.

at least, leads to an understanding of the scope of the problem, if not the problem itself. In economic theory, for example, it is customary to use *ceteris paribus* (all other things remaining equal) as a simple way of controlling the unknowns to reveal the social and economic behavior of individuals or groups. Similarly, with GIS, the real world can be taken in pieces or snapshots and projected on the computer screen with the underlying assumption that only the variables that are being studied will be shown in relation to other nearby variables that might be affecting the key variable. The simplified view of the real world adopted by GIS is often termed a model. What GIS represents are essentially abstract models of selected aspects of the real world. Aerial photographs, satellite images, census data, and particularly maps contain inherent simplification or assumptions that are syntheses of data. As the synthesizer, GIS transforms the three-dimensional real world spatial data and projects it on a two-dimensional flat screen. The level of detail in the map is not only limited to what will be shown (model of spatial form) but also how it will be shown (model of spatial processes) to exemplify the problem in the best way. The model of spatial form is the representation of structures and the dispersion of features in a geographical space. For example, river can be shown in lines or using polygons (shapes) depending on how detailed the parts of the real world we would like to acknowledge for our purposes. The model of spatial processes entails describing the relationship or real world processes in terms of physical process (cornfields, houses, floods), human processes (movement and interaction of people and or places; example, new shopping center and its effects on street congestions), and decision-making process (choosing the alternative and weighting the priorities). Whereas simplification may have been the initial goal for building a model, without sound research methodology the whole process of knowledge formation through maps can be highly complex and dangerously misleading.

The fact that millions of points on Earth have to be accurately projected on computer screen is a phenomenal task. It not only requires *smart* software to engineer the geographical language but also plenty of hardware (especially for data storage and processing of data) to display it on a screen.

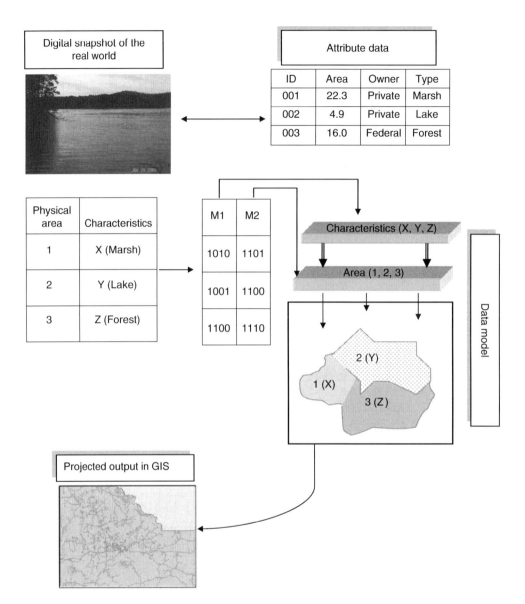

FIGURE 41.1 Transformation of real world into GIS model.

Therefore, to minimize errors in identifying the problem, just as an economist or biologist might want to control for variables that are unrelated or unknown to the model (problem), a GIS user will control for objects or geographical phenomenon that fits best to explain the phenomenon. Figure 41.1 shows a schematic diagram of how the real world may be transformed in GIS to produce a digitized model. The complexity (or noises) of the real world has been simplified (through digital transformation of binary codes) with lines and polygons (shapes) to show the relevant attributes (lake, marshes, forests, etc.) that would be used to explain the model.

The art of handling the model is a large part of what GIS might be able to do. Figure 41.2 is a Choropleth* map of a neighborhood of central Birmingham, Alabama by block groups with

---

* Choropleth map is a thematic map that displays a quantitative attribute using ordinal classes. A grades series of shades is used to indicate increasing values of the variable.

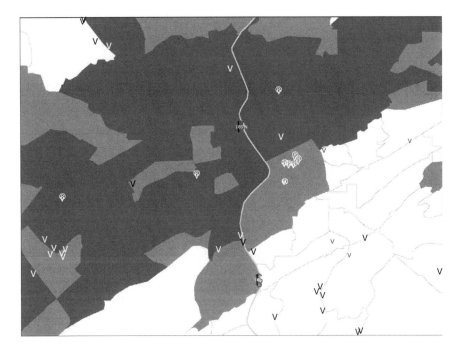

FIGURE 41.2 Black population distribution by block groups, Birmingham, AL (Data: U.S. Bureau of Census, 2000).

concentration of Black population shaded from lighter (white) to darker grey (less than 8 percent; 9–23 percent; and 24 percent and higher respectively). Hospitals and shopping areas have been overlaid on top of the Black population (by block groups) layer. The map highlight that the majority of the hospitals and shopping areas are outside the Black populated areas and with the exception of two, all hospitals in the map-view are on the right of Interstate 65. Similar socioeconomic profiles and snapshots depicted through maps can be used to generate multiple hypotheses about neighborhoods in the area.

Decision making using maps in general is more of an art* than science.[†] The classic demonstration of map-based decision making is Dr. John Snow's investigation of cholera in Victorian London in 1854 (for details, see http://www.ph.ucla.edu/epi/snow.html). John Snow plotted the locations of incidences of cholera against the location of water pumps, and through the process of elimination found how the center of the epidemic seemed to focus on a certain neighborhood and was most concentrated in the households that clustered around the specific water pump. The field of epidemiology began as John Snow used mapping to identify the contaminated source. A map of just the water pumps or incidences of cholera alone would have been of little value. Following the water pump network and incidence revealed the contaminated source. Ecological linkage approach to solving social problems is of tremendous value to social scientists who utilize GIS for socioeconomic data analysis. According to Tobler's *First Law of Geography* (1976) all things are related but nearby things are more related than distant things. This phenomenon is common to many of the problems and issues that can be adequately answered with the help of GIS. However, there is danger in perceiving GIS as a technique that can solve problems (even if the problems are common to us).

---

* The art is described here as a nonrational approach—a skill that comes from the experience of working with the data in context. The *artist* takes advantage of this skill to make decisions from visual inspection by naked eye. After all, it is generally accepted that the human information processing system has strong insight to visualization and an exceptional ability to recognize structure and relationships.

[†] The scientific skill can be described as knowing the technique (set of rational options) of arriving at a decision.

Because data is not generally uniform across one jurisdiction (for example, median income in a census tract does not mean each individual in the tract has that income), ecological fallacy (data for the aggregate is applied to individuals) is a common problem when using GIS. Models in GIS need additional care than other types of data models that do not address the spatial reference.*

The prescribed method of research using GIS can be described in two steps. The first step involves asking the right question about the location and setting up the agenda. Consistent with Simon's (1979) view of three stages of decision making, namely, (i) gathering intelligence on decision criteria, (ii) designing options to choose from, and (iii) the choice; decision makers can utilize GIS maps to (a) formulate the question or problem, (b) explore and evaluate alternative plan of action (for solving the problem), and (c) evaluate a reduced set of competing alternatives. After formalizing the research model (agenda) the second step relates to cartography—the study and practice of creating maps as an accurate representation of real life phenomenon. A brief explanation of the two steps follows

41.4   GIS RESEARCH: STEP 1—MODEL BUILDING

Perhaps what matters most in using GIS as a research tool is to ask the question "where" prior to asking the question "why." Location must be a determinant factor in GIS decision making. If we are trying to fight crime, GIS should be used to find where the crime occurred (incidence) before we can delve into the idea of why such a crime took place. This is because GIS should first direct us where to look for the problem. The question of why comes after we have found where we might expect to find the most plausible answer to the question. Decision making using GIS involves asking the basic question about the "where" factor, i.e., the location—Where is the best site for the industrial park given criteria set by the stakeholders? Where one might expect the prevalence of a particular type of disease? Where is the highest concentration of voters or nonvoters? Where is the high growth area (related to traffic congestion etc)? Where are the high property values (or people with high income) located? Clearly GIS finds its most use in models where location plays a primary role. A community that is seeking to improve the quality of life for their community should prepare to ask the right questions relevant to quality of life:

* Where have the crimes occurred in the past five years?
* Which houses have been sold in the last five years?
* What parts of the streets or sidewalks need maintenance?
* What is age distribution of the neighborhood population?
* What is the income distribution of the neighborhood population?
* Identify parks and recreation facilities in the neighborhood.
* Identify distance to emergency services (Fire, police, hospitals, etc.) and lead time for arrival.
* Individual property values.
* Traffic (number of cars within a specific time period) along the main arteries of the neighborhood.

The relative quality of life of the neighborhood can be presented using the above information. The characteristics of the neighborhood depicted through the maps can adequately describe the quality of health for the neighborhood and identify problem areas that need to be addressed. Through the use of GIS, the common medium of map could be used as a tool to help experts from different backgrounds exchange ideas and compare possible solutions. Because GIS allows diverse viewpoints to be presented through a common platform (maps), it has received wide appeal as a

---

* This issue has been addressed in the later part of this chapter.

participatory tool in problem solving and hypothesis generation (Carver et al., 1997; Craig et al., 2002). As GIS scholars, Longley et al. (2005) observe, "By building representation [models using GIS], we humans can assemble far more knowledge about the planet than we could as individuals." (p. 61).

The methodology for preparing the research agenda should be followed in stages. The schematic diagram shown in Figure 41.3 describes the five steps in GIS decision-making process.

41.5 STEP 2: CARTOGRAPHY—MAPMAKING

Maps have been used for centuries for navigation purposes. The utility of the tool largely depended on how accurately it represented the real world—the roads, waterways, land-use, and direction.

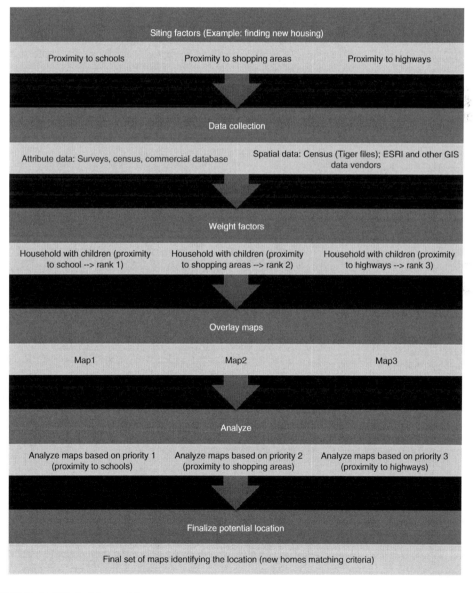

FIGURE 41.3 GIS decision making process.

During times of war it was the primary tool for forming strategies as well as to mislead opponents. Today such uses continue, however, in digital form and through static or real-time simulation. In the digital world, where data manipulation could be virtually infinite, GIS adds a revolutionary idea of mapping for human consumption. Through GIS mapmaking now is relatively a painless endeavor. This allows mass production of wrong maps (see Monmonier, 1996) open to interpretation by novice users. Because of the nature of the problem of GIS today, it is not enough to be satisfied with a knowledgeable and sound research model. It is equally important to have a good understanding of mapmaking.

Visualization (of maps) presupposes a good understanding of how to present the model over a flat computer screen. In most cases how to create maps (technique) supersedes the underlying science behind mapmaking (spatial analysis or spatial logic). For example, maps that show landfills in a neighborhood can be powerfully described with appropriate colors and schemes—a discussion more pertinent in cartography. However to look for answers to questions like proximity of houses from landfills, would require more than the technique but some basic understanding of the science of GIS. Digital maps have to be projected to the correct coordinate system and the spatial attributes clearly delineated to reflect the correct measurement from the landfills. In other words, just like a social scientist who needs to hypothesize a model prior to his or her analysis (studying relationship using raw data), a GIS specialist needs to develop a geographic model, in addition to the research model, to make the correct assessment of the real-world phenomenon.

In general, geographic model building is the primary task for two types of GIS users: (1) cartographers and (2) geographic information analysts. The field of cartography is devoted to the theory of mapping, a process by which maps are created using spatial data. Cartography primarily deals with drawings and graphics and aims to improve the visualization of maps so that they can easily be communicated. It requires a certain amount of artistic skill as well as intuition so that maps can be presented in ways that are appealing and easy-to-understand, and at the same time, ensuring the integrity of the maps (as accurate and best reflection of the real-world phenomenon). Most cartographic models are temporally static, because they represent spatial features at a fixed point or points of time. Geographic information analysis on the other hand, can be described as a study of maps that is devoted to spatial analysis under a GIS environment. Its primary focus is the transformation of real life space into a GIS environment and understanding relationships between spaces (spatial analysis). The idea behind the science is to deal with the continuous variable (space) and finding the best means (through statistical probability) to describe temporal or discrete relationships through GIS. Concepts such as spatial autocorrelation, modifiable areal units, ecological fallacy, distance, and adjacency, etc., are the focus of discussion among geographic information analysis (see O'Sullivan and Unwin, 2002) which is beyond the scope of our discussion in this chapter. We will limit our discussion to mainly cartography and visualization.

41.6 VISUALIZATION

Relationship between maps and GIS is that of a tool and the product. GIS is the tool that produces maps. Although GIS is the tool that aides map creation through manipulation of spatial data, maps are final products for visualization of spatial data. With digital cartography visualization has taken another meaning. With new software and hardware connected to GIS, better visualization tools are being developed for understanding, analyzing, and exploring spatial data (maps). The functionality of GIS now extends beyond mapping to scientific visualization techniques or cartographic visualization (MacEachren, 1994).

Because visualization becomes a reality after the map is made, we must ensure beforehand what the map will be used for. Visualization can be strategically used to fulfill three independent purposes (MacEachren, 1994): (1) to present spatial information, answering "what is?" or "where is?" type questions. The cartographic discipline offers design rules to answer such questions; (2) to analyze and manipulate known data to reveal spatial relationships. Questions like "what is the best site?"

or "what is the fastest route?" can be answered; (3) finally, visualization can be used for exploratory purposes to find what may not be known. One might consider combining satellite images or remote sensing data to raw data in answering questions like, "what is the nature of the data set as far as other data sets that are available?" "Which data set is likely to be most promising in finding the solution to the problem (like, finding ancient cities underground or finding oil, or soil erosion, etc.)?"

Data can be organized in three different ways: by time (or temporal), by themes (or thematic), and by location (or spatial). GIS uses the space as the common denominator to describe data. It is the key ingredient to mapmaking. Therefore, it must be treated as an endogenous variable within the mapping scheme.* To describe a theme like crime for example, GIS uses location of the crime as common denominator to identify crime hot spots and the temporal dimension of the crime. Although all dimensions of the data are critical to the explanation of the problem, GIS builds on the spatial dimension to transform data into information (maps). With the development of GIS spatial data handling have been significant in recent years. GIS has introduced integration of the spatial data from different kinds of sources including aerial photographs, remote sensing, and paper maps.

To implement better visualization of maps, researchers have introduced ways in which maps can be presented and interpreted. According to Robinson et al. (1995) to create maps we must pay attention to the following issues:

1. Establish the purpose of the maps: The purpose of the map is directly related to who will be using the maps. An engineer looking at the highways will look for a different set of maps than a traveler who is interested in finding places.
2. Defining scale: Define the scale at which the map is to be produced. In simple terms how small will be the size of the real world on the computer screen. According to Martin (1996) a scale can be defined as the ration of a distance on the map to the corresponding distance on the ground. For example, if the scale is expressed as a ratio 1:550,000 a 1 cm line on the map represents 550,000 cm in the real world.
3. Selection of features: Select the features (buildings, rivers, boundaries, populations) from the real world which must be depicted on the map. Whether to show a building with a point or a polygon (shape) depends on the scale and scope of the map. Similarly a city can be shown with a point or a polygon depending on whether the map will be used at national or regional scales.
4. Limit details: Generalization of features helps conceptualize a map better than having greater details presented on a single map. Which features will be generalized depends on the focus of the map or what should be eye-catching at first sight. A map showing crimes in a neighborhood may not need the level of detail about type of houses (with distinct colors) than a generic point of location of the houses.
5. Projection of the maps: For the GIS user to project the spherical world (three dimension) on a flat screen (two dimension), they must approximate the true shape of the Earth. There are different types of projections that can be used. All of them will have errors (distortions from the real world) due to transformation from three dimensions to two-dimensional flat screen or paper map but can achieve the desired results depending on the goal of the map.
6. Geographic coordinates: Just as the three-dimensional globe has to be projected on a two-dimension flat map, features on Earth's surface also need to be located on the flat surface. This is known as spatial referencing. In general, geographic coordinate or latitude and longitude (x, y) are the most widely used geo-referencing method.
7. Labels and legends: A map is better than thousand words—the map must tell the story through appropriate labeling, legends, and texts. The description per se depends on the

---

* The difference between spatial and nonspatial data is like knowing the characteristics of the house but not knowing where it is located. Without the knowledge of space (house number or latitude and longitude) the data in question cannot be used with GIS. For example without knowing the house number or nearby location, the house cannot be mapped.

attribute data—the nonspatial data associated with points, line, and polygons. For example, the attribute data of crime hot spots, in addition to location of the crime, can include the type and time of the crime. The neighborhood houses can be categorized by value of the houses, family size, age group, income, etc.

Step 1 (model building) and Step 2 (mapmaking) both require certain set of skills that are independent of each other. Although mapmaking skills can be acquired through training and experience, model building may require more than training the knowledge of the discipline (theory) upon which the model will be based. Ideally to conduct research with GIS one must expect researchers to have both the skills. Although this is a difficult challenge, the situation is similar to statistical applications few decades ago. As GIS becomes an integral part of Research Method curriculum in policy science such combined skill will become commonplace as well as desirable among our future generation of graduate students.

41.6.1 USE OF SOCIOECONOMIC DATA IN GIS

One of the primary uses of GIS among social scientists is mapping socioeconomic characteristics of the population. Population data is most commonly related to geographical locations by reference to areal geographies such as census zones, electoral districts, political jurisdictions, or regular grid squares. Generally, these are the only areal units from which individual population data is collected (through census, surveys, or sample of population) and aggregated to provide summary values for individual areal units. One of the essential limitations of areal units is that they are imposed rather than natural. Natural areas such as that of woodland on a land-use map or the surface outcrop of a particular geological formation (cornfield, ricefield) describe the actual characteristics of the areal unit. On the other hand, artificial areal units or zones such as congressional districts, census tracts, and other political boundaries are made for convenience and therefore deemed imposed (and arbitrary). Any configuration of the imposed boundaries (zones) will result in different aggregation of the individual data. Therefore, each time artificial boundaries are reconfigured it will result in different distribution of characteristics of the newly configured zones, even though there has been no change in underlying population. This problem in geography is known as the modifiable areal unit problem (MAUP). The MAUP had been most prominent in the analysis of socioeconomic and epidemiological data (see Unwin, 1981; Openshaw and Alvandies, 1999; Nakaya, 2000). For example, it is not possible to measure the percent of high school graduates at a single point; this percentage must be calculated within a defined area.* It is the selection of these artificial boundaries and their use in analysis that produces the MAUP. According to Martin (1999) "Most artificial boundaries are designed to cover the entire land surface and therefore include extensive areas of unpopulated land, leading to wide variation in population density between areas." (p. 73).

The apparent simplicity of maps as visual description of data should not blind us to its many obvious and not obvious deficiencies including ecological fallacy (Openshaw, 1984) that is associated with MAUP. Ecological fallacy occurs when data for a given area under study is applied to the individuals within those areas. Income for a census tract is an aggregate for all income reported by individual households living within the census tract zone. Dividing the total income in the tract by total population will give the average income that one might expect in the tract. It is an ecological fallacy to assume that all the individuals within the census tract have that level of income because the average income is derived from a range of incomes. Figure 41.4 compares percent occupied housing unit data (number of occupied housing units by households) for two maps of two separate zones, census tracts, and block groups, with same classification and shades for each category of classes. It shows what is classified by tracts (less than 43 percent or 44–73 percent or 74 percent and higher occupied housing units) may not be the right classification for block groups. Some of the areas by tracts that show less than 43 percent occupied housing units within the central city area

---

* Note that satellite images and aerial photographs do not have such limitations because it will capture the exact number of people and objects as seen from Earth.

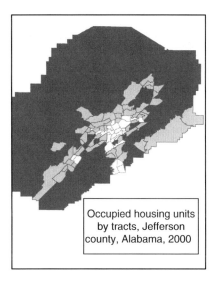
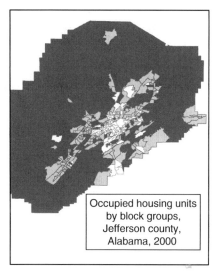

Data source: ESRI data and
maps for ArcGIS 9.2.
Redlands, California: ESRI, 2006.

FIGURE 41.4 Occupied housing units by tracts showing MAUP, Jefferson County, AL (Data: U.S. bureau of census, 2000).

(middle of the county) actually show 44–73 percent or higher in block groups. The reverse is also true for some of the areas.

One way to overcome the problem is to avoid comparisons using different types of areal units (use all tracts or all block groups). However, if possible it is always better to use smaller areal units (block groups instead of tracts or addresses instead of blocks, etc.) for analysis. This may not be possible for most of the socioeconomic data that is available under the public domain. Despite some of the limitations of data related to MAUP, a careful observer should always be cognizant of the limitations of area-based data and appropriately design the model to utilize GIS for sound decisions. Analyzing spatial distribution can be a tricky problem; some useful visual comparison tools are explained below.

41.6.2 LOCATION QUOTIENT

Visual comparison of maps is a complicated task particularly in the absence of a viable measuring tool. The inferred association between two maps (or location) is more likely due to the visual appeal and due to the technique of mapping than the realities of underlying geography. It is important that likes should be compared with the likes and the class interval and the number used are the same. The result is often subjective. Today objectivity demands numerical values for comparison. Numerical comparison of maps (to measure the strength of association) is receiving wide attention in GIS. Spatial analysis literature identifies the comparison of an observed pattern to a theoretically derived pattern to assess how closely the observed pattern fits to reality. Known as the coefficient of areal correspondence (Ca) such measures are ratios of the areas covered by two or more phenomena over total area covered by the phenomena (Unwin, 1981). The range of Ca is between 0 and 1. If the distributions of the phenomenon are independent of each other the Ca value is 0, while exactly coincident ones give a value of 1.

Location quotient (LQ) is a similar concept as coefficient of areal correspondence. However, rather than measuring the actual area covering the phenomenon LQs measure the activity covering an area.

They are ratios that compare concentration of a resource or activity (such as employment, income, mortality, etc.) in a defined area to that of a larger aggregate area or standard. It has received wide appeal among economic development practitioners interested in identifying concentrations of industrial or economic activity in one location relative to the larger (standard) base. For example the LQ of an activity or event, say mortality i, in a county for a particular year can be expressed as

$$LQ_i = (C_i/C_t)/(S_i/S_t)$$

where

    LQ_i = Location quotient (of mortality) in county i
    C_i = Number of deaths in county i
    C_t = Total population in county i
    S_i = Number of deaths in state i
    S_t = Total population in state i

The range for LQ is between 0 and 1. LQ = 1 would signify the location (county) has the same percentage (or proportion) of the activity as the Standard Base (rest of the state). If LQ < 1 then the location has less than proportionate share of the activity, whereas LQ > 1 implies a greater proportionate concentration of that activity. Figure 41.5 shows LQ for mortality by county in

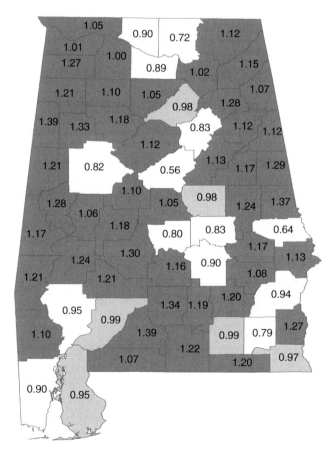

FIGURE 41.5 Location quotient (LQ) of mortality for Alabama by County (Data: ESRI data and maps for ArcGIS 9.2, Redland, CA, ESRI 2006).

Alabama in 1990. Although majority of the counties have LQ > 1 (higher concentration of deaths than rest of counties in the state), some counties had disproportionately higher or lower concentration of mortality.

The LQ ratios can also be modified to calculate residual activity (number of births minus number of deaths) over residual activity in the base area. The LQ range in this case would be between −1 and +1 with perfect negative LQ would signify perfect dissimilarity (concentration below the normal in the area) than average in the standard base. On the other hand +1 will indicate greater than average concentration of the activity.

41.7 COMMUNITY DISTRESS INDEX

The community distress index (CDI) is a method of identifying the socioeconomic condition of a geographical area using a combination of socioeconomic distress indicators of the given population living in that area (Haque and Telfair, 2000; Telfair et al., 2003). Developing one single index from several different distress indicators gives a comprehensive profile of the socioeconomic condition of the area that may be used for comparison across areas of interest. Haque and Telfair (2000) identified clients with sickle-cell disease in North Carolina and geo-coded* the locations where the clients lived. Census data was collected for these locations by tracts and then interpolated to zip codes. To identify the poor socioeconomic condition of an area, an index was developed for each zip code where clients lived. A CDI was developed with the following variables: (1) percent Black population below poverty, (2) percent Black not beyond 12th grade education, (3) percent Black not in labor force, (4) percent Black unemployed, and (5) Black per-capita income.[†] Each census variable was classified into groups representing low, medium, or high distress conditions (such as low, medium, and high poverty zip codes; and similar categories for other variables by zip code) (see Table 41.2).

By summing up the five socioeconomic indices, the CDI was calculated. A higher CDI score in this case would signify worse socioeconomic condition of an area. Similar indices can be produced using a combination of socioeconomic indicators that show positive attributes (glass half full) of a community. The Index of Economic Health (Glasmeier and Kurt, 1999) produced for the Appalachian Regional Commission measures spatial and temporal patterns of distressed status as a composite of income, unemployment, share of transfer payments to total income, and labor force participation rates.

41.7.1 CLUSTER ANALYSIS—MORAN'S I

Moran's I is a weighted correlation coefficient used to detect departures from spatial randomness. In other words, given a set of features and an associated attribute, it evaluates whether the pattern expressed is clustered, dispersed, or random. By plotting the Z score (measures of standard deviation) the tool calculates the Moran's I Index value and a Z score evaluating the significance of the index value. In general, a Moran's Index value near +1.0 indicates clustering (positive spatial autocorrelation), whereas an index value near −1.0 indicates dispersion (negative spatial autocorrelation). It is a weighted product–moment correlation coefficient, where the weights reflect geographic proximity. The high–high and low–low locations (positive local spatial autocorrelation) are typically referred to as spatial clusters, whereas the high–low and low–high locations (negative local spatial autocorrelation) are termed spatial outliers.

Assuming the null hypothesis of no clustering the Z score should be between −1.96 and +1.96 standard deviations for 95 percent confidence level. However, if the Z score falls outside the

---

* A process by which GIS is used to match the location of an attribute (home or business address) to a map.
[†] As SCD predominantly occur in Black population, Black population data has been used to develop the community distress index.

TABLE 41.2
Community Distress Index

Variables	Definition	Code
Income	Black per-capita income	Very low = Less than \$4,000 (= 4) Low = \$4,001–\$7,300 (= 3) Medium = \$7,301–\$11,999 (= 2) High = \$12,000 and above (= 1)
Education	Percentage Black not beyond high school education	High = 34 percent and above (= 3) Medium = 26–33 percent (= 2) Low = 0–25 percent (= 1)
Poverty	Percentage Black below poverty	High = 31 percent and above (= 4) Medium = 21–30 percent (= 3) Low = 11–20 percent (= 2) Very low = 10 percent and less (= 1)
Unemployment	Percentage Black unemployed	High = 8 percent and above (= 3) Medium = 4–7 percent (= 2) Low = 0–3 percent (= 1)
Not in labor force	Percentage Black not in labor force	High = 32 percent and above (= 4) Medium = 21–31 percent (= 3) Low = 11–20 percent (= 2) Very low = 0–10 percent (= 1)
Community index = sum (1 through 5)	Higher the index would mean worse socioeconomic condition as explained by the five variables (Range = 0–18)	High distress = 14 and above Medium distress = 9–13 Low distress = 0–8

95 percent confidence range (for example −2.5 or +5.4), we can reject the null to confirm that the exhibited clustering is too unusual to be due to random chance. Using ArcGIS ArcTool's Anselin Moran's I spatial statistics (ArcGIS, 2006) a test for spatial autocorrelation in mortality is shown in Figure 41.6.

The map shows identifiable clusters of mortality in Alabama in 1999. Although the clustering is not statistically significant, from the distribution of Z score it appears clustering of mortality rates in rural parts of Alabama, particularly in the Black-belt area (southwest shaded darker grey) where mortality is high. Additional data tests can be conducted to find the significance of this clustering.

41.8 IMPLICATION OF GIS-BASED RESEARCH

Sound research methodology is fundamental to understanding the socioeconomic problems of today. By portraying real-world data as maps, GIS provide unparalleled power to analyze social, economic, and political circumstances. The use of GIS in political reapportionment and redistricting provides powerful evidence of its value as the most efficient tool for that purpose. Indeed GIS promises abound; so are the challenges. The subsequent abuse of this tool reminds us of the dangers and responsibilities of using GIS in a representative democracy (see Pickles, 1995; Monmonier, 2001; Haque, 2003). Particularly, because of government's ability to have access to critical geo-referenced data that is not available in the public domain, in the absence technocrats* with responsible values dealing with diversity and individual freedom, GIS could necessarily be used to manipulate policy directions or to meet purposeful ends of government and individuals. In addition,

---

* GIS users in government and business who deal with private data.

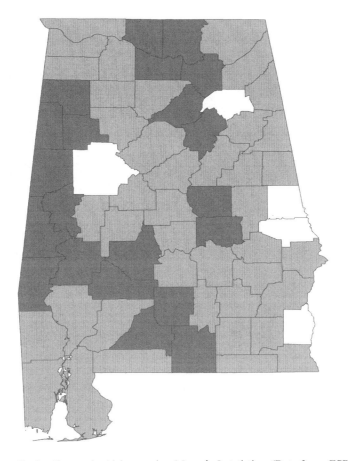

FIGURE 41.6 Mortality by County in Alabana using Moran's I statistics. (Data from: ESRI Data and Maps for ArcGIS 9.2, ESRI, Redlands, CA, 2006.)

as consumers demand more from data, private vendors will scramble to supply them, raising serious concerns about violation of civil liberties and citizen's rights to privacy, including data integrity (see Haque, 2001; Monmonier, 2002). In a more positive side however, as GIS becomes a commonplace in the academia, citizens will become more aware of the known abuses of GIS and subsequently make GIS users more responsible. Moreover as GIS is rapidly growing over the internet sphere, making it accessible to general public, such concerns should fade.

41.9 CONCLUSION

A large part of GIS today is not about making maps but interpreting them. This is where GIS analyst needs the most attention. In recent years the Center for Spatially Integrated Social Science (http://www.csiss.org/clearinghouse/) has taken a leap in advancing the understanding of spatial reasoning and ways it could be used with socioeconomic data. Spatial analysis software such as GeoDa is available free over the internet. In addition large-scale remote sensing data along with high resolution satellite images over the internet has opened a new community of GIS enthusiasts.* Public participation geographic information systems (PPGIS) use GIS as an empowering tool by

---

* Popularity of Google Earth over the internet has made GIS and GPS (Global Positioning System) tools an acceptable communication tool for the global community.

connecting space to people via online and offline GIS users around the world. It may not be far from now when the global GIS communities can realistically participate in critical decisions in housing, zoning, health, racism, environmental equity, and sustainable developmental projects (See, Craig et al., 2005). PPGIS opens avenues for marginalized communities to take control of the decision-making process before the technical details are finalized. Just as GIS promises to bring our global socioeconomic issues to our desktop, it also challenges us to move away from the "reality" of the real-world to the abstract two-dimensional domain. The limitation of transforming the real world to a flat screen is reasonably obvious, yet powerful substitute for making qualitatively better decisions that affect our larger societies in the twenty-first century.

REFERENCES

ArcGIS, 2006. *Arcgis Version 9.2* [computer software], Redland, California: ESRI.

Berry, J.K. 1993. *Beyond Mapping: Concepts, Algorithms, and Issues in GIS*. Fort Collins, Colorado: GIS World Books.

Carver, S., Blacke, M., Turton, I., and Duke-Williams, O. 1997. Open spatial decision-making; evaluating the potential of the World Wide Web. In: Kemp, Z. (Ed.) *Innovations in GIS 4*. London: Taylor & Francis, pp. 267–278.

Craig, W., Harris, T.M., and Weiner, D. (Eds.). 2005. *Community Participation and Geographic Information Systems*. New York: Taylor & Francis.

Getting Started with GIS. (n.d.) Who uses GIS and why. Retrieved from http://www.gis.rgs.org/10.html on August 9, 2005.

Glasmeier, A.K. and Kurt, G.F. 1999. *Building on past experiences: Creating a new future for distressed counties. Appalachian regional commission report*, Institute for Policy Research and Evaluation, Pennsylvania State University. (Accessed online, January, 2007: http://www.arc.gov/index.do?nodeId = 1374).

Haque, A. 2001. GIS, public service and the issue of democratic governance. *Public Administration Review*, 61(3): 259–265.

Haque, A. 2003. Information technology, GIS, and democratic values: Ethical implications for IT professionals in public service. *Journal of Ethics and Technology*, 5: 39–48.

Haque, A. and Telfair, J. 2000. Socioeconomic distress and health status: The urban–rural dichotomy of services utilization for people with sickle cell disorder in North Carolina. *Journal of Rural Health*, 16 (1): 43–55.

http://www.ph.ucla.edu/epi/snow.html (n.d.). John Snow: A historical giant in epidemiology. Accessed, July 2006.

Longley, P., Goodchild, M., Maguire, D., and Rhind, D. (Eds.). 2005. *Geographic Information Systems and Science* (2nd ed.). New York: John Wiley & Sons.

MacEachren, A.M. 1994. Visualization in modern Cartography: Setting the agenda. In MacEachren, A.M. and Taylor, D.R.F. (Eds.), *Visualization In Modern Cartography*. Oxford: Pergamon Press, pp. 1–12.

Martin, D.J. 1996. *Geographical Information Systems and Their Socioeconomic Applications* (2nd ed.). London: Routledge.

Martin, D.J. 1999. Spatial representation: The social scientist perspective. In Longley, P., Goodchild, M., Maguire, D., and Rhind, D. (Eds.), *Geographic Information Systems: Principles and Technical Issues*. Vol. 1, 2nd ed. New York: John Wiley & Sons Inc, pp. 71–80.

Monmonier, M. 1996. *How to Lie with Maps* (2nd ed.). Chicago, Illinois: University of Chicago Press.

Monmonier, M. 2001. *Bushmanders and Bullwinkles: How Politicians Manipulate Electronic Maps and Census Data to Win Elections*. Chicago, Illinois: University of Chicago Press.

Monmonier, M. 2002. *Spying with Maps: Surveillance Technologies and the Future of Privacy*. Chicago, Illinois: University of Chicago Press.

Nakaya, T. 2000. An information statistical approach to the modifiable areal unit problem in incidence rate maps. *Environment and Planning*, 32 (1): 91–109.

Openshaw, S. 1984. *The Modifiable Areal Unity Problem. Concepts and Techniques in Modern Geography*. Vol. 38. Norwich, United Kingdom: GeoBooks.

Openshaw, S. and Alvandies, S. 1999. Applying geocomputation to the analysis of spatial distributions. In Longley, P., Goodchild, M., Maguire, D., and Rhind, D. (Eds.), *Geographic Information Systems: Principles and Technical Issues*. Vol. 1, 2nd ed. New York: John Wiley & Sons Inc, pp. 267–282.

O'Sullivan, D. and Unwin, D. 2002. *Geographic Information Analysis*. New Jersey: John Wiley & Sons Inc.

Pickles, M. 1995. *Ground Truth: The Social Implications of Geographic Information Systems*. New York: Guilford Press.

Robinson, A.H., Morrison, J.L., Muehrecke, P.C., Kimerling, A.J., Guptill, S.C. 1995. *Elements of Cartography* (6th ed.). New York: Wiley.

Simon, H. 1979. Rational decision making in business. *American Economic Review*, 69: 493–513.

Telfair, J., Haque, A., Etienne, M., Tang, S., and Strasser, S. 2003. Urban and rural differences of access to and utilization of services among persons with sickle cell disease in Alabama. *Public Health Registry*, 118 (1): 27–37.

Tobler, W.R. 1976. Spatial interaction patterns. *Journal of Environmental Systems*, 6: 271–301.

Unwin, D. 1981. *Introductory Spatial Analysis*. New York: Methuen & Co.

Part VIII

Reporting, Presentation, and Teaching

42 Presenting Quantitative Research Results

Jane E. Miller

CONTENTS

42.1 INTRODUCTION

42.1.1 Overview of Writing about Quantitative Research Results

Writing about statistical analyses is a common task for public administrators and other types of quantitative analysts. Results of such analyses inform decisions of government and nonprofit agencies every day, included in documents such as research papers, grant proposals, policy briefs, consultant's reports, and oral presentations. Despite this apparently widespread need, few people are formally trained to write about numbers. Communications specialists learn to write for varied audiences, but rarely are taught to deal with statistical analyses. Quantitative researchers learn to calculate statistics and interpret the findings, but rarely are taught to describe them in ways that are comprehensible to readers with different levels of quantitative expertise or interest.

In this chapter, I show how to apply expository writing techniques and principles for quantitative writing, illustrated with examples based on topics related to public administration. Using these examples, I demonstrate how to tell a clear story with numbers as evidence, introducing the question, describing individual facts in context, and finally relating the entire body of evidence back to the original question. I demonstrate several basic principles for describing numeric patterns: choosing the right tools to present numeric information; creating self-contained tables and charts; reporting and interpreting numbers; writing about statistical significance; specifying direction and magnitude of an association; and summarizing patterns. I illustrate these principles with examples of "poor," "better," and "best" descriptions—samples of ineffective writing annotated to point out weaknesses, followed by concrete examples and explanations of improved presentation. Using these guidelines, writers can learn to present a coherent quantitative inquiry, with numbers playing a fundamental but unobtrusive role.

42.1.2 AUDIENCE CONSIDERATIONS

Results of quantitative analyses are of interest to a spectrum of audiences, including

- Legislators, members of nonprofit organizations, the general public, and other "applied audiences" who may have little statistical training but want to understand and apply results of statistical analyses about issues that matter to them
- Readers of a professional journal, who often vary substantially in their familiarity with statistics
- Reviewers for a grant proposal or article, some of whom are experts on your topic but not the methods, others of whom are experts in advanced statistical methods but not your topic

Clearly, these audiences require very different approaches to writing about statistics. When writing for statistically trained readers, explain not only the methods and findings but also how those methods fit your question and how the findings add to the body of knowledge on the topic. Avoid common pitfalls such as over-reliance on equations and jargon, tables full of acronyms from computerized databases, or writing about statistics in generalities without helping readers see how those statistics fit your specific topic and data.

When writing for an applied audience, give greater prominence to the research question, reduce the emphasis on technical details of data and methods, and translate your results to show how they apply to real-world issues of interest to that audience. Rephrase statistical terminology to focus on the underlying ideas, show how the concepts apply to your particular topic, and resist the urge to include equations or Greek symbols. For readers who are interested in the technical details, provide a citation to the scientific papers or reports on your analysis. Simplify tables and charts, replacing standard errors or test statistics with p-values, symbols, or color to denote statistically significant findings. See Nelson et al. (2002) and Miller (2005) for guidelines on how to adapt your writing to suit nonstatistical audiences, including formats such as issue briefs and chartbooks.

42.2 NUMBERS AS EVIDENCE

Writing about a statistical analysis is similar to writing a legal argument. In the opening statement, a lawyer raises the major questions to be addressed during the trial and gives a general introduction to the characters and events in question. To build a compelling case, he then presents specific facts collected and analyzed using standard methods of inquiry. If innovative or unusual methods were used, he introduces experts to describe and justify those techniques. He presents individual facts, and then ties them to other evidence to demonstrate patterns or themes. He may submit exhibits such as diagrams or physical evidence to supplement or clarify the facts. He cites previous cases that have established precedents and standards in the field and discusses how they do or do not apply to the current case. Finally, in the closing argument he summarizes conclusions based on the complete body of evidence, restating the critical points but with far less detail than in the evidence portion of the trial.

Follow the same general structure as you write your quantitative story line for a research paper, grant proposal, or presentation. The introduction to a research paper parallels the opening argument of a trial; the data and methods and results sections mirror the evidence portion of the trial; and the discussion and conclusions of the paper parallel a lawyer's closing argument. Open your paper by introducing the overarching questions before describing the detailed statistical findings, just as a lawyer outlines the big picture before introducing specific testimony or other evidence to the jury. In the methods section, describe and justify your methods of data collection and analysis. In the results section, systematically introduce and explain the numeric evidence in your exhibits—tables, charts, maps, or other diagrams—building a logical sequence of analyses. Close the paper by summarizing your findings and connecting them back to the initial questions and previous studies of related topics.

42.2.1 WRITING THE INTRODUCTION

As you write about quantitative research results, apply standard expository writing techniques for organizing that material. In the introduction, ask the question in plain English, mentioning the broad questions you seek to answer with the numbers that follow. If a lawyer starts talking about a specific fingerprint or piece of DNA without having first outlined the basic facts of the crime and its context, a jury will have a hard time understanding where that evidence fits in the overall case. Consider an introduction to an analysis of the effects of a residential mobility experiment:

Poor: (No introductory sentence.) "In 1994–1995, movers scored 0.26 on a measure of danger in their neighborhood." *This version jumps directly to presenting data without orienting the audience to the topic and objectives, so it will be difficult for them to see what those numbers mean.*

Better: "How do movers versus stayers compare in Yonkers in 1994–1995?" *This version uses a rhetorical question to introduce the context (where and when), and the groups to be compared. However, it does not specify the outcomes to be considered or explain that the analysis is of an experimental study.*

Best: "This analysis investigates the effects of the Moving to Opportunity (MTO) residential mobility experiment, comparing a range of neighborhood and housing quality measures for low-income adults in public housing who moved to low-poverty neighborhoods to those who stayed in their original, high-poverty neighborhoods (Table 42.1). 'Movers' were chosen by lottery from among those who applied for the program in the Yonkers, New York area in the mid-1990s." *This version sets the context, mentions the outcomes (neighborhood and housing quality), and the key explanatory factor (lottery-assigned residential status), and refers to the table where results are shown.*

42.2.2 ORGANIZING THE RESULTS SECTION

In the results section, methodically review the statistical evidence, with separate paragraphs or sections for each major question. Use introductory and transition sentences to keep readers oriented to the logical flow of the analysis and the purpose of the numbers, just as an effective lawyer helps the jury understand where each fact or piece of evidence fits in the overall case. Good introductory and transition sentences are especially important when presenting a series of charts and tables, each of which addresses one part of your analysis. For instance, in their analysis of the residential mobility experiment introduced above, Fauth and colleagues (2004) present bivariate statistics on

TABLE 42.1

Individual Background Characteristics, Neighborhood, and Housing Characteristics of Movers and Stayers, Yonkers Residential Mobility Program, 1994–1995

| | Residential Status | | | |
	Movers ($n=173$)	Stayers ($n=142$)	All ($n=315$)	χ^2 or F^a
Background characteristics				
Age (mean years)	36.69	34.07	35.51	6.45**
Female	97%	96%	97%	0.41
Latino	31%	25%	28%	1.07
At least high school education	67%	53%	61%	6.62**
Female household head	76%	85%	80%	4.39*
Mean number of children in household	1.72	2.01	1.85	6.04*
Neighborhood or housing				
Danger (3 items)	0.26	1.29	0.72	144.11***
Number of victimizations in past year (1 item)	0.12	0.32	0.21	9.21*
Disorder (5 items)	0.15	1.41	0.72	796.17***
Cohesion (4 items)	0.62	0.40	0.52	43.48***
Resources (5 items)	3.05	2.89	2.98	4.90*
Housing problems (5 items)	0.20	0.54	0.35	54.40***

Adapted from Fauth, R.C., Leventhal, T., and Brooks-Gunn, J., *Social Sci. Med.*, 59, 2271, 2004, Table 1.

[a] χ^2 statistic reported for difference in categorical variable between movers and stayers; *F*-statistic for difference in continuous variable.

* $p < .05$;

** $p < .01$;

*** $p < .001$.

demographic characteristics and measures of neighborhood and housing quality outcomes for movers and stayers (Table 42.1) before presenting multivariate models of each of those six outcomes (Table 42.2).

As you move from one topic to another, introduce it before presenting the associated numeric evidence, using paragraphs to organize the material and transition sentences to guide the reader from one major point to another.

Poor: "In the 1994–1995 Yonkers Residential Mobility Program, movers averaged 0.26 on the danger scale, as against 1.29 among stayers ($p < .001$; Table 42.1). (Separate sentences reporting values of the other five neighborhood/housing items for movers and stayers from Table 42.1.) In a multivariate model controlling for age, Latino ethnicity, high school graduate, female-headed households, and number of children in households, movers were -0.99 compared to stayers on the danger scale ($p < .001$; Table 42.2). (Separate sentences reporting coefficients on 'mover' for each of the other outcomes.)" *This description simply lists statistics from each of several tables without explaining how they relate to one another or how the statistics address the initial research question.*

Better: (Transition sentence from a paragraph describing Table 42.1, to a second paragraph describing Table 42.2.) "In bivariate comparisons, each of the six neighborhood and housing outcomes were more favorable among movers than stayers in the 1994–1995 Yonkers Residential Mobility Program (Table 42.1). However, all of the observed differences in background characteristics would be expected to favor better outcomes among movers than stayers regardless of where they live. For example, older age, two-parent households, better education, and smaller families

TABLE 42.2

Results from Ordinary Least Squares Models of Six Neighborhood Characteristics and Housing Quality Measures, Yonkers Residential Mobility Program, 1994–1995

Independent Variable	Dependent Variable					
	Danger	Victimization	Disorder	Cohesion	Resources	Housing Problems
Mover	−0.99***	−0.19**	−1.25***	0.21***	0.13	−0.30***
Age (years)	0.01	0.00	0.00	0.00	0.00	0.00
Latino	0.16	0.00	−0.02	−0.01	0.09	−0.19***
High school graduate	0.06	0.07	0.04	0.02	0.05	−0.06
Female-headed household	−0.27*	−0.01	0.02	−0.03	−0.05	0.07
Number of children in household	0.05	0.07*	0.05*	−0.01	0.00	0.03
R^2	0.34	0.05	0.73	0.14	0.02	0.20

* $p < .05$;
** $p < .01$;
*** $p < .001$.

Source: Adapted from Fauth, R.C., Leventhal, T., and Brooks-Gunn, J., *Social Sci. Med.*, 59, 2271, 2004, Table 3.

are often associated with better resources than younger, female-headed, less-educated, and larger families. Hence multivariate models are needed to control for those characteristics to measure the net effect of moving versus staying." *By starting a new paragraph and section to present evidence from the multivariate model, this version signals a second step in the investigation. The first sentence summarizes the conclusions of the preceding section (on bivariate differences in demographic characteristics of movers and stayers). The next few sentences explain why these findings necessitate multivariate analyses of the effects of the MTO experiment on the neighborhood and housing outcomes. Subheadings such as "Demographic differences between movers and stayers," and "Multivariate analyses of neighborhood and housing outcomes" could be used to provide further guidance through the different parts of the analysis.*

42.2.3 Writing the Conclusion

As in a standard expository writing essay, the conclusion of a quantitative research paper should bring the narrative full circle, summarizing how the evidence answers the major questions posed in the introduction, comparing findings with previous studies, and discussing program, policy, and research implications (Miller, 2004, 2005; Pyrczak and Bruce, 2000). Specific examples are provided later in this chapter, after the section on writing about numeric results.

42.3 FUNDAMENTALS FOR WRITING ABOUT NUMBERS

Having covered the broad organizing principles for writing a well-organized research paper, I now turn to some important details of writing about numbers.

42.3.1 Set the Context

Context is essential for all types of writing. Few stories are told without conveying "who, what, when, and where," or "the W's" as they are known in journalism Without them your audience cannot interpret your numbers and will probably assume that your data describes everyone in the current time and place (e.g., the entire population of the United States in 2006). If you encounter data without the W's attached, either track down the contextual information and report it, or do not use those facts.

To set the context for your statistics, begin with a topic sentence that introduces the characters (variables, in a statistical paper) and the W's, each of which requires only a few words or a short phrase that can be easily incorporated into the sentence with the numbers.

Poor: "Income was $20,120." *From this statement, readers cannot tell the time, place, or subgroup (e.g., age group or region) to whom the income statistic pertains. From the units ($), they might guess it was for the United States, but Canada also uses dollars as their monetary unit.*

Better: "Income in the United States was $20,120 (U.S. Census Bureau, 1999)." *This version conveys the location but not the date or subgroup.*

Best: "In 1998, per capita income in the United States was $20,120 (U.S. Census Bureau, 1999)." *This statement conveys when, where, what, and who in a short, simple, sentence.*

If you are writing a description of numeric patterns that spans several paragraphs, occasionally mention the W's again. For longer descriptions, this will occur naturally as the comparisons you make vary from one paragraph to the next. In a detailed analysis of income patterns, you might compare mean income for different age groups, family structures, and racial groups in the same time and place, mean income in other places or other times, and to the cost of living. Discuss each of these points in separate sentences or paragraphs, with introductory topic phrases or sentences stating the purpose and context of the comparison. Then incorporate the pertinent W's into the introductory sentence or the sentence reporting and comparing the numbers.

42.3.2 SPECIFY UNITS

An important aspect of "what" you are reporting is the units in which it was measured. There are different systems of measurement for virtually everything we quantify—distance (miles or kilometers), weight (pounds or kilograms), volume (gallons or liters), temperature (Fahrenheit or Celsius), and monetary value (e.g., dollars or euros or yen), to name a few. Unit of analysis also varies, from individuals to families to towns, states, or nations, for example. Make a note of the units for any numeric facts you collect from other sources so you can use and interpret them correctly. Then incorporate units of observation and measurement into the sentence with the pertinent numbers.

"In 1998, per capita income in the United States was $20,120 (U.S. Census Bureau, 1999)." *This sentence includes information on units of measurement (dollars), units of observation (per capita means "for each person").*

42.4 CHOOSING TOOLS TO PRESENT NUMBERS

42.4.1 TOOLS TO PRESENT NUMBERS

The main tools for presenting quantitative information—prose, charts, and tables—have different, albeit sometimes overlapping, advantages and disadvantages. Prose is the best choice for introducing topics, describing patterns and explaining how statistics answer the research question. In addition to sentences and paragraphs in the main text, prose can be used in footnotes or appendixes to present and explain a few numbers or a calculation. However, prose is a lousy way to organize a lot of numbers (such as mean values for each of 20 variables) because the numbers get lost among the words needed to report the units and specify the context for each number.

In contrast, tables and charts are excellent ways to organize many numbers. Tables use a grid to present numbers in a predictable way, guided by labels and notes within the table. Likewise, charts use axis labels, legends, and notes to lead the audience through a systematic understanding of the value being presented. Tables are preferred to charts for presenting precise numeric values, such as if your readers will be using your paper as a source of data for their own calculations and comparisons. A chart version is often helpful for portraying the general size and shape of

TABLE 42.3

Percentage of Respondents Who Said Abortion Should be Legal under Specified Circumstances, by Topic and Gender, 2000 U.S. General Social Survey

	Both Genders	Male	Female	p-Value
Health reasons				
Woman's health seriously endangered by the pregnancy	88.2	90.5	86.5	0.08
Woman pregnant as a result of rape	80.8	84.1	78.2	0.03
Strong chance of defect in the baby	79.8	82.7	77.5	0.07
Social reasons or preference				
Married and does not want any more children	44.4	44.4	44.4	0.99
The woman wants it for any reason	43.7	42.8	44.8	0.49
Not married and does not want to marry the man	42.5	42.1	42.8	0.84

Source: ICPSR, *General Social Survey, 1972–2000 Cumulative Codebook.* Available online at http://webapp.icpsr.umich.edu/GSS/. Accessed June 2007.

patterns, making it easy to see whether trend lines are rising or falling, or which values exceed others and by how much (Miller, 2007).

For instance, Table 42.3 and Figure 42.1 present data from an analysis of attitudes about circumstances under which abortion should be legal (ICPSR, 2004), sorted into theoretical groupings and then descending empirical order. Both the table and chart compare the rates of agreement for men and for women across six different circumstances. From the chart, it is clear that rates of agreement are higher for health than social reasons for both genders, and that the direction of the gender difference is reversed for health (men > women) than for social reasons (women > men).

42.4.2 CREATING SELF-CONTAINED TABLES AND CHARTS

Create each of your tables or charts to be self-contained, so that readers can interpret them without reference to the text.

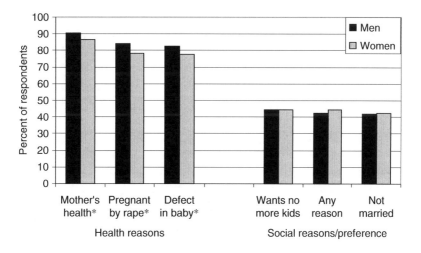

FIGURE 42.1 Agreement and legal abortion under specified circumstances, by gender of respondent and topic, 2000 U.S. General Social Survey. (*Indicates that the difference between men and women is significant at $p < 0.05$.)

- Write a title to reflect the specific contents of that table or chart, conveying how it is different from other tables and charts in the paper. Use the W's as a checklist to ensure that you identify the topic, context, and methods for that table or chart.
- In the row and column labels of a table, or the axis labels and legend of a chart, provide a short, informative phrase to identify each variable, along with its units of measurement or categories.
- Use footnotes to define terms, abbreviations, and symbols, and to identify the data source.

Table 42.4 is a poor version of Table 42.1, annotated with footnotes to point out the many weak aspects of the table's construction and labeling. Table 42.1 is the better version of the same table, allowing readers to interpret every number in the table using only the information therein.

See Miller (2005) for suggestions on structure and labeling of univariate, bivariate, and multivariate tables; see Morgan et al. (2002) for examples of how to create tables to present a variety of types of statistics commonly used in the social sciences.

TABLE 42.4
Descriptive Statistics[a]

| Variables[b, c, d] | Residential Status | | | |
	Movers ($n=173$)	Stayers ($n=142$)	Total ($n=315$)	Sig[e]
Age	36.69	34.07	35.51	6.45**[f]
GENDER[g]	97	96	97	0.41
LATINO	31	25	28	1.07
HSPLUS	67	53	61	6.62**
FEMHHH	76	85	80	4.39*
AVGNKIDS	1.72	2.01	1.85	6.04*
DANGER	0.26	1.29	0.72	144.11***
NUMVICS	0.12	0.32	0.21	9.21*
DISORDER	0.15	1.41	0.72	796.17***
COHSN	0.62	0.40	0.52	43.48***
RSCES	3.05	2.89	2.98	4.90*
HSGQUAL	0.20	0.54	0.35	54.40***

[a] The title is very vague, not specifying the topics or context (W's) of the information in the table.

[b] All variables are lumped together in a single block, without differentiating background (demographic) variables from neighborhood and housing measures (outcomes).

[c] The identities of the variables is obscured by use of acronyms. Readers are not going to use your database, so they do not need to know your acronyms for the variables.

[d] Units of measurement are not specified for any of the variables, making the values difficult to interpret.

[e] The column label fails to identify the type of inferential statistical information, such as whether the numbers are standard errors or test statistics, and if the latter, the name of the test statistic (e.g., F-, t-, or chi-square statistic).

[f] Symbols used to denote levels of statistical significance ("*," "**," and "***") are not explained.

[g] Gender is a categorical variable, but the identity of category shown is unspecified; e.g., is the number reported for "gender" the percentage female or percentage male?

Source: Adapted from Fauth, R.C., Leventhal, T., and Brooks-Gunn, J., *Social Sci. Med.*, 59, 2271, 2004.

42.5   COMPARING TWO OR MORE NUMBERS

Comparing two or more numbers is an extremely common task when writing about quantitative findings, whether contrasting two income statistics in your introduction or conclusions, or describing the relationship between two variables such as income and access to health care in your results section. This section presents four principles to help you write more effectively about such contrasts: (1) reporting and interpreting numbers, (2) conveying results of inferential statistical tests, (3) specifying direction and magnitude of an association, and (4) summarizing patterns involving many numbers. Examples and wording for both bivariate and multivariate analyses are included.

42.5.1   REPORT AND INTERPRET

As you present evidence to test your hypotheses, both report and interpret the numbers. Reporting the numbers you work with is an important first step toward writing effective numeric descriptions. By including the numbers in the text, table or chart, you give your audience the raw materials with which to perform additional calculations or to compare your data with that for other times, places, or groups.

However, if you stop there, you leave it to your readers to figure out how those data answer the question at hand. An isolated number or scientific fact that has not been introduced or explained leaves its explication entirely to your audience. Those who are not familiar with your topic are unlikely to know which comparisons to make or to have the information for those comparisons immediately at hand. Consequently, after reporting the raw data, interpret it. To help readers grasp the meaning of the numbers you report, provide the relevant data and explain the comparisons. Consider an introduction to a report on health care costs in the United States, where you want to illustrate why these expenditures are of concern.

Poor: "In 1998, total expenditures on health care in the United States were estimated to be more than $1.1 trillion (Centers for Medicare and Medicaid Services, 2004)." *From this sentence, it is difficult to assess whether total U.S. expenditures on health care are high or low, stable or changing quickly. To most people, $1.1 trillion sounds like a lot of money, but a key question is "compared to what?" If they knew total national expenditures, they could do a benchmark calculation, but you will make the point more directly if you do that calculation for them.*

Better: "In 1998, total expenditures on health care in the United States were estimated to be more than $1.1 trillion, equivalent to $4,178 for each person (Centers for Medicare and Medicaid Services, 2004)." *This simple translation of total expenditures into a per capita figure takes a large number that is difficult for many people to fathom and converts it into one they can relate to.*

Best: "In the United States, per capita health expenditures averaged $4,108 in the 1990s, equivalent to 13.0 percent of gross domestic product (GDP)—a higher share of GDP than in any other country in the same period. In comparison, Switzerland—the country with the second highest per capita health expenditures—spent approximately $3,835 per person, or 10.4 percent of its GDP. No other country exceeded $3,000 per capita on health expenditures (World Bank, 2001)." *This description reveals that health care expenditures in the United States were the highest of any country and compares it to those in the next highest country.*

Although it is important to interpret quantitative information, it is also essential to report the original data upon which they are based. If you only present a ratio or percentage change, for example, you will have painted an incomplete picture. Suppose a report states that the number of homicides in the United States was 60 percent higher in 1994 than in 1985, but does not report the number of homicides for either year. A 60 percent increase is consistent with many possible combinations: 10 and 16, 1,000 and 1,600, or 100,000 and 160,000 homicides, for example. The first pair of numbers suggests a very low incidence of homicide, the last pair an extremely high rate. Unless the rates themselves are mentioned, you cannot determine whether the nation has nearly eradicated homicide or faces a huge homicide problem. Furthermore, you cannot compare homicide statistics from other times or places.

42.5.2 REPORT STATISTICAL SIGNIFICANCE

Statistical significance is a formal way of assessing whether observed associations are likely to be explained by chance alone. In the absence of disclaimers about lack of statistical significance, readers tend to interpret reported associations as "real" and may use them to explain certain patterns or to generate solutions to problems, especially if the association has been shown to be causal.

Many academic journals specify that you use a table to report statistical test results for all variables, but then limit your text description to only those results that are statistically significant, in most cases using $p < .05$ as the criterion. See examples of how to report statistical significance in the results section under "Specify direction and magnitude" below. Emphasizing statistically significant findings is especially important if you are investigating several different independent variables, such as estimating a multivariate model of how a variety of state-level policy, programmatic, and socioeconomic factors affect take-up in the State Children's Health Insurance Program (SCHIP; see exercises, Table 42.6). If only some traits are statistically significant, focus your discussion on those rather than giving equal prominence to all factors. This approach helps readers answer the main question behind the analysis: which factors can help improve SCHIP take-up the most?

The $p < .05$ rule notwithstanding, a finding that is not statistically significant can be highly salient if that result pertains to the main variable you are investigating. If the lack of statistical significance runs contrary to theory or previously reported results, report the numbers, size of the association, and the lack of statistical significance. In such situations, the lack of a difference between groups answers a key question in the analysis; so highlight it in the concluding section of the work. For more guidelines on writing about statistical significance, see Miller (2005), chapters 3 and 10.

42.5.3 SPECIFY DIRECTION AND MAGNITUDE

Writing about numbers often involves portraying associations between two or more variables. To describe an association, explain both its shape and size rather than simply stating whether the variables are correlated. In other words, which value is higher and how much higher? For instance, which group is older—movers or stayers? How much older? Is a trend rising, falling, or level (direction)? Was the trend steep or shallow (magnitude)?

For ordinal, interval, or ratio variables such as age group or year for which the values have an inherent numeric order, direction of association can also be described in terms of positive (direct) or negative (inverse) associations. For nominal variables such as gender, race, geographic region, or marital status that are classified into categories with no inherent order, describe direction of association by specifying which category has the highest or lowest value and how other categories compare.

Poor: "Household head is negatively associated with residential status ($p < .05$; Table 42.1)." *Household headship and residential status have no directionality, so this sentence cannot be interpreted.*

Better: "Stayers were more likely than movers to have a female household head ($p < .05$; Table 42.1)." *This version identifies the type of household that was most likely to stay, and names the other category against which it is being compared.*

An association can be large—a given change in one variable is associated with a big change in the other variable—or small—a given change in one variable is associated with a small change in the other. If several factors are each associated with chances of moving, knowing which have the strongest association can help identify which attributes to target.

42.5.3.1　Direction and Magnitude for Bivariate Associations

For bivariate associations, describing the size of an association is usually quite straightforward. The size of a difference between two values can be calculated in any of several ways, including absolute difference (subtracting one value from the other), relative difference or ratio (dividing one value by the other), or percentage difference or change. To decide which of these alternatives to use as you write, read similar comparisons in the literature for your field. As you describe the sizes of differences between values, mention the pertinent units, whether the original units of measurement (as in subtraction) or multiples (as for ratios). See Miller (2005) chapter 8 for suggestions on how to choose among and write about results of these different types of quantitative comparison.

Poor: "Men and women have different attitudes about legal abortion (Table 42.3)." *This sentence does not convey which gender is more likely to support legal abortion.*

Better: "Men are more likely than women to agree that abortion should be legal if a woman became pregnant by rape (Table 42.3)." *Although this version specifies the direction of the associations, the size of the association is still unclear.*

Best: "Men are about six percentage points more likely than women to agree that abortion should be legal if a woman became pregnant by rape (84 percent versus 78 percent, $p = 0.03$; Table 42.3)." *This version explains the direction, size, and statistical significance level of the association between gender and agreement with legal abortion under circumstances of rape.*

42.5.3.2　Direction and Magnitude for Multivariate Associations

The same general principles for reporting associations apply equally to describing results of multivariate statistical models. In the next few paragraphs, I provide a quick overview of how to interpret coefficients from ordinary least squares (OLS) and logistic regression. For an excellent intuitive description of multivariate regression, see Allison (1999); for a more detailed treatment about how to write about such models, see Miller (2005) chapter 9.

Report detailed coefficients and statistical significance information from multivariate models in a table, following the guidelines earlier in this chapter for effective titles, row and column labels, interior cells, and footnotes. A few special considerations for multivariate tables:

- In the title, name the type of statistical model, the dependent variable and its units or coding, and a phrase summarizing the concepts captured by the independent variables.
- Label each column of effect estimates to convey whether it contains standardized or unstandardized coefficients, log-odds or odds ratios, etc.
- Label columns of statistical test results to identify which variant is presented—t-statistic, standard error, p-value, etc.

42.5.3.2.1　Ordinary Least Squares Regression

Ordinary least squares regression (also known as linear regression) is used to estimate the association of one or more independent variables with a continuous dependent variable such as income in dollars or number of criminal victimizations. Coefficients (also known as "effect estimates," "parameter estimates," or "β's") on continuous and categorical independent variables are interpreted differently from one another.

For a continuous independent variable, the unstandardized coefficient from an OLS regression is an estimate of the slope of the relationship between the independent and dependent variables: the marginal effect of a one-unit increase in that independent variable on the dependent variable, holding constant all other variables in the model.* In tables and text that report OLS coefficients, specify the units in which the dependent and independent variables are measured. Unstandardized

---

* A standardized coefficient estimates the effect of a one-standard-deviation increase in the independent variable on the dependent variable, where that effect is measured in standard deviation units of the dependent variable.

OLS coefficients are in the same units as the dependent variable: "For each additional child in the household, there were on average 0.07 more victimizations ($p < .05$; Table 42.2)."

With categorical variables such as race/ethnicity, one category is selected as the reference (or "omitted") category and is the basis of comparison for the other categories of that variable.* The OLS coefficients on "Latino" measure the absolute difference in the dependent variable compared to blacks (the reference category in the Yonkers study), taking into account the other variables in the model. In the text, specify the reference group as the basis of comparison as you report the coefficients for categorical variables, and mention the units of the dependent variable. "Latinos averaged 0.19 fewer housing problems than blacks ($p < .001$; Table 42.2)." To reduce chances of misinterpretation of coefficients on categorical variables, label the dummy variables in your data set, text, tables, and charts to reflect the values they represent, e.g., "Latino" not "ethnicity."

42.5.3.2.2 Logistic Regression

Logistic regression (or logit model) is used to estimate the effects of several variables on a categorical dependent variable such as winning an election or being born low birth weight. The coefficient for a continuous variable in a logit model measures the marginal effect of a one-unit increase in the independent variable on the dependent variable—controlling for the other variables in the model. For instance, Table 42.5 presents the log-odds of low birth weight (LBW) among U.S. infants according to race or ethnicity, gender, and several socioeconomic characteristics of the family.

Many audiences find it easier to assess the effect size from logit models using the odds ratio rather than the log-odds because odds ratios are interpretable as simple multiples or can be easily transformed into percentage differences (Miller, 2005). Consequently, the odds ratio (also known as the "relative odds") often is presented instead of, or in addition to, the log-odds, as in Table 42.5. The odds ratio (OR) is calculated by exponentiating the logit coefficient: odds ratio $= e^{\beta} = e^{\text{log-odds}}$. A positive log-odds corresponds to an odds ratio greater than 1.0, or higher odds of LBW than the reference category. For example, the "mother smoked during pregnancy" coefficient of 0.33 translates to an odds ratio of 1.39 ($= e^{(0.33)}$). A negative log-odds corresponds to an odds ratio less than 1.0, or lower odds of LBW, e.g., boys compared to girls (OR $= 0.94$).

The odds ratio on a continuous independent variable is an estimate of the change in relative odds of the event for a one-unit increase in the independent variable. For example, the odds of LBW are 0.992 times as high for each additional year of mother's age, equivalent to a decrease of eight tenths of 1 percent in risk of LBW for a one-year increase in mother's age. The odds ratio for a dummy variable compares the risk of the event under study in that group to those in the reference category: "infants born to mothers who smoked had 1.39 times the odds of LBW of those born to nonsmokers."

42.5.4 SUMMARIZE PATTERNS

Often answering a research question requires describing a pattern involving many numbers, such as trends in homicides for each of three age groups over several decades, or rates of violent crime by type of offense and region in the United States. Typically, the data for such patterns are reported in tables and charts, which provide an efficient way to organize lots of numbers. If you only provide a table or chart, however, you leave it to your audience to figure out for themselves what that evidence says. An important step in telling a clear story with numbers as evidence is to summarize the patterns shown in your tables and charts, and relate them back to the substantive question at hand. Use prose to describe the general relationship in the table or chart—the forest, not the individual trees. If readers want to know the number of homicides for a particular date and age group, they can look it up in the associated chart.

---

* Dummy variables (also known as "binary," "dichotomous," or "indicator" variables) are defined for each of the other categories, each coded 1 if the characteristic applies to that case, and 0 otherwise. A dummy variable is not defined for the reference group (hence the name "omitted category"), resulting in $(n-1)$ dummies for an n-category variable. Cases in the reference category will have a value of 0 for each of the dummy variables pertaining to that categorical variable.

TABLE 42.5

Estimated Odds Ratios (OR) and 95 Percent Confidence Interval (CI) from a Logistic Regression of Low Birth Weight, United States, 1988–1994

	Log-Odds (β_k)	Odds Ratio (OR)	95 Percent CI for OR
Intercept	−2.03		
Race/Hispanic origin (Non-Hispanic white)[a]			
Non-Hispanic black	0.38	1.46	1.23–1.74
Mexican American	0.36	1.43	1.15–1.78
Boy	−0.02	0.98	0.86–1.12
Mother's education (College+)			
Less than high school	0.51	1.67	1.36–2.05
High school graduate	0.31	1.37	1.14–1.63
Mother's age at child's birth (years)	−0.008	0.99	0.98–1.01
Income-to-poverty ratio (IPR)[b]	−0.26	0.77	0.65–0.91
IPR^2	0.019	1.02	0.99–1.05
Mother smoked during pregnancy	0.33	1.39	1.20–1.62

$N = 9{,}813$. Wald chi-square statistic (df) = 236.68 (9); −2 Log L = 6,130.4; −2 Log L for null model = 6,377.9.

[a] Reference categories in parentheses.

[b] IPR is family income divided by the federal poverty level for a family of comparable size and age composition.

Note: Results weighted to population levels using sampling weights from the NHANES III (U.S. DHHS 1997).

Low birth weight <2,500 grams or 5.5 pounds.

Source: U.S. Department of Health and Human Services. *National Health and Nutrition Examination Survey, III, 1988–1994.* CD-ROM Series 11, no. 1. National Center for Health Statistics, Centers for Disease Control and Prevention, Hyattsville, MD, 1997.

When summarizing a table or chart, inexperienced writers often make one of two opposite mistakes: (1) they report every single number from the table or chart in their description or (2) they pick a few arbitrary numbers to contrast in sentence form without considering whether those numbers represent an underlying general pattern. Neither approach adds much to the information presented in the table or chart, and both can confuse or mislead the audience. Paint the big picture, rather than reiterating all of the little details. Link the evidence back to the substantive question, in the case of Figure 42.1, considering how abortion attitudes differ by gender and circumstances. Describe broad patterns with a few simple statements, pointing out similarities and differences across groups.

Here is a mantra I devised to guide you through the steps of writing an effective description of a pattern involving three or more numbers: "generalization, example, exceptions" or "GEE" for short. The idea is to identify and describe the general shape of a pattern, give a representative numeric example to illustrate that pattern, and then explain and illustrate any exceptions. This approach can also be used to summarize findings of previous studies, identifying consensus and pointing out discrepancies.

42.5.4.1 Generalization

For a generalization, come up with a description that characterizes a relationship among most, if not all, of the numbers. If the pattern fits most of the groups most of the time, it is a generalization.

The few numbers or associations that do not fit are your exceptions (see below). For the patterns shown in Figure 42.1, the generalization might read:

> The share of adults who agree that abortion should be legal differs substantially according to both circumstances of the abortion and gender of the respondent. As shown in Figure 42.1, respondents in the 2000 General Social Survey were much more likely to say a legal abortion should be available under each of the three health circumstances than for any of the three social or preference reasons.

The first sentence introduces the concepts (attitudes about abortion under different circumstances) and the groups to be compared (the two genders). The second sentence summarizes the direction of the first general pattern, and names the figure in which the associated numbers appear. No numbers yet—that comes in the second step.

Note that these patterns are much easier to recognize and describe because the reasons were grouped into conceptual categories in the chart (health reasons on the left, social reasons on the right) rather than listed in alphabetical or arbitrary order. As you create your tables and charts, anticipate the conceptual or empirical contrasts you plan to write about, and use those principles to organize the variables in the table or chart (Miller, 2007).

42.5.4.2 Example

Having described a generalizable pattern in intuitive language, illustrate it with numbers from your table or chart. This step anchors your generalization to the specific numbers upon which it is based. It ties the prose and table or chart together. By reporting a few illustrative numbers, you implicitly show your audience where in the table or chart those numbers come from as well as the shape and size of comparison involved. They can then test whether the pattern applies to other times, groups, or places using other data from the table or chart. To illustrate the above generalization:

> For example, respondents were about twice as likely to agree that it should be possible for a pregnant woman to obtain a legal abortion if her health is seriously endangered by the pregnancy than if 'the woman wants an abortion for any reason' (90 percent and 45 percent, respectively).

This sentence reports the direction and magnitude of one relationship that fits the generalization introduced above.

42.5.4.3 Exceptions

Sometimes you will be lucky enough that your generalizations capture all the relevant variation in your data. If you are working with real-world data, however, often there will be important exceptions to the general pattern you have sketched. Tiny blips can usually be ignored, but if some parts of a table or chart depart substantially from your generalization, describe those departures.

When portraying an exception, explain its overall shape and how it differs from the generalization you have described and illustrated in your preceding sentences. Is it higher or lower? By how much? If a trend, is it moving toward or away from the pattern you are contrasting it against? In other words, describe both direction and magnitude of the difference between the generalization and the exception. Use phrases such as "however" or "on the other hand" to differentiate an exception from a generalization; "conversely" or "on the contrary" can be used to point out when one pattern is the opposite direction of another. Finally, provide numeric examples from the table or chart to illustrate the exception.

> Although men are slightly more likely than women to agree with abortion for each of the health reasons, the reverse is true for each of the social reasons.

By using the words "although" and "reverse," this description helps readers to see the different directions of the gender pattern of agreement with abortion for health versus social reasons. This pattern could then be illustrated with a numeric example.

This particular exception occurred in terms of direction, with men more likely than women to agree with abortion for one set of reasons, but the opposite pattern for the other set of reasons. Other types of exceptions can occur in magnitude, such as wider gaps for some items (attitudes about abortion concerning women who became pregnant by rape) than others (wants no more kids). Exceptions can also be in terms of statistical significance, as when all but one association is statistically significant (Table 42.2).

42.6 WRITING THE DISCUSSION AND CONCLUSION

Having presented the individual pieces of evidence, a lawyer must summarize how that evidence, taken together, incriminates or eliminates a particular suspect of the criminal charges. Likewise, in the concluding section of a paper, explain whether the collective body of statistical evidence supports or refutes your hypothesis.

In contrast to the results section of a scientific paper, where individual pieces of numeric evidence are reviewed in detail, the discussion and conclusion section should relate that evidence back to the larger research question, comparing broad conclusions against hypotheses posed at the beginning of the work and results from related studies. Rather than repeat precise numeric estimates and results of statistical tests from the results section, use verbal descriptions or approximate numeric values, rounding to the nearest whole multiple or familiar fraction. In the discussion section, use phrases such as "were statistically significant" or "was not associated" in lieu of detailed inferential statistical test results such as test statistics, standard errors, or p-values.

Poor: "Multivariate analysis of data from the Yonkers Residential Mobility Program showed that even when the effects of potential confounders were taken into account, danger was 0.99 units lower, victimization 0.19 units lower, disorder 1.25 units lower, and housing problems 0.30 units lower among movers than stayers. In addition, multivariate models of cohesion and resources showed that both were better among movers (+.21 and +.13, respectively), although the difference in resources was not statistically significant." *This version merely restates the statistics from the results section of the paper, adding nothing to what has already been demonstrated and failing to put the evidence back in the "big picture" of the main research question.*

Better: "The study by Fauth and colleagues demonstrates that low-income families who moved into low-poverty neighborhoods were appreciably better off than those who remained in their original neighborhoods on each of six measures of housing and neighborhood quality. These benefits persisted even when possible confounding factors were taken into account, suggesting that differences were due to moving per se rather than differences in background traits of those who moved versus those who stayed." *This paragraph brings the analysis full circle, relating the statistical evidence back to the original question about the possible beneficial effects of moving out of high poverty areas, but without the detailed numeric evidence. The conclusion could then be fleshed out with possible explanations for these patterns and comparison against other studies of residential mobility experiments, as well as implications for programs or policy.*

Unlike the results section, which is devoted almost exclusively to reporting and analyzing data from within your own study, a discussion and conclusions section often incorporates numeric information from other studies. These statistics might be used (1) to evaluate whether the current findings are consistent with previous research, (2) to provide perspective on the importance of the research question, (3) to apply numbers from other sources of background information that place the findings of the current study in context, or (4) to offer ideas about underlying reasons for observed patterns, generating hypotheses to be tested empirically in later studies.

Finally, to help put your findings back into real world context, discuss the implications for policy and practice, identifying groups at particular risk or aspects of programs that worked (or did not work), for instance. If your intended audience includes researchers, also include a discussion of research implications, such as new questions raised by your findings, and strengths and limitations of your study; see Miller (2004) or Pyrczak and Bruce (2000) for guidelines.

42.7 SUMMARY

In summary, writing an effective paper, talk, or grant proposal about an application of statistical methods to topics in public policy or administration involves integrating good expository writing techniques with principles for presenting numeric evidence. As you write about statistical findings, craft a logical narrative with a beginning, middle, and end. In the introduction, ask the question in plain English, mentioning the specific concepts under study. In the results section, systematically review the statistical evidence using introductory and transition sentences to keep readers oriented to the logical flow of the analysis. Finally, close by placing the statistical conclusions in the larger context of the original question. These approaches will help yield a clear story with numbers as evidence.

EXERCISES

1. Based on the information in Table 42.1 about the study by Fauth et al. (2004):
   a. Write a sentence reporting the direction, magnitude, and statistical significance of the association between residential status and number of children in the household.
   b. Write a sentence reporting the direction, magnitude, and statistical significance of the association between residential status and having at least a high school education.
2. Based on the information in Table 42.1, write a paragraph comparing neighborhood or housing quality of movers versus stayers, using the GEE approach. (Hint: Consider whether there are theoretical groupings of the six outcome measures that could help you simplify the description.)
3. (Advanced) Write a description of the findings in Table 42.2 from the study by Fauth et al. (2004), using the GEE (generalization, example, exception) approach to summarize findings across the six dependent variables.
4. (Advanced) Table 42.6 shows results of a study of family, programmatic, and state socio-economic factors associated with enrollment in the State Children's Health Insurance Program (SCHIP). Answer the following questions based on that table.
   a. What is the dependent variable in the model? What is its theoretically possible range?
   b. Write a sentence reporting the direction, size, and statistical significance of the coefficient on a required SCHIP premium. Comment on the substantive importance of that change.
   c. Suppose the poverty rate among children under age five years is expected to rise by five percentage points over the next year. By how much would SCHIP take-up be predicted to change based on this model, holding all other variables constant?
   d. Write a sentence reporting the direction, size, and statistical significance of the coefficient on required face-to-face interview.
   e. Write a sentence explaining whether there was a time trend in SCHIP enrollment during the study period.

ACKNOWLEDGMENT

This chapter is adapted from material in *The Chicago Guide to Writing about Multivariate Analysis*. Chicago: The University of Chicago Press. © 2005 by The University of Chicago. All rights reserved.

TABLE 42.6

Linear Probability Model of the Proportion of Eligible Children Who Enroll in SCHIP[a], by SCHIP Program Characteristics and State Economic Characteristics, U.S. 2003–2004

Variable[b]	Coefficient	Standard Error
Intercept	0.444	0.055
SCHIP program structure		
SCHIP separate program	0.078**	0.023
Parental coverage	0.028*	0.015
Monthly SCHIP premium (*1,000) ($)	−0.132**	0.050
SCHIP eligibility/application process		
# Months w/o coverage to be eligible	−0.007*	0.003
Have presumptive eligibility	0.019	0.015
Asset test	−0.022	0.044
Required face-to-face interview	−0.040*	0.018
SCHIP information and assistance		
Have phone application help	0.034**	0.007
Have family Web site	0.010	0.012
State economic characteristics		
Area unemployment rate (percent)	0.022**	0.003
Avg. state employee share of premium for employer-based coverage (*1,000) ($)	0.115*	0.051
Poverty rate for children <5 years (percent)	0.002	0.003
Poverty rate for children 5–18 years (percent)	−0.003	0.002
Year 2004	0.027*	0.013
R^2	0.173	
F-statistic	221.22	
N	25,107	

Note: Children in families with income below 200 percent of the federal poverty level (FPL) without other health insurance.

[a] SCHIP: State Children's Health Insurance Program.

[b] Model also controls for gender, race, and age of child, urban residence, parental education, family income or FPL, marital status, and parents' employment status.

* $p < .05$;
** $p < .01$.

REFERENCES

Allison, P.D. 1999. *Multiple Regression: A Primer*. Thousand Oaks, California: Sage Publications.

Centers for Medicare and Medicaid Services, Office of the Actuary, National Health Statistics Group, Department of Health and Human Services. 2004. Table 1. National Health Expenditures, Aggregate and Per Capita Amounts, Percent Distribution, and Average Annual Percent Growth, by Source of Funds: Selected Calendar Years 1980–2002.

Fauth, R.C., Leventhal, T., and Brooks-Gunn, J. 2004. Short-term effects of moving from public housing in poor to middle-class neighborhoods on low-income, minority adults' outcomes. *Social Science and Medicine, 59,* 2271–2284.

ICPSR. 2004. *General Social Survey, 1972–2000 Cumulative Codebook*. Available online at http://webapp.icpsr.umich.edu/GSS/. Accessed June 2007.

Miller, J.E. 2004. *The Chicago Guide to Writing about Numbers*. Chicago, Illinois: University of Chicago Press.

Miller, J.E. 2005. *The Chicago Guide to Writing about Multivariate Analysis*. Chicago, Illinois: University of Chicago Press.

Miller, J.E. 2007. Organizing data in tables and charts: Different criteria for different tasks. *Teaching Statistics*, 29(3), 98–101.

Morgan, S.E., Reichert, T., and Harrison, T.R. 2002. *From Numbers to Words: Reporting Statistical Results for the Social Sciences*. Boston, Massachusetts: Allyn and Bacon.

Nelson, D.E., Brownson, R.C., Remington, P.L., and Parvanta, C. (Eds.). 2002. *Communicating Public Health Information Effectively: A Guide for Practitioners*. Washington, DC: American Public Health Association.

Pyrczak, F. and Bruce, R.R. 2000. *Writing Empirical Research Reports: A Guide for Students of the Social and Behavioral Sciences*, third edition. Los Angeles, California: Pyrczak Publishing.

U.S. Bureau of the Census. 1999. Comparison of summary measures of income by selected characteristics: 1989, 1997, and 1998. Available online at http://www.census.gov/hhes/income/income98/in98sum.html.

U.S. Dept. of Health and Human Services. 1997. *National Health and Nutrition Examination Survey, III, 1988–1994*. CD-ROM Series 11, no. 1. Hyattsville, Maryland: National Center for Health Statistics, Centers for Disease Control and Prevention.

World Bank. 2001. *2001 World Development Indicators: Health Expenditure, Service, and Use*. Herndon, Virginia: World Bank.

43 Styles of Scholarship in Public Administration

Kyle Farmbry and Lamar Vernon Bennett

CONTENTS

43.1   INTRODUCTION

As both a relatively young discipline, and one that draws upon a number of other disciplines, the field of public administration is open to a number of factors that impact its research agendas. The process through which research agendas emerge in the field is shaped by public administration's interdisciplinary nature, and the fact that many of the questions selected for exploration are framed by political, social, and economic occurrences at a given time. Because of the wide-scale public impact of the field, understanding both the problems and the questions public administration researchers ask is of utmost importance.

Despite the fact that research agendas on political and administrative issues impact every component of our lives, research in public administration has fallen under some criticism for lack of rigor and relevance. As a result, various scholars have engaged in reviews of various articles in search of processes for analyzing the development of scholarship in the field. Stallings and Ferris (1988) for example engaged in a study in trends in PA research for the 45 year span of 1940–1984. By examining research as it appeared in five-year intervals, they found that the status of research changed little over the time-span they examined. One of their concerns worth noting is a significant lack of research in the area of causal analysis within the field of administrative research. As they observe, "Little causal analysis or theory testing has taken place over the years, and causal analysis, significantly more frequent now than in previous decades, comprises only a small proportion of current research" (584). More recently, Gill and Meier (2000) noted challenges in the field by noting that "Public administration research has fallen notably behind research in related fields in terms of methodological sophistication. This hinders the development of empirical investigations into substantive questions of interest to practitioners and academics." The observations of these researchers speak to the need for greater disciplinary reflection on the field.

The purpose of this chapter is to address this need for an examination of factors related to the emergence of research agendas within public administration. Our examination is framed in several stages. We begin with an exploration of the role of theory in shaping the inquiry processes. We attempt to ground this exploration in both research agendas related to public administration as well as within the larger social science inquiry processes. We continue with an exploration of the historical evolution of the field of public administration and the resulting context for the shaping of questions. From what is frequently viewed as the founding era in the field, to the present day, we explore the interplay between historic events and the shape of inquiry. Next, we examine a snapshot of research, drawing upon a sample of articles within public administration over the past several years. From this examination, we build a typology of current research in the field, and attempt to identify current perspectives and trends in research. We close with a reexamination of key factors related to research, with the purpose of examining where and how styles of scholarship emerge within public administration.

43.2 THEORETICAL CONTEXT

We begin our examination of foundations for research processes through an exploration of the purpose of theory as it pertains to research. Several primary areas frame our discussion. First, are matters surrounding the purpose of theory. In our view, theory provides a framework from which to ask questions about a situation. As we write, numerous societal issues, such as social security reform, rising crime in communities, and rapidly increasing disparities between communities, confront researchers and form parts of political and administrative agendas. Traditional approaches to research on these issues within the discipline of public administration, are frequently focused on the political/administrative implications, but not on the theoretical underpinnings. Theory provides a deeper context for issues and the shaping of future questions. At the core, theory provides a critical point of departure for a number of questions related to strategies for exploring an inquiry-based process or exercise.

The value proposition of theory providing a deeper context for the shaping of questions is complicated by the fact that many current practitioners in the field do not maintain an interest in framing questions within a theoretical grounding. Thus, from a point of concern for this chapter, questions related to theory are focused on matters pertaining to the development of critical research questions for practitioners, researchers, and students in the field. Our initial premise related to theory relates then, to the notion in a prescriptive context. As a discipline, we pay far too little attention to the role of theory in shaping our research agendas. Ultimately, we feel this is a condition that individuals engaged with crafting administrative inquiry should seek to address by encouraging reflection on the theoretical undertones to research agendas that might be explored.

The second area for exploration is grounded in questions related to the role of positivism in shaping social science inquiry. Our strategies of developing hypotheses, exploring the null, and frequently framing our work in rigorous quantitative methods, helps to establish a methodological base for the field that drives many of the questions we ask and our methods for exploring such questions. The process of inquiry that shapes the natural and social sciences, and shapes many of the more positivist approaches, can be traced to the theories proposed by Rene Descartes in the seventeenth century (Descartes et al., 1985). Descartes shaped a foundation for the sciences based on a sense of absolutism that was derived from an inquiry process based initially on a system of doubt and critical inquiry of assumptions underlying the foundation of knowledge at a particular time. Prior to Descartes, theology provided the foundation for knowledge. As a result of his writings however, scientific processes found themselves focused on systems of philosophy-grounded proofs. This shift helped ultimately to build a foundation for the sciences, which helped to build the latter evolution of various positivistic forms of the natural and the social sciences.

Nonpositivistic approaches however, have also played a major role in shaping theories and basic inquiry in the social sciences, particularly as they have provided a foundation for exploring matters related to developing other research foundations. Such approaches ultimately shaped a framework that led to the development of such fields of inquiry as phenomenology and other approaches to understand the interpretative bases of meaning that underlies systems and approaches in various perspectives. These perspectives, in turn, helped to frame approaches to inquiry that influence the shaping of research agendas that seek to understand from a more antipositivist stance. Inquiry and scholarship thus, if assumed from a traditional Cartesian perspective, is focused on applying perspectives aimed at inquiry focused on proving or disproving notions. If from a nonpositivist approach, the focus is not so much to prove or disprove, as merely seeking to interpret a given reality. Both perspectives ground, through theoretical conceptualizations and frameworks, much of the development of the social sciences.

The third area for exploration as we reflect on the role of theory in the inquiry process stems from public administration's interdisciplinary nature. Public administration is influenced by a number of areas, including political philosophy, economics, and sociology. The notion of an interdisciplinary field has received some attention in recent years. Fish (1994) for example reflects on the challenges of interdisciplinarity, a notion he argues has surfaced in academic discourse as a critical attack on specialized approaches within academic disciplines. Interdisciplinary research, he argues, is grounded frequently in a form of "antiprofessionalism," or an "indictment of the narrow special interests that stake out a field of inquiry and then colonize it with a view toward nothing more than serving their own selfish needs." Such observations raise questions about the foundation of scholarly agendas in the field as being grounded in one particular discipline or within a set of disciplines that have wide-ranging foundations.

How ultimately then do these notions of theory impact the evolution and type of scholarship in the field of public administration? We have attempted to address this question in this section first, with a discussion of theory as a frequently overlooked component of our field—one that ultimately provides a context for helping to shape the foundation from which questions are frequently structured. We then continued with an exploration of foundations of positivist-based scientific inquiry as well as some of the foundations for antipositivist frameworks that also shaped much of the inquiry process in the social sciences. We conclude with an examination of the question of the interdisciplinary role of public administration and its impact on the shaping of the field. With these foundations noted, we now turn to the development of inquiry in the field using the interplay of history and the formulation of research agendas.

43.3 HISTORICAL CONTEXT

The emergence of research agendas reflect various social, political, and economic dynamics of a given time period. It is for this reason that we ground part of our exploration of the inquiry process in public administration through a lens that builds off of the historical context through which the field has evolved. We have framed the discussion of a historical context along five historical eras that shaped the field of American public administration stretching from its founding era in the 1880s to the present. Through a brief analysis of these periods, we hope to provide a foundation for further understanding history's impact upon the framing of scholarship in our field.

Table 43.1 provides an overview of the frameworks for the various time periods and the impact of historical incidents in these periods on the shaping of research agendas and questions during that time period.

43.4 PUBLIC ADMINISTRATION FOUNDING-ERA IMPACTS ON SCHOLARSHIP

The emergence of research agendas in relation to administrative agendas and issues during the period 1880–1920, a period frequently referred to as the founding era in public administration,

TABLE 43.1
Historical Eras

Time Period	Key Incidents	Key Research Paradigms
Founding era 1880–1920	Urbanization, industrialization, and immigration, emergence of the social sciences	Municipal research, general social sciences—anthropology, sociology, etc.
Scholarship and growth of government 1920–1945	New deal era, WWII, founding of ASPA	Governmental infrastructure needs, legitimacy of governmental growth, efficiency in processes
Post-war era 1946–1970	Post-war notions of affluence, war on poverty/ great society, implementation of PPBS Rational approaches to government Emergence of the policy sciences	Rationalism, humanistic inquiry, quantitative policy processes/foundations
Legitimacy 1970–1990	Watergate, reflections on the war on poverty war in Vietnam	Ethics, evaluation research
Current crises 1990–present	Changes in global balance of powers (Post WWII)	Civil society, democratization, new public management, quasi-governmental/business influences

coincided with the emergence of American approaches to exploring the social sciences. The influences on public administration research can be founded in some of the basic foundations that were emerging in the field of American social science research at the time. The early years of social science's evolution in the United States were grounded initially in many of the German historical models for examining the social sciences. However, as Ross (1992) points out, within time, a set of characteristics that very much defined the American social sciences evolved and began to take root in how we began to explore various points of inquiry. As she considers these characteristics, she defines them with having a practical bent, a limited historical perspective, and a focus on technocratic approaches. As she notes, "to foreign and domestic critics, these characteristics make American social science ahistorical and scientist, lacking in appreciation of historical difference and complexity" (xii). This early period of public administration scholarship, by being influenced by emerging processes within the social sciences as a whole, can ultimately be viewed as having been influenced by processes that were focused on issues of practicality, ahistoricism, and technocism.

The period was also influenced heavily by the evolution of various agendas that intersected with various social and economic phenomena of the time. First was rapid urbanization. The early 1900s saw a shift in settlement patterns in the United States, which resulted in the nation transforming from being a rural nation to an urban one. With increasing populations in urban settings, questions arose on the impact of such urban dynamics on the framing of agendas for research. Service delivery in such areas, particularly when they were balanced with pressures and dynamics of urban change helped to influence such efforts. Many of the people moving into settings were people who had immigrated to the United States, and in particular to urban settings. Research questions, then, at times focused upon several of the factors that both distinguished these communities from other communities. In many cases, questions emerged regarding the potential impact and change resulting from such demographic shifts.

With industrial processes came both changes in demographic settlement patterns (people moving into industrial centers), and factors related to questions surrounding management patterns. Taylorism and its focus on scientific processes was the direct result of industrial patterns of the era. Research agendas, within the emergent field of public administration were frequently shaped, as was the case of much of the work in the management sciences with approaches and patterns related to structures in such management systems. Industrialization and its related fields of engineering led to the engagement of various rational processes, or in the case of Taylor's work, the engagement of scientific principles to organizational approaches. The emergence of such principles and approaches led to the further emergence of various approaches and models related to various processes of management that examined Tayloristic principles as related to the management of individuals in industrial-influenced workplaces.

The founding of the New York Bureau of Municipal Research in 1906 initiated many of the early processes of inquiry in the field of public administration. The initial work of the Bureau, focusing on systematically surveying the streets of Manhattan, provided the initiation of systematic processes for analyzing public services for the ultimate goal of improvement. The questions explored by the Bureau, and several of the organizations that grew out of its work helped to focus emergent research on the development of methods of examining the practices that would lead to systematic municipal management.

There is some debate related to the goals of the founders of the New York Bureau of Municipal Research. Some criticism was noted that questions underscoring their scholarship were focused on identifying best practices for the management of administrative challenges and problems. Other observations noted that some of the challenges and explorations were focused on the development of mechanisms for managing the multitudes of people who were moving into the urban environments. Authors such as Wiebe (1967) and Schiesl (1977) argue that much of focus of reform during the Progressive era—from which the bureau emerged—was focused on minimizing the roles of the poor and the immigrant groups that were finding their ways into cities en masse.

43.5 SCHOLARSHIP AND THE GROWTH OF GOVERNMENT 1920–1945

The period of 1920–1945 was largely driven by the continued growth of government and government processes, as well as several discussions related to government and its role in society. The era began with perspectives of government having a relatively limited role. It ended with a rapid expansion of government (and a corresponding role of government). With such expansion arose numerous agendas exploring the role of government and the scope of its powers, particularly at the executive level. Both new-deal era policies and the infrastructure needed to address new-deal era policies shaped the emergence of various research agendas—largely from a structural perspective, and based on the needs of various entities at the time. How various emergent programs should have been shaped during this era, was a component of the factors related to the development and shaping of various research agendas.

The period of the depression led to a number of questions related to the role of government in addressing many of the social ailments of the time correlating to the emergence of poverty in many communities. Numerous agencies were formed, and with them came questions related to strategies for both responding to the social needs they sought to address and to deal with questions related to the growing governmental infrastructure that coincided with their development. The period also helped to move the inquiry generation process, as related to issues facing government out of a realm that was influenced heavily by nongovernmental organizations such as the New York Bureau of Municipal Research, into an area where governmental organizations shaped the research agendas. The President's Committee on Administrative Management in 1937 was an early example of government stepping into the role of direct research sponsor on issues of the improvement of systems and plans. This role of government as a sponsor of research was replicated by municipalities, states, and other governmental entities in numerous other systems.

The late 1920s saw the establishment of several entities that helped to further build a community of practitioners and scholars in the field of public administration—many of whom shaped endeavors related to research processes. In 1929, the International City Managers Association was formed. Shortly thereafter, the American Municipal Association (later to become the National League of Cities), established a community of practitioners and scholars on items related to the development of research agendas that further examined urban systems and processes. Much of the emphasis of this organization was still with a focus on identifying administrative practices that worked and were framed in an efficient manner.

The founding of The American Society for Public Administration (ASPA) in 1939, helped to further frame a context for shaping research agendas and develop a community of individuals involved with inquiry in the field. Ultimately through forming what became a professional society, driven largely by member interests, ASPA was able to garner from practitioners and scholars questions about the performance of government, and ultimately helped to frame the advance of the research agendas in the field. As a result, questions that guided the scholarship process were found in research generated by practitioners and scholars of governance processes.

The Second World War ushered in a series of questions related to the development of research agendas in the field. Much of the focus during the war era explored concepts of efficiency—as both scarcity of resources, and the goal of winning the war focused much of the combined energy of various sectors. As a result, various entities focused related questions of maximizing resources for various goals. The period also helped to frame a scientific/technical approach to addressing many of the challenges that existed during the war era, and helped to transfer some of these activities to the post-war era. Ultimately, the period shifted to a degree to one where scientific/technical notions ultimately influenced and impacted the development of the war effort. Science played several roles throughout the war, and as a result, played a role in war-resultant research processes.

43.6 POST-WAR ERA—1946–1970

The post-war era saw several major factors that influenced the development of research agendas in the fields of public administration and public affairs. First, this was a period in which scientific/technical notions became further grounded in research and practice. The enhanced grounding of these factors were shaped largely by an emergent view of the role of science and rationalism in framing the debate on roles of administrative and political processes. Herbert Simon's work which integrated notions of bounded rationality into administrative processes helped to frame several of these notions of research and development in the administrative and policy fields.

Second were areas of research that focused on issues of humanism and humanistic inquiry. In the United States, much of the research focused on questions that examined the integration of ideals related to the type of society we ultimately wanted to be in the light of the type of society that we felt we had. The 1940s, with the gradual introduction of humanistic questions into social science discourse allowed for the emergence of strategies that ultimately shifted the perspectives of the process of diversity vis-à-vis the administrative state. The work of Gunnar Myrdal's research team in the exploration of the dilemma of race in American society provided an example of some of the questions that were explored in the late 1940s and that ultimately had an impact upon scholarly evolution both in the wider social sciences and later in the intersection of such areas as political/administrative theories and theories of social equity. The humanistic exercise in inquiry also took another method in surfacing, especially as scholars who had been part of the Frankfurt School began to integrate into various institutions of higher education in the United States. Their arrival initiated the development of critical processes of reflecting upon the status of our society and ultimately raised a number of positions from which questions of critical inquiry could be framed and articulated. Their work ultimately resulted in areas of critical inquiry in the field of administrative research theory.

The third was the development of a university infrastructure, which stemmed from the demand for higher education resulting from the rapid influx of former servicemen onto campuses due to the GI Bill. The Bill's impact, first in creating a demand for degrees in higher education, ultimately had a role in shaping other approaches in development of infrastructures for higher education. Ultimately as the resulting national university infrastructure was developed, so was the capacity for exploring various research agendas in numerous fields of research, including public administration.

University growth ultimately enabled the further development of locations for the incubation of inquiry processes. Today, if one were to examine research where agendas within the field of public administration are housed, an overwhelming majority would be people within schools that emerged in the years following and resulting from the GI Bill.

The fourth area is linked into the rise of the policy sciences, an area of research that was linked with the emergence and development of the policy sciences. Lerner and Lasswell's book *The Policy Sciences* (1951), in particular Lasswell's contribution to the publication—a chapter entitled "The policy orientation," helped to shape a notion of the policy sciences that was grounded in a normative and problem-oriented approach to thinking about public policy. This approach helped to shape much of the policy debate for years following. Part of Laswell's argument was grounded in a concept of identifying new strategies for engaging the policy sciences through the development of institutions that would help with the framing of policy orientations. Laswell's work found itself launching a framework for defining and claiming a positional stance for various areas within the policy arena—from the political sciences to economics that would help to shape the development of many of the approaches to policy that emerged.

With the rise of President Johnson's War on Poverty and Great Society programs, there were numerous notions related to the development of research as part of a larger policy process. Such an emergence linked in a number of issues pertaining to the diversity of the policy roles and procedures. The mid-1960s provided a crucial turning point in the development and shift in research formulation agendas. In 1965, President Johnson formally endorsed the Planning–Programming–Budgeting System (PPBS) as the strategy for implementing various evaluation mechanisms into program design and development plans in the years. This helped both to formulate new evaluation policies and procedures and gave rise to a "science" of evaluation processes. This process, adapted largely from strategies introduced to the defense department by Robert McNamara, was grounded in leveraging rational approaches to the development of a research strategy.

Such approaches to frame research also received the guidance of several research institutions to help with the formulation processes. First, federal agencies such as the Office of Economic Opportunity (OEO) provided support to all different levels to help frame research with a focus on research related to poverty as impacted by various OEO policies. Second, the time period saw the emergence of several schools of policy research that helped to support the growth of various public policy methods and approaches for shaping inquiry that were grounded in rigorous quantitative and economic frameworks for inquiry. Because many of these schools were supported by OEO funding streams, a significant amount of the research they generated was focused on matters of poverty and poverty alleviation.

43.7 1970–1990—LEGITIMIZING GOVERNMENT PROCESSES

The period of 1970–1990 was one of legitimacy building for government processes within the disciplines. The period began with numerous research agendas driven by evaluation and research questions, many of which were the result of policy frameworks that had emerged both in response to social planning processes of the war on poverty, and as a result of mechanisms and strategies related to the development of new processes for the evaluation of social policies that came as a result of the policy schools that emerged during the 1960s.

The concept of ethics became a second area that had evolved into a research area of its own during the era, and had a role in framing questions of legitimacy in governmental processes. Driven largely by the era of Watergate, this issue of ethics began to greatly impact the research agendas of the era. As a result, numerous articles began to appear within several of the public administration associated journals exploring challenges of ethics as they surfaced in various research fields. Ultimately, ethics-focused research became a framework for grounding various approaches for research as an instrument for legitimacy development.

The 1980s saw the increasing visibility of a number of policy research institutions or think tanks that have had a significant impact on the emergence of policy research. For many of these institutions, the question of research agendas was framed largely for the purpose of influencing and shaping policy. These think tanks that played a major role in formulating research on various policy issues for political frameworks, shaped numerous processes and mechanisms for policy development. Ultimately, these institutions helped to introduce into the field of research notions of policy agenda setting from a position of advocating one perspective over another.

Several of these policy institutions found themselves critical of the roles of the size of administrative systems, in particular those at the federal level. The work of these organizations coincided with what some practitioners saw as an attack on federal systems by Reagan-era policies. Research then, particularly as generated from within the community of those involved in the field of public administration, began to respond in two ways. First, agendas were framed to demonstrate both the relevance and effectiveness of government—particularly at the federal level. Second, was to develop approaches that would leverage opportunities to engage strategies for agency development that might emerge in the private or nonprofit sectors to address public needs.

43.8 CURRENT CRISES—1990s TO THE PRESENT

Our perspective on the final era that we examine is on the development of various administrative processes vis-à-vis the state and factors related to crises or dramatic changes that have both emerged, and that we argue provide a foundation for the emergence of various research agendas. The first area that we explore pertains to many of the geopolitical transitions at the time. Changes within the Soviet Union that emerged in the late 1980s and early 1990s along with the democratization of various Soviet-bloc states as well as nations in Southern Africa were primary components of such changes. As a result, the early to mid-1990s saw an emergence of literature on the growth of research pertaining to administrative research in the realm of transitional democracies and the establishment of new state structures. With geopolitical dynamics of the era, there have been a number of changes in nongovernmental structures and processes to explore such change. Scholarship impacted by these transitions focused on transitional governance issues and processes of ensuring factors were addressed in light of transitional occurrences.

The second area consisted of a crisis of the welfare state. This crisis focused on challenges that emerged with the development of realizations of challenges that various welfare state systems were rapidly shifting, and also focused on resultant questions pertaining to the development and growth of state-related processes. As we wrestle with further questions related to an aging populations, social security needs, and housing concerns, there is an ongoing challenge related to the growth of such challenges that the state faces in addressing the concerns of people. This crisis of the welfare state saw the shaping of numerous questions in relation to the evolution of welfare reform policies, health care systems, and other systems that are integrated to safety net concerns. As government was seen as increasingly less able to handle many of the challenges related to expectations of the state research began to focus on factors pertaining to the development and shifting of the government and its level of ability in addressing various concerns related to safety in various communities. Today, numerous research questions generated are focused on many of these challenges in relation to state systems or processes.

43.9 EXPLORATION OF CURRENT LITERATURE

An exploration of recent literature in the field provides our third method for exploring the issue of emergence and framing scholarly activities in public administration. To explore the issue of inquiry type, we examined issues of *Public Administration Review* for the five-year period of 2000–2005, with a goal of identifying the foundations of various research agendas in the journal. We selected *Public Administration Review* largely because of its role as a central journal in the field of public

TABLE 43.2
Typology of Research

Type I: Evaluation of systems and processes	Type II: Presentation and testing of theories
Type III: Case-based, grounded research	Type IV: Concept clarification

administration—and one that includes various subcategories within the field. From annual indices, we identified topical areas where there were the greatest number of articles generated in the five-year period. Nine areas were identified. They included budget and finance, bureaucracy, performance measurement, citizen participation, ethics, comparative public administration, international, federal government, and privatization. The Appendix provides a list of the 39 articles examined as we conducted this analysis.

As indicated in Table 43.2, we categorize four types of research selected from our analysis of the articles: evaluation of various systems and processes, the presentation and testing of theories, case-based or case-grounded, and clarification of concepts. The first area, focusing on the evaluation of various systems and processes, examined issues of system improvement or the framing of various inventories of systems and processes. An example of research in this type is work by Page (2004), which examined the processes implemented by individuals engaged in collaboration and attempts to manage the expectations of various stakeholders in collaborative relations. Another example is provided by Rubenstein, Schwartz, and Stiefel's (2003) work examining the benefits and usage of raw performance measures and of performance measures that have been adjusted in what ultimately amounts to as an evaluation of processes for using adjusted performance measures as a means for enhancing agency performance. Finally, Rubin and Bartle's (2005) work, examining gender-responsive budgeting, provides a mechanism for building into budgeting processes factors related to the challenges and opportunities related to gender-responsive budgeting. In each of these cases, the articles are focused on some strategy of evaluating the impact of processes and systems as they stand, as well as examining mechanisms for enhancing agency processes, whether in the area of enhancing collaborative abilities, performance management, or budgeting processes.

The second area included the presentation and testing of theories. Here, authors proposed new theoretical perspectives or adaptations of older theoretical systems or processes. These articles tend to be grounded more in history than many of the other types of research, and in many cases help to frame prescriptive discussions about the direction of general trends in the profession. Haque's (2001) examination of the challenge to the concept of publicness in the field of public service, largely as a result of increasing trends toward market-driven modes of service delivery, provides one example of the theoretical explorations we examined. Cooper's (2004) call for more focused research in the field of administrative ethics, provides another example of some of the theoretical work in the field. Cooper's proposing of some of the more pressing questions that might frame a discussion related to ethics within this article, provides a foundation for later work that might appear related to ethics in the field of public administration.

Third is research that we will categorize as case-based or grounded in applied realities from the experiences of practitioners. Here, situations are either directly drawn upon to build lessons from a wider set of applications, or particular political or administrative trends are drawn upon to frame research agendas. Ryan's (2004) work, examining the challenges stemming from decentralization in Costa Rica presents an overview of some of the challenges related to decentralization and the impact upon reform. The vital components of this work, as applied to explorations of traditional case utility, is that there is an application of theory to a wider contextual framework than the specific case examined. The issue of applicability in a wider context is applied in Beck, Asenova, and Dickson's (2005) work examining the bovine spongiform encephalopathy outbreak in the United Kingdom in the late 1990s as a means of examining factors related to governance, and elements of specialization as a means of better assessing risk factors. Finally, in some cases, such as Gooden and Bailey's (2001) work examining the job retention impacts of welfare to work employees in the years following the 1997 implementation of the Welfare to Work initiative, agendas set in a political or administrative framework shape the foundation for inquiry processes. In this case, the implementation of Welfare to Work provided a context for Gooden and Bailey to explore the impact of the initiative in a wider context.

Fourth is research that attempts to clarify particular concepts. In these instances, authors examine notions that are incorporated in current discussions in administrative/political realms, but that are open to further interpretation in meaning. Work by Bevir and O'Brien (2001), in which they examine in-depth the philosophies of the New Labour party, help to provide for the readers a greater understanding of the approaches to governance articulated by the Britain's New Labour politicians. Yang's (2005) work examining trust as related to citizenship involvement provides not only clarification related to the notion of trust, but also, examines notions of trust as framed from the perspectives of administrators as they view citizens. His exploration of how much administrators actually trust citizens is helpful in framing conceptualizations of notions of trust. Finally, Newman, Jackson, and Baker's (2003) work examining sexual harassment in the federal workplace both helps examine conceptualizations of sexual harassment, and provides clarity under some of the factors that might enable it to happen in particular workplace settings.

Ultimately, these four areas help to provide a beginning of a typology for exploring some of the commonalities in research questions and issues that are explored in the course of exploring research as it has surfaced in the past several years in the field of public administration. By no means is this typology the final and exhaustive framework for the analysis of emergent literature in the field. We propose it merely as a starting point for further categorizations.

43.10 CONCLUSIONS

Through the years, there has been a degree of criticism in the field of public administration, surrounding in particular, notions of academic rigor and potential impact of research in the field. Explorations of scholarship within the field must take into consideration these criticisms. We have attempted to examine approaches to understanding dynamics related to inquiry in the field by exploring in detail factors related to the framing of research agendas.

We have attempted to explore in detail various concepts related to the development and exploration of processes through which research questions and agendas in the field of public administration are generated. We began with an examination of the roles of theory in framing research processes. We call in this section for a more attentive approach by those who are shaping inquiry processes for the development of comprehension of theory's role in framing research agendas.

Next, we examined the historical evolution of the field, with an examination of various stages of history in the evolution of the field and parallel research agendas as they have evolved over time and focusing for distinct periods of time. Our focus was on five eras of administrative history, with a focus on exploring the interplay of historical events on the development of approaches to research.

We continue with an examination of articles that have appeared within the field of public administration between 2000 and 2005, with an emphasis upon articles that have appeared in the journal *Public Administration Review*. From the examination, we were ultimately able to propose a typology of research categories within the field. Our typology identified four areas of research type: evaluation of systems and processes, case-based and grounded research, the presentation of theories, and concept clarification. Our hope is that this typology might be used to frame for further reflection on inquiry in the field.

If, ultimately, the criticism of research in the field of public administration—as observed by Gill and Meier, Stallings and Ferris, and others—is valid, the evolution of research in public administration will require further scholarly reflection. Such reflection will need to focus on the exploration of various mechanisms related to the further development of research and its further legitimization in a larger community of inquiry.

REFERENCES

Adams, B. 2004. Public meetings and the democratic process. *Public Administration Review*, *64*(1), 43–54.

Alasdair, R. 2003. In the eye of the storm? Societal aging and the future of public-service reform. *Public Administration Review*, *63*(6), 720–733.

Beck, M., Asenova, D., and Dickson, G. 2005. Public administration, science, and risk assessment: A case study of the U.K. bovine spongiform encephalopathy crisis. *Public Administration Review*, *65*(4), 396–408.

Bevir, M. and O'Brien, D. 2001. New labour and the public sector in Britain. *Public Administration Review*, *61*(5), 535–547.

Bowling, C.J., Cho, C., and Wright, D.S. 2004. Establishing a continuum from minimizing to maximizing bureaucrats: State agency head preferences for governmental expansion—A typology of administrator growth postures, 1964–1998. *Public Administration Review*, *64*(4), 489–499.

Brady, F.N. 2003. "Publics" administration and the ethics of particularity. *Public Administration Review*, *63*(5), 525–534.

Cooper, T.L. 2004. Big questions in administrative ethics: A need for focused, collaborative effort. *Public Administration Review*, *64*(4), 395–407.

Czarniawska, B. 2002. Remembering while forgetting: The role of automorphism in city management in Warsaw. *Public Administration Review*, *62*(2), 63–173.

Descartes, R., Cottingham, J., Stoothoff, R., and Murdoch, D. 1985. *The Philosophical Writings of Descartes*. New York: Cambridge University Press.

Dolan, J. 2002. The budget minimizing bureaucrat? Empirical evidence from the senior executive service. *Public Administration Review*, *62*(1), 42–50.

Durant, R.F. and Legge, Jr., J.S. 2002. Politics, public opinion, and privatization in France: Assessing the calculus of consent for market reforms. *Public Administration Review*, *62*(3), 307–323.

Fish, S. 1994. *There is No Such Thing as Free Speech: And It Is a Good Thing Too*. New York: Oxford University Press.

Ghere, R.K. 2001. Probing the strategic intricacies of public–private partnership: The patent as a comparative reference. *Public Administration Review*, *61*(4), 441–451.

Gill, J. and Meier, K. 2000. Public administration research and practice: A methodological manifesto. *Journal of Public Administration Research and Theory*, *10*(1), 157–199.

Gooden, S.T. and Bailey, M. 2001. Welfare and work: Job retention outcomes of federal welfare-to-work employees. *Public Administration Review*, *61*(1), 83–91.

Gormley, Jr., W.T. 2001. Moralists, pragmatists, and rogues: Bureaucrats in modern mysteries. *Public Administration Review*, *61*(5), 535–547.

Halvorsen, K.E. 2003. Assessing the effects of public participation. *Public Administration Review*, *63*(5), 535–543.

Hambleton, R. and Sweeting, D. 2004. U.S.-style leadership for English local government. *Public Administration Review*, *64*(4), 474–488.

Haque, M.S. 2001. The diminishing publicness of public service under the current mode of governance. *Public Administration Review*, *61*(1), 65–82.

Heinrich, C.J. 2002. Outcomes-based performance management in the public sector: Implications for government accountability and effectiveness. *Public Administration Review*, *62*(6), 712–725.

Hoffman, S. and Cassell, M. 2002. What are the federal home loan banks up to? Emerging views of purpose among institutional leadership. *Public Administration Review*, *62*(4), 83–91.

Holliday, I. and Wong, L. 2003. Social policy under one country, two systems: Institutional dynamics in China and Hong Kong since 1997. *Public Administration Review*, *63*(3), 269–282.

Kaufman, H. 2001. Major players: Bureaucracies in American government. *Public Administration Review*, *61*(1), 18–42.

Keating, E.G. and Gates, S.M. 2002. Working capital fund pricing policies: Lessons from defense finance and accounting service expenditure and workload data. *Public Administration Review*, *62*(1), 73–81.

Kelly, J.M. 2005. The dilemma of the unsatisfied customer in a market model of public administration. *Public Administration Review*, *65*(1), 76–84.

de Lancer Julnes, P. and Holzer, M. 2001. Promoting the utilization of performance measures in public organizations: An empirical study of factors affecting adoption and implementation. *Public Administration Review*, *61*(6), 693–708.

Lerner, D. and Lasswell, H.D. (Eds). 1951. *The Policy Sciences: Recent Developments in Scope and Methods.* Stanford: Stanford University Press.

Melkers, J.E. and Willoughby, K.G. 2001. Budgeters' views of state performance-budgeting systems. *Public Administration Review, 61*(1), 54–64.

Miller, G.J., Yeager, S.J., Hildreth, W.B., and Rabin, J. 2005. How financial managers deal with ethical stress. *Public Administration Review, 65*(3), 301–312.

Newman, M.A., Jackson, R.A., and Baker, D.D. 2003. Sexual harassment in the federal workplace. *Public Administration Review, 63*(4), 472–483.

O'Toole, L.J. and Meier, K.J. 2004. Parkinson's law and the new public management? Contracting determinants and service quality consequences in public education. *Public Administration Review, 64*(3), 342–352.

Page, S. 2004. Measuring accountability for results in interagency collaboratives. *Public Administration Review, 64*(5), 591–606.

Painter, M. 2005. Transforming the administrative state: Reform in Hong Kong and the future of the developmental state. *Public Administration Review, 65*(3), 335–346.

Ross, D. 1992. *The Origins of American Social Science.* New York: Cambridge University Press.

Rubenstein, R., Schwartz, A.E., and Stiefel, L. 2003. Better than raw: A guide to measuring organizational performance with adjusted performance measures. *Public Administration Review, 63*(5), 607–615.

Rubin, M.M. and Bartle, J.R. 2005. Integrating gender into government budgets: A new perspective. *Public Administration Review, 65*(3), 259–272.

Ryan, J.J. 2004. Decentralization and democratic instability: The case of Costa Rica. *Public Administration Review, 64*(1), 1–91.

Schachter, H.L. and Liu, R. 2005. Policy development and new immigrant communities: A case study of citizen input in defining transit problems. *Public Administration Review, 65*(5), 614–623.

Schiesl, M. 1977. *The Politics of Efficiency.* California: University of California Press.

Segal, L. 2002. Roadblocks in reforming corrupt agencies: The case of the New York city school custodians. *Public Administration Review, 62*(4), 445–460.

Stallings, R.A. and Ferris, J. 1988. Public administration research: Work in PAR, 1940–1984. *Public Administration Review, 48*(1), 580–587.

Stewart, J. and Kringas, P. 2003. Change management—Strategy and values in six agencies from the Australian public service. *Public Administration Review, 63*(6), 675–688.

Van Slyke, D.M. 2003. The mythology of privatization in contracting for social services. *Public Administration Review, 63*(3), 296–315.

Vigoda, E. 2002. From responsiveness to collaboration: Governance, citizens, and the next generation of public administration. *Public Administration Review, 62*(5), 527–540.

Warner, B.E. 2001. John Stuart Mill's theory of bureaucracy within representative government: Balancing competence and participation. *Public Administration Review, 61*(4), 403–413.

Wiebe, R. 1967. *The Search for Order, 1877–1920.* New York: Hill and Wang.

Yang, K. 2005. Public administrators' trust in citizens: A missing link in citizen involvement efforts. *Public Administration Review, 65*(3), 273–285.

Appendix: Articles Used in This Analysis

Author	Year	Title	Area
Type I research: Evaluation of various systems and processes			
Melkers and Willoughby	2001	Budgeters' views of state performance-budgeting systems	Budget/Finance
Keating and Gates	2002	Working capital fund pricing policies: Lessons from defense finance and accounting service expenditure and workload data	Budget/Finance
O'Toole and Meier	2004	Parkinson's law and the new public management? Contracting determinants and service quality consequences in public education	Bureaucracy
Bowling, Cho, and Wright	2004	Establishing a continuum from minimizing to maximizing bureaucrats: State agency head preferences for governmental expansion—A typology of administrator growth postures, 1964–1998	Budget/Finance
Marks Rubin	2005	Integrating gender into government budgets: A new perspective	Budget/Finance
de Lancer Julnes and Holzer	2001	Promoting the utilization of performance measures in public organizations: An empirical study of factors affecting adoption and implementation	Performance Measurement
Rubenstein, Schwartz, and Stiefel	2003	Better than raw: A guide to measuring organizational performance with adjusted performance measures	Performance Measurement
Page	2004	Measuring accountability for results in interagency collaboratives	Performance Measurement
Type II research: The presentation and testing of theories			
Dolan	2002	The budget minimizing bureaucrat? Empirical evidence from the senior executive service	Bureaucracy
Warner	2001	John Stuart Mill's theory of bureaucracy within representative government: Balancing competence and participation	Citizen Participation
Vigoda	2002	From responsiveness to collaboration: Governance, citizens, and the next generation of public administration	Citizen Participation
Halvorsen	2003	Assessing the effects of public participation	Citizen Participation
Haque	2001	The diminishing publicness of public service under the current mode of governance	Comparative
Brady	2003	"Publics" administration and the ethics of particularity	Ethics
Cooper	2004	Big questions in administrative ethics: A need for focused, collaborative effort	Ethics
Kelly	2005	The dilemma of the unsatisfied customer in a market model of public administration	Performance Measurement

(continued)

(*Continued*)

Author	Year	Title	Area
Czarniawska	2002	Remembering while forgetting: The role of automorphism in city management in Warsaw	International
Gormley	2001	Moralists, pragmatists, and rogues: Bureaucrats in modern mysteries	Ethics
Kaufman	2001	Major players: Bureaucracies in American government	Bureaucracy
Type III research: Case-based or case-grounded			
Segal	2002	Roadblocks in reforming corrupt agencies: The case of the New York city school custodians	Bureaucracy
Stewart and Kringas	2003	Change management—Strategy and values in six agencies from the Australian public service	International
Ryan	2004	Decentralization and democratic instability: The case of Costa Rica	International
Beck, Asenova, and Dickson	2005	Public administration, science, and risk assessment: A case study of the U.K. bovine spongiform encephalopathy crisis	International
Holliday and Wong	2003	Social policy under one country, two systems: Institutional dynamics in China and Hong Kong since 1997	International
Alasdair	2003	In the eye of the storm? Societal aging and the future of public-service reform	Budget/Finance
Painter	2005	Transforming the administrative state: Reform in Hong Kong and the future of the developmental state	International
Durant and Legge	2002	Politics, public opinion, and privatization in France: Assessing the calculus of consent for market reforms	Privatization
Schachter and Liu	2005	Policy development and new immigrant communities: A case study of citizen input in defining transit problems	Citizen Participation
Gooden and Bailey	2001	Welfare and work: Job retention outcomes of federal welfare-to-work employees	Federal Government
Hambleton and Sweeting	2004	U.S.-style leadership for English local government	Comparative
Type IV research: Clarification of concepts			
Adams	2004	Public meetings and the democratic process	Citizen Participation
Yang	2005	Public administrators' trust in citizens: A missing link in citizen involvement efforts	Citizen Participation
Miller, Yeager, Hildreth, and Rabin	2005	How financial managers deal with ethical stress	Ethics
Heinrich	2002	Outcomes-based performance management in the public sector: Implications for government accountability and effectiveness	Performance Management
Hoffman and Cassell	2002	What are the federal home loan banks up to? Emerging views of purpose among institutional leadership	Federal Government
Newman, Jackson, and Baker	2003	Sexual harassment in the federal workplace	Federal Government
Bevir and O'Brien	2001	New Labour and the public sector in Britain	International
Ghere	2001	Probing the strategic intricacies of public–private partnership: The patent as a comparative reference	Privatization
Van Slyke	2003	The mythology of privatization in contracting for social services	Privatization

44 Making the Translation: Strategies for Effective Data Presentation

Marc Holzer, Kathryn Kloby, and Aroon Manoharan

CONTENTS

44.1 INTRODUCTION

Measuring performance and communicating the results of government programs and service efforts is a critical task for public managers. The goals of data collection and presentation should be twofold. First, performance information has the capacity to improve management decision making. Second, it provides an opportunity to connect management decisions to the expectations of citizens and their elected surrogates. Managers must, therefore, translate performance information and other data from technical terms and spreadsheets to graphics and narratives that highlight patterns and explain results for a broad public audience.

This chapter will address techniques and strategies for presenting data. Drawing from the experiences of government agencies, of collaborations between government and nonprofit organizations, and of nonprofit organizations that work independently to determine how government measures up to citizen expectations, we present useful and tested techniques for data presentation. We begin with the mechanics of graphical presentation, when such techniques are appropriate and how they should be presented. Our aim is to present guidelines for data presentation, as well as additional techniques that build a contextual envelope around data so as to improve communication of government efforts to the public. We conclude with some exemplary cases of performance reporting that serve as working models for making the translation from quantitative data to a more holistic view for the assessment of government performance.

44.2   GRAPHICAL PRESENTATION TECHNIQUES

Many user-friendly statistical software and publishing programs permit a broad range of possibilities when preparing reports with data and graphical illustrations. Instead of reiterating those
capacities, we present guidelines for reporting via visual aids and graphics. The most frequently
used types of graphical presentations are pie charts, bar graphs, histograms, line graphs, and
statistical maps.

44.2.1   PIE CHARTS

Pie charts are used to represent the relative proportions of each component, category, or classification of data. This type of graph is used primarily for nominal-level or categorical data (i.e., data that
is categorical such as gender, race, and ethnicity), as well as for ordinal level data (i.e., level of
citizen satisfaction, level of awareness of program offerings). A pie chart is generally circular in
shape and is divided into different portions, with each slice representing a percentage or "slice" of
the data (O'Sullivan et al., 2006). Overall, pie charts should be used when there are no more than
five components to be compared, and when there are substantial differences across the data
(Roberts, 1992; Statistics Canada, 2006).* In addition, a pie chart should be constructed with the
largest slice placed at the twelve o'clock position and other portions following in a clockwise
direction (O'Sullivan et al., 2006). For example, Figure 44.1 presents a pie chart reported in
the 2005 Performance Report of the Capitol Corridor Joint Powers Authority in California
(Capitol Corridors Joint Powers Authority, 2005).

   This chart clearly communicates relative proportions of various types of riders who use the
Capitol Corridor intercity train between San Jose and Sacramento, California. Each slice of the pie
illustrates key reasons why riders utilize Capitol Corridor services. The largest portion, showing
55 percent as traveling to work or business related purposes, is followed by the second-largest
portion of travel for leisure purposes (37 percent) in a clockwise direction. The graphic is easy to
read and understand as there are only four slices, with substantial differences in size between each
component.

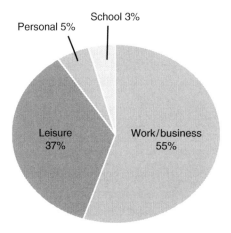

FIGURE 44.1 Rider profile—Reason for using the capitol corridor.

---

* Statistics Canada is an informative source for administrators interested in effective graphical presentation of data. For more
  on piecharts, refer to http://www.statcan.ca/english/edu/power/ch9/piecharts/pie.htm

44.2.2 Bar Charts

Bar charts are useful for assisting a reader in making comparisons across the attributes of variables. The variables are represented along one axis while bars of equal width and length proportional to the frequency are represented along the other axis (O'Sullivan et al., 2006). Unlike pie charts, bar charts can be used to represent any type of data, as well as changes in data trends over time.

Bar charts may be either horizontal or vertical, depending on the number of variables, the length and width of the bars used, and the variations in frequency (O'Sullivan et al., 2006). Vertical bar charts are more frequently used to depict changes in magnitude. They are typically used to represent data that describes components, frequency distributions, and time-series trends (Rutchik, 1998). An example of a vertical bar graph from the research bureau's report on citizen satisfaction with municipal services and quality of life in Worcester 2005 is shown in Figure 44.2.

Figure 44.2 illustrates the results of a citizen survey regarding citizen perceptions of vacant or abandoned buildings in neighborhoods in the city of Worchester, Massachusetts. The categorized respondents' opinions are represented along the X-axis while the frequency is expressed as percentages along the Y-axis. According to Figure 44.2, an overwhelming majority of nearly 83 percent do not consider the vacant or abandoned buildings a problem in the neighborhoods.

Horizontal bar charts can also be used to compare the same data as shown on vertical bar charts. Although they are used less frequently as compared to vertical bar charts, they are preferred when a wider space is required for text labeling. They are more effective when no more than nine bars are compared (Statistics Canada, 2006).* It is generally recommended that the bars are arranged in descending order, with the longest bar placed at the top, as shown below in Figure 44.3.

The horizontal bar chart is used to show citizen perceptions of traffic-related problems (Tri-State Transportation Campaign, 2006). The longest bar, representing the highest reported traffic-related problem, is placed at the top of the bar chart, with the others following in a descending order. This information is shown with a horizontal bar chart, as the length of the text wording is too long to fit on the X-axis in a vertical graph.

Bar charts can also be used to depict the increase or decrease in frequency of a variable over time. Figure 44.4 shows a typical application of bar charts in depicting the net change of different variables over two time periods (Boston Indicators Project, 2004).

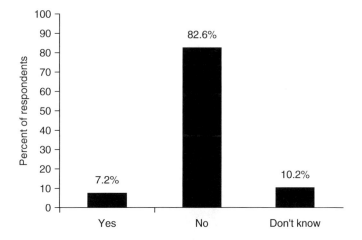

FIGURE 44.2 Are vacant or abandoned buildings a problem in your neighborhood? (Citywide, $n = 2091$).

---

* For more on bar graphs, refer to Statcan http://www.statcan.ca/english/edu/power/ch9/bargraph/bar.htm

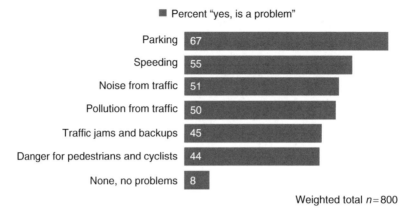

FIGURE 44.3 Traffic-related problems in "your neighborhood".

Figure 44.4 shows the change in the payroll employment in various industries over a span of ten years, divided into two periods: 1994–2001 and 2001–2004. The industries are represented along the *X*-axis while the frequency is represented in thousands along the *Y*-axis in both the positive and negative directions. The positive *Y*-axis shows the increase in employment, while the negative *Y*-axis shows the decrease in employment in thousands. The most significant change is

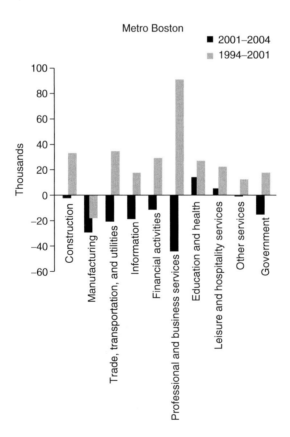

FIGURE 44.4 Payroll employment by industry net change, 1994–2004 metro Boston. (From U.S. Bureau of Labor Statistics, State, and Area Employment. Data for Boston CMSA.)

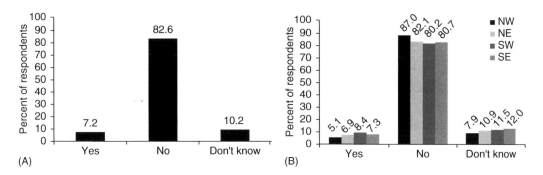

FIGURE 44.5 Are vacant or abandoned buildings a problem in your neighborhood? (Citywide, $n = 2091$). (A) Simple bar chart and (B) Clustered bar chart.

recorded in the professional and business services sector, with employment increasing by about 90,000 during 1994–2001. In the period 2001–2004, however, that sector experienced a decrease in employment of at least 45,000.

Cluster bar charts are used to compare two or more measures over time or space. Both horizontal and vertical bar charts can be used in all cases, with the only caveat that horizontal bar charts should have more space between them (Rutchik, 1998). Figure 44.5 shows the results of a citizen survey regarding perceptions of vacant or abandoned buildings (Worcester Regional Research Bureau, 2005):

Overall, the simple bar chart (on the left) shows that a majority of citizens do not perceive abandoned buildings as a problem in their neighborhood. The clustered bar chart (on right) offers more precision to a reader as it further disaggregates the data by comparing citizen opinions by geographical areas in Worcester.

44.2.3 HISTOGRAMS

The histogram is a useful graphic for showing a distribution of data with both continuous and discrete categories. Discrete data includes, for example, the population of a city, number of affordable housing units, number of riders on public transit, expenditures of the city government, or revenue of the public transit service (Lind et al., 2005). It is generally recommended that this type of graphic should be used when a data set consists of more than 100 observations. The histogram is particularly useful for identifying extremes or outliers in data (Statistics Canada, 2006). Figure 44.6 shows the inaccuracies in cost estimates in 258 transportation projects (Flyvbjerg et al., 2002).

The percentage of cost escalation of the transportation projects is represented on the X-axis and the frequency percentage is represented on the Y-axis. The largest percentage of cost escalation ranges between 0 and 20 percent, which consists of about 37 percent of the projects.

44.2.4 LINE GRAPHS

Line graphs are effective tools for underscoring changes in the frequency of a variable over a given period of time (O'Sullivan et al., 2006). The X-axis usually represents increments of time, while the Y-axis shows the frequencies or percentages. Figure 44.7 provides a good example of an application of a line chart from the Kentucky Metro Annual Performance Report (Georgia Regional Transportation Authority, 2005).

This graph depicts highway fatality rates per 100 million vehicle miles traveled in the city of Atlanta, Georgia, in comparison with state and national statistics from 1998 to 2004. According to the graph, the fatality rate per 100 million vehicle miles traveled in Atlanta was 1.05 in 2004, which was significantly lower than the state and the national benchmarks. A review of such trends also

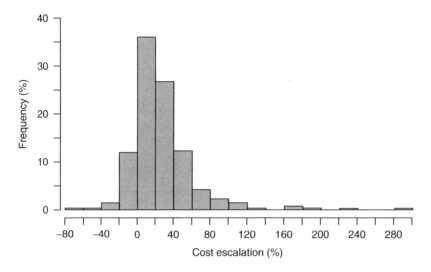

FIGURE 44.6 Transportation infrastructure projects ($N = 258$).

permits public administrators and other officials to establish baselines and targets that are realistic in relation to past occurrences.

In general, administrators should keep clarity in mind when constructing line graphs. Including too many lines of data (more than five) runs the risk of confusion and noise (Rutchik, 1998). Ideally, comparisons should also be made for more than two years of data.

44.2.5 STATISTICAL MAPS

Statistical maps are useful in depicting the frequency and the change in frequency of a variable over different geographical areas. These areas are mostly defined by political boundaries and differ in

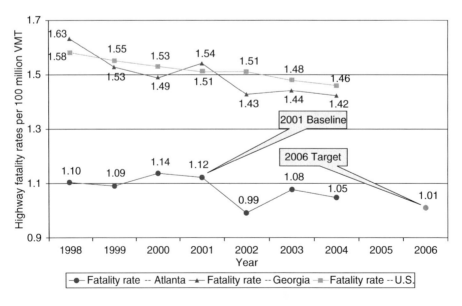

FIGURE 44.7 Line graph showing the relationship between fatality rates and miles traveled. (From 2005 Transportation Metropolitan Atlanta Performance report.)

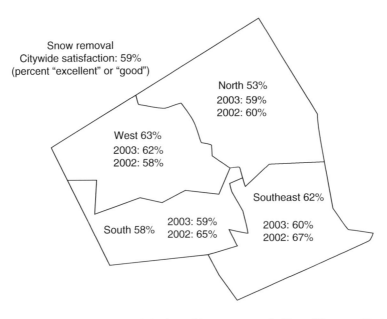

Snow removal
Citywide satisfaction: 59%
(percent "excellent" or "good")

North 53%
2003: 59%
2002: 60%

West 63%
2003: 62%
2002: 58%

Southeast 62%

South 58% | 2003: 59% | 2003: 60%
2002: 65% | 2002: 67%

FIGURE 44.8 Statistical map of citizen satisfaction with snow removal. (From Worcester Regional Research Bureau: Citizen satisfaction with municipal services: 2004 Survey.)

terms of the population and population density. Thus, care needs to be taken to ensure that the frequency of the variable is measured in terms of rates, percentages, and ratios, and not just in absolute numbers (Rutchik, 1998). Figure 44.8, for example, presents citywide citizen satisfaction with snow removal and satisfaction by neighborhood for the current year (2004) and previous years (2002 and 2003) (Worcester Regional Research Bureau, 2004).

Disaggregated and presented by neighborhood, citizens and government officials can see how neighborhood assessments differ in comparison to each other and to the citywide level of satisfaction. Furthermore, change in satisfaction by neighborhood can be viewed over time.

44.3 WORKING MODELS AND EXAMPLES

There are a number of exemplars that can serve as useful resources and models for data presentation. Listed below are a few organizations that are exceptional models for measuring and reporting performance, as well as for assisting governments to measure up to citizen expectations through collaborative measurement of service quality and citizen perceptions.

44.3.1 FAIRFAX COUNTY

Fairfax County (http://www.fairfaxcounty.gov/), Virginia, is lauded by professional associations and prestigious institutions for its performance measurement and reporting achievements. In 2005, for example, the International City or County Management Association gave Fairfax County its highest performance measurement award, the Certificate of Distinction, in recognition of county efforts to incorporate performance data into decision making, sustain the program through training and process improvement, and share lessons learned with others. Furthermore, research findings of the Government Performance Project (2001) of 40 counties nationwide showed Fairfax as the highest ranking jurisdiction in the areas of financial, human resource and capital management, information technology, and managing for results.

Fairfax reports are available online, serving as a resource for public managers in search of ways to develop multiple measures of county agency performance (efficiency, outputs, and outcomes).

Budget documents present quantitative information clearly as the information is used to highlight trends that impact county funding, present the broader vision of county services via strategic goals and program objectives, and provide narrative to explain patterns in the data and variations in performance (McGuire and Kloby, 2007). The Web site also offers a range of manuals for conducting citizen surveys and measuring performance, as well as citizen guides for navigating the budget.

44.3.2 BOSTON INDICATORS PROJECT

The Boston Indicators Project (http://www.tbf.org/indicatorsProject/) coordinates its efforts with the city of Boston, the Boston Redevelopment Authority, and the Metropolitan Area Planning Council. Part of the project's goal is to present government performance in the context of broader social, demographic, and economic trends. The aim is to find ways to foster collaboration across sectors, rather than having the burden of solving problems fall to elected officials and public servants that implement city government programs and services.

The Boston Indicators Project Web site presents performance information for key government services, including public health, transportation, public safety, and other areas. In particular, Web site visitors are offered a comprehensive view of public safety in the city of Boston. Structured by the categories of goals, indicator measures, and how are we doing? citizens are presented with information as to the impact of Homeland Security requirements on local public safety resources, city efforts to achieve emergency preparedness, and Boston crime trends in comparison to other cities. The frequencies and types of reported crimes are presented per 1000 residents in Boston neighborhoods. Citizen survey results graphically highlight citizen perception of crime, as well as the levels of respect and trust between residents and Boston police officers. The impact of crime prevention efforts through civic and social networks, programs for children and youth, and other activities are demonstrated with clear explanations and graphics. Data sets are also made available for download.

The Boston Indicators Report, available online, is a biennial publication that highlights government performance in the context of a large urban city in a dynamically changing environment. The report presents issues such as the importance of global and regional thinking; long-term trends affecting Boston, such as changing demographics and the economy; the cost of inaction; possible scenarios for the future; and strategies for acting locally through a civic agenda. Other Web site offerings include information-sharing features such as the Hub of Innovation, a data portal that includes links to other data-rich sites in the United States and globally.

44.3.3 MINNESOTA MILESTONES

This initiative is useful for public managers in search of effective data presentation, as well as techniques to show progress. Minnesota Milestones (http://www.mnplan.state.mn.us/mm/) was established in 1991 to help the State of Minnesota create a future as envisioned by the public. It works to show progress toward meeting long-term strategic goals for the state in key areas such as the economy, the natural environment, community life, children and families, education, health, and quality of government. The Web site offers strategies for public managers to show progress, rather than just indicating that performance targets have not been met. Serving as a data clearinghouse, school, district, and county data is readily available, as well as other data sets and reports. Visitors are able to compare data within a region and across the state, and to create maps showing county comparisons.

44.3.4 WORCESTER REGIONAL RESEARCH BUREAU

The Worcester Regional Research Bureau (http://www.wrrb.org/) serves the public interest of the Greater Worcester region by conducting independent, nonpartisan research and analysis of public policy issues to promote informed public debate and decision making. Its goal is to educate both citizens and public officials about local public policy issues and to suggest directions toward their resolution that would ultimately contribute to greater efficiency and accountability on the part of local governments. To fulfill its mission, The Research Bureau prepares studies and sponsors forums on municipal and regional issues, and disseminates the results. In serving the community for almost 22 years, The Research Bureau has prepared more than 130 reports and sponsored more than 135 forums that address public policy issues of short and long-term consequence to the region.

The Research Bureau's Center for Community Performance Measurement (CCPM) has worked with citizens and government officials to benchmark municipal and community performance in the goals of Worcester's strategic plan: to improve economic development, public education and youth services, municipal and neighborhood services, and public safety. CCPM publishes annual reports for each of the five areas that provide data and information which can be used by citizens, government officials, community leaders, and neighborhood organizations to improve Worcester. The reports are framed with key questions that help government leaders and citizens interpret results. Questions ask: Why is this important? How does Worcester perform? What does this mean for Worcester? These questions are addressed with narratives and easy to interpret charts and graphics in reports that are available online.

44.4 CONCLUSION

As public administrators work to measure the efforts of their public organizations, it is just as important that they communicate those measures to a range of stakeholders: citizens, clients, legislators, partners, the media, etc. Measurement is only useful to the extent that it is the basis for an analytical discussion in which discourse is driven by data rather than subjective, personal experiences. Excellent presentation of data is more likely to lead to productive discussions, and ultimately performance improvement of essential services, helping governments to "deliver as promised."

It is, therefore, necessary to master techniques for effectively communicating progress and achievements. Off the shelf software can facilitate the technical aspects of reporting, but cannot address the subtleties and sensitivities that we have addressed above. Our goal was multifaceted: to present guidelines for the graphical display of quantitative information; to identify key organizations known for their efforts to measure and report government performance, thereby encouraging replication in other jurisdictions; and to underscore clarity of communication as a necessary criterion.

REFERENCES

The Boston Indicators Project. 2004. A summary of the Boston indicators report 2002–2004. Retrieved on Nov 11, 2006 from www.tbf.org/uploadedFiles/Indicators2004.pdf.

The Capitol Corridors Joint Powers Authority. 2005. Rider reasons for using the capitol corridor. 2005 Performance Report. Retrieved on Nov 11, 2006, from www.capitolcorridor.org/included/docs/ccjpa/perfreport05.pdf.

Flyvbjerg, B., Holm, M.S., and Buhl, S. 2002. Underestimating costs in public works projects. *Journal of the American Planning Association*, 68(3), 279–295.

Georgia Regional Transportation Authority. 2005. Transportation metropolitan Atlanta performance report. Retrieved on Nov 11, 2006 from www.grta.org/news_section/2005_publications/2005%20Transportation %20MAP%20Report%20Final%20Body.pdf.

Lind, A.D., Marchal, G.W., and Wathen, A.S. 2005. *Basic Statistics for Business & Economics*, *International Edition*. New York: McGraw-Hill.

McGuire, A. and Kloby, K. 2007. Fairfax measures up: Key factors for the design and implementation. In Callahan, K. (Ed.), *Elements of Effective Governance: Measurement, Accountability, Participation*. New York: Taylor & Francis.

O'Sullivan, E., Rassel, G.R., and Berner, M. 2006. *Research Methods in Public Administration*. New York: Longman Publishers.

Roberts, R.A. 1992. Graphic displays of data. In Holzer, M. (Ed.), *Public Productivity Handbook*. New York: Marcel Dekker Publishers, pp. 603–623.

Rutchik, H.R. 1998. EIA Guidelines for statistical graphs. Retrieved on Nov 6, 2006 from http://www.eia.doe. gov/neic/graphs/preface.htm.

Statistics Canada. 2006. Retrieved on Nov 5, 2006 from http://www.statcan.ca/english/edu/power/ ch9/first9.htm.

Tri-State Transportation Campaign. 2006. New Yorkers on traffic and transportation: Key findings telephone survey of 800 New York City residents. Retrieved on Nov 11, 2006 from www.tstc.org/press/ 2006/TSTC_transportation_opinion_survey.pdf.

The Worcester Regional Research Bureau. 2004. Citizen satisfaction with municipal services: 2004 Survey. Retrieved on Nov 11, 2006 from www.wrrb.org/reports/CCPM-04-08.pdf.

The Worcester Regional Research Bureau. 2005. Citizen satisfaction with municipal services and quality of life in Worcester: 2005 Survey. Retrieved on Nov 11, 2006 from www.wrrb.org/reports/CCPM-06-02.pdf.

45 Influencing the Policy Process: Making Performance Reports Relevant to Citizens

Kathe Callahan

CONTENTS

Edward R. Tufte, a professor emeritus at Yale University and one of the world's leading experts on the visual presentation of information, believes that the 1986 explosion of the space shuttle Challenger can be partially blamed on the poorly designed presentations to NASA officials about the potential failure of O-rings in cold weather [1–3]. Tufte felt that if the potential risk had been presented properly, decision makers would have understood the extreme risk involved and would have postponed the launch. Tufte's perspective reflects a rational point of view that ignores the political pressures that influenced NASA's decision to launch, but it is a critical perspective, nevertheless, and one that reflects the importance of data presentation. Every day, public administrators rely on good data to inform decisions and shape public policy. Granted, lives may not be at stake, but if the data does not tell the story it is supposed to tell, or if it is misleading, ill-informed decisions will be made. Citizens rely on data communicated by policy analysts and public administrators to inform them about the outcomes and results of policy initiatives. Information, communicated effectively, enables

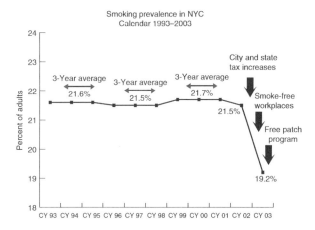

FIGURE 45.1 New York City's mayor's management report. (From http://www.nyc.gov/html/ops/html/mmr/mmr.shtml.)

citizens to engage in meaningful dialogue with their neighbors, elected officials and public administrators about the quality of public sector services.

Critical to the success of any policy initiative is the way the information is communicated. No matter how good the policy or program is, it is only as good as the information that is communicated. Overly technical and detailed reporting is too complicated for most people to comprehend. While at the same time, oversimplified data that fails to inform the reader is of little value. Unfortunately, more often than not, the presentation of quantitative data fails to communicate information clearly or efficiently. According to Stephen Few, the founder of Perceptual Edge, a consulting firm that specializes in information design for analysis and communication, all too often data presentations try to impress the reader rather than inform the reader and they entertain when they should explain [4]. Many data displays are difficult to read because they are filled with too much information, and the tables and graphs can often be misleading. There are numerous examples of misleading and confusing data presentations, not only in the public sector, but the private sector as well. A classic example of a misleading data presentation appears in Figure 45.1. In an effort to show dramatic results from public policy initiatives implemented in an effort to decrease the prevalence of smoking in New York City (e.g., tax increase on tobacco, smoke-free workplaces, and a free patch program) the graph in Figure 45.1 shows a steep decline in the prevalence of adults who smoke. Upon quick glance, a reader might think, "Wow, these policies really brought about significant change." However, upon closer inspection, the reader would see that the steep decline on the graph reflects a drop of 2.3 points (from 21.5 to 19.2 percent, or a drop of 10.7 percent). Data effectively communicated through visual displays can be far more powerful than words. One image, properly designed, can communicate what word and numbers alone may fail to convey. For example, Figure 45.2 accurately and efficiently conveys the rising property tax burden in the greater New York area. A wealth of information is depicted using very few numbers and words.

Because people process data in different ways, a varied format that includes a narrative, traditional tabular reporting, as well as the use of graphs and pictures will enhance the value of the information being communicated and increase the likelihood that it will be utilized. The communication should be simple and straightforward, and should take advantage of various communication strategies, including newsletters, newspapers, reports, public meetings, cable television, e-mail, and Web sites. In many cases, multiple levels of reporting may be necessary: A detailed profile of performance that includes numerous indicators might be necessary for an internal report, while a

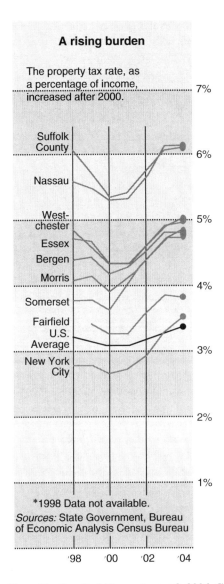

A rising burden

The property tax rate, as a percentage of income, increased after 2000.

7%

Suffolk County

6%

Nassau

West-chester

5%

Essex

Bergen

Morris

4%

Somerset

Fairfield
U.S. Average

3%

New York City

2%

1%

*1998 Data not available.
Sources: State Government, Bureau of Economic Analysis Census Bureau

'98   '00   '02   '04

FIGURE 45.2 A rising burden. (From *The New York Times*, August 8, 2006, Gain in income is offset by rise in property taxes.)

summary of the most essential, and socially relevant, indicators is communicated externally to citizens, the media, and elected officials.

Internal performance reports, communicated at all levels of an organization, allow staff members to know if their performance is on target or off course. Are policy and organizational goals being met? If off course, decisions about mid-course corrections can be made. If on target, acknowledgement of the achievement can be made and discussions surrounding what needs to be done to remain on course can be generated. When performance is reported on a regular basis and in a timely fashion throughout the entire organization, different departments or units are able to see how they contribute to the implementation of public policy initiatives as well as the realization of organizational goals. In addition, they can see areas where services are duplicated and identify areas for possible coordination of services. External reports inform citizens, elected officials, the media, the business community and other stakeholders about performance gains and losses, and enable interested, and informed, stakeholders to hold government accountable for its performance and expenditure of public resources. Effective communication with the public on a regular basis increases transparency, accountability, and ultimately trust in government.

A good public performance report should appear more than once a year. Yes, the splashy annual report is important for a variety of reasons—it highlights significant achievements, can be used as a public relations tool to generate media coverage and can secure political and financial support—but reporting performance data only once a year is not sufficient. Individual organizations need to determine what timeframe makes the most sense for them. A large city serving over a million people a year might want to report performance data more frequently than a smaller community. And, communities addressing critical issues in education or public health may choose to report on these areas more frequently to better develop an understanding of patterns and trends. Policy areas that are not problematic can be reported less frequently. Again, it is up to the agency or organization to determine what frequency makes the most sense. Reports issued too frequently can result in data overload. Too much data can overwhelm citizens and decision makers. Too much information can actually mask the problems as well as the achievements. The purpose of reporting performance data is to provide easy access to information that promotes problem-solving discussions, raises questions, resolves critical issues, inspires managerial thinking, and ultimately improves government performance.

CCAF-FCVI, Inc., a national, nonprofit research and education foundation in Canada, has spent more than 20 years researching public sector governance, accountability, management, and auditing. In 2002, after a multiyear public performance reporting program, CCAF published *Reporting Principles: Taking Public Performance Reporting to a New Level,* in which they present nine principles for performance reporting that support critical thinking, discussion, and action. In the introduction to their report, Jean-Pierre Boisclair, the president of the foundation, states, "This document aims to help government advance the quality of their formal reporting on performance, in keeping with the results-oriented and values-based approaches they are taking. Better communication, understanding and transparency of performance are crucial to the success of government efforts to improve their operations and improve public confidence in them" [5]. Their recommendations include

1. Focus on the few critical aspects of performance that add value.
2. In doing so, look forward as well as back; at a minimum, identify and explain goals and expectations, and relate the results achieved to previously established expectations.
3. Explain key strategic risks and their influence on policy choices and performance expectations. Relate results achieved to the risks and level of risk accepted.
4. Explain key considerations affecting capacity to sustain or improve results and meet expectations.
5. Explain other factors critical to the successful implementation of strategies or to understanding performance.
6. Integrate financial and nonfinancial information to show how resources and strategies influence results.
7. Provide comparative information about past performance and about the performance of similar organizations when doing so would significantly enhance the clarity and usefulness of the information reported.
8. Present credible quantitative and qualitative information that has been fairly interpreted.
9. Disclose the basis for reporting, including the selection process for the few critical aspects of performance, any changes in the way that performance is measured or presented, and the basis on which those responsible for the report feel confident in the reliability of the information being reported.

45.1 WHAT TO INCLUDE IN A PERFORMANCE REPORT?

Before compiling data and writing a report you need to think about your message and your target audience. What is it you want to say and who do you want reach with the information? You want to make sure your message is clear and communicated at a level that your target audience will easily comprehend. Data should be understood accurately and efficiently. A reader should not have to spend time figuring out what a chart or graph is trying to convey. Charts and graphs should simplify, not complicate the message. A good performance report can, and should, stimulate intelligent conversation about the policy process, including the outcomes and strategies that ultimately lead to improved performance and better quality programs. In order for intelligent conversation to take place, for managerial thinking to be inspired, for informed policy decision making to take place and for citizens to be able to hold government accountable, results must be effectively communicated on a regular basis. The data reported should provide a balanced and comprehensive picture of program goals and objectives, the results achieved, the clients served, the costs incurred and it should do so in a way that is easy to understand.

Before deciding what information to include in a performance report, an organization should consider the needs and expectations of its audience. Who is the intended audience? Employees, citizens, elected officials, other stakeholders? Is it a document for internal use, external use, or both? How will the information be used? What is the nature of the data? What information should be reported? Which formats are best for displaying the data and making it user friendly? Some data can be displayed as raw numbers, others as averages, percentages, or ratios. What level of aggregation makes sense? Which criteria should be used in deciding what performance measures to select for reporting? Which criteria should be used in deciding how performance measures are to be communicated? How can the report foster informed and continuous use of the data?

A good format to follow for a formal report is one put forth by the Government Accounting Standards Board (GASB). The board acknowledges that most governments will be unable to meet all the suggested criteria, but contends that this fact should not discourage them. Instead, GASB encourages public organizations to use the criteria outlined here and suggests that when they cannot provide the data for a specific category, they explore the reasons why and then figure out what needs to be done to report on those criteria in the future. In doing this, public organizations make an effort to continually improve the quality of their performance reporting. A detailed report, prepared by GASB, *Reporting Performance Information: Suggested Criteria for Effective Communication*, can be obtained on their Web site [6].

45.1.1 CRITERION 1: EXPLANATION OF PURPOSE AND SCOPE OF THE INFORMATION

The purpose and scope of the report should be communicated up front. What is the information intended to communicate? Who is the intended audience? What level of detail is presented? What programs or services are included? When readers have answers to these questions, they can quickly determine whether the information is of significance to them. The purpose could be stated as "communicating this information meets the organization's commitment to manage for results and be open and accountable." Depending on the intended audience, the purpose could be stated as "the publication of this information is intended to improve public accountability and assist citizens in making decisions." As far as scope is concerned, an explanation as to why certain data has been selected for inclusion should be made—"Information included in this report highlights our most significant achievements as well as our greatest challenges." Major programs, such as one that comprise the largest allocation of resources, or critical programs, which are identified as being of significant importance, are typically included in performance reports. For example, the city of Portland, Oregon, in their annual report on government performance indicates the report's scope and limitations: "As illustrated below, the nine services covered in this report comprise about 79% of the

City's budget and 86% of its staff. These services are generally considered the most visible and most important services provided to the public.''

45.1.2 Criterion 2: Statement of Major Goals and Objectives

A concise statement about the organization's mission, goals, and objectives should answer the following questions:

1. What is the organization trying to accomplish?
2. How do its programs attempt to achieve results?
3. Who benefits?

Readers need to understand what an organization does, why it exists, and what it intends to accomplish. The relationship between organizational objectives and policy objectives should be evident. Readers also need to see how the mission is articulated through its goals and objectives. This provides a basis for determining whether the outcomes and results achieved contribute to the accomplishment of the stated goals and objectives and whether the performance information offers a basis for assessing the effectiveness of the organization in meeting its objectives. By clearly stating its mission, goals, and objectives, the organization ensures that the reader can easily determine whether the performance data being reported is relevant to what the organization is trying to accomplish. For example, in Table 45.1, the New York City Police Department (NYPD) clearly states its mission and directly links that mission to four primary values, or goals, for the department to realize. On the CD-ROM that accompanies this book you will find the complete report prepared by the NYPD that organizes performance indicators around this mission and value statement. The police department does not overwhelm the reader with too much information and the indicators are organized under objectives that will help them realize their mission, such as enhance the safety and security of the public, improve the quality of life for city residents, enhance traffic safety, and improve police and community relations.

45.1.3 Criterion 3: Involvement in the Establishment of the Goals and Objectives

A statement indicating who was involved in the establishment of the goals and objectives is helpful in communicating whether citizens, elected officials, management, employees, and other interested stakeholders were involved in the development of the goals and objectives. If not clearly stated, it is

---

TABLE 45.1
Mission Statement and Values for the New York City Police Department

About the NYPD

Mission

The Mission of the New York City Police Department is to enhance the quality of life in our city by working in partnership with the community and in accordance with constitutional rights to enforce the laws, preserve the peace, reduce fear, and provide for a safe environment.

Values

In partnership with the community, we pledge to

• Protect the lives and property of our fellow citizens and impartially enforce the law.
• Fight crime both by preventing it and by aggressively pursuing violators of the law.
• Maintain a higher standard of integrity than is generally expected of others because so much is expected of us.
• Value human life, respect the dignity of each individual and render our services with courtesy and civility.

Source: http://www.nyc.gov/html/nypd/html/mission.html.

---

safe to assume the goals and objectives were developed by the administration with little input from the people who will likely benefit from, or be accountable for, the service provision. As the GAB report clearly states, "By suggesting a disclosure about the involvement of both citizens and elected officials, this criterion recognizes the balance in government between citizen engagement and representative democracy. The addition of management and employees adds further balance by disclosing how those actually responsible for the results of the programs and services are involved in setting forth what they are expected to achieve" [7].

For example, Albuquerque, New Mexico, clearly states how the goals and desired community conditions were formulated: "As a result of Community Goals Forums... goals and the resulting community conditions were developed by several hundred citizens. These goals and desired conditions were formally adopted by the City Council and approved by the Mayor" [8].

45.1.4 Criterion 4: Multiple Levels of Reporting

The way performance data is presented really matters, and utilizing one approach and providing one level of information is a format that is bound to fail. One level of reporting does not reflect the diverse use of performance reports. People have different needs, interests, levels of understanding, and purposes for performance information, so it is important to communicate the performance information at various levels of detail. One individual might only want summary data that provides an overall picture of what the organization does and how well it delivers results. Another might want more detailed information about a specific program, let's say parks and recreation, and would want to see data on park usage, dollars spent, and level of satisfaction of park users. Another person might want that information broken down by individual parks or neighborhoods and desire information on the demographics of park users—how many elderly, young children, women, Latinos, and organized sports leagues utilize the parks on a regular basis? To satisfy the multiple needs of multiple users, effective reports should present performance information at multiple levels of detail. Reporting information in this way acknowledges the various levels of interest, knowledge, and analytical sophistication.

A good way to present performance information is to begin with an overview, followed by an introductory summary, then information about specific programs and services, and finally performance data broken down by specific activities or demographic characteristics. Some organizations present performance information as internal and external reports, with the internal-level reports providing excruciatingly detailed information for managers and staff, and an external report that simplifies and summarizes the detailed information for public consumption.

The Mayor's Office of Operations in New York City provides performance data on a neighborhood basis through a program called My Neighborhood Statistics. My Neighborhood Statistics lets New York City residents know how City agencies are performing in their neighborhood by viewing locally mapped performance information. Residents just enter a street address or intersection, and color-shaded maps pop up that allow for easy comparison of highs and lows in different neighborhoods. In addition to plotting an address or intersection, maps can be reconfigured based on the location of community boards, police precincts, or school districts. The Web site provides year-to-year neighborhood and citywide comparisons for agency performance data, as well as month-to-month and citywide comparisons for select services requested through the 311 Citizen Service Center. The 311 statistics, based on calls received through the 311 hotline, typically center on complaints surrounding parking violations, noise complaints, and restaurants and bars violating the smoking law. Users can search for performance information by thematic agency groupings, such as health, education, and human services, or public safety and legal affairs. Performance indicators under health, education, and human services include such things as infant mortality, deaths due to drug abuse, number of persons receiving food stamps, substantiated child abuse cases, or percentage of students meeting or exceeding national standards in math and English. Public safety and legal affairs includes indicators that include the number of civilian fire fatalities, average response time to critical crimes in progress, and the number of assaults and burglaries. The user just has to keep on clicking to peel away the layers and get at more program- or neighborhood-specific data. In addition, the neighborhood statistics data can be saved and opened in several different spreadsheet programs so that the information can be analyzed and further communicated. A link to My Neighborhood Statistics is provided on the CD-ROM that accompanies this book.

45.1.5 CRITERION 5: ANALYSIS OF RESULTS AND CHALLENGES

This section of a report provides a summary of the major management challenges confronting the organization. It provides evidence that the key decision makers within the organization have analyzed the performance information and what it means to the organization. This analysis summarizes significant achievements and the reasons behind those achievements. These achievements should be goal related and tied to policy initiatives. For example, a drop in the crime rate could be attributed to a new community policing strategy, or an increase in the high school graduation rate could be attributed to a revised curriculum. This section should also outline the challenges confronting the organization and the strategies that will be undertaken to address the challenges. According to the GASB report, "An executive or management analysis provides users with condensed information about the general performance of the organization that they can use to select areas that they wish to investigate in more detail. It also provides a basis for assessing whether the organization has been making overall progress in achieving its objectives and what challenges have been identified that will affect results" [9].

The Jacksonville Community Council, Inc. (JCCI) a nonpartisan civic organization in Northeast Florida successfully utilizes performance data and performance reports to analyze results, articulate problems and improve the overall quality of life in Jacksonville and the surrounding area. Over the years they have brought diverse groups of people together to gather data, track trends and collectively improve community conditions through a collaborative project called the Jacksonville Indicators for Progress [10]. Community indicators are reported annually to inform the public about the progress that has been made and identifies areas in need of attention. For example, several indicators recently illustrated that the infrastructure in older neighborhoods was in significant decline. This finding prompted citizens to establish a study committee that focused on what the citizens call "Neighborhoods at the Tipping Point" in an effort to identify the stress factors contributing to the decline as well as the resources and tools needed to strengthen neighborhoods before conditions worsen.

45.1.6 CRITERION 6: FOCUS ON KEY MEASURES

The performance report should focus on a few key measures that are critical to goal attainment in the organization that effectively communicate outcomes and results. Just because data is available and makes a terrific-looking graph does not mean it should be included in a report. A recent report by the Government Accountability Office (GAO) looked at the overwhelming amount of data collected and reported by federal agencies as a result of the Government Performance and Results Act (GPRA). GAO researchers found that while federal agencies are collecting more data to comply with GPRA, managers are not using the additional information to inform decision making and improve the effectiveness of their agency's performance [11]. "Nearly 10 years have passed since the Government Performance and Results Act (GPRA) was enacted. Agencies spend an inordinate amount of time preparing reports to comply with it, producing volumes of information of questionable value. If one were to stack up all the GPRA documents produced for Congress last year, the pile would measure over a yard high. Policy makers would need to wade through reams of paper to find a few kernels of useful information" [12]. Theodore Poister and Gregory Streib, professors at the Andrew Young School of Policy Studies at Georgia State University refer to this as the DRIP syndrome – data rich, information poor [13]. Too much data can be overwhelming. To avoid DRIP, and other problems associated with too much information, it is critical for public administrators to identify the key measures that communicate critical results to citizens and other interested stakeholders. These

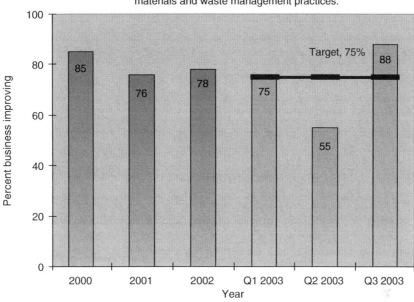

FIGURE 45.3 King County Department of Public Health. (From King County Managing for Results, www. metrokc.gov/exec/perform.)

key measures should address both the failures and successes of specific programs. Of course, this is easier said than done. How does a public manager make the decision on what data to include? State and local governments provide a myriad of services that are often complex, and a few key measures fail to capture the results. The best advice is to report on the most critical areas—the services that are most visible, the ones that require the most funding, the programs that have the most profound impact on constituents. Organizations should attempt to achieve a balance between the number of services reported on and the capability of readers to understand and act on the information. The key measures should be outcome measures that reflect how well an organization did in realizing its goals. Too much information about too many things confuses rather than clarifies, and as a result the report overwhelms readers rather than informing them.

Selecting just a few measures to report is difficult because the expected outputs and outcomes of government activities are not always clear and because user interests and needs are so diverse. It is important to be rigorous in the selection of the measures that will be reported and explaining how the measures were selected and why they were included is a good idea. Sometimes an explanation of the measure and what it means is equally important. King County, Washington, does a terrific job of communicating a few key measures of performance with an explanation of what each measures means. In Figure 45.3 the King County Department of Public Health explains the meaning of an outcome measure for improving their hazardous waste management practices.

45.1.7 CRITERION 7: RELIABLE INFORMATION

To instill confidence in the performance information communicated, the source of the information should be made clear. How was the data collected, and who collected it? Is the data derived from agency records? Was it collected through a survey? Does the data come from an outside source (e.g., census data, uniform crime reports)? It is important that the information itself be verifiable and free from bias, and it should accurately represent what it is intended to represent. If questions exist about the reliability of the information, but the data in question is the most appropriate data to include, a statement addressing the concerns surrounding the data should be included. For example, Prince William County, Virginia, in their Service Efforts and Accomplishments Report, include a statement that indicates the data reported was reviewed and discussed in focus groups comprised of executive management, agency management, and staff to question unusual variances in the data, but that it was not possible for them to fully analyze or address every variable. In essence, they did their best to insure the reliability of the data, but were unable to verify all of the data contained in the report. Likewise, when data has been reviewed by the audit division staff, or some other review body, the report should clearly state that the accuracy and reliability of the data was checked and briefly, in a sentence or two, explain how that was done. The bottom line is simple as this: The performance information presented should be fair, accurate, consistent, relevant, reliable, and understandable.

45.1.8 CRITERION 8: RELEVANT MEASURES OF RESULTS

The two Rs are most important—relevance and results. Relevance relates to mission, goals, and objectives. To what degree has the organization achieved its mission, goals, and objectives? Does the performance information provided answer that question? Outcome measures communicate results and should be the primary focus, but the report should also include input, output, efficiency, and productivity measures, or what is sometimes referred to as a "family of measures." This really is the heart of the report. The Worcester Regional Research Bureau, in Worcester, Massachusetts, does an outstanding job reporting on the quality of local government services through its Center for Community Performance Measurement (CCPM). For the last four years the CCPM has been measuring and reporting on the status of public education, in addition to other areas of municipal services such as public safety and economic development. With public education, CCPM looks at same five performance indicators year after year: attendance and drop out rates, student mobility, family involvement, post-graduate placement and standardized test scores. There are numerous other indicators to measure and report, yet they stick to the five most relevant measures. In doing so, they enable annual comparisons to be made and they can measure performance by asking themselves what has changed from last year, what have they accomplished, and what challenges remain? Figure 45.4 reports on the

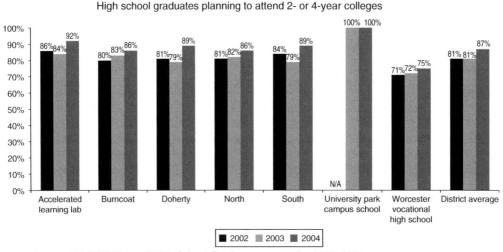

Source: MA DOE Plans of High School Graduates reports for 2002–2004.

FIGURE 45.4

(continued)

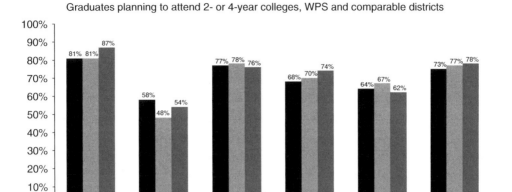

Source: MA DOE Plans of High School Graduates reports for 2002–2004.

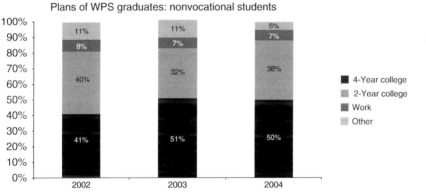

Source: MA DOE Plans of High School Graduates reports for 2002–2004.

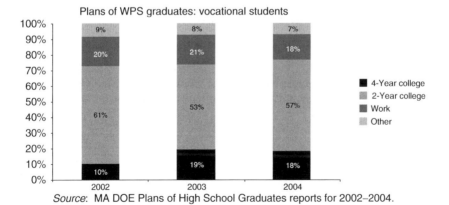

Source: MA DOE Plans of High School Graduates reports for 2002–2004.

FIGURE 45.4 (continued)   Worcester, Massachusetts post-graduate placement. (From Worcester Regional Research Bureau, http://www.wrrb.org/reports/CCPM-06–01.pdf.)

indicator post-graduate placement. The report tells the reader why this indicator is important, describes the trend in Worcester, graphically displays the trend in four charts, and then explains what this means for Worcester.

45.1.9 Criterion 9: Resources Used and Efficiency

Performance reporting should focus primarily on communicating the results, or outcomes, of programs and activities, but in addition to reporting what has been achieved, the costs associated with delivering the desired results need to be communicated. Public organizations are accountable for results and for the efficient and effective use of public resources. Citizens, as well as other stakeholders, want to be assured that they are receiving value for their tax dollar. Public managers are expected to deliver quality services at a reasonable cost, and these costs should be clearly communicated. To provide a complete picture, performance information should include data about the resources expended. The cost of providing a service and achieving a specific outcome can be communicated in a variety of ways. The unit cost of delivering a meal to the homebound, or paving a mile of roadway, or processing an application can be communicated. This is referred to as an efficiency measure. Productivity measures can also communicate costs: the number of meals a driver delivers in a day, or the number of miles one work crew paves in a day, or the number of applications an intake officer processes in an hour. Cost effectiveness can be communicated as the number of meals delivered by each driver that were on time and still hot, or the percent of applications processed in an hour that are complete and accurate. Expenditures or inputs can be communicated in a variety of ways as well. The total expenditures for each division can be provided, as can the total personnel expenditures or the total number of employees needed to provide the services measured.

Montgomery County, Maryland, reports on a "family" of measures, including input, output, efficiency, service quality, and outcome. Combined, these measures provide a comprehensive view of program performance from multiple perspectives. Figure 45.5 shows the family of measures for the civil cases heard in circuit court. Efficiency is communicated as the number of cases terminated per staff member on an annual basis and the average cost per case.

Reporting on results without relating them to the resources used to achieve those results provides an incomplete picture. To inspire managerial thinking and engage the public in meaningful discussions about the expectations and outcomes of the public sector programs, the costs associated with service delivery need to be clearly communicated.

The Straphangers Campaign in New York City measures the efficiency of city subways in a unique way that speaks directly to the value of service received for each dollar spent. The Straphangers developed a weighted index that measures the quality of subway service based on the aspects of service deemed most important by subway riders: frequency of service, reliability of service, likelihood that a rider will get a seat during rush hour, the cleanliness of the car, and the quality of the in-car announcements. Using this index the Straphangers Campaign is able to calculate the value of a ride on each subway line as rated by subway riders. So, for example, a rider pays $2.00 to ride the A line. Service on this line is sporadic—the train is scheduled to come more often than most subway line, but it arrives with below-average regularity, the cars break down at a higher rate than the average, however, a rider is more likely to get a seat and their in car announcements are above average. According to the Straphanger rating, the A line is tied for 11th place out of the 22 subway lines rated in 2006 and as such riders on the A line receive $1.00 worth of value for their $2.00 fare. Figure 45.6 shows how quality and performance are communicated in an attractive and easy-to-understand format. Linking performance to the value of a service is complicated, yet the Straphangers Campaign does an excellent job communicating the dollar value of the service provided.

45.1.10 Criterion 10: Citizen and Customer Perceptions

The perception of citizens and customers should be communicated to complement the objective measures of performance in a performance report. Managerial measures of performance capture one aspect of performance and, when combined with measures that capture how satisfied citizens are with the quality of services in their community or how well a customer was treated in a particular office, provide a much better picture of service quality. For example, a performance report on a

CIRCUIT COURT					
PROGRAM: Management and Adjudication of Civil Cases			**PROGRAM ELEMENT:**		
PROGRAM MISSION: To administer justice in a fair, timely, and efficient manner when adjudicating civil matters					
COMMUNITY OUTCOMES SUPPORTED: • Provide for fair and timely administration of justice • Foster respect for the law					
PROGRAM MEASURES	FY01 ACTUAL	FY02 ACTUAL	FY03 ACTUAL	FY04 BUDGET	FY05 CE REC
Outcomes/Results:					
Civil judgments entered	1,141	1,176	1,330	1,176	1,176
Civil cases terminated (resolved)[a]	12,188	11,668	12,029	11,668	11,668
Civil cases resolved through Alternative Dispute Resolution	470	432	472	432	432
Service Quality:					
Average time to dispose of civil cases[b] (days)					
Track NT - Little or no trial time necessary (*target - 165 days*)[c]	114	116	130	165	165
Track 0 - No discovery necessary (*target - 167 days*)	131	141	141	167	167
Track 2 - 1/2 to 1 day trial estimate (*target - 271 days*)	208	202	199	271	271
Track 3 - 1 to 3 day trial estimate (*target - 416 days*)	327	306	309	416	416
Track 4 - 3 day trial or more (*target - 481 days*)	413	431	389	481	481
Overall average time for disposition of civil cases (all cases and tracks)	187	184	189	233	233
Efficiency:					
Cases terminated per staff year (civil, criminal, family, and juvenile)[d]	298	327	335	334	351
Average cost per case terminated (civil, criminal, family, and juvenile) ($)[d]	247	248	258	258	274
Workload/Outputs:					
Civil cases filed[g]	12,040	11,866	11,893	11,870	11,870
Civil hearings held	5,581	5,496	5,798	5,781	5,781
Civil trials by jury	203	166	166	166	166
Civil trials by judge	187	146	166	166	166
Civil cases ordered to Alternative Dispute Resolution	542	504	577	490	490
Civil cases filed as a percentage of total Circuit Court filings	37.5	33.0	33.0	31.0	31.0
Total Circuit Court filings (civil, criminal, family, and juvenile)	32,119	35,915	36,038	37,889	37,889
Total Circuit Court terminations (civil, criminal, family, and juvenile)[d]	32,242	35,773	36,175	38,078	38,078
Inputs:					
Workyears[d,e]	108.3	109.3	108.1	[f]100.0	103.2
Expenditures ($000)[d,e]	7,978	8,879	9,326	9,541	9,926

Notes:

[a]Civil terminations include cases that are tried, dismissed, settled, or administratively closed due to lack of prosecution.

[b]For civil cases, the disposition time is measured from initial filing to disposition (i.e., trial, settlement, or dismissal).

[c]The figures in italics represent targets (guidelines) for the time to dispose of civil cases when using the given track. Cases that were formerly classified as Track 1 represent family cases and are reported under the "Management and Adjudication of Family Cases" program.

[d]Workyears, expenditures, and the corresponding efficiency measures include the processing of civil, criminal, family, *and* juvenile cases because it is not feasible to separate expenditures and workyears by type of case. (Staff responsibilities and case processing are not organized by type of case: one person may process several types of cases.) Because workyears and expenditures cannot be split by type of case, both efficiency measures are based on *all* Circuit Court terminations: civil, criminal, family, and juvenile (this total is shown for reference under "Workload/Outputs").

[e]Expenditures include the Family Grant. The Juvenile Division is partially funded by the Family Grant.

[f]The State of Maryland assumed the funding for the judicial law clerks, resulting in a permanent decrease in workyears for FY04.

[g]Civil filing data includes the Register of Wills caseload.

EXPLANATION:

One of the Circuit Court's primary functions is the adjudication of civil cases. The Court has integrated the Differentiated Case Management (DCM) concept into the daily operations of all units supporting the Circuit Court's functions. DCM is an approach designed to improve the efficiency of case processing and reduce the demand for judicial intervention (continuances, hearings, etc.) at every phase of litigation. Mechanisms have been designed to avoid multiple court appearances and assure the timely provision of resources for the expeditious processing and resolution of cases on each track.

The results for the average time to dispose of cases are based on cases that were disposed in the fiscal years indicated, regardless of the date on which a case was filed. Timely case termination based upon track guidelines depends upon the availability of sufficient resource levels in the Circuit and District Courts, the Public Defender's Office, Parole and Probation, and the State's Attorney. Criminal litigation takes precedence over civil litigation as criminal cases must be tried within 180 days from the Rule 4-215 hearing.

PROGRAM PARTNERS IN SUPPORT OF OUTCOMES: Clerk of the Circuit Court, Maryland and Montgomery County bar associations.

MAJOR RELATED PLANS AND GUIDELINES: State legislative mandates, Maryland Rules of Procedure, Maryland Annotated Code, Montgomery County Code, Court of Appeals of Maryland.

FIGURE 45.5 Montgomery County, Maryland Circuit Court–efficiency measures. (From Montgomery Measures Up, www.montgomerycountymd.gov.)

police department that includes both crime rates and measures of how safe citizens feel in their neighborhood is more powerful than a report that just includes crime rates. Likewise, a performance report for a motor vehicle inspection station that includes data on the number of cars inspected in an hour, the average wait time, and the level of customer satisfaction with the service provided tells

Straphangers Campaign
Ⓐ SUBWAY LINE PROFILE

Straphangers Campaign MetroCard Rating $1.00

The A line ranks tied for 11th out of the 22 subway lines rated by the Straphangers Campaign. Our ranking is based on the MTA New York City Transit data below, using a method described at www.straphangers.org.

The A line is scheduled to come more often than most subway lines. . .

Scheduled minutes between weekday trains
as of January 2006

	AM Rush	Noon	PM Rush	Overnight
A line	4:45	7:30	5	20
System average	5:33	8:26	5:48	20

and arrives with below-average regularity.

% of trains arriving at regular intervals
(without gaps in service or train "bunching")
between 6 a.m. and 9 p.m.

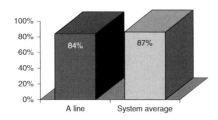

Cars on the A line break down more often than those on the average line.

Average miles traveled between delays
caused by mechanical failures, 2005

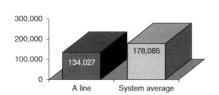

You're more likely to get a seat on the A line.

% of passengers with seats at most crowded point
during rush hour

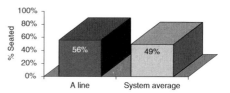

The A line is less clean than average...

% of cars with 'light or no interior dirtiness'
as defined by NYC Transit

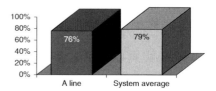

but performs better than average on in-car announcements.

% of cars with correct announcements
(as defined by NYC transit)

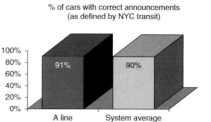

Suggestions? Complaints? Call the A line superintendent at (212) 712-3706.

FIGURE 45.6 Straphangers campaign—A-line subway profile. (From Straphangers Campaign, www.straphangers.org.)

more about the quality of the service provided than only reporting on the number of cars inspected in an hour.

Citizen and customer satisfaction can be measured in a variety of ways, such as tracking complaints and/or comments and convening focus groups, but the most common way to assess citizen and customer satisfaction is through a survey. Ideally, survey data should be collected, and reported, on a regular basis so that perceptions over time can be tracked and compared.

When communicating performance information collected through a survey, it is important to mention how the data was collected, the sample size, and the response rate. The limitations of survey data should also be discussed, such as the nonresponse bias on the external validity and generalizability of the results. It can become overwhelming to report on the level of citizen or customer satisfaction with every service provided, and for some services it may be confusing, or misleading, to report on citizen and customer satisfaction. Again, as with all performance information, data collected through citizen and customer surveys should only be communicated if it adds clarity to a report. If it fills a gap, or strengthens a managerial measure, it should be included. If the usefulness of the measure is questionable, and it just adds clutter, it should not be reported.

The Oregon Progress Board, an independent state planning and oversight agency, is responsible for monitoring the state's strategic plan. The board publishes the Oregon Benchmarks on an annual basis, and in an effort to gauge how the state is doing, reports on a variety of performance measures, including citizen satisfaction. Figure 45.7 communicates citizen satisfaction with police services, including the overall satisfaction with police services by neighborhood and feelings of safety, both during the day and at night, and provides comparative data over a four-year period.

45.1.11 CRITERION 11: COMPARISON FOR ASSESSING PERFORMANCE

Comparison data provides a frame of reference for assessing performance information. Comparative data enables the user to see whether performance is improving, remaining stable, or declining over time. How did the program do this year compared to last? When performance targets are established, performance information can be compared to that target. Did the school meet its 90 percent graduation rate? If comparisons are made with similar organizations, demographically comparable communities, or national standards, a determination of quality can be made. How good is the organization doing compared with similar organizations? Are the citizens in El Paso more satisfied with their schools than the citizens in San Antonio? How does police response time in Richmond compare to the national average?

Harry Hatry, one of the nation's leading experts on performance measurement, identifies the following as major types of benchmarks, or data used to make comparisons for a particular reporting period:

- Performance in the previous period
- Performance of similar organizational units or geographical areas
- Outcomes for different workload or customer groups
- A recognized general standard
- Performance of other jurisdictions or the private sector
- Different service delivery practices
- Targets established at the beginning of the performance period [14]

Hatry uses a sports metaphor to explain the need for comparing performance measures: "Unless you are keeping score, it is difficult to know if you are winning or losing" [15]. Sports team managers need to know the strengths and weaknesses of their players to determine what changes or adjustments need to be made to keep the team competitive. Just look at the data kept on the performance of baseball players: earned runs average (ERA), runs batted in (RBI), on base percentage (OBP), number of pitches thrown, speed of pitches thrown, number of games played, and so forth. And in football the performance data is just as plentiful: passing yardage, rushing yardage, fumbles lost, interceptions, third down conversions, and the list goes on. The data is widely disseminated, and comparisons of performance can be made between players, teams, leagues, and conferences; comparisons can be made over time as well. How well did the Yankees do this season compared to last? Like managers of sports teams, managers of public organizations need similar information to assess the performance of their organization and ultimately improve it.

Bureau of Police

CITIZEN SATISFACTION   Citizens say they feel safer in their neighborhoods during the day and night over the last 10 years. As with City services in general, they also report a decline in overall satisfaction with police services.

CITIZENS: OVERALL POLICE SERVICE, 2005
(percent "good" or "very good")

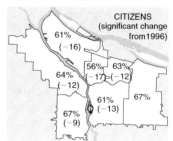

All areas report less satisfaction with the Bureau in 2005 than in 1996, with six reporting significant changes as shown on the accompanying map. The largest decline is in the Inner Northeast (17 percent).

BUSINESSES: OVERALL POLICE SERVICE, 2005
(percent "good" or "very good")

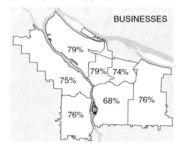

Like last year, businesses continue to rate police services higher than residents. The average rating was 74 percent "good" or "very good" for businesses, compared to 63 percent for residents. Businesses in the North rate Police services the highest, while businesses in Southeast rate them lowest.

- ■ "bad" or "very bad"
- □ "neither"
- ▨ "good" or "very good"

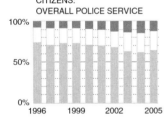

CITIZENS: OVERALL POLICE SERVICE

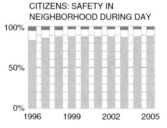

CITIZENS: SAFETY IN NEIGHBORHOOD DURING DAY

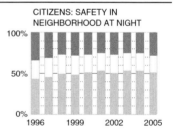

CITIZENS: SAFETY IN NEIGHBORHOOD AT NIGHT

FIGURE 45.7 Portland, Oregon, citizen satisfaction with police service. (From Oregon Progress Board, www. oregon.gov.)

When comparing performance to similar organizations or jurisdictions, it is important to compare apples to apples. There will always be differences in operating procedures, technologies, staffing patterns, level of service, and type of customer served, but obviously, the more similar the communities and organizations, the more powerful the comparison. For example, when comparing annual circulation per capita for public libraries, it is important to note that some of the variation in circulation could be due to such factors as hours of operation, the number of branch libraries, the size and scope of the library holdings, as well as the economic or demographic characteristics of the population served.

The International City/County Management Association (ICMA) recently introduced the Virginia Performance Consortium, where 27 cities and counties in Virginia will participate in a statewide performance consortium. ICMA coordinates a national Center for Performance Measurement, and 15 service areas measured in the nationwide program will be used as the comparative data for the Virginia project. These core measures will provide the regional consortium with a uniform and broad set of measures to compare their performance and identify high performers and effective practices. No overall ranking or formal rating will be assigned, although informally a ranking is bound to happen, and this can spark competition and generate improvements in service delivery. ICMA states the goals in this way:

*   Identify similarities and differences in performance on specific measures within the region (as well as compare regional performance to performance nationwide).
*   Identify high-performing jurisdictions on particular measures (or clusters of related measures) to identify key factors contributing to high performance (e.g., effective practices, leading practices) [16].

The Oregon benchmarks again provide an excellent illustration of performance reporting (Figure 45.8), this time using comparison data over time, between neighborhoods and with others; a six-city average of crimes per 1,000 residents.

45.1.12 CRITERION 12: FACTORS AFFECTING RESULTS/EXPLANATORY INFORMATION

The results of services provided by public organizations are not only affected by factors within the organization itself, like staffing patterns, the technology available, delays in acquiring supplies, or the size of the budget, but they are likely to be affected by factors outside of the organization, such as the weather or the changing demographics of the population served. When communicating performance, an organization should explain the factors that contributed to, or inhibited, performance. This information provides a context for understanding the performance reported. Can the improvement over last year's performance be attributed to the utilization of a new technology or additional resources? Can the decline in performance be attributed to a growing at-risk population or the infrastructure damage incurred by Hurricane Katrina? Whatever the factors, internal or external, the information needs to be communicated so that their impact on performance can be discussed and understood.

Prince William County provides a "comments" section for each performance indicator reported. The example provided in Figure 45.9 communicates why Prince William County has fewer full-time employees per thousand residents when compared to other counties in Virginia.

45.1.13 CRITERION 13: AGGREGATION AND DISAGGREGATION OF INFORMATION

Information communicated at only one level of aggregation can paint a misleading picture of performance. For example, statewide averages of student achievement can hide critical differences among students based on racial and ethnic backgrounds, just as citywide averages of emergency response time can mask the discrepancy in response time in different neighborhoods. Generally speaking, aggregate data should be presented in the summary or overview of a report; disaggregate data, based on geography or demographics, should be communicated at a more detailed level in the report. It is quite common to see performance information communicated by geographic area (neighborhood, census tract, school district), service unit (regional office, school, hospital), and demographic characteristic (income level, age, race, gender). Disaggregated information allows for comparisons and enhances the usefulness of the information. Managerial thinking is inspired when differences in outcomes based on neighborhoods or specific populations can be seen. Why are

BUREAU GOAL:
Reduce crime and the fear
of crime

Over the past ten years, the City's crime rate has declined considerably.

The reduction in both property and person crime rates appears to be part of a larger national trend. Portland's trend mirrors that of our six comparison cities. However, while the decline in person crimes has been continuous, property crimes are trending upward.

| | CRIMES PER 1,000 | |
	PROPERTY	PERSON
2000	67.3	10.7
2001	72.8	8.5
2002	73.0	8.4
2003	77.7	8.1
2004	76.0	7.3
5 years:	+31%	−32%
10 years:	−20%	−59%

Crime clearance rates remain fairly steady. The number of reported crimes per detective, however, is high compared to other cities, as Audit Services found in a recent audit.

The Bureau has responded quickly to high priority calls, exceeding the response time goal for four of the past five years.

BUREAU GOAL:
Improve the quality of life in
neighborhoods

SAFETY IN NEIGHBORHOOD DURING DAY, 2005 (percent "safe" or "very safe")

More residents report feeling safe in their neighborhoods both during the day and at night over the last 10 years. Most areas of the City report gains in feelings of safety in their neighborhoods, with three reporting significant increases.

In addition, the number of drug houses complained about has decreased approximately 51 percent over the last 10 years.

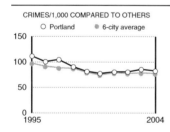

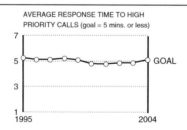

FIGURE 45.8 Portland Oregon, trends over time and neighborhood comparisons. (From Oregon Progress Board, www.oregon.gov.)

residents of the Central Ward more satisfied with city services than residents of the South Ward? What contributes to the achievement gap between Asian and Latino students? Why do trains on the A line break down more often than trains on the D line?

The level or aggregation can be determined by the nature of the data available and by the intended audience. Performance information should be easy to understand and should resonate with the reader. People want to see how the information relates to them personally; thus, information communicated at the neighborhood or district level or on the basis of race, gender, or age carries greater impact than information communicated at a broad or generic level. Performance reports

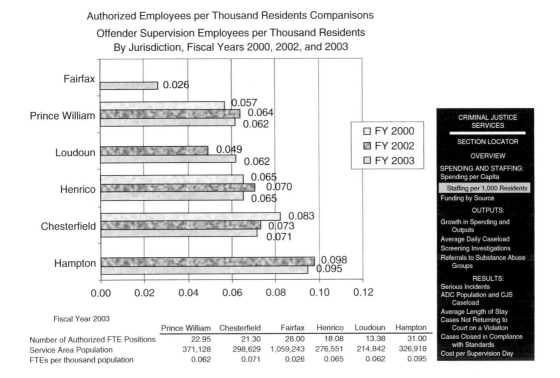

Authorized Employees per Thousand Residents Companisons

Offender Supervision Employees per Thousand Residents
By Jurisdiction, Fiscal Years 2000, 2002, and 2003

Fiscal Year 2003	Prince William	Chesterfield	Fairfax	Henrico	Loudoun	Hampton
Number of Authorized FTE Positions	22.95	21.30	28.00	18.08	13.38	31.00
Service Area Population	371,128	298,629	1,059,243	276,551	214,842	326,918
FTEs per thousand population	0.062	0.071	0.026	0.065	0.062	0.095

Compared to Other Jurisdictions:

♦ Of the six jurisdictions reporting supervision FTEs, Henrico, Hampton, and Chesterfield had a higher number of FTEs per 1,000 residents than Prince William, Fairfax, and Loudoun. Only Fairfax has a lower rate of staffing per thousand residents than Prince William.

Comments:

♦ The number of FTEs in a program is driven in part by availability of funding support and caseload (the number of cases each probation officer handles). Although Prince William has relatively fewer FTEs per thousand residents, additional resources are spent on contract workers and services. Prince William hires hourly interns to assist officers and also provides many services in-house (such as substance abuse services and anger management). Also, OCJS offers extended evening office hours in addition to the standard government hours. Other localities may not offer additional office hours.

FIGURE 45.9 Prince William county explanatory comments. (From Service Efforts and Accomplishment Report, www.co.prince-william.va.us.)

should include a variety of key measures reported at aggregate and disaggregate levels. Again, reports should strive for balance and clarity. Too much aggregate data fails to adequately inform, and too much disaggregation can overwhelm the reader.

The New Jersey Department of Education publishes an annual school report card that communicates performance information on the public schools. Statewide data is available, as is district-wide and school-specific data. The examples provided here show statewide results on the High School Proficiency Assessment in math and English (Figure 45.10) and a breakdown of student performance on the math portion of the test based on gender, race, and income (Figure 45.11).

45.1.14 Criterion 14: Consistency, Easy Access, and Regular and Timely Reporting

Consistency in communication means measuring and reporting the same indicators in the same way over the same time period. Doing this increases the ease in understanding what is being communicated and enhances the reader's and the organization's ability to make comparisons over time.

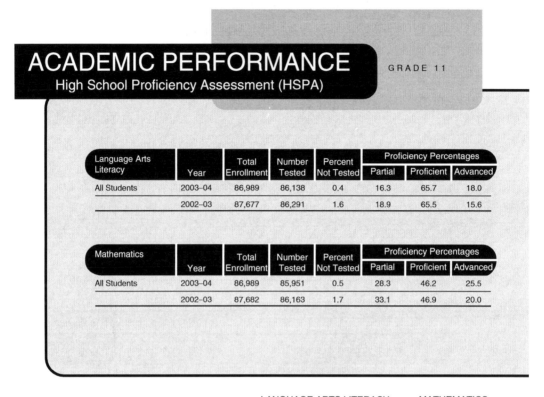

ACADEMIC PERFORMANCE
High School Proficiency Assessment (HSPA)

GRADE 11

Language Arts Literacy	Year	Total Enrollment	Number Tested	Percent Not Tested	Proficiency Percentages		
					Partial	Proficient	Advanced
All Students	2003–04	86,989	86,138	0.4	16.3	65.7	18.0
	2002–03	87,677	86,291	1.6	18.9	65.5	15.6

Mathematics	Year	Total Enrollment	Number Tested	Percent Not Tested	Proficiency Percentages		
					Partial	Proficient	Advanced
All Students	2003–04	86,989	85,951	0.5	28.3	46.2	25.5
	2002–03	87,682	86,163	1.7	33.1	46.9	20.0

LANGUAGE ARTS LITERACY

ADVANCED 18.0%
PARTIAL 16.3%
PROFICIENT 65.7%

ALL STUDENTS
2003–2004

MATHEMATICS

ADVANCED 25.5%
PARTIAL 28.3%
PROFICIENT 46.2%

ALL STUDENTS
2003–2004

No Child
LEFT BEHIND

New Jersey
Department of Education
2004
NCLB State Report Card

FIGURE 45.10 Aggregate performance information. (From New Jersey Department of Education, http://education.state.nj.us/rc/nclb04/state04.)

Consistency does not mean that changes cannot be made. Changes in the way measures are calculated or presented can be a good thing as long as the changes are recognized and explained. The recommendation for consistent reporting is to say that once a workable format has been

ACADEMIC PERFORMANCE
High School Proficiency Assessment (HSPA)

GRADE 11

Language Arts Literacy 2003–2004	Total Enrollment	Number Tested	Percent Not Tested	Proficiency Percentages		
				Partial	Proficient	Advanced
Students with Disabilities	12,611	12,274	2.7	55.8	41.1	3.1
Limited English Proficient Students	2,459	2,426	1.3	74.0	25.4	0.7
Male	43,768	43,262	1.2	19.7	67.4	12.9
Female	43,080	42,745	0.8	12.7	64.1	23.2
White	55,238	54,900	1.0	9.5	68.3	22.1
Black	12,698	12,407	2.3	32.3	62.4	5.2
Asian & Pacific Islander	6,178	6,147	0.5	10.6	59.4	30.1
American Indian/Alaskan Native	157	157	0	21.7	52.9	5.1
Hispanic	11,455	11,296	1.4	32.4	61.1	6.5
Other Race	1,263	1,231	2.5	34.9	56.9	8.2
Migrant Students	13	13	*	*	*	*
Economically Disadvantaged	13,004	12,772	1.8	35.8	59.5	4.7

The state standard for Adequate Yearly Progress (AYP) for language arts literacy is 73% proficient for the school and each subgroup.

LANGUAGE
ARTS
RESULTS

No Child
LEFT BEHIND

New Jersey
Department of Education
2004
NCLB State Report Card

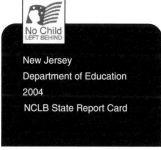

FIGURE 45.11 Disaggregate performance information. (From New Jersey Department of Education, http://education.state.nj.us/rc/nclb04/state04.)

developed and communicated, it should be utilized on a regular basis. Readers of the report should not have to decipher a new format, or read instructions on how to use the report each time it is published. Performance reports should keep acronyms, jargon, and abbreviations to a minimum.

Visual techniques such as headings, graphs, maps, tables, and photographs should be used to simplify and clarify what is being communicated. The information should be presented in a recognizable and practical format that communicates in a way that makes sense and aids understanding.

Performance information should be broadly communicated through a variety of formats to increase its accessibility. Performance information can be disseminated in a various ways. The most familiar format is the annual report, typically printed in full color on expensive paper. A more affordable print version can be realized with a newsletter or newspaper format. As Internet access increases and Web-based applications are easier to use, more and more public organizations are turning to computers to communicate their performance. Technology has the potential to take performance reporting to a new level. Performance information can be kept current, manipulated, and presented in visually appealing formats that can bring data to life. With technology a greater volume of data is available for those who have interest in more detailed performance reporting. Mapping can be used to graphically depict performance on a variety of levels, from global performance to reporting by zip code and street address.

In terms of accessibility, people should know where and how to look for performance information. It should not require an advanced degree to access information from a Web site or to obtain a print copy. The New York City Mayor's Management Report is easy to access through the nyc. gov Web site. Links are provided so that readers can easily access certain sections of the report, and a phone number and URL (Web site address) are provided for those who want to obtain a printed copy of the report. In addition to ease of access, information should be provided in a timely fashion and on a regular basis. The Internet has made access and timeliness easier to achieve; however, all too often information provided on a Web site can be out of date. Many Web sites accessed for this chapter presented 2001 data as the most current information.

Regular and timely reporting of information increases the likelihood that the information will be accessed and used to enhance decision making and increase accountability. At a minimum, performance information should be communicated on an annual basis and linked to the budget and planning process. Information that is communicated more frequently can be acted upon in a more responsive fashion. Some public managers insist that performance information be communicated on a monthly or quarterly basis. The City of Baltimore requires reporting on a biweekly basis. According to the mayor, the frequency of reporting increases the urgency of the situation and allows for improvements in service delivery throughout the year. If the city only looked at performance every year at budget time, the mayor said he would be old and gray before anything would change. Granted, it is not necessary to provide external reports on such a frequent basis; annual reports to citizens and customers may be sufficient. However, if performance information is tracked and reported on a Web site, interested stakeholders could have access to real-time data whenever they want it.

45.2   REPORTING FORMATS

As demonstrated with the various examples provided in this chapter, performance can be communicated using a variety of formats. Some performance information can be communicated effectively in a simple spreadsheet. Spreadsheets are obviously useful for communicating revenue and expenditures, but they are also effective for comparing performance over time, and for setting targets, national standards, and other organizations of jurisdictions. Spreadsheets are easy to use, access, and export. They are also economical to produce and easy to update. Entering too much information on a spreadsheet is a common problem, with all those potential rows and columns to fill. When using spreadsheets, the aim should be for balance and clarity.

Graphs have the advantage of quickly communicating performance information and are especially useful for showing trends over time and the comparison of performance to other organizations or units. Graphical displays are easily absorbed and understood, and people are likely to remember them more vividly than raw numbers. It is much easier to understand and recall performance over time with a line graph, and comparisons to other organizations are easier to communicate with a bar graph than with words and numbers. Common graphical displays include pie charts, bar graphs, and line graphs, but organizations are increasingly introducing creative graphs, maps, and pictorial displays to their performance reports. For example, the Straphangers Campaign utilizes common bar graphs as well as a picture of a MetroCard with the dollar value of the service provided (Figure 45.6). Staying with New York City, the Fund for the City of New York uses maps to communicate and compare street smoothness, and the Mayor's Office of Operations utilizes maps that enable residents to compare the quality of city services in their neighborhood with the quality of city services in other neighborhoods. Creative displays attract attention to the data being communicated in a way that is relatively easy to understand. The CD-ROM that accompanies this book contains several examples of high quality reporting, including the Straphangers Campaign, Boston Community Indicators Project and New York City's My Neighborhood Statistics.

It is important to remember that a significant amount of time and resources went into the design and implementation of the performance measurement system. Failing to effectively communicate the findings is a tremendous waste. Effectively communicated performance information helps organizations determine what steps need to be taken or what changes must be made to improve service. Effective communication can help organizations identify the conditions under which a program is doing well or poorly, stimulate discussion on what can be done to improve performance and pinpoint factors that contribute to high performance so they can be replicated in other areas. Performance information can generate questions regarding service delivery that can help staff develop and carry out improvement strategies, as well as provide clues to underlying problems. Well-thought out and well-designed reports educate and inform citizens so that they can become more involved in the decision-making processes of government. A well-written report that is widely disseminated to the public enables the public to raise intelligent questions and hold government accountable for results. Again, referring to what the expert has to say, Harry Hatry suggests that organizations perform a systematic examination of performance data on a regular basis that includes the following steps:

1. Examine changes over time.
2. Examine comparison data to assess where performance is good, fair, or poor.
3. Compare the program's outcomes to those of similar programs; look for best practices.
4. Use exception reporting—that is, look particularly at indicator values that fall outside the target range.
5. Obtain and examine explanatory information.
6. Determine whether the data on major types of performance indicators is consistent with each other.
7. Focus individual outcome indicators on areas in which the program or agency has particular responsibility or influence.
8. Examine multiple outcomes together to obtain a more comprehensive perspective on overall performance.
9. Use past performance data to trigger trials of new procedures and to help evaluate their success later [17].

45.3   WEB-BASED REPORTING

The Internet and Web-based reporting expands the opportunity to communicate real time data in creative and interactive ways. Possibly the most advanced use of technology in reporting performance data is the United Nations Development Program (UNDP) Millennium Development Goals project (MDG). (Data and reports can be found at http://www.undp.org/mdg/.) The millennium goals were adopted in 2005 as a blueprint for promoting poverty reduction, education, maternal health, and gender equality, while at the same time combating child mortality and AIDS. Among other things, the MDG monitors and reports on the international progress toward the attainment of the goals. It is difficult to capture in words what the various data displays communicate, but it is well worth a look at their Web site, and in particular go to gapminder.org for an interactive presentation of the data collected for the 2005 Human Development Report. Although the UNDP effort reflects an advanced use of technology, other efforts mentioned in this chapter also utilize sophisticated Web-based reporting. The New York City Straphangers' Campaign and My Neighborhood Statistics sites allow viewers to look at current performance data and make comparisons by subway lines and by neighborhood. When utilizing the Internet to communicate data, public administrators must recognize that not everyone has access to computers. And many people who do have access might not have the advanced software, or high speed capacity, necessary to view data. Until the digital divide is comprehensively addressed, data and reports should be made available in a variety of formats. New York City clearly states that hard copies of reports are available to all those interested in exploring the data more fully.

45.4 CONCLUSION

Communicating the results of government programs is an integral part of good government. It demonstrates transparency, fosters communication and promotes accountability. Performance information that is communicated in a simple and straightforward manner has the potential to bring about improvements. When stakeholders can act on the performance information—whether it's to improve processes and procedures, request additional funding, hold elected and appointed officials accountable, celebrate accomplishments, motivate employees, or inspire managerial thinking—the value of a performance measurement system is realized. When performance information is reported within government, it supports better decision making, fosters cohesion through the communication of a shared sense of purpose, and promotes organizational learning. The bottom line is simply this: communicating results helps government perform better. When results are effectively communicated to the public, information about performance promotes dialogue, helps build confidence in government, and serves to strengthen the accountability relationship between government and the people they serve.

PROBLEMS

1. This chapter reviewed the essential elements of a good performance report. Utilizing the criteria outlined in this chapter, evaluate the performance reports of any of the following:
   a. The community where you live
   b. The college or university you attend
   c. The agency or organization where you work, or would like to work (a comparison of public and private sector organizations could prove interesting)
       How effective was their reporting? What aspects of the report were particularly compelling? Where did they fall short? What recommendations can you make to improve the report and make it more meaningful to citizens?
2. The Straphangers Campaign, in New York City, was commended for their creative and graphic style of communicating results. Explore their full report, found at their Web site straphangers.org and on the CD-ROM provided with this book. How might you replicate/modify/adapt their style of reporting in another public or nonprofit organization. Pay particular attention to the graphics and their ability to communicate dollar value based on the quality of service provided. In addition to developing a similar reporting mechanism, discuss the challenges in doing so.
3. The importance of comparison data and the ability to compare the performance of your agency or community over time, to comparable communities or agencies, to national standards was one of the reporting criteria presented in this chapter. Using one of the communities or organizations

you identified for problem 1, think about how you might use comparison data to communicate the performance of your community or agency. What type of comparisons would you make and how might you report those comparisons?

REFERENCES

1. Tufte, E. 1990. *Envisioning Quantitative Information*. Graphics Press, Cheshire, Connecticut.
2. Tufte, E. 2001. *The Visual Display of Quantitative Information*. Graphics Press, Cheshire, Connecticut.
3. Tufte, E. 2003. *The Cognitive Style of PowerPoint*. Graphics Press, Cheshire, Connecticut.
4. Few, S. 2004. Common mistakes in data presentation, *Intelligent Enterprise*, 35–39, August 7, intelligententerprise.com.
5. CCAF-FCVI, 2002. *Reporting Principles: Taking Public Performance Reporting to a New Level*. CCAF-FCVI, Inc., Ottawa, Ontario, Canada.
6. Government Accounting Standards Board (GASB), 2003. *Reporting Performance Information: Suggested Criteria for Effective Communication*, www.seagov.org/sea_gasb_project/suggested_criteria_report.pdf, August 3.
7. GASB, *Reporting Performance Information*, p. 53.
8. http://www.cabq.gov/progress/pdf/IPC-letter.pdf. City of Albuquerque, accessed March 7.
9. GASB, *Reporting Performance Information*, p. 69.
10. Jacksonville Community Council 2006. www.jcci.org, accessed March 7.
11. Government Accountability Office 2005. *Managing for Results: Enhancing Agency Use of Performance Information for Management Decision Making*, September GAO-05-927.
12. Frederickson, H.G. 2005. Coming to account, *PA Times*, 28(5), p. 11.
13. Poister, T.H. and Streib, G. 1999. Performance measurement in municipal government: assessing the state of the practice, *Public Administration Review*, 59(4), 325–335.
14. Hatry, H. 1999. *Performance Measurement: Getting Results*, Urban Institute Press, Washington, DC, p. 119.
15. Hatry, H. 1999. *Performance Measurement, Getting Results*. Urban Institute, Washington, DC, p. 1.
16. International City/County management Association, www.icma.org/performance.
17. Hatry, H. 1999. *Performance Measurement: Getting Results*, Urban Institute, Washington, DC, p. 132.

RECOMMENDED READINGS AND REPORTS

1. The work of Edward Tufte can be found at http://www.edwardtufte.com/tufte/. In addition to complete information on his publications, Dr. Tufte offers a one-day course, at locations across the country, on effective ways to present data and information.
2. Additional information on CCAF-FCVI, Inc., the Canadian research and education foundation that completed a multi-year program on performance reporting can be found at www.ccaf-fcvi.com.
3. The definitive source on performance reporting: Hatry, H., *Performance Measurement: Getting Results*, Washington, D.C., The Urban Institute Press, 1999.
4. Three new books on performance measurement and citizen involvement:
   a. Berman, B.C., *Listening to the Public: Adding the Voices of the People to Government Performance Measurement and Reporting*, Fund For the City of New York, January 2006.
   b. Epstein, P., Coates, P., and Wray, L., *Results that Matter: Improving Communities by Engaging Citizens, Measuring Performance and Getting Things Done*, Jossey-Bass, San Francisco, 2006.
   c. Callahan, K., *Elements of Effective Governance: Measurement, Accountability and Participation*, Taylor & Francis, 2007.
5. Robert Behn's Public Management Report http://www.ksg.harvard.edu/thebehnreport/.

46 Applying for Research Grants

Neil De Haan

CONTENTS

46.1 INTRODUCTION

Congratulations! You have mastered most, if not all, of the chapters in this handbook. You have an intriguing research question, a great research design and a detailed plan as to how you will collect your data, analyze the results, and prepare a report. However, there will be costs involved, such as mailings and printing, and there are the opportunity costs for your time and the time of your research colleagues and associates. How will these costs be paid for? And would it not be nice to send the leaders of your organization—the provost, dean, or executive director—some funds to pay for the space, telephone, computer, and supervisory and support staff that are also related to the costs of your research? Why should you settle for doing it all without any additional compensation and no reimbursement of costs? After all, when you reach out to the auto mechanic, the plumber, the dry cleaner, hair dresser, and computer technician, they all want compensation for their services, and rightly so. How about you and your work as a researcher?

46.2 AVAILABILITY OF FUNDS

The good news is that there are funds available for research. The bad news is that the competition for these funds is intense and the availability for funds for research in the field of public administration is much less than in many other fields, such as health care, medicine, and education. In most cases the pursuit of these funds requires the preparation of an application that follows a required or generally accepted format. The application, if it is to be funded, must be outstanding—an A+ and not just an A, particularly if the application comes from a new or beginning researcher or is being submitted by an organization which is not necessarily a well-known entity. These funds to support your research efforts may be available from the federal or state government, quasi-public organizations, foundations, or individuals. In some cases local or regional governments may have funds available to support your research agenda.

Writing some 20 years ago as a program officer for the Ford Foundation, Crossland (1995) noted that there are generally three common sources of funds for first-time faculty members to get support for their research—the institutions where they are employed, public sources, and private sources (Crossland, p. 236). The researcher's institution might have available research funds, and the place to start is your Department or your organization's office of research and development. In either case, expect very tough competition for limited funds. The second source is the public sector, particularly the federal government, and this chapter will be offering Internet-based strategies on hour to pursue these funds. The third source is the private sector, including individuals, corporations, special-purpose nonprofit agencies, and broad-based philanthropies or foundations conducting regular, ongoing grant programs (Crossland, p. 236). Once we have established a format for a basic research grant application, we will also examine these private sources of funds for research.

46.3   FORMAT FOR THE RESEARCH PROJECT DESCRIPTION

Most applications for grant funding follow a similar format. There are differences, however, in an application for social action-type grants in contrast to research grants. The social action-type application, described by Browning's popular book and on the Foundation Center's Web site, usually consists of an abstract, needs assessment or problem statement, a conceptual context, goals and objectives, methods and a budget, and an evaluation component (Kiritz, 1980; Browning, 2005). A research-type application usually consists of an introduction, background or need, goals and objectives, program narrative which includes the research design, methodologies, and procedures, significance, and qualifications and resources (Argon, 228).

Table 46.1 displays these components for each of the two major types of grant applications—social action type and research type.

Writing as the Director of the Office of Research Services in the B.S.D. Pritzker School of Medicine, University of Chicago, Judith, K. Argon gives some definition and content to the key components of a research grant proposal (1995). She begins her descriptions with the observation that the two most essential aspects of a successful proposal are "a powerful new idea or project and a clear, convincing, and compelling presentation." (p. 226) Ogden and Goldberg (1995, p. 4), with a focus on raising money for research in the life sciences, make a claim which we also endorse: The basic principles of seeking and managing grants apply to virtually all research proposals. These principles are

---

TABLE 46.1

Components of Grant Applications—Social Action and Research

Social Action Grant	Research Grant
1. Abstract	1. Abstract
2. Needs assessment or problem statement	2. Introduction background or need
3. Conceptual context	3. Research question
4. Goals and objectives	4. Goals and objectives and hypotheses
5. Methods	5. Program narrative
	Research design
	Methodologies
	Procedures
6. Evaluation	6. Significance (i.e., Why this research matters)
7. Budget and budget narrative	7. Qualifications and special resources
	8. Budget and budget narrative
	9. Bibliography

- An obviously qualified, expert, productive investigator
- A proposal tailored to the funding source and its review
- A literate, focused, well-organized, interesting proposal
- An important hypothesis effectively tested
- State-of-the-art science

Argon describes the introduction as "a coherent and interesting preview to the project description" (p. 227). The background or need section, she says, describes "the background of your project, the state of the field, and the recent evolution of the field." She suggests that this section should "also critically evaluate existing knowledge and identify the need or gap that your project is expected to fill" (pp. 227–228). Therefore, as pointed out by Przeworski and Salomon, in order to establish the context "it is essential that the proposal summarize the current state of knowledge and provide an up-to-date, comprehensive bibliography." (p. 4 of 11)

The section on goals and objectives plays an important role in the research proposal as it does in the social action proposal. Topics in this section for the research proposal include the basic hypothesis to be tested, the long-term objectives, and the anticipated results, outcomes or accomplishments of your research project (Argon, p. 228).

The program narrative, called the heart of the proposal, consists of the research design, methodologies, and procedures. Przeworski and Salomon make two suggestions about this section. First, "the proposal must specify the research operations you will undertake and the way you will interpret the results of these operations in terms of your central problem." Second, they suggest that a methodology is "not just a list of research tasks but an argument as to why these tasks add up to the best attack on the problem." (p. 8 of 11)

The significance section must make clear the value of the research project and its potential impact and its expected outcome (Argon, p. 228). Ogden and Goldberg suggest that the prose in this section must be sharply focused to show that the research project is important, interesting, and that there is a high probability of success (p. 89). In the qualifications and resources section, you will discuss "your qualifications and the qualifications of your team as well as the special resources—facilities and equipment—you have at your disposal" (Argon, p. 228). You can use this section, Argon suggests, "to convince the reviewers that your particular university is the right place to conduct this project."

How do you get to the first or second draft of the application which includes these components? Reif-Lehrer (1989) suggests that you start with a planning process in which you ask some key questions, such like the ones we have displayed in Table 46.2.

46.4 PROJECT BUDGET AND BUDGET JUSTIFICATION

The budget and the budget justification usually include direct and indirect costs (Argon, pp. 230–321). Most funding sources give directions for a well-developed and well-justified budget. Direct costs, as described by Argon, are "those that can be specifically identified with a particular project and are easily tracked and accounted for" (p. 230). These direct costs include salaries and wages for project personnel, materials, and equipment, travel associated with the project, telephone and Internet charges, computer costs, and publication charges. Indirect costs, Argon points out, are "those incurred for common or joint objectives and that therefore cannot be identified specifically with a particular project." (p. 230) In other words, indirect costs are costs that will occur even without your research project. Examples of costs that are generally covered by indirect costs are the costs for maintenance and operations of a building, library costs, departmental administration and university administration. Argon also gives other examples, such as "accounting, sponsored projects, grants, and contacts management, personnel, purchasing, and plant accounting" (p. 230). Not all funding sources recognize indirect costs, others set a limit (e.g., ten percent) and federal and most State agencies require an approved indirect cost rate, which the organization receives based on a detailed indirect cost proposal and, in most cases, extensive negotiations.

TABLE 46.2

Questions to Ask during the Planning Process

Component	Questions to Answer
Background/Need	Are you and your team aware of what's been done in this and related fields?
Goals and Objectives	What is the long-range goal?
	What are the specific objectives?
	Do the specific objectives lead toward accomplishment of the long-range goal?
Narrative	What is the hypothesis to be tested or question to be answered?
Research design	Is the methodology "state-of-the-art?"
Methodologies	How long will the work take?
Procedures	What are the expected results?
	What are your contingency plans in case you hit a "snag?"
	Where will the work be carried out (i.e., project site)?
Significance	Is the work original?
	How will the project benefit your institution?
	How will the project benefit society?
Qualifications and resources	Who will do the work?
	What is the reputation of the grantee and his or her team?
	Why should the granting agency let you do the project (i.e., What are your unique qualifications)?
Budget and budget narrative	How much will the project cost (budget) and why (budget justification)?
	What is the cost/benefit ratio for the project?
	What other funds are available to support your project?

Source: Based on Reif-Lehrer, L., in *Writing a Successful Grant Application*, Jones and Bartlet Publishers, Boston, 1989, 78–79.

Figure 46.2 gives a very simple example for a research grant budget that was funded by the Association for Institutional Research (AIR), which also gives detailed instructions and guidelines on its Web site (www.airweb.org). With regard to salaries and wages, most funding sources recognize salaries of staff and faculty which constitute appropriate direct costs and may be requested in proportion to the effort devoted to the project. As explained by the guidelines of the AIR, research is usually regarded as one of the normal functions of institutional research staff and faculty members at institutions of higher education. Compensation for time normally spent on research within the term of appointment is deemed to be included within the staff or faculty members' regular institutional salary. In the case of AIR, grant funds may not be used to augment the total salary or rate of salary of staff or faculty members during the period covered by the term of their appointment, or to reimburse staff or faculty members for consulting or other time in addition to regular full-time institutional salary covering the same general period of employment. In the case of these restrictions, many faculty members will budget for a summer salary as part of their research grants. Other funding sources often take a different view, so it is important to ascertain the funding source's policies on this important issue.

46.5   SAMPLE RESEARCH PROPOSAL

Lessons to be learned for writing a grant application for research in public administration can come from different fields, and the Web site of the AIR is an excellent example. The AIR, with support from the United States Department of Education and the National Center for Education Statistics (NCES), has developed several grant programs, with goals to enhance the quality of institutional research in postsecondary education and provide professional development opportunities to individuals in the area of institutional research in the United States. AIR's Web site offers a link to research grant proposals, including a grant for $25,776 which went to principal investigator Marvin Titus, Ph.D., Assistant Professor, North Carolina State University.

Starting with a project summary for a proposed study with a title which should interest most of us—"Examining the Private Benefit of Graduate Education: A Two-Stage Approach," Titus (2004) explains in the opening summary that his study is different from previous research in several ways: its focus is on the marginal private benefit, it will draw from cultural, social, and capital theories, and it "will address self-selection in graduate school, and the implications of controlling for this process." (2004, p. ii) Figure 46.1 displays the proposal's table of contents.

As is evident from the table of contents (Figure 46.1), Titus uses five pages to describe the essence of his proposal. In the research design section, he offers his two research questions: "(1) Do variables, measuring cultural and social capital, predict whether individuals attend graduate school? In other words, what variables reflecting cultural and social capital help to explain self-selection? (2) After taking into account self-selection, what is the private marginal return to an advanced degree, by degree type?" Having covered the research design in one half page, Titus explains that his data will come from the 1993 Bachelor's and Beyond Longitudinal Study, which is a restricted database sponsored by the National Center for Education Statistics (NCES). The

Project summary

Table of contents

Project summary

A. Statement of the problem 1
B. Proposal of work 4
    Research design 4
    Data 4
    Conceptual model 5
    Variables—first stage 6
    Variables—second stage 8
    Analysis 9
C. Dissemination plan 10
D. Description of policy relevance 11
E. Discussion of innovative concepts 12
    of project
F. Discussion of audience to whom the
    the project will be important 13

References cited 14

Biographical sketch 21

Budget and budget justification...............................26

Current and pending support 28

Facilities, equipment and other resources 29

Special information and supplementary
documentation 30

FIGURE 46.1 Sample table of contents for a research grant application. (From Titus, M.A., Examining the private benefit of graduate education: a two-stage approach. Available as of December 26, 2006 at http://www.airweb.org/images/209-Titus%20Marvin.pdf.)

next step is the description of the conceptual model, which relies on citing about ten sources. Titus explains that "this study uses a comprehensive conceptual model that incorporates rationale from cultural, social, and human capital theories to examine the private benefits of graduate education." (p. 5)

Having covered the conceptual model in one page, the proposal describes the variables in two and a half pages. In the first stage of the analysis, he says, "the independent variables will include several measures of cultural and social capital." The two measures of cultural capital are parental educational attainment and whether the language that is most often spoken in the home is English (yes or no). The proposal explains that it will use exploratory factor analysis to construct several composite measures, with the view towards measuring social capital through "variables reflecting parental involvement in graduate education, and the extent to which social networks that promote graduate enrollment exist." Titus cites about 17 sources to describe his approach to the variables and explains, for example, that as a result of prior research, he will include gender, race or ethnicity, and family income as predictors of earnings. Using very precise language, Titus explains that in the second stage of analysis, "the dependent variable will be continuous and defined as the natural log of annual earnings." The proposal's one page description of the Analysis is the most technical of all the sections, reflecting competence in statistical models, as described elsewhere in this handbook.

This research proposal informs the process of writing a research grant proposal, because it balances technical language inherent in the research with commonsense language that will appeal to the less-technically astute person who might have a role in the decision whether or not to fund the proposal. For example, the one paragraph for description of policy relevance acknowledges the fact that "institutions are increasingly being asked to provide accountability indicators reflecting graduate school outcomes," and sets forth the claim that "this research will inform campus leaders and higher education policy makers with regard to the predictors of the marginal benefit of an advanced degree." (p. 11)

This proposal addresses the other key components, such as dissemination, policy, innovative concepts, and target audience, with clear and concise paragraphs. The budget and budget justification for this proposal are also very instructive to those who are pursuing research grants in other fields, such as public administration. The proposal's budget of $25,776, as displayed in Figure 46.2,

Senior personnel	
Principal investigator (2 months summer salary)	$ 12,889
Other personnel	
Hourly graduate students	
($20/h × 10 h/week × 28 weeks)	$ 5,600
Fringe benefits	
Faculty (23 percent)	$ 2,964
Graduate student hourly rate (8.45 percent)	$ 473
Travel	
To attend mandatory AIR conference	$ 1,800
Conference attendance for dissemination of results	$ 1,800
Other direct costs	
Publication costs/dissemination & research supplies	$ 250
Total direct costs (A through G)	$ 25,776
Total direct	$ 25,776

FIGURE 46.2 Sample research grant proposal budget and budget justification. (From Titus, M.A. Examining the private benefit of graduate education: a two-stage approach. Association for Institutional Research Grant Proposal, 2004, 6. Available as of December 26, 2006 at http://www.airweb.org/images/209-Titus%20Marvin.pdf.)

requests specific line items that, if funded, would be of substantial benefit to many researchers starting out in their areas of research. The budget will cover two months of the principal investigator's salary during the summer, 280 hours to pay a graduate assistant at $20 per hour, related fringe benefit costs for both individuals, travel funds for two national conferences, and duplication costs for the interim and final reports. In this budget there are no indirect costs which can be claimed by the sponsoring institution.

46.6   CRITERIA FOR A WINNING PROPOSAL

Grants writers affiliated with the Social Science Research Council underscore the importance of perfecting the art of writing proposals (Przeworski and Salomon, 2006). Suggesting that the writing of proposals for research funding is a "peculiar facet of North American academic culture," the writers point out that a proposal's overt function is to persuade a committee of scholars that the "project shines with the three kinds of merit all disciplines value, namely conceptual innovation, methodological rigor, and rich, substantive content." (p. 1) In order to meet these criteria, as well as to overcome barriers such as "incomprehension among disciplines" and "proposals that reflect unlike social and academic circumstances," Przeworski and Salomon suggest that the proposal writer must provide clear answers to three questions which are constantly in the minds of the readers who review proposals:

- What are we going to learn as a result of the proposed project that we do not know now?
- Why is it worth knowing?
- How will we know that the conclusions are valid? (p. 2)

To rise above the competition, the writers suggest that you "say what you have to say immediately, crisply, and forcefully." They recommend that you use the opening paragraph or the first page "to grab the reviewer's attention." That is the moment, they say, "to overstate, rather than understate, your point or question." Caveats and conditions, they suggest, can be added later. Przeworski and Salomon claim that the best way to begin a proposal is with questions that are clearly posed or with stating your central point, hypothesis, or interpretation. They encourage the proposal writer to "leave the reviewer with something to remember: some message that will remain after reading many other proposals and discussing them for hours and hours." (p. 3)

Argon (1995) rightly observes that "your completed proposal should read smoothly, with elegant transitions from paragraph to paragraph, section to section." She challenges the grant writers to produce a research proposal which is "well-written and appropriately ordered" so that it can captivate the reader "with its order, logic, and importance." (p. 229) We advocate that you ask a colleague to review your proposal using the criteria in Table 46.3, and that you take this crucial step well before the deadline, so that you will have sufficient time to make necessary changes.

46.7   WHAT CAN BE LEARNED FROM RESEARCH FUNDING IN BIOMEDICINE

Even if your research agenda is in public administration, much still can be learned from manuals and information pertaining to money for research in the life sciences. Writing about competitively funded biomedical research grants from the National Institutes of Health (NIH), Ogden and Goldberg (1995) support our claim that the "principles of grantsmanship" apply to "virtually all research proposals." These principles include what we have already emphasized: (1) a proposal tailored to the funding source; (2) a literate, focused, well-organized, interesting proposal; and (3) an important hypothesis effectively tested (p. 4).

GrantsNet is an Internet portable available through the U.S. Department of Health and Human Services (2006) on the Internet at http://www.hhs.gov/grantsnet/. This portal leads to the research dollars available through the National Institutes of Health (NIH). Research dollars in the life

TABLE 46.3
Review Criteria for the First or Second Drafts

Criteria: My Research Proposal	Yes	No	Does Not Apply
1. Has a clearly articulated needs statement			
2. Is there sufficient attention given to related research by others?			
3. Are the purposes of the study clear and sufficiently detailed?			
4. Describes how my proposal fits into the field of public administration and how it will advance it.			
5. Has a clearly articulated hypothesis.			
6. Is the proposal well-coordinated and clearly related to a central focus?			
7. Will the study design provide the data needed to achieve the aims of the project?			
8. Is the sampling design appropriate? Have you justified the sample size?			
9. Have you spelled out the major dependent and independent variables?			
10. Demonstrates the importance of the research project.			
11. Are the specific tasks clearly related to personnel, time, and budget?			
12. Is there sufficient time commitment by the principal investigators?			

Source: Based on Argon, J.K., in Deneef, A. Leigh and Craufurd, D. Goodwin (Eds.), *The Academic's Handbook*. Duke University Press, Durham, 1995, 229; Reif-Lehrer, L., Second Edition. *Writing a Successful Grant Application*. Jones and Bartlett Publishers, Boston, 1989, 146–148.

sciences in 1993 totaled $30 billion, with thirty-two percent being available from the 21 grant-making components of the National Institute of Health, seven percent from other federal and military sources, fifty percent from industry, and eleven percent from other sources, mainly foundations (Ogden and Goldberg, p. 3). The past decade has seen a significant increase in research funds for medicine and related fields. In the federal Fiscal Year 2006 the NIH level of funding alone was $28.4 billion, which reflects a threefold increase of funding during the past 14 years (Zerhouni, 2006). The GrantsNet portal provides a convenient and user-friendly point and click method of accessing information that is divided into seven sections: (1) Introduction to HHS Grants, (2) funding opportunities, (3) application process, (4) HHS Grant process overview, (5) grant policies and regulations, (6) tracking obligated grant funds, and (7) additional grant resources (USDHHS, GrantsNet, p. 1).

To get started, for example, you can locate the NIH guide, which will link you to the NIH Guide for Grants and Contracts, or you can access the link directly at http://grants.nih.gov/grants. This Web page gives you links to definitions and more information, requests for applications (RFAs), program announcements (PAs), recent policies and guidelines, and new announcements for the week. Other links available from this page are funding opportunities, NIH forms and applications, submission dates and deadlines, submitting your grant application, and resources for grant applications. If you connect with the resources link, you will have access to getting started at NIH, grant writing tips sheets, glossary of NIH terms, NIH acronym list, information for new grantees, the office of extramural research outreach activities, and resources for new investigators.

If you had searched for "public policy" in funding opportunities and notices in mid 2006, for example, you will have been directed to about 20 opportunities, including program announcement (PA) number PA-05-036 from the National Institute on Aging entitled Retirement Economics. This PA is instructive to researchers in public administration in many ways, including its broad range of research interests, the amount of the research funds available, and the types of grants available. The PA encompassed "research on the work and retirement decisions that people make at older ages and the health and economic circumstances of individuals as they evolve before retirement, at the time that work transitions take place, and throughout retirement." As stated by the PA, this research is

TABLE 46.4

Research Objectives for PA-05-036, Retirement Objectives

Research Objectives, PA-05-036

1. The determinants of retirement behavior
2. The variation in work patterns in later life
3. The evolution of health and economic circumstances of individuals
4. Time use and life satisfaction before and during retirement
5. The implications of retirement trends
6. Retirement expectations
7. International comparisons of retirement
8. The development of innovative retirement modeling techniques

about "the complex interrelationships between work, economic circumstances, public policy, health, and other aspects of later life." Researchers in public administration should be able to enter this area of research with a strong competitive advantage. Table 46.4 summarizes the possible research objectives, which includes determining the factors in retirement behavior and life circumstances and describing retirement trends and expectations.

To convince our readers of the relevance of the NIH grant research material researchers in the field of public administration, let us take a closer look at what PA-05-036 says about the review criteria for this proposal. According to the Web page:

The NIH R21 exploratory/developmental grant is a mechanism for supporting novel scientific ideas or new model systems, tools, or technologies that have the potential to significantly advance our knowledge or the status of health-related research. Because the Research Plan is limited to 15 pages, an exploratory/developmental grant application need not have extensive background material or preliminary information as one might normally expect in an R01 application. Accordingly, reviewers will focus their evaluation on the conceptual framework, the level of innovation, and the potential to significantly advance our knowledge or understanding. Reviewers will place less emphasis on methodological details and certain indicators traditionally used in evaluating the scientific merit of R01 applications, including supportive preliminary data. Appropriate justification for the proposed work can be provided through literature citations, data from other sources, or, when available, from investigator-generated data. Preliminary data are not required for R21 applications; however, they may be included if available.

What, you may ask, is the RO1 or the R21? The NIH Web site provides the answer. The Research Project Grant (R01) is the original and historically oldest grant mechanism used by NIH, dating back to 1968. The R01 provides support for health-related research and development based on the mission of the NIH. R01s can be investigator initiated or can be in response to a program announcement or request for application. The NIH awards R01 grants to organizations of all types (universities, colleges, small businesses, for-profit, foreign, and domestic, faith-based, etc.) and the R01 mechanism allows an investigator to define the scientific focus or objective of the research based on a particular area of interest and competence. Although the principal investigator writes the grant application and is responsible for conducting the research, the applicant is the research organization. The Research Project (R01) grant is an award made to support a discrete, specified, circumscribed project to be performed by the named investigators in an area representing the investigators' specific interest and competencies, based on the mission of the NIH.

The R21 is intended to encourage exploratory or developmental research projects by providing support for the early and conceptual stages of development. Initiatives can be obtained in the NIH Guide for Grants and Contracts at http://grants.nih.gov/grants/guide/index.html and by consulting with NIH staff. In some cases those announcements may specify different application character-istics, review criteria, and receipt dates.

The PA for investigator-initiated R21 applications can be found at http://grants.nih.gov/grants/guide/pa-files/PA-06-181.html. The R21 mechanism is intended to encourage new, explora-tory, and developmental research projects by providing support for the early stages of their development. For example, such projects could assess the feasibility of a novel area of investigation or a new experimental system that has the potential to enhance health-related research. These studies may involve considerable risk but may lead to a breakthrough in a particular area, or to the development of novel techniques, agents, methodologies, models or applications that could have major impact on a field of biomedical, behavioral, or clinical research. The combined budget for direct costs for the two-year project period may not exceed $275,000.

The Web page also provides criteria which will be used, also suggesting that "an application does not need to be strong in all categories to be judged likely to have major scientific impact and thus deserve a high priority score. For example, an investigator may propose to carry out important work that by its nature is not innovative but is essential to move a field forward." As found on the Web page (http://grants.nih.gov/grants/guide/pa-files/PA-06-236.html#SectionV), the criteria are:

Significance: Does this study address an important problem? If the aims of the application are achieved, how will scientific knowledge or clinical practice be advanced? What will be the effect of these studies on the concepts, methods, technologies, treatments, services, or preventative interven-tions that drive this field?

Approach: Are the conceptual or clinical framework, design, methods, and analyses adequately developed, well integrated, well reasoned, and appropriate to the aims of the project? Does the applicant acknowledge potential problem areas and consider alternative tactics?

Innovation: Is the project original and innovative? For example: Does the project challenge existing paradigms or clinical practice; address an innovative hypothesis or critical barrier to progress in the field? Does the project develop or employ novel concepts, approaches, methodologies, tools, or technologies for this area?

Investigators: Are the investigators appropriately trained and well suited to carry out this work? Is the work proposed appropriate to the experience level of the principal investigator and other researchers? Does the investigative team bring complementary and integrated expertise to the project (if applicable)?

Environment: Does the scientific environment in which the work will be done contribute to the probability of success? Do the proposed studies benefit from unique features of the scientific environment, or subject populations, or employ useful collaborative arrangements? Is there evidence of institutional support?

During the process of pursuing federal research grants, and certainly upon the award of a federal grant, we recommend that you visit Know Net, which can be accessed at http://www.knownet.hhs.gov. Know Net is a knowledge management, e-learning, and performance support system for federal agencies, state, and local governments, contractors, grantees, and citizens. The Web site provides information on key business functions in the federal government, such as acquisition, finance, grants, and logistics, as well as audit resolution, cost policy, performance management, and real property management. In short, Know Net utilizes a novel approach by providing a direct, timely, and usable connection between the practitioner and the laws, regulations, and policies of the federal government.

46.8 FUNDING SOURCES

Professor Jon Harrison's Web site opens up a huge array of Web-based resources that inform and support our search for research grants. This outstanding portal, located at http://www.lib.msu.edu/harris23/grants/, will link you to most of the Internet resources that you could possibly need to search for research grants and to properly and skillfully prepare and submit your applications.

(If this link does not work for you, do an Internet search for "Michigan State University and Jon Harrison.") Part one of the Web site, designed for users of the Michigan State University Libraries, is still a very valuable resource for everyone interested in grants, because it provides a wide-ranging, comprehensive bibliography of resources, many of which can be found in other University libraries, as well. Part two lists and summarizes grant-related resources available on the World Wide Web, using 34 different categories. For example, if you visit the first category, "Academic Funding Newsletters and Current Awareness Services," you will be linked to many journals and newsletters that are appropriate for your pursuit of research dollars. If you visit category 19, "Academic Research and Development Links," you will be introduced to University research oriented organizations and their Web sites, such as the Association of Professional Researcher's for Advancement (APRA), the National Council of University Research Administrators (NCURA), and the Society of Research Administrators (SRA) International.

Although Crossland's essay is over 20 years old, his words are wise counsel for the researcher, particularly the new entrant looking for research funds. Crossland (1995) offers many specific instructions and excellent hints and tips, and he warns that "the odds are that your requests for foundation support will be rejected." (p. 244) He does add, however, that you should not be easily discouraged even though your first foundation grant "very likely will be the most difficult to secure." (p. 245)

Crossland acknowledges that there are about 50 foundations that have "reasonably broad objectives, operate on the national scene, have full-time professional staffs, and evince interest in higher education activities." (p. 238) The foundations which he names as fitting in this category are displayed in Table 46.5, along their Web site addresses. Crossland suggests that a researcher should become familiar with these foundations, and in today's Internet-based world, it is easy to do so. However, he suggests that researchers who are new in academe will not be involved with these foundations, because "you probably will be seeking support from smaller, local, less well-known potential funders." (p. 238)

Some foundations suggest that you begin with a letter of inquiry. For example, the Carnegie Corporation of New York, which expects that the Corporation's grant making will total more than $80 million during fiscal year 2005–2006, advises that, after you take a quiz for eligibility, your letter of inquiry should address the following points, per its Web site (http://www.carnegie.org/sub/program/grantletter/html):

TABLE 46.5
Thirteen Large Foundations in the United States which Support Research

Foundation	Uniform Resource Locator (URL)
Carnegie Corporation of New York	http://www.carnegie.org
ExxonMobil Foundation	www.exxonmobil.com/Corporate/Citizenship/ Corp_citizenship_Com_foundations.asp
Ford Foundation	http://www.fordfound.og
The William and Flora Hewlett Foundation	http://www.hewlett.org
The Robert Wood Johnson Foundation	http://www.rwjf.org
W.K. Kellogg Foundation	http://www.wkkf.org
The Kresge Foundation	http://www.kresge.org
Eli Lilly and Company Foundation	http://www.lilly.com/products/access/foundation.html
The John, D. and Catherine, T. MacArthur Foundation	http://www.macfound.org
The Andrew W. Mellon Foundation	http://www.mellon.org
The Pew Charitable Trusts	http://pewtrusts.com
The Rockefeller Foundation	http://www.rockfound.org
Alfred P. Sloan Foundation	http://www.sloan.org

1. What problem does your project address? Why is this issue significant? What is the relationship of the problem or issue to the corporation's current program interests as noted in its Information Pamphlet and Web site?
2. What strengths and skills do your organization and personnel bring to this project? What makes your organization the right one to conduct this project?
3. Who will lead the project? Identify key personnel and attach resumes.
4. What do you intend to demonstrate or prove? What means will you use? If the project is already under way, what have you accomplished so far?
5. If you are requesting funding from the Carnegie Corporation for a component of a larger project, specify which activities you are requesting the corporation to fund and how they relate to the larger project.
6. What outcomes do you expect, both immediate and long term?
7. If you have requested funds from other sources (or plan to), please list those sources and note the status of your request.
8. What plans do you have to disseminate information to the public about your project?

The Ford Foundation also suggests that a request for a grant begin with a brief letter of inquiry to its New York office. The Foundation's Web page (http://www.fordfound.org/about/guideline. cfm) also points out that its funds are limited in relation to the great number of worthwhile proposals received. For example, in 2004 the foundation received about 41,000 grant requests and made 2,091 grants. The William and Flora Hewlett Foundation uses an online letter of inquiry (http://www. hewlett.org/Grantseekers/ShortLOI.htm). The format is quite simple, but it is apparent that the foundation limits the number of inquiries by restricting the areas for which it receives requests.

The Robert Wood Johnson Foundation (RWJF) is the largest American foundation which is dedicated solely to health care. In 2005, RWJF awarded 959 grants and contracts providing $369.5 million in support of programs and projects to improve health and health care of all Americans. According to its Web site (http://www.rwjf.org/applications/firsttimeapplicants.jhtml), RWJF funds projects in addiction prevention and treatment, building human capital, childhood obesity, disparities, health insurance coverage, nursing, public health, quality health care, tobacco use and exposure, and vulnerable populations. The projects that RWJF funds include service demonstrations, gathering, and monitoring of health-related statistics, public education, training, and fellowship programs, policy analysis, health services research, technical assistance, communication activities, and evaluations. RWJF reports that most of its grants are solicited, as they are awarded in response to calls for proposals (CFPs). However, about 25 percent of its funds are awarded to unsolicited proposals, according to its Web site. (Based on its 959 awards in 2005, that is about 240 unsolicited approvals per year.)

The W.K. Kellogg Foundation (www.wkkf.org) lists five areas of interest for its grants in the United States: Health, Food Systems and Rural Development, Youth, and Education, Philanthropy, and Volunteerism, the Greater Battle Creek, Michigan area, and Learning Opportunities. WKKF reports that research is funded only as part of a broader program, such as investigating the effects of a Foundation-funded project. The foundation prefers that grant applicants submit their proposals electronically by using the foundation's online application, which allows you to choose between two alternatives—submit a letter of inquiry or submit a preproposal. The format for the letter of inquiry is made up of components which are very similar to the key proposal items which we have seen throughout this chapter: project name, project overview, project goals, project objectives, rationale, project activities, anticipated outcomes, and target geographic area. The preproposal online is very similar, adding items such as a sustainability plan and a list of collaborating organizations.

The Kresge Foundation, according to its Web site (www.kresge.org) is a $3 billion national foundation that builds stronger nonprofit organizations—catalyzing their growth, helping them connect with their stakeholders, and challenging them grants that leverage greater support. Half of each Kresge Science Initiative grant is applied toward the purchase of scientific equipment.

The other half supports an endowment restricted to the future maintenance and replacement of the equipment.

The Andrew W. Mellon Foundation has three of six areas of interest that might be of relevance to public administration: higher education and scholarship, scholarly communications, and research in information technology. If public administration is viewed in a very broad sense, the foundation's three other areas of interest might also be seen within the purview of public administration: Museums and Art Conservation, Performing Arts, and Conservation and the Environment. The Web site (http://www.mellon.org/scholarly.html) warns, however, that the foundation is rarely able to respond positively to unsolicited requests and suggests that prospective applicants explore their ideas with program staff in a short e-mail describing the project and the budget. As is the case for all of the foundations listed in Table 46.4, the Mellon Foundation's Web site (http://www.mellon.org/research.html) is truly worth the visit, and in the case of the Mellon Foundation's site, if for no other reason than to be briefed on the foundation's own research, including the Bowen-Rudenstein study of PhD programs (*In Pursuit of the PhD*) and, in addition, the 1992 study of research libraries (*University Libraries and Scholarly Communication*), which led to the creation of JSTOR.

The Pew Charitable Trusts serves the public interest by providing information, advancing policy solutions, and supporting civic life. According to its Web site (www.pewtrusts.com), the Trusts will invest $248 million in fiscal year 2007 to provide organizations and citizens with fact-based research and practical solutions for challenging issues. The foundation joins the other foundations, as described above, in its inability to respond to many unsolicited funding inquiries, which in FY2005 numbered over 2000. Because the foundation can respond to only a very few, its Web site indicates that "we hope that our expanded program descriptions and guidelines will enable would-be applicants whose projects fall outside our funding priorities to direct their efforts toward more promising funding prospects." The foundation encourages the applicant to consult the Trusts' program staff for assistance (www.pewtrusts.com/grants/index.cfm).

The Rockefeller Foundation's Web site (http://www.rockfound.org) makes it very clear that the foundation is really not interested in unsolicited funding requests. It points out that "Rockefeller Foundation officers rarely provide funding in response to unsolicited proposals." However, the foundation does provide a mechanism to send a brief letter of inquiry either electronically or by U.S. Mail, if, after carefully reading the foundation's Guide for Grantmaking (http://www.rockfound.org/Grantmaking/Funding/Programs), you think your organization's project aligns with the foundation's strategic goals.

The foundation's broad areas of interest are agriculture, arts and culture, health, employment, housing and education, and globalization. As a courtesy to its audience and stakeholders, some of whom may be you and me, desperately trying to obtain funds for a research project, the Rockefeller Foundation's Web site offers a Web page packed with valuable links. These links, as displayed in Table 46.6, might "inform the process" of seeking financial support for your project, which the authors of the Web site, recognize "can be time-consuming and even frustrating."

A visit to the Web site for the Alfred P. Sloan Foundation (http://ww.sloan.org) will be encouraging to the researchers and practitioners in public administration, who may have become disillusioned in reading this chapter with the daunting task of securing funds for research in public administration. The foundation's programs of interest are science and technology, standards of living and economic performance, education careers in science and technology, selected national issues, and the civic program. In its description of the 40 or so projects that make up a sub-program in standard of living and economic performance, entitled "Making Municipal Governments More Responsive to Their Citizens," the many themes and issues within the field of public administration ring loud and clear (http://sloan.org/programs/PerformanceMeasurementandReporting.shtml). A broad range of organizations and universities are also represented in this group. The Web site reports that "grant requests can be made at any time for support of activities related to Foundation program areas and interests." The Foundation has no deadlines or standard forms, and concise,

TABLE 46.6
Other Philanthropic Resources

Organization	Uniform Resource Locator (URL)
The Foundation Center	http://www.fdncenter.org
Forum of Regional Associations of Grant Makers	http://www.givingforum.org
Independent sector	http://www.independentsector.org
Council on Foundations	http://www.cof.org
Chronicle of Philanthropy	http://www.philanthropy.com
Yahoo—Philanthropy	http://www.dir.yahoo.com/Society_and_Culture/Issues_ and_Causes/Philanthropy
Guidestar	http://www.guidestar.org
Women & Philanthropy	http://www.womenphi.org
National Science Foundation	http://www.nsf.gov/funding/research_edu_community.jsp
Association of Small Foundation	http://www.smallfoundations.org
Grantmakers for Effective Organizations	http://www.geofundes.org
Center for Family Philanthropy	http://www.ncfp.org
The ePhilanthropy Foundation	http://www.ephilanthropy.org/site/PageServer

Source: http://www.rockfound.org.

well-organized proposals are preferred, with a limit of 20 pages. This foundation also recommends that the application process can begin with a letter of inquiry.

Table 46.6 gives us a comprehensive set of references for financial resources that might be available among private foundations. Certainly we should not forget about potential gifts from individual donors, and these benefactors might best be reached through the personnel of your organization's development office. We should always be mindful of the fact that over half of all philanthropy comes from the giving by individuals.

A comprehensive approach to federal research dollars can be initiated through two government portals on the Internet: www.//firstgov.gov and www.//grants.gov. Assisting us in tracking government grants can be a very reliable and timely resource—the business daily *Federal Register*. You can arrange for the *Federal Register's* table of contents, with links to pdf files for each set of regulations, to be e-mailed to you on a daily basis by registering with the listserv located at http://listserv.access.gpo.gov.

Of course, your State government must also be monitored and we encourage you to do so by way of the Internet. Other organizations worthy of pursuit are the World Bank and the United Nations. Another familiar spot for you should be your organization's office of research and development. It is predictable that your organization's development team will be able to legitimately tell you that they are busy. However, keep in mind that it pays to be heard and the squeaky wheel usually gets the grease.

46.9   FINAL LESSONS TO BE LEARNED

The final lessons to be learned remind us that, despite the changes introduced in recent years with regard to electronic submissions and Internet-based information, there are proposal writing basics, as we have seen, and there are also other details that must be attended to in the pursuit and management of research grant dollars. As previously reported, Argon's contribution to *The Academic's Handbook's* Part V, "Funding Academic Research," has emphasized many basics of preparing a grant application for research. Argon's chapter, "Securing Funding from Federal

---

TABLE 46.7

Additional Items in the Proposal Package

Items for the Proposal Package in Addition to the Project Description

1. Cover sheet
2. Project summary or abstract
3. Curriculum vitae (CV)
4. Budget and budget narrative
5. Certificates and representations, assurances, and checklists

---

Sources," also points us to additional details that must be addressed in either the proposal or preaward stage.

Table 46.7 lists these additional items. Of course, as pointed out by Argon, it is important to read the solicitation carefully, because additional elements do vary widely. For example, many federal agencies have developed unique and individual cover sheets and others use a standard form. However, with the introduction of electronic submissions, as found on the federal portal for grants, www.grants.gov, the requirement for a cover sheet is changing. The project summary, or abstract, however, continues to function as a "succinct and self-contained summary of the proposed work," (p. 230) and it is a valuable exercise to save sufficient time in your grant writing venture to prepare an excellent summary after all your writing has been completed.

Argon reminds us that a curriculum vitae (CV) of everyone who will assume major responsibility for the project should be included in the proposal package. It is wise to have a long version and a short version of each CV and to have the CV's in digital form, because the guidelines for these required documents often limit the length to two pages or so and they often require them to be uploaded as part of the electronic submission.

We have already covered the budget and the budget narrative. Argon gives key insights into important aspects of the budget process for federal grants and contracts. For example, she points to the federal guidelines in the Office of Management and Budget (OMB), which publishes circulars specifically for the preparation and management of budgets and grants by universities, hospitals, local governments, nonprofit organizations, and for-profit companies. Argon points out that "if a cost is included in the cost pools that make up the institution's indirect cost rate, the same cost may not appear as a direct cost." (p. 231)

With regard to certifications and representations, assurances, and checklists, Argon notes that "federal law requires that an institution certify that it is in compliance with an array of federal regulations before an award can be made." (p. 231) Making sure that the appropriate representative of your organization can and will sign for your proposal, therefore, is one of the many reasons why it is necessary for you "to learn and follow the internal requirements of your institution." (p. 231)

Finally, the Web site for the Agency for Healthcare Research and Quality in the U.S. Department of Health and Human Services (http://www.ahcpr.gov/fund/apptime.htm) reminds us to determine the human subjects requirement in order to comply with our institution's internal review board. This federal Web site also reminds us a basic in writing: "Be sure to allow time for others to review, edit, and proofread the application."

46.10 FINAL SUMMARY

We started this chapter with good news and bad news regarding dollars for research grants in the field of public administration. Yes, there is funding available, but, unfortunately the dollars are limited and very competitive. Therefore, a research grant application, starting with its abstract and including its descriptions of the background and need, its goals and objectives, the program narrative that describes the research design, methodologies, and procedures, as well as its statements on significance, qualifications, and resources, and the budget and its narrative—all of these must be of superior quality.

In order to present a powerful new idea in a clear, convincing, and compelling presentation (Argon, p. 226), it is wise to start with a disciplined planning process (Table 46.2) and end with a thorough self-evaluation exercise of your complete narrative (Table 46.3). By examining some of the funding sources in the field of health care, we demonstrated and supported our claim that the principles of grant writing and management apply to virtually all research proposals.

Furthermore, the federal government provides useful and essential portals to its funding opportunities, including research grants, through various Internet portals, including GrantsNet and Web sites such as www.//firstgov.gov and www.//grants.gov. Funding opportunities with national foundations (Tables 46.4 and 46.5) are essential to the pursuit of research funds, but your local and regional foundations, as well as individuals in your organization's network of influence—people who have a heart and interest in your work and have the financial capacity to make significant gifts—certainly should not be overlooked.

Finally, drafting, editing, and getting input from others, all of which takes time, must be an essential part of your efforts to win grant dollars for your research work and agenda.

REFERENCES

Argon, J.K. 1995. Seeking funding from federal sources. In Deneef, A.L. and Craufurd, D.G. (Eds.), *The Academic's Handbook*. Durham, North Carolina: Duke University Press, pp. 219—235.

Browning, B. 2005. *Grant Writing for Dummies*. Second Edition. Indianapolis, Indiana: Wiley Publishing.

Crossland, F.E. 1995. New academics and the quest for private funds. In Deneef, A.L. and Craufurd, D.G. (Eds.) *The Academic's Handbook*, Second Edition. Durham, North Carolina: Duke University Press, pp. 237–248.

Kiritz, N.J. 1980. *Program Planning & Proposal Writing*. Los Angeles, California: Grantsmanship Center.

Ogden, T.E. and Goldberg, I.A. 1995. *Research Proposals, A Guide to Success*, Second Edition. New York: Raven Press.

Przeworski, A. and Salomon, F. 2006. The art of writing proposals: Some candid suggestions for applicants to social science research council competitions. Web site of the Social Science Research Council. Available as of December 26, 2006 at http://www.ssrc.org/fellowships. (See the Art of Writing Proposals link.)

Reif-Lehrer, L. 1989. *Writing a Successful Grant Application*, Second Edition. Boston: Jones and Bartlett Publishers.

Titus, M.A. 2004. Examining the private benefit of graduate education: A two-stage approach. Association for Institutional Research Grant Proposal. Available as of July 1, 2007 at http://www.airweb.org/images/209-Titus%20Marvin.pdf.

U.S. Department of Health and Human Services. 2006. GrantsNet. An Internet portal for grants information for the United States Department of Health and Human Services. Available as of July 1, 2007 at http://www.hhs.gov/grantsnet/

Zerhouni, Dr. E.A. 2006. Fiscal year budget 2007 budget request house subcommittee on labor—HHS-education appropriations. Available as of December 26, 2006 at http://www.nih.gov/about/director/budgetrequest/fy2007/directorsbudgetrequest.htm.

ADDITIONAL SOURCES OF INFORMATION

Baron, R.A. 1987. Research grants: A practical guide. In Zanna, M.P. and John, M.D. (Eds.), *The Complete Academic: A Practical Guide for the Beginning Social Scientist*. New York: Random House, pp. 151–169.

Booth, W.C., Colomb, G.G., and Williams, J.M. 2003. *The Craft of Research*. Chicago, Illinois: The University of Chicago Press.

Geever, J.C. 2004. *Guide to Proposal Writing*. New York: The Foundation Center.

Jackson, M., Broom, C.A., Vogelsang-Coombs, V., and Harris, J. 1999. *Performance Measurement*. Washington, D.C.: American Society for Public Administration.

Schladweiler, K. (Ed.). 2001. *Guide to Grantseeking on the Web*. New York: The Foundation Center.

Index

PGIL2020USA